SECOND EDITION

Fluent Python
Clear, Concise, and Effective Programming

Luciano Ramalho

Beijing · Boston · Farnham · Sebastopol · Tokyo

Fluent Python

by Luciano Ramalho

Copyright © 2022 Luciano Ramalho. All rights reserved.

Published by O'Reilly Media, Inc., 1005 Gravenstein Highway North, Sebastopol, CA 95472.

O'Reilly books may be purchased for educational, business, or sales promotional use. Online editions are also available for most titles (*http://oreilly.com*). For more information, contact our corporate/institutional sales department: 800-998-9938 or *corporate@oreilly.com*.

Acquisitions Editor: Amanda Quinn
Development Editor: Jeff Bleiel
Production Editor: Daniel Elfanbaum
Copyeditor: Sonia Saruba
Proofreader: Kim Cofer

Indexer: Judith McConville
Interior Designer: David Futato
Cover Designer: Karen Montgomery
Illustrator: Kate Dullea

April 2022:   Second Edition

Revision History for the Second Edition
2022-03-31:   First Release

See *http://oreilly.com/catalog/errata.csp?isbn=9781492056355* for release details.

978-1-492-05635-5

[LSI]

Para Marta, com todo o meu amor.

Table of Contents

Preface.. xix

Part I.   Data Structures

1. The Python Data Model.. 3
What's New in This Chapter   4
A Pythonic Card Deck   5
How Special Methods Are Used   8
Emulating Numeric Types   9
String Representation   12
Boolean Value of a Custom Type   13
Collection API   14
Overview of Special Methods   15
Why len Is Not a Method   17
Chapter Summary   18
Further Reading   18

2. An Array of Sequences.. 21
What's New in This Chapter   22
Overview of Built-In Sequences   22
List Comprehensions and Generator Expressions   25
List Comprehensions and Readability   25
Listcomps Versus map and filter   27
Cartesian Products   27
Generator Expressions   29
Tuples Are Not Just Immutable Lists   30
Tuples as Records   30

Tuples as Immutable Lists	32
Comparing Tuple and List Methods	34
Unpacking Sequences and Iterables	35
Using * to Grab Excess Items	36
Unpacking with * in Function Calls and Sequence Literals	37
Nested Unpacking	37
Pattern Matching with Sequences	39
Pattern Matching Sequences in an Interpreter	43
Slicing	47
Why Slices and Ranges Exclude the Last Item	47
Slice Objects	48
Multidimensional Slicing and Ellipsis	49
Assigning to Slices	50
Using + and * with Sequences	50
Building Lists of Lists	51
Augmented Assignment with Sequences	53
A += Assignment Puzzler	54
list.sort Versus the sorted Built-In	56
When a List Is Not the Answer	59
Arrays	59
Memory Views	62
NumPy	64
Deques and Other Queues	67
Chapter Summary	70
Further Reading	71
3. Dictionaries and Sets. **77**
What's New in This Chapter	78
Modern dict Syntax	78
dict Comprehensions	79
Unpacking Mappings	80
Merging Mappings with |	80
Pattern Matching with Mappings	81
Standard API of Mapping Types	83
What Is Hashable	84
Overview of Common Mapping Methods	85
Inserting or Updating Mutable Values	87
Automatic Handling of Missing Keys	90
defaultdict: Another Take on Missing Keys	90
The __missing__ Method	91
Inconsistent Usage of __missing__ in the Standard Library	94
Variations of dict	95

collections.OrderedDict   95
collections.ChainMap   95
collections.Counter   96
shelve.Shelf   97
Subclassing UserDict Instead of dict   97
Immutable Mappings   99
Dictionary Views   101
Practical Consequences of How dict Works   102
Set Theory   103
Set Literals   105
Set Comprehensions   106
Practical Consequences of How Sets Work   107
Set Operations   107
Set Operations on dict Views   110
Chapter Summary   112
Further Reading   113

4. Unicode Text Versus Bytes.   117
What's New in This Chapter   118
Character Issues   118
Byte Essentials   120
Basic Encoders/Decoders   123
Understanding Encode/Decode Problems   125
Coping with UnicodeEncodeError   125
Coping with UnicodeDecodeError   126
SyntaxError When Loading Modules with Unexpected Encoding   128
How to Discover the Encoding of a Byte Sequence   128
BOM: A Useful Gremlin   129
Handling Text Files   131
Beware of Encoding Defaults   134
Normalizing Unicode for Reliable Comparisons   140
Case Folding   142
Utility Functions for Normalized Text Matching   143
Extreme "Normalization": Taking Out Diacritics   144
Sorting Unicode Text   148
Sorting with the Unicode Collation Algorithm   150
The Unicode Database   151
Finding Characters by Name   151
Numeric Meaning of Characters   153
Dual-Mode str and bytes APIs   155
str Versus bytes in Regular Expressions   155
str Versus bytes in os Functions   157

Chapter Summary   157
Further Reading   158

5. Data Class Builders **163**
What's New in This Chapter   164
Overview of Data Class Builders   164
  Main Features   167
Classic Named Tuples   169
Typed Named Tuples   172
Type Hints 101   173
  No Runtime Effect   173
  Variable Annotation Syntax   174
  The Meaning of Variable Annotations   175
More About @dataclass   179
  Field Options   180
  Post-init Processing   183
  Typed Class Attributes   185
  Initialization Variables That Are Not Fields   186
  @dataclass Example: Dublin Core Resource Record   187
Data Class as a Code Smell   190
  Data Class as Scaffolding   191
  Data Class as Intermediate Representation   191
Pattern Matching Class Instances   192
  Simple Class Patterns   192
  Keyword Class Patterns   193
  Positional Class Patterns   194
Chapter Summary   195
Further Reading   196

6. Object References, Mutability, and Recycling **201**
What's New in This Chapter   202
Variables Are Not Boxes   202
Identity, Equality, and Aliases   204
  Choosing Between == and is   206
  The Relative Immutability of Tuples   207
Copies Are Shallow by Default   208
  Deep and Shallow Copies of Arbitrary Objects   211
Function Parameters as References   213
  Mutable Types as Parameter Defaults: Bad Idea   214
  Defensive Programming with Mutable Parameters   216
del and Garbage Collection   219
Tricks Python Plays with Immutables   221

Chapter Summary   223
Further Reading   224

Part II.   Functions as Objects

7. Functions as First-Class Objects. 231
    What's New in This Chapter   232
    Treating a Function Like an Object   232
    Higher-Order Functions   234
      Modern Replacements for map, filter, and reduce   235
    Anonymous Functions   236
    The Nine Flavors of Callable Objects   237
    User-Defined Callable Types   239
    From Positional to Keyword-Only Parameters   240
      Positional-Only Parameters   242
    Packages for Functional Programming   243
      The operator Module   243
      Freezing Arguments with functools.partial   247
    Chapter Summary   249
    Further Reading   250

8. Type Hints in Functions. 253
    What's New in This Chapter   254
    About Gradual Typing   254
    Gradual Typing in Practice   255
      Starting with Mypy   256
      Making Mypy More Strict   257
      A Default Parameter Value   258
      Using None as a Default   260
    Types Are Defined by Supported Operations   261
    Types Usable in Annotations   266
      The Any Type   266
      Simple Types and Classes   269
      Optional and Union Types   270
      Generic Collections   271
      Tuple Types   274
      Generic Mappings   277
      Abstract Base Classes   278
      Iterable   280
      Parameterized Generics and TypeVar   282
      Static Protocols   287

Callable   292
NoReturn   295
Annotating Positional Only and Variadic Parameters   295
Imperfect Typing and Strong Testing   296
Chapter Summary   298
Further Reading   299

9. Decorators and Closures. 305
What's New in This Chapter   306
Decorators 101   306
When Python Executes Decorators   308
Registration Decorators   310
Variable Scope Rules   310
Closures   313
The nonlocal Declaration   317
Variable Lookup Logic   318
Implementing a Simple Decorator   319
How It Works   320
Decorators in the Standard Library   322
Memoization with functools.cache   322
Using lru_cache   325
Single Dispatch Generic Functions   326
Parameterized Decorators   331
A Parameterized Registration Decorator   331
The Parameterized Clock Decorator   334
A Class-Based Clock Decorator   337
Chapter Summary   338
Further Reading   338

10. Design Patterns with First-Class Functions. 343
What's New in This Chapter   344
Case Study: Refactoring Strategy   344
Classic Strategy   344
Function-Oriented Strategy   349
Choosing the Best Strategy: Simple Approach   352
Finding Strategies in a Module   353
Decorator-Enhanced Strategy Pattern   355
The Command Pattern   357
Chapter Summary   359
Further Reading   360

Part III. Classes and Protocols

11. A Pythonic Object. **365**
What's New in This Chapter   366
Object Representations   366
Vector Class Redux   367
An Alternative Constructor   370
classmethod Versus staticmethod   371
Formatted Displays   372
A Hashable Vector2d   376
Supporting Positional Pattern Matching   379
Complete Listing of Vector2d, Version 3   380
Private and "Protected" Attributes in Python   384
Saving Memory with __slots__   386
   Simple Measure of __slot__ Savings   389
   Summarizing the Issues with __slots__   390
Overriding Class Attributes   391
Chapter Summary   393
Further Reading   394

12. Special Methods for Sequences. **399**
What's New in This Chapter   400
Vector: A User-Defined Sequence Type   400
Vector Take #1: Vector2d Compatible   401
Protocols and Duck Typing   404
Vector Take #2: A Sliceable Sequence   405
   How Slicing Works   406
   A Slice-Aware __getitem__   408
Vector Take #3: Dynamic Attribute Access   409
Vector Take #4: Hashing and a Faster ==   413
Vector Take #5: Formatting   420
Chapter Summary   427
Further Reading   428

13. Interfaces, Protocols, and ABCs. **433**
The Typing Map   434
What's New in This Chapter   435
Two Kinds of Protocols   436
Programming Ducks   438
   Python Digs Sequences   438
   Monkey Patching: Implementing a Protocol at Runtime   440
   Defensive Programming and "Fail Fast"   442

Goose Typing   444
   Subclassing an ABC   449
   ABCs in the Standard Library   451
   Defining and Using an ABC   453
   ABC Syntax Details   459
   Subclassing an ABC   460
   A Virtual Subclass of an ABC   462
   Usage of register in Practice   465
   Structural Typing with ABCs   466
Static Protocols   468
   The Typed double Function   468
   Runtime Checkable Static Protocols   470
   Limitations of Runtime Protocol Checks   473
   Supporting a Static Protocol   474
   Designing a Static Protocol   476
   Best Practices for Protocol Design   478
   Extending a Protocol   479
   The numbers ABCs and Numeric Protocols   480
Chapter Summary   483
Further Reading   484

14. Inheritance: For Better or for Worse. 489
What's New in This Chapter   490
The super() Function   490
Subclassing Built-In Types Is Tricky   492
Multiple Inheritance and Method Resolution Order   496
Mixin Classes   502
   Case-Insensitive Mappings   502
Multiple Inheritance in the Real World   504
   ABCs Are Mixins Too   504
   ThreadingMixIn and ForkingMixIn   505
   Django Generic Views Mixins   506
   Multiple Inheritance in Tkinter   509
Coping with Inheritance   512
   Favor Object Composition over Class Inheritance   512
   Understand Why Inheritance Is Used in Each Case   512
   Make Interfaces Explicit with ABCs   513
   Use Explicit Mixins for Code Reuse   513
   Provide Aggregate Classes to Users   513
   Subclass Only Classes Designed for Subclassing   514
   Avoid Subclassing from Concrete Classes   515
   Tkinter: The Good, the Bad, and the Ugly   515

    Chapter Summary   516
    Further Reading   517

15. More About Type Hints. **523**
    What's New in This Chapter   523
    Overloaded Signatures   524
      Max Overload   525
      Takeaways from Overloading max   529
    TypedDict   530
    Type Casting   538
    Reading Type Hints at Runtime   541
      Problems with Annotations at Runtime   542
      Dealing with the Problem   544
    Implementing a Generic Class   545
      Basic Jargon for Generic Types   548
    Variance   548
      An Invariant Dispenser   549
      A Covariant Dispenser   550
      A Contravariant Trash Can   551
      Variance Review   553
    Implementing a Generic Static Protocol   556
    Chapter Summary   558
    Further Reading   559

16. Operator Overloading. **565**
    What's New in This Chapter   566
    Operator Overloading 101   566
    Unary Operators   567
    Overloading + for Vector Addition   570
    Overloading * for Scalar Multiplication   576
    Using @ as an Infix Operator   578
    Wrapping-Up Arithmetic Operators   580
    Rich Comparison Operators   581
    Augmented Assignment Operators   584
    Chapter Summary   589
    Further Reading   591

Part IV.   Control Flow

17. Iterators, Generators, and Classic Coroutines. **597**
    What's New in This Chapter   598

A Sequence of Words 598
Why Sequences Are Iterable: The iter Function 600
    Using iter with a Callable 602
Iterables Versus Iterators 603
Sentence Classes with __iter__ 607
    Sentence Take #2: A Classic Iterator 607
    Don't Make the Iterable an Iterator for Itself 609
    Sentence Take #3: A Generator Function 610
    How a Generator Works 611
Lazy Sentences 614
    Sentence Take #4: Lazy Generator 614
    Sentence Take #5: Lazy Generator Expression 616
When to Use Generator Expressions 617
An Arithmetic Progression Generator 619
    Arithmetic Progression with itertools 622
Generator Functions in the Standard Library 623
Iterable Reducing Functions 634
Subgenerators with yield from 636
    Reinventing chain 637
    Traversing a Tree 638
Generic Iterable Types 643
Classic Coroutines 645
    Example: Coroutine to Compute a Running Average 647
    Returning a Value from a Coroutine 650
    Generic Type Hints for Classic Coroutines 654
Chapter Summary 656
Further Reading 656

18. with, match, and else Blocks. 661
What's New in This Chapter 662
Context Managers and with Blocks 662
    The contextlib Utilities 667
    Using @contextmanager 668
Pattern Matching in lis.py: A Case Study 673
    Scheme Syntax 673
    Imports and Types 675
    The Parser 675
    The Environment 677
    The REPL 679
    The Evaluator 680
    Procedure: A Class Implementing a Closure 689
    Using OR-patterns 690

  Do This, Then That: else Blocks Beyond if   691
  Chapter Summary   693
  Further Reading   694

19. **Concurrency Models in Python.** **699**
  What's New in This Chapter   700
  The Big Picture   700
  A Bit of Jargon   701
    Processes, Threads, and Python's Infamous GIL   703
  A Concurrent Hello World   705
    Spinner with Threads   705
    Spinner with Processes   708
    Spinner with Coroutines   710
    Supervisors Side-by-Side   715
  The Real Impact of the GIL   717
    Quick Quiz   717
  A Homegrown Process Pool   720
    Process-Based Solution   722
    Understanding the Elapsed Times   722
    Code for the Multicore Prime Checker   723
    Experimenting with More or Fewer Processes   727
    Thread-Based Nonsolution   728
  Python in the Multicore World   729
    System Administration   730
    Data Science   731
    Server-Side Web/Mobile Development   732
    WSGI Application Servers   734
    Distributed Task Queues   736
  Chapter Summary   737
  Further Reading   738
    Concurrency with Threads and Processes   738
    The GIL   740
    Concurrency Beyond the Standard Library   740
    Concurrency and Scalability Beyond Python   742

20. **Concurrent Executors.** **747**
  What's New in This Chapter   747
  Concurrent Web Downloads   748
    A Sequential Download Script   750
    Downloading with concurrent.futures   753
    Where Are the Futures?   755
  Launching Processes with concurrent.futures   758

    Multicore Prime Checker Redux   759
    Experimenting with Executor.map   762
    Downloads with Progress Display and Error Handling   766
      Error Handling in the flags2 Examples   770
      Using futures.as_completed   773
    Chapter Summary   776
    Further Reading   776

21. Asynchronous Programming. **779**
    What's New in This Chapter   780
    A Few Definitions   781
    An asyncio Example: Probing Domains   782
      Guido's Trick to Read Asynchronous Code   784
    New Concept: Awaitable   785
    Downloading with asyncio and HTTPX   786
      The Secret of Native Coroutines: Humble Generators 789
      The All-or-Nothing Problem   790
    Asynchronous Context Managers   790
    Enhancing the asyncio Downloader   792
      Using asyncio.as_completed and a Thread   793
      Throttling Requests with a Semaphore   795
      Making Multiple Requests for Each Download   799
    Delegating Tasks to Executors   801
    Writing asyncio Servers   803
      A FastAPI Web Service   805
      An asyncio TCP Server   808
    Asynchronous Iteration and Asynchronous Iterables 815
      Asynchronous Generator Functions   816
      Async Comprehensions and Async Generator Expressions 822
    async Beyond asyncio: Curio   825
    Type Hinting Asynchronous Objects   828
    How Async Works and How It Doesn't   829
      Running Circles Around Blocking Calls   829
      The Myth of I/O-Bound Systems   830
      Avoiding CPU-Bound Traps   830
    Chapter Summary   831
    Further Reading   832

Part V. Metaprogramming

22. Dynamic Attributes and Properties. 839

What's New in This Chapter   840
Data Wrangling with Dynamic Attributes   840
  Exploring JSON-Like Data with Dynamic Attributes   842
  The Invalid Attribute Name Problem   846
  Flexible Object Creation with __new__   847
Computed Properties   849
  Step 1: Data-Driven Attribute Creation   850
  Step 2: Property to Retrieve a Linked Record   852
  Step 3: Property Overriding an Existing Attribute   856
  Step 4: Bespoke Property Cache   857
  Step 5: Caching Properties with functools   859
Using a Property for Attribute Validation   861
  LineItem Take #1: Class for an Item in an Order   861
  LineItem Take #2: A Validating Property   862
A Proper Look at Properties   864
  Properties Override Instance Attributes   865
  Property Documentation   868
Coding a Property Factory   869
Handling Attribute Deletion   872
Essential Attributes and Functions for Attribute Handling   873
  Special Attributes that Affect Attribute Handling   874
  Built-In Functions for Attribute Handling   874
  Special Methods for Attribute Handling   875
Chapter Summary   877
Further Reading   878

23. Attribute Descriptors. 883

What's New in This Chapter   884
Descriptor Example: Attribute Validation   884
  LineItem Take #3: A Simple Descriptor   884
  LineItem Take #4: Automatic Naming of Storage Attributes 891
  LineItem Take #5: A New Descriptor Type   893
Overriding Versus Nonoverriding Descriptors   896
  Overriding Descriptors   898
  Overriding Descriptor Without __get__   899
  Nonoverriding Descriptor   900
  Overwriting a Descriptor in the Class   901
Methods Are Descriptors   902
Descriptor Usage Tips   904

Descriptor Docstring and Overriding Deletion   906
Chapter Summary   907
Further Reading   908

24. Class Metaprogramming.. **911**
What's New in This Chapter   912
Classes as Objects   912
type: The Built-In Class Factory   913
A Class Factory Function   915
Introducing __init_subclass__   918
    Why __init_subclass__ Cannot Configure __slots__   925
Enhancing Classes with a Class Decorator   926
What Happens When: Import Time Versus Runtime   929
    Evaluation Time Experiments   930
Metaclasses 101   935
    How a Metaclass Customizes a Class   937
    A Nice Metaclass Example   938
    Metaclass Evaluation Time Experiment   941
A Metaclass Solution for Checked   946
Metaclasses in the Real World   951
    Modern Features Simplify or Replace Metaclasses   951
    Metaclasses Are Stable Language Features   952
    A Class Can Only Have One Metaclass   952
    Metaclasses Should Be Implementation Details   953
A Metaclass Hack with __prepare__   954
Wrapping Up   956
Chapter Summary   957
Further Reading   958

Afterword.. **963**

Index.. **967**

Preface

Here's the plan: when someone uses a feature you don't understand, simply shoot them. This is easier than learning something new, and before too long the only living coders will be writing in an easily understood, tiny subset of Python 0.9.6 <wink>.[1]

—Tim Peters, legendary core developer and author of *The Zen of Python*

"Python is an easy to learn, powerful programming language." Those are the first words of the official Python 3.10 tutorial (*https://fpy.li/p-2*). That is true, but there is a catch: because the language is easy to learn and put to use, many practicing Python programmers leverage only a fraction of its powerful features.

An experienced programmer may start writing useful Python code in a matter of hours. As the first productive hours become weeks and months, a lot of developers go on writing Python code with a very strong accent carried from languages learned before. Even if Python is your first language, often in academia and in introductory books it is presented while carefully avoiding language-specific features.

As a teacher introducing Python to programmers experienced in other languages, I see another problem that this book tries to address: we only miss stuff we know about. Coming from another language, anyone may guess that Python supports regular expressions, and look that up in the docs. But if you've never seen tuple unpacking or descriptors before, you will probably not search for them, and you may end up not using those features just because they are specific to Python.

This book is not an A-to-Z exhaustive reference of Python. Its emphasis is on the language features that are either unique to Python or not found in many other popular languages. This is also mostly a book about the core language and some of its libraries. I will rarely talk about packages that are not in the standard library, even though the Python package index now lists more than 60,000 libraries, and many of them are incredibly useful.

---

1 Message to the comp.lang.python Usenet group, Dec. 23, 2002: "Acrimony in c.l.p" (*https://fpy.li/p-1*).

Who This Book Is For

This book was written for practicing Python programmers who want to become proficient in Python 3. I tested the examples in Python 3.10—most of them also in Python 3.9 and 3.8. When an example requires Python 3.10, it should be clearly marked.

If you are not sure whether you know enough Python to follow along, review the topics of the official Python tutorial (*https://fpy.li/p-3*). Topics covered in the tutorial will not be explained here, except for some features that are new.

Who This Book Is Not For

If you are just learning Python, this book is going to be hard to follow. Not only that, if you read it too early in your Python journey, it may give you the impression that every Python script should leverage special methods and metaprogramming tricks. Premature abstraction is as bad as premature optimization.

Five Books in One

I recommend that everyone read Chapter 1, "The Python Data Model". The core audience for this book should not have trouble jumping directly to any part in this book after Chapter 1, but often I assume you've read preceding chapters in each specific part. Think of Parts I through V as books within the book.

I tried to emphasize using what is available before discussing how to build your own. For example, in Part I, Chapter 2 covers sequence types that are ready to use, including some that don't get a lot of attention, like `collections.deque`. Building user-defined sequences is only addressed in Part III, where we also see how to leverage the abstract base classes (ABCs) from `collections.abc`. Creating your own ABCs is discussed even later in Part III, because I believe it's important to be comfortable using an ABC before writing your own.

This approach has a few advantages. First, knowing what is ready to use can save you from reinventing the wheel. We use existing collection classes more often than we implement our own, and we can give more attention to the advanced usage of available tools by deferring the discussion on how to create new ones. We are also more likely to inherit from existing ABCs than to create a new ABC from scratch. And finally, I believe it is easier to understand the abstractions after you've seen them in action.

The downside of this strategy is the forward references scattered throughout the chapters. I hope these will be easier to tolerate now that you know why I chose this path.

How the Book Is Organized

Here are the main topics in each part of the book:

Part I, "Data Structures"
> Chapter 1 introduces the Python Data Model and explains why the special methods (e.g., `__repr__`) are the key to the consistent behavior of objects of all types. Special methods are covered in more detail throughout the book. The remaining chapters in this part cover the use of collection types: sequences, mappings, and sets, as well as the str versus bytes split—the cause of much celebration among Python 3 users and much pain for Python 2 users migrating their codebases. Also covered are the high-level class builders in the standard library: named tuple factories and the `@dataclass` decorator. Pattern matching—new in Python 3.10—is covered in sections in Chapters 2, 3, and 5, which discuss sequence patterns, mapping patterns, and class patterns. The last chapter in Part I is about the life cycle of objects: references, mutability, and garbage collection.

Part II, "Functions as Objects"
> Here we talk about functions as first-class objects in the language: what that means, how it affects some popular design patterns, and how to implement function decorators by leveraging closures. Also covered here is the general concept of callables in Python, function attributes, introspection, parameter annotations, and the new `nonlocal` declaration in Python 3. Chapter 8 introduces the major new topic of type hints in function signatures.

Part III, "Classes and Protocols"
> Now the focus is on building classes "by hand"—as opposed to using the class builders covered in Chapter 5. Like any Object-Oriented (OO) language, Python has its particular set of features that may or may not be present in the language in which you and I learned class-based programming. The chapters explain how to build your own collections, abstract base classes (ABCs), and protocols, as well as how to cope with multiple inheritance, and how to implement operator overloading—when that makes sense. Chapter 15 continues the coverage of type hints.

Part IV, "Control Flow"
> Covered in this part are the language constructs and libraries that go beyond traditional control flow with conditionals, loops, and subroutines. We start with generators, then visit context managers and coroutines, including the challenging but powerful new `yield from` syntax. Chapter 18 includes a significant example using pattern matching in a simple but functional language interpreter. Chapter 19, "Concurrency Models in Python" is a new chapter presenting an overview of alternatives for concurrent and parallel processing in Python, their limitations, and how software architecture allows Python to operate at web scale. I rewrote

the chapter about *asynchronous programming* to emphasize core language features—e.g., `await`, `async dev`, `async for`, and `async with`, and show how they are used with *asyncio* and other frameworks.

Part V, "Metaprogramming"

This part starts with a review of techniques for building classes with attributes created dynamically to handle semi-structured data, such as JSON datasets. Next, we cover the familiar properties mechanism, before diving into how object attribute access works at a lower level in Python using descriptors. The relationship among functions, methods, and descriptors is explained. Throughout Part V, the step-by-step implementation of a field validation library uncovers subtle issues that lead to the advanced tools of the final chapter: class decorators and metaclasses.

Hands-On Approach

Often we'll use the interactive Python console to explore the language and libraries. I feel it is important to emphasize the power of this learning tool, particularly for those readers who've had more experience with static, compiled languages that don't provide a read-eval-print loop (REPL).

One of the standard Python testing packages, `doctest` (*https://fpy.li/doctest*), works by simulating console sessions and verifying that the expressions evaluate to the responses shown. I used `doctest` to check most of the code in this book, including the console listings. You don't need to use or even know about `doctest` to follow along: the key feature of doctests is that they look like transcripts of interactive Python console sessions, so you can easily try out the demonstrations yourself.

Sometimes I will explain what we want to accomplish by showing a doctest before the code that makes it pass. Firmly establishing what is to be done before thinking about how to do it helps focus our coding effort. Writing tests first is the basis of test-driven development (TDD), and I've also found it helpful when teaching. If you are unfamiliar with `doctest`, take a look at its documentation (*https://fpy.li/doctest*) and this book's example code repository (*https://fpy.li/code*).

I also wrote unit tests for some of the larger examples using *pytest*—which I find easier to use and more powerful than the *unittest* module in the standard library. You'll find that you can verify the correctness of most of the code in the book by typing `python3 -m doctest example_script.py` or `pytest` in the command shell of your OS. The *pytest.ini* configuration at the root of the example code repository (*https://fpy.li/code*) ensures that doctests are collected and executed by the `pytest` command.

Soapbox: My Personal Perspective

I have been using, teaching, and debating Python since 1998, and I enjoy studying and comparing programming languages, their design, and the theory behind them. At the end of some chapters, I have added "Soapbox" sidebars with my own perspective about Python and other languages. Feel free to skip these if you are not into such discussions. Their content is completely optional.

Companion Website: fluentpython.com

Covering new features—like type hints, data classes, and pattern matching—made this second edition almost 30% larger than the first. To keep the book luggable, I moved some content to *fluentpython.com*. You will find links to articles I published there in several chapters. Some sample chapters are also in the companion website. The full text is available online (*https://fpy.li/p-4*) at the O'Reilly Learning (*https://fpy.li/p-5*) subscription service. The example code repository is on GitHub (*https://fpy.li/code*).

Conventions Used in This Book

The following typographical conventions are used in this book:

Italic
: Indicates new terms, URLs, email addresses, filenames, and file extensions.

`Constant width`
: Used for program listings, as well as within paragraphs to refer to program elements such as variable or function names, databases, data types, environment variables, statements, and keywords.

: Note that when a line break falls within a `constant_width` term, a hyphen is not added—it could be misunderstood as part of the term.

`Constant width bold`
: Shows commands or other text that should be typed literally by the user.

`Constant width italic`
: Shows text that should be replaced with user-supplied values or by values determined by context.

This element signifies a tip or suggestion.

This element signifies a general note.

This element indicates a warning or caution.

Using Code Examples

Every script and most code snippets that appear in the book are available in the Fluent Python code repository on GitHub at *https://fpy.li/code*.

If you have a technical question or a problem using the code examples, please send email to *bookquestions@oreilly.com*.

This book is here to help you get your job done. In general, if example code is offered with this book, you may use it in your programs and documentation. You do not need to contact us for permission unless you're reproducing a significant portion of the code. For example, writing a program that uses several chunks of code from this book does not require permission. Selling or distributing examples from O'Reilly books does require permission. Answering a question by citing this book and quoting example code does not require permission. Incorporating a significant amount of example code from this book into your product's documentation does require permission.

We appreciate, but generally do not require, attribution. An attribution usually includes the title, author, publisher, and ISBN, e.g., "*Fluent Python*, 2nd ed., by Luciano Ramalho (O'Reilly). Copyright 2022 Luciano Ramalho, 978-1-492-05635-5."

If you feel your use of code examples falls outside fair use or the permission given above, feel free to contact us at *permissions@oreilly.com*.

O'Reilly Online Learning

 For more than 40 years, *O'Reilly Media* has provided technology and business training, knowledge, and insight to help companies succeed.

Our unique network of experts and innovators share their knowledge and expertise through books, articles, and our online learning platform. O'Reilly's online learning platform gives you on-demand access to live training courses, in-depth learning paths, interactive coding environments, and a vast collection of text and video from O'Reilly and 200+ other publishers. For more information, visit *http://oreilly.com*.

How to Contact Us

Please address comments and questions concerning this book to the publisher:

O'Reilly Media, Inc.
1005 Gravenstein Highway North
Sebastopol, CA 95472
800-998-9938 (in the United States or Canada)
707-829-0515 (international or local)
707-829-0104 (fax)

We have a web page for this book, where we list errata, examples, and any additional information. You can access this page at *https://fpy.li/p-4*.

Email *bookquestions@oreilly.com* to comment or ask technical questions about this book.

For news and information about our books and courses, visit *http://oreilly.com*.

Find us on Facebook: *http://facebook.com/oreilly*.

Follow us on Twitter: *https://twitter.com/oreillymedia*.

Watch us on YouTube: *http://www.youtube.com/oreillymedia*.

Acknowledgments

I did not expect updating a Python book five years later to be such a major undertaking, but it was. Marta Mello, my beloved wife, was always there when I needed her. My dear friend Leonardo Rochael helped me from the earliest writing to the final technical review, including consolidating and double-checking the feedback from the other tech reviewers, readers, and editors. I honestly don't know if I'd have made it without your support, Marta and Leo. Thank you so much!

Jürgen Gmach, Caleb Hattingh, Jess Males, Leonardo Rochael, and Miroslav Šedivý were the outstanding technical review team for the second edition. They reviewed the whole book. Bill Behrman, Bruce Eckel, Renato Oliveira, and Rodrigo Bernardo Pimentel reviewed specific chapters. Their many suggestions from different perspectives made the book much better.

Many readers sent corrections or made other contributions during the early release phase, including: Guilherme Alves, Christiano Anderson, Konstantin Baikov, K. Alex Birch, Michael Boesl, Lucas Brunialti, Sergio Cortez, Gino Crecco, Chukwuerika Dike, Juan Esteras, Federico Fissore, Will Frey, Tim Gates, Alexander Hagerman, Chen Hanxiao, Sam Hyeong, Simon Ilincev, Parag Kalra, Tim King, David Kwast, Tina Lapine, Wanpeng Li, Guto Maia, Scott Martindale, Mark Meyer, Andy McFarland, Chad McIntire, Diego Rabatone Oliveira, Francesco Piccoli, Meredith Rawls, Michael Robinson, Federico Tula Rovaletti, Tushar Sadhwani, Arthur Constantino Scardua, Randal L. Schwartz, Avichai Sefati, Guannan Shen, William Simpson, Vivek Vashist, Jerry Zhang, Paul Zuradzki—and others who did not want to be named, sent corrections after I delivered the draft, or are omitted because I failed to record their names—sorry.

During my research, I learned about typing, concurrency, pattern matching, and metaprogramming while interacting with Michael Albert, Pablo Aguilar, Kaleb Barrett, David Beazley, J. S. O. Bueno, Bruce Eckel, Martin Fowler, Ivan Levkivskyi, Alex Martelli, Peter Norvig, Sebastian Rittau, Guido van Rossum, Carol Willing, and Jelle Zijlstra.

O'Reilly editors Jeff Bleiel, Jill Leonard, and Amelia Blevins made suggestions that improved the flow of the book in many places. Jeff Bleiel and production editor Danny Elfanbaum supported me throughout this long marathon.

The insights and suggestions of every one of them made the book better and more accurate. Inevitably, there will still be bugs of my own creation in the final product. I apologize in advance.

Finally, I want to extend my heartfelt thanks to my colleagues at Thoughtworks Brazil —and especially to my sponsor, Alexey Bôas—who supported this project in many ways, all the way.

Of course, everyone who helped me understand Python and write the first edition now deserves double thanks. There would be no second edition without a successful first.

Acknowledgments for the First Edition

The Bauhaus chess set by Josef Hartwig is an example of excellent design: beautiful, simple, and clear. Guido van Rossum, son of an architect and brother of a master font designer, created a masterpiece of language design. I love teaching Python because it is beautiful, simple, and clear.

Alex Martelli and Anna Ravenscroft were the first people to see the outline of this book and encouraged me to submit it to O'Reilly for publication. Their books taught me idiomatic Python and are models of clarity, accuracy, and depth in technical writing. Alex's 6,200+ Stack Overflow posts (*https://fpy.li/p-7*) are a fountain of insights about the language and its proper use.

Martelli and Ravenscroft were also technical reviewers of this book, along with Lennart Regebro and Leonardo Rochael. Everyone in this outstanding technical review team has at least 15 years of Python experience, with many contributions to high-impact Python projects in close contact with other developers in the community. Together they sent me hundreds of corrections, suggestions, questions, and opinions, adding tremendous value to the book. Victor Stinner kindly reviewed Chapter 21, bringing his expertise as an `asyncio` maintainer to the technical review team. It was a great privilege and a pleasure to collaborate with them over these past several months.

Editor Meghan Blanchette was an outstanding mentor, helping me improve the organization and flow of the book, letting me know when it was boring, and keeping me from delaying even more. Brian MacDonald edited chapters in Part II while Meghan was away. I enjoyed working with them, and with everyone I've contacted at O'Reilly, including the Atlas development and support team (Atlas is the O'Reilly book publishing platform, which I was fortunate to use to write this book).

Mario Domenech Goulart provided numerous, detailed suggestions starting with the first early release. I also received valuable feedback from Dave Pawson, Elias Dorneles, Leonardo Alexandre Ferreira Leite, Bruce Eckel, J. S. Bueno, Rafael Gonçalves, Alex Chiaranda, Guto Maia, Lucas Vido, and Lucas Brunialti.

Over the years, a number of people urged me to become an author, but the most persuasive were Rubens Prates, Aurelio Jargas, Rudá Moura, and Rubens Altimari. Mauricio Bussab opened many doors for me, including my first real shot at writing a book. Renzo Nuccitelli supported this writing project all the way, even if that meant a slow start for our partnership at *python.pro.br*.

The wonderful Brazilian Python community is knowledgeable, generous, and fun. The Python Brasil group (*https://fpy.li/p-9*) has thousands of people, and our national conferences bring together hundreds, but the most influential in my journey as a Pythonista were Leonardo Rochael, Adriano Petrich, Daniel Vainsencher, Rodrigo RBP Pimentel, Bruno Gola, Leonardo Santagada, Jean Ferri, Rodrigo Senra, J. S.

Bueno, David Kwast, Luiz Irber, Osvaldo Santana, Fernando Masanori, Henrique Bastos, Gustavo Niemayer, Pedro Werneck, Gustavo Barbieri, Lalo Martins, Danilo Bellini, and Pedro Kroger.

Dorneles Tremea was a great friend (incredibly generous with his time and knowledge), an amazing hacker, and the most inspiring leader of the Brazilian Python Association. He left us too early.

My students over the years taught me a lot through their questions, insights, feedback, and creative solutions to problems. Érico Andrei and Simples Consultoria made it possible for me to focus on being a Python teacher for the first time.

Martijn Faassen was my Grok mentor and shared invaluable insights with me about Python and Neanderthals. His work and that of Paul Everitt, Chris McDonough, Tres Seaver, Jim Fulton, Shane Hathaway, Lennart Regebro, Alan Runyan, Alexander Limi, Martijn Pieters, Godefroid Chapelle, and others from the Zope, Plone, and Pyramid planets have been decisive in my career. Thanks to Zope and surfing the first web wave, I was able to start making a living with Python in 1998. José Octavio Castro Neves was my partner in the first Python-centric software house in Brazil.

I have too many gurus in the wider Python community to list them all, but besides those already mentioned, I am indebted to Steve Holden, Raymond Hettinger, A.M. Kuchling, David Beazley, Fredrik Lundh, Doug Hellmann, Nick Coghlan, Mark Pilgrim, Martijn Pieters, Bruce Eckel, Michele Simionato, Wesley Chun, Brandon Craig Rhodes, Philip Guo, Daniel Greenfeld, Audrey Roy, and Brett Slatkin for teaching me new and better ways to teach Python.

Most of these pages were written in my home office and in two labs: CoffeeLab and Garoa Hacker Clube. CoffeeLab (*https://fpy.li/p-10*) is the caffeine-geek headquarters in Vila Madalena, São Paulo, Brazil. Garoa Hacker Clube (*https://fpy.li/p-11*) is a hackerspace open to all: a community lab where anyone can freely try out new ideas.

The Garoa community provided inspiration, infrastructure, and slack. I think Aleph would enjoy this book.

My mother, Maria Lucia, and my father, Jairo, always supported me in every way. I wish he was here to see the book; I am glad I can share it with her.

My wife, Marta Mello, endured 15 months of a husband who was always working, but remained supportive and coached me through some critical moments in the project when I feared I might drop out of the marathon.

Thank you all, for everything.

## PART I

Data Structures

## CHAPTER 1

The Python Data Model

Guido's sense of the aesthetics of language design is amazing. I've met many fine language designers who could build theoretically beautiful languages that no one would ever use, but Guido is one of those rare people who can build a language that is just slightly less theoretically beautiful but thereby is a joy to write programs in.

—Jim Hugunin, creator of Jython, cocreator of AspectJ, and architect of the .Net DLR[1]

One of the best qualities of Python is its consistency. After working with Python for a while, you are able to start making informed, correct guesses about features that are new to you.

However, if you learned another object-oriented language before Python, you may find it strange to use len(collection) instead of collection.len(). This apparent oddity is the tip of an iceberg that, when properly understood, is the key to everything we call *Pythonic*. The iceberg is called the Python Data Model, and it is the API that we use to make our own objects play well with the most idiomatic language features.

You can think of the data model as a description of Python as a framework. It formalizes the interfaces of the building blocks of the language itself, such as sequences, functions, iterators, coroutines, classes, context managers, and so on.

When using a framework, we spend a lot of time coding methods that are called by the framework. The same happens when we leverage the Python Data Model to build new classes. The Python interpreter invokes special methods to perform basic object operations, often triggered by special syntax. The special method names are always

---

1 "Story of Jython" (*https://fpy.li/1-1*), written as a foreword to *Jython Essentials* by Samuele Pedroni and Noel Rappin (O'Reilly).

written with leading and trailing double underscores. For example, the syntax `obj[key]` is supported by the `__getitem__` special method. In order to evaluate `my_collection[key]`, the interpreter calls `my_collection.__getitem__(key)`.

We implement special methods when we want our objects to support and interact with fundamental language constructs such as:

- Collections
- Attribute access
- Iteration (including asynchronous iteration using `async for`)
- Operator overloading
- Function and method invocation
- String representation and formatting
- Asynchronous programming using `await`
- Object creation and destruction
- Managed contexts using the `with` or `async with` statements

Magic and Dunder

The term *magic method* is slang for special method, but how do we talk about a specific method like `__getitem__`? I learned to say "dunder-getitem" from author and teacher Steve Holden. "Dunder" is a shortcut for "double underscore before and after." That's why the special methods are also known as *dunder methods*. The "Lexical Analysis" (*https://fpy.li/1-3*) chapter of *The Python Language Reference* warns that "*Any* use of `__*__` names, in any context, that does not follow explicitly documented use, is subject to breakage without warning."

What's New in This Chapter

This chapter had few changes from the first edition because it is an introduction to the Python Data Model, which is quite stable. The most significant changes are:

- Special methods supporting asynchronous programming and other new features, added to the tables in "Overview of Special Methods" on page 15.
- Figure 1-2 showing the use of special methods in "Collection API" on page 14, including the `collections.abc.Collection` abstract base class introduced in Python 3.6.

Also, here and throughout this second edition I adopted the *f-string* syntax introduced in Python 3.6, which is more readable and often more convenient than the older string formatting notations: the `str.format()` method and the `%` operator.

 One reason to still use `my_fmt.format()` is when the definition of `my_fmt` must be in a different place in the code than where the formatting operation needs to happen. For instance, when `my_fmt` has multiple lines and is better defined in a constant, or when it must come from a configuration file, or from the database. Those are real needs, but don't happen very often.

A Pythonic Card Deck

Example 1-1 is simple, but it demonstrates the power of implementing just two special methods, `__getitem__` and `__len__`.

Example 1-1. A deck as a sequence of playing cards

```
import collections

Card = collections.namedtuple('Card', ['rank', 'suit'])

class FrenchDeck:
    ranks = [str(n) for n in range(2, 11)] + list('JQKA')
    suits = 'spades diamonds clubs hearts'.split()

    def __init__(self):
        self._cards = [Card(rank, suit) for suit in self.suits
                                        for rank in self.ranks]

    def __len__(self):
        return len(self._cards)

    def __getitem__(self, position):
        return self._cards[position]
```

The first thing to note is the use of `collections.namedtuple` to construct a simple class to represent individual cards. We use `namedtuple` to build classes of objects that are just bundles of attributes with no custom methods, like a database record. In the example, we use it to provide a nice representation for the cards in the deck, as shown in the console session:

```
>>> beer_card = Card('7', 'diamonds')
>>> beer_card
Card(rank='7', suit='diamonds')
```

But the point of this example is the FrenchDeck class. It's short, but it packs a punch. First, like any standard Python collection, a deck responds to the len() function by returning the number of cards in it:

```
>>> deck = FrenchDeck()
>>> len(deck)
52
```

Reading specific cards from the deck—say, the first or the last—is easy, thanks to the __getitem__ method:

```
>>> deck[0]
Card(rank='2', suit='spades')
>>> deck[-1]
Card(rank='A', suit='hearts')
```

Should we create a method to pick a random card? No need. Python already has a function to get a random item from a sequence: random.choice. We can use it on a deck instance:

```
>>> from random import choice
>>> choice(deck)
Card(rank='3', suit='hearts')
>>> choice(deck)
Card(rank='K', suit='spades')
>>> choice(deck)
Card(rank='2', suit='clubs')
```

We've just seen two advantages of using special methods to leverage the Python Data Model:

- Users of your classes don't have to memorize arbitrary method names for standard operations. ("How to get the number of items? Is it .size(), .length(), or what?")
- It's easier to benefit from the rich Python standard library and avoid reinventing the wheel, like the random.choice function.

But it gets better.

Because our __getitem__ delegates to the [] operator of self._cards, our deck automatically supports slicing. Here's how we look at the top three cards from a brand-new deck, and then pick just the aces by starting at index 12 and skipping 13 cards at a time:

```
>>> deck[:3]
[Card(rank='2', suit='spades'), Card(rank='3', suit='spades'),
Card(rank='4', suit='spades')]
>>> deck[12::13]
[Card(rank='A', suit='spades'), Card(rank='A', suit='diamonds'),
Card(rank='A', suit='clubs'), Card(rank='A', suit='hearts')]
```

Just by implementing the __getitem__ special method, our deck is also iterable:

```
>>> for card in deck:  # doctest: +ELLIPSIS
...     print(card)
Card(rank='2', suit='spades')
Card(rank='3', suit='spades')
Card(rank='4', suit='spades')
...
```

We can also iterate over the deck in reverse:

```
>>> for card in reversed(deck):  # doctest: +ELLIPSIS
...     print(card)
Card(rank='A', suit='hearts')
Card(rank='K', suit='hearts')
Card(rank='Q', suit='hearts')
...
```

Ellipsis in doctests

Whenever possible, I extracted the Python console listings in this book from doctest (*https://fpy.li/doctest*) to ensure accuracy. When the output was too long, the elided part is marked by an ellipsis (...), like in the last line in the preceding code. In such cases, I used the # doctest: +ELLIPSIS directive to make the doctest pass. If you are trying these examples in the interactive console, you may omit the doctest comments altogether.

Iteration is often implicit. If a collection has no __contains__ method, the in operator does a sequential scan. Case in point: in works with our FrenchDeck class because it is iterable. Check it out:

```
>>> Card('Q', 'hearts') in deck
True
>>> Card('7', 'beasts') in deck
False
```

How about sorting? A common system of ranking cards is by rank (with aces being highest), then by suit in the order of spades (highest), hearts, diamonds, and clubs (lowest). Here is a function that ranks cards by that rule, returning 0 for the 2 of clubs and 51 for the ace of spades:

```
suit_values = dict(spades=3, hearts=2, diamonds=1, clubs=0)

def spades_high(card):
    rank_value = FrenchDeck.ranks.index(card.rank)
    return rank_value * len(suit_values) + suit_values[card.suit]
```

Given spades_high, we can now list our deck in order of increasing rank:

```
>>> for card in sorted(deck, key=spades_high):  # doctest: +ELLIPSIS
...         print(card)
Card(rank='2', suit='clubs')
Card(rank='2', suit='diamonds')
Card(rank='2', suit='hearts')
... (46 cards omitted)
Card(rank='A', suit='diamonds')
Card(rank='A', suit='hearts')
Card(rank='A', suit='spades')
```

Although FrenchDeck implicitly inherits from the object class, most of its functionality is not inherited, but comes from leveraging the data model and composition. By implementing the special methods __len__ and __getitem__, our FrenchDeck behaves like a standard Python sequence, allowing it to benefit from core language features (e.g., iteration and slicing) and from the standard library, as shown by the examples using random.choice, reversed, and sorted. Thanks to composition, the __len__ and __getitem__ implementations can delegate all the work to a list object, self._cards.

How About Shuffling?

As implemented so far, a FrenchDeck cannot be shuffled because it is *immutable*: the cards and their positions cannot be changed, except by violating encapsulation and handling the _cards attribute directly. In Chapter 13, we will fix that by adding a one-line __setitem__ method.

How Special Methods Are Used

The first thing to know about special methods is that they are meant to be called by the Python interpreter, and not by you. You don't write my_object.__len__(). You write len(my_object) and, if my_object is an instance of a user-defined class, then Python calls the __len__ method you implemented.

But the interpreter takes a shortcut when dealing for built-in types like list, str, bytearray, or extensions like the NumPy arrays. Python variable-sized collections written in C include a struct[2] called PyVarObject, which has an ob_size field holding the number of items in the collection. So, if my_object is an instance of one of those built-ins, then len(my_object) retrieves the value of the ob_size field, and this is much faster than calling a method.

---

2 A C struct is a record type with named fields.

More often than not, the special method call is implicit. For example, the statement `for i in x:` actually causes the invocation of `iter(x)`, which in turn may call `x.__iter__()` if that is available, or use `x.__getitem__()`, as in the `FrenchDeck` example.

Normally, your code should not have many direct calls to special methods. Unless you are doing a lot of metaprogramming, you should be implementing special methods more often than invoking them explicitly. The only special method that is frequently called by user code directly is `__init__` to invoke the initializer of the superclass in your own `__init__` implementation.

If you need to invoke a special method, it is usually better to call the related built-in function (e.g., `len`, `iter`, `str`, etc.). These built-ins call the corresponding special method, but often provide other services and—for built-in types—are faster than method calls. See, for example, "Using iter with a Callable" on page 602 in Chapter 17.

In the next sections, we'll see some of the most important uses of special methods:

- Emulating numeric types
- String representation of objects
- Boolean value of an object
- Implementing collections

Emulating Numeric Types

Several special methods allow user objects to respond to operators such as +. We will cover that in more detail in Chapter 16, but here our goal is to further illustrate the use of special methods through another simple example.

We will implement a class to represent two-dimensional vectors—that is, Euclidean vectors like those used in math and physics (see Figure 1-1).

The built-in `complex` type can be used to represent two-dimensional vectors, but our class can be extended to represent *n*-dimensional vectors. We will do that in Chapter 17.

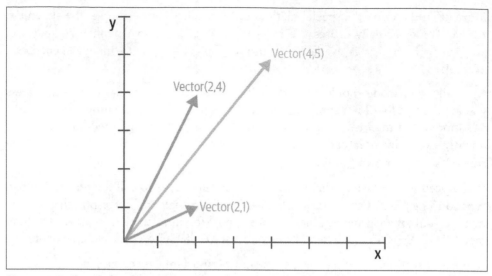

Figure 1-1. Example of two-dimensional vector addition; Vector(2, 4) + Vector(2, 1) results in Vector(4, 5).

We will start designing the API for such a class by writing a simulated console session that we can use later as a doctest. The following snippet tests the vector addition pictured in Figure 1-1:

```
>>> v1 = Vector(2, 4)
>>> v2 = Vector(2, 1)
>>> v1 + v2
Vector(4, 5)
```

Note how the + operator results in a new Vector, displayed in a friendly format at the console.

The abs built-in function returns the absolute value of integers and floats, and the magnitude of complex numbers, so to be consistent, our API also uses abs to calculate the magnitude of a vector:

```
>>> v = Vector(3, 4)
>>> abs(v)
5.0
```

We can also implement the * operator to perform scalar multiplication (i.e., multiplying a vector by a number to make a new vector with the same direction and a multiplied magnitude):

```
>>> v * 3
Vector(9, 12)
>>> abs(v * 3)
15.0
```

Example 1-2 is a Vector class implementing the operations just described, through the use of the special methods __repr__, __abs__, __add__, and __mul__.

Example 1-2. A simple two-dimensional vector class

```
"""
vector2d.py: a simplistic class demonstrating some special methods

It is simplistic for didactic reasons. It lacks proper error handling,
especially in the ``__add__`` and ``__mul__`` methods.

This example is greatly expanded later in the book.

Addition::

    >>> v1 = Vector(2, 4)
    >>> v2 = Vector(2, 1)
    >>> v1 + v2
    Vector(4, 5)

Absolute value::

    >>> v = Vector(3, 4)
    >>> abs(v)
    5.0

Scalar multiplication::

    >>> v * 3
    Vector(9, 12)
    >>> abs(v * 3)
    15.0

"""


import math

class Vector:

    def __init__(self, x=0, y=0):
        self.x = x
        self.y = y

    def __repr__(self):
        return f'Vector({self.x!r}, {self.y!r})'

    def __abs__(self):
        return math.hypot(self.x, self.y)

    def __bool__(self):
```

```
        return bool(abs(self))

    def __add__(self, other):
        x = self.x + other.x
        y = self.y + other.y
        return Vector(x, y)

    def __mul__(self, scalar):
        return Vector(self.x * scalar, self.y * scalar)
```

We implemented five special methods in addition to the familiar __init__. Note that none of them is directly called within the class or in the typical usage of the class illustrated by the doctests. As mentioned before, the Python interpreter is the only frequent caller of most special methods.

Example 1-2 implements two operators: + and *, to show basic usage of __add__ and __mul__. In both cases, the methods create and return a new instance of Vector, and do not modify either operand—self or other are merely read. This is the expected behavior of infix operators: to create new objects and not touch their operands. I will have a lot more to say about that in Chapter 16.

> As implemented, Example 1-2 allows multiplying a Vector by a number, but not a number by a Vector, which violates the commutative property of scalar multiplication. We will fix that with the special method __rmul__ in Chapter 16.

In the following sections, we discuss the other special methods in Vector.

String Representation

The __repr__ special method is called by the repr built-in to get the string representation of the object for inspection. Without a custom __repr__, Python's console would display a Vector instance <Vector object at 0x10e100070>.

The interactive console and debugger call repr on the results of the expressions evaluated, as does the %r placeholder in classic formatting with the % operator, and the !r conversion field in the new format string syntax (*https://fpy.li/1-4*) used in *f-strings* the str.format method.

Note that the *f-string* in our __repr__ uses !r to get the standard representation of the attributes to be displayed. This is good practice, because it shows the crucial difference between Vector(1, 2) and Vector('1', '2')—the latter would not work in the context of this example, because the constructor's arguments should be numbers, not str.

The string returned by __repr__ should be unambiguous and, if possible, match the source code necessary to re-create the represented object. That is why our Vector representation looks like calling the constructor of the class (e.g., Vector(3, 4)).

In contrast, __str__ is called by the str() built-in and implicitly used by the print function. It should return a string suitable for display to end users.

Sometimes same string returned by __repr__ is user-friendly, and you don't need to code __str__ because the implementation inherited from the object class calls __repr__ as a fallback. Example 5-2 is one of several examples in this book with a custom __str__.

> Programmers with prior experience in languages with a toString method tend to implement __str__ and not __repr__. If you only implement one of these special methods in Python, choose __repr__.
>
> "What is the difference between __str__ and __repr__ in Python?" (*https://fpy.li/1-5*) is a Stack Overflow question with excellent contributions from Pythonistas Alex Martelli and Martijn Pieters.

Boolean Value of a Custom Type

Although Python has a bool type, it accepts any object in a Boolean context, such as the expression controlling an if or while statement, or as operands to and, or, and not. To determine whether a value x is *truthy* or *falsy*, Python applies bool(x), which returns either True or False.

By default, instances of user-defined classes are considered truthy, unless either __bool__ or __len__ is implemented. Basically, bool(x) calls x.__bool__() and uses the result. If __bool__ is not implemented, Python tries to invoke x.__len__(), and if that returns zero, bool returns False. Otherwise bool returns True.

Our implementation of __bool__ is conceptually simple: it returns False if the magnitude of the vector is zero, True otherwise. We convert the magnitude to a Boolean using bool(abs(self)) because __bool__ is expected to return a Boolean. Outside of __bool__ methods, it is rarely necessary to call bool() explicitly, because any object can be used in a Boolean context.

Note how the special method __bool__ allows your objects to follow the truth value testing rules defined in the "Built-in Types" chapter (*https://fpy.li/1-6*) of *The Python Standard Library* documentation.

A faster implementation of `Vector.__bool__` is this:

```
def __bool__(self):
    return bool(self.x or self.y)
```

This is harder to read, but avoids the trip through abs, `__abs__`, the squares, and square root. The explicit conversion to `bool` is needed because `__bool__` must return a Boolean, and `or` returns either operand as is: `x or y` evaluates to `x` if that is truthy, otherwise the result is `y`, whatever that is.

Collection API

Figure 1-2 documents the interfaces of the essential collection types in the language. All the classes in the diagram are ABCs—*abstract base classes*. ABCs and the `collections.abc` module are covered in Chapter 13. The goal of this brief section is to give a panoramic view of Python's most important collection interfaces, showing how they are built from special methods.

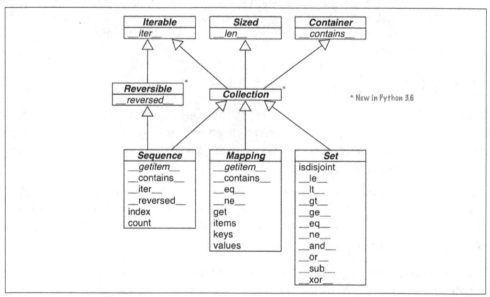

Figure 1-2. UML class diagram with fundamental collection types. Method names in italic are abstract, so they must be implemented by concrete subclasses such as `list` and `dict`. The remaining methods have concrete implementations, therefore subclasses can inherit them.

Each of the top ABCs has a single special method. The `Collection` ABC (new in Python 3.6) unifies the three essential interfaces that every collection should implement:

- **Iterable** to support `for`, unpacking (*https://fpy.li/1-7*), and other forms of iteration
- **Sized** to support the `len` built-in function
- **Container** to support the `in` operator

Python does not require concrete classes to actually inherit from any of these ABCs. Any class that implements `__len__` satisfies the `Sized` interface.

Three very important specializations of `Collection` are:

- **Sequence**, formalizing the interface of built-ins like `list` and `str`
- **Mapping**, implemented by `dict`, `collections.defaultdict`, etc.
- **Set**, the interface of the `set` and `frozenset` built-in types

Only `Sequence` is `Reversible`, because sequences support arbitrary ordering of their contents, while mappings and sets do not.

 Since Python 3.7, the `dict` type is officially "ordered," but that only means that the key insertion order is preserved. You cannot rearrange the keys in a `dict` however you like.

All the special methods in the `Set` ABC implement infix operators. For example, `a & b` computes the intersection of sets a and b, and is implemented in the `__and__` special method.

The next two chapters will cover standard library sequences, mappings, and sets in detail.

Now let's consider the major categories of special methods defined in the Python Data Model.

Overview of Special Methods

The "Data Model" chapter (*https://fpy.li/dtmodel*) of *The Python Language Reference* lists more than 80 special method names. More than half of them implement arithmetic, bitwise, and comparison operators. As an overview of what is available, see the following tables.

Table 1-1 shows special method names, excluding those used to implement infix operators or core math functions like `abs`. Most of these methods will be covered throughout the book, including the most recent additions: asynchronous special methods such as __anext__ (added in Python 3.5), and the class customization hook, __init_subclass__ (from Python 3.6).

Table 1-1. Special method names (operators excluded)

Category	Method names
String/bytes representation	`__repr__` `__str__` `__format__` `__bytes__` `__fspath__`
Conversion to number	`__bool__` `__complex__` `__int__` `__float__` `__hash__` `__index__`
Emulating collections	`__len__` `__getitem__` `__setitem__` `__delitem__` `__contains__`
Iteration	`__iter__` `__aiter__` `__next__` `__anext__` `__reversed__`
Callable or coroutine execution	`__call__` `__await__`
Context management	`__enter__` `__exit__` `__aexit__` `__aenter__`
Instance creation and destruction	`__new__` `__init__` `__del__`
Attribute management	`__getattr__` `__getattribute__` `__setattr__` `__delattr__` `__dir__`
Attribute descriptors	`__get__` `__set__` `__delete__` `__set_name__`
Abstract base classes	`__instancecheck__` `__subclasscheck__`
Class metaprogramming	`__prepare__` `__init_subclass__` `__class_getitem__` `__mro_entries__`

Infix and numerical operators are supported by the special methods listed in Table 1-2. Here the most recent names are __matmul__, __rmatmul__, and __imatmul__, added in Python 3.5 to support the use of @ as an infix operator for matrix multiplication, as we'll see in Chapter 16.

Table 1-2. Special method names and symbols for operators

Operator category	Symbols	Method names
Unary numeric	`-  +  abs()`	`__neg__` `__pos__` `__abs__`
Rich comparison	`<  <=  ==  !=  >  >=`	`__lt__` `__le__` `__eq__` `__ne__` `__gt__` `__ge__`
Arithmetic	`+  -  *  /  //  %  @` `divmod()  round()  **` `pow()`	`__add__` `__sub__` `__mul__` `__truediv__` `__floordiv__` `__mod__` `__matmul__` `__divmod__` `__round__` `__pow__`
Reversed arithmetic	(arithmetic operators with swapped operands)	`__radd__` `__rsub__` `__rmul__` `__rtruediv__` `__rfloordiv__` `__rmod__` `__rmatmul__` `__rdivmod__` `__rpow__`
Augmented assignment arithmetic	`+=  -=  *=  /=  //=  %=` `@=  **=`	`__iadd__` `__isub__` `__imul__` `__itruediv__` `__ifloordiv__` `__imod__` `__imatmul__` `__ipow__`

Operator category	Symbols	Method names
Bitwise	`&` `|` `^` `<<` `>>` `~`	`__and__` `__or__` `__xor__` `__lshift__` `__rshift__` `__invert__`
Reversed bitwise	(bitwise operators with swapped operands)	`__rand__` `__ror__` `__rxor__` `__rlshift__` `__rrshift__`
Augmented assignment bitwise	`&=` `|=` `^=` `<<=` `>>=`	`__iand__` `__ior__` `__ixor__` `__ilshift__` `__irshift__`

Python calls a reversed operator special method on the second operand when the corresponding special method on the first operand cannot be used. Augmented assignments are shortcuts combining an infix operator with variable assignment, e.g., a += b.

Chapter 16 explains reversed operators and augmented assignment in detail.

Why len Is Not a Method

I asked this question to core developer Raymond Hettinger in 2013, and the key to his answer was a quote from "The Zen of Python" (*https://fpy.li/1-8*): "practicality beats purity." In "How Special Methods Are Used" on page 8, I described how `len(x)` runs very fast when x is an instance of a built-in type. No method is called for the built-in objects of CPython: the length is simply read from a field in a C struct. Getting the number of items in a collection is a common operation and must work efficiently for such basic and diverse types as `str`, `list`, `memoryview`, and so on.

In other words, `len` is not called as a method because it gets special treatment as part of the Python Data Model, just like `abs`. But thanks to the special method `__len__`, you can also make `len` work with your own custom objects. This is a fair compromise between the need for efficient built-in objects and the consistency of the language. Also from "The Zen of Python": "Special cases aren't special enough to break the rules."

If you think of `abs` and `len` as unary operators, you may be more inclined to forgive their functional look and feel, as opposed to the method call syntax one might expect in an object-oriented language. In fact, the ABC language—a direct ancestor of Python that pioneered many of its features—had an `#` operator that was the equivalent of `len` (you'd write `#s`). When used as an infix operator, written `x#s`, it counted the occurrences of x in s, which in Python you get as `s.count(x)`, for any sequence s.

Chapter Summary

By implementing special methods, your objects can behave like the built-in types, enabling the expressive coding style the community considers Pythonic.

A basic requirement for a Python object is to provide usable string representations of itself, one used for debugging and logging, another for presentation to end users. That is why the special methods `__repr__` and `__str__` exist in the data model.

Emulating sequences, as shown with the FrenchDeck example, is one of the most common uses of the special methods. For example, database libraries often return query results wrapped in sequence-like collections. Making the most of existing sequence types is the subject of Chapter 2. Implementing your own sequences will be covered in Chapter 12, when we create a multidimensional extension of the Vector class.

Thanks to operator overloading, Python offers a rich selection of numeric types, from the built-ins to `decimal.Decimal` and `fractions.Fraction`, all supporting infix arithmetic operators. The *NumPy* data science libraries support infix operators with matrices and tensors. Implementing operators—including reversed operators and augmented assignment—will be shown in Chapter 16 via enhancements of the Vector example.

The use and implementation of the majority of the remaining special methods of the Python Data Model are covered throughout this book.

Further Reading

The "Data Model" chapter (*https://fpy.li/dtmodel*) of *The Python Language Reference* is the canonical source for the subject of this chapter and much of this book.

Python in a Nutshell, 3rd ed. by Alex Martelli, Anna Ravenscroft, and Steve Holden (O'Reilly) has excellent coverage of the data model. Their description of the mechanics of attribute access is the most authoritative I've seen apart from the actual C source code of CPython. Martelli is also a prolific contributor to Stack Overflow, with more than 6,200 answers posted. See his user profile at Stack Overflow (*https://fpy.li/1-9*).

David Beazley has two books covering the data model in detail in the context of Python 3: *Python Essential Reference*, 4th ed. (Addison-Wesley), and *Python Cookbook*, 3rd ed. (O'Reilly), coauthored with Brian K. Jones.

The Art of the Metaobject Protocol (MIT Press) by Gregor Kiczales, Jim des Rivieres, and Daniel G. Bobrow explains the concept of a metaobject protocol, of which the Python Data Model is one example.

Soapbox

Data Model or Object Model?

What the Python documentation calls the "Python Data Model," most authors would say is the "Python object model." Martelli, Ravenscroft, and Holden's *Python in a Nutshell*, 3rd ed., and David Beazley's *Python Essential Reference*, 4th ed. are the best books covering the Python Data Model, but they refer to it as the "object model." On Wikipedia, the first definition of "object model" (*https://fpy.li/1-10*) is: "The properties of objects in general in a specific computer programming language." This is what the Python Data Model is about. In this book, I will use "data model" because the documentation favors that term when referring to the Python object model, and because it is the title of the chapter of *The Python Language Reference* (*https://fpy.li/dtmodel*) most relevant to our discussions.

Muggle Methods

The Original Hacker's Dictionary (*https://fpy.li/1-11*) defines *magic* as "yet unexplained, or too complicated to explain" or "a feature not generally publicized which allows something otherwise impossible."

The Ruby community calls their equivalent of the special methods *magic methods*. Many in the Python community adopt that term as well. I believe the special methods are the opposite of magic. Python and Ruby empower their users with a rich metaobject protocol that is fully documented, enabling muggles like you and me to emulate many of the features available to core developers who write the interpreters for those languages.

In contrast, consider Go. Some objects in that language have features that are magic, in the sense that we cannot emulate them in our own user-defined types. For example, Go arrays, strings, and maps support the use brackets for item access, as in a[i]. But there's no way to make the [] notation work with a new collection type that you define. Even worse, Go has no user-level concept of an iterable interface or an iterator object, therefore its for/range syntax is limited to supporting five "magic" built-in types, including arrays, strings, and maps.

Maybe in the future, the designers of Go will enhance its metaobject protocol. But currently, it is much more limited than what we have in Python or Ruby.

Metaobjects

The Art of the Metaobject Protocol (AMOP) is my favorite computer book title. But I mention it because the term *metaobject protocol* is useful to think about the Python Data Model and similar features in other languages. The *metaobject* part refers to the objects that are the building blocks of the language itself. In this context, *protocol* is a synonym of *interface*. So a *metaobject protocol* is a fancy synonym for object model: an API for core language constructs.

A rich metaobject protocol enables extending a language to support new programming paradigms. Gregor Kiczales, the first author of the *AMOP* book, later became a pioneer in aspect-oriented programming and the initial author of AspectJ, an extension of Java implementing that paradigm. Aspect-oriented programming is much easier to implement in a dynamic language like Python, and some frameworks do it. The most important example is *zope.interface* (*https://fpy.li/1-12*), part of the framework on which the Plone content management (*https://fpy.li/1-13*) system is built.

## CHAPTER 2

An Array of Sequences

> As you may have noticed, several of the operations mentioned work equally for texts, lists and tables. Texts, lists and tables together are called 'trains'. [...] The FOR command also works generically on trains.
>
> —Leo Geurts, Lambert Meertens, and Steven Pembertonm, *ABC Programmer's Handbook*[1]

Before creating Python, Guido was a contributor to the ABC language—a 10-year research project to design a programming environment for beginners. ABC introduced many ideas we now consider "Pythonic": generic operations on different types of sequences, built-in tuple and mapping types, structure by indentation, strong typing without variable declarations, and more. It's no accident that Python is so user-friendly.

Python inherited from ABC the uniform handling of sequences. Strings, lists, byte sequences, arrays, XML elements, and database results share a rich set of common operations, including iteration, slicing, sorting, and concatenation.

Understanding the variety of sequences available in Python saves us from reinventing the wheel, and their common interface inspires us to create APIs that properly support and leverage existing and future sequence types.

Most of the discussion in this chapter applies to sequences in general, from the familiar list to the str and bytes types added in Python 3. Specific topics on lists, tuples, arrays, and queues are also covered here, but the specifics of Unicode strings and byte sequences appear in Chapter 4. Also, the idea here is to cover sequence types that are ready to use. Creating your own sequence types is the subject of Chapter 12.

---

1 Leo Geurts, Lambert Meertens, and Steven Pemberton, *ABC Programmer's Handbook*, p. 8. (Bosko Books).

These are the main topics this chapter will cover:

- List comprehensions and the basics of generator expressions
- Using tuples as records versus using tuples as immutable lists
- Sequence unpacking and sequence patterns
- Reading from slices and writing to slices
- Specialized sequence types, like arrays and queues

What's New in This Chapter

The most important update in this chapter is "Pattern Matching with Sequences" on page 39. That's the first time the new pattern matching feature of Python 3.10 appears in this second edition.

Other changes are not updates but improvements over the first edition:

- New diagram and description of the internals of sequences, contrasting containers and flat sequences
- Brief comparison of the performance and storage characteristics of list versus tuple
- Caveats of tuples with mutable elements, and how to detect them if needed

I moved coverage of named tuples to "Classic Named Tuples" on page 169 in Chapter 5, where they are compared to typing.NamedTuple and @dataclass.

 To make room for new content and keep the page count within reason, the section "Managing Ordered Sequences with Bisect" from the first edition is now a post (*https://fpy.li/bisect*) in the *fluentpython.com* companion website.

Overview of Built-In Sequences

The standard library offers a rich selection of sequence types implemented in C:

Container sequences
Can hold items of different types, including nested containers. Some examples: list, tuple, and collections.deque.

Flat sequences
Hold items of one simple type. Some examples: str, bytes, and array.array.

A *container sequence* holds references to the objects it contains, which may be of any type, while a *flat sequence* stores the value of its contents in its own memory space, not as distinct Python objects. See Figure 2-1.

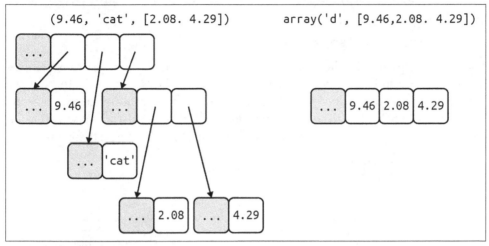

Figure 2-1. Simplified memory diagrams for a tuple *and an* array, *each with three items. Gray cells represent the in-memory header of each Python object—not drawn to proportion. The* tuple *has an array of references to its items. Each item is a separate Python object, possibly holding references to other Python objects, like that two-item list. In contrast, the Python* array *is a single object, holding a C language array of three doubles.*

Thus, flat sequences are more compact, but they are limited to holding primitive machine values like bytes, integers, and floats.

Every Python object in memory has a header with metadata. The simplest Python object, a float, has a value field and two metadata fields:

- ob_refcnt: the object's reference count
- ob_type: a pointer to the object's type
- ob_fval: a C double holding the value of the float

On a 64-bit Python build, each of those fields takes 8 bytes. That's why an array of floats is much more compact than a tuple of floats: the array is a single object holding the raw values of the floats, while the tuple consists of several objects—the tuple itself and each float object contained in it.

Another way of grouping sequence types is by mutability:

Mutable sequences
For example, `list`, `bytearray`, `array.array`, and `collections.deque`.

Immutable sequences
For example, `tuple`, `str`, and `bytes`.

Figure 2-2 helps visualize how mutable sequences inherit all methods from immutable sequences, and implement several additional methods. The built-in concrete sequence types do not actually subclass the `Sequence` and `MutableSequence` abstract base classes (ABCs), but they are *virtual subclasses* registered with those ABCs—as we'll see in Chapter 13. Being virtual subclasses, `tuple` and `list` pass these tests:

```
>>> from collections import abc
>>> issubclass(tuple, abc.Sequence)
True
>>> issubclass(list, abc.MutableSequence)
True
```

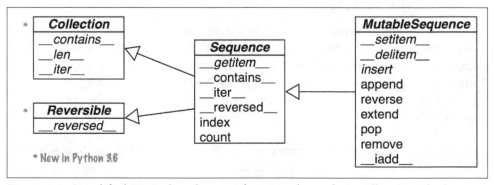

Figure 2-2. Simplified UML class diagram for some classes from collections.abc (superclasses are on the left; inheritance arrows point from subclasses to superclasses; names in italic are abstract classes and abstract methods).

Keep in mind these common traits: mutable versus immutable; container versus flat. They are helpful to extrapolate what you know about one sequence type to others.

The most fundamental sequence type is the `list`: a mutable container. I expect you are very familiar with lists, so we'll jump right into list comprehensions, a powerful way of building lists that is sometimes underused because the syntax may look unusual at first. Mastering list comprehensions opens the door to generator expressions, which—among other uses—can produce elements to fill up sequences of any type. Both are the subject of the next section.

List Comprehensions and Generator Expressions

A quick way to build a sequence is using a list comprehension (if the target is a `list`) or a generator expression (for other kinds of sequences). If you are not using these syntactic forms on a daily basis, I bet you are missing opportunities to write code that is more readable and often faster at the same time.

If you doubt my claim that these constructs are "more readable," read on. I'll try to convince you.

 For brevity, many Python programmers refer to list comprehensions as *listcomps*, and generator expressions as *genexps*. I will use these words as well.

List Comprehensions and Readability

Here is a test: which do you find easier to read, Example 2-1 or Example 2-2?

Example 2-1. Build a list of Unicode code points from a string

```
>>> symbols = '$¢£¥€¤'
>>> codes = []
>>> for symbol in symbols:
...     codes.append(ord(symbol))
...
>>> codes
[36, 162, 163, 165, 8364, 164]
```

Example 2-2. Build a list of Unicode code points from a string, using a listcomp

```
>>> symbols = '$¢£¥€¤'
>>> codes = [ord(symbol) for symbol in symbols]
>>> codes
[36, 162, 163, 165, 8364, 164]
```

Anybody who knows a little bit of Python can read Example 2-1. However, after learning about listcomps, I find Example 2-2 more readable because its intent is explicit.

A for loop may be used to do lots of different things: scanning a sequence to count or pick items, computing aggregates (sums, averages), or any number of other tasks. The code in Example 2-1 is building up a list. In contrast, a listcomp is more explicit. Its goal is always to build a new list.

Of course, it is possible to abuse list comprehensions to write truly incomprehensible code. I've seen Python code with listcomps used just to repeat a block of code for its side effects. If you are not doing something with the produced list, you should not use that syntax. Also, try to keep it short. If the list comprehension spans more than two lines, it is probably best to break it apart or rewrite it as a plain old for loop. Use your best judgment: for Python, as for English, there are no hard-and-fast rules for clear writing.

Syntax Tip

In Python code, line breaks are ignored inside pairs of [ ], { }, or ( ). So you can build multiline lists, listcomps, tuples, dictionaries, etc., without using the \ line continuation escape, which doesn't work if you accidentally type a space after it. Also, when those delimiter pairs are used to define a literal with a comma-separated series of items, a trailing comma will be ignored. So, for example, when coding a multiline list literal, it is thoughtful to put a comma after the last item, making it a little easier for the next coder to add one more item to that list, and reducing noise when reading diffs.

Local Scope Within Comprehensions and Generator Expressions

In Python 3, list comprehensions, generator expressions, and their siblings set and dict comprehensions, have a local scope to hold the variables assigned in the for clause.

However, variables assigned with the "Walrus operator" := remain accessible after those comprehensions or expressions return—unlike local variables in a function. PEP 572—Assignment Expressions (*https://fpy.li/pep572*) defines the scope of the target of := as the enclosing function, unless there is a global or nonlocal declaration for that target.[2]

```
>>> x = 'ABC'
>>> codes = [ord(x) for x in x]
>>> x  ❶
'ABC'
>>> codes
[65, 66, 67]
>>> codes = [last := ord(c) for c in x]
>>> last  ❷
67
>>> c  ❸
Traceback (most recent call last):
```

---

2 Thanks to reader Tina Lapine for pointing this out.

```
    File "<stdin>", line 1, in <module>
NameError: name 'c' is not defined
```

❶ x was not clobbered: it's still bound to 'ABC'.

❷ last remains.

❸ c is gone; it existed only inside the listcomp.

List comprehensions build lists from sequences or any other iterable type by filtering and transforming items. The filter and map built-ins can be composed to do the same, but readability suffers, as we will see next.

Listcomps Versus map and filter

Listcomps do everything the map and filter functions do, without the contortions of the functionally challenged Python lambda. Consider Example 2-3.

Example 2-3. The same list built by a listcomp and a map/filter composition

```
>>> symbols = '$¢£¥€¤'
>>> beyond_ascii = [ord(s) for s in symbols if ord(s) > 127]
>>> beyond_ascii
[162, 163, 165, 8364, 164]
>>> beyond_ascii = list(filter(lambda c: c > 127, map(ord, symbols)))
>>> beyond_ascii
[162, 163, 165, 8364, 164]
```

I used to believe that map and filter were faster than the equivalent listcomps, but Alex Martelli pointed out that's not the case—at least not in the preceding examples. The *02-array-seq/listcomp_speed.py* (*https://fpy.li/2-1*) script in the *Fluent Python* code repository (*https://fpy.li/code*) is a simple speed test comparing listcomp with filter/map.

I'll have more to say about map and filter in Chapter 7. Now we turn to the use of listcomps to compute Cartesian products: a list containing tuples built from all items from two or more lists.

Cartesian Products

Listcomps can build lists from the Cartesian product of two or more iterables. The items that make up the Cartesian product are tuples made from items from every input iterable. The resulting list has a length equal to the lengths of the input iterables multiplied. See Figure 2-3.

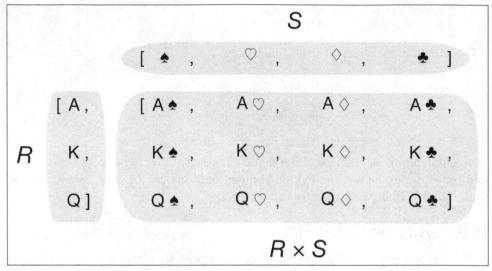

Figure 2-3. The Cartesian product of 3 card ranks and 4 suits is a sequence of 12 pairings.

For example, imagine you need to produce a list of T-shirts available in two colors and three sizes. Example 2-4 shows how to produce that list using a listcomp. The result has six items.

Example 2-4. Cartesian product using a list comprehension

```
>>> colors = ['black', 'white']
>>> sizes = ['S', 'M', 'L']
>>> tshirts = [(color, size) for color in colors for size in sizes]    ❶
>>> tshirts
[('black', 'S'), ('black', 'M'), ('black', 'L'), ('white', 'S'),
 ('white', 'M'), ('white', 'L')]
>>> for color in colors:    ❷
...     for size in sizes:
...         print((color, size))
...
('black', 'S')
('black', 'M')
('black', 'L')
('white', 'S')
('white', 'M')
('white', 'L')
>>> tshirts = [(color, size) for size in sizes        ❸
...                          for color in colors]
>>> tshirts
[('black', 'S'), ('white', 'S'), ('black', 'M'), ('white', 'M'),
 ('black', 'L'), ('white', 'L')]
```

❶ This generates a list of tuples arranged by color, then size.

❷ Note how the resulting list is arranged as if the for loops were nested in the same order as they appear in the listcomp.

❸ To get items arranged by size, then color, just rearrange the for clauses; adding a line break to the listcomp makes it easier to see how the result will be ordered.

In Example 1-1 (Chapter 1), I used the following expression to initialize a card deck with a list made of 52 cards from all 13 ranks of each of the 4 suits, sorted by suit, then rank:

```
self._cards = [Card(rank, suit) for suit in self.suits
                                for rank in self.ranks]
```

Listcomps are a one-trick pony: they build lists. To generate data for other sequence types, a genexp is the way to go. The next section is a brief look at genexps in the context of building sequences that are not lists.

Generator Expressions

To initialize tuples, arrays, and other types of sequences, you could also start from a listcomp, but a genexp (generator expression) saves memory because it yields items one by one using the iterator protocol instead of building a whole list just to feed another constructor.

Genexps use the same syntax as listcomps, but are enclosed in parentheses rather than brackets.

Example 2-5 shows basic usage of genexps to build a tuple and an array.

Example 2-5. Initializing a tuple and an array from a generator expression

```
>>> symbols = '$¢£¥€¤'
>>> tuple(ord(symbol) for symbol in symbols)  ❶
(36, 162, 163, 165, 8364, 164)
>>> import array
>>> array.array('I', (ord(symbol) for symbol in symbols))  ❷
array('I', [36, 162, 163, 165, 8364, 164])
```

❶ If the generator expression is the single argument in a function call, there is no need to duplicate the enclosing parentheses.

❷ The array constructor takes two arguments, so the parentheses around the generator expression are mandatory. The first argument of the array constructor defines the storage type used for the numbers in the array, as we'll see in "Arrays" on page 59.

Example 2-6 uses a genexp with a Cartesian product to print out a roster of T-shirts of two colors in three sizes. In contrast with Example 2-4, here the six-item list of T-shirts is never built in memory: the generator expression feeds the for loop producing one item at a time. If the two lists used in the Cartesian product had a thousand items each, using a generator expression would save the cost of building a list with a million items just to feed the for loop.

Example 2-6. Cartesian product in a generator expression

```
>>> colors = ['black', 'white']
>>> sizes = ['S', 'M', 'L']
>>> for tshirt in (f'{c} {s}' for c in colors for s in sizes):  ❶
...     print(tshirt)
...
black S
black M
black L
white S
white M
white L
```

❶ The generator expression yields items one by one; a list with all six T-shirt variations is never produced in this example.

 Chapter 17 explains how generators work in detail. Here the idea was just to show the use of generator expressions to initialize sequences other than lists, or to produce output that you don't need to keep in memory.

Now we move on to the other fundamental sequence type in Python: the tuple.

Tuples Are Not Just Immutable Lists

Some introductory texts about Python present tuples as "immutable lists," but that is short selling them. Tuples do double duty: they can be used as immutable lists and also as records with no field names. This use is sometimes overlooked, so we will start with that.

Tuples as Records

Tuples hold records: each item in the tuple holds the data for one field, and the position of the item gives its meaning.

If you think of a tuple just as an immutable list, the quantity and the order of the items may or may not be important, depending on the context. But when using a tuple as a collection of fields, the number of items is usually fixed and their order is always important.

Example 2-7 shows tuples used as records. Note that in every expression, sorting the tuple would destroy the information because the meaning of each field is given by its position in the tuple.

Example 2-7. Tuples used as records

```
>>> lax_coordinates = (33.9425, -118.408056)      ❶
>>> city, year, pop, chg, area = ('Tokyo', 2003, 32_450, 0.66, 8014)   ❷
>>> traveler_ids = [('USA', '31195855'), ('BRA', 'CE342567'),   ❸
...     ('ESP', 'XDA205856')]
>>> for passport in sorted(traveler_ids):    ❹
...     print('%s/%s' % passport)     ❺
...
BRA/CE342567
ESP/XDA205856
USA/31195855
>>> for country, _ in traveler_ids:    ❻
...     print(country)
...
USA
BRA
ESP
```

❶ Latitude and longitude of the Los Angeles International Airport.

❷ Data about Tokyo: name, year, population (thousands), population change (%), and area (km²).

❸ A list of tuples of the form (country_code, passport_number).

❹ As we iterate over the list, passport is bound to each tuple.

❺ The % formatting operator understands tuples and treats each item as a separate field.

❻ The for loop knows how to retrieve the items of a tuple separately—this is called "unpacking." Here we are not interested in the second item, so we assign it to _, a dummy variable.

In general, using _ as a dummy variable is just a convention. It's just a strange but valid variable name. However, in a match/case statement, _ is a wildcard that matches any value but is not bound to a value. See "Pattern Matching with Sequences" on page 39. And in the Python console, the result of the preceding command is assigned to _—unless the result is None.

We often think of records as data structures with named fields. Chapter 5 presents two ways of creating tuples with named fields.

But often, there's no need to go through the trouble of creating a class just to name the fields, especially if you leverage unpacking and avoid using indexes to access the fields. In Example 2-7, we assigned ('Tokyo', 2003, 32_450, 0.66, 8014) to city, year, pop, chg, area in a single statement. Then, the % operator assigned each item in the passport tuple to the corresponding slot in the format string in the print argument. Those are two examples of *tuple unpacking*.

The term *tuple unpacking* is widely used by Pythonistas, but *iterable unpacking* is gaining traction, as in the title of PEP 3132 — Extended Iterable Unpacking (*https://fpy.li/2-2*).

"Unpacking Sequences and Iterables" on page 35 presents a lot more about unpacking not only tuples, but sequences and iterables in general.

Now let's consider the tuple class as an immutable variant of the list class.

Tuples as Immutable Lists

The Python interpreter and standard library make extensive use of tuples as immutable lists, and so should you. This brings two key benefits:

Clarity
When you see a tuple in code, you know its length will never change.

Performance
A tuple uses less memory than a list of the same length, and it allows Python to do some optimizations.

However, be aware that the immutability of a tuple only applies to the references contained in it. References in a tuple cannot be deleted or replaced. But if one of those references points to a mutable object, and that object is changed, then the value of the tuple changes. The next snippet illustrates this point by creating two tuples—a and b—which are initially equal. Figure 2-4 represents the initial layout of the b tuple in memory.

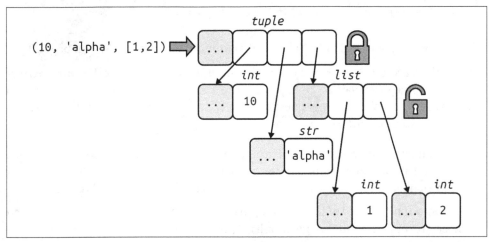

Figure 2-4. The content of the tuple itself is immutable, but that only means the references held by the tuple will always point to the same objects. However, if one of the referenced objects is mutable—like a list—its content may change.

When the last item in b is changed, b and a become different:

```
>>> a = (10, 'alpha', [1, 2])
>>> b = (10, 'alpha', [1, 2])
>>> a == b
True
>>> b[-1].append(99)
>>> a == b
False
>>> b
(10, 'alpha', [1, 2, 99])
```

Tuples with mutable items can be a source of bugs. As we'll see in "What Is Hashable" on page 84, an object is only hashable if its value cannot ever change. An unhashable tuple cannot be inserted as a dict key, or a set element.

If you want to determine explicitly if a tuple (or any object) has a fixed value, you can use the hash built-in to create a fixed function like this:

```
>>> def fixed(o):
...     try:
...         hash(o)
...     except TypeError:
...         return False
...     return True
...
>>> tf = (10, 'alpha', (1, 2))
>>> tm = (10, 'alpha', [1, 2])
>>> fixed(tf)
True
```

```
>>> fixed(tm)
False
```

We explore this issue further in "The Relative Immutability of Tuples" on page 207.

Despite this caveat, tuples are widely used as immutable lists. They offer some performance advantages explained by Python core developer Raymond Hettinger in a StackOverflow answer to the question: "Are tuples more efficient than lists in Python?" (*https://fpy.li/2-3*). To summarize, Hettinger wrote:

- To evaluate a tuple literal, the Python compiler generates bytecode for a tuple constant in one operation; but for a list literal, the generated bytecode pushes each element as a separate constant to the data stack, and then builds the list.

- Given a tuple t, tuple(t) simply returns a reference to the same t. There's no need to copy. In contrast, given a list l, the list(l) constructor must create a new copy of l.

- Because of its fixed length, a tuple instance is allocated the exact memory space it needs. Instances of list, on the other hand, are allocated with room to spare, to amortize the cost of future appends.

- The references to the items in a tuple are stored in an array in the tuple struct, while a list holds a pointer to an array of references stored elsewhere. The indirection is necessary because when a list grows beyond the space currently allocated, Python needs to reallocate the array of references to make room. The extra indirection makes CPU caches less effective.

Comparing Tuple and List Methods

When using a tuple as an immutable variation of list, it is good to know how similar their APIs are. As you can see in Table 2-1, tuple supports all list methods that do not involve adding or removing items, with one exception—tuple lacks the __reversed__ method. However, that is just for optimization; reversed(my_tuple) works without it.

Table 2-1. Methods and attributes found in list or tuple (methods implemented by object are omitted for brevity)

	list	tuple	
s.__add__(s2)	•	•	s + s2—concatenation
s.__iadd__(s2)	•		s += s2—in-place concatenation
s.append(e)	•		Append one element after last
s.clear()	•		Delete all items
s.__contains__(e)	•	•	e in s
s.copy()	•		Shallow copy of the list

	list	tuple	
s.count(e)	•	•	Count occurrences of an element
s.__delitem__(p)	•		Remove item at position p
s.extend(it)	•		Append items from iterable it
s.__getitem__(p)	•	•	s[p]—get item at position
s.__getnewargs__()		•	Support for optimized serialization with pickle
s.index(e)	•	•	Find position of first occurrence of e
s.insert(p, e)	•		Insert element e before the item at position p
s.__iter__()	•	•	Get iterator
s.__len__()	•	•	len(s)—number of items
s.__mul__(n)	•	•	s * n—repeated concatenation
s.__imul__(n)	•		s *= n—in-place repeated concatenation
s.__rmul__(n)	•	•	n * s—reversed repeated concatenation[a]
s.pop([p])	•		Remove and return last item or item at optional position p
s.remove(e)	•		Remove first occurrence of element e by value
s.reverse()	•		Reverse the order of the items in place
s.__reversed__()	•		Get iterator to scan items from last to first
s.__setitem__(p, e)	•		s[p] = e—put e in position p, overwriting existing item[b]
s.sort([key], [reverse])	•		Sort items in place with optional keyword arguments key and reverse

[a] Reversed operators are explained in Chapter 16.
[b] Also used to overwrite a subsequence. See "Assigning to Slices" on page 50.

Now let's switch to an important subject for idiomatic Python programming: tuple, list, and iterable unpacking.

Unpacking Sequences and Iterables

Unpacking is important because it avoids unnecessary and error-prone use of indexes to extract elements from sequences. Also, unpacking works with any iterable object as the data source—including iterators, which don't support index notation ([ ]). The only requirement is that the iterable yields exactly one item per variable in the receiving end, unless you use a star (*) to capture excess items, as explained in "Using * to Grab Excess Items" on page 36.

The most visible form of unpacking is *parallel assignment*; that is, assigning items from an iterable to a tuple of variables, as you can see in this example:

```
>>> lax_coordinates = (33.9425, -118.408056)
>>> latitude, longitude = lax_coordinates  # unpacking
>>> latitude
```

```
33.9425
>>> longitude
-118.408056
```

An elegant application of unpacking is swapping the values of variables without using a temporary variable:

```
>>> b, a = a, b
```

Another example of unpacking is prefixing an argument with * when calling a function:

```
>>> divmod(20, 8)
(2, 4)
>>> t = (20, 8)
>>> divmod(*t)
(2, 4)
>>> quotient, remainder = divmod(*t)
>>> quotient, remainder
(2, 4)
```

The preceding code shows another use of unpacking: allowing functions to return multiple values in a way that is convenient to the caller. As another example, the os.path.split() function builds a tuple (path, last_part) from a filesystem path:

```
>>> import os
>>> _, filename = os.path.split('/home/luciano/.ssh/id_rsa.pub')
>>> filename
'id_rsa.pub'
```

Another way of using just some of the items when unpacking is to use the * syntax, as we'll see right away.

Using * to Grab Excess Items

Defining function parameters with *args to grab arbitrary excess arguments is a classic Python feature.

In Python 3, this idea was extended to apply to parallel assignment as well:

```
>>> a, b, *rest = range(5)
>>> a, b, rest
(0, 1, [2, 3, 4])
>>> a, b, *rest = range(3)
>>> a, b, rest
(0, 1, [2])
>>> a, b, *rest = range(2)
>>> a, b, rest
(0, 1, [])
```

In the context of parallel assignment, the * prefix can be applied to exactly one variable, but it can appear in any position:

```
>>> a, *body, c, d = range(5)
>>> a, body, c, d
(0, [1, 2], 3, 4)
>>> *head, b, c, d = range(5)
>>> head, b, c, d
([0, 1], 2, 3, 4)
```

Unpacking with * in Function Calls and Sequence Literals

PEP 448—Additional Unpacking Generalizations (*https://fpy.li/pep448*) introduced more flexible syntax for iterable unpacking, best summarized in "What's New In Python 3.5" (*https://fpy.li/2-4*).

In function calls, we can use * multiple times:

```
>>> def fun(a, b, c, d, *rest):
...     return a, b, c, d, rest
...
>>> fun(*[1, 2], 3, *range(4, 7))
(1, 2, 3, 4, (5, 6))
```

The * can also be used when defining list, tuple, or set literals, as shown in these examples from "What's New In Python 3.5" (*https://fpy.li/2-4*):

```
>>> *range(4), 4
(0, 1, 2, 3, 4)
>>> [*range(4), 4]
[0, 1, 2, 3, 4]
>>> {*range(4), 4, *(5, 6, 7)}
{0, 1, 2, 3, 4, 5, 6, 7}
```

PEP 448 introduced similar new syntax for **, which we'll see in "Unpacking Mappings" on page 80.

Finally, a powerful feature of tuple unpacking is that it works with nested structures.

Nested Unpacking

The target of an unpacking can use nesting, e.g., (a, b, (c, d)). Python will do the right thing if the value has the same nesting structure. Example 2-8 shows nested unpacking in action.

Example 2-8. Unpacking nested tuples to access the longitude

```
metro_areas = [
    ('Tokyo', 'JP', 36.933, (35.689722, 139.691667)),    ❶
    ('Delhi NCR', 'IN', 21.935, (28.613889, 77.208889)),
    ('Mexico City', 'MX', 20.142, (19.433333, -99.133333)),
    ('New York-Newark', 'US', 20.104, (40.808611, -74.020386)),
    ('São Paulo', 'BR', 19.649, (-23.547778, -46.635833)),
]
```

```python
def main():
    print(f'{"":15} | {"latitude":>9} | {"longitude":>9}')
    for name, _, _, (lat, lon) in metro_areas:  ❷
        if lon <= 0:  ❸
            print(f'{name:15} | {lat:9.4f} | {lon:9.4f}')

if __name__ == '__main__':
    main()
```

❶ Each tuple holds a record with four fields, the last of which is a coordinate pair.

❷ By assigning the last field to a nested tuple, we unpack the coordinates.

❸ The `lon <= 0:` test selects only cities in the Western hemisphere.

The output of Example 2-8 is:

```
                | latitude | longitude
Mexico City     |  19.4333 |  -99.1333
New York-Newark |  40.8086 |  -74.0204
São Paulo       | -23.5478 |  -46.6358
```

The target of an unpacking assignment can also be a list, but good use cases are rare. Here is the only one I know: if you have a database query that returns a single record (e.g., the SQL code has a `LIMIT 1` clause), then you can unpack and at the same time make sure there's only one result with this code:

```python
>>> [record] = query_returning_single_row()
```

If the record has only one field, you can get it directly, like this:

```python
>>> [[field]] = query_returning_single_row_with_single_field()
```

Both of these could be written with tuples, but don't forget the syntax quirk that single-item tuples must be written with a trailing comma. So the first target would be `(record,)` and the second `((field,),)`. In both cases you get a silent bug if you forget a comma.[3]

Now let's study pattern matching, which supports even more powerful ways to unpack sequences.

---

3 Thanks to tech reviewer Leonardo Rochael for this example.

Pattern Matching with Sequences

The most visible new feature in Python 3.10 is pattern matching with the `match/case` statement proposed in PEP 634—Structural Pattern Matching: Specification (*https://fpy.li/pep634*).

 Python core developer Carol Willing wrote the excellent introduction to pattern matching in the "Structural Pattern Matching" (*https://fpy.li/2-6*) section of "What's New In Python 3.10" (*https://fpy.li/2-7*). You may want to read that quick overview. In this book, I chose to split the coverage of pattern matching over different chapters, depending on the pattern types: "Pattern Matching with Mappings" on page 81 and "Pattern Matching Class Instances" on page 192. An extended example is in "Pattern Matching in lis.py: A Case Study" on page 673.

Here is a first example of `match/case` handling sequences. Imagine you are designing a robot that accepts commands sent as sequences of words and numbers, like BEEPER 440 3. After splitting into parts and parsing the numbers, you'd have a message like `['BEEPER', 440, 3]`. You could use a method like this to handle such messages:

Example 2-9. Method from an imaginary Robot class

```python
def handle_command(self, message):
    match message:  ❶
        case ['BEEPER', frequency, times]:  ❷
            self.beep(times, frequency)
        case ['NECK', angle]:  ❸
            self.rotate_neck(angle)
        case ['LED', ident, intensity]:  ❹
            self.leds[ident].set_brightness(ident, intensity)
        case ['LED', ident, red, green, blue]:  ❺
            self.leds[ident].set_color(ident, red, green, blue)
        case _:  ❻
            raise InvalidCommand(message)
```

❶ The expression after the `match` keyword is the *subject*. The subject is the data that Python will try to match to the patterns in each `case` clause.

❷ This pattern matches any subject that is a sequence with three items. The first item must be the string `'BEEPER'`. The second and third item can be anything, and they will be bound to the variables `frequency` and `times`, in that order.

❸ This matches any subject with two items, the first being `'NECK'`.

❹ This will match a subject with three items starting with `'LED'`. If the number of items does not match, Python proceeds to the next `case`.

❺ Another sequence pattern starting with `'LED'`, now with five items—including the `'LED'` constant.

❻ This is the default `case`. It will match any subject that did not match a previous pattern. The `_` variable is special, as we'll soon see.

On the surface, `match/case` may look like the `switch/case` statement from the C language—but that's only half the story.[4] One key improvement of `match` over `switch` is *destructuring*—a more advanced form of unpacking. Destructuring is a new word in the Python vocabulary, but it is commonly used in the documentation of languages that support pattern matching—like Scala and Elixir.

As a first example of destructuring, Example 2-10 shows part of Example 2-8 rewritten with `match/case`.

Example 2-10. Destructuring nested tuples—requires Python ≥ 3.10

```python
metro_areas = [
    ('Tokyo', 'JP', 36.933, (35.689722, 139.691667)),
    ('Delhi NCR', 'IN', 21.935, (28.613889, 77.208889)),
    ('Mexico City', 'MX', 20.142, (19.433333, -99.133333)),
    ('New York-Newark', 'US', 20.104, (40.808611, -74.020386)),
    ('São Paulo', 'BR', 19.649, (-23.547778, -46.635833)),
]

def main():
    print(f'{"":15} | {"latitude":>9} | {"longitude":>9}')
    for record in metro_areas:
        match record:  ❶
            case [name, _, _, (lat, lon)] if lon <= 0:  ❷
                print(f'{name:15} | {lat:9.4f} | {lon:9.4f}')
```

❶ The subject of this `match` is `record`— i.e., each of the tuples in `metro_areas`.

❷ A `case` clause has two parts: a pattern and an optional guard with the `if` keyword.

In general, a sequence pattern matches the subject if:

---

4 In my view, a sequence of `if/elif/elif/.../else` blocks is a fine replacement for `switch/case`. It doesn't suffer from the fallthrough (*https://fpy.li/2-8*) and dangling else (*https://fpy.li/2-9*) problems that some language designers irrationally copied from C—decades after they were widely known as the cause of countless bugs.

1. The subject is a sequence *and*;
2. The subject and the pattern have the same number of items *and*;
3. Each corresponding item matches, including nested items.

For example, the pattern [name, _, _, (lat, lon)] in Example 2-10 matches a sequence with four items, and the last item must be a two-item sequence.

Sequence patterns may be written as tuples or lists or any combination of nested tuples and lists, but it makes no difference which syntax you use: in a sequence pattern, square brackets and parentheses mean the same thing. I wrote the pattern as a list with a nested 2-tuple just to avoid repeating brackets or parentheses in Example 2-10.

A sequence pattern can match instances of most actual or virtual subclasses of collections.abc.Sequence, with the exception of str, bytes, and bytearray.

Instances of str, bytes, and bytearray are not handled as sequences in the context of match/case. A match subject of one of those types is treated as an "atomic" value—like the integer 987 is treated as one value, not a sequence of digits. Treating those three types as sequences could cause bugs due to unintended matches. If you want to treat an object of those types as a sequence subject, convert it in the match clause. For example, see tuple(phone) in the following:

```
match tuple(phone):
    case ['1', *rest]:  # North America and Caribbean
        ...
    case ['2', *rest]:  # Africa and some territories
        ...
    case ['3' | '4', *rest]:  # Europe
        ...
```

In the standard library, these types are compatible with sequence patterns:

```
list     memoryview   array.array
tuple    range        collections.deque
```

Unlike unpacking, patterns don't destructure iterables that are not sequences (such as iterators).

The _ symbol is special in patterns: it matches any single item in that position, but it is never bound to the value of the matched item. Also, the _ is the only variable that can appear more than once in a pattern.

You can bind any part of a pattern with a variable using the as keyword:

```
case [name, _, _, (lat, lon) as coord]:
```

Given the subject ['Shanghai', 'CN', 24.9, (31.1, 121.3)], the preceding pattern will match, and set the following variables:

Variable	Set Value
name	'Shanghai'
lat	31.1
lon	121.3
coord	(31.1, 121.3)

We can make patterns more specific by adding type information. For example, the following pattern matches the same nested sequence structure as the previous example, but the first item must be an instance of str, and both items in the 2-tuple must be instances of float:

```
case [str(name), _, _, (float(lat), float(lon))]:
```

 The expressions str(name) and float(lat) look like constructor calls, which we'd use to convert name and lat to str and float. But in the context of a pattern, that syntax performs a runtime type check: the preceding pattern will match a four-item sequence in which item 0 must be a str, and item 3 must be a pair of floats. Additionally, the str in item 0 will be bound to the name variable, and the floats in item 3 will be bound to lat and lon, respectively. So, although str(name) borrows the syntax of a constructor call, the semantics are completely different in the context of a pattern. Using arbitrary classes in patterns is covered in "Pattern Matching Class Instances" on page 192.

On the other hand, if we want to match any subject sequence starting with a str, and ending with a nested sequence of two floats, we can write:

```
case [str(name), *_, (float(lat), float(lon))]:
```

The *_ matches any number of items, without binding them to a variable. Using *extra instead of *_ would bind the items to extra as a list with 0 or more items.

The optional guard clause starting with if is evaluated only if the pattern matches, and can reference variables bound in the pattern, as in Example 2-10:

```
match record:
    case [name, _, _, (lat, lon)] if lon <= 0:
        print(f'{name:15} | {lat:9.4f} | {lon:9.4f}')
```

The nested block with the print statement runs only if the pattern matches and the guard expression is *truthy*.

Destructuring with patterns is so expressive that sometimes a match with a single `case` can make code simpler. Guido van Rossum has a collection of `case/match` examples, including one that he titled "A very deep iterable and type match with extraction" (*https://fpy.li/2-10*).

Example 2-10 is not an improvement over Example 2-8. It's just an example to contrast two ways of doing the same thing. The next example shows how pattern matching contributes to clear, concise, and effective code.

Pattern Matching Sequences in an Interpreter

Peter Norvig of Stanford University wrote *lis.py* (*https://fpy.li/2-11*): an interpreter for a subset of the Scheme dialect of the Lisp programming language in 132 lines of beautiful and readable Python code. I took Norvig's MIT-licensed source and updated it to Python 3.10 to showcase pattern matching. In this section, we'll compare a key part of Norvig's code—which uses `if/elif` and unpacking—with a rewrite using `match/case`.

The two main functions of *lis.py* are `parse` and `evaluate`.[5] The parser takes Scheme parenthesized expressions and returns Python lists. Here are two examples:

```
>>> parse('(gcd 18 45)')
['gcd', 18, 45]
>>> parse('''
... (define double
...     (lambda (n)
...         (* n 2)))
... ''')
['define', 'double', ['lambda', ['n'], ['*', 'n', 2]]]
```

The evaluator takes lists like these and executes them. The first example is calling a `gcd` function with 18 and 45 as arguments. When evaluated, it computes the greatest common divisor of the arguments: 9. The second example is defining a function named `double` with a parameter n. The body of the function is the expression (* n 2). The result of calling a function in Scheme is the value of the last expression in its body.

Our focus here is destructuring sequences, so I will not explain the evaluator actions. See "Pattern Matching in lis.py: A Case Study" on page 673 to learn more about how *lis.py* works.

Example 2-11 shows Norvig's evaluator with minor changes, abbreviated to show only the sequence patterns.

---

5 The latter is named `eval` in Norvig's code; I renamed it to avoid confusion with Python's `eval` built-in.

Example 2-11. Matching patterns without match/case

```
def evaluate(exp: Expression, env: Environment) -> Any:
    "Evaluate an expression in an environment."
    if isinstance(exp, Symbol):        # variable reference
        return env[exp]
    # ... lines omitted
    elif exp[0] == 'quote':            # (quote exp)
        (_, x) = exp
        return x
    elif exp[0] == 'if':               # (if test conseq alt)
        (_, test, consequence, alternative) = exp
        if evaluate(test, env):
            return evaluate(consequence, env)
        else:
            return evaluate(alternative, env)
    elif exp[0] == 'lambda':           # (lambda (parm…) body…)
        (_, parms, *body) = exp
        return Procedure(parms, body, env)
    elif exp[0] == 'define':
        (_, name, value_exp) = exp
        env[name] = evaluate(value_exp, env)
    # ... more lines omitted
```

Note how each elif clause checks the first item of the list, and then unpacks the list, ignoring the first item. The extensive use of unpacking suggests that Norvig is a fan of pattern matching, but he wrote that code originally for Python 2 (though it now works with any Python 3).

Using match/case in Python ≥ 3.10, we can refactor evaluate as shown in Example 2-12.

Example 2-12. Pattern matching with match/case—requires Python ≥ 3.10

```
def evaluate(exp: Expression, env: Environment) -> Any:
    "Evaluate an expression in an environment."
    match exp:
    # ... lines omitted
        case ['quote', x]:                        ❶
            return x
        case ['if', test, consequence, alternative]:    ❷
            if evaluate(test, env):
                return evaluate(consequence, env)
            else:
                return evaluate(alternative, env)
        case ['lambda', [*parms], *body] if body:       ❸
            return Procedure(parms, body, env)
        case ['define', Symbol() as name, value_exp]:   ❹
            env[name] = evaluate(value_exp, env)
        # ... more lines omitted
```

```
    case _:  ❺
        raise SyntaxError(lispstr(exp))
```

❶ Match if subject is a two-item sequence starting with `'quote'`.

❷ Match if subject is a four-item sequence starting with `'if'`.

❸ Match if subject is a sequence of three or more items starting with `'lambda'`. The guard ensures that body is not empty.

❹ Match if subject is a three-item sequence starting with `'define'`, followed by an instance of `Symbol`.

❺ It is good practice to have a catch-all `case`. In this example, if exp doesn't match any of the patterns, the expression is malformed, and I raise `SyntaxError`.

Without a catch-all, the whole `match` statement does nothing when a subject does not match any case—and this can be a silent failure.

Norvig deliberately avoided error checking in *lis.py* to keep the code easy to understand. With pattern matching, we can add more checks and still keep it readable. For example, in the `'define'` pattern, the original code does not ensure that `name` is an instance of `Symbol`—that would require an `if` block, an `isinstance` call, and more code. Example 2-12 is shorter and safer than Example 2-11.

Alternative patterns for lambda

This is the syntax of `lambda` in Scheme, using the syntactic convention that the suffix ... means the element may appear zero or more times:

```
(lambda (parms...) body1 body2...)
```

A simple pattern for the lambda case `'lambda'` would be this:

```
        case ['lambda', parms, *body] if body:
```

However, that matches any value in the `parms` position, including the first `'x'` in this invalid subject:

```
['lambda', 'x', ['*', 'x', 2]]
```

The nested list after the `lambda` keyword in Scheme holds the names of the formal parameters for the function, and it must be a list even if it has only one element. It may also be an empty list, if the function takes no parameters—like Python's `random.random()`.

In Example 2-12, I made the `'lambda'` pattern safer using a nested sequence pattern:

```
case ['lambda', [*parms], *body] if body:
    return Procedure(parms, body, env)
```

In a sequence pattern, * can appear only once per sequence. Here we have two sequences: the outer and the inner.

Adding the characters [*] around parms made the pattern look more like the Scheme syntax it handles, and gave us an additional structural check.

Shortcut syntax for function definition

Scheme has an alternative define syntax to create a named function without using a nested lambda. This is the syntax:

```
(define (name parm…) body1 body2…)
```

The define keyword is followed by a list with the name of the new function and zero or more parameter names. After that list comes the function body with one or more expressions.

Adding these two lines to the match takes care of the implementation:

```
case ['define', [Symbol() as name, *parms], *body] if body:
    env[name] = Procedure(parms, body, env)
```

I'd place that case after the other define case in Example 2-12. The order between the define cases is irrelevant in this example because no subject can match both of these patterns: the second element must be a Symbol in the original define case, but it must be a sequence starting with a Symbol in the define shortcut for function definition.

Now consider how much work we'd have adding support for this second define syntax without the help of pattern matching in Example 2-11. The match statement does a lot more than the switch in C-like languages.

Pattern matching is an example of declarative programming: the code describes "what" you want to match, instead of "how" to match it. The shape of the code follows the shape of the data, as Table 2-2 illustrates.

Table 2-2. Some Scheme syntactic forms and case patterns to handle them

Scheme syntax	Sequence pattern
(quote exp)	['quote', exp]
(if test conseq alt)	['if', test, conseq, alt]
(lambda (parms…) body1 body2…)	['lambda', [*parms], *body] if body
(define name exp)	['define', Symbol() as name, exp]
(define (name parms…) body1 body2…)	['define', [Symbol() as name, *parms], *body] if body

I hope this refactoring of Norvig's `evaluate` with pattern matching convinced you that `match/case` can make your code more readable and safer.

 We'll see more of *lis.py* in "Pattern Matching in lis.py: A Case Study" on page 673, when we'll review the complete `match/case` example in `evaluate`. If you want to learn more about Norvig's *lis.py*, read his wonderful post "(How to Write a (Lisp) Interpreter (in Python))" (*https://fpy.li/2-12*).

This concludes our first tour of unpacking, destructuring, and pattern matching with sequences. We'll cover other types of patterns in later chapters.

Every Python programmer knows that sequences can be sliced using the `s[a:b]` syntax. We now turn to some less well-known facts about slicing.

Slicing

A common feature of `list`, `tuple`, `str`, and all sequence types in Python is the support of slicing operations, which are more powerful than most people realize.

In this section, we describe the *use* of these advanced forms of slicing. Their implementation in a user-defined class will be covered in Chapter 12, in keeping with our philosophy of covering ready-to-use classes in this part of the book, and creating new classes in Part III.

Why Slices and Ranges Exclude the Last Item

The Pythonic convention of excluding the last item in slices and ranges works well with the zero-based indexing used in Python, C, and many other languages. Some convenient features of the convention are:

- It's easy to see the length of a slice or range when only the stop position is given: `range(3)` and `my_list[:3]` both produce three items.
- It's easy to compute the length of a slice or range when start and stop are given: just subtract `stop - start`.
- It's easy to split a sequence in two parts at any index x, without overlapping: simply get `my_list[:x]` and `my_list[x:]`. For example:

```
>>> l = [10, 20, 30, 40, 50, 60]
>>> l[:2]  # split at 2
[10, 20]
>>> l[2:]
[30, 40, 50, 60]
>>> l[:3]  # split at 3
[10, 20, 30]
```

```
>>> l[3:]
[40, 50, 60]
```

The best arguments for this convention were written by the Dutch computer scientist Edsger W. Dijkstra (see the last reference in "Further Reading" on page 71).

Now let's take a close look at how Python interprets slice notation.

Slice Objects

This is no secret, but worth repeating just in case: s[a:b:c] can be used to specify a stride or step c, causing the resulting slice to skip items. The stride can also be negative, returning items in reverse. Three examples make this clear:

```
>>> s = 'bicycle'
>>> s[::3]
'bye'
>>> s[::-1]
'elcycib'
>>> s[::-2]
'eccb'
```

Another example was shown in Chapter 1 when we used deck[12::13] to get all the aces in the unshuffled deck:

```
>>> deck[12::13]
[Card(rank='A', suit='spades'), Card(rank='A', suit='diamonds'),
Card(rank='A', suit='clubs'), Card(rank='A', suit='hearts')]
```

The notation a:b:c is only valid within [ ] when used as the indexing or subscript operator, and it produces a slice object: slice(a, b, c). As we will see in "How Slicing Works" on page 406, to evaluate the expression seq[start:stop:step], Python calls seq.__getitem__(slice(start, stop, step)). Even if you are not implementing your own sequence types, knowing about slice objects is useful because it lets you assign names to slices, just like spreadsheets allow naming of cell ranges.

Suppose you need to parse flat-file data like the invoice shown in Example 2-13. Instead of filling your code with hardcoded slices, you can name them. See how readable this makes the for loop at the end of the example.

Example 2-13. Line items from a flat-file invoice

```
>>> invoice = """
... 0.....6...............................40........52...55........
... 1909  Pimoroni PiBrella                    $17.50    3    $52.50
... 1489  6mm Tactile Switch x20                $4.95    2     $9.90
... 1510  Panavise Jr. - PV-201                $28.00    1    $28.00
... 1601  PiTFT Mini Kit 320x240               $34.95    1    $34.95
... """
```

```
>>> SKU = slice(0, 6)
>>> DESCRIPTION = slice(6, 40)
>>> UNIT_PRICE = slice(40, 52)
>>> QUANTITY =  slice(52, 55)
>>> ITEM_TOTAL = slice(55, None)
>>> line_items = invoice.split('\n')[2:]
>>> for item in line_items:
...     print(item[UNIT_PRICE], item[DESCRIPTION])
...
    $17.50   Pimoroni PiBrella
     $4.95   6mm Tactile Switch x20
    $28.00   Panavise Jr. - PV-201
    $34.95   PiTFT Mini Kit 320x240
```

We'll come back to slice objects when we discuss creating your own collections in "Vector Take #2: A Sliceable Sequence" on page 405. Meanwhile, from a user perspective, slicing includes additional features such as multidimensional slices and ellipsis (...) notation. Read on.

Multidimensional Slicing and Ellipsis

The [] operator can also take multiple indexes or slices separated by commas. The __getitem__ and __setitem__ special methods that handle the [] operator simply receive the indices in a[i, j] as a tuple. In other words, to evaluate a[i, j], Python calls a.__getitem__((i, j)).

This is used, for instance, in the external NumPy package, where items of a two-dimensional numpy.ndarray can be fetched using the syntax a[i, j] and a two-dimensional slice obtained with an expression like a[m:n, k:l]. Example 2-22 later in this chapter shows the use of this notation.

Except for memoryview, the built-in sequence types in Python are one-dimensional, so they support only one index or slice, and not a tuple of them.[6]

The ellipsis—written with three full stops (...) and not … (Unicode U+2026)—is recognized as a token by the Python parser. It is an alias to the Ellipsis object, the single instance of the ellipsis class.[7] As such, it can be passed as an argument to functions and as part of a slice specification, as in f(a, ..., z) or a[i:...]. NumPy uses ... as a shortcut when slicing arrays of many dimensions; for example,

---

6 In "Memory Views" on page 62 we show that specially constructed memory views can have more than one dimension.

7 No, I did not get this backwards: the ellipsis class name is really all lowercase, and the instance is a built-in named Ellipsis, just like bool is lowercase but its instances are True and False.

if x is a four-dimensional array, x[i, ...] is a shortcut for x[i, :, :, :,]. See "NumPy quickstart" (*https://fpy.li/2-13*) to learn more about this.

At the time of this writing, I am unaware of uses of Ellipsis or multidimensional indexes and slices in the Python standard library. If you spot one, let me know. These syntactic features exist to support user-defined types and extensions such as NumPy.

Slices are not just useful to extract information from sequences; they can also be used to change mutable sequences in place—that is, without rebuilding them from scratch.

Assigning to Slices

Mutable sequences can be grafted, excised, and otherwise modified in place using slice notation on the lefthand side of an assignment statement or as the target of a del statement. The next few examples give an idea of the power of this notation:

```
>>> l = list(range(10))
>>> l
[0, 1, 2, 3, 4, 5, 6, 7, 8, 9]
>>> l[2:5] = [20, 30]
>>> l
[0, 1, 20, 30, 5, 6, 7, 8, 9]
>>> del l[5:7]
>>> l
[0, 1, 20, 30, 5, 8, 9]
>>> l[3::2] = [11, 22]
>>> l
[0, 1, 20, 11, 5, 22, 9]
>>> l[2:5] = 100  ❶
Traceback (most recent call last):
  File "<stdin>", line 1, in <module>
TypeError: can only assign an iterable
>>> l[2:5] = [100]
>>> l
[0, 1, 100, 22, 9]
```

❶ When the target of the assignment is a slice, the righthand side must be an iterable object, even if it has just one item.

Every coder knows that concatenation is a common operation with sequences. Introductory Python tutorials explain the use of + and * for that purpose, but there are some subtle details on how they work, which we cover next.

Using + and * with Sequences

Python programmers expect that sequences support + and *. Usually both operands of + must be of the same sequence type, and neither of them is modified, but a new sequence of that same type is created as result of the concatenation.

To concatenate multiple copies of the same sequence, multiply it by an integer. Again, a new sequence is created:

```
>>> l = [1, 2, 3]
>>> l * 5
[1, 2, 3, 1, 2, 3, 1, 2, 3, 1, 2, 3, 1, 2, 3]
>>> 5 * 'abcd'
'abcdabcdabcdabcdabcd'
```

Both + and * always create a new object, and never change their operands.

 Beware of expressions like a * n when a is a sequence containing mutable items, because the result may surprise you. For example, trying to initialize a list of lists as my_list = [[]] * 3 will result in a list with three references to the same inner list, which is probably not what you want.

The next section covers the pitfalls of trying to use * to initialize a list of lists.

Building Lists of Lists

Sometimes we need to initialize a list with a certain number of nested lists—for example, to distribute students in a list of teams or to represent squares on a game board. The best way of doing so is with a list comprehension, as in Example 2-14.

Example 2-14. A list with three lists of length 3 can represent a tic-tac-toe board

```
>>> board = [['_'] * 3 for i in range(3)]  ❶
>>> board
[['_', '_', '_'], ['_', '_', '_'], ['_', '_', '_']]
>>> board[1][2] = 'X'  ❷
>>> board
[['_', '_', '_'], ['_', '_', 'X'], ['_', '_', '_']]
```

❶ Create a list of three lists of three items each. Inspect the structure.

❷ Place a mark in row 1, column 2, and check the result.

A tempting, but wrong, shortcut is doing it like Example 2-15.

Example 2-15. A list with three references to the same list is useless

```
>>> weird_board = [['_'] * 3] * 3  ❶
>>> weird_board
[['_', '_', '_'], ['_', '_', '_'], ['_', '_', '_']]
>>> weird_board[1][2] = 'O'  ❷
```

```
>>> weird_board
[['_', '_', 'O'], ['_', '_', 'O'], ['_', '_', 'O']]
```

❶ The outer list is made of three references to the same inner list. While it is unchanged, all seems right.

❷ Placing a mark in row 1, column 2, reveals that all rows are aliases referring to the same object.

The problem with Example 2-15 is that, in essence, it behaves like this code:

```
row = ['_'] * 3
board = []
for i in range(3):
    board.append(row)   ❶
```

❶ The same row is appended three times to board.

On the other hand, the list comprehension from Example 2-14 is equivalent to this code:

```
>>> board = []
>>> for i in range(3):
...     row = ['_'] * 3   ❶
...     board.append(row)
...
>>> board
[['_', '_', '_'], ['_', '_', '_'], ['_', '_', '_']]
>>> board[2][0] = 'X'
>>> board   ❷
[['_', '_', '_'], ['_', '_', '_'], ['X', '_', '_']]
```

❶ Each iteration builds a new row and appends it to board.

❷ Only row 2 is changed, as expected.

 If either the problem or the solution in this section is not clear to you, relax. Chapter 6 was written to clarify the mechanics and pitfalls of references and mutable objects.

So far we have discussed the use of the plain + and * operators with sequences, but there are also the += and *= operators, which produce very different results, depending on the mutability of the target sequence. The following section explains how that works.

Augmented Assignment with Sequences

The augmented assignment operators += and *= behave quite differently, depending on the first operand. To simplify the discussion, we will focus on augmented addition first (+=), but the concepts also apply to *= and to other augmented assignment operators.

The special method that makes += work is __iadd__ (for "in-place addition").

However, if __iadd__ is not implemented, Python falls back to calling __add__. Consider this simple expression:

```
>>> a += b
```

If a implements __iadd__, that will be called. In the case of mutable sequences (e.g., list, bytearray, array.array), a will be changed in place (i.e., the effect will be similar to a.extend(b)). However, when a does not implement __iadd__, the expression a += b has the same effect as a = a + b: the expression a + b is evaluated first, producing a new object, which is then bound to a. In other words, the identity of the object bound to a may or may not change, depending on the availability of __iadd__.

In general, for mutable sequences, it is a good bet that __iadd__ is implemented and that += happens in place. For immutable sequences, clearly there is no way for that to happen.

What I just wrote about += also applies to *=, which is implemented via __imul__. The __iadd__ and __imul__ special methods are discussed in Chapter 16. Here is a demonstration of *= with a mutable sequence and then an immutable one:

```
>>> l = [1, 2, 3]
>>> id(l)
4311953800    ❶
>>> l *= 2
>>> l
[1, 2, 3, 1, 2, 3]
>>> id(l)
4311953800    ❷
>>> t = (1, 2, 3)
>>> id(t)
4312681568    ❸
>>> t *= 2
>>> id(t)
4301348296    ❹
```

❶ ID of the initial list.

❷ After multiplication, the list is the same object, with new items appended.

❸ ID of the initial tuple.

❹ After multiplication, a new tuple was created.

Repeated concatenation of immutable sequences is inefficient, because instead of just appending new items, the interpreter has to copy the whole target sequence to create a new one with the new items concatenated.[8]

We've seen common use cases for +=. The next section shows an intriguing corner case that highlights what "immutable" really means in the context of tuples.

A += Assignment Puzzler

Try to answer without using the console: what is the result of evaluating the two expressions in Example 2-16?[9]

Example 2-16. A riddle

```
>>> t = (1, 2, [30, 40])
>>> t[2] += [50, 60]
```

What happens next? Choose the best answer:

A. t becomes (1, 2, [30, 40, 50, 60]).

B. TypeError is raised with the message 'tuple' object does not support item assignment.

C. Neither.

D. Both A and B.

When I saw this, I was pretty sure the answer was B, but it's actually D, "Both A and B"! Example 2-17 is the actual output from a Python 3.9 console.[10]

---

8 str is an exception to this description. Because string building with += in loops is so common in real codebases, CPython is optimized for this use case. Instances of str are allocated in memory with extra room, so that concatenation does not require copying the whole string every time.

9 Thanks to Leonardo Rochael and Cesar Kawakami for sharing this riddle at the 2013 PythonBrasil Conference.

10 Readers suggested that the operation in the example can be done with t[2].extend([50,60]), without errors. I am aware of that, but my intent is to show the strange behavior of the += operator in this case.

Example 2-17. The unexpected result: item t2 is changed and an exception is raised

```
>>> t = (1, 2, [30, 40])
>>> t[2] += [50, 60]
Traceback (most recent call last):
  File "<stdin>", line 1, in <module>
TypeError: 'tuple' object does not support item assignment
>>> t
(1, 2, [30, 40, 50, 60])
```

Online Python Tutor (*https://fpy.li/2-14*) is an awesome online tool to visualize how Python works in detail. Figure 2-5 is a composite of two screenshots showing the initial and final states of the tuple t from Example 2-17.

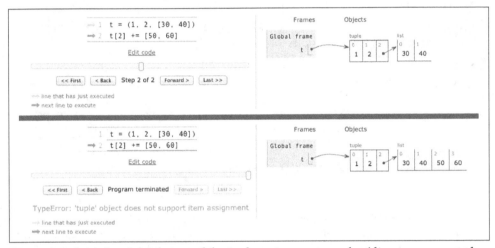

Figure 2-5. Initial and final state of the tuple assignment puzzler (diagram generated by Online Python Tutor).

If you look at the bytecode Python generates for the expression s[a] += b (Example 2-18), it becomes clear how that happens.

Example 2-18. Bytecode for the expression s[a] += b

```
>>> dis.dis('s[a] += b')
  1           0 LOAD_NAME               0 (s)
              3 LOAD_NAME               1 (a)
              6 DUP_TOP_TWO
              7 BINARY_SUBSCR                   ❶
              8 LOAD_NAME               2 (b)
             11 INPLACE_ADD                     ❷
             12 ROT_THREE
             13 STORE_SUBSCR                    ❸
             14 LOAD_CONST              0 (None)
             17 RETURN_VALUE
```

❶ Put the value of s[a] on TOS (Top Of Stack).

❷ Perform TOS += b. This succeeds if TOS refers to a mutable object (it's a list, in Example 2-17).

❸ Assign s[a] = TOS. This fails if s is immutable (the t tuple in Example 2-17).

This example is quite a corner case—in 20 years using Python, I have never seen this strange behavior actually bite somebody.

I take three lessons from this:

- Avoid putting mutable items in tuples.
- Augmented assignment is not an atomic operation—we just saw it throwing an exception after doing part of its job.
- Inspecting Python bytecode is not too difficult, and can be helpful to see what is going on under the hood.

After witnessing the subtleties of using + and * for concatenation, we can change the subject to another essential operation with sequences: sorting.

list.sort Versus the sorted Built-In

The list.sort method sorts a list in place—that is, without making a copy. It returns None to remind us that it changes the receiver[11] and does not create a new list. This is an important Python API convention: functions or methods that change an object in place should return None to make it clear to the caller that the receiver was changed, and no new object was created. Similar behavior can be seen, for example, in the random.shuffle(s) function, which shuffles the mutable sequence s in place, and returns None.

 The convention of returning None to signal in-place changes has a drawback: we cannot cascade calls to those methods. In contrast, methods that return new objects (e.g., all str methods) can be cascaded in the fluent interface style. See Wikipedia's "Fluent interface" entry (*https://fpy.li/2-15*) for further description of this topic.

In contrast, the built-in function sorted creates a new list and returns it. It accepts any iterable object as an argument, including immutable sequences and generators

---

11 Receiver is the target of a method call, the object bound to self in the method body.

(see Chapter 17). Regardless of the type of iterable given to `sorted`, it always returns a newly created list.

Both `list.sort` and `sorted` take two optional, keyword-only arguments:

`reverse`
> If `True`, the items are returned in descending order (i.e., by reversing the comparison of the items). The default is `False`.

`key`
> A one-argument function that will be applied to each item to produce its sorting key. For example, when sorting a list of strings, `key=str.lower` can be used to perform a case-insensitive sort, and `key=len` will sort the strings by character length. The default is the identity function (i.e., the items themselves are compared).

> You can also use the optional keyword parameter `key` with the `min()` and `max()` built-ins and with other functions from the standard library (e.g., `itertools.groupby()` and `heapq.nlargest()`).

Here are a few examples to clarify the use of these functions and keyword arguments. The examples also demonstrate that Python's sorting algorithm is stable (i.e., it preserves the relative ordering of items that compare equally):[12]

```
>>> fruits = ['grape', 'raspberry', 'apple', 'banana']
>>> sorted(fruits)
['apple', 'banana', 'grape', 'raspberry']    ❶
>>> fruits
['grape', 'raspberry', 'apple', 'banana']    ❷
>>> sorted(fruits, reverse=True)
['raspberry', 'grape', 'banana', 'apple']    ❸
>>> sorted(fruits, key=len)
['grape', 'apple', 'banana', 'raspberry']    ❹
>>> sorted(fruits, key=len, reverse=True)
['raspberry', 'banana', 'grape', 'apple']    ❺
>>> fruits
['grape', 'raspberry', 'apple', 'banana']    ❻
>>> fruits.sort()                             ❼
>>> fruits
['apple', 'banana', 'grape', 'raspberry']    ❽
```

---

12 Python's main sorting algorithm is named Timsort after its creator, Tim Peters. For a bit of Timsort trivia, see the "Soapbox" on page 73.

❶ This produces a new list of strings sorted alphabetically.[13]

❷ Inspecting the original list, we see it is unchanged.

❸ This is the previous "alphabetical" ordering, reversed.

❹ A new list of strings, now sorted by length. Because the sorting algorithm is stable, "grape" and "apple," both of length 5, are in the original order.

❺ These are the strings sorted by length in descending order. It is not the reverse of the previous result because the sorting is stable, so again "grape" appears before "apple."

❻ So far, the ordering of the original `fruits` list has not changed.

❼ This sorts the list in place, and returns `None` (which the console omits).

❽ Now `fruits` is sorted.

 By default, Python sorts strings lexicographically by character code. That means ASCII uppercase letters will come before lowercase letters, and non-ASCII characters are unlikely to be sorted in a sensible way. "Sorting Unicode Text" on page 148 covers proper ways of sorting text as humans would expect.

Once your sequences are sorted, they can be very efficiently searched. A binary search algorithm is already provided in the `bisect` module of the Python standard library. That module also includes the `bisect.insort` function, which you can use to make sure that your sorted sequences stay sorted. You'll find an illustrated introduction to the `bisect` module in the "Managing Ordered Sequences with Bisect" (*https://fpy.li/ bisect*) post in the *fluentpython.com* companion website.

Much of what we have seen so far in this chapter applies to sequences in general, not just lists or tuples. Python programmers sometimes overuse the `list` type because it is so handy—I know I've done it. For example, if you are processing large lists of numbers, you should consider using arrays instead. The remainder of the chapter is devoted to alternatives to lists and tuples.

---

13 The words in this example are sorted alphabetically because they are 100% made of lowercase ASCII characters. See the warning after the example.

When a List Is Not the Answer

The list type is flexible and easy to use, but depending on specific requirements, there are better options. For example, an array saves a lot of memory when you need to handle millions of floating-point values. On the other hand, if you are constantly adding and removing items from opposite ends of a list, it's good to know that a deque (double-ended queue) is a more efficient FIFO[14] data structure.

 If your code frequently checks whether an item is present in a collection (e.g., item in my_collection), consider using a set for my_collection, especially if it holds a large number of items. Sets are optimized for fast membership checking. They are also iterable, but they are not sequences because the ordering of set items is unspecified. We cover them in Chapter 3.

For the remainder of this chapter, we discuss mutable sequence types that can replace lists in many cases, starting with arrays.

Arrays

If a list only contains numbers, an array.array is a more efficient replacement. Arrays support all mutable sequence operations (including .pop, .insert, and .extend), as well as additional methods for fast loading and saving, such as .frombytes and .tofile.

A Python array is as lean as a C array. As shown in Figure 2-1, an array of float values does not hold full-fledged float instances, but only the packed bytes representing their machine values—similar to an array of double in the C language. When creating an array, you provide a typecode, a letter to determine the underlying C type used to store each item in the array. For example, b is the typecode for what C calls a signed char, an integer ranging from –128 to 127. If you create an array('b'), then each item will be stored in a single byte and interpreted as an integer. For large sequences of numbers, this saves a lot of memory. And Python will not let you put any number that does not match the type for the array.

Example 2-19 shows creating, saving, and loading an array of 10 million floating-point random numbers.

---

14 First in, first out—the default behavior of queues.

Example 2-19. Creating, saving, and loading a large array of floats

```
>>> from array import array  ❶
>>> from random import random
>>> floats = array('d', (random() for i in range(10**7)))  ❷
>>> floats[-1]  ❸
0.07802343889111107
>>> fp = open('floats.bin', 'wb')
>>> floats.tofile(fp)  ❹
>>> fp.close()
>>> floats2 = array('d')  ❺
>>> fp = open('floats.bin', 'rb')
>>> floats2.fromfile(fp, 10**7)  ❻
>>> fp.close()
>>> floats2[-1]  ❼
0.07802343889111107
>>> floats2 == floats  ❽
True
```

❶ Import the array type.

❷ Create an array of double-precision floats (typecode 'd') from any iterable object —in this case, a generator expression.

❸ Inspect the last number in the array.

❹ Save the array to a binary file.

❺ Create an empty array of doubles.

❻ Read 10 million numbers from the binary file.

❼ Inspect the last number in the array.

❽ Verify that the contents of the arrays match.

As you can see, array.tofile and array.fromfile are easy to use. If you try the example, you'll notice they are also very fast. A quick experiment shows that it takes about 0.1 seconds for array.fromfile to load 10 million double-precision floats from a binary file created with array.tofile. That is nearly 60 times faster than reading the numbers from a text file, which also involves parsing each line with the float built-in. Saving with array.tofile is about seven times faster than writing one float per line in a text file. In addition, the size of the binary file with 10 million doubles is 80,000,000 bytes (8 bytes per double, zero overhead), while the text file has 181,515,739 bytes for the same data.

For the specific case of numeric arrays representing binary data, such as raster images, Python has the `bytes` and `bytearray` types discussed in Chapter 4.

We wrap up this section on arrays with Table 2-3, comparing the features of `list` and `array.array`.

Table 2-3. Methods and attributes found in `list` or `array` (deprecated array methods and those also implemented by object are omitted for brevity)

	list	array	
`s.__add__(s2)`	●	●	`s + s2`—concatenation
`s.__iadd__(s2)`	●	●	`s += s2`—in-place concatenation
`s.append(e)`	●	●	Append one element after last
`s.byteswap()`		●	Swap bytes of all items in array for endianness conversion
`s.clear()`	●		Delete all items
`s.__contains__(e)`	●	●	`e in s`
`s.copy()`	●		Shallow copy of the list
`s.__copy__()`		●	Support for `copy.copy`
`s.count(e)`	●	●	Count occurrences of an element
`s.__deepcopy__()`		●	Optimized support for `copy.deepcopy`
`s.__delitem__(p)`	●	●	Remove item at position p
`s.extend(it)`	●	●	Append items from iterable `it`
`s.frombytes(b)`		●	Append items from byte sequence interpreted as packed machine values
`s.fromfile(f, n)`		●	Append n items from binary file f interpreted as packed machine values
`s.fromlist(l)`		●	Append items from list; if one causes `TypeError`, none are appended
`s.__getitem__(p)`	●	●	`s[p]`—get item or slice at position
`s.index(e)`	●	●	Find position of first occurrence of e
`s.insert(p, e)`	●	●	Insert element e before the item at position p
`s.itemsize`		●	Length in bytes of each array item
`s.__iter__()`	●	●	Get iterator
`s.__len__()`	●	●	`len(s)`—number of items
`s.__mul__(n)`	●	●	`s * n`—repeated concatenation
`s.__imul__(n)`	●	●	`s *= n`—in-place repeated concatenation
`s.__rmul__(n)`	●	●	`n * s`—reversed repeated concatenation[a]
`s.pop([p])`	●	●	Remove and return item at position p (default: last)
`s.remove(e)`	●	●	Remove first occurrence of element e by value
`s.reverse()`	●	●	Reverse the order of the items in place
`s.__reversed__()`	●		Get iterator to scan items from last to first
`s.__setitem__(p, e)`	●	●	`s[p] = e`—put e in position p, overwriting existing item or slice

	list	array	
s.sort([key], [reverse])	●		Sort items in place with optional keyword arguments key and reverse
s.tobytes()		●	Return items as packed machine values in a bytes object
s.tofile(f)		●	Save items as packed machine values to binary file f
s.tolist()		●	Return items as numeric objects in a list
s.typecode		●	One-character string identifying the C type of the items

[a] Reversed operators are explained in Chapter 16.

 As of Python 3.10, the array type does not have an in-place sort method like list.sort(). If you need to sort an array, use the built-in sorted function to rebuild the array:

```
a = array.array(a.typecode, sorted(a))
```

To keep a sorted array sorted while adding items to it, use the bisect.insort (*https://fpy.li/2-16*) function.

If you do a lot of work with arrays and don't know about memoryview, you're missing out. See the next topic.

Memory Views

The built-in memoryview class is a shared-memory sequence type that lets you handle slices of arrays without copying bytes. It was inspired by the NumPy library (which we'll discuss shortly in "NumPy" on page 64). Travis Oliphant, lead author of NumPy, answers the question, "When should a memoryview be used?" (*https://fpy.li/2-17*) like this:

> A memoryview is essentially a generalized NumPy array structure in Python itself (without the math). It allows you to share memory between data-structures (things like PIL images, SQLite databases, NumPy arrays, etc.) without first copying. This is very important for large data sets.

Using notation similar to the array module, the memoryview.cast method lets you change the way multiple bytes are read or written as units without moving bits around. memoryview.cast returns yet another memoryview object, always sharing the same memory.

Example 2-20 shows how to create alternate views on the same array of 6 bytes, to operate on it as a 2×3 matrix or a 3×2 matrix.

Example 2-20. Handling 6 bytes of memory as 1×6, 2×3, and 3×2 views

```
>>> from array import array
>>> octets = array('B', range(6))   ❶
>>> m1 = memoryview(octets)   ❷
>>> m1.tolist()
[0, 1, 2, 3, 4, 5]
>>> m2 = m1.cast('B', [2, 3])   ❸
>>> m2.tolist()
[[0, 1, 2], [3, 4, 5]]
>>> m3 = m1.cast('B', [3, 2])   ❹
>>> m3.tolist()
[[0, 1], [2, 3], [4, 5]]
>>> m2[1,1] = 22   ❺
>>> m3[1,1] = 33   ❻
>>> octets   ❼
array('B', [0, 1, 2, 33, 22, 5])
```

❶ Build array of 6 bytes (typecode `'B'`).

❷ Build `memoryview` from that array, then export it as a list.

❸ Build new `memoryview` from that previous one, but with 2 rows and 3 columns.

❹ Yet another `memoryview`, now with 3 rows and 2 columns.

❺ Overwrite byte in `m2` at row 1, column 1 with 22.

❻ Overwrite byte in `m3` at row 1, column 1 with 33.

❼ Display original array, proving that the memory was shared among `octets`, `m1`, `m2`, and `m3`.

The awesome power of `memoryview` can also be used to corrupt. Example 2-21 shows how to change a single byte of an item in an array of 16-bit integers.

Example 2-21. Changing the value of a 16-bit integer array item by poking one of its bytes

```
>>> numbers = array.array('h', [-2, -1, 0, 1, 2])
>>> memv = memoryview(numbers)   ❶
>>> len(memv)
5
>>> memv[0]   ❷
-2
>>> memv_oct = memv.cast('B')   ❸
>>> memv_oct.tolist()   ❹
[254, 255, 255, 255, 0, 0, 1, 0, 2, 0]
```

```
>>> memv_oct[5] = 4    ❺
>>> numbers
array('h', [-2, -1, 1024, 1, 2])    ❻
```

❶ Build memoryview from array of 5 16-bit signed integers (typecode 'h').

❷ memv sees the same 5 items in the array.

❸ Create memv_oct by casting the elements of memv to bytes (typecode 'B').

❹ Export elements of memv_oct as a list of 10 bytes, for inspection.

❺ Assign value 4 to byte offset 5.

❻ Note the change to numbers: a 4 in the most significant byte of a 2-byte unsigned integer is 1024.

> You'll find an example of inspecting memoryview with the struct package at *fluentpython.com*: "Parsing binary records with struct" (*https://fpy.li/2-18*).

Meanwhile, if you are doing advanced numeric processing in arrays, you should be using the NumPy libraries. We'll take a brief look at them right away.

NumPy

Throughout this book, I make a point of highlighting what is already in the Python standard library so you can make the most of it. But NumPy is so awesome that a detour is warranted.

For advanced array and matrix operations, NumPy is the reason why Python became mainstream in scientific computing applications. NumPy implements multi-dimensional, homogeneous arrays and matrix types that hold not only numbers but also user-defined records, and provides efficient element-wise operations.

SciPy is a library, written on top of NumPy, offering many scientific computing algorithms from linear algebra, numerical calculus, and statistics. SciPy is fast and reliable because it leverages the widely used C and Fortran codebase from the Netlib Repository (*https://fpy.li/2-19*). In other words, SciPy gives scientists the best of both worlds: an interactive prompt and high-level Python APIs, together with industrial-strength number-crunching functions optimized in C and Fortran.

As a very brief NumPy demo, Example 2-22 shows some basic operations with two-dimensional arrays.

Example 2-22. Basic operations with rows and columns in a `numpy.ndarray`

```
>>> import numpy as np  ❶
>>> a = np.arange(12)   ❷
>>> a
array([ 0,  1,  2,  3,  4,  5,  6,  7,  8,  9, 10, 11])
>>> type(a)
<class 'numpy.ndarray'>
>>> a.shape  ❸
(12,)
>>> a.shape = 3, 4  ❹
>>> a
array([[ 0,  1,  2,  3],
       [ 4,  5,  6,  7],
       [ 8,  9, 10, 11]])
>>> a[2]  ❺
array([ 8,  9, 10, 11])
>>> a[2, 1]  ❻
9
>>> a[:, 1]  ❼
array([1, 5, 9])
>>> a.transpose()  ❽
array([[ 0,  4,  8],
       [ 1,  5,  9],
       [ 2,  6, 10],
       [ 3,  7, 11]])
```

❶ Import NumPy, after installing (it's not in the Python standard library). Conventionally, numpy is imported as np.

❷ Build and inspect a `numpy.ndarray` with integers 0 to 11.

❸ Inspect the dimensions of the array: this is a one-dimensional, 12-element array.

❹ Change the shape of the array, adding one dimension, then inspecting the result.

❺ Get row at index 2.

❻ Get element at index 2, 1.

❼ Get column at index 1.

❽ Create a new array by transposing (swapping columns with rows).

NumPy also supports high-level operations for loading, saving, and operating on all elements of a `numpy.ndarray`:

```
>>> import numpy
>>> floats = numpy.loadtxt('floats-10M-lines.txt')  ❶
```

```
>>> floats[-3:]  ❷
array([ 3016362.69195522,    535281.10514262,   4566560.44373946])
>>> floats *= .5  ❸
>>> floats[-3:]
array([ 1508181.34597761,    267640.55257131,   2283280.22186973])
>>> from time import perf_counter as pc  ❹
>>> t0 = pc(); floats /= 3; pc() - t0  ❺
0.03690556302899495
>>> numpy.save('floats-10M', floats)  ❻
>>> floats2 = numpy.load('floats-10M.npy', 'r+')  ❼
>>> floats2 *= 6
>>> floats2[-3:]  ❽
memmap([ 3016362.69195522,    535281.10514262,   4566560.44373946])
```

❶ Load 10 million floating-point numbers from a text file.

❷ Use sequence slicing notation to inspect the last three numbers.

❸ Multiply every element in the floats array by .5 and inspect the last three elements again.

❹ Import the high-resolution performance measurement timer (available since Python 3.3).

❺ Divide every element by 3; the elapsed time for 10 million floats is less than 40 milliseconds.

❻ Save the array in a *.npy* binary file.

❼ Load the data as a memory-mapped file into another array; this allows efficient processing of slices of the array even if it does not fit entirely in memory.

❽ Inspect the last three elements after multiplying every element by 6.

This was just an appetizer.

NumPy and SciPy are formidable libraries, and are the foundation of other awesome tools such as the Pandas (*https://fpy.li/2-20*)—which implements efficient array types that can hold nonnumeric data and provides import/export functions for many different formats, like *.csv*, *.xls*, SQL dumps, HDF5, etc.—and scikit-learn (*https://fpy.li/2-21*), currently the most widely used Machine Learning toolset. Most NumPy and SciPy functions are implemented in C or C++, and can leverage all CPU cores because they release Python's GIL (Global Interpreter Lock). The Dask (*https://fpy.li/dask*) project supports parallelizing NumPy, Pandas, and scikit-learn processing across clusters of machines. These packages deserve entire books about them. This is not one of those books. But no overview of Python sequences would be complete without at least a quick look at NumPy arrays.

Having looked at flat sequences—standard arrays and NumPy arrays—we now turn to a completely different set of replacements for the plain old list: queues.

Deques and Other Queues

The .append and .pop methods make a list usable as a stack or a queue (if you use .append and .pop(0), you get FIFO behavior). But inserting and removing from the head of a list (the 0-index end) is costly because the entire list must be shifted in memory.

The class collections.deque is a thread-safe double-ended queue designed for fast inserting and removing from both ends. It is also the way to go if you need to keep a list of "last seen items" or something of that nature, because a deque can be bounded —i.e., created with a fixed maximum length. If a bounded deque is full, when you add a new item, it discards an item from the opposite end. Example 2-23 shows some typical operations performed on a deque.

Example 2-23. Working with a deque

```
>>> from collections import deque
>>> dq = deque(range(10), maxlen=10)    ❶
>>> dq
deque([0, 1, 2, 3, 4, 5, 6, 7, 8, 9], maxlen=10)
>>> dq.rotate(3)    ❷
>>> dq
deque([7, 8, 9, 0, 1, 2, 3, 4, 5, 6], maxlen=10)
>>> dq.rotate(-4)
>>> dq
deque([1, 2, 3, 4, 5, 6, 7, 8, 9, 0], maxlen=10)
>>> dq.appendleft(-1)    ❸
>>> dq
deque([-1, 1, 2, 3, 4, 5, 6, 7, 8, 9], maxlen=10)
>>> dq.extend([11, 22, 33])    ❹
>>> dq
deque([3, 4, 5, 6, 7, 8, 9, 11, 22, 33], maxlen=10)
>>> dq.extendleft([10, 20, 30, 40])    ❺
>>> dq
deque([40, 30, 20, 10, 3, 4, 5, 6, 7, 8], maxlen=10)
```

❶ The optional maxlen argument sets the maximum number of items allowed in this instance of deque; this sets a read-only maxlen instance attribute.

❷ Rotating with n > 0 takes items from the right end and prepends them to the left; when n < 0 items are taken from left and appended to the right.

❸ Appending to a deque that is full (`len(d) == d.maxlen`) discards items from the other end; note in the next line that the 0 is dropped.

❹ Adding three items to the right pushes out the leftmost -1, 1, and 2.

❺ Note that `extendleft(iter)` works by appending each successive item of the `iter` argument to the left of the deque, therefore the final position of the items is reversed.

Table 2-4 compares the methods that are specific to `list` and `deque` (removing those that also appear in `object`).

Note that `deque` implements most of the `list` methods, and adds a few that are specific to its design, like `popleft` and `rotate`. But there is a hidden cost: removing items from the middle of a `deque` is not as fast. It is really optimized for appending and popping from the ends.

The `append` and `popleft` operations are atomic, so `deque` is safe to use as a FIFO queue in multithreaded applications without the need for locks.

Table 2-4. Methods implemented in `list` or `deque` (those that are also implemented by `object` are omitted for brevity)

	list	deque	
s.__add__(s2)	●		s + s2—concatenation
s.__iadd__(s2)	●	●	s += s2—in-place concatenation
s.append(e)	●	●	Append one element to the right (after last)
s.appendleft(e)		●	Append one element to the left (before first)
s.clear()	●	●	Delete all items
s.__contains__(e)	●		e in s
s.copy()	●		Shallow copy of the list
s.__copy__()		●	Support for copy.copy (shallow copy)
s.count(e)	●	●	Count occurrences of an element
s.__delitem__(p)	●	●	Remove item at position p
s.extend(i)	●	●	Append items from iterable i to the right
s.extendleft(i)		●	Append items from iterable i to the left
s.__getitem__(p)	●	●	s[p]—get item or slice at position
s.index(e)	●		Find position of first occurrence of e
s.insert(p, e)	●		Insert element e before the item at position p
s.__iter__()	●	●	Get iterator
s.__len__()	●	●	len(s)—number of items

	list	deque	
s.__mul__(n)	●		s * n—repeated concatenation
s.__imul__(n)	●		s *= n—in-place repeated concatenation
s.__rmul__(n)	●		n * s—reversed repeated concatenation[a]
s.pop()	●	●	Remove and return last item[b]
s.popleft()		●	Remove and return first item
s.remove(e)	●	●	Remove first occurrence of element e by value
s.reverse()	●	●	Reverse the order of the items in place
s.__reversed__()	●	●	Get iterator to scan items from last to first
s.rotate(n)		●	Move n items from one end to the other
s.__setitem__(p, e)	●	●	s[p] = e—put e in position p, overwriting existing item or slice
s.sort([key], [reverse])	●		Sort items in place with optional keyword arguments key and reverse

[a] Reversed operators are explained in Chapter 16.

[b] a_list.pop(p) allows removing from position p, but deque does not support that option.

Besides deque, other Python standard library packages implement queues:

queue

This provides the synchronized (i.e., thread-safe) classes SimpleQueue, Queue, LifoQueue, and PriorityQueue. These can be used for safe communication between threads. All except SimpleQueue can be bounded by providing a max size argument greater than 0 to the constructor. However, they don't discard items to make room as deque does. Instead, when the queue is full, the insertion of a new item blocks—i.e., it waits until some other thread makes room by taking an item from the queue, which is useful to throttle the number of live threads.

multiprocessing

Implements its own unbounded SimpleQueue and bounded Queue, very similar to those in the queue package, but designed for interprocess communication. A specialized multiprocessing.JoinableQueue is provided for task management.

asyncio

Provides Queue, LifoQueue, PriorityQueue, and JoinableQueue with APIs inspired by the classes in the queue and multiprocessing modules, but adapted for managing tasks in asynchronous programming.

heapq

In contrast to the previous three modules, heapq does not implement a queue class, but provides functions like heappush and heappop that let you use a mutable sequence as a heap queue or priority queue.

This ends our overview of alternatives to the list type, and also our exploration of sequence types in general—except for the particulars of str and binary sequences, which have their own chapter (Chapter 4).

Chapter Summary

Mastering the standard library sequence types is a prerequisite for writing concise, effective, and idiomatic Python code.

Python sequences are often categorized as mutable or immutable, but it is also useful to consider a different axis: flat sequences and container sequences. The former are more compact, faster, and easier to use, but are limited to storing atomic data such as numbers, characters, and bytes. Container sequences are more flexible, but may surprise you when they hold mutable objects, so you need to be careful to use them correctly with nested data structures.

Unfortunately, Python has no foolproof immutable container sequence type: even "immutable" tuples can have their values changed when they contain mutable items like lists or user-defined objects.

List comprehensions and generator expressions are powerful notations to build and initialize sequences. If you are not yet comfortable with them, take the time to master their basic usage. It is not hard, and soon you will be hooked.

Tuples in Python play two roles: as records with unnamed fields and as immutable lists. When using a tuple as an immutable list, remember that a tuple value is only guaranteed to be fixed if all the items in it are also immutable. Calling hash(t) on a tuple is a quick way to assert that its value is fixed. A TypeError will be raised if t contains mutable items.

When a tuple is used as a record, tuple unpacking is the safest, most readable way of extracting the fields of the tuple. Beyond tuples, * works with lists and iterables in many contexts, and some of its use cases appeared in Python 3.5 with PEP 448— Additional Unpacking Generalizations (*https://fpy.li/pep448*). Python 3.10 introduced pattern matching with match/case, supporting more powerful unpacking, known as destructuring.

Sequence slicing is a favorite Python syntax feature, and it is even more powerful than many realize. Multidimensional slicing and ellipsis (...) notation, as used in NumPy, may also be supported by user-defined sequences. Assigning to slices is a very expressive way of editing mutable sequences.

Repeated concatenation as in seq * n is convenient and, with care, can be used to initialize lists of lists containing immutable items. Augmented assignment with += and *= behaves differently for mutable and immutable sequences. In the latter case, these operators necessarily build new sequences. But if the target sequence is mutable, it is usually changed in place—but not always, depending on how the sequence is implemented.

The sort method and the sorted built-in function are easy to use and flexible, thanks to the optional key argument: a function to calculate the ordering criterion. By the way, key can also be used with the min and max built-in functions.

Beyond lists and tuples, the Python standard library provides array.array. Although NumPy and SciPy are not part of the standard library, if you do any kind of numerical processing on large sets of data, studying even a small part of these libraries can take you a long way.

We closed by visiting the versatile and thread-safe collections.deque, comparing its API with that of list in Table 2-4 and mentioning other queue implementations in the standard library.

Further Reading

Chapter 1, "Data Structures," of the *Python Cookbook*, 3rd ed. (O'Reilly) by David Beazley and Brian K. Jones, has many recipes focusing on sequences, including "Recipe 1.11. Naming a Slice," from which I learned the trick of assigning slices to variables to improve readability, illustrated in our Example 2-13.

The second edition of the *Python Cookbook* was written for Python 2.4, but much of its code works with Python 3, and a lot of the recipes in Chapters 5 and 6 deal with sequences. The book was edited by Alex Martelli, Anna Ravenscroft, and David Ascher, and it includes contributions by dozens of Pythonistas. The third edition was rewritten from scratch, and focuses more on the semantics of the language—particularly what has changed in Python 3—while the older volume emphasizes pragmatics (i.e., how to apply the language to real-world problems). Even though some of the second edition solutions are no longer the best approach, I honestly think it is worthwhile to have both editions of the *Python Cookbook* on hand.

The official Python "Sorting HOW TO" (*https://fpy.li/2-22*) has several examples of advanced tricks for using sorted and list.sort.

PEP 3132—Extended Iterable Unpacking (*https://fpy.li/2-2*) is the canonical source to read about the new use of *extra syntax on the lefthand side of parallel assignments. If you'd like a glimpse of Python evolving, "Missing * unpacking generalizations" (*https://fpy.li/2-24*) is a bug tracker issue proposing enhancements to the iterable unpacking notation. PEP 448—Additional Unpacking Generalizations (*https://fpy.li/pep448*) resulted from the discussions in that issue.

As I mentioned in "Pattern Matching with Sequences" on page 39, Carol Willing's "Structural Pattern Matching" (*https://fpy.li/2-6*) section of "What's New In Python 3.10" (*https://fpy.li/2-7*) is a great introduction to this major new feature in about 1,400 words (that's less than 5 pages when Firefox makes a PDF from the HTML). PEP 636—Structural Pattern Matching: Tutorial (*https://fpy.li/pep636*) is also good, but longer. The same PEP 636 includes "Appendix A—Quick Intro" (*https://fpy.li/2-27*). It is shorter than Willing's intro because it omits high-level considerations about why pattern matching is good for you. If you need more arguments to convince yourself or others that pattern matching is good for Python, read the 22-page PEP 635—Structural Pattern Matching: Motivation and Rationale (*https://fpy.li/pep635*).

Eli Bendersky's blog post "Less copies in Python with the buffer protocol and memoryviews" (*https://fpy.li/2-28*) includes a short tutorial on `memoryview`.

There are numerous books covering NumPy in the market, and many don't mention "NumPy" in the title. Two examples are the open access *Python Data Science Handbook* (*https://fpy.li/2-29*) by Jake VanderPlas, and the second edition of Wes McKinney's *Python for Data Analysis*.

"NumPy is all about vectorization." That is the opening sentence of Nicolas P. Rougier's open access book *From Python to NumPy* (*https://fpy.li/2-31*). Vectorized operations apply mathematical functions to all elements of an array without an explicit loop written in Python. They can operate in parallel, using special vector instructions in modern CPUs, leveraging multiple cores or delegating to the GPU, depending on the library. The first example in Rougier's book shows a speedup of 500 times after refactoring a nice Pythonic class using a generator method, into a lean and mean function calling a couple of NumPy vector functions.

To learn how to use `deque` (and other collections), see the examples and practical recipes in "Container datatypes" (*https://fpy.li/collec*) in the Python documentation.

The best defense of the Python convention of excluding the last item in ranges and slices was written by Edsger W. Dijkstra himself, in a short memo titled "Why Numbering Should Start at Zero" (*https://fpy.li/2-32*). The subject of the memo is mathematical notation, but it's relevant to Python because Dijkstra explains with rigor and humor why a sequence like 2, 3, …, 12 should always be expressed as $2 \leq i < 13$. All other reasonable conventions are refuted, as is the idea of letting each user choose a convention. The title refers to zero-based indexing, but the memo is really about why it is desirable that `'ABCDE'[1:3]` means `'BC'` and not `'BCD'` and why it makes perfect sense to write `range(2, 13)` to produce 2, 3, 4, …, 12. By the way, the memo is a handwritten note, but it's beautiful and totally readable. Dijkstra's handwriting is so clear that someone created a font (*https://fpy.li/2-33*) out of his notes.

Soapbox

The Nature of Tuples

In 2012, I presented a poster about the ABC language at PyCon US. Before creating Python, Guido van Rossum had worked on the ABC interpreter, so he came to see my poster. Among other things, we talked about the ABC *compounds*, which are clearly the predecessors of Python tuples. Compounds also support parallel assignment and are used as composite keys in dictionaries (or *tables*, in ABC parlance). However, compounds are not sequences. They are not iterable and you cannot retrieve a field by index, much less slice them. You either handle the compound as whole or extract the individual fields using parallel assignment, that's all.

I told Guido that these limitations make the main purpose of compounds very clear: they are just records without field names. His response: "Making tuples behave as sequences was a hack."

This illustrates the pragmatic approach that made Python more practical and more successful than ABC. From a language implementer perspective, making tuples behave as sequences costs little. As a result, the main use case for tuples as records is not so obvious, but we gained immutable lists—even if their type is not as clearly named as `frozenlist`.

Flat Versus Container Sequences

To highlight the different memory models of the sequence types, I used the terms *container sequence* and *flat sequence*. The "container" word is from the "Data Model" documentation (*https://fpy.li/2-34*):

> Some objects contain references to other objects; these are called containers.

I used the term "container sequence" to be specific, because there are containers in Python that are not sequences, like `dict` and `set`. Container sequences can be nested because they may contain objects of any type, including their own type.

On the other hand, *flat sequences* are sequence types that cannot be nested because they only hold simple atomic types like integers, floats, or characters.

I adopted the term *flat sequence* because I needed something to contrast with "container sequence."

Despite the previous use of the word "containers" in the official documentation, there is an abstract class in `collections.abc` called `Container`. That ABC has just one method, `__contains__`—the special method behind the `in` operator. This means that strings and arrays, which are not containers in the traditional sense, are virtual subclasses of `Container` because they implement `__contains__`. This is just one more example of humans using a word to mean different things. In this book I'll write "container" with lowercase letters to mean "an object that contains references to other objects," and `Container` with a capitalized initial in a single-spaced font to refer to `collections.abc.Container`.

Mixed-Bag Lists

Introductory Python texts emphasize that lists can contain objects of mixed types, but in practice that feature is not very useful: we put items in a list to process them later, which implies that all items should support at least some operation in common (i.e., they should all "quack" whether or not they are genetically 100% ducks). For example, you can't sort a list in Python 3 unless the items in it are comparable:

```
>>> l = [28, 14, '28', 5, '9', '1', 0, 6, '23', 19]
>>> sorted(l)
Traceback (most recent call last):
  File "<stdin>", line 1, in <module>
TypeError: unorderable types: str() < int()
```

Unlike lists, tuples often hold items of different types. That's natural: if each item in a tuple is a field, then each field may have a different type.

key Is Brilliant

The optional key argument of `list.sort`, `sorted`, `max`, and `min` is a great idea. Other languages force you to provide a two-argument comparison function like the deprecated `cmp(a, b)` function in Python 2. Using key is both simpler and more efficient. It's simpler because you just define a one-argument function that retrieves or calculates whatever criterion you want to use to sort your objects; this is easier than writing a two-argument function to return –1, 0, 1. It is also more efficient because the key function is invoked only once per item, while the two-argument comparison is called every time the sorting algorithm needs to compare two items. Of course, Python also has to compare the keys while sorting, but that comparison is done in optimized C code and not in a Python function that you wrote.

By the way, using key we can sort a mixed bag of numbers and number-like strings. We just need to decide whether we want to treat all items as integers or strings:

```
>>> l = [28, 14, '28', 5, '9', '1', 0, 6, '23', 19]
>>> sorted(l, key=int)
[0, '1', 5, 6, '9', 14, 19, '23', 28, '28']
>>> sorted(l, key=str)
[0, '1', 14, 19, '23', 28, '28', 5, 6, '9']
```

Oracle, Google, and the Timbot Conspiracy

The sorting algorithm used in `sorted` and `list.sort` is Timsort, an adaptive algorithm that switches from insertion sort to merge sort strategies, depending on how ordered the data is. This is efficient because real-world data tends to have runs of sorted items. There is a Wikipedia article (*https://fpy.li/2-35*) about it.

Timsort was first used in CPython in 2002. Since 2009, Timsort is also used to sort arrays in both standard Java and Android, a fact that became widely known when Oracle used some of the code related to Timsort as evidence of Google infringement of Sun's intellectual property. For example, see this order by Judge William Alsup (*https://fpy.li/2-36*) from 2012. In 2021, the US Supreme Court ruled Google's use of Java code as "fair use."

Timsort was invented by Tim Peters, a Python core developer so prolific that he is believed to be an AI, the Timbot. You can read about that conspiracy theory in "Python Humor" (*https://fpy.li/2-37*). Tim also wrote "The Zen of Python": `import this`.

## CHAPTER 3

Dictionaries and Sets

Python is basically dicts wrapped in loads of syntactic sugar.

—Lalo Martins, early digital nomad and Pythonista

We use dictionaries in all our Python programs. If not directly in our code, then indirectly because the `dict` type is a fundamental part of Python's implementation. Class and instance attributes, module namespaces, and function keyword arguments are some of the core Python constructs represented by dictionaries in memory. The `__builtins__.__dict__` stores all built-in types, objects, and functions.

Because of their crucial role, Python dicts are highly optimized—and continue to get improvements. *Hash tables* are the engines behind Python's high-performance dicts.

Other built-in types based on hash tables are `set` and `frozenset`. These offer richer APIs and operators than the sets you may have encountered in other popular languages. In particular, Python sets implement all the fundamental operations from set theory, like union, intersection, subset tests, etc. With them, we can express algorithms in a more declarative way, avoiding lots of nested loops and conditionals.

Here is a brief outline of this chapter:

- Modern syntax to build and handle `dicts` and mappings, including enhanced unpacking and pattern matching
- Common methods of mapping types
- Special handling for missing keys
- Variations of `dict` in the standard library
- The `set` and `frozenset` types
- Implications of hash tables in the behavior of sets and dictionaries

What's New in This Chapter

Most changes in this second edition cover new features related to mapping types:

- "Modern dict Syntax" on page 78 covers enhanced unpacking syntax and different ways of merging mappings—including the | and |= operators supported by dicts since Python 3.9.

- "Pattern Matching with Mappings" on page 81 illustrates handling mappings with match/case, since Python 3.10.

- "collections.OrderedDict" on page 95 now focuses on the small but still relevant differences between dict and OrderedDict—considering that dict keeps the key insertion order since Python 3.6.

- New sections on the view objects returned by dict.keys, dict.items, and dict.values: "Dictionary Views" on page 101 and "Set Operations on dict Views" on page 110.

The underlying implementation of dict and set still relies on hash tables, but the dict code has two important optimizations that save memory and preserve the insertion order of the keys in dict. "Practical Consequences of How dict Works" on page 102 and "Practical Consequences of How Sets Work" on page 107 summarize what you need to know to use them well.

 After adding more than 200 pages in this second edition, I moved the optional section "Internals of sets and dicts" (*https://fpy.li/hashint*) to the *fluentpython.com* companion website. The updated and expanded 18-page post (*https://fpy.li/hashint*) includes explanations and diagrams about:

- The hash table algorithm and data structures, starting with its use in set, which is simpler to understand.

- The memory optimization that preserves key insertion order in dict instances (since Python 3.6).

- The key-sharing layout for dictionaries holding instance attributes—the __dict__ of user-defined objects (optimization implemented in Python 3.3).

Modern dict Syntax

The next sections describe advanced syntax features to build, unpack, and process mappings. Some of these features are not new in the language, but may be new to you. Others require Python 3.9 (like the | operator) or Python 3.10 (like match/case). Let's start with one of the best and oldest of these features.

dict Comprehensions

Since Python 2.7, the syntax of listcomps and genexps was adapted to `dict` comprehensions (and `set` comprehensions as well, which we'll soon visit). A *dictcomp* (dict comprehension) builds a `dict` instance by taking `key:value` pairs from any iterable. Example 3-1 shows the use of `dict` comprehensions to build two dictionaries from the same list of tuples.

Example 3-1. Examples of `dict` comprehensions

```
>>> dial_codes = [                                                      ❶
...     (880, 'Bangladesh'),
...     (55,  'Brazil'),
...     (86,  'China'),
...     (91,  'India'),
...     (62,  'Indonesia'),
...     (81,  'Japan'),
...     (234, 'Nigeria'),
...     (92,  'Pakistan'),
...     (7,   'Russia'),
...     (1,   'United States'),
... ]
>>> country_dial = {country: code for code, country in dial_codes}      ❷
>>> country_dial
{'Bangladesh': 880, 'Brazil': 55, 'China': 86, 'India': 91, 'Indonesia': 62,
'Japan': 81, 'Nigeria': 234, 'Pakistan': 92, 'Russia': 7, 'United States': 1}
>>> {code: country.upper()                                              ❸
...     for country, code in sorted(country_dial.items())
...     if code < 70}
{55: 'BRAZIL', 62: 'INDONESIA', 7: 'RUSSIA', 1: 'UNITED STATES'}
```

❶ An iterable of key-value pairs like `dial_codes` can be passed directly to the `dict` constructor, but...

❷ ...here we swap the pairs: `country` is the key, and `code` is the value.

❸ Sorting `country_dial` by name, reversing the pairs again, uppercasing values, and filtering items with `code < 70`.

If you're used to listcomps, dictcomps are a natural next step. If you aren't, the spread of the comprehension syntax means it's now more profitable than ever to become fluent in it.

Unpacking Mappings

PEP 448—Additional Unpacking Generalizations (*https://fpy.li/pep448*) enhanced the support of mapping unpackings in two ways, since Python 3.5.

First, we can apply ** to more than one argument in a function call. This works when keys are all strings and unique across all arguments (because duplicate keyword arguments are forbidden):

```
>>> def dump(**kwargs):
...     return kwargs
...
>>> dump(**{'x': 1}, y=2, **{'z': 3})
{'x': 1, 'y': 2, 'z': 3}
```

Second, ** can be used inside a dict literal—also multiple times:

```
>>> {'a': 0, **{'x': 1}, 'y': 2, **{'z': 3, 'x': 4}}
{'a': 0, 'x': 4, 'y': 2, 'z': 3}
```

In this case, duplicate keys are allowed. Later occurrences overwrite previous ones—see the value mapped to x in the example.

This syntax can also be used to merge mappings, but there are other ways. Please read on.

Merging Mappings with |

Python 3.9 supports using | and |= to merge mappings. This makes sense, since these are also the set union operators.

The | operator creates a new mapping:

```
>>> d1 = {'a': 1, 'b': 3}
>>> d2 = {'a': 2, 'b': 4, 'c': 6}
>>> d1 | d2
{'a': 2, 'b': 4, 'c': 6}
```

Usually the type of the new mapping will be the same as the type of the left operand —d1 in the example—but it can be the type of the second operand if user-defined types are involved, according to the operator overloading rules we explore in Chapter 16.

To update an existing mapping in place, use |=. Continuing from the previous example, d1 was not changed, but now it is:

```
>>> d1
{'a': 1, 'b': 3}
>>> d1 |= d2
>>> d1
{'a': 2, 'b': 4, 'c': 6}
```

If you need to maintain code to run on Python 3.8 or earlier, the "Motivation" (*https://fpy.li/3-1*) section of PEP 584—Add Union Operators To dict (*https://fpy.li/pep584*) provides a good summary of other ways to merge mappings.

Now let's see how pattern matching applies to mappings.

Pattern Matching with Mappings

The `match/case` statement supports subjects that are mapping objects. Patterns for mappings look like `dict` literals, but they can match instances of any actual or virtual subclass of `collections.abc.Mapping`.[1]

In Chapter 2 we focused on sequence patterns only, but different types of patterns can be combined and nested. Thanks to destructuring, pattern matching is a powerful tool to process records structured like nested mappings and sequences, which we often need to read from JSON APIs and databases with semi-structured schemas, like MongoDB, EdgeDB, or PostgreSQL. Example 3-2 demonstrates that. The simple type hints in `get_creators` make it clear that it takes a `dict` and returns a `list`.

Example 3-2. creator.py: `get_creators()` extracts names of creators from media records

```
def get_creators(record: dict) -> list:
    match record:
        case {'type': 'book', 'api': 2, 'authors': [*names]}:  ❶
            return names
        case {'type': 'book', 'api': 1, 'author': name}:  ❷
            return [name]
        case {'type': 'book'}:  ❸
            raise ValueError(f"Invalid 'book' record: {record!r}")
        case {'type': 'movie', 'director': name}:  ❹
            return [name]
        case _:  ❺
            raise ValueError(f'Invalid record: {record!r}')
```

---

[1] A virtual subclass is any class registered by calling the `.register()` method of an ABC, as explained in "A Virtual Subclass of an ABC" on page 462. A type implemented via Python/C API is also eligible if a specific marker bit is set. See `Py_TPFLAGS_MAPPING` (*https://fpy.li/3-2*).

❶ Match any mapping with `'type': 'book'`, `'api'` :2, and an `'authors'` key mapped to a sequence. Return the items in the sequence, as a new `list`.

❷ Match any mapping with `'type': 'book'`, `'api'` :1, and an `'author'` key mapped to any object. Return the object inside a `list`.

❸ Any other mapping with `'type': 'book'` is invalid, raise `ValueError`.

❹ Match any mapping with `'type': 'movie'` and a `'director'` key mapped to a single object. Return the object inside a `list`.

❺ Any other subject is invalid, raise `ValueError`.

Example 3-2 shows some useful practices for handling semi-structured data such as JSON records:

- Include a field describing the kind of record (e.g., `'type': 'movie'`)
- Include a field identifying the schema version (e.g., `'api': 2'`) to allow for future evolution of public APIs
- Have `case` clauses to handle invalid records of a specific type (e.g., `'book'`), as well as a catch-all

Now let's see how `get_creators` handles some concrete doctests:

```
>>> b1 = dict(api=1, author='Douglas Hofstadter',
...           type='book', title='Gödel, Escher, Bach')
>>> get_creators(b1)
['Douglas Hofstadter']
>>> from collections import OrderedDict
>>> b2 = OrderedDict(api=2, type='book',
...         title='Python in a Nutshell',
...         authors='Martelli Ravenscroft Holden'.split())
>>> get_creators(b2)
['Martelli', 'Ravenscroft', 'Holden']
>>> get_creators({'type': 'book', 'pages': 770})
Traceback (most recent call last):
    ...
ValueError: Invalid 'book' record: {'type': 'book', 'pages': 770}
>>> get_creators('Spam, spam, spam')
Traceback (most recent call last):
    ...
ValueError: Invalid record: 'Spam, spam, spam'
```

Note that the order of the keys in the patterns is irrelevant, even if the subject is an `OrderedDict` as b2.

In contrast with sequence patterns, mapping patterns succeed on partial matches. In the doctests, the b1 and b2 subjects include a 'title' key that does not appear in any 'book' pattern, yet they match.

There is no need to use **extra to match extra key-value pairs, but if you want to capture them as a dict, you can prefix one variable with **. It must be the last in the pattern, and **_ is forbidden because it would be redundant. A simple example:

```
>>> food = dict(category='ice cream', flavor='vanilla', cost=199)
>>> match food:
...     case {'category': 'ice cream', **details}:
...         print(f'Ice cream details: {details}')
...
Ice cream details: {'flavor': 'vanilla', 'cost': 199}
```

In "Automatic Handling of Missing Keys" on page 90 we'll study defaultdict and other mappings where key lookups via __getitem__ (i.e., d[key]) succeed because missing items are created on the fly. In the context of pattern matching, a match succeeds only if the subject already has the required keys at the top of the match statement.

> The automatic handling of missing keys is not triggered because pattern matching always uses the d.get(key, sentinel) method —where the default sentinel is a special marker value that cannot occur in user data.

Moving on from syntax and structure, let's study the API of mappings.

Standard API of Mapping Types

The collections.abc module provides the Mapping and MutableMapping ABCs describing the interfaces of dict and similar types. See Figure 3-1.

The main value of the ABCs is documenting and formalizing the standard interfaces for mappings, and serving as criteria for isinstance tests in code that needs to support mappings in a broad sense:

```
>>> my_dict = {}
>>> isinstance(my_dict, abc.Mapping)
True
>>> isinstance(my_dict, abc.MutableMapping)
True
```

Using `isinstance` with an ABC is often better than checking whether a function argument is of the concrete `dict` type, because then alternative mapping types can be used. We'll discuss this in detail in Chapter 13.

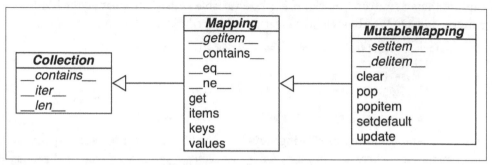

Figure 3-1. Simplified UML class diagram for the `MutableMapping` and its superclasses from `collections.abc` (inheritance arrows point from subclasses to superclasses; names in italic are abstract classes and abstract methods).

To implement a custom mapping, it's easier to extend `collections.UserDict`, or to wrap a `dict` by composition, instead of subclassing these ABCs. The `collections.UserDict` class and all concrete mapping classes in the standard library encapsulate the basic `dict` in their implementation, which in turn is built on a hash table. Therefore, they all share the limitation that the keys must be *hashable* (the values need not be hashable, only the keys). If you need a refresher, the next section explains.

What Is Hashable

Here is part of the definition of hashable adapted from the Python *Glossary* (*https://fpy.li/3-3*):

> An object is hashable if it has a hash code which never changes during its lifetime (it needs a `__hash__()` method), and can be compared to other objects (it needs an `__eq__()` method). Hashable objects which compare equal must have the same hash code.[2]

Numeric types and flat immutable types `str` and `bytes` are all hashable. Container types are hashable if they are immutable and all contained objects are also hashable.

---

2 The Python *Glossary* (*https://fpy.li/3-3*) entry for "hashable" uses the term "hash value" instead of *hash code*. I prefer *hash code* because that is a concept often discussed in the context of mappings, where items are made of keys and values, so it may be confusing to mention the hash code as a value. In this book, I only use *hash code*.

A frozenset is always hashable, because every element it contains must be hashable by definition. A tuple is hashable only if all its items are hashable. See tuples tt, tl, and tf:

```
>>> tt = (1, 2, (30, 40))
>>> hash(tt)
8027212646858338501
>>> tl = (1, 2, [30, 40])
>>> hash(tl)
Traceback (most recent call last):
  File "<stdin>", line 1, in <module>
TypeError: unhashable type: 'list'
>>> tf = (1, 2, frozenset([30, 40]))
>>> hash(tf)
-4118419923444501110
```

The hash code of an object may be different depending on the version of Python, the machine architecture, and because of a *salt* added to the hash computation for security reasons.[3] The hash code of a correctly implemented object is guaranteed to be constant only within one Python process.

User-defined types are hashable by default because their hash code is their id(), and the __eq__() method inherited from the object class simply compares the object IDs. If an object implements a custom __eq__() that takes into account its internal state, it will be hashable only if its __hash__() always returns the same hash code. In practice, this requires that __eq__() and __hash__() only take into account instance attributes that never change during the life of the object.

Now let's review the API of the most commonly used mapping types in Python: dict, defaultdict, and OrderedDict.

Overview of Common Mapping Methods

The basic API for mappings is quite rich. Table 3-1 shows the methods implemented by dict and two popular variations: defaultdict and OrderedDict, both defined in the collections module.

---

3 See PEP 456—Secure and interchangeable hash algorithm (*https://fpy.li/pep456*) to learn about the security implications and solutions adopted.

Table 3-1. Methods of the mapping types dict, collections.defaultdict, *and* collec
tions.OrderedDict *(common object methods omitted for brevity); optional arguments are
enclosed in [...]*

	dict	defaultdict	OrderedDict	
d.clear()	●	●	●	Remove all items
d.__contains__(k)	●	●	●	k in d
d.copy()	●	●	●	Shallow copy
d.__copy__()		●		Support for copy.copy(d)
d.default_factory		●		Callable invoked by __missing__ to set missing values[a]
d.__delitem__(k)	●	●	●	del d[k]—remove item with key k
d.fromkeys(it, [ini tial])	●	●	●	New mapping from keys in iterable, with optional initial value (defaults to None)
d.get(k, [default])	●	●	●	Get item with key k, return default or None if missing
d.__getitem__(k)	●	●	●	d[k]—get item with key k
d.items()	●	●	●	Get *view* over items—(key, value) pairs
d.__iter__()	●	●	●	Get iterator over keys
d.keys()	●	●	●	Get *view* over keys
d.__len__()	●	●	●	len(d)—number of items
d.__missing__(k)		●		Called when __getitem__ cannot find the key
d.move_to_end(k, [last])			●	Move k first or last position (last is True by default)
d.__or__(other)	●	●	●	Support for d1 | d2 to create new dict merging d1 and d2 (Python ≥ 3.9)
d.__ior__(other)	●	●	●	Support for d1 |= d2 to update d1 with d2 (Python ≥ 3.9)
d.pop(k, [default])	●	●	●	Remove and return value at k, or default or None if missing
d.popitem()	●	●	●	Remove and return the last inserted item as (key, value) [b]
d.__reversed__()	●	●	●	Support for reverse(d)—returns iterator for keys from last to first inserted.
d.__ror__(other)	●	●	●	Support for other | dd— reversed union operator (Python ≥ 3.9)[c]

	dict	defaultdict	OrderedDict	
d.setdefault(k, [default])	•	•	•	If k in d, return d[k]; else set d[k] = default and return it
d.__setitem__(k, v)	•	•	•	d[k] = v—put v at k
d.update(m, [**kwargs])	•	•	•	Update d with items from mapping or iterable of (key, value) pairs
d.values()	•	•	•	Get *view* over values

^a default_factory is not a method, but a callable attribute set by the end user when a defaultdict is instantiated.
^b OrderedDict.popitem(last=False) removes the first item inserted (FIFO). The last keyword argument is not supported in dict or defaultdict as recently as Python 3.10b3.
^c Reversed operators are explained in Chapter 16.

The way d.update(m) handles its first argument m is a prime example of *duck typing*: it first checks whether m has a keys method and, if it does, assumes it is a mapping. Otherwise, update() falls back to iterating over m, assuming its items are (key, value) pairs. The constructor for most Python mappings uses the logic of update() internally, which means they can be initialized from other mappings or from any iterable object producing (key, value) pairs.

A subtle mapping method is setdefault(). It avoids redundant key lookups when we need to update the value of an item in place. The next section shows how to use it.

Inserting or Updating Mutable Values

In line with Python's *fail-fast* philosophy, dict access with d[k] raises an error when k is not an existing key. Pythonistas know that d.get(k, default) is an alternative to d[k] whenever a default value is more convenient than handling KeyError. However, when you retrieve a mutable value and want to update it, there is a better way.

Consider a script to index text, producing a mapping where each key is a word, and the value is a list of positions where that word occurs, as shown in Example 3-3.

Example 3-3. Partial output from Example 3-4 processing the "Zen of Python"; each line shows a word and a list of occurrences coded as pairs: (line_number, column_number)

```
$ python3 index0.py zen.txt
a [(19, 48), (20, 53)]
Although [(11, 1), (16, 1), (18, 1)]
ambiguity [(14, 16)]
and [(15, 23)]
are [(21, 12)]
aren [(10, 15)]
at [(16, 38)]
bad [(19, 50)]
```

```
be [(15, 14), (16, 27), (20, 50)]
beats [(11, 23)]
Beautiful [(3, 1)]
better [(3, 14), (4, 13), (5, 11), (6, 12), (7, 9), (8, 11), (17, 8), (18, 25)]
...
```

Example 3-4 is a suboptimal script written to show one case where dict.get is not the best way to handle a missing key. I adapted it from an example by Alex Martelli.[4]

Example 3-4. index0.py uses dict.get *to fetch and update a list of word occurrences from the index (a better solution is in Example 3-5)*

```
"""Build an index mapping word -> list of occurrences"""

import re
import sys

WORD_RE = re.compile(r'\w+')

index = {}
with open(sys.argv[1], encoding='utf-8') as fp:
    for line_no, line in enumerate(fp, 1):
        for match in WORD_RE.finditer(line):
            word = match.group()
            column_no = match.start() + 1
            location = (line_no, column_no)
            # this is ugly; coded like this to make a point
            occurrences = index.get(word, [])      ❶
            occurrences.append(location)           ❷
            index[word] = occurrences              ❸

# display in alphabetical order
for word in sorted(index, key=str.upper):          ❹
    print(word, index[word])
```

❶ Get the list of occurrences for word, or [ ] if not found.

❷ Append new location to occurrences.

❸ Put changed occurrences into index dict; this entails a second search through the index.

---

4 The original script appears in slide 41 of Martelli's "Re-learning Python" presentation (*https://fpy.li/3-5*). His script is actually a demonstration of dict.setdefault, as shown in our Example 3-5.

❹ In the key= argument of sorted, I am not calling str.upper, just passing a reference to that method so the sorted function can use it to normalize the words for
sorting.[5]

The three lines dealing with occurrences in Example 3-4 can be replaced by a single
line using dict.setdefault. Example 3-5 is closer to Alex Martelli's code.

Example 3-5. index.py uses `dict.setdefault` *to fetch and update a list of word
occurrences from the index in a single line; contrast with Example 3-4*

```
"""Build an index mapping word -> list of occurrences"""

import re
import sys

WORD_RE = re.compile(r'\w+')

index = {}
with open(sys.argv[1], encoding='utf-8') as fp:
    for line_no, line in enumerate(fp, 1):
        for match in WORD_RE.finditer(line):
            word = match.group()
            column_no = match.start() + 1
            location = (line_no, column_no)
            index.setdefault(word, []).append(location)  ❶

# display in alphabetical order
for word in sorted(index, key=str.upper):
    print(word, index[word])
```

❶ Get the list of occurrences for word, or set it to [] if not found; setdefault
returns the value, so it can be updated without requiring a second search.

In other words, the end result of this line…

```
my_dict.setdefault(key, []).append(new_value)
```

…is the same as running…

```
if key not in my_dict:
    my_dict[key] = []
my_dict[key].append(new_value)
```

…except that the latter code performs at least two searches for key—three if it's not
found—while setdefault does it all with a single lookup.

---

5 This is an example of using a method as a first-class function, the subject of Chapter 7.

A related issue, handling missing keys on any lookup (and not only when inserting), is the subject of the next section.

Automatic Handling of Missing Keys

Sometimes it is convenient to have mappings that return some made-up value when a missing key is searched. There are two main approaches to this: one is to use a defaultdict instead of a plain dict. The other is to subclass dict or any other mapping type and add a __missing__ method. Both solutions are covered next.

defaultdict: Another Take on Missing Keys

A collections.defaultdict instance creates items with a default value on demand whenever a missing key is searched using d[k] syntax. Example 3-6 uses default dict to provide another elegant solution to the word index task from Example 3-5.

Here is how it works: when instantiating a defaultdict, you provide a callable to produce a default value whenever __getitem__ is passed a nonexistent key argument.

For example, given a defaultdict created as dd = defaultdict(list), if 'new-key' is not in dd, the expression dd['new-key'] does the following steps:

1. Calls list() to create a new list.
2. Inserts the list into dd using 'new-key' as key.
3. Returns a reference to that list.

The callable that produces the default values is held in an instance attribute named default_factory.

Example 3-6. index_default.py: using defaultdict instead of the setdefault method

```
"""Build an index mapping word -> list of occurrences"""

import collections
import re
import sys

WORD_RE = re.compile(r'\w+')

index = collections.defaultdict(list)     ❶
with open(sys.argv[1], encoding='utf-8') as fp:
    for line_no, line in enumerate(fp, 1):
        for match in WORD_RE.finditer(line):
            word = match.group()
            column_no = match.start() + 1
            location = (line_no, column_no)
```

```
        index[word].append(location)  ❷
```

```
# display in alphabetical order
for word in sorted(index, key=str.upper):
    print(word, index[word])
```

❶ Create a `defaultdict` with the `list` constructor as `default_factory`.

❷ If `word` is not initially in the `index`, the `default_factory` is called to produce the missing value, which in this case is an empty `list` that is then assigned to `index[word]` and returned, so the `.append(location)` operation always succeeds.

If no `default_factory` is provided, the usual `KeyError` is raised for missing keys.

 The `default_factory` of a `defaultdict` is only invoked to provide default values for `__getitem__` calls, and not for the other methods. For example, if `dd` is a `defaultdict`, and `k` is a missing key, `dd[k]` will call the `default_factory` to create a default value, but `dd.get(k)` still returns `None`, and `k in dd` is `False`.

The mechanism that makes `defaultdict` work by calling `default_factory` is the `__missing__` special method, a feature that we discuss next.

The __missing__ Method

Underlying the way mappings deal with missing keys is the aptly named `__missing__` method. This method is not defined in the base `dict` class, but `dict` is aware of it: if you subclass `dict` and provide a `__missing__` method, the standard `dict.__getitem__` will call it whenever a key is not found, instead of raising `KeyError`.

Suppose you'd like a mapping where keys are converted to `str` when looked up. A concrete use case is a device library for IoT,[6] where a programmable board with general-purpose I/O pins (e.g., a Raspberry Pi or an Arduino) is represented by a `Board` class with a `my_board.pins` attribute, which is a mapping of physical pin identifiers to pin software objects. The physical pin identifier may be just a number or a string like `"A0"` or `"P9_12"`. For consistency, it is desirable that all keys in `board.pins` are strings, but it is also convenient looking up a pin by number, as in `my_arduino.pin[13]`, so that beginners are not tripped when they want to blink the LED on pin 13 of their Arduinos. Example 3-7 shows how such a mapping would work.

---

6 One such library is *Pingo.io* (*https://fpy.li/3-6*), no longer under active development.

Example 3-7. When searching for a nonstring key, `StrKeyDict0` converts it to `str` when it is not found

Tests for item retrieval using `d[key]` notation::

```
>>> d = StrKeyDict0([('2', 'two'), ('4', 'four')])
>>> d['2']
'two'
>>> d[4]
'four'
>>> d[1]
Traceback (most recent call last):
  ...
KeyError: '1'
```

Tests for item retrieval using `d.get(key)` notation::

```
>>> d.get('2')
'two'
>>> d.get(4)
'four'
>>> d.get(1, 'N/A')
'N/A'
```

Tests for the `in` operator::

```
>>> 2 in d
True
>>> 1 in d
False
```

Example 3-8 implements a class `StrKeyDict0` that passes the preceding doctests.

> A better way to create a user-defined mapping type is to subclass `collections.UserDict` instead of `dict` (as we will do in Example 3-9). Here we subclass `dict` just to show that `__miss ing__` is supported by the built-in `dict.__getitem__` method.

Example 3-8. `StrKeyDict0` converts nonstring keys to `str` on lookup (see tests in Example 3-7)

```
class StrKeyDict0(dict):  ❶

    def __missing__(self, key):
        if isinstance(key, str):  ❷
            raise KeyError(key)
        return self[str(key)]  ❸
```

```
def get(self, key, default=None):
    try:
        return self[key]  ❹
    except KeyError:
        return default  ❺

def __contains__(self, key):
    return key in self.keys() or str(key) in self.keys()  ❻
```

❶ StrKeyDict0 inherits from dict.

❷ Check whether key is already a str. If it is, and it's missing, raise KeyError.

❸ Build str from key and look it up.

❹ The get method delegates to __getitem__ by using the self[key] notation; that gives the opportunity for our __missing__ to act.

❺ If a KeyError was raised, __missing__ already failed, so we return the default.

❻ Search for unmodified key (the instance may contain non-str keys), then for a str built from the key.

Take a moment to consider why the test isinstance(key, str) is necessary in the __missing__ implementation.

Without that test, our __missing__ method would work OK for any key k—str or not str—whenever str(k) produced an existing key. But if str(k) is not an existing key, we'd have an infinite recursion. In the last line of __missing__, self[str(key)] would call __getitem__, passing that str key, which in turn would call __missing__ again.

The __contains__ method is also needed for consistent behavior in this example, because the operation k in d calls it, but the method inherited from dict does not fall back to invoking __missing__. There is a subtle detail in our implementation of __contains__: we do not check for the key in the usual Pythonic way—k in my_dict —because str(key) in self would recursively call __contains__. We avoid this by explicitly looking up the key in self.keys().

A search like k in my_dict.keys() is efficient in Python 3 even for very large mappings because dict.keys() returns a view, which is similar to a set, as we'll see in "Set Operations on dict Views" on page 110. However, remember that k in my_dict does the same job, and is faster because it avoids the attribute lookup to find the .keys method.

I had a specific reason to use self.keys() in the __contains__ method in Example 3-8. The check for the unmodified key—key in self.keys()—is necessary for correctness because StrKeyDict0 does not enforce that all keys in the dictionary must be of type str. Our only goal with this simple example is to make searching "friendlier" and not enforce types.

 User-defined classes derived from standard library mappings may or may not use __missing__ as a fallback in their implementations of __getitem__, get, or __contains__, as explained in the next section.

Inconsistent Usage of __missing__ in the Standard Library

Consider the following scenarios, and how the missing key lookups are affected:

dict *subclass*
A subclass of dict implementing only __missing__ and no other method. In this case, __missing__ may be called only on d[k], which will use the __getitem__ inherited from dict.

collections.UserDict *subclass*
Likewise, a subclass of UserDict implementing only __missing__ and no other method. The get method inherited from UserDict calls __getitem__. This means __missing__ may be called to handle lookups with d[k] and d.get(k).

abc.Mapping *subclass with the simplest possible* __getitem__
A minimal subclass of abc.Mapping implementing __missing__ and the required abstract methods, including an implementation of __getitem__ that does not call __missing__. The __missing__ method is never triggered in this class.

abc.Mapping *subclass with* __getitem__ *calling* __missing__
A minimal subclass of abc.Mapping implementing __missing__ and the required abstract methods, including an implementation of __getitem__ that calls __miss ing__. The __missing__ method is triggered in this class for missing key lookups made with d[k], d.get(k), and k in d.

See *missing.py* (*https://fpy.li/3-7*) in the example code repository for demonstrations of the scenarios described here.

The four scenarios just described assume minimal implementations. If your subclass implements __getitem__, get, and __contains__, then you can make those methods use __missing__ or not, depending on your needs. The point of this section is to show that you must be careful when subclassing standard library mappings to use __missing__, because the base classes support different behaviors by default.

Don't forget that the behavior of setdefault and update is also affected by key lookup. And finally, depending on the logic of your __missing__, you may need to implement special logic in __setitem__, to avoid inconsistent or surprising behavior. We'll see an example of this in "Subclassing UserDict Instead of dict" on page 97.

So far we have covered the dict and defaultdict mapping types, but the standard library comes with other mapping implementations, which we discuss next.

Variations of dict

In this section is an overview of mapping types included in the standard library, besides defaultdict, already covered in "defaultdict: Another Take on Missing Keys" on page 90.

collections.OrderedDict

Now that the built-in dict also keeps the keys ordered since Python 3.6, the most common reason to use OrderedDict is writing code that is backward compatible with earlier Python versions. Having said that, Python's documentation lists some remaining differences between dict and OrderedDict, which I quote here—only reordering the items for relevance in daily use:

- The equality operation for OrderedDict checks for matching order.
- The popitem() method of OrderedDict has a different signature. It accepts an optional argument to specify which item is popped.
- OrderedDict has a move_to_end() method to efficiently reposition an element to an endpoint.
- The regular dict was designed to be very good at mapping operations. Tracking insertion order was secondary.
- OrderedDict was designed to be good at reordering operations. Space efficiency, iteration speed, and the performance of update operations were secondary.
- Algorithmically, OrderedDict can handle frequent reordering operations better than dict. This makes it suitable for tracking recent accesses (for example, in an LRU cache).

collections.ChainMap

A ChainMap instance holds a list of mappings that can be searched as one. The lookup is performed on each input mapping in the order it appears in the constructor call, and succeeds as soon as the key is found in one of those mappings. For example:

```
>>> d1 = dict(a=1, b=3)
>>> d2 = dict(a=2, b=4, c=6)
>>> from collections import ChainMap
>>> chain = ChainMap(d1, d2)
>>> chain['a']
1
>>> chain['c']
6
```

The ChainMap instance does not copy the input mappings, but holds references to them. Updates or insertions to a ChainMap only affect the first input mapping. Continuing from the previous example:

```
>>> chain['c'] = -1
>>> d1
{'a': 1, 'b': 3, 'c': -1}
>>> d2
{'a': 2, 'b': 4, 'c': 6}
```

ChainMap is useful to implement interpreters for languages with nested scopes, where each mapping represents a scope context, from the innermost enclosing scope to the outermost scope. The "ChainMap objects" section of the collections docs (*https://fpy.li/3-8*) has several examples of ChainMap usage, including this snippet inspired by the basic rules of variable lookup in Python:

```
import builtins
pylookup = ChainMap(locals(), globals(), vars(builtins))
```

Example 18-14 shows a ChainMap subclass used to implement an interpreter for a subset of the Scheme programming language.

collections.Counter

A mapping that holds an integer count for each key. Updating an existing key adds to its count. This can be used to count instances of hashable objects or as a multiset (discussed later in this section). Counter implements the + and - operators to combine tallies, and other useful methods such as most_common([n]), which returns an ordered list of tuples with the *n* most common items and their counts; see the documentation (*https://fpy.li/3-9*). Here is Counter used to count letters in words:

```
>>> ct = collections.Counter('abracadabra')
>>> ct
Counter({'a': 5, 'b': 2, 'r': 2, 'c': 1, 'd': 1})
>>> ct.update('aaaaazzz')
>>> ct
Counter({'a': 10, 'z': 3, 'b': 2, 'r': 2, 'c': 1, 'd': 1})
>>> ct.most_common(3)
[('a', 10), ('z', 3), ('b', 2)]
```

Note that the `'b'` and `'r'` keys are tied in third place, but `ct.most_common(3)` shows only three counts.

To use `collections.Counter` as a multiset, pretend each key is an element in the set, and the count is the number of occurrences of that element in the set.

shelve.Shelf

The `shelve` module in the standard library provides persistent storage for a mapping of string keys to Python objects serialized in the `pickle` binary format. The curious name of `shelve` makes sense when you realize that pickle jars are stored on shelves.

The `shelve.open` module-level function returns a `shelve.Shelf` instance—a simple key-value DBM database backed by the `dbm` module, with these characteristics:

- `shelve.Shelf` subclasses `abc.MutableMapping`, so it provides the essential methods we expect of a mapping type.
- In addition, `shelve.Shelf` provides a few other I/O management methods, like `sync` and `close`.
- A `Shelf` instance is a context manager, so you can use a `with` block to make sure it is closed after use.
- Keys and values are saved whenever a new value is assigned to a key.
- The keys must be strings.
- The values must be objects that the `pickle` module can serialize.

The documentation for the shelve (*https://fpy.li/3-10*), dbm (*https://fpy.li/3-11*), and pickle (*https://fpy.li/3-12*) modules provides more details and some caveats.

 Python's `pickle` is easy to use in the simplest cases, but has several drawbacks. Read Ned Batchelder's "Pickle's nine flaws" (*https://fpy.li/3-13*) before adopting any solution involving `pickle`. In his post, Ned mentions other serialization formats to consider.

`OrderedDict`, `ChainMap`, `Counter`, and `Shelf` are ready to use but can also be customized by subclassing. In contrast, `UserDict` is intended only as a base class to be extended.

Subclassing UserDict Instead of dict

It's better to create a new mapping type by extending `collections.UserDict` rather than `dict`. We realize that when we try to extend our `StrKeyDict0` from Example 3-8 to make sure that any keys added to the mapping are stored as `str`.

The main reason why it's better to subclass `UserDict` rather than `dict` is that the built-in has some implementation shortcuts that end up forcing us to override methods that we can just inherit from `UserDict` with no problems.[7]

Note that `UserDict` does not inherit from `dict`, but uses composition: it has an internal `dict` instance, called `data`, which holds the actual items. This avoids undesired recursion when coding special methods like __setitem__, and simplifies the coding of __contains__, compared to Example 3-8.

Thanks to `UserDict`, `StrKeyDict` (Example 3-9) is more concise than `StrKeyDict0` (Example 3-8), but it does more: it stores all keys as `str`, avoiding unpleasant surprises if the instance is built or updated with data containing nonstring keys.

Example 3-9. StrKeyDict always converts nonstring keys to str on insertion, update, and lookup

```
import collections


class StrKeyDict(collections.UserDict):  ❶

    def __missing__(self, key):  ❷
        if isinstance(key, str):
            raise KeyError(key)
        return self[str(key)]

    def __contains__(self, key):
        return str(key) in self.data  ❸

    def __setitem__(self, key, item):
        self.data[str(key)] = item  ❹
```

❶ `StrKeyDict` extends `UserDict`.

❷ __missing__ is exactly as in Example 3-8.

❸ __contains__ is simpler: we can assume all stored keys are `str`, and we can check on `self.data` instead of invoking `self.keys()` as we did in `StrKeyDict0`.

❹ __setitem__ converts any key to a `str`. This method is easier to overwrite when we can delegate to the `self.data` attribute.

---

7 The exact problem with subclassing `dict` and other built-ins is covered in "Subclassing Built-In Types Is Tricky" on page 492.

Because UserDict extends abc.MutableMapping, the remaining methods that make StrKeyDict a full-fledged mapping are inherited from UserDict, MutableMapping, or Mapping. The latter have several useful concrete methods, in spite of being abstract base classes (ABCs). The following methods are worth noting:

MutableMapping.update

This powerful method can be called directly but is also used by __init__ to load the instance from other mappings, from iterables of (key, value) pairs, and keyword arguments. Because it uses self[key] = value to add items, it ends up calling our implementation of __setitem__.

Mapping.get

In StrKeyDict0 (Example 3-8), we had to code our own get to return the same results as __getitem__, but in Example 3-9 we inherited Mapping.get, which is implemented exactly like StrKeyDict0.get (see the Python source code (*https://fpy.li/3-14*)).

 Antoine Pitrou authored PEP 455—Adding a key-transforming dictionary to collections (*https://fpy.li/pep455*) and a patch to enhance the collections module with a TransformDict, that is more general than StrKeyDict and preserves the keys as they are provided, before the transformation is applied. PEP 455 was rejected in May 2015—see Raymond Hettinger's rejection message (*https://fpy.li/3-15*). To experiment with TransformDict, I extracted Pitrou's patch from issue18986 (*https://fpy.li/3-16*) into a standalone module (*03-dict-set/transformdict.py* (*https://fpy.li/3-17*)) in the *Fluent Python* second edition code repository (*https://fpy.li/code*)).

We know there are immutable sequence types, but how about an immutable mapping? Well, there isn't a real one in the standard library, but a stand-in is available. That's next.

Immutable Mappings

The mapping types provided by the standard library are all mutable, but you may need to prevent users from changing a mapping by accident. A concrete use case can be found, again, in a hardware programming library like *Pingo*, mentioned in "The __missing__ Method" on page 91: the board.pins mapping represents the physical GPIO pins on the device. As such, it's useful to prevent inadvertent updates to board.pins because the hardware can't be changed via software, so any change in the mapping would make it inconsistent with the physical reality of the device.

The types module provides a wrapper class called MappingProxyType, which, given a mapping, returns a mappingproxy instance that is a read-only but dynamic proxy for the original mapping. This means that updates to the original mapping can be seen in the mappingproxy, but changes cannot be made through it. See Example 3-10 for a brief demonstration.

Example 3-10. MappingProxyType builds a read-only mappingproxy instance from a dict

```
>>> from types import MappingProxyType
>>> d = {1: 'A'}
>>> d_proxy = MappingProxyType(d)
>>> d_proxy
mappingproxy({1: 'A'})
>>> d_proxy[1]   ❶
'A'
>>> d_proxy[2] = 'x'   ❷
Traceback (most recent call last):
  File "<stdin>", line 1, in <module>
TypeError: 'mappingproxy' object does not support item assignment
>>> d[2] = 'B'
>>> d_proxy   ❸
mappingproxy({1: 'A', 2: 'B'})
>>> d_proxy[2]
'B'
>>>
```

❶ Items in d can be seen through d_proxy.

❷ Changes cannot be made through d_proxy.

❸ d_proxy is dynamic: any change in d is reflected.

Here is how this could be used in practice in the hardware programming scenario: the constructor in a concrete Board subclass would fill a private mapping with the pin objects, and expose it to clients of the API via a public .pins attribute implemented as a mappingproxy. That way the clients would not be able to add, remove, or change pins by accident.

Next, we'll cover views—which allow high-performance operations on a dict, without unnecessary copying of data.

Dictionary Views

The `dict` instance methods `.keys()`, `.values()`, and `.items()` return instances of classes called `dict_keys`, `dict_values`, and `dict_items`, respectively. These dictionary views are read-only projections of the internal data structures used in the `dict` implementation. They avoid the memory overhead of the equivalent Python 2 methods that returned lists duplicating data already in the target `dict`, and they also replace the old methods that returned iterators.

Example 3-11 shows some basic operations supported by all dictionary views.

Example 3-11. The `.values()` method returns a view of the values in a `dict`

```
>>> d = dict(a=10, b=20, c=30)
>>> values = d.values()
>>> values
dict_values([10, 20, 30])   ❶
>>> len(values)   ❷
3
>>> list(values)   ❸
[10, 20, 30]
>>> reversed(values)   ❹
<dict_reversevalueiterator object at 0x10e9e7310>
>>> values[0]   ❺
Traceback (most recent call last):
  File "<stdin>", line 1, in <module>
TypeError: 'dict_values' object is not subscriptable
```

❶ The `repr` of a view object shows its content.

❷ We can query the `len` of a view.

❸ Views are iterable, so it's easy to create lists from them.

❹ Views implement `__reversed__`, returning a custom iterator.

❺ We can't use [ ] to get individual items from a view.

A view object is a dynamic proxy. If the source `dict` is updated, you can immediately see the changes through an existing view. Continuing from Example 3-11:

```
>>> d['z'] = 99
>>> d
{'a': 10, 'b': 20, 'c': 30, 'z': 99}
>>> values
dict_values([10, 20, 30, 99])
```

The classes `dict_keys`, `dict_values`, and `dict_items` are internal: they are not available via `__builtins__` or any standard library module, and even if you get a reference to one of them, you can't use it to create a view from scratch in Python code:

```
>>> values_class = type({}.values())
>>> v = values_class()
Traceback (most recent call last):
  File "<stdin>", line 1, in <module>
TypeError: cannot create 'dict_values' instances
```

The `dict_values` class is the simplest dictionary view—it implements only the `__len__`, `__iter__`, and `__reversed__` special methods. In addition to these methods, `dict_keys` and `dict_items` implement several set methods, almost as many as the `frozenset` class. After we cover sets, we'll have more to say about `dict_keys` and `dict_items` in "Set Operations on dict Views" on page 110.

Now let's see some rules and tips informed by the way `dict` is implemented under the hood.

Practical Consequences of How dict Works

The hash table implementation of Python's `dict` is very efficient, but it's important to understand the practical effects of this design:

- Keys must be hashable objects. They must implement proper `__hash__` and `__eq__` methods as described in "What Is Hashable" on page 84.

- Item access by key is very fast. A `dict` may have millions of keys, but Python can locate a key directly by computing the hash code of the key and deriving an index offset into the hash table, with the possible overhead of a small number of tries to find a matching entry.

- Key ordering is preserved as a side effect of a more compact memory layout for `dict` in CPython 3.6, which became an official language feature in 3.7.

- Despite its new compact layout, dicts inevitably have a significant memory overhead. The most compact internal data structure for a container would be an array of pointers to the items.[8] Compared to that, a hash table needs to store more data per entry, and Python needs to keep at least one-third of the hash table rows empty to remain efficient.

- To save memory, avoid creating instance attributes outside of the `__init__` method.

---

8 That's how tuples are stored.

That last tip about instance attributes comes from the fact that Python's default behavior is to store instance attributes in a special __dict__ attribute, which is a dict attached to each instance.[9] Since PEP 412—Key-Sharing Dictionary (*https://fpy.li/ pep412*) was implemented in Python 3.3, instances of a class can share a common hash table, stored with the class. That common hash table is shared by the __dict__ of each new instance that has the same attributes names as the first instance of that class when __init__ returns. Each instance __dict__ can then hold only its own attribute values as a simple array of pointers. Adding an instance attribute after __init__ forces Python to create a new hash table just for the __dict__ of that one instance (which was the default behavior for all instances before Python 3.3). According to PEP 412, this optimization reduces memory use by 10% to 20% for object-oriented programs.

The details of the compact layout and key-sharing optimizations are rather complex. For more, please read "Internals of sets and dicts" (*https://fpy.li/hashint*) at *fluentpython.com*.

Now let's dive into sets.

Set Theory

Sets are not new in Python, but are still somewhat underused. The set type and its immutable sibling frozenset first appeared as modules in the Python 2.3 standard library, and were promoted to built-ins in Python 2.6.

> In this book, I use the word "set" to refer both to set and frozen set. When talking specifically about the set class, I use constant width font: set.

A set is a collection of unique objects. A basic use case is removing duplication:

```
>>> l = ['spam', 'spam', 'eggs', 'spam', 'bacon', 'eggs']
>>> set(l)
{'eggs', 'spam', 'bacon'}
>>> list(set(l))
['eggs', 'spam', 'bacon']
```

---

9 Unless the class has a __slots__ attribute, as explained in "Saving Memory with __slots__" on page 386.

If you want to remove duplicates but also preserve the order of the first occurrence of each item, you can now use a plain dict to do it, like this:

```
>>> dict.fromkeys(l).keys()
dict_keys(['spam', 'eggs', 'bacon'])
>>> list(dict.fromkeys(l).keys())
['spam', 'eggs', 'bacon']
```

Set elements must be hashable. The set type is not hashable, so you can't build a set with nested set instances. But frozenset is hashable, so you can have frozenset elements inside a set.

In addition to enforcing uniqueness, the set types implement many set operations as infix operators, so, given two sets a and b, a | b returns their union, a & b computes the intersection, a - b the difference, and a ^ b the symmetric difference. Smart use of set operations can reduce both the line count and the execution time of Python programs, at the same time making code easier to read and reason about—by removing loops and conditional logic.

For example, imagine you have a large set of email addresses (the haystack) and a smaller set of addresses (the needles) and you need to count how many needles occur in the haystack. Thanks to set intersection (the & operator) you can code that in a simple line (see Example 3-12).

Example 3-12. Count occurrences of needles in a haystack, both of type set

```
found = len(needles & haystack)
```

Without the intersection operator, you'd have to write Example 3-13 to accomplish the same task as Example 3-12.

Example 3-13. Count occurrences of needles in a haystack (same end result as Example 3-12)

```
found = 0
for n in needles:
    if n in haystack:
        found += 1
```

Example 3-12 runs slightly faster than Example 3-13. On the other hand, Example 3-13 works for any iterable objects needles and haystack, while Example 3-12 requires that both be sets. But, if you don't have sets on hand, you can always build them on the fly, as shown in Example 3-14.

Example 3-14. Count occurrences of needles in a haystack; these lines work for any iterable types

```
found = len(set(needles) & set(haystack))

# another way:
found = len(set(needles).intersection(haystack))
```

Of course, there is an extra cost involved in building the sets in Example 3-14, but if either the needles or the haystack is already a set, the alternatives in Example 3-14 may be cheaper than Example 3-13.

Any one of the preceding examples are capable of searching 1,000 elements in a haystack of 10,000,000 items in about 0.3 milliseconds—that's close to 0.3 microseconds per element.

Besides the extremely fast membership test (thanks to the underlying hash table), the set and frozenset built-in types provide a rich API to create new sets or, in the case of set, to change existing ones. We will discuss the operations shortly, but first a note about syntax.

Set Literals

The syntax of set literals—{1}, {1, 2}, etc.—looks exactly like the math notation, with one important exception: there's no literal notation for the empty set, so we must remember to write set().

Syntax Quirk

Don't forget that to create an empty set, you should use the constructor without an argument: set(). If you write {}, you're creating an empty dict—this hasn't changed in Python 3.

In Python 3, the standard string representation of sets always uses the {...} notation, except for the empty set:

```
>>> s = {1}
>>> type(s)
<class 'set'>
>>> s
{1}
>>> s.pop()
1
>>> s
set()
```

Literal set syntax like {1, 2, 3} is both faster and more readable than calling the constructor (e.g., set([1, 2, 3])). The latter form is slower because, to evaluate it, Python has to look up the set name to fetch the constructor, then build a list, and finally pass it to the constructor. In contrast, to process a literal like {1, 2, 3}, Python runs a specialized BUILD_SET bytecode.[10]

There is no special syntax to represent frozenset literals—they must be created by calling the constructor. The standard string representation in Python 3 looks like a frozenset constructor call. Note the output in the console session:

```
>>> frozenset(range(10))
frozenset({0, 1, 2, 3, 4, 5, 6, 7, 8, 9})
```

Speaking of syntax, the idea of listcomps was adapted to build sets as well.

Set Comprehensions

Set comprehensions (*setcomps*) were added way back in Python 2.7, together with the dictcomps that we saw in "dict Comprehensions" on page 79. Example 3-15 shows how.

Example 3-15. Build a set of Latin-1 characters that have the word "SIGN" in their Unicode names

```
>>> from unicodedata import name  ❶
>>> {chr(i) for i in range(32, 256) if 'SIGN' in name(chr(i),'')}  ❷
{'§', '=', '¢', '#', '¤', '<', '¥', 'µ', '×', '$', '¶', '£', '©',
'°', '+', '÷', '±', '>', '¬', '®', '%'}
```

❶ Import name function from unicodedata to obtain character names.

❷ Build set of characters with codes from 32 to 255 that have the word 'SIGN' in their names.

The order of the output changes for each Python process, because of the salted hash mentioned in "What Is Hashable" on page 84.

Syntax matters aside, let's now consider the behavior of sets.

---

10 This may be interesting, but is not super important. The speed up will happen only when a set literal is evaluated, and that happens at most once per Python process—when a module is initially compiled. If you're curious, import the dis function from the dis module and use it to disassemble the bytecodes for a set literal—e.g., dis('{1}')—and a set call—dis('set([1])')

Practical Consequences of How Sets Work

The `set` and `frozenset` types are both implemented with a hash table. This has these effects:

- Set elements must be hashable objects. They must implement proper `__hash__` and `__eq__` methods as described in "What Is Hashable" on page 84.
- Membership testing is very efficient. A set may have millions of elements, but an element can be located directly by computing its hash code and deriving an index offset, with the possible overhead of a small number of tries to find a matching element or exhaust the search.
- Sets have a significant memory overhead, compared to a low-level array pointers to its elements—which would be more compact but also much slower to search beyond a handful of elements.
- Element ordering depends on insertion order, but not in a useful or reliable way. If two elements are different but have the same hash code, their position depends on which element is added first.
- Adding elements to a set may change the order of existing elements. That's because the algorithm becomes less efficient if the hash table is more than two-thirds full, so Python may need to move and resize the table as it grows. When this happens, elements are reinserted and their relative ordering may change.

See "Internals of sets and dicts" (*https://fpy.li/hashint*) at *fluentpython.com* for details.

Let's now review the rich assortment of operations provided by sets.

Set Operations

Figure 3-2 gives an overview of the methods you can use on mutable and immutable sets. Many of them are special methods that overload operators, such as & and >=. Table 3-2 shows the math set operators that have corresponding operators or methods in Python. Note that some operators and methods perform in-place changes on the target set (e.g., &=, `difference_update`, etc.). Such operations make no sense in the ideal world of mathematical sets, and are not implemented in `frozenset`.

The infix operators in Table 3-2 require that both operands be sets, but all other methods take one or more iterable arguments. For example, to produce the union of four collections, a, b, c, and d, you can call a.union(b, c, d), where a must be a set, but b, c, and d can be iterables of any type that produce hashable items. If you need to create a new set with the union of four iterables, instead of updating an existing set, you can write {*a, *b, *c, *d} since Python 3.5 thanks to PEP 448—Additional Unpacking Generalizations (*https://fpy.li/pep448*).

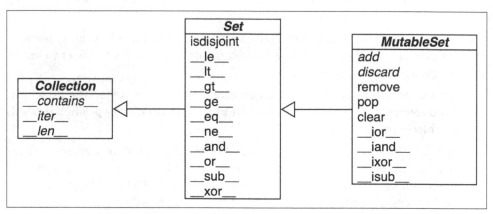

Figure 3-2. Simplified UML class diagram for MutableSet *and its superclasses from* collections.abc *(names in italic are abstract classes and abstract methods; reverse operator methods omitted for brevity).*

Table 3-2. Mathematical set operations: these methods either produce a new set or update the target set in place, if it's mutable

Math symbol	Python operator	Method	Description
S∩Z	s & z	s.__and__(z)	Intersection of s and z
	z & s	s.__rand__(z)	Reversed & operator
		s.intersection(it, …)	Intersection of s and all sets built from iterables it, etc.
	s &= z	s.__iand__(z)	s updated with intersection of s and z
		s.intersection_update(it, …)	s updated with intersection of s and all sets built from iterables it, etc.
S∪Z	s | z	s.__or__(z)	Union of s and z
	z | s	s.__ror__(z)	Reversed |
		s.union(it, …)	Union of s and all sets built from iterables it, etc.

Math symbol	Python operator	Method	Description
	s |= z	s.__ior__(z)	s updated with union of s and z
		s.update(it, ...)	s updated with union of s and all sets built from iterables it, etc.
S\Z	s - z	s.__sub__(z)	Relative complement or difference between s and z
	z - s	s.__rsub__(z)	Reversed - operator
		s.difference(it, ...)	Difference between s and all sets built from iterables it, etc.
	s -= z	s.__isub__(z)	s updated with difference between s and z
		s.difference_update(it, ...)	s updated with difference between s and all sets built from iterables it, etc.
SΔZ	s ^ z	s.__xor__(z)	Symmetric difference (the complement of the intersection s & z)
	z ^ s	s.__rxor__(z)	Reversed ^ operator
		s.symmetric_difference(it)	Complement of s & set(it)
	s ^= z	s.__ixor__(z)	s updated with symmetric difference of s and z
		s.symmetric_difference_update(it, ...)	s updated with symmetric difference of s and all sets built from iterables it, etc.

Table 3-3 lists set predicates: operators and methods that return True or False.

Table 3-3. Set comparison operators and methods that return a bool

Math symbol	Python operator	Method	Description
S∩Z=∅		s.isdisjoint(z)	s and z are disjoint (no elements in common)
e∈S	e in s	s.__contains__(e)	Element e is a member of s
S⊆Z	s <= z	s.__le__(z)	s is a subset of the z set
		s.issubset(it)	s is a subset of the set built from the iterable it
S⊂Z	s < z	s.__lt__(z)	s is a proper subset of the z set
S⊇Z	s >= z	s.__ge__(z)	s is a superset of the z set
		s.issuperset(it)	s is a superset of the set built from the iterable it
S⊃Z	s > z	s.__gt__(z)	s is a proper superset of the z set

In addition to the operators and methods derived from math set theory, the set types implement other methods of practical use, summarized in Table 3-4.

Table 3-4. Additional set methods

	set	frozenset	
s.add(e)	•		Add element e to s
s.clear()	•		Remove all elements of s
s.copy()	•	•	Shallow copy of s
s.discard(e)	•		Remove element e from s if it is present
s.__iter__()	•	•	Get iterator over s
s.__len__()	•	•	len(s)
s.pop()	•		Remove and return an element from s, raising KeyError if s is empty
s.remove(e)	•		Remove element e from s, raising KeyError if e not in s

This completes our overview of the features of sets. As promised in "Dictionary Views" on page 101, we'll now see how two of the dictionary view types behave very much like a frozenset.

Set Operations on dict Views

Table 3-5 shows that the view objects returned by the dict methods .keys() and .items() are remarkably similar to frozenset.

Table 3-5. Methods implemented by frozenset, dict_keys, and dict_items

	frozenset	dict_keys	dict_items	Description
s.__and__(z)	•	•	•	s & z (intersection of s and z)
s.__rand__(z)	•	•	•	Reversed & operator
s.__contains__()	•	•	•	e in s
s.copy()	•			Shallow copy of s
s.difference(it, …)	•			Difference between s and iterables it, etc.
s.intersection(it, …)	•			Intersection of s and iterables it, etc.
s.isdisjoint(z)	•	•	•	s and z are disjoint (no elements in common)
s.issubset(it)	•			s is a subset of iterable it
s.issuperset(it)	•			s is a superset of iterable it
s.__iter__()	•	•	•	Get iterator over s
s.__len__()	•	•	•	len(s)
s.__or__(z)	•	•	•	s | z (union of s and z)
s.__ror__()	•	•	•	Reversed | operator
s.__reversed__()		•	•	Get iterator over s in reverse order
s.__rsub__(z)	•	•	•	Reversed - operator
s.__sub__(z)	•	•	•	s - z (difference between s and z)

	frozenset	dict_keys	dict_items	Description
`s.symmetric_differ ence(it)`	•			Complement of s & set(it)
`s.union(it, …)`	•			Union of s and iterables it, etc.
`s.__xor__()`	•	•	•	s ^ z (symmetric difference of s and z)
`s.__rxor__()`	•	•	•	Reversed ^ operator

In particular, `dict_keys` and `dict_items` implement the special methods to support the powerful set operators & (intersection), | (union), - (difference), and ^ (symmetric difference).

For example, using & is easy to get the keys that appear in two dictionaries:

```
>>> d1 = dict(a=1, b=2, c=3, d=4)
>>> d2 = dict(b=20, d=40, e=50)
>>> d1.keys() & d2.keys()
{'b', 'd'}
```

Note that the return value of & is a `set`. Even better: the set operators in dictionary views are compatible with `set` instances. Check this out:

```
>>> s = {'a', 'e', 'i'}
>>> d1.keys() & s
{'a'}
>>> d1.keys() | s
{'a', 'c', 'b', 'd', 'i', 'e'}
```

A `dict_items` view only works as a set if all values in the `dict` are hashable. Attempting set operations on a `dict_items` view with an unhashable value raises `TypeError: unhashable type 'T'`, with `T` as the type of the offending value.

On the other hand, a `dict_keys` view can always be used as a set, because every key is hashable—by definition.

Using set operators with views will save a lot of loops and ifs when inspecting the contents of dictionaries in your code. Let Python's efficient implementation in C work for you!

With this, we can wrap up this chapter.

Chapter Summary

Dictionaries are a keystone of Python. Over the years, the familiar {k1: v1, k2: v2} literal syntax was enhanced to support unpacking with **, pattern matching, as well as dict comprehensions.

Beyond the basic dict, the standard library offers handy, ready-to-use specialized mappings like defaultdict, ChainMap, and Counter, all defined in the collections module. With the new dict implementation, OrderedDict is not as useful as before, but should remain in the standard library for backward compatibility—and has specific characteristics that dict doesn't have, such as taking into account key ordering in == comparisons. Also in the collections module is the UserDict, an easy to use base class to create custom mappings.

Two powerful methods available in most mappings are setdefault and update. The setdefault method can update items holding mutable values—for example, in a dict of list values—avoiding a second search for the same key. The update method allows bulk insertion or overwriting of items from any other mapping, from iterables providing (key, value) pairs, and from keyword arguments. Mapping constructors also use update internally, allowing instances to be initialized from mappings, iterables, or keyword arguments. Since Python 3.9, we can also use the |= operator to update a mapping, and the | operator to create a new one from the union of two mappings.

A clever hook in the mapping API is the __missing__ method, which lets you customize what happens when a key is not found when using the d[k] syntax that invokes __getitem__.

The collections.abc module provides the Mapping and MutableMapping abstract base classes as standard interfaces, useful for runtime type checking. The Mapping ProxyType from the types module creates an immutable façade for a mapping you want to protect from accidental change. There are also ABCs for Set and MutableSet.

Dictionary views were a great addition in Python 3, eliminating the memory overhead of the Python 2 .keys(), .values(), and .items() methods that built lists duplicating data in the target dict instance. In addition, the dict_keys and dict_items classes support the most useful operators and methods of frozenset.

Further Reading

In The Python Standard Library documentation, "collections—Container datatypes" (*https://fpy.li/collec*), includes examples and practical recipes with several mapping types. The Python source code for the module *Lib/collections/__init__.py* is a great reference for anyone who wants to create a new mapping type or grok the logic of the existing ones. Chapter 1 of the *Python Cookbook*, 3rd ed. (O'Reilly) by David Beazley and Brian K. Jones has 20 handy and insightful recipes with data structures—the majority using `dict` in clever ways.

Greg Gandenberger advocates for the continued use of `collections.OrderedDict`, on the grounds that "explicit is better than implicit," backward compatibility, and the fact that some tools and libraries assume the ordering of `dict` keys is irrelevant—his post: "Python Dictionaries Are Now Ordered. Keep Using OrderedDict" (*https://fpy.li/3-18*).

PEP 3106—Revamping dict.keys(), .values() and .items() (*https://fpy.li/pep3106*) is where Guido van Rossum presented the dictionary views feature for Python 3. In the abstract, he wrote that the idea came from the Java Collections Framework.

PyPy (*https://fpy.li/3-19*) was the first Python interpreter to implement Raymond Hettinger's proposal of compact dicts, and they blogged about it in "Faster, more memory efficient and more ordered dictionaries on PyPy" (*https://fpy.li/3-20*), acknowledging that a similar layout was adopted in PHP 7, described in PHP's new hashtable implementation (*https://fpy.li/3-21*). It's always great when creators cite prior art.

At PyCon 2017, Brandon Rhodes presented "The Dictionary Even Mightier" (*https://fpy.li/3-22*), a sequel to his classic animated presentation "The Mighty Dictionary" (*https://fpy.li/3-23*)—including animated hash collisions! Another up-to-date, but more in-depth video on the internals of Python's `dict` is "Modern Dictionaries" (*https://fpy.li/3-24*) by Raymond Hettinger, where he tells that after initially failing to sell compact dicts to the CPython core devs, he lobbied the PyPy team, they adopted it, the idea gained traction, and was finally contributed (*https://fpy.li/3-25*) to CPython 3.6 by INADA Naoki. For all details, check out the extensive comments in the CPython code for *Objects/dictobject.c* (*https://fpy.li/3-26*) and the design document *Objects/dictnotes.txt* (*https://fpy.li/3-27*).

The rationale for adding sets to Python is documented in PEP 218—Adding a Built-In Set Object Type (*https://fpy.li/pep218*). When PEP 218 was approved, no special literal syntax was adopted for sets. The `set` literals were created for Python 3 and backported to Python 2.7, along with `dict` and `set` comprehensions. At PyCon 2019, I presented "Set Practice: learning from Python's set types" (*https://fpy.li/3-29*) describing use cases of sets in real programs, covering their API design, and the implementation of `uintset` (*https://fpy.li/3-30*), a set class for integer elements using a bit vector instead of a hash table, inspired by an example in Chapter 6 of the excellent *The Go Programming Language* (*http://gopl.io*), by Alan Donovan and Brian Kernighan (Addison-Wesley).

IEEE's *Spectrum* magazine has a story about Hans Peter Luhn, a prolific inventor who patented a punched card deck to select cocktail recipes depending on ingredients available, among other diverse inventions including…hash tables! See "Hans Peter Luhn and the Birth of the Hashing Algorithm" (*https://fpy.li/3-31*).

Soapbox

Syntactic Sugar

My friend Geraldo Cohen once remarked that Python is "simple and correct."

Programming language purists like to dismiss syntax as unimportant.

> Syntactic sugar causes cancer of the semicolon.
>> —Alan Perlis

Syntax is the user interface of a programming language, so it does matter in practice.

Before finding Python, I did some web programming using Perl and PHP. The syntax for mappings in these languages is very useful, and I badly miss it whenever I have to use Java or C.

A good literal syntax for mappings is very convenient for configuration, table-driven implementations, and to hold data for prototyping and testing. That's one lesson the designers of Go learned from dynamic languages. The lack of a good way to express structured data in code pushed the Java community to adopt the verbose and overly complex XML as a data format.

JSON was proposed as "The Fat-Free Alternative to XML" (*https://fpy.li/3-32*) and became a huge success, replacing XML in many contexts. A concise syntax for lists and dictionaries makes an excellent data interchange format.

PHP and Ruby imitated the hash syntax from Perl, using => to link keys to values. JavaScript uses : like Python. Why use two characters when one is readable enough?

JSON came from JavaScript, but it also happens to be an almost exact subset of Python syntax. JSON is compatible with Python except for the spelling of the values true, false, and null.

Armin Ronacher tweeted (*https://fpy.li/3-33*) that he likes to hack Python's global namespace to add JSON-compatible aliases for Python's True, False, and None so he can paste JSON directly in the console. The basic idea:

```
>>> true, false, null = True, False, None
>>> fruit = {
...     "type": "banana",
...     "avg_weight": 123.2,
...     "edible_peel": false,
...     "species": ["acuminata", "balbisiana", "paradisiaca"],
...     "issues": null,
... }
>>> fruit
{'type': 'banana', 'avg_weight': 123.2, 'edible_peel': False,
'species': ['acuminata', 'balbisiana', 'paradisiaca'], 'issues': None}
```

The syntax everybody now uses for exchanging data is Python's dict and list syntax. Now we have the nice syntax with the convenience of preserved insertion order.

Simple and correct.

## CHAPTER 4

Unicode Text Versus Bytes

> Humans use text. Computers speak bytes.
>
> —Esther Nam and Travis Fischer, "Character Encoding and Unicode in Python"[1]

Python 3 introduced a sharp distinction between strings of human text and sequences of raw bytes. Implicit conversion of byte sequences to Unicode text is a thing of the past. This chapter deals with Unicode strings, binary sequences, and the encodings used to convert between them.

Depending on the kind of work you do with Python, you may think that understanding Unicode is not important. That's unlikely, but anyway there is no escaping the `str` versus `byte` divide. As a bonus, you'll find that the specialized binary sequence types provide features that the "all-purpose" Python 2 `str` type did not have.

In this chapter, we will visit the following topics:

- Characters, code points, and byte representations
- Unique features of binary sequences: `bytes`, `bytearray`, and `memoryview`
- Encodings for full Unicode and legacy character sets
- Avoiding and dealing with encoding errors
- Best practices when handling text files
- The default encoding trap and standard I/O issues
- Safe Unicode text comparisons with normalization

---

1 Slide 12 of PyCon 2014 talk "Character Encoding and Unicode in Python" (slides (*https://fpy.li/4-1*), video (*https://fpy.li/4-2*)).

- Utility functions for normalization, case folding, and brute-force diacritic removal
- Proper sorting of Unicode text with `locale` and the *pyuca* library
- Character metadata in the Unicode database
- Dual-mode APIs that handle `str` and `bytes`

What's New in This Chapter

Support for Unicode in Python 3 has been comprehensive and stable, so the most notable addition is "Finding Characters by Name" on page 151, describing a utility for searching the Unicode database—a great way to find circled digits and smiling cats from the command line.

One minor change worth mentioning is the Unicode support on Windows, which is better and simpler since Python 3.6, as we'll see in "Beware of Encoding Defaults" on page 134.

Let's start with the not-so-new, but fundamental concepts of characters, code points, and bytes.

For the second edition, I expanded the section about the `struct` module and published it online at "Parsing binary records with struct" (*https://fpy.li/4-3*), in the *fluentpython.com* companion website.

There you will also find "Building Multi-character Emojis" (*https://fpy.li/4-4*), describing how to make country flags, rainbow flags, people with different skin tones, and diverse family icons by combining Unicode characters.

Character Issues

The concept of "string" is simple enough: a string is a sequence of characters. The problem lies in the definition of "character."

In 2021, the best definition of "character" we have is a Unicode character. Accordingly, the items we get out of a Python 3 `str` are Unicode characters, just like the items of a `unicode` object in Python 2—and not the raw bytes we got from a Python 2 `str`.

The Unicode standard explicitly separates the identity of characters from specific byte representations:

- The identity of a character—its *code point*—is a number from 0 to 1,114,111 (base 10), shown in the Unicode standard as 4 to 6 hex digits with a "U+" prefix, from U+0000 to U+10FFFF. For example, the code point for the letter A is U+0041, the Euro sign is U+20AC, and the musical symbol G clef is assigned to code point U+1D11E. About 13% of the valid code points have characters assigned to them in Unicode 13.0.0, the standard used in Python 3.10.0b4.

- The actual bytes that represent a character depend on the *encoding* in use. An encoding is an algorithm that converts code points to byte sequences and vice versa. The code point for the letter A (U+0041) is encoded as the single byte \x41 in the UTF-8 encoding, or as the bytes \x41\x00 in UTF-16LE encoding. As another example, UTF-8 requires three bytes—\xe2\x82\xac—to encode the Euro sign (U+20AC), but in UTF-16LE the same code point is encoded as two bytes: \xac\x20.

Converting from code points to bytes is *encoding*; converting from bytes to code points is *decoding*. See Example 4-1.

Example 4-1. Encoding and decoding

```
>>> s = 'café'
>>> len(s)   ❶
4
>>> b = s.encode('utf8')   ❷
>>> b
b'caf\xc3\xa9'   ❸
>>> len(b)   ❹
5
>>> b.decode('utf8')   ❺
'café'
```

❶ The str 'café' has four Unicode characters.

❷ Encode str to bytes using UTF-8 encoding.

❸ bytes literals have a b prefix.

❹ bytes b has five bytes (the code point for "é" is encoded as two bytes in UTF-8).

❺ Decode bytes to str using UTF-8 encoding.

If you need a memory aid to help distinguish .decode() from .encode(), convince yourself that byte sequences can be cryptic machine core dumps, while Unicode str objects are "human" text. Therefore, it makes sense that we *decode* bytes to str to get human-readable text, and we *encode* str to bytes for storage or transmission.

Although the Python 3 str is pretty much the Python 2 unicode type with a new name, the Python 3 bytes is not simply the old str renamed, and there is also the closely related bytearray type. So it is worthwhile to take a look at the binary sequence types before advancing to encoding/decoding issues.

Byte Essentials

The new binary sequence types are unlike the Python 2 str in many regards. The first thing to know is that there are two basic built-in types for binary sequences: the immutable bytes type introduced in Python 3 and the mutable bytearray, added way back in Python 2.6.[2] The Python documentation sometimes uses the generic term "byte string" to refer to both bytes and bytearray. I avoid that confusing term.

Each item in bytes or bytearray is an integer from 0 to 255, and not a one-character string like in the Python 2 str. However, a slice of a binary sequence always produces a binary sequence of the same type—including slices of length 1. See Example 4-2.

Example 4-2. A five-byte sequence as bytes and as bytearray

```
>>> cafe = bytes('café', encoding='utf_8')  ❶
>>> cafe
b'caf\xc3\xa9'
>>> cafe[0]  ❷
99
>>> cafe[:1]  ❸
b'c'
>>> cafe_arr = bytearray(cafe)
>>> cafe_arr  ❹
bytearray(b'caf\xc3\xa9')
>>> cafe_arr[-1:]  ❺
bytearray(b'\xa9')
```

❶ bytes can be built from a str, given an encoding.

❷ Each item is an integer in range(256).

---

2 Python 2.6 and 2.7 also had bytes, but it was just an alias to the str type.

---

❸ Slices of bytes are also bytes—even slices of a single byte.

❹ There is no literal syntax for bytearray: they are shown as bytearray() with a bytes literal as argument.

❺ A slice of bytearray is also a bytearray.

 The fact that my_bytes[0] retrieves an int but my_bytes[:1] returns a bytes sequence of length 1 is only surprising because we are used to Python's str type, where s[0] == s[:1]. For all other sequence types in Python, 1 item is not the same as a slice of length 1.

Although binary sequences are really sequences of integers, their literal notation reflects the fact that ASCII text is often embedded in them. Therefore, four different displays are used, depending on each byte value:

- For bytes with decimal codes 32 to 126—from space to ~ (tilde)—the ASCII character itself is used.

- For bytes corresponding to tab, newline, carriage return, and \, the escape sequences \t, \n, \r, and \\ are used.

- If both string delimiters ' and " appear in the byte sequence, the whole sequence is delimited by ', and any ' inside are escaped as \'.[3]

- For other byte values, a hexadecimal escape sequence is used (e.g., \x00 is the null byte).

That is why in Example 4-2 you see b'caf\xc3\xa9': the first three bytes b'caf' are in the printable ASCII range, the last two are not.

Both bytes and bytearray support every str method except those that do formatting (format, format_map) and those that depend on Unicode data, including case fold, isdecimal, isidentifier, isnumeric, isprintable, and encode. This means that you can use familiar string methods like endswith, replace, strip, translate, upper, and dozens of others with binary sequences—only using bytes and not str arguments. In addition, the regular expression functions in the re module also work

---

3 Trivia: the ASCII "single quote" character that Python uses by default as the string delimiter is actually named APOSTROPHE in the Unicode standard. The real single quotes are asymmetric: left is U+2018 and right is U+2019.

on binary sequences, if the regex is compiled from a binary sequence instead of a str. Since Python 3.5, the % operator works with binary sequences again.[4]

Binary sequences have a class method that str doesn't have, called fromhex, which builds a binary sequence by parsing pairs of hex digits optionally separated by spaces:

```
>>> bytes.fromhex('31 4B CE A9')
b'1K\xce\xa9'
```

The other ways of building bytes or bytearray instances are calling their constructors with:

- A str and an encoding keyword argument
- An iterable providing items with values from 0 to 255
- An object that implements the buffer protocol (e.g., bytes, bytearray, memory view, array.array) that copies the bytes from the source object to the newly created binary sequence

> Until Python 3.5, it was also possible to call bytes or bytearray with a single integer to create a binary sequence of that size initialized with null bytes. This signature was deprecated in Python 3.5 and removed in Python 3.6. See PEP 467—Minor API improvements for binary sequences (https://fpy.li/pep467).

Building a binary sequence from a buffer-like object is a low-level operation that may involve type casting. See a demonstration in Example 4-3.

Example 4-3. Initializing bytes from the raw data of an array

```
>>> import array
>>> numbers = array.array('h', [-2, -1, 0, 1, 2])  ❶
>>> octets = bytes(numbers)  ❷
>>> octets
b'\xfe\xff\xff\xff\x00\x00\x01\x00\x02\x00'  ❸
```

❶ Typecode 'h' creates an array of short integers (16 bits).

❷ octets holds a copy of the bytes that make up numbers.

❸ These are the 10 bytes that represent the 5 short integers.

---

4 It did not work in Python 3.0 to 3.4, causing much pain to developers dealing with binary data. The reversal is documented in PEP 461—Adding % formatting to bytes and bytearray (https://fpy.li/pep461).

Creating a bytes or bytearray object from any buffer-like source will always copy the bytes. In contrast, memoryview objects let you share memory between binary data structures, as we saw in "Memory Views" on page 62.

After this basic exploration of binary sequence types in Python, let's see how they are converted to/from strings.

Basic Encoders/Decoders

The Python distribution bundles more than 100 *codecs* (encoder/decoders) for text to byte conversion and vice versa. Each codec has a name, like 'utf_8', and often aliases, such as 'utf8', 'utf-8', and 'U8', which you can use as the encoding argument in functions like open(), str.encode(), bytes.decode(), and so on. Example 4-4 shows the same text encoded as three different byte sequences.

Example 4-4. The string "El Niño" encoded with three codecs producing very different byte sequences

```
>>> for codec in ['latin_1', 'utf_8', 'utf_16']:
...     print(codec, 'El Niño'.encode(codec), sep='\t')
...
latin_1 b'El Ni\xf1o'
utf_8   b'El Ni\xc3\xb1o'
utf_16  b'\xff\xfeE\x00l\x00 \x00N\x00i\x00\xf1\x00o\x00'
```

Figure 4-1 demonstrates a variety of codecs generating bytes from characters like the letter "A" through the G-clef musical symbol. Note that the last three encodings are variable-length, multibyte encodings.

char.	code point	ascii	latin1	cp1252	cp437	gb2312	utf-8	utf-16le
A	U+0041	41	41	41	41	41	41	41 00
¿	U+00BF	*	BF	BF	A8	*	C2 BF	BF 00
Ã	U+00C3	*	C3	C3	*	*	C3 83	C3 00
á	U+00E1	*	E1	E1	A0	A8 A2	C3 A1	E1 00
Ω	U+03A9	*	*	*	EA	A6 B8	CE A9	A9 03
௬	U+06BF	*	*	*	*	*	DA BF	BF 06
"	U+201C	*	*	93	*	A1 B0	E2 80 9C	1C 20
€	U+20AC	*	*	80	*	*	E2 82 AC	AC 20
┌	U+250C	*	*	*	DA	A9 B0	E2 94 8C	0C 25
气	U+6C14	*	*	*	*	C6 F8	E6 B0 94	14 6C
氣	U+6C23	*	*	*	*	*	E6 B0 A3	23 6C
𝄞	U+1D11E	*	*	*	*	*	F0 9D 84 9E	34 D8 1E DD

Figure 4-1. Twelve characters, their code points, and their byte representation (in hex) in 7 different encodings (asterisks indicate that the character cannot be represented in that encoding).

All those asterisks in Figure 4-1 make clear that some encodings, like ASCII and even the multibyte GB2312, cannot represent every Unicode character. The UTF encodings, however, are designed to handle every Unicode code point.

The encodings shown in Figure 4-1 were chosen as a representative sample:

`latin1` *a.k.a.* `iso8859_1`
> Important because it is the basis for other encodings, such as `cp1252` and Unicode itself (note how the `latin1` byte values appear in the `cp1252` bytes and even in the code points).

`cp1252`
> A useful `latin1` superset created by Microsoft, adding useful symbols like curly quotes and € (euro); some Windows apps call it "ANSI," but it was never a real ANSI standard.

`cp437`
> The original character set of the IBM PC, with box drawing characters. Incompatible with `latin1`, which appeared later.

`gb2312`
> Legacy standard to encode the simplified Chinese ideographs used in mainland China; one of several widely deployed multibyte encodings for Asian languages.

`utf-8`
> The most common 8-bit encoding on the web, by far, as of July 2021, "W[3]Techs: Usage statistics of character encodings for websites" (*https://fpy.li/4-5*) claims that 97% of sites use UTF-8, up from 81.4% when I wrote this paragraph in the first edition of this book in September 2014.

`utf-16le`
> One form of the UTF 16-bit encoding scheme; all UTF-16 encodings support code points beyond U+FFFF through escape sequences called "surrogate pairs."

 UTF-16 superseded the original 16-bit Unicode 1.0 encoding—UCS-2—way back in 1996. UCS-2 is still used in many systems despite being deprecated since the last century because it only supports code points up to U+FFFF. As of 2021, more than 57% of the allocated code points are above U+FFFF, including the all-important emojis.

With this overview of common encodings now complete, we move to handling issues in encoding and decoding operations.

Understanding Encode/Decode Problems

Although there is a generic UnicodeError exception, the error reported by Python is usually more specific: either a UnicodeEncodeError (when converting str to binary sequences) or a UnicodeDecodeError (when reading binary sequences into str). Loading Python modules may also raise SyntaxError when the source encoding is unexpected. We'll show how to handle all of these errors in the next sections.

 The first thing to note when you get a Unicode error is the exact type of the exception. Is it a UnicodeEncodeError, a UnicodeDeco deError, or some other error (e.g., SyntaxError) that mentions an encoding problem? To solve the problem, you have to understand it first.

Coping with UnicodeEncodeError

Most non-UTF codecs handle only a small subset of the Unicode characters. When converting text to bytes, if a character is not defined in the target encoding, Unico deEncodeError will be raised, unless special handling is provided by passing an errors argument to the encoding method or function. The behavior of the error handlers is shown in Example 4-5.

Example 4-5. Encoding to bytes: success and error handling

```
>>> city = 'São Paulo'
>>> city.encode('utf_8')   ❶
b'S\xc3\xa3o Paulo'
>>> city.encode('utf_16')
b'\xff\xfeS\x00\xe3\x00o\x00 \x00P\x00a\x00u\x00l\x00o\x00'
>>> city.encode('iso8859_1')   ❷
b'S\xe3o Paulo'
>>> city.encode('cp437')   ❸
Traceback (most recent call last):
  File "<stdin>", line 1, in <module>
  File "/.../lib/python3.4/encodings/cp437.py", line 12, in encode
    return codecs.charmap_encode(input,errors,encoding_map)
UnicodeEncodeError: 'charmap' codec can't encode character '\xe3' in
position 1: character maps to <undefined>
>>> city.encode('cp437', errors='ignore')   ❹
b'So Paulo'
>>> city.encode('cp437', errors='replace')   ❺
b'S?o Paulo'
>>> city.encode('cp437', errors='xmlcharrefreplace')   ❻
b'S&#227;o Paulo'
```

❶ The UTF encodings handle any `str`.

❷ `iso8859_1` also works for the `'São Paulo'` string.

❸ `cp437` can't encode the `'ã'` ("a" with tilde). The default error handler —`'strict'`—raises `UnicodeEncodeError`.

❹ The `error='ignore'` handler skips characters that cannot be encoded; this is usually a very bad idea, leading to silent data loss.

❺ When encoding, `error='replace'` substitutes unencodable characters with `'?'`; data is also lost, but users will get a clue that something is amiss.

❻ `'xmlcharrefreplace'` replaces unencodable characters with an XML entity. If you can't use UTF, and you can't afford to lose data, this is the only option.

 The `codecs` error handling is extensible. You may register extra strings for the `errors` argument by passing a name and an error handling function to the `codecs.register_error` function. See the `codecs.register_error` documentation (*https://fpy.li/4-6*).

ASCII is a common subset to all the encodings that I know about, therefore encoding should always work if the text is made exclusively of ASCII characters. Python 3.7 added a new boolean method `str.isascii()` (*https://fpy.li/4-7*) to check whether your Unicode text is 100% pure ASCII. If it is, you should be able to encode it to bytes in any encoding without raising `UnicodeEncodeError`.

Coping with UnicodeDecodeError

Not every byte holds a valid ASCII character, and not every byte sequence is valid UTF-8 or UTF-16; therefore, when you assume one of these encodings while converting a binary sequence to text, you will get a `UnicodeDecodeError` if unexpected bytes are found.

On the other hand, many legacy 8-bit encodings like `'cp1252'`, `'iso8859_1'`, and `'koi8_r'` are able to decode any stream of bytes, including random noise, without reporting errors. Therefore, if your program assumes the wrong 8-bit encoding, it will silently decode garbage.

Garbled characters are known as gremlins or mojibake (文字化け —Japanese for "transformed text").

Example 4-6 illustrates how using the wrong codec may produce gremlins or a UnicodeDecodeError.

Example 4-6. Decoding from str to bytes: success and error handling

```
>>> octets = b'Montr\xe9al'  ❶
>>> octets.decode('cp1252')  ❷
'Montréal'
>>> octets.decode('iso8859_7')  ❸
'Montrιal'
>>> octets.decode('koi8_r')  ❹
'MontrИal'
>>> octets.decode('utf_8')  ❺
Traceback (most recent call last):
  File "<stdin>", line 1, in <module>
UnicodeDecodeError: 'utf-8' codec can't decode byte 0xe9 in position 5:
invalid continuation byte
>>> octets.decode('utf_8', errors='replace')  ❻
'Montr�al'
```

❶ The word "Montréal" encoded as latin1; '\xe9' is the byte for "é".

❷ Decoding with Windows 1252 works because it is a superset of latin1.

❸ ISO-8859-7 is intended for Greek, so the '\xe9' byte is misinterpreted, and no error is issued.

❹ KOI8-R is for Russian. Now '\xe9' stands for the Cyrillic letter "И".

❺ The 'utf_8' codec detects that octets is not valid UTF-8, and raises UnicodeDecodeError.

❻ Using 'replace' error handling, the \xe9 is replaced by "�" (code point U+FFFD), the official Unicode REPLACEMENT CHARACTER intended to represent unknown characters.

SyntaxError When Loading Modules with Unexpected Encoding

UTF-8 is the default source encoding for Python 3, just as ASCII was the default for Python 2. If you load a *.py* module containing non-UTF-8 data and no encoding declaration, you get a message like this:

```
SyntaxError: Non-UTF-8 code starting with '\xe1' in file ola.py on line
    1, but no encoding declared; see https://python.org/dev/peps/pep-0263/
    for details
```

Because UTF-8 is widely deployed in GNU/Linux and macOS systems, a likely scenario is opening a *.py* file created on Windows with cp1252. Note that this error happens even in Python for Windows, because the default encoding for Python 3 source is UTF-8 across all platforms.

To fix this problem, add a magic coding comment at the top of the file, as shown in Example 4-7.

Example 4-7. ola.py: "Hello, World!" in Portuguese

```
# coding: cp1252

print('Olá, Mundo!')
```

> Now that Python 3 source code is no longer limited to ASCII and defaults to the excellent UTF-8 encoding, the best "fix" for source code in legacy encodings like 'cp1252' is to convert them to UTF-8 already, and not bother with the coding comments. If your editor does not support UTF-8, it's time to switch.

Suppose you have a text file, be it source code or poetry, but you don't know its encoding. How do you detect the actual encoding? Answers in the next section.

How to Discover the Encoding of a Byte Sequence

How do you find the encoding of a byte sequence? Short answer: you can't. You must be told.

Some communication protocols and file formats, like HTTP and XML, contain headers that explicitly tell us how the content is encoded. You can be sure that some byte streams are not ASCII because they contain byte values over 127, and the way UTF-8 and UTF-16 are built also limits the possible byte sequences.

Leo's Hack for Guessing UTF-8 Decoding

(The next paragraphs come from a note left by tech reviewer Leonardo Rochael in the draft of this book.)

The way UTF-8 was designed, it's almost impossible for a random sequence of bytes, or even a nonrandom sequence of bytes coming from a non-UTF-8 encoding, to be decoded accidentally as garbage in UTF-8, instead of raising `UnicodeDecodeError`.

The reasons for this are that UTF-8 escape sequences never use ASCII characters, and these escape sequences have bit patterns that make it very hard for random data to be valid UTF-8 by accident.

So if you can decode some bytes containing codes > 127 as UTF-8, it's probably UTF-8.

In dealing with Brazilian online services, some of which were attached to legacy back-ends, I've had, on occasion, to implement a decoding strategy of trying to decode via UTF-8 and treat a `UnicodeDecodeError` by decoding via `cp1252`. It was ugly but effective.

However, considering that human languages also have their rules and restrictions, once you assume that a stream of bytes is human *plain text*, it may be possible to sniff out its encoding using heuristics and statistics. For example, if b'\x00' bytes are common, it is probably a 16- or 32-bit encoding, and not an 8-bit scheme, because null characters in plain text are bugs. When the byte sequence b'\x20\x00' appears often, it is more likely to be the space character (U+0020) in a UTF-16LE encoding, rather than the obscure U+2000 EN QUAD character—whatever that is.

That is how the package "Chardet—The Universal Character Encoding Detector" (*https://fpy.li/4-8*) works to guess one of more than 30 supported encodings. *Chardet* is a Python library that you can use in your programs, but also includes a command-line utility, `chardetect`. Here is what it reports on the source file for this chapter:

```
$ chardetect 04-text-byte.asciidoc
04-text-byte.asciidoc: utf-8 with confidence 0.99
```

Although binary sequences of encoded text usually don't carry explicit hints of their encoding, the UTF formats may prepend a byte order mark to the textual content. That is explained next.

BOM: A Useful Gremlin

In Example 4-4, you may have noticed a couple of extra bytes at the beginning of a UTF-16 encoded sequence. Here they are again:

```
>>> u16 = 'El Niño'.encode('utf_16')
>>> u16
b'\xff\xfeE\x00l\x00 \x00N\x00i\x00\xf1\x00o\x00'
```

The bytes are b'\xff\xfe'. That is a *BOM*—byte-order mark—denoting the "little-endian" byte ordering of the Intel CPU where the encoding was performed.

On a little-endian machine, for each code point the least significant byte comes first: the letter 'E', code point U+0045 (decimal 69), is encoded in byte offsets 2 and 3 as 69 and 0:

```
>>> list(u16)
[255, 254, 69, 0, 108, 0, 32, 0, 78, 0, 105, 0, 241, 0, 111, 0]
```

On a big-endian CPU, the encoding would be reversed; 'E' would be encoded as 0 and 69.

To avoid confusion, the UTF-16 encoding prepends the text to be encoded with the special invisible character ZERO WIDTH NO-BREAK SPACE (U+FEFF). On a little-endian system, that is encoded as b'\xff\xfe' (decimal 255, 254). Because, by design, there is no U+FFFE character in Unicode, the byte sequence b'\xff\xfe' must mean the ZERO WIDTH NO-BREAK SPACE on a little-endian encoding, so the codec knows which byte ordering to use.

There is a variant of UTF-16—UTF-16LE—that is explicitly little-endian, and another one explicitly big-endian, UTF-16BE. If you use them, a BOM is not generated:

```
>>> u16le = 'El Niño'.encode('utf_16le')
>>> list(u16le)
[69, 0, 108, 0, 32, 0, 78, 0, 105, 0, 241, 0, 111, 0]
>>> u16be = 'El Niño'.encode('utf_16be')
>>> list(u16be)
[0, 69, 0, 108, 0, 32, 0, 78, 0, 105, 0, 241, 0, 111]
```

If present, the BOM is supposed to be filtered by the UTF-16 codec, so that you only get the actual text contents of the file without the leading ZERO WIDTH NO-BREAK SPACE. The Unicode standard says that if a file is UTF-16 and has no BOM, it should be assumed to be UTF-16BE (big-endian). However, the Intel x86 architecture is little-endian, so there is plenty of little-endian UTF-16 with no BOM in the wild.

This whole issue of endianness only affects encodings that use words of more than one byte, like UTF-16 and UTF-32. One big advantage of UTF-8 is that it produces the same byte sequence regardless of machine endianness, so no BOM is needed. Nevertheless, some Windows applications (notably Notepad) add the BOM to UTF-8 files anyway—and Excel depends on the BOM to detect a UTF-8 file, otherwise it assumes the content is encoded with a Windows code page. This UTF-8 encoding with BOM is called UTF-8-SIG in Python's codec registry. The character U+FEFF encoded in UTF-8-SIG is the three-byte sequence b'\xef\xbb\xbf'. So if a file starts with those three bytes, it is likely to be a UTF-8 file with a BOM.

Caleb's Tip about UTF-8-SIG

Caleb Hattingh—one of the tech reviewers—suggests always using the UTF-8-SIG codec when reading UTF-8 files. This is harmless because UTF-8-SIG reads files with or without a BOM correctly, and does not return the BOM itself. When writing, I recommend using UTF-8 for general interoperability. For example, Python scripts can be made executable in Unix systems if they start with the comment: #!/usr/bin/env python3. The first two bytes of the file must be b'#!' for that to work, but the BOM breaks that convention. If you have a specific requirement to export data to apps that need the BOM, use UTF-8-SIG but be aware that Python's codecs documentation (*https://fpy.li/4-9*) says: "In UTF-8, the use of the BOM is discouraged and should generally be avoided."

We now move on to handling text files in Python 3.

Handling Text Files

The best practice for handling text I/O is the "Unicode sandwich" (Figure 4-2).[5] This means that bytes should be decoded to str as early as possible on input (e.g., when opening a file for reading). The "filling" of the sandwich is the business logic of your program, where text handling is done exclusively on str objects. You should never be encoding or decoding in the middle of other processing. On output, the str are encoded to bytes as late as possible. Most web frameworks work like that, and we rarely touch bytes when using them. In Django, for example, your views should output Unicode str; Django itself takes care of encoding the response to bytes, using UTF-8 by default.

Python 3 makes it easier to follow the advice of the Unicode sandwich, because the open() built-in does the necessary decoding when reading and encoding when writing files in text mode, so all you get from my_file.read() and pass to my_file.write(text) are str objects.

Therefore, using text files is apparently simple. But if you rely on default encodings, you will get bitten.

---

5 I first saw the term "Unicode sandwich" in Ned Batchelder's excellent "Pragmatic Unicode" talk (*https://fpy.li/4-10*) at US PyCon 2012.

The Unicode sandwich

bytes → str   Decode bytes on input,

100% str   process text only,

str → bytes   encode text on output.

Figure 4-2. Unicode sandwich: current best practice for text processing.

Consider the console session in Example 4-8. Can you spot the bug?

Example 4-8. A platform encoding issue (if you try this on your machine, you may or may not see the problem)

```
>>> open('cafe.txt', 'w', encoding='utf_8').write('café')
4
>>> open('cafe.txt').read()
'cafÃ©'
```

The bug: I specified UTF-8 encoding when writing the file but failed to do so when reading it, so Python assumed Windows default file encoding—code page 1252—and the trailing bytes in the file were decoded as characters 'Ã©' instead of 'é'.

I ran Example 4-8 on Python 3.8.1, 64 bits, on Windows 10 (build 18363). The same statements running on recent GNU/Linux or macOS work perfectly well because their default encoding is UTF-8, giving the false impression that everything is fine. If the encoding argument was omitted when opening the file to write, the locale default encoding would be used, and we'd read the file correctly using the same encoding. But then this script would generate files with different byte contents depending on the platform or even depending on locale settings in the same platform, creating compatibility problems.

Code that has to run on multiple machines or on multiple occasions should never depend on encoding defaults. Always pass an explicit encoding= argument when opening text files, because the default may change from one machine to the next, or from one day to the next.

A curious detail in Example 4-8 is that the write function in the first statement reports that four characters were written, but in the next line five characters are read. Example 4-9 is an extended version of Example 4-8, explaining that and other details.

Example 4-9. Closer inspection of Example 4-8 running on Windows reveals the bug and how to fix it

```
>>> fp = open('cafe.txt', 'w', encoding='utf_8')
>>> fp  ❶
<_io.TextIOWrapper name='cafe.txt' mode='w' encoding='utf_8'>
>>> fp.write('café')  ❷
4
>>> fp.close()
>>> import os
>>> os.stat('cafe.txt').st_size  ❸
5
>>> fp2 = open('cafe.txt')
>>> fp2  ❹
<_io.TextIOWrapper name='cafe.txt' mode='r' encoding='cp1252'>
>>> fp2.encoding  ❺
'cp1252'
>>> fp2.read()  ❻
'cafÃ©'
>>> fp3 = open('cafe.txt', encoding='utf_8')  ❼
>>> fp3
<_io.TextIOWrapper name='cafe.txt' mode='r' encoding='utf_8'>
>>> fp3.read()  ❽
'café'
>>> fp4 = open('cafe.txt', 'rb')  ❾
>>> fp4  ❿
<_io.BufferedReader name='cafe.txt'>
>>> fp4.read()  ⓫
b'caf\xc3\xa9'
```

❶ By default, open uses text mode and returns a TextIOWrapper object with a specific encoding.

❷ The write method on a TextIOWrapper returns the number of Unicode characters written.

❸ os.stat says the file has 5 bytes; UTF-8 encodes 'é' as 2 bytes, 0xc3 and 0xa9.

❹ Opening a text file with no explicit encoding returns a TextIOWrapper with the encoding set to a default from the locale.

❺ A TextIOWrapper object has an encoding attribute that you can inspect: cp1252 in this case.

❻ In the Windows cp1252 encoding, the byte 0xc3 is an "Ã" (A with tilde), and 0xa9 is the copyright sign.

❼ Opening the same file with the correct encoding.

❽ The expected result: the same four Unicode characters for `'café'`.

❾ The `'rb'` flag opens a file for reading in binary mode.

❿ The returned object is a `BufferedReader` and not a `TextIOWrapper`.

⓫ Reading that returns bytes, as expected.

 Do not open text files in binary mode unless you need to analyze the file contents to determine the encoding—even then, you should be using Chardet instead of reinventing the wheel (see "How to Discover the Encoding of a Byte Sequence" on page 128). Ordinary code should only use binary mode to open binary files, like raster images.

The problem in Example 4-9 has to do with relying on a default setting while opening a text file. There are several sources for such defaults, as the next section shows.

Beware of Encoding Defaults

Several settings affect the encoding defaults for I/O in Python. See the *default_encodings.py* script in Example 4-10.

Example 4-10. Exploring encoding defaults

```
import locale
import sys

expressions = """
        locale.getpreferredencoding()
        type(my_file)
        my_file.encoding
        sys.stdout.isatty()
        sys.stdout.encoding
        sys.stdin.isatty()
        sys.stdin.encoding
        sys.stderr.isatty()
        sys.stderr.encoding
        sys.getdefaultencoding()
        sys.getfilesystemencoding()
    """
```

```
my_file = open('dummy', 'w')

for expression in expressions.split():
    value = eval(expression)
    print(f'{expression:>30} -> {value!r}')
```

The output of Example 4-10 on GNU/Linux (Ubuntu 14.04 to 19.10) and macOS (10.9 to 10.14) is identical, showing that UTF-8 is used everywhere in these systems:

```
$ python3 default_encodings.py
 locale.getpreferredencoding() -> 'UTF-8'
                type(my_file) -> <class '_io.TextIOWrapper'>
              my_file.encoding -> 'UTF-8'
          sys.stdout.isatty() -> True
         sys.stdout.encoding -> 'utf-8'
           sys.stdin.isatty() -> True
          sys.stdin.encoding -> 'utf-8'
          sys.stderr.isatty() -> True
         sys.stderr.encoding -> 'utf-8'
      sys.getdefaultencoding() -> 'utf-8'
   sys.getfilesystemencoding() -> 'utf-8'
```

On Windows, however, the output is Example 4-11.

Example 4-11. Default encodings on Windows 10 PowerShell (output is the same on cmd.exe)

```
> chcp  ❶
Active code page: 437
> python default_encodings.py  ❷
 locale.getpreferredencoding() -> 'cp1252'  ❸
                type(my_file) -> <class '_io.TextIOWrapper'>
              my_file.encoding -> 'cp1252'  ❹
          sys.stdout.isatty() -> True      ❺
         sys.stdout.encoding -> 'utf-8'    ❻
           sys.stdin.isatty() -> True
          sys.stdin.encoding -> 'utf-8'
          sys.stderr.isatty() -> True
         sys.stderr.encoding -> 'utf-8'
      sys.getdefaultencoding() -> 'utf-8'
   sys.getfilesystemencoding() -> 'utf-8'
```

❶ chcp shows the active code page for the console: 437.

❷ Running *default_encodings.py* with output to console.

❸ locale.getpreferredencoding() is the most important setting.

❹ Text files use locale.getpreferredencoding() by default.

❺ The output is going to the console, so `sys.stdout.isatty()` is `True`.

❻ Now, `sys.stdout.encoding` is not the same as the console code page reported by chcp!

Unicode support in Windows itself, and in Python for Windows, got better since I wrote the first edition of this book. Example 4-11 used to report four different encodings in Python 3.4 on Windows 7. The encodings for `stdout`, `stdin`, and `stderr` used to be the same as the active code page reported by the chcp command, but now they're all `utf-8` thanks to PEP 528—Change Windows console encoding to UTF-8 (*https://fpy.li/pep528*) implemented in Python 3.6, and Unicode support in Power-Shell in *cmd.exe* (since Windows 1809 from October 2018).[6] It's weird that chcp and `sys.stdout.encoding` say different things when `stdout` is writing to the console, but it's great that now we can print Unicode strings without encoding errors on Windows—unless the user redirects output to a file, as we'll soon see. That does not mean all your favorite emojis will appear in the console: that also depends on the font the console is using.

Another change was PEP 529—Change Windows filesystem encoding to UTF-8 (*https://fpy.li/pep529*), also implemented in Python 3.6, which changed the filesystem encoding (used to represent names of directories and files) from Microsoft's proprietary MBCS to UTF-8.

However, if the output of Example 4-10 is redirected to a file, like this:

```
Z:\>python default_encodings.py > encodings.log
```

then, the value of `sys.stdout.isatty()` becomes `False`, and `sys.stdout.encoding` is set by `locale.getpreferredencoding()`, `'cp1252'` in that machine—but `sys.stdin.encoding` and `sys.stderr.encoding` remain `utf-8`.

 In Example 4-12 I use the `'\N{}'` escape for Unicode literals, where we write the official name of the character inside the `\N{}`. It's rather verbose, but explicit and safe: Python raises `SyntaxError` if the name doesn't exist—much better than writing a hex number that could be wrong, but you'll only find out much later. You'd probably want to write a comment explaining the character codes anyway, so the verbosity of `\N{}` is easy to accept.

This means that a script like Example 4-12 works when printing to the console, but may break when output is redirected to a file.

---

6 Source: "Windows Command-Line: Unicode and UTF-8 Output Text Buffer" (*https://fpy.li/4-11*).

Example 4-12. stdout_check.py

```python
import sys
from unicodedata import name

print(sys.version)
print()
print('sys.stdout.isatty():', sys.stdout.isatty())
print('sys.stdout.encoding:', sys.stdout.encoding)
print()

test_chars = [
    '\N{HORIZONTAL ELLIPSIS}',      # exists in cp1252, not in cp437
    '\N{INFINITY}',                 # exists in cp437, not in cp1252
    '\N{CIRCLED NUMBER FORTY TWO}', # not in cp437 or in cp1252
]

for char in test_chars:
    print(f'Trying to output {name(char)}:')
    print(char)
```

Example 4-12 displays the result of `sys.stdout.isatty()`, the value of `sys.stdout.encoding`, and these three characters:

- `'…'` HORIZONTAL ELLIPSIS—exists in CP 1252 but not in CP 437.

- `'∞'` INFINITY—exists in CP 437 but not in CP 1252.

- `'㊷'` CIRCLED NUMBER FORTY TWO—doesn't exist in CP 1252 or CP 437.

When I run *stdout_check.py* on PowerShell or *cmd.exe*, it works as captured in Figure 4-3.

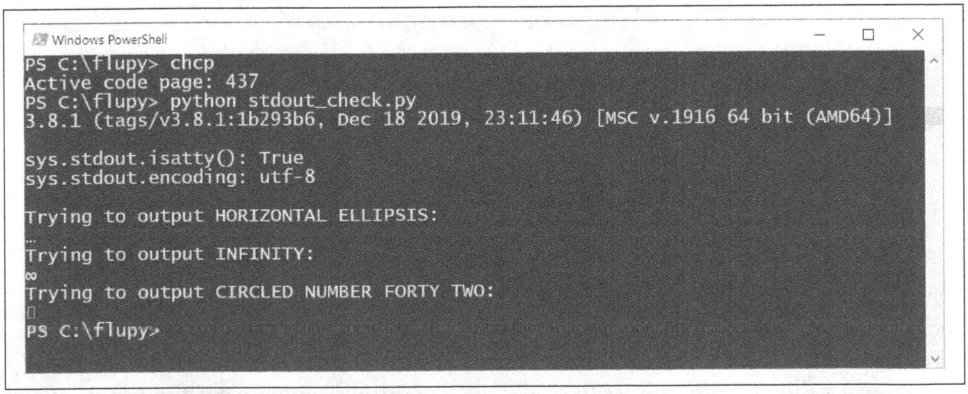

Figure 4-3. Running stdout_check.py on PowerShell.

Despite chcp reporting the active code as 437, `sys.stdout.encoding` is UTF-8, so the HORIZONTAL ELLIPSIS and INFINITY both output correctly. The CIRCLED NUMBER FORTY TWO is replaced by a rectangle, but no error is raised. Presumably it is recognized as a valid character, but the console font doesn't have the glyph to display it.

However, when I redirect the output of *stdout_check.py* to a file, I get Figure 4-4.

```
Windows PowerShell                                           —  □  ×
PS C:\flupy> python stdout_check.py > out.txt
Traceback (most recent call last):
  File "stdout_check.py", line 18, in <module>
    print(char)
  File "C:\Users\luciano\AppData\Local\Programs\Python\Python38\lib\encodings\cp
1252.py", line 19, in encode
    return codecs.charmap_encode(input,self.errors,encoding_table)[0]
UnicodeEncodeError: 'charmap' codec can't encode character '\u221e' in position
0: character maps to <undefined>
PS C:\flupy> type .\out.txt
3.8.1 (tags/v3.8.1:1b293b6, Dec 18 2019, 23:11:46) [MSC v.1916 64 bit (AMD64)]

sys.stdout.isatty(): False
sys.stdout.encoding: cp1252

Trying to output HORIZONTAL ELLIPSIS:
à
Trying to output INFINITY:
PS C:\flupy>
```

Figure 4-4. Running stdout_check.py on PowerShell, redirecting output.

The first problem demonstrated by Figure 4-4 is the `UnicodeEncodeError` mentioning character `'\u221e'`, because `sys.stdout.encoding` is `'cp1252'`—a code page that doesn't have the INFINITY character.

Reading *out.txt* with the `type` command—or a Windows editor like VS Code or Sublime Text—shows that instead of HORIZONTAL ELLIPSIS, I got `'à'` (LATIN SMALL LETTER A WITH GRAVE). As it turns out, the byte value 0x85 in CP 1252 means `'…'`, but in CP 437 the same byte value represents `'à'`. So it seems the active code page does matter, not in a sensible or useful way, but as partial explanation of a bad Unicode experience.

I used a laptop configured for the US market, running Windows 10 OEM to run these experiments. Windows versions localized for other countries may have different encoding configurations. For example, in Brazil the Windows console uses code page 850 by default—not 437.

To wrap up this maddening issue of default encodings, let's give a final look at the different encodings in Example 4-11:

- If you omit the `encoding` argument when opening a file, the default is given by `locale.getpreferredencoding()` (`'cp1252'` in Example 4-11).

- The encoding of `sys.stdout|stdin|stderr` used to be set by the `PYTHONIOENCOD ING` (*https://fpy.li/4-12*) environment variable before Python 3.6—now that variable is ignored, unless `PYTHONLEGACYWINDOWSSTDIO` (*https://fpy.li/4-13*) is set to a nonempty string. Otherwise, the encoding for standard I/O is UTF-8 for interactive I/O, or defined by `locale.getpreferredencoding()` if the output/input is redirected to/from a file.

- `sys.getdefaultencoding()` is used internally by Python in implicit conversions of binary data to/from `str`. Changing this setting is not supported.

- `sys.getfilesystemencoding()` is used to encode/decode filenames (not file contents). It is used when `open()` gets a `str` argument for the filename; if the filename is given as a `bytes` argument, it is passed unchanged to the OS API.

 On GNU/Linux and macOS, all of these encodings are set to UTF-8 by default, and have been for several years, so I/O handles all Unicode characters. On Windows, not only are different encodings used in the same system, but they are usually code pages like `'cp850'` or `'cp1252'` that support only ASCII, with 127 additional characters that are not the same from one encoding to the other. Therefore, Windows users are far more likely to face encoding errors unless they are extra careful.

To summarize, the most important encoding setting is that returned by `locale.get preferredencoding()`: it is the default for opening text files and for `sys.stdout/ stdin/stderr` when they are redirected to files. However, the documentation (*https://fpy.li/4-14*) reads (in part):

`locale.getpreferredencoding(do_setlocale=True)`
  Return the encoding used for text data, according to user preferences. User preferences are expressed differently on different systems, and might not be available programmatically on some systems, so this function only returns a guess. [...]

Therefore, the best advice about encoding defaults is: do not rely on them.

You will avoid a lot of pain if you follow the advice of the Unicode sandwich and always are explicit about the encodings in your programs. Unfortunately, Unicode is painful even if you get your `bytes` correctly converted to `str`. The next two sections cover subjects that are simple in ASCII-land, but get quite complex on planet Unicode: text normalization (i.e., converting text to a uniform representation for comparisons) and sorting.

Normalizing Unicode for Reliable Comparisons

String comparisons are complicated by the fact that Unicode has combining characters: diacritics and other marks that attach to the preceding character, appearing as one when printed.

For example, the word "café" may be composed in two ways, using four or five code points, but the result looks exactly the same:

```
>>> s1 = 'café'
>>> s2 = 'cafe\N{COMBINING ACUTE ACCENT}'
>>> s1, s2
('café', 'café')
>>> len(s1), len(s2)
(4, 5)
>>> s1 == s2
False
```

Placing COMBINING ACUTE ACCENT (U+0301) after "e" renders "é". In the Unicode standard, sequences like 'é' and 'e\u0301' are called "canonical equivalents," and applications are supposed to treat them as the same. But Python sees two different sequences of code points, and considers them not equal.

The solution is unicodedata.normalize(). The first argument to that function is one of four strings: 'NFC', 'NFD', 'NFKC', and 'NFKD'. Let's start with the first two.

Normalization Form C (NFC) composes the code points to produce the shortest equivalent string, while NFD decomposes, expanding composed characters into base characters and separate combining characters. Both of these normalizations make comparisons work as expected, as the next example shows:

```
>>> from unicodedata import normalize
>>> s1 = 'café'
>>> s2 = 'cafe\N{COMBINING ACUTE ACCENT}'
>>> len(s1), len(s2)
(4, 5)
>>> len(normalize('NFC', s1)), len(normalize('NFC', s2))
(4, 4)
>>> len(normalize('NFD', s1)), len(normalize('NFD', s2))
(5, 5)
>>> normalize('NFC', s1) == normalize('NFC', s2)
True
>>> normalize('NFD', s1) == normalize('NFD', s2)
True
```

Keyboard drivers usually generate composed characters, so text typed by users will be in NFC by default. However, to be safe, it may be good to normalize strings with normalize('NFC', user_text) before saving. NFC is also the normalization form recommended by the W3C in "Character Model for the World Wide Web: String Matching and Searching" (*https://fpy.li/4-15*).

Some single characters are normalized by NFC into another single character. The symbol for the ohm (Ω) unit of electrical resistance is normalized to the Greek upper-case omega. They are visually identical, but they compare as unequal, so it is essential to normalize to avoid surprises:

```
>>> from unicodedata import normalize, name
>>> ohm = '\u2126'
>>> name(ohm)
'OHM SIGN'
>>> ohm_c = normalize('NFC', ohm)
>>> name(ohm_c)
'GREEK CAPITAL LETTER OMEGA'
>>> ohm == ohm_c
False
>>> normalize('NFC', ohm) == normalize('NFC', ohm_c)
True
```

The other two normalization forms are NFKC and NFKD, where the letter K stands for "compatibility." These are stronger forms of normalization, affecting the so-called "compatibility characters." Although one goal of Unicode is to have a single "canonical" code point for each character, some characters appear more than once for compatibility with preexisting standards. For example, the MICRO SIGN, µ (U+00B5), was added to Unicode to support round-trip conversion to latin1, which includes it, even though the same character is part of the Greek alphabet with code point U+03BC (GREEK SMALL LETTER MU). So, the micro sign is considered a "compatibility character."

In the NFKC and NFKD forms, each compatibility character is replaced by a "compatibility decomposition" of one or more characters that are considered a "preferred" representation, even if there is some formatting loss—ideally, the formatting should be the responsibility of external markup, not part of Unicode. To exemplify, the compatibility decomposition of the one-half fraction '½' (U+00BD) is the sequence of three characters '1/2', and the compatibility decomposition of the micro sign 'µ' (U +00B5) is the lowercase mu 'µ' (U+03BC).[7]

Here is how the NFKC works in practice:

```
>>> from unicodedata import normalize, name
>>> half = '\N{VULGAR FRACTION ONE HALF}'
>>> print(half)
½
>>> normalize('NFKC', half)
'1/2'
```

---

7 Curiously, the micro sign is considered a "compatibility character," but the ohm symbol is not. The end result is that NFC doesn't touch the micro sign but changes the ohm symbol to capital omega, while NFKC and NFKD change both the ohm and the micro into Greek characters.

```
>>> for char in normalize('NFKC', half):
...     print(char, name(char), sep='\t')
...
1 DIGIT ONE
/ FRACTION SLASH
2 DIGIT TWO
>>> four_squared = '4²'
>>> normalize('NFKC', four_squared)
'42'
>>> micro = 'µ'
>>> micro_kc = normalize('NFKC', micro)
>>> micro, micro_kc
('µ', 'µ')
>>> ord(micro), ord(micro_kc)
(181, 956)
>>> name(micro), name(micro_kc)
('MICRO SIGN', 'GREEK SMALL LETTER MU')
```

Although '1/2' is a reasonable substitute for '½', and the micro sign is really a lowercase Greek mu, converting '4²' to '42' changes the meaning. An application could store '4²' as '4²', but the normalize function knows nothing about formatting. Therefore, NFKC or NFKD may lose or distort information, but they can produce convenient intermediate representations for searching and indexing.

Unfortunately, with Unicode everything is always more complicated than it first seems. For the VULGAR FRACTION ONE HALF, the NFKC normalization produced 1 and 2 joined by FRACTION SLASH, instead of SOLIDUS, a.k.a. "slash"—the familiar character with ASCII code decimal 47. Therefore, searching for the three-character ASCII sequence '1/2' would not find the normalized Unicode sequence.

 NFKC and NFKD normalization cause data loss and should be applied only in special cases like search and indexing, and not for permanent storage of text.

When preparing text for searching or indexing, another operation is useful: case folding, our next subject.

Case Folding

Case folding is essentially converting all text to lowercase, with some additional transformations. It is supported by the str.casefold() method.

For any string s containing only latin1 characters, s.casefold() produces the same result as s.lower(), with only two exceptions—the micro sign 'µ' is changed to the

Greek lowercase mu (which looks the same in most fonts) and the German Eszett or "sharp s" (ß) becomes "ss":

```
>>> micro = 'µ'
>>> name(micro)
'MICRO SIGN'
>>> micro_cf = micro.casefold()
>>> name(micro_cf)
'GREEK SMALL LETTER MU'
>>> micro, micro_cf
('µ', 'μ')
>>> eszett = 'ß'
>>> name(eszett)
'LATIN SMALL LETTER SHARP S'
>>> eszett_cf = eszett.casefold()
>>> eszett, eszett_cf
('ß', 'ss')
```

There are nearly 300 code points for which `str.casefold()` and `str.lower()` return different results.

As usual with anything related to Unicode, case folding is a hard issue with plenty of linguistic special cases, but the Python core team made an effort to provide a solution that hopefully works for most users.

In the next couple of sections, we'll put our normalization knowledge to use developing utility functions.

Utility Functions for Normalized Text Matching

As we've seen, NFC and NFD are safe to use and allow sensible comparisons between Unicode strings. NFC is the best normalized form for most applications. `str.case fold()` is the way to go for case-insensitive comparisons.

If you work with text in many languages, a pair of functions like `nfc_equal` and `fold_equal` in Example 4-13 are useful additions to your toolbox.

Example 4-13. normeq.py: normalized Unicode string comparison

```
"""
Utility functions for normalized Unicode string comparison.

Using Normal Form C, case sensitive:

    >>> s1 = 'café'
    >>> s2 = 'cafe\u0301'
    >>> s1 == s2
    False
    >>> nfc_equal(s1, s2)
    True
```

```
>>> nfc_equal('A', 'a')
False
```

Using Normal Form C with case folding:

```
>>> s3 = 'Straße'
>>> s4 = 'strasse'
>>> s3 == s4
False
>>> nfc_equal(s3, s4)
False
>>> fold_equal(s3, s4)
True
>>> fold_equal(s1, s2)
True
>>> fold_equal('A', 'a')
True

    """

from unicodedata import normalize

def nfc_equal(str1, str2):
    return normalize('NFC', str1) == normalize('NFC', str2)

def fold_equal(str1, str2):
    return (normalize('NFC', str1).casefold() ==
            normalize('NFC', str2).casefold())
```

Beyond Unicode normalization and case folding—which are both part of the Unicode standard—sometimes it makes sense to apply deeper transformations, like changing 'café' into 'cafe'. We'll see when and how in the next section.

Extreme "Normalization": Taking Out Diacritics

The Google Search secret sauce involves many tricks, but one of them apparently is ignoring diacritics (e.g., accents, cedillas, etc.), at least in some contexts. Removing diacritics is not a proper form of normalization because it often changes the meaning of words and may produce false positives when searching. But it helps coping with some facts of life: people sometimes are lazy or ignorant about the correct use of diacritics, and spelling rules change over time, meaning that accents come and go in living languages.

Outside of searching, getting rid of diacritics also makes for more readable URLs, at least in Latin-based languages. Take a look at the URL for the Wikipedia article about the city of São Paulo:

```
https://en.wikipedia.org/wiki/S%C3%A3o_Paulo
```

The %C3%A3 part is the URL-escaped, UTF-8 rendering of the single letter "ã" ("a" with tilde). The following is much easier to recognize, even if it is not the right spelling:

```
https://en.wikipedia.org/wiki/Sao_Paulo
```

To remove all diacritics from a str, you can use a function like Example 4-14.

Example 4-14. simplify.py: function to remove all combining marks

```
import unicodedata
import string


def shave_marks(txt):
    """Remove all diacritic marks"""
    norm_txt = unicodedata.normalize('NFD', txt)  ❶
    shaved = ''.join(c for c in norm_txt
                     if not unicodedata.combining(c))  ❷
    return unicodedata.normalize('NFC', shaved)  ❸
```

❶ Decompose all characters into base characters and combining marks.

❷ Filter out all combining marks.

❸ Recompose all characters.

Example 4-15 shows a couple of uses of shave_marks.

Example 4-15. Two examples using shave_marks from Example 4-14

```
>>> order = '"Herr Voß: • ½ cup of Œtker™ caffè latte • bowl of açaí."'
>>> shave_marks(order)
'"Herr Voß: • ½ cup of Œtker™ caffe latte • bowl of acai."'  ❶
>>> Greek = 'Ζέφυρος, Zéfiro'
>>> shave_marks(Greek)
'Ζεφυρος, Zefiro'  ❷
```

❶ Only the letters "è", "ç", and "í" were replaced.

❷ Both "έ" and "é" were replaced.

The function shave_marks from Example 4-14 works all right, but maybe it goes too far. Often the reason to remove diacritics is to change Latin text to pure ASCII, but shave_marks also changes non-Latin characters—like Greek letters—which will never become ASCII just by losing their accents. So it makes sense to analyze each base character and to remove attached marks only if the base character is a letter from the Latin alphabet. This is what Example 4-16 does.

Example 4-16. Function to remove combining marks from Latin characters (import statements are omitted as this is part of the simplify.py module from Example 4-14)

```python
def shave_marks_latin(txt):
    """Remove all diacritic marks from Latin base characters"""
    norm_txt = unicodedata.normalize('NFD', txt)   ❶
    latin_base = False
    preserve = []
    for c in norm_txt:
        if unicodedata.combining(c) and latin_base:   ❷
            continue  # ignore diacritic on Latin base char
        preserve.append(c)                               ❸
        # if it isn't a combining char, it's a new base char
        if not unicodedata.combining(c):                 ❹
            latin_base = c in string.ascii_letters
    shaved = ''.join(preserve)
    return unicodedata.normalize('NFC', shaved)   ❺
```

❶ Decompose all characters into base characters and combining marks.

❷ Skip over combining marks when base character is Latin.

❸ Otherwise, keep current character.

❹ Detect new base character and determine if it's Latin.

❺ Recompose all characters.

An even more radical step would be to replace common symbols in Western texts (e.g., curly quotes, em dashes, bullets, etc.) into ASCII equivalents. This is what the function asciize does in Example 4-17.

Example 4-17. Transform some Western typographical symbols into ASCII (this snippet is also part of simplify.py from Example 4-14)

```python
single_map = str.maketrans("""‚ƒ„ˆ‹''""•––˜""",   ❶
                           """'f"^<'''"---~>""")

multi_map = str.maketrans({   ❷
    '€': 'EUR',
    '…': '...',
    'Æ': 'AE',
    'æ': 'ae',
    'Œ': 'OE',
    'œ': 'oe',
```

```
        '™': '(TM)',
        '‰': '<per mille>',
        '†': '**',
        '‡': '***',
})

multi_map.update(single_map)    ❸


def dewinize(txt):
    """Replace Win1252 symbols with ASCII chars or sequences"""
    return txt.translate(multi_map)    ❹


def asciize(txt):
    no_marks = shave_marks_latin(dewinize(txt))    ❺
    no_marks = no_marks.replace('ß', 'ss')    ❻
    return unicodedata.normalize('NFKC', no_marks)    ❼
```

❶ Build mapping table for char-to-char replacement.

❷ Build mapping table for char-to-string replacement.

❸ Merge mapping tables.

❹ dewinize does not affect ASCII or latin1 text, only the Microsoft additions to latin1 in cp1252.

❺ Apply dewinize and remove diacritical marks.

❻ Replace the Eszett with "ss" (we are not using case fold here because we want to preserve the case).

❼ Apply NFKC normalization to compose characters with their compatibility code points.

Example 4-18 shows asciize in use.

Example 4-18. Two examples using asciize from Example 4-17

```
>>> order = '"Herr Voß: • ½ cup of Œtker™ caffè latte • bowl of açaí."'
>>> dewinize(order)
'"Herr Voß: - ½ cup of OEtker(TM) caffè latte - bowl of açaí."'    ❶
>>> asciize(order)
'"Herr Voss: - 1/2 cup of OEtker(TM) caffe latte - bowl of acai."'    ❷
```

❶ `dewinize` replaces curly quotes, bullets, and ™ (trademark symbol).

❷ `asciize` applies `dewinize`, drops diacritics, and replaces the `'ß'`.

> Different languages have their own rules for removing diacritics. For example, Germans change the `'ü'` into `'ue'`. Our `asciize` function is not as refined, so it may or not be suitable for your language. It works acceptably for Portuguese, though.

To summarize, the functions in *simplify.py* go way beyond standard normalization and perform deep surgery on the text, with a good chance of changing its meaning. Only you can decide whether to go so far, knowing the target language, your users, and how the transformed text will be used.

This wraps up our discussion of normalizing Unicode text.

Now let's sort out Unicode sorting.

Sorting Unicode Text

Python sorts sequences of any type by comparing the items in each sequence one by one. For strings, this means comparing the code points. Unfortunately, this produces unacceptable results for anyone who uses non-ASCII characters.

Consider sorting a list of fruits grown in Brazil:

```
>>> fruits = ['caju', 'atemoia', 'cajá', 'açaí', 'acerola']
>>> sorted(fruits)
['acerola', 'atemoia', 'açaí', 'caju', 'cajá']
```

Sorting rules vary for different locales, but in Portuguese and many languages that use the Latin alphabet, accents and cedillas rarely make a difference when sorting.[8] So "cajá" is sorted as "caja," and must come before "caju."

The sorted `fruits` list should be:

```
['açaí', 'acerola', 'atemoia', 'cajá', 'caju']
```

The standard way to sort non-ASCII text in Python is to use the `locale.strxfrm` function which, according to the `locale` module docs (*https://fpy.li/4-16*), "transforms a string to one that can be used in locale-aware comparisons."

---

8 Diacritics affect sorting only in the rare case when they are the only difference between two words—in that case, the word with a diacritic is sorted after the plain word.

To enable `locale.strxfrm`, you must first set a suitable locale for your application, and pray that the OS supports it. The sequence of commands in Example 4-19 may work for you.

Example 4-19. locale_sort.py: using the `locale.strxfrm` function as the sort key

```
import locale
my_locale = locale.setlocale(locale.LC_COLLATE, 'pt_BR.UTF-8')
print(my_locale)
fruits = ['caju', 'atemoia', 'cajá', 'açaí', 'acerola']
sorted_fruits = sorted(fruits, key=locale.strxfrm)
print(sorted_fruits)
```

Running Example 4-19 on GNU/Linux (Ubuntu 19.10) with the `pt_BR.UTF-8` locale installed, I get the correct result:

```
'pt_BR.UTF-8'
['açaí', 'acerola', 'atemoia', 'cajá', 'caju']
```

So you need to call `setlocale(LC_COLLATE, «your_locale»)` before using `locale.strxfrm` as the key when sorting.

There are some caveats, though:

- Because locale settings are global, calling `setlocale` in a library is not recommended. Your application or framework should set the locale when the process starts, and should not change it afterward.

- The locale must be installed on the OS, otherwise `setlocale` raises a `locale.Error: unsupported locale setting` exception.

- You must know how to spell the locale name.

- The locale must be correctly implemented by the makers of the OS. I was successful on Ubuntu 19.10, but not on macOS 10.14. On macOS, the call `setlo cale(LC_COLLATE, 'pt_BR.UTF-8')` returns the string `'pt_BR.UTF-8'` with no complaints. But `sorted(fruits, key=locale.strxfrm)` produced the same incorrect result as `sorted(fruits)` did. I also tried the `fr_FR`, `es_ES`, and `de_DE` locales on macOS, but `locale.strxfrm` never did its job.[9]

So the standard library solution to internationalized sorting works, but seems to be well supported only on GNU/Linux (perhaps also on Windows, if you are an expert). Even then, it depends on locale settings, creating deployment headaches.

---

9 Again, I could not find a solution, but did find other people reporting the same problem. Alex Martelli, one of the tech reviewers, had no problem using `setlocale` and `locale.strxfrm` on his Macintosh with macOS 10.9. In summary: your mileage may vary.

Fortunately, there is a simpler solution: the *pyuca* library, available on *PyPI*.

Sorting with the Unicode Collation Algorithm

James Tauber, prolific Django contributor, must have felt the pain and created *pyuca* (*https://fpy.li/4-17*), a pure-Python implementation of the Unicode Collation Algorithm (UCA). Example 4-20 shows how easy it is to use.

Example 4-20. Using the `pyuca.Collator.sort_key` *method*

```
>>> import pyuca
>>> coll = pyuca.Collator()
>>> fruits = ['caju', 'atemoia', 'cajá', 'açaí', 'acerola']
>>> sorted_fruits = sorted(fruits, key=coll.sort_key)
>>> sorted_fruits
['açaí', 'acerola', 'atemoia', 'cajá', 'caju']
```

This is simple and works on GNU/Linux, macOS, and Windows, at least with my small sample.

pyuca does not take the locale into account. If you need to customize the sorting, you can provide the path to a custom collation table to the `Collator()` constructor. Out of the box, it uses *allkeys.txt* (*https://fpy.li/4-18*), which is bundled with the project. That's just a copy of the Default Unicode Collation Element Table from *Unicode.org* (*https://fpy.li/4-19*).

PyICU: Miro's Recommendation for Unicode Sorting

(Tech reviewer Miroslav Šedivý is a polyglot and an expert on Unicode. This is what he wrote about *pyuca*.)

pyuca has one sorting algorithm that does not respect the sorting order in individual languages. For instance, Ä in German is between A and B, while in Swedish it comes after Z. Have a look at PyICU (*https://fpy.li/4-20*) that works like locale without changing the locale of the process. It is also needed if you want to change the case of iİ/ıI in Turkish. PyICU includes an extension that must be compiled, so it may be harder to install in some systems than *pyuca*, which is just Python.

By the way, that collation table is one of the many data files that comprise the Unicode database, our next subject.

The Unicode Database

The Unicode standard provides an entire database—in the form of several structured text files—that includes not only the table mapping code points to character names, but also metadata about the individual characters and how they are related. For example, the Unicode database records whether a character is printable, is a letter, is a decimal digit, or is some other numeric symbol. That's how the str methods isalpha, isprintable, isdecimal, and isnumeric work. str.casefold also uses information from a Unicode table.

> The unicodedata.category(char) function returns the two-letter category of char from the Unicode database. The higher-level str methods are easier to use. For example, label.isalpha() (*https://fpy.li/4-21*) returns True if every character in label belongs to one of these categories: Lm, Lt, Lu, Ll, or Lo. To learn what those codes mean, see "General Category" (*https://fpy.li/4-22*) in the English Wikipedia's "Unicode character property" article (*https://fpy.li/4-23*).

Finding Characters by Name

The unicodedata module has functions to retrieve character metadata, including unicodedata.name(), which returns a character's official name in the standard. Figure 4-5 demonstrates that function.[10]

```
>>> from unicodedata import name
>>> name('A')
'LATIN CAPITAL LETTER A'
>>> name('ã')
'LATIN SMALL LETTER A WITH TILDE'
>>> name('♛')
'BLACK CHESS QUEEN'
>>> name('😸')
'GRINNING CAT FACE WITH SMILING EYES'
```

Figure 4-5. Exploring unicodedata.name() in the Python console.

You can use the name() function to build apps that let users search for characters by name. Figure 4-6 demonstrates the *cf.py* command-line script that takes one or more

---

10 That's an image—not a code listing—because emojis are not well supported by O'Reilly's digital publishing toolchain as I write this.

words as arguments, and lists the characters that have those words in their official Unicode names. The full source code for *cf.py* is in Example 4-21.

```
$ ./cf.py cat smiling
U+1F638  😸       GRINNING CAT FACE WITH SMILING EYES
U+1F63A  😺       SMILING CAT FACE WITH OPEN MOUTH
U+1F63B  😻       SMILING CAT FACE WITH HEART-SHAPED EYES
```

Figure 4-6. Using cf.py to find smiling cats.

 Emoji support varies widely across operating systems and apps. In recent years the macOS terminal offers the best support for emojis, followed by modern GNU/Linux graphic terminals. Windows *cmd.exe* and PowerShell now support Unicode output, but as I write this section in January 2020, they still don't display emojis—at least not "out of the box." Tech reviewer Leonardo Rochael told me about a new, open source Windows Terminal by Microsoft (*https://fpy.li/4-24*), which may have better Unicode support than the older Microsoft consoles. I did not have time to try it.

In Example 4-21, note the `if` statement in the `find` function using the `.issubset()` method to quickly test whether all the words in the `query` set appear in the list of words built from the character's name. Thanks to Python's rich set API, we don't need a nested `for` loop and another `if` to implement this check.

Example 4-21. cf.py: the character finder utility

```
#!/usr/bin/env python3
import sys
import unicodedata

START, END = ord(' '), sys.maxunicode + 1              ❶

def find(*query_words, start=START, end=END):          ❷
    query = {w.upper() for w in query_words}           ❸
    for code in range(start, end):
        char = chr(code)                               ❹
        name = unicodedata.name(char, None)            ❺
        if name and query.issubset(name.split()):      ❻
            print(f'U+{code:04X}\t{char}\t{name}')      ❼

def main(words):
    if words:
        find(*words)
    else:
        print('Please provide words to find.')
```

```
if __name__ == '__main__':
    main(sys.argv[1:])
```

❶ Set defaults for the range of code points to search.

❷ find accepts query_words and optional keyword-only arguments to limit the range of the search, to facilitate testing.

❸ Convert query_words into a set of uppercased strings.

❹ Get the Unicode character for code.

❺ Get the name of the character, or None if the code point is unassigned.

❻ If there is a name, split it into a list of words, then check that the query set is a subset of that list.

❼ Print out line with code point in U+9999 format, the character, and its name.

The unicodedata module has other interesting functions. Next, we'll see a few that are related to getting information from characters that have numeric meaning.

Numeric Meaning of Characters

The unicodedata module includes functions to check whether a Unicode character represents a number and, if so, its numeric value for humans—as opposed to its code point number. Example 4-22 shows the use of unicodedata.name() and unicode data.numeric(), along with the .isdecimal() and .isnumeric() methods of str.

Example 4-22. Demo of Unicode database numerical character metadata (callouts describe each column in the output)

```
import unicodedata
import re

re_digit = re.compile(r'\d')

sample = '1\xbc\xb2\u0969\u136b\u216b\u2466\u2480\u3285'

for char in sample:
    print(f'U+{ord(char):04x}',                          ❶
          char.center(6),                                 ❷
          're_dig' if re_digit.match(char) else '-',      ❸
          'isdig' if char.isdigit() else '-',             ❹
          'isnum' if char.isnumeric() else '-',           ❺
          f'{unicodedata.numeric(char):5.2f}',            ❻
```

```
                    unicodedata.name(char),                    ❼
                    sep='\t')
```

❶ Code point in U+0000 format.

❷ Character centralized in a str of length 6.

❸ Show re_dig if character matches the r'\d' regex.

❹ Show isdig if char.isdigit() is True.

❺ Show isnum if char.isnumeric() is True.

❻ Numeric value formatted with width 5 and 2 decimal places.

❼ Unicode character name.

Running Example 4-22 gives you Figure 4-7, if your terminal font has all those glyphs.

```
$ python3 numerics_demo.py
U+0031    1      re_dig  isdig   isnum    1.00   DIGIT ONE
U+00bc    ¼      -       -       isnum    0.25   VULGAR FRACTION ONE QUARTER
U+00b2    ²      -       isdig   isnum    2.00   SUPERSCRIPT TWO
U+0969    ३      re_dig  isdig   isnum    3.00   DEVANAGARI DIGIT THREE
U+136b    ፫      -       isdig   isnum    3.00   ETHIOPIC DIGIT THREE
U+216b    XII    -       -       isnum   12.00   ROMAN NUMERAL TWELVE
U+2466    ⑦      -       isdig   isnum    7.00   CIRCLED DIGIT SEVEN
U+2480    ⒀      -       -       isnum   13.00   PARENTHESIZED NUMBER THIRTEEN
U+3285    ㊅      -       -       isnum    6.00   CIRCLED IDEOGRAPH SIX
$
```

Figure 4-7. macOS terminal showing numeric characters and metadata about them; re_dig means the character matches the regular expression r'\d'.

The sixth column of Figure 4-7 is the result of calling unicodedata.numeric(char) on the character. It shows that Unicode knows the numeric value of symbols that represent numbers. So if you want to create a spreadsheet application that supports Tamil digits or Roman numerals, go for it!

Figure 4-7 shows that the regular expression r'\d' matches the digit "1" and the Devanagari digit 3, but not some other characters that are considered digits by the isdigit function. The re module is not as savvy about Unicode as it could be. The new `regex` module available on PyPI was designed to eventually replace `re` and provides better Unicode support.[11] We'll come back to the `re` module in the next section.

Throughout this chapter we've used several `unicodedata` functions, but there are many more we did not cover. See the standard library documentation for the `unicode data` module (*https://fpy.li/4-25*).

Next we'll take a quick look at dual-mode APIs offering functions that accept `str` or `bytes` arguments with special handling depending on the type.

Dual-Mode str and bytes APIs

Python's standard library has functions that accept `str` or `bytes` arguments and behave differently depending on the type. Some examples can be found in the `re` and `os` modules.

str Versus bytes in Regular Expressions

If you build a regular expression with `bytes`, patterns such as `\d` and `\w` only match ASCII characters; in contrast, if these patterns are given as `str`, they match Unicode digits or letters beyond ASCII. Example 4-23 and Figure 4-8 compare how letters, ASCII digits, superscripts, and Tamil digits are matched by `str` and `bytes` patterns.

Example 4-23. ramanujan.py: compare behavior of simple str and bytes regular expressions

```
import re

re_numbers_str = re.compile(r'\d+')        ❶
re_words_str = re.compile(r'\w+')
re_numbers_bytes = re.compile(rb'\d+')     ❷
re_words_bytes = re.compile(rb'\w+')

text_str = ("Ramanujan saw \u0be7\u0bed\u0be8\u0bef"   ❸
            " as 1729 = 1³ + 12³ = 9³ + 10³.")          ❹

text_bytes = text_str.encode('utf_8')       ❺

print(f'Text\n  {text_str!r}')
print('Numbers')
print('  str  :', re_numbers_str.findall(text_str))       ❻
print('  bytes:', re_numbers_bytes.findall(text_bytes))   ❼
print('Words')
```

---

11 Although it was not better than `re` at identifying digits in this particular sample.

```
print('  str   :', re_words_str.findall(text_str))        ❽
print('  bytes:', re_words_bytes.findall(text_bytes))     ❾
```

❶ The first two regular expressions are of the str type.

❷ The last two are of the bytes type.

❸ Unicode text to search, containing the Tamil digits for 1729 (the logical line continues until the right parenthesis token).

❹ This string is joined to the previous one at compile time (see "2.4.2. String literal concatenation" (*https://fpy.li/4-26*) in *The Python Language Reference*).

❺ A bytes string is needed to search with the bytes regular expressions.

❻ The str pattern r'\d+' matches the Tamil and ASCII digits.

❼ The bytes pattern rb'\d+' matches only the ASCII bytes for digits.

❽ The str pattern r'\w+' matches the letters, superscripts, Tamil, and ASCII digits.

❾ The bytes pattern rb'\w+' matches only the ASCII bytes for letters and digits.

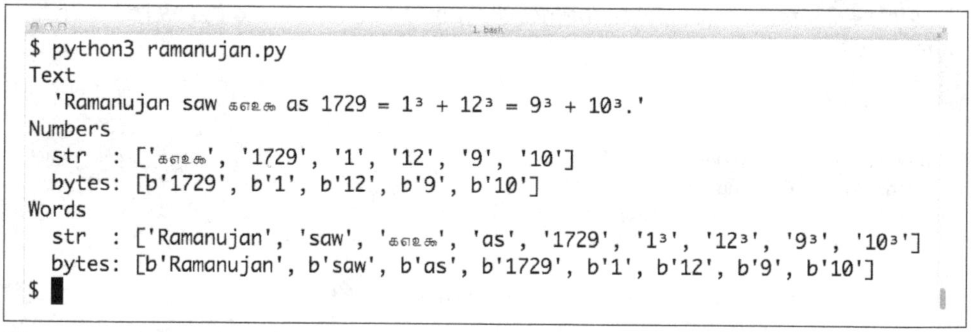

```
$ python3 ramanujan.py
Text
  'Ramanujan saw ௧௭௨௯ as 1729 = 1³ + 12³ = 9³ + 10³.'
Numbers
  str   : ['௧௭௨௯', '1729', '1', '12', '9', '10']
  bytes: [b'1729', b'1', b'12', b'9', b'10']
Words
  str   : ['Ramanujan', 'saw', '௧௭௨௯', 'as', '1729', '1³', '12³', '9³', '10³']
  bytes: [b'Ramanujan', b'saw', b'as', b'1729', b'1', b'12', b'9', b'10']
$ ▊
```

Figure 4-8. Screenshot of running ramanujan.py from Example 4-23.

Example 4-23 is a trivial example to make one point: you can use regular expressions on str and bytes, but in the second case, bytes outside the ASCII range are treated as nondigits and nonword characters.

For str regular expressions, there is a re.ASCII flag that makes \w, \W, \b, \B, \d, \D, \s, and \S perform ASCII-only matching. See the documentation of the re module (*https://fpy.li/4-27*) for full details.

Another important dual-mode module is os.

str Versus bytes in os Functions

The GNU/Linux kernel is not Unicode savvy, so in the real world you may find filenames made of byte sequences that are not valid in any sensible encoding scheme, and cannot be decoded to str. File servers with clients using a variety of OSes are particularly prone to this problem.

In order to work around this issue, all os module functions that accept filenames or pathnames take arguments as str or bytes. If one such function is called with a str argument, the argument will be automatically converted using the codec named by sys.getfilesystemencoding(), and the OS response will be decoded with the same codec. This is almost always what you want, in keeping with the Unicode sandwich best practice.

But if you must deal with (and perhaps fix) filenames that cannot be handled in that way, you can pass bytes arguments to the os functions to get bytes return values. This feature lets you deal with any file or pathname, no matter how many gremlins you may find. See Example 4-24.

Example 4-24. listdir with str and bytes arguments and results

```
>>> os.listdir('.')   ❶
['abc.txt', 'digits-of-n.txt']
>>> os.listdir(b'.')   ❷
[b'abc.txt', b'digits-of-\xcf\x80.txt']
```

❶ The second filename is "digits-of-π.txt" (with the Greek letter pi).

❷ Given a byte argument, listdir returns filenames as bytes: b'\xcf\x80' is the UTF-8 encoding of the Greek letter pi.

To help with manual handling of str or bytes sequences that are filenames or pathnames, the os module provides special encoding and decoding functions os.fsen code(name_or_path) and os.fsdecode(name_or_path). Both of these functions accept an argument of type str, bytes, or an object implementing the os.PathLike interface since Python 3.6.

Unicode is a deep rabbit hole. Time to wrap up our exploration of str and bytes.

Chapter Summary

We started the chapter by dismissing the notion that 1 character == 1 byte. As the world adopts Unicode, we need to keep the concept of text strings separated from the binary sequences that represent them in files, and Python 3 enforces this separation.

After a brief overview of the binary sequence data types—bytes, bytearray, and memoryview—we jumped into encoding and decoding, with a sampling of important codecs, followed by approaches to prevent or deal with the infamous UnicodeEnco deError, UnicodeDecodeError, and the SyntaxError caused by wrong encoding in Python source files.

We then considered the theory and practice of encoding detection in the absence of metadata: in theory, it can't be done, but in practice the Chardet package pulls it off pretty well for a number of popular encodings. Byte order marks were then presented as the only encoding hint commonly found in UTF-16 and UTF-32 files—sometimes in UTF-8 files as well.

In the next section, we demonstrated opening text files, an easy task except for one pitfall: the encoding= keyword argument is not mandatory when you open a text file, but it should be. If you fail to specify the encoding, you end up with a program that manages to generate "plain text" that is incompatible across platforms, due to conflicting default encodings. We then exposed the different encoding settings that Python uses as defaults and how to detect them. A sad realization for Windows users is that these settings often have distinct values within the same machine, and the values are mutually incompatible; GNU/Linux and macOS users, in contrast, live in a happier place where UTF-8 is the default pretty much everywhere.

Unicode provides multiple ways of representing some characters, so normalizing is a prerequisite for text matching. In addition to explaining normalization and case folding, we presented some utility functions that you may adapt to your needs, including drastic transformations like removing all accents. We then saw how to sort Unicode text correctly by leveraging the standard locale module—with some caveats—and an alternative that does not depend on tricky locale configurations: the external *pyuca* package.

We leveraged the Unicode database to program a command-line utility to search for characters by name—in 28 lines of code, thanks to the power of Python. We glanced at other Unicode metadata, and had a brief overview of dual-mode APIs where some functions can be called with str or bytes arguments, producing different results.

Further Reading

Ned Batchelder's 2012 PyCon US talk "Pragmatic Unicode, or, How Do I Stop the Pain?" (*https://fpy.li/4-28*) was outstanding. Ned is so professional that he provides a full transcript of the talk along with the slides and video.

"Character encoding and Unicode in Python: How to (╯°□°)╯ ︵ ┻━┻ with dignity" (slides (*https://fpy.li/4-1*), video (*https://fpy.li/4-2*)) was the excellent PyCon 2014 talk by Esther Nam and Travis Fischer, where I found this chapter's pithy epigraph: "Humans use text. Computers speak bytes."

Lennart Regebro—one of the technical reviewers for the first edition of this book—shares his "Useful Mental Model of Unicode (UMMU)" in the short post "Unconfusing Unicode: What Is Unicode?" (*https://fpy.li/4-31*). Unicode is a complex standard, so Lennart's UMMU is a really useful starting point.

The official "Unicode HOWTO" (*https://fpy.li/4-32*) in the Python docs approaches the subject from several different angles, from a good historic intro, to syntax details, codecs, regular expressions, filenames, and best practices for Unicode-aware I/O (i.e., the Unicode sandwich), with plenty of additional reference links from each section. Chapter 4, "Strings" (*https://fpy.li/4-33*), of Mark Pilgrim's awesome book *Dive into Python 3* (*https://fpy.li/4-34*) (Apress) also provides a very good intro to Unicode support in Python 3. In the same book, Chapter 15 (*https://fpy.li/4-35*) describes how the Chardet library was ported from Python 2 to Python 3, a valuable case study given that the switch from the old `str` to the new `bytes` is the cause of most migration pains, and that is a central concern in a library designed to detect encodings.

If you know Python 2 but are new to Python 3, Guido van Rossum's "What's New in Python 3.0" (*https://fpy.li/4-36*) has 15 bullet points that summarize what changed, with lots of links. Guido starts with the blunt statement: "Everything you thought you knew about binary data and Unicode has changed." Armin Ronacher's blog post "The Updated Guide to Unicode on Python" (*https://fpy.li/4-37*) is deep and highlights some of the pitfalls of Unicode in Python 3 (Armin is not a big fan of Python 3).

Chapter 2, "Strings and Text," of the *Python Cookbook*, 3rd ed. (O'Reilly), by David Beazley and Brian K. Jones, has several recipes dealing with Unicode normalization, sanitizing text, and performing text-oriented operations on byte sequences. Chapter 5 covers files and I/O, and it includes "Recipe 5.17. Writing Bytes to a Text File," showing that underlying any text file there is always a binary stream that may be accessed directly when needed. Later in the cookbook, the `struct` module is put to use in "Recipe 6.11. Reading and Writing Binary Arrays of Structures."

Nick Coghlan's "Python Notes" blog has two posts very relevant to this chapter: "Python 3 and ASCII Compatible Binary Protocols" (*https://fpy.li/4-38*) and "Processing Text Files in Python 3" (*https://fpy.li/4-39*). Highly recommended.

A list of encodings supported by Python is available at "Standard Encodings" (*https://fpy.li/4-40*) in the `codecs` module documentation. If you need to get that list programmatically, see how it's done in the */Tools/unicode/listcodecs.py* (*https://fpy.li/4-41*) script that comes with the CPython source code.

The books *Unicode Explained* by Jukka K. Korpela (O'Reilly) and *Unicode Demystified* (*https://fpy.li/4-43*) by Richard Gillam (Addison-Wesley) are not Python-specific but were very helpful as I studied Unicode concepts. *Programming with Unicode* (*https://fpy.li/4-44*) by Victor Stinner is a free, self-published book (Creative

Commons BY-SA) covering Unicode in general, as well as tools and APIs in the context of the main operating systems and a few programming languages, including Python.

The W3C pages "Case Folding: An Introduction" (*https://fpy.li/4-45*) and "Character Model for the World Wide Web: String Matching" (*https://fpy.li/4-15*) cover normalization concepts, with the former being a gentle introduction and the latter a working group note written in dry standard-speak—the same tone of the "Unicode Standard Annex #15—Unicode Normalization Forms" (*https://fpy.li/4-47*). The "Frequently Asked Questions, Normalization" (*https://fpy.li/4-48*) section from *Unicode.org* is more readable, as is the "NFC FAQ" (*https://fpy.li/4-50*) by Mark Davis—author of several Unicode algorithms and president of the Unicode Consortium at the time of this writing.

In 2016, the Museum of Modern Art (MoMA) in New York added to its collection the original emoji (*https://fpy.li/4-51*), the 176 emojis designed by Shigetaka Kurita in 1999 for NTT DOCOMO—the Japanese mobile carrier. Going further back in history, *Emojipedia* (*https://fpy.li/4-52*) published "Correcting the Record on the First Emoji Set" (*https://fpy.li/4-53*), crediting Japan's SoftBank for the earliest known emoji set, deployed in cell phones in 1997. SoftBank's set is the source of 90 emojis now in Unicode, including U+1F4A9 (PILE OF POO). Matthew Rothenberg's *emoji-tracker.com* (*https://fpy.li/4-54*) is a live dashboard showing counts of emoji usage on Twitter, updated in real time. As I write this, FACE WITH TEARS OF JOY (U+1F602) is the most popular emoji on Twitter, with more than 3,313,667,315 recorded occurrences.

Soapbox

Non-ASCII Names in Source Code: Should You Use Them?

Python 3 allows non-ASCII identifiers in source code:

```
>>> ação = 'PBR'   # ação = stock
>>> ε = 10**-6     # ε = epsilon
```

Some people dislike the idea. The most common argument to stick with ASCII identifiers is to make it easy for everyone to read and edit code. That argument misses the point: you want your source code to be readable and editable by its intended audience, and that may not be "everyone." If the code belongs to a multinational corporation or is open source and you want contributors from around the world, the identifiers should be in English, and then all you need is ASCII.

But if you are a teacher in Brazil, your students will find it easier to read code that uses Portuguese variable and function names, correctly spelled. And they will have no difficulty typing the cedillas and accented vowels on their localized keyboards.

Now that Python can parse Unicode names and UTF-8 is the default source encoding, I see no point in coding identifiers in Portuguese without accents, as we used to do in Python 2 out of necessity—unless you need the code to run on Python 2 also. If the names are in Portuguese, leaving out the accents won't make the code more readable to anyone.

This is my point of view as a Portuguese-speaking Brazilian, but I believe it applies across borders and cultures: choose the human language that makes the code easier to read by the team, then use the characters needed for correct spelling.

What Is "Plain Text"?

For anyone who deals with non-English text on a daily basis, "plain text" does not imply "ASCII." The Unicode Glossary (*https://fpy.li/4-55*) defines *plain text* like this:

> Computer-encoded text that consists only of a sequence of code points from a given standard, with no other formatting or structural information.

That definition starts very well, but I don't agree with the part after the comma. HTML is a great example of a plain-text format that carries formatting and structural information. But it's still plain text because every byte in such a file is there to represent a text character, usually using UTF-8. There are no bytes with nontext meaning, as you can find in a *.png* or *.xls* document where most bytes represent packed binary values like RGB values and floating-point numbers. In plain text, numbers are represented as sequences of digit characters.

I am writing this book in a plain-text format called—ironically—AsciiDoc (*https://fpy.li/4-56*), which is part of the toolchain of O'Reilly's excellent Atlas book publishing platform (*https://fpy.li/4-57*). AsciiDoc source files are plain text, but they are UTF-8, not ASCII. Otherwise, writing this chapter would have been really painful. Despite the name, AsciiDoc is just great.

The world of Unicode is constantly expanding and, at the edges, tool support is not always there. Not all characters I wanted to show were available in the fonts used to render the book. That's why I had to use images instead of listings in several examples in this chapter. On the other hand, the Ubuntu and macOS terminals display most Unicode text very well—including the Japanese characters for the word "mojibake": 文字化け.

How Are str Code Points Represented in RAM?

The official Python docs avoid the issue of how the code points of a str are stored in memory. It is really an implementation detail. In theory, it doesn't matter: whatever the internal representation, every str must be encoded to bytes on output.

In memory, Python 3 stores each str as a sequence of code points using a fixed number of bytes per code point, to allow efficient direct access to any character or slice.

Since Python 3.3, when creating a new `str` object, the interpreter checks the characters in it and chooses the most economic memory layout that is suitable for that particular `str`: if there are only characters in the `latin1` range, that `str` will use just one byte per code point. Otherwise, two or four bytes per code point may be used, depending on the `str`. This is a simplification; for the full details, look up PEP 393—Flexible String Representation (*https://fpy.li/pep393*).

The flexible string representation is similar to the way the `int` type works in Python 3: if the integer fits in a machine word, it is stored in one machine word. Otherwise, the interpreter switches to a variable-length representation like that of the Python 2 `long` type. It is nice to see the spread of good ideas.

However, we can always count on Armin Ronacher to find problems in Python 3. He explained to me why that was not such as great idea in practice: it takes a single RAT (U+1F400) to inflate an otherwise all-ASCII text into a memory-hogging array using four bytes per character, when one byte would suffice for each character except the RAT. In addition, because of all the ways Unicode characters combine, the ability to quickly retrieve an arbitrary character by position is overrated—and extracting arbitrary slices from Unicode text is naïve at best, and often wrong, producing mojibake. As emojis become more popular, these problems will only get worse.

## CHAPTER 5

Data Class Builders

Data classes are like children. They are okay as a starting point, but to participate as a grownup object, they need to take some responsibility.

—Martin Fowler and Kent Beck[1]

Python offers a few ways to build a simple class that is just a collection of fields, with little or no extra functionality. That pattern is known as a "data class"—and `data classes` is one of the packages that supports this pattern. This chapter covers three different class builders that you may use as shortcuts to write data classes:

`collections.namedtuple`
> The simplest way—available since Python 2.6.

`typing.NamedTuple`
> An alternative that requires type hints on the fields—since Python 3.5, with `class` syntax added in 3.6.

`@dataclasses.dataclass`
> A class decorator that allows more customization than previous alternatives, adding lots of options and potential complexity—since Python 3.7.

After covering those class builders, we will discuss why *Data Class* is also the name of a code smell: a coding pattern that may be a symptom of poor object-oriented design.

---

1 From *Refactoring*, first edition, Chapter 3, "Bad Smells in Code, Data Class" section, page 87 (Addison-Wesley).

typing.TypedDict may seem like another data class builder. It uses similar syntax and is described right after typing.NamedTuple in the typing module documentation (*https://fpy.li/5-1*) for Python 3.9.

However, TypedDict does not build concrete classes that you can instantiate. It's just syntax to write type hints for function parameters and variables that will accept mapping values used as records, with keys as field names. We'll see them in Chapter 15, "TypedDict" on page 530.

What's New in This Chapter

This chapter is new in the second edition of *Fluent Python*. The section "Classic Named Tuples" on page 169 appeared in Chapter 2 of the first edition, but the rest of the chapter is completely new.

We begin with a high-level overview of the three class builders.

Overview of Data Class Builders

Consider a simple class to represent a geographic coordinate pair, as shown in Example 5-1.

Example 5-1. class/coordinates.py

```
class Coordinate:

    def __init__(self, lat, lon):
        self.lat = lat
        self.lon = lon
```

That Coordinate class does the job of holding latitude and longitude attributes. Writing the __init__ boilerplate becomes old real fast, especially if your class has more than a couple of attributes: each of them is mentioned three times! And that boilerplate doesn't buy us basic features we'd expect from a Python object:

```
>>> from coordinates import Coordinate
>>> moscow = Coordinate(55.76, 37.62)
>>> moscow
<coordinates.Coordinate object at 0x107142f10>    ❶
>>> location = Coordinate(55.76, 37.62)
>>> location == moscow    ❷
False
>>> (location.lat, location.lon) == (moscow.lat, moscow.lon)    ❸
True
```

❶ __repr__ inherited from object is not very helpful.

❷ Meaningless ==; the __eq__ method inherited from object compares object IDs.

❸ Comparing two coordinates requires explicit comparison of each attribute.

The data class builders covered in this chapter provide the necessary __init__, __repr__, and __eq__ methods automatically, as well as other useful features.

 None of the class builders discussed here depend on inheritance to do their work. Both collections.namedtuple and typing.Name dTuple build classes that are tuple subclasses. @dataclass is a class decorator that does not affect the class hierarchy in any way. Each of them uses different metaprogramming techniques to inject methods and data attributes into the class under construction.

Here is a Coordinate class built with namedtuple—a factory function that builds a subclass of tuple with the name and fields you specify:

```
>>> from collections import namedtuple
>>> Coordinate = namedtuple('Coordinate', 'lat lon')
>>> issubclass(Coordinate, tuple)
True
>>> moscow = Coordinate(55.756, 37.617)
>>> moscow
Coordinate(lat=55.756, lon=37.617)  ❶
>>> moscow == Coordinate(lat=55.756, lon=37.617)  ❷
True
```

❶ Useful __repr__.

❷ Meaningful __eq__.

The newer typing.NamedTuple provides the same functionality, adding a type annotation to each field:

```
>>> import typing
>>> Coordinate = typing.NamedTuple('Coordinate',
...     [('lat', float), ('lon', float)])
>>> issubclass(Coordinate, tuple)
True
>>> typing.get_type_hints(Coordinate)
{'lat': <class 'float'>, 'lon': <class 'float'>}
```

A typed named tuple can also be constructed with the fields given as keyword arguments, like this:

```
Coordinate = typing.NamedTuple('Coordinate', lat=float, lon=float)
```

This is more readable, and also lets you provide the mapping of fields and types as **fields_and_types.

Since Python 3.6, typing.NamedTuple can also be used in a class statement, with type annotations written as described in PEP 526—Syntax for Variable Annotations (*https://fpy.li/pep526*). This is much more readable, and makes it easy to override methods or add new ones. Example 5-2 is the same Coordinate class, with a pair of float attributes and a custom __str__ to display a coordinate formatted like 55.8°N, 37.6°E.

Example 5-2. typing_namedtuple/coordinates.py

```python
from typing import NamedTuple

class Coordinate(NamedTuple):
    lat: float
    lon: float

    def __str__(self):
        ns = 'N' if self.lat >= 0 else 'S'
        we = 'E' if self.lon >= 0 else 'W'
        return f'{abs(self.lat):.1f}°{ns}, {abs(self.lon):.1f}°{we}'
```

Although NamedTuple appears in the class statement as a superclass, it's actually not. typing.NamedTuple uses the advanced functionality of a metaclass[2] to customize the creation of the user's class. Check this out:

```
>>> issubclass(Coordinate, typing.NamedTuple)
False
>>> issubclass(Coordinate, tuple)
True
```

In the __init__ method generated by typing.NamedTuple, the fields appear as parameters in the same order they appear in the class statement.

Like typing.NamedTuple, the dataclass decorator supports PEP 526 (*https://fpy.li/pep526*) syntax to declare instance attributes. The decorator reads the variable annotations and automatically generates methods for your class. For comparison, check

---

2 Metaclasses are one of the subjects covered in Chapter 24, "Class Metaprogramming".

out the equivalent `Coordinate` class written with the help of the `dataclass` decorator, as shown in Example 5-3.

Example 5-3. dataclass/coordinates.py

```
from dataclasses import dataclass

@dataclass(frozen=True)
class Coordinate:
    lat: float
    lon: float

    def __str__(self):
        ns = 'N' if self.lat >= 0 else 'S'
        we = 'E' if self.lon >= 0 else 'W'
        return f'{abs(self.lat):.1f}°{ns}, {abs(self.lon):.1f}°{we}'
```

Note that the body of the classes in Example 5-2 and Example 5-3 are identical—the difference is in the `class` statement itself. The `@dataclass` decorator does not depend on inheritance or a metaclass, so it should not interfere with your own use of these mechanisms.[3] The `Coordinate` class in Example 5-3 is a subclass of `object`.

Main Features

The different data class builders have a lot in common, as summarized in Table 5-1.

Table 5-1. Selected features compared across the three data class builders; x stands for an instance of a data class of that kind

	namedtuple	NamedTuple	dataclass
mutable instances	NO	NO	YES
class statement syntax	NO	YES	YES
construct dict	x._asdict()	x._asdict()	dataclasses.asdict(x)
get field names	x._fields	x._fields	[f.name for f in dataclasses.fields(x)]
get defaults	x._field_defaults	x._field_defaults	[f.default for f in dataclasses.fields(x)]
get field types	N/A	x.__annotations__	x.__annotations__
new instance with changes	x._replace(...)	x._replace(...)	dataclasses.replace(x, ...)
new class at runtime	namedtuple(...)	NamedTuple(...)	dataclasses.make_dataclass(...)

---

3 Class decorators are covered in Chapter 24, "Class Metaprogramming," along with metaclasses. Both are ways of customizing class behavior beyond what is possible with inheritance.

The classes built by `typing.NamedTuple` and `@dataclass` have an `__annotations__` attribute holding the type hints for the fields. However, reading from `__annotations__` directly is not recommended. Instead, the recommended best practice to get that information is to call `inspect.get_annotations(MyClass)` (*https://fpy.li/5-2*) (added in Python 3.10) or `typing.get_type_hints(MyClass)` (*https://fpy.li/5-3*) (Python 3.5 to 3.9). That's because those functions provide extra services, like resolving forward references in type hints. We'll come back to this issue much later in the book, in "Problems with Annotations at Runtime" on page 542.

Now let's discuss those main features.

Mutable instances

A key difference between these class builders is that `collections.namedtuple` and `typing.NamedTuple` build `tuple` subclasses, therefore the instances are immutable. By default, `@dataclass` produces mutable classes. But the decorator accepts a keyword argument `frozen`—shown in Example 5-3. When `frozen=True`, the class will raise an exception if you try to assign a value to a field after the instance is initialized.

Class statement syntax

Only `typing.NamedTuple` and `dataclass` support the regular `class` statement syntax, making it easier to add methods and docstrings to the class you are creating.

Construct dict

Both named tuple variants provide an instance method (`._asdict`) to construct a `dict` object from the fields in a data class instance. The `dataclasses` module provides a function to do it: `dataclasses.asdict`.

Get field names and default values

All three class builders let you get the field names and default values that may be configured for them. In named tuple classes, that metadata is in the `._fields` and `._fields_defaults` class attributes. You can get the same metadata from a `data class` decorated class using the `fields` function from the `dataclasses` module. It returns a tuple of `Field` objects that have several attributes, including `name` and `default`.

Get field types

Classes defined with the help of `typing.NamedTuple` and `@dataclass` have a mapping of field names to type the __annotations__ class attribute. As mentioned, use the `typing.get_type_hints` function instead of reading __annotations__ directly.

New instance with changes

Given a named tuple instance x, the call `x._replace(**kwargs)` returns a new instance with some attribute values replaced according to the keyword arguments given. The `dataclasses.replace(x, **kwargs)` module-level function does the same for an instance of a `dataclass` decorated class.

New class at runtime

Although the `class` statement syntax is more readable, it is hardcoded. A framework may need to build data classes on the fly, at runtime. For that, you can use the default function call syntax of `collections.namedtuple`, which is likewise supported by `typing.NamedTuple`. The `dataclasses` module provides a `make_dataclass` function for the same purpose.

After this overview of the main features of the data class builders, let's focus on each of them in turn, starting with the simplest.

Classic Named Tuples

The `collections.namedtuple` function is a factory that builds subclasses of `tuple` enhanced with field names, a class name, and an informative __repr__. Classes built with `namedtuple` can be used anywhere where tuples are needed, and in fact many functions of the Python standard library that are used to return tuples now return named tuples for convenience, without affecting the user's code at all.

> Each instance of a class built by `namedtuple` takes exactly the same amount of memory as a tuple because the field names are stored in the class.

Example 5-4 shows how we could define a named tuple to hold information about a city.

Example 5-4. Defining and using a named tuple type

```
>>> from collections import namedtuple
>>> City = namedtuple('City', 'name country population coordinates')  ❶
```

```
>>> tokyo = City('Tokyo', 'JP', 36.933, (35.689722, 139.691667))  ❷
>>> tokyo
City(name='Tokyo', country='JP', population=36.933, coordinates=(35.689722,
139.691667))
>>> tokyo.population  ❸
36.933
>>> tokyo.coordinates
(35.689722, 139.691667)
>>> tokyo[1]
'JP'
```

❶ Two parameters are required to create a named tuple: a class name and a list of field names, which can be given as an iterable of strings or as a single space-delimited string.

❷ Field values must be passed as separate positional arguments to the constructor (in contrast, the tuple constructor takes a single iterable).

❸ You can access the fields by name or position.

As a tuple subclass, City inherits useful methods such as __eq__ and the special methods for comparison operators—including __lt__, which allows sorting lists of City instances.

A named tuple offers a few attributes and methods in addition to those inherited from the tuple. Example 5-5 shows the most useful: the _fields class attribute, the class method _make(iterable), and the _asdict() instance method.

Example 5-5. Named tuple attributes and methods (continued from the previous example)

```
>>> City._fields  ❶
('name', 'country', 'population', 'location')
>>> Coordinate = namedtuple('Coordinate', 'lat lon')
>>> delhi_data = ('Delhi NCR', 'IN', 21.935, Coordinate(28.613889, 77.208889))
>>> delhi = City._make(delhi_data)  ❷
>>> delhi._asdict()  ❸
{'name': 'Delhi NCR', 'country': 'IN', 'population': 21.935,
'location': Coordinate(lat=28.613889, lon=77.208889)}
>>> import json
>>> json.dumps(delhi._asdict())  ❹
'{"name": "Delhi NCR", "country": "IN", "population": 21.935,
"location": [28.613889, 77.208889]}'
```

❶ ._fields is a tuple with the field names of the class.

❷ ._make() builds City from an iterable; City(*delhi_data) would do the same.

❸ ._asdict() returns a dict built from the named tuple instance.

❹ ._asdict() is useful to serialize the data in JSON format, for example.

 The _asdict method returned an OrderedDict until Python 3.7. Since Python 3.8, it returns a simple dict—which is OK now that we can rely on key insertion order. If you must have an Ordered Dict, the _asdict documentation (*https://fpy.li/5-4*) recommends building one from the result: OrderedDict(x._asdict()).

Since Python 3.7, namedtuple accepts the defaults keyword-only argument providing an iterable of N default values for each of the N rightmost fields of the class. Example 5-6 shows how to define a Coordinate named tuple with a default value for a reference field.

Example 5-6. Named tuple attributes and methods, continued from Example 5-5

```
>>> Coordinate = namedtuple('Coordinate', 'lat lon reference', defaults=['WGS84'])
>>> Coordinate(0, 0)
Coordinate(lat=0, lon=0, reference='WGS84')
>>> Coordinate._field_defaults
{'reference': 'WGS84'}
```

In "Class statement syntax" on page 168, I mentioned it's easier to code methods with the class syntax supported by typing.NamedTuple and @dataclass. You can also add methods to a namedtuple, but it's a hack. Skip the following box if you're not interested in hacks.

Hacking a namedtuple to Inject a Method

Recall how we built the Card class in Example 1-1 in Chapter 1:

```
Card = collections.namedtuple('Card', ['rank', 'suit'])
```

Later in Chapter 1, I wrote a spades_high function for sorting. It would be nice if that logic was encapsulated in a method of Card, but adding spades_high to Card without the benefit of a class statement requires a quick hack: define the function and then assign it to a class attribute. Example 5-7 shows how.

Example 5-7. frenchdeck.doctest: Adding a class attribute and a method to Card, the namedtuple from "A Pythonic Card Deck" on page 5

```
>>> Card.suit_values = dict(spades=3, hearts=2, diamonds=1, clubs=0)   ❶
>>> def spades_high(card):                                             ❷
...     rank_value = FrenchDeck.ranks.index(card.rank)
```

```
...        suit_value = card.suit_values[card.suit]
...        return rank_value * len(card.suit_values) + suit_value
...
>>> Card.overall_rank = spades_high                               ❸
>>> lowest_card = Card('2', 'clubs')
>>> highest_card = Card('A', 'spades')
>>> lowest_card.overall_rank()                                    ❹
0
>>> highest_card.overall_rank()
51
```

❶ Attach a class attribute with values for each suit.

❷ spades_high will become a method; the first argument doesn't need to be named self. Anyway, it will get the receiver when called as a method.

❸ Attach the function to the Card class as a method named overall_rank.

❹ It works!

For readability and future maintenance, it's much better to code methods inside a class statement. But it's good to know this hack is possible, because it may come in handy.[4]

This was a small detour to showcase the power of a dynamic language.

Now let's check out the typing.NamedTuple variation.

Typed Named Tuples

The Coordinate class with a default field from Example 5-6 can be written using typing.NamedTuple, as shown in Example 5-8.

Example 5-8. typing_namedtuple/coordinates2.py

```
from typing import NamedTuple

class Coordinate(NamedTuple):
    lat: float              ❶
    lon: float
    reference: str = 'WGS84'   ❷
```

---

4 If you know Ruby, you know that injecting methods is a well-known but controversial technique among Rubyists. In Python, it's not as common, because it doesn't work with any built-in type—str, list, etc. I consider this limitation of Python a blessing.

❶ Every instance field must be annotated with a type.

❷ The `reference` instance field is annotated with a type and a default value.

Classes built by `typing.NamedTuple` don't have any methods beyond those that `col lections.namedtuple` also generates—and those that are inherited from `tuple`. The only difference is the presence of the `__annotations__` class attribute—which Python completely ignores at runtime.

Given that the main feature of `typing.NamedTuple` are the type annotations, we'll take a brief look at them before resuming our exploration of data class builders.

Type Hints 101

Type hints—a.k.a. type annotations—are ways to declare the expected type of function arguments, return values, variables, and attributes.

The first thing you need to know about type hints is that they are not enforced at all by the Python bytecode compiler and interpreter.

 This is a very brief introduction to type hints, just enough to make sense of the syntax and meaning of the annotations used in `typ ing.NamedTuple` and `@dataclass` declarations. We will cover type hints for function signatures in Chapter 8 and more advanced annotations in Chapter 15. Here we'll mostly see hints with simple built-in types, such as `str`, `int`, and `float`, which are probably the most common types used to annotate fields of data classes.

No Runtime Effect

Think about Python type hints as "documentation that can be verified by IDEs and type checkers."

That's because type hints have no impact on the runtime behavior of Python programs. Check out Example 5-9.

Example 5-9. Python does not enforce type hints at runtime

```
>>> import typing
>>> class Coordinate(typing.NamedTuple):
...     lat: float
...     lon: float
...
>>> trash = Coordinate('Ni!', None)
>>> print(trash)
Coordinate(lat='Ni!', lon=None)     ❶
```

❶ I told you: no type checking at runtime!

If you type the code of Example 5-9 in a Python module, it will run and display a meaningless `Coordinate`, with no error or warning:

```
$ python3 nocheck_demo.py
Coordinate(lat='Ni!', lon=None)
```

The type hints are intended primarily to support third-party type checkers, like Mypy (*https://fpy.li/mypy*) or the PyCharm IDE (*https://fpy.li/5-5*) built-in type checker. These are static analysis tools: they check Python source code "at rest," not running code.

To see the effect of type hints, you must run one of those tools on your code—like a linter. For instance, here is what Mypy has to say about the previous example:

```
$ mypy nocheck_demo.py
nocheck_demo.py:8: error: Argument 1 to "Coordinate" has
incompatible type "str"; expected "float"
nocheck_demo.py:8: error: Argument 2 to "Coordinate" has
incompatible type "None"; expected "float"
```

As you can see, given the definition of `Coordinate`, Mypy knows that both arguments to create an instance must be of type `float`, but the assignment to `trash` uses a `str` and None.[5]

Now let's talk about the syntax and meaning of type hints.

Variable Annotation Syntax

Both `typing.NamedTuple` and `@dataclass` use the syntax of variable annotations defined in PEP 526 (*https://fpy.li/pep526*). This is a quick introduction to that syntax in the context defining attributes in `class` statements.

The basic syntax of variable annotation is:

```
var_name: some_type
```

The "Acceptable type hints" section in PEP 484 (*https://fpy.li/5-6*) explains what are acceptable types, but in the context of defining a data class, these types are more likely to be useful:

- A concrete class, for example, `str` or `FrenchDeck`
- A parameterized collection type, like `list[int]`, `tuple[str, float]`, etc.

---

5 In the context of type hints, None is not the `NoneType` singleton, but an alias for `NoneType` itself. This is strange when we stop to think about it, but appeals to our intuition and makes function return annotations easier to read in the common case of functions that return None.

- typing.Optional, for example, Optional[str]—to declare a field that can be a str or None

You can also initialize the variable with a value. In a typing.NamedTuple or @data class declaration, that value will become the default for that attribute if the corresponding argument is omitted in the constructor call:

```
var_name: some_type = a_value
```

The Meaning of Variable Annotations

We saw in "No Runtime Effect" on page 173 that type hints have no effect at runtime. But at import time—when a module is loaded—Python does read them to build the __annotations__ dictionary that typing.NamedTuple and @dataclass then use to enhance the class.

We'll start this exploration with a simple class in Example 5-10, so that we can later see what extra features are added by typing.NamedTuple and @dataclass.

Example 5-10. meaning/demo_plain.py: a plain class with type hints

```
class DemoPlainClass:
    a: int             ❶
    b: float = 1.1     ❷
    c = 'spam'         ❸
```

❶ a becomes an entry in __annotations__, but is otherwise discarded: no attribute named a is created in the class.

❷ b is saved as an annotation, and also becomes a class attribute with value 1.1.

❸ c is just a plain old class attribute, not an annotation.

We can verify that in the console, first reading the __annotations__ of the Demo PlainClass, then trying to get its attributes named a, b, and c:

```
>>> from demo_plain import DemoPlainClass
>>> DemoPlainClass.__annotations__
{'a': <class 'int'>, 'b': <class 'float'>}
>>> DemoPlainClass.a
Traceback (most recent call last):
  File "<stdin>", line 1, in <module>
AttributeError: type object 'DemoPlainClass' has no attribute 'a'
>>> DemoPlainClass.b
1.1
>>> DemoPlainClass.c
'spam'
```

Note that the `__annotations__` special attribute is created by the interpreter to record the type hints that appear in the source code—even in a plain class.

The a survives only as an annotation. It doesn't become a class attribute because no value is bound to it.[6] The b and c are stored as class attributes because they are bound to values.

None of those three attributes will be in a new instance of `DemoPlainClass`. If you create an object `o = DemoPlainClass()`, `o.a` will raise `AttributeError`, while `o.b` and `o.c` will retrieve the class attributes with values `1.1` and `'spam'`—that's just normal Python object behavior.

Inspecting a typing.NamedTuple

Now let's examine a class built with `typing.NamedTuple` (Example 5-11), using the same attributes and annotations as `DemoPlainClass` from Example 5-10.

Example 5-11. meaning/demo_nt.py: a class built with `typing.NamedTuple`

```python
import typing

class DemoNTClass(typing.NamedTuple):
    a: int              ❶
    b: float = 1.1      ❷
    c = 'spam'          ❸
```

❶ a becomes an annotation and also an instance attribute.

❷ b is another annotation, and also becomes an instance attribute with default value `1.1`.

❸ c is just a plain old class attribute; no annotation will refer to it.

Inspecting the `DemoNTClass`, we get:

```python
>>> from demo_nt import DemoNTClass
>>> DemoNTClass.__annotations__
{'a': <class 'int'>, 'b': <class 'float'>}
>>> DemoNTClass.a
<_collections._tuplegetter object at 0x101f0f940>
>>> DemoNTClass.b
<_collections._tuplegetter object at 0x101f0f8b0>
>>> DemoNTClass.c
'spam'
```

---

6 Python has no concept of *undefined*, one of the silliest mistakes in the design of JavaScript. Thank Guido!

Here we have the same annotations for a and b as we saw in Example 5-10. But typ
ing.NamedTuple creates a and b class attributes. The c attribute is just a plain class
attribute with the value 'spam'.

The a and b class attributes are *descriptors*—an advanced feature covered in Chapter 23. For now, think of them as similar to property getters: methods that don't
require the explicit call operator () to retrieve an instance attribute. In practice, this
means a and b will work as read-only instance attributes—which makes sense when
we recall that DemoNTClass instances are just fancy tuples, and tuples are immutable.

DemoNTClass also gets a custom docstring:

```
>>> DemoNTClass.__doc__
'DemoNTClass(a, b)'
```

Let's inspect an instance of DemoNTClass:

```
>>> nt = DemoNTClass(8)
>>> nt.a
8
>>> nt.b
1.1
>>> nt.c
'spam'
```

To construct nt, we need to give at least the a argument to DemoNTClass. The constructor also takes a b argument, but it has a default value of 1.1, so it's optional. The
nt object has the a and b attributes as expected; it doesn't have a c attribute, but
Python retrieves it from the class, as usual.

If you try to assign values to nt.a, nt.b, nt.c, or even nt.z, you'll get Attribute
Error exceptions with subtly different error messages. Try that and reflect on the
messages.

Inspecting a class decorated with dataclass

Now, we'll examine Example 5-12.

Example 5-12. meaning/demo_dc.py: a class decorated with @dataclass

```
from dataclasses import dataclass

@dataclass
class DemoDataClass:
    a: int           ❶
    b: float = 1.1   ❷
    c = 'spam'       ❸
```

❶ a becomes an annotation and also an instance attribute controlled by a descriptor.

❷ b is another annotation, and also becomes an instance attribute with a descriptor and a default value 1.1.

❸ c is just a plain old class attribute; no annotation will refer to it.

Now let's check out __annotations__, __doc__, and the a, b, c attributes on Demo DataClass:

```
>>> from demo_dc import DemoDataClass
>>> DemoDataClass.__annotations__
{'a': <class 'int'>, 'b': <class 'float'>}
>>> DemoDataClass.__doc__
'DemoDataClass(a: int, b: float = 1.1)'
>>> DemoDataClass.a
Traceback (most recent call last):
  File "<stdin>", line 1, in <module>
AttributeError: type object 'DemoDataClass' has no attribute 'a'
>>> DemoDataClass.b
1.1
>>> DemoDataClass.c
'spam'
```

The __annotations__ and __doc__ are not surprising. However, there is no attribute named a in DemoDataClass—in contrast with DemoNTClass from Example 5-11, which has a descriptor to get a from the instances as read-only attributes (that mysterious <_collections._tuplegetter>). That's because the a attribute will only exist in instances of DemoDataClass. It will be a public attribute that we can get and set, unless the class is frozen. But b and c exist as class attributes, with b holding the default value for the b instance attribute, while c is just a class attribute that will not be bound to the instances.

Now let's see how a DemoDataClass instance looks:

```
>>> dc = DemoDataClass(9)
>>> dc.a
9
>>> dc.b
1.1
>>> dc.c
'spam'
```

Again, a and b are instance attributes, and c is a class attribute we get via the instance.

As mentioned, DemoDataClass instances are mutable—and no type checking is done at runtime:

```
>>> dc.a = 10
>>> dc.b = 'oops'
```

We can do even sillier assignments:

```
>>> dc.c = 'whatever'
>>> dc.z = 'secret stash'
```

Now the dc instance has a c attribute—but that does not change the c class attribute. And we can add a new z attribute. This is normal Python behavior: regular instances can have their own attributes that don't appear in the class.[7]

More About @dataclass

We've only seen simple examples of @dataclass use so far. The decorator accepts several keyword arguments. This is its signature:

```
@dataclass(*, init=True, repr=True, eq=True, order=False,
           unsafe_hash=False, frozen=False)
```

The * in the first position means the remaining parameters are keyword-only. Table 5-2 describes them.

Table 5-2. Keyword parameters accepted by the @dataclass decorator

Option	Meaning	Default	Notes
init	Generate __init__	True	Ignored if __init__ is implemented by user.
repr	Generate __repr__	True	Ignored if __repr__ is implemented by user.
eq	Generate __eq__	True	Ignored if __eq__ is implemented by user.
order	Generate __lt__, __le__, __gt__, __ge__	False	If True, raises exceptions if eq=False, or if any of the comparison methods that would be generated are defined or inherited.
unsafe_hash	Generate __hash__	False	Complex semantics and several caveats—see: dataclass documentation (*https://fpy.li/5-7*).
frozen	Make instances "immutable"	False	Instances will be reasonably safe from accidental change, but not really immutable.[a]

[a] @dataclass emulates immutability by generating __setattr__ and __delattr__, which raise data class.FrozenInstanceError—a subclass of AttributeError—when the user attempts to set or delete a field.

---

7 Setting an attribute after __init__ defeats the __dict__ key-sharing memory optimization mentioned in "Practical Consequences of How dict Works" on page 102.

The defaults are really the most useful settings for common use cases. The options you are more likely to change from the defaults are:

`frozen=True`
> Protects against accidental changes to the class instances.

`order=True`
> Allows sorting of instances of the data class.

Given the dynamic nature of Python objects, it's not too hard for a nosy programmer to go around the protection afforded by `frozen=True`. But the necessary tricks should be easy to spot in a code review.

If the `eq` and `frozen` arguments are both `True`, `@dataclass` produces a suitable `__hash__` method, so the instances will be hashable. The generated `__hash__` will use data from all fields that are not individually excluded using a field option we'll see in "Field Options" on page 180. If `frozen=False` (the default), `@dataclass` will set `__hash__` to `None`, signalling that the instances are unhashable, therefore overriding `__hash__` from any superclass.

PEP 557—Data Classes (*https://fpy.li/pep557*) has this to say about `unsafe_hash`:

> Although not recommended, you can force Data Classes to create a `__hash__` method with `unsafe_hash=True`. This might be the case if your class is logically immutable but can nonetheless be mutated. This is a specialized use case and should be considered carefully.

I will leave `unsafe_hash` at that. If you feel you must use that option, check the `data classes.dataclass` documentation (*https://fpy.li/5-7*).

Further customization of the generated data class can be done at a field level.

Field Options

We've already seen the most basic field option: providing (or not) a default value with the type hint. The instance fields you declare will become parameters in the generated `__init__`. Python does not allow parameters without defaults after parameters with defaults, therefore after you declare a field with a default value, all remaining fields must also have default values.

Mutable default values are a common source of bugs for beginning Python developers. In function definitions, a mutable default value is easily corrupted when one invocation of the function mutates the default, changing the behavior of further invocations—an issue we'll explore in "Mutable Types as Parameter Defaults: Bad Idea" on page 214 (Chapter 6). Class attributes are often used as default attribute values for instances, including in data classes. And `@dataclass` uses the default values in the

type hints to generate parameters with defaults for __init__. To prevent bugs, @data
class rejects the class definition in Example 5-13.

Example 5-13. dataclass/club_wrong.py: this class raises ValueError

```
@dataclass
class ClubMember:
    name: str
    guests: list = []
```

If you load the module with that ClubMember class, this is what you get:

```
$ python3 club_wrong.py
Traceback (most recent call last):
  File "club_wrong.py", line 4, in <module>
    class ClubMember:
  ...several lines omitted...
ValueError: mutable default <class 'list'> for field guests is not allowed:
use default_factory
```

The ValueError message explains the problem and suggests a solution: use
default_factory. Example 5-14 shows how to correct ClubMember.

Example 5-14. dataclass/club.py: this ClubMember definition works

```
from dataclasses import dataclass, field

@dataclass
class ClubMember:
    name: str
    guests: list = field(default_factory=list)
```

In the guests field of Example 5-14, instead of a literal list, the default value is set by
calling the dataclasses.field function with default_factory=list.

The default_factory parameter lets you provide a function, class, or any other callable, which will be invoked with zero arguments to build a default value each time an
instance of the data class is created. This way, each instance of ClubMember will have
its own list—instead of all instances sharing the same list from the class, which is
rarely what we want and is often a bug.

 It's good that @dataclass rejects class definitions with a list
default value in a field. However, be aware that it is a partial solution that only applies to list, dict, and set. Other mutable values
used as defaults will not be flagged by @dataclass. It's up to you to
understand the problem and remember to use a default factory to
set mutable default values.

If you browse the dataclasses (*https://fpy.li/5-9*) module documentation, you'll see a list field defined with a novel syntax, as in Example 5-15.

Example 5-15. dataclass/club_generic.py: this ClubMember definition is more precise

```
from dataclasses import dataclass, field

@dataclass
class ClubMember:
    name: str
    guests: list[str] = field(default_factory=list)  ❶
```

❶ list[str] means "a list of str."

The new syntax list[str] is a parameterized generic type: since Python 3.9, the list built-in accepts that bracket notation to specify the type of the list items.

 Prior to Python 3.9, the built-in collections did not support generic type notation. As a temporary workaround, there are corresponding collection types in the typing module. If you need a parameterized list type hint in Python 3.8 or earlier, you must import the List type from typing and use it: List[str]. For more about this issue, see "Legacy Support and Deprecated Collection Types" on page 272.

We'll cover generics in Chapter 8. For now, note that Examples 5-14 and 5-15 are both correct, and the Mypy type checker does not complain about either of those class definitions.

The difference is that guests: list means that guests can be a list of objects of any kind, while guests: list[str] says that guests must be a list in which every item is a str. This will allow the type checker to find (some) bugs in code that puts invalid items in the list, or that read items from it.

The default_factory is likely to be the most common option of the field function, but there are several others, listed in Table 5-3.

Table 5-3. Keyword arguments accepted by the field function

Option	Meaning	Default
default	Default value for field	_MISSING_TYPE[a]
default_factory	0-parameter function used to produce a default	_MISSING_TYPE
init	Include field in parameters to __init__	True
repr	Include field in __repr__	True

Option	Meaning	Default
compare	Use field in comparison methods __eq__, __lt__, etc.	True
hash	Include field in __hash__ calculation	None[b]
metadata	Mapping with user-defined data; ignored by the @dataclass	None

[a] dataclass._MISSING_TYPE is a sentinel value indicating the option was not provided. It exists so we can set None as an actual default value, a common use case.

[b] The option hash=None means the field will be used in __hash__ only if compare=True.

The default option exists because the field call takes the place of the default value in the field annotation. If you want to create an athlete field with a default value of False, and also omit that field from the __repr__ method, you'd write this:

```
@dataclass
class ClubMember:
    name: str
    guests: list = field(default_factory=list)
    athlete: bool = field(default=False, repr=False)
```

Post-init Processing

The __init__ method generated by @dataclass only takes the arguments passed and assigns them—or their default values, if missing—to the instance attributes that are instance fields. But you may need to do more than that to initialize the instance. If that's the case, you can provide a __post_init__ method. When that method exists, @dataclass will add code to the generated __init__ to call __post_init__ as the last step.

Common use cases for __post_init__ are validation and computing field values based on other fields. We'll study a simple example that uses __post_init__ for both of these reasons.

First, let's look at the expected behavior of a ClubMember subclass named HackerClub Member, as described by doctests in Example 5-16.

Example 5-16. dataclass/hackerclub.py: doctests for HackerClubMember

```
"""
``Hacker ClubMember`` objects accept an optional ``handle`` argument::

    >>> anna = HackerClubMember('Anna Ravenscroft', handle='AnnaRaven')
    >>> anna
    HackerClubMember(name='Anna Ravenscroft', guests=[], handle='AnnaRaven')

If ``handle`` is omitted, it's set to the first part of the member's name::
```

```
>>> leo = HackerClubMember('Leo Rochael')
>>> leo
HackerClubMember(name='Leo Rochael', guests=[], handle='Leo')

Members must have a unique handle. The following ``leo2`` will not be created,
because its ``handle`` would be 'Leo', which was taken by ``leo``::

    >>> leo2 = HackerClubMember('Leo DaVinci')
    Traceback (most recent call last):
      ...
    ValueError: handle 'Leo' already exists.

To fix, ``leo2`` must be created with an explicit ``handle``::

    >>> leo2 = HackerClubMember('Leo DaVinci', handle='Neo')
    >>> leo2
    HackerClubMember(name='Leo DaVinci', guests=[], handle='Neo')
"""
```

Note that we must provide `handle` as a keyword argument, because `HackerClubMem`ber inherits `name` and `guests` from `ClubMember`, and adds the `handle` field. The generated docstring for `HackerClubMember` shows the order of the fields in the constructor call:

```
>>> HackerClubMember.__doc__
"HackerClubMember(name: str, guests: list = <factory>, handle: str = '')"
```

Here, `<factory>` is a short way of saying that some callable will produce the default value for `guests` (in our case, the factory is the `list` class). The point is: to provide a `handle` but no `guests`, we must pass `handle` as a keyword argument.

The "Inheritance" section of the `dataclasses` module documentation (*https://fpy.li/ 5-10*) explains how the order of the fields is computed when there are several levels of inheritance.

 In Chapter 14 we'll talk about misusing inheritance, particularly when the superclasses are not abstract. Creating a hierarchy of data classes is usually a bad idea, but it served us well here to make Example 5-17 shorter, focusing on the `handle` field declaration and `__post_init__` validation.

Example 5-17 shows the implementation.

Example 5-17. dataclass/hackerclub.py: code for `HackerClubMember`

```
from dataclasses import dataclass
from club import ClubMember
```

```
@dataclass
class HackerClubMember(ClubMember):                          ❶
    all_handles = set()                                      ❷
    handle: str = ''                                         ❸

    def __post_init__(self):
        cls = self.__class__                                 ❹
        if self.handle == '':                                ❺
            self.handle = self.name.split()[0]
        if self.handle in cls.all_handles:                   ❻
            msg = f'handle {self.handle!r} already exists.'
            raise ValueError(msg)
        cls.all_handles.add(self.handle)                     ❼
```

❶ HackerClubMember extends ClubMember.

❷ all_handles is a class attribute.

❸ handle is an instance field of type str with an empty string as its default value;
    this makes it optional.

❹ Get the class of the instance.

❺ If self.handle is the empty string, set it to the first part of name.

❻ If self.handle is in cls.all_handles, raise ValueError.

❼ Add the new handle to cls.all_handles.

Example 5-17 works as intended, but is not satisfactory to a static type checker. Next,
we'll see why, and how to fix it.

Typed Class Attributes

If we type check Example 5-17 with Mypy, we are reprimanded:

```
$ mypy hackerclub.py
hackerclub.py:37: error: Need type annotation for "all_handles"
(hint: "all_handles: Set[<type>] = ...")
Found 1 error in 1 file (checked 1 source file)
```

Unfortunately, the hint provided by Mypy (version 0.910 as I review this) is not helpful in the context of @dataclass usage. First, it suggests using Set, but I am using
Python 3.9 so I can use set—and avoid importing Set from typing. More importantly, if we add a type hint like set[…] to all_handles, @dataclass will find that
annotation and make all_handles an instance field. We saw this happening in
"Inspecting a class decorated with dataclass" on page 177.

The workaround defined in PEP 526—Syntax for Variable Annotations (*https://fpy.li/ 5-11*) is ugly. To code a class variable with a type hint, we need to use a pseudotype named `typing.ClassVar`, which leverages the generics [ ] notation to set the type of the variable and also declare it a class attribute.

To make the type checker and `@dataclass` happy, this is how we are supposed to declare `all_handles` in Example 5-17:

```
all_handles: ClassVar[set[str]] = set()
```

That type hint is saying:

> `all_handles` is a class attribute of type `set-of-str`, with an empty `set` as its default value.

To code that annotation, we must import `ClassVar` from the `typing` module.

The `@dataclass` decorator doesn't care about the types in the annotations, except in two cases, and this is one of them: if the type is `ClassVar`, an instance field will not be generated for that attribute.

The other case where the type of the field is relevant to `@dataclass` is when declaring *init-only variables*, our next topic.

Initialization Variables That Are Not Fields

Sometimes you may need to pass arguments to `__init__` that are not instance fields. Such arguments are called *init-only variables* by the `dataclasses` documentation (*https://fpy.li/initvar*). To declare an argument like that, the `dataclasses` module provides the pseudotype `InitVar`, which uses the same syntax of `typing.ClassVar`. The example given in the documentation is a data class that has a field initialized from a database, and the database object must be passed to the constructor.

Example 5-18 shows the code that illustrates the "Init-only variables" section (*https:// fpy.li/initvar*).

Example 5-18. Example from the `dataclasses` (https://fpy.li/initvar) module documentation

```
@dataclass
class C:
    i: int
    j: int = None
    database: InitVar[DatabaseType] = None

    def __post_init__(self, database):
        if self.j is None and database is not None:
            self.j = database.lookup('j')
```

```
c = C(10, database=my_database)
```

Note how the database attribute is declared. InitVar will prevent @dataclass from treating database as a regular field. It will not be set as an instance attribute, and the dataclasses.fields function will not list it. However, database will be one of the arguments that the generated __init__ will accept, and it will be also passed to __post_init__. If you write that method, you must add a corresponding argument to the method signature, as shown in Example 5-18.

This rather long overview of @dataclass covered the most useful features—some of them appeared in previous sections, like "Main Features" on page 167 where we covered all three data class builders in parallel. The dataclasses documentation (*https:// fpy.li/initvar*) and PEP 526—Syntax for Variable Annotations (*https://fpy.li/pep526*) have all the details.

In the next section, I present a longer example with @dataclass.

@dataclass Example: Dublin Core Resource Record

Often, classes built with @dataclass will have more fields than the very short examples presented so far. Dublin Core (*https://fpy.li/5-12*) provides the foundation for a more typical @dataclass example.

> The Dublin Core Schema is a small set of vocabulary terms that can be used to describe digital resources (video, images, web pages, etc.), as well as physical resources such as books or CDs, and objects like artworks.[8]
>
> —Dublin Core on Wikipedia

The standard defines 15 optional fields; the Resource class in Example 5-19 uses 8 of them.

Example 5-19. dataclass/resource.py: code for Resource, a class based on Dublin Core terms

```
from dataclasses import dataclass, field
from typing import Optional
from enum import Enum, auto
from datetime import date


class ResourceType(Enum):    ❶
    BOOK = auto()
```

---

8 Source: Dublin Core (*https://fpy.li/5-13*) article in the English Wikipedia.

```
    EBOOK = auto()
    VIDEO = auto()


@dataclass
class Resource:
    """Media resource description."""
    identifier: str                                        ❷
    title: str = '<untitled>'                              ❸
    creators: list[str] = field(default_factory=list)
    date: Optional[date] = None                            ❹
    type: ResourceType = ResourceType.BOOK                 ❺
    description: str = ''
    language: str = ''
    subjects: list[str] = field(default_factory=list)
```

❶ This Enum will provide type-safe values for the `Resource.type` field.

❷ `identifier` is the only required field.

❸ `title` is the first field with a default. This forces all fields below to provide defaults.

❹ The value of `date` can be a `datetime.date` instance, or `None`.

❺ The `type` field default is `ResourceType.BOOK`.

Example 5-20 shows a doctest to demonstrate how a `Resource` record appears in code.

Example 5-20. dataclass/resource.py: code for Resource, a class based on Dublin Core terms

```
>>> description = 'Improving the design of existing code'
>>> book = Resource('978-0-13-475759-9', 'Refactoring, 2nd Edition',
...     ['Martin Fowler', 'Kent Beck'], date(2018, 11, 19),
...     ResourceType.BOOK, description, 'EN',
...     ['computer programming', 'OOP'])
>>> book  # doctest: +NORMALIZE_WHITESPACE
Resource(identifier='978-0-13-475759-9', title='Refactoring, 2nd Edition',
creators=['Martin Fowler', 'Kent Beck'], date=datetime.date(2018, 11, 19),
type=<ResourceType.BOOK: 1>, description='Improving the design of existing code',
language='EN', subjects=['computer programming', 'OOP'])
```

The `__repr__` generated by `@dataclass` is OK, but we can make it more readable. This is the format we want from `repr(book)`:

```
>>> book  # doctest: +NORMALIZE_WHITESPACE
Resource(
```

```
        identifier = '978-0-13-475759-9',
        title = 'Refactoring, 2nd Edition',
        creators = ['Martin Fowler', 'Kent Beck'],
        date = datetime.date(2018, 11, 19),
        type = <ResourceType.BOOK: 1>,
        description = 'Improving the design of existing code',
        language = 'EN',
        subjects = ['computer programming', 'OOP'],
    )
```

Example 5-21 is the code of __repr__ to produce the format shown in the last snippet. This example uses dataclass.fields to get the names of the data class fields.

Example 5-21. dataclass/resource_repr.py: code for __repr__ method implemented in the Resource class from Example 5-19

```
def __repr__(self):
    cls = self.__class__
    cls_name = cls.__name__
    indent = ' ' * 4
    res = [f'{cls_name}(']                              ❶
    for f in fields(cls):                               ❷
        value = getattr(self, f.name)                   ❸
        res.append(f'{indent}{f.name} = {value!r},')    ❹

    res.append(')')                                     ❺
    return '\n'.join(res)                               ❻
```

❶ Start the res list to build the output string with the class name and open parenthesis.

❷ For each field f in the class…

❸ …get the named attribute from the instance.

❹ Append an indented line with the name of the field and repr(value)—that's what the !r does.

❺ Append closing parenthesis.

❻ Build a multiline string from res and return it.

With this example inspired by the soul of Dublin, Ohio, we conclude our tour of Python's data class builders.

Data classes are handy, but your project may suffer if you overuse them. The next section explains.

Data Class as a Code Smell

Whether you implement a data class by writing all the code yourself or leveraging one of the class builders described in this chapter, be aware that it may signal a problem in your design.

In *Refactoring: Improving the Design of Existing Code*, 2nd ed. (Addison-Wesley), Martin Fowler and Kent Beck present a catalog of "code smells"—patterns in code that may indicate the need for refactoring. The entry titled "Data Class" starts like this:

> These are classes that have fields, getting and setting methods for fields, and nothing else. Such classes are dumb data holders and are often being manipulated in far too much detail by other classes.

In Fowler's personal website, there's an illuminating post titled "Code Smell" (*https://fpy.li/5-14*). The post is very relevant to our discussion because he uses *data class* as one example of a code smell and suggests how to deal with it. Here is the post, reproduced in full.[9]

Code Smell

By Martin Fowler

A code smell is a surface indication that usually corresponds to a deeper problem in the system. The term was first coined by Kent Beck while helping me with my *Refactoring* book (*https://fpy.li/5-15*).

The quick definition above contains a couple of subtle points. Firstly, a smell is by definition something that's quick to spot—or sniffable as I've recently put it. A long method is a good example of this—just looking at the code and my nose twitches if I see more than a dozen lines of Java.

The second is that smells don't always indicate a problem. Some long methods are just fine. You have to look deeper to see if there is an underlying problem there—smells aren't inherently bad on their own—they are often an indicator of a problem rather than the problem themselves.

The best smells are something that's easy to spot and most of the time lead you to really interesting problems. Data classes (classes with all data and no behavior) are good examples of this. You look at them and ask yourself what behavior should be in this class. Then you start refactoring to move that behavior in there. Often simple

---

9 I am fortunate to have Martin Fowler as a colleague at Thoughtworks, so it took just 20 minutes to get his permission.

questions and initial refactorings can be the vital step in turning anemic objects into something that really has class.

One of the nice things about smells is that it's easy for inexperienced people to spot them, even if they don't know enough to evaluate if there's a real problem or to correct them. I've heard of lead developers who will pick a "smell of the week" and ask people to look for the smell and bring it up with the senior members of the team. Doing it one smell at a time is a good way of gradually teaching people on the team to be better programmers.

The main idea of object-oriented programming is to place behavior and data together in the same code unit: a class. If a class is widely used but has no significant behavior of its own, it's possible that code dealing with its instances is scattered (and even duplicated) in methods and functions throughout the system—a recipe for maintenance headaches. That's why Fowler's refactorings to deal with a data class involve bringing responsibilities back into it.

Taking that into account, there are a couple of common scenarios where it makes sense to have a data class with little or no behavior.

Data Class as Scaffolding

In this scenario, the data class is an initial, simplistic implementation of a class to jump-start a new project or module. With time, the class should get its own methods, instead of relying on methods of other classes to operate on its instances. Scaffolding is temporary; eventually your custom class may become fully independent from the builder you used to start it.

Python is also used for quick problem solving and experimentation, and then it's OK to leave the scaffolding in place.

Data Class as Intermediate Representation

A data class can be useful to build records about to be exported to JSON or some other interchange format, or to hold data that was just imported, crossing some system boundary. Python's data class builders all provide a method or function to convert an instance to a plain dict, and you can always invoke the constructor with a dict used as keyword arguments expanded with **. Such a dict is very close to a JSON record.

In this scenario, the data class instances should be handled as immutable objects—even if the fields are mutable, you should not change them while they are in this intermediate form. If you do, you're losing the key benefit of having data and behavior close together. When importing/exporting requires changing values, you should implement your own builder methods instead of using the given "as dict" methods or standard constructors.

Now we change the subject to see how to write patterns that match instances of arbitrary classes, and not just the sequences and mappings we've seen in "Pattern Matching with Sequences" on page 39 and "Pattern Matching with Mappings" on page 81.

Pattern Matching Class Instances

Class patterns are designed to match class instances by type and—optionally—by attributes. The subject of a class pattern can be any class instance, not only instances of data classes.[10]

There are three variations of class patterns: simple, keyword, and positional. We'll study them in that order.

Simple Class Patterns

We've already seen an example with simple class patterns used as subpatterns in "Pattern Matching with Sequences" on page 39:

```
case [str(name), _, _, (float(lat), float(lon))]:
```

That pattern matches a four-item sequence where the first item must be an instance of str, and the last item must be a 2-tuple with two instances of float.

The syntax for class patterns looks like a constructor invocation. The following is a class pattern that matches float values without binding a variable (the case body can refer to x directly if needed):

```
match x:
    case float():
        do_something_with(x)
```

But this is likely to be a bug in your code:

```
match x:
    case float:  # DANGER!!!
        do_something_with(x)
```

In the preceding example, case float: matches any subject, because Python sees float as a variable, which is then bound to the subject.

---

10 I put this content here because it is the earliest chapter focusing on user-defined classes, and I thought pattern matching with classes was too important to wait until Part II of the book. My philosophy: it's more important to know how to use classes than to define classes.

The simple pattern syntax of `float(x)` is a special case that applies only to nine blessed built-in types, listed at the end of the "Class Patterns" (*https://fpy.li/5-16*) section of PEP 634—Structural Pattern Matching: Specification:

```
bytes   dict   float   frozenset   int   list   set   str   tuple
```

In those classes, the variable that looks like a constructor argument—e.g., the `x` in `float(x)`—is bound to the whole subject instance or the part of the subject that matches a subpattern, as exemplified by `str(name)` in the sequence pattern we saw earlier:

```
case [str(name), _, _, (float(lat), float(lon))]:
```

If the class is not one of those nine blessed built-ins, then the argument-like variables represent patterns to be matched against attributes of an instance of that class.

Keyword Class Patterns

To understand how to use keyword class patterns, consider the following `City` class and five instances in Example 5-22.

Example 5-22. City class and a few instances

```python
import typing

class City(typing.NamedTuple):
    continent: str
    name: str
    country: str


cities = [
    City('Asia', 'Tokyo', 'JP'),
    City('Asia', 'Delhi', 'IN'),
    City('North America', 'Mexico City', 'MX'),
    City('North America', 'New York', 'US'),
    City('South America', 'São Paulo', 'BR'),
]
```

Given those definitions, the following function would return a list of Asian cities:

```python
def match_asian_cities():
    results = []
    for city in cities:
        match city:
            case City(continent='Asia'):
                results.append(city)
    return results
```

The pattern `City(continent='Asia')` matches any `City` instance where the continent attribute value is equal to `'Asia'`, regardless of the values of the other attributes.

If you want to collect the value of the `country` attribute, you could write:

```
def match_asian_countries():
    results = []
    for city in cities:
        match city:
            case City(continent='Asia', country=cc):
                results.append(cc)
    return results
```

The pattern `City(continent='Asia', country=cc)` matches the same Asian cities as before, but now the `cc` variable is bound to the `country` attribute of the instance. This also works if the pattern variable is called `country` as well:

```
    match city:
        case City(continent='Asia', country=country):
            results.append(country)
```

Keyword class patterns are very readable, and work with any class that has public instance attributes, but they are somewhat verbose.

Positional class patterns are more convenient in some cases, but they require explicit support by the class of the subject, as we'll see next.

Positional Class Patterns

Given the definitions from Example 5-22, the following function would return a list of Asian cities, using a positional class pattern:

```
def match_asian_cities_pos():
    results = []
    for city in cities:
        match city:
            case City('Asia'):
                results.append(city)
    return results
```

The pattern `City('Asia')` matches any `City` instance where the first attribute value is `'Asia'`, regardless of the values of the other attributes.

If you want to collect the value of the `country` attribute, you could write:

```
def match_asian_countries_pos():
    results = []
    for city in cities:
        match city:
            case City('Asia', _, country):
                results.append(country)
    return results
```

The pattern City('Asia', _, country) matches the same cities as before, but now the country variable is bound to the third attribute of the instance.

I've mentioned "first" or "third" attribute, but what does that really mean?

What makes City or any class work with positional patterns is the presence of a special class attribute named __match_args__, which the class builders in this chapter automatically create. This is the value of __match_args__ in the City class:

```
>>> City.__match_args__
('continent', 'name', 'country')
```

As you can see, __match_args__ declares the names of the attributes in the order they will be used in positional patterns.

In "Supporting Positional Pattern Matching" on page 379 we'll write code to define __match_args__ for a class we'll create without the help of a class builder.

 You can combine keyword and positional arguments in a pattern. Some, but not all, of the instance attributes available for matching may be listed in __match_args__. Therefore, sometimes you may need to use keyword arguments in addition to positional arguments in a pattern.

Time for a chapter summary.

Chapter Summary

The main topic of this chapter was the data class builders collections.namedtuple, typing.NamedTuple, and dataclasses.dataclass. We saw that each generates data classes from descriptions provided as arguments to a factory function, or from class statements with type hints in the case of the latter two. In particular, both named tuple variants produce tuple subclasses, adding only the ability to access fields by name, and providing a _fields class attribute listing the field names as a tuple of strings.

Next we studied the main features of the three class builders side by side, including how to extract instance data as a dict, how to get the names and default values of fields, and how to make a new instance from an existing one.

This prompted our first look into type hints, particularly those used to annotate attributes in a class statement, using the notation introduced in Python 3.6 with PEP 526—Syntax for Variable Annotations (*https://fpy.li/pep526*). Probably the most surprising aspect of type hints in general is the fact that they have no effect at all at runtime. Python remains a dynamic language. External tools, like Mypy, are needed to take advantage of typing information to detect errors via static analysis of the source code. After a basic overview of the syntax from PEP 526, we studied the effect of annotations in a plain class and in classes built by `typing.NamedTuple` and `@dataclass`.

Next, we covered the most commonly used features provided by `@dataclass` and the `default_factory` option of the `dataclasses.field` function. We also looked into the special pseudotype hints `typing.ClassVar` and `dataclasses.InitVar` that are important in the context of data classes. This main topic concluded with an example based on the Dublin Core Schema, which illustrated how to use `dataclasses.fields` to iterate over the attributes of a `Resource` instance in a custom `__repr__`.

Then, we warned against possible abuse of data classes defeating a basic principle of object-oriented programming: data and the functions that touch it should be together in the same class. Classes with no logic may be a sign of misplaced logic.

In the last section, we saw how pattern matching works with subjects that are instances of any class—not just classes built with the class builders presented in this chapter.

Further Reading

Python's standard documentation for the data class builders we covered is very good, and has quite a few small examples.

For `@dataclass` in particular, most of PEP 557—Data Classes (*https://fpy.li/pep557*) was copied into the `dataclasses` (*https://fpy.li/5-9*) module documentation. But PEP 557 (*https://fpy.li/pep557*) has a few very informative sections that were not copied, including "Why not just use namedtuple?" (*https://fpy.li/5-18*), "Why not just use typing.NamedTuple?" (*https://fpy.li/5-19*), and the "Rationale" section (*https://fpy.li/5-20*), which concludes with this Q&A:

> Where is it not appropriate to use Data Classes?
>
> API compatibility with tuples or dicts is required. Type validation beyond that provided by PEPs 484 and 526 is required, or value validation or conversion is required.
>
> —Eric V. Smith, PEP 557 "Rationale"

Over at *RealPython.com*, Geir Arne Hjelle wrote a very complete "Ultimate guide to data classes in Python 3.7" (*https://fpy.li/5-22*).

At PyCon US 2018, Raymond Hettinger presented "Dataclasses: The code generator to end all code generators" (video) (*https://fpy.li/5-23*).

For more features and advanced functionality, including validation, the *attrs* project (*https://fpy.li/5-24*) led by Hynek Schlawack appeared years before `dataclasses`, and offers more features, promising to "bring back the joy of writing classes by relieving you from the drudgery of implementing object protocols (aka dunder methods)."

The influence of *attrs* on @dataclass is acknowledged by Eric V. Smith in PEP 557. This probably includes Smith's most important API decision: the use of a class decorator instead of a base class and/or a metaclass to do the job.

Glyph—founder of the Twisted project—wrote an excellent introduction to *attrs* in "The One Python Library Everyone Needs" (*https://fpy.li/5-25*). The *attrs* documentation includes a discussion of alternatives (*https://fpy.li/5-26*).

Book author, instructor, and mad computer scientist Dave Beazley wrote *cluegen* (*https://fpy.li/5-27*), yet another data class generator. If you've seen any of Dave's talks, you know he is a master of metaprogramming Python from first principles. So I found it inspiring to learn from the *cluegen README.md* file the concrete use case that motivated him to write an alternative to Python's @dataclass, and his philosophy of presenting an approach to solve the problem, in contrast to providing a tool: the tool may be quicker to use at first, but the approach is more flexible and can take you as far as you want to go.

Regarding *data class* as a code smell, the best source I found was Martin Fowler's book *Refactoring*, 2nd ed. This newest version is missing the quote from the epigraph of this chapter, "Data classes are like children...," but otherwise it's the best edition of Fowler's most famous book, particularly for Pythonistas because the examples are in modern JavaScript, which is closer to Python than Java—the language of the first edition.

The website *Refactoring Guru* (*https://fpy.li/5-28*) also has a description of the data class code smell (*https://fpy.li/5-29*).

Soapbox

The entry for "Guido" (*https://fpy.li/5-30*) in "The Jargon File" is about Guido van Rossum. It says, among other things:

> Mythically, Guido's most important attribute besides Python itself is Guido's time machine, a device he is reputed to possess because of the unnerving frequency with which user requests for new features have been met with the response "I just implemented that last night..."

For the longest time, one of the missing pieces in Python's syntax has been a quick, standard way to declare instance attributes in a class. Many object-oriented languages have that. Here is part of a Point class definition in Smalltalk:

```
Object subclass: #Point
    instanceVariableNames: 'x y'
    classVariableNames: ''
    package: 'Kernel-BasicObjects'
```

The second line lists the names of the instance attributes x and y. If there were class attributes, they would be in the third line.

Python has always offered an easy way to declare class attributes, if they have an initial value. But instance attributes are much more common, and Python coders have been forced to look into the __init__ method to find them, always afraid that there may be instance attributes created elsewhere in the class—or even created by external functions or methods of other classes.

Now we have @dataclass, yay!

But they bring their own problems.

First, when you use @dataclass, type hints are not optional. We've been promised for the last seven years, since PEP 484—Type Hints (*https://fpy.li/pep484*) that they would always be optional. Now we have a major new language feature that requires them. If you don't like the whole static typing trend, you may want to use attrs (*https://fpy.li/5-24*) instead.

Second, the PEP 526 (*https://fpy.li/pep526*) syntax for annotating instance and class attributes reverses the established convention of class statements: everything declared at the top-level of a class block was a class attribute (methods are class attributes, too). With PEP 526 and @dataclass, any attribute declared at the top level with a type hint becomes an instance attribute:

```
@dataclass
class Spam:
    repeat: int  # instance attribute
```

Here, repeat is also an instance attribute:

```
@dataclass
class Spam:
    repeat: int = 99  # instance attribute
```

But if there are no type hints, suddenly you are back in the good old times when declarations at the top level of the class belong to the class only:

```
@dataclass
class Spam:
    repeat = 99  # class attribute!
```

Finally, if you want to annotate that class attribute with a type, you can't use regular types because then it will become an instance attribute. You must resort to that pseudotype ClassVar annotation:

```
@dataclass
class Spam:
    repeat: ClassVar[int] = 99  # aargh!
```

Here we are talking about the exception to the exception to the rule. This seems rather unPythonic to me.

I did not take part in the discussions leading to PEP 526 or PEP 557—Data Classes (*https://fpy.li/pep557*), but here is an alternative syntax that I'd like to see:

```
@dataclass
class HackerClubMember:
    .name: str                                     ❶
    .guests: list = field(default_factory=list)
    .handle: str = ''

    all_handles = set()                            ❷
```

❶ Instance attributes must be declared with a . prefix.

❷ Any attribute name that doesn't have a . prefix is a class attribute (as they always have been).

The language grammar would have to change to accept that. I find this quite readable, and it avoids the exception-to-the-exception issue.

I wish I could borrow Guido's time machine to go back to 2017 and sell this idea to the core team.

## CHAPTER 6

Object References, Mutability, and Recycling

"You are sad," the Knight said in an anxious tone: "let me sing you a song to comfort you. [...] The name of the song is called 'HADDOCKS' EYES'."

"Oh, that's the name of the song, is it?" Alice said, trying to feel interested.

"No, you don't understand," the Knight said, looking a little vexed. "That's what the name is CALLED. The name really IS 'THE AGED AGED MAN.'"

> —Adapted from Lewis Carroll, *Through the Looking-Glass, and What Alice Found There*

Alice and the Knight set the tone of what we will see in this chapter. The theme is the distinction between objects and their names. A name is not the object; a name is a separate thing.

We start the chapter by presenting a metaphor for variables in Python: variables are labels, not boxes. If reference variables are old news to you, the analogy may still be handy if you need to explain aliasing issues to others.

We then discuss the concepts of object identity, value, and aliasing. A surprising trait of tuples is revealed: they are immutable but their values may change. This leads to a discussion of shallow and deep copies. References and function parameters are our next theme: the problem with mutable parameter defaults and the safe handling of mutable arguments passed by clients of our functions.

The last sections of the chapter cover garbage collection, the del command, and a selection of tricks that Python plays with immutable objects.

This is a rather dry chapter, but its topics lie at the heart of many subtle bugs in real Python programs.

What's New in This Chapter

The topics covered here are very fundamental and stable. There were no changes worth mentioning in this second edition.

I added an example of using `is` to test for a sentinel object, and a warning about misuses of the `is` operator at the end of "Choosing Between == and is" on page 206.

This chapter used to be in Part IV, but I decided to bring it up earlier because it works better as an ending to Part II, "Data Structures," than an opening to "Object-Oriented Idioms."

 The section on "Weak References" from the first edition of this book is now a post at *fluentpython.com* (*https://fpy.li/weakref*).

Let's start by unlearning that a variable is like a box where you store data.

Variables Are Not Boxes

In 1997, I took a summer course on Java at MIT. The professor, Lynn Stein,[1] made the point that the usual "variables as boxes" metaphor actually hinders the understanding of reference variables in object-oriented languages. Python variables are like reference variables in Java; a better metaphor is to think of variables as labels with names attached to objects. The next example and figure will help you understand why.

Example 6-1 is a simple interaction that the "variables as boxes" idea cannot explain. Figure 6-1 illustrates why the box metaphor is wrong for Python, while sticky notes provide a helpful picture of how variables actually work.

Example 6-1. Variables a and b hold references to the same list, not copies of the list

```
>>> a = [1, 2, 3]     ❶
>>> b = a             ❷
>>> a.append(4)       ❸
>>> b                 ❹
[1, 2, 3, 4]
```

---

1 Lynn Andrea Stein is an award-winning computer science educator who currently teaches at Olin College of Engineering (*https://fpy.li/6-1*).

❶ Create a list [1, 2, 3] and bind the variable a to it.

❷ Bind the variable b to the same value that a is referencing.

❸ Modify the list referenced by a, by appending another item.

❹ You can see the effect via the b variable. If we think of b as a box that stored a copy of the [1, 2, 3] from the a box, this behavior makes no sense.

Figure 6-1. If you imagine variables are like boxes, you can't make sense of assignment in Python; instead, think of variables as sticky notes, and Example 6-1 becomes easy to explain.

Therefore, the b = a statement does not copy the contents of box a into box b. It attaches the label b to the object that already has the label a.

Prof. Stein also spoke about assignment in a very deliberate way. For example, when talking about a seesaw object in a simulation, she would say: "Variable s is assigned to the seesaw," but never "The seesaw is assigned to variable s." With reference variables, it makes much more sense to say that the variable is assigned to an object, and not the other way around. After all, the object is created before the assignment. Example 6-2 proves that the righthand side of an assignment happens first.

Since the verb "to assign" is used in contradictory ways, a useful alternative is "to bind": Python's assignment statement x = … binds the x name to the object created or referenced on the righthand side. And the object must exist before a name can be bound to it, as Example 6-2 proves.

Example 6-2. Variables are bound to objects only after the objects are created

```
>>> class Gizmo:
...     def __init__(self):
...         print(f'Gizmo id: {id(self)}')
...
>>> x = Gizmo()
```

```
Gizmo id: 4301489152  ❶
>>> y = Gizmo() * 10  ❷
Gizmo id: 4301489432  ❸
Traceback (most recent call last):
  File "<stdin>", line 1, in <module>
TypeError: unsupported operand type(s) for *: 'Gizmo' and 'int'
>>>
>>> dir()  ❹
['Gizmo', '__builtins__', '__doc__', '__loader__', '__name__',
'__package__', '__spec__', 'x']
```

❶ The output `Gizmo id: …` is a side effect of creating a `Gizmo` instance.

❷ Multiplying a `Gizmo` instance will raise an exception.

❸ Here is proof that a second `Gizmo` was actually instantiated before the multiplication was attempted.

❹ But variable y was never created, because the exception happened while the righthand side of the assignment was being evaluated.

> To understand an assignment in Python, read the righthand side first: that's where the object is created or retrieved. After that, the variable on the left is bound to the object, like a label stuck to it. Just forget about the boxes.

Because variables are mere labels, nothing prevents an object from having several labels assigned to it. When that happens, you have *aliasing*, our next topic.

Identity, Equality, and Aliases

Lewis Carroll is the pen name of Prof. Charles Lutwidge Dodgson. Mr. Carroll is not only equal to Prof. Dodgson, they are one and the same. Example 6-3 expresses this idea in Python.

Example 6-3. charles and lewis refer to the same object

```
>>> charles = {'name': 'Charles L. Dodgson', 'born': 1832}
>>> lewis = charles  ❶
>>> lewis is charles
True
>>> id(charles), id(lewis)  ❷
(4300473992, 4300473992)
>>> lewis['balance'] = 950  ❸
```

```
>>> charles
{'name': 'Charles L. Dodgson', 'born': 1832, 'balance': 950}
```

❶ lewis is an alias for charles.

❷ The is operator and the id function confirm it.

❸ Adding an item to lewis is the same as adding an item to charles.

However, suppose an impostor—let's call him Dr. Alexander Pedachenko—claims he is Charles L. Dodgson, born in 1832. His credentials may be the same, but Dr. Pedachenko is not Prof. Dodgson. Figure 6-2 illustrates this scenario.

Figure 6-2. charles and lewis are bound to the same object; alex is bound to a separate object of equal value.

Example 6-4 implements and tests the alex object depicted in Figure 6-2.

Example 6-4. alex and charles compare equal, but alex is not charles

```
>>> alex = {'name': 'Charles L. Dodgson', 'born': 1832, 'balance': 950}   ❶
>>> alex == charles   ❷
True
>>> alex is not charles   ❸
True
```

❶ alex refers to an object that is a replica of the object assigned to charles.

❷ The objects compare equal because of the __eq__ implementation in the dict class.

❸ But they are distinct objects. This is the Pythonic way of writing the negative identity comparison: a is not b.

Example 6-3 is an example of *aliasing*. In that code, lewis and charles are aliases: two variables bound to the same object. On the other hand, alex is not an alias for `charles`: these variables are bound to distinct objects. The objects bound to `alex` and `charles` have the same *value*—that's what `==` compares—but they have different identities.

In *The Python Language Reference*, "3.1. Objects, values and types" (*https://fpy.li/6-2*) states:

> An object's identity never changes once it has been created; you may think of it as the object's address in memory. The `is` operator compares the identity of two objects; the `id()` function returns an integer representing its identity.

The real meaning of an object's ID is implementation dependent. In CPython, `id()` returns the memory address of the object, but it may be something else in another Python interpreter. The key point is that the ID is guaranteed to be a unique integer label, and it will never change during the life of the object.

In practice, we rarely use the `id()` function while programming. Identity checks are most often done with the `is` operator, which compares the object IDs, so our code doesn't need to call `id()` explicitly. Next, we'll talk about `is` versus `==`.

 For tech reviewer Leonardo Rochael, the most frequent use for `id()` is while debugging, when the `repr()` of two objects look alike, but you need to understand whether two references are aliases or point to separate objects. If the references are in different contexts —such as different stack frames—using the `is` operator may not be viable.

Choosing Between == and is

The `==` operator compares the values of objects (the data they hold), while `is` compares their identities.

While programming, we often care more about values than object identities, so `==` appears more frequently than `is` in Python code.

However, if you are comparing a variable to a singleton, then it makes sense to use `is`. By far, the most common case is checking whether a variable is bound to `None`. This is the recommended way to do it:

    x is None

And the proper way to write its negation is:

    x is not None

`None` is the most common singleton we test with `is`. Sentinel objects are another example of singletons we test with `is`. Here is one way to create and test a sentinel object:

```
END_OF_DATA = object()
# ... many lines
def traverse(...):
    # ... more lines
    if node is END_OF_DATA:
        return
    # etc.
```

The `is` operator is faster than `==`, because it cannot be overloaded, so Python does not have to find and invoke special methods to evaluate it, and computing is as simple as comparing two integer IDs. In contrast, `a == b` is syntactic sugar for `a.__eq__(b)`. The `__eq__` method inherited from `object` compares object IDs, so it produces the same result as `is`. But most built-in types override `__eq__` with more meaningful implementations that actually take into account the values of the object attributes. Equality may involve a lot of processing—for example, when comparing large collections or deeply nested structures.

 Usually we are more interested in object equality than identity. Checking for `None` is the *only* common use case for the `is` operator. Most other uses I see while reviewing code are wrong. If you are not sure, use `==`. It's usually what you want, and also works with `None`—albeit not as fast.

To wrap up this discussion of identity versus equality, we'll see that the famously immutable `tuple` is not as unchanging as you may expect.

The Relative Immutability of Tuples

Tuples, like most Python collections—lists, dicts, sets, etc.—are containers: they hold references to objects.[2] If the referenced items are mutable, they may change even if the tuple itself does not. In other words, the immutability of tuples really refers to the physical contents of the `tuple` data structure (i.e., the references it holds), and does not extend to the referenced objects.

Example 6-5 illustrates the situation in which the value of a tuple changes as a result of changes to a mutable object referenced in it. What can never change in a tuple is the identity of the items it contains.

---

2 In contrast, flat sequences like `str`, `bytes`, and `array.array` don't contain references but directly hold their contents—characters, bytes, and numbers—in contiguous memory.

Example 6-5. t1 and t2 initially compare equal, but changing a mutable item inside tuple t1 makes it different

```
>>> t1 = (1, 2, [30, 40])    ❶
>>> t2 = (1, 2, [30, 40])    ❷
>>> t1 == t2    ❸
True
>>> id(t1[-1])    ❹
4302515784
>>> t1[-1].append(99)    ❺
>>> t1
(1, 2, [30, 40, 99])
>>> id(t1[-1])    ❻
4302515784
>>> t1 == t2    ❼
False
```

❶ t1 is immutable, but t1[-1] is mutable.

❷ Build a tuple t2 whose items are equal to those of t1.

❸ Although distinct objects, t1 and t2 compare equal, as expected.

❹ Inspect the identity of the list at t1[-1].

❺ Modify the t1[-1] list in place.

❻ The identity of t1[-1] has not changed, only its value.

❼ t1 and t2 are now different.

This relative immutability of tuples is behind the riddle "A += Assignment Puzzler" on page 54. It's also the reason why some tuples are unhashable, as we've seen in "What Is Hashable" on page 84.

The distinction between equality and identity has further implications when you need to copy an object. A copy is an equal object with a different ID. But if an object contains other objects, should the copy also duplicate the inner objects, or is it OK to share them? There's no single answer. Read on for a discussion.

Copies Are Shallow by Default

The easiest way to copy a list (or most built-in mutable collections) is to use the built-in constructor for the type itself. For example:

```
>>> l1 = [3, [55, 44], (7, 8, 9)]
>>> l2 = list(l1)    ❶
```

```
>>> l2
[3, [55, 44], (7, 8, 9)]
>>> l2 == l1   ❷
True
>>> l2 is l1   ❸
False
```

❶ list(l1) creates a copy of l1.

❷ The copies are equal...

❸ ...but refer to two different objects.

For lists and other mutable sequences, the shortcut l2 = l1[:] also makes a copy.

However, using the constructor or [:] produces a *shallow copy* (i.e., the outermost container is duplicated, but the copy is filled with references to the same items held by the original container). This saves memory and causes no problems if all the items are immutable. But if there are mutable items, this may lead to unpleasant surprises.

In Example 6-6, we create a shallow copy of a list containing another list and a tuple, and then make changes to see how they affect the referenced objects.

 If you have a connected computer on hand, I highly recommend watching the interactive animation for Example 6-6 at the Online Python Tutor (*https://fpy.li/6-3*). As I write this, direct linking to a prepared example at *pythontutor.com* is not working reliably, but the tool is awesome, so taking the time to copy and paste the code is worthwhile.

Example 6-6. Making a shallow copy of a list containing another list; copy and paste this code to see it animated at the Online Python Tutor

```
l1 = [3, [66, 55, 44], (7, 8, 9)]
l2 = list(l1)          ❶
l1.append(100)         ❷
l1[1].remove(55)       ❸
print('l1:', l1)
print('l2:', l2)
l2[1] += [33, 22]      ❹
l2[2] += (10, 11)      ❺
print('l1:', l1)
print('l2:', l2)
```

❶ l2 is a shallow copy of l1. This state is depicted in Figure 6-3.

❷ Appending 100 to l1 has no effect on l2.

❸ Here we remove 55 from the inner list l1[1]. This affects l2 because l2[1] is bound to the same list as l1[1].

❹ For a mutable object like the list referred by l2[1], the operator += changes the list in place. This change is visible at l1[1], which is an alias for l2[1].

❺ += on a tuple creates a new tuple and rebinds the variable l2[2] here. This is the same as doing l2[2] = l2[2] + (10, 11). Now the tuples in the last position of l1 and l2 are no longer the same object. See Figure 6-4.

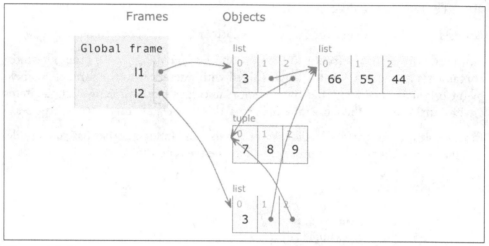

Figure 6-3. Program state immediately after the assignment l2 = list(l1) in Example 6-6. l1 and l2 refer to distinct lists, but the lists share references to the same inner list object [66, 55, 44] and tuple (7, 8, 9). (Diagram generated by the Online Python Tutor.)

The output of Example 6-6 is Example 6-7, and the final state of the objects is depicted in Figure 6-4.

Example 6-7. Output of Example 6-6

```
l1: [3, [66, 44], (7, 8, 9), 100]
l2: [3, [66, 44], (7, 8, 9)]
l1: [3, [66, 44, 33, 22], (7, 8, 9), 100]
l2: [3, [66, 44, 33, 22], (7, 8, 9, 10, 11)]
```

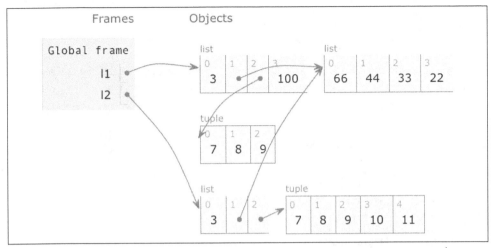

Figure 6-4. Final state of l1 and l2: they still share references to the same list object, now containing [66, 44, 33, 22], but the operation l2[2] += (10, 11) created a new tuple with content (7, 8, 9, 10, 11), unrelated to the tuple (7, 8, 9) referenced by l1[2]. (Diagram generated by the Online Python Tutor.)

It should be clear now that shallow copies are easy to make, but they may or may not be what you want. How to make deep copies is our next topic.

Deep and Shallow Copies of Arbitrary Objects

Working with shallow copies is not always a problem, but sometimes you need to make deep copies (i.e., duplicates that do not share references of embedded objects). The copy module provides the deepcopy and copy functions that return deep and shallow copies of arbitrary objects.

To illustrate the use of copy() and deepcopy(), Example 6-8 defines a simple class, Bus, representing a school bus that is loaded with passengers and then picks up or drops off passengers on its route.

Example 6-8. Bus picks up and drops off passengers

```
class Bus:

    def __init__(self, passengers=None):
        if passengers is None:
            self.passengers = []
        else:
            self.passengers = list(passengers)

    def pick(self, name):
        self.passengers.append(name)
```

```
    def drop(self, name):
        self.passengers.remove(name)
```

Now, in the interactive Example 6-9, we will create a bus object (bus1) and two clones—a shallow copy (bus2) and a deep copy (bus3)—to observe what happens as bus1 drops off a student.

Example 6-9. Effects of using copy versus deepcopy

```
>>> import copy
>>> bus1 = Bus(['Alice', 'Bill', 'Claire', 'David'])
>>> bus2 = copy.copy(bus1)
>>> bus3 = copy.deepcopy(bus1)
>>> id(bus1), id(bus2), id(bus3)
(4301498296, 4301499416, 4301499752)    ❶
>>> bus1.drop('Bill')
>>> bus2.passengers
['Alice', 'Claire', 'David']            ❷
>>> id(bus1.passengers), id(bus2.passengers), id(bus3.passengers)
(4302658568, 4302658568, 4302657800)    ❸
>>> bus3.passengers
['Alice', 'Bill', 'Claire', 'David']    ❹
```

❶ Using copy and deepcopy, we create three distinct Bus instances.

❷ After bus1 drops 'Bill', he is also missing from bus2.

❸ Inspection of the passengers attributes shows that bus1 and bus2 share the same list object, because bus2 is a shallow copy of bus1.

❹ bus3 is a deep copy of bus1, so its passengers attribute refers to another list.

Note that making deep copies is not a simple matter in the general case. Objects may have cyclic references that would cause a naïve algorithm to enter an infinite loop. The deepcopy function remembers the objects already copied to handle cyclic references gracefully. This is demonstrated in Example 6-10.

Example 6-10. Cyclic references: b refers to a, and then is appended to a; deepcopy still manages to copy a

```
>>> a = [10, 20]
>>> b = [a, 30]
>>> a.append(b)
>>> a
[10, 20, [[...], 30]]
>>> from copy import deepcopy
```

```
>>> c = deepcopy(a)
>>> c
[10, 20, [[...], 30]]
```

Also, a deep copy may be too deep in some cases. For example, objects may refer to external resources or singletons that should not be copied. You can control the behavior of both copy and deepcopy by implementing the __copy__() and __deepcopy__() special methods, as described in the copy module documentation (*https://fpy.li/6-4*).

The sharing of objects through aliases also explains how parameter passing works in Python, and the problem of using mutable types as parameter defaults. These issues will be covered next.

Function Parameters as References

The only mode of parameter passing in Python is *call by sharing*. That is the same mode used in most object-oriented languages, including JavaScript, Ruby, and Java (this applies to Java reference types; primitive types use call by value). Call by sharing means that each formal parameter of the function gets a copy of each reference in the arguments. In other words, the parameters inside the function become aliases of the actual arguments.

The result of this scheme is that a function may change any mutable object passed as a parameter, but it cannot change the identity of those objects (i.e., it cannot altogether replace an object with another). Example 6-11 shows a simple function using += on one of its parameters. As we pass numbers, lists, and tuples to the function, the actual arguments passed are affected in different ways.

Example 6-11. A function may change any mutable object it receives

```
>>> def f(a, b):
...     a += b
...     return a
...
>>> x = 1
>>> y = 2
>>> f(x, y)
3
>>> x, y    ❶
(1, 2)
>>> a = [1, 2]
>>> b = [3, 4]
>>> f(a, b)
[1, 2, 3, 4]
>>> a, b    ❷
([1, 2, 3, 4], [3, 4])
```

```
>>> t = (10, 20)
>>> u = (30, 40)
>>> f(t, u)  ❸
(10, 20, 30, 40)
>>> t, u
((10, 20), (30, 40))
```

❶ The number x is unchanged.

❷ The list a is changed.

❸ The tuple t is unchanged.

Another issue related to function parameters is the use of mutable values for defaults, as discussed next.

Mutable Types as Parameter Defaults: Bad Idea

Optional parameters with default values are a great feature of Python function definitions, allowing our APIs to evolve while remaining backward compatible. However, you should avoid mutable objects as default values for parameters.

To illustrate this point, in Example 6-12, we take the Bus class from Example 6-8 and change its __init__ method to create HauntedBus. Here we tried to be clever, and instead of having a default value of passengers=None, we have passengers=[], thus avoiding the if in the previous __init__. This "cleverness" gets us into trouble.

Example 6-12. A simple class to illustrate the danger of a mutable default

```
class HauntedBus:
    """A bus model haunted by ghost passengers"""

    def __init__(self, passengers=[]):  ❶
        self.passengers = passengers  ❷

    def pick(self, name):
        self.passengers.append(name)  ❸

    def drop(self, name):
        self.passengers.remove(name)
```

❶ When the passengers argument is not passed, this parameter is bound to the default list object, which is initially empty.

❷ This assignment makes self.passengers an alias for passengers, which is itself an alias for the default list, when no passengers argument is given.

---

❸ When the methods .remove() and .append() are used with self.passengers, we are actually mutating the default list, which is an attribute of the function object.

Example 6-13 shows the eerie behavior of the HauntedBus.

Example 6-13. Buses haunted by ghost passengers

```
>>> bus1 = HauntedBus(['Alice', 'Bill'])  ❶
>>> bus1.passengers
['Alice', 'Bill']
>>> bus1.pick('Charlie')
>>> bus1.drop('Alice')
>>> bus1.passengers  ❷
['Bill', 'Charlie']
>>> bus2 = HauntedBus()  ❸
>>> bus2.pick('Carrie')
>>> bus2.passengers
['Carrie']
>>> bus3 = HauntedBus()  ❹
>>> bus3.passengers  ❺
['Carrie']
>>> bus3.pick('Dave')
>>> bus2.passengers  ❻
['Carrie', 'Dave']
>>> bus2.passengers is bus3.passengers  ❼
True
>>> bus1.passengers  ❽
['Bill', 'Charlie']
```

❶ bus1 starts with a two-passenger list.

❷ So far, so good: no surprises with bus1.

❸ bus2 starts empty, so the default empty list is assigned to self.passengers.

❹ bus3 also starts empty, again the default list is assigned.

❺ The default is no longer empty!

❻ Now Dave, picked by bus3, appears in bus2.

❼ The problem: bus2.passengers and bus3.passengers refer to the same list.

❽ But bus1.passengers is a distinct list.

The problem is that HauntedBus instances that don't get an initial passenger list end up sharing the same passenger list among themselves.

Such bugs may be subtle. As Example 6-13 demonstrates, when a HauntedBus is instantiated with passengers, it works as expected. Strange things happen only when a HauntedBus starts empty, because then self.passengers becomes an alias for the default value of the passengers parameter. The problem is that each default value is evaluated when the function is defined—i.e., usually when the module is loaded—and the default values become attributes of the function object. So if a default value is a mutable object, and you change it, the change will affect every future call of the function.

After running the lines in Example 6-13, you can inspect the HauntedBus.__init__ object and see the ghost students haunting its __defaults__ attribute:

```
>>> dir(HauntedBus.__init__)  # doctest: +ELLIPSIS
['__annotations__', '__call__', ..., '__defaults__', ...]
>>> HauntedBus.__init__.__defaults__
(['Carrie', 'Dave'],)
```

Finally, we can verify that bus2.passengers is an alias bound to the first element of the HauntedBus.__init__.__defaults__ attribute:

```
>>> HauntedBus.__init__.__defaults__[0] is bus2.passengers
True
```

The issue with mutable defaults explains why None is commonly used as the default value for parameters that may receive mutable values. In Example 6-8, __init__ checks whether the passengers argument is None. If it is, self.passengers is bound to a new empty list. If passengers is not None, the correct implementation binds a copy of that argument to self.passengers. The next section explains why copying the argument is a good practice.

Defensive Programming with Mutable Parameters

When you are coding a function that receives a mutable parameter, you should carefully consider whether the caller expects the argument passed to be changed.

For example, if your function receives a dict and needs to modify it while processing it, should this side effect be visible outside of the function or not? Actually it depends on the context. It's really a matter of aligning the expectation of the coder of the function and that of the caller.

The last bus example in this chapter shows how a TwilightBus breaks expectations by sharing its passenger list with its clients. Before studying the implementation, see in Example 6-14 how the TwilightBus class works from the perspective of a client of the class.

Example 6-14. Passengers disappear when dropped by a TwilightBus

```
>>> basketball_team = ['Sue', 'Tina', 'Maya', 'Diana', 'Pat']  ❶
>>> bus = TwilightBus(basketball_team)  ❷
>>> bus.drop('Tina')  ❸
>>> bus.drop('Pat')
>>> basketball_team  ❹
['Sue', 'Maya', 'Diana']
```

❶ basketball_team holds five student names.

❷ A TwilightBus is loaded with the team.

❸ The bus drops one student, then another.

❹ The dropped passengers vanished from the basketball team!

TwilightBus violates the "Principle of least astonishment," a best practice of interface design.[3] It surely is astonishing that when the bus drops a student, their name is removed from the basketball team roster.

Example 6-15 is the implementation TwilightBus and an explanation of the problem.

Example 6-15. A simple class to show the perils of mutating received arguments

```
class TwilightBus:
    """A bus model that makes passengers vanish"""

    def __init__(self, passengers=None):
        if passengers is None:
            self.passengers = []  ❶
        else:
            self.passengers = passengers  ❷

    def pick(self, name):
        self.passengers.append(name)

    def drop(self, name):
        self.passengers.remove(name)  ❸
```

---

3 See *Principle of least astonishment (https://fpy.li/6-5)* in the English Wikipedia.

❶ Here we are careful to create a new empty list when `passengers` is None.

❷ However, this assignment makes `self.passengers` an alias for `passengers`, which is itself an alias for the actual argument passed to `__init__` (i.e., `basket ball_team` in Example 6-14).

❸ When the methods `.remove()` and `.append()` are used with `self.passengers`, we are actually mutating the original list received as an argument to the constructor.

The problem here is that the bus is aliasing the list that is passed to the constructor. Instead, it should keep its own passenger list. The fix is simple: in `__init__`, when the `passengers` parameter is provided, `self.passengers` should be initialized with a copy of it, as we did correctly in Example 6-8:

```
def __init__(self, passengers=None):
    if passengers is None:
        self.passengers = []
    else:
        self.passengers = list(passengers)  ❶
```

❶ Make a copy of the `passengers` list, or convert it to a `list` if it's not one.

Now our internal handling of the passenger list will not affect the argument used to initialize the bus. As a bonus, this solution is more flexible: now the argument passed to the `passengers` parameter may be a `tuple` or any other iterable, like a `set` or even database results, because the `list` constructor accepts any iterable. As we create our own list to manage, we ensure that it supports the necessary `.remove()` and `.append()` operations we use in the `.pick()` and `.drop()` methods.

 Unless a method is explicitly intended to mutate an object received as an argument, you should think twice before aliasing the argument object by simply assigning it to an instance variable in your class. If in doubt, make a copy. Your clients will be happier. Of course, making a copy is not free: there is a cost in CPU and memory. However, an API that causes subtle bugs is usually a bigger problem than one that is a little slower or uses more resources.

Now let's talk about one of the most misunderstood of Python's statements: `del`.

del and Garbage Collection

> Objects are never explicitly destroyed; however, when they become unreachable they may be garbage-collected.
>
> —"Data Model" chapter of *The Python Language Reference*

The first strange fact about del is that it's not a function, it's a statement. We write del x and not del(x)—although the latter also works, but only because the expressions x and (x) usually mean the same thing in Python.

The second surprising fact is that del deletes references, not objects. Python's garbage collector may discard an object from memory as an indirect result of del, if the deleted variable was the last reference to the object. Rebinding a variable may also cause the number of references to an object to reach zero, causing its destruction.

```
>>> a = [1, 2]    ❶
>>> b = a         ❷
>>> del a         ❸
>>> b             ❹
[1, 2]
>>> b = [3]       ❺
```

❶ Create object [1, 2] and bind a to it.

❷ Bind b to the same [1, 2] object.

❸ Delete reference a.

❹ [1, 2] was not affected, because b still points to it.

❺ Rebinding b to a different object removes the last remaining reference to [1, 2]. Now the garbage collector can discard that object.

 There is a __del__ special method, but it does not cause the disposal of the instance, and should not be called by your code. __del__ is invoked by the Python interpreter when the instance is about to be destroyed to give it a chance to release external resources. You will seldom need to implement __del__ in your own code, yet some Python programmers spend time coding it for no good reason. The proper use of __del__ is rather tricky. See the __del__ special method documentation (*https://fpy.li/6-6*) in the "Data Model" chapter of *The Python Language Reference*.

In CPython, the primary algorithm for garbage collection is reference counting. Essentially, each object keeps count of how many references point to it. As soon as that *refcount* reaches zero, the object is immediately destroyed: CPython calls the __del__ method on the object (if defined) and then frees the memory allocated to the object. In CPython 2.0, a generational garbage collection algorithm was added to detect groups of objects involved in reference cycles—which may be unreachable even with outstanding references to them, when all the mutual references are contained within the group. Other implementations of Python have more sophisticated garbage collectors that do not rely on reference counting, which means the __del__ method may not be called immediately when there are no more references to the object. See "PyPy, Garbage Collection, and a Deadlock" (*https://fpy.li/6-7*) by A. Jesse Jiryu Davis for discussion of improper and proper use of __del__.

To demonstrate the end of an object's life, Example 6-16 uses weakref.finalize to register a callback function to be called when an object is destroyed.

Example 6-16. Watching the end of an object when no more references point to it

```
>>> import weakref
>>> s1 = {1, 2, 3}
>>> s2 = s1          ❶
>>> def bye():       ❷
...     print('...like tears in the rain.')
...
>>> ender = weakref.finalize(s1, bye)   ❸
>>> ender.alive    ❹
True
>>> del s1
>>> ender.alive    ❺
True
>>> s2 = 'spam'    ❻
...like tears in the rain.
>>> ender.alive
False
```

❶ s1 and s2 are aliases referring to the same set, {1, 2, 3}.

❷ This function must not be a bound method of the object about to be destroyed or otherwise hold a reference to it.

❸ Register the bye callback on the object referred by s1.

❹ The .alive attribute is True before the finalize object is called.

❺ As discussed, del did not delete the object, just the s1 reference to it.

❻ Rebinding the last reference, s2, makes {1, 2, 3} unreachable. It is destroyed, the bye callback is invoked, and ender.alive becomes False.

The point of Example 6-16 is to make explicit that del does not delete objects, but objects may be deleted as a consequence of being unreachable after del is used.

You may be wondering why the {1, 2, 3} object was destroyed in Example 6-16. After all, the s1 reference was passed to the finalize function, which must have held on to it in order to monitor the object and invoke the callback. This works because finalize holds a *weak reference* to {1, 2, 3}. Weak references to an object do not increase its reference count. Therefore, a weak reference does not prevent the target object from being garbage collected. Weak references are useful in caching applications because you don't want the cached objects to be kept alive just because they are referenced by the cache.

Weak references is a very specialized topic. That's why I chose to skip it in this second edition. Instead, I published "Weak References" on *fluentpython.com* (*https://fpy.li/weakref*).

Tricks Python Plays with Immutables

This optional section discusses some Python details that are not really important for *users* of Python, and that may not apply to other Python implementations or even future versions of CPython. Nevertheless, I've seen people stumble upon these corner cases and then start using the is operator incorrectly, so I felt they were worth mentioning.

I was surprised to learn that, for a tuple t, t[:] does not make a copy, but returns a reference to the same object. You also get a reference to the same tuple if you write tuple(t).[4] Example 6-17 proves it.

Example 6-17. A tuple built from another is actually the same exact tuple

```
>>> t1 = (1, 2, 3)
>>> t2 = tuple(t1)
>>> t2 is t1        ❶
True
>>> t3 = t1[:]
>>> t3 is t1        ❷
True
```

---

4 This is clearly documented. Type help(tuple) in the Python console to read: "If the argument is a tuple, the return value is the same object." I thought I knew everything about tuples before writing this book.

❶ t1 and t2 are bound to the same object.

❷ And so is t3.

The same behavior can be observed with instances of str, bytes, and frozenset. Note that a frozenset is not a sequence, so fs[:] does not work if fs is a frozenset. But fs.copy() has the same effect: it cheats and returns a reference to the same object, and not a copy at all, as Example 6-18 shows.[5]

Example 6-18. String literals may create shared objects

```
>>> t1 = (1, 2, 3)
>>> t3 = (1, 2, 3)  ❶
>>> t3 is t1  ❷
False
>>> s1 = 'ABC'
>>> s2 = 'ABC'  ❸
>>> s2 is s1  ❹
True
```

❶ Creating a new tuple from scratch.

❷ t1 and t3 are equal, but not the same object.

❸ Creating a second str from scratch.

❹ Surprise: a and b refer to the same str!

The sharing of string literals is an optimization technique called *interning*. CPython uses a similar technique with small integers to avoid unnecessary duplication of numbers that appear frequently in programs like 0, 1, –1, etc. Note that CPython does not intern all strings or integers, and the criteria it uses to do so is an undocumented implementation detail.

 Never depend on str or int interning! Always use == instead of is to compare strings or integers for equality. Interning is an optimization for internal use of the Python interpreter.

---

5 The harmless lie of having the copy method not copying anything is justified by interface compatibility: it makes frozenset more compatible with set. Anyway, it makes no difference to the end user whether two identical immutable objects are the same or are copies.

The tricks discussed in this section, including the behavior of `frozenset.copy()`, are harmless "lies" that save memory and make the interpreter faster. Do not worry about them, they should not give you any trouble because they only apply to immutable types. Probably the best use of these bits of trivia is to win bets with fellow Pythonistas.[6]

Chapter Summary

Every Python object has an identity, a type, and a value. Only the value of an object may change over time.[7]

If two variables refer to immutable objects that have equal values (`a == b` is `True`), in practice it rarely matters if they refer to copies or are aliases referring to the same object, because the value of an immutable object does not change, with one exception. The exception being immutable collections such as tuples: if an immutable collection holds references to mutable items, then its value may actually change when the value of a mutable item changes. In practice, this scenario is not so common. What never changes in an immutable collection are the identities of the objects within. The `frozenset` class does not suffer from this problem because it can only hold hashable elements, and the value of hashable objects cannot ever change, by definition.

The fact that variables hold references has many practical consequences in Python programming:

- Simple assignment does not create copies.
- Augmented assignment with += or *= creates new objects if the lefthand variable is bound to an immutable object, but may modify a mutable object in place.
- Assigning a new value to an existing variable does not change the object previously bound to it. This is called a rebinding: the variable is now bound to a different object. If that variable was the last reference to the previous object, that object will be garbage collected.

---

6 A terrible use for this information would be to ask about it when interviewing candidates or authoring questions for "certification" exams. There are countless more important and useful facts to check for Python knowledge.

7 Actually the type of an object may be changed by merely assigning a different class to its __class__ attribute, but that is pure evil and I regret writing this footnote.

- Function parameters are passed as aliases, which means the function may change any mutable object received as an argument. There is no way to prevent this, except making local copies or using immutable objects (e.g., passing a tuple instead of a list).

- Using mutable objects as default values for function parameters is dangerous because if the parameters are changed in place, then the default is changed, affecting every future call that relies on the default.

In CPython, objects are discarded as soon as the number of references to them reaches zero. They may also be discarded if they form groups with cyclic references but not outside references.

In some situations, it may be useful to hold a reference to an object that will not—by itself—keep an object alive. One example is a class that wants to keep track of all its current instances. This can be done with weak references, a low-level mechanism underlying the more useful collections WeakValueDictionary, WeakKeyDictionary, WeakSet, and the finalize function from the weakref module. For more on this, please see "Weak References" at *fluentpython.com* (*https://fpy.li/weakref*).

Further Reading

The "Data Model" chapter (*https://fpy.li/dtmodel*) of *The Python Language Reference* starts with a clear explanation of object identities and values.

Wesley Chun, author of the *Core Python* series of books, presented Understanding Python's Memory Model, Mutability, and Methods (*https://fpy.li/6-8*) at EuroPython 2011, covering not only the theme of this chapter but also the use of special methods.

Doug Hellmann wrote the posts "copy – Duplicate Objects" (*https://fpy.li/6-9*) and "weakref—Garbage-Collectable References to Objects" (*https://fpy.li/6-10*) covering some of the topics we just discussed.

More information on the CPython generational garbage collector can be found in the gc module documentation (*https://fpy.li/6-11*), which starts with the sentence "This module provides an interface to the optional garbage collector." The "optional" qualifier here may be surprising, but the "Data Model" chapter (*https://fpy.li/dtmodel*) also states:

> An implementation is allowed to postpone garbage collection or omit it altogether—it is a matter of implementation quality how garbage collection is implemented, as long as no objects are collected that are still reachable.

Pablo Galindo wrote more in-depth treatment of Python's GC in "Design of CPython's Garbage Collector" (*https://fpy.li/6-12*) in the *Python Developer's Guide* (*https://fpy.li/6-13*), aimed at new and experienced contributors to the CPython implementation.

The CPython 3.4 garbage collector improved handling of objects with a __del__ method, as described in PEP 442—Safe object finalization (*https://fpy.li/6-14*).

Wikipedia has an article about string interning (*https://fpy.li/6-15*), mentioning the use of this technique in several languages, including Python.

Wikipedia also as an article on "Haddocks' Eyes" (*https://fpy.li/6-16*), the Lewis Carroll song I quoted at the top of this chapter. The Wikipedia editors wrote that the lyrics are used in works on logic and philosophy "to elaborate on the symbolic status of the concept of *name*: a name as identification marker may be assigned to anything, including another name, thus introducing different levels of symbolization."

Soapbox

Equal Treatment to All Objects

I learned Java before I discovered Python. The == operator in Java never felt right to me. It is much more common for programmers to care about equality than identity, but for objects (not primitive types), the Java == compares references, and not object values. Even for something as basic as comparing strings, Java forces you to use the .equals method. Even then, there is another catch: if you write a.equals(b) and a is null, you get a null pointer exception. The Java designers felt the need to overload + for strings, so why not go ahead and overload == as well?

Python gets this right. The == operator compares object values; is compares references. And because Python has operator overloading, == works sensibly with all objects in the standard library, including None, which is a proper object, unlike Java's null.

And of course, you can define __eq__ in your own classes to decide what == means for your instances. If you don't override __eq__, the method inherited from object compares object IDs, so the fallback is that every instance of a user-defined class is considered different.

These are some of the things that made me switch from Java to Python as soon as I finished reading *The Python Tutorial* one afternoon in September 1998.

Mutability

This chapter would not be necessary if all Python objects were immutable. When you are dealing with unchanging objects, it makes no difference whether variables hold the actual objects or references to shared objects. If a == b is true, and neither object

---

can change, they might as well be the same. That's why string interning is safe. Object identity becomes important only when objects are mutable.

In "pure" functional programming, all data is immutable: appending to a collection actually creates a new collection. Elixir is one easy to learn, practical functional language in which all built-in types are immutable, including lists.

Python, however, is not a functional language, much less a pure one. Instances of user-defined classes are mutable by default in Python—as in most object-oriented languages. When creating your own objects, you have to be extra careful to make them immutable, if that is a requirement. Every attribute of the object must also be immutable, otherwise you end up with something like the tuple: immutable as far as object IDs go, but the value of a tuple may change if it holds a mutable object.

Mutable objects are also the main reason why programming with threads is so hard to get right: threads mutating objects without proper synchronization produce corrupted data. Excessive synchronization, on the other hand, causes deadlocks. The Erlang language and platform—which includes Elixir—was designed to maximize uptime in highly concurrent, distributed applications such as telecommunications switches. Naturally, they chose immutable data by default.

Object Destruction and Garbage Collection

There is no mechanism in Python to directly destroy an object, and this omission is actually a great feature: if you could destroy an object at any time, what would happen to existing references pointing to it?

Garbage collection in CPython is done primarily by reference counting, which is easy to implement, but is prone to memory leaking when there are reference cycles, so with version 2.0 (October 2000) a generational garbage collector was implemented, and it is able to dispose of unreachable objects kept alive by reference cycles.

But the reference counting is still there as a baseline, and it causes the immediate disposal of objects with zero references. This means that, in CPython—at least for now —it's safe to write this:

```
open('test.txt', 'wt', encoding='utf-8').write('1, 2, 3')
```

That code is safe because the reference count of the file object will be zero after the write method returns, and Python will immediately close the file before destroying the object representing it in memory. However, the same line is not safe in Jython or IronPython that use the garbage collector of their host runtimes (the Java VM and the .NET CLR), which are more sophisticated but do not rely on reference counting and may take longer to destroy the object and close the file. In all cases, including CPython, the best practice is to explicitly close the file, and the most reliable way of doing it is using the with statement, which guarantees that the file will be closed even if exceptions are raised while it is open. Using with, the previous snippet becomes:

```
with open('test.txt', 'wt', encoding='utf-8') as fp:
    fp.write('1, 2, 3')
```

If you are into the subject of garbage collectors, you may want to read Thomas Perl's paper "Python Garbage Collector Implementations: CPython, PyPy and GaS" (*https://fpy.li/6-17*), from which I learned the bit about the safety of the open().write() in CPython.

Parameter Passing: Call by Sharing

A popular way of explaining how parameter passing works in Python is the phrase: "Parameters are passed by value, but the values are references." This is not wrong, but causes confusion because the most common parameter passing modes in older languages are *call by value* (the function gets a copy of the argument) and *call by reference* (the function gets a pointer to the argument). In Python, the function gets a copy of the arguments, but the arguments are always references. So the value of the referenced objects may be changed, if they are mutable, but their identity cannot. Also, because the function gets a copy of the reference in an argument, rebinding it in the function body has no effect outside of the function. I adopted the term *call by sharing* after reading up on the subject in *Programming Language Pragmatics*, 3rd ed., by Michael L. Scott (Morgan Kaufmann), section "8.3.1: Parameter Modes."

## PART II

Functions as Objects

Functions as First-Class Objects

I have never considered Python to be heavily influenced by functional languages, no matter what people say or think. I was much more familiar with imperative languages such as C and Algol 68 and although I had made functions first-class objects, I didn't view Python as a functional programming language.

— Guido van Rossum, Python BDFL[1]

Functions in Python are first-class objects. Programming language researchers define a "first-class object" as a program entity that can be:

- Created at runtime
- Assigned to a variable or element in a data structure
- Passed as an argument to a function
- Returned as the result of a function

Integers, strings, and dictionaries are other examples of first-class objects in Python —nothing fancy here. Having functions as first-class objects is an essential feature of functional languages, such as Clojure, Elixir, and Haskell. However, first-class functions are so useful that they've been adopted by popular languages like JavaScript, Go, and Java (since JDK 8), none of which claim to be "functional languages."

This chapter and most of Part III explore the practical applications of treating functions as objects.

---

1 "Origins of Python's 'Functional' Features" (*https://fpy.li/7-1*), from Guido's *The History of Python* blog.

The term "first-class functions" is widely used as shorthand for "functions as first-class objects." It's not ideal because it implies an "elite" among functions. In Python, all functions are first-class.

What's New in This Chapter

The section "The Nine Flavors of Callable Objects" on page 237 was titled "The Seven Flavors of Callable Objects" in the first edition of this book. The new callables are native coroutines and asynchronous generators, introduced in Python 3.5 and 3.6, respectively. Both are covered in Chapter 21, but they are mentioned here along with the other callables for completeness.

"Positional-Only Parameters" on page 242 is a new section, covering a feature added in Python 3.8.

I moved the discussion of runtime access to function annotations to "Reading Type Hints at Runtime" on page 541. When I wrote the first edition, PEP 484—Type Hints (*https://fpy.li/pep484*) was still under consideration, and people used annotations in different ways. Since Python 3.5, annotations should conform to PEP 484. Therefore, the best place to cover them is when discussing type hints.

The first edition of this book had sections about the introspection of function objects that were too low-level and distracted from the main subject of this chapter. I merged those sections into a post titled "Introspection of Function Parameters" at *fluentpython.com* (*https://fpy.li/7-2*).

Now let's see why Python functions are full-fledged objects.

Treating a Function Like an Object

The console session in Example 7-1 shows that Python functions are objects. Here we create a function, call it, read its __doc__ attribute, and check that the function object itself is an instance of the function class.

Example 7-1. Create and test a function, then read its __doc__ and check its type

```
>>> def factorial(n):  ❶
...     """returns n!"""
...     return 1 if n < 2 else n * factorial(n - 1)
...
>>> factorial(42)
1405006117752879898543142606244511569936384000000000
```

```
>>> factorial.__doc__   ❷
'returns n!'
>>> type(factorial)   ❸
<class 'function'>
```

❶ This is a console session, so we're creating a function at "runtime."

❷ __doc__ is one of several attributes of function objects.

❸ factorial is an instance of the function class.

The __doc__ attribute is used to generate the help text of an object. In the Python console, the command help(factorial) will display a screen like Figure 7-1.

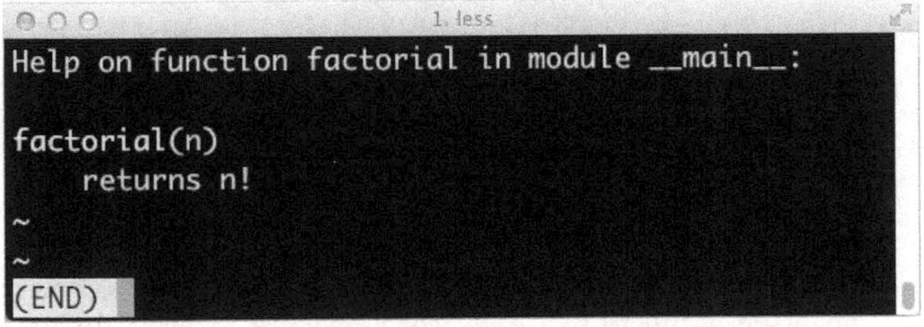

Figure 7-1. Help screen for factorial; the text is built from the __doc__ attribute of the function.

Example 7-2 shows the "first class" nature of a function object. We can assign it a variable fact and call it through that name. We can also pass factorial as an argument to the map (*https://fpy.li/7-3*) function. Calling map(function, iterable) returns an iterable where each item is the result of calling the first argument (a function) to successive elements of the second argument (an iterable), range(10) in this example.

Example 7-2. Use factorial through a different name, and pass factorial as an argument

```
>>> fact = factorial
>>> fact
<function factorial at 0x...>
>>> fact(5)
120
>>> map(factorial, range(11))
<map object at 0x...>
>>> list(map(factorial, range(11)))
[1, 1, 2, 6, 24, 120, 720, 5040, 40320, 362880, 3628800]
```

Having first-class functions enables programming in a functional style. One of the hallmarks of functional programming (*https://fpy.li/7-4*) is the use of higher-order functions, our next topic.

Higher-Order Functions

A function that takes a function as an argument or returns a function as the result is a *higher-order function*. One example is `map`, shown in Example 7-2. Another is the built-in function `sorted`: the optional key argument lets you provide a function to be applied to each item for sorting, as we saw in "list.sort Versus the sorted Built-In" on page 56. For example, to sort a list of words by length, pass the `len` function as the key, as in Example 7-3.

Example 7-3. Sorting a list of words by length

```
>>> fruits = ['strawberry', 'fig', 'apple', 'cherry', 'raspberry', 'banana']
>>> sorted(fruits, key=len)
['fig', 'apple', 'cherry', 'banana', 'raspberry', 'strawberry']
>>>
```

Any one-argument function can be used as the key. For example, to create a rhyme dictionary it might be useful to sort each word spelled backward. In Example 7-4, note that the words in the list are not changed at all; only their reversed spelling is used as the sort criterion, so that the berries appear together.

Example 7-4. Sorting a list of words by their reversed spelling

```
>>> def reverse(word):
...     return word[::-1]
>>> reverse('testing')
'gnitset'
>>> sorted(fruits, key=reverse)
['banana', 'apple', 'fig', 'raspberry', 'strawberry', 'cherry']
>>>
```

In the functional programming paradigm, some of the best known higher-order functions are `map`, `filter`, `reduce`, and `apply`. The `apply` function was deprecated in Python 2.3 and removed in Python 3 because it's no longer necessary. If you need to call a function with a dynamic set of arguments, you can write `fn(*args, **kwargs)` instead of `apply(fn, args, kwargs)`.

The `map`, `filter`, and `reduce` higher-order functions are still around, but better alternatives are available for most of their use cases, as the next section shows.

Modern Replacements for map, filter, and reduce

Functional languages commonly offer the map, filter, and reduce higher-order functions (sometimes with different names). The map and filter functions are still built-ins in Python 3, but since the introduction of list comprehensions and generator expressions, they are not as important. A listcomp or a genexp does the job of map and filter combined, but is more readable. Consider Example 7-5.

Example 7-5. Lists of factorials produced with map and filter compared to alternatives coded as list comprehensions

```
>>> list(map(factorial, range(6)))   ❶
[1, 1, 2, 6, 24, 120]
>>> [factorial(n) for n in range(6)]   ❷
[1, 1, 2, 6, 24, 120]
>>> list(map(factorial, filter(lambda n: n % 2, range(6))))   ❸
[1, 6, 120]
>>> [factorial(n) for n in range(6) if n % 2]   ❹
[1, 6, 120]
>>>
```

❶ Build a list of factorials from 0! to 5!.

❷ Same operation, with a list comprehension.

❸ List of factorials of odd numbers up to 5!, using both map and filter.

❹ List comprehension does the same job, replacing map and filter, and making lambda unnecessary.

In Python 3, map and filter return generators—a form of iterator—so their direct substitute is now a generator expression (in Python 2, these functions returned lists, therefore their closest alternative was a listcomp).

The reduce function was demoted from a built-in in Python 2 to the functools module in Python 3. Its most common use case, summation, is better served by the sum built-in available since Python 2.3 was released in 2003. This is a big win in terms of readability and performance (see Example 7-6).

Example 7-6. Sum of integers up to 99 performed with reduce and sum

```
>>> from functools import reduce   ❶
>>> from operator import add   ❷
>>> reduce(add, range(100))   ❸
4950
>>> sum(range(100))   ❹
```

```
4950
>>>
```

❶ Starting with Python 3.0, reduce is no longer a built-in.

❷ Import add to avoid creating a function just to add two numbers.

❸ Sum integers up to 99.

❹ Same task with sum—no need to import and call reduce and add.

 The common idea of sum and reduce is to apply some operation to successive items in a series, accumulating previous results, thus reducing a series of values to a single value.

Other reducing built-ins are all and any:

all(iterable)
> Returns True if there are no falsy elements in the iterable; all([]) returns True.

any(iterable)
> Returns True if any element of the iterable is truthy; any([]) returns False.

I give a fuller explanation of reduce in "Vector Take #4: Hashing and a Faster ==" on page 413 where an ongoing example provides a meaningful context for the use of this function. The reducing functions are summarized later in the book when iterables are in focus, in "Iterable Reducing Functions" on page 634.

To use a higher-order function, sometimes it is convenient to create a small, . one-off function. That is why anonymous functions exist. We'll cover them next.

Anonymous Functions

The lambda keyword creates an anonymous function within a Python expression.

However, the simple syntax of Python limits the body of lambda functions to be pure expressions. In other words, the body cannot contain other Python statements such as while, try, etc. Assignment with = is also a statement, so it cannot occur in a lambda. The new assignment expression syntax using := can be used—but if you need it, your lambda is probably too complicated and hard to read, and it should be refactored into a regular function using def.

The best use of anonymous functions is in the context of an argument list for a higher-order function. For example, Example 7-7 is the rhyme index example from Example 7-4 rewritten with lambda, without defining a reverse function.

Example 7-7. Sorting a list of words by their reversed spelling using lambda

```
>>> fruits = ['strawberry', 'fig', 'apple', 'cherry', 'raspberry', 'banana']
>>> sorted(fruits, key=lambda word: word[::-1])
['banana', 'apple', 'fig', 'raspberry', 'strawberry', 'cherry']
>>>
```

Outside the limited context of arguments to higher-order functions, anonymous functions are rarely useful in Python. The syntactic restrictions tend to make nontrivial lambdas either unreadable or unworkable. If a lambda is hard to read, I strongly advise you follow Fredrik Lundh's refactoring advice.

Fredrik Lundh's lambda Refactoring Recipe

If you find a piece of code hard to understand because of a lambda, Fredrik Lundh suggests this refactoring procedure:

1. Write a comment explaining what the heck that lambda does.
2. Study the comment for a while, and think of a name that captures the essence of the comment.
3. Convert the lambda to a def statement, using that name.
4. Remove the comment.

These steps are quoted from the "Functional Programming HOWTO" (*https://fpy.li/ 7-5*), a must read.

The lambda syntax is just syntactic sugar: a lambda expression creates a function object just like the def statement. That is just one of several kinds of callable objects in Python. The following section reviews all of them.

The Nine Flavors of Callable Objects

The call operator () may be applied to other objects besides functions. To determine whether an object is callable, use the callable() built-in function. As of Python 3.9, the data model documentation (*https://fpy.li/7-6*) lists nine callable types:

User-defined functions

Created with def statements or lambda expressions.

Built-in functions

A function implemented in C (for CPython), like len or time.strftime.

Built-in methods

Methods implemented in C, like dict.get.

Methods

Functions defined in the body of a class.

Classes

When invoked, a class runs its __new__ method to create an instance, then __init__ to initialize it, and finally the instance is returned to the caller. Because there is no new operator in Python, calling a class is like calling a function.[2]

Class instances

If a class defines a __call__ method, then its instances may be invoked as functions—that's the subject of the next section.

Generator functions

Functions or methods that use the yield keyword in their body. When called, they return a generator object.

Native coroutine functions

Functions or methods defined with async def. When called, they return a coroutine object. Added in Python 3.5.

Asynchronous generator functions

Functions or methods defined with async def that have yield in their body. When called, they return an asynchronous generator for use with async for. Added in Python 3.6.

Generators, native coroutines, and asynchronous generator functions are unlike other callables in that their return values are never application data, but objects that require further processing to yield application data or perform useful work. Generator functions return iterators. Both are covered in Chapter 17. Native coroutine functions and asynchronous generator functions return objects that only work with the help of an asynchronous programming framework, such as *asyncio*. They are the subject of Chapter 21.

---

2 Calling a class usually creates an instance of that same class, but other behaviors are possible by overriding __new__. We'll see an example of this in "Flexible Object Creation with __new__" on page 847.

Given the variety of existing callable types in Python, the safest way to determine whether an object is callable is to use the `callable()` built-in:

```
>>> abs, str, 'Ni!'
(<built-in function abs>, <class 'str'>, 'Ni!')
>>> [callable(obj) for obj in (abs, str, 'Ni!')]
[True, True, False]
```

We now move on to building class instances that work as callable objects.

User-Defined Callable Types

Not only are Python functions real objects, but arbitrary Python objects may also be made to behave like functions. Implementing a `__call__` instance method is all it takes.

Example 7-8 implements a `BingoCage` class. An instance is built from any iterable, and stores an internal `list` of items, in random order. Calling the instance pops an item.[3]

Example 7-8. bingocall.py: A BingoCage does one thing: picks items from a shuffled list

```
import random

class BingoCage:

    def __init__(self, items):
        self._items = list(items)      ❶
        random.shuffle(self._items)    ❷

    def pick(self):                    ❸
        try:
            return self._items.pop()
        except IndexError:
            raise LookupError('pick from empty BingoCage')  ❹

    def __call__(self):                ❺
        return self.pick()
```

---

3 Why build a `BingoCage` when we already have `random.choice`? The `choice` function may return the same item multiple times, because the picked item is not removed from the collection given. Calling `BingoCage` never returns duplicate results—as long as the instance is filled with unique values.

❶ `__init__` accepts any iterable; building a local copy prevents unexpected side effects on any `list` passed as an argument.

❷ `shuffle` is guaranteed to work because `self._items` is a `list`.

❸ The main method.

❹ Raise exception with custom message if `self._items` is empty.

❺ Shortcut to `bingo.pick()`: `bingo()`.

Here is a simple demo of Example 7-8. Note how a `bingo` instance can be invoked as a function, and the `callable()` built-in recognizes it as a callable object:

```
>>> bingo = BingoCage(range(3))
>>> bingo.pick()
1
>>> bingo()
0
>>> callable(bingo)
True
```

A class implementing `__call__` is an easy way to create function-like objects that have some internal state that must be kept across invocations, like the remaining items in the `BingoCage`. Another good use case for `__call__` is implementing decorators. Decorators must be callable, and it is sometimes convenient to "remember" something between calls of the decorator (e.g., for memoization—caching the results of expensive computations for later use) or to split a complex implementation into separate methods.

The functional approach to creating functions with internal state is to use closures. Closures, as well as decorators, are the subject of Chapter 9.

Now let's explore the powerful syntax Python offers to declare function parameters and pass arguments into them.

From Positional to Keyword-Only Parameters

One of the best features of Python functions is the extremely flexible parameter handling mechanism. Closely related are the use of * and ** to unpack iterables and mappings into separate arguments when we call a function. To see these features in action, see the code for Example 7-9 and tests showing its use in Example 7-10.

Example 7-9. tag generates HTML elements; a keyword-only argument class_ is used to pass "class" attributes as a workaround because class is a keyword in Python

```python
def tag(name, *content, class_=None, **attrs):
    """Generate one or more HTML tags"""
    if class_ is not None:
        attrs['class'] = class_
    attr_pairs = (f' {attr}="{value}"' for attr, value
                    in sorted(attrs.items()))
    attr_str = ''.join(attr_pairs)
    if content:
        elements = (f'<{name}{attr_str}>{c}</{name}>'
                    for c in content)
        return '\n'.join(elements)
    else:
        return f'<{name}{attr_str} />'
```

The tag function can be invoked in many ways, as Example 7-10 shows.

Example 7-10. Some of the many ways of calling the tag function from Example 7-9

```
>>> tag('br')  ❶
'<br />'
>>> tag('p', 'hello')  ❷
'<p>hello</p>'
>>> print(tag('p', 'hello', 'world'))
<p>hello</p>
<p>world</p>
>>> tag('p', 'hello', id=33)  ❸
'<p id="33">hello</p>'
>>> print(tag('p', 'hello', 'world', class_='sidebar'))  ❹
<p class="sidebar">hello</p>
<p class="sidebar">world</p>
>>> tag(content='testing', name="img")  ❺
'<img content="testing" />'
>>> my_tag = {'name': 'img', 'title': 'Sunset Boulevard',
...           'src': 'sunset.jpg', 'class': 'framed'}
>>> tag(**my_tag)  ❻
'<img class="framed" src="sunset.jpg" title="Sunset Boulevard" />'
```

❶ A single positional argument produces an empty tag with that name.

❷ Any number of arguments after the first are captured by *content as a tuple.

❸ Keyword arguments not explicitly named in the tag signature are captured by **attrs as a dict.

❹ The class_ parameter can only be passed as a keyword argument.

❺ The first positional argument can also be passed as a keyword.

❻ Prefixing the `my_tag` dict with `**` passes all its items as separate arguments, which are then bound to the named parameters, with the remaining caught by `**attrs`. In this case we can have a `'class'` key in the arguments `dict`, because it is a string, and does not clash with the `class` reserved word.

Keyword-only arguments are a feature of Python 3. In Example 7-9, the `class_` parameter can only be given as a keyword argument—it will never capture unnamed positional arguments. To specify keyword-only arguments when defining a function, name them after the argument prefixed with `*`. If you don't want to support variable positional arguments but still want keyword-only arguments, put a `*` by itself in the signature, like this:

```
>>> def f(a, *, b):
...     return a, b
...
>>> f(1, b=2)
(1, 2)
>>> f(1, 2)
Traceback (most recent call last):
  File "<stdin>", line 1, in <module>
TypeError: f() takes 1 positional argument but 2 were given
```

Note that keyword-only arguments do not need to have a default value: they can be mandatory, like b in the preceding example.

Positional-Only Parameters

Since Python 3.8, user-defined function signatures may specify positional-only parameters. This feature always existed for built-in functions, such as `divmod(a, b)`, which can only be called with positional parameters, and not as `divmod(a=10, b=4)`.

To define a function requiring positional-only parameters, use `/` in the parameter list.

This example from "What's New In Python 3.8" (*https://fpy.li/7-7*) shows how to emulate the `divmod` built-in function:

```
def divmod(a, b, /):
    return (a // b, a % b)
```

All arguments to the left of the `/` are positional-only. After the `/`, you may specify other arguments, which work as usual.

The / in the parameter list is a syntax error in Python 3.7 or earlier.

For example, consider the `tag` function from Example 7-9. If we want the `name` parameter to be positional only, we can add a / after it in the function signature, like this:

```
def tag(name, /, *content, class_=None, **attrs):
    ...
```

You can find other examples of positional-only parameters in "What's New In Python 3.8" (*https://fpy.li/7-7*) and in PEP 570 (*https://fpy.li/pep570*).

After diving into Python's flexible argument declaration features, the remainder of this chapter covers the most useful packages in the standard library for programming in a functional style.

Packages for Functional Programming

Although Guido makes it clear that he did not design Python to be a functional programming language, a functional coding style can be used to good extent, thanks to first-class functions, pattern matching, and the support of packages like `operator` and `functools`, which we cover in the next two sections.

The operator Module

Often in functional programming it is convenient to use an arithmetic operator as a function. For example, suppose you want to multiply a sequence of numbers to calculate factorials without using recursion. To perform summation, you can use `sum`, but there is no equivalent function for multiplication. You could use `reduce`—as we saw in "Modern Replacements for map, filter, and reduce" on page 235—but this requires a function to multiply two items of the sequence. Example 7-11 shows how to solve this using `lambda`.

Example 7-11. Factorial implemented with reduce and an anonymous function

```
from functools import reduce

def factorial(n):
    return reduce(lambda a, b: a*b, range(1, n+1))
```

The operator module provides function equivalents for dozens of operators so you don't have to code trivial functions like lambda a, b: a*b. With it, we can rewrite Example 7-11 as Example 7-12.

Example 7-12. Factorial implemented with reduce and operator.mul

```
from functools import reduce
from operator import mul

def factorial(n):
    return reduce(mul, range(1, n+1))
```

Another group of one-trick lambdas that operator replaces are functions to pick items from sequences or read attributes from objects: itemgetter and attrgetter are factories that build custom functions to do that.

Example 7-13 shows a common use of itemgetter: sorting a list of tuples by the value of one field. In the example, the cities are printed sorted by country code (field 1). Essentially, itemgetter(1) creates a function that, given a collection, returns the item at index 1. That's easier to write and read than lambda fields: fields[1], which does the same thing.

Example 7-13. Demo of itemgetter to sort a list of tuples (data from Example 2-8)

```
>>> metro_data = [
...     ('Tokyo', 'JP', 36.933, (35.689722, 139.691667)),
...     ('Delhi NCR', 'IN', 21.935, (28.613889, 77.208889)),
...     ('Mexico City', 'MX', 20.142, (19.433333, -99.133333)),
...     ('New York-Newark', 'US', 20.104, (40.808611, -74.020386)),
...     ('São Paulo', 'BR', 19.649, (-23.547778, -46.635833)),
... ]
>>>
>>> from operator import itemgetter
>>> for city in sorted(metro_data, key=itemgetter(1)):
...     print(city)
...
('São Paulo', 'BR', 19.649, (-23.547778, -46.635833))
('Delhi NCR', 'IN', 21.935, (28.613889, 77.208889))
('Tokyo', 'JP', 36.933, (35.689722, 139.691667))
('Mexico City', 'MX', 20.142, (19.433333, -99.133333))
('New York-Newark', 'US', 20.104, (40.808611, -74.020386))
```

If you pass multiple index arguments to itemgetter, the function it builds will return tuples with the extracted values, which is useful for sorting on multiple keys:

```
>>> cc_name = itemgetter(1, 0)
>>> for city in metro_data:
...     print(cc_name(city))
```

```
...
('JP', 'Tokyo')
('IN', 'Delhi NCR')
('MX', 'Mexico City')
('US', 'New York-Newark')
('BR', 'São Paulo')
>>>
```

Because `itemgetter` uses the `[]` operator, it supports not only sequences but also mappings and any class that implements `__getitem__`.

A sibling of `itemgetter` is `attrgetter`, which creates functions to extract object attributes by name. If you pass `attrgetter` several attribute names as arguments, it also returns a tuple of values. In addition, if any argument name contains a . (dot), `attrgetter` navigates through nested objects to retrieve the attribute. These behaviors are shown in Example 7-14. This is not the shortest console session because we need to build a nested structure to showcase the handling of dotted attributes by `attrgetter`.

Example 7-14. Demo of `attrgetter` to process a previously defined list of `namedtuple` called `metro_data` (the same list that appears in Example 7-13)

```
>>> from collections import namedtuple
>>> LatLon = namedtuple('LatLon', 'lat lon')     ❶
>>> Metropolis = namedtuple('Metropolis', 'name cc pop coord')     ❷
>>> metro_areas = [Metropolis(name, cc, pop, LatLon(lat, lon))     ❸
...     for name, cc, pop, (lat, lon) in metro_data]
>>> metro_areas[0]
Metropolis(name='Tokyo', cc='JP', pop=36.933, coord=LatLon(lat=35.689722,
lon=139.691667))
>>> metro_areas[0].coord.lat     ❹
35.689722
>>> from operator import attrgetter
>>> name_lat = attrgetter('name', 'coord.lat')     ❺
>>>
>>> for city in sorted(metro_areas, key=attrgetter('coord.lat')):     ❻
...     print(name_lat(city))     ❼
...
('São Paulo', -23.547778)
('Mexico City', 19.433333)
('Delhi NCR', 28.613889)
('Tokyo', 35.689722)
('New York-Newark', 40.808611)
```

❶ Use `namedtuple` to define `LatLon`.

❷ Also define `Metropolis`.

❸ Build `metro_areas` list with `Metropolis` instances; note the nested tuple unpacking to extract `(lat, lon)` and use them to build the `LatLon` for the `coord` attribute of `Metropolis`.

❹ Reach into element `metro_areas[0]` to get its latitude.

❺ Define an `attrgetter` to retrieve the `name` and the `coord.lat` nested attribute.

❻ Use `attrgetter` again to sort list of cities by latitude.

❼ Use the `attrgetter` defined in ❺ to show only the city name and latitude.

Here is a partial list of functions defined in `operator` (names starting with _ are omitted, because they are mostly implementation details):

```
>>> [name for name in dir(operator) if not name.startswith('_')]
['abs', 'add', 'and_', 'attrgetter', 'concat', 'contains',
'countOf', 'delitem', 'eq', 'floordiv', 'ge', 'getitem', 'gt',
'iadd', 'iand', 'iconcat', 'ifloordiv', 'ilshift', 'imatmul',
'imod', 'imul', 'index', 'indexOf', 'inv', 'invert', 'ior',
'ipow', 'irshift', 'is_', 'is_not', 'isub', 'itemgetter',
'itruediv', 'ixor', 'le', 'length_hint', 'lshift', 'lt', 'matmul',
'methodcaller', 'mod', 'mul', 'ne', 'neg', 'not_', 'or_', 'pos',
'pow', 'rshift', 'setitem', 'sub', 'truediv', 'truth', 'xor']
```

Most of the 54 names listed are self-evident. The group of names prefixed with i and the name of another operator—e.g., iadd, iand, etc.—correspond to the augmented assignment operators—e.g., +=, &=, etc. These change their first argument in place, if it is mutable; if not, the function works like the one without the i prefix: it simply returns the result of the operation.

Of the remaining `operator` functions, `methodcaller` is the last we will cover. It is somewhat similar to `attrgetter` and `itemgetter` in that it creates a function on the fly. The function it creates calls a method by name on the object given as argument, as shown in Example 7-15.

Example 7-15. Demo of `methodcaller`: second test shows the binding of extra arguments

```
>>> from operator import methodcaller
>>> s = 'The time has come'
>>> upcase = methodcaller('upper')
>>> upcase(s)
'THE TIME HAS COME'
>>> hyphenate = methodcaller('replace', ' ', '-')
>>> hyphenate(s)
'The-time-has-come'
```

The first test in Example 7-15 is there just to show `methodcaller` at work, but if you need to use the `str.upper` as a function, you can just call it on the `str` class and pass a string as an argument, like this:

```
>>> str.upper(s)
'THE TIME HAS COME'
```

The second test in Example 7-15 shows that `methodcaller` can also do a partial application to freeze some arguments, like the `functools.partial` function does. That is our next subject.*Bold Text*opmod07

Freezing Arguments with functools.partial

The `functools` module provides several higher-order functions. We saw `reduce` in "Modern Replacements for map, filter, and reduce" on page 235. Another is `partial`: given a callable, it produces a new callable with some of the arguments of the original callable bound to predetermined values. This is useful to adapt a function that takes one or more arguments to an API that requires a callback with fewer arguments. Example 7-16 is a trivial demonstration.

Example 7-16. Using `partial` to use a two-argument function where a one-argument callable is required

```
>>> from operator import mul
>>> from functools import partial
>>> triple = partial(mul, 3)   ❶
>>> triple(7)   ❷
21
>>> list(map(triple, range(1, 10)))   ❸
[3, 6, 9, 12, 15, 18, 21, 24, 27]
```

❶ Create new `triple` function from `mul`, binding the first positional argument to 3.

❷ Test it.

❸ Use `triple` with `map`; `mul` would not work with `map` in this example.

A more useful example involves the `unicode.normalize` function that we saw in "Normalizing Unicode for Reliable Comparisons" on page 140. If you work with text from many languages, you may want to apply `unicode.normalize('NFC', s)` to any string `s` before comparing or storing it. If you do that often, it's handy to have an `nfc` function to do so, as in Example 7-17.

Example 7-17. Building a convenient Unicode normalizing function with `partial`

```
>>> import unicodedata, functools
>>> nfc = functools.partial(unicodedata.normalize, 'NFC')
>>> s1 = 'café'
>>> s2 = 'cafe\u0301'
>>> s1, s2
('café', 'café')
>>> s1 == s2
False
>>> nfc(s1) == nfc(s2)
True
```

`partial` takes a callable as first argument, followed by an arbitrary number of positional and keyword arguments to bind.

Example 7-18 shows the use of `partial` with the `tag` function from Example 7-9, to freeze one positional argument and one keyword argument.

Example 7-18. Demo of `partial` *applied to the function* `tag` *from Example 7-9*

```
>>> from tagger import tag
>>> tag
<function tag at 0x10206d1e0>      ❶
>>> from functools import partial
>>> picture = partial(tag, 'img', class_='pic-frame')      ❷
>>> picture(src='wumpus.jpeg')
'<img class="pic-frame" src="wumpus.jpeg" />'      ❸
>>> picture
functools.partial(<function tag at 0x10206d1e0>, 'img', class_='pic-frame')      ❹
>>> picture.func      ❺
<function tag at 0x10206d1e0>
>>> picture.args
('img',)
>>> picture.keywords
{'class_': 'pic-frame'}
```

❶ Import `tag` from Example 7-9 and show its ID.

❷ Create the `picture` function from `tag` by fixing the first positional argument with `'img'` and the `class_` keyword argument with `'pic-frame'`.

❸ `picture` works as expected.

❹ partial() returns a functools.partial object.[4]

❺ A functools.partial object has attributes providing access to the original function and the fixed arguments.

The functools.partialmethod function does the same job as partial, but is designed to work with methods.

The functools module also includes higher-order functions designed to be used as function decorators, such as cache and singledispatch, among others. Those functions are covered in Chapter 9, which also explains how to implement custom decorators.

Chapter Summary

The goal of this chapter was to explore the first-class nature of functions in Python. The main ideas are that you can assign functions to variables, pass them to other functions, store them in data structures, and access function attributes, allowing frameworks and tools to act on that information.

Higher-order functions, a staple of functional programming, are common in Python. The sorted, min, and max built-ins, and functools.partial are examples of commonly used higher-order functions in the language. Using map, filter, and reduce is not as common as it used to be, thanks to list comprehensions (and similar constructs like generator expressions) and the addition of reducing built-ins like sum, all, and any.

Callables come in nine different flavors since Python 3.6, from the simple functions created with lambda to instances of classes implementing __call__. Generators and coroutines are also callable, although their behavior is very different from other callables. All callables can be detected by the callable() built-in. Callables offer rich syntax for declaring formal parameters, including keyword-only parameters, positional-only parameters, and annotations.

Lastly, we covered some functions from the operator module and functools.partial, which facilitate functional programming by minimizing the need for the functionally challenged lambda syntax.

---

4 The source code (*https://fpy.li/7-9*) for *functools.py* reveals that functools.partial is implemented in C and is used by default. If that is not available, a pure-Python implementation of partial is available since Python 3.4.

Further Reading

The next chapters continue our exploration of programming with function objects. Chapter 8 is devoted to type hints in function parameters and return values. Chapter 9 dives into function decorators—a special kind of higher-order function—and the closure mechanism that makes them work. Chapter 10 shows how first-class functions can simplify some classic object-oriented design patterns.

In *The Python Language Reference*, "3.2. The standard type hierarchy" (*https://fpy.li/ 7-10*) presents the nine callable types, along with all the other built-in types.

Chapter 7 of the *Python Cookbook*, 3rd ed. (O'Reilly), by David Beazley and Brian K. Jones, is an excellent complement to the current chapter as well as Chapter 9 of this book, covering mostly the same concepts with a different approach.

See PEP 3102—Keyword-Only Arguments (*https://fpy.li/pep3102*) if you are interested in the rationale and use cases for that feature.

A great introduction to functional programming in Python is A. M. Kuchling's "Python Functional Programming HOWTO" (*https://fpy.li/7-5*). The main focus of that text, however, is the use of iterators and generators, which are the subject of Chapter 17.

The StackOverflow question "Python: Why is functools.partial necessary?" (*https:// fpy.li/7-12*) has a highly informative (and funny) reply by Alex Martelli, coauthor of the classic *Python in a Nutshell* (O'Reilly).

Reflecting on the question "Is Python a functional language?", I created one of my favorite talks, "Beyond Paradigms," which I presented at PyCaribbean, PyBay, and PyConDE. See the slides (*https://fpy.li/7-13*) and video (*https://fpy.li/7-14*) from the Berlin presentation—where I met Miroslav Šedivý and Jürgen Gmach, two of the technical reviewers of this book.

Soapbox

Is Python a Functional Language?

Sometime in the year 2000 I attended a Zope workshop at Zope Corporation in the United States when Guido van Rossum dropped by the classroom (he was not the instructor). In the Q&A that followed, somebody asked him which features of Python were borrowed from other languages. Guido's answer: "Everything that is good in Python was stolen from other languages."

Shriram Krishnamurthi, professor of Computer Science at Brown University, starts his "Teaching Programming Languages in a Post-Linnaean Age" paper (*https://fpy.li/ 7-15*) with this:

> Programming language "paradigms" are a moribund and tedious legacy of a bygone age. Modern language designers pay them no respect, so why do our courses slavishly adhere to them?

In that paper, Python is mentioned by name in this passage:

> What else to make of a language like Python, Ruby, or Perl? Their designers have no patience for the niceties of these Linnaean hierarchies; they borrow features as they wish, creating mélanges that utterly defy characterization.

Krishnamurthi argues that instead of trying to classify languages in some taxonomy, it's more useful to consider them as aggregations of features. His ideas inspired my talk "Beyond Paradigms," mentioned at the end of "Further Reading" on page 250.

Even if it was not Guido's goal, endowing Python with first-class functions opened the door to functional programming. In his post, "Origins of Python's *Functional Features*" (*https://fpy.li/7-1*), he says that map, filter, and reduce were the motivation for adding lambda to Python in the first place. All of these features were contributed together by Amrit Prem for Python 1.0 in 1994, according to Misc/HISTORY (*https://fpy.li/7-17*) in the CPython source code.

Functions like map, filter, and reduce first appeared in Lisp, the original functional language. However, Lisp does not limit what can be done inside a lambda, because everything in Lisp is an expression. Python uses a statement-oriented syntax in which expressions cannot contain statements, and many language constructs are statements —including try/catch, which is what I miss most often when writing lambdas. This is the price to pay for Python's highly readable syntax.[5] Lisp has many strengths, but readability is not one of them.

Ironically, stealing the list comprehension syntax from another functional language— Haskell—significantly diminished the need for map and filter, and also for lambda.

Besides the limited anonymous function syntax, the biggest obstacle to wider adoption of functional programming idioms in Python is the lack of tail-call elimination, an optimization that allows memory-efficient computation of a function that makes a recursive call at the "tail" of its body. In another blog post, "Tail Recursion Elimination" (*https://fpy.li/7-18*), Guido gives several reasons why such optimization is not a good fit for Python. That post is a great read for the technical arguments, but even more so because the first three and most important reasons given are usability issues. It is no accident that Python is a pleasure to use, learn, and teach. Guido made it so.

So there you have it: Python is not, by design, a functional language—whatever that means. Python just borrows a few good ideas from functional languages.

---

5 There is also the problem of lost indentation when pasting code to web forums, but I digress.

The Problem with Anonymous Functions

Beyond the Python-specific syntax constraints, anonymous functions have a serious drawback in any language: they have no name.

I am only half joking here. Stack traces are easier to read when functions have names. Anonymous functions are a handy shortcut, people have fun coding with them, but sometimes they get carried away—especially if the language and environment encourage deep nesting of anonymous functions, like JavaScript on Node.js do. Lots of nested anonymous functions make debugging and error handling hard. Asynchronous programming in Python is more structured, perhaps because the limited `lambda` syntax prevents its abuse and forces a more explicit approach. Promises, futures, and deferreds are concepts used in modern asynchronous APIs. Along with coroutines, they provide an escape from the so-called "callback hell." I promise to write more about asynchronous programming in the future, but this subject must be deferred to Chapter 21.

## CHAPTER 8

Type Hints in Functions

It should also be emphasized that **Python will remain a dynamically typed language, and the authors have no desire to ever make type hints mandatory, even by convention.**

— Guido van Rossum, Jukka Lehtosalo, and Łukasz Langa, PEP 484—Type Hints[1]

Type hints are the biggest change in the history of Python since the unification of types and classes (*https://fpy.li/descr101*) in Python 2.2, released in 2001. However, type hints do not benefit all Python users equally. That's why they should always be optional.

PEP 484—Type Hints (*https://fpy.li/pep484*) introduced syntax and semantics for explicit type declarations in function arguments, return values, and variables. The goal is to help developer tools find bugs in Python codebases via static analysis, i.e., without actually running the code through tests.

The main beneficiaries are professional software engineers using IDEs (Integrated Development Environments) and CI (Continuous Integration). The cost-benefit analysis that makes type hints attractive to that group does not apply to all users of Python.

Python's user base is much wider than that. It includes scientists, traders, journalists, artists, makers, analysts, and students in many fields—among others. For most of them, the cost of learning type hints is likely higher—unless they already know a language with static types, subtyping, and generics. The benefits will be lower for many of those users, given how they interact with Python, and the smaller size of their codebases and teams—often "teams" of one. Python's default dynamic typing is

---

1 PEP 484—Type Hints (*https://fpy.li/8-1*), "Rationale and Goals"; bold emphasis retained from the original.

simpler and more expressive when writing code for exploring data and ideas, as in data science, creative computing, and learning,

This chapter focuses on Python's type hints in function signatures. Chapter 15 explores type hints in the context of classes, and other typing module features.

The major topics in this chapter are:

- A hands-on introduction to gradual typing with Mypy
- The complementary perspectives of duck typing and nominal typing
- Overview of the main categories of types that can appear in annotations—this is about 60% of the chapter
- Type hinting variadic parameters (*args, **kwargs)
- Limitations and downsides of type hints and static typing

What's New in This Chapter

This chapter is completely new. Type hints appeared in Python 3.5 after I wrapped up the first edition of *Fluent Python*.

Given the limitations of a static type system, the best idea of PEP 484 was to introduce a *gradual type system*. Let's begin by defining what that means.

About Gradual Typing

PEP 484 introduced a *gradual type system* to Python. Other languages with gradual type systems are Microsoft's TypeScript, Dart (the language of the Flutter SDK, created by Google), and Hack (a dialect of PHP supported by Facebook's HHVM virtual machine). The Mypy type checker itself started as a language: a gradually typed dialect of Python with its own interpreter. Guido van Rossum convinced the creator of Mypy, Jukka Lehtosalo, to make it a tool for checking annotated Python code.

A gradual type system:

Is optional

By default, the type checker should not emit warnings for code that has no type hints. Instead, the type checker assumes the Any type when it cannot determine the type of an object. The Any type is considered compatible with all other types.

Does not catch type errors at runtime

Type hints are used by static type checkers, linters, and IDEs to raise warnings. They do not prevent inconsistent values from being passed to functions or assigned to variables at runtime.

Does not enhance performance

Type annotations provide data that could, in theory, allow optimizations in the generated bytecode, but such optimizations are not implemented in any Python runtime that I am aware in of July 2021.[2]

The best usability feature of gradual typing is that annotations are always optional.

With static type systems, most type constraints are easy to express, many are cumbersome, some are hard, and a few are impossible.[3] You may very well write an excellent piece of Python code, with good test coverage and passing tests, but still be unable to add type hints that satisfy a type checker. That's OK; just leave out the problematic type hints and ship it!

Type hints are optional at all levels: you can have entire packages with no type hints, you can silence the type checker when you import one of those packages into a module where you use type hints, and you can add special comments to make the type checker ignore specific lines in your code.

Seeking 100% coverage of type hints is likely to stimulate type hinting without proper thought, only to satisfy the metric. It will also prevent teams from making the most of the power and flexibility of Python. Code without type hints should naturally be accepted when annotations would make an API less user-friendly, or unduly complicate its implementation.

Gradual Typing in Practice

Let's see how gradual typing works in practice, starting with a simple function and gradually adding type hints to it, guided by Mypy.

---

2 A just-in-time compiler like the one in PyPy has much better data than type hints: it monitors the Python program as it runs, detects the concrete types in use, and generates optimized machine code for those concrete types.

3 For example, recursive types are not supported as of July 2021—see typing module issue #182, Define a JSON type (*https://fpy.li/8-2*) and Mypy issue #731, Support recursive types (*https://fpy.li/8-3*).

There are several Python type checkers compatible with PEP 484, including Google's pytype (*https://fpy.li/8-4*), Microsoft's Pyright (*https://fpy.li/8-5*), Facebook's Pyre (*https://fpy.li/8-6*)—in addition to type checkers embedded in IDEs such as PyCharm. I picked Mypy (*https://fpy.li/mypy*) for the examples because it's the best known. However, one of the others may be a better fit for some projects or teams. Pytype, for example, is designed to handle codebases with no type hints and still provide useful advice. It is more lenient than Mypy, and can also generate annotations for your code.

We will annotate a `show_count` function that returns a string with a count and a singular or plural word, depending on the count:

```
>>> show_count(99, 'bird')
'99 birds'
>>> show_count(1, 'bird')
'1 bird'
>>> show_count(0, 'bird')
'no birds'
```

Example 8-1 shows the source code of `show_count`, without annotations.

Example 8-1. show_count from messages.py without type hints

```
def show_count(count, word):
    if count == 1:
        return f'1 {word}'
    count_str = str(count) if count else 'no'
    return f'{count_str} {word}s'
```

Starting with Mypy

To begin type checking, I run the `mypy` command on the *messages.py* module:

```
…/no_hints/ $ pip install mypy
[lots of messages omitted...]
…/no_hints/ $ mypy messages.py
Success: no issues found in 1 source file
```

Mypy with default settings finds no problem with Example 8-1.

I am using Mypy 0.910, the most recent release as I review this in July 2021. The Mypy "Introduction" (*https://fpy.li/8-7*) warns that it "is officially beta software. There will be occasional changes that break backward compatibility." Mypy is giving me at least one report that is not the same I got when I wrote this chapter in April 2020. By the time you read this, you may get different results than shown here.

If a function signature has no annotations, Mypy ignores it by default—unless configured otherwise.

For Example 8-2, I also have `pytest` unit tests. This is the code in *messages_test.py*.

Example 8-2. messages_test.py without type hints

```
from pytest import mark

from messages import show_count

@mark.parametrize('qty, expected', [
    (1, '1 part'),
    (2, '2 parts'),
])
def test_show_count(qty, expected):
    got = show_count(qty, 'part')
    assert got == expected


def test_show_count_zero():
    got = show_count(0, 'part')
    assert got == 'no parts'
```

Now let's add type hints, guided by Mypy.

Making Mypy More Strict

The command-line option `--disallow-untyped-defs` makes Mypy flag any function definition that does not have type hints for all its parameters and for its return value.

Using `--disallow-untyped-defs` on the test file produces three errors and a note:

```
.../no_hints/ $ mypy --disallow-untyped-defs messages_test.py
messages.py:14: error: Function is missing a type annotation
messages_test.py:10: error: Function is missing a type annotation
messages_test.py:15: error: Function is missing a return type annotation
messages_test.py:15: note: Use "-> None" if function does not return a value
Found 3 errors in 2 files (checked 1 source file)
```

For the first steps with gradual typing, I prefer to use another option: `--disallow-incomplete-defs`. Initially, it tells me nothing:

```
.../no_hints/ $ mypy --disallow-incomplete-defs messages_test.py
Success: no issues found in 1 source file
```

Now I can add just the return type to `show_count` in *messages.py*:

```
def show_count(count, word) -> str:
```

This is enough to make Mypy look at it. Using the same command line as before to check *messages_test.py* will lead Mypy to look at *messages.py* again:

```
.../no_hints/ $ mypy --disallow-incomplete-defs messages_test.py
messages.py:14: error: Function is missing a type annotation
for one or more arguments
Found 1 error in 1 file (checked 1 source file)
```

Now I can gradually add type hints function by function, without getting warnings about functions that I haven't annotated. This is a fully annotated signature that satisfies Mypy:

```
def show_count(count: int, word: str) -> str:
```

> Instead of typing command-line options like `--disallow-incomplete-defs`, you can save your favorite as described in the Mypy configuration file (*https://fpy.li/8-8*) documentation. You can have global settings and per-module settings. Here is a simple *mypy.ini* to get started:
>
> ```
> [mypy]
> python_version = 3.9
> warn_unused_configs = True
> disallow_incomplete_defs = True
> ```

A Default Parameter Value

The `show_count` function in Example 8-1 only works with regular nouns. If the plural can't be spelled by appending an `'s'`, we should let the user provide the plural form, like this:

```
>>> show_count(3, 'mouse', 'mice')
'3 mice'
```

Let's do a little "type-driven development." First we add a test that uses that third argument. Don't forget to add the return type hint to the test function, otherwise Mypy will not check it.

```
def test_irregular() -> None:
    got = show_count(2, 'child', 'children')
    assert got == '2 children'
```

Mypy detects the error:

```
.../hints_2/ $ mypy messages_test.py
messages_test.py:22: error: Too many arguments for "show_count"
Found 1 error in 1 file (checked 1 source file)
```

Now I edit `show_count`, adding the optional `plural` parameter in Example 8-3.

Example 8-3. showcount from hints_2/messages.py with an optional parameter

```
def show_count(count: int, singular: str, plural: str = '') -> str:
    if count == 1:
```

```
        return f'1 {singular}'
    count_str = str(count) if count else 'no'
    if not plural:
        plural = singular + 's'
    return f'{count_str} {plural}'
```

Now Mypy reports "Success."

 Here is one typing mistake that Python does not catch. Can you spot it?

```
def hex2rgb(color=str) -> tuple[int, int, int]:
```

Mypy's error report is not very helpful:

```
colors.py:24: error: Function is missing a type
    annotation for one or more arguments
```

The type hint for the `color` argument should be `color: str`. I wrote `color=str`, which is not an annotation: it sets the default value of `color` to `str`.

In my experience, it's a common mistake and easy to overlook, especially in complicated type hints.

The following details are considered good style for type hints:

- No space between the parameter name and the `:`; one space after the `:`
- Spaces on both sides of the `=` that precedes a default parameter value

On the other hand, PEP 8 says there should be no spaces around the `=` if there is no type hint for that particular parameter.

Code Style: Use flake8 and blue

Instead of memorizing such silly rules, use tools like *flake8* (*https://fpy.li/8-9*) and *blue* (*https://fpy.li/8-10*). *flake8* reports on code styling, among many other issues, and *blue* rewrites source code according to (most) rules embedded in the *black* (*https://fpy.li/8-11*) code formatting tool.

Given the goal of enforcing a "standard" coding style, *blue* is better than *black* because it follows Python's own style of using single quotes by default, double quotes as an alternative:

```
>>> "I prefer single quotes"
'I prefer single quotes'
```

The preference for single quotes is embedded in `repr()`, among other places in CPython. The *doctest* (*https://fpy.li/doctest*) module depends on `repr()` using single quotes by default.

One of the authors of *blue* is Barry Warsaw (*https://fpy.li/8-12*), coauthor of PEP 8, Python core developer since 1994, and a member of Python's Steering Council from 2019 to present (July 2021). We are in very good company when we choose single quotes by default.

If you must use *black*, use the `black -S` option. Then it will leave your quotes as they are.

Using None as a Default

In Example 8-3, the parameter `plural` is annotated as `str`, and the default value is `''`, so there is no type conflict.

I like that solution, but in other contexts `None` is a better default. If the optional parameter expects a mutable type, then `None` is the only sensible default—as we saw in "Mutable Types as Parameter Defaults: Bad Idea" on page 214.

To have `None` as the default for the `plural` parameter, here is what the signature would look like:

```
from typing import Optional

def show_count(count: int, singular: str, plural: Optional[str] = None) -> str:
```

Let's unpack that:

- `Optional[str]` means `plural` may be a `str` or `None`.
- You must explicitly provide the default value = `None`.

If you don't assign a default value to `plural`, the Python runtime will treat it as a required parameter. Remember: at runtime, type hints are ignored.

Note that we need to import `Optional` from the `typing` module. When importing types, it's good practice to use the syntax `from typing import X` to reduce the length of the function signatures.

 `Optional` is not a great name, because that annotation does not make the parameter optional. What makes it optional is assigning a default value to the parameter. `Optional[str]` just means: the type of this parameter may be `str` or `NoneType`. In the Haskell and Elm languages, a similar type is named `Maybe`.

Now that we've had a first practical view of gradual typing, let's consider what the concept of *type* means in practice.

Types Are Defined by Supported Operations

> There are many definitions of the concept of type in the literature. Here we assume
> that type is a set of values and a set of functions that one can apply to these values.
>
> —PEP 483—The Theory of Type Hints

In practice, it's more useful to consider the set of supported operations as the defining characteristic of a type.[4]

For example, from the point of view of applicable operations, what are the valid types for x in the following function?

```
def double(x):
    return x * 2
```

The x parameter type may be numeric (`int`, `complex`, `Fraction`, `numpy.uint32`, etc.) but it may also be a sequence (`str`, `tuple`, `list`, `array`), an N-dimensional `numpy.array`, or any other type that implements or inherits a `__mul__` method that accepts an `int` argument.

However, consider this annotated `double`. Please ignore the missing return type for now, let's focus on the parameter type:

```
from collections import abc

def double(x: abc.Sequence):
    return x * 2
```

A type checker will reject that code. If you tell Mypy that x is of type `abc.Sequence`, it will flag x * 2 as an error because the `Sequence` ABC (*https://fpy.li/8-13*) does not implement or inherit the `__mul__` method. At runtime, that code will work with concrete sequences such as `str`, `tuple`, `list`, `array`, etc., as well as numbers, because at runtime the type hints are ignored. But the type checker only cares about what is explicitly declared, and `abc.Sequence` has no `__mul__`.

That's why the title of this section is "Types Are Defined by Supported Operations." The Python runtime accepts any object as the x argument for both versions of the double function. The computation x * 2 may work, or it may raise `TypeError` if the operation is not supported by x. In contrast, Mypy will declare x * 2 as wrong while

---

4 Python doesn't provide syntax to control the set of possible values for a type—except in `Enum` types. For example, using type hints you can't define `Quantity` as an integer between 1 and 1000, or `AirportCode` as a 3-letter combination. NumPy offers `uint8`, `int16`, and other machine-oriented numeric types, but in the Python standard library we only have types with very small sets of values (`NoneType`, `bool`) or extremely large sets (`float`, `int`, `str`, all possible tuples, etc.).

analyzing the annotated `double` source code, because it's an unsupported operation for the declared type: `x: abc.Sequence`.

In a gradual type system, we have the interplay of two different views of types:

Duck typing

The view adopted by Smalltalk—the pioneering object-oriented language—as well as Python, JavaScript, and Ruby. Objects have types, but variables (including parameters) are untyped. In practice, it doesn't matter what the declared type of the object is, only what operations it actually supports. If I can invoke `birdie.quack()`, then `birdie` is a duck in this context. By definition, duck typing is only enforced at runtime, when operations on objects are attempted. This is more flexible than *nominal typing*, at the cost of allowing more errors at runtime.[5]

Nominal typing

The view adopted by C++, Java, and C#, supported by annotated Python. Objects and variables have types. But objects only exist at runtime, and the type checker only cares about the source code where variables (including parameters) are annotated with type hints. If `Duck` is a subclass of `Bird`, you can assign a `Duck` instance to a parameter annotated as `birdie: Bird`. But in the body of the function, the type checker considers the call `birdie.quack()` illegal, because `birdie` is nominally a `Bird`, and that class does not provide the `.quack()` method. It doesn't matter if the actual argument at runtime is a `Duck`, because nominal typing is enforced statically. The type checker doesn't run any part of the program, it only reads the source code. This is more rigid than *duck typing*, with the advantage of catching some bugs earlier in a build pipeline, or even as the code is typed in an IDE.

Example 8-4 is a silly example that contrasts duck typing and nominal typing, as well as static type checking and runtime behavior.[6]

Example 8-4. birds.py

```
class Bird:
    pass

class Duck(Bird):     ❶
```

---

5 Duck typing is an implicit form of *structural typing*, which Python ≥ 3.8 also supports with the introduction of `typing.Protocol`. This is covered later in this chapter—in "Static Protocols" on page 287—with more details in Chapter 13.

6 Inheritance is often overused and hard to justify in examples that are realistic yet simple, so please accept this animal example as a quick illustration of subtyping.

```
    def quack(self):
        print('Quack!')

def alert(birdie):        ❷
    birdie.quack()

def alert_duck(birdie: Duck) -> None:    ❸
    birdie.quack()

def alert_bird(birdie: Bird) -> None:    ❹
    birdie.quack()
```

❶ Duck is a subclass of Bird.

❷ alert has no type hints, so the type checker ignores it.

❸ alert_duck takes one argument of type Duck.

❹ alert_bird takes one argument of type Bird.

Type checking *birds.py* with Mypy, we see a problem:

```
.../birds/ $ mypy birds.py
birds.py:16: error: "Bird" has no attribute "quack"
Found 1 error in 1 file (checked 1 source file)
```

Just by analyzing the source code, Mypy sees that alert_bird is problematic: the type hint declares the birdie parameter with type Bird, but the body of the function calls birdie.quack()—and the Bird class has no such method.

Now let's try to use the birds module in *daffy.py* in Example 8-5.

Example 8-5. daffy.py

```
from birds import *

daffy = Duck()
alert(daffy)          ❶
alert_duck(daffy)     ❷
alert_bird(daffy)     ❸
```

❶ Valid call, because alert has no type hints.

❷ Valid call, because alert_duck takes a Duck argument, and daffy is a Duck.

❸ Valid call, because alert_bird takes a Bird argument, and daffy is also a Bird—the superclass of Duck.

Running Mypy on *daffy.py* raises the same error about the `quack` call in the `alert_bird` function defined in *birds.py*:

```
.../birds/ $ mypy daffy.py
birds.py:16: error: "Bird" has no attribute "quack"
Found 1 error in 1 file (checked 1 source file)
```

But Mypy sees no problem with *daffy.py* itself: the three function calls are OK.

Now, if you run *daffy.py*, this is what you get:

```
.../birds/ $ python3 daffy.py
Quack!
Quack!
Quack!
```

Everything works! Duck typing FTW!

At runtime, Python doesn't care about declared types. It uses duck typing only. Mypy flagged an error in `alert_bird`, but calling it with `daffy` works fine at runtime. This may surprise many Pythonistas at first: a static type checker will sometimes find errors in programs that we know will execute.

However, if months from now you are tasked with extending the silly bird example, you may be grateful for Mypy. Consider this *woody.py* module, which also uses `birds`, in Example 8-6.

Example 8-6. woody.py

```
from birds import *

woody = Bird()
alert(woody)
alert_duck(woody)
alert_bird(woody)
```

Mypy finds two errors while checking *woody.py*:

```
.../birds/ $ mypy woody.py
birds.py:16: error: "Bird" has no attribute "quack"
woody.py:5: error: Argument 1 to "alert_duck" has incompatible type "Bird";
expected "Duck"
Found 2 errors in 2 files (checked 1 source file)
```

The first error is in *birds.py*: the `birdie.quack()` call in `alert_bird`, which we've seen before. The second error is in *woody.py*: woody is an instance of `Bird`, so the call `alert_duck(woody)` is invalid because that function requires a `Duck`. Every `Duck` is a `Bird`, but not every `Bird` is a `Duck`.

At runtime, none of the calls in *woody.py* succeed. The succession of failures is best illustrated in a console session with callouts in Example 8-7.

Example 8-7. Runtime errors and how Mypy could have helped

```
>>> from birds import *
>>> woody = Bird()
>>> alert(woody)  ❶
Traceback (most recent call last):
  ...
AttributeError: 'Bird' object has no attribute 'quack'
>>>
>>> alert_duck(woody)  ❷
Traceback (most recent call last):
  ...
AttributeError: 'Bird' object has no attribute 'quack'
>>>
>>> alert_bird(woody)  ❸
Traceback (most recent call last):
  ...
AttributeError: 'Bird' object has no attribute 'quack'
```

❶ Mypy could not detect this error because there are no type hints in `alert`.

❷ Mypy reported the problem: `Argument 1 to "alert_duck" has incompatible type "Bird"; expected "Duck"`.

❸ Mypy has been telling us since Example 8-4 that the body of the `alert_bird` function is wrong: `"Bird" has no attribute "quack"`.

This little experiment shows that duck typing is easier to get started and is more flexible, but allows unsupported operations to cause errors at runtime. Nominal typing detects errors before runtime, but sometimes can reject code that actually runs—such as the call `alert_bird(daffy)` in Example 8-5. Even if it sometimes works, the `alert_bird` function is misnamed: its body does require an object that supports the `.quack()` method, which `Bird` doesn't have.

In this silly example, the functions are one-liners. But in real code they could be longer; they could pass the `birdie` argument to more functions, and the origin of the `birdie` argument could be many function calls away, making it hard to pinpoint the cause of a runtime error. The type checker prevents many such errors from ever happening at runtime.

The value of type hints is questionable in the tiny examples that fit in a book. The benefits grow with the size of the codebase. That's why companies with millions of lines of Python code—like Dropbox, Google, and Facebook—invested in teams and tools to support the company-wide adoption of type hints, and have significant and increasing portions of their Python codebases type checked in their CI pipelines.

In this section we explored the relationship of types and operations in duck typing and nominal typing, starting with the simple `double()` function—which we left without proper type hints. Now we will tour the most important types used for annotating functions. We'll see a good way to add type hints to `double()` when we reach "Static Protocols" on page 287. But before we get to that, there are more fundamental types to know.

Types Usable in Annotations

Pretty much any Python type can be used in type hints, but there are restrictions and recommendations. In addition, the `typing` module introduced special constructs with semantics that are sometimes surprising.

This section covers all the major types you can use with annotations:

- `typing.Any`
- Simple types and classes
- `typing.Optional` and `typing.Union`
- Generic collections, including tuples and mappings
- Abstract base classes
- Generic iterables
- Parameterized generics and `TypeVar`
- `typing.Protocols`—the key to *static duck typing*
- `typing.Callable`
- `typing.NoReturn`—a good way to end this list

We'll cover each of these in turn, starting with a type that is strange, apparently useless, but crucially important.

The Any Type

The keystone of any gradual type system is the `Any` type, also known as the *dynamic type*. When a type checker sees an untyped function like this:

```python
def double(x):
    return x * 2
```

it assumes this:

```python
def double(x: Any) -> Any:
    return x * 2
```

That means the x argument and the return value can be of any type, including different types. Any is assumed to support every possible operation.

Contrast Any with `object`. Consider this signature:

```
def double(x: object) -> object:
```

This function also accepts arguments of every type, because every type is a *subtype-of* `object`.

However, a type checker will reject this function:

```
def double(x: object) -> object:
    return x * 2
```

The problem is that `object` does not support the `__mul__` operation. This is what Mypy reports:

```
.../birds/ $ mypy double_object.py
double_object.py:2: error: Unsupported operand types for * ("object" and "int")
Found 1 error in 1 file (checked 1 source file)
```

More general types have narrower interfaces, i.e., they support fewer operations. The `object` class implements fewer operations than `abc.Sequence`, which implements fewer operations than `abc.MutableSequence`, which implements fewer operations than `list`.

But Any is a magic type that sits at the top and the bottom of the type hierarchy. It's simultaneously the most general type—so that an argument `n: Any` accepts values of every type—and the most specialized type, supporting every possible operation. At least, that's how the type checker understands Any.

Of course, no type can support every possible operation, so using Any prevents the type checker from fulfilling its core mission: detecting potentially illegal operations before your program crashes with a runtime exception.

Subtype-of versus consistent-with

Traditional object-oriented nominal type systems rely on the is *subtype-of* relationship. Given a class T1 and a subclass T2, then T2 is *subtype-of* T1.

Consider this code:

```
class T1:
    ...

class T2(T1):
    ...

def f1(p: T1) -> None:
    ...
```

```
o2 = T2()

f1(o2)  # OK
```

The call `f1(o2)` is an application of the Liskov Substitution Principle—LSP. Barbara Liskov[7] actually defined *is subtype-of* in terms of supported operations: if an object of type T2 substitutes an object of type T1 and the program still behaves correctly, then T2 is *subtype-of* T1.

Continuing from the previous code, this shows a violation of the LSP:

```
def f2(p: T2) -> None:
    ...

o1 = T1()

f2(o1)  # type error
```

From the point of view of supported operations, this makes perfect sense: as a subclass, T2 inherits and must support all operations that T1 does. So an instance of T2 can be used anywhere an instance of T1 is expected. But the reverse is not necessarily true: T2 may implement additional methods, so an instance of T1 may not be used everywhere an instance of T2 is expected. This focus on supported operations is reflected in the name *behavioral subtyping* (*https://fpy.li/8-15*), also used to refer to the LSP.

In a gradual type system, there is another relationship: *consistent-with*, which applies wherever *subtype-of* applies, with special provisions for type Any.

The rules for *consistent-with* are:

1. Given T1 and a subtype T2, then T2 is *consistent-with* T1 (Liskov substitution).

2. Every type is *consistent-with* Any: you can pass objects of every type to an argument declared of type Any.

3. Any is *consistent-with* every type: you can always pass an object of type Any where an argument of another type is expected.

Considering the previous definitions of the objects o1 and o2, here are examples of valid code, illustrating rules #2 and #3:

```
def f3(p: Any) -> None:
    ...
```

---

7 MIT Professor, programming language designer, and Turing Award recipient. Wikipedia: Barbara Liskov (*https://fpy.li/8-14*).

```
o0 = object()
o1 = T1()
o2 = T2()

f3(o0)  #
f3(o1)  #  all OK: rule #2
f3(o2)  #

def f4():  # implicit return type: `Any`
    ...

o4 = f4()  # inferred type: `Any`

f1(o4)  #
f2(o4)  #  all OK: rule #3
f3(o4)  #
```

Every gradual type system needs a wildcard type like Any.

> The verb "to infer" is a fancy synomym for "to guess," used in the context of type analysis. Modern type checkers in Python and other languages don't require type annotations everywhere because they can infer the type of many expressions. For example, if I write x = len(s) * 10, the type checker doesn't need an explicit local declaration to know that x is an int, as long as it can find type hints for the len built-in.

Now we can explore the rest of the types used in annotations.

Simple Types and Classes

Simple types like int, float, str, and bytes may be used directly in type hints. Concrete classes from the standard library, external packages, or user defined—French Deck, Vector2d, and Duck—may also be used in type hints.

Abstract base classes are also useful in type hints. We'll get back to them as we study collection types, and in "Abstract Base Classes" on page 278.

Among classes, *consistent-with* is defined like *subtype-of*: a subclass is *consistent-with* all its superclasses.

However, "practicality beats purity," so there is an important exception, which I discuss in the following tip.

int Is Consistent-With complex

There is no nominal subtype relationship between the built-in types int, float, and complex: they are direct subclasses of object. But PEP 484 declares (*https://fpy.li/cardxvi*) that int is *consistent-with* float, and float is *consistent-with* complex. It makes sense in practice: int implements all operations that float does, and int implements additional ones as well—bitwise operations like &, |, <<, etc. The end result is: int is *consistent-with* complex. For i = 3, i.real is 3, and i.imag is 0.

Optional and Union Types

We saw the Optional special type in "Using None as a Default" on page 260. It solves the problem of having None as a default, as in this example from that section:

```
from typing import Optional

def show_count(count: int, singular: str, plural: Optional[str] = None) -> str:
```

The construct Optional[str] is actually a shortcut for Union[str, None], which means the type of plural may be str or None.

Better Syntax for Optional and Union in Python 3.10

We can write str | bytes instead of Union[str, bytes] since Python 3.10. It's less typing, and there's no need to import Optional or Union from typing. Contrast the old and new syntax for the type hint of the plural parameter of show_count:

```
plural: Optional[str] = None     # before
plural: str | None = None        # after
```

The | operator also works with isinstance and issubclass to build the second argument: isinstance(x, int | str). For more, see PEP 604—Complementary syntax for Union[] (*https://fpy.li/pep604*).

The ord built-in function's signature is a simple example of Union—it accepts str or bytes, and returns an int:[8]

```
def ord(c: Union[str, bytes]) -> int: ...
```

Here is an example of a function that takes a str, but may return a str or a float:

---

[8] To be more precise, ord only accepts str or bytes with len(s) == 1. But the type system currently can't express this constraint.

```
from typing import Union

def parse_token(token: str) -> Union[str, float]:
    try:
        return float(token)
    except ValueError:
        return token
```

If possible, avoid creating functions that return Union types, as they put an extra bur-den on the user—forcing them to check the type of the returned value at runtime to know what to do with it. But the parse_token in the preceding code is a reasonable use case in the context of a simple expression evaluator.

 In "Dual-Mode str and bytes APIs" on page 155, we saw functions that accept either str or bytes arguments, but return str if the argument was str or bytes if the arguments was bytes. In those cases, the return type is determined by the input type, so Union is not an accurate solution. To properly annotate such functions, we need a type variable—presented in "Parameterized Generics and TypeVar" on page 282—or overloading, which we'll see in "Overloa-ded Signatures" on page 524.

Union[] requires at least two types. Nested Union types have the same effect as a flat-tened Union. So this type hint:

```
Union[A, B, Union[C, D, E]]
```

is the same as:

```
Union[A, B, C, D, E]
```

Union is more useful with types that are not consistent among themselves. For exam-ple: Union[int, float] is redundant because int is *consistent-with* float. If you just use float to annotate the parameter, it will accept int values as well.

Generic Collections

Most Python collections are heterogeneous. For example, you can put any mixture of different types in a list. However, in practice that's not very useful: if you put objects in a collection, you are likely to want to operate on them later, and usually this means they must share at least one common method.[9]

Generic types can be declared with type parameters to specify the type of the items they can handle.

---

9 In ABC—the language that most influenced the initial design of Python—each list was constrained to accept values of a single type: the type of the first item you put into it.

For example, a `list` can be parameterized to constrain the type of the elements in it, as you can see in Example 8-8.

Example 8-8. `tokenize` with type hints for Python ≥ 3.9

```
def tokenize(text: str) -> list[str]:
    return text.upper().split()
```

In Python ≥ 3.9, it means that `tokenize` returns a `list` where every item is of type `str`.

The annotations `stuff: list` and `stuff: list[Any]` mean the same thing: `stuff` is a list of objects of any type.

> If you are using Python 3.8 or earlier, the concept is the same, but you need more code to make it work—as explained in the optional box "Legacy Support and Deprecated Collection Types" on page 272.

PEP 585—Type Hinting Generics In Standard Collections (*https://fpy.li/8-16*) lists collections from the standard library accepting generic type hints. The following list shows only those collections that use the simplest form of generic type hint, `container[item]`:

`list`	`collections.deque`	`abc.Sequence`	`abc.MutableSequence`
`set`	`abc.Container`	`abc.Set`	`abc.MutableSet`
`frozenset`	`abc.Collection`		

The `tuple` and mapping types support more complex type hints, as we'll see in their respective sections.

As of Python 3.10, there is no good way to annotate `array.array`, taking into account the `typecode` constructor argument, which determines whether integers or floats are stored in the array. An even harder problem is how to type check integer ranges to prevent `OverflowError` at runtime when adding elements to arrays. For example, an `array` with `typecode='B'` can only hold `int` values from 0 to 255. Currently, Python's static type system is not up to this challenge.

Legacy Support and Deprecated Collection Types

(You may skip this box if you only use Python 3.9 or later.)

For Python 3.7 and 3.8, you need a `__future__` import to make the `[]` notation work with built-in collections such as `list`, as shown in Example 8-9.

Example 8-9. tokenize with type hints for Python ≥ 3.7

```
from __future__ import annotations

def tokenize(text: str) -> list[str]:
    return text.upper().split()
```

The __future__ import does not work with Python 3.6 or earlier. Example 8-10 shows how to annotate tokenize in a way that works with Python ≥ 3.5.

Example 8-10. tokenize with type hints for Python ≥ 3.5

```
from typing import List

def tokenize(text: str) -> List[str]:
    return text.upper().split()
```

To provide the initial support for generic type hints, the authors of PEP 484 created dozens of generic types in the typing module. Table 8-1 shows some of them. For the full list, visit the *typing* (*https://fpy.li/typing*) documentation.

Table 8-1. Some collection types and their type hint equivalents

Collection	Type hint equivalent
list	typing.List
set	typing.Set
frozenset	typing.FrozenSet
collections.deque	typing.Deque
collections.abc.MutableSequence	typing.MutableSequence
collections.abc.Sequence	typing.Sequence
collections.abc.Set	typing.AbstractSet
collections.abc.MutableSet	typing.MutableSet

PEP 585—Type Hinting Generics In Standard Collections (*https://fpy.li/pep585*) started a multiyear process to improve the usability of generic type hints. We can summarize that process in four steps:

1. Introduce from __future__ import annotations in Python 3.7 to enable the use of standard library classes as generics with list[str] notation.

2. Make that behavior the default in Python 3.9: list[str] now works without the future import.

3. Deprecate all the redundant generic types from the `typing` module.[10] Deprecation warnings will not be issued by the Python interpreter because type checkers should flag the deprecated types when the checked program targets Python 3.9 or newer.

4. Remove those redundant generic types in the first version of Python released five years after Python 3.9. At the current cadence, that could be Python 3.14, a.k.a Python Pi.

Now let's see how to annotate generic tuples.

Tuple Types

There are three ways to annotate tuple types:

- Tuples as records
- Tuples as records with named fields
- Tuples as immutable sequences

Tuples as records

If you're using a `tuple` as a record, use the `tuple` built-in and declare the types of the fields within [ ].

For example, the type hint would be `tuple[str, float, str]` to accept a tuple with city name, population, and country: (`'Shanghai'`, `24.28`, `'China'`).

Consider a function that takes a pair of geographic coordinates and returns a Geohash (*https://fpy.li/8-18*), used like this:

```
>>> shanghai = 31.2304, 121.4737
>>> geohash(shanghai)
'wtw3sjq6q'
```

Example 8-11 shows how `geohash` is defined, using the `geolib` package from PyPI.

Example 8-11. coordinates.py with the geohash function

```
from geolib import geohash as gh  # type: ignore  ❶

PRECISION = 9
```

---

10 One of my contributions to the `typing` module documentation was to add dozens of deprecation warnings as I reorganized the entries below "Module Contents" (*https://fpy.li/8-17*) into subsections, under the supervision of Guido van Rossum.

```
def geohash(lat_lon: tuple[float, float]) -> str:  ❷
    return gh.encode(*lat_lon, PRECISION)
```

❶ This comment stops Mypy from reporting that the `geolib` package doesn't have type hints.

❷ `lat_lon` parameter annotated as a `tuple` with two `float` fields.

 For Python < 3.9, import and use `typing.Tuple` in type hints. It is deprecated but will remain in the standard library at least until 2024.

Tuples as records with named fields

To annotate a tuple with many fields, or specific types of tuple your code uses in many places, I highly recommend using `typing.NamedTuple`, as seen in Chapter 5. Example 8-12 shows a variation of Example 8-11 with `NamedTuple`.

Example 8-12. coordinates_named.py with the NamedTuple Coordinate and the geo hash function

```
from typing import NamedTuple

from geolib import geohash as gh  # type: ignore

PRECISION = 9

class Coordinate(NamedTuple):
    lat: float
    lon: float

def geohash(lat_lon: Coordinate) -> str:
    return gh.encode(*lat_lon, PRECISION)
```

As explained in "Overview of Data Class Builders" on page 164, `typing.NamedTuple` is a factory for `tuple` subclasses, so `Coordinate` is *consistent-with* `tuple[float, float]` but the reverse is not true—after all, `Coordinate` has extra methods added by `NamedTuple`, like `._asdict()`, and could also have user-defined methods.

In practice, this means that it is type safe to pass a `Coordinate` instance to the `dis play` function defined in the following:

```
def display(lat_lon: tuple[float, float]) -> str:
    lat, lon = lat_lon
    ns = 'N' if lat >= 0 else 'S'
```

```
    ew = 'E' if lon >= 0 else 'W'
    return f'{abs(lat):0.1f}°{ns}, {abs(lon):0.1f}°{ew}'
```

Tuples as immutable sequences

To annotate tuples of unspecified length that are used as immutable lists, you must specify a single type, followed by a comma and ... (that's Python's ellipsis token, made of three periods, not Unicode U+2026—HORIZONTAL ELLIPSIS).

For example, `tuple[int, ...]` is a tuple with `int` items.

The ellipsis indicates that any number of elements >= 1 is acceptable. There is no way to specify fields of different types for tuples of arbitrary length.

The annotations `stuff: tuple[Any, ...]` and `stuff: tuple` mean the same thing: `stuff` is a tuple of unspecified length with objects of any type.

Here is a `columnize` function that transforms a sequence into a table of rows and cells in the form of a list of tuples with unspecified lengths. This is useful to display items in columns, like this:

```
>>> animals = 'drake fawn heron ibex koala lynx tahr xerus yak zapus'.split()
>>> table = columnize(animals)
>>> table
[('drake', 'koala', 'yak'), ('fawn', 'lynx', 'zapus'), ('heron', 'tahr'),
 ('ibex', 'xerus')]
>>> for row in table:
...     print(''.join(f'{word:10}' for word in row))
...
drake     koala     yak
fawn      lynx      zapus
heron     tahr
ibex      xerus
```

Example 8-13 shows the implementation of `columnize`. Note the return type:

```
list[tuple[str, ...]]
```

Example 8-13. columnize.py returns a list of tuples of strings

```
from collections.abc import Sequence

def columnize(
    sequence: Sequence[str], num_columns: int = 0
) -> list[tuple[str, ...]]:
    if num_columns == 0:
        num_columns = round(len(sequence) ** 0.5)
    num_rows, reminder = divmod(len(sequence), num_columns)
    num_rows += bool(reminder)
    return [tuple(sequence[i::num_rows]) for i in range(num_rows)]
```

Generic Mappings

Generic mapping types are annotated as `MappingType[KeyType, ValueType]`. The built-in `dict` and the mapping types in `collections` and `collections.abc` accept that notation in Python ≥ 3.9. For earlier versions, you must use `typing.Dict` and other mapping types from the `typing` module, as described in "Legacy Support and Deprecated Collection Types" on page 272.

Example 8-14 shows a practical use of a function returning an inverted index (*https://fpy.li/8-19*) to search Unicode characters by name—a variation of Example 4-21 more suitable for server-side code that we'll study in Chapter 21.

Given starting and ending Unicode character codes, `name_index` returns a `dict[str, set[str]]`, which is an inverted index mapping each word to a set of characters that have that word in their names. For example, after indexing ASCII characters from 32 to 64, here are the sets of characters mapped to the words `'SIGN'` and `'DIGIT'`, and how to find the character named `'DIGIT EIGHT'`:

```
>>> index = name_index(32, 65)
>>> index['SIGN']
{'$', '>', '=', '+', '<', '%', '#'}
>>> index['DIGIT']
{'8', '5', '6', '2', '3', '0', '1', '4', '7', '9'}
>>> index['DIGIT'] & index['EIGHT']
{'8'}
```

Example 8-14 shows the source code for *charindex.py* with the `name_index` function. Besides a `dict[]` type hint, this example has three features appearing for the first time in the book.

Example 8-14. charindex.py

```python
import sys
import re
import unicodedata
from collections.abc import Iterator

RE_WORD = re.compile(r'\w+')
STOP_CODE = sys.maxunicode + 1

def tokenize(text: str) -> Iterator[str]:  ❶
    """return iterable of uppercased words"""
    for match in RE_WORD.finditer(text):
        yield match.group().upper()

def name_index(start: int = 32, end: int = STOP_CODE) -> dict[str, set[str]]:
    index: dict[str, set[str]] = {}  ❷
    for char in (chr(i) for i in range(start, end)):
        if name := unicodedata.name(char, ''):  ❸
```

```
        for word in tokenize(name):
            index.setdefault(word, set()).add(char)
    return index
```

❶ tokenize is a generator function. Chapter 17 is about generators.

❷ The local variable index is annotated. Without the hint, Mypy says: Need type annotation for 'index' (hint: "index: dict[<type>, <type>] = ..."}.

❸ I used the walrus operator := in the if condition. It assigns the result of the uni codedata.name() call to name, and the whole expression evaluates to that result. When the result is ' ', that's falsy, and the index is not updated.[11]

 When using a dict as a record, it is common to have all keys of the str type, with values of different types depending on the keys. That is covered in "TypedDict" on page 530.

Abstract Base Classes

> Be conservative in what you send, be liberal in what you accept.
>
> —Postel's law, a.k.a. the Robustness Principle

Table 8-1 lists several abstract classes from collections.abc. Ideally, a function should accept arguments of those abstract types—or their typing equivalents before Python 3.9—and not concrete types. This gives more flexibility to the caller.

Consider this function signature:

```
from collections.abc import Mapping

def name2hex(name: str, color_map: Mapping[str, int]) -> str:
```

Using abc.Mapping allows the caller to provide an instance of dict, defaultdict, ChainMap, a UserDict subclass, or any other type that is a *subtype-of* Mapping.

In contrast, consider this signature:

```
def name2hex(name: str, color_map: dict[str, int]) -> str:
```

Now color_map must be a dict or one of its subtypes, such as defaultDict or OrderedDict. In particular, a subclass of collections.UserDict would not pass the type check for color_map, despite being the recommended way to create

---

11 I use := when it makes sense in a few examples, but I don't cover it in the book. Please see PEP 572—Assignment Expressions (*https://fpy.li/pep572*) for all the gory details.

user-defined mappings, as we saw in "Subclassing UserDict Instead of dict" on page 97. Mypy would reject a UserDict or an instance of a class derived from it, because UserDict is not a subclass of dict; they are siblings. Both are subclasses of abc.MutableMapping.[12]

Therefore, in general it's better to use abc.Mapping or abc.MutableMapping in parameter type hints, instead of dict (or typing.Dict in legacy code). If the name2hex function doesn't need to mutate the given color_map, the most accurate type hint for color_map is abc.Mapping. That way, the caller doesn't need to provide an object that implements methods like setdefault, pop, and update, which are part of the MutableMapping interface, but not of Mapping. This has to do with the second part of Postel's law: "Be liberal in what you accept."

Postel's law also tells us to be conservative in what we send. The return value of a function is always a concrete object, so the return type hint should be a concrete type, as in the example from "Generic Collections" on page 271—which uses list[str]:

```
def tokenize(text: str) -> list[str]:
    return text.upper().split()
```

Under the entry of typing.List (*https://fpy.li/8-20*), the Python documentation says:

> Generic version of list. Useful for annotating return types. To annotate arguments it is preferred to use an abstract collection type such as Sequence or Iterable.

A similar comment appears in the entries for typing.Dict (*https://fpy.li/8-21*) and typing.Set (*https://fpy.li/8-22*).

Remember that most ABCs from collections.abc and other concrete classes from collections, as well as built-in collections, support generic type hint notation like collections.deque[str] starting with Python 3.9. The corresponding typing collections are only needed to support code written in Python 3.8 or earlier. The full list of classes that became generic appears in the "Implementation" (*https://fpy.li/8-16*) section of PEP 585—Type Hinting Generics In Standard Collections (*https://fpy.li/pep585*).

To wrap up our discussion of ABCs in type hints, we need to talk about the numbers ABCs.

---

12 Actually, dict is a virtual subclass of abc.MutableMapping. The concept of a virtual subclass is explained in Chapter 13. For now, know that issubclass(dict, abc.MutableMapping) is True, despite the fact that dict is implemented in C and does not inherit anything from abc.MutableMapping, but only from object.

The fall of the numeric tower

The numbers (*https://fpy.li/8-24*) package defines the so-called *numeric tower* described in PEP 3141—A Type Hierarchy for Numbers (*https://fpy.li/pep3141*). The tower is linear hierarchy of ABCs, with Number at the top:

- Number
- Complex
- Real
- Rational
- Integral

Those ABCs work perfectly well for runtime type checking, but they are not supported for static type checking. The "Numeric Tower" (*https://fpy.li/cardxvi*) section of PEP 484 rejects the numbers ABCs and dictates that the built-in types complex, float, and int should be treated as special cases, as explained in "int Is Consistent-With complex" on page 270.

We'll come back to this issue in "The numbers ABCs and Numeric Protocols" on page 480, in Chapter 13, which is devoted to contrasting protocols and ABCs.

In practice, if you want to annotate numeric arguments for static type checking, you have a few options:

1. Use one of the concrete types int, float, or complex—as recommended by PEP 488.
2. Declare a union type like Union[float, Decimal, Fraction].
3. If you want to avoid hardcoding concrete types, use numeric protocols like Sup portsFloat, covered in "Runtime Checkable Static Protocols" on page 470.

The upcoming section "Static Protocols" on page 287 is a prerequisite for understanding the numeric protocols.

Meanwhile, let's get to one of the most useful ABCs for type hints: Iterable.

Iterable

The typing.List (*https://fpy.li/8-20*) documentation I just quoted recommends Sequence and Iterable for function parameter type hints.

One example of the Iterable argument appears in the math.fsum function from the standard library:

```
def fsum(__seq: Iterable[float]) -> float:
```

Stub Files and the Typeshed Project

As of Python 3.10, the standard library has no annotations, but Mypy, PyCharm, etc. can find the necessary type hints in the Typeshed (*https://fpy.li/8-26*) project, in the form of *stub files*: special source files with a *.pyi* extension that have annotated function and method signatures, without the implementation—much like header files in C.

The signature for `math.fsum` is in */stdlib/2and3/math.pyi* (*https://fpy.li/8-27*). The leading underscores in __seq are a PEP 484 convention for positional-only parameters, explained in "Annotating Positional Only and Variadic Parameters" on page 295.

Example 8-15 is another example using an `Iterable` parameter that produces items that are `tuple[str, str]`. Here is how the function is used:

```
>>> l33t = [('a', '4'), ('e', '3'), ('i', '1'), ('o', '0')]
>>> text = 'mad skilled noob powned leet'
>>> from replacer import zip_replace
>>> zip_replace(text, l33t)
'm4d sk1ll3d n00b p0wn3d l33t'
```

Example 8-15 shows how it's implemented.

Example 8-15. replacer.py

```
from collections.abc import Iterable

FromTo = tuple[str, str]  ❶

def zip_replace(text: str, changes: Iterable[FromTo]) -> str:  ❷
    for from_, to in changes:
        text = text.replace(from_, to)
    return text
```

❶ FromTo is a *type alias*: I assigned `tuple[str, str]` to FromTo, to make the signature of `zip_replace` more readable.

❷ changes needs to be an `Iterable[FromTo]`; that's the same as `Iterable[tuple[str, str]]`, but shorter and easier to read.

Explicit TypeAlias in Python 3.10

PEP 613—Explicit Type Aliases (*https://fpy.li/pep613*) introduced a special type, TypeAlias, to make the assignments that create type aliases more visible and easier to type check. Starting with Python 3.10, this is the preferred way to create type aliases:

```
from typing import TypeAlias

FromTo: TypeAlias = tuple[str, str]
```

abc.Iterable versus abc.Sequence

Both `math.fsum` and `replacer.zip_replace` must iterate over the entire `Iterable` arguments to return a result. Given an endless iterable such as the `itertools.cycle` generator as input, these functions would consume all memory and crash the Python process. Despite this potential danger, it is fairly common in modern Python to offer functions that accept an `Iterable` input even if they must process it completely to return a result. That gives the caller the option of providing input data as a generator instead of a prebuilt sequence, potentially saving a lot of memory if the number of input items is large.

On the other hand, the `columnize` function from Example 8-13 needs a `Sequence` parameter, and not an `Iterable`, because it must get the `len()` of the input to compute the number of rows up front.

Like `Sequence`, `Iterable` is best used as a parameter type. It's too vague as a return type. A function should be more precise about the concrete type it returns.

Closely related to `Iterable` is the `Iterator` type, used as a return type in Example 8-14. We'll get back to it in Chapter 17, which is about generators and classic iterators.

Parameterized Generics and TypeVar

A parameterized generic is a generic type, written as `list[T]`, where `T` is a type variable that will be bound to a specific type with each usage. This allows a parameter type to be reflected on the result type.

Example 8-16 defines `sample`, a function that takes two arguments: a `Sequence` of elements of type `T`, and an `int`. It returns a `list` of elements of the same type `T`, picked at random from the first argument.

Example 8-16 shows the implementation.

Example 8-16. sample.py

```
from collections.abc import Sequence
from random import shuffle
from typing import TypeVar

T = TypeVar('T')

def sample(population: Sequence[T], size: int) -> list[T]:
    if size < 1:
        raise ValueError('size must be >= 1')
    result = list(population)
    shuffle(result)
    return result[:size]
```

Here are two examples of why I used a type variable in `sample`:

- If called with a tuple of type `tuple[int, ...]`—which is *consistent-with* `Sequence[int]`—then the type parameter is `int`, so the return type is `list[int]`.

- If called with a `str`—which is *consistent-with* `Sequence[str]`—then the type parameter is `str`, so the return type is `list[str]`.

Why Is TypeVar Needed?

The authors of PEP 484 wanted to introduce type hints by adding the `typing` module and not changing anything else in the language. With clever metaprogramming they could make the `[]` operator work on classes like `Sequence[T]`. But the name of the `T` variable inside the brackets must be defined somewhere—otherwise the Python interpreter would need deep changes to support generic type notation as special use of `[]`. That's why the `typing.TypeVar` constructor is needed: to introduce the variable name in the current namespace. Languages such as Java, C#, and TypeScript don't require the name of type variable to be declared beforehand, so they have no equivalent of Python's `TypeVar` class.

Another example is the `statistics.mode` function from the standard library, which returns the most common data point from a series.

Here is one usage example from the documentation (*https://fpy.li/8-28*):

```
>>> mode([1, 1, 2, 3, 3, 3, 3, 4])
3
```

Without using a `TypeVar`, `mode` could have the signature shown in Example 8-17.

Example 8-17. mode_float.py: mode that operates on float and subtypes[13]

```
from collections import Counter
from collections.abc import Iterable

def mode(data: Iterable[float]) -> float:
    pairs = Counter(data).most_common(1)
    if len(pairs) == 0:
        raise ValueError('no mode for empty data')
    return pairs[0][0]
```

Many uses of mode involve int or float values, but Python has other numerical types, and it is desirable that the return type follows the element type of the given Iterable. We can improve that signature using TypeVar. Let's start with a simple, but wrong, parameterized signature:

```
from collections.abc import Iterable
from typing import TypeVar

T = TypeVar('T')

def mode(data: Iterable[T]) -> T:
```

When it first appears in the signature, the type parameter T can be any type. The second time it appears, it will mean the same type as the first.

Therefore, every iterable is *consistent-with* Iterable[T], including iterables of unhashable types that collections.Counter cannot handle. We need to restrict the possible types assigned to T. We'll see two ways of doing that in the next two sections.

Restricted TypeVar

TypeVar accepts extra positional arguments to restrict the type parameter. We can improve the signature of mode to accept specific number types, like this:

```
from collections.abc import Iterable
from decimal import Decimal
from fractions import Fraction
from typing import TypeVar

NumberT = TypeVar('NumberT', float, Decimal, Fraction)

def mode(data: Iterable[NumberT]) -> NumberT:
```

That's better than before, and it was the signature for mode in the *statistics.pyi* (*https://fpy.li/8-30*) stub file on typeshed on May 25, 2020.

---

[13] The implementation here is simpler than the one in the Python standard library statistics (*https://fpy.li/8-29*) module.

However, the `statistics.mode` (*https://fpy.li/8-28*) documentation includes this example:

```
>>> mode(["red", "blue", "blue", "red", "green", "red", "red"])
'red'
```

In a hurry, we could just add `str` to the `NumberT` definition:

```
NumberT = TypeVar('NumberT', float, Decimal, Fraction, str)
```

That certainly works, but `NumberT` is badly misnamed if it accepts `str`. More importantly, we can't keep listing types forever, as we realize `mode` can deal with them. We can do better with another feature of `TypeVar`, introduced next.

Bounded TypeVar

Looking at the body of `mode` in Example 8-17, we see that the `Counter` class is used for ranking. `Counter` is based on `dict`, therefore the element type of the `data` iterable must be hashable.

At first, this signature may seem to work:

```
from collections.abc import Iterable, Hashable

def mode(data: Iterable[Hashable]) -> Hashable:
```

Now the problem is that the type of the returned item is `Hashable`: an ABC that implements only the __hash__ method. So the type checker will not let us do anything with the return value except call `hash()` on it. Not very useful.

The solution is another optional parameter of `TypeVar`: the bound keyword parameter. It sets an upper boundary for the acceptable types. In Example 8-18, we have `bound=Hashable`, which means the type parameter may be `Hashable` or any *subtype-of* it.[14]

Example 8-18. mode_hashable.py: same as Example 8-17, with a more flexible signature

```
from collections import Counter
from collections.abc import Iterable, Hashable
from typing import TypeVar

HashableT = TypeVar('HashableT', bound=Hashable)

def mode(data: Iterable[HashableT]) -> HashableT:
```

---

14 I contributed this solution to typeshed, and that's how `mode` is annotated on *statistics.pyi* (*https://fpy.li/8-32*) as of May 26, 2020.

```
    pairs = Counter(data).most_common(1)
    if len(pairs) == 0:
        raise ValueError('no mode for empty data')
    return pairs[0][0]
```

To summarize:

- A restricted type variable will be set to one of the types named in the TypeVar declaration.
- A bounded type variable will be set to the inferred type of the expression—as long as the inferred type is *consistent-with* the boundary declared in the bound= keyword argument of TypeVar.

 It is unfortunate that the keyword argument to declare a bounded TypeVar is named bound=, because the verb "to bind" is commonly used to mean setting the value of a variable, which in the reference semantics of Python is best described as binding a name to the value. It would have been less confusing if the keyword argument was named boundary=.

The typing.TypeVar constructor has other optional parameters—covariant and contravariant—that we'll cover in Chapter 15, "Variance" on page 548.

Let's conclude this introduction to TypeVar with AnyStr.

The AnyStr predefined type variable

The typing module includes a predefined TypeVar named AnyStr. It's defined like this:

```
AnyStr = TypeVar('AnyStr', bytes, str)
```

AnyStr is used in many functions that accept either bytes or str, and return values of the given type.

Now, on to typing.Protocol, a new feature of Python 3.8 that can support more Pythonic use of type hints.

Static Protocols

In object-oriented programming, the concept of a "protocol" as an informal interface is as old as Smalltalk, and is an essential part of Python from the beginning. However, in the context of type hints, a protocol is a typing.Protocol subclass defining an interface that a type checker can verify. Both kinds of protocols are covered in Chapter 13. This is just a brief introduction in the context of function annotations.

The Protocol type, as presented in PEP 544—Protocols: Structural subtyping (static duck typing) (*https://fpy.li/pep544*), is similar to interfaces in Go: a protocol type is defined by specifying one or more methods, and the type checker verifies that those methods are implemented where that protocol type is required.

In Python, a protocol definition is written as a typing.Protocol subclass. However, classes that *implement* a protocol don't need to inherit, register, or declare any relationship with the class that *defines* the protocol. It's up to the type checker to find the available protocol types and enforce their usage.

Here is a problem that can be solved with the help of Protocol and TypeVar. Suppose you want to create a function top(it, n) that returns the largest n elements of the iterable it:

```
>>> top([4, 1, 5, 2, 6, 7, 3], 3)
[7, 6, 5]
>>> l = 'mango pear apple kiwi banana'.split()
>>> top(l, 3)
['pear', 'mango', 'kiwi']
>>>
>>> l2 = [(len(s), s) for s in l]
>>> l2
[(5, 'mango'), (4, 'pear'), (5, 'apple'), (4, 'kiwi'), (6, 'banana')]
>>> top(l2, 3)
[(6, 'banana'), (5, 'mango'), (5, 'apple')]
```

A parameterized generic top would look like what's shown in Example 8-19.

Example 8-19. top function with an undefined T type parameter

```
def top(series: Iterable[T], length: int) -> list[T]:
    ordered = sorted(series, reverse=True)
    return ordered[:length]
```

The problem is how to constrain T? It cannot be Any or object, because the series must work with sorted. The sorted built-in actually accepts Iterable[Any], but that's because the optional parameter key takes a function that computes an arbitrary sort key from each element. What happens if you give `sorted` a list of plain objects but don't provide a `key` argument? Let's try that:

```
>>> l = [object() for _ in range(4)]
>>> l
[<object object at 0x10fc2fca0>, <object object at 0x10fc2fbb0>,
<object object at 0x10fc2fbc0>, <object object at 0x10fc2fbd0>]
>>> sorted(l)
Traceback (most recent call last):
  File "<stdin>", line 1, in <module>
TypeError: '<' not supported between instances of 'object' and 'object'
```

The error message shows that `sorted` uses the < operator on the elements of the iterable. Is this all it takes? Let's do another quick experiment:[15]

```
>>> class Spam:
...     def __init__(self, n): self.n = n
...     def __lt__(self, other): return self.n < other.n
...     def __repr__(self): return f'Spam({self.n})'
...
>>> l = [Spam(n) for n in range(5, 0, -1)]
>>> l
[Spam(5), Spam(4), Spam(3), Spam(2), Spam(1)]
>>> sorted(l)
[Spam(1), Spam(2), Spam(3), Spam(4), Spam(5)]
```

That confirms it: I can sort a list of `Spam` because `Spam` implements `__lt__`—the special method that supports the < operator.

So the `T` type parameter in Example 8-19 should be limited to types that implement `__lt__`. In Example 8-18 we needed a type parameter that implemented `__hash__`, so we were able to use `typing.Hashable` as the upper bound for the type parameter. But now there is no suitable type in `typing` or `abc` to use, so we need to create it.

Example 8-20 shows the new `SupportsLessThan` type, a `Protocol`.

Example 8-20. comparable.py: definition of a SupportsLessThan Protocol type

```
from typing import Protocol, Any

class SupportsLessThan(Protocol):    ❶
    def __lt__(self, other: Any) -> bool: ...    ❷
```

❶   A protocol is a subclass of `typing.Protocol`.

---

15 How wonderful it is to open an interactive console and rely on duck typing to explore language features like I just did. I badly miss this kind of exploration when I use languages that don't support it.

❷ The body of the protocol has one or more method definitions, with ... in their bodies.

A type T is *consistent-with* a protocol P if T implements all the methods defined in P, with matching type signatures.

Given SupportsLessThan, we can now define this working version of top in Example 8-21.

Example 8-21. top.py: definition of the top function using a TypeVar with bound=Sup portsLessThan

```python
from collections.abc import Iterable
from typing import TypeVar

from comparable import SupportsLessThan

LT = TypeVar('LT', bound=SupportsLessThan)

def top(series: Iterable[LT], length: int) -> list[LT]:
    ordered = sorted(series, reverse=True)
    return ordered[:length]
```

Let's test-drive top. Example 8-22 shows part of a test suite for use with pytest. It tries calling top first with a generator expression that yields tuple[int, str], and then with a list of object. With the list of object, we expect to get a TypeError exception.

Example 8-22. top_test.py: partial listing of the test suite for top

```python
from collections.abc import Iterator
from typing import TYPE_CHECKING  ❶

import pytest

from top import top

# several lines omitted

def test_top_tuples() -> None:
    fruit = 'mango pear apple kiwi banana'.split()
    series: Iterator[tuple[int, str]] = (  ❷
        (len(s), s) for s in fruit)
    length = 3
    expected = [(6, 'banana'), (5, 'mango'), (5, 'apple')]
    result = top(series, length)
    if TYPE_CHECKING:  ❸
        reveal_type(series)  ❹
```

```
        reveal_type(expected)
        reveal_type(result)
    assert result == expected

# intentional type error
def test_top_objects_error() -> None:
    series = [object() for _ in range(4)]
    if TYPE_CHECKING:
        reveal_type(series)
    with pytest.raises(TypeError) as excinfo:
        top(series, 3)  ❺
    assert "'<' not supported" in str(excinfo.value)
```

❶ The typing.TYPE_CHECKING constant is always False at runtime, but type check-ers pretend it is True when they are type checking.

❷ Explicit type declaration for the series variable, to make the Mypy output easier to read.[16]

❸ This if prevents the next three lines from executing when the test runs.

❹ reveal_type() cannot be called at runtime, because it is not a regular function but a Mypy debugging facility—that's why there is no import for it. Mypy will output one debugging message for each reveal_type() pseudofunction call, showing the inferred type of the argument.

❺ This line will be flagged as an error by Mypy.

The preceding tests pass—but they would pass anyway, with or without type hints in *top.py*. More to the point, if I check that test file with Mypy, I see that the TypeVar is working as intended. See the mypy command output in Example 8-23.

 As of Mypy 0.910 (July 2021), the output of reveal_type does not show precisely the types I declared in some cases, but compatible types instead. For example, I did not use typing.Iterator but used abc.Iterator. Please ignore this detail. The Mypy output is still useful. I will pretend this issue of Mypy is fixed when discussing the output.

---

16 Without this type hint, Mypy would infer the type of series as Generator[Tuple[builtins.int, buil tins.str*], None, None], which is verbose but *consistent-with* Iterator[tuple[int, str]], as we'll see in "Generic Iterable Types" on page 643.

Example 8-23. Output of mypy top_test.py (lines split for readability)

```
…/comparable/ $ mypy top_test.py
top_test.py:32: note:
    Revealed type is "typing.Iterator[Tuple[builtins.int, builtins.str]]" ❶
top_test.py:33: note:
    Revealed type is "builtins.list[Tuple[builtins.int, builtins.str]]"
top_test.py:34: note:
    Revealed type is "builtins.list[Tuple[builtins.int, builtins.str]]" ❷
top_test.py:41: note:
    Revealed type is "builtins.list[builtins.object*]" ❸
top_test.py:43: error:
    Value of type variable "LT" of "top" cannot be "object" ❹
Found 1 error in 1 file (checked 1 source file)
```

❶ In `test_top_tuples`, `reveal_type(series)` shows it is an `Iterator[tuple[int, str]]`—which I explicitly declared.

❷ `reveal_type(result)` confirms that the type returned by the `top` call is what I wanted: given the type of `series`, the `result` is `list[tuple[int, str]]`.

❸ In `test_top_objects_error`, `reveal_type(series)` shows it is `list[object*]`. Mypy puts a `*` after any type that was inferred: I did not annotate the type of `series` in this test.

❹ Mypy flags the error that this test intentionally triggers: the element type of the `Iterable series` cannot be `object` (it must be of type `SupportsLessThan`).

A key advantage of a protocol type over ABCs is that a type doesn't need any special declaration to be *consistent-with* a protocol type. This allows a protocol to be created leveraging preexisting types, or types implemented in code that we do not control. I don't need to derive or register `str`, `tuple`, `float`, `set`, etc. with `SupportsLessThan` to use them where a `SupportsLessThan` parameter is expected. They only need to implement `__lt__`. And the type checker will still be able do its job, because `SupportsLessThan` is explicitly defined as a `Protocol`—in contrast with the implicit protocols that are common with duck typing, which are invisible to the type checker.

The special `Protocol` class was introduced in PEP 544—Protocols: Structural subtyping (static duck typing) (*https://fpy.li/pep544*). Example 8-21 demonstrates why this feature is known as *static duck typing*: the solution to annotate the `series` parameter of `top` was to say "The nominal type of `series` doesn't matter, as long as it implements the `__lt__` method." Python's duck typing always allowed us to say that implicitly, leaving static type checkers clueless. A type checker can't read CPython's source code in C, or perform console experiments to find out that `sorted` only requires that the elements support `<`.

Now we can make duck typing explicit for static type checkers. That's why it makes sense to say that `typing.Protocol` gives us *static duck typing*.[17]

There's more to see about `typing.Protocol`. We'll come back to it in Part IV, where Chapter 13 contrasts structural typing, duck typing, and ABCs—another approach to formalizing protocols. In addition, "Overloaded Signatures" on page 524 (Chapter 15) explains how to declare overloaded function signatures with `@typing.overload`, and includes an extensive example using `typing.Protocol` and a bounded `TypeVar`.

 `typing.Protocol` makes it possible to annotate the `double` function presented in "Types Are Defined by Supported Operations" on page 261 without losing functionality. The key is to define a protocol class with the `__mul__` method. I invite you to do that as an exercise. The solution appears in "The Typed `double` Function" on page 468 (Chapter 13).

Callable

To annotate callback parameters or callable objects returned by higher-order functions, the `collections.abc` module provides the `Callable` type, available in the `typing` module for those not yet using Python 3.9. A `Callable` type is parameterized like this:

```
Callable[[ParamType1, ParamType2], ReturnType]
```

The parameter list—`[ParamType1, ParamType2]`—can have zero or more types.

Here is an example in the context of a `repl` function, part of a simple interactive interpreter we'll see in "Pattern Matching in lis.py: A Case Study" on page 673:[18]

```
def repl(input_fn: Callable[[Any], str] = input) -> None:
```

During normal usage, the `repl` function uses Python's `input` built-in to read expressions from the user. However, for automated testing or for integration with other input sources, `repl` accepts an optional `input_fn` parameter: a `Callable` with the same parameter and return types as `input`.

The built-in `input` has this signature on typeshed:

```
def input(__prompt: Any = ...) -> str: ...
```

The `input` signature is *consistent-with* this `Callable` type hint:

---

17 I don't know who invented the term *static duck typing*, but it became more popular with the Go language, which has interface semantics that are more like Python's protocols than the nominal interfaces of Java.

18 REPL stands for Read-Eval-Print-Loop, the basic behavior of interactive interpreters.

```
Callable[[Any], str]
```

There is no syntax to annotate optional or keyword argument types. The documentation (*https://fpy.li/8-34*) of `typing.Callable` says "such function types are rarely used
as callback types." If you need a type hint to match a function with a flexible signature, replace the whole parameter list with . . .—like this:

```
Callable[..., ReturnType]
```

The interaction of generic type parameters with a type hierarchy introduces a new
typing concept: variance.

Variance in Callable types

Imagine a temperature control system with a simple `update` function as shown in
Example 8-24. The `update` function calls the `probe` function to get the current temperature, and calls `display` to show the temperature to the user. Both `probe` and `dis
play` are passed as arguments to `update` for didactic reasons. The goal of the example
is to contrast two `Callable` annotations: one with a return type, the other with a
parameter type.

Example 8-24. Illustrating variance.

```
from collections.abc import Callable

def update(              ❶
        probe: Callable[[], float],       ❷
        display: Callable[[float], None]  ❸
    ) -> None:
    temperature = probe()
    # imagine lots of control code here
    display(temperature)

def probe_ok() -> int:   ❹
    return 42

def display_wrong(temperature: int) -> None:  ❺
    print(hex(temperature))

update(probe_ok, display_wrong)  # type error  ❻

def display_ok(temperature: complex) -> None:  ❼
    print(temperature)

update(probe_ok, display_ok)  # OK  ❽
```

❶ update takes two callables as arguments.

❷ probe must be a callable that takes no arguments and returns a `float`.

❸ `display` takes a `float` argument and returns `None`.

❹ `probe_ok` is *consistent-with* `Callable[[], float]` because returning an `int` does not break code that expects a `float`.

❺ `display_wrong` is not *consistent-with* `Callable[[float], None]` because there's no guarantee that a function that expects an `int` can handle a `float`; for example, Python's `hex` function accepts an `int` but rejects a `float`.

❻ Mypy flags this line because `display_wrong` is incompatible with the type hint in the `display` parameter of `update`.

❼ `display_ok` is *consistent-with* `Callable[[float], None]` because a function that accepts a `complex` can also handle a `float` argument.

❽ Mypy is happy with this line.

To summarize, it's OK to provide a callback that returns an `int` when the code expects a callback that returns a `float`, because an `int` value can always be used where a `float` is expected.

Formally, we say that `Callable[[], int]` is *subtype-of* `Callable[[], float]`—as `int` is *subtype-of* `float`. This means that `Callable` is *covariant* on the return type because the *subtype-of* relationship of the types `int` and `float` is in the same direction as the relationship of the `Callable` types that use them as return types.

On the other hand, it's a type error to provide a callback that takes a `int` argument when a callback that handles a `float` is required.

Formally, `Callable[[int], None]` is not a *subtype-of* `Callable[[float], None]`. Although `int` is *subtype-of* `float`, in the parameterized `Callable` type the relationship is reversed: `Callable[[float], None]` is *subtype-of* `Callable[[int], None]`. Therefore we say that `Callable` is *contravariant* on the declared parameter types.

"Variance" on page 548 in Chapter 15 explains variance with more details and examples of invariant, covariant, and contravariant types.

For now, rest assured that most parameterized generic types are *invariant*, therefore simpler. For example, if I declare scores: list[float], that tells me exactly what I can assign to scores. I can't assign objects declared as list[int] or list[complex]:

- A list[int] object is not acceptable because it cannot hold float values which my code may need to put into scores.
- A list[complex] object is not acceptable because my code may need to sort scores to find the median, but complex does not provide __lt__, therefore list[complex] is not sortable.

Now we get to the last special type we'll cover in this chapter.

NoReturn

This is a special type used only to annotate the return type of functions that never return. Usually, they exist to raise exceptions. There are dozens of such functions in the standard library.

For example, sys.exit() raises SystemExit to terminate the Python process.

Its signature in typeshed is:

```
def exit(__status: object = ...) -> NoReturn: ...
```

The __status parameter is positional only, and it has a default value. Stub files don't spell out the default values, they use ... instead. The type of __status is object, which means it may also be None, therefore it would be redundant to mark it Optional[object].

In Chapter 24, Example 24-6 uses NoReturn in the __flag_unknown_attrs, a method designed to produce a user-friendly and comprehensive error message, and then raise AttributeError.

The last section in this epic chapter is about positional and variadic parameters.

Annotating Positional Only and Variadic Parameters

Recall the tag function from Example 7-9. The last time we saw its signature was in "Positional-Only Parameters" on page 242:

```
def tag(name, /, *content, class_=None, **attrs):
```

Here is tag, fully annotated, written in several lines—a common convention for long signatures, with line breaks the way the *blue* (*https://fpy.li/8-10*) formatter would do it:

```
from typing import Optional

def tag(
    name: str,
    /,
    *content: str,
    class_: Optional[str] = None,
    **attrs: str,
) -> str:
```

Note the type hint *content: str for the arbitrary positional parameters; this means all those arguments must be of type str. The type of the content local variable in the function body will be tuple[str, ...].

The type hint for the arbitrary keyword arguments is **attrs: str in this example, therefore the type of attrs inside the function will be dict[str, str]. For a type hint like **attrs: float, the type of attrs in the function would be dict[str, float].``

If the attrs parameter must accept values of different types, you'll need to use a Union[] or Any: **attrs: Any.

The / notation for positional-only parameters is only available in Python ≥ 3.8. In Python 3.7 or earlier, that's a syntax error. The PEP 484 convention (*https://fpy.li/ 8-36*) is to prefix each positional-only parameter name with two underscores. Here is the tag signature again, now in two lines, using the PEP 484 convention:

```
from typing import Optional

def tag(__name: str, *content: str, class_: Optional[str] = None,
        **attrs: str) -> str:
```

Mypy understands and enforces both ways of declaring positional-only parameters.

To close this chapter, let's briefly consider the limits of type hints and the static type system they support.

Imperfect Typing and Strong Testing

Maintainers of large corporate codebases report that many bugs are found by static type checkers and fixed more cheaply than if the bugs were discovered only after the code is running in production. However, it's essential to note that automated testing was standard practice and widely adopted long before static typing was introduced in the companies that I know about.

Even in the contexts where they are most beneficial, static typing cannot be trusted as the ultimate arbiter of correctness. It's not hard to find:

False positives
> Tools report type errors on code that is correct.

False negatives
> Tools don't report type errors on code that is incorrect.

Also, if we are forced to type check everything, we lose some of the expressive power of Python:

- Some handy features can't be statically checked; for example, argument unpacking like `config(**settings)`.
- Advanced features like properties, descriptors, metaclasses, and metaprogramming in general are poorly supported or beyond comprehension for type checkers.
- Type checkers lag behind Python releases, rejecting or even crashing while analyzing code with new language features—for more than a year in some cases.

Common data constraints cannot be expressed in the type system—even simple ones. For example, type hints are unable to ensure "quantity must be an integer > 0" or "label must be a string with 6 to 12 ASCII letters." In general, type hints are not helpful to catch errors in business logic.

Given those caveats, type hints cannot be the mainstay of software quality, and making them mandatory without exception would amplify the downsides.

Consider a static type checker as one of the tools in a modern CI pipeline, along with test runners, linters, etc. The point of a CI pipeline is to reduce software failures, and automated tests catch many bugs that are beyond the reach of type hints. Any code you can write in Python, you can test in Python—with or without type hints.

> The title and conclusion of this section were inspired by Bruce Eckel's article "Strong Typing vs. Strong Testing" (*https://fpy.li/ 8-37*), also published in the anthology *The Best Software Writing I* (*https://fpy.li/8-38*), edited by Joel Spolsky (Apress). Bruce is a fan of Python and author of books about C++, Java, Scala, and Kotlin. In that post, he tells how he was a static typing advocate until he learned Python and concluded: "If a Python program has adequate unit tests, it can be as robust as a C++, Java, or C# program with adequate unit tests (although the tests in Python will be faster to write)."

This wraps up our coverage of Python's type hints for now. They are also the main focus of Chapter 15, which covers generic classes, variance, overloaded signatures, type casting, and more. Meanwhile, type hints will make guest appearances in several examples throughout the book.

Chapter Summary

We started with a brief introduction to the concept of gradual typing and then switched to a hands-on approach. It's hard to see how gradual typing works without a tool that actually reads the type hints, so we developed an annotated function guided by Mypy error reports.

Back to the idea of gradual typing, we explored how it is a hybrid of Python's traditional duck typing and the nominal typing more familiar to users of Java, C++, and other statically typed languages.

Most of the chapter was devoted to presenting the major groups of types used in annotations. Many of the types we covered are related to familiar Python object types, such as collections, tuples, and callables—extended to support generic notation like Sequence[float]. Many of those types are temporary surrogates implemented in the typing module before the standard types were changed to support generics in Python 3.9.

Some of the types are special entities. Any, Optional, Union, and NoReturn have nothing to do with actual objects in memory, but exist only in the abstract domain of the type system.

We studied parameterized generics and type variables, which bring more flexibility to type hints without sacrificing type safety.

Parameterized generics become even more expressive with the use of Protocol. Because it appeared only in Python 3.8, Protocol is not widely used yet—but it is hugely important. Protocol enables static duck typing: the essential bridge between Python's duck-typed core and the nominal typing that allows static type checkers to catch bugs.

While covering some of these types, we experimented with Mypy to see type checking errors and inferred types with the help of Mypy's magic reveal_type() function.

The final section covered how to annotate positional-only and variadic parameters.

Type hints are a complex and evolving topic. Fortunately, they are an optional feature. Let us keep Python accessible to the widest user base and stop preaching that all Python code should have type hints—as I've seen in public sermons by typing evangelists.

Our BDFL[19] emeritus led this push toward type hints in Python, so it's only fair that this chapter starts and ends with his words:

> I wouldn't like a version of Python where I was morally obligated to add type hints all the time. I really do think that type hints have their place but there are also plenty of times that it's not worth it, and it's so wonderful that you can choose to use them.[20]
>
> —Guido van Rossum

Further Reading

Bernát Gábor wrote in his excellent post, "The state of type hints in Python" (*https:// fpy.li/8-41*):

> Type hints should be used whenever unit tests are worth writing.

I am a big fan of testing, but I also do a lot of exploratory coding. When I am exploring, tests and type hints are not helpful. They are a drag.

Gábor's post is one of the best introductions to Python's type hints that I found, along with Geir Arne Hjelle's "Python Type Checking (Guide)" (*https://fpy.li/8-42*). "Hypermodern Python Chapter 4: Typing" (*https://fpy.li/8-43*) by Claudio Jolowicz is a shorter introduction that also covers runtime type checking validation.

For deeper coverage, the Mypy documentation (*https://fpy.li/8-44*) is the best source. It is valuable regardless of the type checker you are using, because it has tutorial and reference pages about Python typing in general—not just about the Mypy tool itself. There you will also find a handy cheat sheets (*https://fpy.li/8-45*) and a very useful page about common issues and solutions (*https://fpy.li/8-46*).

The `typing` (*https://fpy.li/typing*) module documentation is a good quick reference, but it doesn't go into much detail. PEP 483—The Theory of Type Hints (*https://fpy.li/ pep483*) includes a deep explanation about variance, using `Callable` to illustrate contravariance. The ultimate references are the PEP documents related to typing. There are more than 20 of them already. The intended audience of PEPs are Python core developers and Python's Steering Council, so they assume a lot of prior knowledge and are certainly not light reading.

As mentioned, Chapter 15 covers more typing topics, and "Further Reading" on page 559 provides additional references, including Table 15-1, listing typing PEPs approved or under discussion as of late 2021.

---

19 "Benevolent Dictator For Life." See Guido van van Rossum on the "Origin of BDFL" (*https://fpy.li/bdfl*).

20 From the YouTube video, "Type Hints by Guido van Rossum (March 2015)" (*https://fpy.li/8-39*). Quote starts at 13'40" (*https://fpy.li/8-40*). I did some light editing for clarity.

"Awesome Python Typing" (*https://fpy.li/8-47*) is a valuable collection of links to tools and references.

Soapbox

Just Ride

> Forget the ultralight, uncomfortable bikes, flashy jerseys, clunky shoes that clip onto tiny pedals, the grinding out of endless miles. Instead, ride like you did when you were a kid—just get on your bike and discover the pure joy of riding it.
>
> —Grant Petersen, *Just Ride: A Radically Practical Guide to Riding Your Bike* (Workman Publishing)

If coding is not your whole profession, but a useful tool in your profession, or something you do to learn, tinker, and enjoy, you probably don't need type hints any more than most bikers need shoes with stiff soles and metal cleats.

Just code.

The Cognitive Effect of Typing

I worry about the effect type hints will have on Python coding style.

I agree that users of most APIs benefit from type hints. But Python attracted me—among other reasons—because it provides functions that are so powerful that they replace entire APIs, and we can write similarly powerful functions ourselves. Consider the max() (*https://fpy.li/8-48*) built-in. It's powerful, yet easy to understand. But I will show in "Max Overload" on page 525 that it takes 14 lines of type hints to properly annotate it—not counting a typing.Protocol and a few TypeVar definitions to support those type hints.

I am concerned that strict enforcement of type hints in libraries will discourage programmers from even considering writing such functions in the future.

According to the English Wikipedia, "linguistic relativity" (*https://fpy.li/8-49*)—a.k.a. the Sapir–Whorf hypothesis— is a "principle claiming that the structure of a language affects its speakers' world view or cognition." Wikipedia further explains:

- The *strong* version says that language *determines* thought and that linguistic categories limit and determine cognitive categories.
- The *weak* version says that linguistic categories and usage only *influence* thought and decisions.

Linguists generally agree the strong version is false, but there is empirical evidence supporting the weak version.

I am not aware of specific studies with programming languages, but in my experience they've had a big impact on how I approach problems. The first programming language I used professionally was Applesoft BASIC in the age of 8-bit computers. Recursion was not directly supported by BASIC—you had to roll your own call stack to use it. So I never considered using recursive algorithms or data structures. I knew at some conceptual level such things existed, but they weren't part of my problem-solving toolbox.

Decades later when I started with Elixir, I enjoyed solving problems with recursion and overused it—until I discovered that many of my solutions would be simpler if I used existing functions from the Elixir Enum and Stream modules. I learned that idiomatic Elixir application-level code rarely has explicit recursive calls, but uses enums and streams that implement recursion under the hood.

Linguistic relativity could explain the widespread idea (also unproven) that learning different programming languages makes you a better programmer, particularly when the languages support different programming paradigms. Practicing Elixir made me more likely to apply functional patterns when I write Python or Go code.

Now, back to Earth.

The requests package would probably have a very different API if Kenneth Reitz was determined (or told by his boss) to annotate all its functions. His goal was to write an API that was easy to use, flexible, and powerful. He succeeded, given the amazing popularity of requests—in May 2020, it's #4 on PyPI Stats (*https://fpy.li/8-50*), with 2.6 million downloads a day. #1 is urllib3, a dependency of requests.

In 2017, the requests maintainers decided (*https://fpy.li/8-51*) not to spend their time writing type hints. One of the maintainers, Cory Benfield, had written an e-mail (*https://fpy.li/8-52*) stating:

> I think that libraries with *Pythonic* APIs are the least likely to take up this typing system because it will provide the least value to them.

In that message, Benfield gave this extreme example of a tentative type definition for the files keyword argument of requests.request() (*https://fpy.li/8-53*):

```
Optional[
  Union[
    Mapping[
      basestring,
      Union[
        Tuple[basestring, Optional[Union[basestring, file]]],
        Tuple[basestring, Optional[Union[basestring, file]],
              Optional[basestring]],
        Tuple[basestring, Optional[Union[basestring, file]],
              Optional[basestring], Optional[Headers]]
      ]
    ],
    Iterable[
```

```
      Tuple[
        basestring,
        Union[
          Tuple[basestring, Optional[Union[basestring, file]]],
          Tuple[basestring, Optional[Union[basestring, file]],
                Optional[basestring]],
          Tuple[basestring, Optional[Union[basestring, file]],
                Optional[basestring], Optional[Headers]]
        ]
      ]
    ]
  ]
```

And that assumes this definition:

```
Headers = Union[
  Mapping[basestring, basestring],
  Iterable[Tuple[basestring, basestring]],
]
```

Do you think `requests` would be the way it is if the maintainers insisted on 100% type hint coverage? SQLAlchemy is another important package that doesn't play well with type hints.

What makes these libraries great is embracing the dynamic nature of Python.

While there are benefits to type hints, there is also a price to pay.

First, there is the significant investment of understanding how the type system works. That's a one-time cost.

But there is also a recurring cost, forever.

We lose some of the expressive power of Python if we insist on type checking everything. Beautiful features like argument unpacking—e.g., `config(**settings)`—are beyond comprehension for type checkers.

If you want to have a call like `config(**settings)` type checked, you must spell every argument out. That brings me memories of Turbo Pascal code I wrote 35 years ago.

Libraries that use metaprogramming are hard or impossible to annotate. Surely metaprogramming can be abused, but it's also what makes many Python packages a joy to use.

If type hints are mandated top-down without exceptions in large companies, I bet soon we'll see people using code generation to reduce boilerplate in Python source-code—a common practice with less dynamic languages.

For some projects and contexts, type hints just don't make sense. Even in contexts where they mostly make sense, they don't make sense all the time. Any reasonable policy about the use of type hints must have exceptions.

Alan Kay, the Turing Award laureate who pioneered object-oriented programming, once said:

> Some people are completely religious about type systems and as a mathematician I love the idea of type systems, but nobody has ever come up with one that has enough scope.[21]

Thank Guido for optional typing. Let's use it as intended, and not aim to annotate everything into strict conformity to a coding style that looks like Java 1.5.

Duck Typing FTW

Duck typing fits my brain, and static duck typing is a good compromise allowing static type checking without losing a lot of flexibility that some nominal type systems only provide with a lot of complexity—if ever.

Before PEP 544, this whole idea of type hints seemed utterly unPythonic to me. I was very glad to see `typing.Protocol` land in Python. It brings balance to the force.

Generics or Specifics?

From a Python perspective, the typing usage of the term "generic" is backward. Common meanings of "generic" are "applicable to an entire class or group" or "without a brand name."

Consider `list` versus `list[str]`. The first is generic: it accepts any object. The second is specific: it only accepts `str`.

The term makes sense in Java, though. Before Java 1.5, all Java collections (except the magic `array`) were "specific": they could only hold `Object` references, so we had to cast the items that came out of a collection to use them. With Java 1.5, collections got type parameters, and became "generic."

---

21 Source: "A Conversation with Alan Kay" (*https://fpy.li/8-54*).

## CHAPTER 9

Decorators and Closures

There's been a number of complaints about the choice of the name "decorator" for this feature. The major one is that the name is not consistent with its use in the GoF book.[1] The name *decorator* probably owes more to its use in the compiler area—a syntax tree is walked and annotated.

—PEP 318—Decorators for Functions and Methods

Function decorators let us "mark" functions in the source code to enhance their behavior in some way. This is powerful stuff, but mastering it requires understanding closures—which is what we get when functions capture variables defined outside of their bodies.

The most obscure reserved keyword in Python is `nonlocal`, introduced in Python 3.0. You can have a profitable life as a Python programmer without ever using it if you adhere to a strict regimen of class-centered object orientation. However, if you want to implement your own function decorators, you must understand closures, and then the need for `nonlocal` becomes obvious.

Aside from their application in decorators, closures are also essential for any type of programming using callbacks, and for coding in a functional style when it makes sense.

The end goal of this chapter is to explain exactly how function decorators work, from the simplest registration decorators to the rather more complicated parameterized ones. However, before we reach that goal we need to cover:

---

1 That's the 1995 *Design Patterns* book by the so-called Gang of Four (Gamma et al., Addison-Wesley).

- How Python evaluates decorator syntax
- How Python decides whether a variable is local
- Why closures exist and how they work
- What problem is solved by `nonlocal`

With this grounding, we can tackle further decorator topics:

- Implementing a well-behaved decorator
- Powerful decorators in the standard library: `@cache`, `@lru_cache`, and `@single dispatch`
- Implementing a parameterized decorator

What's New in This Chapter

The caching decorator `functools.cache`—new in Python 3.9—is simpler than the traditional `functools.lru_cache`, so I present it first. The latter is covered in "Using lru_cache" on page 325, including the simplified form added in Python 3.8.

"Single Dispatch Generic Functions" on page 326 was expanded and now uses type hints, the preferred way to use `functools.singledispatch` since Python 3.7.

"Parameterized Decorators" on page 331 now includes a class-based example, Example 9-27.

I moved Chapter 10, "Design Patterns with First-Class Functions" to the end of Part II to improve the flow of the book. "Decorator-Enhanced Strategy Pattern" on page 355 is now in that chapter, along with other variations of the Strategy design pattern using callables.

We start with a very gentle introduction to decorators, and then proceed with the rest of the items listed in the chapter opening.

Decorators 101

A decorator is a callable that takes another function as an argument (the decorated function).

A decorator may perform some processing with the decorated function, and returns it or replaces it with another function or callable object.[2]

---

[2] If you replace "function" with "class" in the previous sentence, you have a brief description of what a class decorator does. Class decorators are covered in Chapter 24.

In other words, assuming an existing decorator named decorate, this code:

```
@decorate
def target():
    print('running target()')
```

has the same effect as writing this:

```
def target():
    print('running target()')

target = decorate(target)
```

The end result is the same: at the end of either of these snippets, the target name is bound to whatever function is returned by decorate(target)—which may be the function initially named target, or may be a different function.

To confirm that the decorated function is replaced, see the console session in Example 9-1.

Example 9-1. A decorator usually replaces a function with a different one

```
>>> def deco(func):
...     def inner():
...         print('running inner()')
...     return inner       ❶
...
>>> @deco
... def target():          ❷
...     print('running target()')
...
>>> target()               ❸
running inner()
>>> target                 ❹
<function deco.<locals>.inner at 0x10063b598>
```

❶   deco returns its inner function object.

❷   target is decorated by deco.

❸   Invoking the decorated target actually runs inner.

❹   Inspection reveals that target is a now a reference to inner.

Strictly speaking, decorators are just syntactic sugar. As we just saw, you can always simply call a decorator like any regular callable, passing another function. Sometimes that is actually convenient, especially when doing *metaprogramming*—changing program behavior at runtime.

Three essential facts make a good summary of decorators:

- A decorator is a function or another callable.
- A decorator may replace the decorated function with a different one.
- Decorators are executed immediately when a module is loaded.

Now let's focus on the third point.

When Python Executes Decorators

A key feature of decorators is that they run right after the decorated function is defined. That is usually at *import time* (i.e., when a module is loaded by Python). Consider *registration.py* in Example 9-2.

Example 9-2. The registration.py module

```
registry = []  ❶

def register(func):  ❷
    print(f'running register({func})')  ❸
    registry.append(func)  ❹
    return func  ❺

@register  ❻
def f1():
    print('running f1()')

@register
def f2():
    print('running f2()')

def f3():  ❼
    print('running f3()')

def main():  ❽
    print('running main()')
    print('registry ->', registry)
    f1()
    f2()
    f3()

if __name__ == '__main__':
    main()  ❾
```

❶ registry will hold references to functions decorated by @register.

❷ register takes a function as an argument.

---

❸   Display what function is being decorated, for demonstration.

❹   Include `func` in `registry`.

❺   Return `func`: we must return a function; here we return the same received as argument.

❻   `f1` and `f2` are decorated by `@register`.

❼   `f3` is not decorated.

❽   `main` displays the `registry`, then calls `f1()`, `f2()`, and `f3()`.

❾   `main()` is only invoked if *registration.py* runs as a script.

The output of running *registration.py* as a script looks like this:

```
$ python3 registration.py
running register(<function f1 at 0x100631bf8>)
running register(<function f2 at 0x100631c80>)
running main()
registry -> [<function f1 at 0x100631bf8>, <function f2 at 0x100631c80>]
running f1()
running f2()
running f3()
```

Note that `register` runs (twice) before any other function in the module. When `register` is called, it receives the decorated function object as an argument—for example, `<function f1 at 0x100631bf8>`.

After the module is loaded, the `registry` list holds references to the two decorated functions: `f1` and `f2`. These functions, as well as `f3`, are only executed when explicitly called by `main`.

If *registration.py* is imported (and not run as a script), the output is this:

```
>>> import registration
running register(<function f1 at 0x10063b1e0>)
running register(<function f2 at 0x10063b268>)
```

At this time, if you inspect `registry`, this is what you see:

```
>>> registration.registry
[<function f1 at 0x10063b1e0>, <function f2 at 0x10063b268>]
```

The main point of Example 9-2 is to emphasize that function decorators are executed as soon as the module is imported, but the decorated functions only run when they are explicitly invoked. This highlights the difference between what Pythonistas call *import time* and *runtime*.

Registration Decorators

Considering how decorators are commonly employed in real code, Example 9-2 is unusual in two ways:

- The decorator function is defined in the same module as the decorated functions. A real decorator is usually defined in one module and applied to functions in other modules.

- The `register` decorator returns the same function passed as an argument. In practice, most decorators define an inner function and return it.

Even though the `register` decorator in Example 9-2 returns the decorated function unchanged, that technique is not useless. Similar decorators are used in many Python frameworks to add functions to some central registry—for example, a registry mapping URL patterns to functions that generate HTTP responses. Such registration decorators may or may not change the decorated function.

We will see a registration decorator applied in "Decorator-Enhanced Strategy Pattern" on page 355 (Chapter 10).

Most decorators do change the decorated function. They usually do it by defining an inner function and returning it to replace the decorated function. Code that uses inner functions almost always depends on closures to operate correctly. To understand closures, we need to take a step back and review how variable scopes work in Python.

Variable Scope Rules

In Example 9-3, we define and test a function that reads two variables: a local variable a—defined as function parameter—and variable b that is not defined anywhere in the function.

Example 9-3. Function reading a local and a global variable

```
>>> def f1(a):
...     print(a)
...     print(b)
...
>>> f1(3)
3
Traceback (most recent call last):
  File "<stdin>", line 1, in <module>
  File "<stdin>", line 3, in f1
NameError: global name 'b' is not defined
```

The error we got is not surprising. Continuing from Example 9-3, if we assign a value to a global b and then call f1, it works:

```
>>> b = 6
>>> f1(3)
3
6
```

Now, let's see an example that may surprise you.

Take a look at the f2 function in Example 9-4. Its first two lines are the same as f1 in Example 9-3, then it makes an assignment to b. But it fails at the second print, before the assignment is made.

Example 9-4. Variable b is local, because it is assigned a value in the body of the function

```
>>> b = 6
>>> def f2(a):
...     print(a)
...     print(b)
...     b = 9
...
>>> f2(3)
3
Traceback (most recent call last):
  File "<stdin>", line 1, in <module>
  File "<stdin>", line 3, in f2
UnboundLocalError: local variable 'b' referenced before assignment
```

Note that the output starts with 3, which proves that the print(a) statement was executed. But the second one, print(b), never runs. When I first saw this I was surprised, thinking that 6 should be printed, because there is a global variable b and the assignment to the local b is made after print(b).

But the fact is, when Python compiles the body of the function, it decides that b is a local variable because it is assigned within the function. The generated bytecode reflects this decision and will try to fetch b from the local scope. Later, when the call f2(3) is made, the body of f2 fetches and prints the value of the local variable a, but when trying to fetch the value of local variable b, it discovers that b is unbound.

This is not a bug, but a design choice: Python does not require you to declare variables, but assumes that a variable assigned in the body of a function is local. This is much better than the behavior of JavaScript, which does not require variable declarations either, but if you do forget to declare that a variable is local (with var), you may clobber a global variable without knowing.

If we want the interpreter to treat b as a global variable and still assign a new value to it within the function, we use the global declaration:

```
>>> b = 6
>>> def f3(a):
...     global b
...     print(a)
...     print(b)
...     b = 9
...
>>> f3(3)
3
6
>>> b
9
```

In the preceding examples, we can see two scopes in action:

The module global scope
Made of names assigned to values outside of any class or function block.

The f3 function local scope
Made of names assigned to values as parameters, or directly in the body of the function.

There is one other scope where variables can come from, which we call *nonlocal* and is fundamental for closures; we'll see it in a bit.

After this closer look at how variable scopes work in Python, we can tackle closures in the next section, "Closures" on page 313. If you are curious about the bytecode differences between the functions in Examples 9-3 and 9-4, see the following sidebar.

Comparing Bytecodes

The dis module provides an easy way to disassemble the bytecode of Python functions. Read Examples 9-5 and 9-6 to see the bytecodes for f1 and f2 from Examples 9-3 and 9-4.

Example 9-5. Disassembly of the f1 function from Example 9-3

```
>>> from dis import dis
>>> dis(f1)
  2           0 LOAD_GLOBAL          0 (print)  ❶
              3 LOAD_FAST            0 (a)  ❷
              6 CALL_FUNCTION        1 (1 positional, 0 keyword pair)
              9 POP_TOP

  3          10 LOAD_GLOBAL          0 (print)
             13 LOAD_GLOBAL          1 (b)  ❸
             16 CALL_FUNCTION        1 (1 positional, 0 keyword pair)
```

```
                    19  POP_TOP
                    20  LOAD_CONST        0 (None)
                    23  RETURN_VALUE
```

❶ Load global name `print`.

❷ Load *local* name `a`.

❸ Load global name `b`.

Contrast the bytecode for `f1` shown in Example 9-5 with the bytecode for `f2` in Example 9-6.

Example 9-6. Disassembly of the f2 function from Example 9-4

```
>>> dis(f2)
  2            0  LOAD_GLOBAL       0 (print)
               3  LOAD_FAST         0 (a)
               6  CALL_FUNCTION     1 (1 positional, 0 keyword pair)
               9  POP_TOP

  3           10  LOAD_GLOBAL       0 (print)
              13  LOAD_FAST         1 (b)  ❶
              16  CALL_FUNCTION     1 (1 positional, 0 keyword pair)
              19  POP_TOP

  4           20  LOAD_CONST        1 (9)
              23  STORE_FAST        1 (b)
              26  LOAD_CONST        0 (None)
              29  RETURN_VALUE
```

❶ Load *local* name `b`. This shows that the compiler considers `b` a local variable, even if the assignment to `b` occurs later, because the nature of the variable—whether it is local or not—cannot change in the body of the function.

The CPython virtual machine (VM) that runs the bytecode is a stack machine, so LOAD and POP operations refer to the stack. It is beyond the scope of this book to further describe the Python opcodes, but they are documented along with the `dis` module in "dis—Disassembler for Python bytecode" (*https://fpy.li/9-1*).

Closures

In the blogosphere, closures are sometimes confused with anonymous functions. Many confuse them because of the parallel history of those features: defining functions inside functions is not so common or convenient, until you have anonymous functions. And closures only matter when you have nested functions. So a lot of people learn both concepts at the same time.

Actually, a closure is a function—let's call it f—with an extended scope that encompasses variables referenced in the body of f that are not global variables or local variables of f. Such variables must come from the local scope of an outer function that encompasses f.

It does not matter whether the function is anonymous or not; what matters is that it can access nonglobal variables that are defined outside of its body.

This is a challenging concept to grasp, and is better approached through an example.

Consider an avg function to compute the mean of an ever-growing series of values; for example, the average closing price of a commodity over its entire history. Every day a new price is added, and the average is computed taking into account all prices so far.

Starting with a clean slate, this is how avg could be used:

```
>>> avg(10)
10.0
>>> avg(11)
10.5
>>> avg(12)
11.0
```

Where does avg come from, and where does it keep the history of previous values?

For starters, Example 9-7 is a class-based implementation.

Example 9-7. average_oo.py: a class to calculate a running average

```
class Averager():

    def __init__(self):
        self.series = []

    def __call__(self, new_value):
        self.series.append(new_value)
        total = sum(self.series)
        return total / len(self.series)
```

The Averager class creates instances that are callable:

```
>>> avg = Averager()
>>> avg(10)
10.0
>>> avg(11)
10.5
>>> avg(12)
11.0
```

Now, Example 9-8 is a functional implementation, using the higher-order function make_averager.

Example 9-8. average.py: a higher-order function to calculate a running average

```
def make_averager():
    series = []

    def averager(new_value):
        series.append(new_value)
        total = sum(series)
        return total / len(series)

    return averager
```

When invoked, make_averager returns an averager function object. Each time an averager is called, it appends the passed argument to the series, and computes the current average, as shown in Example 9-9.

Example 9-9. Testing Example 9-8

```
>>> avg = make_averager()
>>> avg(10)
10.0
>>> avg(11)
10.5
>>> avg(15)
12.0
```

Note the similarities of the examples: we call Averager() or make_averager() to get a callable object avg that will update the historical series and calculate the current mean. In Example 9-7, avg is an instance of Averager, and in Example 9-8, it is the inner function, averager. Either way, we just call avg(n) to include n in the series and get the updated mean.

It's obvious where the avg of the Averager class keeps the history: the self.series instance attribute. But where does the avg function in the second example find the series?

Note that series is a local variable of make_averager because the assignment series = [] happens in the body of that function. But when avg(10) is called, make_averager has already returned, and its local scope is long gone.

Within averager, series is a *free variable*. This is a technical term meaning a variable that is not bound in the local scope. See Figure 9-1.

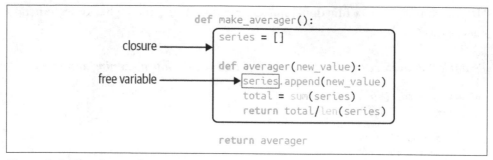

Figure 9-1. The closure for averager extends the scope of that function to include the binding for the free variable series.

Inspecting the returned averager object shows how Python keeps the names of local and free variables in the __code__ attribute that represents the compiled body of the function. Example 9-10 demonstrates.

Example 9-10. Inspecting the function created by make_averager in Example 9-8

```
>>> avg.__code__.co_varnames
('new_value', 'total')
>>> avg.__code__.co_freevars
('series',)
```

The value for series is kept in the __closure__ attribute of the returned function avg. Each item in avg.__closure__ corresponds to a name in avg. __code__ .co_freevars. These items are cells, and they have an attribute called cell_con tents where the actual value can be found. Example 9-11 shows these attributes.

Example 9-11. Continuing from Example 9-9

```
>>> avg.__code__.co_freevars
('series',)
>>> avg.__closure__
(<cell at 0x107a44f78: list object at 0x107a91a48>,)
>>> avg.__closure__[0].cell_contents
[10, 11, 12]
```

To summarize: a closure is a function that retains the bindings of the free variables that exist when the function is defined, so that they can be used later when the function is invoked and the defining scope is no longer available.

Note that the only situation in which a function may need to deal with external variables that are nonglobal is when it is nested in another function and those variables are part of the local scope of the outer function.

The nonlocal Declaration

Our previous implementation of `make_averager` was not efficient. In Example 9-8, we stored all the values in the historical series and computed their sum every time `averager` was called. A better implementation would only store the total and the number of items so far, and compute the mean from these two numbers.

Example 9-12 is a broken implementation, just to make a point. Can you see where it breaks?

Example 9-12. A broken higher-order function to calculate a running average without keeping all history

```
def make_averager():
    count = 0
    total = 0

    def averager(new_value):
        count += 1
        total += new_value
        return total / count

    return averager
```

If you try Example 9-12, here is what you get:

```
>>> avg = make_averager()
>>> avg(10)
Traceback (most recent call last):
  ...
UnboundLocalError: local variable 'count' referenced before assignment
>>>
```

The problem is that the statement `count += 1` actually means the same as `count = count + 1`, when `count` is a number or any immutable type. So we are actually assigning to `count` in the body of `averager`, and that makes it a local variable. The same problem affects the `total` variable.

We did not have this problem in Example 9-8 because we never assigned to the `series` name; we only called `series.append` and invoked `sum` and `len` on it. So we took advantage of the fact that lists are mutable.

But with immutable types like numbers, strings, tuples, etc., all you can do is read, never update. If you try to rebind them, as in `count = count + 1`, then you are implicitly creating a local variable `count`. It is no longer a free variable, and therefore it is not saved in the closure.

To work around this, the `nonlocal` keyword was introduced in Python 3. It lets you declare a variable as a free variable even when it is assigned within the function. If a new value is assigned to a `nonlocal` variable, the binding stored in the closure is changed. A correct implementation of our newest `make_averager` looks like Example 9-13.

Example 9-13. Calculate a running average without keeping all history (fixed with the use of `nonlocal`)

```python
def make_averager():
    count = 0
    total = 0

    def averager(new_value):
        nonlocal count, total
        count += 1
        total += new_value
        return total / count

    return averager
```

After studying the use of `nonlocal`, let's summarize how Python's variable lookup works.

Variable Lookup Logic

When a function is defined, the Python bytecode compiler determines how to fetch a variable x that appears in it, based on these rules:[3]

- If there is a `global` x declaration, x comes from and is assigned to the x global variable module.[4]

- If there is a `nonlocal` x declaration, x comes from and is assigned to the x local variable of the nearest surrounding function where x is defined.

- If x is a parameter or is assigned a value in the function body, then x is the local variable.

- If x is referenced but is not assigned and is not a parameter:

  — x will be looked up in the local scopes of the surrounding function bodies (nonlocal scopes).

---

3 Thanks to tech reviewer Leonardo Rochael for suggesting this summary.

4 Python does not have a program global scope, only module global scopes.

— If not found in surrounding scopes, it will be read from the module global scope.

— If not found in the global scope, it will be read from __builtins__.__dict__.

Now that we have Python closures covered, we can effectively implement decorators with nested functions.

Implementing a Simple Decorator

Example 9-14 is a decorator that clocks every invocation of the decorated function and displays the elapsed time, the arguments passed, and the result of the call.

Example 9-14. clockdeco0.py: simple decorator to show the running time of functions

```
import time


def clock(func):
    def clocked(*args):    ❶
        t0 = time.perf_counter()
        result = func(*args)    ❷
        elapsed = time.perf_counter() - t0
        name = func.__name__
        arg_str = ', '.join(repr(arg) for arg in args)
        print(f'[{elapsed:0.8f}s] {name}({arg_str}) -> {result!r}')
        return result
    return clocked    ❸
```

❶ Define inner function clocked to accept any number of positional arguments.

❷ This line only works because the closure for clocked encompasses the func free variable.

❸ Return the inner function to replace the decorated function.

Example 9-15 demonstrates the use of the clock decorator.

Example 9-15. Using the clock decorator

```
import time
from clockdeco0 import clock


@clock
def snooze(seconds):
    time.sleep(seconds)


@clock
```

```
def factorial(n):
    return 1 if n < 2 else n*factorial(n-1)

if __name__ == '__main__':
    print('*' * 40, 'Calling snooze(.123)')
    snooze(.123)
    print('*' * 40, 'Calling factorial(6)')
    print('6! =', factorial(6))
```

The output of running Example 9-15 looks like this:

```
$ python3 clockdeco_demo.py
**************************************** Calling snooze(.123)
[0.12363791s] snooze(0.123) -> None
**************************************** Calling factorial(6)
[0.00000095s] factorial(1) -> 1
[0.00002408s] factorial(2) -> 2
[0.00003934s] factorial(3) -> 6
[0.00005221s] factorial(4) -> 24
[0.00006390s] factorial(5) -> 120
[0.00008297s] factorial(6) -> 720
6! = 720
```

How It Works

Remember that this code:

```
@clock
def factorial(n):
    return 1 if n < 2 else n*factorial(n-1)
```

actually does this:

```
def factorial(n):
    return 1 if n < 2 else n*factorial(n-1)

factorial = clock(factorial)
```

So, in both examples, clock gets the factorial function as its func argument (see Example 9-14). It then creates and returns the clocked function, which the Python interpreter assigns to factorial (behind the scenes, in the first example). In fact, if you import the clockdeco_demo module and check the __name__ of factorial, this is what you get:

```
>>> import clockdeco_demo
>>> clockdeco_demo.factorial.__name__
'clocked'
>>>
```

So factorial now actually holds a reference to the clocked function. From now on, each time factorial(n) is called, clocked(n) gets executed. In essence, clocked does the following:

1. Records the initial time t0.

2. Calls the original `factorial` function, saving the result.

3. Computes the elapsed time.

4. Formats and displays the collected data.

5. Returns the result saved in step 2.

This is the typical behavior of a decorator: it replaces the decorated function with a new function that accepts the same arguments and (usually) returns whatever the decorated function was supposed to return, while also doing some extra processing.

In *Design Patterns* by Gamma et al., the short description of the decorator pattern starts with: "Attach additional responsibilities to an object dynamically." Function decorators fit that description. But at the implementation level, Python decorators bear little resemblance to the classic decorator described in the original *Design Patterns* work. "Soapbox" on page 340 has more on this subject.

The `clock` decorator implemented in Example 9-14 has a few shortcomings: it does not support keyword arguments, and it masks the __name__ and __doc__ of the decorated function. Example 9-16 uses the `functools.wraps` decorator to copy the relevant attributes from `func` to `clocked`. Also, in this new version, keyword arguments are correctly handled.

Example 9-16. clockdeco.py: an improved clock decorator

```
import time
import functools


def clock(func):
    @functools.wraps(func)
    def clocked(*args, **kwargs):
        t0 = time.perf_counter()
        result = func(*args, **kwargs)
        elapsed = time.perf_counter() - t0
        name = func.__name__
        arg_lst = [repr(arg) for arg in args]
        arg_lst.extend(f'{k}={v!r}' for k, v in kwargs.items())
        arg_str = ', '.join(arg_lst)
        print(f'[{elapsed:0.8f}s] {name}({arg_str}) -> {result!r}')
        return result
    return clocked
```

`functools.wraps` is just one of the ready-to-use decorators in the standard library. In the next section, we'll meet the most impressive decorator that `functools` provides: `cache`.

Decorators in the Standard Library

Python has three built-in functions that are designed to decorate methods: `property`, `classmethod`, and `staticmethod`. We'll discuss `property` in "Using a Property for Attribute Validation" on page 861 and the others in "classmethod Versus staticmethod" on page 371.

In Example 9-16 we saw another important decorator: `functools.wraps`, a helper for building well-behaved decorators. Some of the most interesting decorators in the standard library are `cache`, `lru_cache`, and `singledispatch`—all from the `functools` module. We'll cover them next.

Memoization with functools.cache

The `functools.cache` decorator implements *memoization*:[5] an optimization technique that works by saving the results of previous invocations of an expensive function, avoiding repeat computations on previously used arguments.

`functools.cache` was added in Python 3.9. If you need to run these examples in Python 3.8, replace `@cache` with `@lru_cache`. For prior versions of Python, you must invoke the decorator, writing `@lru_cache()`, as explained in "Using lru_cache" on page 325.

A good demonstration is to apply `@cache` to the painfully slow recursive function to generate the *n*th number in the Fibonacci sequence, as shown in Example 9-17.

Example 9-17. The very costly recursive way to compute the nth number in the Fibonacci series

```
from clockdeco import clock


@clock
def fibonacci(n):
    if n < 2:
        return n
```

---

5 To clarify, this is not a typo: *memoization* (*https://fpy.li/9-2*) is a computer science term vaguely related to "memorization," but not the same.

```
    return fibonacci(n - 2) + fibonacci(n - 1)


if __name__ == '__main__':
    print(fibonacci(6))
```

Here is the result of running *fibo_demo.py*. Except for the last line, all output is generated by the clock decorator:

```
$ python3 fibo_demo.py
[0.00000042s] fibonacci(0) -> 0
[0.00000049s] fibonacci(1) -> 1
[0.00006115s] fibonacci(2) -> 1
[0.00000031s] fibonacci(1) -> 1
[0.00000035s] fibonacci(0) -> 0
[0.00000030s] fibonacci(1) -> 1
[0.00001084s] fibonacci(2) -> 1
[0.00002074s] fibonacci(3) -> 2
[0.00009189s] fibonacci(4) -> 3
[0.00000029s] fibonacci(1) -> 1
[0.00000027s] fibonacci(0) -> 0
[0.00000029s] fibonacci(1) -> 1
[0.00000959s] fibonacci(2) -> 1
[0.00001905s] fibonacci(3) -> 2
[0.00000026s] fibonacci(0) -> 0
[0.00000029s] fibonacci(1) -> 1
[0.00000997s] fibonacci(2) -> 1
[0.00000028s] fibonacci(1) -> 1
[0.00000030s] fibonacci(0) -> 0
[0.00000031s] fibonacci(1) -> 1
[0.00001019s] fibonacci(2) -> 1
[0.00001967s] fibonacci(3) -> 2
[0.00003876s] fibonacci(4) -> 3
[0.00006670s] fibonacci(5) -> 5
[0.00016852s] fibonacci(6) -> 8
8
```

The waste is obvious: fibonacci(1) is called eight times, fibonacci(2) five times, etc. But adding just two lines to use cache, performance is much improved. See Example 9-18.

Example 9-18. Faster implementation using caching

```
import functools

from clockdeco import clock


@functools.cache    ❶
@clock    ❷
def fibonacci(n):
```

```
if n < 2:
    return n
return fibonacci(n - 2) + fibonacci(n - 1)


if __name__ == '__main__':
    print(fibonacci(6))
```

❶ This line works with Python 3.9 or later. See "Using lru_cache" on page 325 for alternatives supporting earlier versions of Python.

❷ This is an example of stacked decorators: @cache is applied on the function returned by @clock.

Stacked Decorators

To make sense of stacked decorators, recall that the @ is syntax sugar for applying the decorator function to the function below it. If there's more than one decorator, they behave like nested function calls. This:

```
@alpha
@beta
def my_fn():
    ...
```

is the same as this:

```
my_fn = alpha(beta(my_fn))
```

In other words, the beta decorator is applied first, and the function it returns is then passed to alpha.

Using cache in Example 9-18, the fibonacci function is called only once for each value of n:

```
$ python3 fibo_demo_lru.py
[0.00000043s] fibonacci(0) -> 0
[0.00000054s] fibonacci(1) -> 1
[0.00006179s] fibonacci(2) -> 1
[0.00000070s] fibonacci(3) -> 2
[0.00007366s] fibonacci(4) -> 3
[0.00000057s] fibonacci(5) -> 5
[0.00008479s] fibonacci(6) -> 8
8
```

In another test, to compute fibonacci(30), Example 9-18 made the 31 calls needed in 0.00017s (total time), while the uncached Example 9-17 took 12.09s on an Intel Core i7 notebook, because it called fibonacci(1) 832,040 times, in a total of 2,692,537 calls.

All the arguments taken by the decorated function must be *hashable*, because the underlying lru_cache uses a dict to store the results, and the keys are made from the positional and keyword arguments used in the calls.

Besides making silly recursive algorithms viable, @cache really shines in applications that need to fetch information from remote APIs.

> functools.cache can consume all available memory if there is a very large number of cache entries. I consider it more suitable for use in short-lived command-line scripts. In long-running processes, I recommend using functools.lru_cache with a suitable maxsize parameter, as explained in the next section.

Using lru_cache

The functools.cache decorator is actually a simple wrapper around the older functools.lru_cache function, which is more flexible and compatible with Python 3.8 and earlier versions.

The main advantage of @lru_cache is that its memory usage is bounded by the maxsize parameter, which has a rather conservative default value of 128—which means the cache will hold at most 128 entries at any time.

The acronym LRU stands for Least Recently Used, meaning that older entries that have not been read for a while are discarded to make room for new ones.

Since Python 3.8, lru_cache can be applied in two ways. This is how to use it in the simplest way:

```
@lru_cache
def costly_function(a, b):
    ...
```

The other way—available since Python 3.2—is to invoke it as a function, with ():

```
@lru_cache()
def costly_function(a, b):
    ...
```

In both cases, the default parameters would be used. These are:

maxsize=128
: Sets the maximum number of entries to be stored. After the cache is full, the least recently used entry is discarded to make room for each new entry. For optimal performance, maxsize should be a power of 2. If you pass maxsize=None, the LRU logic is disabled, so the cache works faster but entries are never discarded, which may consume too much memory. That's what @functools.cache does.

```
typed=False
```
Determines whether the results of different argument types are stored separately. For example, in the default setting, float and integer arguments that are considered equal are stored only once, so there would be a single entry for the calls `f(1)` and `f(1.0)`. If `typed=True`, those arguments would produce different entries, possibly storing distinct results.

Here is an example invoking `@lru_cache` with nondefault parameters:

```
@lru_cache(maxsize=2**20, typed=True)
def costly_function(a, b):
    ...
```

Now let's study another powerful decorator: `functools.singledispatch`.

Single Dispatch Generic Functions

Imagine we are creating a tool to debug web applications. We want to generate HTML displays for different types of Python objects.

We could start with a function like this:

```
import html

def htmlize(obj):
    content = html.escape(repr(obj))
    return f'<pre>{content}</pre>'
```

That will work for any Python type, but now we want to extend it to generate custom displays for some types. Some examples:

str
Replace embedded newline characters with `'<br/>\n'` and use `<p>` tags instead of `<pre>`.

int
Show the number in decimal and hexadecimal (with a special case for `bool`).

list
Output an HTML list, formatting each item according to its type.

float *and* Decimal
Output the value as usual, but also in the form of a fraction (why not?).

The behavior we want is shown in Example 9-19.

Example 9-19. htmlize() generates HTML tailored to different object types

```
>>> htmlize({1, 2, 3})  ❶
'<pre>{1, 2, 3}</pre>'
>>> htmlize(abs)
'<pre>&lt;built-in function abs&gt;</pre>'
>>> htmlize('Heimlich & Co.\n- a game')  ❷
'<p>Heimlich &amp; Co.<br/>\n- a game</p>'
>>> htmlize(42)  ❸
'<pre>42 (0x2a)</pre>'
>>> print(htmlize(['alpha', 66, {3, 2, 1}]))  ❹
<ul>
<li><p>alpha</p></li>
<li><pre>66 (0x42)</pre></li>
<li><pre>{1, 2, 3}</pre></li>
</ul>
>>> htmlize(True)  ❺
'<pre>True</pre>'
>>> htmlize(fractions.Fraction(2, 3))  ❻
'<pre>2/3</pre>'
>>> htmlize(2/3)  ❼
'<pre>0.6666666666666666 (2/3)</pre>'
>>> htmlize(decimal.Decimal('0.02380952'))
'<pre>0.02380952 (1/42)</pre>'
```

❶ The original function is registered for object, so it serves as a catch-all to handle argument types that don't match the other implementations.

❷ str objects are also HTML-escaped but wrapped in <p></p>, with <br/> line breaks inserted before each '\n'.

❸ An int is shown in decimal and hexadecimal, inside <pre></pre>.

❹ Each list item is formatted according to its type, and the whole sequence is rendered as an HTML list.

❺ Although bool is an int subtype, it gets special treatment.

❻ Show Fraction as a fraction.

❼ Show float and Decimal with an approximate fractional equivalent.

Function singledispatch

Because we don't have Java-style method overloading in Python, we can't simply create variations of htmlize with different signatures for each data type we want to handle differently. A possible solution in Python would be to turn htmlize into a dispatch function, with a chain of `if/elif/…` or `match/case/…` calling specialized functions like `htmlize_str`, `htmlize_int`, etc. This is not extensible by users of our module, and is unwieldy: over time, the `htmlize` dispatcher would become too big, and the coupling between it and the specialized functions would be very tight.

The `functools.singledispatch` decorator allows different modules to contribute to the overall solution, and lets you easily provide specialized functions even for types that belong to third-party packages that you can't edit. If you decorate a plain function with `@singledispatch`, it becomes the entry point for a *generic function*: a group of functions to perform the same operation in different ways, depending on the type of the first argument. This is what is meant by the term *single dispatch*. If more arguments were used to select the specific functions, we'd have *multiple dispatch*. Example 9-20 shows how.

 `functools.singledispatch` exists since Python 3.4, but it only supports type hints since Python 3.7. The last two functions in Example 9-20 illustrate the syntax that works in all versions of Python since 3.4.

Example 9-20. `@singledispatch` creates a custom `@htmlize.register` to bundle several functions into a generic function

```python
from functools import singledispatch
from collections import abc
import fractions
import decimal
import html
import numbers

@singledispatch  ❶
def htmlize(obj: object) -> str:
    content = html.escape(repr(obj))
    return f'<pre>{content}</pre>'

@htmlize.register  ❷
def _(text: str) -> str:  ❸
    content = html.escape(text).replace('\n', '<br/>\n')
    return f'<p>{content}</p>'

@htmlize.register  ❹
def _(seq: abc.Sequence) -> str:
    inner = '</li>\n<li>'.join(htmlize(item) for item in seq)
    return '<ul>\n<li>' + inner + '</li>\n</ul>'

@htmlize.register  ❺
def _(n: numbers.Integral) -> str:
    return f'<pre>{n} (0x{n:x})</pre>'
```

```
@htmlize.register      ⑥
def _(n: bool) -> str:
    return f'<pre>{n}</pre>'


@htmlize.register(fractions.Fraction)      ⑦
def _(x) -> str:
    frac = fractions.Fraction(x)
    return f'<pre>{frac.numerator}/{frac.denominator}</pre>'


@htmlize.register(decimal.Decimal)      ⑧
@htmlize.register(float)
def _(x) -> str:
    frac = fractions.Fraction(x).limit_denominator()
    return f'<pre>{x} ({frac.numerator}/{frac.denominator})</pre>'
```

❶ @singledispatch marks the base function that handles the object type.

❷ Each specialized function is decorated with @«base».register.

❸ The type of the first argument given at runtime determines when this particular function definition will be used. The name of the specialized functions is irrelevant; _ is a good choice to make this clear.[6]

❹ For each additional type to get special treatment, register a new function with a matching type hint in the first parameter.

❺ The numbers ABCs are useful for use with singledispatch.[7]

❻ bool is a *subtype-of* numbers.Integral, but the singledispatch logic seeks the implementation with the most specific matching type, regardless of the order they appear in the code.

---

6 Unfortunately, Mypy 0.770 complains when it sees multiple functions with the same name.

7 Despite the warning in "The fall of the numeric tower" on page 280, the number ABCs are not deprecated and you find them in Python 3 code.

❼ If you don't want to, or cannot, add type hints to the decorated function, you can pass a type to the `@«base».register` decorator. This syntax works in Python 3.4 or later.

❽ The `@«base».register` decorator returns the undecorated function, so it's possible to stack them to register two or more types on the same implementation.[8]

When possible, register the specialized functions to handle ABCs (abstract classes) such as `numbers.Integral` and `abc.MutableSequence`, instead of concrete implementations like `int` and `list`. This allows your code to support a greater variety of compatible types. For example, a Python extension can provide alternatives to the `int` type with fixed bit lengths as subclasses of `numbers.Integral`.[9]

 Using ABCs or `typing.Protocol` with `@singledispatch` allows your code to support existing or future classes that are actual or virtual subclasses of those ABCs, or that implement those protocols. The use of ABCs and the concept of a virtual subclass are subjects of Chapter 13.

A notable quality of the `singledispatch` mechanism is that you can register specialized functions anywhere in the system, in any module. If you later add a module with a new user-defined type, you can easily provide a new custom function to handle that type. And you can write custom functions for classes that you did not write and can't change.

`singledispatch` is a well-thought-out addition to the standard library, and it offers more features than I can describe here. PEP 443—Single-dispatch generic functions (*https://fpy.li/pep443*) is a good reference, but it doesn't mention the use of type hints, which were added later. The `functools` module documentation has improved and has more up-to-date coverage with several examples in its `singledispatch` (*https://fpy.li/9-4*) entry.

---

8 Maybe one day you'll also be able to express this with single unparameterized `@htmlize.register` and type hint using `Union`, but when I tried, Python raised a `TypeError` with a message saying that `Union` is not a class. So, although PEP 484 *syntax* is supported by `@singledispatch`, the *semantics* are not there yet.

9 NumPy, for example, implements several machine-oriented integer and floating-point (*https://fpy.li/9-3*) types.

@singledispatch is not designed to bring Java-style method overloading to Python. A single class with many overloaded variations of a method is better than a single function with a lengthy stretch of if/elif/elif/elif blocks. But both solutions are flawed because they concentrate too much responsibility in a single code unit—the class or the function. The advantage of @singledispatch is supporting modular extension: each module can register a specialized function for each type it supports. In a realistic use case, you would not have all the implementations of generic functions in the same module as in Example 9-20.

We've seen some decorators that take arguments, for example, @lru_cache() and htmlize.register(float), created by @singledispatch in Example 9-20. The next section shows how to build decorators that accept parameters.

Parameterized Decorators

When parsing a decorator in source code, Python takes the decorated function and passes it as the first argument to the decorator function. So how do you make a decorator accept other arguments? The answer is: make a decorator factory that takes those arguments and returns a decorator, which is then applied to the function to be decorated. Confusing? Sure. Let's start with an example based on the simplest decorator we've seen: register in Example 9-21.

Example 9-21. Abridged registration.py module from Example 9-2, repeated here for convenience

```
registry = []

def register(func):
    print(f'running register({func})')
    registry.append(func)
    return func

@register
def f1():
    print('running f1()')

print('running main()')
print('registry ->', registry)
f1()
```

A Parameterized Registration Decorator

To make it easy to enable or disable the function registration performed by register, we'll make it accept an optional active parameter which, if False, skips registering the decorated function. Example 9-22 shows how. Conceptually, the new `register` function is not a decorator but a decorator factory. When called, it returns the actual decorator that will be applied to the target function.

Example 9-22. To accept parameters, the new `register` decorator must be called as a function

```
registry = set()  ❶

def register(active=True):  ❷
    def decorate(func):  ❸
        print('running register'
                f'(active={active})->decorate({func})')
        if active:  ❹
            registry.add(func)
        else:
            registry.discard(func)  ❺

        return func  ❻
    return decorate  ❼

@register(active=False)  ❽
def f1():
    print('running f1()')

@register()  ❾
def f2():
    print('running f2()')

def f3():
    print('running f3()')
```

❶ `registry` is now a `set`, so adding and removing functions is faster.

❷ `register` takes an optional keyword argument.

❸ The `decorate` inner function is the actual decorator; note how it takes a function as an argument.

❹ Register `func` only if the `active` argument (retrieved from the closure) is `True`.

❺ If not `active` and `func in registry`, remove it.

❻ Because `decorate` is a decorator, it must return a function.

❼ `register` is our decorator factory, so it returns `decorate`.

❽ The `@register` factory must be invoked as a function, with the desired parameters.

❾ If no parameters are passed, `register` must still be called as a function—`@regis ter()`—i.e., to return the actual decorator, `decorate`.

The main point is that `register()` returns `decorate`, which is then applied to the decorated function.

The code in Example 9-22 is in a *registration_param.py* module. If we import it, this is what we get:

```
>>> import registration_param
running register(active=False)->decorate(<function f1 at 0x10063c1e0>)
running register(active=True)->decorate(<function f2 at 0x10063c268>)
>>> registration_param.registry
[<function f2 at 0x10063c268>]
```

Note how only the f2 function appears in the `registry`; f1 does not appear because `active=False` was passed to the `register` decorator factory, so the `decorate` that was applied to f1 did not add it to the `registry`.

If, instead of using the @ syntax, we used `register` as a regular function, the syntax needed to decorate a function f would be `register()(f)` to add f to the `registry`, or `register(active=False)(f)` to not add it (or remove it). See Example 9-23 for a demo of adding and removing functions to the `registry`.

Example 9-23. Using the registration_param module listed in Example 9-22

```
>>> from registration_param import *
running register(active=False)->decorate(<function f1 at 0x10073c1e0>)
running register(active=True)->decorate(<function f2 at 0x10073c268>)
>>> registry  ❶
{<function f2 at 0x10073c268>}
>>> register()(f3)  ❷
running register(active=True)->decorate(<function f3 at 0x10073c158>)
<function f3 at 0x10073c158>
>>> registry  ❸
{<function f3 at 0x10073c158>, <function f2 at 0x10073c268>}
>>> register(active=False)(f2)  ❹
running register(active=False)->decorate(<function f2 at 0x10073c268>)
<function f2 at 0x10073c268>
>>> registry  ❺
{<function f3 at 0x10073c158>}
```

❶ When the module is imported, f2 is in the `registry`.

❷ The `register()` expression returns `decorate`, which is then applied to f3.

❸ The previous line added f3 to the `registry`.

❹ This call removes f2 from the `registry`.

❺ Confirm that only f3 remains in the `registry`.

The workings of parameterized decorators are fairly involved, and the one we've just discussed is simpler than most. Parameterized decorators usually replace the decorated function, and their construction requires yet another level of nesting. Now we will explore the architecture of one such function pyramid.

The Parameterized Clock Decorator

In this section, we'll revisit the `clock` decorator, adding a feature: users may pass a format string to control the output of the clocked function report. See Example 9-24.

 For simplicity, Example 9-24 is based on the initial `clock` implementation from Example 9-14, and not the improved one from Example 9-16 that uses `@functools.wraps`, adding yet another function layer.

Example 9-24. Module clockdeco_param.py: the parameterized clock decorator

```
import time

DEFAULT_FMT = '[{elapsed:0.8f}s] {name}({args}) -> {result}'

def clock(fmt=DEFAULT_FMT):  ❶
    def decorate(func):  ❷
        def clocked(*_args):  ❸
            t0 = time.perf_counter()
            _result = func(*_args)  ❹
            elapsed = time.perf_counter() - t0
            name = func.__name__
            args = ', '.join(repr(arg) for arg in _args)  ❺
            result = repr(_result)  ❻
            print(fmt.format(**locals()))  ❼
            return _result  ❽
        return clocked  ❾
    return decorate  ❿

if __name__ == '__main__':

    @clock()  ⓫
    def snooze(seconds):
        time.sleep(seconds)
```

```
for i in range(3):
    snooze(.123)
```

❶ clock is our parameterized decorator factory.

❷ decorate is the actual decorator.

❸ clocked wraps the decorated function.

❹ _result is the actual result of the decorated function.

❺ _args holds the actual arguments of clocked, while args is str used for display.

❻ result is the str representation of _result, for display.

❼ Using **locals() here allows any local variable of clocked to be referenced in the fmt.[10]

❽ clocked will replace the decorated function, so it should return whatever that function returns.

❾ decorate returns clocked.

❿ clock returns decorate.

⓫ In this self test, clock() is called without arguments, so the decorator applied will use the default format str.

If you run Example 9-24 from the shell, this is what you get:

```
$ python3 clockdeco_param.py
[0.12412500s] snooze(0.123) -> None
[0.12411904s] snooze(0.123) -> None
[0.12410498s] snooze(0.123) -> None
```

To exercise the new functionality, let's have a look at Examples 9-25 and 9-26, which are two other modules using clockdeco_param, and the outputs they generate.

---

10 Tech reviewer Miroslav Šedivý noted: "It also means that code linters will complain about unused variables since they tend to ignore uses of locals()." Yes, that's yet another example of how static checking tools discourage the use of the dynamic features that attracted me and countless programmers to Python in the first place. To make the linter happy, I could spell out each local variable twice in the call: fmt.format(elapsed=elapsed, name=name, args=args, result=result). I'd rather not. If you use static checking tools, it's very important to know when to ignore them.

Example 9-25. clockdeco_param_demo1.py

```
import time
from clockdeco_param import clock

@clock('{name}: {elapsed}s')
def snooze(seconds):
    time.sleep(seconds)

for i in range(3):
    snooze(.123)
```

Output of Example 9-25:

```
$ python3 clockdeco_param_demo1.py
snooze: 0.12414693832397461s
snooze: 0.1241159439086914s
snooze: 0.12412118911743164s
```

Example 9-26. clockdeco_param_demo2.py

```
import time
from clockdeco_param import clock

@clock('{name}({args}) dt={elapsed:0.3f}s')
def snooze(seconds):
    time.sleep(seconds)

for i in range(3):
    snooze(.123)
```

Output of Example 9-26:

```
$ python3 clockdeco_param_demo2.py
snooze(0.123) dt=0.124s
snooze(0.123) dt=0.124s
snooze(0.123) dt=0.124s
```

Lennart Regebro—a technical reviewer for the first edition—argues that decorators are best coded as classes implementing __call__, and not as functions like the examples in this chapter. I agree that approach is better for nontrivial decorators, but to explain the basic idea of this language feature, functions are easier to understand. See "Further Reading" on page 338, in particular, Graham Dumpleton's blog and wrapt module for industrial-strength techniques when building decorators.

The next section shows an example in the style recommended by Regebro and Dumpleton.

A Class-Based Clock Decorator

As a final example, Example 9-27 lists the implementation of a parameterized `clock`
decorator implemented as a class with `__call__`. Contrast Example 9-24 with
Example 9-27. Which one do you prefer?

*Example 9-27. Module clockdeco_cls.py: parameterized clock decorator implemented as
class*

```
import time

DEFAULT_FMT = '[{elapsed:0.8f}s] {name}({args}) -> {result}'

class clock:  ❶
    def __init__(self, fmt=DEFAULT_FMT):  ❷
        self.fmt = fmt

    def __call__(self, func):  ❸
        def clocked(*_args):
            t0 = time.perf_counter()
            _result = func(*_args)  ❹
            elapsed = time.perf_counter() - t0
            name = func.__name__
            args = ', '.join(repr(arg) for arg in _args)
            result = repr(_result)
            print(self.fmt.format(**locals()))
            return _result
        return clocked
```

❶ Instead of a `clock` outer function, the `clock` class is our parameterized decorator
factory. I named it with a lowercase c to make clear that this implementation is a
drop-in replacement for the one in Example 9-24.

❷ The argument passed in the `clock(my_format)` is assigned to the `fmt` parameter
here. The class constructor returns an instance of `clock`, with `my_format` stored
in `self.fmt`.

❸ `__call__` makes the `clock` instance callable. When invoked, the instance replaces
the decorated function with `clocked`.

❹ `clocked` wraps the decorated function.

This ends our exploration of function decorators. We'll see class decorators in
Chapter 24.

Chapter Summary

We covered some difficult terrain in this chapter. I tried to make the journey as smooth as possible, but we definitely entered the realm of metaprogramming.

We started with a simple `@register` decorator without an inner function, and finished with a parameterized `@clock()` involving two levels of nested functions.

Registration decorators, though simple in essence, have real applications in Python frameworks. We will apply the registration idea in one implementation of the Strategy design pattern in Chapter 10.

Understanding how decorators actually work required covering the difference between *import time* and *runtime*, then diving into variable scoping, closures, and the new `nonlocal` declaration. Mastering closures and `nonlocal` is valuable not only to build decorators, but also to code event-oriented programs for GUIs or asynchronous I/O with callbacks, and to adopt a functional style when it makes sense.

Parameterized decorators almost always involve at least two nested functions, maybe more if you want to use `@functools.wraps` to produce a decorator that provides better support for more advanced techniques. One such technique is stacked decorators, which we saw in Example 9-18. For more sophisticated decorators, a class-based implementation may be easier to read and maintain.

As examples of parameterized decorators in the standard library, we visited the powerful `@cache` and `@singledispatch` from the `functools` module.

Further Reading

Item #26 of Brett Slatkin's *Effective Python*, 2nd ed. (*https://fpy.li/effectpy*) (Addison-Wesley), covers best practices for function decorators and recommends always using `functools.wraps`—which we saw in Example 9-16.[11]

Graham Dumpleton has a series of in-depth blog posts (*https://fpy.li/9-5*) about techniques for implementing well-behaved decorators, starting with "How you implemented your Python decorator is wrong" (*https://fpy.li/9-6*). His deep expertise in this matter is also nicely packaged in the `wrapt` (*https://fpy.li/9-7*) module he wrote to simplify the implementation of decorators and dynamic function wrappers, which support introspection and behave correctly when further decorated, when applied to methods, and when used as attribute descriptors. Chapter 23 in Part III is about descriptors.

---

11 I wanted to make the code as simple as possible, so I did not follow Slatkin's excellent advice in all examples.

Chapter 9, "Metaprogramming" (*https://fpy.li/9-8*), of the *Python Cookbook*, 3rd ed. by David Beazley and Brian K. Jones (O'Reilly), has several recipes, from elementary decorators to very sophisticated ones, including one that can be called as a regular decorator or as a decorator factory, e.g., @clock or @clock(). That's "Recipe 9.6. Defining a Decorator That Takes an Optional Argument" in that cookbook.

Michele Simionato authored a package aiming to "simplify the usage of decorators for the average programmer, and to popularize decorators by showing various nontrivial examples," according to the docs. It's available on PyPI as the decorator package (*https://fpy.li/9-9*).

Created when decorators were still a new feature in Python, the Python Decorator Library wiki page (*https://fpy.li/9-10*) has dozens of examples. Because that page started years ago, some of the techniques shown have been superseded, but the page is still an excellent source of inspiration.

"Closures in Python" (*https://fpy.li/9-11*) is a short blog post by Fredrik Lundh that explains the terminology of closures.

PEP 3104—Access to Names in Outer Scopes (*https://fpy.li/9-12*) describes the introduction of the nonlocal declaration to allow rebinding of names that are neither local nor global. It also includes an excellent overview of how this issue is resolved in other dynamic languages (Perl, Ruby, JavaScript, etc.) and the pros and cons of the design options available to Python.

On a more theoretical level, PEP 227—Statically Nested Scopes (*https://fpy.li/9-13*) documents the introduction of lexical scoping as an option in Python 2.1 and as a standard in Python 2.2, explaining the rationale and design choices for the implementation of closures in Python.

PEP 443 (*https://fpy.li/9-14*) provides the rationale and a detailed description of the single-dispatch generic functions' facility. An old (March 2005) blog post by Guido van Rossum, "Five-Minute Multimethods in Python" (*https://fpy.li/9-15*), walks through an implementation of generic functions (a.k.a. multimethods) using decorators. His code supports multiple-dispatch (i.e., dispatch based on more than one positional argument). Guido's multimethods code is interesting, but it's a didactic example. For a modern, production-ready implementation of multiple dispatch generic functions, check out Reg (*https://fpy.li/9-16*) by Martijn Faassen—author of the model-driven and REST-savvy Morepath (*https://fpy.li/9-17*) web framework.

Soapbox

Dynamic Scope Versus Lexical Scope

The designer of any language with first-class functions faces this issue: being a first-class object, a function is defined in a certain scope but may be invoked in other scopes. The question is: how to evaluate the free variables? The first and simplest answer is "dynamic scope." This means that free variables are evaluated by looking into the environment where the function is invoked.

If Python had dynamic scope and no closures, we could improvise avg—similar to Example 9-8—like this:

```
>>> ### this is not a real Python console session! ###
>>> avg = make_averager()
>>> series = []         ❶
>>> avg(10)
10.0
>>> avg(11)             ❷
10.5
>>> avg(12)
11.0
>>> series = [1]        ❸
>>> avg(5)
3.0
```

❶ Before using avg, we have to define series = [] ourselves, so we must know that averager (inside make_averager) refers to a list named series.

❷ Behind the scenes, series accumulates the values to be averaged.

❸ When series = [1] is executed, the previous list is lost. This could happen by accident, when handling two independent running averages at the same time.

Functions should be opaque, with their implementation hidden from users. But with dynamic scope, if a function uses free variables, the programmer has to know its internals to set up an environment where it works correctly. After years of struggling with the LaTeX document preparation language, the excellent *Practical LaTeX* book by George Grätzer (Springer) taught me that LaTeX variables use dynamic scope. That's why they were so confusing to me!

Emacs Lisp also uses dynamic scope, at least by default. See "Dynamic Binding" (*https://fpy.li/9-18*) in the Emacs Lisp manual for a short explanation.

Dynamic scope is easier to implement, which is probably why it was the path taken by John McCarthy when he created Lisp, the first language to have first-class functions. Paul Graham's article "The Roots of Lisp" (*https://fpy.li/9-19*) is an accessible explanation of John McCarthy's original paper about the Lisp language, "Recursive Functions of Symbolic Expressions and Their Computation by Machine, Part I" (*https://fpy.li/9-20*). McCarthy's paper is a masterpiece as great as Beethoven's 9th Symphony. Paul Graham translated it for the rest of us, from mathematics to English and running code.

Paul Graham's commentary explains how tricky dynamic scoping is. Quoting from "The Roots of Lisp":

> It's an eloquent testimony to the dangers of dynamic scope that even the very first example of higher-order Lisp functions was broken because of it. It may be that McCarthy was not fully aware of the implications of dynamic scope in 1960. Dynamic scope remained in Lisp implementations for a surprisingly long time—until Sussman and Steele developed Scheme in 1975. Lexical scope does not complicate the definition of eval very much, but it may make compilers harder to write.

Today, lexical scope is the norm: free variables are evaluated considering the environment where the function is defined. Lexical scope complicates the implementation of languages with first-class functions, because it requires the support of closures. On the other hand, lexical scope makes source code easier to read. Most languages invented since Algol have lexical scope. One notable exception is JavaScript, where the special variable this is confusing because it can be lexically or dynamically scoped, depending on how the code is written (*https://fpy.li/9-21*).

For many years, Python lambdas did not provide closures, contributing to the bad name of this feature among functional-programming geeks in the blogosphere. This was fixed in Python 2.2 (December 2001), but the blogosphere has a long memory. Since then, lambda is embarrassing only because of its limited syntax.

Python Decorators and the Decorator Design Pattern

Python function decorators fit the general description of decorator given by Gamma et al. in *Design Patterns*: "Attach additional responsibilities to an object dynamically. Decorators provide a flexible alternative to subclassing for extending functionality."

At the implementation level, Python decorators do not resemble the classic decorator design pattern, but an analogy can be made.

In the design pattern, Decorator and Component are abstract classes. An instance of a concrete decorator wraps an instance of a concrete component in order to add behaviors to it. Quoting from *Design Patterns*:

> The decorator conforms to the interface of the component it decorates so that its presence is transparent to the component's clients. The decorator forwards requests to the component and may perform additional actions (such as drawing a border) before or after forwarding. Transparency lets you nest decorators recursively, thereby allowing an unlimited number of added responsibilities." (p. 175)

In Python, the decorator function plays the role of a concrete Decorator subclass, and the inner function it returns is a decorator instance. The returned function wraps the function to be decorated, which is analogous to the component in the design pattern. The returned function is transparent because it conforms to the interface of the component by accepting the same arguments. It forwards calls to the component and may perform additional actions either before or after it. Borrowing from the previous citation, we can adapt the last sentence to say that "Transparency lets you stack decorators, thereby allowing an unlimited number of added behaviors."

Note that I am not suggesting that function decorators should be used to implement the decorator pattern in Python programs. Although this can be done in specific situations, in general the decorator pattern is best implemented with classes to represent the decorator and the components it will wrap.

## CHAPTER 10

Design Patterns with First-Class Functions

Conformity to patterns is not a measure of goodness.

—Ralph Johnson, coauthor of the *Design Patterns* classic[1]

In software engineering, a *design pattern* (*https://fpy.li/10-1*) is a general recipe for solving a common design problem. You don't need to know design patterns to follow this chapter. I will explain the patterns used in the examples.

The use of design patterns in programming was popularized by the landmark book *Design Patterns: Elements of Reusable Object-Oriented Software* (Addison-Wesley) by Erich Gamma, Richard Helm, Ralph Johnson, and John Vlissides—a.k.a. "the Gang of Four." The book is a catalog of 23 patterns consisting of arrangements of classes exemplified with code in C++, but assumed to be useful in other object-oriented languages as well.

Although design patterns are language independent, that does not mean every pattern applies to every language. For example, Chapter 17 will show that it doesn't make sense to emulate the recipe of the Iterator (*https://fpy.li/10-2*) pattern in Python, because the pattern is embedded in the language and ready to use in the form of generators—which don't need classes to work, and require less code than the classic recipe.

The authors of *Design Patterns* acknowledge in their introduction that the implementation language determines which patterns are relevant:

> The choice of programming language is important because it influences one's point of view. Our patterns assume Smalltalk/C++-level language features, and that choice

---

1 From a slide in the talk "Root Cause Analysis of Some Faults in Design Patterns," presented by Ralph Johnson at IME/CCSL, Universidade de São Paulo, Nov. 15, 2014.

determines what can and cannot be implemented easily. If we assumed procedural languages, we might have included design patterns called "Inheritance," "Encapsulation," and "Polymorphism." Similarly, some of our patterns are supported directly by the less common object-oriented languages. CLOS has multi-methods, for example, which lessen the need for a pattern such as Visitor.[2]

In his 1996 presentation, "Design Patterns in Dynamic Languages" (*https://fpy.li/ norvigdp*), Peter Norvig states that 16 out of the 23 patterns in the original *Design Patterns* book become either "invisible or simpler" in a dynamic language (slide 9). He's talking about the Lisp and Dylan languages, but many of the relevant dynamic features are also present in Python. In particular, in the context of languages with first-class functions, Norvig suggests rethinking the classic patterns known as Strategy, Command, Template Method, and Visitor.

The goal of this chapter is to show how—in some cases—functions can do the same work as classes, with code that is more readable and concise. We will refactor an implementation of Strategy using functions as objects, removing a lot of boilerplate code. We'll also discuss a similar approach to simplifying the Command pattern.

What's New in This Chapter

I moved this chapter to the end of Part III so I could apply a registration decorator in "Decorator-Enhanced Strategy Pattern" on page 355 and also use type hints in the examples. Most type hints used in this chapter are not complicated, and they do help with readability.

Case Study: Refactoring Strategy

Strategy is a good example of a design pattern that can be simpler in Python if you leverage functions as first-class objects. In the following section, we describe and implement Strategy using the "classic" structure described in *Design Patterns*. If you are familiar with the classic pattern, you can skip to "Function-Oriented Strategy" on page 349 where we refactor the code using functions, significantly reducing the line count.

Classic Strategy

The UML class diagram in Figure 10-1 depicts an arrangement of classes that exemplifies the Strategy pattern.

---

2 Quoted from page 4 of *Design Patterns*.

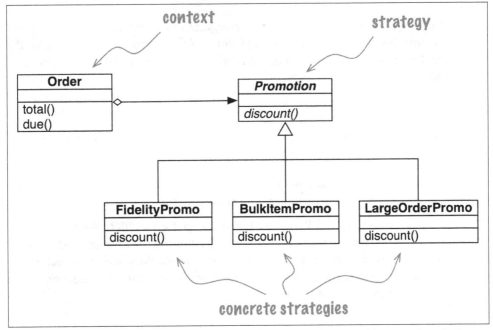

Figure 10-1. UML class diagram for order discount processing implemented with the Strategy design pattern.

The Strategy pattern is summarized like this in *Design Patterns*:

> Define a family of algorithms, encapsulate each one, and make them interchangeable. Strategy lets the algorithm vary independently from clients that use it.

A clear example of Strategy applied in the ecommerce domain is computing discounts to orders according to the attributes of the customer or inspection of the ordered items.

Consider an online store with these discount rules:

- Customers with 1,000 or more fidelity points get a global 5% discount per order.
- A 10% discount is applied to each line item with 20 or more units in the same order.
- Orders with at least 10 distinct items get a 7% global discount.

For brevity, let's assume that only one discount may be applied to an order.

The UML class diagram for the Strategy pattern is depicted in Figure 10-1. Its participants are:

Context

Provides a service by delegating some computation to interchangeable components that implement alternative algorithms. In the ecommerce example, the context is an `Order`, which is configured to apply a promotional discount according to one of several algorithms.

Strategy

The interface common to the components that implement the different algorithms. In our example, this role is played by an abstract class called `Promotion`.

Concrete strategy

One of the concrete subclasses of Strategy. `FidelityPromo`, `BulkPromo`, and `LargeOrderPromo` are the three concrete strategies implemented.

The code in Example 10-1 follows the blueprint in Figure 10-1. As described in *Design Patterns*, the concrete strategy is chosen by the client of the context class. In our example, before instantiating an order, the system would somehow select a promotional discount strategy and pass it to the `Order` constructor. The selection of the strategy is outside the scope of the pattern.

Example 10-1. Implementation of the `Order` class with pluggable discount strategies

```python
from abc import ABC, abstractmethod
from collections.abc import Sequence
from decimal import Decimal
from typing import NamedTuple, Optional


class Customer(NamedTuple):
    name: str
    fidelity: int


class LineItem(NamedTuple):
    product: str
    quantity: int
    price: Decimal

    def total(self) -> Decimal:
        return self.price * self.quantity


class Order(NamedTuple):  # the Context
    customer: Customer
    cart: Sequence[LineItem]
    promotion: Optional['Promotion'] = None

    def total(self) -> Decimal:
        totals = (item.total() for item in self.cart)
```

```python
        return sum(totals, start=Decimal(0))

    def due(self) -> Decimal:
        if self.promotion is None:
            discount = Decimal(0)
        else:
            discount = self.promotion.discount(self)
        return self.total() - discount

    def __repr__(self):
        return f'<Order total: {self.total():.2f} due: {self.due():.2f}>'


class Promotion(ABC):  # the Strategy: an abstract base class
    @abstractmethod
    def discount(self, order: Order) -> Decimal:
        """Return discount as a positive dollar amount"""


class FidelityPromo(Promotion):  # first Concrete Strategy
    """5% discount for customers with 1000 or more fidelity points"""

    def discount(self, order: Order) -> Decimal:
        rate = Decimal('0.05')
        if order.customer.fidelity >= 1000:
            return order.total() * rate
        return Decimal(0)


class BulkItemPromo(Promotion):  # second Concrete Strategy
    """10% discount for each LineItem with 20 or more units"""

    def discount(self, order: Order) -> Decimal:
        discount = Decimal(0)
        for item in order.cart:
            if item.quantity >= 20:
                discount += item.total() * Decimal('0.1')
        return discount


class LargeOrderPromo(Promotion):  # third Concrete Strategy
    """7% discount for orders with 10 or more distinct items"""

    def discount(self, order: Order) -> Decimal:
        distinct_items = {item.product for item in order.cart}
        if len(distinct_items) >= 10:
            return order.total() * Decimal('0.07')
        return Decimal(0)
```

Note that in Example 10-1, I coded `Promotion` as an abstract base class (ABC) to use the `@abstractmethod` decorator and make the pattern more explicit.

Example 10-2 shows doctests used to demonstrate and verify the operation of a module implementing the rules described earlier.

Example 10-2. Sample usage of Order class with different promotions applied

```
>>> joe = Customer('John Doe', 0)  ❶
>>> ann = Customer('Ann Smith', 1100)
>>> cart = (LineItem('banana', 4, Decimal('.5')),  ❷
...         LineItem('apple', 10, Decimal('1.5')),
...         LineItem('watermelon', 5, Decimal(5)))
>>> Order(joe, cart, FidelityPromo())  ❸
<Order total: 42.00 due: 42.00>
>>> Order(ann, cart, FidelityPromo())  ❹
<Order total: 42.00 due: 39.90>
>>> banana_cart = (LineItem('banana', 30, Decimal('.5')),  ❺
...                LineItem('apple', 10, Decimal('1.5')))
>>> Order(joe, banana_cart, BulkItemPromo())  ❻
<Order total: 30.00 due: 28.50>
>>> long_cart = tuple(LineItem(str(sku), 1, Decimal(1))  ❼
...                   for sku in range(10))
>>> Order(joe, long_cart, LargeOrderPromo())  ❽
<Order total: 10.00 due: 9.30>
>>> Order(joe, cart, LargeOrderPromo())
<Order total: 42.00 due: 42.00>
```

❶ Two customers: joe has 0 fidelity points, ann has 1,100.

❷ One shopping cart with three line items.

❸ The FidelityPromo promotion gives no discount to joe.

❹ ann gets a 5% discount because she has at least 1,000 points.

❺ The banana_cart has 30 units of the "banana" product and 10 apples.

❻ Thanks to the BulkItemPromo, joe gets a $1.50 discount on the bananas.

❼ long_cart has 10 different items at $1.00 each.

❽ joe gets a 7% discount on the whole order because of LargerOrderPromo.

Example 10-1 works perfectly well, but the same functionality can be implemented with less code in Python by using functions as objects. The next section shows how.

Function-Oriented Strategy

Each concrete strategy in Example 10-1 is a class with a single method, discount. Furthermore, the strategy instances have no state (no instance attributes). You could say they look a lot like plain functions, and you would be right. Example 10-3 is a refactoring of Example 10-1, replacing the concrete strategies with simple functions and removing the Promo abstract class. Only small adjustments are needed in the Order class.[3]

Example 10-3. Order class with discount strategies implemented as functions

```
from collections.abc import Sequence
from dataclasses import dataclass
from decimal import Decimal
from typing import Optional, Callable, NamedTuple


class Customer(NamedTuple):
    name: str
    fidelity: int


class LineItem(NamedTuple):
    product: str
    quantity: int
    price: Decimal

    def total(self):
        return self.price * self.quantity

@dataclass(frozen=True)
class Order:  # the Context
    customer: Customer
    cart: Sequence[LineItem]
    promotion: Optional[Callable[['Order'], Decimal]] = None  ❶

    def total(self) -> Decimal:
        totals = (item.total() for item in self.cart)
        return sum(totals, start=Decimal(0))

    def due(self) -> Decimal:
        if self.promotion is None:
```

---

3 I had to reimplement Order with @dataclass due to a bug in Mypy. You may ignore this detail, because this class works with NamedTuple as well, just like in Example 10-1. If Order is a NamedTuple, Mypy 0.910 crashes when checking the type hint for promotion. I tried adding # type ignore to that specific line, but Mypy crashed anyway. Mypy handles the same type hint correctly if Order is built with @dataclass. Issue #9397 (*https://fpy.li/10-3*) is unresolved as of July 19, 2021. Hopefully it will be fixed by the time you read this.

```
            discount = Decimal(0)
        else:
            discount = self.promotion(self)   ❷
        return self.total() - discount

    def __repr__(self):
        return f'<Order total: {self.total():.2f} due: {self.due():.2f}>'
```

❸

```
def fidelity_promo(order: Order) -> Decimal:   ❹
    """5% discount for customers with 1000 or more fidelity points"""
    if order.customer.fidelity >= 1000:
        return order.total() * Decimal('0.05')
    return Decimal(0)


def bulk_item_promo(order: Order) -> Decimal:
    """10% discount for each LineItem with 20 or more units"""
    discount = Decimal(0)
    for item in order.cart:
        if item.quantity >= 20:
            discount += item.total() * Decimal('0.1')
    return discount


def large_order_promo(order: Order) -> Decimal:
    """7% discount for orders with 10 or more distinct items"""
    distinct_items = {item.product for item in order.cart}
    if len(distinct_items) >= 10:
        return order.total() * Decimal('0.07')
    return Decimal(0)
```

❶ This type hint says: promotion may be None, or it may be a callable that takes an Order argument and returns a Decimal.

❷ To compute a discount, call the self.promotion callable, passing self as an argument. See the following tip for the reason.

❸ No abstract class.

❹ Each strategy is a function.

Why self.promotion(self)?

In the `Order` class, `promotion` is not a method. It's an instance attribute that happens to be callable. So the first part of the expression, `self.promotion`, retrieves that callable. To invoke it, we must provide an instance of `Order`, which in this case is `self`. That's why `self` appears twice in that expression.

"Methods Are Descriptors" on page 902 will explain the mechanism that binds methods to instances automatically. It does not apply to `promotion` because it is not a method.

The code in Example 10-3 is shorter than Example 10-1. Using the new `Order` is also a bit simpler, as shown in the Example 10-4 doctests.

Example 10-4. Sample usage of `Order` class with promotions as functions

```
>>> joe = Customer('John Doe', 0)  ❶
>>> ann = Customer('Ann Smith', 1100)
>>> cart = [LineItem('banana', 4, Decimal('.5')),
...         LineItem('apple', 10, Decimal('1.5')),
...         LineItem('watermelon', 5, Decimal(5))]
>>> Order(joe, cart, fidelity_promo)  ❷
<Order total: 42.00 due: 42.00>
>>> Order(ann, cart, fidelity_promo)
<Order total: 42.00 due: 39.90>
>>> banana_cart = [LineItem('banana', 30, Decimal('.5')),
...                LineItem('apple', 10, Decimal('1.5'))]
>>> Order(joe, banana_cart, bulk_item_promo)  ❸
<Order total: 30.00 due: 28.50>
>>> long_cart = [LineItem(str(item_code), 1, Decimal(1))
...              for item_code in range(10)]
>>> Order(joe, long_cart, large_order_promo)
<Order total: 10.00 due: 9.30>
>>> Order(joe, cart, large_order_promo)
<Order total: 42.00 due: 42.00>
```

❶ Same test fixtures as Example 10-1.

❷ To apply a discount strategy to an `Order`, just pass the promotion function as an argument.

❸ A different promotion function is used here and in the next test.

Note the callouts in Example 10-4—there is no need to instantiate a new promotion object with each new order: the functions are ready to use.

It is interesting to note that in *Design Patterns*, the authors suggest: "Strategy objects often make good flyweights."[4] A definition of the Flyweight pattern in another part of that work states: "A flyweight is a shared object that can be used in multiple contexts simultaneously."[5] The sharing is recommended to reduce the cost of creating a new concrete strategy object when the same strategy is applied over and over again with every new context—with every new Order instance, in our example. So, to overcome a drawback of the Strategy pattern—its runtime cost—the authors recommend applying yet another pattern. Meanwhile, the line count and maintenance cost of your code are piling up.

A thornier use case, with complex concrete strategies holding internal state, may require all the pieces of the Strategy and Flyweight design patterns combined. But often concrete strategies have no internal state; they only deal with data from the context. If that is the case, then by all means use plain old functions instead of coding single-method classes implementing a single-method interface declared in yet another class. A function is more lightweight than an instance of a user-defined class, and there is no need for Flyweight because each strategy function is created just once per Python process when it loads the module. A plain function is also "a shared object that can be used in multiple contexts simultaneously."

Now that we have implemented the Strategy pattern with functions, other possibilities emerge. Suppose you want to create a "metastrategy" that selects the best available discount for a given Order. In the following sections we study additional refactorings that implement this requirement using a variety of approaches that leverage functions and modules as objects.

Choosing the Best Strategy: Simple Approach

Given the same customers and shopping carts from the tests in Example 10-4, we now add three additional tests in Example 10-5.

Example 10-5. The best_promo function applies all discounts and returns the largest

```
>>> Order(joe, long_cart, best_promo)      ❶
<Order total: 10.00 due: 9.30>
>>> Order(joe, banana_cart, best_promo)    ❷
<Order total: 30.00 due: 28.50>
>>> Order(ann, cart, best_promo)           ❸
<Order total: 42.00 due: 39.90>
```

---

4 See page 323 of *Design Patterns*.

5 Ibid., p. 196.

❶ best_promo selected the larger_order_promo for customer joe.

❷ Here joe got the discount from bulk_item_promo for ordering lots of bananas.

❸ Checking out with a simple cart, best_promo gave loyal customer ann the discount for the fidelity_promo.

The implementation of best_promo is very simple. See Example 10-6.

Example 10-6. best_promo finds the maximum discount iterating over a list of functions

```
promos = [fidelity_promo, bulk_item_promo, large_order_promo]  ❶


def best_promo(order: Order) -> Decimal:  ❷
    """Compute the best discount available"""
    return max(promo(order) for promo in promos)  ❸
```

❶ promos: list of the strategies implemented as functions.

❷ best_promo takes an instance of Order as argument, as do the other *_promo functions.

❸ Using a generator expression, we apply each of the functions from promos to the order, and return the maximum discount computed.

Example 10-6 is straightforward: promos is a list of functions. Once you get used to the idea that functions are first-class objects, it naturally follows that building data structures holding functions often makes sense.

Although Example 10-6 works and is easy to read, there is some duplication that could lead to a subtle bug: to add a new promotion strategy, we need to code the function and remember to add it to the promos list, or else the new promotion will work when explicitly passed as an argument to Order, but will not be considered by best_promotion.

Read on for a couple of solutions to this issue.

Finding Strategies in a Module

Modules in Python are also first-class objects, and the standard library provides several functions to handle them. The built-in globals is described as follows in the Python docs:

```
globals()
```
> Return a dictionary representing the current global symbol table. This is always
> the dictionary of the current module (inside a function or method, this is the
> module where it is defined, not the module from which it is called).

Example 10-7 is a somewhat hackish way of using globals to help best_promo automatically find the other available *_promo functions.

Example 10-7. The promos list is built by introspection of the module global namespace

```python
from decimal import Decimal
from strategy import Order
from strategy import (
    fidelity_promo, bulk_item_promo, large_order_promo  ❶
)

promos = [promo for name, promo in globals().items()      ❷
                if name.endswith('_promo') and            ❸
                    name != 'best_promo'                  ❹
]


def best_promo(order: Order) -> Decimal:                  ❺
    """Compute the best discount available"""
    return max(promo(order) for promo in promos)
```

❶ Import the promotion functions so they are available in the global namespace.[6]

❷ Iterate over each item in the dict returned by globals().

❸ Select only values where the name ends with the _promo suffix and…

❹ …filter out best_promo itself, to avoid an infinite recursion when best_promo is
called.

❺ No changes in best_promo.

Another way of collecting the available promotions would be to create a module and
put all the strategy functions there, except for best_promo.

In Example 10-8, the only significant change is that the list of strategy functions
is built by introspection of a separate module called promotions. Note that

---

6 flake8 and VS Code both complain that these names are imported but not used. By definition, static analysis
tools cannot understand the dynamic nature of Python. If we heed every advice from such tools, we'll soon be
writing grim and verbose Java-like code with Python syntax.

Example 10-8 depends on importing the promotions module as well as inspect, which provides high-level introspection functions.

Example 10-8. The promos list is built by introspection of a new promotions module

```
from decimal import Decimal
import inspect

from strategy import Order
import promotions


promos = [func for _, func in inspect.getmembers(promotions, inspect.isfunction)]


def best_promo(order: Order) -> Decimal:
    """Compute the best discount available"""
    return max(promo(order) for promo in promos)
```

The function inspect.getmembers returns the attributes of an object—in this case, the promotions module—optionally filtered by a predicate (a boolean function). We use inspect.isfunction to get only the functions from the module.

Example 10-8 works regardless of the names given to the functions; all that matters is that the promotions module contains only functions that calculate discounts given orders. Of course, this is an implicit assumption of the code. If someone were to create a function with a different signature in the promotions module, then best_promo would break while trying to apply it to an order.

We could add more stringent tests to filter the functions, by inspecting their arguments for instance. The point of Example 10-8 is not to offer a complete solution, but to highlight one possible use of module introspection.

A more explicit alternative to dynamically collecting promotional discount functions would be to use a simple decorator. That's next.

Decorator-Enhanced Strategy Pattern

Recall that our main issue with Example 10-6 is the repetition of the function names in their definitions and then in the promos list used by the best_promo function to determine the highest discount applicable. The repetition is problematic because someone may add a new promotional strategy function and forget to manually add it to the promos list—in which case, best_promo will silently ignore the new strategy, introducing a subtle bug in the system. Example 10-9 solves this problem with the technique covered in "Registration Decorators" on page 310.

Example 10-9. The promos list is filled by the Promotion decorator

```python
Promotion = Callable[[Order], Decimal]

promos: list[Promotion] = []  ❶


def promotion(promo: Promotion) -> Promotion:  ❷
    promos.append(promo)
    return promo


def best_promo(order: Order) -> Decimal:
    """Compute the best discount available"""
    return max(promo(order) for promo in promos)  ❸


@promotion  ❹
def fidelity(order: Order) -> Decimal:
    """5% discount for customers with 1000 or more fidelity points"""
    if order.customer.fidelity >= 1000:
        return order.total() * Decimal('0.05')
    return Decimal(0)


@promotion
def bulk_item(order: Order) -> Decimal:
    """10% discount for each LineItem with 20 or more units"""
    discount = Decimal(0)
    for item in order.cart:
        if item.quantity >= 20:
            discount += item.total() * Decimal('0.1')
    return discount


@promotion
def large_order(order: Order) -> Decimal:
    """7% discount for orders with 10 or more distinct items"""
    distinct_items = {item.product for item in order.cart}
    if len(distinct_items) >= 10:
        return order.total() * Decimal('0.07')
    return Decimal(0)
```

❶ The promos list is a module global, and starts empty.

❷ Promotion is a registration decorator: it returns the promo function unchanged, after appending it to the promos list.

❸ No changes needed to best_promo, because it relies on the promos list.

➍ Any function decorated by @promotion will be added to promos.

This solution has several advantages over the others presented before:

- The promotion strategy functions don't have to use special names—no need for the _promo suffix.

- The @promotion decorator highlights the purpose of the decorated function, and also makes it easy to temporarily disable a promotion: just comment out the decorator.

- Promotional discount strategies may be defined in other modules, anywhere in the system, as long as the @promotion decorator is applied to them.

In the next section, we discuss Command—another design pattern that is sometimes implemented via single-method classes when plain functions would do.

The Command Pattern

Command is another design pattern that can be simplified by the use of functions passed as arguments. Figure 10-2 shows the arrangement of classes in the Command pattern.

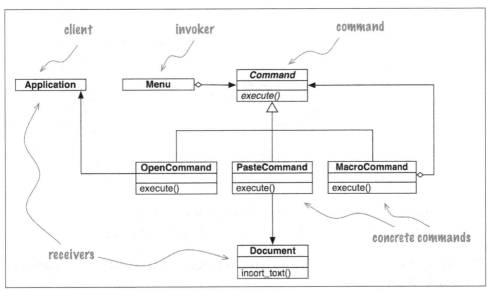

Figure 10-2. UML class diagram for menu-driven text editor implemented with the Command design pattern. Each command may have a different receiver: the object that implements the action. For PasteCommand, the receiver is the Document. For OpenCom mand, the receiver is the application.

The goal of Command is to decouple an object that invokes an operation (the invoker) from the provider object that implements it (the receiver). In the example from *Design Patterns*, each invoker is a menu item in a graphical application, and the receivers are the document being edited or the application itself.

The idea is to put a Command object between the two, implementing an interface with a single method, execute, which calls some method in the receiver to perform the desired operation. That way the invoker does not need to know the interface of the receiver, and different receivers can be adapted through different Command subclasses. The invoker is configured with a concrete command and calls its execute method to operate it. Note in Figure 10-2 that MacroCommand may store a sequence of commands; its execute() method calls the same method in each command stored.

Quoting from *Design Patterns*, "Commands are an object-oriented replacement for callbacks." The question is: do we need an object-oriented replacement for callbacks? Sometimes yes, but not always.

Instead of giving the invoker a Command instance, we can simply give it a function. Instead of calling command.execute(), the invoker can just call command(). The Macro Command can be implemented with a class implementing __call__. Instances of MacroCommand would be callables, each holding a list of functions for future invocation, as implemented in Example 10-10.

Example 10-10. Each instance of MacroCommand has an internal list of commands

```
class MacroCommand:
    """A command that executes a list of commands"""

    def __init__(self, commands):
        self.commands = list(commands)  ❶

    def __call__(self):
        for command in self.commands:  ❷
            command()
```

❶ Building a list from the commands arguments ensures that it is iterable and keeps a local copy of the command references in each MacroCommand instance.

❷ When an instance of MacroCommand is invoked, each command in self.commands is called in sequence.

More advanced uses of the Command pattern—to support undo, for example—may require more than a simple callback function. Even then, Python provides a couple of alternatives that deserve consideration:

- A callable instance like `MacroCommand` in Example 10-10 can keep whatever state is necessary, and provide extra methods in addition to `__call__`.
- A closure can be used to hold the internal state of a function between calls.

This concludes our rethinking of the Command pattern with first-class functions. At a high level, the approach here was similar to the one we applied to Strategy: replacing with callables the instances of a participant class that implemented a single-method interface. After all, every Python callable implements a single-method interface, and that method is named `__call__`.

Chapter Summary

As Peter Norvig pointed out a couple of years after the classic *Design Patterns* book appeared, "16 of 23 patterns have qualitatively simpler implementation in Lisp or Dylan than in C++ for at least some uses of each pattern" (slide 9 of Norvig's "Design Patterns in Dynamic Languages" presentation (*https://fpy.li/10-4*)). Python shares some of the dynamic features of the Lisp and Dylan languages, in particular, first-class functions, our focus in this part of the book.

From the same talk quoted at the start of this chapter, in reflecting on the 20th anniversary of *Design Patterns: Elements of Reusable Object-Oriented Software*, Ralph Johnson has stated that one of the failings of the book is: "Too much emphasis on patterns as end-points instead of steps in the design process."[7] In this chapter, we used the Strategy pattern as a starting point: a working solution that we could simplify using first-class functions.

In many cases, functions or callable objects provide a more natural way of implementing callbacks in Python than mimicking the Strategy or the Command patterns as described by Gamma, Helm, Johnson, and Vlissides in *Design Patterns*. The refactoring of Strategy and the discussion of Command in this chapter are examples of a more general insight: sometimes you may encounter a design pattern or an API that requires that components implement an interface with a single method, and that method has a generic-sounding name such as "execute," "run," or "do_it." Such patterns or APIs often can be implemented with less boilerplate code in Python using functions as first-class objects.

---

7 "Root Cause Analysis of Some Faults in Design Patterns," presented by Johnson at IME-USP, November 15, 2014.

Further Reading

"Recipe 8.21. Implementing the Visitor Pattern," in the *Python Cookbook*, 3rd ed., presents an elegant implementation of the Visitor pattern in which a `NodeVisitor` class handles methods as first-class objects.

On the general topic of design patterns, the choice of readings for the Python programmer is not as broad as what is available to other language communities.

Learning Python Design Patterns, by Gennadiy Zlobin (Packt), is the only book that I have seen entirely devoted to patterns in Python. But Zlobin's work is quite short (100 pages) and covers 8 of the original 23 design patterns.

Expert Python Programming, by Tarek Ziadé (Packt), is one of the best intermediate-level Python books in the market, and its final chapter, "Useful Design Patterns," presents several of the classic patterns from a Pythonic perspective.

Alex Martelli has given several talks about Python design patterns. There is a video of his EuroPython 2011 presentation (*https://fpy.li/10-5*) and a set of slides on his personal website (*https://fpy.li/10-6*). I've found different slide decks and videos over the years, of varying lengths, so it is worthwhile to do a thorough search for his name with the words "Python Design Patterns." A publisher told me Martelli is working on a book about this subject. I will certainly get it when it comes out.

There are many books about design patterns in the context of Java, but among them the one I like most is *Head First Design Patterns*, 2nd ed., by Eric Freeman and Elisabeth Robson (O'Reilly). It explains 16 of the 23 classic patterns. If you like the wacky style of the *Head First* series and need an introduction to this topic, you will love that work. It is Java-centric, but the second edition was updated to reflect the addition of first-class functions in Java, making some of the examples closer to code we'd write in Python.

For a fresh look at patterns from the point of view of a dynamic language with duck typing and first-class functions, *Design Patterns in Ruby* by Russ Olsen (Addison-Wesley) has many insights that are also applicable to Python. In spite of their many syntactic differences, at the semantic level Python and Ruby are closer to each other than to Java or C++.

In "Design Patterns in Dynamic Languages" (*https://fpy.li/norvigdp*) (slides), Peter Norvig shows how first-class functions (and other dynamic features) make several of the original design patterns either simpler or unnecessary.

The introduction of the original *Design Patterns* book by Gamma et al. is worth the price of the book—more than the catalog of 23 patterns, which includes recipes ranging from very important to rarely useful. The widely quoted design principles,

"Program to an interface, not an implementation" and "Favor object composition over class inheritance," both come from that introduction.

The application of patterns to design originated with the architect Christopher Alexander et al., presented in the book *A Pattern Language* (Oxford University Press). Alexander's idea is to create a standard vocabulary allowing teams to share common design decisions while designing buildings. M. J. Dominus wrote "'Design Patterns' Aren't" (*https://fpy.li/10-7*), an intriguing slide deck and postscript text arguing that Alexander's original vision of patterns is more profound, more human, and also applicable to software engineering.

Soapbox

Python has first-class functions and first-class types, features that Norvig claims affect 10 of the 23 patterns (slide 10 of "Design Patterns in Dynamic Languages" (*https://fpy.li/norvigdp*)). In Chapter 9, we saw that Python also has generic functions ("Single Dispatch Generic Functions" on page 326), a limited form of the CLOS multimethods that Gamma et al. suggest as a simpler way to implement the classic Visitor pattern. Norvig, on the other hand, says that multimethods simplify the Builder pattern (slide 10). Matching design patterns to language features is not an exact science.

In classrooms around the world, design patterns are frequently taught using Java examples. I've heard more than one student claim that they were led to believe that the original design patterns are useful in any implementation language. It turns out that the "classic" 23 patterns from *Design Patterns* apply to "classic" Java very well in spite of being originally presented mostly in the context of C++—a few have Smalltalk examples in the book. But that does not mean every one of those patterns applies equally well in any language. The authors are explicit right at the beginning of their book that "some of our patterns are supported directly by the less common object-oriented languages" (recall full quote on the first page of this chapter).

The Python bibliography about design patterns is very thin, compared to that of Java, C++, or Ruby. In "Further Reading" on page 360 I mentioned *Learning Python Design Patterns* by Gennadiy Zlobin, which was published as recently as November 2013. In contrast, Russ Olsen's *Design Patterns in Ruby* was published in 2007 and has 384 pages—284 more than Zlobin's work.

Now that Python is becoming increasingly popular in academia, let's hope more will be written about design patterns in the context of this language. Also, Java 8 introduced method references and anonymous functions, and those highly anticipated features are likely to prompt fresh approaches to patterns in Java—recognizing that as languages evolve, so must our understanding of how to apply the classic design patterns.

The *call* of the Wild

As we collaborated to put the final touches to this book, tech reviewer Leonardo Rochael wondered:

If functions have a __call__ method, and methods are also callable, do __call__ methods also have a __call__ method?

I don't know if his discovery is useful, but it is a fun fact:

```
>>> def turtle():
...         return 'eggs'
...
>>> turtle()
'eggs'
>>> turtle.__call__()
'eggs'
>>> turtle.__call__.__call__()
'eggs'
>>> turtle.__call__.__call__.__call__()
'eggs'
>>> turtle.__call__.__call__.__call__.__call__()
'eggs'
>>> turtle.__call__.__call__.__call__.__call__.__call__()
'eggs'
>>> turtle.__call__.__call__.__call__.__call__.__call__.__call__()
'eggs'
>>> turtle.__call__.__call__.__call__.__call__.__call__.__call__.__call__()
'eggs'
```

Turtles all the way down (*https://fpy.li/10-8*)!

## PART III

Classes and Protocols

## CHAPTER 11

A Pythonic Object

For a library or framework to be Pythonic is to make it as easy and natural as possible for a Python programmer to pick up how to perform a task.

—Martijn Faassen, creator of Python and JavaScript frameworks.[1]

Thanks to the Python Data Model, your user-defined types can behave as naturally as the built-in types. And this can be accomplished without inheritance, in the spirit of *duck typing*: you just implement the methods needed for your objects to behave as expected.

In previous chapters, we studied the behavior of many built-in objects. We will now build user-defined classes that behave as real Python objects. Your application classes probably don't need and should not implement as many special methods as the examples in this chapter. But if you are writing a library or a framework, the programmers who will use your classes may expect them to behave like the classes that Python provides. Fulfilling that expectation is one way of being "Pythonic."

This chapter starts where Chapter 1 ended, by showing how to implement several special methods that are commonly seen in Python objects of many different types.

In this chapter, we will see how to:

- Support the built-in functions that convert objects to other types (e.g., `repr()`, `bytes()`, `complex()`, etc.)
- Implement an alternative constructor as a class method
- Extend the format mini-language used by f-strings, the `format()` built-in, and the `str.format()` method

---

1 From Faassen's blog post, "What is Pythonic?" (*https://fpy.li/11-1*)

- Provide read-only access to attributes
- Make an object hashable for use in sets and as `dict` keys
- Save memory with the use of `__slots__`

We'll do all that as we develop `Vector2d`, a simple two-dimensional Euclidean vector type. This code will be the foundation of an N-dimensional vector class in Chapter 12.

The evolution of the example will be paused to discuss two conceptual topics:

- How and when to use the `@classmethod` and `@staticmethod` decorators
- Private and protected attributes in Python: usage, conventions, and limitations

What's New in This Chapter

I added a new epigraph and a few words in the second paragraph of the chapter to address the concept of "Pythonic"—which was only discussed at the very end in the first edition.

"Formatted Displays" on page 372 was updated to mention f-strings, introduced in Python 3.6. It's a small change because f-strings support the same formatting mini-language as the `format()` built-in and the `str.format()` method, so any previously implemented `__format__` methods simply work with f-strings.

The rest of the chapter barely changed—the special methods are mostly the same since Python 3.0, and the core ideas appeared in Python 2.2.

Let's get started with the object representation methods.

Object Representations

Every object-oriented language has at least one standard way of getting a string representation from any object. Python has two:

`repr()`
> Return a string representing the object as the developer wants to see it. It's what you get when the Python console or a debugger shows an object.

`str()`
> Return a string representing the object as the user wants to see it. It's what you get when you `print()` an object.

The special methods `__repr__` and `__str__` support `repr()` and `str()`, as we saw in Chapter 1.

There are two additional special methods to support alternative representations of objects: __bytes__ and __format__. The __bytes__ method is analogous to __str__: it's called by bytes() to get the object represented as a byte sequence. Regarding __format__, it is used by f-strings, by the built-in function format(), and by the str.format() method. They call obj.__format__(format_spec) to get string displays of objects using special formatting codes. We'll cover __bytes__ in the next example, and __format__ after that.

 If you're coming from Python 2, remember that in Python 3 __repr__, __str__, and __format__ must always return Unicode strings (type str). Only __bytes__ is supposed to return a byte sequence (type bytes).

Vector Class Redux

In order to demonstrate the many methods used to generate object representations, we'll use a Vector2d class similar to the one we saw in Chapter 1. We will build on it in this and future sections. Example 11-1 illustrates the basic behavior we expect from a Vector2d instance.

Example 11-1. Vector2d instances have several representations

```
>>> v1 = Vector2d(3, 4)
>>> print(v1.x, v1.y)    ❶
3.0 4.0
>>> x, y = v1    ❷
>>> x, y
(3.0, 4.0)
>>> v1    ❸
Vector2d(3.0, 4.0)
>>> v1_clone = eval(repr(v1))    ❹
>>> v1 == v1_clone    ❺
True
>>> print(v1)    ❻
(3.0, 4.0)
>>> octets = bytes(v1)    ❼
>>> octets
b'd\\x00\\x00\\x00\\x00\\x00\\x00\\x08@\\x00\\x00\\x00\\x00\\x00\\x00\\x10@'
>>> abs(v1)    ❽
5.0
>>> bool(v1), bool(Vector2d(0, 0))    ❾
(True, False)
```

❶ The components of a `Vector2d` can be accessed directly as attributes (no getter method calls).

❷ A `Vector2d` can be unpacked to a tuple of variables.

❸ The `repr` of a `Vector2d` emulates the source code for constructing the instance.

❹ Using `eval` here shows that the `repr` of a `Vector2d` is a faithful representation of its constructor call.[2]

❺ `Vector2d` supports comparison with `==`; this is useful for testing.

❻ `print` calls `str`, which for `Vector2d` produces an ordered pair display.

❼ `bytes` uses the `__bytes__` method to produce a binary representation.

❽ `abs` uses the `__abs__` method to return the magnitude of the `Vector2d`.

❾ `bool` uses the `__bool__` method to return `False` for a `Vector2d` of zero magnitude or `True` otherwise.

`Vector2d` from Example 11-1 is implemented in *vector2d_v0.py* (Example 11-2). The code is based on Example 1-2, except for the methods for the + and * operations, which we'll see later in Chapter 16. We'll add the method for == since it's useful for testing. At this point, `Vector2d` uses several special methods to provide operations that a Pythonista expects in a well-designed object.

Example 11-2. vector2d_v0.py: methods so far are all special methods

```
from array import array
import math


class Vector2d:
    typecode = 'd'    ❶

    def __init__(self, x, y):
        self.x = float(x)    ❷
        self.y = float(y)

    def __iter__(self):
        return (i for i in (self.x, self.y))    ❸
```

---

2 I used eval to clone the object here just to make a point about repr; to clone an instance, the copy.copy function is safer and faster.

```
def __repr__(self):
    class_name = type(self).__name__
    return '{}({!r}, {!r})'.format(class_name, *self)   ❹

def __str__(self):
    return str(tuple(self))   ❺

def __bytes__(self):
    return (bytes([ord(self.typecode)]) +   ❻
            bytes(array(self.typecode, self)))   ❼

def __eq__(self, other):
    return tuple(self) == tuple(other)   ❽

def __abs__(self):
    return math.hypot(self.x, self.y)   ❾

def __bool__(self):
    return bool(abs(self))   ❿
```

❶ typecode is a class attribute we'll use when converting Vector2d instances to/from bytes.

❷ Converting x and y to float in __init__ catches errors early, which is helpful in case Vector2d is called with unsuitable arguments.

❸ __iter__ makes a Vector2d iterable; this is what makes unpacking work (e.g, x, y = my_vector). We implement it simply by using a generator expression to yield the components one after the other.[3]

❹ __repr__ builds a string by interpolating the components with {!r} to get their repr; because Vector2d is iterable, *self feeds the x and y components to format.

❺ From an iterable Vector2d, it's easy to build a tuple for display as an ordered pair.

❻ To generate bytes, we convert the typecode to bytes and concatenate…

❼ …bytes converted from an array built by iterating over the instance.

---

3 This line could also be written as yield self.x; yield.self.y. I have a lot more to say about the __iter__ special method, generator expressions, and the yield keyword in Chapter 17.

⑧ To quickly compare all components, build tuples out of the operands. This works for operands that are instances of `Vector2d`, but has issues. See the following warning.

⑨ The magnitude is the length of the hypotenuse of the right triangle formed by the x and y components.

⑩ `__bool__` uses `abs(self)` to compute the magnitude, then converts it to `bool`, so `0.0` becomes `False`, nonzero is `True`.

> Method `__eq__` in Example 11-2 works for `Vector2d` operands but also returns `True` when comparing `Vector2d` instances to other iterables holding the same numeric values (e.g., `Vector(3, 4) == [3, 4]`). This may be considered a feature or a bug. Further discussion needs to wait until Chapter 16, when we cover operator overloading.

We have a fairly complete set of basic methods, but we still need a way to rebuild a `Vector2d` from the binary representation produced by `bytes()`.

An Alternative Constructor

Since we can export a `Vector2d` as bytes, naturally we need a method that imports a `Vector2d` from a binary sequence. Looking at the standard library for inspiration, we find that `array.array` has a class method named `.frombytes` that suits our purpose —we saw it in "Arrays" on page 59. We adopt its name and use its functionality in a class method for `Vector2d` in *vector2d_v1.py* (Example 11-3).

Example 11-3. Part of vector2d_v1.py: this snippet shows only the frombytes class method, added to the Vector2d definition in vector2d_v0.py (Example 11-2)

```
@classmethod  ❶
def frombytes(cls, octets):  ❷
    typecode = chr(octets[0])  ❸
    memv = memoryview(octets[1:]).cast(typecode)  ❹
    return cls(*memv)  ❺
```

❶ The `classmethod` decorator modifies a method so it can be called directly on a class.

❷ No `self` argument; instead, the class itself is passed as the first argument—conventionally named `cls`.

❸ Read the `typecode` from the first byte.

❹ Create a `memoryview` from the `octets` binary sequence and use the `typecode` to cast it.[4]

❺ Unpack the `memoryview` resulting from the cast into the pair of arguments needed for the constructor.

I just used a `classmethod` decorator and it is very Python specific, so let's have a word about it.

classmethod Versus staticmethod

The `classmethod` decorator is not mentioned in the Python tutorial, and neither is `staticmethod`. Anyone who has learned OO in Java may wonder why Python has both of these decorators and not just one of them.

Let's start with `classmethod`. Example 11-3 shows its use: to define a method that operates on the class and not on instances. `classmethod` changes the way the method is called, so it receives the class itself as the first argument, instead of an instance. Its most common use is for alternative constructors, like `frombytes` in Example 11-3. Note how the last line of `frombytes` actually uses the `cls` argument by invoking it to build a new instance: `cls(*memv)`.

In contrast, the `staticmethod` decorator changes a method so that it receives no special first argument. In essence, a static method is just like a plain function that happens to live in a class body, instead of being defined at the module level. Example 11-4 contrasts the operation of `classmethod` and `staticmethod`.

Example 11-4. Comparing behaviors of `classmethod` and `staticmethod`

```
>>> class Demo:
...     @classmethod
...     def klassmeth(*args):
...         return args        ❶
...     @staticmethod
...     def statmeth(*args):
...         return args        ❷
...
>>> Demo.klassmeth()           ❸
(<class '__main__.Demo'>,)
>>> Demo.klassmeth('spam')
```

---

4 We had a brief introduction to `memoryview`, explaining its `.cast` method, in "Memory Views" on page 62.

```
(<class '__main__.Demo'>, 'spam')
>>> Demo.statmeth()        ❹
()
>>> Demo.statmeth('spam')
('spam',)
```

❶ klassmeth just returns all positional arguments.

❷ statmeth does the same.

❸ No matter how you invoke it, Demo.klassmeth receives the Demo class as the first argument.

❹ Demo.statmeth behaves just like a plain old function.

> The classmethod decorator is clearly useful, but good use cases for staticmethod are very rare in my experience. Maybe the function is closely related even if it never touches the class, so you may want to place it nearby in the code. Even then, defining the function right before or after the class in the same module is close enough most of the time.[5]

Now that we've seen what classmethod is good for (and that staticmethod is not very useful), let's go back to the issue of object representation and see how to support formatted output.

Formatted Displays

The f-strings, the format() built-in function, and the str.format() method delegate the actual formatting to each type by calling their .__format__(format_spec) method. The format_spec is a formatting specifier, which is either:

- The second argument in format(my_obj, format_spec), or
- Whatever appears after the colon in a replacement field delimited with {} inside an f-string or the fmt in fmt.str.format()

---

5 Leonardo Rochael, one of the technical reviewers of this book, disagrees with my low opinion of staticmethod, and recommends the blog post "The Definitive Guide on How to Use Static, Class or Abstract Methods in Python" (https://fpy.li/11-2) by Julien Danjou as a counterargument. Danjou's post is very good; I do recommend it. But it wasn't enough to change my mind about staticmethod. You'll have to decide for yourself.

For example:

```
>>> brl = 1 / 4.82  # BRL to USD currency conversion rate
>>> brl
0.20746887966804978
>>> format(brl, '0.4f')   ❶
'0.2075'
>>> '1 BRL = {rate:0.2f} USD'.format(rate=brl)   ❷
'1 BRL = 0.21 USD'
>>> f'1 USD = {1 / brl:0.2f} BRL'   ❸
'1 USD = 4.82 BRL'
```

❶ Formatting specifier is '0.4f'.

❷ Formatting specifier is '0.2f'. The rate part in the replacement field is not part of the formatting specifier. It determines which keyword argument of .format() goes into that replacement field.

❸ Again, the specifier is '0.2f'. The 1 / brl expression is not part of it.

The second and third callouts make an important point: a format string such as '{0.mass:5.3e}' actually uses two separate notations. The '0.mass' to the left of the colon is the field_name part of the replacement field syntax, and it can be an arbitrary expression in an f-string. The '5.3e' after the colon is the formatting specifier. The notation used in the formatting specifier is called the Format Specification Mini-Language (*https://fpy.li/11-3*).

If f-strings, format(), and str.format() are new to you, classroom experience tells me it's best to study the format() built-in function first, which uses just the Format Specification Mini-Language (*https://fpy.li/fmtspec*). After you get the gist of that, read "Formatted string literals" (*https://fpy.li/11-4*) and "Format String Syntax" (*https://fpy.li/11-5*) to learn about the {:} replacement field notation, used in f-strings and the str.format() method (including the !s, !r, and !a conversion flags). F-strings don't make str.format() obsolete: most of the time f-strings solve the problem, but sometimes it's better to specify the formatting string elsewhere, and not where it will be rendered.

A few built-in types have their own presentation codes in the Format Specification Mini-Language. For example—among several other codes—the int type supports b and x for base 2 and base 16 output, respectively, while float implements f for a fixed-point display and % for a percentage display:

```
>>> format(42, 'b')
'101010'
```

```
>>> format(2 / 3, '.1%')
'66.7%'
```

The Format Specification Mini-Language is extensible because each class gets to interpret the format_spec argument as it likes. For instance, the classes in the date time module use the same format codes in the strftime() functions and in their __format__ methods. Here are a couple of examples using the format() built-in and the str.format() method:

```
>>> from datetime import datetime
>>> now = datetime.now()
>>> format(now, '%H:%M:%S')
'18:49:05'
>>> "It's now {:%I:%M %p}".format(now)
"It's now 06:49 PM"
```

If a class has no __format__, the method inherited from object returns str(my_object). Because Vector2d has a __str__, this works:

```
>>> v1 = Vector2d(3, 4)
>>> format(v1)
'(3.0, 4.0)'
```

However, if you pass a format specifier, object.__format__ raises TypeError:

```
>>> format(v1, '.3f')
Traceback (most recent call last):
  ...
TypeError: non-empty format string passed to object.__format__
```

We will fix that by implementing our own format mini-language. The first step will be to assume the format specifier provided by the user is intended to format each float component of the vector. This is the result we want:

```
>>> v1 = Vector2d(3, 4)
>>> format(v1)
'(3.0, 4.0)'
>>> format(v1, '.2f')
'(3.00, 4.00)'
>>> format(v1, '.3e')
'(3.000e+00, 4.000e+00)'
```

Example 11-5 implements __format__ to produce the displays just shown.

Example 11-5. Vector2d.__format__ method, take #1

```
# inside the Vector2d class

def __format__(self, fmt_spec=''):
    components = (format(c, fmt_spec) for c in self)   ❶
    return '({}, {})'.format(*components)              ❷
```

❶ Use the `format` built-in to apply the `fmt_spec` to each vector component, building an iterable of formatted strings.

❷ Plug the formatted strings in the formula `'(x, y)'`.

Now let's add a custom formatting code to our mini-language: if the format specifier ends with a `'p'`, we'll display the vector in polar coordinates: `<r, θ>`, where `r` is the magnitude and θ (theta) is the angle in radians. The rest of the format specifier (whatever comes before the `'p'`) will be used as before.

 When choosing the letter for the custom format code, I avoided overlapping with codes used by other types. In Format Specification Mini-Language (*https://fpy.li/11-3*), we see that integers use the codes `'bcdoxXn'`, floats use `'eEfFgGn%'`, and strings use `'s'`. So I picked `'p'` for polar coordinates. Because each class interprets these codes independently, reusing a code letter in a custom format for a new type is not an error, but may be confusing to users.

To generate polar coordinates, we already have the `__abs__` method for the magnitude, and we'll code a simple `angle` method using the `math.atan2()` function to get the angle. This is the code:

```
# inside the Vector2d class

def angle(self):
    return math.atan2(self.y, self.x)
```

With that, we can enhance our `__format__` to produce polar coordinates. See Example 11-6.

Example 11-6. Vector2d.__format__ method, take #2, now with polar coordinates

```
def __format__(self, fmt_spec=''):
    if fmt_spec.endswith('p'):          ❶
        fmt_spec = fmt_spec[:-1]        ❷
        coords = (abs(self), self.angle())   ❸
        outer_fmt = '<{}, {}>'          ❹
    else:
        coords = self                   ❺
        outer_fmt - '({}, {})'          ❻
    components = (format(c, fmt_spec) for c in coords)   ❼
    return outer_fmt.format(*components)   ❽
```

❶ Format ends with `'p'`: use polar coordinates.

❷ Remove `'p'` suffix from `fmt_spec`.

❸ Build `tuple` of polar coordinates: `(magnitude, angle)`.

❹ Configure outer format with angle brackets.

❺ Otherwise, use `x, y` components of `self` for rectangular coordinates.

❻ Configure outer format with parentheses.

❼ Generate iterable with components as formatted strings.

❽ Plug formatted strings into outer format.

With Example 11-6, we get results similar to these:

```
>>> format(Vector2d(1, 1), 'p')
'<1.4142135623730951, 0.7853981633974483>'
>>> format(Vector2d(1, 1), '.3ep')
'<1.414e+00, 7.854e-01>'
>>> format(Vector2d(1, 1), '0.5fp')
'<1.41421, 0.78540>'
```

As this section shows, it's not hard to extend the Format Specification Mini-Language to support user-defined types.

Now let's move to a subject that's not just about appearances: we will make our `Vector2d` hashable, so we can build sets of vectors, or use them as `dict` keys.

A Hashable Vector2d

As defined, so far our `Vector2d` instances are unhashable, so we can't put them in a set:

```
>>> v1 = Vector2d(3, 4)
>>> hash(v1)
Traceback (most recent call last):
  ...
TypeError: unhashable type: 'Vector2d'
>>> set([v1])
Traceback (most recent call last):
  ...
TypeError: unhashable type: 'Vector2d'
```

To make a `Vector2d` hashable, we must implement `__hash__` (`__eq__` is also required, and we already have it). We also need to make vector instances immutable, as we've seen in "What Is Hashable" on page 84.

Right now, anyone can do v1.x = 7, and there is nothing in the code to suggest that changing a Vector2d is forbidden. This is the behavior we want:

```
>>> v1.x, v1.y
(3.0, 4.0)
>>> v1.x = 7
Traceback (most recent call last):
  ...
AttributeError: can't set attribute
```

We'll do that by making the x and y components read-only properties in Example 11-7.

Example 11-7. vector2d_v3.py: only the changes needed to make Vector2d immutable are shown here; see full listing in Example 11-11

```python
class Vector2d:
    typecode = 'd'

    def __init__(self, x, y):
        self.__x = float(x)    ❶
        self.__y = float(y)

    @property    ❷
    def x(self):    ❸
        return self.__x    ❹

    @property    ❺
    def y(self):
        return self.__y

    def __iter__(self):
        return (i for i in (self.x, self.y))    ❻

    # remaining methods: same as previous Vector2d
```

❶ Use exactly two leading underscores (with zero or one trailing underscore) to make an attribute private.[6]

❷ The @property decorator marks the getter method of a property.

❸ The getter method is named after the public property it exposes: x.

❹ Just return self.__x.

---

6 The pros and cons of private attributes are the subject of the upcoming "Private and 'Protected' Attributes in Python" on page 384.

❺ Repeat the same formula for y property.

❻ Every method that just reads the x, y components can stay as it was, reading the public properties via self.x and self.y instead of the private attribute, so this listing omits the rest of the code for the class.

Vector.x and Vector.y are examples of read-only properties. Read/write properties will be covered in Chapter 22, where we dive deeper into @property.

Now that our vectors are reasonably safe from accidental mutation, we can implement the __hash__ method. It should return an int and ideally take into account the hashes of the object attributes that are also used in the __eq__ method, because objects that compare equal should have the same hash. The __hash__ special method documentation (*https://fpy.li/11-7*) suggests computing the hash of a tuple with the components, so that's what we do in Example 11-8.

Example 11-8. vector2d_v3.py: implementation of hash

```
# inside class Vector2d:

def __hash__(self):
    return hash((self.x, self.y))
```

With the addition of the __hash__ method, we now have hashable vectors:

```
>>> v1 = Vector2d(3, 4)
>>> v2 = Vector2d(3.1, 4.2)
>>> hash(v1), hash(v2)
(1079245023883434373, 1994163070182233067)
>>> {v1, v2}
{Vector2d(3.1, 4.2), Vector2d(3.0, 4.0)}
```

It's not strictly necessary to implement properties or otherwise protect the instance attributes to create a hashable type. Implementing __hash__ and __eq__ correctly is all it takes. But the value of a hashable object is never supposed to change, so this provided a good excuse to talk about read-only properties.

If you are creating a type that has a sensible scalar numeric value, you may also implement the __int__ and __float__ methods, invoked by the int() and float() constructors, which are used for type coercion in some contexts. There is also a __complex__ method to support the complex() built-in constructor. Perhaps Vec tor2d should provide __complex__, but I'll leave that as an exercise for you.

Supporting Positional Pattern Matching

So far, Vector2d instances are compatible with keyword class patterns—covered in "Keyword Class Patterns" on page 193.

In Example 11-9, all of these keyword patterns work as expected.

Example 11-9. Keyword patterns for Vector2d subjects—requires Python 3.10

```
def keyword_pattern_demo(v: Vector2d) -> None:
    match v:
        case Vector2d(x=0, y=0):
            print(f'{v!r} is null')
        case Vector2d(x=0):
            print(f'{v!r} is vertical')
        case Vector2d(y=0):
            print(f'{v!r} is horizontal')
        case Vector2d(x=x, y=y) if x==y:
            print(f'{v!r} is diagonal')
        case _:
            print(f'{v!r} is awesome')
```

However, if you try to use a positional pattern like this:

```
        case Vector2d(_, 0):
            print(f'{v!r} is horizontal')
```

you get:

```
    TypeError: Vector2d() accepts 0 positional sub-patterns (1 given)
```

To make Vector2d work with positional patterns, we need to add a class attribute named __match_args__ , listing the instance attributes in the order they will be used for positional pattern matching:

```
    class Vector2d:
        __match_args__ = ('x', 'y')

        # etc...
```

Now we can save a few keystrokes when writing patterns to match Vector2d subjects, as you can see in Example 11-10.

Example 11-10. Positional patterns for Vector2d subjects—requires Python 3.10

```
def positional_pattern_demo(v: Vector2d) -> None:
    match v:
```

```
        case Vector2d(0, 0):
            print(f'{v!r} is null')
        case Vector2d(0):
            print(f'{v!r} is vertical')
        case Vector2d(_, 0):
            print(f'{v!r} is horizontal')
        case Vector2d(x, y) if x==y:
            print(f'{v!r} is diagonal')
        case _:
            print(f'{v!r} is awesome')
```

The __match_args__ class attribute does not need to include all public instance attributes. In particular, if the class __init__ has required and optional arguments that are assigned to instance attributes, it may be reasonable to name the required arguments in __match_args__, but not the optional ones.

Let's step back and review what we've coded so far in Vector2d.

Complete Listing of Vector2d, Version 3

We have been working on Vector2d for a while, showing just snippets, so Example 11-11 is a consolidated, full listing of *vector2d_v3.py*, including the doctests I used when developing it.

Example 11-11. vector2d_v3.py: the full monty

```
"""
A two-dimensional vector class

    >>> v1 = Vector2d(3, 4)
    >>> print(v1.x, v1.y)
    3.0 4.0
    >>> x, y = v1
    >>> x, y
    (3.0, 4.0)
    >>> v1
    Vector2d(3.0, 4.0)
    >>> v1_clone = eval(repr(v1))
    >>> v1 == v1_clone
    True
    >>> print(v1)
    (3.0, 4.0)
    >>> octets = bytes(v1)
    >>> octets
    b'd\\x00\\x00\\x00\\x00\\x00\\x00\\x08@\\x00\\x00\\x00\\x00\\x00\\x00\\x10@'
    >>> abs(v1)
    5.0
    >>> bool(v1), bool(Vector2d(0, 0))
    (True, False)
```

Test of `` `.frombytes()` `` class method:

```
>>> v1_clone = Vector2d.frombytes(bytes(v1))
>>> v1_clone
Vector2d(3.0, 4.0)
>>> v1 == v1_clone
True
```

Tests of `` `format()` `` with Cartesian coordinates:

```
>>> format(v1)
'(3.0, 4.0)'
>>> format(v1, '.2f')
'(3.00, 4.00)'
>>> format(v1, '.3e')
'(3.000e+00, 4.000e+00)'
```

Tests of the `` `angle` `` method::

```
>>> Vector2d(0, 0).angle()
0.0
>>> Vector2d(1, 0).angle()
0.0
>>> epsilon = 10**-8
>>> abs(Vector2d(0, 1).angle() - math.pi/2) < epsilon
True
>>> abs(Vector2d(1, 1).angle() - math.pi/4) < epsilon
True
```

Tests of `` `format()` `` with polar coordinates:

```
>>> format(Vector2d(1, 1), 'p')  # doctest:+ELLIPSIS
'<1.414213..., 0.785398...>'
>>> format(Vector2d(1, 1), '.3ep')
'<1.414e+00, 7.854e-01>'
>>> format(Vector2d(1, 1), '0.5fp')
'<1.41421, 0.78540>'
```

Tests of `x` and `y` read-only properties:

```
>>> v1.x, v1.y
(3.0, 4.0)
>>> v1.x = 123
Traceback (most recent call last):
  ...
AttributeError: can't set attribute 'x'
```

Tests of hashing:

```
>>> v1 = Vector2d(3, 4)
>>> v2 = Vector2d(3.1, 4.2)
>>> len({v1, v2})
2
```

"""

```python
from array import array
import math

class Vector2d:
    __match_args__ = ('x', 'y')

    typecode = 'd'

    def __init__(self, x, y):
        self.__x = float(x)
        self.__y = float(y)

    @property
    def x(self):
        return self.__x

    @property
    def y(self):
        return self.__y

    def __iter__(self):
        return (i for i in (self.x, self.y))

    def __repr__(self):
        class_name = type(self).__name__
        return '{}({!r}, {!r})'.format(class_name, *self)

    def __str__(self):
        return str(tuple(self))

    def __bytes__(self):
        return (bytes([ord(self.typecode)]) +
                bytes(array(self.typecode, self)))

    def __eq__(self, other):
        return tuple(self) == tuple(other)

    def __hash__(self):
        return hash((self.x, self.y))

    def __abs__(self):
```

```
        return math.hypot(self.x, self.y)

    def __bool__(self):
        return bool(abs(self))

    def angle(self):
        return math.atan2(self.y, self.x)

    def __format__(self, fmt_spec=''):
        if fmt_spec.endswith('p'):
            fmt_spec = fmt_spec[:-1]
            coords = (abs(self), self.angle())
            outer_fmt = '<{}, {}>'
        else:
            coords = self
            outer_fmt = '({}, {})'
        components = (format(c, fmt_spec) for c in coords)
        return outer_fmt.format(*components)

    @classmethod
    def frombytes(cls, octets):
        typecode = chr(octets[0])
        memv = memoryview(octets[1:]).cast(typecode)
        return cls(*memv)
```

To recap, in this and the previous sections, we saw some essential special methods that you may want to implement to have a full-fledged object.

You should only implement these special methods if your application needs them. End users don't care if the objects that make up the application are "Pythonic" or not.

On the other hand, if your classes are part of a library for other Python programmers to use, you can't really guess what they will do with your objects, and they may expect more of the "Pythonic" behaviors we are describing.

As coded in Example 11-11, Vector2d is a didactic example with a laundry list of special methods related to object representation, not a template for every user-defined class.

In the next section, we'll take a break from Vector2d to discuss the design and drawbacks of the private attribute mechanism in Python—the double-underscore prefix in self.__x.

Private and "Protected" Attributes in Python

In Python, there is no way to create private variables like there is with the `private` modifier in Java. What we have in Python is a simple mechanism to prevent accidental overwriting of a "private" attribute in a subclass.

Consider this scenario: someone wrote a class named `Dog` that uses a `mood` instance attribute internally, without exposing it. You need to subclass `Dog` as `Beagle`. If you create your own `mood` instance attribute without being aware of the name clash, you will clobber the `mood` attribute used by the methods inherited from `Dog`. This would be a pain to debug.

To prevent this, if you name an instance attribute in the form `__mood` (two leading underscores and zero or at most one trailing underscore), Python stores the name in the instance `__dict__` prefixed with a leading underscore and the class name, so in the `Dog` class, `__mood` becomes `_Dog__mood`, and in `Beagle` it's `_Beagle__mood`. This language feature goes by the lovely name of *name mangling*.

Example 11-12 shows the result in the `Vector2d` class from Example 11-7.

Example 11-12. Private attribute names are "mangled" by prefixing the _ and the class name

```
>>> v1 = Vector2d(3, 4)
>>> v1.__dict__
{'_Vector2d__y': 4.0, '_Vector2d__x': 3.0}
>>> v1._Vector2d__x
3.0
```

Name mangling is about safety, not security: it's designed to prevent accidental access and not malicious prying. Figure 11-1 illustrates another safety device.

Anyone who knows how private names are mangled can read the private attribute directly, as the last line of Example 11-12 shows—that's actually useful for debugging and serialization. They can also directly assign a value to a private component of a `Vector2d` by writing `v1._Vector2d__x = 7`. But if you are doing that in production code, you can't complain if something blows up.

The name mangling functionality is not loved by all Pythonistas, and neither is the skewed look of names written as `self.__x`. Some prefer to avoid this syntax and use just one underscore prefix to "protect" attributes by convention (e.g., `self._x`). Critics of the automatic double-underscore mangling suggest that concerns about accidental attribute clobbering should be addressed by naming conventions. Ian Bicking —creator of pip, virtualenv, and other projects—wrote:

Never, ever use two leading underscores. This is annoyingly private. If name clashes are a concern, use explicit name mangling instead (e.g., _MyThing_blahblah). This is essentially the same thing as double-underscore, only it's transparent where double underscore obscures.[7]

Figure 11-1. A cover on a switch is a safety device, not a security one: it prevents accidents, not sabotage.

The single underscore prefix has no special meaning to the Python interpreter when used in attribute names, but it's a very strong convention among Python programmers that you should not access such attributes from outside the class.[8] It's easy to respect the privacy of an object that marks its attributes with a single _, just as it's easy respect the convention that variables in ALL_CAPS should be treated as constants.

Attributes with a single _ prefix are called "protected" in some corners of the Python documentation.[9] The practice of "protecting" attributes by convention with the form self._x is widespread, but calling that a "protected" attribute is not so common. Some even call that a "private" attribute.

---

7 From the "Paste Style Guide" (*https://fpy.li/11-8*).

8 In modules, a single _ in front of a top-level name does have an effect: if you write from mymod import *, the names with a _ prefix are not imported from mymod. However, you can still write from mymod import _priva tefunc. This is explained in the *Python Tutorial*, section 6.1., "More on Modules" (*https://fpy.li/11-9*).

9 One example is in the gettext module docs (*https://fpy.li/11-10*).

To conclude: the `Vector2d` components are "private" and our `Vector2d` instances are "immutable"—with scare quotes—because there is no way to make them really private and immutable.[10]

We'll now come back to our `Vector2d` class. In the next section, we cover a special attribute (not a method) that affects the internal storage of an object, with potentially huge impact on the use of memory but little effect on its public interface: `__slots__`.

Saving Memory with __slots__

By default, Python stores the attributes of each instance in a `dict` named `__dict__`. As we saw in "Practical Consequences of How dict Works" on page 102, a `dict` has a significant memory overhead—even with the optimizations mentioned in that section. But if you define a class attribute named `__slots__` holding a sequence of attribute names, Python uses an alternative storage model for the instance attributes: the attributes named in `__slots__` are stored in a hidden array or references that use less memory than a `dict`. Let's see how that works through simple examples, starting with Example 11-13.

Example 11-13. The `Pixel` class uses `__slots__`

```
>>> class Pixel:
...     __slots__ = ('x', 'y')  ❶
...
>>> p = Pixel()  ❷
>>> p.__dict__  ❸
Traceback (most recent call last):
  ...
AttributeError: 'Pixel' object has no attribute '__dict__'
>>> p.x = 10  ❹
>>> p.y = 20
>>> p.color = 'red'  ❺
Traceback (most recent call last):
  ...
AttributeError: 'Pixel' object has no attribute 'color'
```

❶ `__slots__` must be present when the class is created; adding or changing it later has no effect. The attribute names may be in a `tuple` or `list`, but I prefer a `tuple` to make it clear there's no point in changing it.

---

10 If this state of affairs depresses you, and makes you wish Python was more like Java in this regard, don't read my discussion of the relative strength of the Java `private` modifier in "Soapbox" on page 396.

❷ Create an instance of `Pixel`, because we see the effects of `__slots__` on the instances.

❸ First effect: instances of `Pixel` have no `__dict__`.

❹ Set the `p.x` and `p.y` attributes normally.

❺ Second effect: trying to set an attribute not listed in `__slots__` raises `AttributeError`.

So far, so good. Now let's create a subclass of `Pixel` in Example 11-14 to see the counterintuitive side of `__slots__`.

Example 11-14. The `OpenPixel` is a subclass of `Pixel`

```
>>> class OpenPixel(Pixel):    ❶
...     pass
...
>>> op = OpenPixel()
>>> op.__dict__    ❷
{}
>>> op.x = 8    ❸
>>> op.__dict__    ❹
{}
>>> op.x    ❺
8
>>> op.color = 'green'    ❻
>>> op.__dict__    ❼
{'color': 'green'}
```

❶ `OpenPixel` declares no attributes of its own.

❷ Surprise: instances of `OpenPixel` have a `__dict__`.

❸ If you set attribute `x` (named in the `__slots__` of the base class `Pixel`)...

❹ ...it is not stored in the instance `__dict__`...

❺ ...but it is stored in the hidden array of references in the instance.

❻ If you set an attribute not named in the `__slots__`...

❼ ...it is stored in the instance `__dict__`.

Example 11-14 shows that the effect of __slots__ is only partially inherited by a subclass. To make sure that instances of a subclass have no __dict__, you must declare __slots__ again in the subclass.

If you declare __slots__ = () (an empty tuple), then the instances of the subclass will have no __dict__ and will only accept the attributes named in the __slots__ of the base class.

If you want a subclass to have additional attributes, name them in __slots__, as shown in Example 11-15.

Example 11-15. The ColorPixel, another subclass of Pixel

```
>>> class ColorPixel(Pixel):
...     __slots__ = ('color',)   ❶
>>> cp = ColorPixel()
>>> cp.__dict__   ❷
Traceback (most recent call last):
  ...
AttributeError: 'ColorPixel' object has no attribute '__dict__'
>>> cp.x = 2
>>> cp.color = 'blue'   ❸
>>> cp.flavor = 'banana'
Traceback (most recent call last):
  ...
AttributeError: 'ColorPixel' object has no attribute 'flavor'
```

❶ Essentially, __slots__ of the superclasses are added to the __slots__ of the current class. Don't forget that single-item tuples must have a trailing comma.

❷ ColorPixel instances have no __dict__.

❸ You can set the attributes declared in the __slots__ of this class and superclasses, but no other.

It's possible to "save memory and eat it too": if you add the '__dict__' name to the __slots__ list, your instances will keep attributes named in __slots__ in the per-instance array of references, but will also support dynamically created attributes, which will be stored in the usual __dict__. This is necessary if you want to use the @cached_property decorator (covered in "Step 5: Caching Properties with functools" on page 859).

Of course, having '__dict__' in __slots__ may entirely defeat its purpose, depending on the number of static and dynamic attributes in each instance and how they are used. Careless optimization is worse than premature optimization: you add complexity but may not get any benefit.

Another special per-instance attribute that you may want to keep is __weakref__, necessary for an object to support weak references (mentioned briefly in "del and Garbage Collection" on page 219). That attribute exists by default in instances of user-defined classes. However, if the class defines __slots__, and you need the instances to be targets of weak references, then you need to include '__weakref__' among the attributes named in __slots__.

Now let's see the effect of adding __slots__ to Vector2d.

Simple Measure of __slot__ Savings

Example 11-16 shows the implementation of __slots__ in Vector2d.

Example 11-16. vector2d_v3_slots.py: the __slots__ attribute is the only addition to Vector2d

```
class Vector2d:
    __match_args__ = ('x', 'y')    ❶
    __slots__ = ('__x', '__y')    ❷

    typecode = 'd'
    # methods are the same as previous version
```

❶ __match_args__ lists the public attribute names for positional pattern matching.

❷ In contrast, __slots__ lists the names of the instance attributes, which in this case are private attributes.

To measure the memory savings, I wrote the *mem_test.py* script. It takes the name of a module with a Vector2d class variant as command-line argument, and uses a list comprehension to build a list with 10,000,000 instances of Vector2d. In the first run shown in Example 11-17, I use vector2d_v3.Vector2d (from Example 11-7); in the second run, I use the version with __slots__ from Example 11-16.

Example 11-17. mem_test.py creates 10 million Vector2d instances using the class defined in the named module

```
$ time python3 mem_test.py vector2d_v3
Selected Vector2d type: vector2d_v3.Vector2d
Creating 10,000,000 Vector2d instances
Initial RAM usage:      6,983,680
  Final RAM usage:  1,666,535,424

real 0m11.990s
user 0m10.861s
sys 0m0.978s
```

```
$ time python3 mem_test.py vector2d_v3_slots
Selected Vector2d type: vector2d_v3_slots.Vector2d
Creating 10,000,000 Vector2d instances
Initial RAM usage:      6,995,968
  Final RAM usage:    577,839,104

real 0m8.381s
user 0m8.006s
sys 0m0.352s
```

As Example 11-17 reveals, the RAM footprint of the script grows to 1.55 GiB when
instance __dict__ is used in each of the 10 million Vector2d instances, but that is
reduced to 551 MiB when Vector2d has a __slots__ attribute. The __slots__ version is also faster. The *mem_test.py* script in this test basically deals with loading a
module, checking memory usage, and formatting results. You can find its source
code in the *fluentpython/example-code-2e* repository (*https://fpy.li/11-11*).

 If you are handling millions of objects with numeric data, you
should really be using NumPy arrays (see "NumPy" on page 64),
which are not only memory efficient but have highly optimized
functions for numeric processing, many of which operate on the
entire array at once. I designed the Vector2d class just to provide
context when discussing special methods, because I try to avoid
vague foo and bar examples when I can.

Summarizing the Issues with __slots__

The __slots__ class attribute may provide significant memory savings if properly
used, but there are a few caveats:

- You must remember to redeclare __slots__ in each subclass to prevent their
  instances from having __dict__.

- Instances will only be able to have the attributes listed in __slots__, unless you
  include '__dict__' in __slots__ (but doing so may negate the memory
  savings).

- Classes using __slots__ cannot use the @cached_property decorator, unless
  they explicitly name '__dict__' in __slots__.

- Instances cannot be targets of weak references, unless you add '__weakref__' in
  __slots__.

The last topic in this chapter has to do with overriding a class attribute in instances
and subclasses.

Overriding Class Attributes

A distinctive feature of Python is how class attributes can be used as default values for instance attributes. In Vector2d there is the typecode class attribute. It's used twice in the __bytes__ method, but we read it as self.typecode by design. Because Vector2d instances are created without a typecode attribute of their own, self.typecode will get the Vector2d.typecode class attribute by default.

But if you write to an instance attribute that does not exist, you create a new instance attribute—e.g., a typecode instance attribute—and the class attribute by the same name is untouched. However, from then on, whenever the code handling that instance reads self.typecode, the instance typecode will be retrieved, effectively shadowing the class attribute by the same name. This opens the possibility of customizing an individual instance with a different typecode.

The default Vector2d.typecode is 'd', meaning each vector component will be represented as an 8-byte double precision float when exporting to bytes. If we set the typecode of a Vector2d instance to 'f' prior to exporting, each component will be exported as a 4-byte single precision float. Example 11-18 demonstrates.

 We are discussing adding a custom instance attribute, therefore Example 11-18 uses the Vector2d implementation without __slots__, as listed in Example 11-11.

Example 11-18. Customizing an instance by setting the typecode attribute that was formerly inherited from the class

```
>>> from vector2d_v3 import Vector2d
>>> v1 = Vector2d(1.1, 2.2)
>>> dumpd = bytes(v1)
>>> dumpd
b'd\x9a\x99\x99\x99\x99\x99\xf1?\x9a\x99\x99\x99\x99\x99\x01@'
>>> len(dumpd)    ❶
17
>>> v1.typecode = 'f'    ❷
>>> dumpf = bytes(v1)
>>> dumpf
b'f\xcd\xcc\x8c?\xcd\xcc\x0c@'
>>> len(dumpf)    ❸
9
>>> Vector2d.typecode    ❹
'd'
```

❶ Default `bytes` representation is 17 bytes long.

❷ Set `typecode` to `'f'` in the v1 instance.

❸ Now the `bytes` dump is 9 bytes long.

❹ `Vector2d.typecode` is unchanged; only the v1 instance uses typecode `'f'`.

Now it should be clear why the `bytes` export of a `Vector2d` is prefixed by the type code: we wanted to support different export formats.

If you want to change a class attribute, you must set it on the class directly, not through an instance. You could change the default `typecode` for all instances (that don't have their own `typecode`) by doing this:

```
>>> Vector2d.typecode = 'f'
```

However, there is an idiomatic Python way of achieving a more permanent effect, and being more explicit about the change. Because class attributes are public, they are inherited by subclasses, so it's common practice to subclass just to customize a class data attribute. The Django class-based views use this technique extensively. Example 11-19 shows how.

Example 11-19. The ShortVector2d is a subclass of Vector2d, which only overwrites the default typecode

```
>>> from vector2d_v3 import Vector2d
>>> class ShortVector2d(Vector2d):   ❶
...     typecode = 'f'
...
>>> sv = ShortVector2d(1/11, 1/27)   ❷
>>> sv
ShortVector2d(0.09090909090909091, 0.037037037037037035)   ❸
>>> len(bytes(sv))   ❹
9
```

❶ Create `ShortVector2d` as a `Vector2d` subclass just to overwrite the `typecode` class attribute.

❷ Build `ShortVector2d` instance sv for demonstration.

❸ Inspect the `repr` of sv.

❹ Check that the length of the exported bytes is 9, not 17 as before.

This example also explains why I did not hardcode the `class_name` in `Vector2d.__repr__`, but instead got it from `type(self).__name__`, like this:

```
# inside class Vector2d:

    def __repr__(self):
        class_name = type(self).__name__
        return '{}({!r}, {!r})'.format(class_name, *self)
```

If I had hardcoded the class_name, subclasses of Vector2d like ShortVector2d would have to overwrite __repr__ just to change the class_name. By reading the name from the type of the instance, I made __repr__ safer to inherit.

This ends our coverage of building a simple class that leverages the data model to play well with the rest of Python: offering different object representations, providing a custom formatting code, exposing read-only attributes, and supporting hash() to integrate with sets and mappings.

Chapter Summary

The aim of this chapter was to demonstrate the use of special methods and conventions in the construction of a well-behaved Pythonic class.

Is *vector2d_v3.py* (shown in Example 11-11) more Pythonic than *vector2d_v0.py* (shown in Example 11-2)? The Vector2d class in *vector2d_v3.py* certainly exhibits more Python features. But whether the first or the last Vector2d implementation is suitable depends on the context where it would be used. Tim Peter's "Zen of Python" says:

> Simple is better than complex.

An object should be as simple as the requirements dictate—and not a parade of language features. If the code is for an application, then it should focus on what is needed to support the end users, not more. If the code is for a library for other programmers to use, then it's reasonable to implement special methods supporting behaviors that Pythonistas expect. For example, __eq__ may not be necessary to support a business requirement, but it makes the class easier to test.

My goal in expanding the Vector2d code was to provide context for discussing Python special methods and coding conventions. The examples in this chapter have demonstrated several of the special methods we first saw in Table 1-1 (Chapter 1):

- String/bytes representation methods: __repr__, __str__, __format__, and __bytes__
- Methods for reducing an object to a number: __abs__, __bool__, and __hash__
- The __eq__ operator, to support testing and hashing (along with __hash__)

While supporting conversion to bytes, we also implemented an alternative constructor, Vector2d.frombytes(), which provided the context for discussing the decorators @classmethod (very handy) and @staticmethod (not so useful, module-level functions are simpler). The frombytes method was inspired by its namesake in the array.array class.

We saw that the Format Specification Mini-Language (*https://fpy.li/fmtspec*) is extensible by implementing a __format__ method that parses a format_spec provided to the format(obj, format_spec) built-in or within replacement fields '{:«for mat_spec»}' in f-strings or strings used with the str.format() method.

In preparation to make Vector2d instances hashable, we made an effort to make them immutable, at least preventing accidental changes by coding the x and y attributes as private, and exposing them as read-only properties. We then implemented __hash__ using the recommended technique of xor-ing the hashes of the instance attributes.

We then discussed the memory savings and the caveats of declaring a __slots__ attribute in Vector2d. Because using __slots__ has side effects, it really makes sense only when handling a very large number of instances—think millions of instances, not just thousands. In many such cases, using pandas (*https://fpy.li/pandas*) may be the best option.

The last topic we covered was the overriding of a class attribute accessed via the instances (e.g., self.typecode). We did that first by creating an instance attribute, and then by subclassing and overwriting at the class level.

Throughout the chapter, I mentioned how design choices in the examples were informed by studying the API of standard Python objects. If this chapter can be summarized in one sentence, this is it:

> To build Pythonic objects, observe how real Python objects behave.
>
> —Ancient Chinese proverb

Further Reading

This chapter covered several special methods of the data model, so naturally the primary references are the same as the ones provided in Chapter 1, which gave a high-level view of the same topic. For convenience, I'll repeat those four earlier recommendations here, and add a few other ones:

The "Data Model" chapter (https://fpy.li/dtmodel) of The Python Language Reference
    Most of the methods we used in this chapter are documented in "3.3.1. Basic customization" (*https://fpy.li/11-12*).

Python in a Nutshell, 3rd ed., by Alex Martelli, Anna Ravenscroft, and Steve Holden
Covers the special methods in depth.

Python Cookbook, 3rd ed., by David Beazley and Brian K. Jones
Modern Python practices demonstrated through recipes. Chapter 8, "Classes and Objects," in particular has several solutions related to discussions in this chapter.

Python Essential Reference, 4th ed., by David Beazley
Covers the data model in detail, even if only Python 2.6 and 3.0 are covered (in the fourth edition). The fundamental concepts are all the same and most of the Data Model APIs haven't changed at all since Python 2.2, when built-in types and user-defined classes were unified.

In 2015—the year I finished the first edition of *Fluent Python*—Hynek Schlawack started the `attrs` package. From the `attrs` documentation:

> `attrs` is the Python package that will bring back the **joy** of **writing classes** by relieving you from the drudgery of implementing object protocols (aka dunder methods).

I mentioned `attrs` as a more powerful alternative to `@dataclass` in "Further Reading" on page 196. The data class builders from Chapter 5 as well as `attrs` automatically equip your classes with several special methods. But knowing how to code those special methods yourself is still essential to understand what those packages do, to decide whether you really need them, and to override the methods they generate—when necessary.

In this chapter, we saw every special method related to object representation, except `__index__` and `__fspath__`. We'll discuss `__index__` in Chapter 12, "A Slice-Aware `__getitem__`" on page 408. I will not cover `__fspath__`. To learn about it, see PEP 519 —Adding a file system path protocol (*https://fpy.li/pep519*).

An early realization of the need for distinct string representations for objects appeared in Smalltalk. The 1996 article "How to Display an Object as a String: print-String and displayString" (*https://fpy.li/11-13*) by Bobby Woolf discusses the implementation of the `printString` and `displayString` methods in that language. From that article, I borrowed the pithy descriptions "the way the developer wants to see it" and "the way the user wants to see it" when defining `repr()` and `str()` in "Object Representations" on page 366.

Soapbox

Properties Help Reduce Up-Front Costs

In the initial versions of `Vector2d`, the `x` and `y` attributes were public, as are all Python instance and class attributes by default. Naturally, users of vectors need to access its components. Although our vectors are iterable and can be unpacked into a pair of variables, it's also desirable to write `my_vector.x` and `my_vector.y` to get each component.

When we felt the need to avoid accidental updates to the `x` and `y` attributes, we implemented properties, but nothing changed elsewhere in the code and in the public interface of `Vector2d`, as verified by the doctests. We are still able to access `my_vector.x` and `my_vector.y`.

This shows that we can always start our classes in the simplest possible way, with public attributes, because when (or if) we later need to impose more control with getters and setters, these can be implemented through properties without changing any of the code that already interacts with our objects through the names (e.g., `x` and `y`) that were initially simple public attributes.

This approach is the opposite of that encouraged by the Java language: a Java programmer cannot start with simple public attributes and only later, if needed, implement properties, because they don't exist in the language. Therefore, writing getters and setters is the norm in Java—even when those methods do nothing useful —because the API cannot evolve from simple public attributes to getters and setters without breaking all code that uses those attributes.

In addition, as Martelli, Ravenscroft, and Holden point out in *Python in a Nutshell*, 3rd ed., typing getter/setter calls everywhere is goofy. You have to write stuff like:

```
>>> my_object.set_foo(my_object.get_foo() + 1)
```

Just to do this:

```
>>> my_object.foo += 1
```

Ward Cunningham, inventor of the wiki and an Extreme Programming pioneer, recommends asking: "What's the simplest thing that could possibly work?" The idea is to focus on the goal.[11] Implementing setters and getters up-front is a distraction from the goal. In Python, we can simply use public attributes, knowing we can change them to properties later, if the need arises.

---

11 See the "Simplest Thing that Could Possibly Work: A Conversation with Ward Cunningham, Part V" (*https://fpy.li/11-14*).

Safety Versus Security in Private Attributes

> Perl doesn't have an infatuation with enforced privacy. It would prefer that you stayed out of its living room because you weren't invited, not because it has a shotgun.
>
> —Larry Wall, creator of Perl

Python and Perl are polar opposites in many regards, but Guido and Larry seem to agree on object privacy.

Having taught Python to many Java programmers over the years, I've found a lot of them put too much faith in the privacy guarantees that Java offers. As it turns out, the Java `private` and `protected` modifiers normally provide protection against accidents only (i.e., safety). They only offer security against malicious intent if the application is specially configured and deployed on top of a Java SecurityManager (*https://fpy.li/ 11-15*), and that seldom happens in practice, even in security conscious corporate settings.

To prove my point, I like to show this Java class (Example 11-20).

Example 11-20. Confidential.java: a Java class with a private field named `secret`

```
public class Confidential {

    private String secret = "";

    public Confidential(String text) {
        this.secret = text.toUpperCase();
    }
}
```

In Example 11-20, I store the `text` in the `secret` field after converting it to uppercase, just to make it obvious that whatever is in that field will be in all caps.

The actual demonstration consists of running *expose.py* with Jython. That script uses introspection ("reflection" in Java parlance) to get the value of a private field. The code is in Example 11-21.

Example 11-21. expose.py: Jython code to read the content of a private field in another class

```
#!/usr/bin/env jython
# NOTE: Jython is still Python 2.7 in late2020

import Confidential

message = Confidential('top secret text')
secret_field = Confidential.getDeclaredField('secret')
secret_field.setAccessible(True)  # break the lock!
print 'message.secret =', secret_field.get(message)
```

If you run Example 11-21, this is what you get:

```
$ jython expose.py
message.secret = TOP SECRET TEXT
```

The string `'TOP SECRET TEXT'` was read from the `secret` private field of the `Confidential` class.

There is no black magic here: *expose.py* uses the Java reflection API to get a reference to the private field named `'secret'`, and then calls `'secret_field.setAccessible(True)'` to make it readable. The same thing can be done with Java code, of course (but it takes more than three times as many lines to do it; see the file *Expose.java* (*https://fpy.li/11-16*) in the _Fluent Python_ code repository).

The crucial call `.setAccessible(True)` will fail only if the Jython script or the Java main program (e.g., `Expose.class`) is running under the supervision of a Security-Manager (*https://fpy.li/11-15*). But in the real world, Java applications are rarely deployed with a SecurityManager—except for Java applets when they were still supported by browsers.

My point is: in Java too, access control modifiers are mostly about safety and not security, at least in practice. So relax and enjoy the power Python gives you. Use it responsibly.

## CHAPTER 12

Special Methods for Sequences

Don't check whether it *is*-a duck: check whether it *quacks*-like-a duck, *walks*-like-a duck, etc., etc., depending on exactly what subset of duck-like behavior you need to play your language-games with. (`comp.lang.python`, Jul. 26, 2000)

 —Alex Martelli

In this chapter, we will create a class to represent a multidimensional `Vector` class—a significant step up from the two-dimensional `Vector2d` of Chapter 11. `Vector` will behave like a standard Python immutable flat sequence. Its elements will be floats, and it will support the following by the end of this chapter:

- Basic sequence protocol: `__len__` and `__getitem__`
- Safe representation of instances with many items
- Proper slicing support, producing new `Vector` instances
- Aggregate hashing, taking into account every contained element value
- Custom formatting language extension

We'll also implement dynamic attribute access with `__getattr__` as a way of replacing the read-only properties we used in `Vector2d`—although this is not typical of sequence types.

The code-intensive presentation will be interrupted by a conceptual discussion about the idea of protocols as an informal interface. We'll talk about how protocols and *duck typing* are related, and its practical implications when you create your own types.

What's New in This Chapter

There are no major changes in this chapter. There is a new, brief discussion of the typing.Protocol in a tip box near the end of "Protocols and Duck Typing" on page 404.

In "A Slice-Aware __getitem__" on page 408, the implementation of __getitem__ in Example 12-6 is more concise and robust than the example in the first edition, thanks to duck typing and operator.index. This change carried over to later implementations of Vector in this chapter and in Chapter 16.

Let's get started.

Vector: A User-Defined Sequence Type

Our strategy to implement Vector will be to use composition, not inheritance. We'll store the components in an array of floats, and will implement the methods needed for our Vector to behave like an immutable flat sequence.

But before we implement the sequence methods, let's make sure we have a baseline implementation of Vector that is compatible with our earlier Vector2d class—except where such compatibility would not make sense.

Vector Applications Beyond Three Dimensions

Who needs a vector with 1,000 dimensions? N-dimensional vectors (with large values of N) are widely used in information retrieval, where documents and text queries are represented as vectors, with one dimension per word. This is called the Vector space model (*https://fpy.li/12-1*). In this model, a key relevance metric is the cosine similarity (i.e., the cosine of the angle between the vector representing the query and the vector representing the document). As the angle decreases, the cosine approaches the maximum value of 1, and so does the relevance of the document to the query.

Having said that, the Vector class in this chapter is a didactic example and we'll not do much math here. Our goal is just to demonstrate some Python special methods in the context of a sequence type.

NumPy and SciPy are the tools you need for real-world vector math. The PyPI package gensim (*https://fpy.li/12-2*), by Radim Řehůřek, implements vector space modeling for natural language processing and information retrieval, using NumPy and SciPy.

Vector Take #1: Vector2d Compatible

The first version of `Vector` should be as compatible as possible with our earlier `Vector2d` class.

However, by design, the `Vector` constructor is not compatible with the `Vector2d` constructor. We could make `Vector(3, 4)` and `Vector(3, 4, 5)` work, by taking arbitrary arguments with `*args` in `__init__`, but the best practice for a sequence constructor is to take the data as an iterable argument in the constructor, like all built-in sequence types do. Example 12-1 shows some ways of instantiating our new `Vector` objects.

Example 12-1. Tests of Vector.__init__ and Vector.__repr__

```
>>> Vector([3.1, 4.2])
Vector([3.1, 4.2])
>>> Vector((3, 4, 5))
Vector([3.0, 4.0, 5.0])
>>> Vector(range(10))
Vector([0.0, 1.0, 2.0, 3.0, 4.0, ...])
```

Apart from a new constructor signature, I made sure every test I did with `Vector2d` (e.g., `Vector2d(3, 4)`) passed and produced the same result with a two-component `Vector([3, 4])`.

 When a `Vector` has more than six components, the string produced by `repr()` is abbreviated with ... as seen in the last line of Example 12-1. This is crucial in any collection type that may contain a large number of items, because `repr` is used for debugging— and you don't want a single large object to span thousands of lines in your console or log. Use the `reprlib` module to produce limited-length representations, as in Example 12-2. The `reprlib` module was named `repr` in Python 2.7.

Example 12-2 lists the implementation of our first version of `Vector` (this example builds on the code shown in Examples 11-2 and 11-3).

Example 12-2. vector_v1.py: derived from vector2d_v1.py

```
from array import array
import reprlib
import math


class Vector:
```

```
    typecode = 'd'

    def __init__(self, components):
        self._components = array(self.typecode, components)  ❶

    def __iter__(self):
        return iter(self._components)  ❷

    def __repr__(self):
        components = reprlib.repr(self._components)  ❸
        components = components[components.find('['):-1]  ❹
        return f'Vector({components})'

    def __str__(self):
        return str(tuple(self))

    def __bytes__(self):
        return (bytes([ord(self.typecode)]) +
                bytes(self._components))  ❺

    def __eq__(self, other):
        return tuple(self) == tuple(other)

    def __abs__(self):
        return math.hypot(*self)  ❻

    def __bool__(self):
        return bool(abs(self))

    @classmethod
    def frombytes(cls, octets):
        typecode = chr(octets[0])
        memv = memoryview(octets[1:]).cast(typecode)
        return cls(memv)  ❼
```

❶ The self._components instance "protected" attribute will hold an array with the Vector components.

❷ To allow iteration, we return an iterator over self._components.[1]

❸ Use reprlib.repr() to get a limited-length representation of self._components (e.g., array('d', [0.0, 1.0, 2.0, 3.0, 4.0, ...])).

❹ Remove the array('d', prefix, and the trailing) before plugging the string into a Vector constructor call.

---

1 The iter() function is covered in Chapter 17, along with the __iter__ method.

❺ Build a bytes object directly from `self._components`.

❻ Since Python 3.8, `math.hypot` accepts N-dimensional points. I used this expression before: `math.sqrt(sum(x * x for x in self))`.

❼ The only change needed from the earlier `frombytes` is in the last line: we pass the `memoryview` directly to the constructor, without unpacking with `*` as we did before.

The way I used `reprlib.repr` deserves some elaboration. That function produces safe representations of large or recursive structures by limiting the length of the output string and marking the cut with `'...'`. I wanted the repr of a Vector to look like `Vector([3.0, 4.0, 5.0])` and not `Vector(array('d', [3.0, 4.0, 5.0]))`, because the fact that there is an `array` inside a Vector is an implementation detail. Because these constructor calls build identical Vector objects, I prefer the simpler syntax using a `list` argument.

When coding `__repr__`, I could have produced the simplified `components` display with this expression: `reprlib.repr(list(self._components))`. However, this would be wasteful, as I'd be copying every item from `self._components` to a `list` just to use the `list` repr. Instead, I decided to apply `reprlib.repr` to the `self._components` array directly, and then chop off the characters outside of the `[]`. That's what the second line of `__repr__` does in Example 12-2.

> Because of its role in debugging, calling `repr()` on an object should never raise an exception. If something goes wrong inside your implementation of `__repr__`, you must deal with the issue and do your best to produce some serviceable output that gives the user a chance of identifying the receiver (`self`).

Note that the `__str__`, `__eq__`, and `__bool__` methods are unchanged from `Vector2d`, and only one character was changed in `frombytes` (a `*` was removed in the last line). This is one of the benefits of making the original `Vector2d` iterable.

By the way, we could have subclassed Vector from Vector2d, but I chose not to do it for two reasons. First, the incompatible constructors really make subclassing not advisable. I could work around that with some clever parameter handling in `__init__`, but the second reason is more important: I want Vector to be a standalone example of a class implementing the sequence protocol. That's what we'll do next, after a discussion of the term *protocol*.

Protocols and Duck Typing

As early as Chapter 1, we saw that you don't need to inherit from any special class to create a fully functional sequence type in Python; you just need to implement the methods that fulfill the sequence protocol. But what kind of protocol are we talking about?

In the context of object-oriented programming, a protocol is an informal interface, defined only in documentation and not in code. For example, the sequence protocol in Python entails just the __len__ and __getitem__ methods. Any class Spam that implements those methods with the standard signature and semantics can be used anywhere a sequence is expected. Whether Spam is a subclass of this or that is irrelevant; all that matters is that it provides the necessary methods. We saw that in Example 1-1, reproduced here in Example 12-3.

Example 12-3. Code from Example 1-1, reproduced here for convenience

```
import collections

Card = collections.namedtuple('Card', ['rank', 'suit'])

class FrenchDeck:
    ranks = [str(n) for n in range(2, 11)] + list('JQKA')
    suits = 'spades diamonds clubs hearts'.split()

    def __init__(self):
        self._cards = [Card(rank, suit) for suit in self.suits
                                        for rank in self.ranks]

    def __len__(self):
        return len(self._cards)

    def __getitem__(self, position):
        return self._cards[position]
```

The FrenchDeck class in Example 12-3 takes advantage of many Python facilities because it implements the sequence protocol, even if that is not declared anywhere in the code. An experienced Python coder will look at it and understand that it *is* a sequence, even if it subclasses object. We say it *is* a sequence because it *behaves* like one, and that is what matters.

This became known as *duck typing*, after Alex Martelli's post quoted at the beginning of this chapter.

Because protocols are informal and unenforced, you can often get away with implementing just part of a protocol, if you know the specific context where a class will be used. For example, to support iteration, only __getitem__ is required; there is no need to provide __len__.

 With PEP 544—Protocols: Structural subtyping (static duck typing) (*https://fpy.li/pep544*), Python 3.8 supports *protocol classes*: typing constructs, which we studied in "Static Protocols" on page 287. This new use of the word protocol in Python has a related but different meaning. When I need to differentiate them, I write *static protocol* to refer to the protocols formalized in protocol classes, and *dynamic protocol* for the traditional sense. One key difference is that static protocol implementations must provide all methods defined in the protocol class. "Two Kinds of Protocols" on page 436 in Chapter 13 has more details.

We'll now implement the sequence protocol in Vector, initially without proper support for slicing, but later adding that.

Vector Take #2: A Sliceable Sequence

As we saw with the FrenchDeck example, supporting the sequence protocol is really easy if you can delegate to a sequence attribute in your object, like our self._compo nents array. These __len__ and __getitem__ one-liners are a good start:

```
class Vector:
    # many lines omitted
    # ...

    def __len__(self):
        return len(self._components)

    def __getitem__(self, index):
        return self._components[index]
```

With these additions, all of these operations now work:

```
>>> v1 = Vector([3, 4, 5])
>>> len(v1)
3
>>> v1[0], v1[-1]
(3.0, 5.0)
>>> v7 = Vector(range(7))
>>> v7[1:4]
array('d', [1.0, 2.0, 3.0])
```

As you can see, even slicing is supported—but not very well. It would be better if a slice of a Vector was also a Vector instance and not an array. The old FrenchDeck class has a similar problem: when you slice it, you get a list. In the case of Vector, a lot of functionality is lost when slicing produces plain arrays.

Consider the built-in sequence types: every one of them, when sliced, produces a new instance of its own type, and not of some other type.

To make Vector produce slices as Vector instances, we can't just delegate the slicing to array. We need to analyze the arguments we get in __getitem__ and do the right thing.

Now, let's see how Python turns the syntax my_seq[1:3] into arguments for my_seq.__getitem__(...).

How Slicing Works

A demo is worth a thousand words, so take a look at Example 12-4.

Example 12-4. Checking out the behavior of __getitem__ and slices

```
>>> class MySeq:
...     def __getitem__(self, index):
...         return index  ❶
...
>>> s = MySeq()
>>> s[1]  ❷
1
>>> s[1:4]  ❸
slice(1, 4, None)
>>> s[1:4:2]  ❹
slice(1, 4, 2)
>>> s[1:4:2, 9]  ❺
(slice(1, 4, 2), 9)
>>> s[1:4:2, 7:9]  ❻
(slice(1, 4, 2), slice(7, 9, None))
```

❶ For this demonstration, __getitem__ merely returns whatever is passed to it.

❷ A single index, nothing new.

❸ The notation 1:4 becomes slice(1, 4, None).

❹ slice(1, 4, 2) means start at 1, stop at 4, step by 2.

❺ Surprise: the presence of commas inside the [] means __getitem__ receives a tuple.

❻ The tuple may even hold several slice objects.

Now let's take a closer look at slice itself in Example 12-5.

Example 12-5. Inspecting the attributes of the slice *class*

```
>>> slice ❶
<class 'slice'>
>>> dir(slice) ❷
['__class__', '__delattr__', '__dir__', '__doc__', '__eq__',
 '__format__', '__ge__', '__getattribute__', '__gt__',
 '__hash__', '__init__', '__le__', '__lt__', '__ne__',
 '__new__', '__reduce__', '__reduce_ex__', '__repr__',
 '__setattr__', '__sizeof__', '__str__', '__subclasshook__',
 'indices', 'start', 'step', 'stop']
```

❶ slice is a built-in type (we saw it first in "Slice Objects" on page 48).

❷ Inspecting a slice, we find the data attributes start, stop, and step, and an indices method.

In Example 12-5, calling dir(slice) reveals an indices attribute, which turns out to be a very interesting but little-known method. Here is what help(slice.indices) reveals:

S.indices(len) -> (start, stop, stride)
> Assuming a sequence of length len, calculate the start and stop indices, and the stride length of the extended slice described by S. Out-of-bounds indices are clipped just like they are in a normal slice.

In other words, indices exposes the tricky logic that's implemented in the built-in sequences to gracefully handle missing or negative indices and slices that are longer than the original sequence. This method produces "normalized" tuples of nonnegative start, stop, and stride integers tailored to a sequence of the given length.

Here are a couple of examples, considering a sequence of len == 5, e.g., 'ABCDE':

```
>>> slice(None, 10, 2).indices(5) ❶
(0, 5, 2)
>>> slice(-3, None, None).indices(5) ❷
(2, 5, 1)
```

❶ 'ABCDE'[:10:2] is the same as 'ABCDE'[0:5:2].

❷ 'ABCDE'[-3:] is the same as 'ABCDE'[2:5:1].

In our Vector code, we'll not need the slice.indices() method because when we get a slice argument we'll delegate its handling to the _components array. But if you can't count on the services of an underlying sequence, this method can be a huge time saver.

Now that we know how to handle slices, let's take a look at the improved Vec tor.__getitem__ implementation.

A Slice-Aware __getitem__

Example 12-6 lists the two methods needed to make Vector behave as a sequence: __len__ and __getitem__ (the latter now implemented to handle slicing correctly).

Example 12-6. Part of vector_v2.py: __len__ and __getitem__ methods added to Vector class from vector_v1.py (see Example 12-2)

```
def __len__(self):
    return len(self._components)

def __getitem__(self, key):
    if isinstance(key, slice):        ❶
        cls = type(self)              ❷
        return cls(self._components[key])    ❸
    index = operator.index(key)       ❹
    return self._components[index]    ❺
```

❶ If the key argument is a slice...

❷ ...get the class of the instance (i.e., Vector) and...

❸ ...invoke the class to build another Vector instance from a slice of the _components array.

❹ If we can get an index from key...

❺ ...return the specific item from _components.

The operator.index() function calls the __index__ special method. The function and the special method were defined in PEP 357—Allowing Any Object to be Used for Slicing (*https://fpy.li/pep357*), proposed by Travis Oliphant to allow any of the numerous types of integers in NumPy to be used as indexes and slice arguments. The key difference between operator.index() and int() is that the former is intended for this specific purpose. For example, int(3.14) returns 3, but opera tor.index(3.14) raises TypeError because a float should not be used as an index.

Excessive use of isinstance may be a sign of bad OO design, but handling slices in __getitem__ is a justified use case. In the first edition, I also used an isinstance test on key to test if it was an integer. Using operator.index avoids this test, and raises Type Error with a very informative message if we can't get the index from key. See the last error message from Example 12-7.

Once the code in Example 12-6 is added to the Vector class, we have proper slicing behavior, as Example 12-7 demonstrates.

Example 12-7. Tests of enhanced Vector.__getitem__ from Example 12-6

```
>>> v7 = Vector(range(7))
>>> v7[-1]  ❶
6.0
>>> v7[1:4]  ❷
Vector([1.0, 2.0, 3.0])
>>> v7[-1:]  ❸
Vector([6.0])
>>> v7[1,2]  ❹
Traceback (most recent call last):
  ...
TypeError: 'tuple' object cannot be interpreted as an integer
```

❶ An integer index retrieves just one component value as a float.

❷ A slice index creates a new Vector.

❸ A slice of len == 1 also creates a Vector.

❹ Vector does not support multidimensional indexing, so a tuple of indices or slices raises an error.

Vector Take #3: Dynamic Attribute Access

In the evolution from Vector2d to Vector, we lost the ability to access vector components by name (e.g., v.x, v.y). We are now dealing with vectors that may have a large number of components. Still, it may be convenient to access the first few components with shortcut letters such as x, y, z instead of v[0], v[1], and v[2].

Here is the alternative syntax we want to provide for reading the first four components of a vector:

```
>>> v = Vector(range(10))
>>> v.x
0.0
```

```
>>> v.y, v.z, v.t
(1.0, 2.0, 3.0)
```

In `Vector2d`, we provided read-only access to x and y using the `@property` decorator (Example 11-7). We could write four properties in `Vector`, but it would be tedious. The `__getattr__` special method provides a better way.

The `__getattr__` method is invoked by the interpreter when attribute lookup fails. In simple terms, given the expression `my_obj.x`, Python checks if the `my_obj` instance has an attribute named x; if not, the search goes to the class (`my_obj.__class__`), and then up the inheritance graph.[2] If the x attribute is not found, then the `__getattr__` method defined in the class of `my_obj` is called with `self` and the name of the attribute as a string (e.g., `'x'`).

Example 12-8 lists our `__getattr__` method. Essentially it checks whether the attribute being sought is one of the letters xyzt and if so, returns the corresponding vector component.

Example 12-8. Part of vector_v3.py: `__getattr__` method added to the `Vector` class

```
__match_args__ = ('x', 'y', 'z', 't')  ❶

def __getattr__(self, name):
    cls = type(self)  ❷
    try:
        pos = cls.__match_args__.index(name)  ❸
    except ValueError:  ❹
        pos = -1
    if 0 <= pos < len(self._components):  ❺
        return self._components[pos]
    msg = f'{cls.__name__!r} object has no attribute {name!r}'  ❻
    raise AttributeError(msg)
```

❶ Set `__match_args__` to allow positional pattern matching on the dynamic attributes supported by `__getattr__`.[3]

❷ Get the `Vector` class for later use.

---

2 Attribute lookup is more complicated than this; we'll see the gory details in Part V. For now, this simplified explanation will do.

3 Although `__match_args__` exists to support pattern matching in Python 3.10, setting this attribute is harmless in previous versions of Python. In the first edition of this book, I named it `shortcut_names`. With the new name it does double duty: it supports positional patterns in case clauses, and it holds the names of the dynamic attributes supported by special logic in `__getattr__` and `__setattr__`.

---

❸ Try to get the position of `name` in `__match_args__`.

❹ `.index(name)` raises `ValueError` when `name` is not found; set `pos` to `-1`. (I'd rather use a method like `str.find` here, but `tuple` doesn't implement it.)

❺ If the `pos` is within range of the available components, return the component.

❻ If we get this far, raise `AttributeError` with a standard message text.

It's not hard to implement `__getattr__`, but in this case it's not enough. Consider the bizarre interaction in Example 12-9.

Example 12-9. Inappropriate behavior: assigning to v.x raises no error, but introduces an inconsistency

```
>>> v = Vector(range(5))
>>> v
Vector([0.0, 1.0, 2.0, 3.0, 4.0])
>>> v.x        ❶
0.0
>>> v.x = 10   ❷
>>> v.x        ❸
10
>>> v
Vector([0.0, 1.0, 2.0, 3.0, 4.0])   ❹
```

❶ Access element v[0] as v.x.

❷ Assign new value to v.x. This should raise an exception.

❸ Reading v.x shows the new value, 10.

❹ However, the vector components did not change.

Can you explain what is happening? In particular, why does v.x return 10 the second time if that value is not in the vector components array? If you don't know right off the bat, study the explanation of `__getattr__` given right before Example 12-8. It's a bit subtle, but a very important foundation to understand a lot of what comes later in the book.

After you've given it some thought, proceed and we'll explain exactly what happened.

The inconsistency in Example 12-9 was introduced because of the way `__getattr__` works: Python only calls that method as a fallback, when the object does not have the named attribute. However, after we assign v.x = 10, the v object now has an x attribute, so `__getattr__` will no longer be called to retrieve v.x: the interpreter will just return the value 10 that is bound to v.x. On the other hand, our implementation of __getattr__ pays no attention to instance attributes other than self._compo nents, from where it retrieves the values of the "virtual attributes" listed in __match_args__.

We need to customize the logic for setting attributes in our Vector class in order to avoid this inconsistency.

Recall that in the latest Vector2d examples from Chapter 11, trying to assign to the .x or .y instance attributes raised AttributeError. In Vector, we want the same excep tion with any attempt at assigning to all single-letter lowercase attribute names, just to avoid confusion. To do that, we'll implement __setattr__, as listed in Example 12-10.

Example 12-10. Part of vector_v3.py: __setattr__ method in the Vector class

```python
def __setattr__(self, name, value):
    cls = type(self)
    if len(name) == 1:                                      ❶
        if name in cls.__match_args__:                      ❷
            error = 'readonly attribute {attr_name!r}'
        elif name.islower():                                ❸
            error = "can't set attributes 'a' to 'z' in {cls_name!r}"
        else:
            error = ''                                      ❹
        if error:                                           ❺
            msg = error.format(cls_name=cls.__name__, attr_name=name)
            raise AttributeError(msg)
    super().__setattr__(name, value)                        ❻
```

❶ Special handling for single-character attribute names.

❷ If name is one of __match_args__, set specific error message.

❸ If name is lowercase, set error message about all single-letter names.

❹ Otherwise, set blank error message.

❺ If there is a nonblank error message, raise AttributeError.

❻ Default case: call __setattr__ on superclass for standard behavior.

The super() function provides a way to access methods of super-classes dynamically, a necessity in a dynamic language supporting multiple inheritance like Python. It's used to delegate some task from a method in a subclass to a suitable method in a superclass, as seen in Example 12-10. There is more about super in "Multiple Inheritance and Method Resolution Order" on page 496.

While choosing the error message to display with AttributeError, my first check was the behavior of the built-in complex type, because they are immutable and have a pair of data attributes, real and imag. Trying to change either of those in a complex instance raises AttributeError with the message "can't set attribute". On the other hand, trying to set a read-only attribute protected by a property as we did in "A Hashable Vector2d" on page 376 produces the message "read-only attribute". I drew inspiration from both wordings to set the error string in __setitem__, but was more explicit about the forbidden attributes.

Note that we are not disallowing setting all attributes, only single-letter, lowercase ones, to avoid confusion with the supported read-only attributes x, y, z, and t.

Knowing that declaring __slots__ at the class level prevents setting new instance attributes, it's tempting to use that feature instead of implementing __setattr__ as we did. However, because of all the caveats discussed in "Summarizing the Issues with __slots__" on page 390, using __slots__ just to prevent instance attribute creation is not recommended. __slots__ should be used only to save memory, and only if that is a real issue.

Even without supporting writing to the Vector components, here is an important takeaway from this example: very often when you implement __getattr__, you need to code __setattr__ as well, to avoid inconsistent behavior in your objects.

If we wanted to allow changing components, we could implement __setitem__ to enable v[0] = 1.1 and/or __setattr__ to make v.x = 1.1 work. But Vector will remain immutable because we want to make it hashable in the coming section.

Vector Take #4: Hashing and a Faster ==

Once more we get to implement a __hash__ method. Together with the existing __eq__, this will make Vector instances hashable.

The __hash__ in Vector2d (Example 11-8) computed the hash of a tuple built with the two components, self.x and self.y. Now we may be dealing with thousands of components, so building a tuple may be too costly. Instead, I will apply the ^ (xor) operator to the hashes of every component in succession, like this: v[0] ^ v[1] ^ v[2]. That is what the functools.reduce function is for. Previously I said that reduce is not as popular as before,[4] but computing the hash of all vector components is a good use case for it. Figure 12-1 depicts the general idea of the reduce function.

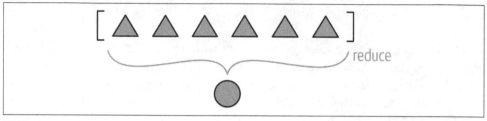

Figure 12-1. Reducing functions—reduce, sum, any, all—produce a single aggregate result from a sequence or from any finite iterable object.

So far we've seen that functools.reduce() can be replaced by sum(), but now let's properly explain how it works. The key idea is to reduce a series of values to a single value. The first argument to reduce() is a two-argument function, and the second argument is an iterable. Let's say we have a two-argument function fn and a list lst. When you call reduce(fn, lst), fn will be applied to the first pair of elements—fn(lst[0], lst[1])—producing a first result, r1. Then fn is applied to r1 and the next element—fn(r1, lst[2])—producing a second result, r2. Now fn(r2, lst[3]) is called to produce r3 ... and so on until the last element, when a single result, rN, is returned.

Here is how you could use reduce to compute 5! (the factorial of 5):

```
>>> 2 * 3 * 4 * 5  # the result we want: 5! == 120
120
>>> import functools
>>> functools.reduce(lambda a,b: a*b, range(1, 6))
120
```

Back to our hashing problem, Example 12-11 shows the idea of computing the aggregate xor by doing it in three ways: with a for loop and two reduce calls.

Example 12-11. Three ways of calculating the accumulated xor of integers from 0 to 5

```
>>> n = 0
>>> for i in range(1, 6):    ❶
...     n ^= i
...
```

---

[4] The sum, any, and all cover the most common uses of reduce. See the discussion in "Modern Replacements for map, filter, and reduce" on page 235.

```
>>> n
1
>>> import functools
>>> functools.reduce(lambda a, b: a^b, range(6))    ❷
1
>>> import operator
>>> functools.reduce(operator.xor, range(6))    ❸
1
```

❶ Aggregate xor with a `for` loop and an accumulator variable.

❷ `functools.reduce` using an anonymous function.

❸ `functools.reduce` replacing custom `lambda` with `operator.xor`.

From the alternatives in Example 12-11, the last one is my favorite, and the `for` loop comes second. What is your preference?

As seen in "The operator Module" on page 243, `operator` provides the functionality of all Python infix operators in function form, lessening the need for `lambda`.

To code `Vector.__hash__` in my preferred style, we need to import the `functools` and `operator` modules. Example 12-12 shows the relevant changes.

Example 12-12. Part of vector_v4.py: two imports and __hash__ method added to the Vector class from vector_v3.py

```
from array import array
import reprlib
import math
import functools    ❶
import operator    ❷


class Vector:
    typecode = 'd'

    # many lines omitted in book listing...

    def __eq__(self, other):    ❸
        return tuple(self) == tuple(other)

    def __hash__(self):
        hashes = (hash(x) for x in self._components)    ❹
        return functools.reduce(operator.xor, hashes, 0)    ❺

    # more lines omitted...
```

❶ Import `functools` to use `reduce`.

❷ Import `operator` to use `xor`.

❸ No change to `__eq__`; I listed it here because it's good practice to keep `__eq__` and `__hash__` close in source code, because they need to work together.

❹ Create a generator expression to lazily compute the hash of each component.

❺ Feed `hashes` to `reduce` with the `xor` function to compute the aggregate hash code; the third argument, 0, is the initializer (see the next warning).

 When using `reduce`, it's good practice to provide the third argument, `reduce(function, iterable, initializer)`, to prevent this exception: `TypeError: reduce() of empty sequence with no initial value` (excellent message: explains the problem and how to fix it). The `initializer` is the value returned if the sequence is empty and is used as the first argument in the reducing loop, so it should be the identity value of the operation. As examples, for +, |, ^ the `initializer` should be 0, but for *, & it should be 1.

As implemented, the `__hash__` method in Example 12-12 is a perfect example of a map-reduce computation (Figure 12-2).

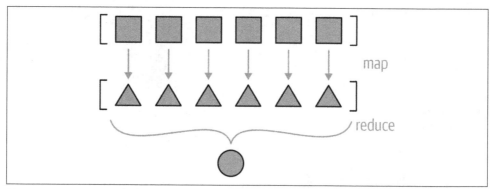

Figure 12-2. Map-reduce: apply function to each item to generate a new series (map), then compute the aggregate (reduce).

The mapping step produces one hash for each component, and the reduce step aggregates all hashes with the `xor` operator. Using `map` instead of a *genexp* makes the mapping step even more visible:

```
def __hash__(self):
    hashes = map(hash, self._components)
    return functools.reduce(operator.xor, hashes)
```

 The solution with map would be less efficient in Python 2, where the map function builds a new list with the results. But in Python 3, map is lazy: it creates a generator that yields the results on demand, thus saving memory—just like the generator expression we used in the __hash__ method of Example 12-8.

While we are on the topic of reducing functions, we can replace our quick implementation of __eq__ with another one that will be cheaper in terms of processing and memory, at least for large vectors. As introduced in Example 11-2, we have this very concise implementation of __eq__:

```
def __eq__(self, other):
    return tuple(self) == tuple(other)
```

This works for Vector2d and for Vector—it even considers Vector([1, 2]) equal to (1, 2), which may be a problem, but we'll overlook that for now.[5] But for Vector instances that may have thousands of components, it's very inefficient. It builds two tuples copying the entire contents of the operands just to use the __eq__ of the tuple type. For Vector2d (with only two components), it's a good shortcut, but not for the large multidimensional vectors. A better way of comparing one Vector to another Vector or iterable would be Example 12-13.

Example 12-13. The Vector.__eq__ implementation using zip in a for loop for more efficient comparison

```
def __eq__(self, other):
    if len(self) != len(other):      ❶
        return False
    for a, b in zip(self, other):    ❷
        if a != b:                   ❸
            return False
    return True                      ❹
```

❶ If the len of the objects are different, they are not equal.

❷ zip produces a generator of tuples made from the items in each iterable argument. See "The Awesome zip" on page 418 if zip is new to you. In ❶, the len

---

5 We will seriously consider the matter of Vector([1, 2]) == (1, 2) in "Operator Overloading 101" on page 566.

comparison is needed because zip stops producing values without warning as soon as one of the inputs is exhausted.

❸ As soon as two components are different, exit returning False.

❹ Otherwise, the objects are equal.

 The zip function is named after the zipper fastener because the physical device works by interlocking pairs of teeth taken from both zipper sides, a good visual analogy for what zip(left, right) does. No relation to compressed files.

Example 12-13 is efficient, but the all function can produce the same aggregate computation of the for loop in one line: if all comparisons between corresponding components in the operands are True, the result is True. As soon as one comparison is False, all returns False. Example 12-14 shows how __eq__ looks using all.

Example 12-14. The Vector.__eq__ implementation using zip and all: same logic as Example 12-13

```
def __eq__(self, other):
    return len(self) == len(other) and all(a == b for a, b in zip(self, other))
```

Note that we first check that the operands have equal length, because zip will stop at the shortest operand.

Example 12-14 is the implementation we choose for __eq__ in *vector_v4.py*.

The Awesome zip

Having a for loop that iterates over items without fiddling with index variables is great and prevents lots of bugs, but demands some special utility functions. One of them is the zip built-in, which makes it easy to iterate in parallel over two or more iterables by returning tuples that you can unpack into variables, one for each item in the parallel inputs. See Example 12-15.

Example 12-15. The zip built-in at work

```
>>> zip(range(3), 'ABC')  ❶
<zip object at 0x10063ae48>
>>> list(zip(range(3), 'ABC'))  ❷
[(0, 'A'), (1, 'B'), (2, 'C')]
>>> list(zip(range(3), 'ABC', [0.0, 1.1, 2.2, 3.3]))  ❸
[(0, 'A', 0.0), (1, 'B', 1.1), (2, 'C', 2.2)]
```

```
>>> from itertools import zip_longest    ❹
>>> list(zip_longest(range(3), 'ABC', [0.0, 1.1, 2.2, 3.3], fillvalue=-1))
[(0, 'A', 0.0), (1, 'B', 1.1), (2, 'C', 2.2), (-1, -1, 3.3)]
```

❶ `zip` returns a generator that produces tuples on demand.

❷ Build a `list` just for display; usually we iterate over the generator.

❸ `zip` stops without warning when one of the iterables is exhausted.

❹ The `itertools.zip_longest` function behaves differently: it uses an optional `fillvalue` (None by default) to complete missing values so it can generate tuples until the last iterable is exhausted.

New zip() Option in Python 3.10

I wrote in the first edition of this book that `zip` silently stopping at the shortest iterable was surprising—not a good trait for an API. Silently ignoring part of the input can cause subtle bugs. Instead, `zip` should raise `ValueError` if the iterables are not all of the same length, which is what happens when unpacking an iterable to a tuple of variables of different length —in line with Python's *fail fast* policy. PEP 618—Add Optional Length-Checking To zip (*https://fpy.li/pep618*) added an optional `strict` argument to `zip` to make it behave in that way. It is implemented in Python 3.10.

The `zip` function can also be used to transpose a matrix represented as nested iterables. For example:

```
>>> a = [(1, 2, 3),
...      (4, 5, 6)]
>>> list(zip(*a))
[(1, 4), (2, 5), (3, 6)]
>>> b = [(1, 2),
...      (3, 4),
...      (5, 6)]
>>> list(zip(*b))
[(1, 3, 5), (2, 4, 6)]
```

If you want to grok `zip`, spend some time figuring out how these examples work.

The `enumerate` built-in is another generator function often used in `for` loops to avoid direct handling of index variables. If you're not familiar with `enumerate`, you should definitely check it out in the "Built-in functions" documentation (*https://fpy.li/12-3*). The `zip` and `enumerate` built-ins, along with several other generator functions in the standard library, are covered in "Generator Functions in the Standard Library" on page 623.

We wrap up this chapter by bringing back the __format__ method from Vector2d to Vector.

Vector Take #5: Formatting

The __format__ method of Vector will resemble that of Vector2d, but instead of providing a custom display in polar coordinates, Vector will use spherical coordinates—also known as "hyperspherical" coordinates, because now we support n dimensions, and spheres are "hyperspheres" in 4D and beyond.[6] Accordingly, we'll change the custom format suffix from 'p' to 'h'.

 As we saw in "Formatted Displays" on page 372, when extending the Format Specification Mini-Language (*https://fpy.li/fmtspec*), it's best to avoid reusing format codes supported by built-in types. In particular, our extended mini-language also uses the float formatting codes 'eEfFgGn%' in their original meaning, so we definitely must avoid these. Integers use 'bcdoxXn' and strings use 's'. I picked 'p' for Vector2d polar coordinates. Code 'h' for hyperspherical coordinates is a good choice.

For example, given a Vector object in 4D space (len(v) == 4), the 'h' code will produce a display like <r, Φ_1, Φ_2, Φ_3>, where r is the magnitude (abs(v)), and the remaining numbers are the angular components Φ_1, Φ_2, Φ_3.

Here are some samples of the spherical coordinate format in 4D, taken from the doctests of *vector_v5.py* (see Example 12-16):

```
>>> format(Vector([-1, -1, -1, -1]), 'h')
'<2.0, 2.0943951023931957, 2.186276035465284, 3.9269908169872414>'
>>> format(Vector([2, 2, 2, 2]), '.3eh')
'<4.000e+00, 1.047e+00, 9.553e-01, 7.854e-01>'
>>> format(Vector([0, 1, 0, 0]), '0.5fh')
'<1.00000, 1.57080, 0.00000, 0.00000>'
```

Before we can implement the minor changes required in __format__, we need to code a pair of support methods: angle(n) to compute one of the angular coordinates (e.g., Φ_1), and angles() to return an iterable of all angular coordinates. I will not

---

6 The Wolfram Mathworld website has an article on hypersphere (*https://fpy.li/12-4*); on Wikipedia, "hypersphere" redirects to the "*n*-sphere" entry (*https://fpy.li/nsphere*).

describe the math here; if you're curious, Wikipedia's "*n*-sphere" entry (*https://fpy.li/ nsphere*) has the formulas I used to calculate the spherical coordinates from the Cartesian coordinates in the `Vector` components array.

Example 12-16 is a full listing of *vector_v5.py* consolidating all we've implemented since "Vector Take #1: Vector2d Compatible" on page 401 and introducing custom formatting.

Example 12-16. vector_v5.py: doctests and all code for the final `Vector` class; callouts highlight additions needed to support __format__

```
"""
A multidimensional ``Vector`` class, take 5

A ``Vector`` is built from an iterable of numbers::

    >>> Vector([3.1, 4.2])
    Vector([3.1, 4.2])
    >>> Vector((3, 4, 5))
    Vector([3.0, 4.0, 5.0])
    >>> Vector(range(10))
    Vector([0.0, 1.0, 2.0, 3.0, 4.0, ...])


Tests with two dimensions (same results as ``vector2d_v1.py``)::

    >>> v1 = Vector([3, 4])
    >>> x, y = v1
    >>> x, y
    (3.0, 4.0)
    >>> v1
    Vector([3.0, 4.0])
    >>> v1_clone = eval(repr(v1))
    >>> v1 == v1_clone
    True
    >>> print(v1)
    (3.0, 4.0)
    >>> octets = bytes(v1)
    >>> octets
    b'd\\x00\\x00\\x00\\x00\\x00\\x00\\x08@\\x00\\x00\\x00\\x00\\x00\\x00\\x10@'
    >>> abs(v1)
    5.0
    >>> bool(v1), bool(Vector([0, 0]))
    (True, False)


Test of ``.frombytes()`` class method:

    >>> v1_clone = Vector.frombytes(bytes(v1))
    >>> v1_clone
```

```
Vector([3.0, 4.0])
>>> v1 == v1_clone
True
```

Tests with three dimensions::

```
>>> v1 = Vector([3, 4, 5])
>>> x, y, z = v1
>>> x, y, z
(3.0, 4.0, 5.0)
>>> v1
Vector([3.0, 4.0, 5.0])
>>> v1_clone = eval(repr(v1))
>>> v1 == v1_clone
True
>>> print(v1)
(3.0, 4.0, 5.0)
>>> abs(v1)  # doctest:+ELLIPSIS
7.071067811...
>>> bool(v1), bool(Vector([0, 0, 0]))
(True, False)
```

Tests with many dimensions::

```
>>> v7 = Vector(range(7))
>>> v7
Vector([0.0, 1.0, 2.0, 3.0, 4.0, ...])
>>> abs(v7)  # doctest:+ELLIPSIS
9.53939201...
```

Test of ``.__bytes__`` and ``.frombytes()`` methods::

```
>>> v1 = Vector([3, 4, 5])
>>> v1_clone = Vector.frombytes(bytes(v1))
>>> v1_clone
Vector([3.0, 4.0, 5.0])
>>> v1 == v1_clone
True
```

Tests of sequence behavior::

```
>>> v1 = Vector([3, 4, 5])
>>> len(v1)
3
>>> v1[0], v1[len(v1)-1], v1[-1]
(3.0, 5.0, 5.0)
```

Test of slicing::

```
>>> v7 = Vector(range(7))
>>> v7[-1]
6.0
>>> v7[1:4]
Vector([1.0, 2.0, 3.0])
>>> v7[-1:]
Vector([6.0])
>>> v7[1,2]
Traceback (most recent call last):
  ...
TypeError: 'tuple' object cannot be interpreted as an integer
```

Tests of dynamic attribute access::

```
>>> v7 = Vector(range(10))
>>> v7.x
0.0
>>> v7.y, v7.z, v7.t
(1.0, 2.0, 3.0)
```

Dynamic attribute lookup failures::

```
>>> v7.k
Traceback (most recent call last):
  ...
AttributeError: 'Vector' object has no attribute 'k'
>>> v3 = Vector(range(3))
>>> v3.t
Traceback (most recent call last):
  ...
AttributeError: 'Vector' object has no attribute 't'
>>> v3.spam
Traceback (most recent call last):
  ...
AttributeError: 'Vector' object has no attribute 'spam'
```

Tests of hashing::

```
>>> v1 = Vector([3, 4])
>>> v2 = Vector([3.1, 4.2])
>>> v3 = Vector([3, 4, 5])
>>> v6 = Vector(range(6))
>>> hash(v1), hash(v3), hash(v6)
(7, 2, 1)
```

Most hash codes of non-integers vary from a 32-bit to 64-bit CPython build::

```
>>> import sys
>>> hash(v2) == (384307168202284039 if sys.maxsize > 2**32 else 357915986)
True
```

Tests of ``format()`` with Cartesian coordinates in 2D::

```
>>> v1 = Vector([3, 4])
>>> format(v1)
'(3.0, 4.0)'
>>> format(v1, '.2f')
'(3.00, 4.00)'
>>> format(v1, '.3e')
'(3.000e+00, 4.000e+00)'
```

Tests of ``format()`` with Cartesian coordinates in 3D and 7D::

```
>>> v3 = Vector([3, 4, 5])
>>> format(v3)
'(3.0, 4.0, 5.0)'
>>> format(Vector(range(7)))
'(0.0, 1.0, 2.0, 3.0, 4.0, 5.0, 6.0)'
```

Tests of ``format()`` with spherical coordinates in 2D, 3D and 4D::

```
>>> format(Vector([1, 1]), 'h')  # doctest:+ELLIPSIS
'<1.414213..., 0.785398...>'
>>> format(Vector([1, 1]), '.3eh')
'<1.414e+00, 7.854e-01>'
>>> format(Vector([1, 1]), '0.5fh')
'<1.41421, 0.78540>'
>>> format(Vector([1, 1, 1]), 'h')  # doctest:+ELLIPSIS
'<1.73205..., 0.95531..., 0.78539...>'
>>> format(Vector([2, 2, 2]), '.3eh')
'<3.464e+00, 9.553e-01, 7.854e-01>'
>>> format(Vector([0, 0, 0]), '0.5fh')
'<0.00000, 0.00000, 0.00000>'
>>> format(Vector([-1, -1, -1, -1]), 'h')  # doctest:+ELLIPSIS
'<2.0, 2.09439..., 2.18627..., 3.92699...>'
>>> format(Vector([2, 2, 2, 2]), '.3eh')
'<4.000e+00, 1.047e+00, 9.553e-01, 7.854e-01>'
>>> format(Vector([0, 1, 0, 0]), '0.5fh')
'<1.00000, 1.57080, 0.00000, 0.00000>'
"""


from array import array
import reprlib
import math
import functools
import operator
```

```
import itertools  ❶

class Vector:
    typecode = 'd'

    def __init__(self, components):
        self._components = array(self.typecode, components)

    def __iter__(self):
        return iter(self._components)

    def __repr__(self):
        components = reprlib.repr(self._components)
        components = components[components.find('['):-1]
        return f'Vector({components})'

    def __str__(self):
        return str(tuple(self))

    def __bytes__(self):
        return (bytes([ord(self.typecode)]) +
                bytes(self._components))

    def __eq__(self, other):
        return (len(self) == len(other) and
                all(a == b for a, b in zip(self, other)))

    def __hash__(self):
        hashes = (hash(x) for x in self)
        return functools.reduce(operator.xor, hashes, 0)

    def __abs__(self):
        return math.hypot(*self)

    def __bool__(self):
        return bool(abs(self))

    def __len__(self):
        return len(self._components)

    def __getitem__(self, key):
        if isinstance(key, slice):
            cls = type(self)
            return cls(self._components[key])
        index = operator.index(key)
        return self._components[index]

    __match_args__ = ('x', 'y', 'z', 't')

    def __getattr__(self, name):
        cls = type(self)
```

```
        try:
            pos = cls.__match_args__.index(name)
        except ValueError:
            pos = -1
        if 0 <= pos < len(self._components):
            return self._components[pos]
        msg = f'{cls.__name__!r} object has no attribute {name!r}'
        raise AttributeError(msg)

    def angle(self, n):  ❷
        r = math.hypot(*self[n:])
        a = math.atan2(r, self[n-1])
        if (n == len(self) - 1) and (self[-1] < 0):
            return math.pi * 2 - a
        else:
            return a

    def angles(self):  ❸
        return (self.angle(n) for n in range(1, len(self)))

    def __format__(self, fmt_spec=''):
        if fmt_spec.endswith('h'):  # hyperspherical coordinates
            fmt_spec = fmt_spec[:-1]
            coords = itertools.chain([abs(self)],
                                     self.angles())  ❹
            outer_fmt = '<{}>'  ❺
        else:
            coords = self
            outer_fmt = '({})'  ❻
        components = (format(c, fmt_spec) for c in coords)  ❼
        return outer_fmt.format(', '.join(components))  ❽

    @classmethod
    def frombytes(cls, octets):
        typecode = chr(octets[0])
        memv = memoryview(octets[1:]).cast(typecode)
        return cls(memv)
```

❶ Import `itertools` to use `chain` function in `__format__`.

❷ Compute one of the angular coordinates, using formulas adapted from the *n*-sphere article (*https://fpy.li/nsphere*).

❸ Create a generator expression to compute all angular coordinates on demand.

❹ Use `itertools.chain` to produce *genexp* to iterate seamlessly over the magnitude and the angular coordinates.

❺ Configure a spherical coordinate display with angular brackets.

---

❻ Configure a Cartesian coordinate display with parentheses.

❼ Create a generator expression to format each coordinate item on demand.

❽ Plug formatted components separated by commas inside brackets or parentheses.

 We are making heavy use of generator expressions in __format__, angle, and angles, but our focus here is in providing __format__ to bring Vector to the same implementation level as Vector2d. When we cover generators in Chapter 17, we'll use some of the code in Vector as examples, and then the generator tricks will be explained in detail.

This concludes our mission for this chapter. The Vector class will be enhanced with infix operators in Chapter 16, but our goal here was to explore techniques for coding special methods that are useful in a wide variety of collection classes.

Chapter Summary

The Vector example in this chapter was designed to be compatible with Vector2d, except for the use of a different constructor signature accepting a single iterable argument, just like the built-in sequence types do. The fact that Vector behaves as a sequence just by implementing __getitem__ and __len__ prompted a discussion of protocols, the informal interfaces used in duck-typed languages.

We then looked at how the my_seq[a:b:c] syntax works behind the scenes, by creating a slice(a, b, c) object and handing it to __getitem__. Armed with this knowledge, we made Vector respond correctly to slicing, by returning new Vector instances, just like a Pythonic sequence is expected to do.

The next step was to provide read-only access to the first few Vector components using notation such as my_vec.x. We did it by implementing __getattr__. Doing that opened the possibility of tempting the user to assign to those special components by writing my_vec.x = 7, revealing a potential bug. We fixed it by implementing __setattr__ as well, to forbid assigning values to single-letter attributes. Very often, when you code a __getattr__ you need to add __setattr__ too, in order to avoid inconsistent behavior.

Implementing the __hash__ function provided the perfect context for using func tools.reduce, because we needed to apply the xor operator ^ in succession to the hashes of all Vector components to produce an aggregate hash code for the whole

Vector. After applying reduce in __hash__, we used the all reducing built-in to create a more efficient __eq__ method.

The last enhancement to Vector was to reimplement the __format__ method from Vector2d by supporting spherical coordinates as an alternative to the default Cartesian coordinates. We used quite a bit of math and several generators to code __format__ and its auxiliary functions, but these are implementation details—and we'll come back to the generators in Chapter 17. The goal of that last section was to support a custom format, thus fulfilling the promise of a Vector that could do everything a Vector2d did, and more.

As we did in Chapter 11, here we often looked at how standard Python objects behave, to emulate them and provide a "Pythonic" look-and-feel to Vector.

In Chapter 16, we will implement several infix operators on Vector. The math will be much simpler than in the angle() method here, but exploring how infix operators work in Python is a great lesson in OO design. But before we get to operator overloading, we'll step back from working on one class and look at organizing multiple classes with interfaces and inheritance, the subjects of Chapters 13 and 14.

Further Reading

Most special methods covered in the Vector example also appear in the Vector2d example from Chapter 11, so the references in "Further Reading" on page 394 are all relevant here.

The powerful reduce higher-order function is also known as fold, accumulate, aggregate, compress, and inject. For more information, see Wikipedia's "Fold (higher-order function)" article (*https://fpy.li/12-5*), which presents applications of that higher-order function with emphasis on functional programming with recursive data structures. The article also includes a table listing fold-like functions in dozens of programming languages.

"What's New in Python 2.5" (*https://fpy.li/12-6*) has a short explanation of __index__, designed to support __getitem__ methods, as we saw in "A Slice-Aware __getitem__" on page 408. PEP 357—Allowing Any Object to be Used for Slicing (*https://fpy.li/pep357*) details the need for it from the perspective of an implementor of a C-extension—Travis Oliphant, the primary creator of NumPy. Oliphant's many contributions to Python made it a leading scientific computing language, which then positioned it to lead the way in machine learning applications.

Soapbox

Protocols as Informal Interfaces

Protocols are not an invention of Python. The Smalltalk team, which also coined the expression "object-oriented," used "protocol" as a synonym for what we now call interfaces. Some Smalltalk programming environments allowed programmers to tag a group of methods as a protocol, but that was merely a documentation and navigation aid, and not enforced by the language. That's why I believe "informal interface" is a reasonable short explanation for "protocol" when I speak to an audience that is more familiar with formal (and compiler enforced) interfaces.

Established protocols naturally evolve in any language that uses dynamic typing, that is, when type checking is done at runtime because there is no static type information in method signatures and variables. Ruby is another important object-oriented language that has dynamic typing and uses protocols.

In the Python documentation, you can often tell when a protocol is being discussed when you see language like "a file-like object." This is a quick way of saying "something that behaves sufficiently like a file, by implementing the parts of the file interface that are relevant in the context."

You may think that implementing only part of a protocol is sloppy, but it has the advantage of keeping things simple. Section 3.3 (*https://fpy.li/12-7*) of the "Data Model" chapter suggests:

> When implementing a class that emulates any built-in type, it is important that the emulation only be implemented to the degree that it makes sense for the object being modeled. For example, some sequences may work well with retrieval of individual elements, but extracting a slice may not make sense.

When we don't need to code nonsense methods just to fulfill some overdesigned interface contract and keep the compiler happy, it becomes easier to follow the KISS principle (*https://fpy.li/12-8*).

On the other hand, if you want to use a type checker to verify your protocol implementations, then a stricter definition of protocol is required. That's what `typing.Protocol` provides.

I'll have more to say about protocols and interfaces in Chapter 13, where they are the main focus.

Origins of Duck Typing

I believe the Ruby community, more than any other, helped popularize the term "duck typing," as they preached to the Java masses. But the expression has been used in Python discussions before either Ruby or Python were "popular." According to Wikipedia, an early example of the duck analogy in object-oriented programming is a message to the Python-list by Alex Martelli from July 26, 2000: "polymorphism (was Re: Type checking in python?)" (*https://fpy.li/12-9*). That's where the quote at the beginning of this chapter comes from. If you are curious about the literary origins of the "duck typing" term, and the applications of this OO concept in many languages, check out Wikipedia's "Duck typing" entry (*https://fpy.li/12-10*).

A Safe __format__, with Enhanced Usability

While implementing __format__, I did not take any precautions regarding Vector instances with a very large number of components, as we did in __repr__ using reprlib. The reasoning is that repr() is for debugging and logging, so it must always generate some serviceable output, while __format__ is used to display output to end users who presumably want to see the entire Vector. If you think this is dangerous, then it would be cool to implement a further extension to the Format Specifier Mini-Language.

Here is how I'd do it: by default, any formatted Vector would display a reasonable but limited number of components, say 30. If there are more elements than that, the default behavior would be similar to what the reprlib does: chop the excess and put ... in its place. However, if the format specifier ended with the special * code, meaning "all," then the size limitation would be disabled. So a user who's unaware of the problem of very long displays will not be bitten by it by accident. But if the default limitation becomes a nuisance, then the presence of the ... could lead the user to search the documentation and discover the * formatting code.

The Search for a Pythonic Sum

There's no single answer to "What is Pythonic?" just as there's no single answer to "What is beautiful?" Saying, as I often do, that it means using "idiomatic Python" is not 100% satisfactory, because what may be "idiomatic" for you may not be for me. One thing I know: "idiomatic" does not mean using the most obscure language features.

In the Python-list (*https://fpy.li/12-11*), there's a thread titled "Pythonic Way to Sum n-th List Element?" from April 2003 (*https://fpy.li/12-12*). It's relevant to our discussion of reduce in this chapter.

The original poster, Guy Middleton, asked for an improvement on this solution, stating he did not like to use lambda:[7]

```
>>> my_list = [[1, 2, 3], [40, 50, 60], [9, 8, 7]]
>>> import functools
>>> functools.reduce(lambda a, b: a+b, [sub[1] for sub in my_list])
60
```

---

[7] I adapted the code for this presentation: in 2003, reduce was a built-in, but in Python 3 we need to import it; also, I replaced the names x and y with my_list and sub, for sub-list.

That code uses lots of idioms: lambda, reduce, and a list comprehension. It would probably come last in a popularity contest, because it offends people who hate lambda and those who despise list comprehensions—pretty much both sides of a divide.

If you're going to use lambda, there's probably no reason to use a list comprehension —except for filtering, which is not the case here.

Here is a solution of my own that will please the lambda lovers:

```
>>> functools.reduce(lambda a, b: a + b[1], my_list, 0)
60
```

I did not take part in the original thread, and I wouldn't use that in real code, because I don't like lambda too much myself, but I wanted to show an example without a list comprehension.

The first answer came from Fernando Perez, creator of IPython, highlighting that NumPy supports *n*-dimensional arrays and *n*-dimensional slicing:

```
>>> import numpy as np
>>> my_array = np.array(my_list)
>>> np.sum(my_array[:, 1])
60
```

I think Perez's solution is cool, but Guy Middleton praised this next solution, by Paul Rubin and Skip Montanaro:

```
>>> import operator
>>> functools.reduce(operator.add, [sub[1] for sub in my_list], 0)
60
```

Then Evan Simpson asked, "What's wrong with this?":

```
>>> total = 0
>>> for sub in my_list:
...     total += sub[1]
...
>>> total
60
```

Lots of people agreed that was quite Pythonic. Alex Martelli went as far as saying that's probably how Guido would code it.

I like Evan Simpson's code, but I also like David Eppstein's comment on it:

> If you want the sum of a list of items, you should write it in a way that looks like "the sum of a list of items," not in a way that looks like "loop over these items, maintain another variable t, perform a sequence of additions." Why do we have high-level languages if not to express our intentions at a higher level and let the language worry about what low-level operations are needed to implement it?

Then Alex Martelli comes back to suggest:

> "The sum" is so frequently needed that I wouldn't mind at all if Python singled it out as a built-in. But "reduce(operator.add, …)" just isn't a great way to express it, in my opinion (and yet as an old APL'er, and FP-liker, I *should* like it—but I don't).

Alex goes on to suggest a sum( ) function, which he contributed. It became a built-in in Python 2.3, released only three months after that conversation took place. So Alex's preferred syntax became the norm:

```
>>> sum([sub[1] for sub in my_list])
60
```

By the end of the next year (November 2004), Python 2.4 was launched with generator expressions, providing what is now in my opinion the most Pythonic answer to Guy Middleton's original question:

```
>>> sum(sub[1] for sub in my_list)
60
```

This is not only more readable than reduce but also avoids the trap of the empty sequence: sum([]) is 0, simple as that.

In the same conversation, Alex Martelli suggests the reduce built-in in Python 2 was more trouble than it was worth, because it encouraged coding idioms that were hard to explain. He was most convincing: the function was demoted to the functools module in Python 3.

Still, functools.reduce has its place. It solved the problem of our Vector.__hash__ in a way that I would call Pythonic.

## CHAPTER 13

Interfaces, Protocols, and ABCs

> Program to an interface, not an implementation.
>
> —Gamma, Helm, Johnson, Vlissides, First Principle of Object-Oriented Design[1]

Object-oriented programming is all about interfaces. The best approach to understanding a type in Python is knowing the methods it provides—its interface—as discussed in "Types Are Defined by Supported Operations" on page 261 (Chapter 8).

Depending on the programming language, we have one or more ways of defining and using interfaces. Since Python 3.8, we have four ways. They are depicted in the *Typing Map* (Figure 13-1). We can summarize them like this:

Duck typing
Python's default approach to typing from the beginning. We've been studying duck typing since Chapter 1.

Goose typing
The approach supported by abstract base classes (ABCs) since Python 2.6, which relies on runtime checks of objects against ABCs. *Goose typing* is a major subject in this chapter.

Static typing
The traditional approach of statically-typed languages like C and Java; supported since Python 3.5 by the typing module, and enforced by external type checkers compliant with PEP 484—Type Hints (*https://fpy.li/pep484*). This is not the theme of this chapter. Most of Chapter 8 and the upcoming Chapter 15 are about static typing.

---

1 *Design Patterns: Elements of Reusable Object-Oriented Software*, "Introduction," p. 18.

Static duck typing

An approach made popular by the Go language; supported by subclasses of typ ing.Protocol—new in Python 3.8—also enforced by external type checkers. We first saw this in "Static Protocols" on page 287 (Chapter 8).

The Typing Map

The four typing approaches depicted in Figure 13-1 are complementary: they have different pros and cons. It doesn't make sense to dismiss any of them.

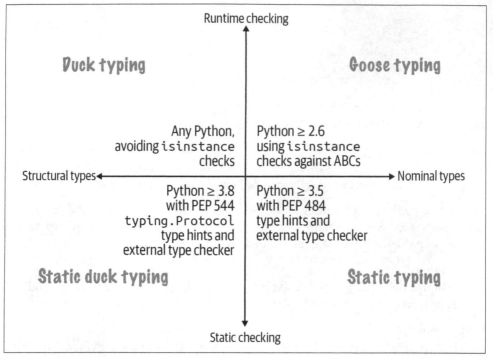

Figure 13-1. The top half describes runtime type checking approaches using just the Python interpreter; the bottom requires an external static type checker such as MyPy or an IDE like PyCharm. The left quadrants cover typing based on the object's structure— i.e., the methods provided by the object, regardless of the name of its class or super-classes; the right quadrants depend on objects having explicitly named types: the name of the object's class, or the name of its superclasses.

Each of these four approaches rely on interfaces to work, but static typing can be done—poorly—using only concrete types instead of interface abstractions like protocols and abstract base classes. This chapter is about duck typing, goose typing, and static duck typing—typing disciplines that revolve around interfaces.

This chapter is split in four main sections, addressing three of the four quadrants in the Typing Map (Figure 13-1):

- "Two Kinds of Protocols" on page 436 compares the two forms of structural typing with protocols—i.e., the lefthand side of the Typing Map.

- "Programming Ducks" on page 438 dives deeper into Python's usual duck typing, including how to make it safer while preserving its major strength: flexibility.

- "Goose Typing" on page 444 explains the use of ABCs for stricter runtime type checking. This is the longest section, not because it's more important, but because there are more sections about duck typing, static duck typing, and static typing elsewhere in the book.

- "Static Protocols" on page 468 covers usage, implementation, and design of `typing.Protocol` subclasses—useful for static and runtime type checking.

What's New in This Chapter

This chapter was heavily edited and is about 24% longer than the corresponding Chapter 11 in the first edition of *Fluent Python*. Although some sections and many paragraphs are the same, there's a lot of new content. These are the highlights:

- The chapter introduction and the Typing Map (Figure 13-1) are new. That's the key to most new content in this chapter—and all other chapters related to typing in Python ≥ 3.8.

- "Two Kinds of Protocols" on page 436 explains the similarities and differences between dynamic and static protocols.

- "Defensive Programming and 'Fail Fast'" on page 442 mostly reproduces content from the first edition, but was updated and now has a section title to highlight its importance.

- "Static Protocols" on page 468 is all new. It builds on the initial presentation in "Static Protocols" on page 287 (Chapter 8).

- Updated class diagrams of `collections.abc` in Figures 13-2, 13-3, and 13-4 to include the `Collection` ABC, from Python 3.6.

The first edition of *Fluent Python* had a section encouraging use of the `numbers` ABCs for goose typing. In "The numbers ABCs and Numeric Protocols" on page 480, I explain why you should use numeric static protocols from the `typing` module instead, if you plan to use static type checkers as well as runtime checks in the style of goose typing.

Two Kinds of Protocols

The word *protocol* has different meanings in computer science depending on context. A network protocol such as HTTP specifies commands that a client can send to a server, such as GET, PUT, and HEAD. We saw in "Protocols and Duck Typing" on page 404 that an object protocol specifies methods which an object must provide to fulfill a role. The FrenchDeck example in Chapter 1 demonstrated one object protocol, the sequence protocol: the methods that allow a Python object to behave as a sequence.

Implementing a full protocol may require several methods, but often it is OK to implement only part of it. Consider the Vowels class in Example 13-1.

Example 13-1. Partial sequence protocol implementation with __getitem__

```
>>> class Vowels:
...     def __getitem__(self, i):
...         return 'AEIOU'[i]
...
>>> v = Vowels()
>>> v[0]
'A'
>>> v[-1]
'U'
>>> for c in v: print(c)
...
A
E
I
O
U
>>> 'E' in v
True
>>> 'Z' in v
False
```

Implementing __getitem__ is enough to allow retrieving items by index, and also to support iteration and the in operator. The __getitem__ special method is really the key to the sequence protocol. Take a look at this entry from the *Python/C API Reference Manual*, "Sequence Protocol" section (*https://fpy.li/13-2*):

int PySequence_Check(PyObject *o)
> Return 1 if the object provides sequence protocol, and 0 otherwise. Note that it returns 1 for Python classes with a __getitem__() method unless they are dict subclasses [...].

We expect a sequence to also support len(), by implementing __len__. Vowels has no __len__ method, but it still behaves as a sequence in some contexts. And that may be enough for our purposes. That is why I like to say that a protocol is an "informal interface." That is also how protocols are understood in Smalltalk, the first object-oriented programming environment to use that term.

Except in pages about network programming, most uses of the word "protocol" in the Python documentation refer to these informal interfaces.

Now, with the adoption of PEP 544—Protocols: Structural subtyping (static duck typing) (*https://fpy.li/pep544*) in Python 3.8, the word "protocol" has another meaning in Python—closely related, but different. As we saw in "Static Protocols" on page 287 (Chapter 8), PEP 544 allows us to create subclasses of typing.Protocol to define one or more methods that a class must implement (or inherit) to satisfy a static type checker.

When I need to be specific, I will adopt these terms:

Dynamic protocol
> The informal protocols Python always had. Dynamic protocols are implicit, defined by convention, and described in the documentation. Python's most important dynamic protocols are supported by the interpreter itself, and are documented in the "Data Model" chapter (*https://fpy.li/dtmodel*) of *The Python Language Reference*.

Static protocol
> A protocol as defined by PEP 544—Protocols: Structural subtyping (static duck typing) (*https://fpy.li/pep544*), since Python 3.8. A static protocol has an explicit definition: a typing.Protocol subclass.

There are two key differences between them:

- An object may implement only part of a dynamic protocol and still be useful; but to fulfill a static protocol, the object must provide every method declared in the protocol class, even if your program doesn't need them all.
- Static protocols can be verified by static type checkers, but dynamic protocols can't.

Both kinds of protocols share the essential characteristic that a class never needs to declare that it supports a protocol by name, i.e., by inheritance.

In addition to static protocols, Python provides another way of defining an explicit interface in code: an abstract base class (ABC).

The rest of this chapter covers dynamic and static protocols, as well as ABCs.

Programming Ducks

Let's start our discussion of dynamic protocols with two of the most important in Python: the sequence and iterable protocols. The interpreter goes out of its way to handle objects that provide even a minimal implementation of those protocols, as the next section explains.

Python Digs Sequences

The philosophy of the Python Data Model is to cooperate with essential dynamic protocols as much as possible. When it comes to sequences, Python tries hard to work with even the simplest implementations.

Figure 13-2 shows how the `Sequence` interface is formalized as an ABC. The Python interpreter and built-in sequences like `list`, `str`, etc., do not rely on that ABC at all. I am using it only to describe what a full-fledged `Sequence` is expected to support.

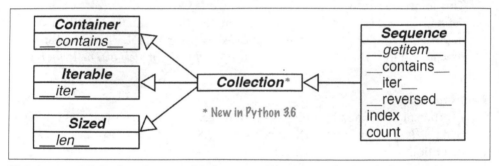

Figure 13-2. UML class diagram for the `Sequence` ABC and related abstract classes from `collections.abc`. Inheritance arrows point from a subclass to its superclasses. Names in italic are abstract methods. Before Python 3.6, there was no `Collection` ABC—Sequence was a direct subclass of `Container`, `Iterable`, and `Sized`.

 Most ABCs in the `collections.abc` module exist to formalize interfaces that are implemented by built-in objects and are implicitly supported by the interpreter—both of which predate the ABCs themselves. The ABCs are useful as starting points for new classes, and to support explicit type checking at runtime (a.k.a. *goose typing*) as well as type hints for static type checkers.

Studying Figure 13-2, we see that a correct subclass of `Sequence` must implement `__getitem__` and `__len__` (from `Sized`). All the other methods in `Sequence` are concrete, so subclasses can inherit their implementations—or provide better ones.

Now, recall the `Vowels` class in Example 13-1. It does not inherit from `abc.Sequence` and it only implements `__getitem__`.

There is no __iter__ method, yet Vowels instances are iterable because—as a fallback —if Python finds a __getitem__ method, it tries to iterate over the object by calling that method with integer indexes starting with 0. Because Python is smart enough to iterate over Vowels instances, it can also make the in operator work even when the __contains__ method is missing: it does a sequential scan to check if an item is present.

In summary, given the importance of sequence-like data structures, Python manages to make iteration and the in operator work by invoking __getitem__ when __iter__ and __contains__ are unavailable.

The original FrenchDeck from Chapter 1 does not subclass abc.Sequence either, but it does implement both methods of the sequence protocol: __getitem__ and __len__. See Example 13-2.

Example 13-2. A deck as a sequence of cards (same as Example 1-1)

```python
import collections

Card = collections.namedtuple('Card', ['rank', 'suit'])

class FrenchDeck:
    ranks = [str(n) for n in range(2, 11)] + list('JQKA')
    suits = 'spades diamonds clubs hearts'.split()

    def __init__(self):
        self._cards = [Card(rank, suit) for suit in self.suits
                                        for rank in self.ranks]

    def __len__(self):
        return len(self._cards)

    def __getitem__(self, position):
        return self._cards[position]
```

Several of the examples in Chapter 1 work because of the special treatment Python gives to anything vaguely resembling a sequence. The iterable protocol in Python represents an extreme form of duck typing: the interpreter tries two different methods to iterate over objects.

To be clear, the behaviors I described in this section are implemented in the interpreter itself, mostly in C. They do not depend on methods from the Sequence ABC. For example, the concrete methods __iter__ and __contains__ in the Sequence class emulate the built-in behaviors of the Python interpreter. If you are curious, check the source code of these methods in *Lib/_collections_abc.py* (*https://fpy.li/13-3*).

Now let's study another example emphasizing the dynamic nature of protocols—and why static type checkers have no chance of dealing with them.

Monkey Patching: Implementing a Protocol at Runtime

Monkey patching is dynamically changing a module, class, or function at runtime, to add features or fix bugs. For example, the gevent networking library monkey patches parts of Python's standard library to allow lightweight concurrency without threads or async/await.[2]

The FrenchDeck class from Example 13-2 is missing an essential feature: it cannot be shuffled. Years ago when I first wrote the FrenchDeck example, I did implement a shuffle method. Later I had a Pythonic insight: if a FrenchDeck acts like a sequence, then it doesn't need its own shuffle method because there is already random.shuf fle, documented (*https://fpy.li/13-6*) as "Shuffle the sequence *x* in place."

The standard random.shuffle function is used like this:

```
>>> from random import shuffle
>>> l = list(range(10))
>>> shuffle(l)
>>> l
[5, 2, 9, 7, 8, 3, 1, 4, 0, 6]
```

> When you follow established protocols, you improve your chances of leveraging existing standard library and third-party code, thanks to duck typing.

However, if we try to shuffle a FrenchDeck instance, we get an exception, as in Example 13-3.

Example 13-3. random.shuffle cannot handle FrenchDeck

```
>>> from random import shuffle
>>> from frenchdeck import FrenchDeck
>>> deck = FrenchDeck()
>>> shuffle(deck)
Traceback (most recent call last):
  File "<stdin>", line 1, in <module>
  File ".../random.py", line 265, in shuffle
    x[i], x[j] = x[j], x[i]
TypeError: 'FrenchDeck' object does not support item assignment
```

---

2 The "Monkey patch" (*https://fpy.li/13-4*) article on Wikipedia has a funny example in Python.

The error message is clear: 'FrenchDeck' object does not support item assign ment. The problem is that shuffle operates *in place*, by swapping items inside the collection, and FrenchDeck only implements the *immutable* sequence protocol. Mutable sequences must also provide a __setitem__ method.

Because Python is dynamic, we can fix this at runtime, even at the interactive console. Example 13-4 shows how to do it.

Example 13-4. Monkey patching FrenchDeck to make it mutable and compatible with random.shuffle (continuing from Example 13-3)

```
>>> def set_card(deck, position, card):  ❶
...     deck._cards[position] = card
...
>>> FrenchDeck.__setitem__ = set_card  ❷
>>> shuffle(deck)  ❸
>>> deck[:5]
[Card(rank='3', suit='hearts'), Card(rank='4', suit='diamonds'), Card(rank='4',
suit='clubs'), Card(rank='7', suit='hearts'), Card(rank='9', suit='spades')]
```

❶ Create a function that takes deck, position, and card as arguments.

❷ Assign that function to an attribute named __setitem__ in the FrenchDeck class.

❸ deck can now be shuffled because I added the necessary method of the mutable sequence protocol.

The signature of the __setitem__ special method is defined in *The Python Language Reference* in "3.3.6. Emulating container types" (*https://fpy.li/13-7*). Here I named the arguments deck, position, card—and not self, key, value as in the language reference—to show that every Python method starts life as a plain function, and naming the first argument self is merely a convention. This is OK in a console session, but in a Python source file it's much better to use self, key, and value as documented.

The trick is that set_card knows that the deck object has an attribute named _cards, and _cards must be a mutable sequence. The set_card function is then attached to the FrenchDeck class as the __setitem__ special method. This is an example of *monkey patching*: changing a class or module at runtime, without touching the source code. Monkey patching is powerful, but the code that does the actual patching is very tightly coupled with the program to be patched, often handling private and undocu-mented attributes.

Besides being an example of monkey patching, Example 13-4 highlights the dynamic nature of protocols in dynamic duck typing: random.shuffle doesn't care about the class of the argument, it only needs the object to implement methods from the mutable sequence protocol. It doesn't even matter if the object was "born" with the necessary methods or if they were somehow acquired later.

Duck typing doesn't need to be wildly unsafe or hard to debug. The next section shows some useful code patterns to detect dynamic protocols without resorting to explicit checks.

Defensive Programming and "Fail Fast"

Defensive programming is like defensive driving: a set of practices to enhance safety even when faced with careless programmers—or drivers.

Many bugs cannot be caught except at runtime—even in mainstream statically typed languages.[3] In a dynamically typed language, "fail fast" is excellent advice for safer and easier-to-maintain programs. Failing fast means raising runtime errors as soon as possible, for example, rejecting invalid arguments right a the beginning of a function body.

Here is one example: when you write code that accepts a sequence of items to process internally as a list, don't enforce a list argument by type checking. Instead, take the argument and immediately build a list from it. One example of this code pattern is the __init__ method in Example 13-10, later in this chapter:

```python
def __init__(self, iterable):
    self._balls = list(iterable)
```

That way you make your code more flexible, because the list() constructor handles any iterable that fits in memory. If the argument is not iterable, the call will fail fast with a very clear TypeError exception, right when the object is initialized. If you want to be more explicit, you can wrap the list() call with try/except to customize the error message—but I'd use that extra code only on an external API, because the problem would be easy to see for maintainers of the codebase. Either way, the offending call will appear near the end of the traceback, making it straightforward to fix. If you don't catch the invalid argument in the class constructor, the program will blow up later, when some other method of the class needs to operate on self._balls and it is not a list. Then the root cause will be harder to find.

Of course, calling list() on the argument would be bad if the data shouldn't be copied, either because it's too large or because the function, by design, needs to change it in place for the benefit of the caller, like random.shuffle does. In that case, a runtime check like isinstance(x, abc.MutableSequence) would be the way to go.

---

3 That's why automated testing is necessary.

If you are afraid to get an infinite generator—not a common issue—you can begin by calling len() on the argument. This would reject iterators, while safely dealing with tuples, arrays, and other existing or future classes that fully implement the Sequence interface. Calling len() is usually very cheap, and an invalid argument will raise an error immediately.

On the other hand, if any iterable is acceptable, then call iter(x) as soon as possible to obtain an iterator, as we'll see in "Why Sequences Are Iterable: The iter Function" on page 600. Again, if x is not iterable, this will fail fast with an easy-to-debug exception.

In the cases I just described, a type hint could catch some problems earlier, but not all problems. Recall that the type Any is *consistent-with* every other type. Type inference may cause a variable to be tagged with the Any type. When that happens, the type checker is in the dark. In addition, type hints are not enforced at runtime. Fail fast is the last line of defense.

Defensive code leveraging duck types can also include logic to handle different types without using isinstance() or hasattr() tests.

One example is how we might emulate the handling of the field_names argument in collections.namedtuple (*https://fpy.li/13-8*): field_names accepts a single string with identifiers separated by spaces or commas, or a sequence of identifiers. Example 13-5 shows how I'd do it using duck typing.

Example 13-5. Duck typing to handle a string or an iterable of strings

```
try:  ❶
    field_names = field_names.replace(',', ' ').split()  ❷
except AttributeError:  ❸
    pass  ❹
field_names = tuple(field_names)  ❺
if not all(s.isidentifier() for s in field_names):  ❻
    raise ValueError('field_names must all be valid identifiers')
```

❶ Assume it's a string (EAFP = it's easier to ask forgiveness than permission).

❷ Convert commas to spaces and split the result into a list of names.

❸ Sorry, field_names doesn't quack like a str: it has no .replace, or it returns something we can't .split.

❹ If AttributeError was raised, then field_names is not a str and we assume it was already an iterable of names.

❺ To make sure it's an iterable and to keep our own copy, create a tuple out of what we have. A `tuple` is more compact than `list`, and it also prevents my code from changing the names by mistake.

❻ Use `str.isidentifier` to ensure every name is valid.

Example 13-5 shows one situation where duck typing is more expressive than static type hints. There is no way to spell a type hint that says "`field_names` must be a string of identifiers separated by spaces or commas." This is the relevant part of the `namedtuple` signature on typeshed (see the full source at *stdlib/3/collections/__init__.pyi* (*https://fpy.li/13-9*)):

```
def namedtuple(
    typename: str,
    field_names: Union[str, Iterable[str]],
    *,
    # rest of signature omitted
```

As you can see, `field_names` is annotated as `Union[str, Iterable[str]]`, which is OK as far as it goes, but is not enough to catch all possible problems.

After reviewing dynamic protocols, we move to a more explicit form of runtime type checking: goose typing.

Goose Typing

> An abstract class represents an interface.
>
> —Bjarne Stroustrup, creator of C++[4]

Python doesn't have an `interface` keyword. We use abstract base classes (ABCs) to define interfaces for explicit type checking at runtime—also supported by static type checkers.

The *Python Glossary* entry for abstract base class (*https://fpy.li/13-10*) has a good explanation of the value they bring to duck-typed languages:

> Abstract base classes complement duck typing by providing a way to define interfaces when other techniques like `hasattr()` would be clumsy or subtly wrong (for example, with magic methods). ABCs introduce virtual subclasses, which are classes that don't inherit from a class but are still recognized by `isinstance()` and `issubclass()`; see the abc module documentation.[5]

---

4 Bjarne Stroustrup, *The Design and Evolution of C++*, p. 278 (Addison-Wesley).

5 Retrieved October 18, 2020.

Goose typing is a runtime type checking approach that leverages ABCs. I will let Alex Martelli explain in "Waterfowl and ABCs" on page 445.

 I am very grateful to my friends Alex Martelli and Anna Ravenscroft. I showed them the first outline of *Fluent Python* at OSCON 2013, and they encouraged me to submit it for publication with O'Reilly. Both later contributed with thorough tech reviews. Alex was already the most cited person in this book, and then he offered to write this essay. Take it away, Alex!

Waterfowl and ABCs

By Alex Martelli

I've been credited on Wikipedia (*https://fpy.li/13-11*) for helping spread the helpful meme and sound-bite "*duck typing*" (i.e, ignoring an object's actual type, focusing instead on ensuring that the object implements the method names, signatures, and semantics required for its intended use).

In Python, this mostly boils down to avoiding the use of `isinstance` to check the object's type (not to mention the even worse approach of checking, for example, whether `type(foo) is bar`—which is rightly anathema as it inhibits even the simplest forms of inheritance!).

The overall *duck typing* approach remains quite useful in many contexts—and yet, in many others, an often preferable one has evolved over time. And herein lies a tale...

In recent generations, the taxonomy of genus and species (including, but not limited to, the family of waterfowl known as Anatidae) has mostly been driven by *phenetics*—an approach focused on similarities of morphology and behavior...chiefly, *observable* traits. The analogy to "duck typing" was strong.

However, parallel evolution can often produce similar traits, both morphological and behavioral ones, among species that are actually unrelated, but just happened to evolve in similar, though separate, ecological niches. Similar "accidental similarities" happen in programming, too—for example, consider the classic object-oriented programming example:

```
class Artist:
    def draw(self): ...

class Gunslinger:
    def draw(self): ...

class Lottery:
    def draw(self): ...
```

Clearly, the mere existence of a method named draw, callable without arguments, is far from sufficient to assure us that two objects x and y, such that x.draw() and y.draw() can be called, are in any way exchangeable or abstractly equivalent—nothing about the similarity of the semantics resulting from such calls can be inferred. Rather, we need a knowledgeable programmer to somehow positively *assert* that such an equivalence holds at some level!

In biology (and other disciplines), this issue has led to the emergence (and, on many facets, the dominance) of an approach that's an alternative to phenetics, known as *cladistics*—focusing taxonomical choices on characteristics that are inherited from common ancestors, rather than ones that are independently evolved. (Cheap and rapid DNA sequencing can make cladistics highly practical in many more cases in recent years.)

For example, sheldgeese (once classified as being closer to other geese) and shelducks (once classified as being closer to other ducks) are now grouped together within the subfamily Tadornidae (implying they're closer to each other than to any other Anatidae, as they share a closer common ancestor). Furthermore, DNA analysis has shown, in particular, that the white-winged wood duck is not as close to the Muscovy duck (the latter being a shelduck) as similarity in looks and behavior had long suggested—so the wood duck was reclassified into its own genus, and entirely out of the subfamily!

Does this matter? It depends on the context! For such purposes as deciding how best to cook a waterfowl once you've bagged it, for example, specific observable traits (not all of them—plumage, for example, is de minimis in such a context), mostly texture and flavor (old-fashioned phenetics!), may be far more relevant than cladistics. But for other issues, such as susceptibility to different pathogens (whether you're trying to raise waterfowl in captivity, or preserve them in the wild), DNA closeness can matter much more.

So, by very loose analogy with these taxonomic revolutions in the world of waterfowls, I'm recommending supplementing (not entirely replacing—in certain contexts it shall still serve) good old *duck typing* with…*goose typing*!

What *goose typing* means is: isinstance(obj, cls) is now just fine…as long as cls is an abstract base class—in other words, cls's metaclass is abc.ABCMeta.

You can find many useful existing abstract classes in collections.abc (and additional ones in the numbers module of *The Python Standard Library*).[6]

---

6 You can also, of course, define your own ABCs—but I would discourage all but the most advanced Pythonistas from going that route, just as I would discourage them from defining their own custom metaclasses…and even for said "most advanced Pythonistas," those of us sporting deep mastery of every fold and crease in the language, these are not tools for frequent use. Such "deep metaprogramming," if ever appropriate, is intended for authors of broad frameworks meant to be independently extended by vast numbers of separate development teams…less than 1% of "most advanced Pythonistas" may ever need that! — A.M.

Among the many conceptual advantages of ABCs over concrete classes (e.g., Scott Meyer's "all non-leaf classes should be abstract"; see Item 33 (*https://fpy.li/13-12*) in his book, *More Effective C++*, Addison-Wesley), Python's ABCs add one major practical advantage: the `register` class method, which lets end-user code "declare" that a certain class becomes a "virtual" subclass of an ABC (for this purpose, the registered class must meet the ABC's method name and signature requirements, and more importantly, the underlying semantic contract—but it need not have been developed with any awareness of the ABC, and in particular need not inherit from it!). This goes a long way toward breaking the rigidity and strong coupling that make inheritance something to use with much more caution than typically practiced by most object-oriented programmers.

Sometimes you don't even need to register a class for an ABC to recognize it as a subclass!

That's the case for the ABCs whose essence boils down to a few special methods. For example:

```
>>> class Struggle:
...     def __len__(self): return 23
...
>>> from collections import abc
>>> isinstance(Struggle(), abc.Sized)
True
```

As you see, `abc.Sized` recognizes `Struggle` as "a subclass," with no need for registration, as implementing the special method named `__len__` is all it takes (it's supposed to be implemented with the proper syntax—callable without arguments—and semantics—returning a nonnegative integer denoting an object's "length"; any code that implements a specially named method, such as `__len__`, with arbitrary, non-compliant syntax and semantics has much worse problems anyway).

So, here's my valediction: whenever you're implementing a class embodying any of the concepts represented in the ABCs in `numbers`, `collections.abc`, or other framework you may be using, be sure (if needed) to subclass it from, or register it into, the corresponding ABC. At the start of your programs using some library or framework defining classes which have omitted to do that, perform the registrations yourself; then, when you must check for (most typically) an argument being, e.g, "a sequence," check whether:

```
isinstance(the_arg, collections.abc.Sequence)
```

And, *don't* define custom ABCs (or metaclasses) in production code. If you feel the urge to do so, I'd bet it's likely to be a case of the "all problems look like a nail"–syndrome for somebody who just got a shiny new hammer—you (and future maintainers of your code) will be much happier sticking with straightforward and simple code, eschewing such depths. *Valē!*

To summarize, *goose typing* entails:

- Subclassing from ABCs to make it explicit that you are implementing a previously defined interface.

- Runtime type checking using ABCs instead of concrete classes as the second argument for `isinstance` and `issubclass`.

Alex makes the point that inheriting from an ABC is more than implementing the required methods: it's also a clear declaration of intent by the developer. That intent can also be made explicit through registering a virtual subclass.

 Details of using `register` are covered in "A Virtual Subclass of an ABC" on page 462, later in this chapter. For now, here is a brief example: given the FrenchDeck class, if I want it to pass a check like `issubclass(FrenchDeck, Sequence)`, I can make it a *virtual subclass* of the Sequence ABC with these lines:

```
from collections.abc import Sequence
Sequence.register(FrenchDeck)
```

The use of `isinstance` and `issubclass` becomes more acceptable if you are checking against ABCs instead of concrete classes. If used with concrete classes, type checks limit polymorphism—an essential feature of object-oriented programming. But with ABCs these tests are more flexible. After all, if a component does not implement an ABC by subclassing—but does implement the required methods—it can always be registered after the fact so it passes those explicit type checks.

However, even with ABCs, you should beware that excessive use of `isinstance` checks may be a *code smell*—a symptom of bad OO design.

It's usually *not* OK to have a chain of `if/elif/elif` with `isinstance` checks performing different actions depending on the type of object: you should be using polymorphism for that—i.e., design your classes so that the interpreter dispatches calls to the proper methods, instead of you hardcoding the dispatch logic in `if/elif/elif` blocks.

On the other hand, it's OK to perform an `isinstance` check against an ABC if you must enforce an API contract: "Dude, you have to implement this if you want to call me," as technical reviewer Lennart Regebro put it. That's particularly useful in systems that have a plug-in architecture. Outside of frameworks, duck typing is often simpler and more flexible than type checks.

Finally, in his essay, Alex reinforces more than once the need for restraint in the creation of ABCs. Excessive use of ABCs would impose ceremony in a language that became popular because it is practical and pragmatic. During the *Fluent Python* review process, Alex wrote in an e-mail:

> ABCs are meant to encapsulate very general concepts, abstractions, introduced by a framework—things like "a sequence" and "an exact number." [Readers] most likely don't need to write any new ABCs, just use existing ones correctly, to get 99.9% of the benefits without serious risk of misdesign.

Now let's see goose typing in practice.

Subclassing an ABC

Following Martelli's advice, we'll leverage an existing ABC, collections.MutableSe quence, before daring to invent our own. In Example 13-6, FrenchDeck2 is explicitly declared a subclass of collections.MutableSequence.

Example 13-6. frenchdeck2.py: FrenchDeck2, a subclass of collections.MutableSe quence

```python
from collections import namedtuple, abc

Card = namedtuple('Card', ['rank', 'suit'])

class FrenchDeck2(abc.MutableSequence):
    ranks = [str(n) for n in range(2, 11)] + list('JQKA')
    suits = 'spades diamonds clubs hearts'.split()

    def __init__(self):
        self._cards = [Card(rank, suit) for suit in self.suits
                                        for rank in self.ranks]

    def __len__(self):
        return len(self._cards)

    def __getitem__(self, position):
        return self._cards[position]

    def __setitem__(self, position, value):  ❶
        self._cards[position] = value

    def __delitem__(self, position):  ❷
        del self._cards[position]

    def insert(self, position, value):  ❸
        self._cards.insert(position, value)
```

❶ __setitem__ is all we need to enable shuffling...

❷ ...but subclassing MutableSequence forces us to implement __delitem__, an abstract method of that ABC.

❸ We are also required to implement insert, the third abstract method of MutableSequence.

Python does not check for the implementation of the abstract methods at import time (when the *frenchdeck2.py* module is loaded and compiled), but only at runtime when we actually try to instantiate FrenchDeck2. Then, if we fail to implement any of the abstract methods, we get a TypeError exception with a message such as "Can't instantiate abstract class FrenchDeck2 with abstract methods __delitem__, insert". That's why we must implement __delitem__ and insert, even if our FrenchDeck2 examples do not need those behaviors: the MutableSequence ABC demands them.

As Figure 13-3 shows, not all methods of the Sequence and MutableSequence ABCs are abstract.

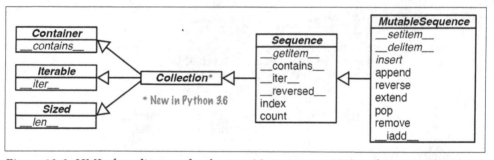

Figure 13-3. UML class diagram for the MutableSequence ABC and its superclasses from collections.abc (inheritance arrows point from subclasses to ancestors; names in italic are abstract classes and abstract methods).

To write FrenchDeck2 as a subclass of MutableSequence, I had to pay the price of implementing __delitem__ and insert, which my examples did not require. In return, FrenchDeck2 inherits five concrete methods from Sequence: __contains__, __iter__, __reversed__, index, and count. From MutableSequence, it gets another six methods: append, reverse, extend, pop, remove, and __iadd__—which supports the += operator for in place concatenation.

The concrete methods in each collections.abc ABC are implemented in terms of the public interface of the class, so they work without any knowledge of the internal structure of instances.

As the coder of a concrete subclass, you may be able to override methods inherited from ABCs with more efficient implementations. For example, `__contains__` works by doing a sequential scan of the sequence, but if your concrete sequence keeps its items sorted, you can write a faster `__contains__` that does a binary search using the `bisect` (*https://fpy.li/13-13*) function from the standard library. See "Managing Ordered Sequences with Bisect" (*https://fpy.li/bisect*) at *fluentpython.com* to learn more about it.

To use ABCs well, you need to know what's available. We'll review the `collections` ABCs next.

ABCs in the Standard Library

Since Python 2.6, the standard library provides several ABCs. Most are defined in the `collections.abc` module, but there are others. You can find ABCs in the `io` and `numbers` packages, for example. But the most widely used are in `collections.abc`.

There are two modules named abc in the standard library. Here we are talking about `collections.abc`. To reduce loading time, since Python 3.4 that module is implemented outside of the `collections` package—in *Lib/_collections_abc.py* (*https://fpy.li/13-14*)—so it's imported separately from `collections`. The other abc module is just abc (i.e., *Lib/abc.py* (*https://fpy.li/13-15*)) where the abc.ABC class is defined. Every ABC depends on the abc module, but we don't need to import it ourselves except to create a brand-new ABC.

Figure 13-4 is a summary UML class diagram (without attribute names) of 17 ABCs defined in `collections.abc`. The documentation of `collections.abc` has a nice table (*https://fpy.li/13-16*) summarizing the ABCs, their relationships, and their abstract and concrete methods (called "mixin methods"). There is plenty of multiple inheritance going on in Figure 13-4. We'll devote most of Chapter 14 to multiple inheritance, but for now it's enough to say that it is usually not a problem when ABCs are concerned.[7]

---

7 Multiple inheritance was *considered harmful* and excluded from Java, except for interfaces: Java interfaces can extend multiple interfaces, and Java classes can implement multiple interfaces.

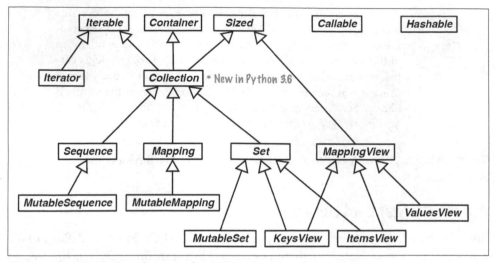

Figure 13-4. UML class diagram for ABCs in `collections.abc`.

Let's review the clusters in Figure 13-4:

`Iterable, Container, Sized`
> Every collection should either inherit from these ABCs or implement compatible protocols. `Iterable` supports iteration with `__iter__`, `Container` supports the in operator with `__contains__`, and `Sized` supports `len()` with `__len__`.

`Collection`
> This ABC has no methods of its own, but was added in Python 3.6 to make it easier to subclass from `Iterable`, `Container`, and `Sized`.

`Sequence, Mapping, Set`
> These are the main immutable collection types, and each has a mutable subclass. A detailed diagram for `MutableSequence` is in Figure 13-3; for `MutableMapping` and `MutableSet`, see Figures 3-1 and 3-2 in Chapter 3.

`MappingView`
> In Python 3, the objects returned from the mapping methods `.items()`, `.keys()`, and `.values()` implement the interfaces defined in `ItemsView`, `KeysView`, and `ValuesView`, respectively. The first two also implement the rich interface of `Set`, with all the operators we saw in "Set Operations" on page 107.

`Iterator`
> Note that iterator subclasses `Iterable`. We discuss this further in Chapter 17.

`Callable, Hashable`

These are not collections, but `collections.abc` was the first package to define ABCs in the standard library, and these two were deemed important enough to be included. They support type checking objects that must be callable or hashable.

For callable detection, the `callable(obj)` built-in function is more convenient than `insinstance(obj, Callable)`.

If `insinstance(obj, Hashable)` returns `False`, you can be certain that `obj` is not hashable. But if the return is `True`, it may be a false positive. The next box explains.

---

isinstance with Hashable and Iterable Can Be Misleading

It's easy to misinterpret the results of the `isinstance` and `issubclass` tests against the `Hashable` and `Iterable` ABCs.

If `isinstance(obj, Hashable)` returns `True`, that only means that the class of `obj` implements or inherits `__hash__`. But if `obj` is a tuple containing unhashable items, then `obj` is not hashable, despite the positive result of the `isinstance` check. Tech reviewer Jürgen Gmach pointed out that duck typing provides the most accurate way to determine if an instance is hashable: call `hash(obj)`. That call will raise `TypeError` if `obj` is not hashable.

On the other hand, even when `isinstance(obj, Iterable)` returns `False`, Python may still be able to iterate over `obj` using `__getitem__` with 0-based indices, as we saw in Chapter 1 and "Python Digs Sequences" on page 438. The documentation for `collections.abc.Iterable` (*https://fpy.li/13-17*) states:

> The only reliable way to determine whether an object is iterable is to call `iter(obj)`.

After looking at some existing ABCs, let's practice goose typing by implementing an ABC from scratch and putting it to use. The goal here is not to encourage everyone to start creating ABCs left and right, but to learn how to read the source code of the ABCs you'll find in the standard library and other packages.

Defining and Using an ABC

This warning appeared in the "Interfaces" chapter of the first edition of *Fluent Python*:

> ABCs, like descriptors and metaclasses, are tools for building frameworks. Therefore, only a small minority of Python developers can create ABCs without imposing unreasonable limitations and needless work on fellow programmers.

Now ABCs have more potential use cases in type hints to support static typing. As discussed in "Abstract Base Classes" on page 278, using ABCs instead of concrete types in function argument type hints gives more flexibility to the caller.

To justify creating an ABC, we need to come up with a context for using it as an extension point in a framework. So here is our context: imagine you need to display advertisements on a website or a mobile app in random order, but without repeating an ad before the full inventory of ads is shown. Now let's assume we are building an ad management framework called ADAM. One of its requirements is to support user-provided nonrepeating random-picking classes.[8] To make it clear to ADAM users what is expected of a "nonrepeating random-picking" component, we'll define an ABC.

In the literature about data structures, "stack" and "queue" describe abstract interfaces in terms of physical arrangements of objects. I will follow suit and use a real-world metaphor to name our ABC: bingo cages and lottery blowers are machines designed to pick items at random from a finite set, without repeating, until the set is exhausted.

The ABC will be named Tombola, after the Italian name of bingo and the tumbling container that mixes the numbers.

The Tombola ABC has four methods. The two abstract methods are:

.load(…)
Put items into the container.

.pick()
Remove one item at random from the container, returning it.

The concrete methods are:

.loaded()
Return True if there is at least one item in the container.

.inspect()
Return a tuple built from the items currently in the container, without changing its contents (the internal ordering is not preserved).

Figure 13-5 shows the Tombola ABC and three concrete implementations.

---

8 Perhaps the client needs to audit the randomizer; or the agency wants to provide a rigged one. You never know…

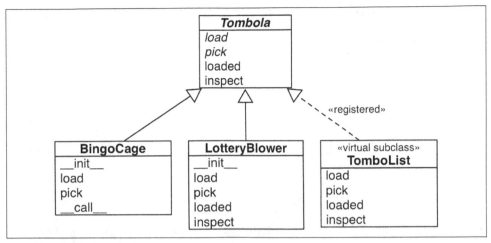

Figure 13-5. UML diagram for an ABC and three subclasses. The name of the Tombola ABC and its abstract methods are written in italics, per UML conventions. The dashed arrow is used for interface implementation—here I am using it to show that TomboList not only implements the Tombola interface, but is also registered as virtual subclass of Tombola—as we will see later in this chapter.[9]

Example 13-7 shows the definition of the Tombola ABC.

Example 13-7. tombola.py: Tombola is an ABC with two abstract methods and two concrete methods

```python
import abc

class Tombola(abc.ABC):  ❶

    @abc.abstractmethod
    def load(self, iterable):  ❷
        """Add items from an iterable."""

    @abc.abstractmethod
    def pick(self):  ❸
        """Remove item at random, returning it.

        This method should raise `LookupError` when the instance is empty.
        """

    def loaded(self):  ❹
        """Return `True` if there's at least 1 item, `False` otherwise."""
```

---

9 «registered» and «virtual subclass» are not standard UML terms. I am using them to represent a class relationship that is specific to Python.

```
            return bool(self.inspect())    ❺

    def inspect(self):
        """Return a sorted tuple with the items currently inside."""
        items = []
        while True:    ❻
            try:
                items.append(self.pick())
            except LookupError:
                break
        self.load(items)    ❼
        return tuple(items)
```

❶ To define an ABC, subclass abc.ABC.

❷ An abstract method is marked with the @abstractmethod decorator, and often its body is empty except for a docstring.[10]

❸ The docstring instructs implementers to raise LookupError if there are no items to pick.

❹ An ABC may include concrete methods.

❺ Concrete methods in an ABC must rely only on the interface defined by the ABC (i.e., other concrete or abstract methods or properties of the ABC).

❻ We can't know how concrete subclasses will store the items, but we can build the inspect result by emptying the Tombola with successive calls to .pick()…

❼ …then use .load(…) to put everything back.

---

10 Before ABCs existed, abstract methods would raise NotImplementedError to signal that subclasses were responsible for their implementation. In Smalltalk-80, abstract method bodies would invoke subclassRespon sibility, a method inherited from object that would produce an error with the message, "My subclass should have overridden one of my messages."

An abstract method can actually have an implementation. Even if it does, subclasses will still be forced to override it, but they will be able to invoke the abstract method with super(), adding functionality to it instead of implementing from scratch. See the abc module documentation (*https://fpy.li/13-18*) for details on @abstractmethod usage.

The code for the .inspect() method in Example 13-7 is silly, but it shows that we can rely on .pick() and .load(…) to inspect what's inside the Tombola by picking all items and loading them back—without knowing how the items are actually stored. The point of this example is to highlight that it's OK to provide concrete methods in ABCs, as long as they only depend on other methods in the interface. Being aware of their internal data structures, concrete subclasses of Tombola may always override .inspect() with a smarter implementation, but they don't have to.

The .loaded() method in Example 13-7 has one line, but it's expensive: it calls .inspect() to build the tuple just to apply bool() on it. This works, but a concrete subclass can do much better, as we'll see.

Note that our roundabout implementation of .inspect() requires that we catch a LookupError thrown by self.pick(). The fact that self.pick() may raise LookupError is also part of its interface, but there is no way to make this explicit in Python, except in the documentation (see the docstring for the abstract pick method in Example 13-7).

I chose the LookupError exception because of its place in the Python hierarchy of exceptions in relation to IndexError and KeyError, the most likely exceptions to be raised by the data structures used to implement a concrete Tombola. Therefore, implementations can raise LookupError, IndexError, KeyError, or a custom subclass of LookupError to comply. See Figure 13-6.

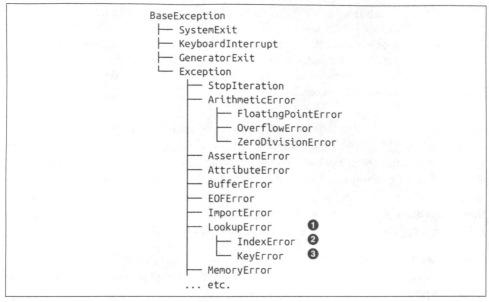

```
                     BaseException
                       ├── SystemExit
                       ├── KeyboardInterrupt
                       ├── GeneratorExit
                       └── Exception
                              ├── StopIteration
                              ├── ArithmeticError
                              │      ├── FloatingPointError
                              │      ├── OverflowError
                              │      └── ZeroDivisionError
                              ├── AssertionError
                              ├── AttributeError
                              ├── BufferError
                              ├── EOFError
                              ├── ImportError
                              ├── LookupError          ❶
                              │      ├── IndexError     ❷
                              │      └── KeyError       ❸
                              ├── MemoryError
                         ... etc.
```

Figure 13-6. Part of the Exception class hierarchy.[11]

❶ LookupError is the exception we handle in Tombola.inspect.

❷ IndexError is the LookupError subclass raised when we try to get an item from a sequence with an index beyond the last position.

❸ KeyError is raised when we use a nonexistent key to get an item from a mapping.

We now have our very own Tombola ABC. To witness the interface checking performed by an ABC, let's try to fool Tombola with a defective implementation in Example 13-8.

Example 13-8. A fake Tombola doesn't go undetected

```
>>> from tombola import Tombola
>>> class Fake(Tombola):    ❶
...     def pick(self):
...         return 13
...
>>> Fake    ❷
<class '__main__.Fake'>
>>> f = Fake()    ❸
Traceback (most recent call last):
```

---

11 The complete tree is in section "5.4. Exception hierarchy" of *The Python Standard Library* docs.

```
  File "<stdin>", line 1, in <module>
TypeError: Can't instantiate abstract class Fake with abstract method load
```

❶ Declare Fake as a subclass of Tombola.

❷ The class was created, no errors so far.

❸ TypeError is raised when we try to instantiate Fake. The message is very clear:
    Fake is considered abstract because it failed to implement load, one of the
    abstract methods declared in the Tombola ABC.

So we have our first ABC defined, and we put it to work validating a class. We'll soon
subclass the Tombola ABC, but first we must cover some ABC coding rules.

ABC Syntax Details

The standard way to declare an ABC is to subclass abc.ABC or any other ABC.

Besides the ABC base class, and the @abstractmethod decorator, the abc module
defines the @abstractclassmethod, @abstractstaticmethod, and @abstractprop
erty decorators. However, these last three were deprecated in Python 3.3, when it
became possible to stack decorators on top of @abstractmethod, making the others
redundant. For example, the preferred way to declare an abstract class method is:

```
class MyABC(abc.ABC):
    @classmethod
    @abc.abstractmethod
    def an_abstract_classmethod(cls, ...):
        pass
```

> The order of stacked function decorators matters, and in the case
> of @abstractmethod, the documentation is explicit:
>
> > When abstractmethod() is applied in combination with
> > other method descriptors, it should be applied as the
> > innermost decorator...[12]
>
> In other words, no other decorator may appear between @abstract
> method and the def statement.

Now that we've got these ABC syntax issues covered, let's put Tombola to use by
implementing two concrete descendants of it.

---

[12] The @abc.abstractmethod (*https://fpy.li/13-19*) entry in the abc module documentation (*https://fpy.li/13-20*).

Subclassing an ABC

Given the Tombola ABC, we'll now develop two concrete subclasses that satisfy its interface. These classes were pictured in Figure 13-5, along with the virtual subclass to be discussed in the next section.

The BingoCage class in Example 13-9 is a variation of Example 7-8 using a better randomizer. This BingoCage implements the required abstract methods load and pick.

Example 13-9. bingo.py: BingoCage is a concrete subclass of Tombola

```python
import random

from tombola import Tombola


class BingoCage(Tombola):  ❶

    def __init__(self, items):
        self._randomizer = random.SystemRandom()  ❷
        self._items = []
        self.load(items)  ❸

    def load(self, items):
        self._items.extend(items)
        self._randomizer.shuffle(self._items)  ❹

    def pick(self):  ❺
        try:
            return self._items.pop()
        except IndexError:
            raise LookupError('pick from empty BingoCage')

    def __call__(self):  ❻
        self.pick()
```

❶ This BingoCage class explicitly extends Tombola.

❷ Pretend we'll use this for online gaming. random.SystemRandom implements the random API on top of the os.urandom(…) function, which provides random bytes "suitable for cryptographic use," according to the os module docs (*https://fpy.li/ 13-21*).

❸ Delegate initial loading to the .load(…) method.

❹ Instead of the plain random.shuffle() function, we use the .shuffle() method of our SystemRandom instance.

❺ pick is implemented as in Example 7-8.

❻ __call__ is also from Example 7-8. It's not needed to satisfy the Tombola interface, but there's no harm in adding extra methods.

BingoCage inherits the expensive loaded and the silly inspect methods from Tombola. Both could be overridden with much faster one-liners, as in Example 13-10. The point is: we can be lazy and just inherit the suboptimal concrete methods from an ABC. The methods inherited from Tombola are not as fast as they could be for BingoCage, but they do provide correct results for any Tombola subclass that correctly implements pick and load.

Example 13-10 shows a very different but equally valid implementation of the Tombola interface. Instead of shuffling the "balls" and popping the last, LottoBlower pops from a random position.

Example 13-10. lotto.py: LottoBlower is a concrete subclass that overrides the inspect and loaded methods from Tombola

```python
import random

from tombola import Tombola


class LottoBlower(Tombola):

    def __init__(self, iterable):
        self._balls = list(iterable)  ❶

    def load(self, iterable):
        self._balls.extend(iterable)

    def pick(self):
        try:
            position = random.randrange(len(self._balls))  ❷
        except ValueError:
            raise LookupError('pick from empty LottoBlower')
        return self._balls.pop(position)  ❸

    def loaded(self):  ❹
        return bool(self._balls)

    def inspect(self):  ❺
        return tuple(self._balls)
```

❶ The initializer accepts any iterable: the argument is used to build a list.

❷ The `random.randrange(…)` function raises `ValueError` if the range is empty, so we catch that and throw `LookupError` instead, to be compatible with `Tombola`.

❸ Otherwise the randomly selected item is popped from `self._balls`.

❹ Override `loaded` to avoid calling `inspect` (as `Tombola.loaded` does in Example 13-7). We can make it faster by working with `self._balls` directly—no need to build a whole new `tuple`.

❺ Override `inspect` with a one-liner.

Example 13-10 illustrates an idiom worth mentioning: in `__init__`, `self._balls` stores `list(iterable)` and not just a reference to `iterable` (i.e., we did not merely assign `self._balls = iterable`, aliasing the argument). As mentioned in "Defensive Programming and 'Fail Fast'" on page 442, this makes our `LottoBlower` flexible because the `iterable` argument may be any iterable type. At the same time, we make sure to store its items in a `list` so we can `pop` items. And even if we always get lists as the `iterable` argument, `list(iterable)` produces a copy of the argument, which is a good practice considering we will be removing items from it and the client might not expect that the provided list will be changed.[13]

We now come to the crucial dynamic feature of goose typing: declaring virtual subclasses with the `register` method.

A Virtual Subclass of an ABC

An essential characteristic of goose typing—and one reason why it deserves a water-fowl name—is the ability to register a class as a *virtual subclass* of an ABC, even if it does not inherit from it. When doing so, we promise that the class faithfully implements the interface defined in the ABC—and Python will believe us without checking. If we lie, we'll be caught by the usual runtime exceptions.

This is done by calling a `register` class method on the ABC. The registered class then becomes a virtual subclass of the ABC, and will be recognized as such by `issubclass`, but it does not inherit any methods or attributes from the ABC.

---

13 "Defensive Programming with Mutable Parameters" on page 216 in Chapter 6 was devoted to the aliasing issue we just avoided here.

Virtual subclasses do not inherit from their registered ABCs, and are not checked for conformance to the ABC interface at any time, not even when they are instantiated. Also, static type checkers can't handle virtual subclasses at this time. For details, see Mypy issue 2922—ABCMeta.register support (*https://fpy.li/13-22*).

The `register` method is usually invoked as a plain function (see "Usage of register in Practice" on page 465), but it can also be used as a decorator. In Example 13-11, we use the decorator syntax and implement `TomboList`, a virtual subclass of `Tombola`, depicted in Figure 13-7.

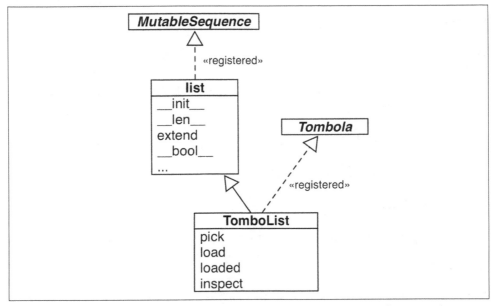

Figure 13-7. UML class diagram for the TomboList, a real subclass of list and a virtual subclass of Tombola.

Example 13-11. tombolist.py: class TomboList is a virtual subclass of Tombola

```
from random import randrange

from tombola import Tombola

@Tombola.register        ❶
class TomboList(list):   ❷

    def pick(self):
        if self:         ❸
            position = randrange(len(self))
            return self.pop(position)   ❹
```

```
        else:
            raise LookupError('pop from empty TomboList')

    load = list.extend    ❺

    def loaded(self):
        return bool(self)    ❻

    def inspect(self):
        return tuple(self)

# Tombola.register(TomboList)    ❼
```

❶ Tombolist is registered as a virtual subclass of Tombola.

❷ Tombolist extends list.

❸ Tombolist inherits its boolean behavior from list, and that returns True if the list is not empty.

❹ Our pick calls self.pop, inherited from list, passing a random item index.

❺ Tombolist.load is the same as list.extend.

❻ loaded delegates to bool.[14]

❼ It's always possible to call register in this way, and it's useful to do so when you need to register a class that you do not maintain, but which does fulfill the interface.

Note that because of the registration, the functions issubclass and isinstance act as if TomboList is a subclass of Tombola:

```
>>> from tombola import Tombola
>>> from tombolist import TomboList
>>> issubclass(TomboList, Tombola)
True
>>> t = TomboList(range(100))
>>> isinstance(t, Tombola)
True
```

---

14 The same trick I used with load() doesn't work with loaded(), because the list type does not implement __bool__, the method I'd have to bind to loaded. The bool() built-in doesn't need __bool__ to work because it can also use __len__. See "4.1. Truth Value Testing" (*https://fpy.li/13-23*) in the "Built-in Types" chapter of the Python documentation.

However, inheritance is guided by a special class attribute named __mro__—the Method Resolution Order. It basically lists the class and its superclasses in the order Python uses to search for methods.[15] If you inspect the __mro__ of TomboList, you'll see that it lists only the "real" superclasses—list and object:

```
>>> TomboList.__mro__
(<class 'tombolist.TomboList'>, <class 'list'>, <class 'object'>)
```

Tombola is not in TomboList.__mro__, so TomboList does not inherit any methods from Tombola.

This concludes our Tombola ABC case study. In the next section, we'll address how the register ABC function is used in the wild.

Usage of register in Practice

In Example 13-11, we used Tombola.register as a class decorator. Prior to Python 3.3, register could not be used like that—it had to be called as a plain function after the class definition, as suggested by the comment at the end of Example 13-11. However, even now, it's more widely deployed as a function to register classes defined elsewhere. For example, in the source code (*https://fpy.li/13-24*) for the collections.abc module, the built-in types tuple, str, range, and memoryview are registered as virtual subclasses of Sequence, like this:

```
Sequence.register(tuple)
Sequence.register(str)
Sequence.register(range)
Sequence.register(memoryview)
```

Several other built-in types are registered to ABCs in *_collections_abc.py*. Those registrations happen only when that module is imported, which is OK because you'll have to import it anyway to get the ABCs. For example, you need to import MutableMapping from collections.abc to perform a check like isinstance(my_dict, MutableMapping).

Subclassing an ABC or registering with an ABC are both explicit ways of making our classes pass issubclass checks—as well as isinstance checks, which also rely on issubclass. But some ABCs support structural typing as well. The next section explains.

---

15 There is a whole section explaining the __mro__ class attribute in "Multiple Inheritance and Method Resolution Order" on page 496. Right now, this quick explanation will do.

Structural Typing with ABCs

ABCs are mostly used with nominal typing. When a class Sub explicitly inherits from AnABC, or is registered with AnABC, the name of AnABC is linked to the Sub class—and that's how at runtime, issubclass(AnABC, Sub) returns True.

In contrast, structural typing is about looking at the structure of an object's public interface to determine its type: an object is *consistent-with* a type if it implements the methods defined in the type.[16] Dynamic and static duck typing are two approaches to structural typing.

It turns out that some ABCs also support structural typing. In his essay, "Waterfowl and ABCs" on page 445, Alex shows that a class can be recognized as a subclass of an ABC even without registration. Here is his example again, with an added test using issubclass:

```
>>> class Struggle:
...     def __len__(self): return 23
...
>>> from collections import abc
>>> isinstance(Struggle(), abc.Sized)
True
>>> issubclass(Struggle, abc.Sized)
True
```

Class Struggle is considered a subclass of abc.Sized by the issubclass function (and, consequently, by isinstance as well) because abc.Sized implements a special class method named __subclasshook__.

The __subclasshook__ for Sized checks whether the class argument has an attribute named __len__. If it does, then it is considered a virtual subclass of Sized. See Example 13-12.

Example 13-12. Definition of Sized from the source code of Lib/_collections_abc.py (https://fpy.li/13-25)

```
class Sized(metaclass=ABCMeta):

    __slots__ = ()

    @abstractmethod
    def __len__(self):
        return 0

    @classmethod
```

---

16 The concept of type consistency was explained in "Subtype-of versus consistent-with" on page 267.

```
def __subclasshook__(cls, C):
    if cls is Sized:
        if any("__len__" in B.__dict__ for B in C.__mro__):  ❶
            return True  ❷
    return NotImplemented  ❸
```

❶ If there is an attribute named __len__ in the __dict__ of any class listed in C.__mro__ (i.e., C and its superclasses)...

❷ ...return True, signaling that C is a virtual subclass of Sized.

❸ Otherwise return NotImplemented to let the subclass check proceed.

> If you are interested in the details of the subclass check, see the source code for the ABCMeta.__subclasscheck__ method in Python 3.6: *Lib/abc.py* (*https://fpy.li/13-26*). Beware: it has lots of ifs and two recursive calls. In Python 3.7, Ivan Levkivskyi and Inada Naoki rewrote in C most of the logic for the abc module, for better performance. See Python issue #31333 (*https://fpy.li/13-27*). The current implementation of ABCMeta.__subclasscheck__ simply calls _abc_subclasscheck. The relevant C source code is in *cpython/Modules/_abc.c#L605* (*https://fpy.li/13-28*).

That's how __subclasshook__ allows ABCs to support structural typing. You can formalize an interface with an ABC, you can make isinstance checks against that ABC, and still have a completely unrelated class pass an issubclass check because it implements a certain method (or because it does whatever it takes to convince a __subclasshook__ to vouch for it).

Is it a good idea to implement __subclasshook__ in our own ABCs? Probably not. All the implementations of __subclasshook__ I've seen in the Python source code are in ABCs like Sized that declare just one special method, and they simply check for that special method name. Given their "special" status, you can be pretty sure that any method named __len__ does what you expect. But even in the realm of special methods and fundamental ABCs, it can be risky to make such assumptions. For example, mappings implement __len__, __getitem__, and __iter__, but they are rightly not considered subtypes of Sequence, because you can't retrieve items using integer offsets or slices. That's why the abc.Sequence (*https://fpy.li/13-29*) class does not implement __subclasshook__.

For ABCs that you and I may write, a __subclasshook__ would be even less dependable. I am not ready to believe that any class named Spam that implements or inherits load, pick, inspect, and loaded is guaranteed to behave as a Tombola. It's better to let the programmer affirm it by subclassing Spam from Tombola, or registering it with

`Tombola.register(Spam)`. Of course, your `__subclasshook__` could also check method signatures and other features, but I just don't think it's worthwhile.

Static Protocols

 Static protocols were introduced in "Static Protocols" on page 287 (Chapter 8). I considered delaying all coverage of protocols until this chapter, but decided that the initial presentation of type hints in functions had to include protocols because duck typing is an essential part of Python, and static type checking without protocols doesn't handle Pythonic APIs very well.

We will wrap up this chapter by illustrating static protocols with two simple examples, and a discussion of numeric ABCs and protocols. Let's start by showing how a static protocol makes it possible to annotate and type check the double() function we first saw in "Types Are Defined by Supported Operations" on page 261.

The Typed double Function

When introducing Python to programmers more used to statically typed languages, one of my favorite examples is this simple double function:

```
>>> def double(x):
...     return x * 2
...
>>> double(1.5)
3.0
>>> double('A')
'AA'
>>> double([10, 20, 30])
[10, 20, 30, 10, 20, 30]
>>> from fractions import Fraction
>>> double(Fraction(2, 5))
Fraction(4, 5)
```

Before static protocols were introduced, there was no practical way to add type hints to double without limiting its possible uses.[17]

---

17 OK, double() is not very useful, except as an example. But the Python standard library has many functions that could not be properly annotated before static protocols were added in Python 3.8. I helped fix a couple of bugs in *typeshed* by adding type hints using protocols. For example, the pull request that fixed "Should Mypy warn about potential invalid arguments to max?" (*https://fpy.li/shed4051*) leveraged a _SupportsLessThan protocol, which I used to enhance the annotations for max, min, sorted, and list.sort.

Thanks to duck typing, `double` works even with types from the future, such as the enhanced `Vector` class that we'll see in "Overloading * for Scalar Multiplication" on page 576 (Chapter 16):

```
>>> from vector_v7 import Vector
>>> double(Vector([11.0, 12.0, 13.0]))
Vector([22.0, 24.0, 26.0])
```

The initial implementation of type hints in Python was a nominal type system: the name of a type in an annotation had to match the name of the type of the actual arguments—or the name of one of its superclasses. Since it's impossible to name all types that implement a protocol by supporting the required operations, duck typing could not be described by type hints before Python 3.8.

Now, with `typing.Protocol` we can tell Mypy that `double` takes an argument x that supports x * 2. Example 13-13 shows how.

Example 13-13. double_protocol.py: definition of double using a Protocol

```
from typing import TypeVar, Protocol

T = TypeVar('T')  ❶

class Repeatable(Protocol):
    def __mul__(self: T, repeat_count: int) -> T: ...  ❷

RT = TypeVar('RT', bound=Repeatable)  ❸

def double(x: RT) -> RT:  ❹
    return x * 2
```

❶ We'll use this T in the `__mul__` signature.

❷ `__mul__` is the essence of the `Repeatable` protocol. The `self` parameter is usually not annotated—its type is assumed to be the class. Here we use T to make sure the result type is the same as the type of `self`. Also, note that `repeat_count` is limited to `int` in this protocol.

❸ The RT type variable is bounded by the `Repeatable` protocol: the type checker will require that the actual type implements `Repeatable`.

❹ Now the type checker is able to verify that the x parameter is an object that can be multiplied by an integer, and the return value has the same type as x.

This example shows why PEP 544 (*https://fpy.li/pep544*) is titled "Protocols: Structural subtyping (static duck typing)." The nominal type of the actual argument x given to double is irrelevant as long as it quacks—that is, as long as it implements __mul__.

Runtime Checkable Static Protocols

In the Typing Map (Figure 13-1), `typing.Protocol` appears in the static checking area—the bottom half of the diagram. However, when defining a `typing.Protocol` subclass, you can use the `@runtime_checkable` decorator to make that protocol support `isinstance`/`issubclass` checks at runtime. This works because `typing.Protocol` is an ABC, therefore it supports the __subclasshook__ we saw in "Structural Typing with ABCs" on page 466.

As of Python 3.9, the `typing` module includes seven ready-to-use protocols that are runtime checkable. Here are two of them, quoted directly from the `typing` documentation (*https://fpy.li/13-30*):

class typing.SupportsComplex
 An ABC with one abstract method, __complex__.

class typing.SupportsFloat
 An ABC with one abstract method, __float__.

These protocols are designed to check numeric types for "convertibility": if an object o implements __complex__, then you should be able to get a `complex` by invoking `complex(o)`—because the __complex__ special method exists to support the `complex()` built-in function.

Example 13-14 shows the source code (*https://fpy.li/13-31*) for the `typing.Supports Complex` protocol.

Example 13-14. typing.SupportsComplex protocol source code

```
@runtime_checkable
class SupportsComplex(Protocol):
    """An ABC with one abstract method __complex__."""
    __slots__ = ()

    @abstractmethod
    def __complex__(self) -> complex:
        pass
```

The key is the __complex__ abstract method.[18] During static type checking, an object will be considered *consistent-with* the SupportsComplex protocol if it implements a __complex__ method that takes only self and returns a complex.

Thanks to the @runtime_checkable class decorator applied to SupportsComplex, that protocol can also be used with isinstance checks in Example 13-15.

Example 13-15. Using SupportsComplex at runtime

```
>>> from typing import SupportsComplex
>>> import numpy as np
>>> c64 = np.complex64(3+4j)    ❶
>>> isinstance(c64, complex)    ❷
False
>>> isinstance(c64, SupportsComplex)    ❸
True
>>> c = complex(c64)    ❹
>>> c
(3+4j)
>>> isinstance(c, SupportsComplex)    ❺
False
>>> complex(c)
(3+4j)
```

❶ complex64 is one of five complex number types provided by NumPy.

❷ None of the NumPy complex types subclass the built-in complex.

❸ But NumPy's complex types implement __complex__, so they comply with the SupportsComplex protocol.

❹ Therefore, you can create built-in complex objects from them.

❺ Sadly, the complex built-in type does not implement __complex__, although complex(c) works fine if c is a complex.

As a result of that last point, if you want to test whether an object c is a complex or SupportsComplex, you can provide a tuple of types as the second argument to isinstance, like this:

```
isinstance(c, (complex, SupportsComplex))
```

---

18 The __slots__ attribute is irrelevant to the current discussion—it's an optimization we covered in "Saving Memory with __slots__" on page 386.

An alternative would be to use the `Complex` ABC, defined in the `numbers` module. The built-in `complex` type and the NumPy `complex64` and `complex128` types are all registered as virtual subclasses of `numbers.Complex`, therefore this works:

```
>>> import numbers
>>> isinstance(c, numbers.Complex)
True
>>> isinstance(c64, numbers.Complex)
True
```

I recommended using the `numbers` ABCs in the first edition of *Fluent Python*, but now that's no longer good advice, because those ABCs are not recognized by the static type checkers, as we'll see in "The numbers ABCs and Numeric Protocols" on page 480.

In this section I wanted to demonstrate that a runtime checkable protocol works with `isinstance`, but it turns out this is example not a particularly good use case of `isinstance`, as the sidebar "Duck Typing Is Your Friend" on page 472 explains.

 If you're using an external type checker, there is one advantage of explicit `isinstance` checks: when you write an `if` statement where the condition is `isinstance(o, MyType)`, then Mypy can infer that inside the `if` block, the type of the `o` object is *consistent-with* `MyType`.

Duck Typing Is Your Friend

Very often at runtime, duck typing is the best approach for type checking: instead of calling `isinstance` or `hasattr`, just try the operations you need to do on the object, and handle exceptions as needed. Here is a concrete example.

Continuing the previous discussion—given an object `o` that I need to use as a complex number, this would be one approach:

```
if isinstance(o, (complex, SupportsComplex)):
    # do something that requires `o` to be convertible to complex
else:
    raise TypeError('o must be convertible to complex')
```

The goose typing approach would be to use the `numbers.Complex` ABC:

```
if isinstance(o, numbers.Complex):
    # do something with `o`, an instance of `Complex`
else:
    raise TypeError('o must be an instance of Complex')
```

However, I prefer to leverage duck typing and do this using the EAFP principle—it's easier to ask for forgiveness than permission:

```
    try:
        c = complex(o)
    except TypeError as exc:
        raise TypeError('o must be convertible to complex') from exc
```

And, if all you're going to do is raise a TypeError anyway, then I'd omit the try/ except/raise statements and just write this:

```
    c = complex(o)
```

In this last case, if o is not an acceptable type, Python will raise an exception with a very clear message. For example, this is what I get if o is a tuple:

```
    TypeError: complex() first argument must be a string or a number, not 'tuple'
```

I find the duck typing approach much better in this case.

Now that we've seen how to use static protocols at runtime with preexisting types like complex and numpy.complex64, we need to discuss the limitations of runtime checkable protocols.

Limitations of Runtime Protocol Checks

We've seen that type hints are generally ignored at runtime, and this also affects the use of isinstance or issubclass checks against static protocols.

For example, any class with a __float__ method is considered—at runtime—a virtual subclass of SupportsFloat, even if the __float__ method does not return a float.

Check out this console session:

```
>>> import sys
>>> sys.version
'3.9.5 (v3.9.5:0a7dcbdb13, May  3 2021, 13:17:02) \n[Clang 6.0 (clang-600.0.57)]'
>>> c = 3+4j
>>> c.__float__
<method-wrapper '__float__' of complex object at 0x10a16c590>
>>> c.__float__()
Traceback (most recent call last):
  File "<stdin>", line 1, in <module>
TypeError: can't convert complex to float
```

In Python 3.9, the complex type does have a __float__ method, but it exists only to raise a TypeError with an explicit error message. If that __float__ method had annotations, the return type would be NoReturn—which we saw in "NoReturn" on page 295.

But type hinting `complex.__float__` on *typeshed* would not solve this problem because Python's runtime generally ignores type hints—and can't access the *typeshed* stub files anyway.

Continuing from the previous Python 3.9 session:

```
>>> from typing import SupportsFloat
>>> c = 3+4j
>>> isinstance(c, SupportsFloat)
True
>>> issubclass(complex, SupportsFloat)
True
```

So we have misleading results: the runtime checks against `SupportsFloat` suggest that you can convert a `complex` to `float`, but in fact that raises a type error.

 The specific isssue with the `complex` type is fixed in Python 3.10.0b4 with the removal of the `complex.__float__` method.

But the overall issue remains: `isinstance`/`issubclass` checks only look at the presence or absence of methods, without checking their signatures, much less their type annotations. And this is not about to change, because such type checks at runtime would have an unacceptable performance cost.[19]

Now let's see how to implement a static protocol in a user-defined class.

Supporting a Static Protocol

Recall the `Vector2d` class we built in Chapter 11. Given that a `complex` number and a `Vector2d` instance both consist of a pair of floats, it makes sense to support conversion from `Vector2d` to `complex`.

Example 13-16 shows the implementation of the `__complex__` method to enhance the last version of `Vector2d` we saw in Example 11-11. For completeness, we can support the inverse operation with a `fromcomplex` class method to build a `Vector2d` from a `complex`.

---

[19] Thanks to Ivan Levkivskyi, coauthor of PEP 544 (*https://fpy.li/pep544*) (on Protocols), for pointing out that type checking is not just a matter of checking whether the type of x is T: it's about determining that the type of x is *consistent-with* T, which may be expensive. It's no wonder that Mypy takes a few seconds to type check even short Python scripts.

Example 13-16. vector2d_v4.py: methods for converting to and from `complex`

```python
def __complex__(self):
    return complex(self.x, self.y)

@classmethod
def fromcomplex(cls, datum):
    return cls(datum.real, datum.imag)  ❶
```

❶ This assumes that `datum` has `.real` and `.imag` attributes. We'll see a better implementation in Example 13-17.

Given the preceding code, and the `__abs__` method the `Vector2d` already had in Example 11-11, we get these features:

```python
>>> from typing import SupportsComplex, SupportsAbs
>>> from vector2d_v4 import Vector2d
>>> v = Vector2d(3, 4)
>>> isinstance(v, SupportsComplex)
True
>>> isinstance(v, SupportsAbs)
True
>>> complex(v)
(3+4j)
>>> abs(v)
5.0
>>> Vector2d.fromcomplex(3+4j)
Vector2d(3.0, 4.0)
```

For runtime type checking, Example 13-16 is fine, but for better static coverage and error reporting with Mypy, the `__abs__`, `__complex__`, and `fromcomplex` methods should get type hints, as shown in Example 13-17.

Example 13-17. vector2d_v5.py: adding annotations to the methods under study

```python
def __abs__(self) -> float:  ❶
    return math.hypot(self.x, self.y)

def __complex__(self) -> complex:  ❷
    return complex(self.x, self.y)

@classmethod
def fromcomplex(cls, datum: SupportsComplex) -> Vector2d:  ❸
    c = complex(datum)  ❹
    return cls(c.real, c.imag)
```

❶ The `float` return annotation is needed, otherwise Mypy infers `Any`, and doesn't check the body of the method.

❷ Even without the annotation, Mypy was able to infer that this returns a `complex`. The annotation prevents a warning, depending on your Mypy configuration.

❸ Here `SupportsComplex` ensures the `datum` is convertible.

❹ This explicit conversion is necessary, because the `SupportsComplex` type does not declare `.real` and `.imag` attributes, used in the next line. For example, `Vector2d` doesn't have those attributes, but implements `__complex__`.

The return type of `fromcomplex` can be `Vector2d` if `from __future__ import anno tations` appears at the top of the module. That import causes type hints to be stored as strings, without being evaluated at import time, when function definitions are evaluated. Without the `__future__` import of `annotations`, `Vector2d` is an invalid reference at this point (the class is not fully defined yet) and should be written as a string: `'Vector2d'`, as if it were a forward reference. This `__future__` import was introduced in PEP 563—Postponed Evaluation of Annotations (*https://fpy.li/pep563*), implemented in Python 3.7. That behavior was scheduled to become default in 3.10, but the change was delayed to a later version.[20] When that happens, the import will be redundant, but harmless.

Next, let's see how to create—and later, extend—a new static protocol.

Designing a Static Protocol

While studying goose typing, we saw the `Tombola` ABC in "Defining and Using an ABC" on page 453. Here we'll see how to define a similar interface using a static protocol.

The `Tombola` ABC specifies two methods: `pick` and `load`. We could define a static protocol with these two methods as well, but I learned from the Go community that single-method protocols make static duck typing more useful and flexible. The Go standard library has several interfaces like `Reader`, an interface for I/O that requires just a `read` method. After a while, if you realize a more complete protocol is required, you can combine two or more protocols to define a new one.

Using a container that picks items at random may or may not require reloading the container, but it certainly needs a method to do the actual pick, so that's the method I

---

20 Read the Python Steering Council decision (*https://fpy.li/13-32*) on python-dev.

will choose for the minimal `RandomPicker` protocol. The code for that protocol is in Example 13-18, and its use is demonstrated by tests in Example 13-19.

Example 13-18. randompick.py: definition of RandomPicker

```
from typing import Protocol, runtime_checkable, Any

@runtime_checkable
class RandomPicker(Protocol):
    def pick(self) -> Any: ...
```

 The `pick` method returns Any. In "Implementing a Generic Static Protocol" on page 556, we will see how to make `RandomPicker` a generic type with a parameter to let users of the protocol specify the return type of the `pick` method.

Example 13-19. randompick_test.py: RandomPicker in use

```
import random
from typing import Any, Iterable, TYPE_CHECKING

from randompick import RandomPicker        ❶

class SimplePicker:                        ❷
    def __init__(self, items: Iterable) -> None:
        self._items = list(items)
        random.shuffle(self._items)

    def pick(self) -> Any:                 ❸
        return self._items.pop()

def test_isinstance() -> None:             ❹
    popper: RandomPicker = SimplePicker([1])   ❺
    assert isinstance(popper, RandomPicker)    ❻

def test_item_type() -> None:              ❼
    items = [1, 2]
    popper = SimplePicker(items)
    item = popper.pick()
    assert item in items
    if TYPE_CHECKING:
        reveal_type(item)                  ❽
    assert isinstance(item, int)
```

❶ It's not necessary to import the static protocol to define a class that implements it. Here I imported `RandomPicker` only to use it on `test_isinstance` later.

❷ `SimplePicker` implements `RandomPicker`—but it does not subclass it. This is static duck typing in action.

❸ `Any` is the default return type, so this annotation is not strictly necessary, but it does make it more clear that we are implementing the `RandomPicker` protocol as defined in Example 13-18.

❹ Don't forget to add `-> None` hints to your tests if you want Mypy to look at them.

❺ I added a type hint for the `popper` variable to show that Mypy understands that `SimplePicker` is *consistent-with*.

❻ This test proves that an instance of `SimplePicker` is also an instance of `Random Picker`. This works because of the `@runtime_checkable` decorator applied to `RandomPicker`, and because `SimplePicker` has a `pick` method as required.

❼ This test invokes the `pick` method from a `SimplePicker`, verifies that it returns one of the items given to `SimplePicker`, and then does static and runtime checks on the returned item.

❽ This line generates a note in the Mypy output.

As we saw in Example 8-22, `reveal_type` is a "magic" function recognized by Mypy. That's why it is not imported and we can only call it inside `if` blocks protected by `typing.TYPE_CHECKING`, which is only `True` in the eyes of a static type checker, but is `False` at runtime.

Both tests in Example 13-19 pass. Mypy does not see any errors in that code either, and shows the result of the `reveal_type` on the `item` returned by `pick`:

```
$ mypy randompick_test.py
randompick_test.py:24: note: Revealed type is 'Any'
```

Having created our first protocol, let's study some advice on the matter.

Best Practices for Protocol Design

After 10 years of experience with static duck typing in Go, it is clear that narrow protocols are more useful—often such protocols have a single method, rarely more than a couple of methods. Martin Fowler wrote a post defining *role interface* (*https://fpy.li/ 13-33*), a useful idea to keep in mind when designing protocols.

Also, sometimes you see a protocol defined near the function that uses it—that is, defined in "client code" instead of being defined in a library. This is makes it easy to create new types to call that function, which is good for extensibility and testing with mocks.

The practices of narrow protocols and client-code protocols both avoid unnecessary tight coupling, in line with the Interface Segregation Principle (*https://fpy.li/13-34*), which we can summarize as "Clients should not be forced to depend upon interfaces that they do not use."

The page "Contributing to typeshed" (*https://fpy.li/13-35*) recommends this naming convention for static protocols (the following three points are quoted verbatim):

- Use plain names for protocols that represent a clear concept (e.g., `Iterator`, `Container`).
- Use `SupportsX` for protocols that provide callable methods (e.g., `SupportsInt`, `SupportsRead`, `SupportsReadSeek`).[21]
- Use `HasX` for protocols that have readable and/or writable attributes or getter/setter methods (e.g., `HasItems`, `HasFileno`).

The Go standard library has a naming convention that I like: for single method protocols, if the method name is a verb, append "-er" or "-or" to make it a noun. For example, instead of `SupportsRead`, have `Reader`. More examples include `Formatter`, `Animator`, and `Scanner`. For inspiration, see "Go (Golang) Standard Library Interfaces (Selected)" (*https://fpy.li/13-36*) by Asuka Kenji.

One good reason to create minimalistic protocols is the ability to extend them later, if needed. We'll now see that it's not hard to create a derived protocol with an additional method.

Extending a Protocol

As I mentioned at the start of the previous section, Go developers advocate to err on the side of minimalism when defining interfaces—their name for static protocols. Many of the most widely used Go interfaces have a single method.

When practice reveals that a protocol with more methods is useful, instead of adding methods to the original protocol, it's better to derive a new protocol from it. Extending a static protocol in Python has a few caveats, as Example 13-20 shows.

---

21 Every method is callable, so this guideline doesn't say much. Perhaps "provide one or two methods"? Anyway, it's a guideline, not a strict rule.

Example 13-20. randompickload.py: extending RandomPicker

```python
from typing import Protocol, runtime_checkable
from randompick import RandomPicker

@runtime_checkable  ❶
class LoadableRandomPicker(RandomPicker, Protocol):  ❷
    def load(self, Iterable) -> None: ...  ❸
```

❶ If you want the derived protocol to be runtime checkable, you must apply the decorator again—its behavior is not inherited.[22]

❷ Every protocol must explicitly name `typing.Protocol` as one of its base classes in addition to the protocol we are extending. This is different from the way inheritance works in Python.[23]

❸ Back to "regular" object-oriented programming: we only need to declare the method that is new in this derived protocol. The `pick` method declaration is inherited from `RandomPicker`.

This concludes the final example of defining and using a static protocol in this chapter.

To wrap the chapter, we'll go over numeric ABCs and their possible replacement with numeric protocols.

The numbers ABCs and Numeric Protocols

As we saw in "The fall of the numeric tower" on page 280, the ABCs in the `numbers` package of the standard library work fine for runtime type checking.

If you need to check for an integer, you can use `isinstance(x, numbers.Integral)` to accept `int`, `bool` (which subclasses `int`) or other integer types that are provided by external libraries that register their types as virtual subclasses of the `numbers` ABCs. For example, NumPy has 21 integer types (*https://fpy.li/13-39*)—as well as several variations of floating-point types registered as `numbers.Real`, and complex numbers with various bit widths registered as `numbers.Complex`.

---

22 For details and rationale, please see the section about `@runtime_checkable` (*https://fpy.li/13-37*) in PEP 544—Protocols: Structural subtyping (static duck typing).

23 Again, please read "Merging and extending protocols" (*https://fpy.li/13-38*) in PEP 544 for details and rationale.

Somewhat surprisingly, decimal.Decimal is not registered as a virtual subclass of numbers.Real. The reason is that, if you need the precision of Decimal in your program, then you want to be protected from accidental mixing of decimals with floating-point numbers that are less precise.

Sadly, the numeric tower was not designed for static type checking. The root ABC— numbers.Number—has no methods, so if you declare x: Number, Mypy will not let you do arithmetic or call any methods on x.

If the numbers ABCs are not supported, what are the options?

A good place to look for typing solutions is the *typeshed* project. As part of the Python standard library, the statistics module has a corresponding *statistics.pyi* (*https://fpy.li/13-40*) stub file with type hints for on *typeshed*. There you'll find the following definitions, which are used to annotate several functions:

```
_Number = Union[float, Decimal, Fraction]
_NumberT = TypeVar('_NumberT', float, Decimal, Fraction)
```

That approach is correct, but limited. It does not support numeric types outside of the standard library, which the numbers ABCs do support at runtime—when the numeric types are registered as virtual subclasses.

The current trend is to recommend the numeric protocols provided by the typing module, which we discussed in "Runtime Checkable Static Protocols" on page 470.

Unfortunately, at runtime, the numeric protocols may let you down. As mentioned in "Limitations of Runtime Protocol Checks" on page 473, the complex type in Python 3.9 implements __float__, but the method exists only to raise TypeError with an explicit message: "can't convert complex to float." It implements __int__ as well, for the same reason. The presence of those methods makes isinstance return misleading results in Python 3.9. In Python 3.10, the methods of complex that unconditionally raised TypeError were removed.[24]

On the other hand, NumPy's complex types implement __float__ and __int__ methods that work, only issuing a warning when each of them is used for the first time:

```
>>> import numpy as np
>>> cd = np.cdouble(3+4j)
>>> cd
(3+4j)
>>> float(cd)
```

---

24 See Issue #41974—Remove complex.__float__, complex.__floordiv__, etc (*https://fpy.li/13-41*).

```
<stdin>:1: ComplexWarning: Casting complex values to real
discards the imaginary part
3.0
```

The opposite problem also happens: built-ins `complex`, `float`, and `int`, and also `numpy.float16` and `numpy.uint8`, don't have a `__complex__` method, so `isin stance(x, SupportsComplex)` returns `False` for them.[25] The NumPy complex types, such as `np.complex64`, do implement `__complex__` to convert to a built-in `complex`.

However, in practice, the `complex()` built-in constructor handles instances of all these types with no errors or warnings:

```
>>> import numpy as np
>>> from typing import SupportsComplex
>>> sample = [1+0j, np.complex64(1+0j), 1.0, np.float16(1.0), 1, np.uint8(1)]
>>> [isinstance(x, SupportsComplex) for x in sample]
[False, True, False, False, False, False]
>>> [complex(x) for x in sample]
[(1+0j), (1+0j), (1+0j), (1+0j), (1+0j), (1+0j)]
```

This shows that `isinstance` checks against `SupportsComplex` suggest that those conversions to `complex` would fail, but they all succeed. In the typing-sig mailing list, Guido van Rossum pointed out that the built-in `complex` accepts a single argument, and that's why those conversions work.

On the other hand, Mypy accepts arguments of all those six types in a call to a `to_complex()` function defined like this:

```
def to_complex(n: SupportsComplex) -> complex:
    return complex(n)
```

As I write this, NumPy has no type hints, so its number types are all `Any`.[26] On the other hand, Mypy is somehow "aware" that the built-in `int` and `float` can be converted to `complex`, even though on *typeshed* only the built-in `complex` class has a `__complex__` method.[27]

In conclusion, although numeric types should not be hard to type check, the current situation is this: the type hints PEP 484 eschews (*https://fpy.li/cardxvi*) the numeric tower and implicitly recommends that type checkers hardcode the subtype relationships among built-in `complex`, `float`, and `int`. Mypy does that, and it also pragmatically accepts that `int` and `float` are *consistent-with* `SupportsComplex`, even though they don't implement `__complex__`.

---

25 I did not test all the other float and integer variants NumPy offers.

26 The NumPy number types are all registered against the appropriate `numbers` ABCs, which Mypy ignores.

27 That's a well-meaning lie on the part of typeshed: as of Python 3.9, the built-in `complex` type does not actually have a `__complex__` method.

I only found unexpected results when using `isinstance` checks with numeric `Supports*` protocols while experimenting with conversions to or from `complex`. If you don't use complex numbers, you can rely on those protocols instead of the `numbers` ABCs.

The main takeaways for this section are:

- The `numbers` ABCs are fine for runtime type checking, but unsuitable for static typing.
- The numeric static protocols `SupportsComplex`, `SupportsFloat`, etc. work well for static typing, but are unreliable for runtime type checking when complex numbers are involved.

We are now ready for a quick review of what we saw in this chapter.

Chapter Summary

The Typing Map (Figure 13-1) is the key to making sense of this chapter. After a brief introduction to the four approaches to typing, we contrasted dynamic and static protocols, which respectively support duck typing and static duck typing. Both kinds of protocols share the essential characteristic that a class is never required to explicitly declare support for any specific protocol. A class supports a protocol simply by implementing the necessary methods.

The next major section was "Programming Ducks" on page 438, where we explored the lengths to which the Python interpreter goes to make the sequence and iterable dynamic protocols work, including partial implementations of both. We then saw how a class can be made to implement a protocol at runtime through the addition of extra methods via monkey patching. The duck typing section ended with hints for defensive programming, including detection of structural types without explicit `isin stance` or `hasattr` checks using `try/except` and failing fast.

After Alex Martelli introduced goose typing in "Waterfowl and ABCs" on page 445, we saw how to subclass existing ABCs, surveyed important ABCs in the standard library, and created an ABC from scratch, which we then implemented by traditional subclassing and by registration. To close this section, we saw how the `__subclass hook__` special method enables ABCs to support structural typing by recognizing unrelated classes that provide methods fulfilling the interface defined in the ABC.

The last major section was "Static Protocols" on page 468, where we resumed coverage of static duck typing, which started in Chapter 8, in "Static Protocols" on page 287. We saw how the `@runtime_checkable` decorator also leverages `__subclass hook__` to support structural typing at runtime—even though the best use of static protocols is with static type checkers, which can take into account type hints to make structural typing more reliable. Next we talked about the design and coding of a static protocol and how to extend it. The chapter ended with "The numbers ABCs and Numeric Protocols" on page 480, which tells the sad story of the derelict state of the numeric tower and a few existing shortcomings of the proposed alternative: the numeric static protocols such as SupportsFloat and others added to the typing module in Python 3.8.

The main message of this chapter is that we have four complementary ways of programming with interfaces in modern Python, each with different advantages and drawbacks. You are likely to find suitable use cases for each typing scheme in any modern Python codebase of significant size. Rejecting any one of these approaches will make your work as a Python programmer harder than it needs to be.

Having said that, Python achieved widespread popularity while supporting only duck typing. Other popular languages such as JavaScript, PHP, and Ruby, as well as Lisp, Smalltalk, Erlang, and Clojure—not popular but very influential—are all languages that had and still have tremendous impact by leveraging the power and simplicity of duck typing.

Further Reading

For a quick look at typing pros and cons, as well as the importance of typing.Protocol for the health of statically checked codebases, I highly recommend Glyph Lefkowitz's post "I Want A New Duck: typing.Protocol and the future of duck typing" (*https://fpy.li/13-42*). I also learned a lot from his post "Interfaces and Protocols" (*https://fpy.li/13-43*), comparing typing.Protocol and zope.interface—an earlier mechanism for defining interfaces in loosely coupled plug-in systems, used by the Plone CMS (*https://fpy.li/13-44*), the Pyramid web framework (*https://fpy.li/13-45*), and the Twisted (*https://fpy.li/13-46*) asynchronous programming framework, a project founded by Glyph.[28]

Great books about Python have—almost by definition—great coverage of duck typing. Two of my favorite Python books had updates released after the first edition of *Fluent Python*: *The Quick Python Book*, 3rd ed., (Manning), by Naomi Ceder; and *Python in a Nutshell*, 3rd ed., by Alex Martelli, Anna Ravenscroft, and Steve Holden (O'Reilly).

For a discussion of the pros and cons of dynamic typing, see Guido van Rossum's interview with Bill Venners in "Contracts in Python: A Conversation with Guido van Rossum, Part IV" (*https://fpy.li/13-47*). An insightful and balanced take on this

---

28 Thanks to tech reviewer Jürgen Gmach for recommending the "Interfaces and Protocols" post.

debate is Martin Fowler's post "Dynamic Typing" (*https://fpy.li/13-48*). He also wrote "Role Interface" (*https://fpy.li/13-33*), which I mentioned in "Best Practices for Protocol Design" on page 478. Although it is not about duck typing, that post is highly relevant for Python protocol design, as he contrasts narrow role interfaces with the broader public interfaces of classes in general.

The Mypy documentation is often the best source of information for anything related to static typing in Python, including static duck typing, addressed in their "Protocols and structural subtyping" chapter (*https://fpy.li/13-50*).

The remaining references are all about goose typing. Beazley and Jones's *Python Cookbook*, 3rd ed. (O'Reilly) has a section about defining an ABC (Recipe 8.12). The book was written before Python 3.4, so they don't use the now preferred syntax of declaring ABCs by subclassing from abc.ABC (instead, they use the metaclass keyword, which we'll only really need in Chapter 24). Apart from this small detail, the recipe covers the major ABC features very well.

The Python Standard Library by Example by Doug Hellmann (Addison-Wesley), has a chapter about the abc module. It's also available on the web in Doug's excellent *PyMOTW*—Python Module of the Week (*https://fpy.li/13-51*). Hellmann also uses the old style of ABC declaration: PluginBase(metaclass=abc.ABCMeta) instead of the simpler PluginBase(abc.ABC) available since Python 3.4.

When using ABCs, multiple inheritance is not only common but practically inevitable, because each of the fundamental collection ABCs—Sequence, Mapping, and Set —extends Collection, which in turn extends multiple ABCs (see Figure 13-4). Therefore, Chapter 14 is an important follow-up to this one.

PEP 3119—Introducing Abstract Base Classes (*https://fpy.li/13-52*) gives the rationale for ABCs. PEP 3141—A Type Hierarchy for Numbers (*https://fpy.li/13-53*) presents the ABCs of the numbers module (*https://fpy.li/13-54*), but the discussion in the Mypy issue #3186 "int is not a Number?" (*https://fpy.li/13-55*) includes some arguments about why the numeric tower is unsuitable for static type checking. Alex Waygood wrote a comprehensive answer on StackOverflow (*https://fpy.li/13-56*), discussing ways to annotate numeric types. I'll keep watching Mypy issue #3186 (*https://fpy.li/ 13-55*) for the next chapters of this saga, hoping for a happy ending that will make static typing and goose typing compatible—as they should be.

Soapbox

The MVP Journey of Python Static Typing

I work for Thoughtworks, a worldwide leader in Agile software development. At Thoughtworks, we often recommend that our clients should aim to create and deploy MVPs: minimal viable products: "a simple version of a product that is given to users in order to validate the key business assumptions," as defined by my colleague Paulo Caroli in "Lean Inception" (*https://fpy.li/13-58*), a post in Martin Fowler's collective blog (*https://fpy.li/13-59*).

Guido van Rossum and the other core developers who designed and implemented static typing have followed an MVP strategy since 2006. First, PEP 3107—Function Annotations (*https://fpy.li/pep3107*) was implemented in Python 3.0 with very limited semantics: just syntax to attach annotations to function parameters and returns. This was done explicitly to allow for experimentation and collect feedback—key benefits of an MVP.

Eight years later, PEP 484—Type Hints (*https://fpy.li/pep484*) was proposed and approved. Its implementation in Python 3.5 required no changes in the language or standard library—except for adding the `typing` module, on which no other part of the standard library depended. PEP 484 supported only nominal types with generics —similar to Java—but with the actual static checking done by external tools. Important features were missing, like variable annotations, generic built-in types, and protocols. Despite those limitations, this typing MVP was valuable enough to attract investment and adoption by companies with very large Python codebases, like Dropbox, Google, and Facebook; as well as support from professional IDEs, like PyCharm (*https://fpy.li/13-60*), Wing (*https://fpy.li/13-61*), and VS Code (*https://fpy.li/13-62*).

PEP 526—Syntax for Variable Annotations (*https://fpy.li/pep526*) was the first evolutionary step that required changes to the interpreter in Python 3.6. More changes to the Python 3.7 interpreter were made to support PEP 563—Postponed Evaluation of Annotations (*https://fpy.li/pep563*) and PEP 560—Core support for typing module and generic types (*https://fpy.li/pep560*), which allowed built-in and standard library collections to accept generic type hints out of the box in Python 3.9, thanks to PEP 585—Type Hinting Generics In Standard Collections (*https://fpy.li/pep585*).

During those years, some Python users—including me—were underwhelmed by the typing support. After I learned Go, the lack of static duck typing in Python was incomprehensible, in a language where duck typing had always been a core strength.

But that is the nature of MVPs: they may not satisfy all potential users, but they can be implemented with less effort, and guide further development with feedback from actual usage in the field.

If there is one thing we all learned from Python 3, it's that incremental progress is safer than big-bang releases. I am glad we did not have to wait for Python 4—if it ever comes—to make Python more attractive to large enterprises, where the benefits of static typing outweigh the added complexity.

Typing Approaches in Popular Languages

Figure 13-8 is a variation of the Typing Map (Figure 13-1) with the names of a few popular languages that support each of the typing approaches.

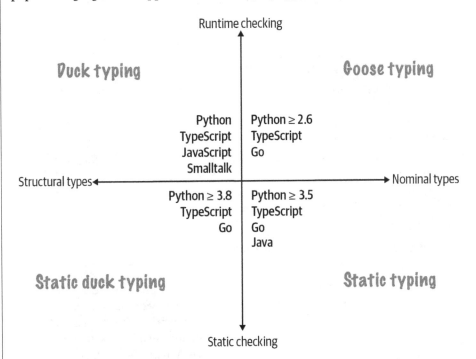

Figure 13-8. Four approaches to type checking and some languages that support them.

TypeScript and Python ≥ 3.8 are the only languages in my small and arbitrary sample that support all four approaches.

Go is clearly a statically typed language in the Pascal tradition, but it pioneered static duck typing—at least among languages that are widely used today. I also put Go in the goose typing quadrant because of its type assertions, which allow checking and adapting to different types at runtime.

If I had to draw a similar diagram in the year 2000, only the duck typing and the static typing quadrants would have languages in them. I am not aware of languages that supported static duck typing or goose typing 20 years ago. The fact that each of the four quadrants has at least three popular languages suggests that a lot of people see value in each of the four approaches to typing.

Monkey Patching

Monkey patching has a bad reputation. If abused, it can lead to systems that are hard to understand and maintain. The patch is usually tightly coupled with its target, making it brittle. Another problem is that two libraries that apply monkey patches may step on each other's toes, with the second library to run destroying patches of the first.

But monkey patching can also be useful, for example, to make a class implement a protocol at runtime. The Adapter design pattern solves the same problem by implementing a whole new class.

It's easy to monkey patch Python code, but there are limitations. Unlike Ruby and JavaScript, Python does not let you monkey patch the built-in types. I actually consider this an advantage, because you can be certain that a str object will always have those same methods. This limitation reduces the chance that external libraries apply conflicting patches.

Metaphors and Idioms in Interfaces

A metaphor fosters understanding by making constraints and affordances clear. That's the value of the words "stack" and "queue" in describing those fundamental data structures: they make clear which operations are allowed, i.e., how items can be added or removed. On the other hand, Alan Cooper et al. write in *About Face, the Essentials of Interaction Design*, 4th ed. (Wiley):

> Strict adherence to metaphors ties interfaces unnecessarily tightly to the workings of the physical world.

He's referring to user interfaces, but the admonition applies to APIs as well. But Cooper does grant that when a "truly appropriate" metaphor "falls on our lap," we can use it (he writes "falls on our lap" because it's so hard to find fitting metaphors that you should not spend time actively looking for them). I believe the bingo machine imagery I used in this chapter is appropriate and I stand by it.

About Face is by far the best book about UI design I've read—and I've read a few. Letting go of metaphors as a design paradigm, and replacing it with "idiomatic interfaces" was the most valuable thing I learned from Cooper's work.

In *About Face*, Cooper does not deal with APIs, but the more I think about his ideas, the more I see how they apply to Python. The fundamental protocols of the language are what Cooper calls "idioms." Once we learn what a "sequence" is, we can apply that knowledge in different contexts. This is a main theme of *Fluent Python*: highlighting the fundamental idioms of the language, so your code is concise, effective, and readable—for a fluent Pythonista.

## CHAPTER 14

Inheritance: For Better or for Worse

[...] we needed a better theory about inheritance entirely (and still do). For example, inheritance and instancing (which is a kind of inheritance) muddles both pragmatics (such as factoring code to save space) and semantics (used for way too many tasks such as: specialization, generalization, speciation, etc.).

—Alan Kay, "The Early History of Smalltalk"[1]

This chapter is about inheritance and subclassing. I will assume a basic understanding of these concepts, which you may know from reading *The Python Tutorial* (*https://fpy.li/14-2*) or from experience with another mainstream object-oriented language, such as Java, C#, or C++. Here we'll focus on four characteristics of Python:

- The `super()` function
- The pitfalls of subclassing from built-in types
- Multiple inheritance and method resolution order
- Mixin classes

Multiple inheritance is the ability of a class to have more than one base class. C++ supports it; Java and C# don't. Many consider multiple inheritance more trouble than it's worth. It was deliberately left out of Java after its perceived abuse in early C++ codebases.

---

1 Alan Kay, "The Early History of Smalltalk," in SIGPLAN Not. 28, 3 (March 1993), 69–95. Also available online (*https://fpy.li/14-1*). Thanks to my friend Christiano Anderson, who shared this reference as I was writing this chapter.

This chapter introduces multiple inheritance for those who have never used it, and provides some guidance on how to cope with single or multiple inheritance if you must use it.

As of 2021, there is a significant backlash against overuse of inheritance in general—not only multiple inheritance—because superclasses and subclasses are tightly coupled. Tight coupling means that changes to one part of the program may have unexpected and far-reaching effects in other parts, making systems brittle and hard to understand.

However, we have to maintain existing systems designed with complex class hierarchies, or use frameworks that force us to use inheritance—even multiple inheritance sometimes.

I will illustrate practical uses of multiple inheritance with the standard library, the Django web framework, and the Tkinter GUI toolkit.

What's New in This Chapter

There are no new Python features related to the subject of this chapter, but I heavily edited it based on feedback from technical reviewers of the second edition, especially Leonardo Rochael and Caleb Hattingh.

I wrote a new opening section focusing on the `super()` built-in function, and changed the examples in "Multiple Inheritance and Method Resolution Order" on page 496 for a deeper exploration of how `super()` works to support *cooperative multiple inheritance*.

"Mixin Classes" on page 502 is also new. "Multiple Inheritance in the Real World" on page 504 was reorganized and covers simpler mixin examples from the standard library, before the complex Django and the complicated Tkinter hierarchies.

As the chapter title suggests, the caveats of inheritance have always been one of the main themes of this chapter. But more and more developers consider it so problematic that I've added a couple of paragraphs about avoiding inheritance to the end of "Chapter Summary" on page 516 and "Further Reading" on page 517.

We'll start with an overview of the mysterious `super()` function.

The super() Function

Consistent use the of the `super()` built-in function is essential for maintainable object-oriented Python programs.

When a subclass overrides a method of a superclass, the overriding method usually needs to call the corresponding method of the superclass. Here's the recommended

---

way to do it, from an example in the *collections* module documentation, section "OrderedDict Examples and Recipes" (*https://fpy.li/14-3*):[2]

```
class LastUpdatedOrderedDict(OrderedDict):
    """Store items in the order they were last updated"""

    def __setitem__(self, key, value):
        super().__setitem__(key, value)
        self.move_to_end(key)
```

To do its job, `LastUpdatedOrderedDict` overrides `__setitem__` to:

1. Use `super().__setitem__` to call that method on the superclass, to let it insert or update the key/value pair.

2. Call `self.move_to_end` to ensure the updated key is in the last position.

Invoking an overridden `__init__` method is particularly important to allow superclasses to do their part in initializing the instance.

> If you learned object-oriented programming in Java, you may recall that a Java constructor method automatically calls the no-argument constructor of the superclass. Python doesn't do this. You must get used to writing this pattern:
>
> ```
> def __init__(self, a, b) :
>     super().__init__(a, b)
>     ... # more initialization code
> ```

You may have seen code that doesn't use `super()`, but instead calls the method directly on the superclass, like this:

```
class NotRecommended(OrderedDict):
    """This is a counter example!"""

    def __setitem__(self, key, value):
        OrderedDict.__setitem__(self, key, value)
        self.move_to_end(key)
```

This alternative works in this particular case, but is not recommended for two reasons. First, it hardcodes the base class. The name `OrderedDict` appears in the `class` statement and also inside `__setitem__`. If in the future someone changes the `class` statement to change the base class or add another one, they may forget to update the body of `__setitem__`, introducing a bug.

---

2 I only changed the docstring in the example, because the original is misleading. It says: "Store items in the order the keys were last added," but that is not what the clearly named `LastUpdatedOrderedDict` does.

The second reason is that `super` implements logic to handle class hierarchies with multiple inheritance. We'll come back to that in "Multiple Inheritance and Method Resolution Order" on page 496. To conclude this refresher about `super`, it is useful to review how we had to call it in Python 2, because the old signature with two arguments is revealing:

```
class LastUpdatedOrderedDict(OrderedDict):
    """This code works in Python 2 and Python 3"""

    def __setitem__(self, key, value):
        super(LastUpdatedOrderedDict, self).__setitem__(key, value)
        self.move_to_end(key)
```

Both arguments of `super` are now optional. The Python 3 bytecode compiler automatically provides them by inspecting the surrounding context when `super()` is invoked in a method. The arguments are:

type
> The start of the search path for the superclass implementing the desired method. By default, it is the class that owns the method where the `super()` call appears.

object_or_type
> The object (for instance method calls) or class (for class method calls) to be the receiver of the method call. By default, it is `self` if the `super()` call happens in an instance method.

Whether you or the compiler provides those arguments, the `super()` call returns a dynamic proxy object that finds a method (such as `__setitem__` in the example) in a superclass of the `type` parameter, and binds it to the `object_or_type`, so that we don't need to pass the receiver (`self`) explicitly when invoking the method.

In Python 3, you can still explicitly provide the first and second arguments to `super()`.[3] But they are needed only in special cases, such as skipping over part of the MRO for testing or debugging, or for working around undesired behavior in a superclass.

Now let's discuss the caveats when subclassing built-in types.

Subclassing Built-In Types Is Tricky

It was not possible to subclass built-in types such as `list` or `dict` in the earliest versions of Python. Since Python 2.2, it's possible, but there is a major caveat: the code of

---

[3] It is also possible to provide only the first argument, but this not useful and may soon be deprecated, with the blessing of Guido van Rossum who created `super()` in the first place. See the discussion at "Is it time to deprecate unbound super methods?" (*https://fpy.li/14-4*).

the built-ins (written in C) usually does not call methods overridden by user-defined classes. A good short description of the problem is in the documentation for PyPy, in the "Differences between PyPy and CPython" section, "Subclasses of built-in types" (*https://fpy.li/pypydif*):

> Officially, CPython has no rule at all for when exactly overridden method of subclasses of built-in types get implicitly called or not. As an approximation, these methods are never called by other built-in methods of the same object. For example, an overridden __getitem__() in a subclass of dict will not be called by e.g. the built-in get() method.

Example 14-1 illustrates the problem.

Example 14-1. Our __setitem__ override is ignored by the __init__ and __update__ methods of the built-in dict

```
>>> class DoppelDict(dict):
...     def __setitem__(self, key, value):
...         super().__setitem__(key, [value] * 2)  ❶
...
>>> dd = DoppelDict(one=1)  ❷
>>> dd
{'one': 1}
>>> dd['two'] = 2  ❸
>>> dd
{'one': 1, 'two': [2, 2]}
>>> dd.update(three=3)  ❹
>>> dd
{'three': 3, 'one': 1, 'two': [2, 2]}
```

❶ DoppelDict.__setitem__ duplicates values when storing (for no good reason, just to have a visible effect). It works by delegating to the superclass.

❷ The __init__ method inherited from dict clearly ignored that __setitem__ was overridden: the value of 'one' is not duplicated.

❸ The [] operator calls our __setitem__ and works as expected: 'two' maps to the duplicated value [2, 2].

❹ The update method from dict does not use our version of __setitem__ either: the value of 'three' was not duplicated.

This built-in behavior is a violation of a basic rule of object-oriented programming: the search for methods should always start from the class of the receiver (self), even when the call happens inside a method implemented in a superclass. This is what is called "late binding," which Alan Kay—of Smalltalk fame—considers a key feature of object-oriented programming: in any call of the form x.method(), the exact method to be called must be determined at runtime, based on the class of the receiver x.[4] This sad state of affairs contributes to the issues we saw in "Inconsistent Usage of __missing__ in the Standard Library" on page 94.

The problem is not limited to calls within an instance—whether self.get() calls self.__getitem__()—but also happens with overridden methods of other classes that should be called by the built-in methods. Example 14-2 is adapted from the PyPy documentation (*https://fpy.li/14-5*).

Example 14-2. The __getitem__ of AnswerDict is bypassed by dict.update

```
>>> class AnswerDict(dict):
...     def __getitem__(self, key):  ❶
...         return 42
...
>>> ad = AnswerDict(a='foo')  ❷
>>> ad['a']  ❸
42
>>> d = {}
>>> d.update(ad)  ❹
>>> d['a']  ❺
'foo'
>>> d
{'a': 'foo'}
```

❶ AnswerDict.__getitem__ always returns 42, no matter what the key.

❷ ad is an AnswerDict loaded with the key-value pair ('a', 'foo').

❸ ad['a'] returns 42, as expected.

❹ d is an instance of plain dict, which we update with ad.

❺ The dict.update method ignored our AnswerDict.__getitem__.

---

4 It is interesting to note that C++ has the notion of virtual and nonvirtual methods. Virtual methods are late bound, but nonvirtual methods are bound at compile time. Although every method that we can write in Python is late bound like a virtual method, built-in objects written in C seem to have nonvirtual methods by default, at least in CPython.

Subclassing built-in types like dict or list or str directly is error-prone because the built-in methods mostly ignore user-defined overrides. Instead of subclassing the built-ins, derive your classes from the collections (*https://fpy.li/14-6*) module using UserDict, UserList, and UserString, which are designed to be easily extended.

If you subclass collections.UserDict instead of dict, the issues exposed in Examples 14-1 and 14-2 are both fixed. See Example 14-3.

Example 14-3. DoppelDict2 and AnswerDict2 work as expected because they extend UserDict and not dict

```
>>> import collections
>>>
>>> class DoppelDict2(collections.UserDict):
...     def __setitem__(self, key, value):
...         super().__setitem__(key, [value] * 2)
...
>>> dd = DoppelDict2(one=1)
>>> dd
{'one': [1, 1]}
>>> dd['two'] = 2
>>> dd
{'two': [2, 2], 'one': [1, 1]}
>>> dd.update(three=3)
>>> dd
{'two': [2, 2], 'three': [3, 3], 'one': [1, 1]}
>>>
>>> class AnswerDict2(collections.UserDict):
...     def __getitem__(self, key):
...         return 42
...
>>> ad = AnswerDict2(a='foo')
>>> ad['a']
42
>>> d = {}
>>> d.update(ad)
>>> d['a']
42
>>> d
{'a': 42}
```

As an experiment to measure the extra work required to subclass a built-in, I rewrote the StrKeyDict class from Example 3-9 to subclass dict instead of UserDict. In order to make it pass the same suite of tests, I had to implement __init__, get, and update because the versions inherited from dict refused to cooperate with the overridden __missing__, __contains__, and __setitem__. The UserDict subclass from

Example 3-9 has 16 lines, while the experimental dict subclass ended up with 33 lines.[5]

To be clear: this section covered an issue that applies only to method delegation within the C language code of the built-in types, and only affects classes derived directly from those types. If you subclass a base class coded in Python, such as UserDict or MutableMapping, you will not be troubled by this.[6]

Now let's focus on an issue that arises with multiple inheritance: if a class has two superclasses, how does Python decide which attribute to use when we call super().attr, but both superclasses have an attribute with that name?

Multiple Inheritance and Method Resolution Order

Any language implementing multiple inheritance needs to deal with potential naming conflicts when superclasses implement a method by the same name. This is called the "diamond problem," illustrated in Figure 14-1 and Example 14-4.

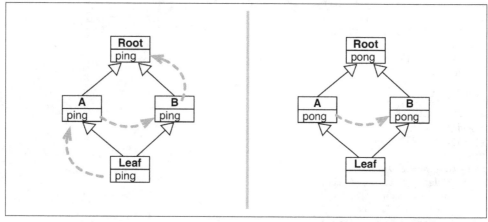

Figure 14-1. Left: Activation sequence for the leaf1.ping() call. Right: Activation sequence for the leaf1.pong() call.

Example 14-4. diamond.py: classes Leaf, A, B, Root form the graph in Figure 14-1

```
class Root:  ❶
    def ping(self):
```

---

5 If you are curious, the experiment is in the *14-inheritance/strkeydict_dictsub.py* (*https://fpy.li/14-7*) file in the *fluentpython/example-code-2e* (*https://fpy.li/code*) repository.

6 By the way, in this regard, PyPy behaves more "correctly" than CPython, at the expense of introducing a minor incompatibility. See "Differences between PyPy and CPython" (*https://fpy.li/14-5*) for details.

```
        print(f'{self}.ping() in Root')

    def pong(self):
        print(f'{self}.pong() in Root')

    def __repr__(self):
        cls_name = type(self).__name__
        return f'<instance of {cls_name}>'

class A(Root):  ❷
    def ping(self):
        print(f'{self}.ping() in A')
        super().ping()

    def pong(self):
        print(f'{self}.pong() in A')
        super().pong()

class B(Root):  ❸
    def ping(self):
        print(f'{self}.ping() in B')
        super().ping()

    def pong(self):
        print(f'{self}.pong() in B')

class Leaf(A, B):  ❹
    def ping(self):
        print(f'{self}.ping() in Leaf')
        super().ping()
```

❶ Root provides ping, pong, and __repr__ to make the output easier to read.

❷ The ping and pong methods in class A both call super().

❸ Only the ping method in class B calls super().

❹ Class Leaf implements only ping, and it calls super().

Now let's see the effect of calling the ping and pong methods on an instance of Leaf (Example 14-5).

Example 14-5. Doctests for calling ping and pong on a Leaf object

```
>>> leaf1 = Leaf()  ❶
>>> leaf1.ping()    ❷
<instance of Leaf>.ping() in Leaf
```

```
<instance of Leaf>.ping() in A
<instance of Leaf>.ping() in B
<instance of Leaf>.ping() in Root

>>> leaf1.pong()        ❸
<instance of Leaf>.pong() in A
<instance of Leaf>.pong() in B
```

❶ leaf1 is an instance of Leaf.

❷ Calling leaf1.ping() activates the ping methods in Leaf, A, B, and Root, because the ping methods in the first three classes call super().ping().

❸ Calling leaf1.pong() activates pong in A via inheritance, which then calls super.pong(), activating B.pong.

The activation sequences shown in Example 14-5 and Figure 14-1 are determined by two factors:

- The method resolution order of the Leaf class.
- The use of super() in each method.

Every class has an attribute called __mro__ holding a tuple of references to the super-classes in method resolution order, from the current class all the way to the object class.[7] For the Leaf class, this is the __mro__:

```
>>> Leaf.__mro__  # doctest:+NORMALIZE_WHITESPACE
    (<class 'diamond1.Leaf'>, <class 'diamond1.A'>, <class 'diamond1.B'>,
     <class 'diamond1.Root'>, <class 'object'>)
```

Looking at Figure 14-1, you may think the MRO describes a breadth-first search (*https://fpy.li/14-9*), but that's just a coincidence for that particular class hierarchy. The MRO is computed by a published algorithm called C3. Its use in Python is detailed in Michele Simionato's "The Python 2.3 Method Resolution Order" (*https://fpy.li/14-10*). It's a challenging read, but Simionato writes: "unless you make strong use of multiple inheritance and you have non-trivial hierarchies, you don't need to understand the C3 algorithm, and you can easily skip this paper."

---

7 Classes also have a .mro() method, but that's an advanced feature of metaclass programming, mentioned in "Classes as Objects" on page 912. The content of the __mro__ attribute is what matters during normal usage of a class.

The MRO only determines the activation order, but whether a particular method will be activated in each of the classes depends on whether each implementation calls super() or not.

Consider the experiment with the pong method. The Leaf class does not override it, therefore calling leaf1.pong() activates the implementation in the next class of Leaf.__mro__: the A class. Method A.pong calls super().pong(). The B class is next in the MRO, therefore B.pong is activated. But that method doesn't call super().pong(), so the activation sequence ends here.

The MRO takes into account not only the inheritance graph but also the order in which superclasses are listed in a subclass declaration. In other words, if in *diamond.py* (Example 14-4) the Leaf class was declared as Leaf(B, A), then class B would appear before A in Leaf.__mro__. This would affect the activation order of the ping methods, and would also cause leaf1.pong() to activate B.pong via inheritance, but A.pong and Root.pong would never run, because B.pong doesn't call super().

When a method calls super(), it is a *cooperative method*. Cooperative methods enable *cooperative multiple inheritance*. These terms are intentional: in order to work, multiple inheritance in Python requires the active cooperation of the methods involved. In the B class, ping cooperates, but pong does not.

 A noncooperative method can be the cause of subtle bugs. Many coders reading Example 14-4 may expect that when method A.pong calls super.pong(), that will ultimately activate Root.pong. But if B.pong is activated before, it drops the ball. That's why it is recommended that every method m of a nonroot class should call super().m().

Cooperative methods must have compatible signatures, because you never know whether A.ping will be called before or after B.ping. The activation sequence depends on the order of A and B in the declaration of each subclass that inherits from both.

Python is a dynamic language, so the interaction of super() with the MRO is also dynamic. Example 14-6 shows a surprising result of this dynamic behavior.

Example 14-6. diamond2.py: classes to demonstrate the dynamic nature of super()

```
from diamond import A    ❶

class U():    ❷
    def ping(self):
        print(f'{self}.ping() in U')
        super().ping()    ❸
```

```
class LeafUA(U, A):    ❹
    def ping(self):
        print(f'{self}.ping() in LeafUA')
        super().ping()
```

❶   Class A comes from *diamond.py* (Example 14-4).

❷   Class U is unrelated to A or Root from the diamond module.

❸   What does super().ping() do? Answer: it depends. Read on.

❹   LeafUA subclasses U and A in this order.

If you create an instance of U and try to call ping, you get an error:

```
>>> u = U()
>>> u.ping()
Traceback (most recent call last):
  ...
AttributeError: 'super' object has no attribute 'ping'
```

The 'super' object returned by super() has no attribute 'ping' because the MRO
of U has two classes: U and object, and the latter has no attribute named 'ping'.

However, the U.ping method is not completely hopeless. Check this out:

```
>>> leaf2 = LeafUA()
>>> leaf2.ping()
<instance of LeafUA>.ping() in LeafUA
<instance of LeafUA>.ping() in U
<instance of LeafUA>.ping() in A
<instance of LeafUA>.ping() in Root
>>> LeafUA.__mro__    # doctest:+NORMALIZE_WHITESPACE
(<class 'diamond2.LeafUA'>, <class 'diamond2.U'>,
 <class 'diamond.A'>, <class 'diamond.Root'>, <class 'object'>)
```

The super().ping() call in LeafUA activates U.ping, which cooperates by calling
super().ping() too, activating A.ping, and eventually Root.ping.

Note the base classes of LeafUA are (U, A) in that order. If instead the bases were
(A, U), then leaf2.ping() would never reach U.ping, because the super().ping()
in A.ping would activate Root.ping, and that method does not call super().

In a real program, a class like U could be a *mixin class*: a class intended to be used
together with other classes in multiple inheritance, to provide additional functionality. We'll study that shortly, in "Mixin Classes" on page 502.

To wrap up this discussion of the MRO, Figure 14-2 illustrates part of the complex multiple inheritance graph of the Tkinter GUI toolkit from the Python standard library.

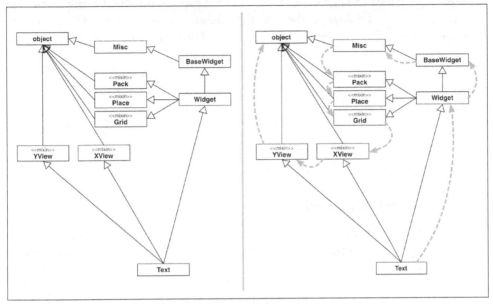

Figure 14-2. Left: UML diagram of the Tkinter Text *widget class and superclasses. Right: The long and winding path of* Text.__mro__ *is drawn with dashed arrows.*

To study the picture, start at the Text class at the bottom. The Text class implements a full-featured, multiline editable text widget. It provides rich functionality in itself, but also inherits many methods from other classes. The lefthand side shows a plain UML class diagram. On the right, it's decorated with arrows showing the MRO, as listed in Example 14-7 with the help of a print_mro convenience function.

Example 14-7. MRO of tkinter.Text

```
>>> def print_mro(cls):
...     print(', '.join(c.__name__ for c in cls.__mro__))
>>> import tkinter
>>> print_mro(tkinter.Text)
Text, Widget, BaseWidget, Misc, Pack, Place, Grid, XView, YView, object
```

Now let's talk about mixins.

Mixin Classes

A mixin class is designed to be subclassed together with at least one other class in a multiple inheritance arrangement. A mixin is not supposed to be the only base class of a concrete class, because it does not provide all the functionality for a concrete object, but only adds or customizes the behavior of child or sibling classes.

 Mixin classes are a convention with no explicit language support in Python and C++. Ruby allows the explicit definition and use of modules that work as mixins—collections of methods that may be included to add functionality to a class. C#, PHP, and Rust implement traits, which are also an explicit form of mixin.

Let's see a simple but handy example of a mixin class.

Case-Insensitive Mappings

Example 14-8 shows UpperCaseMixin, a class designed to provide case-insensitive access to mappings with string keys, by uppercasing those keys when they are added or looked up.

Example 14-8. uppermixin.py: UpperCaseMixin supports case-insensitive mappings

```python
import collections

def _upper(key):  ❶
    try:
        return key.upper()
    except AttributeError:
        return key

class UpperCaseMixin:  ❷
    def __setitem__(self, key, item):
        super().__setitem__(_upper(key), item)

    def __getitem__(self, key):
        return super().__getitem__(_upper(key))

    def get(self, key, default=None):
        return super().get(_upper(key), default)

    def __contains__(self, key):
        return super().__contains__(_upper(key))
```

❶ This helper function takes a key of any type, and tries to return `key.upper()`; if that fails, it returns the key unchanged.

❷ The mixin implements four essential methods of mappings, always calling `super()`, with the key uppercased, if possible.

Since every method ot `UpperCaseMixin` calls `super()`, this mixin depends on a sibling class that implements or inherits methods with the same signature. To make its contribution, a mixin usually needs to appear before other classes in the MRO of a subclass that uses it. In practice, that means mixins must appear first in the tuple of base classes in a class declaration. Example 14-9 shows two examples.

Example 14-9. uppermixin.py: two classes that use UpperCaseMixin

```
class UpperDict(UpperCaseMixin, collections.UserDict):    ❶
    pass

class UpperCounter(UpperCaseMixin, collections.Counter):    ❷
    """Specialized 'Counter' that uppercases string keys"""    ❸
```

❶ `UpperDict` needs no implementation of its own, but `UpperCaseMixin` must be the first base class, otherwise the methods from `UserDict` would be called instead.

❷ `UpperCaseMixin` also works with `Counter`.

❸ Instead of `pass`, it's better to provide a docstring to satisfy the need for a body in the `class` statement syntax.

Here are some doctests from *uppermixin.py* (*https://fpy.li/14-11*), for `UpperDict`:

```
>>> d = UpperDict([('a', 'letter A'), (2, 'digit two')])
>>> list(d.keys())
['A', 2]
>>> d['b'] = 'letter B'
>>> 'b' in d
True
>>> d['a'], d.get('B')
('letter A', 'letter B')
>>> list(d.keys())
['A', 2, 'B']
```

And a quick demonstration of `UpperCounter`:

```
>>> c = UpperCounter('BaNanA')
>>> c.most_common()
[('A', 3), ('N', 2), ('B', 1)]
```

UpperDict and UpperCounter seem almost magical, but I had to carefully study the code of UserDict and Counter to make UpperCaseMixin work with them.

For example, my first version of UpperCaseMixin did not provide the get method. That version worked with UserDict but not with Counter. The UserDict class inherits get from collections.abc.Mapping, and that get calls __getitem__, which I implemented. But keys were not uppercased when an UpperCounter was loaded upon __init__. That happened because Counter.__init__ uses Counter.update, which in turn relies on the get method inherited from dict. However, the get method in the dict class does not call __getitem__. This is the heart of the issue discussed in "Inconsistent Usage of __missing__ in the Standard Library" on page 94. It is also a stark reminder of the brittle and puzzling nature of programs leveraging inheritance, even at a small scale.

The next section covers several examples of multiple inheritance, often featuring mixin classes.

Multiple Inheritance in the Real World

In the *Design Patterns* book,[8] almost all the code is in C++, but the only example of multiple inheritance is the Adapter pattern. In Python, multiple inheritance is not the norm either, but there are important examples that I will comment on in this section.

ABCs Are Mixins Too

In the Python standard library, the most visible use of multiple inheritance is the collections.abc package. That is not controversial: after all, even Java supports multiple inheritance of interfaces, and ABCs are interface declarations that may optionally provide concrete method implementations.[9]

Python's official documentation of collections.abc (*https://fpy.li/14-13*) uses the term *mixin method* for the concrete methods implemented in many of the collection ABCs. The ABCs that provide mixin methods play two roles: they are interface definitions and also mixin classes. For example, the implementation of collections.UserDict (*https://fpy.li/14-14*) relies on several of the mixin methods provided by collections.abc.MutableMapping.

---

8 Erich Gamma, Richard Helm, Ralph Johnson, and John Vlissides, *Design Patterns: Elements of Reusable Object-Oriented Software* (Addison-Wesley).

9 As previously mentioned, Java 8 allows interfaces to provide method implementations as well. The new feature is called "Default Methods" (*https://fpy.li/14-12*) in the official Java Tutorial.

ThreadingMixIn and ForkingMixIn

The *http.server* (*https://fpy.li/14-15*) package provides HTTPServer and Threa
dingHTTPServer classes. The latter was added in Python 3.7. Its documentation says:

class http.server.ThreadingHTTPServer(*server_address, RequestHandlerClass*)
> This class is identical to HTTPServer but uses threads to handle requests by using
> the ThreadingMixIn. This is useful to handle web browsers pre-opening sockets,
> on which HTTPServer would wait indefinitely.

This is the complete source code (*https://fpy.li/14-16*) for the ThreadingHTTPServer
class in Python 3.10:

```
class ThreadingHTTPServer(socketserver.ThreadingMixIn, HTTPServer):
    daemon_threads = True
```

The source code (*https://fpy.li/14-17*) of socketserver.ThreadingMixIn has 38
lines, including comments and docstrings. Example 14-10 shows a summary of its
implementation.

Example 14-10. Part of Lib/socketserver.py in Python 3.10

```
class ThreadingMixIn:
    """Mixin class to handle each request in a new thread."""

    # 8 lines omitted in book listing

    def process_request_thread(self, request, client_address):  ❶
        ... # 6 lines omitted in book listing

    def process_request(self, request, client_address):  ❷
        ... # 8 lines omitted in book listing

    def server_close(self):  ❸
        super().server_close()
        self._threads.join()
```

❶ process_request_thread does not call super() because it is a new method, not
an override. Its implementation calls three instance methods that HTTPServer
provides or inherits.

❷ This overrides the process_request method that HTTPServer inherits from sock
etserver.BaseServer, starting a thread and delegating the actual work to pro
cess_request_thread running in that thread. It does not call super().

❸ server_close calls super().server_close() to stop taking requests, then waits
for the threads started by process_request to finish their jobs.

The `ThreadingMixIn` appears in the `socketserver` (*https://fpy.li/14-18*) module documentation next to `ForkingMixin`. The latter is designed to support concurrent servers based on `os.fork()` (*https://fpy.li/14-19*), an API for launching a child process, available in POSIX (*https://fpy.li/14-20*)-compliant Unix-like systems.

Django Generic Views Mixins

 You don't need to know Django to follow this section. I am using a small part of the framework as a practical example of multiple inheritance, and I will try to give all the necessary background, assuming you have some experience with server-side web development in any language or framework.

In Django, a view is a callable object that takes a `request` argument—an object representing an HTTP request—and returns an object representing an HTTP response. The different responses are what interests us in this discussion. They can be as simple as a redirect response, with no content body, or as complex as a catalog page in an online store, rendered from an HTML template and listing multiple merchandise with buttons for buying, and links to detail pages.

Originally, Django provided a set of functions, called generic views, that implemented some common use cases. For example, many sites need to show search results that include information from numerous items, with the listing spanning multiple pages, and for each item a link to a page with detailed information about it. In Django, a list view and a detail view are designed to work together to solve this problem: a list view renders search results, and a detail view produces a page for each individual item.

However, the original generic views were functions, so they were not extensible. If you needed to do something similar but not exactly like a generic list view, you'd have to start from scratch.

The concept of class-based views was introduced in Django 1.3, along with a set of generic view classes organized as base classes, mixins, and ready-to-use concrete classes. In Django 3.2, the base classes and mixins are in the `base` module of the `django.views.generic` package, pictured in Figure 14-3. At the top of the diagram we see two classes that take care of very distinct responsibilities: `View` and `TemplateResponseMixin`.

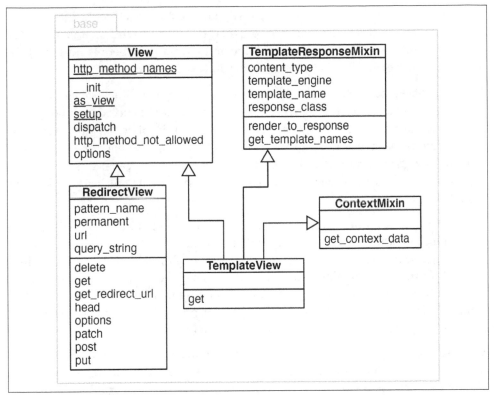

Figure 14-3. UML class diagram for the `django.views.generic.base` *module.*

A great resource to study these classes is the *Classy Class-Based Views* (*https://fpy.li/14-21*) website, where you can easily navigate through them, see all methods in each class (inherited, overridden, and added methods), view diagrams, browse their documentation, and jump to their source code on GitHub (*https://fpy.li/14-22*).

View is the base class of all views (it could be an ABC), and it provides core functionality like the dispatch method, which delegates to "handler" methods like get, head, post, etc., implemented by concrete subclasses to handle the different HTTP verbs.[10] The RedirectView class inherits only from View, and you can see that it implements get, head, post, etc.

Concrete subclasses of View are supposed to implement the handler methods, so why aren't those methods part of the View interface? The reason: subclasses are free to

---

10 Django programmers know that the as_view class method is the most visible part of the View interface, but it's not relevant to us here.

implement just the handlers they want to support. A `TemplateView` is used only to display content, so it only implements `get`. If an HTTP `POST` request is sent to a `TemplateView`, the inherited `View.dispatch` method checks that there is no post handler, and produces an HTTP `405 Method Not Allowed` response.[11]

The `TemplateResponseMixin` provides functionality that is of interest only to views that need to use a template. A `RedirectView`, for example, has no content body, so it has no need of a template and it does not inherit from this mixin. `TemplateResponseMixin` provides behaviors to `TemplateView` and other template-rendering views, such as `ListView`, `DetailView`, etc., defined in the `django.views.generic` subpackages. Figure 14-4 depicts the `django.views.generic.list` module and part of the base module.

For Django users, the most important class in Figure 14-4 is `ListView`, which is an aggregate class, with no code at all (its body is just a docstring). When instantiated, a `ListView` has an `object_list` instance attribute through which the template can iterate to show the page contents, usually the result of a database query returning multiple objects. All the functionality related to generating this iterable of objects comes from the `MultipleObjectMixin`. That mixin also provides the complex pagination logic—to display part of the results in one page and links to more pages.

Suppose you want to create a view that will not render a template, but will produce a list of objects in JSON format. That's why the `BaseListView` exists. It provides an easy-to-use extension point that brings together `View` and `MultipleObjectMixin` functionality, without the overhead of the template machinery.

The Django class-based views API is a better example of multiple inheritance than Tkinter. In particular, it is easy to make sense of its mixin classes: each has a well-defined purpose, and they are all named with the *…Mixin* suffix.

---

11 If you are into design patterns, you'll notice that the Django dispatch mechanism is a dynamic variation of the Template Method pattern (*https://fpy.li/14-23*). It's dynamic because the `View` class does not force subclasses to implement all handlers, but `dispatch` checks at runtime if a concrete handler is available for the specific request.

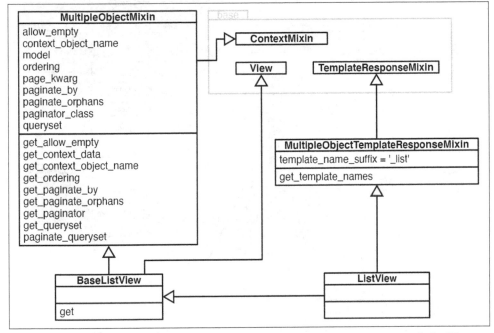

Figure 14-4. UML class diagram for the `django.views.generic.list` module. Here the three classes of the base module are collapsed (see Figure 14-3). The `ListView` class has no methods or attributes: it's an aggregate class.

Class-based views were not universally embraced by Django users. Many do use them in a limited way, as opaque boxes, but when it's necessary to create something new, a lot of Django coders continue writing monolithic view functions that take care of all those responsibilities, instead of trying to reuse the base views and mixins.

It does take some time to learn how to leverage class-based views and how to extend them to fulfill specific application needs, but I found that it was worthwhile to study them. They eliminate a lot of boilerplate code, make it easier to reuse solutions, and even improve team communication—for example, by defining standard names to templates, and to the variables passed to template contexts. Class-based views are Django views "on rails."

Multiple Inheritance in Tkinter

An extreme example of multiple inheritance in Python's standard library is the Tkinter GUI toolkit (*https://fpy.li/14-24*). I used part of the Tkinter widget hierarchy to illustrate the MRO in Figure 14-2. Figure 14-5 shows all the widget classes in the tkinter base package (there are more widgets in the tkinter.ttk subpackage (*https://fpy.li/14-25*)).

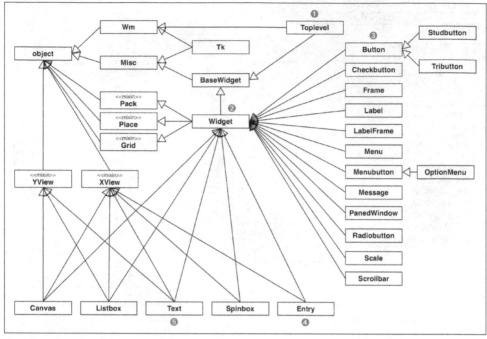

Figure 14-5. Summary UML diagram for the Tkinter GUI class hierarchy; classes tagged «mixin» are designed to provide concrete methods to other classes via multiple inheritance.

Tkinter is 25 years old as I write this. It is not an example of current best practices. But it shows how multiple inheritance was used when coders did not appreciate its drawbacks. And it will serve as a counterexample when we cover some good practices in the next section.

Consider these classes from Figure 14-5:

❶ `Toplevel`: The class of a top-level window in a Tkinter application.

❷ `Widget`: The superclass of every visible object that can be placed on a window.

❸ `Button`: A plain button widget.

❹ `Entry`: A single-line editable text field.

❺ `Text`: A multiline editable text field.

Here are the MROs of those classes, displayed by the `print_mro` function from Example 14-7:

```
>>> import tkinter
>>> print_mro(tkinter.Toplevel)
Toplevel, BaseWidget, Misc, Wm, object
```

```
>>> print_mro(tkinter.Widget)
Widget, BaseWidget, Misc, Pack, Place, Grid, object
>>> print_mro(tkinter.Button)
Button, Widget, BaseWidget, Misc, Pack, Place, Grid, object
>>> print_mro(tkinter.Entry)
Entry, Widget, BaseWidget, Misc, Pack, Place, Grid, XView, object
>>> print_mro(tkinter.Text)
Text, Widget, BaseWidget, Misc, Pack, Place, Grid, XView, YView, object
```

 By current standards, the class hierarchy of Tkinter is very deep. Few parts of the Python standard library have more than three or four levels of concrete classes, and the same can be said of the Java class library. However, it is interesting to note that the some of the deepest hierarchies in the Java class library are precisely in the packages related to GUI programming: java.awt (*https://fpy.li/14-26*) and javax.swing (*https://fpy.li/14-27*). Squeak (*https://fpy.li/14-28*), the modern, free version of Smalltalk, includes the powerful and innovative Morphic GUI toolkit, also with a deep class hierarchy. In my experience, GUI toolkits are where inheritance is most useful.

Note how these classes relate to others:

- Toplevel is the only graphical class that does not inherit from Widget, because it is the top-level window and does not behave like a widget; for example, it cannot be attached to a window or frame. Toplevel inherits from Wm, which provides direct access functions of the host window manager, like setting the window title and configuring its borders.

- Widget inherits directly from BaseWidget and from Pack, Place, and Grid. These last three classes are geometry managers: they are responsible for arranging widgets inside a window or frame. Each encapsulates a different layout strategy and widget placement API.

- Button, like most widgets, descends only from Widget, but indirectly from Misc, which provides dozens of methods to every widget.

- Entry subclasses Widget and XView, which support horizontal scrolling.

- Text subclasses from Widget, XView, and YView for vertical scrolling.

We'll now discuss some good practices of multiple inheritance and see whether Tkinter goes along with them.

Coping with Inheritance

What Alan Kay wrote in the epigraph remains true: there's still no general theory about inheritance that can guide practicing programmers. What we have are rules of thumb, design patterns, "best practices," clever acronyms, taboos, etc. Some of these provide useful guidelines, but none of them are universally accepted or always applicable.

It's easy to create incomprehensible and brittle designs using inheritance, even without multiple inheritance. Because we don't have a comprehensive theory, here are a few tips to avoid spaghetti class graphs.

Favor Object Composition over Class Inheritance

The title of this subsection is the second principle of object-oriented design from the *Design Patterns* book,[12] and is the best advice I can offer here. Once you get comfortable with inheritance, it's too easy to overuse it. Placing objects in a neat hierarchy appeals to our sense of order; programmers do it just for fun.

Favoring composition leads to more flexible designs. For example, in the case of the `tkinter.Widget` class, instead of inheriting the methods from all geometry managers, widget instances could hold a reference to a geometry manager, and invoke its methods. After all, a `Widget` should not "be" a geometry manager, but could use the services of one via delegation. Then you could add a new geometry manager without touching the widget class hierarchy and without worrying about name clashes. Even with single inheritance, this principle enhances flexibility, because subclassing is a form of tight coupling, and tall inheritance trees tend to be brittle.

Composition and delegation can replace the use of mixins to make behaviors available to different classes, but cannot replace the use of interface inheritance to define a hierarchy of types.

Understand Why Inheritance Is Used in Each Case

When dealing with multiple inheritance, it's useful to keep straight the reasons why subclassing is done in each particular case. The main reasons are:

- Inheritance of interface creates a subtype, implying an "is-a" relationship. This is best done with ABCs.

- Inheritance of implementation avoids code duplication by reuse. Mixins can help with this.

---

12 The principle appears on p. 20 of the introduction to the book.

In practice, both uses are often simultaneous, but whenever you can make the intent clear, do it. Inheritance for code reuse is an implementation detail, and it can often be replaced by composition and delegation. On the other hand, interface inheritance is the backbone of a framework. Interface inheritance should use only ABCs as base classes, if possible.

Make Interfaces Explicit with ABCs

In modern Python, if a class is intended to define an interface, it should be an explicit ABC or a `typing.Protocol` subclass. An ABC should subclass only `abc.ABC` or other ABCs. Multiple inheritance of ABCs is not problematic.

Use Explicit Mixins for Code Reuse

If a class is designed to provide method implementations for reuse by multiple unrelated subclasses, without implying an "is-a" relationship, it should be an explicit *mixin class*. Conceptually, a mixin does not define a new type; it merely bundles methods for reuse. A mixin should never be instantiated, and concrete classes should not inherit only from a mixin. Each mixin should provide a single specific behavior, implementing few and very closely related methods. Mixins should avoid keeping any internal state; i.e., a mixin class should not have instance attributes.

There is no formal way in Python to state that a class is a mixin, so it is highly recommended that they are named with a `Mixin` suffix.

Provide Aggregate Classes to Users

> A class that is constructed primarily by inheriting from mixins and does not add its own structure or behavior is called an *aggregate class*.
>
> —Booch et al.[13]

If some combination of ABCs or mixins is particularly useful to client code, provide a class that brings them together in a sensible way.

For example, here is the complete source code (*https://fpy.li/14-29*) for the Django `ListView` class on the bottom right of Figure 14-4:

```
class ListView(MultipleObjectTemplateResponseMixin, BaseListView):
    """
    Render some list of objects, set by `self.model` or `self.queryset`.
    `self.queryset` can actually be any iterable of items, not just a queryset.
    """
```

---

13 Grady Booch et al., *Object-Oriented Analysis and Design with Applications*, 3rd ed. (Addison-Wesley), p. 109.

The body of `ListView` is empty, but the class provides a useful service: it brings together a mixin and a base class that should be used together.

Another example is `tkinter.Widget` (*https://fpy.li/14-30*), which has four base classes and no methods or attributes of its own—just a docstring. Thanks to the `Widget` aggregate class, we can create new a widget with the required mixins, without having to figure out in which order they should be declared to work as intended.

Note that aggregate classes don't have to be completely empty, but they often are.

Subclass Only Classes Designed for Subclassing

In one comment about this chapter, technical reviewer Leonardo Rochael suggested the following warning.

> Subclassing any complex class and overriding its methods is error-prone because the superclass methods may ignore the subclass overrides in unexpected ways. As much as possible, avoid overriding methods, or at least restrain yourself to subclassing classes which are designed to be easily extended, and only in the ways in which they were designed to be extended.

That's great advice, but how do we know whether or how a class was designed to be extended?

The first answer is documentation (sometimes in the form of docstrings or even comments in code). For example, Python's `socketserver` (*https://fpy.li/14-31*) package is described as "a framework for network servers." Its `BaseServer` (*https://fpy.li/14-32*) class is designed for subclassing, as the name suggests. More importantly, the documentation and the docstring (*https://fpy.li/14-33*) in the source code of the class explicitly note which of its methods are intended to be overridden by subclasses.

In Python ≥ 3.8, a new way of making those design constraints explicit is provided by PEP 591—Adding a final qualifier to typing (*https://fpy.li/pep591*). The PEP introduces a `@final` (*https://fpy.li/14-34*) decorator that can be applied to classes or individual methods, so that IDEs or type checkers can report misguided attempts to subclass those classes or override those methods.[14]

---

14 PEP 591 also introduces a `Final` (*https://fpy.li/14-35*) annotation for variables or attributes that should not be reassigned or overridden.

Avoid Subclassing from Concrete Classes

Subclassing concrete classes is more dangerous than subclassing ABCs and mixins, because instances of concrete classes usually have internal state that can easily be corrupted when you override methods that depend on that state. Even if your methods cooperate by calling super(), and the internal state is held in private attributes using the __x syntax, there are still countless ways a method override can introduce bugs.

In "Waterfowl and ABCs" on page 445, Alex Martelli quotes Scott Meyer's *More Effective C++*, which says: "all non-leaf classes should be abstract." In other words, Meyer recommends that only abstract classes should be subclassed.

If you must use subclassing for code reuse, then the code intended for reuse should be in mixin methods of ABCs or in explicitly named mixin classes.

We will now analyze Tkinter from the point of view of these recommendations.

Tkinter: The Good, the Bad, and the Ugly

Most advice in the previous section is not followed by Tkinter, with the notable exception of "Provide Aggregate Classes to Users" on page 513. Even then, it's not a great example, because composition would probably work better for integrating the geometry managers into Widget, as discussed in "Favor Object Composition over Class Inheritance" on page 512.

Keep in mind that Tkinter has been part of the standard library since Python 1.1 was released in 1994. Tkinter is a layer on top of the excellent Tk GUI toolkit of the Tcl language. The Tcl/Tk combo is not originally object-oriented, so the Tk API is basically a vast catalog of functions. However, the toolkit is object-oriented in its design, if not in its original Tcl implementation.

The docstring of tkinter.Widget starts with the words "Internal class." This suggests that Widget should probably be an ABC. Although Widget has no methods of its own, it does define an interface. Its message is: "You can count on every Tkinter widget providing basic widget methods (__init__, destroy, and dozens of Tk API functions), in addition to the methods of all three geometry managers." We can agree that this is not a great interface definition (it's just too broad), but it is an interface, and Widget "defines" it as the union of the interfaces of its superclasses.

The Tk class, which encapsulates the GUI application logic, inherits from Wm and Misc, neither of which are abstract or mixin (Wm is not a proper mixin because TopLevel subclasses only from it). The name of the Misc class is—by itself—a very strong *code smell*. Misc has more than 100 methods, and all widgets inherit from it. Why is it necessary that every single widget has methods for clipboard handling, text selection, timer management, and the like? You can't really paste into a button or select text from a scrollbar. Misc should be split into several specialized mixin classes, and not all widgets should inherit from every one of those mixins.

To be fair, as a Tkinter user, you don't need to know or use multiple inheritance at all. It's an implementation detail hidden behind the widget classes that you will instantiate or subclass in your own code. But you will suffer the consequences of excessive multiple inheritance when you type dir(tkinter.Button) and try to find the method you need among the 214 attributes listed. And you'll need to face the complexity if you decide to implement a new Tk widget.

 Despite the problems, Tkinter is stable, flexible, and provides a modern look-and-feel if you use the tkinter.ttk package and its themed widgets. Also, some of the original widgets, like Canvas and Text, are incredibly powerful. You can turn a Canvas object into a simple drag-and-drop drawing application in a matter of hours. Tkinter and Tcl/Tk are definitely worth a look if you are interested in GUI programming.

This concludes our tour through the labyrinth of inheritance.

Chapter Summary

This chapter started with a review of the super() function in the context of single inheritance. We then discussed the problem with subclassing built-in types: their native methods implemented in C do not call overridden methods in subclasses, except in very few special cases. That's why, when we need a custom list, dict, or str type, it's easier to subclass UserList, UserDict, or UserString—all defined in the collections module (*https://fpy.li/collec*), which actually wrap the corresponding built-in types and delegate operations to them—three examples of favoring composition over inheritance in the standard library. If the desired behavior is very different from what the built-ins offer, it may be easier to subclass the appropriate ABC from collections.abc (*https://fpy.li/14-13*) and write your own implementation.

The rest of the chapter was devoted to the double-edged sword of multiple inheritance. First we saw how the method resolution order, encoded in the __mro__ class attribute, addresses the problem of potential naming conflicts in inherited methods. We also saw how the super() built-in behaves, sometimes unexpectedly, in hierarchies with multiple inheritance. The behavior of super() is designed to support mixin classes, which we then studied through the simple example of the UpperCase Mixin for case-insensitive mappings.

We saw how multiple inheritance and mixin methods are used in Python's ABCs, as well as in the socketserver threading and forking mixins. More complex uses of multiple inheritance were exemplified by Django's class-based views and the Tkinter GUI toolkit. Although Tkinter is not an example of modern best practices, it is an example of overly complex class hierarchies we may find in legacy systems.

To close the chapter, I presented seven recommendations to cope with inheritance, and applied some of that advice in a commentary of the Tkinter class hierarchy.

Rejecting inheritance—even single inheritance—is a modern trend. One of the most successful languages created in the 21st century is Go. It doesn't have a construct called "class," but you can build types that are structs of encapsulated fields and you can attach methods to those structs. Go allows the definition of interfaces that are checked by the compiler using structural typing, a.k.a. *static duck typing*—very similar to what we now have with protocol types since Python 3.8. Go has special syntax for building types and interfaces by composition, but it does not support inheritance —not even among interfaces.

So perhaps the best advice about inheritance is: avoid it if you can. But often, we don't have a choice: the frameworks we use impose their own design choices.

Further Reading

> When it comes to reading clarity, properly-done composition is superior to inheritance. Since code is much more often read than written, avoid subclassing in general, but especially don't mix the various types of inheritance, and don't use subclassing for code sharing.
>
> —Hynek Schlawack, Subclassing in Python Redux

During the final review of this book, technical reviewer Jürgen Gmach recommended Hynek Schlawack's post "Subclassing in Python Redux" (*https://fpy.li/14-37*)—the source of the preceding quote. Schlawack is the author of the popular *attrs* package, and was a core contributor to the Twisted asynchronous programming framework, a project started by Glyph Lefkowitz in 2002. Over time, the core team realized they had overused subclassing in their design, according to Schlawack. His post is long, and cites other important posts and talks. Highly recommended.

In that same conclusion, Hynek Schlawack wrote: "Don't forget that more often than not, a function is all you need." I agree, and that is precisely why *Fluent Python* covers functions in depth before classes and inheritance. My goal was to show how much you can accomplish with functions leveraging existing classes from the standard library, before creating your own classes.

Subclassing built-ins, the super function, and advanced features like descriptors and metaclasses are all introduced in Guido van Rossum's paper "Unifying types and classes in Python 2.2" (*https://fpy.li/descr101*). Nothing really important has changed in these features since then. Python 2.2 was an amazing feat of language evolution, adding several powerful new features in a coherent whole, without breaking backward compatibility. The new features were 100% opt-in. To use them, we just had to explicitly subclass object—directly or indirectly—to create a so-called "new style class." In Python 3, every class subclasses object.

The *Python Cookbook*, 3rd ed. by David Beazley and Brian K. Jones (O'Reilly) has several recipes showing the use of super() and mixin classes. You can start from the illuminating section "8.7. Calling a Method on a Parent Class" (*https://fpy.li/14-38*), and follow the internal references from there.

Raymond Hettinger's post "Python's super() considered super!" (*https://fpy.li/14-39*) explains the workings of super and multiple inheritance in Python from a positive perspective. It was written in response to "Python's Super is nifty, but you can't use it (Previously: Python's Super Considered Harmful)" (*https://fpy.li/14-40*) by James Knight. Martijn Pieters' response to "How to use super() with one argument?" (*https://fpy.li/14-41*) includes a concise and deep explanation of super, including its relationship with descriptors, a concept we'll only study in Chapter 23. That's the nature of super. It is simple to use in basic use cases, but is a powerful and complex tool that touches some of Python's most advanced dynamic features, rarely found in other languages.

Despite the titles of those posts, the problem is not really the super built-in—which in Python 3 is not as ugly as it was in Python 2. The real issue is multiple inheritance, which is inherently complicated and tricky. Michele Simionato goes beyond criticizing and actually offers a solution in his "Setting Multiple Inheritance Straight" (*https://fpy.li/14-42*): he implements traits, an explict form of mixins that originated in the Self language. Simionato has a long series of blog posts about multiple inheritance in Python, including "The wonders of cooperative inheritance, or using super in Python 3" (*https://fpy.li/14-43*); "Mixins considered harmful," part 1 (*https://fpy.li/14-44*) and part 2 (*https://fpy.li/14-45*); and "Things to Know About Python Super," part 1 (*https://fpy.li/14-46*), part 2 (*https://fpy.li/14-47*), and part 3 (*https://fpy.li/14-48*). The oldest posts use the Python 2 super syntax, but are still relevant.

I read the first edition of Grady Booch et al., *Object-Oriented Analysis and Design*, 3rd ed., and highly recommend it as a general primer on object-oriented thinking, independent of programming language. It is a rare book that covers multiple inheritance without prejudice.

Now more than ever it's fashionable to avoid inheritance, so here are two references about how to do that. Brandon Rhodes wrote "The Composition Over Inheritance Principle" (*https://fpy.li/14-49*), part of his excellent *Python Design Patterns* (*https://fpy.li/14-50*) guide. Augie Fackler and Nathaniel Manista presented "The End Of Object Inheritance & The Beginning Of A New Modularity" (*https://fpy.li/14-51*) at PyCon 2013. Fackler and Manista talk about organizing systems around interfaces and functions that handle objects implementing those interfaces, avoiding the tight coupling and failure modes of classes and inheritance. That reminds me a lot of the Go way, but they advocate it for Python.

Soapbox

Think about the Classes You Really Need

> [We] started to push on the inheritance idea as a way to let novices build on frameworks that could only be designed by experts.
>
> —Alan Kay, "The Early History of Smalltalk"[15]

The vast majority of programmers write applications, not frameworks. Even those who do write frameworks are likely to spend a lot (if not most) of their time writing applications. When we write applications, we normally don't need to code class hierarchies. At most, we write classes that subclass from ABCs or other classes provided by the framework. As application developers, it's very rare that we need to write a class that will act as the superclass of another. The classes we code are almost always leaf classes (i.e., leaves of the inheritance tree).

If, while working as an application developer, you find yourself building multilevel class hierarchies, it's likely that one or more of the following applies:

- You are reinventing the wheel. Go look for a framework or library that provides components you can reuse in your application.
- You are using a badly designed framework. Go look for an alternative.
- You are overengineering. Remember the *KISS principle*.
- You became bored coding applications and decided to start a new framework. Congratulations and good luck!

It's also possible that all of the above apply to your situation: you became bored and decided to reinvent the wheel by building your own overengineered and badly designed framework, which is forcing you to code class after class to solve trivial problems. Hopefully you are having fun, or at least getting paid for it.

Misbehaving Built-Ins: Bug or Feature?

The built-in `dict`, `list`, and `str` types are essential building blocks of Python itself, so they must be fast—any performance issues in them would severely impact pretty much everything else. That's why CPython adopted the shortcuts that cause its built-in methods to misbehave by not cooperating with methods overridden by subclasses.

---

15 Alan Kay, "The Early History of Smalltalk," in SIGPLAN Not. 28, 3 (March 1993), 69–95. Also available online (*https://fpy.li/14-1*). Thanks to my friend Christiano Anderson, who shared this reference as I was writing this chapter.

A possible way out of this dilemma would be to offer two implementations for each of those types: one "internal," optimized for use by the interpreter, and an external, easily extensible one.

But wait, this is what we have already: `UserDict`, `UserList`, and `UserString` are not as fast as the built-ins but are easily extensible. The pragmatic approach taken by CPython means we also get to use, in our own applications, the highly optimized implementations that are hard to subclass. Which makes sense, considering that it's not so often that we need a custom mapping, list, or string, but we use `dict`, `list`, and `str` every day. We just need to be aware of the trade-offs involved.

Inheritance Across Languages

Alan Kay coined the term "object-oriented," and Smalltalk had only single inheritance, although there are forks with various forms of multiple inheritance support, including the modern Squeak and Pharo Smalltalk dialects that support traits—a language construct that fulfills the role of a mixin class, while avoiding some of the issues with multiple inheritance.

The first popular language to implement multiple inheritance was C++, and the feature was abused enough that Java—intended as a C++ replacement—was designed without support for multiple inheritance of implementation (i.e., no mixin classes). That is, until Java 8 introduced default methods that make interfaces very similar to the abstract classes used to define interfaces in C++ and in Python. After Java, probably the most widely deployed JVM language is Scala, and it implements traits.

Other languages supporting traits are the latest stable versions of PHP and Groovy, as well as Rust and Raku—the language formerly known as Perl 6.[16] So it's fair to say that traits are trendy in 2021.

Ruby offers an original take on multiple inheritance: it does not support it, but introduces mixins as a language feature. A Ruby class can include a module in its body, so the methods defined in the module become part of the class implementation. This is a "pure" form of mixin, with no inheritance involved, and it's clear that a Ruby mixin has no influence on the type of the class where it's used. This provides the benefits of mixins, while avoiding many of its usual problems.

Two new object-oriented languages that are getting a lot of attention severely limit inheritance: Go and Julia. Both are about programming "objects," and support polymorphism (*https://fpy.li/14-53*), but they avoid the term "class."

---

16 My friend and technical reviewer Leonardo Rochael explains better than I could: "The continued existence, but persistent lack of arrival, of Perl 6 was draining willpower out of the evolution of Perl itself. Now Perl continues to be developed as a separate language (it's up to version 5.34 as of now) with no shadow of deprecation because of the language formerly known as Perl 6."

Go has no inheritance at all. Julia has a type hierarchy but subtypes cannot inherit structure, only behaviors, and only abstract types can be subtyped. In addition, Julia methods are implemented using multiple dispatch—a more advanced form of the mechanism we saw in "Single Dispatch Generic Functions" on page 326.

## CHAPTER 15

More About Type Hints

I learned a painful lesson that for small programs, dynamic typing is great. For large programs you need a more disciplined approach. And it helps if the language gives you that discipline rather than telling you "Well, you can do whatever you want".

—Guido van Rossum, a fan of Monty Python[1]

This chapter is a sequel to Chapter 8, covering more of Python's gradual type system. The main topics are:

- Overloaded function signatures
- `typing.TypedDict` for type hinting `dicts` used as records
- Type casting
- Runtime access to type hints
- Generic types
  - Declaring a generic class
  - Variance: invariant, covariant, and contravariant types
  - Generic static protocols

What's New in This Chapter

This chapter is new in the second edition of *Fluent Python*. Let's start with overloads.

---

1 From YouTube video of "A Language Creators' Conversation: Guido van Rossum, James Gosling, Larry Wall, and Anders Hejlsberg," streamed live on April 2, 2019. Quote starts at 1:32:05 (*https://fpy.li/15-1*), edited for brevity. Full transcript available at *https://github.com/fluentpython/language-creators*.

Overloaded Signatures

Python functions may accept different combinations of arguments. The @typ ing.overload decorator allows annotating those different combinations. This is particularly important when the return type of the function depends on the type of two or more parameters.

Consider the sum built-in function. This is the text of help(sum):

```
>>> help(sum)
sum(iterable, /, start=0)
    Return the sum of a 'start' value (default: 0) plus an iterable of numbers

    When the iterable is empty, return the start value.
    This function is intended specifically for use with numeric values and may
    reject non-numeric types.
```

The sum built-in is written in C, but *typeshed* has overloaded type hints for it, in *builtins.pyi* (*https://fpy.li/15-2*):

```
@overload
def sum(__iterable: Iterable[_T]) -> Union[_T, int]: ...
@overload
def sum(__iterable: Iterable[_T], start: _S) -> Union[_T, _S]: ...
```

First let's look at the overall syntax of overloads. That's all the code about the sum you'll find in the stub file (*.pyi*). The implementation would be in a different file. The ellipsis (...) has no function other than to fulfill the syntactic requirement for a function body, similar to pass. So *.pyi* files are valid Python files.

As mentioned in "Annotating Positional Only and Variadic Parameters" on page 295, the two leading underscores in __iterable are a PEP 484 convention for positional-only arguments that is enforced by Mypy. It means you can call sum(my_list), but not sum(__iterable = my_list).

The type checker tries to match the given arguments with each overloaded signature, in order. The call sum(range(100), 1000) doesn't match the first overload, because that signature has only one parameter. But it matches the second.

You can also use @overload in a regular Python module, by writing the overloaded signatures right before the function's actual signature and implementation. Example 15-1 shows how sum would appear annotated and implemented in a Python module.

Example 15-1. mysum.py: definition of the sum function with overloaded signatures

```
import functools
import operator
from collections.abc import Iterable
```

```
from typing import overload, Union, TypeVar

T = TypeVar('T')
S = TypeVar('S')  ❶

@overload
def sum(it: Iterable[T]) -> Union[T, int]: ...  ❷
@overload
def sum(it: Iterable[T], /, start: S) -> Union[T, S]: ...  ❸
def sum(it, /, start=0):  ❹
    return functools.reduce(operator.add, it, start)
```

❶ We need this second TypeVar in the second overload.

❷ This signature is for the simple case: sum(my_iterable). The result type may be T —the type of the elements that my_iterable yields—or it may be int if the iterable is empty, because the default value of the start parameter is 0.

❸ When start is given, it can be of any type S, so the result type is Union[T, S]. This is why we need S. If we reused T, then the type of start would have to be the same type as the elements of Iterable[T].

❹ The signature of the actual function implementation has no type hints.

That's a lot of lines to annotate a one-line function. Probably overkill, I know. At least it wasn't a foo function.

If you want to learn about @overload by reading code, *typeshed* has hundreds of examples. On *typeshed*, the stub file (*https://fpy.li/15-3*) for Python's built-ins has 186 overloads as I write this—more than any other in the standard library.

Take Advantage of Gradual Typing

Aiming for 100% of annotated code may lead to type hints that add lots of noise but little value. Refactoring to simplify type hinting can lead to cumbersome APIs. Sometimes it's better to be pragmatic and leave a piece of code without type hints.

The handy APIs we call Pythonic are often hard to annotate. In the next section we'll see an example: six overloads are needed to properly annotate the flexible max built-in function.

Max Overload

It is difficult to add type hints to functions that leverage the powerful dynamic features of Python.

While studying typeshed, I found bug report #4051 (*https://fpy.li/shed4051*): Mypy failed to warn that it is illegal to pass None as one of the arguments to the built-in max() function, or to pass an iterable that at some point yields None. In either case, you get a runtime exception like this one:

```
TypeError: '>' not supported between instances of 'int' and 'NoneType'
```

The documentation of max starts with this sentence:

Return the largest item in an iterable or the largest of two or more arguments.

To me, that's a very intuitive description.

But if I must annotate a function described in those terms, I have to ask: which is it? An iterable or two or more arguments?

The reality is more complicated because max also takes two optional keyword arguments: key and default.

I coded max in Python to make it easier to see the relationship between how it works and the overloaded annotations (the built-in max is in C); see Example 15-2.

Example 15-2. mymax.py: Python rewrite of max function

```python
# imports and definitions omitted, see next listing

MISSING = object()
EMPTY_MSG = 'max() arg is an empty sequence'

# overloaded type hints omitted, see next listing

def max(first, *args, key=None, default=MISSING):
    if args:
        series = args
        candidate = first
    else:
        series = iter(first)
        try:
            candidate = next(series)
        except StopIteration:
            if default is not MISSING:
                return default
            raise ValueError(EMPTY_MSG) from None
    if key is None:
        for current in series:
            if candidate < current:
                candidate = current
    else:
        candidate_key = key(candidate)
        for current in series:
            current_key = key(current)
```

```
            if candidate_key < current_key:
                candidate = current
                candidate_key = current_key
    return candidate
```

The focus of this example is not the logic of max, so I will not spend time with its implementation, other than explaining MISSING. The MISSING constant is a unique object instance used as a sentinel. It is the default value for the default= keyword argument, so that max can accept default=None and still distinguish between these two situations:

1. The user did not provide a value for default=, so it is MISSING, and max raises ValueError if first is an empty iterable.

2. The user provided some value for default=, including None, so max returns that value if first is an empty iterable.

To fix issue #4051 (*https://fpy.li/shed4051*), I wrote the code in Example 15-3.[2]

Example 15-3. mymax.py: top of the module, with imports, definitions, and overloads

```
from collections.abc import Callable, Iterable
from typing import Protocol, Any, TypeVar, overload, Union

class SupportsLessThan(Protocol):
    def __lt__(self, other: Any) -> bool: ...

T = TypeVar('T')
LT = TypeVar('LT', bound=SupportsLessThan)
DT = TypeVar('DT')

MISSING = object()
EMPTY_MSG = 'max() arg is an empty sequence'

@overload
def max(__arg1: LT, __arg2: LT, *args: LT, key: None = ...) -> LT:
    ...
@overload
def max(__arg1: T, __arg2: T, *args: T, key: Callable[[T], LT]) -> T:
    ...
@overload
def max(__iterable: Iterable[LT], *, key: None = ...) -> LT:
    ...
@overload
def max(__iterable: Iterable[T], *, key: Callable[[T], LT]) -> T:
```

---

2 I am grateful to Jelle Zijlstra—a *typeshed* maintainer—who taught me several things, including how to reduce my original nine overloads to six.

```
    ...
@overload
def max(__iterable: Iterable[LT], *, key: None = ...,
        default: DT) -> Union[LT, DT]:
    ...
@overload
def max(__iterable: Iterable[T], *, key: Callable[[T], LT],
        default: DT) -> Union[T, DT]:
    ...
```

My Python implementation of max is about the same length as all those typing imports and declarations. Thanks to duck typing, my code has no isinstance checks, and provides the same error checking as those type hints—but only at runtime, of course.

A key benefit of @overload is declaring the return type as precisely as possible, according to the types of the arguments given. We'll see that benefit next by studying the overloads for max in groups of one or two at a time.

Arguments implementing SupportsLessThan, but key and default not provided

```
@overload
def max(__arg1: LT, __arg2: LT, *_args: LT, key: None = ...) -> LT:
    ...
# ... lines omitted ...
@overload
def max(__iterable: Iterable[LT], *, key: None = ...) -> LT:
    ...
```

In these cases, the inputs are either separate arguments of type LT implementing SupportsLessThan, or an Iterable of such items. The return type of max is the same as the actual arguments or items, as we saw in "Bounded TypeVar" on page 285.

Sample calls that match these overloads:

```
max(1, 2, -3)  # returns 2
max(['Go', 'Python', 'Rust'])  # returns 'Rust'
```

Argument key provided, but no default

```
@overload
def max(__arg1: T, __arg2: T, *_args: T, key: Callable[[T], LT]) -> T:
    ...
# ... lines omitted ...
@overload
def max(__iterable: Iterable[T], *, key: Callable[[T], LT]) -> T:
    ...
```

The inputs can be separate items of any type T or a single Iterable[T], and key= must be a callable that takes an argument of the same type T, and returns a value that implements `SupportsLessThan`. The return type of `max` is the same as the actual arguments.

Sample calls that match these overloads:

```
max(1, 2, -3, key=abs)  # returns -3
max(['Go', 'Python', 'Rust'], key=len)  # returns 'Python'
```

Argument default provided, but no key

```
@overload
def max(__iterable: Iterable[LT], *, key: None = ...,
        default: DT) -> Union[LT, DT]:
    ...
```

The input is an iterable of items of type `LT` implementing `SupportsLessThan`. The `default=` argument is the return value when the `Iterable` is empty. Therefore the return type of `max` must be a `Union` of type `LT` and the type of the `default` argument.

Sample calls that match these overloads:

```
max([1, 2, -3], default=0)  # returns 2
max([], default=None)  # returns None
```

Arguments key and default provided

```
@overload
def max(__iterable: Iterable[T], *, key: Callable[[T], LT],
        default: DT) -> Union[T, DT]:
    ...
```

The inputs are:

- An `Iterable` of items of any type `T`
- Callable that takes an argument of type `T` and returns a value of type `LT` that implements `SupportsLessThan`
- A default value of any type `DT`

The return type of `max` must be a `Union` of type `T` or the type of the `default` argument:

```
max([1, 2, -3], key=abs, default=None)  # returns -3
max([], key=abs, default=None)  # returns None
```

Takeaways from Overloading max

Type hints allow Mypy to flag a call like `max([None, None])` with this error message:

```
mymax_demo.py:109: error: Value of type variable "_LT" of "max"
  cannot be "None"
```

On the other hand, having to write so many lines to support the type checker may discourage people from writing convenient and flexible functions like max. If I had to reinvent the min function as well, I could refactor and reuse most of the implementation of max. But I'd have to copy and paste all overloaded declarations—even though they would be identical for min, except for the function name.

My friend João S. O. Bueno—one of the smartest Python devs I know—tweeted this (*https://fpy.li/15-4*):

> Although it is this hard to express the signature of max—it fits in one's mind quite easily. My understanding is that the expressiveness of annotation markings is very limited, compared to that of Python.

Now let's study the TypedDict typing construct. It is not as useful as I imagined at first, but has its uses. Experimenting with TypedDict demonstrates the limitations of static typing for handling dynamic structures, such as JSON data.

TypedDict

 It's tempting to use TypedDict to protect against errors while handling dynamic data structures like JSON API responses. But the examples here make clear that correct handling of JSON must be done at runtime, and not with static type checking. For runtime checking of JSON-like structures using type hints, check out the *pydantic* (*https://fpy.li/15-5*) package on PyPI.

Python dictionaries are sometimes used as records, with the keys used as field names and field values of different types.

For example, consider a record describing a book in JSON or Python:

```
{"isbn": "0134757599",
 "title": "Refactoring, 2e",
 "authors": ["Martin Fowler", "Kent Beck"],
 "pagecount": 478}
```

Before Python 3.8, there was no good way to annotate a record like that, because the mapping types we saw in "Generic Mappings" on page 277 limit all values to have the same type.

Here are two lame attempts to annotate a record like the preceding JSON object:

Dict[str, Any]
    The values may be of any type.

```
Dict[str, Union[str, int, List[str]]]
```
Hard to read, and doesn't preserve the relationship between field names and their respective field types: `title` is supposed to be a `str`, it can't be an `int` or a `List[str]`.

PEP 589—TypedDict: Type Hints for Dictionaries with a Fixed Set of Keys (*https:// fpy.li/pep589*) addressed that problem. Example 15-4 shows a simple `TypedDict`.

Example 15-4. books.py: the `BookDict` definition

```
from typing import TypedDict

class BookDict(TypedDict):
    isbn: str
    title: str
    authors: list[str]
    pagecount: int
```

At first glance, `typing.TypedDict` may seem like a data class builder, similar to `typing.NamedTuple`—covered in Chapter 5.

The syntactic similarity is misleading. `TypedDict` is very different. It exists only for the benefit of type checkers, and has no runtime effect.

`TypedDict` provides two things:

- Class-like syntax to annotate a `dict` with type hints for the value of each "field."
- A constructor that tells the type checker to expect a `dict` with the keys and values as specified.

At runtime, a `TypedDict` constructor such as `BookDict` is a placebo: it has the same effect as calling the `dict` constructor with the same arguments.

The fact that `BookDict` creates a plain `dict` also means that:

- The "fields" in the pseudoclass definition don't create instance attributes.
- You can't write initializers with default values for the "fields."
- Method definitions are not allowed.

Let's explore the behavior of a `BookDict` at runtime (Example 15-5).

Example 15-5. Using a `BookDict`, but not quite as intended

```
>>> from books import BookDict
>>> pp = BookDict(title='Programming Pearls',    ❶
...               authors='Jon Bentley',          ❷
```

```
...                    isbn='0201657880',
...                    pagecount=256)
>>> pp  ❸
{'title': 'Programming Pearls', 'authors': 'Jon Bentley', 'isbn': '0201657880',
 'pagecount': 256}
>>> type(pp)
<class 'dict'>
>>> pp.title  ❹
Traceback (most recent call last):
  File "<stdin>", line 1, in <module>
AttributeError: 'dict' object has no attribute 'title'
>>> pp['title']
'Programming Pearls'
>>> BookDict.__annotations__  ❺
{'isbn': <class 'str'>, 'title': <class 'str'>, 'authors': typing.List[str],
 'pagecount': <class 'int'>}
```

❶ You can call BookDict like a dict constructor with keyword arguments, or passing a dict argument—including a dict literal.

❷ Oops…I forgot authors takes a list. But gradual typing means no type checking
  at runtime.

❸ The result of calling BookDict is a plain dict…

❹ …therefore you can't read the data using object.field notation.

❺ The type hints are in BookDict.__annotations__, and not in pp.

Without a type checker, TypedDict is as useful as comments: it may help people read
the code, but that's it. In contrast, the class builders from Chapter 5 are useful even if
you don't use a type checker, because at runtime they generate or enhance a custom
class that you can instantiate. They also provide several useful methods or functions
listed in Table 5-1.

Example 15-6 builds a valid BookDict and tries some operations on it. This shows
how TypedDict enables Mypy to catch errors, shown in Example 15-7.

Example 15-6. demo_books.py: legal and illegal operations on a BookDict

```
from books import BookDict
from typing import TYPE_CHECKING

def demo() -> None:  ❶
    book = BookDict(  ❷
        isbn='0134757599',
        title='Refactoring, 2e',
        authors=['Martin Fowler', 'Kent Beck'],
```

```
        pagecount=478
    )
    authors = book['authors']  ❸
    if TYPE_CHECKING:  ❹
        reveal_type(authors)  ❺
    authors = 'Bob'  ❻
    book['weight'] = 4.2
    del book['title']


if __name__ == '__main__':
    demo()
```

❶ Remember to add a return type, so that Mypy doesn't ignore the function.

❷ This is a valid BookDict: all the keys are present, with values of the correct types.

❸ Mypy will infer the type of authors from the annotation for the 'authors' key in BookDict.

❹ typing.TYPE_CHECKING is only True when the program is being type checked. At runtime, it's always false.

❺ The previous if statement prevents reveal_type(authors) from being called at runtime. reveal_type is not a runtime Python function, but a debugging facility provided by Mypy. That's why there is no import for it. See its output in Example 15-7.

❻ The last three lines of the demo function are illegal. They will cause error messages in Example 15-7.

Type checking *demo_books.py* from Example 15-6, we get Example 15-7.

Example 15-7. Type checking demo_books.py

```
.../typeddict/ $ mypy demo_books.py
demo_books.py:13: note: Revealed type is 'built-ins.list[built-ins.str]'  ❶
demo_books.py:14: error: Incompatible types in assignment
                (expression has type "str", variable has type "List[str]")  ❷
demo_books.py:15: error: TypedDict "BookDict" has no key 'weight'  ❸
demo_books.py:16: error: Key 'title' of TypedDict "BookDict" cannot be deleted  ❹
Found 3 errors in 1 file (checked 1 source file)
```

❶ This note is the result of `reveal_type(authors)`.

❷ The type of the `authors` variable was inferred from the type of the `book['au thors']` expression that initialized it. You can't assign a `str` to a variable of type `List[str]`. Type checkers usually don't allow the type of a variable to change.[3]

❸ Cannot assign to a key that is not part of the `BookDict` definition.

❹ Cannot delete a key that is part of the `BookDict` definition.

Now let's see `BookDict` used in function signatures, to type check function calls.

Imagine you need to generate XML from book records, similar to this:

```
<BOOK>
  <ISBN>0134757599</ISBN>
  <TITLE>Refactoring, 2e</TITLE>
  <AUTHOR>Martin Fowler</AUTHOR>
  <AUTHOR>Kent Beck</AUTHOR>
  <PAGECOUNT>478</PAGECOUNT>
</BOOK>
```

If you were writing MicroPython code to be embedded in a tiny microcontroller, you might write a function like what's shown in Example 15-8.[4]

Example 15-8. books.py: to_xml function

```
AUTHOR_ELEMENT = '<AUTHOR>{}</AUTHOR>'

def to_xml(book: BookDict) -> str:    ❶
    elements: list[str] = []    ❷
    for key, value in book.items():
        if isinstance(value, list):    ❸
            elements.extend(
                AUTHOR_ELEMENT.format(n) for n in value)    ❹
        else:
            tag = key.upper()
            elements.append(f'<{tag}>{value}</{tag}>')
    xml = '\n\t'.join(elements)
    return f'<BOOK>\n\t{xml}\n</BOOK>'
```

---

3 As of May 2020, pytype allows it. But its FAQ (*https://fpy.li/15-6*) says it will be disallowed in the future. See the question, "Why didn't pytype catch that I changed the type of an annotated variable?" in the pytype FAQ (*https://fpy.li/15-6*).

4 I prefer to use the lxml (*https://fpy.li/15-8*) package to generate and parse XML: it's easy to get started, full-featured, and fast. Unfortunately, lxml and Python's own *ElementTree* (*https://fpy.li/15-9*) don't fit the limited RAM of my hypothetical microcontroller.

❶ The whole point of the example: using `BookDict` in the function signature.

❷ It's often necessary to annotate collections that start empty, otherwise Mypy can't infer the type of the elements.[5]

❸ Mypy understands `isinstance` checks, and treats `value` as a `list` in this block.

❹ When I used `key == 'authors'` as the condition for the `if` guarding this block, Mypy found an error in this line: `"object" has no attribute "__iter__"`, because it inferred the type of `value` returned from `book.items()` as `object`, which doesn't support the `__iter__` method required by the generator expression. With the `isinstance` check, this works because Mypy knows that `value` is a `list` in this block.

Example 15-9 shows a function that parses a JSON `str` and returns a `BookDict`.

Example 15-9. books_any.py: `from_json` function

```
def from_json(data: str) -> BookDict:
    whatever = json.loads(data)  ❶
    return whatever  ❷
```

❶ The return type of `json.loads()` is Any.[6]

❷ I can return `whatever`—of type Any—because Any is *consistent-with* every type, including the declared return type, `BookDict`.

The second point of Example 15-9 is very important to keep in mind: Mypy will not flag any problem in this code, but at runtime the value in `whatever` may not conform to the `BookDict` structure—in fact, it may not be a `dict` at all!

If you run Mypy with `--disallow-any-expr`, it will complain about the two lines in the body of `from_json`:

```
.../typeddict/ $ mypy books_any.py --disallow-any-expr
books_any.py:30: error: Expression has type "Any"
books_any.py:31: error: Expression has type "Any"
Found 2 errors in 1 file (checked 1 source file)
```

---

5 The Mypy documentation discusses this in its "Common issues and solutions" page (*https://fpy.li/15-10*), in the section, "Types of empty collections" (*https://fpy.li/15-11*).

6 Brett Cannon, Guido van Rossum, and others have been discussing how to type hint `json.loads()` since 2016 in Mypy issue #182: Define a JSON type (*https://fpy.li/15-12*).

Lines 30 and 31 mentioned in the previous snippet are the body of the `from_json` function. We can silence the type error by adding a type hint to the initialization of the `whatever` variable, as in Example 15-10.

Example 15-10. books.py: from_json function with variable annotation

```
def from_json(data: str) -> BookDict:
    whatever: BookDict = json.loads(data)  ❶
    return whatever  ❷
```

❶ `--disallow-any-expr` does not cause errors when an expression of type `Any` is immediately assigned to a variable with a type hint.

❷ Now `whatever` is of type `BookDict`, the declared return type.

 Don't be lulled into a false sense of type safety by Example 15-10! Looking at the code at rest, the type checker cannot predict that `json.loads()` will return anything that resembles a `BookDict`. Only runtime validation can guarantee that.

Static type checking is unable to prevent errors with code that is inherently dynamic, such as `json.loads()`, which builds Python objects of different types at runtime, as Examples 15-11, 15-12, and 15-13 demonstrate.

Example 15-11. demo_not_book.py: from_json returns an invalid BookDict, and to_xml accepts it

```
from books import to_xml, from_json
from typing import TYPE_CHECKING

def demo() -> None:
    NOT_BOOK_JSON = """
        {"title": "Andromeda Strain",
         "flavor": "pistachio",
         "authors": true}
    """
    not_book = from_json(NOT_BOOK_JSON)  ❶
    if TYPE_CHECKING:  ❷
        reveal_type(not_book)
        reveal_type(not_book['authors'])

    print(not_book)  ❸
    print(not_book['flavor'])  ❹

    xml = to_xml(not_book)  ❺
    print(xml)  ❻
```

```
if __name__ == '__main__':
    demo()
```

❶ This line does not produce a valid `BookDict`—see the content of `NOT_BOOK_JSON`.

❷ Let's have Mypy reveal a couple of types.

❸ This should not be a problem: `print` can handle `object` and every other type.

❹ `BookDict` has no `'flavor'` key, but the JSON source does…what will happen?

❺ Remember the signature: `def to_xml(book: BookDict) -> str:`.

❻ What will the XML output look like?

Now we check *demo_not_book.py* with Mypy (Example 15-12).

Example 15-12. Mypy report for demo_not_book.py, reformatted for clarity

```
…/typeddict/ $ mypy demo_not_book.py
demo_not_book.py:12: note: Revealed type is
   'TypedDict('books.BookDict', {'isbn': built-ins.str,
                                 'title': built-ins.str,
                                 'authors': built-ins.list[built-ins.str],
                                 'pagecount': built-ins.int})'   ❶
demo_not_book.py:13: note: Revealed type is 'built-ins.list[built-ins.str]'   ❷
demo_not_book.py:16: error: TypedDict "BookDict" has no key 'flavor'   ❸
Found 1 error in 1 file (checked 1 source file)
```

❶ The revealed type is the nominal type, not the runtime content of `not_book`.

❷ Again, this is the nominal type of `not_book['authors']`, as defined in `BookDict`. Not the runtime type.

❸ This error is for line `print(not_book['flavor'])`: that key does not exist in the nominal type.

Now let's run *demo_not_book.py*, showing the output in Example 15-13.

Example 15-13. Output of running demo_not_book.py

```
…/typeddict/ $ python3 demo_not_book.py
{'title': 'Andromeda Strain', 'flavor': 'pistachio', 'authors': True}   ❶
pistachio   ❷
<BOOK>   ❸
```

```
            <TITLE>Andromeda Strain</TITLE>
            <FLAVOR>pistachio</FLAVOR>
            <AUTHORS>True</AUTHORS>
</BOOK>
```

❶ This is not really a BookDict.

❷ The value of not_book['flavor'].

❸ to_xml takes a BookDict argument, but there is no runtime checking: garbage in, garbage out.

Example 15-13 shows that *demo_not_book.py* outputs nonsense, but has no runtime errors. Using a TypedDict while handling JSON data did not provide much type safety.

If you look at the code for to_xml in Example 15-8 through the lens of duck typing, the argument book must provide an .items() method that returns an iterable of tuples like (key, value) where:

- key must have an .upper() method
- value can be anything

The point of this demonstration: when handling data with a dynamic structure, such as JSON or XML, TypedDict is absolutely not a replacement for data validation at runtime. For that, use *pydantic* (*https://fpy.li/15-5*).

TypedDict has more features, including support for optional keys, a limited form of inheritance, and an alternative declaration syntax. If you want to know more about it, please review PEP 589—TypedDict: Type Hints for Dictionaries with a Fixed Set of Keys (*https://fpy.li/pep589*).

Now let's turn our attention to a function that is best avoided, but sometimes is unavoidable: typing.cast.

Type Casting

No type system is perfect, and neither are the static type checkers, the type hints in the *typeshed* project, or the type hints in the third-party packages that have them.

The typing.cast() special function provides one way to handle type checking malfunctions or incorrect type hints in code we can't fix. The Mypy 0.930 documentation (*https://fpy.li/15-14*) explains:

> Casts are used to silence spurious type checker warnings and give the type checker a little help when it can't quite understand what is going on.

At runtime, `typing.cast` does absolutely nothing. This is its implementation (*https:// fpy.li/15-15*):

```
def cast(typ, val):
    """Cast a value to a type.
    This returns the value unchanged.  To the type checker this
    signals that the return value has the designated type, but at
    runtime we intentionally don't check anything (we want this
    to be as fast as possible).
    """
    return val
```

PEP 484 requires type checkers to "blindly believe" the type stated in the `cast`. The "Casts" section of PEP 484 (*https://fpy.li/15-16*) gives an example where the type checker needs the guidance of `cast`:

```
from typing import cast

def find_first_str(a: list[object]) -> str:
    index = next(i for i, x in enumerate(a) if isinstance(x, str))
    # We only get here if there's at least one string
    return cast(str, a[index])
```

The `next()` call on the generator expression will either return the index of a `str` item or raise `StopIteration`. Therefore, `find_first_str` will always return a `str` if no exception is raised, and `str` is the declared return type.

But if the last line were just `return a[index]`, Mypy would infer the return type as `object` because the `a` argument is declared as `list[object]`. So the `cast()` is required to guide Mypy.[7]

Here is another example with `cast`, this time to correct an outdated type hint for Python's standard library. In Example 21-12, I create an *asyncio* `Server` object and I want to get the address the server is listening to. I coded this line:

```
addr = server.sockets[0].getsockname()
```

But Mypy reported this error:

```
Value of type "Optional[List[socket]]" is not indexable
```

The type hint for `Server.sockets` on *typeshed* in May 2021 is valid for Python 3.6, where the `sockets` attribute could be `None`. But in Python 3.7, `sockets` became a property with a getter that always returns a `list`—which may be empty if the server

---

7 The use of `enumerate` in the example is intended to confuse the type checker. A simpler implementation yielding strings directly instead of going through the `enumerate` index is correctly analyzed by Mypy, and the `cast()` is not needed.

has no sockets. And since Python 3.8, the getter returns a `tuple` (used as an immutable sequence).

Since I can't fix *typeshed* right now,[8] I added a `cast`, like this:

```
from asyncio.trsock import TransportSocket
from typing import cast

# ... many lines omitted ...

    socket_list = cast(tuple[TransportSocket, ...], server.sockets)
    addr = socket_list[0].getsockname()
```

Using `cast` in this case required a couple of hours to understand the problem and read *asyncio* source code to find the correct type of the sockets: the `TransportSocket` class from the undocumented `asyncio.trsock` module. I also had to add two `import` statements and another line of code for readability.[9] But the code is safer.

The careful reader may note that `sockets[0]` could raise `IndexError` if `sockets` is empty. However, as far as I understand `asyncio`, that cannot happen in Example 21-12 because the `server` is ready to accept connections by the time I read its `sockets` attribute, therefore it will not be empty. Anyway, `IndexError` is a runtime error. Mypy can't spot the problem even in a trivial case like `print([][0])`.

 Don't get too comfortable using `cast` to silence Mypy, because Mypy is usually right when it reports an error. If you are using `cast` very often, that's a code smell (*https://fpy.li/15-20*). Your team may be misusing type hints, or you may have low-quality dependencies in your codebase.

Despite the downsides, there are valid uses for `cast`. Here is something Guido van Rossum wrote about it:

> What's wrong with the occasional `cast()` call or `# type: ignore` comment?[10]

---

8 I reported *typeshed* issue #5535 (*https://fpy.li/15-17*), "Wrong type hint for asyncio.base_events.Server sockets attribute." and it was quickly fixed by Sebastian Rittau. However, I decided to keep the example because it illustrates a common use case for `cast`, and the `cast` I wrote is harmless.

9 To be honest, I originally appended a `# type: ignore` comment to the line with `server.sockets[0]` because after a little research I found similar lines the *asyncio* documentation (*https://fpy.li/15-18*) and in a test case (*https://fpy.li/15-19*), so I suspected the problem was not in my code.

10 19 May 2020 message (*https://fpy.li/15-21*) to the typing-sig mailing list.

It is unwise to completely ban the use of `cast`, especially because the other work-arounds are worse:

- `# type: ignore` is less informative.[11]
- Using Any is contagious: since Any is *consistent-with* all types, abusing it may produce cascading effects through type inference, undermining the type checker's ability to detect errors in other parts of the code.

Of course, not all typing mishaps can be fixed with `cast`. Sometimes we need `# type: ignore`, the occasional Any, or even leaving a function without type hints.

Next, let's talk about using annotations at runtime.

Reading Type Hints at Runtime

At import time, Python reads the type hints in functions, classes, and modules, and stores them in attributes named `__annotations__`. For instance, consider the `clip` function in Example 15-14.[12]

Example 15-14. clipannot.py: annotated signature of a `clip` function

```
def clip(text: str, max_len: int = 80) -> str:
```

The type hints are stored as a `dict` in the `__annotations__` attribute of the function:

```
>>> from clip_annot import clip
>>> clip.__annotations__
{'text': <class 'str'>, 'max_len': <class 'int'>, 'return': <class 'str'>}
```

The `'return'` key maps to the return type hint after the `->` symbol in Example 15-14.

Note that the annotations are evaluated by the interpreter at import time, just as parameter default values are also evaluated. That's why the values in the annotations are the Python classes `str` and `int`, and not the strings `'str'` and `'int'`. The import time evaluation of annotations is the standard as of Python 3.10, but that may change if PEP 563 (*https://fpy.li/pep563*) or PEP 649 (*https://fpy.li/pep649*) become the standard behavior.

---

11 The syntax `# type: ignore[code]` allows you to specify which Mypy error code is being silenced, but the codes are not always easy to interpret. See "Error codes" (*https://fpy.li/15-22*) in the Mypy documentation.

12 I will not go into the implementation of `clip`, but you can read the whole module in *clip_annot.py* (*https://fpy.li/15-23*) if you're curious.

Problems with Annotations at Runtime

The increased use of type hints raised two problems:

- Importing modules uses more CPU and memory when many type hints are used.
- Referring to types not yet defined requires using strings instead of actual types.

Both issues are relevant. The first is because of what we just saw: annotations are evaluated by the interpreter at import time and stored in the __annotations__ attribute. Let's focus now on the second issue.

Storing annotations as strings is sometimes required because of the "forward reference" problem: when a type hint needs to refer to a class defined below in the same module. However, a common manifestation of the problem in source code doesn't look like a forward reference at all: that's when a method returns a new object of the same class. Since the class object is not defined until Python completely evaluates the class body, type hints must use the name of the class as a string. Here is an example:

```
class Rectangle:
    # ... lines omitted ...
    def stretch(self, factor: float) -> 'Rectangle':
        return Rectangle(width=self.width * factor)
```

Writing forward referencing type hints as strings is the standard and required practice as of Python 3.10. Static type checkers were designed to deal with that issue from the beginning.

But at runtime, if you write code to read the return annotation for stretch, you will get a string 'Rectangle' instead of a reference to the actual type, the Rectangle class. Now your code needs to figure out what that string means.

The typing module includes three functions and a class categorized as Introspection helpers (*https://fpy.li/15-24*), the most important being typing.get_type_hints. Part of its documentation states:

get_type_hints(obj, globals=None, locals=None, include_extras=False)
> [...] This is often the same as obj.__annotations__. In addition, forward references encoded as string literals are handled by evaluating them in globals and locals namespaces. [...]

 Since Python 3.10, the new inspect.get_annotations(…) (*https://fpy.li/15-25*) function should be used instead of typing.get_type_hints. However, some readers may not be using Python 3.10 yet, so in the examples I'll use typing.get_type_hints, which is available since the typing module was added in Python 3.5.

PEP 563—Postponed Evaluation of Annotations (*https://fpy.li/pep563*) was approved to make it unnecessary to write annotations as strings, and to reduce the runtime costs of type hints. Its main idea is described in these two sentences of the "Abstract" (*https://fpy.li/15-26*):

> This PEP proposes changing function annotations and variable annotations so that they are no longer evaluated at function definition time. Instead, they are preserved in *annotations* in string form.

Beginning with Python 3.7, that's how annotations are handled in any module that starts with this `import` statement:

```
from __future__ import annotations
```

To demonstrate its effect, I put a copy of the same `clip` function from Example 15-14 in a *clip_annot_post.py* module with that `__future__` import line at the top.

At the console, here's what I get when I import that module and read the annotations from `clip`:

```
>>> from clip_annot_post import clip
>>> clip.__annotations__
{'text': 'str', 'max_len': 'int', 'return': 'str'}
```

As you can see, all the type hints are now plain strings, despite the fact they are not written as quoted strings in the definition of `clip` (Example 15-14).

The `typing.get_type_hints` function is able to resolve many type hints, including those in `clip`:

```
>>> from clip_annot_post import clip
>>> from typing import get_type_hints
>>> get_type_hints(clip)
{'text': <class 'str'>, 'max_len': <class 'int'>, 'return': <class 'str'>}
```

Calling `get_type_hints` gives us the real types—even in some cases where the original type hint is written as a quoted string. That's the recommended way to read type hints at runtime.

The PEP 563 behavior was scheduled to become default in Python 3.10, with no `__future__` import needed. However, the maintainers of *FastAPI* and *pydantic* raised the alarm that the change would break their code which relies on type hints at runtime, and cannot use `get_type_hints` reliably.

In the ensuing discussion on the python-dev mailing list, Łukasz Langa—the author of PEP 563—described some limitations of that function:

> [...] it turned out that `typing.get_type_hints()` has limits that make its use in general costly at runtime, and more importantly insufficient to resolve all types. The most common example deals with non-global context in which types are generated (e.g., inner classes, classes within functions, etc.). But one of the crown examples of forward

references: classes with methods accepting or returning objects of their own type, also isn't properly handled by `typing.get_type_hints()` if a class generator is used. There's some trickery we can do to connect the dots but in general it's not great.[13]

Python's Steering Council decided to postpone making PEP 563 the default behavior until Python 3.11 or later, giving more time to developers to come up with a solution that addresses the issues PEP 563 tried to solve, without breaking widespread uses of type hints at runtime. PEP 649—Deferred Evaluation Of Annotations Using Descriptors (*https://fpy.li/pep649*) is under consideration as a possible solution, but a different compromise may be reached.

To summarize: reading type hints at runtime is not 100% reliable as of Python 3.10 and is likely to change in 2022.

 Companies using Python at a very large scale want the benefits of static typing, but they don't want to pay the price for the evaluation of the type hints at import time. Static checking happens at developer workstations and dedicated CI servers, but loading modules happens at a much higher frequency and volume in the production containers, and this cost is not negligible at scale.

This creates tension in the Python community between those who want type hints to be stored as strings only—to reduce the loading costs—versus those who also want to use type hints at runtime, like the creators and users of *pydantic* and *FastAPI*, who would rather have type objects stored instead of having to evaluate those annotations, a challenging task.

Dealing with the Problem

Given the unstable situation at present, if you need to read annotations at runtime, I recommend:

- Avoid reading `__annotations__` directly; instead, use `inspect.get_annotations` (from Python 3.10) or `typing.get_type_hints` (since Python 3.5).

- Write a custom function of your own as a thin wrapper around `inspect.get_annotations` or `typing.get_type_hints`, and have the rest of your codebase call that custom function, so that future changes are localized to a single function.

To demonstrate the second point, here are the first lines of the `Checked` class defined in Example 24-5, which we'll study in Chapter 24:

---

13 Message "PEP 563 in light of PEP 649" (*https://fpy.li/15-27*), posted April 16, 2021.

```
class Checked:
    @classmethod
    def _fields(cls) -> dict[str, type]:
        return get_type_hints(cls)
    # ... more lines ...
```

The `Checked._fields` class method protects other parts of the module from depending directly on `typing.get_type_hints`. If `get_type_hints` changes in the future, requiring additional logic, or you want to replace it with `inspect.get_annotations`, the change is limited to `Checked._fields` and does not affect the rest of your program.

 Given the ongoing discussions and proposed changes for runtime inspection of type hints, the official "Annotations Best Practices" (*https://fpy.li/15-28*) document is required reading, and is likely to be updated on the road to Python 3.11. That how-to was written by Larry Hastings, the author of PEP 649—Deferred Evaluation Of Annotations Using Descriptors (*https://fpy.li/pep649*), an alternative proposal to address the runtime issues raised by PEP 563—Postponed Evaluation of Annotations (*https://fpy.li/pep563*).

The remaining sections of this chapter cover generics, starting with how to define a generic class that can be parameterized by its users.

Implementing a Generic Class

In Example 13-7 we defined the `Tombola` ABC: an interface for classes that work like a bingo cage. The `LottoBlower` class from Example 13-10 is a concrete implementation. Now we'll study a generic version of `LottoBlower` used like in Example 15-15.

Example 15-15. generic_lotto_demo.py: using a generic lottery blower class

```
from generic_lotto import LottoBlower

machine = LottoBlower[int](range(1, 11))  ❶

first = machine.pick()  ❷
remain = machine.inspect()  ❸
```

❶ To instantiate a generic class, we give it an actual type parameter, like `int` here.

❷ Mypy will correctly infer that `first` is an `int`...

❸ ... and that `remain` is a `tuple` of integers.

In addition, Mypy reports violations of the parameterized type with helpful messages, such as what's shown in Example 15-16.

Example 15-16. generic_lotto_errors.py: errors reported by Mypy

```
from generic_lotto import LottoBlower

machine = LottoBlower[int]([1, .2])
## error: List item 1 has incompatible type "float";  ❶
##          expected "int"

machine = LottoBlower[int](range(1, 11))

machine.load('ABC')
## error: Argument 1 to "load" of "LottoBlower"  ❷
##          has incompatible type "str";
##          expected "Iterable[int]"
## note:  Following member(s) of "str" have conflicts:
## note:      Expected:
## note:          def __iter__(self) -> Iterator[int]
## note:      Got:
## note:          def __iter__(self) -> Iterator[str]
```

❶ Upon instantiation of LottoBlower[int], Mypy flags the float.

❷ When calling .load('ABC'), Mypy explains why a str won't do: str.__iter__ returns an Iterator[str], but LottoBlower[int] requires an Iterator[int].

Example 15-17 is the implementation.

Example 15-17. generic_lotto.py: a generic lottery blower class

```
import random

from collections.abc import Iterable
from typing import TypeVar, Generic

from tombola import Tombola

T = TypeVar('T')

class LottoBlower(Tombola, Generic[T]):  ❶

    def __init__(self, items: Iterable[T]) -> None:  ❷
        self._balls = list[T](items)

    def load(self, items: Iterable[T]) -> None:  ❸
        self._balls.extend(items)
```

```
def pick(self) -> T:  ❹
    try:
        position = random.randrange(len(self._balls))
    except ValueError:
        raise LookupError('pick from empty LottoBlower')
    return self._balls.pop(position)

def loaded(self) -> bool:  ❺
    return bool(self._balls)

def inspect(self) -> tuple[T, ...]:  ❻
    return tuple(self._balls)
```

❶ Generic class declarations often use multiple inheritance, because we need to subclass Generic to declare the formal type parameters—in this case, T.

❷ The items argument in __init__ is of type Iterable[T], which becomes Iterable[int] when an instance is declared as LottoBlower[int].

❸ The load method is likewise constrained.

❹ The return type of T now becomes int in a LottoBlower[int].

❺ No type variable here.

❻ Finally, T sets the type of the items in the returned tuple.

 The "User-defined generic types" (https://fpy.li/15-29) section of the typing module documentation is short, presents good examples, and provides a few more details that I do not cover here.

Now that we've seen how to implement a generic class, let's define the terminology to talk about generics.

Basic Jargon for Generic Types

Here are a few definitions that I found useful when studying generics:[14]

Generic type
    A type declared with one or more type variables.
    Examples: `LottoBlower[T]`, `abc.Mapping[KT, VT]`

Formal type parameter
    The type variables that appear in a generic type declaration.
    Example: `KT` and `VT` in the previous example `abc.Mapping[KT, VT]`

Parameterized type
    A type declared with actual type parameters.
    Examples: `LottoBlower[int]`, `abc.Mapping[str, float]`

Actual type parameter
    The actual types given as parameters when a parameterized type is declared.
    Example: the `int` in `LottoBlower[int]`

The next topic is about how to make generic types more flexible, introducing the concepts of covariance, contravariance, and invariance.

Variance

Depending on your experience with generics in other languages, this may be the most challenging section in the book. The concept of variance is abstract, and a rigorous presentation would make this section look like pages from a math book.

In practice, variance is mostly relevant to library authors who want to support new generic container types or provide callback-based APIs. Even then, you can avoid much complexity by supporting only invariant containers—which is mostly what we have now in the Python standard library. So, on a first reading, you can skip the whole section or just read the sections about invariant types.

We first saw the concept of *variance* in "Variance in Callable types" on page 293, applied to parameterized generic `Callable` types. Here we'll expand the concept to cover generic collection types, using a "real world" analogy to make this abstract concept more concrete.

---

14 The terms are from Joshua Bloch's classic book, *Effective Java*, 3rd ed. (Addison-Wesley). The definitions and examples are mine.

Imagine that a school cafeteria has a rule that only juice dispensers can be installed.[15] General beverage dispensers are not allowed because they may serve sodas, which are banned by the school board.[16]

An Invariant Dispenser

Let's try to model the cafeteria scenario with a generic `BeverageDispenser` class that can be parameterized on the type of beverage. See Example 15-18.

Example 15-18. invariant.py: type definitions and `install` function

```python
from typing import TypeVar, Generic

class Beverage:  ❶
    """Any beverage."""

class Juice(Beverage):
    """Any fruit juice."""

class OrangeJuice(Juice):
    """Delicious juice from Brazilian oranges."""

T = TypeVar('T')  ❷

class BeverageDispenser(Generic[T]):  ❸
    """A dispenser parameterized on the beverage type."""
    def __init__(self, beverage: T) -> None:
        self.beverage = beverage

    def dispense(self) -> T:
        return self.beverage

def install(dispenser: BeverageDispenser[Juice]) -> None:  ❹
    """Install a fruit juice dispenser."""
```

❶ Beverage, Juice, and OrangeJuice form a type hierarchy.

❷ Simple TypeVar declaration.

❸ BeverageDispenser is parameterized on the type of beverage.

---

15 I first saw the cafeteria analogy for variance in Erik Meijer's *Foreword* in *The Dart Programming Language* book by Gilad Bracha (Addison-Wesley).

16 Much better than banning books!

❹ install is a module-global function. Its type hint enforces the rule that only a juice dispenser is acceptable.

Given the definitions in Example 15-18, the following code is legal:

```
juice_dispenser = BeverageDispenser(Juice())
install(juice_dispenser)
```

However, this is not legal:

```
beverage_dispenser = BeverageDispenser(Beverage())
install(beverage_dispenser)
## mypy: Argument 1 to "install" has
## incompatible type "BeverageDispenser[Beverage]"
##          expected "BeverageDispenser[Juice]"
```

A dispenser that serves any Beverage is not acceptable because the cafeteria requires a dispenser that is specialized for Juice.

Somewhat surprisingly, this code is also illegal:

```
orange_juice_dispenser = BeverageDispenser(OrangeJuice())
install(orange_juice_dispenser)
## mypy: Argument 1 to "install" has
## incompatible type "BeverageDispenser[OrangeJuice]"
##          expected "BeverageDispenser[Juice]"
```

A dispenser specialized for OrangeJuice is not allowed either. Only BeverageDispenser[Juice] will do. In the typing jargon, we say that BeverageDispenser(Generic[T]) is invariant when BeverageDispenser[OrangeJuice] is not compatible with BeverageDispenser[Juice]—despite the fact that OrangeJuice is a *subtype-of* Juice.

Python mutable collection types—such as list and set—are invariant. The Lotto Blower class from Example 15-17 is also invariant.

A Covariant Dispenser

If we want to be more flexible and model dispensers as a generic class that can accept some beverage type and also its subtypes, we must make it covariant. Example 15-19 shows how we'd declare BeverageDispenser.

Example 15-19. covariant.py: type definitions and install function

```
T_co = TypeVar('T_co', covariant=True)   ❶


class BeverageDispenser(Generic[T_co]):   ❷
    def __init__(self, beverage: T_co) -> None:
        self.beverage = beverage
```

```
    def dispense(self) -> T_co:
        return self.beverage

def install(dispenser: BeverageDispenser[Juice]) -> None:  ❸
    """Install a fruit juice dispenser."""
```

❶ Set covariant=True when declaring the type variable; _co is a conventional suffix for covariant type parameters on *typeshed*.

❷ Use T_co to parameterize the Generic special class.

❸ Type hints for install are the same as in Example 15-18.

The following code works because now both the Juice dispenser and the Orange
Juice dispenser are valid in a covariant BeverageDispenser:

```
juice_dispenser = BeverageDispenser(Juice())
install(juice_dispenser)

orange_juice_dispenser = BeverageDispenser(OrangeJuice())
install(orange_juice_dispenser)
```

But a dispenser for an arbitrary Beverage is not acceptable:

```
beverage_dispenser = BeverageDispenser(Beverage())
install(beverage_dispenser)
## mypy: Argument 1 to "install" has
## incompatible type "BeverageDispenser[Beverage]"
##          expected "BeverageDispenser[Juice]"
```

That's covariance: the subtype relationship of the parameterized dispensers varies in
the same direction as the subtype relationship of the type parameters.

A Contravariant Trash Can

Now we'll model the cafeteria rule for deploying a trash can. Let's assume food and
drinks are served in biodegradable packages, and leftovers as well as single-use uten-
sils are also biodegradable. The trash cans must be suitable for biodegradable refuse.

For the sake of this didactic example, let's make simplifying assumptions to classify trash in a neat hierarchy:

- Refuse is the most general type of trash. All trash is refuse.
- Biodegradable is a specific type of trash that can be decomposed by organisms over time. Some Refuse is not Biodegradable.
- Compostable is a specific type of Biodegradable trash that can be efficiently turned into organic fertilizer in a compost bin or in a composting facility. Not all Biodegradable trash is Compostable in our definition.

In order to model the rule for an acceptable trash can in the cafeteria, we need to introduce the concept of "contravariance" through an example using it, as shown in Example 15-20.

Example 15-20. contravariant.py: type definitions and install function

```python
from typing import TypeVar, Generic

class Refuse:  ❶
    """Any refuse."""

class Biodegradable(Refuse):
    """Biodegradable refuse."""

class Compostable(Biodegradable):
    """Compostable refuse."""

T_contra = TypeVar('T_contra', contravariant=True)  ❷

class TrashCan(Generic[T_contra]):  ❸
    def put(self, refuse: T_contra) -> None:
        """Store trash until dumped."""

def deploy(trash_can: TrashCan[Biodegradable]):
    """Deploy a trash can for biodegradable refuse."""
```

❶ A type hierarchy for refuse: Refuse is the most general type, Compostable is the most specific.

❷ T_contra is a conventional name for a contravariant type variable.

❸ TrashCan is contravariant on the type of refuse.

Given those definitions, these types of trash cans are acceptable:

```
bio_can: TrashCan[Biodegradable] = TrashCan()
deploy(bio_can)

trash_can: TrashCan[Refuse] = TrashCan()
deploy(trash_can)
```

The more general `TrashCan[Refuse]` is acceptable because it can take any kind of refuse, including `Biodegradable`. However, a `TrashCan[Compostable]` will not do, because it cannot take `Biodegradable`:

```
compost_can: TrashCan[Compostable] = TrashCan()
deploy(compost_can)
## mypy: Argument 1 to "deploy" has
## incompatible type "TrashCan[Compostable]"
##           expected "TrashCan[Biodegradable]"
```

Let's summarize the concepts we just saw.

Variance Review

Variance is a subtle property. The following sections recap the concept of invariant, covariant, and contravariant types, and provide some rules of thumb to reason about them.

Invariant types

A generic type `L` is invariant when there is no supertype or subtype relationship between two parameterized types, regardless of the relationship that may exist between the actual parameters. In other words, if `L` is invariant, then `L[A]` is not a supertype or a subtype of `L[B]`. They are inconsistent in both ways.

As mentioned, Python's mutable collections are invariant by default. The `list` type is a good example: `list[int]` is not *consistent-with* `list[float]` and vice versa.

In general, if a formal type parameter appears in type hints of method arguments, and the same parameter appears in method return types, that parameter must be invariant to ensure type safety when updating and reading from the collection.

For example, here is part of the type hints for the `list` built-in on *typeshed* (*https://fpy.li/15-30*):

```
class list(MutableSequence[_T], Generic[_T]):
    @overload
    def __init__(self) -> None: ...
    @overload
    def __init__(self, iterable: Iterable[_T]) -> None: ...
    # ... lines omitted ...
    def append(self, __object: _T) -> None: ...
    def extend(self, __iterable: Iterable[_T]) -> None: ...
```

```
        def pop(self, __index: int = ...) -> _T: ...
        # etc...
```

Note that _T appears in the arguments of __init__, append, and extend, and as the return type of pop. There is no way to make such a class type safe if it is covariant or contravariant in _T.

Covariant types

Consider two types A and B, where B is *consistent-with* A, and neither of them is Any. Some authors use the <: and :> symbols to denote type relationships like this:

A :> B

> A is a *supertype-of* or the same as B.

B <: A

> B is a *subtype-of* or the same as A.

Given A :> B, a generic type C is covariant when C[A] :> C[B].

Note the direction of the :> symbol is the same in both cases where A is to the left of B. Covariant generic types follow the subtype relationship of the actual type parameters.

Immutable containers can be covariant. For example, this is how the typing.Frozen Set class is documented (*https://fpy.li/15-31*) as a covariant with a type variable using the conventional name T_co:

```
    class FrozenSet(frozenset, AbstractSet[T_co]):
```

Applying the :> notation to parameterized types, we have:

```
              float :> int
    frozenset[float] :> frozenset[int]
```

Iterators are another example of covariant generics: they are not read-only collections like a frozenset, but they only produce output. Any code expecting an abc.Itera tor[float] yielding floats can safely use an abc.Iterator[int] yielding integers. Callable types are covariant on the return type for a similar reason.

Contravariant types

Given A :> B, a generic type K is contravariant if K[A] <: K[B].

Contravariant generic types reverse the subtype relationship of the actual type parameters.

The TrashCan class exemplifies this:

```
              Refuse :> Biodegradable
    TrashCan[Refuse] <: TrashCan[Biodegradable]
```

A contravariant container is usually a write-only data structure, also known as a "sink." There are no examples of such collections in the standard library, but there are a few types with contravariant type parameters.

`Callable[[ParamType, …], ReturnType]` is contravariant on the parameter types, but covariant on the `ReturnType`, as we saw in "Variance in Callable types" on page 293. In addition, `Generator` (*https://fpy.li/15-32*), `Coroutine` (*https://fpy.li/typecoro*), and `AsyncGenerator` (*https://fpy.li/15-33*) have one contravariant type parameter. The `Generator` type is described in "Generic Type Hints for Classic Coroutines" on page 654; `Coroutine` and `AsyncGenerator` are described in Chapter 21.

For the present discussion about variance, the main point is that the contravariant formal parameter defines the type of the arguments used to invoke or send data to the object, while different covariant formal parameters define the types of outputs produced by the object—the yield type or the return type, depending on the object. The meanings of "send" and "yield" are explained in "Classic Coroutines" on page 645.

We can derive useful guidelines from these observations of covariant outputs and contravariant inputs.

Variance rules of thumb

Finally, here are a few rules of thumb to reason about when thinking through variance:

- If a formal type parameter defines a type for data that comes out of the object, it can be covariant.
- If a formal type parameter defines a type for data that goes into the object after its initial construction, it can be contravariant.
- If a formal type parameter defines a type for data that comes out of the object and the same parameter defines a type for data that goes into the object, it must be invariant.
- To err on the safe side, make formal type parameters invariant.

`Callable[[ParamType, …], ReturnType]` demonstrates rules #1 and #2: The `Return Type` is covariant, and each `ParamType` is contravariant.

By default, `TypeVar` creates formal parameters that are invariant, and that's how the mutable collections in the standard library are annotated.

"Generic Type Hints for Classic Coroutines" on page 654 continues the present discussion about variance.

Next, let's see how to define generic static protocols, applying the idea of covariance to a couple of new examples.

Implementing a Generic Static Protocol

The Python 3.10 standard library provides a few generic static protocols. One of them is SupportsAbs, implemented like this in the *typing* module (*https://fpy.li/15-34*):

```python
@runtime_checkable
class SupportsAbs(Protocol[T_co]):
    """An ABC with one abstract method __abs__ that is covariant in its
        return type."""
    __slots__ = ()

    @abstractmethod
    def __abs__(self) -> T_co:
        pass
```

T_co is declared according to the naming convention:

```python
T_co = TypeVar('T_co', covariant=True)
```

Thanks to SupportsAbs, Mypy recognizes this code as valid, as you can see in Example 15-21.

Example 15-21. abs_demo.py: use of the generic SupportsAbs protocol

```python
import math
from typing import NamedTuple, SupportsAbs

class Vector2d(NamedTuple):
    x: float
    y: float

    def __abs__(self) -> float:    ❶
        return math.hypot(self.x, self.y)

def is_unit(v: SupportsAbs[float]) -> bool:    ❷
    """'True' if the magnitude of 'v' is close to 1."""
    return math.isclose(abs(v), 1.0)    ❸

assert issubclass(Vector2d, SupportsAbs)    ❹

v0 = Vector2d(0, 1)    ❺
sqrt2 = math.sqrt(2)
v1 = Vector2d(sqrt2 / 2, sqrt2 / 2)
v2 = Vector2d(1, 1)
v3 = complex(.5, math.sqrt(3) / 2)
v4 = 1    ❻

assert is_unit(v0)
assert is_unit(v1)
assert not is_unit(v2)
assert is_unit(v3)
```

```
assert is_unit(v4)

print('OK')
```

❶ Defining __abs__ makes Vector2d *consistent-with* SupportsAbs.

❷ Parameterizing SupportsAbs with float ensures…

❸ …that Mypy accepts abs(v) as the first argument for math.isclose.

❹ Thanks to @runtime_checkable in the definition of SupportsAbs, this is a valid runtime assertion.

❺ The remaining code all passes Mypy checks and runtime assertions.

❻ The int type is also *consistent-with* SupportsAbs. According to *typeshed* (*https://fpy.li/15-35*), int.__abs__ returns an int, which is *consistent-with* the float type parameter declared in the is_unit type hint for the v argument.

Similarly, we can write a generic version of the RandomPicker protocol presented in Example 13-18, which was defined with a single method pick returning Any.

Example 15-22 shows how to make a generic RandomPicker covariant on the return type of pick.

Example 15-22. generic_randompick.py: definition of generic RandomPicker

```
from typing import Protocol, runtime_checkable, TypeVar

T_co = TypeVar('T_co', covariant=True)   ❶

@runtime_checkable
class RandomPicker(Protocol[T_co]):   ❷
    def pick(self) -> T_co: ...   ❸
```

❶ Declare T_co as covariant.

❷ This makes RandomPicker generic with a covariant formal type parameter.

❸ Use T_co as the return type.

The generic `RandomPicker` protocol can be covariant because its only formal parameter is used in a return type.

With this, we can call it a chapter.

Chapter Summary

The chapter started with a simple example of using `@overload`, followed by a much more complex example that we studied in detail: the overloaded signatures required to correctly annotate the `max` built-in function.

The `typing.TypedDict` special construct came next. I chose to cover it here, and not in Chapter 5 where we saw `typing.NamedTuple`, because `TypedDict` is not a class builder; it's merely a way to add type hints to a variable or argument that requires a `dict` with a specific set of string keys, and specific types for each key—which happens when we use a `dict` as a record, often in the context of handling with JSON data. That section was a bit long because using `TypedDict` can give a false sense of security, and I wanted to show how runtime checks and error handling are really inevitable when trying to make statically structured records out of mappings that are dynamic in nature.

Next we talked about `typing.cast`, a function designed to let us guide the work of the type checker. It's important to carefully consider when to use `cast`, because overusing it hinders the type checker.

Runtime access to type hints came next. The key point was to use `typing.get_type_hints` instead of reading the `__annotations__` attribute directly. However, that function may be unreliable with some annotations, and we saw that Python core developers are still working on a way to make type hints usable at runtime, while reducing their impact on CPU and memory usage.

The final sections were about generics, starting with the `LottoBlower` generic class—which we later learned is an invariant generic class. That example was followed by definitions of four basic terms: generic type, formal type parameter, parameterized type, and actual type parameter.

The major topic of variance was presented next, using cafeteria beverage dispensers and trash cans as "real life" examples of invariant, covariant, and contravariant generic types. Next we reviewed, formalized, and further applied those concepts to examples in Python's standard library.

Lastly, we saw how a generic static protocol is defined, first considering the `typing.SupportsAbs` protocol, and then applying the same idea to the `RandomPicker` example, making it more strict than the original protocol from Chapter 13.

Python's type system is a huge and rapidly evolving subject. This chapter is not comprehensive. I chose to focus on topics that are either widely applicable, particularly challenging, or conceptually important and therefore likely to be relevant for a long time.

Further Reading

Python's static type system was complex as initially designed, and is getting more complex with each passing year. Table 15-1 lists all the PEPs that I am aware of as of May 2021. It would take a whole book to cover everything.

*Table 15-1. PEPs about type hints, with links in the titles. PEP with numbers marked with * are important enough to be mentioned in the opening paragraph of the typing documentation (https://fpy.li/typing). Question marks in the Python column indicate PEPs under discussion or not yet implemented; "n/a" appears in informational PEPs with no specific Python version.*

PEP	Title	Python	Year
3107	Function Annotations (*https://fpy.li/pep3107*)	3.0	2006
483*	The Theory of Type Hints (*https://fpy.li/pep483*)	n/a	2014
484*	Type Hints (*https://fpy.li/pep484*)	3.5	2014
482	Literature Overview for Type Hints (*https://fpy.li/pep482*)	n/a	2015
526*	Syntax for Variable Annotations (*https://fpy.li/pep526*)	3.6	2016
544*	Protocols: Structural subtyping (static duck typing) (*https://fpy.li/pep544*)	3.8	2017
557	Data Classes (*https://fpy.li/pep557*)	3.7	2017
560	Core support for typing module and generic types (*https://fpy.li/pep560*)	3.7	2017
561	Distributing and Packaging Type Information (*https://fpy.li/pep561*)	3.7	2017
563	Postponed Evaluation of Annotations (*https://fpy.li/pep563*)	3.7	2017
586*	Literal Types (*https://fpy.li/pep586*)	3.8	2018
585	Type Hinting Generics In Standard Collections (*https://fpy.li/pep585*)	3.9	2019
589*	TypedDict: Type Hints for Dictionaries with a Fixed Set of Keys (*https://fpy.li/pep589*)	3.8	2019
591*	Adding a final qualifier to typing (*https://fpy.li/pep591*)	3.8	2019
593	Flexible function and variable annotations (*https://fpy.li/pep593*)	?	2019
604	Allow writing union types as X | Y (*https://fpy.li/pep604*)	3.10	2019
612	Parameter Specification Variables (*https://fpy.li/pep612*)	3.10	2019
613	Explicit Type Aliases (*https://fpy.li/pep613*)	3.10	2020
645	Allow writing optional types as x? (*https://fpy.li/pep645*)	?	2020
646	Variadic Generics (*https://fpy.li/pep646*)	?	2020
647	User-Defined Type Guards (*https://fpy.li/pep647*)	3.10	2021
649	Deferred Evaluation Of Annotations Using Descriptors (*https://fpy.li/pep649*)	?	2021
655	Marking individual TypedDict items as required or potentially-missing (*https://fpy.li/pep655*)	?	2021

Python's official documentation hardly keeps up with all that, so Mypy's documentation (*https://fpy.li/mypy*) is an essential reference. *Robust Python* by Patrick Viafore (O'Reilly) is the first book with extensive coverage of Python's static type system that I know about, published August 2021. You may be reading the second such book right now.

The subtle topic of variance has its own section in PEP 484 (*https://fpy.li/15-37*), and is also covered in the "Generics" (*https://fpy.li/15-38*) page of Mypy, as well as in its invaluable "Common Issues" (*https://fpy.li/15-39*) page.

PEP 362—Function Signature Object (*https://fpy.li/pep362*) is worth reading if you intend to use the `inspect` module that complements the `typing.get_type_hints` function.

If you are interested in the history of Python, you may like to know that Guido van Rossum posted "Adding Optional Static Typing to Python" (*https://fpy.li/15-40*) on December 23, 2004.

"Python 3 Types in the Wild: A Tale of Two Type Systems" (*https://fpy.li/15-41*) is a research paper by Ingkarat Rak-amnouykit and others from the Rensselaer Polytechnic Institute and IBM TJ Watson Research Center. The paper surveys the use of type hints in open source projects on GitHub, showing that most projects don't use them, and also that most projects that have type hints apparently don't use a type checker. I found most interesting the discussion of the different semantics of Mypy and Google's *pytype*, which they conclude are "essentially two different type systems."

Two seminal papers about gradual typing are Gilad Bracha's "Pluggable Type Systems" (*https://fpy.li/15-42*), and "Static Typing Where Possible, Dynamic Typing When Needed: The End of the Cold War Between Programming Languages" (*https://fpy.li/15-43*) by Eric Meijer and Peter Drayton.[17]

I learned a lot reading the relevant parts of some books about other languages that implement some of the same ideas:

- *Atomic Kotlin* (*https://fpy.li/15-44*) by Bruce Eckel and Svetlana Isakova (Mindview)
- *Effective Java*, 3rd ed., (*https://fpy.li/15-45*) by Joshua Bloch (Addison-Wesley)
- *Programming with Types: TypeScript Examples* (*https://fpy.li/15-46*) by Vlad Riscutia (Manning)
- *Programming TypeScript* (*https://fpy.li/15-47*) by Boris Cherny (O'Reilly)

---

17 As a reader of footnotes, you may recall that I credited Erik Meijer for the cafeteria analogy to explain variance.

- *The Dart Programming Language* (*https://fpy.li/15-48*) by Gilad Bracha (Addison-Wesley)[18]

For some critical views on type systems, I recommend Victor Youdaiken's posts "Bad ideas in type theory" (*https://fpy.li/15-49*) and "Types considered harmful II" (*https://fpy.li/15-50*).

Finally, I was surprised to find "Generics Considered Harmful" (*https://fpy.li/15-51*) by Ken Arnold, a core contributor to Java from the beginning, as well as coauthor of the first four editions of the official *The Java Programming Language* book (Addison-Wesley)—in collaboration with James Gosling, the lead designer of Java.

Sadly, Arnold's criticism applies to Python's static type system as well. While reading the many rules and special cases of the typing PEPs, I was constantly reminded of this passage from Gosling's post:

> Which brings up the problem that I always cite for C++: I call it the "Nth order exception to the exception rule." It sounds like this: "You can do x, except in case y, unless y does z, in which case you can if ..."

Fortunately, Python has a key advantage over Java and C++: an optional type system. We can squelch type checkers and omit type hints when they become too cumbersome.

Soapbox

Typing Rabbit Holes

When using a type checker, we are sometimes forced to discover and import classes we did not need to know about, and our code has no need to reference—except to write type hints. Such classes are undocumented, probably because they are considered implementation details by the authors of the packages. Here are two examples from the standard library.

To use `cast()` in the `server.sockets` example in "Type Casting" on page 538, I had to scour the vast *asyncio* documentation and then browse the source code of several modules in that package to discover the undocumented `TransportSocket` class in the equally undocumented `asyncio.trsock` module. Using `socket.socket` instead of `TransportSocket` would be incorrect, because the latter is explicitly not a subtype of the former, according to a docstring (*https://fpy.li/15-52*) in the source code.

---

18 That book was written for Dart 1. There are significant changes in Dart 2, including in the type system. Nevertheless, Bracha is an important researcher in the field of programming language design, and I found the book valuable for his perspective on the design of Dart.

I fell into a similar rabbit hole when I added type hints to Example 19-13, a simple demonstration of multiprocessing. That example uses SimpleQueue objects, which you get by calling multiprocessing.SimpleQueue(). However, I could not use that name in a type hint, because it turns out that multiprocessing.SimpleQueue is not a class! It's a bound method of the undocumented multiprocessing.BaseContext class, which builds and returns an instance of the SimpleQueue class defined in the undocumented multiprocessing.queues module.

In each of those cases I had to spend a couple of hours to find the right undocumented class to import, just to write a single type hint. This kind of research is part of the job when writing a book. But when writing application code, I'd probably avoid such scavenger hunts for a single offending line and just write # type: ignore. Sometimes that's the only cost-effective solution.

Variance Notation in Other Languages

Variance is a difficult topic, and Python's type hints syntax is not as good as it could be. This is evidenced by this direct quote from PEP 484:

> Covariance or contravariance is not a property of a type variable, but a property of a generic class defined using this variable.[19]

If that is the case, why are covariance and contravariance declared with TypeVar and not on the generic class?

The authors of PEP 484 worked under the severe self-imposed constraint that type hints should be supported without making any change to the interpreter. This required the introduction of TypeVar to define type variables, and also the abuse of [ ] to provide Klass[T] syntax for generics—instead of the Klass<T> notation used in other popular languages, including C#, Java, Kotlin, and TypeScript. None of these languages require type variables to be declared before use.

In addition, the syntax of Kotlin and C# makes it clear whether the type parameter is covariant, contravariant, or invariant exactly where it makes sense: in the class or interface declaration.

In Kotlin, we could declare the BeverageDispenser like this:

```
class BeverageDispenser<out T> {
    // etc...
}
```

The out modifier in the formal type parameter means T is an "output" type, therefore BeverageDispenser is covariant.

---

19 See the last paragraph of the section "Covariance and Contravariance" (*https://fpy.li/15-37*) in PEP 484.

You can probably guess how `TrashCan` would be declared:

```
class TrashCan<in T> {
    // etc...
}
```

Given T as an "input" formal type parameter, then `TrashCan` is contravariant.

If neither `in` nor `out` appear, then the class is invariant on the parameter.

It's easy to recall the "Variance rules of thumb" on page 555 when `out` and `in` are used in the formal type parameters.

This suggests that a good naming convention for covariant and contravariant type variables in Python would be:

```
T_out = TypeVar('T_out', covariant=True)
T_in = TypeVar('T_in', contravariant=True)
```

Then we could define the classes like this:

```
class BeverageDispenser(Generic[T_out]):
    ...

class TrashCan(Generic[T_in]):
    ...
```

Is it too late to change the naming convention established in PEP 484?

## CHAPTER 16

Operator Overloading

There are some things that I kind of feel torn about, like operator overloading. I left out operator overloading as a fairly personal choice because I had seen too many people abuse it in C++.

—James Gosling, creator of Java[1]

In Python, you can compute compound interest using a formula written like this:

```
interest = principal * ((1 + rate) ** periods - 1)
```

Operators that appear between operands, like `1 + rate`, are *infix operators*. In Python, the infix operators can handle any arbitrary type. Thus, if you are dealing with real money, you can make sure that `principal`, `rate`, and `periods` are exact numbers—instances of the Python `decimal.Decimal` class—and that formula will work as written, producing an exact result.

But in Java, if you switch from `float` to `BigDecimal` to get exact results, you can't use infix operators anymore, because they only work with the primitive types. This is the same formula coded to work with `BigDecimal` numbers in Java:

```
BigDecimal interest = principal.multiply(BigDecimal.ONE.add(rate)
                      .pow(periods).subtract(BigDecimal.ONE));
```

It's clear that infix operators make formulas more readable. Operator overloading is necessary to support infix operator notation with user-defined or extension types, such as NumPy arrays. Having operator overloading in a high-level, easy-to-use language was probably a key reason for the huge success of Python in data science, including financial and scientific applications.

---

1 Source: "The C Family of Languages: Interview with Dennis Ritchie, Bjarne Stroustrup, and James Gosling" (*https://fpy.li/16-1*).

In "Emulating Numeric Types" on page 9 (Chapter 1) we saw some trivial implementations of operators in a bare-bones Vector class. The __add__ and __mul__ methods in Example 1-2 were written to show how special methods support operator overloading, but there are subtle problems in their implementations that we overlooked. Also, in Example 11-2, we noted that the Vector2d.__eq__ method considers this to be True: Vector(3, 4) == [3, 4]—which may or not make sense. We will address these matters in this chapter, as well as:

- How an infix operator method should signal it cannot handle an operand
- Using duck typing or goose typing to deal with operands of various types
- The special behavior of the rich comparison operators (e.g., ==, >, <=, etc.)
- The default handling of augmented assignment operators such as +=, and how to overload them

What's New in This Chapter

Goose typing is a key part of Python, but the numbers ABCs are not supported in static typing, so I changed Example 16-11 to use duck typing instead of an explicit isinstance check against numbers.Real.[2]

I covered the @ matrix multiplication operator in the first edition of *Fluent Python* as an upcoming change when 3.5 was still in alpha. Accordingly, that operator is no longer in a side note, but is integrated in the flow of the chapter in "Using @ as an Infix Operator" on page 578. I leveraged goose typing to make the implementation of __matmul__ safer than the one in the first edition, without compromising on flexibility.

"Further Reading" on page 591 now has a couple of new references—including a blog post by Guido van Rossum. I also added mentions of two libraries that showcase effective use of operator overloading outside the domain of mathematics: pathlib and Scapy.

Operator Overloading 101

Operator overloading allows user-defined objects to interoperate with infix operators such as + and |, or unary operators like - and ~. More generally, function invocation

---

[2] The remaining ABCs in Python's standard library are still valuable for goose typing and static typing. The issue with the numbers ABCs is explained in "The numbers ABCs and Numeric Protocols" on page 480.

(()), attribute access (.), and item access/slicing ([]) are also operators in Python, but this chapter covers unary and infix operators.

Operator overloading has a bad name in some circles. It is a language feature that can be (and has been) abused, resulting in programmer confusion, bugs, and unexpected performance bottlenecks. But if used well, it leads to pleasurable APIs and readable code. Python strikes a good balance among flexibility, usability, and safety by imposing some limitations:

- We cannot change the meaning of the operators for the built-in types.
- We cannot create new operators, only overload existing ones.
- A few operators can't be overloaded: is, and, or, not (but the bitwise &, |, ~, can).

In Chapter 12, we already had one infix operator in Vector: ==, supported by the __eq__ method. In this chapter, we'll improve the implementation of __eq__ to better handle operands of types other than Vector. However, the rich comparison operators (==, !=, >, <, >=, <=) are special cases in operator overloading, so we'll start by overloading four arithmetic operators in Vector: the unary - and +, followed by the infix + and *.

Let's start with the easiest topic: unary operators.

Unary Operators

The Python Language Reference, "6.5. Unary arithmetic and bitwise operations" (*https://fpy.li/16-2*) lists three unary operators, shown here with their associated special methods:

-, *implemented by* __neg__
> Arithmetic unary negation. If x is -2 then -x == 2.

+, *implemented by* __pos__
> Arithmetic unary plus. Usually x == +x, but there are a few cases when that's not true. See "When x and +x Are Not Equal" on page 569 if you're curious.

~, *implemented by* __invert__
> Bitwise not, or bitwise inverse of an integer, defined as ~x == -(x+1). If x is 2 then ~x == -3.[3]

---

[3] See *https://en.wikipedia.org/wiki/Bitwise_operation#NOT* for an explanation of the bitwise not.

The "Data Model" chapter (*https://fpy.li/16-3*) of *The Python Language Reference* also lists the abs() built-in function as a unary operator. The associated special method is __abs__, as we've seen before.

It's easy to support the unary operators. Simply implement the appropriate special method, which will take just one argument: self. Use whatever logic makes sense in your class, but stick to the general rule of operators: always return a new object. In other words, do not modify the receiver (self), but create and return a new instance of a suitable type.

In the case of - and +, the result will probably be an instance of the same class as self. For unary +, if the receiver is immutable you should return self; otherwise, return a copy of self. For abs(), the result should be a scalar number.

As for ~, it's difficult to say what would be a sensible result if you're not dealing with bits in an integer. In the *pandas* (*https://fpy.li/pandas*) data analysis package, the tilde negates boolean filtering conditions; see "Boolean indexing" (*https://fpy.li/16-4*) in the *pandas* documentation for examples.

As promised before, we'll implement several new operators on the Vector class from Chapter 12. Example 16-1 shows the __abs__ method we already had in Example 12-16, and the newly added __neg__ and __pos__ unary operator method.

Example 16-1. vector_v6.py: unary operators - and + added to Example 12-16

```
def __abs__(self):
    return math.hypot(*self)

def __neg__(self):
    return Vector(-x for x in self)  ❶

def __pos__(self):
    return Vector(self)  ❷
```

❶ To compute -v, build a new Vector with every component of self negated.

❷ To compute +v, build a new Vector with every component of self.

Recall that Vector instances are iterable, and the Vector.__init__ takes an iterable argument, so the implementations of __neg__ and __pos__ are short and sweet.

We'll not implement __invert__, so if the user tries ~v on a Vector instance, Python will raise TypeError with a clear message: "bad operand type for unary ~: 'Vector'."

The following sidebar covers a curiosity that may help you win a bet about unary + someday.

When x and +x Are Not Equal

Everybody expects that x == +x, and that is true almost all the time in Python, but I found two cases in the standard library where x != +x.

The first case involves the decimal.Decimal class. You can have x != +x if x is a Decimal instance created in an arithmetic context and +x is then evaluated in a context with different settings. For example, x is calculated in a context with a certain precision, but the precision of the context is changed and then +x is evaluated. See Example 16-2 for a demonstration.

Example 16-2. A change in the arithmetic context precision may cause x to differ from +x

```
>>> import decimal
>>> ctx = decimal.getcontext()  ❶
>>> ctx.prec = 40  ❷
>>> one_third = decimal.Decimal('1') / decimal.Decimal('3')  ❸
>>> one_third  ❹
Decimal('0.3333333333333333333333333333333333333333')
>>> one_third == +one_third  ❺
True
>>> ctx.prec = 28  ❻
>>> one_third == +one_third  ❼
False
>>> +one_third  ❽
Decimal('0.3333333333333333333333333333')
```

❶ Get a reference to the current global arithmetic context.

❷ Set the precision of the arithmetic context to 40.

❸ Compute 1/3 using the current precision.

❹ Inspect the result; there are 40 digits after the decimal point.

❺ one_third == +one_third is True.

❻ Lower precision to 28—the default for Decimal arithmetic.

❼ Now one_third == +one_third is False.

❽ Inspect +one_third; there are 28 digits after the '.' here.

The fact is that each occurrence of the expression +one_third produces a new Deci mal instance from the value of one_third, but using the precision of the current arithmetic context.

You can find the second case where x != +x in the collections.Counter documentation (*https://fpy.li/16-5*). The Counter class implements several arithmetic operators, including infix + to add the tallies from two Counter instances. However, for practical reasons, Counter addition discards from the result any item with a negative or zero count. And the prefix + is a shortcut for adding an empty Counter, therefore it produces a new Counter, preserving only the tallies that are greater than zero. See Example 16-3.

Example 16-3. Unary + produces a new Counter without zeroed or negative tallies

```
>>> ct = Counter('abracadabra')
>>> ct
Counter({'a': 5, 'r': 2, 'b': 2, 'd': 1, 'c': 1})
>>> ct['r'] = -3
>>> ct['d'] = 0
>>> ct
Counter({'a': 5, 'b': 2, 'c': 1, 'd': 0, 'r': -3})
>>> +ct
Counter({'a': 5, 'b': 2, 'c': 1})
```

As you can see, +ct returns a counter where all tallies are greater than zero.

Now, back to our regularly scheduled programming.

Overloading + for Vector Addition

The Vector class is a sequence type, and the section "3.3.6. Emulating container types" (*https://fpy.li/16-6*) in the "Data Model" chapter of the official Python documentation says that sequences should support the + operator for concatenation and * for repetition. However, here we will implement + and * as mathematical vector operations, which are a bit harder but more meaningful for a Vector type.

If users want to concatenate or repeat Vector instances, they can convert them to tuples or lists, apply the operator, and convert back—thanks to the fact that Vector is iterable and can be constructed from an iterable:

```
>>> v_concatenated = Vector(list(v1) + list(v2))
>>> v_repeated = Vector(tuple(v1) * 5)
```

Adding two Euclidean vectors results in a new vector in which the components are the pairwise additions of the components of the operands. To illustrate:

```
>>> v1 = Vector([3, 4, 5])
>>> v2 = Vector([6, 7, 8])
>>> v1 + v2
Vector([9.0, 11.0, 13.0])
>>> v1 + v2 == Vector([3 + 6, 4 + 7, 5 + 8])
True
```

What happens if we try to add two Vector instances of different lengths? We could raise an error, but considering practical applications (such as information retrieval), it's better to fill out the shortest Vector with zeros. This is the result we want:

```
>>> v1 = Vector([3, 4, 5, 6])
>>> v3 = Vector([1, 2])
>>> v1 + v3
Vector([4.0, 6.0, 5.0, 6.0])
```

Given these basic requirements, we can implement __add__ like in Example 16-4.

Example 16-4. Vector.__add__ method, take #1

```
# inside the Vector class

def __add__(self, other):
    pairs = itertools.zip_longest(self, other, fillvalue=0.0)  ❶
    return Vector(a + b for a, b in pairs)  ❷
```

❶ pairs is a generator that produces tuples (a, b), where a is from self, and b is from other. If self and other have different lengths, fillvalue supplies the missing values for the shortest iterable.

❷ A new Vector is built from a generator expression, producing one addition for each (a, b) from pairs.

Note how __add__ returns a new Vector instance, and does not change self or other.

 Special methods implementing unary or infix operators should never change the value of the operands. Expressions with such operators are expected to produce results by creating new objects. Only augmented assignment operators may change the first operand (self), as discussed in "Augmented Assignment Operators" on page 584.

Example 16-4 allows adding Vector to a Vector2d, and Vector to a tuple or to any iterable that produces numbers, as Example 16-5 proves.

Example 16-5. Vector.__add__ take #1 supports non-Vector objects, too

```
>>> v1 = Vector([3, 4, 5])
>>> v1 + (10, 20, 30)
Vector([13.0, 24.0, 35.0])
>>> from vector2d_v3 import Vector2d
>>> v2d = Vector2d(1, 2)
>>> v1 + v2d
Vector([4.0, 6.0, 5.0])
```

Both uses of + in Example 16-5 work because __add__ uses `zip_longest(…)`, which can consume any iterable, and the generator expression to build the new `Vector` merely performs `a + b` with the pairs produced by `zip_longest(…)`, so an iterable producing any number items will do.

However, if we swap the operands (Example 16-6), the mixed-type additions fail.

Example 16-6. Vector.__add__ take #1 fails with non-Vector left operands

```
>>> v1 = Vector([3, 4, 5])
>>> (10, 20, 30) + v1
Traceback (most recent call last):
  File "<stdin>", line 1, in <module>
TypeError: can only concatenate tuple (not "Vector") to tuple
>>> from vector2d_v3 import Vector2d
>>> v2d = Vector2d(1, 2)
>>> v2d + v1
Traceback (most recent call last):
  File "<stdin>", line 1, in <module>
TypeError: unsupported operand type(s) for +: 'Vector2d' and 'Vector'
```

To support operations involving objects of different types, Python implements a special dispatching mechanism for the infix operator special methods. Given an expression `a + b`, the interpreter will perform these steps (also see Figure 16-1):

1. If a has __add__, call `a.__add__(b)` and return result unless it's `NotImplemented`.

2. If a doesn't have __add__, or calling it returns `NotImplemented`, check if b has __radd__, then call `b.__radd__(a)` and return result unless it's `NotImplemented`.

3. If b doesn't have __radd__, or calling it returns `NotImplemented`, raise `TypeError` with an *unsupported operand types* message.

The __radd__ method is called the "reflected" or "reversed" version of __add__. I prefer to call them "reversed" special methods.[4]

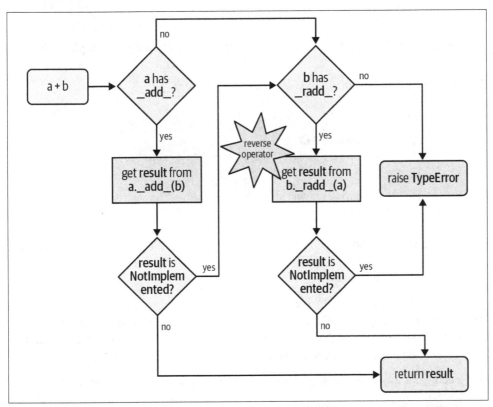

Figure 16-1. Flowchart for computing a + b with __add__ and __radd__.

Therefore, to make the mixed-type additions in Example 16-6 work, we need to implement the Vector.__radd__ method, which Python will invoke as a fallback if the left operand does not implement __add__, or if it does but returns NotImplemented to signal that it doesn't know how to handle the right operand.

---

4 The Python documentation uses both terms. The "Data Model" chapter (*https://fpy.li/dtmodel*) uses "reflected," but "9.1.2.2. Implementing the arithmetic operations" (*https://fpy.li/16-7*) in the numbers module docs mention "forward" and "reverse" methods, and I find this terminology better, because "forward" and "reversed" clearly name each of the directions, while "reflected" doesn't have an obvious opposite.

Do not confuse `NotImplemented` with `NotImplementedError`. The first, `NotImplemented`, is a special singleton value that an infix operator special method should `return` to tell the interpreter it cannot handle a given operand. In contrast, `NotImplementedError` is an exception that stub methods in abstract classes may `raise` to warn that subclasses must implement them.

The simplest implementation of __radd__ that works is shown in Example 16-7.

Example 16-7. The Vector methods __add__ and __radd__

```
# inside the Vector class

def __add__(self, other):  ❶
    pairs = itertools.zip_longest(self, other, fillvalue=0.0)
    return Vector(a + b for a, b in pairs)

def __radd__(self, other):  ❷
    return self + other
```

❶ No changes to __add__ from Example 16-4; listed here because __radd__ uses it.

❷ __radd__ just delegates to __add__.

Often, __radd__ can be as simple as that: just invoke the proper operator, therefore delegating to __add__ in this case. This applies to any commutative operator; + is commutative when dealing with numbers or our vectors, but it's not commutative when concatenating sequences in Python.

If __radd__ simply calls __add__, here is another way to achieve the same effect:

```
def __add__(self, other):
    pairs = itertools.zip_longest(self, other, fillvalue=0.0)
    return Vector(a + b for a, b in pairs)

__radd__ = __add__
```

The methods in Example 16-7 work with Vector objects, or any iterable with numeric items, such as a Vector2d, a tuple of integers, or an array of floats. But if provided with a noniterable object, __add__ raises an exception with a message that is not very helpful, as in Example 16-8.

Example 16-8. Vector.__add__ method needs an iterable operand

```
>>> v1 + 1
Traceback (most recent call last):
  File "<stdin>", line 1, in <module>
```

```
File "vector_v6.py", line 328, in __add__
    pairs = itertools.zip_longest(self, other, fillvalue=0.0)
TypeError: zip_longest argument #2 must support iteration
```

Even worse, we get a misleading message if an operand is iterable but its items cannot be added to the float items in the Vector. See Example 16-9.

Example 16-9. Vector.__add__ method needs an iterable with numeric items

```
>>> v1 + 'ABC'
Traceback (most recent call last):
  File "<stdin>", line 1, in <module>
  File "vector_v6.py", line 329, in __add__
    return Vector(a + b for a, b in pairs)
  File "vector_v6.py", line 243, in __init__
    self._components = array(self.typecode, components)
  File "vector_v6.py", line 329, in <genexpr>
    return Vector(a + b for a, b in pairs)
TypeError: unsupported operand type(s) for +: 'float' and 'str'
```

I tried to add Vector and a str, but the message complains about float and str.

The problems in Examples 16-8 and 16-9 actually go deeper than obscure error messages: if an operator special method cannot return a valid result because of type incompatibility, it should return NotImplemented and not raise TypeError. By returning NotImplemented, you leave the door open for the implementer of the other operand type to perform the operation when Python tries the reversed method call.

In the spirit of duck typing, we will refrain from testing the type of the other operand, or the type of its elements. We'll catch the exceptions and return NotImplemented. If the interpreter has not yet reversed the operands, it will try that. If the reverse method call returns NotImplemented, then Python will raise TypeError with a standard error message like "unsupported operand type(s) for +: *Vector* and *str*."

The final implementation of the special methods for Vector addition is in Example 16-10.

Example 16-10. vector_v6.py: operator + methods added to vector_v5.py (Example 12-16)

```
    def __add__(self, other):
        try:
            pairs = itertools.zip_longest(self, other, fillvalue=0.0)
            return Vector(a + b for a, b in pairs)
        except TypeError:
            return NotImplemented
```

```
def __radd__(self, other):
    return self + other
```

Note that __add__ now catches a TypeError and returns NotImplemented.

 If an infix operator method raises an exception, it aborts the operator dispatch algorithm. In the particular case of TypeError, it is
often better to catch it and return NotImplemented. This allows
the interpreter to try calling the reversed operator method, which
may correctly handle the computation with the swapped operands,
if they are of different types.

At this point, we have safely overloaded the + operator by writing __add__ and
__radd__. We will now tackle another infix operator: *.

Overloading * for Scalar Multiplication

What does Vector([1, 2, 3]) * x mean? If x is a number, that would be a scalar
product, and the result would be a new Vector with each component multiplied by x
—also known as an elementwise multiplication:

```
>>> v1 = Vector([1, 2, 3])
>>> v1 * 10
Vector([10.0, 20.0, 30.0])
>>> 11 * v1
Vector([11.0, 22.0, 33.0])
```

 Another kind of product involving Vector operands would be the
dot product of two vectors—or matrix multiplication, if you take
one vector as a 1 × N matrix and the other as an N × 1 matrix. We
will implement that operator in our Vector class in "Using @ as an
Infix Operator" on page 578.

Back to our scalar product, again we start with the simplest __mul__ and __rmul__
methods that could possibly work:

```
# inside the Vector class

def __mul__(self, scalar):
    return Vector(n * scalar for n in self)

def __rmul__(self, scalar):
    return self * scalar
```

Those methods do work, except when provided with incompatible operands. The
scalar argument has to be a number that when multiplied by a float produces

another float (because our Vector class uses an array of floats internally). So a com plex number will not do, but the scalar can be an int, a bool (because bool is a sub-class of int), or even a fractions.Fraction instance. In Example 16-11, the __mul__ method does not make an explicit type check on scalar, but instead converts it into a float, and returns NotImplemented if that fails. That's a clear example of duck typing.

Example 16-11. vector_v7.py: operator * methods added

```
class Vector:
    typecode = 'd'

    def __init__(self, components):
        self._components = array(self.typecode, components)

    # many methods omitted in book listing, see vector_v7.py
    # in https://github.com/fluentpython/example-code-2e

    def __mul__(self, scalar):
        try:
            factor = float(scalar)
        except TypeError:          ❶
            return NotImplemented  ❷
        return Vector(n * factor for n in self)

    def __rmul__(self, scalar):
        return self * scalar       ❸
```

❶ If scalar cannot be converted to float...

❷ ...we don't know how to handle it, so we return NotImplemented to let Python try __rmul__ on the scalar operand.

❸ In this example, __rmul__ works fine by just performing self * scalar, dele-gating to the __mul__ method.

With Example 16-11, we can multiply Vectors by scalar values of the usual, and not so usual, numeric types:

```
>>> v1 = Vector([1.0, 2.0, 3.0])
>>> 14 * v1
Vector([14.0, 28.0, 42.0])
>>> v1 * True
Vector([1.0, 2.0, 3.0])
>>> from fractions import Fraction
>>> v1 * Fraction(1, 3)
Vector([0.3333333333333333, 0.6666666666666666, 1.0])
```

Now that we can multiply `Vector` by scalars, let's see how to implement `Vector` by `Vector` products.

 In the first edition of *Fluent Python*, I used goose typing in Example 16-11: I checked the `scalar` argument of `__mul__` with `isinstance(scalar, numbers.Real)`. Now I avoid using the `numbers` ABCs because they are not supported by PEP 484, and using types at runtime that cannot also be statically checked seems a bad idea to me.

Alternatively, I could have checked against the `typing.Supports Float` protocol that we saw in "Runtime Checkable Static Protocols" on page 470. I chose duck typing in that example because I think fluent Pythonistas should be comfortable with that coding pattern.

On the other hand, `__matmul__` in Example 16-12 is a good example of goose typing, new in this second edition.

Using @ as an Infix Operator

The `@` sign is well-known as the prefix of function decorators, but since 2015, it can also be used as an infix operator. For years, the dot product was written as `numpy.dot(a, b)` in NumPy. The function call notation makes longer formulas harder to translate from mathematical notation to Python,[5] so the numerical computing community lobbied for PEP 465—A dedicated infix operator for matrix multiplication (*https://fpy.li/pep465*), which was implemented in Python 3.5. Today, you can write a `@` b to compute the dot product of two NumPy arrays.

The `@` operator is supported by the special methods `__matmul__`, `__rmatmul__`, and `__imatmul__`, named for "matrix multiplication." These methods are not used anywhere in the standard library at this time, but are recognized by the interpreter since Python 3.5, so the NumPy team—and the rest of us—can support the `@` operator in user-defined types. The parser was also changed to handle the new operator (a `@` b was a syntax error in Python 3.4).

These simple tests show how `@` should work with `Vector` instances:

```
>>> va = Vector([1, 2, 3])
>>> vz = Vector([5, 6, 7])
>>> va @ vz == 38.0  # 1*5 + 2*6 + 3*7
True
>>> [10, 20, 30] @ vz
```

---

5 See "Soapbox" on page 592 for a discussion of the problem.

```
380.0
>>> va @ 3
Traceback (most recent call last):
...
TypeError: unsupported operand type(s) for @: 'Vector' and 'int'
```

Example 16-12 shows the code of the relevant special methods.

Example 16-12. vector_v7.py: operator @ methods

```
class Vector:
    # many methods omitted in book listing

    def __matmul__(self, other):
        if (isinstance(other, abc.Sized) and  ❶
            isinstance(other, abc.Iterable)):
            if len(self) == len(other):  ❷
                return sum(a * b for a, b in zip(self, other))  ❸
            else:
                raise ValueError('@ requires vectors of equal length.')
        else:
            return NotImplemented

    def __rmatmul__(self, other):
        return self @ other
```

❶ Both operands must implement __len__ and __iter__...

❷ ...and have the same length to allow...

❸ ...a beautiful application of sum, zip, and generator expression.

New zip() Feature in Python 3.10

The zip built-in accepts a strict keyword-only optional argument since Python 3.10. When strict=True, the function raises ValueEr ror when the iterables have different lengths. The default is False. This new strict behavior is in line with Python's *fail fast* (*https:// fpy.li/16-8*) philosophy. In Example 16-12, I'd replace the inner if with a try/except ValueError and add strict=True to the zip call.

Example 16-12 is a good example of *goose typing* in practice. If we tested the other operand against Vector, we'd deny users the flexibility of using lists or arrays as operands to @. As long as one operand is a Vector, our @ implementation supports other operands that are instances of abc.Sized and abc.Iterable. Both of these ABCs implement the __subclasshook__, therefore any object providing __len__ and `__iter__` satisfies our test—no need to actually subclass those ABCs or even register with them, as explained in "Structural Typing with ABCs" on page 466. In particular, our Vector class does not subclass either abc.Sized or abc.Iterable, but it does pass the isinstance checks against those ABCs because it has the necessary methods.

Let's review the arithmetic operators supported by Python, before diving into the special category of "Rich Comparison Operators" on page 581.

Wrapping-Up Arithmetic Operators

Implementing +, *, and @, we saw the most common patterns for coding infix operators. The techniques we described are applicable to all operators listed in Table 16-1 (the in-place operators will be covered in "Augmented Assignment Operators" on page 584).

Table 16-1. Infix operator method names (the in-place operators are used for augmented assignment; comparison operators are in Table 16-2)

Operator	Forward	Reverse	In-place	Description
+	`__add__`	`__radd__`	`__iadd__`	Addition or concatenation
-	`__sub__`	`__rsub__`	`__isub__`	Subtraction
*	`__mul__`	`__rmul__`	`__imul__`	Multiplication or repetition
/	`__truediv__`	`__rtruediv__`	`__itruediv__`	True division
//	`__floordiv__`	`__rfloordiv__`	`__ifloordiv__`	Floor division
%	`__mod__`	`__rmod__`	`__imod__`	Modulo
divmod()	`__divmod__`	`__rdivmod__`	`__idivmod__`	Returns tuple of floor division quotient and modulo
**, pow()	`__pow__`	`__rpow__`	`__ipow__`	Exponentiation[a]
@	`__matmul__`	`__rmatmul__`	`__imatmul__`	Matrix multiplication
&	`__and__`	`__rand__`	`__iand__`	Bitwise and
|	`__or__`	`__ror__`	`__ior__`	Bitwise or
^	`__xor__`	`__rxor__`	`__ixor__`	Bitwise xor
<<	`__lshift__`	`__rlshift__`	`__ilshift__`	Bitwise shift left
>>	`__rshift__`	`__rrshift__`	`__irshift__`	Bitwise shift right

[a] pow takes an optional third argument, modulo: pow(a, b, modulo), also supported by the special methods when invoked directly (e.g., a.`__pow__`(b, modulo)).

The rich comparison operators use a different set of rules.

Rich Comparison Operators

The handling of the rich comparison operators ==, !=, >, <, >=, and <= by the Python interpreter is similar to what we just saw, but differs in two important aspects:

- The same set of methods is used in forward and reverse operator calls. The rules are summarized in Table 16-2. For example, in the case of ==, both the forward and reverse calls invoke __eq__, only swapping arguments; and a forward call to __gt__ is followed by a reverse call to __lt__ with the arguments swapped.

- In the case of == and !=, if the reverse method is missing, or returns NotImplemen ted, Python compares the object IDs instead of raising TypeError.

Table 16-2. Rich comparison operators: reverse methods invoked when the initial method call returns NotImplemented

Group	Infix operator	Forward method call	Reverse method call	Fallback
Equality	a == b	a.__eq__(b)	b.__eq__(a)	Return id(a) == id(b)
	a != b	a.__ne__(b)	b.__ne__(a)	Return not (a == b)
Ordering	a > b	a.__gt__(b)	b.__lt__(a)	Raise TypeError
	a < b	a.__lt__(b)	b.__gt__(a)	Raise TypeError
	a >= b	a.__ge__(b)	b.__le__(a)	Raise TypeError
	a <= b	a.__le__(b)	b.__ge__(a)	Raise TypeError

Given these rules, let's review and improve the behavior of the Vector.__eq__ method, which was coded as follows in *vector_v5.py* (Example 12-16):

```
class Vector:
    # many lines omitted

    def __eq__(self, other):
        return (len(self) == len(other) and
                all(a == b for a, b in zip(self, other)))
```

That method produces the results in Example 16-13.

Example 16-13. Comparing a Vector to a Vector, a Vector2d, and a tuple

```
>>> va = Vector([1.0, 2.0, 3.0])
>>> vb = Vector(range(1, 4))
>>> va == vb     ❶
True
>>> vc = Vector([1, 2])
>>> from vector2d_v3 import Vector2d
>>> v2d = Vector2d(1, 2)
>>> vc == v2d    ❷
```

```
True
>>> t3 = (1, 2, 3)
>>> va == t3   ❸
True
```

❶ Two Vector instances with equal numeric components compare equal.

❷ A Vector and a Vector2d are also equal if their components are equal.

❸ A Vector is also considered equal to a tuple or any iterable with numeric items
   of equal value.

The result in Example 16-13 is probably not desirable. Do we really want a Vector to
be considered equal to a tuple containing the same numbers? I have no hard rule
about this; it depends on the application context. The "Zen of Python" says:

> In the face of ambiguity, refuse the temptation to guess.

Excessive liberality in the evaluation of operands may lead to surprising results, and
programmers hate surprises.

Taking a clue from Python itself, we can see that [1,2] == (1, 2) is False. Therefore, let's be conservative and do some type checking. If the second operand is a
Vector instance (or an instance of a Vector subclass), then use the same logic as the
current __eq__. Otherwise, return NotImplemented and let Python handle that. See
Example 16-14.

Example 16-14. vector_v8.py: improved __eq__ in the Vector class

```
def __eq__(self, other):
    if isinstance(other, Vector):   ❶
        return (len(self) == len(other) and
                all(a == b for a, b in zip(self, other)))
    else:
        return NotImplemented   ❷
```

❶ If the other operand is an instance of Vector (or of a Vector subclass), perform
   the comparison as before.

❷ Otherwise, return NotImplemented.

If you run the tests in Example 16-13 with the new Vector.__eq__ from
Example 16-14, what you get now is shown in Example 16-15.

Example 16-15. Same comparisons as Example 16-13: last result changed

```
>>> va = Vector([1.0, 2.0, 3.0])
>>> vb = Vector(range(1, 4))
>>> va == vb   ❶
True
>>> vc = Vector([1, 2])
>>> from vector2d_v3 import Vector2d
>>> v2d = Vector2d(1, 2)
>>> vc == v2d   ❷
True
>>> t3 = (1, 2, 3)
>>> va == t3   ❸
False
```

❶ Same result as before, as expected.

❷ Same result as before, but why? Explanation coming up.

❸ Different result; this is what we wanted. But why does it work? Read on...

Among the three results in Example 16-15, the first one is no news, but the last two were caused by __eq__ returning NotImplemented in Example 16-14. Here is what happens in the example with a Vector and a Vector2d, vc == v2d, step-by-step:

1. To evaluate vc == v2d, Python calls Vector.__eq__(vc, v2d).

2. Vector.__eq__(vc, v2d) verifies that v2d is not a Vector and returns NotImplemented.

3. Python gets the NotImplemented result, so it tries Vector2d.__eq__(v2d, vc).

4. Vector2d.__eq__(v2d, vc) turns both operands into tuples and compares them: the result is True (the code for Vector2d.__eq__ is in Example 11-11).

As for the comparison va == t3, between Vector and tuple in Example 16-15, the actual steps are:

1. To evaluate va == t3, Python calls Vector.__eq__(va, t3).

2. Vector.__eq__(va, t3) verifies that t3 is not a Vector and returns NotImplemented.

3. Python gets the NotImplemented result, so it tries tuple.__eq__(t3, va).

4. `tuple.__eq__(t3, va)` has no idea what a `Vector` is, so it returns `NotImplemented`.

5. In the special case of `==`, if the reversed call returns `NotImplemented`, Python compares object IDs as a last resort.

We don't need to implement `__ne__` for `!=` because the fallback behavior of `__ne__` inherited from `object` suits us: when `__eq__` is defined and does not return `NotImplemented`, `__ne__` returns that result negated.

In other words, given the same objects we used in Example 16-15, the results for `!=` are consistent:

```
>>> va != vb
False
>>> vc != v2d
False
>>> va != (1, 2, 3)
True
```

The `__ne__` inherited from `object` works like the following code—except that the original is written in C:[6]

```
def __ne__(self, other):
    eq_result = self == other
    if eq_result is NotImplemented:
        return NotImplemented
    else:
        return not eq_result
```

After covering the essentials of infix operator overloading, let's turn to a different class of operators: the augmented assignment operators.

Augmented Assignment Operators

Our `Vector` class already supports the augmented assignment operators `+=` and `*=`. That's because augmented assignment works with immutable receivers by creating new instances and rebinding the lefthand variable.

Example 16-16 shows them in action.

*Example 16-16. Using += and *= with Vector instances*

```
>>> v1 = Vector([1, 2, 3])
>>> v1_alias = v1   ❶
```

---

6 The logic for `object.__eq__` and `object.__ne__` is in function `object_richcompare` in *Objects/typeobject.c* (*https://fpy.li/16-9*) in the CPython source code.

```
>>> id(v1)  ❷
4302860128
>>> v1 += Vector([4, 5, 6])  ❸
>>> v1  ❹
Vector([5.0, 7.0, 9.0])
>>> id(v1)  ❺
4302859904
>>> v1_alias  ❻
Vector([1.0, 2.0, 3.0])
>>> v1 *= 11  ❼
>>> v1  ❽
Vector([55.0, 77.0, 99.0])
>>> id(v1)
4302858336
```

❶ Create an alias so we can inspect the Vector([1, 2, 3]) object later.

❷ Remember the ID of the initial Vector bound to v1.

❸ Perform augmented addition.

❹ The expected result…

❺ …but a new Vector was created.

❻ Inspect v1_alias to confirm the original Vector was not altered.

❼ Perform augmented multiplication.

❽ Again, the expected result, but a new Vector was created.

If a class does not implement the in-place operators listed in Table 16-1, the augmented assignment operators work as syntactic sugar: a += b is evaluated exactly as a = a + b. That's the expected behavior for immutable types, and if you have __add__, then += will work with no additional code.

However, if you do implement an in-place operator method such as __iadd__, that method is called to compute the result of a += b. As the name says, those operators are expected to change the lefthand operand in place, and not create a new object as the result.

The in-place special methods should never be implemented for immutable types like our Vector class. This is fairly obvious, but worth stating anyway.

To show the code of an in-place operator, we will extend the BingoCage class from Example 13-9 to implement __add__ and __iadd__.

We'll call the subclass AddableBingoCage. Example 16-17 is the behavior we want for the + operator.

Example 16-17. The + operator creates a new AddableBingoCage instance

```
>>> vowels = 'AEIOU'
>>> globe = AddableBingoCage(vowels)    ❶
>>> globe.inspect()
('A', 'E', 'I', 'O', 'U')
>>> globe.pick() in vowels    ❷
True
>>> len(globe.inspect())    ❸
4
>>> globe2 = AddableBingoCage('XYZ')    ❹
>>> globe3 = globe + globe2
>>> len(globe3.inspect())    ❺
7
>>> void = globe + [10, 20]    ❻
Traceback (most recent call last):
  ...
TypeError: unsupported operand type(s) for +: 'AddableBingoCage' and 'list'
```

❶ Create a globe instance with five items (each of the vowels).

❷ Pop one of the items, and verify it is one of the vowels.

❸ Confirm that the globe is down to four items.

❹ Create a second instance, with three items.

❺ Create a third instance by adding the previous two. This instance has seven items.

❻ Attempting to add an AddableBingoCage to a list fails with TypeError. That error message is produced by the Python interpreter when our __add__ method returns NotImplemented.

Because an AddableBingoCage is mutable, Example 16-18 shows how it will work when we implement __iadd__.

Example 16-18. An existing AddableBingoCage can be loaded with += (continuing from Example 16-17)

```
>>> globe_orig = globe   ❶
>>> len(globe.inspect())   ❷
4
>>> globe += globe2   ❸
>>> len(globe.inspect())
7
>>> globe += ['M', 'N']   ❹
>>> len(globe.inspect())
9
>>> globe is globe_orig   ❺
True
>>> globe += 1   ❻
Traceback (most recent call last):
  ...
TypeError: right operand in += must be 'Tombola' or an iterable
```

❶ Create an alias so we can check the identity of the object later.

❷ globe has four items here.

❸ An AddableBingoCage instance can receive items from another instance of the same class.

❹ The righthand operand of += can also be any iterable.

❺ Throughout this example, globe has always referred to the same object as globe_orig.

❻ Trying to add a noniterable to an AddableBingoCage fails with a proper error message.

Note that the += operator is more liberal than + with regard to the second operand. With +, we want both operands to be of the same type (AddableBingoCage, in this case), because if we accepted different types, this might cause confusion as to the type of the result. With the +=, the situation is clearer: the lefthand object is updated in place, so there's no doubt about the type of the result.

 I validated the contrasting behavior of + and += by observing how the list built-in type works. Writing my_list + x, you can only concatenate one list to another list, but if you write my_list += x, you can extend the lefthand list with items from any iterable x on the righthand side. This is how the list.extend() method works: it accepts any iterable argument.

Now that we are clear on the desired behavior for `AddableBingoCage`, we can look at its implementation in Example 16-19. Recall that `BingoCage`, from Example 13-9, is a concrete subclass of the `Tombola` ABC from Example 13-7.

Example 16-19. bingoaddable.py: AddableBingoCage extends BingoCage to support + and +=

```
from tombola import Tombola
from bingo import BingoCage


class AddableBingoCage(BingoCage):  ❶

    def __add__(self, other):
        if isinstance(other, Tombola):  ❷
            return AddableBingoCage(self.inspect() + other.inspect())
        else:
            return NotImplemented

    def __iadd__(self, other):
        if isinstance(other, Tombola):
            other_iterable = other.inspect()  ❸
        else:
            try:
                other_iterable = iter(other)  ❹
            except TypeError:  ❺
                msg = ('right operand in += must be '
                       "'Tombola' or an iterable")
                raise TypeError(msg)
        self.load(other_iterable)  ❻
        return self  ❼
```

❶ `AddableBingoCage` extends `BingoCage`.

❷ Our `__add__` will only work with an instance of `Tombola` as the second operand.

❸ In `__iadd__`, retrieve items from `other`, if it is an instance of `Tombola`.

❹ Otherwise, try to obtain an iterator over `other`.[7]

❺ If that fails, raise an exception explaining what the user should do. When possible, error messages should explicitly guide the user to the solution.

---

[7] The `iter` built-in function will be covered in the next chapter. Here I could have used `tuple(other)`, and it would work, but at the cost of building a new `tuple` when all the `.load(…)` method needs is to iterate over its argument.

❻ If we got this far, we can load the `other_iterable` into `self`.

❼ Very important: augmented assignment special methods of mutable objects must return `self`. That's what users expect.

We can summarize the whole idea of in-place operators by contrasting the `return` statements that produce results in __add__ and __iadd__ in Example 16-19:

__add__
The result is produced by calling the constructor `AddableBingoCage` to build a new instance.

__iadd__
The result is produced by returning `self`, after it has been modified.

To wrap up this example, a final observation on Example 16-19: by design, no __radd__ was coded in `AddableBingoCage`, because there is no need for it. The forward method __add__ will only deal with righthand operands of the same type, so if Python is trying to compute a + b, where a is an `AddableBingoCage` and b is not, we return `NotImplemented`—maybe the class of b can make it work. But if the expression is b + a and b is not an `AddableBingoCage`, and it returns `NotImplemented`, then it's better to let Python give up and raise `TypeError` because we cannot handle b.

 In general, if a forward infix operator method (e.g., __mul__) is designed to work only with operands of the same type as `self`, it's useless to implement the corresponding reverse method (e.g., __rmul__) because that, by definition, will only be invoked when dealing with an operand of a different type.

This concludes our exploration of operator overloading in Python.

Chapter Summary

We started this chapter by reviewing some restrictions Python imposes on operator overloading: no redefining of operators in the built-in types themselves, overloading limited to existing operators, with a few operators left out (`is`, `and`, `or`, `not`).

We got down to business with the unary operators, implementing __neg__ and __pos__. Next came the infix operators, starting with +, supported by the __add__ method. We saw that unary and infix operators are supposed to produce results by creating new objects, and should never change their operands. To support operations with other types, we return the `NotImplemented` special value—not an exception—allowing the interpreter to try again by swapping the operands and calling the reverse special method for that operator (e.g., __radd__). The algorithm Python uses to handle infix operators is summarized in the flowchart in Figure 16-1.

Mixing operand types requires detecting operands we can't handle. In this chapter, we did this in two ways: in the duck typing way, we just went ahead and tried the operation, catching a TypeError exception if it happened; later, in __mul__ and __matmul__, we did it with an explicit isinstance test. There are pros and cons to these approaches: duck typing is more flexible, but explicit type checking is more predictable.

In general, libraries should leverage duck typing—opening the door for objects regardless of their types, as long as they support the necessary operations. However, Python's operator dispatch algorithm may produce misleading error messages or unexpected results when combined with duck typing. For this reason, the discipline of type checking using isinstance calls against ABCs is often useful when writing special methods for operator overloading. That's the technique dubbed goose typing by Alex Martelli—which we saw in "Goose Typing" on page 444. Goose typing is a good compromise between flexibility and safety, because existing or future user-defined types can be declared as actual or virtual subclasses of an ABC. In addition, if an ABC implements the __subclasshook__, then objects pass isinstance checks against that ABC by providing the required methods—no subclassing or registration required.

The next topic we covered was the rich comparison operators. We implemented == with __eq__ and discovered that Python provides a handy implementation of != in the __ne__ inherited from the object base class. The way Python evaluates these operators along with >, <, >=, and <= is slightly different, with special logic for choosing the reverse method, and fallback handling for == and !=, which never generate errors because Python compares the object IDs as a last resort.

In the last section, we focused on augmented assignment operators. We saw that Python handles them by default as a combination of plain operator followed by assignment, that is: a += b is evaluated exactly as a = a + b. That always creates a new object, so it works for mutable or immutable types. For mutable objects, we can implement in-place special methods such as __iadd__ for +=, and alter the value of the lefthand operand. To show this at work, we left behind the immutable Vector class and worked on implementing a BingoCage subclass to support += for adding items to the random pool, similar to the way the list built-in supports += as a shortcut for the list.extend() method. While doing this, we discussed how + tends to be stricter than += regarding the types it accepts. For sequence types, + usually requires that both operands are of the same type, while += often accepts any iterable as the righthand operand.

Further Reading

Guido van Rossum wrote a good defense of operator overloading in "Why operators are useful" (*https://fpy.li/16-10*). Trey Hunner blogged "Tuple ordering and deep comparisons in Python" (*https://fpy.li/16-11*), arguing that the rich comparison operators in Python are more flexible and powerful than programmers may realize when coming from other languages.

Operator overloading is one area of Python programming where isinstance tests are common. The best practice around such tests is goose typing, covered in "Goose Typing" on page 444. If you skipped that, make sure to read it.

The main reference for the operator special methods is the "Data Model" chapter (*https://fpy.li/dtmodel*) of the Python documentation. Another relevant reading is "9.1.2.2. Implementing the arithmetic operations" (*https://fpy.li/16-7*) in the numbers module of *The Python Standard Library*.

A clever example of operator overloading appeared in the pathlib (*https://fpy.li/16-13*) package, added in Python 3.4. Its Path class overloads the / operator to build filesystem paths from strings, as shown in this example from the documentation:

```
>>> p = Path('/etc')
>>> q = p / 'init.d' / 'reboot'
>>> q
PosixPath('/etc/init.d/reboot')
```

Another nonarithmetic example of operator overloading is in the Scapy (*https://fpy.li/16-14*) library, used to "send, sniff, dissect, and forge network packets." In Scapy, the / operator builds packets by stacking fields from different network layers. See "Stacking layers" (*https://fpy.li/16-15*) for details.

If you are about to implement comparison operators, study functools.total_order ing. That is a class decorator that automatically generates methods for all rich comparison operators in any class that defines at least a couple of them. See the functools module docs (*https://fpy.li/16-16*).

If you are curious about operator method dispatching in languages with dynamic typing, two seminal readings are "A Simple Technique for Handling Multiple Polymorphism" (*https://fpy.li/16-17*) by Dan Ingalls (member of the original Smalltalk team), and "Arithmetic and Double Dispatching in Smalltalk-80" (*https://fpy.li/16-18*) by Kurt J. Hebel and Ralph Johnson (Johnson became famous as one of the authors of the original *Design Patterns* book). Both papers provide deep insight into the power of polymorphism in languages with dynamic typing, like Smalltalk, Python, and Ruby. Python does not use double dispatching for handling operators as described in those articles. The Python algorithm using forward and reverse operators is easier for user-defined classes to support than double dispatching, but requires special handling by the interpreter. In contrast, classic double dispatching is a general technique you can use in Python or any object-oriented language beyond the specific context of infix operators, and in fact Ingalls, Hebel, and Johnson use very different examples to describe it.

The article, "The C Family of Languages: Interview with Dennis Ritchie, Bjarne Stroustrup, and James Gosling" (*https://fpy.li/16-1*), from which I quoted the epigraph for this chapter, appeared in *Java Report*, 5(7), July 2000, and *C++ Report*, 12(7), July/August 2000, along with two other snippets I used in this chapter's "Soapbox" (next). If you are into programming language design, do yourself a favor and read that interview.

Soapbox

Operator Overloading: Pros and Cons

James Gosling, quoted at the start of this chapter, made the conscious decision to leave operator overloading out when he designed Java. In that same interview ("The C Family of Languages: Interview with Dennis Ritchie, Bjarne Stroustrup, and James Gosling" (*https://fpy.li/16-20*)) he says:

> Probably about 20 to 30 percent of the population think of operator overloading as the spawn of the devil; somebody has done something with operator overloading that has just really ticked them off, because they've used like + for list insertion and it makes life really, really confusing. A lot of that problem stems from the fact that there are only about half a dozen operators you can sensibly overload, and yet there are thousands or millions of operators that people would like to define—so you have to pick, and often the choices conflict with your sense of intuition.

Guido van Rossum picked the middle way in supporting operator overloading: he did not leave the door open for users creating new arbitrary operators like <=> or :-), which prevents a Tower of Babel of custom operators, and allows the Python parser to be simple. Python also does not let you overload the operators of the built-in types, another limitation that promotes readability and predictable performance.

Gosling goes on to say:

> Then there's a community of about 10 percent that have actually used operator overloading appropriately and who really care about it, and for whom it's actually really important; this is almost exclusively people who do numerical work, where the notation is very important to appealing to people's intuition, because they come into it with an intuition about what the + means, and the ability to say "a + b" where a and b are complex numbers or matrices or something really does make sense.

Of course, there are benefits to disallowing operator overloading in a language. I've seen the argument that C is better than C++ for systems programming because operator overloading in C++ can make costly operations seem trivial. Two successful

---

modern languages that compile to binary executables made opposite choices: Go doesn't have operator overloading, but Rust does (*https://fpy.li/16-21*).

But overloaded operators, when used sensibly, do make code easier to read and write. It's a great feature to have in a modern high-level language.

A Glimpse at Lazy Evaluation

If you look closely at the traceback in Example 16-9, you'll see evidence of the *lazy* (*https://fpy.li/16-22*) evaluation of generator expressions. Example 16-20 is that same traceback, now with callouts.

Example 16-20. Same as Example 16-9

```
>>> v1 + 'ABC'
Traceback (most recent call last):
  File "<stdin>", line 1, in <module>
  File "vector_v6.py", line 329, in __add__
    return Vector(a + b for a, b in pairs)  ❶
  File "vector_v6.py", line 243, in __init__
    self._components = array(self.typecode, components)  ❷
  File "vector_v6.py", line 329, in <genexpr>
    return Vector(a + b for a, b in pairs)  ❸
TypeError: unsupported operand type(s) for +: 'float' and 'str'
```

❶ The Vector call gets a generator expression as its components argument. No problem at this stage.

❷ The components genexp is passed to the array constructor. Within the array constructor, Python tries to iterate over the genexp, causing the evaluation of the first item a + b. That's when the TypeError occurs.

❸ The exception propagates to the Vector constructor call, where it is reported.

This shows how the generator expression is evaluated at the latest possible moment, and not where it is defined in the source code.

In contrast, if the Vector constructor was invoked as Vector([a + b for a, b in pairs]), then the exception would happen right there, because the list comprehension tried to build a list to be passed as the argument to the Vector() call. The body of Vector.__init__ would not be reached at all.

Chapter 17 will cover generator expressions in detail, but I did not want to let this accidental demonstration of their lazy nature go unnoticed.

## PART IV

Control Flow

Iterators, Generators, and Classic Coroutines

When I see patterns in my programs, I consider it a sign of trouble. The shape of a program should reflect only the problem it needs to solve. Any other regularity in the code is a sign, to me at least, that I'm using abstractions that aren't powerful enough—often that I'm generating by hand the expansions of some macro that I need to write.

—Paul Graham, Lisp hacker and venture capitalist[1]

Iteration is fundamental to data processing: programs apply computations to data series, from pixels to nucleotides. If the data doesn't fit in memory, we need to fetch the items *lazily*—one at a time and on demand. That's what an iterator does. This chapter shows how the *Iterator* design pattern is built into the Python language so you never need to code it by hand.

Every standard collection in Python is *iterable*. An *iterable* is an object that provides an *iterator*, which Python uses to support operations like:

- for loops
- List, dict, and set comprehensions
- Unpacking assignments
- Construction of collection instances

---

1 From "Revenge of the Nerds" (*https://fpy.li/17-1*), a blog post.

This chapter covers the following topics:

- How Python uses the `iter()` built-in function to handle iterable objects
- How to implement the classic Iterator pattern in Python
- How the classic Iterator pattern can be replaced by a generator function or generator expression
- How a generator function works in detail, with line-by-line descriptions
- Leveraging the general-purpose generator functions in the standard library
- Using `yield from` expressions to combine generators
- Why generators and classic coroutines look alike but are used in very different ways and should not be mixed

What's New in This Chapter

"Subgenerators with yield from" on page 636 grew from one to six pages. It now includes simpler experiments demonstrating the behavior of generators with `yield from`, and an example of traversing a tree data structure, developed step-by-step.

New sections explain the type hints for `Iterable`, `Iterator`, and `Generator` types.

The last major section of this chapter, "Classic Coroutines" on page 645, is a 9-page introduction to a topic that filled a 40-page chapter in the first edition. I updated and moved the "Classic Coroutines" chapter to a post in the companion website (*https://fpy.li/oldcoro*) because it was the most challenging chapter for readers, but its subject matter is less relevant after Python 3.5 introduced native coroutines—which we'll study in Chapter 21.

We'll get started studying how the `iter()` built-in function makes sequences iterable.

A Sequence of Words

We'll start our exploration of iterables by implementing a `Sentence` class: you give its constructor a string with some text, and then you can iterate word by word. The first version will implement the sequence protocol, and it's iterable because all sequences are iterable—as we've seen since Chapter 1. Now we'll see exactly why.

Example 17-1 shows a `Sentence` class that extracts words from a text by index.

Example 17-1. sentence.py: a Sentence as a sequence of words

```
import re
import reprlib
```

```
RE_WORD = re.compile(r'\w+')

class Sentence:

    def __init__(self, text):
        self.text = text
        self.words = RE_WORD.findall(text)    ❶

    def __getitem__(self, index):
        return self.words[index]    ❷

    def __len__(self):    ❸
        return len(self.words)

    def __repr__(self):
        return 'Sentence(%s)' % reprlib.repr(self.text)    ❹
```

❶ `.findall` returns a list with all nonoverlapping matches of the regular expression, as a list of strings.

❷ `self.words` holds the result of `.findall`, so we simply return the word at the given index.

❸ To complete the sequence protocol, we implement `__len__` although it is not needed to make an iterable.

❹ `reprlib.repr` is a utility function to generate abbreviated string representations of data structures that can be very large.[2]

By default, `reprlib.repr` limits the generated string to 30 characters. See the console session in Example 17-2 to see how Sentence is used.

Example 17-2. Testing iteration on a Sentence instance

```
>>> s = Sentence('"The time has come," the Walrus said,')    ❶
>>> s
Sentence('"The time ha... Walrus said,')    ❷
>>> for word in s:    ❸
...     print(word)
The
time
has
come
```

---

2 We first used `reprlib` in "Vector Take #1: Vector2d Compatible" on page 401.

```
the
Walrus
said
>>> list(s)  ❹
['The', 'time', 'has', 'come', 'the', 'Walrus', 'said']
```

❶ A sentence is created from a string.

❷ Note the output of __repr__ using ... generated by reprlib.repr.

❸ Sentence instances are iterable; we'll see why in a moment.

❹ Being iterable, Sentence objects can be used as input to build lists and other iterable types.

In the following pages, we'll develop other Sentence classes that pass the tests in Example 17-2. However, the implementation in Example 17-1 is different from the others because it's also a sequence, so you can get words by index:

```
>>> s[0]
'The'
>>> s[5]
'Walrus'
>>> s[-1]
'said'
```

Python programmers know that sequences are iterable. Now we'll see precisely why.

Why Sequences Are Iterable: The iter Function

Whenever Python needs to iterate over an object x, it automatically calls iter(x).

The iter built-in function:

1. Checks whether the object implements __iter__, and calls that to obtain an iterator.

2. If __iter__ is not implemented, but __getitem__ is, then iter() creates an iterator that tries to fetch items by index, starting from 0 (zero).

3. If that fails, Python raises TypeError, usually saying 'C' object is not iterable, where C is the class of the target object.

That is why all Python sequences are iterable: by definition, they all implement __getitem__. In fact, the standard sequences also implement __iter__, and yours should too, because iteration via __getitem__ exists for backward compatibility and may be gone in the future—although it is not deprecated as of Python 3.10, and I doubt it will ever be removed.

As mentioned in "Python Digs Sequences" on page 438, this is an extreme form of duck typing: an object is considered iterable not only when it implements the special method __iter__, but also when it implements __getitem__. Take a look:

```
>>> class Spam:
...     def __getitem__(self, i):
...         print('->', i)
...         raise IndexError()
...
>>> spam_can = Spam()
>>> iter(spam_can)
<iterator object at 0x10a878f70>
>>> list(spam_can)
-> 0
[]
>>> from collections import abc
>>> isinstance(spam_can, abc.Iterable)
False
```

If a class provides __getitem__, the iter() built-in accepts an instance of that class as iterable and builds an iterator from the instance. Python's iteration machinery will call __getitem__ with indexes starting from 0, and will take an IndexError as a signal that there are no more items.

Note that although spam_can is iterable (its __getitem__ could provide items), it is not recognized as such by an isinstance against abc.Iterable.

In the goose-typing approach, the definition for an iterable is simpler but not as flexible: an object is considered iterable if it implements the __iter__ method. No subclassing or registration is required, because abc.Iterable implements the __subclasshook__, as seen in "Structural Typing with ABCs" on page 466. Here is a demonstration:

```
>>> class GooseSpam:
...     def __iter__(self):
...         pass
...
>>> from collections import abc
>>> issubclass(GooseSpam, abc.Iterable)
True
>>> goose_spam_can = GooseSpam()
>>> isinstance(goose_spam_can, abc.Iterable)
True
```

 As of Python 3.10, the most accurate way to check whether an object x is iterable is to call iter(x) and handle a TypeError exception if it isn't. This is more accurate than using isinstance(x, abc.Iterable), because iter(x) also considers the legacy __getitem__ method, while the Iterable ABC does not.

Explicitly checking whether an object is iterable may not be worthwhile if right after the check you are going to iterate over the object. After all, when the iteration is attempted on a noniterable, the exception Python raises is clear enough: `TypeError: 'C' object is not iterable`. If you can do better than just raising `TypeError`, then do so in a `try/except` block instead of doing an explicit check. The explicit check may make sense if you are holding on to the object to iterate over it later; in this case, catching the error early makes debugging easier.

The `iter()` built-in is more often used by Python itself than by our own code. There's a second way we can use it, but it's not widely known.

Using iter with a Callable

We can call `iter()` with two arguments to create an iterator from a function or any callable object. In this usage, the first argument must be a callable to be invoked repeatedly (with no arguments) to produce values, and the second argument is a *sentinel* (*https://fpy.li/17-2*): a marker value which, when returned by the callable, causes the iterator to raise `StopIteration` instead of yielding the sentinel.

The following example shows how to use `iter` to roll a six-sided die until a 1 is rolled:

```
>>> def d6():
...     return randint(1, 6)
...
>>> d6_iter = iter(d6, 1)
>>> d6_iter
<callable_iterator object at 0x10a245270>
>>> for roll in d6_iter:
...     print(roll)
...
4
3
6
3
```

Note that the `iter` function here returns a `callable_iterator`. The `for` loop in the example may run for a very long time, but it will never display 1, because that is the sentinel value. As usual with iterators, the `d6_iter` object in the example becomes useless once exhausted. To start over, we must rebuild the iterator by invoking `iter()` again.

The documentation for `iter` (*https://fpy.li/17-3*) includes the following explanation and example code:

> One useful application of the second form of `iter()` is to build a block-reader. For example, reading fixed-width blocks from a binary database file until the end of file is reached:

```
from functools import partial

with open('mydata.db', 'rb') as f:
    read64 = partial(f.read, 64)
    for block in iter(read64, b''):
        process_block(block)
```

For clarity, I've added the `read64` assignment, which is not in the original example (*https://fpy.li/17-3*). The `partial()` function is necessary because the callable given to `iter()` must not require arguments. In the example, an empty `bytes` object is the sentinel, because that's what `f.read` returns when there are no more bytes to read.

The next section details the relationship between iterables and iterators.

Iterables Versus Iterators

From the explanation in "Why Sequences Are Iterable: The iter Function" on page 600 we can extrapolate a definition:

iterable

Any object from which the `iter` built-in function can obtain an iterator. Objects implementing an `__iter__` method returning an *iterator* are iterable. Sequences are always iterable, as are objects implementing a `__getitem__` method that accepts 0-based indexes.

It's important to be clear about the relationship between iterables and iterators: Python obtains iterators from iterables.

Here is a simple `for` loop iterating over a `str`. The `str 'ABC'` is the iterable here. You don't see it, but there is an iterator behind the curtain:

```
>>> s = 'ABC'
>>> for char in s:
...     print(char)
...
A
B
C
```

If there was no `for` statement and we had to emulate the `for` machinery by hand with a `while` loop, this is what we'd have to write:

```
>>> s = 'ABC'
>>> it = iter(s)          ❶
>>> while True:
...     try:
...         print(next(it))    ❷
...     except StopIteration:  ❸
...         del it         ❹
...         break          ❺
```

```
...
A
B
C
```

❶ Build an iterator `it` from the iterable.

❷ Repeatedly call `next` on the iterator to obtain the next item.

❸ The iterator raises `StopIteration` when there are no further items.

❹ Release reference to `it`—the iterator object is discarded.

❺ Exit the loop.

`StopIteration` signals that the iterator is exhausted. This exception is handled internally by the `iter()` built-in that is part of the logic of `for` loops and other iteration contexts like list comprehensions, iterable unpacking, etc.

Python's standard interface for an iterator has two methods:

`__next__`
> Returns the next item in the series, raising `StopIteration` if there are no more.

`__iter__`
> Returns `self`; this allows iterators to be used where an iterable is expected, for example, in a `for` loop.

That interface is formalized in the `collections.abc.Iterator` ABC, which declares the `__next__` abstract method, and subclasses `Iterable`—where the abstract `__iter__` method is declared. See Figure 17-1.

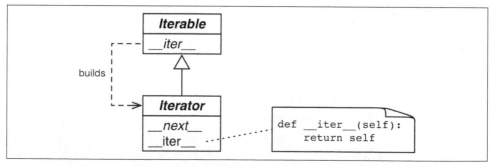

Figure 17-1. The `Iterable` and `Iterator` ABCs. Methods in italic are abstract. A concrete `Iterable.__iter__` should return a new `Iterator` instance. A concrete `Iterator` must implement `__next__`. The `Iterator.__iter__` method just returns the instance itself.

The source code for `collections.abc.Iterator` is in Example 17-3.

Example 17-3. abc.Iterator class; extracted from Lib/_collections_abc.py (https://fpy.li/17-5)

```
class Iterator(Iterable):

    __slots__ = ()

    @abstractmethod
    def __next__(self):
        'Return the next item from the iterator. When exhausted, raise StopIteration'
        raise StopIteration

    def __iter__(self):
        return self

    @classmethod
    def __subclasshook__(cls, C):      ❶
        if cls is Iterator:
            return _check_methods(C, '__iter__', '__next__')      ❷
        return NotImplemented
```

❶ `__subclasshook__` supports structural type checks with `isinstance` and `issub class`. We saw it in "Structural Typing with ABCs" on page 466.

❷ `_check_methods` traverses the `__mro__` of the class to check whether the methods are implemented in its base classes. It's defined in that same *Lib/_collections_abc.py* module. If the methods are implemented, the C class will be recognized as a virtual subclass of `Iterator`. In other words, `issubclass(C, Iterable)` will return `True`.

> The `Iterator` ABC abstract method is `it.__next__()` in Python 3 and `it.next()` in Python 2. As usual, you should avoid calling special methods directly. Just use the `next(it)`: this built-in function does the right thing in Python 2 and 3—which is useful for those migrating codebases from 2 to 3.

The *Lib/types.py* (https://fpy.li/17-6) module source code in Python 3.9 has a comment that says:

```
# Iterators in Python aren't a matter of type but of protocol. A large
# and changing number of builtin types implement *some* flavor of
# iterator. Don't check the type!  Use hasattr to check for both
# "__iter__" and "__next__" attributes instead.
```

In fact, that's exactly what the __subclasshook__ method of the abc.Iterator ABC does.

 Given the advice from *Lib/types.py* and the logic implemented in *Lib/_collections_abc.py*, the best way to check if an object x is an iterator is to call isinstance(x, abc.Iterator). Thanks to Iterator.__subclasshook__, this test works even if the class of x is not a real or virtual subclass of Iterator.

Back to our Sentence class from Example 17-1, you can clearly see how the iterator is built by iter() and consumed by next() using the Python console:

```
>>> s3 = Sentence('Life of Brian')  ❶
>>> it = iter(s3)  ❷
>>> it  # doctest: +ELLIPSIS
<iterator object at 0x...>
>>> next(it)  ❸
'Life'
>>> next(it)
'of'
>>> next(it)
'Brian'
>>> next(it)  ❹
Traceback (most recent call last):
  ...
StopIteration
>>> list(it)  ❺
[]
>>> list(iter(s3))  ❻
['Life', 'of', 'Brian']
```

❶ Create a sentence s3 with three words.

❷ Obtain an iterator from s3.

❸ next(it) fetches the next word.

❹ There are no more words, so the iterator raises a StopIteration exception.

❺ Once exhausted, an iterator will always raise StopIteration, which makes it look like it's empty.

❻ To go over the sentence again, a new iterator must be built.

Because the only methods required of an iterator are __next__ and __iter__, there is no way to check whether there are remaining items, other than to call next() and catch StopIteration. Also, it's not possible to "reset" an iterator. If you need to start over, you need to call iter() on the iterable that built the iterator in the first place. Calling iter() on the iterator itself won't help either, because—as mentioned— Iterator.__iter__ is implemented by returning self, so this will not reset a depleted iterator.

That minimal interface is sensible, because in reality not all iterators are resettable. For example, if an iterator is reading packets from the network, there's no way to rewind it.[3]

The first version of Sentence from Example 17-1 was iterable thanks to the special treatment the iter() built-in gives to sequences. Next, we will implement Sentence variations that implement __iter__ to return iterators.

Sentence Classes with __iter__

The next variations of Sentence implement the standard iterable protocol, first by implementing the Iterator design pattern, and then with generator functions.

Sentence Take #2: A Classic Iterator

The next Sentence implementation follows the blueprint of the classic Iterator design pattern from the *Design Patterns* book. Note that it is not idiomatic Python, as the next refactorings will make very clear. But it is useful to show the distinction between an iterable collection and an iterator that works with it.

The Sentence class in Example 17-4 is iterable because it implements the __iter__ special method, which builds and returns a SentenceIterator. That's how an iterable and an iterator are related.

Example 17-4. sentence_iter.py: Sentence implemented using the Iterator pattern

```
import re
import reprlib

RE_WORD = re.compile(r'\w+')


class Sentence:

    def __init__(self, text):
        self.text = text
        self.words = RE_WORD.findall(text)
```

---

3 Thanks to tech reviewer Leonardo Rochael for this fine example.

```
    def __repr__(self):
        return f'Sentence({reprlib.repr(self.text)})'

    def __iter__(self):  ❶
        return SentenceIterator(self.words)  ❷


class SentenceIterator:

    def __init__(self, words):
        self.words = words  ❸
        self.index = 0  ❹

    def __next__(self):
        try:
            word = self.words[self.index]  ❺
        except IndexError:
            raise StopIteration()  ❻
        self.index += 1  ❼
        return word  ❽

    def __iter__(self):  ❾
        return self
```

❶ The __iter__ method is the only addition to the previous Sentence implementation. This version has no __getitem__, to make it clear that the class is iterable because it implements __iter__.

❷ __iter__ fulfills the iterable protocol by instantiating and returning an iterator.

❸ SentenceIterator holds a reference to the list of words.

❹ self.index determines the next word to fetch.

❺ Get the word at self.index.

❻ If there is no word at self.index, raise StopIteration.

❼ Increment self.index.

❽ Return the word.

❾ Implement self.__iter__.

The code in Example 17-4 passes the tests in Example 17-2.

Note that implementing __iter__ in SentenceIterator is not actually needed for this example to work, but it is the right thing to do: iterators are supposed to implement both `__next__` and `__iter__`, and doing so makes our iterator pass the `issubclass(SentenceIterator, abc.Iterator)` test. If we had subclassed `SentenceIterator` from `abc.Iterator`, we'd inherit the concrete `abc.Iterator.__iter__` method.

That is a lot of work (for us spoiled Python programmers, anyway). Note how most code in `SentenceIterator` deals with managing the internal state of the iterator. Soon we'll see how to avoid that bookkeeping. But first, a brief detour to address an implementation shortcut that may be tempting, but is just wrong.

Don't Make the Iterable an Iterator for Itself

A common cause of errors in building iterables and iterators is to confuse the two. To be clear: iterables have an `__iter__` method that instantiates a new iterator every time. Iterators implement a `__next__` method that returns individual items, and an `__iter__` method that returns `self`.

Therefore, iterators are also iterable, but iterables are not iterators.

It may be tempting to implement `__next__` in addition to `__iter__` in the `Sentence` class, making each `Sentence` instance at the same time an iterable and iterator over itself. But this is rarely a good idea. It's also a common antipattern, according to Alex Martelli who has a lot of experience reviewing Python code at Google.

The "Applicability" section about the Iterator design pattern in the *Design Patterns* book says:

> Use the Iterator pattern
>
> - to access an aggregate object's contents without exposing its internal representation.
> - to support multiple traversals of aggregate objects.
> - to provide a uniform interface for traversing different aggregate structures (that is, to support polymorphic iteration).

To "support multiple traversals," it must be possible to obtain multiple independent iterators from the same iterable instance, and each iterator must keep its own internal state, so a proper implementation of the pattern requires each call to `iter(my_iterable)` to create a new, independent, iterator. That is why we need the `SentenceIterator` class in this example.

Now that the classic Iterator pattern is properly demonstrated, we can let it go. Python incorporated the `yield` keyword from Barbara Liskov's CLU language (*https://fpy.li/17-7*), so we don't need to "generate by hand" the code to implement iterators.

The next sections present more idiomatic versions of Sentence.

Sentence Take #3: A Generator Function

A Pythonic implementation of the same functionality uses a generator, avoiding all the work to implement the SentenceIterator class. A proper explanation of the generator comes right after Example 17-5.

Example 17-5. sentence_gen.py: Sentence implemented using a generator

```python
import re
import reprlib

RE_WORD = re.compile(r'\w+')


class Sentence:

    def __init__(self, text):
        self.text = text
        self.words = RE_WORD.findall(text)

    def __repr__(self):
        return 'Sentence(%s)' % reprlib.repr(self.text)

    def __iter__(self):
        for word in self.words:     ❶
            yield word     ❷
        ❸

# done!  ❹
```

❶ Iterate over self.words.

❷ Yield the current word.

❸ Explicit return is not necessary; the function can just "fall through" and return automatically. Either way, a generator function doesn't raise StopIteration: it simply exits when it's done producing values.[4]

---

[4] When reviewing this code, Alex Martelli suggested the body of this method could simply be return iter(self.words). He is right: the result of calling self.words.__iter__() would also be an iterator, as it should be. However, I used a for loop with yield here to introduce the syntax of a generator function, which requires the yield keyword, as we'll see in the next section. During review of the second edition of this book, Leonardo Rochael suggested yet another shortcut for the body of __iter__: yield from self.words. We'll also cover yield from later in this chapter.

---

❹ No need for a separate iterator class!

Here again we have a different implementation of Sentence that passes the tests in Example 17-2.

Back in the Sentence code in Example 17-4, __iter__ called the SentenceIterator constructor to build an iterator and return it. Now the iterator in Example 17-5 is in fact a generator object, built automatically when the __iter__ method is called, because __iter__ here is a generator function.

A full explanation of generators follows.

How a Generator Works

Any Python function that has the yield keyword in its body is a generator function: a function which, when called, returns a generator object. In other words, a generator function is a generator factory.

> The only syntax distinguishing a plain function from a generator function is the fact that the latter has a yield keyword somewhere in its body. Some argued that a new keyword like gen should be used instead of def to declare generator functions, but Guido did not agree. His arguments are in PEP 255 — Simple Generators (*https://fpy.li/pep255*).[5]

Example 17-6 shows the behavior of a simple generator function.[6]

Example 17-6. A generator function that yields three numbers

```
>>> def gen_123():
...     yield 1    ❶
...     yield 2
...     yield 3
...
>>> gen_123  # doctest: +ELLIPSIS
<function gen_123 at 0x...>    ❷
>>> gen_123()   # doctest: +ELLIPSIS
<generator object gen_123 at 0x...>    ❸
>>> for i in gen_123():    ❹
...     print(i)
```

---

5 Sometimes I add a gen prefix or suffix when naming generator functions, but this is not a common practice. And you can't do that if you're implementing an iterable, of course: the necessary special method must be named __iter__.

6 Thanks to David Kwast for suggesting this example.

```
1
2
3
>>> g = gen_123()  ❺
>>> next(g)  ❻
1
>>> next(g)
2
>>> next(g)
3
>>> next(g)  ❼
Traceback (most recent call last):
  ...
StopIteration
```

❶ The body of a generator function often has yield inside a loop, but not necessarily; here I just repeat yield three times.

❷ Looking closely, we see gen_123 is a function object.

❸ But when invoked, gen_123() returns a generator object.

❹ Generator objects implement the Iterator interface, so they are also iterable.

❺ We assign this new generator object to g, so we can experiment with it.

❻ Because g is an iterator, calling next(g) fetches the next item produced by yield.

❼ When the generator function returns, the generator object raises StopIteration.

A generator function builds a generator object that wraps the body of the function. When we invoke next() on the generator object, execution advances to the next yield in the function body, and the next() call evaluates to the value yielded when the function body is suspended. Finally, the enclosing generator object created by Python raises StopIteration when the function body returns, in accordance with the Iterator protocol.

I find it helpful to be rigorous when talking about values obtained from a generator. It's confusing to say a generator "returns" values. Functions return values. Calling a generator function returns a generator. A generator yields values. A generator doesn't "return" values in the usual way: the return statement in the body of a generator function causes StopIteration to be raised by the generator object. If you return x in the generator, the caller can retrieve the value of x from the StopIteration exception, but usually that is done automatically using the yield from syntax, as we'll see in "Returning a Value from a Coroutine" on page 650.

Example 17-7 makes the interaction between a for loop and the body of the function more explicit.

Example 17-7. A generator function that prints messages when it runs

```
>>> def gen_AB():
...     print('start')
...     yield 'A'            ❶
...     print('continue')
...     yield 'B'            ❷
...     print('end.')        ❸
...
>>> for c in gen_AB():       ❹
...     print('-->', c)      ❺
...
start         ❻
--> A         ❼
continue      ❽
--> B         ❾
end.          ❿
>>>           ⓫
```

❶ The first implicit call to next() in the for loop at ❹ will print 'start' and stop at the first yield, producing the value 'A'.

❷ The second implicit call to next() in the for loop will print 'continue' and stop at the second yield, producing the value 'B'.

❸ The third call to next() will print 'end.' and fall through the end of the function body, causing the generator object to raise StopIteration.

❹ To iterate, the for machinery does the equivalent of g = iter(gen_AB()) to get a generator object, and then next(g) at each iteration.

⑤ The loop prints `-->` and the value returned by `next(g)`. This output will appear only after the output of the `print` calls inside the generator function.

⑥ The text `start` comes from `print('start')` in the generator body.

⑦ `yield 'A'` in the generator body yields the value *A* consumed by the `for` loop, which gets assigned to the `c` variable and results in the output `--> A`.

⑧ Iteration continues with a second call to `next(g)`, advancing the generator body from `yield 'A'` to `yield 'B'`. The text `continue` is output by the second `print` in the generator body.

⑨ `yield 'B'` yields the value *B* consumed by the `for` loop, which gets assigned to the `c` loop variable, so the loop prints `--> B`.

⑩ Iteration continues with a third call to `next(it)`, advancing to the end of the body of the function. The text `end.` appears in the output because of the third `print` in the generator body.

⑪ When the generator function runs to the end, the generator object raises `StopIteration`. The `for` loop machinery catches that exception, and the loop terminates cleanly.

Now hopefully it's clear how `Sentence.__iter__` in Example 17-5 works: `__iter__` is a generator function which, when called, builds a generator object that implements the `Iterator` interface, so the `SentenceIterator` class is no longer needed.

That second version of `Sentence` is more concise than the first, but it's not as lazy as it could be. Nowadays, laziness is considered a good trait, at least in programming languages and APIs. A lazy implementation postpones producing values to the last possible moment. This saves memory and may avoid wasting CPU cycles, too.

We'll build lazy `Sentence` classes next.

Lazy Sentences

The final variations of `Sentence` are lazy, taking advantage of a lazy function from the `re` module.

Sentence Take #4: Lazy Generator

The `Iterator` interface is designed to be lazy: `next(my_iterator)` yields one item at a time. The opposite of lazy is eager: lazy evaluation and eager evaluation are technical terms in programming language theory.

Our Sentence implementations so far have not been lazy because the __init__ eagerly builds a list of all words in the text, binding it to the self.words attribute. This requires processing the entire text, and the list may use as much memory as the text itself (probably more; it depends on how many nonword characters are in the text). Most of this work will be in vain if the user only iterates over the first couple of words. If you wonder, "Is there a lazy way of doing this in Python?" the answer is often "Yes."

The re.finditer function is a lazy version of re.findall. Instead of a list, re.fin diter returns a generator yielding re.MatchObject instances on demand. If there are many matches, re.finditer saves a lot of memory. Using it, our third version of Sentence is now lazy: it only reads the next word from the text when it is needed. The code is in Example 17-8.

Example 17-8. sentence_gen2.py: Sentence implemented using a generator function calling the re.finditer generator function

```
import re
import reprlib

RE_WORD = re.compile(r'\w+')


class Sentence:

    def __init__(self, text):
        self.text = text       ❶

    def __repr__(self):
        return f'Sentence({reprlib.repr(self.text)})'

    def __iter__(self):
        for match in RE_WORD.finditer(self.text):   ❷
            yield match.group()   ❸
```

❶ No need to have a words list.

❷ finditer builds an iterator over the matches of RE_WORD on self.text, yielding MatchObject instances.

❸ match.group() extracts the matched text from the MatchObject instance.

Generators are a great shortcut, but the code can be made even more concise with a generator expression.

Sentence Take #5: Lazy Generator Expression

We can replace simple generator functions like the one in the previous Sentence class (Example 17-8) with a generator expression. As a list comprehension builds lists, a generator expression builds generator objects. Example 17-9 contrasts their behavior.

Example 17-9. The gen_AB generator function is used by a list comprehension, then by a generator expression

```
>>> def gen_AB():  ❶
...     print('start')
...     yield 'A'
...     print('continue')
...     yield 'B'
...     print('end.')
...
>>> res1 = [x*3 for x in gen_AB()]  ❷
start
continue
end.
>>> for i in res1:  ❸
...     print('-->', i)
...
--> AAA
--> BBB
>>> res2 = (x*3 for x in gen_AB())  ❹
>>> res2
<generator object <genexpr> at 0x10063c240>
>>> for i in res2:  ❺
...     print('-->', i)
...
start       ❻
--> AAA
continue
--> BBB
end.
```

❶ This is the same gen_AB function from Example 17-7.

❷ The list comprehension eagerly iterates over the items yielded by the generator object returned by gen_AB(): 'A' and 'B'. Note the output in the next lines: start, continue, end.

❸ This for loop iterates over the res1 list built by the list comprehension.

❹ The generator expression returns res2, a generator object. The generator is not consumed here.

❺ Only when the for loop iterates over res2, this generator gets items from gen_AB. Each iteration of the for loop implicitly calls next(res2), which in turn calls next() on the generator object returned by gen_AB(), advancing it to the next yield.

❻ Note how the output of gen_AB() interleaves with the output of the print in the for loop.

We can use a generator expression to further reduce the code in the Sentence class. See Example 17-10.

Example 17-10. sentence_genexp.py: Sentence implemented using a generator expression

```python
import re
import reprlib

RE_WORD = re.compile(r'\w+')


class Sentence:

    def __init__(self, text):
        self.text = text

    def __repr__(self):
        return f'Sentence({reprlib.repr(self.text)})'

    def __iter__(self):
        return (match.group() for match in RE_WORD.finditer(self.text))
```

The only difference from Example 17-8 is the __iter__ method, which here is not a generator function (it has no yield) but uses a generator expression to build a generator and then returns it. The end result is the same: the caller of __iter__ gets a generator object.

Generator expressions are syntactic sugar: they can always be replaced by generator functions, but sometimes are more convenient. The next section is about generator expression usage.

When to Use Generator Expressions

I used several generator expressions when implementing the Vector class in Example 12-16. Each of these methods has a generator expression: __eq__, __hash__, __abs__, angle, angles, format, __add__, and __mul__. In all those methods, a list comprehension would also work, at the cost of using more memory to store the intermediate list values.

In Example 17-10, we saw that a generator expression is a syntactic shortcut to create a generator without defining and calling a function. On the other hand, generator functions are more flexible: we can code complex logic with multiple statements, and we can even use them as *coroutines*, as we'll see in "Classic Coroutines" on page 645.

For the simpler cases, a generator expression is easier to read at a glance, as the Vector example shows.

My rule of thumb in choosing the syntax to use is simple: if the generator expression spans more than a couple of lines, I prefer to code a generator function for the sake of readability.

Syntax Tip

When a generator expression is passed as the single argument to a function or constructor, you don't need to write a set of parentheses for the function call and another to enclose the generator expression. A single pair will do, like in the Vector call from the __mul__ method in Example 12-16, reproduced here:

```
def __mul__(self, scalar):
    if isinstance(scalar, numbers.Real):
        return Vector(n * scalar for n in self)
    else:
        return NotImplemented
```

However, if there are more function arguments after the generator expression, you need to enclose it in parentheses to avoid a Syntax Error.

The Sentence examples we've seen demonstrate generators playing the role of the classic Iterator pattern: retrieving items from a collection. But we can also use generators to yield values independent of a data source. The next section shows an example.

But first, a short discussion on the overlapping concepts of *iterator* and *generator*.

Contrasting Iterators and Generators

In the official Python documentation and codebase, the terminology around iterators and generators is inconsistent and evolving. I've adopted the following definitions:

iterator
> General term for any object that implements a __next__ method. Iterators are designed to produce data that is consumed by the client code, i.e., the code that drives the iterator via a for loop or other iterative feature, or by explicitly calling

next(it) on the iterator—although this explicit usage is much less common. In practice, most iterators we use in Python are *generators*.

generator
> An iterator built by the Python compiler. To create a generator, we don't implement __next__. Instead, we use the yield keyword to make a *generator function*, which is a factory of *generator objects*. A *generator expression* is another way to build a generator object. Generator objects provide __next__, so they are iterators. Since Python 3.5, we also have *asynchronous generators* declared with async def. We'll study them in Chapter 21, "Asynchronous Programming".

The *Python Glossary* (*https://fpy.li/17-8*) recently introduced the term *generator iterator* (*https://fpy.li/17-9*) to refer to generator objects built by generator functions, while the entry for *generator expression* (*https://fpy.li/17-10*) says it returns an "iterator."

But the objects returned in both cases are generator objects, according to Python:

```
>>> def g():
...     yield 0
...
>>> g()
<generator object g at 0x10e6fb290>
>>> ge = (c for c in 'XYZ')
>>> ge
<generator object <genexpr> at 0x10e936ce0>
>>> type(g()), type(ge)
(<class 'generator'>, <class 'generator'>)
```

An Arithmetic Progression Generator

The classic Iterator pattern is all about traversal: navigating some data structure. But a standard interface based on a method to fetch the next item in a series is also useful when the items are produced on the fly, instead of retrieved from a collection. For example, the range built-in generates a bounded arithmetic progression (AP) of integers. What if you need to generate an AP of numbers of any type, not only integers?

Example 17-11 shows a few console tests of an ArithmeticProgression class we will see in a moment. The signature of the constructor in Example 17-11 is Arithmetic Progression(begin, step[, end]). The complete signature of the range built-in is range(start, stop[, step]). I chose to implement a different signature because the step is mandatory but end is optional in an arithmetic progression. I also changed the argument names from start/stop to begin/end to make it clear that I opted for a different signature. In each test in Example 17-11, I call list() on the result to inspect the generated values.

Example 17-11. Demonstration of an `ArithmeticProgression` class

```
>>> ap = ArithmeticProgression(0, 1, 3)
>>> list(ap)
[0, 1, 2]
>>> ap = ArithmeticProgression(1, .5, 3)
>>> list(ap)
[1.0, 1.5, 2.0, 2.5]
>>> ap = ArithmeticProgression(0, 1/3, 1)
>>> list(ap)
[0.0, 0.3333333333333333, 0.6666666666666666]
>>> from fractions import Fraction
>>> ap = ArithmeticProgression(0, Fraction(1, 3), 1)
>>> list(ap)
[Fraction(0, 1), Fraction(1, 3), Fraction(2, 3)]
>>> from decimal import Decimal
>>> ap = ArithmeticProgression(0, Decimal('.1'), .3)
>>> list(ap)
[Decimal('0'), Decimal('0.1'), Decimal('0.2')]
```

Note that the type of the numbers in the resulting arithmetic progression follows the type of `begin + step`, according to the numeric coercion rules of Python arithmetic. In Example 17-11, you see lists of `int`, `float`, `Fraction`, and `Decimal` numbers. Example 17-12 lists the implementation of the `ArithmeticProgression` class.

Example 17-12. The `ArithmeticProgression` class

```
class ArithmeticProgression:

    def __init__(self, begin, step, end=None):        ❶
        self.begin = begin
        self.step = step
        self.end = end   # None -> "infinite" series

    def __iter__(self):
        result_type = type(self.begin + self.step)    ❷
        result = result_type(self.begin)              ❸
        forever = self.end is None                    ❹
        index = 0
        while forever or result < self.end:           ❺
            yield result                              ❻
            index += 1
            result = self.begin + self.step * index   ❼
```

❶ `__init__` requires two arguments: `begin` and `step`; end is optional, if it's None, the series will be unbounded.

❷ Get the type of adding `self.begin` and `self.step`. For example, if one is `int` and the other is `float`, `result_type` will be `float`.

❸ This line makes a `result` with the same numeric value of `self.begin`, but coerced to the type of the subsequent additions.[7]

❹ For readability, the `forever` flag will be `True` if the `self.end` attribute is `None`, resulting in an unbounded series.

❺ This loop runs `forever` or until the result matches or exceeds `self.end`. When this loop exits, so does the function.

❻ The current `result` is produced.

❼ The next potential result is calculated. It may never be yielded, because the `while` loop may terminate.

In the last line of Example 17-12, instead of adding `self.step` to the previous `result` each time around the loop, I opted to ignore the previous `result` and each new `result` by adding `self.begin` to `self.step` multiplied by `index`. This avoids the cumulative effect of floating-point errors after successive additions. These simple experiments make the difference clear:

```
>>> 100 * 1.1
110.00000000000001
>>> sum(1.1 for _ in range(100))
109.99999999999982
>>> 1000 * 1.1
1100.0
>>> sum(1.1 for _ in range(1000))
1100.0000000000086
```

The `ArithmeticProgression` class from Example 17-12 works as intended, and is a another example of using a generator function to implement the `__iter__` special method. However, if the whole point of a class is to build a generator by implementing `__iter__`, we can replace the class with a generator function. A generator function is, after all, a generator factory.

---

7 In Python 2, there was a `coerce()` built-in function, but it's gone in Python 3. It was deemed unnecessary because the numeric coercion rules are implicit in the arithmetic operator methods. So the best way I could think of to coerce the initial value to be of the same type as the rest of the series was to perform the addition and use its type to convert the result. I asked about this in the Python-list and got an excellent response from Steven D'Aprano (*https://fpy.li/17-11*).

Example 17-13 shows a generator function called `aritprog_gen` that does the same job as `ArithmeticProgression` but with less code. The tests in Example 17-11 all pass if you just call `aritprog_gen` instead of `ArithmeticProgression`.[8]

Example 17-13. The aritprog_gen generator function

```
def aritprog_gen(begin, step, end=None):
    result = type(begin + step)(begin)
    forever = end is None
    index = 0
    while forever or result < end:
        yield result
        index += 1
        result = begin + step * index
```

Example 17-13 is elegant, but always remember: there are plenty of ready-to-use generators in the standard library, and the next section will show a shorter implementation using the `itertools` module.

Arithmetic Progression with itertools

The `itertools` module in Python 3.10 has 20 generator functions that can be combined in a variety of interesting ways.

For example, the `itertools.count` function returns a generator that yields numbers. Without arguments, it yields a series of integers starting with 0. But you can provide optional `start` and `step` values to achieve a result similar to our `aritprog_gen` functions:

```
>>> import itertools
>>> gen = itertools.count(1, .5)
>>> next(gen)
1
>>> next(gen)
1.5
>>> next(gen)
2.0
>>> next(gen)
2.5
```

---

8 The *17-it-generator/* directory in the *Fluent Python* code repository (*https://fpy.li/code*) includes doctests and a script, *aritprog_runner.py*, which runs the tests against all variations of the *aritprog*.py* scripts.

`itertools.count` never stops, so if you call `list(count())`, Python will try to build a `list` that would fill all the memory chips ever made. In practice, your machine will become very grumpy long before the call fails.

On the other hand, there is the `itertools.takewhile` function: it returns a generator that consumes another generator and stops when a given predicate evaluates to `False`. So we can combine the two and write this:

```
>>> gen = itertools.takewhile(lambda n: n < 3, itertools.count(1, .5))
>>> list(gen)
[1, 1.5, 2.0, 2.5]
```

Leveraging `takewhile` and `count`, Example 17-14 is even more concise.

Example 17-14. aritprog_v3.py: this works like the previous aritprog_gen functions

```python
import itertools


def aritprog_gen(begin, step, end=None):
    first = type(begin + step)(begin)
    ap_gen = itertools.count(first, step)
    if end is None:
        return ap_gen
    return itertools.takewhile(lambda n: n < end, ap_gen)
```

Note that `aritprog_gen` in Example 17-14 is not a generator function: it has no `yield` in its body. But it returns a generator, just as a generator function does.

However, recall that `itertools.count` adds the `step` repeatedly, so the floating-point series it produces are not as precise as Example 17-13.

The point of Example 17-14 is: when implementing generators, know what is available in the standard library, otherwise there's a good chance you'll reinvent the wheel. That's why the next section covers several ready-to-use generator functions.

Generator Functions in the Standard Library

The standard library provides many generators, from plain-text file objects providing line-by-line iteration, to the awesome `os.walk` (*https://fpy.li/17 12*) function, which yields filenames while traversing a directory tree, making recursive filesystem searches as simple as a `for` loop.

The `os.walk` generator function is impressive, but in this section I want to focus on general-purpose functions that take arbitrary iterables as arguments and return generators that yield selected, computed, or rearranged items. In the following tables, I summarize two dozen of them, from the built-in, `itertools`, and `functools` modules. For convenience, I grouped them by high-level functionality, regardless of where they are defined.

The first group contains the filtering generator functions: they yield a subset of items produced by the input iterable, without changing the items themselves. Like `take while`, most functions listed in Table 17-1 take a `predicate`, which is a one-argument Boolean function that will be applied to each item in the input to determine whether the item is included in the output.

Table 17-1. Filtering generator functions

Module	Function	Description
itertools	compress(it, selector_it)	Consumes two iterables in parallel; yields items from `it` whenever the corresponding item in `selector_it` is truthy
itertools	dropwhile(predicate, it)	Consumes `it`, skipping items while `predicate` computes truthy, then yields every remaining item (no further checks are made)
(built-in)	filter(predicate, it)	Applies `predicate` to each item of `iterable`, yielding the item if `predicate(item)` is truthy; if `predicate` is None, only truthy items are yielded
itertools	filterfalse(predicate, it)	Same as `filter`, with the `predicate` logic negated: yields items whenever `predicate` computes falsy
itertools	islice(it, stop) or islice(it, start, stop, step=1)	Yields items from a slice of `it`, similar to `s[:stop]` or `s[start:stop:step]` except `it` can be any iterable, and the operation is lazy
itertools	takewhile(predicate, it)	Yields items while `predicate` computes truthy, then stops and no further checks are made

The console listing in Example 17-15 shows the use of all the functions in Table 17-1.

Example 17-15. Filtering generator functions examples

```
>>> def vowel(c):
...     return c.lower() in 'aeiou'
...
>>> list(filter(vowel, 'Aardvark'))
['A', 'a', 'a']
>>> import itertools
>>> list(itertools.filterfalse(vowel, 'Aardvark'))
['r', 'd', 'v', 'r', 'k']
>>> list(itertools.dropwhile(vowel, 'Aardvark'))
['r', 'd', 'v', 'a', 'r', 'k']
>>> list(itertools.takewhile(vowel, 'Aardvark'))
['A', 'a']
>>> list(itertools.compress('Aardvark', (1, 0, 1, 1, 0, 1)))
```

```
['A', 'r', 'd', 'a']
>>> list(itertools.islice('Aardvark', 4))
['A', 'a', 'r', 'd']
>>> list(itertools.islice('Aardvark', 4, 7))
['v', 'a', 'r']
>>> list(itertools.islice('Aardvark', 1, 7, 2))
['a', 'd', 'a']
```

The next group contains the mapping generators: they yield items computed from each individual item in the input iterable—or iterables, in the case of map and star map.[9] The generators in Table 17-2 yield one result per item in the input iterables. If the input comes from more than one iterable, the output stops as soon as the first input iterable is exhausted.

Table 17-2. Mapping generator functions

Module	Function	Description
itertools	accumulate(it, [func])	Yields accumulated sums; if func is provided, yields the result of applying it to the first pair of items, then to the first result and next item, etc.
(built-in)	enumerate(iterable, start=0)	Yields 2-tuples of the form (index, item), where index is counted from start, and item is taken from the iterable
(built-in)	map(func, it1, [it2, …, itN])	Applies func to each item of it, yielding the result; if N iterables are given, func must take N arguments and the iterables will be consumed in parallel
itertools	starmap(func, it)	Applies func to each item of it, yielding the result; the input iterable should yield iterable items iit, and func is applied as func(*iit)

Example 17-16 demonstrates some uses of itertools.accumulate.

Example 17-16. itertools.accumulate generator function examples

```
>>> sample = [5, 4, 2, 8, 7, 6, 3, 0, 9, 1]
>>> import itertools
>>> list(itertools.accumulate(sample))    ❶
[5, 9, 11, 19, 26, 32, 35, 35, 44, 45]
>>> list(itertools.accumulate(sample, min))    ❷
[5, 4, 2, 2, 2, 2, 2, 0, 0, 0]
>>> list(itertools.accumulate(sample, max))    ❸
[5, 5, 5, 8, 8, 8, 8, 8, 9, 9]
>>> import operator
>>> list(itertools.accumulate(sample, operator.mul))    ❹
[5, 20, 40, 320, 2240, 13440, 40320, 0, 0, 0]
```

---

9 Here, the term "mapping" is unrelated to dictionaries, but has to do with the map built-in.

```
>>> list(itertools.accumulate(range(1, 11), operator.mul))
[1, 2, 6, 24, 120, 720, 5040, 40320, 362880, 3628800]  ❺
```

❶ Running sum.

❷ Running minimum.

❸ Running maximum.

❹ Running product.

❺ Factorials from 1! to 10!.

The remaining functions of Table 17-2 are shown in Example 17-17.

Example 17-17. Mapping generator function examples

```
>>> list(enumerate('albatroz', 1))  ❶
[(1, 'a'), (2, 'l'), (3, 'b'), (4, 'a'), (5, 't'), (6, 'r'), (7, 'o'), (8, 'z')]
>>> import operator
>>> list(map(operator.mul, range(11), range(11)))  ❷
[0, 1, 4, 9, 16, 25, 36, 49, 64, 81, 100]
>>> list(map(operator.mul, range(11), [2, 4, 8]))  ❸
[0, 4, 16]
>>> list(map(lambda a, b: (a, b), range(11), [2, 4, 8]))  ❹
[(0, 2), (1, 4), (2, 8)]
>>> import itertools
>>> list(itertools.starmap(operator.mul, enumerate('albatroz', 1)))  ❺
['a', 'll', 'bbb', 'aaaa', 'ttttt', 'rrrrrr', 'ooooooo', 'zzzzzzzz']
>>> sample = [5, 4, 2, 8, 7, 6, 3, 0, 9, 1]
>>> list(itertools.starmap(lambda a, b: b / a,
...      enumerate(itertools.accumulate(sample), 1)))  ❻
[5.0, 4.5, 3.6666666666666665, 4.75, 5.2, 5.333333333333333,
5.0, 4.375, 4.888888888888889, 4.5]
```

❶ Number the letters in the word, starting from 1.

❷ Squares of integers from 0 to 10.

❸ Multiplying numbers from two iterables in parallel: results stop when the short-est iterable ends.

❹ This is what the zip built-in function does.

❺ Repeat each letter in the word according to its place in it, starting from 1.

❻ Running average.

Next, we have the group of merging generators—all of these yield items from multiple input iterables. `chain` and `chain.from_iterable` consume the input iterables sequentially (one after the other), while `product`, `zip`, and `zip_longest` consume the input iterables in parallel. See Table 17-3.

Table 17-3. Generator functions that merge multiple input iterables

Module	Function	Description
itertools	chain(it1, …, itN)	Yields all items from it1, then from it2, etc., seamlessly
itertools	chain.from_iterable(it)	Yields all items from each iterable produced by it, one after the other, seamlessly; it will be an iterable where the items are also iterables, for example, a list of tuples
itertools	product(it1, …, itN, repeat=1)	Cartesian product: yields N-tuples made by combining items from each input iterable, like nested for loops could produce; repeat allows the input iterables to be consumed more than once
(built-in)	zip(it1, …, itN, strict=False)	Yields N-tuples built from items taken from the iterables in parallel, silently stopping when the first iterable is exhausted, unless strict=True is given[a]
itertools	zip_longest(it1, …, itN, fillvalue=None)	Yields N-tuples built from items taken from the iterables in parallel, stopping only when the last iterable is exhausted, filling the blanks with the fillvalue

[a] The strict keyword-only argument is new in Python 3.10. When strict=True, ValueError is raised if any iterable has a different length. The default is False, for backward compatibility.

Example 17-18 shows the use of the `itertools.chain` and `zip` generator functions and their siblings. Recall that the `zip` function is named after the zip fastener or zipper (no relation to compression). Both `zip` and `itertools.zip_longest` were introduced in "The Awesome zip" on page 418.

Example 17-18. Merging generator function examples

```
>>> list(itertools.chain('ABC', range(2)))   ❶
['A', 'B', 'C', 0, 1]
>>> list(itertools.chain(enumerate('ABC')))   ❷
[(0, 'A'), (1, 'B'), (2, 'C')]
>>> list(itertools.chain.from_iterable(enumerate('ABC')))   ❸
[0, 'A', 1, 'B', 2, 'C']
>>> list(zip('ABC', range(5), [10, 20, 30, 40]))   ❹
[('A', 0, 10), ('B', 1, 20), ('C', 2, 30)]
>>> list(itertools.zip_longest('ABC', range(5)))   ❺
[('A', 0), ('B', 1), ('C', 2), (None, 3), (None, 4)]
>>> list(itertools.zip_longest('ABC', range(5), fillvalue='?'))   ❻
[('A', 0), ('B', 1), ('C', 2), ('?', 3), ('?', 4)]
```

❶ chain is usually called with two or more iterables.

❷ chain does nothing useful when called with a single iterable.

❸ But chain.from_iterable takes each item from the iterable, and chains them in sequence, as long as each item is itself iterable.

❹ Any number of iterables can be consumed by zip in parallel, but the generator always stops as soon as the first iterable ends. In Python ≥ 3.10, if the strict=True argument is given and an iterable ends before the others, ValueEr ror is raised.

❺ itertools.zip_longest works like zip, except it consumes all input iterables to the end, padding output tuples with None, as needed.

❻ The fillvalue keyword argument specifies a custom padding value.

The itertools.product generator is a lazy way of computing Cartesian products, which we built using list comprehensions with more than one for clause in "Cartesian Products" on page 27. Generator expressions with multiple for clauses can also be used to produce Cartesian products lazily. Example 17-19 demonstrates itertools.product.

Example 17-19. itertools.product generator function examples

```
>>> list(itertools.product('ABC', range(2)))  ❶
[('A', 0), ('A', 1), ('B', 0), ('B', 1), ('C', 0), ('C', 1)]
>>> suits = 'spades hearts diamonds clubs'.split()
>>> list(itertools.product('AK', suits))  ❷
[('A', 'spades'), ('A', 'hearts'), ('A', 'diamonds'), ('A', 'clubs'),
('K', 'spades'), ('K', 'hearts'), ('K', 'diamonds'), ('K', 'clubs')]
>>> list(itertools.product('ABC'))  ❸
[('A',), ('B',), ('C',)]
>>> list(itertools.product('ABC', repeat=2))  ❹
[('A', 'A'), ('A', 'B'), ('A', 'C'), ('B', 'A'), ('B', 'B'),
('B', 'C'), ('C', 'A'), ('C', 'B'), ('C', 'C')]
>>> list(itertools.product(range(2), repeat=3))
[(0, 0, 0), (0, 0, 1), (0, 1, 0), (0, 1, 1), (1, 0, 0),
(1, 0, 1), (1, 1, 0), (1, 1, 1)]
>>> rows = itertools.product('AB', range(2), repeat=2)
>>> for row in rows: print(row)
...
('A', 0, 'A', 0)
('A', 0, 'A', 1)
('A', 0, 'B', 0)
('A', 0, 'B', 1)
('A', 1, 'A', 0)
```

```
('A', 1, 'A', 1)
('A', 1, 'B', 0)
('A', 1, 'B', 1)
('B', 0, 'A', 0)
('B', 0, 'A', 1)
('B', 0, 'B', 0)
('B', 0, 'B', 1)
('B', 1, 'A', 0)
('B', 1, 'A', 1)
('B', 1, 'B', 0)
('B', 1, 'B', 1)
```

❶ The Cartesian product of a `str` with three characters and a `range` with two integers yields six tuples (because 3 * 2 is 6).

❷ The product of two card ranks (`'AK'`) and four suits is a series of eight tuples.

❸ Given a single iterable, `product` yields a series of one-tuples—not very useful.

❹ The `repeat=N` keyword argument tells the product to consume each input iterable N times.

Some generator functions expand the input by yielding more than one value per input item. They are listed in Table 17-4.

Table 17-4. Generator functions that expand each input item into multiple output items

Module	Function	Description
itertools	combinations(it, out_len)	Yields combinations of out_len items from the items yielded by it
itertools	combinations_with_replacement(it, out_len)	Yields combinations of out_len items from the items yielded by it, including combinations with repeated items
itertools	count(start=0, step=1)	Yields numbers starting at start, incremented by step, indefinitely
itertools	cycle(it)	Yields items from it, storing a copy of each, then yields the entire sequence repeatedly, indefinitely
itertools	pairwise(it)	Yields successive overlapping pairs taken from the input iterable[a]
itertools	permutations(it, out_len=None)	Yields permutations of out_len items from the items yielded by it; by default, out_len is len(list(it))
itertools	repeat(item, [times])	Yields the given item repeatedly, indefinitely unless a number of times is given

[a] `itertools.pairwise` was added in Python 3.10.

The count and repeat functions from itertools return generators that conjure items out of nothing: neither of them takes an iterable as input. We saw iter tools.count in "Arithmetic Progression with itertools" on page 622. The cycle generator makes a backup of the input iterable and yields its items repeatedly. Example 17-20 illustrates the use of count, cycle, pairwise, and repeat.

Example 17-20. count, cycle, pairwise, and repeat

```
>>> ct = itertools.count()  ❶
>>> next(ct)  ❷
0
>>> next(ct), next(ct), next(ct)  ❸
(1, 2, 3)
>>> list(itertools.islice(itertools.count(1, .3), 3))  ❹
[1, 1.3, 1.6]
>>> cy = itertools.cycle('ABC')  ❺
>>> next(cy)
'A'
>>> list(itertools.islice(cy, 7))  ❻
['B', 'C', 'A', 'B', 'C', 'A', 'B']
>>> list(itertools.pairwise(range(7)))  ❼
[(0, 1), (1, 2), (2, 3), (3, 4), (4, 5), (5, 6)]
>>> rp = itertools.repeat(7)  ❽
>>> next(rp), next(rp)
(7, 7)
>>> list(itertools.repeat(8, 4))  ❾
[8, 8, 8, 8]
>>> list(map(operator.mul, range(11), itertools.repeat(5)))  ❿
[0, 5, 10, 15, 20, 25, 30, 35, 40, 45, 50]
```

❶   Build a count generator ct.

❷   Retrieve the first item from ct.

❸   I can't build a list from ct, because ct never stops, so I fetch the next three items.

❹   I can build a list from a count generator if it is limited by islice or takewhile.

❺   Build a cycle generator from 'ABC' and fetch its first item, 'A'.

❻   A list can only be built if limited by islice; the next seven items are retrieved here.

❼   For each item in the input, pairwise yields a 2-tuple with that item and the next —if there is a next item. Available in Python ≥ 3.10.

⑧ Build a `repeat` generator that will yield the number 7 forever.

⑨ A `repeat` generator can be limited by passing the `times` argument: here the number 8 will be produced 4 times.

⑩ A common use of `repeat`: providing a fixed argument in `map`; here it provides the 5 multiplier.

The `combinations`, `combinations_with_replacement`, and `permutations` generator functions—together with `product`—are called the *combinatorics generators* in the `itertools` documentation page (*https://fpy.li/17-13*). There is a close relationship between `itertools.product` and the remaining *combinatoric* functions as well, as Example 17-21 shows.

Example 17-21. Combinatoric generator functions yield multiple values per input item

```
>>> list(itertools.combinations('ABC', 2))  ❶
[('A', 'B'), ('A', 'C'), ('B', 'C')]
>>> list(itertools.combinations_with_replacement('ABC', 2))  ❷
[('A', 'A'), ('A', 'B'), ('A', 'C'), ('B', 'B'), ('B', 'C'), ('C', 'C')]
>>> list(itertools.permutations('ABC', 2))  ❸
[('A', 'B'), ('A', 'C'), ('B', 'A'), ('B', 'C'), ('C', 'A'), ('C', 'B')]
>>> list(itertools.product('ABC', repeat=2))  ❹
[('A', 'A'), ('A', 'B'), ('A', 'C'), ('B', 'A'), ('B', 'B'), ('B', 'C'),
('C', 'A'), ('C', 'B'), ('C', 'C')]
```

❶ All combinations of `len()==2` from the items in `'ABC'`; item ordering in the generated tuples is irrelevant (they could be sets).

❷ All combinations of `len()==2` from the items in `'ABC'`, including combinations with repeated items.

❸ All permutations of `len()==2` from the items in `'ABC'`; item ordering in the generated tuples is relevant.

❹ Cartesian product from `'ABC'` and `'ABC'` (that's the effect of `repeat=2`).

The last group of generator functions we'll cover in this section are designed to yield all items in the input iterables, but rearranged in some way. Here are two functions that return multiple generators: `itertools.groupby` and `itertools.tee`. The other generator function in this group, the `reversed` built-in, is the only one covered in this section that does not accept any iterable as input, but only sequences. This makes sense: because `reversed` will yield the items from last to first, it only works with a sequence with a known length. But it avoids the cost of making a reversed copy of the sequence by yielding each item as needed. I put the itertools.product function together with the *merging* generators in Table 17-3 because they all consume more than one iterable, while the generators in Table 17-5 all accept at most one input iterable.

Table 17-5. Rearranging generator functions

Module	Function	Description
itertools	groupby(it, key=None)	Yields 2-tuples of the form (key, group), where key is the grouping criterion and group is a generator yielding the items in the group
(built-in)	reversed(seq)	Yields items from seq in reverse order, from last to first; seq must be a sequence or implement the __reversed__ special method
itertools	tee(it, n=2)	Yields a tuple of *n* generators, each yielding the items of the input iterable independently

Example 17-22 demonstrates the use of itertools.groupby and the reversed built-in. Note that itertools.groupby assumes that the input iterable is sorted by the grouping criterion, or at least that the items are clustered by that criterion—even if not completely sorted. Tech reviewer Miroslav Šedivý suggested this use case: you can sort the datetime objects chronologically, then groupby weekday to get a group of Monday data, followed by Tuesday data, etc., and then by Monday (of the next week) again, and so on.

Example 17-22. itertools.groupby

```
>>> list(itertools.groupby('LLLLAAGGG'))  ❶
[('L', <itertools._grouper object at 0x102227cc0>),
 ('A', <itertools._grouper object at 0x102227b38>),
 ('G', <itertools._grouper object at 0x102227b70>)]
>>> for char, group in itertools.groupby('LLLLAAAGG'):  ❷
...     print(char, '->', list(group))
...
L -> ['L', 'L', 'L', 'L']
A -> ['A', 'A',]
G -> ['G', 'G', 'G']
>>> animals = ['duck', 'eagle', 'rat', 'giraffe', 'bear',
...            'bat', 'dolphin', 'shark', 'lion']
>>> animals.sort(key=len)  ❸
>>> animals
['rat', 'bat', 'duck', 'bear', 'lion', 'eagle', 'shark',
'giraffe', 'dolphin']
>>> for length, group in itertools.groupby(animals, len):  ❹
...     print(length, '->', list(group))
...
3 -> ['rat', 'bat']
4 -> ['duck', 'bear', 'lion']
5 -> ['eagle', 'shark']
```

```
7 -> ['giraffe', 'dolphin']
>>> for length, group in itertools.groupby(reversed(animals), len):  ❺
...     print(length, '->', list(group))
...
7 -> ['dolphin', 'giraffe']
5 -> ['shark', 'eagle']
4 -> ['lion', 'bear', 'duck']
3 -> ['bat', 'rat']
>>>
```

❶ groupby yields tuples of (key, group_generator).

❷ Handling groupby generators involves nested iteration: in this case, the outer for loop and the inner list constructor.

❸ Sort animals by length.

❹ Again, loop over the key and group pair, to display the key and expand the group into a list.

❺ Here the reverse generator iterates over animals from right to left.

The last of the generator functions in this group is iterator.tee, which has a unique behavior: it yields multiple generators from a single input iterable, each yielding every item from the input. Those generators can be consumed independently, as shown in Example 17-23.

Example 17-23. itertools.tee yields multiple generators, each yielding every item of the input generator

```
>>> list(itertools.tee('ABC'))
[<itertools._tee object at 0x10222abc8>, <itertools._tee object at 0x10222ac08>]
>>> g1, g2 = itertools.tee('ABC')
>>> next(g1)
'A'
>>> next(g2)
'A'
>>> next(g2)
'B'
>>> list(g1)
['B', 'C']
>>> list(g2)
['C']
>>> list(zip(*itertools.tee('ABC')))
[('A', 'A'), ('B', 'B'), ('C', 'C')]
```

Note that several examples in this section used combinations of generator functions. This is a great feature of these functions: because they take generators as arguments and return generators, they can be combined in many different ways.

Now we'll review another group of iterable-savvy functions in the standard library.

Iterable Reducing Functions

The functions in Table 17-6 all take an iterable and return a single result. They are known as "reducing," "folding," or "accumulating" functions. We can implement every one of the built-ins listed here with functools.reduce, but they exist as built-ins because they address some common use cases more easily. A longer explanation about functools.reduce appeared in "Vector Take #4: Hashing and a Faster ==" on page 413.

In the case of all and any, there is an important optimization functools.reduce does not support: all and any short-circuit—i.e., they stop consuming the iterator as soon as the result is determined. See the last test with any in Example 17-24.

Table 17-6. Built-in functions that read iterables and return single values

Module	Function	Description
(built-in)	all(it)	Returns True if all items in it are truthy, otherwise False; all([]) returns True
(built-in)	any(it)	Returns True if any item in it is truthy, otherwise False; any([]) returns False
(built-in)	max(it, [key=,] [default=])	Returns the maximum value of the items in it;[a] key is an ordering function, as in sorted; default is returned if the iterable is empty
(built-in)	min(it, [key=,] [default=])	Returns the minimum value of the items in it.[b] key is an ordering function, as in sorted; default is returned if the iterable is empty
functools	reduce(func, it, [initial])	Returns the result of applying func to the first pair of items, then to that result and the third item, and so on; if given, initial forms the initial pair with the first item
(built-in)	sum(it, start=0)	The sum of all items in it, with the optional start value added (use math.fsum for better precision when adding floats)

[a] May also be called as max(arg1, arg2, ..., [key=?]), in which case the maximum among the arguments is returned.

[b] May also be called as min(arg1, arg2, ..., [key=?]), in which case the minimum among the arguments is returned.

The operation of all and any is exemplified in Example 17-24.

Example 17-24. Results of all and any for some sequences

```
>>> all([1, 2, 3])
True
>>> all([1, 0, 3])
False
>>> all([])
True
>>> any([1, 2, 3])
True
>>> any([1, 0, 3])
True
>>> any([0, 0.0])
False
>>> any([])
False
>>> g = (n for n in [0, 0.0, 7, 8])
>>> any(g)  ❶
True
>>> next(g)  ❷
8
```

❶ any iterated over g until g yielded 7; then any stopped and returned True.

❷ That's why 8 was still remaining.

Another built-in that takes an iterable and returns something else is sorted. Unlike reversed, which is a generator function, sorted builds and returns a new list. After all, every single item of the input iterable must be read so they can be sorted, and the sorting happens in a list, therefore sorted just returns that list after it's done. I mention sorted here because it does consume an arbitrary iterable.

Of course, sorted and the reducing functions only work with iterables that eventually stop. Otherwise, they will keep on collecting items and never return a result.

> If you've gotten this far, you've seen the most important and useful content of this chapter. The remaining sections cover advanced generator features that most of us don't see or need very often, such as the yield from construct and classic coroutines.
>
> There are also sections about type hinting iterables, iterators, and classic coroutines.

The yield from syntax provides a new way of combining generators. That's next.

Subgenerators with yield from

The `yield from` expression syntax was introduced in Python 3.3 to allow a generator to delegate work to a subgenerator.

Before `yield from` was introduced, we used a `for` loop when a generator needed to yield values produced from another generator:

```
>>> def sub_gen():
...     yield 1.1
...     yield 1.2
...
>>> def gen():
...     yield 1
...     for i in sub_gen():
...         yield i
...     yield 2
...
>>> for x in gen():
...     print(x)
...
1
1.1
1.2
2
```

We can get the same result using `yield from`, as you can see in Example 17-25.

Example 17-25. Test-driving `yield from`

```
>>> def sub_gen():
...     yield 1.1
...     yield 1.2
...
>>> def gen():
...     yield 1
...     yield from sub_gen()
...     yield 2
...
>>> for x in gen():
...     print(x)
...
1
1.1
1.2
2
```

In Example 17-25, the `for` loop is the *client code*, gen is the *delegating generator*, and sub_gen is the *subgenerator*. Note that `yield from` pauses gen, and sub_gen takes over until it is exhausted. The values yielded by sub_gen pass through gen directly to the client for loop. Meanwhile, gen is suspended and cannot see the values passing through it. Only when sub_gen is done, gen resumes.

When the subgenerator contains a return statement with a value, that value can be captured in the delegating generator by using yield from as part of an expression. Example 17-26 demonstrates.

Example 17-26. yield from gets the return value of the subgenerator

```
>>> def sub_gen():
...     yield 1.1
...     yield 1.2
...     return 'Done!'
...
>>> def gen():
...     yield 1
...     result = yield from sub_gen()
...     print('<--', result)
...     yield 2
...
>>> for x in gen():
...     print(x)
...
1
1.1
1.2
<-- Done!
2
```

Now that we've seen the basics of yield from, let's study a couple of simple but practical examples of its use.

Reinventing chain

We saw in Table 17-3 that itertools provides a chain generator that yields items from several iterables, iterating over the first, then the second, and so on up to the last. This is a homemade implementation of chain with nested for loops in Python:[10]

```
>>> def chain(*iterables):
...     for it in iterables:
...         for i in it:
...             yield i
...
>>> s = 'ABC'
>>> r = range(3)
```

---

10 chain and most itertools functions are written in C.

```
>>> list(chain(s, r))
['A', 'B', 'C', 0, 1, 2]
```

The chain generator in the preceding code is delegating to each iterable it in turn, by driving each it in the inner for loop. That inner loop can be replaced with a yield from expression, as shown in the next console listing:

```
>>> def chain(*iterables):
...     for i in iterables:
...         yield from i
...
>>> list(chain(s, t))
['A', 'B', 'C', 0, 1, 2]
```

The use of yield from in this example is correct, and the code reads better, but it seems like syntactic sugar with little real gain. Now let's develop a more interesting example.

Traversing a Tree

In this section, we'll see yield from in a script to traverse a tree structure. I will build it in baby steps.

The tree structure for this example is Python's exception hierarchy (*https://fpy.li/ 17-14*). But the pattern can be adapted to show a directory tree or any other tree structure.

Starting from BaseException at level zero, the exception hierarchy is five levels deep as of Python 3.10. Our first baby step is to show level zero.

Given a root class, the tree generator in Example 17-27 yields its name and stops.

Example 17-27. tree/step0/tree.py: yield the name of the root class and stop

```
def tree(cls):
    yield cls.__name__


def display(cls):
    for cls_name in tree(cls):
        print(cls_name)


if __name__ == '__main__':
    display(BaseException)
```

The output of Example 17-27 is just one line:

```
BaseException
```

The next baby step takes us to level 1. The `tree` generator will yield the name of the root class and the names of each direct subclass. The names of the subclasses are indented to reveal the hierarchy. This is the output we want:

```
$ python3 tree.py
BaseException
    Exception
    GeneratorExit
    SystemExit
    KeyboardInterrupt
```

Example 17-28 produces that output.

Example 17-28. tree/step1/tree.py: yield the name of root class and direct subclasses

```
def tree(cls):
    yield cls.__name__, 0                      ❶
    for sub_cls in cls.__subclasses__():       ❷
        yield sub_cls.__name__, 1              ❸


def display(cls):
    for cls_name, level in tree(cls):
        indent = ' ' * 4 * level               ❹
        print(f'{indent}{cls_name}')


if __name__ == '__main__':
    display(BaseException)
```

❶ To support the indented output, yield the name of the class and its level in the hierarchy.

❷ Use the `__subclasses__` special method to get a list of subclasses.

❸ Yield name of subclass and level 1.

❹ Build indentation string of 4 spaces times `level`. At level zero, this will be an empty string.

In Example 17-29, I refactor `tree` to separate the special case of the root class from the subclasses, which are now handled in the `sub_tree` generator. At `yield from`, the `tree` generator is suspended, and `sub_tree` takes over yielding values.

Example 17-29. tree/step2/tree.py: tree yields the root class name, then delegates to sub_tree

```
def tree(cls):
    yield cls.__name__, 0
    yield from sub_tree(cls)              ❶


def sub_tree(cls):
    for sub_cls in cls.__subclasses__():
        yield sub_cls.__name__, 1         ❷


def display(cls):
    for cls_name, level in tree(cls):     ❸
        indent = ' ' * 4 * level
        print(f'{indent}{cls_name}')


if __name__ == '__main__':
    display(BaseException)
```

❶ Delegate to sub_tree to yield the names of the subclasses.

❷ Yield the name of each subclass and level 1. Because of the yield from sub_tree(cls) inside tree, these values bypass the tree generator function completely…

❸ … and are received directly here.

In keeping with the baby steps method, I'll write the simplest code I can imagine to reach level 2. For depth-first (*https://fpy.li/17-15*) tree traversal, after yielding each node in level 1, I want to yield the children of that node in level 2, before resuming level 1. A nested for loop takes care of that, as in Example 17-30.

Example 17-30. tree/step3/tree.py: sub_tree traverses levels 1 and 2 depth-first

```
def tree(cls):
    yield cls.__name__, 0
    yield from sub_tree(cls)


def sub_tree(cls):
    for sub_cls in cls.__subclasses__():
        yield sub_cls.__name__, 1
        for sub_sub_cls in sub_cls.__subclasses__():
            yield sub_sub_cls.__name__, 2
```

```
def display(cls):
    for cls_name, level in tree(cls):
        indent = ' ' * 4 * level
        print(f'{indent}{cls_name}')


if __name__ == '__main__':
    display(BaseException)
```

This is the result of running *step3/tree.py* from Example 17-30:

```
$ python3 tree.py
BaseException
    Exception
        TypeError
        StopAsyncIteration
        StopIteration
        ImportError
        OSError
        EOFError
        RuntimeError
        NameError
        AttributeError
        SyntaxError
        LookupError
        ValueError
        AssertionError
        ArithmeticError
        SystemError
        ReferenceError
        MemoryError
        BufferError
        Warning
    GeneratorExit
    SystemExit
    KeyboardInterrupt
```

You may already know where this is going, but I will stick to baby steps one more time: let's reach level 3 by adding yet another nested for loop. The rest of the program is unchanged, so Example 17-31 shows only the sub_tree generator.

Example 17-31. sub_tree generator from tree/step4/tree.py

```
def sub_tree(cls):
    for sub_cls in cls.__subclasses__():
        yield sub_cls.__name__, 1
        for sub_sub_cls in sub_cls.__subclasses__():
            yield sub_sub_cls.__name__, 2
            for sub_sub_sub_cls in sub_sub_cls.__subclasses__():
                yield sub_sub_sub_cls.__name__, 3
```

There is a clear pattern in Example 17-31. We do a for loop to get the subclasses of level *N*. Each time around the loop, we yield a subclass of level *N*, then start another for loop to visit level *N*+1.

In "Reinventing chain" on page 637, we saw how we can replace a nested for loop driving a generator with yield from on the same generator. We can apply that idea here, if we make sub_tree accept a level parameter, and yield from it recursively, passing the current subclass as the new root class with the next level number. See Example 17-32.

Example 17-32. tree/step5/tree.py: recursive sub_tree goes as far as memory allows

```python
def tree(cls):
    yield cls.__name__, 0
    yield from sub_tree(cls, 1)


def sub_tree(cls, level):
    for sub_cls in cls.__subclasses__():
        yield sub_cls.__name__, level
        yield from sub_tree(sub_cls, level+1)


def display(cls):
    for cls_name, level in tree(cls):
        indent = ' ' * 4 * level
        print(f'{indent}{cls_name}')


if __name__ == '__main__':
    display(BaseException)
```

Example 17-32 can traverse trees of any depth, limited only by Python's recursion limit. The default limit allows 1,000 pending functions.

Any good tutorial about recursion will stress the importance of having a base case to avoid infinite recursion. A base case is a conditional branch that returns without making a recursive call. The base case is often implemented with an if statement. In Example 17-32, sub_tree has no if, but there is an implicit conditional in the for loop: if cls.__subclasses__() returns an empty list, the body of the loop is not executed, therefore no recursive call happens. The base case is when the cls class has no subclasses. In that case, sub_tree yields nothing. It just returns.

Example 17-32 works as intended, but we can make it more concise by recalling the pattern we observed when we reached level 3 (Example 17-31): we yield a subclass with level *N*, then start a nested for loop to visit level *N*+1. In Example 17-32 we replaced that nested loop with `yield from`. Now we can merge `tree` and `sub_tree` into a single generator. Example 17-33 is the last step for this example.

Example 17-33. tree/step6/tree.py: recursive calls of tree pass an incremented level argument

```python
def tree(cls, level=0):
    yield cls.__name__, level
    for sub_cls in cls.__subclasses__():
        yield from tree(sub_cls, level+1)


def display(cls):
    for cls_name, level in tree(cls):
        indent = ' ' * 4 * level
        print(f'{indent}{cls_name}')


if __name__ == '__main__':
    display(BaseException)
```

At the start of "Subgenerators with yield from" on page 636, we saw how `yield from` connects the subgenerator directly to the client code, bypassing the delegating generator. That connection becomes really important when generators are used as coroutines and not only produce but also consume values from the client code, as we'll see in "Classic Coroutines" on page 645.

After this first encounter with `yield from`, let's turn to type hinting iterables and iterators.

Generic Iterable Types

Python's standard library has many functions that accept iterable arguments. In your code, such functions can be annotated like the `zip_replace` function we saw in Example 8-15, using `collections.abc.Iterable` (or `typing.Iterable` if you must support Python 3.8 or earlier, as explained in "Legacy Support and Deprecated Collection Types" on page 272). See Example 17-34.

Example 17-34. replacer.py returns an iterator of tuples of strings

```python
from collections.abc import Iterable

FromTo = tuple[str, str]  ❶

def zip_replace(text: str, changes: Iterable[FromTo]) -> str:  ❷
    for from_, to in changes:
```

```
        text = text.replace(from_, to)
    return text
```

❶ Define type alias; not required, but makes the next type hint more readable. Starting with Python 3.10, FromTo should have a type hint of typing.TypeAlias to clarify the reason for this line: FromTo: TypeAlias = tuple[str, str].

❷ Annotate changes to accept an Iterable of FromTo tuples.

Iterator types don't appear as often as Iterable types, but they are also simple to write. Example 17-35 shows the familiar Fibonacci generator, annotated.

Example 17-35. fibo_gen.py: fibonacci returns a generator of integers

```
from collections.abc import Iterator

def fibonacci() -> Iterator[int]:
    a, b = 0, 1
    while True:
        yield a
        a, b = b, a + b
```

Note that the type Iterator is used for generators coded as functions with yield, as well as iterators written "by hand" as classes with __next__. There is also a collec tions.abc.Generator type (and the corresponding deprecated typing.Generator) that we can use to annotate generator objects, but it is needlessly verbose for genera-tors used as iterators.

Example 17-36, when checked with Mypy, reveals that the Iterator type is really a simplified special case of the Generator type.

Example 17-36. itergentype.py: two ways to annotate iterators

```
from collections.abc import Iterator
from keyword import kwlist
from typing import TYPE_CHECKING

short_kw = (k for k in kwlist if len(k) < 5)  ❶

if TYPE_CHECKING:
    reveal_type(short_kw)  ❷

long_kw: Iterator[str] = (k for k in kwlist if len(k) >= 4)  ❸

if TYPE_CHECKING:  ❹
    reveal_type(long_kw)
```

❶ Generator expression that yields Python keywords with less than 5 characters.

❷ Mypy infers: `typing.Generator[builtins.str*, None, None]`.[11]

❸ This also yields strings, but I added an explicit type hint.

❹ Revealed type: `typing.Iterator[builtins.str]`.

`abc.Iterator[str]` is *consistent-with* `abc.Generator[str, None, None]`, therefore Mypy issues no errors for type checking in Example 17-36.

`Iterator[T]` is a shortcut for `Generator[T, None, None]`. Both annotations mean "a generator that yields items of type `T`, but that does not consume or return values." Generators able to consume and return values are coroutines, our next topic.

Classic Coroutines

 PEP 342—Coroutines via Enhanced Generators (*https://fpy.li/ pep342*) introduced the `.send()` and other features that made it possible to use generators as coroutines. PEP 342 uses the word "coroutine" with the same meaning I am using here.

It is unfortunate that Python's official documentation and standard library now use inconsistent terminology to refer to generators used as coroutines, forcing me to adopt the "classic coroutine" qualifier to contrast with the newer "native coroutine" objects.

After Python 3.5 came out, the trend is to use "coroutine" as a synonym for "native coroutine." But PEP 342 is not deprecated, and classic coroutines still work as originally designed, although they are no longer supported by `asyncio`.

Understanding classic coroutines in Python is confusing because they are actually generators used in a different way. So let's step back and consider another feature of Python that can be used in two ways.

We saw in "Tuples Are Not Just Immutable Lists" on page 30 that we can use `tuple` instances as records or as immutable sequences. When used as a record, a tuple is expected to have a specific number of items, and each item may have a different type. When used as immutable lists, a tuple can have any length, and all items are expected to have the same type. That's why there are two different ways to annotate tuples with type hints:

---

11 As of version 0.910, Mypy still uses the deprecated typing types.

```
# A city record with name, country, and population:
city: tuple[str, str, int]

# An immutable sequence of domain names:
domains: tuple[str, ...]
```

Something similar happens with generators. They are commonly used as iterators, but they can also be used as coroutines. A *coroutine* is really a generator function, created with the yield keyword in its body. And a *coroutine object* is physically a generator object. Despite sharing the same underlying implementation in C, the use cases of generators and coroutines in Python are so different that there are two ways to type hint them:

```
# The `readings` variable can be bound to an iterator
# or generator object that yields `float` items:
readings: Iterator[float]

# The `sim_taxi` variable can be bound to a coroutine
# representing a taxi cab in a discrete event simulation.
# It yields events, receives `float` timestamps, and returns
# the number of trips made during the simulation:
sim_taxi: Generator[Event, float, int]
```

Adding to the confusion, the typing module authors decided to name that type Generator, when in fact it describes the API of a generator object intended to be used as a coroutine, while generators are more often used as simple iterators.

The typing documentation (*https://fpy.li/17-17*) describes the formal type parameters of Generator like this:

```
Generator[YieldType, SendType, ReturnType]
```

The SendType is only relevant when the generator is used as a coroutine. That type parameter is the type of x in the call gen.send(x). It is an error to call .send() on a generator that was coded to behave as an iterator instead of a coroutine. Likewise, ReturnType is only meaningful to annotate a coroutine, because iterators don't return values like regular functions. The only sensible operation on a generator used as an iterator is to call next(it) directly or indirectly via for loops and other forms of iteration. The YieldType is the type of the value returned by a call to next(it).

The Generator type has the same type parameters as typing.Coroutine (*https://fpy.li/typecoro*):

```
Coroutine[YieldType, SendType, ReturnType]
```

The typing.Coroutine documentation (*https://fpy.li/typecoro*) actually says: "The variance and order of type variables correspond to those of Generator." But typing.Coroutine (deprecated) and collections.abc.Coroutine (generic since Python 3.9) are intended to annotate only native coroutines, not classic coroutines. If you want to use type hints with classic coroutines, you'll suffer through the confusion of annotating them as `Generator[YieldType, SendType, ReturnType]`.

David Beazley created some of the best talks and most comprehensive workshops about classic coroutines. In his PyCon 2009 course handout (*https://fpy.li/17-18*), he has a slide titled "Keeping It Straight," which reads:

- Generators produce data for iteration
- Coroutines are consumers of data
- To keep your brain from exploding, don't mix the two concepts together
- Coroutines are not related to iteration
- Note: There is a use of having `yield` produce a value in a coroutine, but it's not tied to iteration.[12]

Now let's see how classic coroutines work.

Example: Coroutine to Compute a Running Average

While discussing closures in Chapter 9, we studied objects to compute a running average. Example 9-7 shows a class and Example 9-13 presents a higher-order function returning a function that keeps the `total` and `count` variables across invocations in a closure. Example 17-37 shows how to do the same with a coroutine.[13]

Example 17-37. coroaverager.py: coroutine to compute a running average

```
from collections.abc import Generator

def averager() -> Generator[float, float, None]:  ❶
    total = 0.0
    count = 0
    average = 0.0
    while True:  ❷
        term = yield average  ❸
        total += term
        count += 1
        average = total/count
```

---

12 Slide 33, "Keeping It Straight," in "A Curious Course on Coroutines and Concurrency" (*https://fpy.li/17-18*).

13 This example is inspired by a snippet from Jacob Holm in the Python-ideas list, message titled "Yield-From: Finalization guarantees" (*https://fpy.li/17-20*). Some variations appear later in the thread, and Holm further explains his thinking in message 003912 (*https://fpy.li/17-21*).

❶ This function returns a generator that yields `float` values, accepts `float` values via `.send()`, and does not return a useful value.[14]

❷ This infinite loop means the coroutine will keep on yielding averages as long as the client code sends values.

❸ The `yield` statement here suspends the coroutine, yields a result to the client, and—later—gets a value sent by the caller to the coroutine, starting another iteration of the infinite loop.

In a coroutine, `total` and `count` can be local variables: no instance attributes or closures are needed to keep the context while the coroutine is suspended waiting for the next `.send()`. That's why coroutines are attractive replacements for callbacks in asynchronous programming—they keep local state between activations.

Example 17-38 runs doctests to show the `averager` coroutine in operation.

Example 17-38. coroaverager.py: doctest for the running average coroutine in Example 17-37

```
>>> coro_avg = averager()   ❶
>>> next(coro_avg)   ❷
0.0
>>> coro_avg.send(10)   ❸
10.0
>>> coro_avg.send(30)
20.0
>>> coro_avg.send(5)
15.0
```

❶ Create the coroutine object.

❷ Start the coroutine. This yields the initial value of `average`: 0.0.

❸ Now we are in business: each call to `.send()` yields the current average.

In Example 17-38, the call `next(coro_avg)` makes the coroutine advance to the `yield`, yielding the initial value for `average`. You can also start the coroutine by calling `coro_avg.send(None)`—this is actually what the `next()` built-in does. But you can't send any value other than None, because the coroutine can only accept a sent

---

14 In fact, it never returns unless some exception breaks the loop. Mypy 0.910 accepts both None and typing
  .NoReturn as the generator return type parameter—but it also accepts str in that position, so apparently it
  can't fully analyze the coroutine code at this time.

value when it is suspended at a `yield` line. Calling `next()` or `.send(None)` to advance to the first `yield` is known as "priming the coroutine."

After each activation, the coroutine is suspended precisely at the `yield` keyword, waiting for a value to be sent. The line `coro_avg.send(10)` provides that value, causing the coroutine to activate. The `yield` expression resolves to the value 10, assigning it to the `term` variable. The rest of the loop updates the `total`, `count`, and `average` variables. The next iteration in the `while` loop yields the `average`, and the coroutine is again suspended at the `yield` keyword.

The attentive reader may be anxious to know how the execution of an `averager` instance (e.g., `coro_avg`) may be terminated, because its body is an infinite loop. We don't usually need to terminate a generator, because it is garbage collected as soon as there are no more valid references to it. If you need to explicitly terminate it, use the `.close()` method, as shown in Example 17-39.

Example 17-39. coroaverager.py: continuing from Example 17-38

```
>>> coro_avg.send(20)   ❶
16.25
>>> coro_avg.close()    ❷
>>> coro_avg.close()    ❸
>>> coro_avg.send(5)    ❹
Traceback (most recent call last):
  ...
StopIteration
```

❶ `coro_avg` is the instance created in Example 17-38.

❷ The `.close()` method raises `GeneratorExit` at the suspended `yield` expression. If not handled in the coroutine function, the exception terminates it. `Generator Exit` is caught by the generator object that wraps the coroutine—that's why we don't see it.

❸ Calling `.close()` on a previously closed coroutine has no effect.

❹ Trying `.send()` on a closed coroutine raises `StopIteration`.

Besides the `.send()` method, PEP 342—Coroutines via Enhanced Generators (*https://fpy.li/pep342*) also introduced a way for a coroutine to return a value. The next section shows how.

Returning a Value from a Coroutine

We'll now study another coroutine to compute an average. This version will not yield partial results. Instead, it returns a tuple with the number of terms and the average. I've split the listing in two parts: Example 17-40 and Example 17-41.

Example 17-40. coroaverager2.py: top of the file

```python
from collections.abc import Generator
from typing import Union, NamedTuple

class Result(NamedTuple):      ❶
    count: int  # type: ignore ❷
    average: float

class Sentinel:  ❸
    def __repr__(self):
        return f'<Sentinel>'

STOP = Sentinel()  ❹

SendType = Union[float, Sentinel]  ❺
```

❶ The `averager2` coroutine in Example 17-41 will return an instance of `Result`.

❷ The `Result` is actually a subclass of `tuple`, which has a `.count()` method that I don't need. The `# type: ignore` comment prevents Mypy from complaining about having a count field.[15]

❸ A class to make a sentinel value with a readable `__repr__`.

❹ The sentinel value that I'll use to make the coroutine stop collecting data and return a result.

❺ I'll use this type alias for the second type parameter of the coroutine `Generator` return type, the `SendType` parameter.

The `SendType` definition also works in Python 3.10, but if you don't need to support earlier versions, it is better to write it like this, after importing `TypeAlias` from typing:

---

15 I considered renaming the field, but count is the best name for the local variable in the coroutine, and is the name I used for this variable in similar examples in the book, so it makes sense to use the same name in the Result field. I don't hesitate to use `# type: ignore` to avoid the limitations and annoyances of static type checkers when submission to the tool would make the code worse or needlessly complicated.

```
SendType: TypeAlias = float | Sentinel
```

Using | instead of typing.Union is so concise and readable that I'd probably not create that type alias, but instead I'd write the signature of averager2 like this:

```
def averager2(verbose: bool=False) -> Generator[None, float | Sentinel, Result]:
```

Now, let's study the coroutine code itself (Example 17-41).

Example 17-41. coroaverager2.py: a coroutine that returns a result value

```
def averager2(verbose: bool = False) -> Generator[None, SendType, Result]:  ❶
    total = 0.0
    count = 0
    average = 0.0
    while True:
        term = yield  ❷
        if verbose:
            print('received:', term)
        if isinstance(term, Sentinel):  ❸
            break
        total += term  ❹
        count += 1
        average = total / count
    return Result(count, average)  ❺
```

❶ For this coroutine, the yield type is None because it does not yield data. It receives data of the SendType and returns a Result tuple when done.

❷ Using yield like this only makes sense in coroutines, which are designed to consume data. This yields None, but receives a term from .send(term).

❸ If the term is a Sentinel, break from the loop. Thanks to this isinstance check…

❹ …Mypy allows me to add term to the total without flagging an error that I can't add a float to an object that may be a float or a Sentinel.

❺ This line will be reached only if a Sentinel is sent to the coroutine.

Now let's see how we can use this coroutine, starting with a simple example that doesn't actually produce a result (Example 17-42).

Example 17-42. coroaverager2.py: doctest showing .cancel()

```
>>> coro_avg = averager2()
>>> next(coro_avg)
>>> coro_avg.send(10)  ❶
```

```
>>> coro_avg.send(30)
>>> coro_avg.send(6.5)
>>> coro_avg.close()     ❷
```

❶ Recall that averager2 does not yield partial results. It yields None, which Python's console omits.

❷ Calling .close() in this coroutine makes it stop but does not return a result, because the GeneratorExit exception is raised at the yield line in the coroutine, so the return statement is never reached.

Now let's make it work in Example 17-43.

Example 17-43. coroaverager2.py: doctest showing StopIteration with a Result

```
>>> coro_avg = averager2()
>>> next(coro_avg)
>>> coro_avg.send(10)
>>> coro_avg.send(30)
>>> coro_avg.send(6.5)
>>> try:
...      coro_avg.send(STOP)     ❶
... except StopIteration as exc:
...      result = exc.value      ❷
...
>>> result     ❸
Result(count=3, average=15.5)
```

❶ Sending the STOP sentinel makes the coroutine break from the loop and return a Result. The generator object that wraps the coroutine then raises StopItera tion.

❷ The StopIteration instance has a value attribute bound to the value of the return statement that terminated the coroutine.

❸ Believe it or not!

This idea of "smuggling" the return value out of the coroutine wrapped in a StopIter ation exception is a bizarre hack. Nevertheless, this bizarre hack is part of PEP 342— Coroutines via Enhanced Generators (*https://fpy.li/pep342*), and is documented with the StopIteration exception (*https://fpy.li/17-22*), and in the "Yield expressions" (*https://fpy.li/17-23*) section of Chapter 6 of *The Python Language Reference* (*https://fpy.li/17-24*).

A delegating generator can get the return value of a coroutine directly using the yield from syntax, as shown in Example 17-44.

Example 17-44. coroaverager2.py: doctest showing StopIteration with a Result

```
>>> def compute():
...     res = yield from averager2(True)     ❶
...     print('computed:', res)     ❷
...     return res     ❸
...
>>> comp = compute()     ❹
>>> for v in [None, 10, 20, 30, STOP]:     ❺
...     try:
...         comp.send(v)     ❻
...     except StopIteration as exc:     ❼
...         result = exc.value
received: 10
received: 20
received: 30
received: <Sentinel>
computed: Result(count=3, average=20.0)
>>> result     ❽
Result(count=3, average=20.0)
```

❶ res will collect the return value of averager2; the yield from machinery retrieves the return value when it handles the StopIteration exception that marks the termination of the coroutine. When True, the verbose parameter makes the coroutine print the value received, to make its operation visible.

❷ Keep an eye out for the output of this line when this generator runs.

❸ Return the result. This will also be wrapped in StopIteration.

❹ Create the delegating coroutine object.

❺ This loop will drive the delegating coroutine.

❻ First value sent is None, to prime the coroutine; last is the sentinel to stop it.

❼ Catch StopIteration to fetch the return value of compute.

❽ After the lines output by averager2 and compute, we get the Result instance.

Even though the examples here don't do much, the code is hard to follow. Driving the coroutine with .send() calls and retrieving results is complicated, except with yield from—but we can only use that syntax inside a delegating generator/coroutine, which must ultimately be driven by some nontrivial code, as shown in Example 17-44.

The previous examples show that using coroutines directly is cumbersome and confusing. Add exception handling and the coroutine .throw() method, and examples become even more convoluted. I won't cover .throw() in this book because—like .send()—it is only useful to drive coroutines "by hand," but I don't recommend doing that, unless you are creating a new coroutine-based framework from scratch.

 If you are interested in deeper coverage of classic coroutines—including the .throw() method—please check out "Classic Coroutines" (*https://fpy.li/oldcoro*) at the *fluentpython.com* companion website. That post includes Python-like pseudocode detailing how yield from drives generators and coroutines, as well as a a small discrete event simulation demonstrating a form of concurrency using coroutines without an asynchronous programming framework.

In practice, productive work with coroutines requires the support of a specialized framework. That is what asyncio provided for classic coroutines way back in Python 3.3. With the advent of native coroutines in Python 3.5, the Python core developers are gradually phasing out support for classic coroutines in asyncio. But the underlying mechanisms are very similar. The async def syntax makes native coroutines easier to spot in code, which is a great benefit. Inside, native coroutines use await instead of yield from to delegate to other coroutines. Chapter 21 is all about that.

Now let's wrap up the chapter with a mind-bending section about covariance and contravariance in type hints for coroutines.

Generic Type Hints for Classic Coroutines

Back in "Contravariant types" on page 554, I mentioned typing.Generator as one of the few standard library types with a contravariant type parameter. Now that we've studied classic coroutines, we are ready to make sense of this generic type.

Here is how typing.Generator was declared (*https://fpy.li/17-25*) in the *typing.py* module of Python 3.6:[16]

```
T_co = TypeVar('T_co', covariant=True)
V_co = TypeVar('V_co', covariant=True)
T_contra = TypeVar('T_contra', contravariant=True)

# many lines omitted
```

---

[16] Since Python 3.7, typing.Generator and other types that correspond to ABCs in collections.abc were refactored with a wrapper around the corresponding ABC, so their generic parameters aren't visible in the *typing.py* source file. That's why I refer to Python 3.6 source code here.

```
class Generator(Iterator[T_co], Generic[T_co, T_contra, V_co],
                extra=_G_base):
```

That generic type declaration means that a `Generator` type hint requires those three type parameters we've seen before:

```
my_coro : Generator[YieldType, SendType, ReturnType]
```

From the type variables in the formal parameters, we see that `YieldType` and `Return Type` are covariant, but `SendType` is contravariant. To understand why, consider that `YieldType` and `ReturnType` are "output" types. Both describe data that comes out of the coroutine object—i.e., the generator object when used as a coroutine object.

It makes sense that these are covariant, because any code expecting a coroutine that yields floats can use a coroutine that yields integers. That's why `Generator` is covariant on its `YieldType` parameter. The same reasoning applies to the `ReturnType` parameter—also covariant.

Using the notation introduced in "Covariant types" on page 554, the covariance of the first and third parameters is expressed by the `:>` symbols pointing in the same direction:

```
                    float :> int
Generator[float, Any, float] :> Generator[int, Any, int]
```

`YieldType` and `ReturnType` are examples of the first rule of "Variance rules of thumb" on page 555:

> 1. If a formal type parameter defines a type for data that comes out of the object, it can be covariant.

On the other hand, `SendType` is an "input" parameter: it is the type of the `value` argument for the `.send(value)` method of the coroutine object. Client code that needs to send floats to a coroutine cannot use a coroutine with `int` as the `SendType` because `float` is not a subtype of `int`. In other words, `float` is not *consistent-with* `int`. But the client can use a coroutine with `complex` as the `SendType`, because `float` is a subtype of `complex`, therefore `float` is *consistent-with* `complex`.

The `:>` notation makes the contravariance of the second parameter visible:

```
                  float :> int
Generator[Any, float, Any] <: Generator[Any, int, Any]
```

This is an example of the second Variance Rule of Thumb:

> 2. If a formal type parameter defines a type for data that goes into the object after its initial construction, it can be contravariant.

This merry discussion of variance completes the longest chapter in the book.

Chapter Summary

Iteration is so deeply embedded in the language that I like to say that Python groks iterators.[17] The integration of the Iterator pattern in the semantics of Python is a prime example of how design patterns are not equally applicable in all programming languages. In Python, a classic Iterator implemented "by hand" as in Example 17-4 has no practical use, except as a didactic example.

In this chapter, we built a few versions of a class to iterate over individual words in text files that may be very long. We saw how Python uses the iter() built-in to create iterators from sequence-like objects. We build a classic iterator as a class with __next__(), and then we used generators to make each successive refactoring of the Sentence class more concise and readable.

We then coded a generator of arithmetic progressions and showed how to leverage the itertools module to make it simpler. An overview of most general-purpose generator functions in the standard library followed.

We then studied yield from expressions in the context of simple generators with the chain and tree examples.

The last major section was about classic coroutines, a topic of waning importance after native coroutines were added in Python 3.5. Although difficult to use in practice, classic coroutines are the foundation of native coroutines, and the yield from expression is the direct precursor of await.

Also covered were type hints for Iterable, Iterator, and Generator types—with the latter providing a concrete and rare example of a contravariant type parameter.

Further Reading

A detailed technical explanation of generators appears in *The Python Language Reference* in "6.2.9. Yield expressions" (*https://fpy.li/17-27*). The PEP where generator functions were defined is PEP 255—Simple Generators (*https://fpy.li/pep255*).

The itertools module documentation (*https://fpy.li/17-28*) is excellent because of all the examples included. Although the functions in that module are implemented in C, the documentation shows how some of them would be written in Python, often by leveraging other functions in the module. The usage examples are also great; for instance, there is a snippet showing how to use the accumulate function to amortize a loan with interest, given a list of payments over time. There is also an "Itertools

---

[17] According to the Jargon file (*https://fpy.li/17-26*), to *grok* is not merely to learn something, but to absorb it so "it becomes part of you, part of your identity."

Recipes" (*https://fpy.li/17-29*) section with additional high-performance functions that use the `itertools` functions as building blocks.

Beyond Python's standard library, I recommend the More Itertools (*https://fpy.li/17-30*) package, which follows the fine `itertools` tradition in providing powerful generators with plenty of examples and some useful recipes.

Chapter 4, "Iterators and Generators," of *Python Cookbook*, 3rd ed., by David Beazley and Brian K. Jones (O'Reilly), has 16 recipes covering this subject from many different angles, focusing on practical applications. It includes some illuminating recipes with `yield from`.

Sebastian Rittau—currently a top contributor of *typeshed*—explains why iterators should be iterable, as he noted in 2006 that, "Java: Iterators are not Iterable" (*https://fpy.li/17-31*).

The `yield from` syntax is explained with examples in the "What's New in Python 3.3" section of PEP 380—Syntax for Delegating to a Subgenerator (*https://fpy.li/17-32*). My post "Classic Coroutines" (*https://fpy.li/oldcoro*) at *fluentpython.com* explains `yield from` in depth, including Python pseudocode of its implementation in C.

David Beazley is the ultimate authority on Python generators and coroutines. The *Python Cookbook*, 3rd ed., (O'Reilly) he coauthored with Brian Jones has numerous recipes with coroutines. Beazley's PyCon tutorials on the subject are famous for their depth and breadth. The first was at PyCon US 2008: "Generator Tricks for Systems Programmers" (*https://fpy.li/17-33*). PyCon US 2009 saw the legendary "A Curious Course on Coroutines and Concurrency" (*https://fpy.li/17-34*) (hard-to-find video links for all three parts: part 1 (*https://fpy.li/17-35*), part 2 (*https://fpy.li/17-36*), and part 3 (*https://fpy.li/17-37*)). His tutorial from PyCon 2014 in Montréal was "Generators: The Final Frontier" (*https://fpy.li/17-38*), in which he tackles more concurrency examples—so it's really more about topics in Chapter 21. Dave can't resist making brains explode in his classes, so in the last part of "The Final Frontier," coroutines replace the classic Visitor pattern in an arithmetic expression evaluator.

Coroutines allow new ways of organizing code, and just as recursion or polymorphism (dynamic dispatch), it takes some time getting used to their possibilities. An interesting example of classic algorithm rewritten with coroutines is in the post "Greedy algorithm with coroutines" (*https://fpy.li/17-39*), by James Powell.

Brett Slatkin's *Effective Python*, 1st ed. (*https://fpy.li/17-40*) (Addison-Wesley) has an excellent short chapter titled "Consider Coroutines to Run Many Functions Concurrently." That chapter is not in the second edition of *Effective Python*, but it is still available online as a sample chapter (*https://fpy.li/17-41*). Slatkin presents the best example of driving coroutines with `yield from` that I've seen: an implementation of John Conway's Game of Life (*https://fpy.li/17-42*) in which coroutines manage the state of each cell as the game runs. I refactored the code for the Game of Life example—separating the functions and classes that implement the game from the testing snippets used in Slatkin's original code. I also rewrote the tests as doctests, so you can see the output of the various coroutines and classes without running the script. The refactored example (*https://fpy.li/17-43*) is posted as a GitHub gist (*https://fpy.li/17-44*).

Soapbox

The Minimalistic Iterator Interface in Python

In the "Implementation" section of the Iterator pattern,[18] the Gang of Four wrote:

> The minimal interface to Iterator consists of the operations First, Next, IsDone, and CurrentItem.

However, that very sentence has a footnote that reads:

> We can make this interface even smaller by merging Next, IsDone, and CurrentItem into a single operation that advances to the next object and returns it. If the traversal is finished, then this operation returns a special value (0, for instance) that marks the end of the iteration.

This is close to what we have in Python: the single method __next__ does the job. But instead of using a sentinel, which could be overlooked by mistake, the StopIteration exception signals the end of the iteration. Simple and correct: that's the Python way.

Pluggable Generators

Anyone who manages large datasets finds many uses for generators. This is the story of the first time I built a practical solution around generators.

Years ago I worked at BIREME, a digital library run by PAHO/WHO (Pan-American Health Organization/World Health Organization) in São Paulo, Brazil. Among the bibliographic datasets created by BIREME are LILACS (Latin American and Caribbean Health Sciences index) and SciELO (Scientific Electronic Library Online), two comprehensive databases indexing the research literature about health sciences produced in the region.

Since the late 1980s, the database system used to manage LILACS is CDS/ISIS, a nonrelational document database created by UNESCO. One of my jobs was to research alternatives for a possible migration of LILACS—and eventually the much larger SciELO—to a modern, open source, document database such as CouchDB or MongoDB. At the time, I wrote a paper explaining the semistructured data model and

---

18 Gamma et. al., *Design Patterns: Elements of Reusable Object-Oriented Software*, p. 261.

different ways to represent CDS/ISIS data with JSON-like records: "From ISIS to CouchDB: Databases and Data Models for Bibliographic Records" (*https://fpy.li/ 17-45*).

As part of that research, I wrote a Python script to read a CDS/ISIS file and write a JSON file suitable for importing to CouchDB or MongoDB. Initially, the script read files in the ISO-2709 format exported by CDS/ISIS. The reading and writing had to be done incrementally because the full datasets were much bigger than main memory. That was easy enough: each iteration of the main for loop read one record from the *.iso* file, massaged it, and wrote it to the *.json* output.

However, for operational reasons, it was deemed necessary that *isis2json.py* supported another CDS/ISIS data format: the binary *.mst* files used in production at BIREME to avoid the costly export to ISO-2709. Now I had a problem: the libraries used to read ISO-2709 and *.mst* files had very different APIs. And the JSON writing loop was already complicated because the script accepted a variety of command-line options to restructure each output record. Reading data using two different APIs in the same for loop where the JSON was produced would be unwieldy.

The solution was to isolate the reading logic into a pair of generator functions: one for each supported input format. In the end, I split the *isis2json.py* script into four functions. You can see the Python 2 source code with dependencies in the *fluentpython/isis2json* (*https://fpy.li/17-46*) repository on GitHub.[19]

Here is a high-level overview of how the script is structured:

main
> The main function uses argparse to read command-line options that configure the structure of the output records. Based on the input filename extension, a suitable generator function is selected to read the data and yield the records, one by one.

iter_iso_records
> This generator function reads *.iso* files (assumed to be in the ISO-2709 format). It takes two arguments: the filename and isis_json_type, one of the options related to the record structure. Each iteration of its for loop reads one record, creates an empty dict, populates it with field data, and yields the dict.

---

19 The code is in Python 2 because one of its optional dependencies is a Java library named *Bruma*, which we can import when we run the script with Jython—which does not yet support Python 3.

`iter_mst_records`

> This other generator functions reads *.mst* files.[20] If you look at the source code for *isis2json.py*, you'll see that it's not as simple as `iter_iso_records`, but its interface and overall structure is the same: it takes a filename and an `isis_json_type` argument and enters a `for` loop, which builds and yields one `dict` per iteration, representing a single record.

`write_json`

> This function performs the actual writing of the JSON records, one at a time. It takes numerous arguments, but the first one—`input_gen`—is a reference to a generator function: either `iter_iso_records` or `iter_mst_records`. The main `for` loop in `write_json` iterates over the dictionaries yielded by the selected `input_gen` generator, restructures it in different ways as determined by the command-line options, and appends the JSON record to the output file.

By leveraging generator functions, I was able to decouple the reading from the writing. Of course, the simplest way to decouple them would be to read all records to memory, then write them to disk. But that was not a viable option because of the size of the datasets. Using generators, the reading and writing is interleaved, so the script can process files of any size. Also, the special logic for reading a record in the different input formats is separated from the logic of restructuring each record for writing.

Now, if we need *isis2json.py* to support an additional input format—say, MARCXML, a DTD used by the US Library of Congress to represent ISO-2709 data—it will be easy to add a third generator function to implement the reading logic, without changing anything in the complicated `write_json` function.

This is not rocket science, but it's a real example where generators enabled an efficient and flexible solution to process databases as a stream of records, keeping memory usage low regardless of the size of the dataset.

---

20 The library used to read the complex *.mst* binary is actually written in Java, so this functionality is only available when *isis2json.py* is executed with the Jython interpreter, version 2.5 or newer. For further details, see the *README.rst* (*https://fpy.li/17-47*) file in the repository. The dependencies are imported inside the generator functions that need them, so the script can run even if only one of the external libraries is available.

with, match, and else Blocks

Context managers may end up being almost as important as the subroutine itself. We've only scratched the surface with them. [...] Basic has a with statement, there are with statements in lots of languages. But they don't do the same thing, they all do something very shallow, they save you from repeated dotted [attribute] lookups, they don't do setup and tear down. Just because it's the same name don't think it's the same thing. The with statement is a very big deal.[1]

—Raymond Hettinger, eloquent Python evangelist

This chapter is about control flow features that are not so common in other languages, and for this reason tend to be overlooked or underused in Python. They are:

- The with statement and context manager protocol
- Pattern matching with match/case
- The else clause in for, while, and try statements

The with statement sets up a temporary context and reliably tears it down, under the control of a context manager object. This prevents errors and reduces boilerplate code, making APIs at the same time safer and easier to use. Python programmers are finding lots of uses for with blocks beyond automatic file closing.

We've seen pattern matching in previous chapters, but here we'll see how the grammar of a language can be expressed as sequence patterns. That observation explains why match/case is an effective tool to create language processors that are easy to understand and extend. We'll study a complete interpreter for a small but functional

---

1 PyCon US 2013 keynote: "What Makes Python Awesome" (*https://fpy.li/18-1*); the part about with starts at 23:00 and ends at 26:15.

subset of the Scheme language. The same ideas could be applied to develop a template language or a DSL (Domain-Specific Language) to encode business rules in a larger system.

The else clause is not a big deal, but it does help convey intention when properly used together with for, while, and try.

What's New in This Chapter

"Pattern Matching in lis.py: A Case Study" on page 673 is a new section.

I updated "The contextlib Utilities" on page 667 to cover a few features of the context lib module added since Python 3.6, and the new parenthesized context managers syntax introduced in Python 3.10.

Let's start with the powerful with statement.

Context Managers and with Blocks

Context manager objects exist to control a with statement, just like iterators exist to control a for statement.

The with statement was designed to simplify some common uses of try/finally, which guarantees that some operation is performed after a block of code, even if the block is terminated by return, an exception, or a sys.exit() call. The code in the finally clause usually releases a critical resource or restores some previous state that was temporarily changed.

The Python community is finding new, creative uses for context managers. Some examples from the standard library are:

- Managing transactions in the sqlite3 module—see "Using the connection as a context manager" (*https://fpy.li/18-2*).
- Safely handling locks, conditions, and semaphores—as described in the thread ing module documentation (*https://fpy.li/18-3*).
- Setting up custom environments for arithmetic operations with Decimal objects —see the decimal.localcontext documentation (*https://fpy.li/18-4*).
- Patching objects for testing—see the unittest.mock.patch function (*https://fpy.li/18-5*).

The context manager interface consists of the __enter__ and __exit__ methods. At the top of the with, Python calls the __enter__ method of the context manager

---

object. When the with block completes or terminates for any reason, Python calls
__exit__ on the context manager object.

The most common example is making sure a file object is closed. Example 18-1 is a
detailed demonstration of using with to close a file.

Example 18-1. Demonstration of a file object as a context manager

```
>>> with open('mirror.py') as fp:    ❶
...     src = fp.read(60)    ❷
...
>>> len(src)
60
>>> fp    ❸
<_io.TextIOWrapper name='mirror.py' mode='r' encoding='UTF-8'>
>>> fp.closed, fp.encoding    ❹
(True, 'UTF-8')
>>> fp.read(60)    ❺
Traceback (most recent call last):
  File "<stdin>", line 1, in <module>
ValueError: I/O operation on closed file.
```

❶   fp is bound to the opened text file because the file's __enter__ method returns
    self.

❷   Read 60 Unicode characters from fp.

❸   The fp variable is still available—with blocks don't define a new scope, as func-
    tions do.

❹   We can read the attributes of the fp object.

❺   But we can't read more text from fp because at the end of the with block, the
    TextIOWrapper.__exit__ method was called, and it closed the file.

The first callout in Example 18-1 makes a subtle but crucial point: the context manager object is the result of evaluating the expression after with, but the value bound
to the target variable (in the as clause) is the result returned by the __enter__
method of the context manager object.

It just happens that the open() function returns an instance of TextIOWrapper, and
its __enter__ method returns self. But in a different class, the __enter__ method
may also return some other object instead of the context manager instance.

When control flow exits the with block in any way, the __exit__ method is invoked
on the context manager object, not on whatever was returned by __enter__.

The as clause of the with statement is optional. In the case of open, we always need it to get a reference to the file, so that we can call methods on it. But some context managers return None because they have no useful object to give back to the user.

Example 18-2 shows the operation of a perfectly frivolous context manager designed to highlight the distinction between the context manager and the object returned by its __enter__ method.

Example 18-2. Test-driving the LookingGlass context manager class

```
>>> from mirror import LookingGlass
>>> with LookingGlass() as what:   ❶
...        print('Alice, Kitty and Snowdrop')   ❷
...        print(what)
...
pordwonS dna yttiK ,ecilA
YKCOWREBBAJ
>>> what   ❸
'JABBERWOCKY'
>>> print('Back to normal.')   ❹
Back to normal.
```

❶   The context manager is an instance of LookingGlass; Python calls __enter__ on the context manager and the result is bound to what.

❷   Print a str, then the value of the target variable what. The output of each print will come out reversed.

❸   Now the with block is over. We can see that the value returned by __enter__, held in what, is the string 'JABBERWOCKY'.

❹   Program output is no longer reversed.

Example 18-3 shows the implementation of LookingGlass.

Example 18-3. mirror.py: code for the LookingGlass context manager class

```
import sys

class LookingGlass:

    def __enter__(self):   ❶
        self.original_write = sys.stdout.write   ❷
        sys.stdout.write = self.reverse_write   ❸
        return 'JABBERWOCKY'   ❹

    def reverse_write(self, text):   ❺
```

```
        self.original_write(text[::-1])

    def __exit__(self, exc_type, exc_value, traceback):  ❻
        sys.stdout.write = self.original_write  ❼
        if exc_type is ZeroDivisionError:  ❽
            print('Please DO NOT divide by zero!')
            return True  ❾
    ❿
```

❶ Python invokes __enter__ with no arguments besides self.

❷ Hold the original sys.stdout.write method, so we can restore it later.

❸ Monkey-patch sys.stdout.write, replacing it with our own method.

❹ Return the 'JABBERWOCKY' string just so we have something to put in the target variable what.

❺ Our replacement to sys.stdout.write reverses the text argument and calls the original implementation.

❻ Python calls __exit__ with None, None, None if all went well; if an exception is raised, the three arguments get the exception data, as described after this example.

❼ Restore the original method to sys.stdout.write.

❽ If the exception is not None and its type is ZeroDivisionError, print a message…

❾ …and return True to tell the interpreter that the exception was handled.

❿ If __exit__ returns None or any *falsy* value, any exception raised in the with block will be propagated.

> When real applications take over standard output, they often want to replace sys.stdout with another file-like object for a while, then switch back to the original. The contextlib.redirect_stdout (*https://fpy.li/18-6*) context manager does exactly that: just pass it the file-like object that will stand in for sys.stdout.

The interpreter calls the __enter__ method with no arguments—beyond the implicit self. The three arguments passed to __exit__ are:

exc_type

   The exception class (e.g., `ZeroDivisionError`).

exc_value

   The exception instance. Sometimes, parameters passed to the exception constructor—such as the error message—can be found in `exc_value.args`.

traceback

   A `traceback` object.[2]

For a detailed look at how a context manager works, see Example 18-4, where
`LookingGlass` is used outside of a `with` block, so we can manually call its `__enter__`
and `__exit__` methods.

Example 18-4. Exercising `LookingGlass` without a `with` block

```
>>> from mirror import LookingGlass
>>> manager = LookingGlass()  ❶
>>> manager  # doctest: +ELLIPSIS
<mirror.LookingGlass object at 0x...>
>>> monster = manager.__enter__()  ❷
>>> monster == 'JABBERWOCKY'  ❸
eurT
>>> monster
'YKCOWREBBAJ'
>>> manager  # doctest: +ELLIPSIS
>... ta tcejbo ssalGgnikooL.rorrim<
>>> manager.__exit__(None, None, None)  ❹
>>> monster
'JABBERWOCKY'
```

❶ Instantiate and inspect the `manager` instance.

❷ Call the manager's `__enter__` method and store result in `monster`.

❸ `monster` is the string `'JABBERWOCKY'`. The `True` identifier appears reversed
   because all output via `stdout` goes through the `write` method we patched in
   `__enter__`.

❹ Call `manager.__exit__` to restore the previous `stdout.write`.

---

2 The three arguments received by `self` are exactly what you get if you call `sys.exc_info()` (*https://fpy.li/18-7*)
  in the `finally` block of a `try/finally` statement. This makes sense, considering that the `with` statement is
  meant to replace most uses of `try/finally`, and calling `sys.exc_info()` was often necessary to determine
  what clean-up action would be required.

Parenthesized Context Managers in Python 3.10

Python 3.10 adopted a new, more powerful parser (*https://fpy.li/ pep617*), allowing new syntax beyond what was possible with the older LL(1) parser (*https://fpy.li/18-8*). One syntax enhancement was to allow parenthesized context managers, like this:

```
with (
    CtxManager1() as example1,
    CtxManager2() as example2,
    CtxManager3() as example3,
):
    ...
```

Prior to 3.10, we'd have to write that as nested with blocks.

The standard library includes the contextlib package with handy functions, classes, and decorators for building, combining, and using context managers.

The contextlib Utilities

Before rolling your own context manager classes, take a look at contextlib—"Utilities for with-statement contexts" (*https://fpy.li/18-9*) in the Python documentation. Maybe what you are about to build already exists, or there is a class or some callable that will make your job easier.

Besides the redirect_stdout context manager mentioned right after Example 18-3, redirect_stderr was added in Python 3.5—it does the same as the former, but for output directed to stderr.

The contextlib package also includes:

closing
    A function to build context managers out of objects that provide a close() method but don't implement the __enter__/__exit__ interface.

suppress
    A context manager to temporarily ignore exceptions given as arguments.

nullcontext
    A context manager that does nothing, to simplify conditional logic around objects that may not implement a suitable context manager. It serves as a stand-in when conditional code before the with block may or may not provide a context manager for the with statement—added in Python 3.7.

The contextlib module provides classes and a decorator that are more widely applicable than the decorators just mentioned:

`@contextmanager`

> A decorator that lets you build a context manager from a simple generator func-tion, instead of creating a class and implementing the interface. See "Using @contextmanager" on page 668.

`AbstractContextManager`

> An ABC that formalizes the context manager interface, and makes it a bit easier to create context manager classes by subclassing—added in Python 3.6.

`ContextDecorator`

> A base class for defining class-based context managers that can also be used as function decorators, running the entire function within a managed context.

`ExitStack`

> A context manager that lets you enter a variable number of context managers. When the `with` block ends, `ExitStack` calls the stacked context managers' `__exit__` methods in LIFO order (last entered, first exited). Use this class when you don't know beforehand how many context managers you need to enter in your `with` block; for example, when opening all files from an arbitrary list of files at the same time.

With Python 3.7, `contextlib` added `AbstractAsyncContextManager`, `@asynccontextmanager`, and `AsyncExitStack`. They are similar to the equivalent utilities without the `async` part of the name, but designed for use with the new `async with` statement, covered in Chapter 21.

The most widely used of these utilities is the `@contextmanager` decorator, so it deserves more attention. That decorator is also interesting because it shows a use for the `yield` statement unrelated to iteration.

Using @contextmanager

The `@contextmanager` decorator is an elegant and practical tool that brings together three distinctive Python features: a function decorator, a generator, and the `with` statement.

Using `@contextmanager` reduces the boilerplate of creating a context manager: instead of writing a whole class with `__enter__`/`__exit__` methods, you just imple-ment a generator with a single `yield` that should produce whatever you want the `__enter__` method to return.

In a generator decorated with `@contextmanager`, `yield` splits the body of the function in two parts: everything before the `yield` will be executed at the beginning of the `with` block when the interpreter calls `__enter__`; the code after `yield` will run when `__exit__` is called at the end of the block.

Example 18-5 replaces the LookingGlass class from Example 18-3 with a generator function.

Example 18-5. mirror_gen.py: a context manager implemented with a generator

```
import contextlib
import sys

@contextlib.contextmanager   ❶
def looking_glass():
    original_write = sys.stdout.write   ❷

    def reverse_write(text):   ❸
        original_write(text[::-1])

    sys.stdout.write = reverse_write   ❹
    yield 'JABBERWOCKY'   ❺
    sys.stdout.write = original_write   ❻
```

❶ Apply the contextmanager decorator.

❷ Preserve the original sys.stdout.write method.

❸ reverse_write can call original_write later because it is available in its closure.

❹ Replace sys.stdout.write with reverse_write.

❺ Yield the value that will be bound to the target variable in the as clause of the with statement. The generator pauses at this point while the body of the with executes.

❻ When control exits the with block, execution continues after the yield; here the original sys.stdout.write is restored.

Example 18-6 shows the looking_glass function in operation.

Example 18-6. Test-driving the looking_glass context manager function

```
>>> from mirror_gen import looking_glass
>>> with looking_glass() as what:   ❶
...     print('Alice, Kitty and Snowdrop')
...     print(what)
...
pordwonS dna yttiK ,ecilA
YKCOWREBBAJ
>>> what
'JABBERWOCKY'
```

```
>>> print('back to normal')
back to normal
```

❶ The only difference from Example 18-2 is the name of the context manager: look
  ing_glass instead of LookingGlass.

The contextlib.contextmanager decorator wraps the function in a class that implements the __enter__ and __exit__ methods.[3]

The __enter__ method of that class:

1. Calls the generator function to get a generator object—let's call it gen.

2. Calls next(gen) to drive it to the yield keyword.

3. Returns the value yielded by next(gen), to allow the user to bind it to a variable
   in the with/as form.

When the with block terminates, the __exit__ method:

1. Checks whether an exception was passed as exc_type; if so, gen.throw(excep
   tion) is invoked, causing the exception to be raised in the yield line inside the
   generator function body.

2. Otherwise, next(gen) is called, resuming the execution of the generator function
   body after the yield.

Example 18-5 has a flaw: if an exception is raised in the body of the with block, the
Python interpreter will catch it and raise it again in the yield expression inside look
ing_glass. But there is no error handling there, so the looking_glass generator will
terminate without ever restoring the original sys.stdout.write method, leaving the
system in an invalid state.

Example 18-7 adds special handling of the ZeroDivisionError exception, making it
functionally equivalent to the class-based Example 18-3.

*Example 18-7. mirror_gen_exc.py: generator-based context manager implementing
exception handling—same external behavior as Example 18-3*

```
import contextlib
import sys


@contextlib.contextmanager
```

---

3 The actual class is named _GeneratorContextManager. If you want to see exactly how it works, read its source
  code (*https://fpy.li/18-10*) in *Lib/contextlib.py* in Python 3.10.

```
def looking_glass():
    original_write = sys.stdout.write

    def reverse_write(text):
        original_write(text[::-1])

    sys.stdout.write = reverse_write
    msg = ''  ❶
    try:
        yield 'JABBERWOCKY'
    except ZeroDivisionError:  ❷
        msg = 'Please DO NOT divide by zero!'
    finally:
        sys.stdout.write = original_write  ❸
        if msg:
            print(msg)  ❹
```

❶ Create a variable for a possible error message; this is the first change in relation to Example 18-5.

❷ Handle ZeroDivisionError by setting an error message.

❸ Undo monkey-patching of sys.stdout.write.

❹ Display error message, if it was set.

Recall that the __exit__ method tells the interpreter that it has handled the exception by returning a truthy value; in that case, the interpreter suppresses the exception. On the other hand, if __exit__ does not explicitly return a value, the interpreter gets the usual None, and propagates the exception. With @contextmanager, the default behavior is inverted: the __exit__ method provided by the decorator assumes any exception sent into the generator is handled and should be suppressed.

> Having a try/finally (or a with block) around the yield is an unavoidable price of using @contextmanager, because you never know what the users of your context manager are going to do inside the with block.[4]

---

4 This tip is quoted literally from a comment by Leonardo Rochael, one of the tech reviewers for this book. Nicely said, Leo!

A little-known feature of @contextmanager is that the generators decorated with it can also be used as decorators themselves.[5] That happens because @contextmanager is implemented with the contextlib.ContextDecorator class.

Example 18-8 shows the looking_glass context manager from Example 18-5 used as decorator.

Example 18-8. The looking_glass context manager also works as a decorator

```
>>> @looking_glass()
... def verse():
...     print('The time has come')
...
>>> verse()  ❶
emoc sah emit ehT
>>> print('back to normal')  ❷
back to normal
```

❶   looking_glass does its job before and after the body of verse runs.

❷   This confirms that the original sys.write was restored.

Contrast Example 18-8 with Example 18-6, where looking_glass is used as a context manager.

An interesting real-life example of @contextmanager outside of the standard library is Martijn Pieters' in-place file rewriting using a context manager (*https://fpy.li/18-11*). Example 18-9 shows how it's used.

Example 18-9. A context manager for rewriting files in place

```
import csv

with inplace(csvfilename, 'r', newline='') as (infh, outfh):
    reader = csv.reader(infh)
    writer = csv.writer(outfh)

    for row in reader:
        row += ['new', 'columns']
        writer.writerow(row)
```

The inplace function is a context manager that gives you two handles—infh and outfh in the example—to the same file, allowing your code to read and write to it at

---

5 At least I and the other technical reviewers didn't know it until Caleb Hattingh told us. Thanks, Caleb!

the same time. It's easier to use than the standard library's `fileinput.input` function (*https://fpy.li/18-12*) (which also provides a context manager, by the way).

If you want to study Martijn's `inplace` source code (listed in the post (*https://fpy.li/18-11*)), find the `yield` keyword: everything before it deals with setting up the context, which entails creating a backup file, then opening and yielding references to the readable and writable file handles that will be returned by the `__enter__` call. The `__exit__` processing after the `yield` closes the file handles and restores the file from the backup if something went wrong.

This concludes our overview of the `with` statement and context managers. Let's turn to `match/case` in the context of a complete example.

Pattern Matching in lis.py: A Case Study

In "Pattern Matching Sequences in an Interpreter" on page 43 we saw examples of sequence patterns extracted from the `evaluate` function of Peter Norvig's *lis.py* interpreter, ported to Python 3.10. In this section I want to give a broader overview of how *lis.py* works, and also explore all the `case` clauses of `evaluate`, explaining not only the patterns but also what the interpreter does in each `case`.

Besides showing more pattern matching, I wrote this section for three reasons:

1. Norvig's *lis.py* is a beautiful example of idiomatic Python code.
2. The simplicity of Scheme is a master class of language design.
3. Learning how an interpreter works gave me a deeper understanding of Python and programming languages in general—interpreted or compiled.

Before looking at the Python code, let's get a little taste of Scheme so you can make sense of this case study—in case you haven't seen Scheme or Lisp before.

Scheme Syntax

In Scheme there is no distinction between expressions and statements, like we have in Python. Also, there are no infix operators. All expressions use prefix notation like `(+ x 13)` instead of `x + 13`. The same prefix notation is used for function calls—e.g., `(gcd x 13)`—and special forms—e.g., `(define x 13)`, which we'd write as the assignment statement `x = 13` in Python. The notation used by Scheme and most Lisp dialects is known as *S-expression*.[6]

---

6 People complain about too many parentheses in Lisp, but thoughtful indentation and a good editor mostly take care of that issue. The main readability problem is using the same `(f …)` notation for function calls and special forms like `(define …)`, `(if …)`, and `(quote …)` that don't behave at all like function calls.

Example 18-10 shows a simple example in Scheme.

Example 18-10. Greatest common divisor in Scheme

```scheme
(define (mod m n)
    (- m (* n (quotient m n))))

(define (gcd m n)
    (if (= n 0)
        m
        (gcd n (mod m n))))

(display (gcd 18 45))
```

Example 18-10 shows three Scheme expressions: two function definitions—mod and gcd—and a call to display, which will output 9, the result of (gcd 18 45). Example 18-11 is the same code in Python (shorter than an English explanation of the recursive *Euclidean algorithm* (*https://fpy.li/18-14*)).

Example 18-11. Same as Example 18-10, written in Python

```python
def mod(m, n):
    return m - (m // n * n)

def gcd(m, n):
    if n == 0:
        return m
    else:
        return gcd(n, mod(m, n))

print(gcd(18, 45))
```

In idiomatic Python, I'd use the % operator instead of reinventing mod, and it would be more efficient to use a while loop instead of recursion. But I wanted to show two function definitions, and make the examples as similar as possible, to help you read the Scheme code.

Scheme has no iterative control flow commands like while or for. Iteration is done with recursion. Note how there are no assignments in the Scheme and Python examples. Extensive use of recursion and minimal use of assignment are hallmarks of programming in a functional style.[7]

---

7 To make iteration through recursion practical and efficient, Scheme and other functional languages implement *proper tail calls*. For more about this, see "Soapbox" on page 695.

Now let's review the code of the Python 3.10 version of *lis.py*. The complete source code with tests is in the *18-with-match/lispy/py3.10/* (*https://fpy.li/18-15*) directory of the GitHub repository *fluentpython/example-code-2e* (*https://fpy.li/code*).

Imports and Types

Example 18-12 shows the first lines of *lis.py*. The use of `TypeAlias` and the `|` type union operator require Python 3.10.

Example 18-12. lis.py: top of the file

```
import math
import operator as op
from collections import ChainMap
from itertools import chain
from typing import Any, TypeAlias, NoReturn

Symbol: TypeAlias = str
Atom: TypeAlias = float | int | Symbol
Expression: TypeAlias = Atom | list
```

The types defined are:

Symbol
>   Just an alias for `str`. In *lis.py*, `Symbol` is used for identifiers; there is no string data type with operations such as slicing, splitting, etc.[8]

Atom
>   A simple syntactic element, such as a number or a `Symbol`—as opposed to a composite structure made of distinct parts, like a list.

Expression
>   The building blocks of Scheme programs are expressions made of atoms and lists, possibly nested.

The Parser

Norvig's parser is 36 lines of code showcasing the power of Python applied to handling the simple recursive syntax of S-expression—without string data, comments, macros, and other features of standard Scheme that make parsing more complicated (Example 18-13).

---

8 But Norvig's second interpreter, *lispy.py* (*https://fpy.li/18-16*), supports strings as a data type, as well as advanced features like syntactic macros, continuations, and proper tail calls. However, *lispy.py* is almost three times longer than *lis.py*—and much harder to understand.

Example 18-13. lis.py: the main parsing functions

```python
def parse(program: str) -> Expression:
    "Read a Scheme expression from a string."
    return read_from_tokens(tokenize(program))

def tokenize(s: str) -> list[str]:
    "Convert a string into a list of tokens."
    return s.replace('(', ' ( ').replace(')', ' ) ').split()

def read_from_tokens(tokens: list[str]) -> Expression:
    "Read an expression from a sequence of tokens."
    # more parsing code omitted in book listing
```

The main function of that group is `parse`, which takes an S-expression as a `str` and returns an `Expression` object, as defined in Example 18-12: an `Atom` or a `list` that may contain more atoms and nested lists.

Norvig uses a smart trick in `tokenize`: he adds spaces before and after each parenthesis in the input and then splits it, resulting in a list of syntactic tokens with `'('` and `')'` as separate tokens. This shortcut works because there is no string type in the little Scheme of *lis.py*, so every `'('` or `')'` is an expression delimiter. The recursive parsing code is in `read_from_tokens`, a 14-line function that you can read in the *fluentpy-thon/example-code-2e* (*https://fpy.li/18-17*) repository. I will skip it because I want to focus on the other parts of the interpreter.

Here are some doctests extracted from *lispy/py3.10/examples_test.py* (*https://fpy.li/18-18*):

```
>>> from lis import parse
>>> parse('1.5')
1.5
>>> parse('ni!')
'ni!'
>>> parse('(gcd 18 45)')
['gcd', 18, 45]
>>> parse('''
... (define double
...     (lambda (n)
...         (* n 2)))
... ''')
['define', 'double', ['lambda', ['n'], ['*', 'n', 2]]]
```

The parsing rules for this subset of Scheme are simple:

1. A token that looks like a number is parsed as a `float` or `int`.

2. Anything else that is not `'('` or `')'` is parsed as a `Symbol`—a `str` to be used as an identifier. This includes source text like `+`, `set!`, and `make-counter` that are valid identifiers in Scheme but not in Python.

---

3. Expressions inside '(' and ')' are recursively parsed as lists containing atoms or as nested lists that may contain atoms and more nested lists.

Using the terminology of the Python interpreter, the output of parse is an AST (Abstract Syntax Tree): a convenient representation of the Scheme program as nested lists forming a tree-like structure, where the outermost list is the trunk, inner lists are the branches, and atoms are the leaves (Figure 18-1).

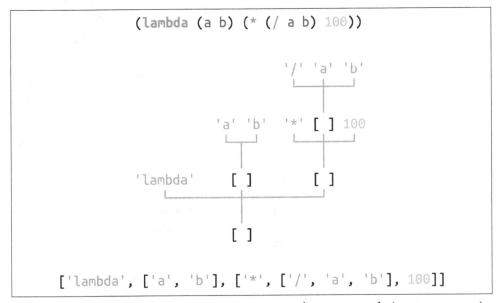

Figure 18-1. A Scheme lambda expression represented as source code (concrete syntax), as a tree, and as a sequence of Python objects (abstract syntax).

The Environment

The Environment class extends collections.ChainMap, adding a change method to update a value inside one of the chained dicts, which ChainMap instances hold in a list of mappings: the self.maps attribute. The change method is needed to support the Scheme (set! …) form, described later; see Example 18-14.

Example 18-14. lis.py: the Environment class

```
class Environment(ChainMap[Symbol, Any]):
    "A ChainMap that allows changing an item in-place."

    def change(self, key: Symbol, value: Any) -> None:
        "Find where key is defined and change the value there."
        for map in self.maps:
            if key in map:
```

```
            map[key] = value  # type: ignore[index]
            return
    raise KeyError(key)
```

Note that the change method only updates existing keys.[9] Trying to change a key that is not found raises KeyError.

This doctest shows how Environment works:

```
>>> from lis import Environment
>>> inner_env = {'a': 2}
>>> outer_env = {'a': 0, 'b': 1}
>>> env = Environment(inner_env, outer_env)
>>> env['a']   ❶
2
>>> env['a'] = 111   ❷
>>> env['c'] = 222
>>> env
Environment({'a': 111, 'c': 222}, {'a': 0, 'b': 1})
>>> env.change('b', 333)   ❸
>>> env
Environment({'a': 111, 'c': 222}, {'a': 0, 'b': 333})
```

❶ When reading values, Environment works as ChainMap: keys are searched in the nested mappings from left to right. That's why the value of a in the outer_env is shadowed by the value in inner_env.

❷ Assigning with [ ] overwrites or inserts new items, but always in the first mapping, inner_env in this example.

❸ env.change('b', 333) seeks the 'b' key and assigns a new value to it in-place, in the outer_env.

Next is the standard_env() function, which builds and returns an Environment loaded with predefined functions, similar to Python's __builtins__ module that is always available (Example 18-15).

Example 18-15. lis.py: standard_env() builds and returns the global environment

```
def standard_env() -> Environment:
    "An environment with some Scheme standard procedures."
    env = Environment()
```

---

9 The # type: ignore[index] comment is there because of *typeshed* issue #6042 (*https://fpy.li/18-19*), which is unresolved as I review this chapter. ChainMap is annotated as MutableMapping, but the type hint in the maps attribute says it's a list of Mapping, indirectly making the whole ChainMap immutable as far as Mypy is concerned.

```
env.update(vars(math))    # sin, cos, sqrt, pi, ...
env.update({
        '+': op.add,
        '-': op.sub,
        '*': op.mul,
        '/': op.truediv,
        # omitted here: more operator definitions
        'abs': abs,
        'append': lambda *args: list(chain(*args)),
        'apply': lambda proc, args: proc(*args),
        'begin': lambda *x: x[-1],
        'car': lambda x: x[0],
        'cdr': lambda x: x[1:],
        # omitted here: more function definitions
        'number?': lambda x: isinstance(x, (int, float)),
        'procedure?': callable,
        'round': round,
        'symbol?': lambda x: isinstance(x, Symbol),
})
return env
```

To summarize, the `env` mapping is loaded with:

- All functions from Python's `math` module
- Selected operators from Python's `op` module
- Simple but powerful functions built with Python's `lambda`
- Python built-ins renamed, like `callable` as `procedure?`, or directly mapped, like `round`

The REPL

Norvig's REPL (read-eval-print-loop) is easy to understand but not user-friendly (see Example 18-16). If no command-line arguments are given to *lis.py*, the `repl()` function is invoked by `main()`—defined at the end of the module. At the `lis.py>` prompt, we must enter correct and complete expressions; if we forget to close one parenthesis, *lis.py* crashes.[10]

---

10 As I studied Norvig's *lis.py* and *lispy.py*, I started a fork named *mylis* (*https://fpy.li/18-20*) that adds some features, including a REPL that accepts partial S-expressions and prompts for the continuation, similar to how Python's REPL knows we are not finished and presents the secondary prompt (`...`) until we enter a complete expression or statement that can be evaluated. *mylis* also handles a few errors gracefully, but it's still easy to crash. It's not nearly as robust as Python's REPL.

Example 18-16. The REPL functions

```
def repl(prompt: str = 'lis.py> ') -> NoReturn:
    "A prompt-read-eval-print loop."
    global_env = Environment({}, standard_env())
    while True:
        ast = parse(input(prompt))
        val = evaluate(ast, global_env)
        if val is not None:
            print(lispstr(val))

def lispstr(exp: object) -> str:
    "Convert a Python object back into a Lisp-readable string."
    if isinstance(exp, list):
        return '(' + ' '.join(map(lispstr, exp)) + ')'
    else:
        return str(exp)
```

Here is a quick explanation about these two functions:

`repl(prompt: str = 'lis.py> ') -> NoReturn`
Calls `standard_env()` to provide built-in functions for the global environment, then enters an infinite loop, reading and parsing each input line, evaluating it in the global environment, and displaying the result—unless it's `None`. The `global_env` may be modified by `evaluate`. For example, when a user defines a new global variable or named function, it is stored in the first mapping of the environment—the empty `dict` in the `Environment` constructor call in the first line of `repl`.

`lispstr(exp: object) -> str`
The inverse function of `parse`: given a Python object representing an expression, `parse` returns the Scheme source code for it. For example, given `['+', 2, 3]`, the result is `'(+ 2 3)'`.

The Evaluator

Now we can appreciate the beauty of Norvig's expression evaluator—made a little prettier with `match/case`. The `evaluate` function in Example 18-17 takes an Expression built by `parse` and an `Environment`.

The body of `evaluate` is a single `match` statement with an expression `exp` as the subject. The `case` patterns express the syntax and semantics of Scheme with amazing clarity.

Example 18-17. evaluate takes an expression and computes its value

```python
KEYWORDS = ['quote', 'if', 'lambda', 'define', 'set!']

def evaluate(exp: Expression, env: Environment) -> Any:
    "Evaluate an expression in an environment."
    match exp:
        case int(x) | float(x):
            return x
        case Symbol(var):
            return env[var]
        case ['quote', x]:
            return x
        case ['if', test, consequence, alternative]:
            if evaluate(test, env):
                return evaluate(consequence, env)
            else:
                return evaluate(alternative, env)
        case ['lambda', [*parms], *body] if body:
            return Procedure(parms, body, env)
        case ['define', Symbol(name), value_exp]:
            env[name] = evaluate(value_exp, env)
        case ['define', [Symbol(name), *parms], *body] if body:
            env[name] = Procedure(parms, body, env)
        case ['set!', Symbol(name), value_exp]:
            env.change(name, evaluate(value_exp, env))
        case [func_exp, *args] if func_exp not in KEYWORDS:
            proc = evaluate(func_exp, env)
            values = [evaluate(arg, env) for arg in args]
            return proc(*values)
        case _:
            raise SyntaxError(lispstr(exp))
```

Let's study each `case` clause and what it does. In some cases I added comments showing an S-expression that would match the pattern when parsed into a Python list. Doctests extracted from *examples_test.py* (*https://fpy.li/18-21*) demonstrate each case.

Evaluating numbers

```python
        case int(x) | float(x):
            return x
```

Subject:
  Instance of `int` or `float`.

Action:
  Return value as is.

Example:
```
>>> from lis import parse, evaluate, standard_env
>>> evaluate(parse('1.5'), {})
1.5
```

Evaluating symbols

```
case Symbol(var):
    return env[var]
```

Subject:

Instance of Symbol, i.e., a str used as an identifier.

Action:

Look up var in env and return its value.

Examples:
```
>>> evaluate(parse('+'), standard_env())
<built-in function add>
>>> evaluate(parse('ni!'), standard_env())
Traceback (most recent call last):
    ...
KeyError: 'ni!'
```

(quote ...)

The quote special form treats atoms and lists as data instead of expressions to be evaluated.

```
# (quote (99 bottles of beer))
case ['quote', x]:
    return x
```

Subject:

List starting with the symbol 'quote', followed by one expression x.

Action:

Return x without evaluating it.

Examples:
```
>>> evaluate(parse('(quote no-such-name)'), standard_env())
'no-such-name'
>>> evaluate(parse('(quote (99 bottles of beer))'), standard_env())
[99, 'bottles', 'of', 'beer']
>>> evaluate(parse('(quote (/ 10 0))'), standard_env())
['/', 10, 0]
```

Without quote, each expression in the test would raise an error:

- no-such-name would be looked up in the environment, raising KeyError

- (99 bottles of beer) cannot be evaluated because the number 99 is not a Symbol naming a special form, operator, or function

- (/ 10 0) would raise ZeroDivisionError

Why Languages Have Reserved Keywords

Although simple, quote cannot be implemented as a function in Scheme. Its special power is to prevent the interpreter from evaluating (f 10) in the expression (quote (f 10)): the result is simply a list with a Symbol and an int. In contrast, in a function call like (abs (f 10)), the interpreter evaluates (f 10) before invoking abs. That's why quote is a reserved keyword: it must be handled as a special form.

In general, reserved keywords are needed:

- To introduce specialized evaluation rules, as in quote and lambda—which don't evaluate any of their subexpressions

- To change the control flow, as in if and function calls—which also have special evaluation rules

- To manage the environment, as in define and set

This is also why Python, and programming languages in general, need reserved keywords. Think about Python's def, if, yield, import, del, and what they do.

(if ...)

```
# (if (< x 0) 0 x)
case ['if', test, consequence, alternative]:
    if evaluate(test, env):
        return evaluate(consequence, env)
    else:
        return evaluate(alternative, env)
```

Subject:

List starting with 'if' followed by three expressions: test, consequence, and alternative.

Action:

Evaluate test:

- If true, evaluate consequence and return its value.

- Otherwise, evaluate alternative and return its value.

Examples:

```
>>> evaluate(parse('(if (= 3 3) 1 0))'), standard_env())
1
>>> evaluate(parse('(if (= 3 4) 1 0))'), standard_env())
0
```

The `consequence` and `alternative` branches must be single expressions. If more than one expression is needed in a branch, you can combine them with (`begin exp1 exp2…`), provided as a function in *lis.py*—see Example 18-15.

(lambda ...)

Scheme's `lambda` form defines anonymous functions. It doesn't suffer from the limitations of Python's `lambda`: any function that can be written in Scheme can be written using the (`lambda …`) syntax.

```
# (lambda (a b) (/ (+ a b) 2))
case ['lambda' [*parms], *body] if body:
    return Procedure(parms, body, env)
```

Subject:

List starting with '`lambda`', followed by:

- List of zero or more parameter names.

- One or more expressions collected in body (the guard ensures that body is not empty).

Action:

Create and return a new `Procedure` instance with the parameter names, the list of expressions as the body, and the current environment.

Example:

```
>>> expr = '(lambda (a b) (* (/ a b) 100))'
>>> f = evaluate(parse(expr), standard_env())
>>> f   # doctest: +ELLIPSIS
<lis.Procedure object at 0x...>
>>> f(15, 20)
75.0
```

The `Procedure` class implements the concept of a closure: a callable object holding parameter names, a function body, and a reference to the environment in which the function is defined. We'll study the code for `Procedure` in a moment.

(define ...)

The `define` keyword is used in two different syntactic forms. The simplest is:

```
# (define half (/ 1 2))
case ['define', Symbol(name), value_exp]:
    env[name] = evaluate(value_exp, env)
```

Subject:

List starting with `'define'`, followed by a `Symbol` and an expression.

Action:

Evaluate the expression and put its value into env, using `name` as key.

Example:

```
>>> global_env = standard_env()
>>> evaluate(parse('(define answer (* 7 6))'), global_env)
>>> global_env['answer']
42
```

The doctest for this `case` creates a `global_env` so that we can verify that `evaluate` puts answer into that `Environment`.

We can use that simple `define` form to create variables or to bind names to anonymous functions, using `(lambda ...)` as the `value_exp`.

Standard Scheme provides a shortcut for defining named functions. That's the second `define` form:

```
# (define (average a b) (/ (+ a b) 2))
case ['define', [Symbol(name), *parms], *body] if body:
    env[name] = Procedure(parms, body, env)
```

Subject:

List starting with `'define'`, followed by:

- A list starting with a `Symbol(name)`, followed by zero or more items collected into a list named `parms`.

- One or more expressions collected in body (the guard ensures that body is not empty).

Action:

- Create a new `Procedure` instance with the parameter names, the list of expressions as the body, and the current environment.

- Put the `Procedure` into env, using `name` as key.

The doctest in Example 18-18 defines a function named % that computes a percentage and adds it to the `global_env`.

Example 18-18. Defining a function named % that computes a percentage

```
>>> global_env = standard_env()
>>> percent = '(define (% a b) (* (/ a b) 100))'
>>> evaluate(parse(percent), global_env)
>>> global_env['%']   # doctest: +ELLIPSIS
<lis.Procedure object at 0x...>
>>> global_env['%'](170, 200)
85.0
```

After calling `evaluate`, we check that `%` is bound to a `Procedure` that takes two numeric arguments and returns a percentage.

The pattern for the second `define` case does not enforce that the items in `parms` are all `Symbol` instances. I'd have to check that before building the `Procedure`, but I didn't—to keep the code as easy to follow as Norvig's.

(set! ...)

The `set!` form changes the value of a previously defined variable.[11]

```
        # (set! n (+ n 1))
        case ['set!', Symbol(name), value_exp]:
            env.change(name, evaluate(value_exp, env))
```

Subject:
    List starting with `'set!'`, followed by a `Symbol` and an expression.

Action:
    Update the value of `name` in `env` with the result of evaluating the expression.

The `Environment.change` method traverses the chained environments from local to global, and updates the first occurrence of `name` with the new value. If we were not implementing the `'set!'` keyword, we could use Python's `ChainMap` as the `Environ ment` type everywhere in this interpreter.

---

11 Assignment is one of the first features taught in many programming tutorials, but `set!` only appears on page 220 of the best known Scheme book, *Structure and Interpretation of Computer Programs*, 2nd ed., (*https:// fpy.li/18-22*) by Abelson et al. (MIT Press), a.k.a. SICP or the "Wizard Book." Coding in a functional style can take us very far without the state changes that are typical of imperative and object-oriented programming.

Python's nonlocal and Scheme's set! Address the Same Issue

The use of the set! form is related to the use of the nonlocal keyword in Python: declaring nonlocal x allows x = 10 to update a previously defined x variable outside of the local scope. Without a nonlocal x declaration, x = 10 will always create a local variable in Python, as we saw in "The nonlocal Declaration" on page 317.

Similarly, (set! x 10) updates a previously defined x that may be outside of the local environment of the function. In contrast, the variable x in (define x 10) is always a local variable, created or updated in the local environment.

Both nonlocal and (set! …) are needed to update program state held in variables within a closure. Example 9-13 demonstrated the use of nonlocal to implement a function to compute a running average, holding an item count and total in a closure. Here is that same idea, written in the Scheme subset of *lis.py*:

```
(define (make-averager)
    (define count 0)
    (define total 0)
    (lambda (new-value)
        (set! count (+ count 1))
        (set! total (+ total new-value))
        (/ total count)
    )
)
(define avg (make-averager))   ❶
(avg 10)   ❷
(avg 11)   ❸
(avg 15)   ❹
```

❶ Creates a new closure with the inner function defined by lambda, and the variables count and total initialized to 0; binds the closure to avg.

❷ Returns 10.0.

❸ Returns 10.5.

❹ Returns 12.0.

The preceding code is one of the tests in *lispy/py3.10/examples_test.py* (*https://fpy.li/ 18-18*).

Now we get to a function call.

Function call

```
# (gcd (* 2 105) 84)
case [func_exp, *args] if func_exp not in KEYWORDS:
    proc = evaluate(func_exp, env)
    values = [evaluate(arg, env) for arg in args]
    return proc(*values)
```

Subject:

List with one or more items.

The guard ensures that func_exp is not one of ['quote', 'if', 'define', 'lambda', 'set!']—listed right before evaluate in Example 18-17.

The pattern matches any list with one or more expressions, binding the first expression to func_exp and the rest to args as a list, which may be empty.

Action:

- Evaluate func_exp to obtain a function proc.

- Evaluate each item in args to build a list of argument values.

- Call proc with the values as separate arguments, returning the result.

Example:

```
>>> evaluate(parse('(% (* 12 14) (- 500 100))'), global_env)
42.0
```

This doctest continues from Example 18-18: it assumes global_env has a function named %. The arguments given to % are arithmetic expressions, to emphasize that the arguments are evaluated before the function is called.

The guard in this case is needed because [func_exp, *args] matches any sequence subject with one or more items. However, if func_exp is a keyword, and the subject did not match any previous case, then it is really a syntax error.

Catch syntax errors

If the subject exp does not match any of the previous cases, the catch-all case raises a SyntaxError:

```
case _:
    raise SyntaxError(lispstr(exp))
```

Here is an example of a malformed (lambda …) reported as a SyntaxError:

```
>>> evaluate(parse('(lambda is not like this)'), standard_env())
Traceback (most recent call last):
  ...
SyntaxError: (lambda is not like this)
```

If the case for function call did not have that guard rejecting keywords, the (lambda is not like this) expression would be handled as a function call, which would raise KeyError because 'lambda' is not part of the environment—just like lambda is not a Python built-in function.

Procedure: A Class Implementing a Closure

The Procedure class could very well be named Closure, because that's what it represents: a function definition together with an environment. The function definition includes the name of the parameters and the expressions that make up the body of the function. The environment is used when the function is called to provide the values of the *free variables*: variables that appear in the body of the function but are not parameters, local variables, or global variables. We saw the concepts of *closure* and *free variable* in "Closures" on page 313.

We learned how to use closures in Python, but now we can dive deeper and see how a closure is implemented in *lis.py*:

```
class Procedure:
    "A user-defined Scheme procedure."

    def __init__(    ❶
        self, parms: list[Symbol], body: list[Expression], env: Environment
    ):
        self.parms = parms    ❷
        self.body = body
        self.env = env

    def __call__(self, *args: Expression) -> Any:    ❸
        local_env = dict(zip(self.parms, args))    ❹
        env = Environment(local_env, self.env)    ❺
        for exp in self.body:    ❻
            result = evaluate(exp, env)
        return result    ❼
```

❶ Called when a function is defined by the lambda or define forms.

❷ Save the parameter names, body expressions, and environment for later use.

❸ Called by proc(*values) in the last line of the case [func_exp, *args] clause.

❹ Build local_env mapping self.parms as local variable names, and the given args as values.

❺ Build a new combined env, putting local_env first, and then self.env—the environment that was saved when the function was defined.

❻ Iterate over each expression in `self.body`, evaluating it in the combined env.

❼ Return the result of the last expression evaluated.

There are a couple of simple functions after `evaluate` in *lis.py* (*https://fpy.li/18-24*): `run` reads a complete Scheme program and executes it, and `main` calls `run` or `repl`, depending on the command line—similar to what Python does. I will not describe those functions because there's nothing new in them. My goals were to share with you the beauty of Norvig's little interpreter, to give more insight into how closures work, and to show how `match/case` is a great addition to Python.

To wrap up this extended section on pattern matching, let's formalize the concept of an OR-pattern.

Using OR-patterns

A series of patterns separated by | is an *OR-pattern* (*https://fpy.li/18-25*): it succeeds if any of the subpatterns succeed. The pattern in "Evaluating numbers" on page 681 is an OR-pattern:

```
case int(x) | float(x):
    return x
```

All subpatterns in an OR-pattern must use the same variables. This restriction is necessary to ensure that the variables are available to the guard expression and the `case` body, regardless of the subpattern that matched.

 In the context of a `case` clause, the | operator has a special meaning. It does not trigger the `__or__` special method, which handles expressions like `a | b` in other contexts, where it is overloaded to perform operations such as set union or integer bitwise-or, depending on the operands.

An OR-pattern is not restricted to appear at the top level of a pattern. You can also use | in subpatterns. For example, if we wanted *lis.py* to accept the Greek letter λ (lambda)[12] as well as the `lambda` keyword, we can rewrite the pattern like this:

```
# (λ (a b) (/ (+ a b) 2) )
case ['lambda' | 'λ', [*parms], *body] if body:
    return Procedure(parms, body, env)
```

---

12 The official Unicode name for λ (U+03BB) is GREEK SMALL LETTER LAMDA. This is not a typo: the character is named "lamda" without the "b" in the Unicode database. According to the English Wikipedia article "Lambda" (*https://fpy.li/18-26*), the Unicode Consortium adopted that spelling because of "preferences expressed by the Greek National Body."

Now we can move to the third and last subject of this chapter: the unusual places where an `else` clause may appear in Python.

Do This, Then That: else Blocks Beyond if

This is no secret, but it is an underappreciated language feature: the `else` clause can be used not only in `if` statements but also in `for`, `while`, and `try` statements.

The semantics of `for/else`, `while/else`, and `try/else` are closely related, but very different from `if/else`. Initially, the word `else` actually hindered my understanding of these features, but eventually I got used to it.

Here are the rules:

`for`

The `else` block will run only if and when the `for` loop runs to completion (i.e., not if the `for` is aborted with a `break`).

`while`

The `else` block will run only if and when the `while` loop exits because the condition became *falsy* (i.e., not if the `while` is aborted with a `break`).

`try`

The `else` block will run only if no exception is raised in the `try` block. The official docs (*https://fpy.li/18-27*) also state: "Exceptions in the `else` clause are not handled by the preceding `except` clauses."

In all cases, the `else` clause is also skipped if an exception or a `return`, `break`, or `continue` statement causes control to jump out of the main block of the compound statement.

 I think `else` is a very poor choice for the keyword in all cases except `if`. It implies an excluding alternative, like, "Run this loop, otherwise do that," but the semantics for `else` in loops is the opposite: "Run this loop, then do that." This suggests `then` as a better keyword—which would also make sense in the `try` context: "Try this, then do that." However, adding a new keyword is a breaking change to the language—not an easy decision to make.

Using `else` with these statements often makes the code easier to read and saves the trouble of setting up control flags or coding extra `if` statements.

The use of `else` in loops generally follows the pattern of this snippet:

```
for item in my_list:
    if item.flavor == 'banana':
```

```
        break
    else:
        raise ValueError('No banana flavor found!')
```

In the case of try/except blocks, else may seem redundant at first. After all, the after_call() in the following snippet will run only if the dangerous_call() does not raise an exception, correct?

```
try:
    dangerous_call()
    after_call()
except OSError:
    log('OSError...')
```

However, doing so puts the after_call() inside the try block for no good reason. For clarity and correctness, the body of a try block should only have the statements that may generate the expected exceptions. This is better:

```
try:
    dangerous_call()
except OSError:
    log('OSError...')
else:
    after_call()
```

Now it's clear that the try block is guarding against possible errors in dangerous_call() and not in after_call(). It's also explicit that after_call() will only execute if no exceptions are raised in the try block.

In Python, try/except is commonly used for control flow, and not just for error handling. There's even an acronym/slogan for that documented in the official Python glossary (*https://fpy.li/18-28*):

EAFP

> Easier to ask for forgiveness than permission. This common Python coding style assumes the existence of valid keys or attributes and catches exceptions if the assumption proves false. This clean and fast style is characterized by the presence of many try and except statements. The technique contrasts with the *LBYL* style common to many other languages such as C.

The glossary then defines LBYL:

LBYL

> Look before you leap. This coding style explicitly tests for pre-conditions before making calls or lookups. This style contrasts with the *EAFP* approach and is characterized by the presence of many if statements. In a multi-threaded environment, the LBYL approach can risk introducing a race condition between "the looking" and "the leaping." For example, the code, if key in mapping: return mapping[key] can fail if another thread removes key from mapping after the test, but before the lookup. This issue can be solved with locks or by using the EAFP approach.

Given the EAFP style, it makes even more sense to know and use else blocks well in try/except statements.

 When the match statement was discussed, some people (including me) thought it should also have an else clause. In the end it was decided that it wasn't needed because case _: does the same job.[13]

Now let's summarize the chapter.

Chapter Summary

This chapter started with context managers and the meaning of the with statement, quickly moving beyond its common use to automatically close opened files. We implemented a custom context manager: the LookingGlass class with the __enter__/__exit__ methods, and saw how to handle exceptions in the __exit__ method. A key point that Raymond Hettinger made in his PyCon US 2013 keynote is that with is not just for resource management; it's a tool for factoring out common setup and teardown code, or any pair of operations that need to be done before and after another procedure.[14]

We reviewed functions in the contextlib standard library module. One of them, the @contextmanager decorator, makes it possible to implement a context manager using a simple generator with one yield—a leaner solution than coding a class with at least two methods. We reimplemented the LookingGlass as a looking_glass generator function, and discussed how to do exception handling when using @contextmanager.

Then we studied Peter Norvig's elegant *lis.py*, a Scheme interpreter written in idiomatic Python, refactored to use match/case in evaluate—the function at the core of any interpreter. Understanding how evaluate works required reviewing a little bit of Scheme, a parser for S-expressions, a simple REPL, and the construction of nested scopes through an Environment subclass of collection.ChainMap. In the end, *lis.py* became a vehicle to explore much more than pattern matching. It shows how the different parts of an interpreter work together, illuminating core features of Python itself: why reserved keywords are necessary, how scoping rules work, and how closures are built and used.

---

13 Watching the discussion in the python-dev mailing list I thought one reason why else was rejected was the lack of consensus on how to indent it within match: should else be indented at the same level as match, or at the same level as case?

14 See slide 21 in "Python is Awesome" (*https://fpy.li/18-29*).

Further Reading

Chapter 8, "Compound Statements," (*https://fpy.li/18-27*) in *The Python Language Reference* says pretty much everything there is to say about else clauses in if, for, while, and try statements. Regarding Pythonic usage of try/except, with or without else, Raymond Hettinger has a brilliant answer to the question "Is it a good practice to use try-except-else in Python?" (*https://fpy.li/18-31*) in StackOverflow. *Python in a Nutshell*, 3rd ed., by Martelli et al., has a chapter about exceptions with an excellent discussion of the EAFP style, crediting computing pioneer Grace Hopper for coining the phrase, "It's easier to ask forgiveness than permission."

The Python Standard Library, Chapter 4, "Built-in Types," has a section devoted to "Context Manager Types" (*https://fpy.li/18-32*). The __enter__/__exit__ special methods are also documented in *The Python Language Reference* in "With Statement Context Managers" (*https://fpy.li/18-33*). Context managers were introduced in PEP 343—The "with" Statement (*https://fpy.li/pep343*).

Raymond Hettinger highlighted the with statement as a "winning language feature" in his PyCon US 2013 keynote (*https://fpy.li/18-29*). He also showed some interesting applications of context managers in his talk, "Transforming Code into Beautiful, Idiomatic Python" (*https://fpy.li/18-35*), at the same conference.

Jeff Preshing's blog post "The Python *with* Statement by Example" (*https://fpy.li/18-36*) is interesting for the examples using context managers with the pycairo graphics library.

The contextlib.ExitStack class is based on an original idea by Nikolaus Rath, who wrote a short post explaining why its useful: "On the Beauty of Python's ExitStack" (*https://fpy.li/18-37*). In that text, Rath submits that ExitStack is similar but more flexible than the defer statement in Go—which I think is one of the best ideas in that language.

Beazley and Jones devised context managers for very different purposes in their *Python Cookbook*, 3rd ed. "Recipe 8.3. Making Objects Support the Context-Management Protocol" implements a LazyConnection class whose instances are context managers that open and close network connections automatically in with blocks. "Recipe 9.22. Defining Context Managers the Easy Way" introduces a context manager for timing code, and another for making transactional changes to a list object: within the with block, a working copy of the list instance is made, and all changes are applied to that working copy. Only when the with block completes without an exception, the working copy replaces the original list. Simple and ingenious.

Peter Norvig describes his small Scheme interpreters in the posts "(How to Write a (Lisp) Interpreter (in Python))" (*https://fpy.li/18-38*) and "(An ((Even Better) Lisp) Interpreter (in Python))" (*https://fpy.li/18-39*). The code for *lis.py* and *lispy.py* is the *norvig/pytudes* (*https://fpy.li/18-40*) repository. My repository *fluentpython/lispy* (*https://fpy.li/18-41*) includes the *mylis* forks of *lis.py*, updated to Python 3.10, with a nicer REPL, command-line integration, examples, more tests, and references for learning more about Scheme. The best Scheme dialect and environment to learn and experiment is Racket (*https://fpy.li/18-42*).

Soapbox

Factoring Out the Bread

In his PyCon US 2013 keynote, "What Makes Python Awesome" (*https://fpy.li/18-1*), Raymond Hettinger says when he first saw the `with` statement proposal he thought it was "a little bit arcane." Initially, I had a similar reaction. PEPs are often hard to read, and PEP 343 is typical in that regard.

Then—Hettinger told us—he had an insight: subroutines are the most important invention in the history of computer languages. If you have sequences of operations like A;B;C and P;B;Q, you can factor out B in a subroutine. It's like factoring out the filling in a sandwich: using tuna with different breads. But what if you want to factor out the bread, to make sandwiches with wheat bread, using a different filling each time? That's what the `with` statement offers. It's the complement of the subroutine. Hettinger went on to say:

> The `with` statement is a very big deal. I encourage you to go out and take this tip of the iceberg and drill deeper. You can probably do profound things with the `with` statement. The best uses of it have not been discovered yet. I expect that if you make good use of it, it will be copied into other languages and all future languages will have it. You can be part of discovering something almost as profound as the invention of the subroutine itself.

Hettinger admits he is overselling the `with` statement. Nevertheless, it is a very useful feature. When he used the sandwich analogy to explain how `with` is the complement to the subroutine, many possibilities opened up in my mind.

If you need to convince anyone that Python is awesome, you should watch Hettinger's keynote. The bit about context managers is from 23:00 to 26:15. But the entire keynote is excellent.

Efficient Recursion with Proper Tail Calls

Standard Scheme implementations are required to provide *proper tail calls* (PTC), to make iteration through recursion a practical alternative to `while` loops in imperative languages. Some writers refer to PTC as *tail call optimization* (TCO); for others, TCO is something different. For more details, see "Tail call" (*https://fpy.li/18-44*) on Wikipedia and "Tail call optimization in ECMAScript 6" (*https://fpy.li/18-45*).

A *tail call* is when a function returns the result of a function call, which may be the same function or not. The gcd examples in Example 18-10 and Example 18-11 make (recursive) tail calls in the *falsy* branch of the if.

On the other hand, this factorial does not make a tail call:

```
def factorial(n):
    if n < 2:
        return 1
    return n * factorial(n - 1)
```

The call to factorial in the last line is not a tail call because the return value is not the result of the recursive call: the result is multiplied by n before it is returned.

Here is an alternative that uses a tail call, and is therefore *tail recursive*:

```
def factorial_tc(n, product=1):
    if n < 1:
        return product
    return factorial_tc(n - 1, product * n)
```

Python does not have PTC, so there's no advantage in writing tail recursive functions. In this case, the first version is shorter and more readable in my opinion. For real-life uses, don't forget that Python has math.factorial, written in C without recursion. The point is that, even in languages that implement PTC, it does not benefit every recursive function, only those that are carefully written to make tail calls.

If PTC is supported by the language, when the interpreter sees a tail call, it jumps into the body of the called function without creating a new stack frame, saving memory. There are also compiled languages that implement PTC, sometimes as an optimization that can be toggled.

There is no universal consensus about the definition of TCO or the value of PTC in languages that were not designed as functional languages from the ground up, like Python or JavaScript. In functional languages, PTC is an expected feature, not merely an optimization that is nice to have. If a language has no iteration mechanism other than recursion, then PTC is necessary for practical usage. Norvig's *lis.py* (*https://fpy.li/18-46*) does not implement PTC, but his more elaborate *lispy.py* (*https://fpy.li/18-16*) interpreter does.

The Case Against Proper Tail Calls in Python and JavaScript

CPython does not implement PTC, and probably never will. Guido van Rossum wrote "Final Words on Tail Calls" (*https://fpy.li/18-48*) to explain why. To summarize, here is a key passage from his post:

> Personally, I think it is a fine feature for some languages, but I don't think it fits Python: the elimination of stack traces for some calls but not others would certainly confuse many users, who have not been raised with tail call religion but might have learned about call semantics by tracing through a few calls in a debugger.

In 2015, PTC was included in the ECMAScript 6 standard for JavaScript. As of October 2021, the interpreter in WebKit implements it (*https://fpy.li/18-49*). WebKit is used by Safari. The JS interpreters in every other major browser don't have PTC, and neither does Node.js, as it relies on the V8 engine that Google maintains for Chrome. Transpilers and polyfills targeting JS, like TypeScript, ClojureScript, and Babel, don't support PTC either, according to this "ECMAScript 6 compatibility table" (*https://fpy.li/18-50*).

I've seen several explanations for the rejection of PTC by the implementers, but the most common is the same that Guido van Rossum mentioned: PTC makes debugging harder for everyone, while benefiting only a minority of people who'd rather use recursion for iteration. For details, see "What happened to proper tail calls in JavaScript?" (*https://fpy.li/18-51*) by Graham Marlow.

There are cases when recursion is the best solution, even in Python without PTC. In a previous post (*https://fpy.li/18-52*) on the subject, Guido wrote:

> [...] a typical Python implementation allows 1000 recursions, which is plenty for non-recursively written code and for code that recourses to traverse, for example, a typical parse tree, but not enough for a recursively written loop over a large list.

I agree with Guido and the majority of JS implementers: PTC is not a good fit for Python or JavaScript. The lack of PTC is the main restriction for writing Python programs in a functional style—more than the limited `lambda` syntax.

If you are curious to see how PTC works in an interpreter with less features (and less code) than Norvig's *lispy.py*, check out *mylis_2* (*https://fpy.li/18-53*). The trick starts with the infinite loop in `evaluate` and the code in the `case` for function calls: that combination makes the intepreter jump into the body of the next `Procedure` without calling `evaluate` recursively during a tail call. Those little interpreters demonstrate the power of abstraction: even though Python does not implement PTC, it's possible and not very hard to write an interpreter, in Python, that does implement PTC. I learned how to do it reading Peter Norvig's code. Thanks for sharing it, professor!

Norvig's Take on evaluate() with Pattern Matching

I shared the code for the Python 3.10 version of *lis.py* with Peter Norvig. He liked the example using pattern matching, but suggested a different solution: instead of the guards I wrote, he would have exactly one `case` per keyword, and have tests within each `case`, to provide more specific `SyntaxError` messages—for example, when a body is empty. This would also make the guard in `case [func_exp, *args] if func_exp not in KEYWORDS:` unnecessary, as every keyword would be handled before the `case` for function calls.

I'll probably follow Norvig's advice when I add more functionality to *mylis* (*https://fpy.li/18-54*). But the way I structured `evaluate` in Example 18-17 has some didactic advantages for this book: the example parallels the implementation with `if/elif/…`

(Example 2-11), the `case` clauses demonstrate more features of pattern matching, and the code is more concise.

## CHAPTER 19

Concurrency Models in Python

Concurrency is about dealing with lots of things at once.

Parallelism is about doing lots of things at once.

Not the same, but related.

One is about structure, one is about execution.

Concurrency provides a way to structure a solution to solve a problem that may (but not necessarily) be parallelizable.

> —Rob Pike, co-inventor of the Go language[1]

This chapter is about how to make Python deal with "lots of things at once." This may involve concurrent or parallel programming—even academics who are keen on jargon disagree on how to use those terms. I will adopt Rob Pike's informal definitions in this chapter's epigraph, but note that I've found papers and books that claim to be about parallel computing but are mostly about concurrency.[2]

Parallelism is a special case of concurrency, in Pike's view. All parallel systems are concurrent, but not all concurrent systems are parallel. In the early 2000s we used single-core machines that handled 100 processes concurrently on GNU Linux. A modern laptop with 4 CPU cores is routinely running more than 200 processes at any given time under normal, casual use. To execute 200 tasks in parallel, you'd need 200 cores. So, in practice, most computing is concurrent and not parallel. The OS

---

1 Slide 8 of the talk "Concurrency Is Not Parallelism" (*https://fpy.li/19-1*).

2 I studied and worked with Prof. Imre Simon, who liked to say there are two major sins in science: using different words to mean the same thing and using one word to mean different things. Imre Simon (1943–2009) was a pioneer of computer science in Brazil who made seminal contributions to Automata Theory and started the field of Tropical Mathematics. He was also an advocate of free software and free culture.

manages hundreds of processes, making sure each has an opportunity to make progress, even if the CPU itself can't do more than four things at once.

This chapter assumes no prior knowledge of concurrent or parallel programming. After a brief conceptual introduction, we will study simple examples to introduce and compare Python's core packages for concurrent programming: threading, multi processing, and asyncio.

The last 30% of the chapter is a high-level overview of third-party tools, libraries, application servers, and distributed task queues—all of which can enhance the performance and scalability of Python applications. These are all important topics, but beyond the scope of a book focused on core Python language features. Nevertheless, I felt it was important to address these themes in this second edition of *Fluent Python*, because Python's fitness for concurrent and parallel computing is not limited to what the standard library provides. That's why YouTube, DropBox, Instagram, Reddit, and others were able to achieve web scale when they started, using Python as their primary language—despite persistent claims that "Python doesn't scale."

What's New in This Chapter

This chapter is new in the second edition of *Fluent Python*. The spinner examples in "A Concurrent Hello World" on page 705 previously were in the chapter about *asyncio*. Here they are improved, and provide the first illustration of Python's three approaches to concurrency: threads, processes, and native coroutines.

The remaining content is new, except for a few paragraphs that originally appeared in the chapters on concurrent.futures and *asyncio*.

"Python in the Multicore World" on page 729 is different from the rest of the book: there are no code examples. The goal is to mention important tools that you may want to study to achieve high-performance concurrency and parallelism beyond what's possible with Python's standard library.

The Big Picture

There are many factors that make concurrent programming hard, but I want to touch on the most basic factor: starting threads or processes is easy enough, but how do you keep track of them?[3]

When you call a function, the calling code is blocked until the function returns. So you know when the function is done, and you can easily get the value it returned. If

---

3 This section was suggested by my friend Bruce Eckel—author of books about Kotlin, Scala, Java, and C++.

the function raises an exception, the calling code can surround the call site with `try/ except` to catch the error.

Those familiar options are not available when you start a thread or process: you don't automatically know when it's done, and getting back results or errors requires setting up some communication channel, such as a message queue.

Additionally, starting a thread or a process is not cheap, so you don't want to start one of them just to perform a single computation and quit. Often you want to amortize the startup cost by making each thread or process into a "worker" that enters a loop and stands by for inputs to work on. This further complicates communications and introduces more questions. How do you make a worker quit when you don't need it anymore? And how do you make it quit without interrupting a job partway, leaving half-baked data and unreleased resources—like open files? Again the usual answers involve messages and queues.

A coroutine is cheap to start. If you start a coroutine using the `await` keyword, it's easy to get a value returned by it, it can be safely cancelled, and you have a clear site to catch exceptions. But coroutines are often started by the asynchronous framework, and that can make them as hard to monitor as threads or processes.

Finally, Python coroutines and threads are not suitable for CPU-intensive tasks, as we'll see.

That's why concurrent programming requires learning new concepts and coding patterns. Let's first make sure we are on the same page regarding some core concepts.

A Bit of Jargon

Here are some terms I will use for the rest of this chapter and the next two:

Concurrency
> The ability to handle multiple pending tasks, making progress one at a time or in parallel (if possible) so that each of them eventually succeeds or fails. A single-core CPU is capable of concurrency if it runs an OS scheduler that interleaves the execution of the pending tasks. Also known as multitasking.

Parallelism
> The ability to execute multiple computations at the same time. This requires a multicore CPU, multiple CPUs, a GPU (*https://fpy.li/19-2*), or multiple computers in a cluster.

Execution unit
> General term for objects that execute code concurrently, each with independent state and call stack. Python natively supports three kinds of execution units: *processes*, *threads*, and *coroutines*.

Process

An instance of a computer program while it is running, using memory and a slice of the CPU time. Modern desktop operating systems routinely manage hundreds of processes concurrently, with each process isolated in its own private memory space. Processes communicate via pipes, sockets, or memory mapped files—all of which can only carry raw bytes. Python objects must be serialized (converted) into raw bytes to pass from one process to another. This is costly, and not all Python objects are serializable. A process can spawn subprocesses, each called a child process. These are also isolated from each other and from the parent. Processes allow *preemptive multitasking*: the OS scheduler *preempts*—i.e., suspends—each running process periodically to allow other processes to run. This means that a frozen process can't freeze the whole system—in theory.

Thread

An execution unit within a single process. When a process starts, it uses a single thread: the main thread. A process can create more threads to operate concurrently by calling operating system APIs. Threads within a process share the same memory space, which holds live Python objects. This allows easy data sharing between threads, but can also lead to corrupted data when more than one thread updates the same object concurrently. Like processes, threads also enable *preemptive multitasking* under the supervision of the OS scheduler. A thread consumes less resources than a process doing the same job.

Coroutine

A function that can suspend itself and resume later. In Python, *classic coroutines* are built from generator functions, and *native coroutines* are defined with `async def`. "Classic Coroutines" on page 645 introduced the concept, and Chapter 21 covers the use of native coroutines. Python coroutines usually run within a single thread under the supervision of an *event loop*, also in the same thread. Asynchronous programming frameworks such as *asyncio*, *Curio*, or *Trio* provide an event loop and supporting libraries for nonblocking, coroutine-based I/O. Coroutines support *cooperative multitasking*: each coroutine must explicitly cede control with the `yield` or `await` keyword, so that another may proceed concurrently (but not in parallel). This means that any blocking code in a coroutine blocks the execution of the event loop and all other coroutines—in contrast with the *preemptive multitasking* supported by processes and threads. On the other hand, each coroutine consumes less resources than a thread or process doing the same job.

Queue

A data structure that lets us put and get items, usually in FIFO order: first in, first out. Queues allow separate execution units to exchange application data and control messages, such as error codes and signals to terminate. The implementation of a queue varies according to the underlying concurrency model: the `queue` package in Python's standard library provides queue classes to support threads, while the `multiprocessing` and `asyncio` packages implement their own queue classes. The `queue` and `asyncio` packages also include queues that are not FIFO: `LifoQueue` and `PriorityQueue`.

Lock

An object that execution units can use to synchronize their actions and avoid corrupting data. While updating a shared data structure, the running code should hold an associated lock. This signals other parts of the program to wait until the lock is released before accessing the same data structure. The simplest type of lock is also known as a mutex (for mutual exclusion). The implementation of a lock depends on the underlying concurrency model.

Contention

Dispute over a limited asset. Resource contention happens when multiple execution units try to access a shared resource—such as a lock or storage. There's also CPU contention, when compute-intensive processes or threads must wait for the OS scheduler to give them a share of the CPU time.

Now let's use some of that jargon to understand concurrency support in Python.

Processes, Threads, and Python's Infamous GIL

Here is how the concepts we just saw apply to Python programming, in 10 points:

1. Each instance of the Python interpreter is a process. You can start additional Python processes using the *multiprocessing* or *concurrent.futures* libraries. Python's *subprocess* library is designed to launch processes to run external programs, regardless of the languages used to write them.

2. The Python interpreter uses a single thread to run the user's program and the memory garbage collector. You can start additional Python threads using the *threading* or *concurrent.futures* libraries.

3. Access to object reference counts and other internal interpreter state is controlled by a lock, the Global Interpreter Lock (GIL). Only one Python thread can hold the GIL at any time. This means that only one thread can execute Python code at any time, regardless of the number of CPU cores.

4. To prevent a Python thread from holding the GIL indefinitely, Python's bytecode interpreter pauses the current Python thread every 5ms by default,[4] releasing the

---

4 Call sys.getswitchinterval() (*https://fpy.li/19-3*) to get the interval; change it with sys.setswitchin terval(s) (*https://fpy.li/19-4*).

GIL. The thread can then try to reacquire the GIL, but if there are other threads waiting for it, the OS scheduler may pick one of them to proceed.

5. When we write Python code, we have no control over the GIL. But a built-in function or an extension written in C—or any language that interfaces at the Python/C API level—can release the GIL while running time-consuming tasks.

6. Every Python standard library function that makes a syscall[5] releases the GIL. This includes all functions that perform disk I/O, network I/O, and time.sleep(). Many CPU-intensive functions in the NumPy/SciPy libraries, as well as the compressing/decompressing functions from the zlib and bz2 modules, also release the GIL.[6]

7. Extensions that integrate at the Python/C API level can also launch other non-Python threads that are not affected by the GIL. Such GIL-free threads generally cannot change Python objects, but they can read from and write to the memory underlying objects that support the buffer protocol (*https://fpy.li/pep3118*), such as bytearray, array.array, and *NumPy* arrays.

8. The effect of the GIL on network programming with Python threads is relatively small, because the I/O functions release the GIL, and reading or writing to the network always implies high latency—compared to reading and writing to memory. Consequently, each individual thread spends a lot of time waiting anyway, so their execution can be interleaved without major impact on the overall throughput. That's why David Beazley says: "Python threads are great at doing nothing."[7]

9. Contention over the GIL slows down compute-intensive Python threads. Sequential, single-threaded code is simpler and faster for such tasks.

10. To run CPU-intensive Python code on multiple cores, you must use multiple Python processes.

Here is a good summary from the threading module documentation:[8]

> **CPython implementation detail**: In CPython, due to the Global Interpreter Lock, only one thread can execute Python code at once (even though certain performance-oriented libraries might overcome this limitation). If you want your application to

---

5 A syscall is a call from user code to a function of the operating system kernel. I/O, timers, and locks are some of the kernel services available through syscalls. To learn more, read the Wikipedia "System call" article (*https://fpy.li/19-5*).

6 The zlib and bz2 modules are specifically mentioned in a python-dev message by Antoine Pitrou (*https://fpy.li/19-6*), who contributed the time-slicing GIL logic to Python 3.2.

7 Source: slide 106 of Beazley's "Generators: The Final Frontier" tutorial (*https://fpy.li/19-7*).

8 Source: last paragraph of the "Thread objects" section (*https://fpy.li/19-8*).

make better use of the computational resources of multicore machines, you are advised to use `multiprocessing` or `concurrent.futures.ProcessPoolExecutor`. However, threading is still an appropriate model if you want to run multiple I/O-bound tasks simultaneously.

The previous paragraph starts with "CPython implementation detail" because the GIL is not part of the Python language definition. The Jython and IronPython implementations don't have a GIL. Unfortunately, both are lagging behind—still tracking Python 2.7. The highly performant PyPy interpreter (*https://fpy.li/19-9*) also has a GIL in its 2.7 and 3.7 versions—the latest as of June 2021.

 This section did not mention coroutines, because by default they share the same Python thread among themselves and with the supervising event loop provided by an asynchronous framework, therefore the GIL does not affect them. It is possible to use multiple threads in an asynchronous program, but the best practice is that one thread runs the event loop and all coroutines, while additional threads carry out specific tasks. This will be explained in "Delegating Tasks to Executors" on page 801.

Enough concepts for now. Let's see some code.

A Concurrent Hello World

During a discussion about threads and how to avoid the GIL, Python contributor Michele Simionato posted an example (*https://fpy.li/19-10*) that is like a concurrent "Hello World": the simplest program to show how Python can "walk and chew gum."

Simionato's program uses `multiprocessing`, but I adapted it to introduce `threading` and `asyncio` as well. Let's start with the `threading` version, which may look familiar if you've studied threads in Java or C.

Spinner with Threads

The idea of the next few examples is simple: start a function that blocks for 3 seconds while animating characters in the terminal to let the user know that the program is "thinking" and not stalled.

The script makes an animated spinner displaying each character in the string `"\|/-"` in the same screen position.[9] When the slow computation finishes, the line with the spinner is cleared and the result is shown: `Answer: 42`.

---

9 Unicode has lots of characters useful for simple animations, like the Braille patterns (*https://fpy.li/19-11*) for example. I used the ASCII characters `"\|/-"` to keep the examples simple.

Figure 19-1 shows the output of two versions of the spinning example: first with threads, then with coroutines. If you're away from the computer, imagine the \ in the last line is spinning.

```
$ python3 spinner_thread.py                    19-concurrency — Python spinner_async.py — 88x9
spinner object: <Thread(Thread-1 (spin), initial)>
Answer: 42
$ python3 spinner_async.py
spinner object: <Task pending name='Task-2' coro=<spin() running at /Users/luciano/flupy
/example-code-2e/19-concurrency/spinner_async.py:11>>
- thinking!
```

Figure 19-1. The scripts spinner_thread.py and spinner_async.py produce similar output: the repr of a spinner object and the text "Answer: 42". In the screenshot, spinner_async.py is still running, and the animated message "/ thinking!" is shown; that line will be replaced by "Answer: 42" after 3 seconds.

Let's review the *spinner_thread.py* script first. Example 19-1 lists the first two functions in the script, and Example 19-2 shows the rest.

Example 19-1. spinner_thread.py: the spin and slow functions

```
import itertools
import time
from threading import Thread, Event

def spin(msg: str, done: Event) -> None:    ❶
    for char in itertools.cycle(r'\|/-'):    ❷
        status = f'\r{char} {msg}'    ❸
        print(status, end='', flush=True)
        if done.wait(.1):    ❹
            break    ❺
    blanks = ' ' * len(status)
    print(f'\r{blanks}\r', end='')    ❻

def slow() -> int:
    time.sleep(3)    ❼
    return 42
```

❶ This function will run in a separate thread. The done argument is an instance of threading.Event, a simple object to synchronize threads.

❷ This is an infinite loop because itertools.cycle yields one character at a time, cycling through the string forever.

❸ The trick for text-mode animation: move the cursor back to the start of the line with the carriage return ASCII control character ('\r').

❹ The `Event.wait(timeout=None)` method returns `True` when the event is set by another thread; if the `timeout` elapses, it returns `False`. The .1s timeout sets the "frame rate" of the animation to 10 FPS. If you want the spinner to go faster, use a smaller timeout.

❺ Exit the infinite loop.

❻ Clear the status line by overwriting with spaces and moving the cursor back to the beginning.

❼ `slow()` will be called by the main thread. Imagine this is a slow API call over the network. Calling `sleep` blocks the main thread, but the GIL is released so the spinner thread can proceed.

 The first important insight of this example is that `time.sleep()` blocks the calling thread but releases the GIL, allowing other Python threads to run.

The `spin` and `slow` functions will execute concurrently. The main thread—the only thread when the program starts—will start a new thread to run `spin` and then call `slow`. By design, there is no API for terminating a thread in Python. You must send it a message to shut down.

The `threading.Event` class is Python's simplest signalling mechanism to coordinate threads. An `Event` instance has an internal boolean flag that starts as `False`. Calling `Event.set()` sets the flag to `True`. While the flag is false, if a thread calls `Event.wait()`, it is blocked until another thread calls `Event.set()`, at which time `Event.wait()` returns `True`. If a timeout in seconds is given to `Event.wait(s)`, this call returns `False` when the timeout elapses, or returns `True` as soon as `Event.set()` is called by another thread.

The `supervisor` function, listed in Example 19-2, uses an `Event` to signal the `spin` function to exit.

Example 19-2. spinner_thread.py: the supervisor and main functions

```python
def supervisor() -> int:  ❶
    done = Event()  ❷
    spinner = Thread(target=spin, args=('thinking!', done))  ❸
    print(f'spinner object: {spinner}')  ❹
    spinner.start()  ❺
    result = slow()  ❻
    done.set()  ❼
```

```
    spinner.join()  ❽
    return result

def main() -> None:
    result = supervisor()  ❾
    print(f'Answer: {result}')

if __name__ == '__main__':
    main()
```

❶ supervisor will return the result of slow.

❷ The threading.Event instance is the key to coordinate the activities of the main thread and the spinner thread, as explained further down.

❸ To create a new Thread, provide a function as the target keyword argument, and positional arguments to the target as a tuple passed via args.

❹ Display the spinner object. The output is <Thread(Thread-1, initial)>, where initial is the state of the thread—meaning it has not started.

❺ Start the spinner thread.

❻ Call slow, which blocks the main thread. Meanwhile, the secondary thread is running the spinner animation.

❼ Set the Event flag to True; this will terminate the for loop inside the spin function.

❽ Wait until the spinner thread finishes.

❾ Run the supervisor function. I wrote separate main and supervisor functions to make this example look more like the asyncio version in Example 19-4.

When the main thread sets the done event, the spinner thread will eventually notice and exit cleanly.

Now let's take a look at a similar example using the multiprocessing package.

Spinner with Processes

The multiprocessing package supports running concurrent tasks in separate Python processes instead of threads. When you create a multiprocessing.Process instance, a whole new Python interpreter is started as a child process in the background. Since each Python process has its own GIL, this allows your program to use all available

CPU cores—but that ultimately depends on the operating system scheduler. We'll see practical effects in "A Homegrown Process Pool" on page 720, but for this simple program it makes no real difference.

The point of this section is to introduce `multiprocessing` and show that its API emulates the `threading` API, making it easy to convert simple programs from threads to processes, as shown in *spinner_proc.py* (Example 19-3).

Example 19-3. spinner_proc.py: only the changed parts are shown; everything else is the same as spinner_thread.py

```python
import itertools
import time
from multiprocessing import Process, Event      ❶
from multiprocessing import synchronize         ❷

def spin(msg: str, done: synchronize.Event) -> None:    ❸

# [snip] the rest of spin and slow functions are unchanged from spinner_thread.py

def supervisor() -> int:
    done = Event()
    spinner = Process(target=spin,               ❹
                      args=('thinking!', done))
    print(f'spinner object: {spinner}')          ❺
    spinner.start()
    result = slow()
    done.set()
    spinner.join()
    return result

# [snip] main function is unchanged as well
```

❶ The basic `multiprocessing` API imitates the `threading` API, but type hints and Mypy expose this difference: `multiprocessing.Event` is a function (not a class like `threading.Event`) which returns a `synchronize.Event` instance...

❷ ...forcing us to import `multiprocessing.synchronize`...

❸ ...to write this type hint.

❹ Basic usage of the `Process` class is similar to `Thread`.

❺ The `spinner` object is displayed as `<Process name='Process-1' parent=14868 initial>`, where 14868 is the process ID of the Python instance running *spinner_proc.py*.

The basic API of threading and multiprocessing are similar, but their implementation is very different, and multiprocessing has a much larger API to handle the added complexity of multiprocess programming. For example, one challenge when converting from threads to processes is how to communicate between processes that are isolated by the operating system and can't share Python objects. This means that objects crossing process boundaries have to be serialized and deserialized, which creates overhead. In Example 19-3, the only data that crosses the process boundary is the Event state, which is implemented with a low-level OS semaphore in the C code underlying the multiprocessing module.[10]

> Since Python 3.8, there's a multiprocessing.shared_memory (*https://fpy.li/19-12*) package in the standard library, but it does not support instances of user-defined classes. Besides raw bytes, the package allows processes to share a ShareableList, a mutable sequence type that can hold a fixed number of items of types int, float, bool, and None, as well as str and bytes up to 10 MB per item. See the ShareableList (*https://fpy.li/19-13*) documentation for more.

Now let's see how the same behavior can be achieved with coroutines instead of threads or processes.

Spinner with Coroutines

> Chapter 21 is entirely devoted to asynchronous programming with coroutines. This is just a high-level introduction to contrast this approach with the threads and processes concurrency models. As such, we will overlook many details.

It is the job of OS schedulers to allocate CPU time to drive threads and processes. In contrast, coroutines are driven by an application-level event loop that manages a queue of pending coroutines, drives them one by one, monitors events triggered by I/O operations initiated by coroutines, and passes control back to the corresponding coroutine when each event happens. The event loop and the library coroutines and the user coroutines all execute in a single thread. Therefore, any time spent in a coroutine slows down the event loop—and all other coroutines.

---

10 The semaphore is a fundamental building block that can be used to implement other synchronization mechanisms. Python provides different semaphore classes for use with threads, processes, and coroutines. We'll see asyncio.Semaphore in "Using asyncio.as_completed and a Thread" on page 793 (Chapter 21).

The coroutine version of the spinner program is easier to understand if we start from the `main` function, then study the `supervisor`. That's what Example 19-4 shows.

Example 19-4. spinner_async.py: the main function and supervisor coroutine

```
def main() -> None:  ❶
    result = asyncio.run(supervisor())  ❷
    print(f'Answer: {result}')

async def supervisor() -> int:  ❸
    spinner = asyncio.create_task(spin('thinking!'))  ❹
    print(f'spinner object: {spinner}')  ❺
    result = await slow()  ❻
    spinner.cancel()  ❼
    return result

if __name__ == '__main__':
    main()
```

❶ `main` is the only regular function defined in this program—the others are coroutines.

❷ The `asyncio.run` function starts the event loop to drive the coroutine that will eventually set the other coroutines in motion. The `main` function will stay blocked until `supervisor` returns. The return value of `supervisor` will be the return value of `asyncio.run`.

❸ Native coroutines are defined with `async def`.

❹ `asyncio.create_task` schedules the eventual execution of `spin`, immediately returning an instance of `asyncio.Task`.

❺ The `repr` of the spinner object looks like `<Task pending name='Task-2' coro=<spin() running at /path/to/spinner_async.py:11>>`.

❻ The `await` keyword calls `slow`, blocking `supervisor` until `slow` returns. The return value of `slow` will be assigned to `result`.

❼ The `Task.cancel` method raises a `CancelledError` exception inside the `spin` coroutine, as we'll see in Example 19-5.

Example 19-4 demonstrates the three main ways of running a coroutine:

```
asyncio.run(coro())
```
Called from a regular function to drive a coroutine object that usually is the entry point for all the asynchronous code in the program, like the supervisor in this example. This call blocks until the body of coro returns. The return value of the run() call is whatever the body of coro returns.

```
asyncio.create_task(coro())
```
Called from a coroutine to schedule another coroutine to execute eventually. This call does not suspend the current coroutine. It returns a Task instance, an object that wraps the coroutine object and provides methods to control and query its state.

```
await coro()
```
Called from a coroutine to transfer control to the coroutine object returned by coro(). This suspends the current coroutine until the body of coro returns. The value of the await expression is whatever the body of coro returns.

 Remember: invoking a coroutine as coro() immediately returns a coroutine object, but does not run the body of the coro function. Driving the body of coroutines is the job of the event loop.

Now let's study the spin and slow coroutines in Example 19-5.

Example 19-5. spinner_async.py: the spin and slow coroutines

```python
import asyncio
import itertools

async def spin(msg: str) -> None:  ❶
    for char in itertools.cycle(r'\|/-'):
        status = f'\r{char} {msg}'
        print(status, flush=True, end='')
        try:
            await asyncio.sleep(.1)  ❷
        except asyncio.CancelledError:  ❸
            break
    blanks = ' ' * len(status)
    print(f'\r{blanks}\r', end='')

async def slow() -> int:
    await asyncio.sleep(3)  ❹
    return 42
```

❶ We don't need the `Event` argument that was used to signal that `slow` had completed its job in *spinner_thread.py* (Example 19-1).

❷ Use `await asyncio.sleep(.1)` instead of `time.sleep(.1)`, to pause without blocking other coroutines. See the experiment after this example.

❸ `asyncio.CancelledError` is raised when the `cancel` method is called on the `Task` controlling this coroutine. Time to exit the loop.

❹ The `slow` coroutine also uses `await asyncio.sleep` instead of `time.sleep`.

Experiment: Break the spinner for an insight

Here is an experiment I recommend to understand how *spinner_async.py* works. Import the `time` module, then go to the `slow` coroutine and replace the line `await asyncio.sleep(3)` with a call to `time.sleep(3)`, like in Example 19-6.

Example 19-6. spinner_async.py: replacing `await asyncio.sleep(3)` *with* `time.sleep(3)`

```
async def slow() -> int:
    time.sleep(3)
    return 42
```

Watching the behavior is more memorable than reading about it. Go ahead, I'll wait.

When you run the experiment, this is what you see:

1. The spinner object is shown, similar to this: `<Task pending name='Task-2' coro=<spin() running at /path/to/spinner_async.py:12>>`.
2. The spinner never appears. The program hangs for 3 seconds.
3. `Answer: 42` is displayed and the program ends.

To understand what is happening, recall that Python code using `asyncio` has only one flow of execution, unless you've explicitly started additional threads or processes. That means only one coroutine executes at any point in time. Concurrency is achieved by control passing from one coroutine to another. In Example 19-7, let's focus on what happens in the `supervisor` and `slow` coroutines during the proposed experiment.

Example 19-7. spinner_async_experiment.py: the `supervisor` *and* `slow` *coroutines*

```
async def slow() -> int:
    time.sleep(3)   ❹
```

```
    return 42

async def supervisor() -> int:
    spinner = asyncio.create_task(spin('thinking!'))   ❶
    print(f'spinner object: {spinner}')   ❷
    result = await slow()   ❸
    spinner.cancel()   ❺
    return result
```

❶ The spinner task is created, to eventually drive the execution of spin.

❷ The display shows the Task is "pending."

❸ The await expression transfers control to the slow coroutine.

❹ time.sleep(3) blocks for 3 seconds; nothing else can happen in the program, because the main thread is blocked—and it is the only thread. The operating system will continue with other activities. After 3 seconds, sleep unblocks, and slow returns.

❺ Right after slow returns, the spinner task is cancelled. The flow of control never reached the body of the spin coroutine.

The *spinner_async_experiment.py* teaches an important lesson, as explained in the following warning.

 Never use time.sleep(…) in asyncio coroutines unless you want to pause your whole program. If a coroutine needs to spend some time doing nothing, it should await asyncio.sleep(DELAY). This yields control back to the asyncio event loop, which can drive other pending coroutines.

Greenlet and gevent

As we discuss concurrency with coroutines, it's important to mention the *greenlet* (*https://fpy.li/19-14*) package, which has been around for many years and is used at scale.[11] The package supports cooperative multitasking through lightweight coroutines—named *greenlets*—that don't require any special syntax such as yield or await, therefore are easier to integrate into existing, sequential codebases. SQL Alchemy 1.4 ORM uses greenlets (*https://fpy.li/19-15*) internally to implement its new asynchronous API (*https://fpy.li/19-16*) compatible with *asyncio*.

---

11 Thanks to tech reviewers Caleb Hattingh and Jürgen Gmach who did not let me overlook *greenlet* and *gevent*.

The *gevent* (*https://fpy.li/19-17*) networking library monkey patches Python's standard `socket` module making it nonblocking by replacing some of its code with greenlets. To a large extent, *gevent* is transparent to the surrounding code, making it easier to adapt sequential applications and libraries—such as database drivers—to perform concurrent network I/O. Numerous open source projects (*https://fpy.li/19-18*) use *gevent*, including the widely deployed *Gunicorn* (*https://fpy.li/gunicorn*)—mentioned in "WSGI Application Servers" on page 734.

Supervisors Side-by-Side

The line count of *spinner_thread.py* and *spinner_async.py* is nearly the same. The `supervisor` functions are the heart of these examples. Let's compare them in detail. Example 19-8 lists only the `supervisor` from Example 19-2.

Example 19-8. spinner_thread.py: the threaded `supervisor` function

```
def supervisor() -> int:
    done = Event()
    spinner = Thread(target=spin,
                     args=('thinking!', done))
    print('spinner object:', spinner)
    spinner.start()
    result = slow()
    done.set()
    spinner.join()
    return result
```

For comparison, Example 19-9 shows the `supervisor` coroutine from Example 19-4.

Example 19-9. spinner_async.py: the asynchronous `supervisor` coroutine

```
async def supervisor() -> int:
    spinner = asyncio.create_task(spin('thinking!'))
    print('spinner object:', spinner)
    result = await slow()
    spinner.cancel()
    return result
```

Here is a summary of the differences and similarities to note between the two `supervisor` implementations:

- An `asyncio.Task` is roughly the equivalent of a `threading.Thread`.
- A `Task` drives a coroutine object, and a `Thread` invokes a callable.
- A coroutine yields control explicitly with the `await` keyword.

- You don't instantiate `Task` objects yourself, you get them by passing a coroutine to `asyncio.create_task(…)`.

- When `asyncio.create_task(…)` returns a `Task` object, it is already scheduled to run, but a `Thread` instance must be explicitly told to run by calling its `start` method.

- In the threaded `supervisor`, `slow` is a plain function and is directly invoked by the main thread. In the asynchronous `supervisor`, `slow` is a coroutine driven by `await`.

- There's no API to terminate a thread from the outside; instead, you must send a signal—like setting the `done Event` object. For tasks, there is the `Task.cancel()` instance method, which raises `CancelledError` at the `await` expression where the coroutine body is currently suspended.

- The `supervisor` coroutine must be started with `asyncio.run` in the `main` function.

This comparison should help you understand how concurrent jobs are orchestrated with *asyncio*, in contrast to how it's done with the `Threading` module, which may be more familiar to you.

One final point related to threads versus coroutines: if you've done any nontrivial programming with threads, you know how challenging it is to reason about the program because the scheduler can interrupt a thread at any time. You must remember to hold locks to protect the critical sections of your program, to avoid getting interrupted in the middle of a multistep operation—which could leave data in an invalid state.

With coroutines, your code is protected against interruption by default. You must explicitly `await` to let the rest of the program run. Instead of holding locks to synchronize the operations of multiple threads, coroutines are "synchronized" by definition: only one of them is running at any time. When you want to give up control, you use `await` to yield control back to the scheduler. That's why it is possible to safely cancel a coroutine: by definition, a coroutine can only be cancelled when it's suspended at an `await` expression, so you can perform cleanup by handling the `Cancel ledError` exception.

The `time.sleep()` call blocks but does nothing. Now we'll experiment with a CPU-intensive call to get a better understanding of the GIL, as well as the effect of CPU-intensive functions in asynchronous code.

The Real Impact of the GIL

In the threading code (Example 19-1), you can replace the `time.sleep(3)` call in the `slow` function with an HTTP client request from your favorite library, and the spinner will keep spinning. That's because a well-designed network library will release the GIL while waiting for the network.

You can also replace the `asyncio.sleep(3)` expression in the `slow` coroutine to `await` for a response from a well-designed asynchronous network library, because such libraries provide coroutines that yield control back to the event loop while waiting for the network. Meanwhile, the spinner will keep spinning.

With CPU-intensive code, the story is different. Consider the function `is_prime` in Example 19-10, which returns `True` if the argument is a prime number, `False` if it's not.

Example 19-10. primes.py: an easy to read primality check, from Python's `ProcessPool Executor` example (https://fpy.li/19-19)

```python
def is_prime(n: int) -> bool:
    if n < 2:
        return False
    if n == 2:
        return True
    if n % 2 == 0:
        return False

    root = math.isqrt(n)
    for i in range(3, root + 1, 2):
        if n % i == 0:
            return False
    return True
```

The call `is_prime(5_000_111_000_222_021)` takes about 3.3s on the company laptop I am using now.[12]

Quick Quiz

Given what we've seen so far, please take the time to consider the following three-part question. One part of the answer is tricky (at least it was for me).

> What would happen to the spinner animation if you made the following changes, assuming that n = 5_000_111_000_222_021—that prime which my machine takes 3.3s to verify:

---

12 It's a 15" MacBook Pro 2018 with a 6-core, 2.2 GHz Intel Core i7 CPU.

1. In *spinner_proc.py*, replace `time.sleep(3)` with a call to `is_prime(n)`?

2. In *spinner_thread.py*, replace `time.sleep(3)` with a call to `is_prime(n)`?

3. In *spinner_async.py*, replace `await asyncio.sleep(3)` with a call to `is_prime(n)`?

Before you run the code or read on, I recommend figuring out the answers on your own. Then, you may want to copy and modify the *spinner_*.py* examples as suggested.

Now the answers, from easier to hardest.

1. Answer for multiprocessing

The spinner is controlled by a child process, so it continues spinning while the primality test is computed by the parent process.[13]

2. Answer for threading

The spinner is controlled by a secondary thread, so it continues spinning while the primality test is computed by the main thread.

I did not get this answer right at first: I was expecting the spinner to freeze because I overestimated the impact of the GIL.

In this particular example, the spinner keeps spinning because Python suspends the running thread every 5ms (by default), making the GIL available to other pending threads. Therefore, the main thread running `is_prime` is interrupted every 5ms, allowing the secondary thread to wake up and iterate once through the `for` loop, until it calls the `wait` method of the `done` event, at which time it will release the GIL. The main thread will then grab the GIL, and the `is_prime` computation will proceed for another 5ms.

This does not have a visible impact on the running time of this specific example, because the `spin` function quickly iterates once and releases the GIL as it waits for the `done` event, so there is not much contention for the GIL. The main thread running `is_prime` will have the GIL most of the time.

We got away with a compute-intensive task using threading in this simple experiment because there are only two threads: one hogging the CPU, and the other waking up only 10 times per second to update the spinner.

---

13 This is true today because you are probably using a modern OS with *preemptive multitasking*. Windows before the NT era and macOS before the OSX era were not "preemptive," therefore any process could take over 100% of the CPU and freeze the whole system. We are not completely free of this kind of problem today but trust this graybeard: this troubled every user in the 1990s, and a hard reset was the only cure.

But if you have two or more threads vying for a lot of CPU time, your program will be slower than sequential code.

3. Answer for asyncio

If you call `is_prime(5_000_111_000_222_021)` in the `slow` coroutine of the *spinner_async.py* example, the spinner will never appear. The effect would be the same we had in Example 19-6, when we replaced `await asyncio.sleep(3)` with `time.sleep(3)`: no spinning at all. The flow of control will pass from `supervisor` to `slow`, and then to `is_prime`. When `is_prime` returns, `slow` returns as well, and `super visor` resumes, cancelling the `spinner` task before it is executed even once. The program appears frozen for about 3s, then shows the answer.

Power Napping with sleep(0)

One way to keep the spinner alive is to rewrite `is_prime` as a coroutine, and periodically call `asyncio.sleep(0)` in an `await` expression to yield control back to the event loop, like in Example 19-11.

Example 19-11. spinner_async_nap.py: `is_prime` is now a coroutine

```python
async def is_prime(n):
    if n < 2:
        return False
    if n == 2:
        return True
    if n % 2 == 0:
        return False

    root = math.isqrt(n)
    for i in range(3, root + 1, 2):
        if n % i == 0:
            return False
        if i % 100_000 == 1:
            await asyncio.sleep(0)    ❶
    return True
```

❶ Sleep once every 50,000 iterations (because the step in the `range` is 2).

Issue #284 (*https://fpy.li/19-20*) in the `asyncio` repository has an informative discussion about the use of `asyncio.sleep(0)`.

However, be aware this will slow down `is_prime`, and—more importantly—will still slow down the event loop and your whole program with it. When I used `await asyncio.sleep(0)` every 100,000 iterations, the spinner was smooth but the program ran in 4.9s on my machine, almost 50% longer than the original `primes.is_prime` function by itself with the same argument (5_000_111_000_222_021).

Using `await asyncio.sleep(0)` should be considered a stopgap measure before you refactor your asynchronous code to delegate CPU-intensive computations to another process. We'll see one way of doing that with `asyncio.loop.run_in_executor` (*https://fpy.li/19-21*), covered in Chapter 21. Another option would be a task queue, which we'll briefly discuss in "Distributed Task Queues" on page 736.

So far, we've only experimented with a single call to a CPU-intensive function. The next section presents concurrent execution of multiple CPU-intensive calls.

A Homegrown Process Pool

 I wrote this section to show the use of multiple processes for CPU-intensive tasks, and the common pattern of using queues to distribute tasks and collect results. Chapter 20 will show a simpler way of distributing tasks to processes: a `ProcessPoolExecutor` from the `concurrent.futures` package, which uses queues internally.

In this section we'll write programs to compute the primality of a sample of 20 integers, from 2 to 9,999,999,999,999,999—i.e., $10^{16} - 1$, or more than 2^{53}. The sample includes small and large primes, as well as composite numbers with small and large prime factors.

The *sequential.py* program provides the performance baseline. Here is a sample run:

```
$ python3 sequential.py
               2  P  0.000001s
 142702110479723  P  0.568328s
 299593572317531  P  0.796773s
3333333333333301  P  2.648625s
3333333333333333     0.000007s
3333335652092209     2.672323s
4444444444444423  P  3.052667s
4444444444444444     0.000001s
4444444488888889     3.061083s
5555553133149889     3.451833s
5555555555555503  P  3.556867s
5555555555555555     0.000007s
6666666666666666     0.000001s
6666666666666719  P  3.781064s
6666667141414921     3.778166s
7777777536340681     4.120069s
7777777777777753  P  4.141530s
7777777777777777     0.000007s
9999999999999917  P  4.678164s
9999999999999999     0.000007s
Total time: 40.31
```

The results are shown in three columns:

- The number to be checked.
- P if it's a prime number, blank if not.
- Elapsed time for checking the primality for that specific number.

In this example, the total time is approximately the sum of the times for each check, but it is computed separately, as you can see in Example 19-12.

Example 19-12. sequential.py: sequential primality check for a small dataset

```python
#!/usr/bin/env python3

"""
sequential.py: baseline for comparing sequential, multiprocessing,
and threading code for CPU-intensive work.
"""

from time import perf_counter
from typing import NamedTuple

from primes import is_prime, NUMBERS

class Result(NamedTuple):  ❶
    prime: bool
    elapsed: float

def check(n: int) -> Result:  ❷
    t0 = perf_counter()
    prime = is_prime(n)
    return Result(prime, perf_counter() - t0)

def main() -> None:
    print(f'Checking {len(NUMBERS)} numbers sequentially:')
    t0 = perf_counter()
    for n in NUMBERS:  ❸
        prime, elapsed = check(n)
        label = 'P' if prime else ' '
        print(f'{n:16}  {label} {elapsed:9.6f}s')

    elapsed = perf_counter() - t0  ❹
    print(f'Total time: {elapsed:.2f}s')

if __name__ == '__main__':
    main()
```

❶ The check function (in the next callout) returns a Result tuple with the boolean value of the is_prime call and the elapsed time.

❷ check(n) calls is_prime(n) and computes the elapsed time to return a Result.

❸ For each number in the sample, we call check and display the result.

❹ Compute and display the total elapsed time.

Process-Based Solution

The next example, *procs.py*, shows the use of multiple processes to distribute the primality checks across multiple CPU cores. These are the times I get with *procs.py*:

```
$ python3 procs.py
Checking 20 numbers with 12 processes:
                2  P  0.000002s
3333333333333333     0.000021s
4444444444444444     0.000002s
5555555555555555     0.000018s
6666666666666666     0.000002s
 142702110479723  P  1.350982s
7777777777777777     0.000009s
 299593572317531  P  1.981411s
9999999999999999     0.000008s
3333333333333301  P  6.328173s
3333335652092209     6.419249s
4444444488888889     7.051267s
4444444444444423  P  7.122004s
5555553133149889     7.412735s
5555555555555503  P  7.603327s
6666666666666719  P  7.934670s
6666667141414921     8.017599s
7777777536340681     8.339623s
7777777777777753  P  8.388859s
9999999999999917  P  8.117313s
20 checks in 9.58s
```

The last line of the output shows that *procs.py* was 4.2 times faster than *sequential.py*.

Understanding the Elapsed Times

Note that the elapsed time in the first column is for checking that specific number. For example, is_prime(7777777777777753) took almost 8.4s to return True. Meanwhile, other processes were checking other numbers in parallel.

There were 20 numbers to check. I wrote *procs.py* to start a number of worker processes equal to the number of CPU cores, as determined by multiprocessing.cpu_count().

The total time in this case is much less than the sum of the elapsed time for the individual checks. There is some overhead in spinning up processes and in inter-process communication, so the end result is that the multiprocess version is only about 4.2 times faster than the sequential. That's good, but a little disappointing considering the code launches 12 processes to use all cores on this laptop.

 The `multiprocessing.cpu_count()` function returns 12 on the MacBook Pro I'm using to write this chapter. It's actually a 6-CPU Core-i7, but the OS reports 12 CPUs because of hyperthreading, an Intel technology which executes 2 threads per core. However, hyperthreading works better when one of the threads is not working as hard as the other thread in the same core—perhaps the first is stalled waiting for data after a cache miss, and the other is crunching numbers. Anyway, there's no free lunch: this laptop performs like a 6-CPU machine for compute-intensive work that doesn't use a lot of memory—like that simple primality test.

Code for the Multicore Prime Checker

When we delegate computing to threads or processes, our code does not call the worker function directly, so we can't simply get a return value. Instead, the worker is driven by the thread or process library, and it eventually produces a result that needs to be stored somewhere. Coordinating workers and collecting results are common uses of queues in concurrent programming—and also in distributed systems.

Much of the new code in *procs.py* has to do with setting up and using queues. The top of the file is in Example 19-13.

 `SimpleQueue` was added to `multiprocessing` in Python 3.9. If you're using an earlier version of Python, you can replace `Simple Queue` with `Queue` in Example 19-13.

Example 19-13. procs.py: multiprocess primality check; imports, types, and functions

```
import sys
from time import perf_counter
from typing import NamedTuple
from multiprocessing import Process, SimpleQueue, cpu_count    ❶
from multiprocessing import queues    ❷

from primes import is_prime, NUMBERS

class PrimeResult(NamedTuple):    ❸
    n: int
```

```
            prime: bool
            elapsed: float

        JobQueue = queues.SimpleQueue[int]    ❹
        ResultQueue = queues.SimpleQueue[PrimeResult]    ❺

        def check(n: int) -> PrimeResult:    ❻
            t0 = perf_counter()
            res = is_prime(n)
            return PrimeResult(n, res, perf_counter() - t0)

        def worker(jobs: JobQueue, results: ResultQueue) -> None:    ❼
            while n := jobs.get():    ❽
                results.put(check(n))    ❾
            results.put(PrimeResult(0, False, 0.0))    ❿

        def start_jobs(
            procs: int, jobs: JobQueue, results: ResultQueue    ⓫
        ) -> None:
            for n in NUMBERS:
                jobs.put(n)    ⓬
            for _ in range(procs):
                proc = Process(target=worker, args=(jobs, results))    ⓭
                proc.start()    ⓮
                jobs.put(0)    ⓯
```

❶ Trying to emulate `threading`, `multiprocessing` provides `multiprocessing.Sim
pleQueue`, but this is a method bound to a predefined instance of a lower-level
`BaseContext` class. We must call this `SimpleQueue` to build a queue, we can't use
it in type hints.

❷ `multiprocessing.queues` has the `SimpleQueue` class we need for type hints.

❸ `PrimeResult` includes the number checked for primality. Keeping `n` together
with the other result fields simplifies displaying results later.

❹ This is a type alias for a `SimpleQueue` that the `main` function (Example 19-14) will
use to send numbers to the processes that will do the work.

❺ Type alias for a second `SimpleQueue` that will collect the results in `main`. The values in the queue will be tuples made of the number to be tested for primality, and
a `Result` tuple.

❻ This is similar to *sequential.py*.

❼ `worker` gets a queue with the numbers to be checked, and another to put results.

❽ In this code, I use the number 0 as a *poison pill*: a signal for the worker to finish. If n is not 0, proceed with the loop.[14]

❾ Invoke the primality check and enqueue `PrimeResult`.

❿ Send back a `PrimeResult(0, False, 0.0)` to let the main loop know that this worker is done.

⓫ `procs` is the number of processes that will compute the prime checks in parallel.

⓬ Enqueue the numbers to be checked in `jobs`.

⓭ Fork a child process for each worker. Each child will run the loop inside its own instance of the `worker` function, until it fetches a 0 from the `jobs` queue.

⓮ Start each child process.

⓯ Enqueue one 0 for each process, to terminate them.

Loops, Sentinels, and Poison Pills

The `worker` function in Example 19-13 follows a common pattern in concurrent programming: looping indefinitely while taking items from a queue and processing each with a function that does the actual work. The loop ends when the queue produces a sentinel value. In this pattern, the sentinel that shuts down the worker is often called a "poison pill."

`None` is often used as a sentinel value, but it may be unsuitable if it can occur in the data stream. Calling `object()` is a common way to get a unique value to use as sentinel. However, that does not work across processes because Python objects must be serialized for inter-process communication, and when you `pickle.dump` and `pickle.load` an instance of `object`, the unpickled instance is distinct from the original: it doesn't compare equal. A good alternative to `None` is the `Ellipsis` built-in object (a.k.a. `...`), which survives serialization without losing its identity.[15]

Python's standard library uses lots of different values (*https://fpy.li/19-22*) as sentinels. PEP 661—Sentinel Values (*https://fpy.li/pep661*) proposes a standard sentinel type. As of September 2021, it's only a draft.

---

14 In this example, 0 is a convenient sentinel. None is also commonly used for that. Using 0 simplifies the type hint for PrimeResult and the code for worker.

15 Surviving serialization without losing our identity is a pretty good life goal.

Now let's study the `main` function of *procs.py* in Example 19-14.

Example 19-14. procs.py: multiprocess primality check; main function

```python
def main() -> None:
    if len(sys.argv) < 2:              ❶
        procs = cpu_count()
    else:
        procs = int(sys.argv[1])

    print(f'Checking {len(NUMBERS)} numbers with {procs} processes:')
    t0 = perf_counter()
    jobs: JobQueue = SimpleQueue()     ❷
    results: ResultQueue = SimpleQueue()
    start_jobs(procs, jobs, results)   ❸
    checked = report(procs, results)   ❹
    elapsed = perf_counter() - t0
    print(f'{checked} checks in {elapsed:.2f}s')   ❺

def report(procs: int, results: ResultQueue) -> int:   ❻
    checked = 0
    procs_done = 0
    while procs_done < procs:          ❼
        n, prime, elapsed = results.get()   ❽
        if n == 0:                     ❾
            procs_done += 1
        else:
            checked += 1               ❿
            label = 'P' if prime else ' '
            print(f'{n:16}  {label} {elapsed:9.6f}s')
    return checked

if __name__ == '__main__':
    main()
```

❶ If no command-line argument is given, set the number of processes to the number of CPU cores; otherwise, create as many processes as given in the first argument.

❷ `jobs` and `results` are the queues described in Example 19-13.

❸ Start `proc` processes to consume `jobs` and post `results`.

❹ Retrieve the results and display them; `report` is defined in ❻.

❺ Display how many numbers were checked and the total elapsed time.

❻ The arguments are the number of `procs` and the queue to post the results.

❼   Loop until all processes are done.

❽   Get one `PrimeResult`. Calling `.get()` on a queue block until there is an item in the queue. It's also possible to make this nonblocking, or set a timeout. See the `SimpleQueue.get` (*https://fpy.li/19-23*) documentation for details.

❾   If n is zero, then one process exited; increment the `procs_done` count.

❿   Otherwise, increment the `checked` count (to keep track of the numbers checked) and display the results.

The results will not come back in the same order the jobs were submitted. That's why I had to put n in each `PrimeResult` tuple. Otherwise, I'd have no way to know which result belonged to each number.

If the main process exits before all subprocesses are done, you may see confusing tracebacks on `FileNotFoundError` exceptions caused by an internal lock in `multiprocessing`. Debugging concurrent code is always hard, and debugging `multiprocessing` is even harder because of all the complexity behind the thread-like façade. Fortunately, the `ProcessPoolExecutor` we'll meet in Chapter 20 is easier to use and more robust.

> Thanks to reader Michael Albert who noticed the code I published during the early release had a *race condition* (*https://fpy.li/19-24*) in Example 19-14. A race condition is a bug that may or may not occur depending on the order of actions performed by concurrent execution units. If "A" happens before "B," all is fine; but it "B" happens first, something goes wrong. That's the race.
>
> If you are curious, this diff shows the bug and how I fixed it: *example-code-2e/commit/2c123057* (*https://fpy.li/19-25*)—but note that I later refactored the example to delegate parts of `main` to the `start_jobs` and `report` functions. There's a *README.md* (*https://fpy.li/19-26*) file in the same directory explaining the problem and the solution.

Experimenting with More or Fewer Processes

You may want try running *procs.py*, passing arguments to set the number of worker processes. For example, this command...

```
$ python3 procs.py 2
```

...will launch two worker processes, producing results almost twice as fast as *sequential.py*—if your machine has at least two cores and is not too busy running other programs.

I ran *procs.py* 12 times with 1 to 20 processes, totaling 240 runs. Then I computed the median time for all runs with the same number of processes, and plotted Figure 19-2.

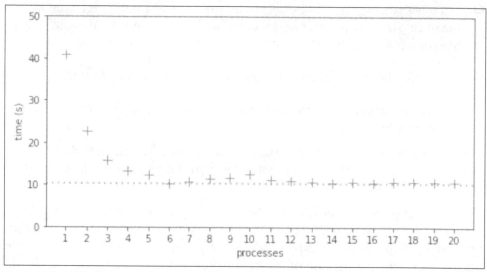

Figure 19-2. Median run times for each number of processes from 1 to 20. Highest median time was 40.81s, with 1 process. Lowest median time was 10.39s, with 6 processes, indicated by the dotted line.

In this 6-core laptop, the lowest median time was with 6 processes: 10.39s—marked by the dotted line in Figure 19-2. I expected the run time to increase after 6 processes due to CPU contention, and it reached a local maximum of 12.51s at 10 processes. I did not expect and I can't explain why the performance improved at 11 processes and remained almost flat from 13 to 20 processes, with median times only slightly higher than the lowest median time at 6 processes.

Thread-Based Nonsolution

I also wrote *threads.py*, a version of *procs.py* using `threading` instead of `multiproc essing`. The code is very similar—as is usually the case when converting simple examples between these two APIs.[16] Due to the GIL and the compute-intensive nature of `is_prime`, the threaded version is slower than the sequential code in Example 19-12, and it gets slower as the number of threads increase, because of CPU contention and the cost of context switching. To switch to a new thread, the OS needs to save CPU registers and update the program counter and stack pointer,

---

16 See *19-concurrency/primes/threads.py* (*https://fpy.li/19-27*) in the *Fluent Python* code repository (*https://fpy.li/code*).

triggering expensive side effects like invalidating CPU caches and possibly even swapping memory pages.[17]

The next two chapters will cover more about concurrent programming in Python, using the high-level *concurrent.futures* library to manage threads and processes (Chapter 20) and the *asyncio* library for asynchronous programming (Chapter 21).

The remaining sections in this chapter aim to answer the question:

> Given the limitations discussed so far, how is Python thriving in a multicore world?

Python in the Multicore World

Consider this citation from the widely quoted article "The Free Lunch Is Over: A Fundamental Turn Toward Concurrency in Software" by Herb Sutter (*https://fpy.li/19-29*):

> The major processor manufacturers and architectures, from Intel and AMD to Sparc and PowerPC, have run out of room with most of their traditional approaches to boosting CPU performance. Instead of driving clock speeds and straight-line instruction throughput ever higher, they are instead turning en masse to hyper-threading and multicore architectures. March 2005. [Available online].

What Sutter calls the "free lunch" was the trend of software getting faster with no additional developer effort because CPUs were executing sequential code faster, year after year. Since 2004, that is no longer true: clock speeds and execution optimizations reached a plateau, and now any significant increase in performance must come from leveraging multiple cores or hyperthreading, advances that only benefit code that is written for concurrent execution.

Python's story started in the early 1990s, when CPUs were still getting exponentially faster at sequential code execution. There was no talk about multicore CPUs except in supercomputers back then. At the time, the decision to have a GIL was a no-brainer. The GIL makes the interpreter faster when running on a single core, and its implementation simpler.[18] The GIL also makes it easier to write simple extensions through the Python/C API.

---

17 To learn more, see "Context switch" (*https://fpy.li/19-28*) in the English Wikipedia.

18 These are probably the same reasons that prompted the creator of the Ruby language, Yukihiro Matsumoto, to use a GIL in his interpreter as well.

I just wrote "simple extensions" because an extension does not need to deal with the GIL at all. A function written in C or Fortran may be hundreds of times faster than the equivalent in Python.[19] Therefore the added complexity of releasing the GIL to leverage multicore CPUs may not be needed in many cases. So we can thank the GIL for many extensions available for Python—and that is certainly one of the key reasons why the language is so popular today.

Despite the GIL, Python is thriving in applications that require concurrent or parallel execution, thanks to libraries and software architectures that work around the limitations of CPython.

Now let's discuss how Python is used in system administration, data science, and server-side application development in the multicore, distributed computing world of 2021.

System Administration

Python is widely used to manage large fleets of servers, routers, load balancers, and network-attached storage (NAS). It's also a leading option in software-defined networking (SDN) and ethical hacking. Major cloud service providers support Python through libraries and tutorials authored by the providers themselves or by their large communities of Python users.

In this domain, Python scripts automate configuration tasks by issuing commands to be carried out by the remote machines, so rarely there are CPU-bound operations to be done. Threads or coroutines are well suited for such jobs. In particular, the concur rent.futures package we'll see in Chapter 20 can be used to perform the same operations on many remote machines at the same time without a lot of complexity.

Beyond the standard library, there are popular Python-based projects to manage server clusters: tools like *Ansible* (*https://fpy.li/19-30*) and *Salt* (*https://fpy.li/19-31*), as well as libraries like *Fabric* (*https://fpy.li/19-32*).

There is also a growing number of libraries for system administration supporting coroutines and asyncio. In 2016, Facebook's Production Engineering team reported (*https://fpy.li/19-33*): "We are increasingly relying on AsyncIO, which was introduced in Python 3.4, and seeing huge performance gains as we move codebases away from Python 2."

---

19 As an exercise in college, I had to implement the LZW compression algorithm in C. But first I wrote it in Python, to check my understanding of the spec. The C version was about 900× faster.

Data Science

Data science—including artificial intelligence—and scientific computing are very well served by Python. Applications in these fields are compute-intensive, but Python users benefit from a vast ecosystem of numeric computing libraries written in C, C++, Fortran, Cython, etc.—many of which are able to leverage multicore machines, GPUs, and/or distributed parallel computing in heterogeneous clusters.

As of 2021, Python's data science ecosystem includes impressive tools such as:

Project Jupyter (https://fpy.li/19-34)
> Two browser-based interfaces—Jupyter Notebook and JupyterLab—that allow users to run and document analytics code potentially running across the network on remote machines. Both are hybrid Python/JavaScript applications, supporting computing kernels written in different languages, all integrated via ZeroMQ—an asynchronous messaging library for distributed applications. The name *Jupyter* actually comes from Julia, Python, and R, the first three languages supported by the Notebook. The rich ecosystem built on top of the Jupyter tools include Bokeh (*https://fpy.li/19-35*), a powerful interactive visualization library that lets users navigate and interact with large datasets or continuously updated streaming data, thanks to the performance of modern JavaScript engines and browsers.

TensorFlow (https://fpy.li/19-36) and PyTorch (https://fpy.li/19-37)
> These are the top two deep learning frameworks, according to O'Reilly's January 2021 report (*https://fpy.li/19-38*) on usage of their learning resources during 2020. Both projects are written in C++, and are able to leverage multiple cores, GPUs, and clusters. They support other languages as well, but Python is their main focus and is used by the majority of their users. TensorFlow was created and is used internally by Google; PyTorch by Facebook.

Dask (https://fpy.li/dask)
> A parallel computing library that can farm out work to local processes or clusters of machines, "tested on some of the largest supercomputers in the world"—as their home page (*https://fpy.li/dask*) states. Dask offers APIs that closely emulate NumPy, pandas, and scikit-learn—the most popular libraries in data science and machine learning today. Dask can be used from JupyterLab or Jupyter Notebook, and leverages Bokeh not only for data visualization but also for an interactive dashboard showing the flow of data and computations across the processes/machines in near real time. Dask is so impressive that I recommend watching a video such as this 15-minute demo (*https://fpy.li/19-39*) in which Matthew Rocklin—a maintainer of the project—shows Dask crunching data on 64 cores distributed in 8 EC2 machines on AWS.

These are only some examples to illustrate how the data science community is creating solutions that leverage the best of Python and overcome the limitations of the CPython runtime.

Server-Side Web/Mobile Development

Python is widely used in web applications and for the backend APIs supporting mobile applications. How is it that Google, YouTube, Dropbox, Instagram, Quora, and Reddit—among others—managed to build Python server-side applications serving hundreds of millions of users 24x7? Again, the answer goes way beyond what Python provides "out of the box."

Before we discuss tools to support Python at scale, I must quote an admonition from the Thoughtworks *Technology Radar*:

> **High performance envy/web scale envy**
>
> We see many teams run into trouble because they have chosen complex tools, frameworks or architectures because they "might need to scale." Companies such as Twitter and Netflix need to support extreme loads and so need these architectures, but they also have extremely skilled development teams able to handle the complexity. Most situations do not require these kinds of engineering feats; teams should keep their *web scale envy* in check in favor of simpler solutions that still get the job done.[20]

At *web scale*, the key is an architecture that allows horizontal scaling. At that point, all systems are distributed systems, and no single programming language is likely to be the right choice for every part of the solution.

Distributed systems is a field of academic research, but fortunately some practitioners have written accessible books anchored on solid research and practical experience. One of them is Martin Kleppmann, the author of *Designing Data-Intensive Applications* (O'Reilly).

Consider Figure 19-3, the first of many architecture diagrams in Kleppmann's book. Here are some components I've seen in Python engagements that I worked on or have firsthand knowledge of:

- Application caches:[21] *memcached, Redis, Varnish*
- Relational databases: *PostgreSQL, MySQL*

---

20 Source: Thoughtworks Technology Advisory Board, *Technology Radar*—November 2015 (*https://fpy.li/ 19-40*).

21 Contrast application caches—used directly by your application code—with HTTP caches, which would be placed on the top edge of Figure 19-3 to serve static assets like images, CSS, and JS files. Content Delivery Networks (CDNs) offer another type of HTTP cache, deployed in data centers closer to the end users of your application.

- Document databases: *Apache CouchDB, MongoDB*
- Full-text indexes: *Elasticsearch, Apache Solr*
- Message queues: *RabbitMQ, Redis*

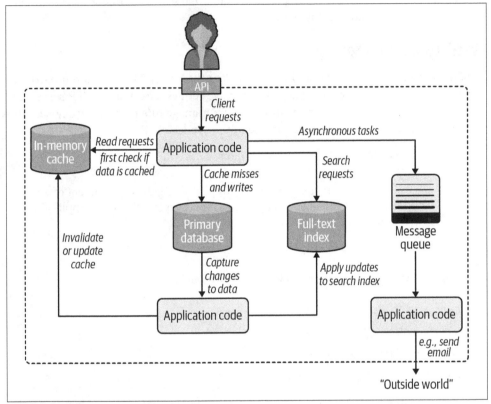

Figure 19-3. One possible architecture for a system combining several components.[22]

There are other industrial-strength open source products in each of those categories. Major cloud providers also offer their own proprietary alternatives.

Kleppmann's diagram is general and language independent—as is his book. For Python server-side applications, two specific components are often deployed:

- An application server to distribute the load among several instances of the Python application. The application server would appear near the top in Figure 19-3, handling client requests before they reached the application code.

---

22 Diagram adapted from Figure 1-1, *Designing Data-Intensive Applications* by Martin Kleppmann (O'Reilly).

- A task queue built around the message queue on the righthand side of Figure 19-3, providing a higher-level, easier-to-use API to distribute tasks to processes running on other machines.

The next two sections explore these components that are recommended best practices in Python server-side deployments.

WSGI Application Servers

WSGI—the Web Server Gateway Interface (*https://fpy.li/pep3333*)—is a standard API for a Python framework or application to receive requests from an HTTP server and send responses to it.[23] WSGI application servers manage one or more processes running your application, maximizing the use of the available CPUs.

Figure 19-4 illustrates a typical WSGI deployment.

 If we wanted to merge the previous pair of diagrams, the content of the dashed rectangle in Figure 19-4 would replace the solid "Application code" rectangle at the top of Figure 19-3.

The best-known application servers in Python web projects are:

- *mod_wsgi* (*https://fpy.li/19-41*)
- *uWSGI* (*https://fpy.li/19-42*)[24]
- *Gunicorn* (*https://fpy.li/gunicorn*)
- *NGINX Unit* (*https://fpy.li/19-43*)

For users of the Apache HTTP server, *mod_wsgi* is the best option. It's as old as WSGI itself, but is actively maintained, and now provides a command-line launcher called `mod_wsgi-express` that makes it easier to configure and more suitable for use in Docker containers.

---

23 Some speakers spell out the WSGI acronym, while others pronounce it as one word rhyming with "whisky."

24 *uWSGI* is spelled with a lowercase "u," but that is pronounced as the Greek letter "μ," so the whole name sounds like "micro-whisky" with a "g" instead of the "k."

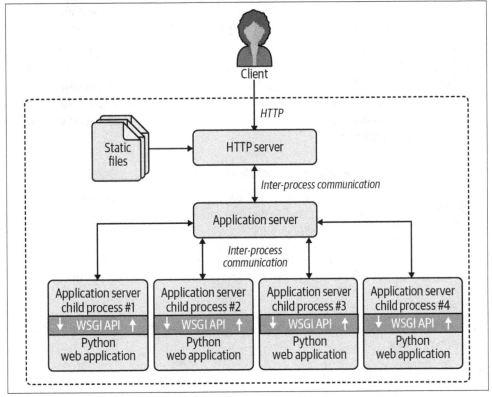

Figure 19-4. Clients connect to an HTTP server that delivers static files and routes other requests to the application server, which forks child processes to run the application code, leveraging multiple CPU cores. The WSGI API is the glue between the application server and the Python application code.

uWSGI and *Gunicorn* are the top choices in recent projects I know about. Both are often used with the *NGINX* HTTP server. *uWSGI* offers a lot of extra functionality, including an application cache, a task queue, cron-like periodic tasks, and many other features. On the flip side, *uWSGI* is much harder to configure properly than *Gunicorn*.[25]

Released in 2018, *NGINX Unit* is a new product from the makers of the well-known *NGINX* HTTP server and reverse proxy.

---

25 Bloomberg engineers Peter Sperl and Ben Green wrote "Configuring uWSGI for Production Deployment" (*https://fpy.li/19-44*), explaining how many of the default settings in *uWSGI* are not suitable for many common deployment scenarios. Sperl presented a summary of their recommendations at EuroPython 2019 (*https://fpy.li/19-45*). Highly recommended for users of *uWSGI*.

mod_wsgi and *Gunicorn* support Python web apps only, while *uWSGI* and *NGINX Unit* work with other languages as well. Please browse their docs to learn more.

The main point: all of these application servers can potentially use all CPU cores on the server by forking multiple Python processes to run traditional web apps written in good old sequential code in *Django, Flask, Pyramid,* etc. This explains why it's been possible to earn a living as a Python web developer without ever studying the `threading`, `multiprocessing`, or `asyncio` modules: the application server handles concurrency transparently.

ASGI—Asynchronous Server Gateway Interface

WSGI is a synchronous API. It doesn't support coroutines with `async`/`await`—the most efficient way to implement WebSockets or HTTP long polling in Python. The ASGI specification (*https://fpy.li/19-46*) is a successor to WSGI, designed for asynchronous Python web frameworks such as *aiohttp, Sanic, FastAPI,* etc., as well as *Django* and *Flask,* which are gradually adding asynchronous functionality.

Now let's turn to another way of bypassing the GIL to achieve higher performance with server-side Python applications.

Distributed Task Queues

When the application server delivers a request to one of the Python processes running your code, your app needs to respond quickly: you want the process to be available to handle the next request as soon as possible. However, some requests demand actions that may take longer—for example, sending email or generating a PDF. That's the problem that distributed task queues are designed to solve.

Celery (*https://fpy.li/19-47*) and *RQ* (*https://fpy.li/19-48*) are the best known open source task queues with Python APIs. Cloud providers also offer their own proprietary task queues.

These products wrap a message queue and offer a high-level API for delegating tasks to workers, possibly running on different machines.

In the context of task queues, the words *producer* and *consumer* are used instead of traditional client/server terminology. For example, a *Django* view handler *produces* job requests, which are put in the queue to be *consumed* by one or more PDF rendering processes.

Quoting directly from *Celery*'s FAQ (*https://fpy.li/19-49*), here are some typical use cases:

- Running something in the background. For example, to finish the web request as soon as possible, then update the users page incrementally. This gives the user the impression of good performance and "snappiness," even though the real work might actually take some time.

- Running something after the web request has finished.

- Making sure something is done, by executing it asynchronously and using retries.

- Scheduling periodic work.

Besides solving these immediate problems, task queues support horizontal scalability. Producers and consumers are decoupled: a producer doesn't call a consumer, it puts a request in a queue. Consumers don't need to know anything about the producers (but the request may include information about the producer, if an acknowledgment is required). Crucially, you can easily add more workers to consume tasks as demand grows. That's why *Celery* and *RQ* are called distributed task queues.

Recall that our simple *procs.py* (Example 19-13) used two queues: one for job requests, the other for collecting results. The distributed architecture of *Celery* and *RQ* uses a similar pattern. Both support using the *Redis* (*https://fpy.li/19-50*) NoSQL database as a message queue and result storage. *Celery* also supports other message queues like *RabbitMQ* or *Amazon SQS*, as well other databases for result storage.

This wraps up our introduction to concurrency in Python. The next two chapters will continue this theme, focusing on the `concurrent.futures` and `asyncio` packages of the standard library.

Chapter Summary

After a bit of theory, this chapter presented the spinner scripts implemented in each of Python's three native concurrency programming models:

- Threads, with the `threading` package
- Processes, with `multiprocessing`
- Asynchronous coroutines with `asyncio`

We then explored the real impact of the GIL with an experiment: changing the spinner examples to compute the primality of a large integer and observe the resulting behavior. This demonstrated graphically that CPU-intensive functions must be avoided in `asyncio`, as they block the event loop. The threaded version of the experiment worked—despite the GIL—because Python periodically interrupts threads, and the example used only two threads: one doing compute-intensive work, and the other driving the animation only 10 times per second. The `multiprocessing` variant worked around the GIL, starting a new process just for the animation, while the main process did the primality check.

The next example, computing several primes, highlighted the difference between mul tiprocessing and threading, proving that only processes allow Python to benefit from multicore CPUs. Python's GIL makes threads worse than sequential code for heavy computations.

The GIL dominates discussions about concurrent and parallel computing in Python, but we should not overestimate its impact. That was the point of "Python in the Multicore World" on page 729. For example, the GIL doesn't affect many use cases of Python in system administration. On the other hand, the data science and server-side development communities have worked around the GIL with industrial-strength solutions tailored to their specific needs. The last two sections mentioned two common elements to support Python server-side applications at scale: WSGI application servers and distributed task queues.

Further Reading

This chapter has an extensive reading list, so I split it into subsections.

Concurrency with Threads and Processes

The *concurrent.futures* library covered in Chapter 20 uses threads, processes, locks, and queues under the hood, but you won't see individual instances of them; they're bundled and managed by the higher-level abstractions of a ThreadPoolExecutor and a ProcessPoolExecutor. If you want to learn more about the practice of concurrent programming with those low-level objects, "An Intro to Threading in Python" (*https://fpy.li/19-51*) by Jim Anderson is a good first read. Doug Hellmann has a chapter titled "Concurrency with Processes, Threads, and Coroutines" on his website (*https://fpy.li/19-52*) and book, *The Python 3 Standard Library by Example* (*https://fpy.li/19-53*) (Addison-Wesley).

Brett Slatkin's *Effective Python* (*https://fpy.li/effectpy*), 2nd ed. (Addison-Wesley), David Beazley's *Python Essential Reference*, 4th ed. (Addison-Wesley), and Martelli et al., *Python in a Nutshell*, 3rd ed. (O'Reilly) are other general Python references with significant coverage of threading and multiprocessing. The vast multiprocessing official documentation includes useful advice in its "Programming guidelines" section (*https://fpy.li/19-54*).

Jesse Noller and Richard Oudkerk contributed the multiprocessing package, introduced in PEP 371—Addition of the multiprocessing package to the standard library (*https://fpy.li/pep371*). The official documentation for the package is a 93 KB *.rst* file (*https://fpy.li/19-55*)—that's about 63 pages—making it one of the longest chapters in the Python standard library.

In *High Performance Python*, 2nd ed., (O'Reilly), authors Micha Gorelick and Ian Ozsvald include a chapter about `multiprocessing` with an example about checking for primes with a different strategy than our *procs.py* example. For each number, they split the range of possible factors—from 2 to `sqrt(n)`—into subranges, and make each worker iterate over one of the subranges. Their divide-and-conquer approach is typical of scientific computing applications where the datasets are huge, and workstations (or clusters) have more CPU cores than users. On a server-side system handling requests from many users, it is simpler and more efficient to let each process work on one computation from start to finish—reducing the overhead of communication and coordination among processes. Besides `multiprocessing`, Gorelick and Ozsvald present many other ways of developing and deploying high-performance data science applications leveraging multiple cores, GPUs, clusters, profilers, and compilers like Cython and Numba. Their last chapter, "Lessons from the Field," is a valuable collection of short case studies contributed by other practitioners of high-performance computing in Python.

Advanced Python Development (*https://fpy.li/19-57*) by Matthew Wilkes (Apress), is a rare book that includes short examples to explain concepts, while also showing how to build a realistic application ready for production: a data aggregator, similar to DevOps monitoring systems or IoT data collectors for distributed sensors. Two chapters in *Advanced Python Development* cover concurrent programming with `thread ing` and `asyncio`.

Jan Palach's *Parallel Programming with Python* (*https://fpy.li/19-58*) (Packt, 2014) explains the core concepts behind concurrency and parallelism, covering Python's standard library as well as *Celery*.

"The Truth About Threads" is the title of Chapter 2 in *Using Asyncio in Python* by Caleb Hattingh (O'Reilly).[26] The chapter covers the benefits and drawbacks of threading—with compelling quotes from several authoritative sources—making it clear that the fundamental challenges of threads have nothing to do with Python or the GIL. Quoting verbatim from page 14 of *Using Asyncio in Python*:

> These themes repeat throughout:
>
> - Threading makes code hard to reason about.
> - Threading is an inefficient model for large-scale concurrency (thousands of concurrent tasks).

If you want to learn the hard way how difficult it is to reason about threads and locks —without risking your job—try the exercises in Allen Downey's workbook, *The Little Book of Semaphores* (*https://fpy.li/19-59*) (Green Tea Press). The exercises in

---

26 Caleb is one of the tech reviewers for this edition of *Fluent Python*.

Downey's book range from easy to very hard to unsolvable, but even the easy ones are eye-opening.

The GIL

If you are intrigued about the GIL, remember we have no control over it from Python code, so the canonical reference is in the C-API documentation: *Thread State and the Global Interpreter Lock* (*https://fpy.li/19-60*). The *Python Library and Extension FAQ* answers: *"Can't we get rid of the Global Interpreter Lock?"* (*https://fpy.li/19-61*). Also worth reading are posts by Guido van Rossum and Jesse Noller (contributor of the `multiprocessing` package), respectively: "It isn't Easy to Remove the GIL" (*https://fpy.li/19-62*) and "Python Threads and the Global Interpreter Lock" (*https://fpy.li/19-63*).

CPython Internals (*https://fpy.li/19-64*) by Anthony Shaw (Real Python) explains the implementation of the CPython 3 interpreter at the C programming level. Shaw's longest chapter is "Parallelism and Concurrency": a deep dive into Python's native support for threads and processes, including managing the GIL from extensions using the C/Python API.

Finally, David Beazley presented a detailed exploration in "Understanding the Python GIL" (*https://fpy.li/19-65*).[27] In slide #54 of the presentation (*https://fpy.li/19-66*), Beazley reports an increase in processing time for a particular benchmark with the new GIL algorithm introduced in Python 3.2. The issue is not significant with real workloads, according to a comment (*https://fpy.li/19-67*) by Antoine Pitrou —who implemented the new GIL algorithm—in the bug report submitted by Beazley: Python issue #7946 (*https://fpy.li/19-68*).

Concurrency Beyond the Standard Library

Fluent Python focuses on core language features and core parts of the standard library. *Full Stack Python* (*https://fpy.li/19-69*) is a great complement to this book: it's about Python's ecosystem, with sections titled "Development Environments," "Data," "Web Development," and "DevOps," among others.

I've already mentioned two books that cover concurrency using the Python standard library that also include significant content on third-party libraries and tools: *High Performance Python*, 2nd ed. and *Parallel Programming with Python*. Francesco Pierfederici's *Distributed Computing with Python* (*https://fpy.li/19-72*) (Packt) covers the standard library and also the use of cloud providers and HPC (High-Performance Computing) clusters.

---

27 Thanks to Lucas Brunialti for sending me a link to this talk.

"Python, Performance, and GPUs" (*https://fpy.li/19-73*) by Matthew Rocklin is "a status update for using GPU accelerators from Python," posted in June 2019.

"Instagram currently features the world's largest deployment of the *Django* web framework, which is written entirely in Python." That's the opening sentence of the blog post, "Web Service Efficiency at Instagram with Python" (*https://fpy.li/19-74*), written by Min Ni—a software engineer at Instagram. The post describes metrics and tools Instagram uses to optimize the efficiency of its Python codebase, as well as detect and diagnose performance regressions as it deploys its back end "30-50 times a day."

Architecture Patterns with Python: Enabling Test-Driven Development, Domain-Driven Design, and Event-Driven Microservices (*https://fpy.li/19-75*) by Harry Percival and Bob Gregory (O'Reilly) presents architectural patterns for Python server-side applications. The authors also made the book freely available online at *cosmicpython.com*.

Two elegant and easy-to-use libraries for parallelizing tasks over processes are *lelo* (*https://fpy.li/19-77*) by João S. O. Bueno and *python-parallelize* (*https://fpy.li/19-78*) by Nat Pryce. The *lelo* package defines a `@parallel` decorator that you can apply to any function to magically make it unblocking: when you call the decorated function, its execution is started in another process. Nat Pryce's *python-parallelize* package provides a `parallelize` generator that distributes the execution of a `for` loop over multiple CPUs. Both packages are built on the *multiprocessing* library.

Python core developer Eric Snow maintains a Multicore Python (*https://fpy.li/19-79*) wiki, with notes about his and other people's efforts to improve Python's support for parallel execution. Snow is the author of PEP 554—Multiple Interpreters in the Stdlib (*https://fpy.li/pep554*). If approved and implemented, PEP 554 lays the groundwork for future enhancements that may eventually allow Python to use multiple cores without the overheads of *multiprocessing*. One of the biggest blockers is the complex interaction between multiple active subinterpreters and extensions that assume a single interpreter.

Mark Shannon—also a Python maintainer—created a useful table (*https://fpy.li/19-80*) comparing concurrent models in Python, referenced in a discussion about subinterpreters between him, Eric Snow, and other developers on the python-dev (*https://fpy.li/19-81*) mailing list. In Shannon's table, the "Ideal CSP" column refers to the theoretical Communicating sequential processes (*https://fpy.li/19-82*) model proposed by Tony Hoare in 1978. Go also allows shared objects, violating an essential constraint of CSP: execution units should communicate through message passing through channels.

Stackless Python (*https://fpy.li/19-83*) (a.k.a. *Stackless*) is a fork of CPython implementing microthreads, which are application-level lightweight threads—as opposed to OS threads. The massively multiplayer online game *EVE Online* (*https://fpy.li/ 19-84*) was built on *Stackless*, and engineers employed by the game company CCP (*https://fpy.li/19-85*) were maintainers of *Stackless* (*https://fpy.li/19-86*) for a while. Some features of *Stackless* were reimplemented in the *Pypy* (*https://fpy.li/19-87*) interpreter and the *greenlet* (*https://fpy.li/19-14*) package, the core technology of the *gevent* (*https://fpy.li/19-17*) networking library, which in turn is the foundation of the *Gunicorn* (*https://fpy.li/gunicorn*) application server.

The actor model of concurrent programming is at the core of the highly scalable Erlang and Elixir languages, and is also the model of the Akka framework for Scala and Java. If you want to try out the actor model in Python, check out the *Thespian* (*https://fpy.li/19-90*) and *Pykka* (*https://fpy.li/19-91*) libraries.

My remaining recommendations have few or zero mentions of Python, but are nevertheless relevant to readers interested in the theme of this chapter.

Concurrency and Scalability Beyond Python

RabbitMQ in Action (*https://fpy.li/19-92*) by Alvaro Videla and Jason J. W. Williams (Manning) is a very well-written introduction to *RabbitMQ* and the Advanced Message Queuing Protocol (AMQP) standard, with examples in Python, PHP, and Ruby. Regardless of the rest of your tech stack, and even if you plan to use *Celery* with *RabbitMQ* under the hood, I recommend this book for its coverage of concepts, motivation, and patterns for distributed message queues, as well as operating and tuning *RabbitMQ* at scale.

I learned a lot reading *Seven Concurrency Models in Seven Weeks* (*https://fpy.li/ 19-93*), by Paul Butcher (Pragmatic Bookshelf), with the eloquent subtitle *When Threads Unravel*. Chapter 1 of the book presents the core concepts and challenges of programming with threads and locks in Java.[28] The remaining six chapters of the book are devoted to what the author considers better alternatives for concurrent and parallel programming, as supported by different languages, tools, and libraries. The examples use Java, Clojure, Elixir, and C (for the chapter about parallel programming with the OpenCL framework (*https://fpy.li/19-94*)). The CSP model is exemplified with Clojure code, although the Go language deserves credit for popularizing that approach. Elixir is the language of the examples illustrating the actor model. A freely available, alternative bonus chapter (*https://fpy.li/19-95*) about actors uses Scala and the Akka framework. Unless you already know Scala, Elixir is a more accessible language to learn and experiment with the actor model and the Erlang/OTP distributed systems platform.

---

28 Python's `threading` and `concurrent.futures` APIs are heavily influenced by the Java standard library.

Unmesh Joshi of Thoughtworks has contributed several pages documenting "Patterns of Distributed Systems" to Martin Fowler's blog (*https://fpy.li/19-96*). The opening page (*https://fpy.li/19-97*) is a great introduction the topic, with links to individual patterns. Joshi is adding patterns incrementally, but what's already there distills years of hard-earned experience in mission-critical systems.

Martin Kleppmann's *Designing Data-Intensive Applications* (O'Reilly) is a rare book written by a practitioner with deep industry experience and advanced academic background. The author worked with large-scale data infrastructure at LinkedIn and two startups, before becoming a researcher of distributed systems at the University of Cambridge. Each chapter in Kleppmann's book ends with an extensive list of references, including recent research results. The book also includes numerous illuminating diagrams and beautiful concept maps.

I was fortunate to be in the audience for Francesco Cesarini's outstanding workshop on the architecture of reliable distributed systems at OSCON 2016: "Designing and architecting for scalability with Erlang/OTP" (video (*https://fpy.li/19-99*) at the O'Reilly Learning Platform). Despite the title, 9:35 into the video, Cesarini explains:

> Very little of what I am going to say will be Erlang-specific […]. The fact remains that Erlang will remove a lot of accidental difficulties to making systems which are resilient and which never fail, and are scalable. So it will be much easier if you do use Erlang, or a language running on the Erlang virtual machine.

That workshop was based on the last four chapters of *Designing for Scalability with Erlang/OTP* (*https://fpy.li/19-100*) by Francesco Cesarini and Steve Vinoski (O'Reilly).

Programming distributed systems is challenging and exciting, but beware of *web-scale envy* (*https://fpy.li/19-40*). The KISS principle (*https://fpy.li/19-102*) remains solid engineering advice.

Check out the paper "Scalability! But at what COST?" (*https://fpy.li/19-103*) by Frank McSherry, Michael Isard, and Derek G. Murray. The authors identified parallel graph-processing systems presented in academic symposia that require hundreds of cores to outperform a "competent single-threaded implementation." They also found systems that "underperform one thread for all of their reported configurations."

Those findings remind me of a classic hacker quip:

> My Perl script is faster than your Hadoop cluster.

Soapbox

To Manage Complexity, We Need Constraints

I learned to program on a TI-58 calculator. Its "language" was similar to assembly. At that level, all "variables" are globals, and you don't have the luxury of structured control flow statements. You have conditional jumps: instructions that take the execution directly to an arbitrary location—ahead or behind the current spot—depending on the value of a CPU register or flag.

Basically you can do anything in assembly, and that's the challenge: there are very few constraints to keep you from making mistakes, and to help maintainers understand the code when changes are needed.

The second language I learned was the unstructured BASIC that came with 8-bit computers—nothing like Visual Basic, which appeared much later. There were FOR, GOSUB, and RETURN statements, but still no concept of local variables. GOSUB did not support parameter passing: it was just a fancy GOTO that put a return line number in a stack so that RETURN had a target to jump to. Subroutines could help themselves to the global data, and put results there too. We had to improvise other forms of control flow with combinations of IF and GOTO—which, again, allowed you to jump to any line of the program.

After a few years of programming with jumps and global variables, I remember the struggle to rewire my brain for "structured programming" when I learned Pascal. Now I had to use control flow statements around blocks of code that have a single entry point. I couldn't jump to any instruction I liked. Global variables were unavoidable in BASIC, but now they were taboo. I needed to rethink the flow of data and explicitly pass arguments to functions.

The next challenge for me was learning object-oriented programming. At its core, object-oriented programming is structured programming with more constraints and polymorphism. Information hiding forces yet another rethink of where data lives. I remember being frustrated more than once because I had to refactor my code so that a method I was writing could get information that was encapsulated in an object that my method could not reach.

Functional programming languages add other constraints, but immutability is the hardest to swallow after decades of imperative programming and object-oriented programming. After we get used to these constraints, we see them as blessings. They make reasoning about the code much easier.

Lack of constraints is the main problem with the threads-and-locks model of concurrent programming. When summarizing Chapter 1 of *Seven Concurrency Models in Seven Weeks*, Paul Butcher wrote:

The greatest weakness of the approach, however, is that threads-and-locks programming is *hard*. It may be easy for a language designer to add them to a language, but they provide us, the poor programmers, with very little help.

Some examples of unconstrained behavior in that model:

- Threads can share access to arbitrary, mutable data structures.
- The scheduler can interrupt a thread at almost any point, including in the middle of a simple operation like a += 1. Very few operations are atomic at the level of source code expressions.
- Locks are usually *advisory*. That's a technical term meaning that you must remember to explicitly hold a lock before updating a shared data structure. If you forget to get the lock, nothing prevents your code from messing up the data while another thread dutifully holds the lock and is updating the same data.

In contrast, consider some constraints enforced by the actor model, in which the execution unit is called an *actor*:[29]

- An actor can have internal state, but cannot share state with other actors.
- Actors can only communicate by sending and receiving messages.
- Messages only hold copies of data, not references to mutable data.
- An actor only handles one message at a time. There is no concurrent execution inside a single actor.

Of course, you can adopt an *actor style* of coding in any language by following these rules. You can also use object-oriented programming idioms in C, and even structured programming patterns in assembly. But doing any of that requires a lot of agreement and discipline among everyone who touches the code.

Managing locks is unnecessary in the actor model, as implemented by Erlang and Elixir, where all data types are immutable.

Threads-and-locks are not going away. I just don't think dealing with such low-level entities is a good use of my time as I write applications—as opposed to kernel modules or databases.

I reserve the right to change my mind, always. But right now, I am convinced that the actor model is the most sensible, general-purpose concurrent programming model available. CSP (Communicating Sequential Processes) is also sensible, but its

---

29 The Erlang community uses the term "process" for actors. In Erlang, each process is a function in its own loop, so they are very lightweight and it's feasible to have millions of them active at once in a single machine —no relation to the heavyweight OS processes we've been talking about elsewhere in this chapter. So here we have examples of the two sins described by Prof. Simon: using different words to mean the same thing, and using one word to mean different things.

implementation in Go leaves out some constraints. The idea in CSP is that coroutines (or *goroutines* in Go) exchange data and synchronize using queues (called *channels* in Go). But Go also supports memory sharing and locks. I've seen a book about Go advocate the use of shared memory and locks instead of channels—in the name of performance. Old habits die hard.

## CHAPTER 20

Concurrent Executors

The people bashing threads are typically system programmers which have in mind use cases that the typical application programmer will never encounter in her life. [...] In 99% of the use cases an application programmer is likely to run into, the simple pattern of spawning a bunch of independent threads and collecting the results in a queue is everything one needs to know.

—Michele Simionato, Python deep thinker[1]

This chapter focuses on the `concurrent.futures.Executor` classes that encapsulate the pattern of "spawning a bunch of independent threads and collecting the results in a queue," described by Michele Simionato. The concurrent executors make this pattern almost trivial to use, not only with threads but also with processes—useful for compute-intensive tasks.

Here I also introduce the concept of *futures*—objects representing the asynchronous execution of an operation, similar to JavaScript promises. This primitive idea is the foundation not only of `concurrent.futures` but also of the `asyncio` package, the subject of Chapter 21.

What's New in This Chapter

I renamed the chapter from "Concurrency with Futures" to "Concurrent Executors" because the executors are the most important high-level feature covered here. Futures are low-level objects, focused on in "Where Are the Futures?" on page 755, but mostly invisible in the rest of the chapter.

---

1 From Michele Simionato's post, "Threads, processes and concurrency in Python: some thoughts" (*https://fpy.li/20-1*), summarized as "Removing the hype around the multicore (non) revolution and some (hopefully) sensible comment about threads and other forms of concurrency."

All the HTTP client examples now use the new *HTTPX* (*https://fpy.li/httpx*) library, which provides synchronous and asynchronous APIs.

The setup for the experiments in "Downloads with Progress Display and Error Handling" on page 766 is now simpler, thanks to the multithreaded server added to the `http.server` (*https://fpy.li/20-2*) package in Python 3.7. Previously, the standard library only had the single-threaded `BaseHttpServer`, which was no good for experimenting with concurrent clients, so I had to resort to external tools in the first edition of this book.

"Launching Processes with concurrent.futures" on page 758 now demonstrates how an executor simplifies the code we saw in "Code for the Multicore Prime Checker" on page 723.

Finally, I moved most of the theory to the new Chapter 19, "Concurrency Models in Python".

Concurrent Web Downloads

Concurrency is essential for efficient network I/O: instead of idly waiting for remote machines, the application should do something else until a response comes back.[2]

To demonstrate with code, I wrote three simple programs to download images of 20 country flags from the web. The first one, *flags.py*, runs sequentially: it only requests the next image when the previous one is downloaded and saved locally. The other two scripts make concurrent downloads: they request several images practically at the same time, and save them as they arrive. The *flags_threadpool.py* script uses the `concurrent.futures` package, while *flags_asyncio.py* uses `asyncio`.

Example 20-1 shows the result of running the three scripts, three times each. I also posted a 73s video on YouTube (*https://fpy.li/20-3*) so you can watch them running while a macOS Finder window displays the flags as they are saved. The scripts are downloading images from *fluentpython.com*, which is behind a CDN, so you may see slower results in the first runs. The results in Example 20-1 were obtained after several runs, so the CDN cache was warm.

Example 20-1. Three typical runs of the scripts flags.py, flags_threadpool.py, and flags_asyncio.py

```
$ python3 flags.py
BD BR CD CN DE EG ET FR ID IN IR JP MX NG PH PK RU TR US VN  ❶
20 flags downloaded in 7.26s  ❷
$ python3 flags.py
```

---

2 Particularly if your cloud provider rents machines by the second, regardless of how busy the CPUs are.

```
BD BR CD CN DE EG ET FR ID IN IR JP MX NG PH PK RU TR US VN
20 flags downloaded in 7.20s
$ python3 flags.py
BD BR CD CN DE EG ET FR ID IN IR JP MX NG PH PK RU TR US VN
20 flags downloaded in 7.09s
$ python3 flags_threadpool.py
DE BD CN JP ID EG NG BR RU CD IR MX US PH FR PK VN IN ET TR
20 flags downloaded in 1.37s    ❸
$ python3 flags_threadpool.py
EG BR FR IN BD JP DE RU PK PH CD MX ID US NG TR CN VN ET IR
20 flags downloaded in 1.60s
$ python3 flags_threadpool.py
BD DE EG CN ID RU IN VN ET MX FR CD NG US JP TR PK BR IR PH
20 flags downloaded in 1.22s
$ python3 flags_asyncio.py    ❹
BD BR IN ID TR DE CN US IR PK PH FR RU NG VN ET MX EG JP CD
20 flags downloaded in 1.36s
$ python3 flags_asyncio.py
RU CN BR IN FR BD TR EG VN IR PH CD ET ID NG DE JP PK MX US
20 flags downloaded in 1.27s
$ python3 flags_asyncio.py
RU IN ID DE BR VN PK MX US IR ET EG NG BD FR CN JP PH CD TR    ❺
20 flags downloaded in 1.42s
```

❶ The output for each run starts with the country codes of the flags as they are downloaded, and ends with a message stating the elapsed time.

❷ It took *flags.py* an average 7.18s to download 20 images.

❸ The average for *flags_threadpool.py* was 1.40s.

❹ For *flags_asyncio.py*, 1.35s was the average time.

❺ Note the order of the country codes: the downloads happened in a different order every time with the concurrent scripts.

The difference in performance between the concurrent scripts is not significant, but they are both more than five times faster than the sequential script—and this is just for the small task of downloading 20 files of a few kilobytes each. If you scale the task to hundreds of downloads, the concurrent scripts can outpace the sequential code by a factor or 20 or more.

> While testing concurrent HTTP clients against public web servers, you may inadvertently launch a denial-of-service (DoS) attack, or be suspected of doing so. In the case of Example 20-1, it's OK to do it because those scripts are hardcoded to make only 20 requests. We'll use Python's `http.server` package to run tests later in this chapter.

Now let's study the implementations of two of the scripts tested in Example 20-1: *flags.py* and *flags_threadpool.py*. I will leave the third script, *flags_asyncio.py*, for Chapter 21, but I wanted to demonstrate all three together to make two points:

1. Regardless of the concurrency constructs you use—threads or coroutines—you'll see vastly improved throughput over sequential code in network I/O operations, if you code it properly.

2. For HTTP clients that can control how many requests they make, there is no significant difference in performance between threads and coroutines.[3]

On to the code.

A Sequential Download Script

Example 20-2 contains the implementation of *flags.py*, the first script we ran in Example 20-1. It's not very interesting, but we'll reuse most of its code and settings to implement the concurrent scripts, so it deserves some attention.

 For clarity, there is no error handling in Example 20-2. We will deal with exceptions later, but here I want to focus on the basic structure of the code, to make it easier to contrast this script with the concurrent ones.

Example 20-2. flags.py: sequential download script; some functions will be reused by the other scripts

```
import time
from pathlib import Path
from typing import Callable

import httpx  ❶

POP20_CC = ('CN IN US ID BR PK NG BD RU JP '
            'MX PH VN ET EG DE IR TR CD FR').split()  ❷

BASE_URL = 'https://www.fluentpython.com/data/flags'  ❸
DEST_DIR = Path('downloaded')                          ❹

def save_flag(img: bytes, filename: str) -> None:      ❺
    (DEST_DIR / filename).write_bytes(img)
```

---

3 For servers that may be hit by many clients, there is a difference: coroutines scale better because they use much less memory than threads, and also reduce the cost of context switching, which I mentioned in "Thread-Based Nonsolution" on page 728.

```python
def get_flag(cc: str) -> bytes:   ❻
    url = f'{BASE_URL}/{cc}/{cc}.gif'.lower()
    resp = httpx.get(url, timeout=6.1,        ❼
                     follow_redirects=True)   ❽
    resp.raise_for_status()   ❾
    return resp.content

def download_many(cc_list: list[str]) -> int:   ❿
    for cc in sorted(cc_list):                  ⓫
        image = get_flag(cc)
        save_flag(image, f'{cc}.gif')
        print(cc, end=' ', flush=True)          ⓬
    return len(cc_list)

def main(downloader: Callable[[list[str]], int]) -> None:   ⓭
    DEST_DIR.mkdir(exist_ok=True)                           ⓮
    t0 = time.perf_counter()                                ⓯
    count = downloader(POP20_CC)
    elapsed = time.perf_counter() - t0
    print(f'\n{count} downloads in {elapsed:.2f}s')

if __name__ == '__main__':
    main(download_many)       ⓰
```

❶ Import the httpx library. It's not part of the standard library, so by convention the import goes after the standard library modules and a blank line.

❷ List of the ISO 3166 country codes for the 20 most populous countries in order of decreasing population.

❸ The directory with the flag images.[4]

❹ Local directory where the images are saved.

❺ Save the img bytes to filename in the DEST_DIR.

❻ Given a country code, build the URL and download the image, returning the binary contents of the response.

❼ It's good practice to add a sensible timeout to network operations, to avoid blocking for several minutes for no good reason.

---

4 The images are originally from the CIA World Factbook (*https://fpy.li/20-4*), a public-domain, US government publication. I copied them to my site to avoid the risk of launching a DOS attack on *cia.gov*.

❽ By default, *HTTPX* does not follow redirects.[5]

❾ There's no error handling in this script, but this method raises an exception if the HTTP status is not in the 2XX range—highly recommended to avoid silent failures.

❿ download_many is the key function to compare with the concurrent implementations.

⓫ Loop over the list of country codes in alphabetical order, to make it easy to see that the ordering is preserved in the output; return the number of country codes downloaded.

⓬ Display one country code at a time in the same line so we can see progress as each download happens. The end=' ' argument replaces the usual line break at the end of each line printed with a space character, so all country codes are displayed progressively in the same line. The flush=True argument is needed because, by default, Python output is line buffered, meaning that Python only displays printed characters after a line break.

⓭ main must be called with the function that will make the downloads; that way, we can use main as a library function with other implementations of download_many in the threadpool and ascyncio examples.

⓮ Create DEST_DIR if needed; don't raise an error if the directory exists.

⓯ Record and report the elapsed time after running the downloader function.

⓰ Call main with the download_many function.

 The *HTTPX* (*https://fpy.li/httpx*) library is inspired by the Pythonic *requests* (*https://fpy.li/20-5*) package, but is built on a more modern foundation. Crucially, *HTTPX* provides synchronous and asynchronous APIs, so we can use it in all HTTP client examples in this chapter and the next. Python's standard library provides the urllib.request module, but its API is synchronous only, and is not user friendly.

---

5 Setting follow_redirects=True is not needed for this example, but I wanted to highlight this important difference between *HTTPX* and *requests*. Also, setting follow_redirects=True in this example gives me flexibility to host the image files elsewhere in the future. I think the *HTTPX* default setting of follow_redirects =False is sensible because unexpected redirects can mask needless requests and complicate error diagnostics.

There's really nothing new to *flags.py*. It serves as a baseline for comparing the other scripts, and I used it as a library to avoid redundant code when implementing them. Now let's see a reimplementation using `concurrent.futures`.

Downloading with concurrent.futures

The main features of the `concurrent.futures` package are the `ThreadPoolExecutor` and `ProcessPoolExecutor` classes, which implement an API to submit callables for execution in different threads or processes, respectively. The classes transparently manage a pool of worker threads or processes, and queues to distribute jobs and collect results. But the interface is very high-level, and we don't need to know about any of those details for a simple use case like our flag downloads.

Example 20-3 shows the easiest way to implement the downloads concurrently, using the `ThreadPoolExecutor.map` method.

Example 20-3. flags_threadpool.py: threaded download script using futures.Thread PoolExecutor

```
from concurrent import futures

from flags import save_flag, get_flag, main    ❶

def download_one(cc: str):    ❷
    image = get_flag(cc)
    save_flag(image, f'{cc}.gif')
    print(cc, end=' ', flush=True)
    return cc

def download_many(cc_list: list[str]) -> int:
    with futures.ThreadPoolExecutor() as executor:        ❸
        res = executor.map(download_one, sorted(cc_list))    ❹

    return len(list(res))                                 ❺

if __name__ == '__main__':
    main(download_many)    ❻
```

❶ Reuse some functions from the `flags` module (Example 20-2).

❷ Function to download a single image; this is what each worker will execute.

❸ Instantiate the `ThreadPoolExecutor` as a context manager; the executor `.__exit__` method will call `executor.shutdown(wait=True)`, which will block until all threads are done.

❹ The `map` method is similar to the `map` built-in, except that the `download_one` function will be called concurrently from multiple threads; it returns a generator that you can iterate to retrieve the value returned by each function call—in this case, each call to `download_one` will return a country code.

❺ Return the number of results obtained. If any of the threaded calls raises an exception, that exception is raised here when the implicit `next()` call inside the `list` constructor tries to retrieve the corresponding return value from the iterator returned by `executor.map`.

❻ Call the `main` function from the `flags` module, passing the concurrent version of `download_many`.

Note that the `download_one` function from Example 20-3 is essentially the body of the `for` loop in the `download_many` function from Example 20-2. This is a common refactoring when writing concurrent code: turning the body of a sequential `for` loop into a function to be called concurrently.

 Example 20-3 is very short because I was able to reuse most functions from the sequential *flags.py* script. One of the best features of `concurrent.futures` is to make it simple to add concurrent execution on top of legacy sequential code.

The `ThreadPoolExecutor` constructor takes several arguments not shown, but the first and most important one is `max_workers`, setting the maximum number of worker threads to be executed. When `max_workers` is `None` (the default), `ThreadPool Executor` decides its value using the following expression—since Python 3.8:

```
max_workers = min(32, os.cpu_count() + 4)
```

The rationale is explained in the `ThreadPoolExecutor` documentation (*https://fpy.li/ 20-6*):

> This default value preserves at least 5 workers for I/O bound tasks. It utilizes at most 32 CPU cores for CPU bound tasks which release the GIL. And it avoids using very large resources implicitly on many-core machines.
>
> `ThreadPoolExecutor` now reuses idle worker threads before starting `max_workers` worker threads too.

To conclude: the computed default for `max_workers` is sensible, and `ThreadPoolExe cutor` avoids starting new workers unnecessarily. Understanding the logic behind `max_workers` may help you decide when and how to set it yourself.

The library is called *concurrency.futures*, yet there are no futures to be seen in Example 20-3, so you may be wondering where they are. The next section explains.

Where Are the Futures?

Futures are core components of `concurrent.futures` and of `asyncio`, but as users of these libraries we sometimes don't see them. Example 20-3 depends on futures behind the scenes, but the code I wrote does not touch them directly. This section is an overview of futures, with an example that shows them in action.

Since Python 3.4, there are two classes named `Future` in the standard library: `concurrent.futures.Future` and `asyncio.Future`. They serve the same purpose: an instance of either `Future` class represents a deferred computation that may or may not have completed. This is somewhat similar to the `Deferred` class in Twisted, the `Future` class in Tornado, and `Promise` in modern JavaScript.

Futures encapsulate pending operations so that we can put them in queues, check whether they are done, and retrieve results (or exceptions) when they become available.

An important thing to know about futures is that you and I should not create them: they are meant to be instantiated exclusively by the concurrency framework, be it `concurrent.futures` or `asyncio`. Here is why: a `Future` represents something that will eventually run, therefore it must be scheduled to run, and that's the job of the framework. In particular, `concurrent.futures.Future` instances are created only as the result of submitting a callable for execution with a `concurrent.futures.Executor` subclass. For example, the `Executor.submit()` method takes a callable, schedules it to run, and returns a `Future`.

Application code is not supposed to change the state of a future: the concurrency framework changes the state of a future when the computation it represents is done, and we can't control when that happens.

Both types of `Future` have a `.done()` method that is nonblocking and returns a Boolean that tells you whether the callable wrapped by that future has executed or not. However, instead of repeatedly asking whether a future is done, client code usually asks to be notified. That's why both `Future` classes have an `.add_done_callback()` method: you give it a callable, and the callable will be invoked with the future as the single argument when the future is done. Be aware that the callback callable will run in the same worker thread or process that ran the function wrapped in the future.

There is also a `.result()` method, which works the same in both classes when the future is done: it returns the result of the callable, or re-raises whatever exception might have been thrown when the callable was executed. However, when the future is not done, the behavior of the result method is very different between the two flavors of Future. In a concurrency.futures.Future instance, invoking f.result() will block the caller's thread until the result is ready. An optional timeout argument can be passed, and if the future is not done in the specified time, the result method raises TimeoutError. The asyncio.Future.result method does not support time-out, and await is the preferred way to get the result of futures in asyncio—but await doesn't work with concurrency.futures.Future instances.

Several functions in both libraries return futures; others use them in their implementation in a way that is transparent to the user. An example of the latter is the Executor.map we saw in Example 20-3: it returns an iterator in which __next__ calls the result method of each future, so we get the results of the futures, and not the futures themselves.

To get a practical look at futures, we can rewrite Example 20-3 to use the concurrent.futures.as_completed (*https://fpy.li/20-7*) function, which takes an iterable of futures and returns an iterator that yields futures as they are done.

Using futures.as_completed requires changes to the download_many function only. The higher-level executor.map call is replaced by two for loops: one to create and schedule the futures, the other to retrieve their results. While we are at it, we'll add a few print calls to display each future before and after it's done. Example 20-4 shows the code for a new download_many function. The code for download_many grew from 5 to 17 lines, but now we get to inspect the mysterious futures. The remaining functions are the same as in Example 20-3.

Example 20-4. flags_threadpool_futures.py: replacing executor.map with executor.submit and futures.as_completed in the download_many function

```python
def download_many(cc_list: list[str]) -> int:
    cc_list = cc_list[:5]  ❶
    with futures.ThreadPoolExecutor(max_workers=3) as executor:  ❷
        to_do: list[futures.Future] = []
        for cc in sorted(cc_list):  ❸
            future = executor.submit(download_one, cc)  ❹
            to_do.append(future)  ❺
            print(f'Scheduled for {cc}: {future}')  ❻

        for count, future in enumerate(futures.as_completed(to_do), 1):  ❼
            res: str = future.result()  ❽
            print(f'{future} result: {res!r}')  ❾

    return count
```

❶ For this demonstration, use only the top five most populous countries.

❷ Set `max_workers` to 3 so we can see pending futures in the output.

❸ Iterate over country codes alphabetically, to make it clear that results will arrive out of order.

❹ `executor.submit` schedules the callable to be executed, and returns a `future` representing this pending operation.

❺ Store each `future` so we can later retrieve them with `as_completed`.

❻ Display a message with the country code and the respective `future`.

❼ `as_completed` yields futures as they are completed.

❽ Get the result of this `future`.

❾ Display the `future` and its result.

Note that the `future.result()` call will never block in this example because the `future` is coming out of `as_completed`. Example 20-5 shows the output of one run of Example 20-4.

Example 20-5. Output of flags_threadpool_futures.py

```
$ python3 flags_threadpool_futures.py
Scheduled for BR: <Future at 0x100791518 state=running>   ❶
Scheduled for CN: <Future at 0x100791710 state=running>
Scheduled for ID: <Future at 0x100791a90 state=running>
Scheduled for IN: <Future at 0x101807080 state=pending>    ❷
Scheduled for US: <Future at 0x101807128 state=pending>
CN <Future at 0x100791710 state=finished returned str> result: 'CN'   ❸
BR ID <Future at 0x100791518 state=finished returned str> result: 'BR'   ❹
<Future at 0x100791a90 state=finished returned str> result: 'ID'
IN <Future at 0x101807080 state=finished returned str> result: 'IN'
US <Future at 0x101807128 state=finished returned str> result: 'US'

5 downloads in 0.70s
```

❶ The futures are scheduled in alphabetical order; the `repr()` of a future shows its state: the first three are `running`, because there are three worker threads.

❷ The last two futures are `pending`, waiting for worker threads.

---

❸ The first CN here is the output of download_one in a worker thread; the rest of the line is the output of download_many.

❹ Here, two threads output codes before download_many in the main thread can display the result of the first thread.

I recommend experimenting with *flags_threadpool_futures.py*. If you run it several times, you'll see the order of the results varying. Increasing max_workers to 5 will increase the variation in the order of the results. Decreasing it to 1 will make this script run sequentially, and the order of the results will always be the order of the submit calls.

We saw two variants of the download script using concurrent.futures: one in Example 20-3 with ThreadPoolExecutor.map and one in Example 20-4 with futures.as_completed. If you are curious about the code for *flags_asyncio.py*, you may peek at Example 21-3 in Chapter 21, where it is explained.

Now let's take a brief look at a simple way to work around the GIL for CPU-bound jobs using concurrent.futures.

Launching Processes with concurrent.futures

The concurrent.futures documentation page (*https://fpy.li/20-8*) is subtitled "Launching parallel tasks." The package enables parallel computation on multicore machines because it supports distributing work among multiple Python processes using the ProcessPoolExecutor class.

Both ProcessPoolExecutor and ThreadPoolExecutor implement the Executor (*https://fpy.li/20-9*) interface, so it's easy to switch from a thread-based to a process-based solution using concurrent.futures.

There is no advantage in using a ProcessPoolExecutor for the flags download example or any I/O-bound job. It's easy to verify this; just change these lines in Example 20-3:

```
def download_many(cc_list: list[str]) -> int:
    with futures.ThreadPoolExecutor() as executor:
```

To this:

```
def download_many(cc_list: list[str]) -> int:
    with futures.ProcessPoolExecutor() as executor:
```

The constructor for ProcessPoolExecutor also has a max_workers parameter, which defaults to None. In that case, the executor limits the number of workers to the number returned by os.cpu_count().

Processes use more memory and take longer to start than threads, so the real value of ProcessPoolExecutor is in CPU-intensive jobs. Let's go back to the primality test example of "A Homegrown Process Pool" on page 720, rewriting it with concurrent.futures.

Multicore Prime Checker Redux

In "Code for the Multicore Prime Checker" on page 723 we studied *procs.py*, a script that checked the primality of some large numbers using multiprocessing. In Example 20-6 we solve the same problem in the *proc_pool.py* program using a Proc essPoolExecutor. From the first import to the main() call at the end, *procs.py* has 43 nonblank lines of code, and *proc_pool.py* has 31—28% shorter.

Example 20-6. proc_pool.py: procs.py rewritten with ProcessPoolExecutor

```python
import sys
from concurrent import futures      ❶
from time import perf_counter
from typing import NamedTuple

from primes import is_prime, NUMBERS

class PrimeResult(NamedTuple):      ❷
    n: int
    flag: bool
    elapsed: float

def check(n: int) -> PrimeResult:
    t0 = perf_counter()
    res = is_prime(n)
    return PrimeResult(n, res, perf_counter() - t0)

def main() -> None:
    if len(sys.argv) < 2:
        workers = None          ❸
    else:
        workers = int(sys.argv[1])

    executor = futures.ProcessPoolExecutor(workers)      ❹
    actual_workers = executor._max_workers  # type: ignore   ❺

    print(f'Checking {len(NUMBERS)} numbers with {actual_workers} processes:')

    t0 = perf_counter()
```

```
    numbers = sorted(NUMBERS, reverse=True)  ❻
    with executor:  ❼
        for n, prime, elapsed in executor.map(check, numbers):  ❽
            label = 'P' if prime else ' '
            print(f'{n:16}  {label} {elapsed:9.6f}s')

    time = perf_counter() - t0
    print(f'Total time: {time:.2f}s')

if __name__ == '__main__':
    main()
```

❶ No need to import multiprocessing, SimpleQueue etc.; concurrent.futures hides all that.

❷ The PrimeResult tuple and the check function are the same as we saw in *procs.py*, but we don't need the queues and the worker function anymore.

❸ Instead of deciding ourselves how many workers to use if no command-line argument was given, we set workers to None and let the ProcessPoolExecutor decide.

❹ Here I build the ProcessPoolExecutor before the with block in ❼ so that I can display the actual number of workers in the next line.

❺ _max_workers is an undocumented instance attribute of a ProcessPoolExecutor. I decided to use it to show the number of workers when the workers variable is None. *Mypy* correctly complains when I access it, so I put the type: ignore comment to silence it.

❻ Sort the numbers to be checked in descending order. This will expose a difference in the behavior of *proc_pool.py* when compared with *procs.py*. See the explanation after this example.

❼ Use the executor as a context manager.

❽ The executor.map call returns the PrimeResult instances returned by check in the same order as the numbers arguments.

If you run Example 20-6, you'll see the results appearing in strict descending order, as shown in Example 20-7. In contrast, the ordering of the output of *procs.py* (shown in "Process-Based Solution" on page 722) is heavily influenced by the difficulty in checking whether each number is a prime. For example, *procs.py* shows the result for

7777777777777777 near the top, because it has a low divisor, 7, so is_prime quickly determines it's not a prime.

In contrast, 7777777536340681 is 88191709^2, so is_prime will take much longer to determine that it's a composite number, and even longer to find out that 7777777777777753 is prime—therefore both of these numbers appear near the end of the output of *procs.py*.

Running *proc_pool.py*, you'll observe not only the descending order of the results, but also that the program will appear to be stuck after showing the result for 9999999999999999.

Example 20-7. Output of proc_pool.py

```
$ ./proc_pool.py
Checking 20 numbers with 12 processes:
9999999999999999      0.000024s   ❶
9999999999999917  P   9.500677s   ❷
7777777777777777      0.000022s   ❸
7777777777777753  P   8.976933s
7777777536340681      8.896149s
6666667141414921      8.537621s
6666666666666719  P   8.548641s
6666666666666666      0.000002s
5555555555555555      0.000017s
5555555555555503  P   8.214086s
5555553133149889      8.067247s
4444444488888889      7.546234s
4444444444444444      0.000002s
4444444444444423  P   7.622370s
3333335652092209      6.724649s
3333333333333333      0.000018s
3333333333333301  P   6.655039s
 299593572317531  P   2.072723s
 142702110479723  P   1.461840s
               2  P   0.000001s
Total time: 9.65s
```

❶ This line appears very quickly.

❷ This line takes more than 9.5s to show up.

❸ All the remaining lines appear almost immediately.

Here is why *proc_pool.py* behaves in that way:

- As mentioned before, `executor.map(check, numbers)` returns the result in the same order as the `numbers` are given.
- By default, *proc_pool.py* uses as many workers as there are CPUs—it's what `ProcessPoolExecutor` does when `max_workers` is `None`. That's 12 processes in this laptop.
- Because we are submitting `numbers` in descending order, the first is 9999999999999999; with 9 as a divisor, it returns quickly.
- The second number is 9999999999999917, the largest prime in the sample. This will take longer than all the others to check.
- Meanwhile, the remaining 11 processes will be checking other numbers, which are either primes or composites with large factors, or composites with very small factors.
- When the worker in charge of 9999999999999917 finally determines that's a prime, all the other processes have completed their last jobs, so the results appear immediately after.

 Although the progress of *proc_pool.py* is not as visible as that of *procs.py*, the overall execution time is practically the same as depicted in Figure 19-2, for the same number of workers and CPU cores.

Understanding how concurrent programs behave is not straightforward, so here's is a second experiment that may help you visualize the operation of `Executor.map`.

Experimenting with Executor.map

Let's investigate `Executor.map`, now using a `ThreadPoolExecutor` with three workers running five callables that output timestamped messages. The code is in Example 20-8, the output in Example 20-9.

Example 20-8. demo_executor_map.py: Simple demonstration of the map method of ThreadPoolExecutor

```
from time import sleep, strftime
from concurrent import futures

def display(*args):    ❶
    print(strftime('[%H:%M:%S]'), end=' ')
    print(*args)
```

```
def loiter(n):  ❷
    msg = '{}loiter({}): doing nothing for {}s...'
    display(msg.format('\t'*n, n, n))
    sleep(n)
    msg = '{}loiter({}): done.'
    display(msg.format('\t'*n, n))
    return n * 10  ❸

def main():
    display('Script starting.')
    executor = futures.ThreadPoolExecutor(max_workers=3)  ❹
    results = executor.map(loiter, range(5))  ❺
    display('results:', results)  ❻
    display('Waiting for individual results:')
    for i, result in enumerate(results):  ❼
        display(f'result {i}: {result}')

if __name__ == '__main__':
    main()
```

❶ This function simply prints whatever arguments it gets, preceded by a timestamp in the format [HH:MM:SS].

❷ loiter does nothing except display a message when it starts, sleep for n seconds, then display a message when it ends; tabs are used to indent the messages according to the value of n.

❸ loiter returns n * 10 so we can see how to collect results.

❹ Create a ThreadPoolExecutor with three threads.

❺ Submit five tasks to the executor. Since there are only three threads, only three of those tasks will start immediately: the calls loiter(0), loiter(1), and loiter(2); this is a nonblocking call.

❻ Immediately display the results of invoking executor.map: it's a generator, as the output in Example 20-9 shows.

❼ The enumerate call in the for loop will implicitly invoke next(results), which in turn will invoke _f.result() on the (internal) _f future representing the first call, loiter(0). The result method will block until the future is done, therefore each iteration in this loop will have to wait for the next result to be ready.

I encourage you to run Example 20-8 and see the display being updated incrementally. While you're at it, play with the max_workers argument for the ThreadPoolExecutor and with the range function that produces the arguments for the executor.map call—or replace it with lists of handpicked values to create different delays.

Example 20-9 shows a sample run of Example 20-8.

Example 20-9. Sample run of demo_executor_map.py from Example 20-8

```
$ python3 demo_executor_map.py
[15:56:50] Script starting.  ❶
[15:56:50] loiter(0): doing nothing for 0s...  ❷
[15:56:50] loiter(0): done.
[15:56:50]      loiter(1): doing nothing for 1s...  ❸
[15:56:50]              loiter(2): doing nothing for 2s...
[15:56:50] results: <generator object result_iterator at 0x106517168>  ❹
[15:56:50]                      loiter(3): doing nothing for 3s...  ❺
[15:56:50] Waiting for individual results:
[15:56:50] result 0: 0  ❻
[15:56:51]      loiter(1): done.  ❼
[15:56:51]                              loiter(4): doing nothing for 4s...
[15:56:51] result 1: 10  ❽
[15:56:52]              loiter(2): done.  ❾
[15:56:52] result 2: 20
[15:56:53]                      loiter(3): done.
[15:56:53] result 3: 30
[15:56:55]                              loiter(4): done.  ❿
[15:56:55] result 4: 40
```

❶   This run started at 15:56:50.

❷   The first thread executes loiter(0), so it will sleep for 0s and return even before the second thread has a chance to start, but YMMV.[6]

❸   loiter(1) and loiter(2) start immediately (because the thread pool has three workers, it can run three functions concurrently).

❹   This shows that the results returned by executor.map is a generator; nothing so far would block, regardless of the number of tasks and the max_workers setting.

---

6 Your mileage may vary: with threads, you never know the exact sequencing of events that should happen nearly at the same time; it's possible that, in another machine, you see loiter(1) starting before loiter(0) finishes, particularly because sleep always releases the GIL, so Python may switch to another thread even if you sleep for 0s.

⑤ Because loiter(0) is done, the first worker is now available to start the fourth thread for loiter(3).

⑥ This is where execution may block, depending on the parameters given to the loiter calls: the __next__ method of the results generator must wait until the first future is complete. In this case, it won't block because the call to loiter(0) finished before this loop started. Note that everything up to this point happened within the same second: 15:56:50.

⑦ loiter(1) is done one second later, at 15:56:51. The thread is freed to start loiter(4).

⑧ The result of loiter(1) is shown: 10. Now the for loop will block waiting for the result of loiter(2).

⑨ The pattern repeats: loiter(2) is done, its result is shown; same with loiter(3).

⑩ There is a 2s delay until loiter(4) is done, because it started at 15:56:51 and did nothing for 4s.

The Executor.map function is easy to use, but often it's preferable to get the results as they are ready, regardless of the order they were submitted. To do that, we need a combination of the Executor.submit method and the futures.as_completed function, as we saw in Example 20-4. We'll come back to this technique in "Using futures.as_completed" on page 773.

 The combination of executor.submit and futures.as_completed is more flexible than executor.map because you can submit different callables and arguments, while executor.map is designed to run the same callable on the different arguments. In addition, the set of futures you pass to futures.as_completed may come from more than one executor—perhaps some were created by a ThreadPoolExecutor instance, while others are from a ProcessPoolExecutor.

In the next section, we will resume the flag download examples with new requirements that will force us to iterate over the results of futures.as_completed instead of using executor.map.

Downloads with Progress Display and Error Handling

As mentioned, the scripts in "Concurrent Web Downloads" on page 748 have no error handling to make them easier to read and to contrast the structure of the three approaches: sequential, threaded, and asynchronous.

In order to test the handling of a variety of error conditions, I created the flags2 examples:

flags2_common.py

    This module contains common functions and settings used by all flags2 examples, including a main function, which takes care of command-line parsing, timing, and reporting results. That is really support code, not directly relevant to the subject of this chapter, so I will not list the source code here, but you can read it in the *fluentpython/example-code-2e* repository: *20-executors/getflags/flags2_common.py* (*https://fpy.li/20-10*).

flags2_sequential.py

    A sequential HTTP client with proper error handling and progress bar display. Its download_one function is also used by flags2_threadpool.py.

flags2_threadpool.py

    Concurrent HTTP client based on futures.ThreadPoolExecutor to demonstrate error handling and integration of the progress bar.

flags2_asyncio.py

    Same functionality as the previous example, but implemented with asyncio and httpx. This will be covered in "Enhancing the asyncio Downloader" on page 792, in Chapter 21.

> **Be Careful when Testing Concurrent Clients**
>
> When testing concurrent HTTP clients on public web servers, you may generate many requests per second, and that's how denial-of-service (DoS) attacks are made. Carefully throttle your clients when hitting public servers. For testing, set up a local HTTP server. See "Setting Up Test Servers" on page 769 for instructions.

The most visible feature of the flags2 examples is that they have an animated, text-mode progress bar implemented with the *tqdm* package (*https://fpy.li/20-11*). I posted a 108s video on YouTube (*https://fpy.li/20-12*) to show the progress bar and contrast the speed of the three flags2 scripts. In the video, I start with the sequential download, but I interrupt it after 32s because it was going to take more than 5 minutes to hit on 676 URLs and get 194 flags. I then run the threaded and asyncio scripts three times each, and every time they complete the job in 6s or less (i.e., more than 60 times faster). Figure 20-1 shows two screenshots: during and after running *flags2_threadpool.py*.

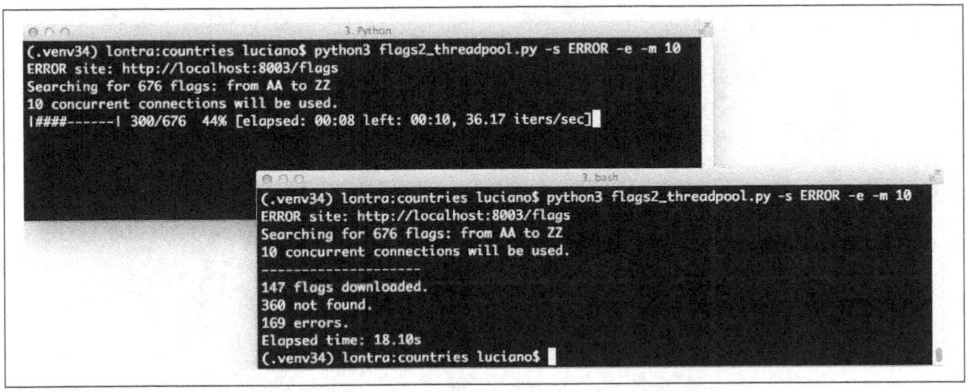

Figure 20-1. Top-left: flags2_threadpool.py running with live progress bar generated by tqdm; bottom-right: same terminal window after the script is finished.

The simplest *tqdm* example appears in an animated *.gif* in the project's *README.md* (*https://fpy.li/20-13*). If you type the following code in the Python console after installing the *tqdm* package, you'll see an animated progress bar where the comment is:

```
>>> import time
>>> from tqdm import tqdm
>>> for i in tqdm(range(1000)):
...     time.sleep(.01)
...
>>> # -> progress bar will appear here <-
```

Besides the neat effect, the tqdm function is also interesting conceptually: it consumes any iterable and produces an iterator which, while it's consumed, displays the progress bar and estimates the remaining time to complete all iterations. To compute that estimate, tqdm needs to get an iterable that has a len, or additionally receive the total= argument with the expected number of items. Integrating tqdm with our flags2 examples provides an opportunity to look deeper into how the concurrent scripts actually work, by forcing us to use the futures.as_completed (*https://fpy.li/20-7*) and the asyncio.as_completed (*https://fpy.li/20-15*) functions so that tqdm can display progress as each future is completed.

The other feature of the flags2 example is a command-line interface. All three scripts accept the same options, and you can see them by running any of the scripts with the -h option. Example 20-10 shows the help text.

Example 20-10. Help screen for the scripts in the flags2 series

```
$ python3 flags2_threadpool.py -h
usage: flags2_threadpool.py [-h] [-a] [-e] [-l N] [-m CONCURRENT] [-s LABEL]
                            [-v]
                            [CC [CC ...]]

Download flags for country codes. Default: top 20 countries by population.

positional arguments:
  CC                    country code or 1st letter (eg. B for BA...BZ)

optional arguments:
  -h, --help            show this help message and exit
  -a, --all             get all available flags (AD to ZW)
  -e, --every           get flags for every possible code (AA...ZZ)
  -l N, --limit N       limit to N first codes
  -m CONCURRENT, --max_req CONCURRENT
                        maximum concurrent requests (default=30)
  -s LABEL, --server LABEL
                        Server to hit; one of DELAY, ERROR, LOCAL, REMOTE
                        (default=LOCAL)
  -v, --verbose         output detailed progress info
```

All arguments are optional. But the `-s`/`--server` is essential for testing: it lets you choose which HTTP server and port will be used in the test. Pass one of these case-insensitive labels to determine where the script will look for the flags:

LOCAL

Use `http://localhost:8000/flags`; this is the default. You should configure a local HTTP server to answer at port 8000. See the following note for instructions.

REMOTE

Use `http://fluentpython.com/data/flags`; that is a public website owned by me, hosted on a shared server. Please do not pound it with too many concurrent requests. The *fluentpython.com* domain is handled by the Cloudflare (*https://fpy.li/20-16*) CDN (Content Delivery Network) so you may notice that the first downloads are slower, but they get faster when the CDN cache warms up.

DELAY

Use `http://localhost:8001/flags`; a server delaying HTTP responses should be listening to port 8001. I wrote *slow_server.py* to make it easier to experiment. You'll find it in the *20-futures/getflags/* directory of the *Fluent Python* code repository (*https://fpy.li/code*). See the following note for instructions.

ERROR

Use `http://localhost:8002/flags`; a server returning some HTTP errors should be listening on port 8002. Instructions are next.

Setting Up Test Servers

If you don't have a local HTTP server for testing, I wrote setup instructions using only Python ≥ 3.9 (no external libraries) in *20-executors/getflags/README.adoc* (*https://fpy.li/20-17*) in the *fluent-python/example-code-2e* (*https://fpy.li/code*) repository. In short, *README.adoc* describes how to use:

`python3 -m http.server`
> The LOCAL server on port 8000

`python3 slow_server.py`
> The DELAY server on port 8001, which adds a random delay of .5s to 5s before each response

`python3 slow_server.py 8002 --error-rate .25`
> The ERROR server on port 8002, which in addition to the random delay, has a 25% chance of returning a "418 I'm a teapot" (*https://fpy.li/20-18*) error response

By default, each *flags2*.py* script will fetch the flags of the 20 most populous countries from the LOCAL server (`http://localhost:8000/flags`) using a default number of concurrent connections, which varies from script to script. Example 20-11 shows a sample run of the *flags2_sequential.py* script using all defaults. To run it, you need a local server, as explained in "Be Careful when Testing Concurrent Clients" on page 766.

Example 20-11. Running flags2_sequential.py with all defaults: LOCAL `site`*, top 20 flags, 1 concurrent connection*

```
$ python3 flags2_sequential.py
LOCAL site: http://localhost:8000/flags
Searching for 20 flags: from BD to VN
1 concurrent connection will be used.
--------------------
20 flags downloaded.
Elapsed time: 0.10s
```

You can select which flags will be downloaded in several ways. Example 20-12 shows how to download all flags with country codes starting with the letters A, B, or C.

Example 20-12. Run flags2_threadpool.py to fetch all flags with country codes prefixes A, B, or C from the DELAY server

```
$ python3 flags2_threadpool.py -s DELAY a b c
DELAY site: http://localhost:8001/flags
Searching for 78 flags: from AA to CZ
```

```
30 concurrent connections will be used.
--------------------
43 flags downloaded.
35 not found.
Elapsed time: 1.72s
```

Regardless of how the country codes are selected, the number of flags to fetch can be limited with the -l/--limit option. Example 20-13 demonstrates how to run exactly 100 requests, combining the -a option to get all flags with -l 100.

Example 20-13. Run flags2_asyncio.py to get 100 flags (-al 100) from the ERROR server, using 100 concurrent requests (-m 100)

```
$ python3 flags2_asyncio.py -s ERROR -al 100 -m 100
ERROR site: http://localhost:8002/flags
Searching for 100 flags: from AD to LK
100 concurrent connections will be used.
--------------------
73 flags downloaded.
27 errors.
Elapsed time: 0.64s
```

That's the user interface of the flags2 examples. Let's see how they are implemented.

Error Handling in the flags2 Examples

The common strategy in all three examples to deal with HTTP errors is that 404 errors (not found) are handled by the function in charge of downloading a single file (download_one). Any other exception propagates to be handled by the down load_many function or the supervisor coroutine—in the asyncio example.

Once more, we'll start by studying the sequential code, which is easier to follow—and mostly reused by the thread pool script. Example 20-14 shows the functions that perform the actual downloads in the *flags2_sequential.py* and *flags2_threadpool.py* scripts.

Example 20-14. flags2_sequential.py: basic functions in charge of downloading; both are reused in flags2_threadpool.py

```
from collections import Counter
from http import HTTPStatus

import httpx
import tqdm  # type: ignore  ❶

from flags2_common import main, save_flag, DownloadStatus  ❷

DEFAULT_CONCUR_REQ = 1
```

```
MAX_CONCUR_REQ = 1

def get_flag(base_url: str, cc: str) -> bytes:
    url = f'{base_url}/{cc}/{cc}.gif'.lower()
    resp = httpx.get(url, timeout=3.1, follow_redirects=True)
    resp.raise_for_status()  ❸
    return resp.content

def download_one(cc: str, base_url: str, verbose: bool = False) -> DownloadStatus:
    try:
        image = get_flag(base_url, cc)
    except httpx.HTTPStatusError as exc:  ❹
        res = exc.response
        if res.status_code == HTTPStatus.NOT_FOUND:
            status = DownloadStatus.NOT_FOUND  ❺
            msg = f'not found: {res.url}'
        else:
            raise  ❻
    else:
        save_flag(image, f'{cc}.gif')
        status = DownloadStatus.OK
        msg = 'OK'

    if verbose:  ❼
        print(cc, msg)

    return status
```

❶ Import the tqdm progress-bar display library, and tell Mypy to skip checking it.[7]

❷ Import a couple of functions and an Enum from the flags2_common module.

❸ Raises HTTPStetusError if the HTTP status code is not in range(200, 300).

❹ download_one catches HTTPStatusError to handle HTTP code 404 specifically...

❺ ...by setting its local status to DownloadStatus.NOT_FOUND; DownloadStatus is an Enum imported from *flags2_common.py*.

❻ Any other HTTPStatusError exception is re-raised to propagate to the caller.

❼ If the -v/--verbose command-line option is set, the country code and status message are displayed; this is how you'll see progress in verbose mode.

---

7 As of September 2021, there are no type hints in the current release of tdqm. That's OK. The world will not end because of that. Thank Guido for optional typing!

Example 20-15 lists the sequential version of the download_many function. This code is straightforward, but it's worth studying to contrast with the concurrent versions coming up. Focus on how it reports progress, handles errors, and tallies downloads.

Example 20-15. flags2_sequential.py: the sequential implementation of download_many

```
def download_many(cc_list: list[str],
                  base_url: str,
                  verbose: bool,
                  _unused_concur_req: int) -> Counter[DownloadStatus]:
    counter: Counter[DownloadStatus] = Counter()  ❶
    cc_iter = sorted(cc_list)  ❷
    if not verbose:
        cc_iter = tqdm.tqdm(cc_iter)  ❸
    for cc in cc_iter:
        try:
            status = download_one(cc, base_url, verbose)  ❹
        except httpx.HTTPStatusError as exc:  ❺
            error_msg = 'HTTP error {resp.status_code} - {resp.reason_phrase}'
            error_msg = error_msg.format(resp=exc.response)
        except httpx.RequestError as exc:  ❻
            error_msg = f'{exc} {type(exc)}'.strip()
        except KeyboardInterrupt:  ❼
            break
        else:  ❽
            error_msg = ''

        if error_msg:
            status = DownloadStatus.ERROR  ❾
        counter[status] += 1              ❿
        if verbose and error_msg:         ⓫
            print(f'{cc} error: {error_msg}')

    return counter  ⓬
```

❶ This Counter will tally the different download outcomes: DownloadStatus.OK, DownloadStatus.NOT_FOUND, or DownloadStatus.ERROR.

❷ cc_iter holds the list of the country codes received as arguments, ordered alphabetically.

❸ If not running in verbose mode, cc_iter is passed to tqdm, which returns an iterator yielding the items in cc_iter while also animating the progress bar.

❹ Make successive calls to download_one.

❺ HTTP status code exceptions raised by `get_flag` and not handled by `down load_one` are handled here.

❻ Other network-related exceptions are handled here. Any other exception will abort the script, because the `flags2_common.main` function that calls `down load_many` has no `try/except`.

❼ Exit the loop if the user hits Ctrl-C.

❽ If no exception escaped `download_one`, clear the error message.

❾ If there was an error, set the local `status` accordingly.

❿ Increment the counter for that `status`.

⓫ In verbose mode, display the error message for the current country code, if any.

⓬ Return `counter` so that `main` can display the numbers in the final report.

We'll now study the refactored thread pool example, *flags2_threadpool.py*.

Using futures.as_completed

In order to integrate the *tqdm* progress bar and handle errors on each request, the *flags2_threadpool.py* script uses `futures.ThreadPoolExecutor` with the `futures.as_completed` function we've already seen. Example 20-16 is the full listing of *flags2_threadpool.py*. Only the `download_many` function is implemented; the other functions are reused from *flags2_common.py* and *flags2_sequential.py*.

Example 20-16. flags2_threadpool.py: full listing

```
from collections import Counter
from concurrent.futures import ThreadPoolExecutor, as_completed

import httpx
import tqdm  # type: ignore

from flags2_common import main, DownloadStatus
from flags2_sequential import download_one    ❶

DEFAULT_CONCUR_REQ = 30   ❷
MAX_CONCUR_REQ = 1000   ❸


def download_many(cc_list: list[str],
                  base_url: str,
```

```
                  verbose: bool,
                  concur_req: int) -> Counter[DownloadStatus]:
    counter: Counter[DownloadStatus] = Counter()
    with ThreadPoolExecutor(max_workers=concur_req) as executor:    ❹
        to_do_map = {}    ❺
        for cc in sorted(cc_list):    ❻
            future = executor.submit(download_one, cc,
                                     base_url, verbose)    ❼
            to_do_map[future] = cc    ❽
        done_iter = as_completed(to_do_map)    ❾
        if not verbose:
            done_iter = tqdm.tqdm(done_iter, total=len(cc_list))    ❿
        for future in done_iter:    ⓫
            try:
                status = future.result()    ⓬
            except httpx.HTTPStatusError as exc:    ⓭
                error_msg = 'HTTP error {resp.status_code} - {resp.reason_phrase}'
                error_msg = error_msg.format(resp=exc.response)
            except httpx.RequestError as exc:
                error_msg = f'{exc} {type(exc)}'.strip()
            except KeyboardInterrupt:
                break
            else:
                error_msg = ''

            if error_msg:
                status = DownloadStatus.ERROR
            counter[status] += 1
            if verbose and error_msg:
                cc = to_do_map[future]    ⓮
                print(f'{cc} error: {error_msg}')

    return counter


if __name__ == '__main__':
    main(download_many, DEFAULT_CONCUR_REQ, MAX_CONCUR_REQ)
```

❶ Reuse download_one from flags2_sequential (Example 20-14).

❷ If the -m/--max_req command-line option is not given, this will be the maximum number of concurrent requests, implemented as the size of the thread pool;
  the actual number may be smaller if the number of flags to download is smaller.

❸ MAX_CONCUR_REQ caps the maximum number of concurrent requests regardless of
  the number of flags to download or the -m/--max_req command-line option. It's
  a safety precaution to avoid launching too many threads with their significant
  memory overhead.

❹ Create the executor with max_workers set to concur_req, computed by the main function as the smaller of: MAX_CONCUR_REQ, the length of cc_list, or the value of the -m/--max_req command-line option. This avoids creating more threads than necessary.

❺ This dict will map each Future instance—representing one download—with the respective country code for error reporting.

❻ Iterate over the list of country codes in alphabetical order. The order of the results will depend on the timing of the HTTP responses more than anything, but if the size of the thread pool (given by concur_req) is much smaller than len(cc_list), you may notice the downloads batched alphabetically.

❼ Each call to executor.submit schedules the execution of one callable and returns a Future instance. The first argument is the callable, the rest are the arguments it will receive.

❽ Store the future and the country code in the dict.

❾ futures.as_completed returns an iterator that yields futures as each task is done.

❿ If not in verbose mode, wrap the result of as_completed with the tqdm function to display the progress bar; because done_iter has no len, we must tell tqdm what is the expected number of items as the total= argument, so tqdm can estimate the work remaining.

⓫ Iterate over the futures as they are completed.

⓬ Calling the result method on a future either returns the value returned by the callable, or raises whatever exception was caught when the callable was executed. This method may block waiting for a resolution, but not in this example because as_completed only returns futures that are done.

⓭ Handle the potential exceptions; the rest of this function is identical to the sequential download_many in Example 20-15), except for the next callout.

⓮ To provide context for the error message, retrieve the country code from the to_do_map using the current future as key. This was not necessary in the sequential version because we were iterating over the list of country codes, so we knew the current cc; here we are iterating over the futures.

Example 20-16 uses an idiom that is very useful with `futures.as_completed`: building a `dict` to map each future to other data that may be useful when the future is completed. Here the `to_do_map` maps each future to the country code assigned to it. This makes it easy to do follow-up processing with the result of the futures, despite the fact that they are produced out of order.

Python threads are well suited for I/O-intensive applications, and the `concurrent.futures` package makes it relatively simple to use for certain use cases. With `ProcessPoolExecutor`, you can also solve CPU-intensive problems on multiple cores —if the computations are "embarrassingly parallel" (*https://fpy.li/20-19*). This concludes our basic introduction to `concurrent.futures`.

Chapter Summary

We started the chapter by comparing two concurrent HTTP clients with a sequential one, demonstrating that the concurrent solutions show significant performance gains over the sequential script.

After studying the first example based on `concurrent.futures`, we took a closer look at future objects, either instances of `concurrent.futures.Future` or `asyncio.Future`, emphasizing what these classes have in common (their differences will be emphasized in Chapter 21). We saw how to create futures by calling `Executor.submit`, and iterate over completed futures with `concurrent.futures.as_completed`.

We then discussed the use of multiple processes with the `concurrent.futures.ProcessPoolExecutor` class, to go around the GIL and use multiple CPU cores to simplify the multicore prime checker we first saw in Chapter 19.

In the following section, we saw how the `concurrent.futures.ThreadPoolExecutor` works with a didactic example, launching tasks that did nothing for a few seconds, except for displaying their status with a timestamp.

Next we went back to the flag downloading examples. Enhancing them with a progress bar and proper error handling prompted further exploration of the `future.as_completed` generator function, showing a common pattern: storing futures in a `dict` to link further information to them when submitting, so that we can use that information when the future comes out of the `as_completed` iterator.

Further Reading

The `concurrent.futures` package was contributed by Brian Quinlan, who presented it in a great talk titled "The Future Is Soon!" (*https://fpy.li/20-20*) at PyCon Australia 2010. Quinlan's talk has no slides; he shows what the library does by typing code directly in the Python console. As a motivating example, the presentation features a short video with XKCD cartoonist/programmer Randall Munroe making an unintended DoS attack on Google Maps to build a colored map of driving times around his city. The formal introduction to the library is PEP 3148 - `futures` - execute computations asynchronously (*https://fpy.li/pep3148*). In the PEP, Quinlan wrote that the `concurrent.futures` library was "heavily influenced by the Java `java.util.concurrent` package."

For additional resources covering `concurrent.futures`, please see Chapter 19. All the references that cover Python's `threading` and `multiprocessing` in "Concurrency with Threads and Processes" on page 738 also cover `concurrent.futures`.

Soapbox

Thread Avoidance

> Concurrency: one of the most difficult topics in computer science (usually best avoided).
>
> —David Beazley, Python instructor and mad scientist[8]

I agree with the apparently contradictory quotes by David Beazley and Michele Simionato at the start of this chapter.

I attended an undergraduate course about concurrency. All we did was POSIX threads (*https://fpy.li/20-22*) programming. What I learned: I don't want to manage threads and locks myself, for the same reason that I don't want to manage memory allocation and deallocation. Those jobs are best carried out by the systems programmers who have the know-how, the inclination, and the time to get them right—hopefully. I am paid to develop applications, not operating systems. I don't need all the fine-grained control of threads, locks, `malloc`, and `free`—see "C dynamic memory allocation" (*https://fpy.li/20-23*).

That's why I think the `concurrent.futures` package is interesting: it treats threads, processes, and queues as infrastructure at your service, not something you have to deal with directly. Of course, it's designed with simple jobs in mind, the so-called embarrassingly parallel problems. But that's a large slice of the concurrency problems we face when writing applications—as opposed to operating systems or database servers, as Simionato points out in that quote.

For "nonembarrassing" concurrency problems, threads and locks are not the answer either. Threads will never disappear at the OS level, but every programming language

---

8 Slide #9 from "A Curious Course on Coroutines and Concurrency" (*https://fpy.li/20-21*) tutorial presented at PyCon 2009.

I've found exciting in the last several years provides higher-level, concurrency abstractions that are easier to use correctly, as the excellent *Seven Concurrency Models in Seven Weeks* (*https://fpy.li/20-24*) book by Paul Butcher demonstrates. Go, Elixir, and Clojure are among them. Erlang—the implementation language of Elixir—is a prime example of a language designed from the ground up with concurrency in mind. Erlang doesn't excite me for a simple reason: I find its syntax ugly. Python spoiled me that way.

José Valim, previously a Ruby on Rails core contributor, designed Elixir with a pleasant, modern syntax. Like Lisp and Clojure, Elixir implements syntactic macros. That's a double-edged sword. Syntactic macros enable powerful DSLs, but the proliferation of sublanguages can lead to incompatible codebases and community fragmentation. Lisp drowned in a flood of macros, with each Lisp shop using its own arcane dialect. Standardizing around Common Lisp resulted in a bloated language. I hope José Valim can inspire the Elixir community to avoid a similar outcome. So far, it's looking good. The Ecto (*https://fpy.li/20-25*) database wrapper and query generator is a joy to use: a great example of using macros to create a flexible yet user-friendly DSL—Domain-Specific Language—for interacting with relational and nonrelational databases.

Like Elixir, Go is a modern language with fresh ideas. But, in some regards, it's a conservative language, compared to Elixir. Go doesn't have macros, and its syntax is simpler than Python's. Go doesn't support inheritance or operator overloading, and it offers fewer opportunities for metaprogramming than Python. These limitations are considered features. They lead to more predictable behavior and performance. That's a big plus in the highly concurrent, mission-critical settings where Go aims to replace C++, Java, and Python.

While Elixir and Go are direct competitors in the high-concurrency space, their design philosophies appeal to different crowds. Both are likely to thrive. But in the history of programming languages, the conservative ones tend to attract more coders.

## CHAPTER 21

Asynchronous Programming

The problem with normal approaches to asynchronous programming is that they're all-or-nothing propositions. You rewrite all your code so none of it blocks or you're just wasting your time.

Alvaro Videla and Jason J. W. Williams, *RabbitMQ in Action*[1]

This chapter addresses three major topics that are closely related:

- Python's `async def`, `await`, `async with`, and `async for` constructs
- Objects supporting those constructs: native coroutines and asynchronous variants of context managers, iterables, generators, and comprehensions
- *asyncio* and other asynchronous libraries

This chapter builds on the ideas of iterables and generators (Chapter 17, in particular "Classic Coroutines" on page 645), context managers (Chapter 18), and general concepts of concurrent programming (Chapter 19).

We'll study concurrent HTTP clients similar to the ones we saw in Chapter 20, rewritten with native coroutines and asynchronous context managers, using the same *HTTPX* library as before, but now through its asynchronous API. We'll also see how to avoid blocking the event loop by delegating slow operations to a thread or process executor.

After the HTTP client examples, we'll see two simple asynchronous server-side applications, one of them using the increasingly popular *FastAPI* framework. Then we'll cover other language constructs enabled by the `async`/`await` keywords:

---

1 Videla & Williams, *RabbitMQ in Action* (Manning), Chapter 4, "Solving Problems with Rabbit: coding and patterns," p. 61.

779

asynchronous generator functions, asynchronous comprehensions, and asynchronous generator expressions. To emphasize the fact that those language features are not tied to *asyncio*, we'll see one example rewritten to use *Curio*—the elegant and innovative asynchronous framework invented by David Beazley.

To wrap up the chapter, I wrote a brief section on the advantages and pitfalls of asynchronous programming.

That's a lot of ground to cover. We only have space for basic examples, but they will illustrate the most important features of each idea.

 The *asyncio* documentation (*https://fpy.li/21-1*) is much better after Yury Selivanov[2] reorganized it, separating the few functions useful to application developers from the low-level API for creators of packages like web frameworks and database drivers.

For book-length coverage of *asyncio*, I recommend *Using Asyncio in Python* by Caleb Hattingh (O'Reilly). Full disclosure: Caleb is one of the tech reviewers of this book.

What's New in This Chapter

When I wrote the first edition of *Fluent Python*, the *asyncio* library was provisional and the `async/await` keywords did not exist. Therefore, I had to update all examples in this chapter. I also created new examples: domain probing scripts, a *FastAPI* web service, and experiments with Python's new asynchronous console mode.

New sections cover language features that did not exist at the time, such as native coroutines, `async with`, `async for`, and the objects that support those constructs.

The ideas in "How Async Works and How It Doesn't" on page 829 reflect hard-earned lessons that I consider essential reading for anyone using asynchronous programming. They may save you a lot of trouble—whether you're using Python or Node.js.

Finally, I removed several paragraphs about `asyncio.Futures`, which is now considered part of the low-level *asyncio* APIs.

---

2 Selivanov implemented `async/await` in Python, and wrote the related PEPs 492 (*https://fpy.li/pep492*), 525 (*https://fpy.li/pep525*), and 530 (*https://fpy.li/pep530*).

A Few Definitions

At the start of "Classic Coroutines" on page 645, we saw that Python 3.5 and later offer three kinds of coroutines:

Native coroutine

A coroutine function defined with `async def`. You can delegate from a native coroutine to another native coroutine using the `await` keyword, similar to how classic coroutines use `yield from`. The `async def` statement always defines a native coroutine, even if the `await` keyword is not used in its body. The `await` keyword cannot be used outside of a native coroutine.[3]

Classic coroutine

A generator function that consumes data sent to it via `my_coro.send(data)` calls, and reads that data by using `yield` in an expression. Classic coroutines can delegate to other classic coroutines using `yield from`. Classic coroutines cannot be driven by `await`, and are no longer supported by *asyncio*.

Generator-based coroutine

A generator function decorated with `@types.coroutine`—introduced in Python 3.5. That decorator makes the generator compatible with the new `await` keyword.

In this chapter, we focus on native coroutines as well as *asynchronous generators*:

Asynchronous generator

A generator function defined with `async def` and using `yield` in its body. It returns an asynchronous generator object that provides `__anext__`, a coroutine method to retrieve the next item.

@asyncio.coroutine has No Future[4]

The `@asyncio.coroutine` decorator for classic coroutines and generator-based coroutines was deprecated in Python 3.8 and is scheduled for removal in Python 3.11, according to Issue 43216 (*https://fpy.li/21-2*). In contrast, `@types.coroutine` should remain, per Issue 36921 (*https://fpy.li/21-3*). It is no longer supported by *asyncio*, but is used in low-level code in the *Curio* and *Trio* asynchronous frameworks.

---

3 There is one exception to this rule: if you run Python with the `-m asyncio` option, you can use `await` directly at the `>>>` prompt to drive a native coroutine. This is explained in "Experimenting with Python's async console" on page 816.

4 Sorry, I could not resist it.

An asyncio Example: Probing Domains

Imagine you are about to start a new blog on Python, and you plan to register a domain using a Python keyword and the *.DEV* suffix—for example: *AWAIT.DEV*. Example 21-1 is a script using *asyncio* to check several domains concurrently. This is the output it produces:

```
$ python3 blogdom.py
  with.dev
+ elif.dev
+ def.dev
  from.dev
  else.dev
  or.dev
  if.dev
  del.dev
+ as.dev
  none.dev
  pass.dev
  true.dev
+ in.dev
+ for.dev
+ is.dev
+ and.dev
+ try.dev
+ not.dev
```

Note that the domains appear unordered. If you run the script, you'll see them displayed one after the other, with varying delays. The + sign indicates your machine was able to resolve the domain via DNS. Otherwise, the domain did not resolve and may be available.[5]

In *blogdom.py*, the DNS probing is done via native coroutine objects. Because the asynchronous operations are interleaved, the time needed to check the 18 domains is much less than checking them sequentially. In fact, the total time is practically the same as the time for the single slowest DNS response, instead of the sum of the times of all responses.

Example 21-1 shows the code for *blogdom.py*.

Example 21-1. blogdom.py: search for domains for a Python blog

```
#!/usr/bin/env python3
import asyncio
import socket
```

---

5 true.dev is available for USD 360/year as I write this. I see that for.dev is registered, but has no DNS configured.

```
from keyword import kwlist

MAX_KEYWORD_LEN = 4  ❶


async def probe(domain: str) -> tuple[str, bool]:  ❷
    loop = asyncio.get_running_loop()  ❸
    try:
        await loop.getaddrinfo(domain, None)  ❹
    except socket.gaierror:
        return (domain, False)
    return (domain, True)


async def main() -> None:  ❺
    names = (kw for kw in kwlist if len(kw) <= MAX_KEYWORD_LEN)  ❻
    domains = (f'{name}.dev'.lower() for name in names)  ❼
    coros = [probe(domain) for domain in domains]  ❽
    for coro in asyncio.as_completed(coros):  ❾
        domain, found = await coro  ❿
        mark = '+' if found else ' '
        print(f'{mark} {domain}')


if __name__ == '__main__':
    asyncio.run(main())  ⓫
```

❶ Set maximum length of keyword for domains, because shorter is better.

❷ `probe` returns a tuple with the domain name and a boolean; `True` means the domain resolved. Returning the domain name will make it easier to display the results.

❸ Get a reference to the `asyncio` event loop, so we can use it next.

❹ The `loop.getaddrinfo(…)` (*https://fpy.li/21-4*) coroutine-method returns a five-part tuple of parameters (*https://fpy.li/21-5*) to connect to the given address using a socket. In this example, we don't need the result. If we got it, the domain resolves; otherwise, it doesn't.

❺ `main` must be a coroutine, so that we can use `await` in it.

❻ Generator to yield Python keywords with length up to `MAX_KEYWORD_LEN`.

❼ Generator to yield domain names with the `.dev` suffix.

⑧ Build a list of coroutine objects by invoking the `probe` coroutine with each `domain` argument.

⑨ `asyncio.as_completed` is a generator that yields coroutines that return the results of the coroutines passed to it in the order they are completed—not the order they were submitted. It's similar to `futures.as_completed`, which we saw in Chapter 20, Example 20-4.

⑩ At this point, we know the coroutine is done because that's how `as_completed` works. Therefore, the `await` expression will not block but we need it to get the result from `coro`. If `coro` raised an unhandled exception, it would be re-raised here.

⑪ `asyncio.run` starts the event loop and returns only when the event loop exits. This is a common pattern for scripts that use `asyncio`: implement `main` as a coroutine, and drive it with `asyncio.run` inside the `if __name__ == '__main__':` block.

> The `asyncio.get_running_loop` function was added in Python 3.7 for use inside coroutines, as shown in `probe`. If there's no running loop, `asyncio.get_running_loop` raises `RuntimeError`. Its implementation is simpler and faster than `asyncio.get_event_loop`, which may start an event loop if necessary. Since Python 3.10, `asyncio.get_event_loop` is deprecated (*https://fpy.li/21-6*) and will eventually become an alias to `asyncio.get_running_loop`.

Guido's Trick to Read Asynchronous Code

There are a lot of new concepts to grasp in *asyncio*, but the overall logic of Example 21-1 is easy to follow if you employ a trick suggested by Guido van Rossum himself: squint and pretend the `async` and `await` keywords are not there. If you do that, you'll realize that coroutines read like plain old sequential functions.

For example, imagine that the body of this coroutine...

```
async def probe(domain: str) -> tuple[str, bool]:
    loop = asyncio.get_running_loop()
    try:
        await loop.getaddrinfo(domain, None)
    except socket.gaierror:
        return (domain, False)
    return (domain, True)
```

...works like the following function, except that it magically never blocks:

```
def probe(domain: str) -> tuple[str, bool]:  # no async
    loop = asyncio.get_running_loop()
    try:
        loop.getaddrinfo(domain, None)  # no await
    except socket.gaierror:
        return (domain, False)
    return (domain, True)
```

Using the syntax await loop.getaddrinfo(...) avoids blocking because await suspends the current coroutine object. For example, during the execution of the probe('if.dev') coroutine, a new coroutine object is created by getad drinfo('if.dev', None). Awaiting it starts the low-level addrinfo query and yields control back to the event loop, not to the probe('if.dev') coroutine, which is suspended. The event loop can then drive other pending coroutine objects, such as probe('or.dev').

When the event loop gets a response for the getaddrinfo('if.dev', None) query, that specific coroutine object resumes and returns control back to the probe('if.dev')—which was suspended at await—and can now handle a possible exception and return the result tuple.

So far, we've only seen asyncio.as_completed and await applied to coroutines. But they handle any *awaitable* object. That concept is explained next.

New Concept: Awaitable

The for keyword works with *iterables*. The await keyword works with *awaitables*.

As an end user of *asyncio*, these are the awaitables you will see on a daily basis:

- A *native coroutine object*, which you get by calling a *native coroutine function*
- An asyncio.Task, which you usually get by passing a coroutine object to asyn cio.create_task()

However, end-user code does not always need to await on a Task. We use asyn cio.create_task(one_coro()) to schedule one_coro for concurrent execution, without waiting for its return. That's what we did with the spinner coroutine in *spinner_async.py* (Example 19-4). If you don't expect to cancel the task or wait for it, there is no need to keep the Task object returned from create_task. Creating the task is enough to schedule the coroutine to run.

In contrast, we use await other_coro() to run other_coro right now and wait for its completion because we need its result before we can proceed. In *spinner_async.py*, the supervisor coroutine did res = await slow() to execute slow and get its result.

When implementing asynchronous libraries or contributing to *asyncio* itself, you may also deal with these lower-level awaitables:

- An object with an __await__ method that returns an iterator; for example, an asyncio.Future instance (asyncio.Task is a subclass of asyncio.Future)
- Objects written in other languages using the Python/C API with a tp_as_async.am_await function, returning an iterator (similar to __await__ method)

Existing codebases may also have one additional kind of awaitable: *generator-based coroutine objects*—which are in the process of being deprecated.

 PEP 492 states (*https://fpy.li/21-7*) that the await expression "uses the yield from implementation with an extra step of validating its argument" and "await only accepts an awaitable." The PEP does not explain that implementation in detail, but refers to PEP 380 (*https://fpy.li/pep380*), which introduced yield from. I posted a detailed explanation in "Classic Coroutines" (*https://fpy.li/oldcoro*), section "The Meaning of yield from" (*https://fpy.li/21-8*), at *fluent-python.com*.

Now let's study the *asyncio* version of a script that downloads a fixed set of flag images.

Downloading with asyncio and HTTPX

The *flags_asyncio.py* script downloads a fixed set of 20 flags from *fluentpython.com*. We first mentioned it in "Concurrent Web Downloads" on page 748, but now we'll study it in detail, applying the concepts we just saw.

As of Python 3.10, *asyncio* only supports TCP and UDP directly, and there are no asynchronous HTTP client or server packages in the standard library. I am using HTTPX (*https://fpy.li/httpx*) in all the HTTP client examples.

We'll explore *flags_asyncio.py* from the bottom up—that is, looking first at the functions that set up the action in Example 21-2.

To make the code easier to read, *flags_asyncio.py* has no error handling. As we introduce `async`/`await`, it's useful to focus on the "happy path" initially, to understand how regular functions and coroutines are arranged in a program. Starting with "Enhancing the asyncio Downloader" on page 792, the examples include error handling and more features.

The *flags_.py* examples from this chapter and Chapter 20 share code and data, so I put them together in the *example-code-2e/20-executors/getflags* (*https://fpy.li/21-9*) directory.

Example 21-2. flags_asyncio.py: startup functions

```python
def download_many(cc_list: list[str]) -> int:      ❶
    return asyncio.run(supervisor(cc_list))        ❷

async def supervisor(cc_list: list[str]) -> int:
    async with AsyncClient() as client:            ❸
        to_do = [download_one(client, cc)
                    for cc in sorted(cc_list)]      ❹
        res = await asyncio.gather(*to_do)          ❺

    return len(res)                                ❻

if __name__ == '__main__':
    main(download_many)
```

❶ This needs to be a plain function—not a coroutine—so it can be passed to and called by the `main` function from the *flags.py* module (Example 20-2).

❷ Execute the event loop driving the `supervisor(cc_list)` coroutine object until it returns. This will block while the event loop runs. The result of this line is whatever `supervisor` returns.

❸ Asynchronous HTTP client operations in `httpx` are methods of `AsyncClient`, which is also an asynchronous context manager: a context manager with asynchronous setup and teardown methods (more about this in "Asynchronous Context Managers" on page 790).

❹ Build a list of coroutine objects by calling the `download_one` coroutine once for each flag to be retrieved.

❺ Wait for the `asyncio.gather` coroutine, which accepts one or more awaitable arguments and waits for all of them to complete, returning a list of results for the given awaitables in the order they were submitted.

❻ supervisor returns the length of the list returned by asyncio.gather.

Now let's review the top of *flags_asyncio.py* (Example 21-3). I reorganized the coroutines so we can read them in the order they are started by the event loop.

Example 21-3. flags_asyncio.py: imports and download functions

```python
import asyncio

from httpx import AsyncClient  ❶

from flags import BASE_URL, save_flag, main  ❷

async def download_one(client: AsyncClient, cc: str):  ❸
    image = await get_flag(client, cc)
    save_flag(image, f'{cc}.gif')
    print(cc, end=' ', flush=True)
    return cc

async def get_flag(client: AsyncClient, cc: str) -> bytes:  ❹
    url = f'{BASE_URL}/{cc}/{cc}.gif'.lower()
    resp = await client.get(url, timeout=6.1,
                            follow_redirects=True)  ❺
    return resp.read()  ❻
```

❶ httpx must be installed—it's not in the standard library.

❷ Reuse code from *flags.py* (Example 20-2).

❸ download_one must be a native coroutine, so it can await on get_flag—which does the HTTP request. Then it displays the code of the downloaded flag, and saves the image.

❹ get_flag needs to receive the AsyncClient to make the request.

❺ The get method of an httpx.AsyncClient instance returns a ClientResponse object that is also an asynchronous context manager.

❻ Network I/O operations are implemented as coroutine methods, so they are driven asynchronously by the asyncio event loop.

For better performance, the save_flag call inside get_flag should be asynchronous, to avoid blocking the event loop. However, *asyncio* does not provide an asynchronous filesystem API at this time— as Node.js does.

"Using asyncio.as_completed and a Thread" on page 793 will show how to delegate save_flag to a thread.

Your code delegates to the httpx coroutines explicitly through await or implicitly through the special methods of the asynchronous context managers, such as Async Client and ClientResponse—as we'll see in "Asynchronous Context Managers" on page 790.

The Secret of Native Coroutines: Humble Generators

A key difference between the classic coroutine examples we saw in "Classic Coroutines" on page 645 and *flags_asyncio.py* is that there are no visible .send() calls or yield expressions in the latter. Your code sits between the *asyncio* library and the asynchronous libraries you are using, such as *HTTPX*. This is illustrated in Figure 21-1.

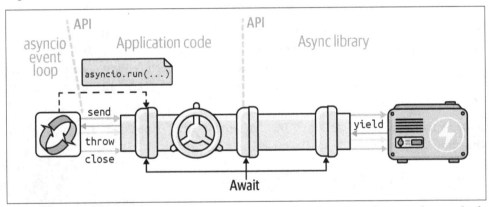

Figure 21-1. In an asynchronous program, a user's function starts the event loop, scheduling an initial coroutine with asyncio.run. Each user's coroutine drives the next with an await expression, forming a channel that enables communication between a library like HTTPX and the event loop.

Under the hood, the asyncio event loop makes the .send calls that drive your coroutines, and your coroutines await on other coroutines, including library coroutines. As mentioned, await borrows most of its implementation from yield from, which also makes .send calls to drive coroutines.

The `await` chain eventually reaches a low-level awaitable, which returns a generator that the event loop can drive in response to events such as timers or network I/O. The low-level awaitables and generators at the end of these `await` chains are implemented deep into the libraries, are not part of their APIs, and may be Python/C extensions.

Using functions like `asyncio.gather` and `asyncio.create_task`, you can start multiple concurrent `await` channels, enabling concurrent execution of multiple I/O operations driven by a single event loop, in a single thread.

The All-or-Nothing Problem

Note that in Example 21-3, I could not reuse the `get_flag` function from *flags.py* (Example 20-2). I had to rewrite it as a coroutine to use the asynchronous API of *HTTPX*. For peak performance with *asyncio*, we must replace every function that does I/O with an asynchronous version that is activated with `await` or `asyncio.cre ate_task`, so that control is given back to the event loop while the function waits for I/O. If you can't rewrite a blocking function as a coroutine, you should run it in a separate thread or process, as we'll see in "Delegating Tasks to Executors" on page 801.

That's why I chose the epigraph for this chapter, which includes this advice: "You rewrite all your code so none of it blocks or you're just wasting your time."

For the same reason, I could not reuse the `download_one` function from *flags_thread-pool.py* (Example 20-3) either. The code in Example 21-3 drives `get_flag` with `await`, so `download_one` must also be a coroutine. For each request, a `download_one` coroutine object is created in `supervisor`, and they are all driven by the `asyncio.gather` coroutine.

Now let's study the `async with` statement that appeared in `supervisor` (Example 21-2) and `get_flag` (Example 21-3).

Asynchronous Context Managers

In "Context Managers and with Blocks" on page 662, we saw how an object can be used to run code before and after the body of a `with` block, if its class provides the `__enter__` and `__exit__` methods.

Now, consider Example 21-4, from the *asyncpg* (*https://fpy.li/21-10*) *asyncio*-compatible PostgreSQL driver documentation on transactions (*https://fpy.li/21-11*).

Example 21-4. Sample code from the documentation of the asyncpg PostgreSQL driver

```
tr = connection.transaction()
await tr.start()
try:
```

```
    await connection.execute("INSERT INTO mytable VALUES (1, 2, 3)")
except:
    await tr.rollback()
    raise
else:
    await tr.commit()
```

A database transaction is a natural fit for the context manager protocol: the transaction has to be started, data is changed with `connection.execute`, and then a rollback or commit must happen, depending on the outcome of the changes.

In an asynchronous driver like *asyncpg*, the setup and wrap-up need to be coroutines so that other operations can happen concurrently. However, the implementation of the classic `with` statement doesn't support coroutines doing the work of `__enter__` or `__exit__`.

That's why PEP 492—Coroutines with async and await syntax (*https://fpy.li/pep492*) introduced the `async with` statement, which works with asynchronous context managers: objects implementing the `__aenter__` and `__aexit__` methods as coroutines.

With `async with`, Example 21-4 can be written like this other snippet from the *asyncpg* documentation (*https://fpy.li/21-11*):

```
async with connection.transaction():
    await connection.execute("INSERT INTO mytable VALUES (1, 2, 3)")
```

In the `asyncpg.Transaction` class (*https://fpy.li/21-13*), the `__aenter__` coroutine method does `await self.start()`, and the `__aexit__` coroutine awaits on private `__rollback` or `__commit` coroutine methods, depending on whether an exception occurred or not. Using coroutines to implement `Transaction` as an asynchronous context manager allows *asyncpg* to handle many transactions concurrently.

Caleb Hattingh on asyncpg

Another really great thing about *asyncpg* is that it also works around PostgreSQL's lack of high-concurrency support (it uses one server-side process per connection) by implementing a connection pool for internal connections to Postgres itself.

This means you don't need additional tools like *pgbouncer* as explained in the *asyncpg* documentation (*https://fpy.li/21-14*).[6]

---

6 This tip is quoted verbatim from a comment by tech reviewer Caleb Hattingh. Thanks, Caleb!

Back to *flags_asyncio.py*, the `AsyncClient` class of `httpx` is an asynchronous context manager, so it can use awaitables in its `__aenter__` and `__aexit__` special coroutine methods.

"Asynchronous generators as context managers" on page 821 shows how to use Python's `contextlib` to create an asynchronous context manager without having to write a class. That explanation comes later in this chapter because of a prerequisite topic: "Asynchronous Generator Functions" on page 816.

We'll now enhance the *asyncio* flag download example with a progress bar, which will lead us to explore a bit more of the *asyncio* API.

Enhancing the asyncio Downloader

Recall from "Downloads with Progress Display and Error Handling" on page 766 that the `flags2` set of examples share the same command-line interface, and they display a progress bar while the downloads are happening. They also include error handling.

I encourage you to play with the `flags2` examples to develop an intuition of how concurrent HTTP clients perform. Use the `-h` option to see the help screen in Example 20-10. Use the `-a`, `-e`, and `-l` command-line options to control the number of downloads, and the `-m` option to set the number of concurrent downloads. Run tests against the LOCAL, REMOTE, DELAY, and ERROR servers. Discover the optimum number of concurrent downloads to maximize throughput against each server. Tweak the options for the test servers, as described in "Setting Up Test Servers" on page 769.

For instance, Example 21-5 shows an attempt to get 100 flags (`-al 100`) from the ERROR server, using 100 concurrent requests (`-m 100`). The 48 errors in the result are either HTTP 418 or time-out errors—the expected (mis)behavior of the *slow_server.py*.

Example 21-5. Running flags2_asyncio.py

```
$ python3 flags2_asyncio.py -s ERROR -al 100 -m 100
ERROR site: http://localhost:8002/flags
Searching for 100 flags: from AD to LK
100 concurrent connections will be used.
100%|████████████████████████████| 100/100 [00:03<00:00, 30.48it/s]
--------------------
 52 flags downloaded.
 48 errors.
Elapsed time: 3.31s
```

Act Responsibly When Testing Concurrent Clients

Even if the overall download time is not much different between the threaded and *asyncio* HTTP clients, *asyncio* can send requests faster, so it's more likely that the server will suspect a DoS attack. To really exercise these concurrent clients at full throttle, please use local HTTP servers for testing, as explained in "Setting Up Test Servers" on page 769.

Now let's see how *flags2_asyncio.py* is implemented.

Using asyncio.as_completed and a Thread

In Example 21-3, we passed several coroutines to `asyncio.gather`, which returns a list with results of the coroutines in the order they were submitted. This means that `asyncio.gather` can only return when all the awaitables are done. However, to update a progress bar, we need to get results as they are done.

Fortunately, there is an `asyncio` equivalent of the `as_completed` generator function we used in the thread pool example with the progress bar (Example 20-16).

Example 21-6 shows the top of the *flags2_asyncio.py* script where the `get_flag` and `download_one` coroutines are defined. Example 21-7 lists the rest of the source, with `supervisor` and `download_many`. This script is longer than *flags_asyncio.py* because of error handling.

Example 21-6. flags2_asyncio.py: top portion of the script; remaining code is in Example 21-7

```
import asyncio
from collections import Counter
from http import HTTPStatus
from pathlib import Path

import httpx
import tqdm  # type: ignore

from flags2_common import main, DownloadStatus, save_flag

# low concurrency default to avoid errors from remote site,
# such as 503 - Service Temporarily Unavailable
DEFAULT_CONCUR_REQ = 5
MAX_CONCUR_REQ = 1000

async def get_flag(client: httpx.AsyncClient,  ❶
                   base_url: str,
                   cc: str) -> bytes:
    url = f'{base_url}/{cc}/{cc}.gif'.lower()
```

```
        resp = await client.get(url, timeout=3.1, follow_redirects=True)  ❷
        resp.raise_for_status()
        return resp.content

async def download_one(client: httpx.AsyncClient,
                       cc: str,
                       base_url: str,
                       semaphore: asyncio.Semaphore,
                       verbose: bool) -> DownloadStatus:
    try:
        async with semaphore:  ❸
            image = await get_flag(client, base_url, cc)
    except httpx.HTTPStatusError as exc:  ❹
        res = exc.response
        if res.status_code == HTTPStatus.NOT_FOUND:
            status = DownloadStatus.NOT_FOUND
            msg = f'not found: {res.url}'
        else:
            raise
    else:
        await asyncio.to_thread(save_flag, image, f'{cc}.gif')  ❺
        status = DownloadStatus.OK
        msg = 'OK'
    if verbose and msg:
        print(cc, msg)
    return status
```

❶ get_flag is very similar to the sequential version in Example 20-14. First difference: it requires the client parameter.

❷ Second and third differences: .get is an AsyncClient method, and it's a coroutine, so we need to await it.

❸ Use the semaphore as an asynchronous context manager so that the program as a
  whole is not blocked; only this coroutine is suspended when the semaphore
  counter is zero. More about this in "Python's Semaphores" on page 795.

❹ The error handling logic is the same as in download_one, from Example 20-14.

❺ Saving the image is an I/O operation. To avoid blocking the event loop, run
  save_flag in a thread.

All network I/O is done with coroutines in *asyncio*, but not file I/O. However, file
I/O is also "blocking"—in the sense that reading/writing files takes thousands of
times longer (*https://fpy.li/21-15*) than reading/writing to RAM. If you're using
Network-Attached Storage (*https://fpy.li/21-16*), it may even involve network I/O
under the covers.

Since Python 3.9, the `asyncio.to_thread` coroutine makes it easy to delegate file I/O to a thread pool provided by *asyncio*. If you need to support Python 3.7 or 3.8, "Delegating Tasks to Executors" on page 801 shows how to add a couple of lines to do it. But first, let's finish our study of the HTTP client code.

Throttling Requests with a Semaphore

Network clients like the ones we are studying should be *throttled* (i.e., limited) to avoid pounding the server with too many concurrent requests.

A *semaphore (https://fpy.li/21-17)* is a synchronization primitive, more flexible than a lock. A semaphore can be held by multiple coroutines, with a configurable maximum number. This makes it ideal to throttle the number of active concurrent coroutines. "Python's Semaphores" on page 795 has more information.

In *flags2_threadpool.py* (Example 20-16), the throttling was done by instantiating the `ThreadPoolExecutor` with the required `max_workers` argument set to `concur_req` in the `download_many` function. In *flags2_asyncio.py*, an `asyncio.Semaphore` is created by the `supervisor` function (shown in Example 21-7) and passed as the `semaphore` argument to `download_one` in Example 21-6.

Python's Semaphores

Computer scientist Edsger W. Dijkstra invented the semaphore (*https://fpy.li/21-17*) in the early 1960s. It's a simple idea, but it's so flexible that most other synchronization objects—such as locks and barriers—can be built on top of semaphores. There are three `Semaphore` classes in Python's standard library: one in `threading`, another in `multiprocessing`, and a third one in `asyncio`. Here we'll describe the latter.

An `asyncio.Semaphore` has an internal counter that is decremented whenever we `await` on the `.acquire()` coroutine method, and incremented when we call the `.release()` method—which is not a coroutine because it never blocks. The initial value of the counter is set when the `Semaphore` is instantiated:

```
semaphore = asyncio.Semaphore(concur_req)
```

Awaiting on `.acquire()` causes no delay when the counter is greater than zero, but if the counter is zero, `.acquire()` suspends the awaiting coroutine until some other coroutine calls `.release()` on the same `Semaphore`, thus incrementing the counter. Instead of using those methods directly, it's safer to use the semaphore as an asynchronous context manager, as I did in Example 21-6, function `download_one`:

```
async with semaphore:
    image = await get_flag(client, base_url, cc)
```

The `Semaphore.__aenter__` coroutine method awaits for `.acquire()`, and its `__aexit__` coroutine method calls `.release()`. That snippet guarantees that no more than `concur_req` instances of `get_flags` coroutines will be active at any time.

Each of the `Semaphore` classes in the standard library has a `BoundedSemaphore` subclass that enforces an additional constraint: the internal counter can never become larger than the initial value when there are more `.release()` than `.acquire()` operations.[7]

Now let's take a look at the rest of the script in Example 21-7.

Example 21-7. flags2_asyncio.py: script continued from Example 21-6

```python
async def supervisor(cc_list: list[str],
                     base_url: str,
                     verbose: bool,
                     concur_req: int) -> Counter[DownloadStatus]:  ❶
    counter: Counter[DownloadStatus] = Counter()
    semaphore = asyncio.Semaphore(concur_req)  ❷
    async with httpx.AsyncClient() as client:
        to_do = [download_one(client, cc, base_url, semaphore, verbose)
                    for cc in sorted(cc_list)]  ❸
        to_do_iter = asyncio.as_completed(to_do)  ❹
        if not verbose:
            to_do_iter = tqdm.tqdm(to_do_iter, total=len(cc_list))  ❺
        error: httpx.HTTPError | None = None  ❻
        for coro in to_do_iter:  ❼
            try:
                status = await coro  ❽
            except httpx.HTTPStatusError as exc:
                error_msg = 'HTTP error {resp.status_code} - {resp.reason_phrase}'
                error_msg = error_msg.format(resp=exc.response)
                error = exc  ❾
            except httpx.RequestError as exc:
                error_msg = f'{exc} {type(exc)}'.strip()
                error = exc  ❿
            except KeyboardInterrupt:
                break

            if error:
                status = DownloadStatus.ERROR  ⓫
                if verbose:
                    url = str(error.request.url)  ⓬
                    cc = Path(url).stem.upper()  ⓭
```

---

7 Thanks to Guto Maia who noted that the concept of a semaphore was not explained when he read the first edition draft for this chapter.

```
                print(f'{cc} error: {error_msg}')
            counter[status] += 1

    return counter

def download_many(cc_list: list[str],
                  base_url: str,
                  verbose: bool,
                  concur_req: int) -> Counter[DownloadStatus]:
    coro = supervisor(cc_list, base_url, verbose, concur_req)
    counts = asyncio.run(coro)  ⓮

    return counts

if __name__ == '__main__':
    main(download_many, DEFAULT_CONCUR_REQ, MAX_CONCUR_REQ)
```

❶ supervisor takes the same arguments as the download_many function, but it cannot be invoked directly from main because it's a coroutine and not a plain function like download_many.

❷ Create an asyncio.Semaphore that will not allow more than concur_req active coroutines among those using this semaphore. The value of concur_req is computed by the main function from *flags2_common.py*, based on command-line options and constants set in each example.

❸ Create a list of coroutine objects, one per call to the download_one coroutine.

❹ Get an iterator that will return coroutine objects as they are done. I did not place this call to as_completed directly in the for loop below because I may need to wrap it with the tqdm iterator for the progress bar, depending on the user's choice for verbosity.

❺ Wrap the as_completed iterator with the tqdm generator function to display progress.

❻ Declare and initialize error with None; this variable will be used to hold an exception beyond the try/except statement, if one is raised.

❼ Iterate over the completed coroutine objects; this loop is similar to the one in download_many in Example 20-16.

❽ await on the coroutine to get its result. This will not block because as_completed only produces coroutines that are done.

❾ This assignment is necessary because the `exc` variable scope is limited to this `except` clause, but I need to preserve its value for later.

❿ Same as before.

⓫ If there was an error, set the `status`.

⓬ In verbose mode, extract the URL from the exception that was raised…

⓭ …and extract the name of the file to display the country code next.

⓮ `download_many` instantiates the `supervisor` coroutine object and passes it to the event loop with `asyncio.run`, collecting the counter `supervisor` returns when the event loop ends.

In Example 21-7, we could not use the mapping of futures to country codes we saw in Example 20-16, because the awaitables returned by `asyncio.as_completed` are the same awaitables we pass into the `as_completed` call. Internally, the *asyncio* machinery may replace the awaitables we provide with others that will, in the end, produce the same results.[8]

 Because I could not use the awaitables as keys to retrieve the country code from a `dict` in case of failure, I had to extract the country code from the exception. To do that, I kept the exception in the `error` variable to retrieve outside of the `try/except` statement. Python is not a block-scoped language: statements such as loops and `try/except` don't create a local scope in the blocks they manage. But if an `except` clause binds an exception to a variable, like the `exc` variables we just saw—that binding only exists within the block inside that particular `except` clause.

This wraps up the discussion of an *asyncio* example functionally equivalent to the *flags2_threadpool.py* we saw earlier.

The next example demonstrates the simple pattern of executing one asynchronous task after another using coroutines. This deserves our attention because anyone with previous experience with JavaScript knows that running one asynchronous function after the other was the reason for the nested coding pattern known as *pyramid of*

---

8 A detailed discussion about this can be found in a thread I started in the python-tulip group, titled "Which other futures may come out of asyncio.as_completed?" (*https://fpy.li/21-19*). Guido responds, and gives insight on the implementation of `as_completed`, as well as the close relationship between futures and coroutines in *asyncio*.

doom (*https://fpy.li/21-20*). The `await` keyword makes that curse go away. That's why `await` is now part of Python and JavaScript.

Making Multiple Requests for Each Download

Suppose you want to save each country flag with the name of the country and the country code, instead of just the country code. Now you need to make two HTTP requests per flag: one to get the flag image itself, the other to get the *metadata.json* file in the same directory as the image—that's where the name of the country is recorded.

Coordinating multiple requests in the same task is easy in the threaded script: just make one request then the other, blocking the thread twice, and keeping both pieces of data (country code and name) in local variables, ready to use when saving the files. If you needed to do the same in an asynchronous script with callbacks, you needed nested functions so that the country code and name were available in their closures until you could save the file, because each callback runs in a different local scope. The `await` keyword provides relief from that, allowing you to drive the asynchronous requests one after the other, sharing the local scope of the driving coroutine.

 If you are doing asynchronous application programming in modern Python with lots of callbacks, you are probably applying old patterns that don't make sense in modern Python. That is justified if you are writing a library that interfaces with legacy or low-level code that does not support coroutines. Anyway, the StackOverflow Q&A, "What is the use case for future.add_done_callback()?" (*https://fpy.li/21-21*) explains why callbacks are needed in low-level code, but are not very useful in Python application-level code these days.

The third variation of the `asyncio` flag downloading script has a few changes:

`get_country`
> This new coroutine fetches the *metadata.json* file for the country code, and gets the name of the country from it.

`download_one`
> This coroutine now uses `await` to delegate to `get_flag` and the new `get_country` coroutine, using the result of the latter to build the name of the file to save.

Let's start with the code for `get_country` (Example 21-8). Note that it is very similar to `get_flag` from Example 21-6.

Example 21-8. flags3_asyncio.py: get_country coroutine

```python
async def get_country(client: httpx.AsyncClient,
                      base_url: str,
                      cc: str) -> str:       ❶
    url = f'{base_url}/{cc}/metadata.json'.lower()
    resp = await client.get(url, timeout=3.1, follow_redirects=True)
    resp.raise_for_status()
    metadata = resp.json()       ❷
    return metadata['country']     ❸
```

❶ This coroutine returns a string with the country name—if all goes well.

❷ metadata will get a Python dict built from the JSON contents of the response.

❸ Return the country name.

Now let's see the modified download_one in Example 21-9, which has only a few lines changed from the same coroutine in Example 21-6.

Example 21-9. flags3_asyncio.py: download_one coroutine

```python
async def download_one(client: httpx.AsyncClient,
                       cc: str,
                       base_url: str,
                       semaphore: asyncio.Semaphore,
                       verbose: bool) -> DownloadStatus:
    try:
        async with semaphore:     ❶
            image = await get_flag(client, base_url, cc)
        async with semaphore:     ❷
            country = await get_country(client, base_url, cc)
    except httpx.HTTPStatusError as exc:
        res = exc.response
        if res.status_code == HTTPStatus.NOT_FOUND:
            status = DownloadStatus.NOT_FOUND
            msg = f'not found: {res.url}'
        else:
            raise
    else:
        filename = country.replace(' ', '_')     ❸
        await asyncio.to_thread(save_flag, image, f'{filename}.gif')
        status = DownloadStatus.OK
        msg = 'OK'
    if verbose and msg:
        print(cc, msg)
    return status
```

❶ Hold the semaphore to await for get_flag…

❷   ...and again for `get_country`.

❸   Use the country name to create a filename. As a command-line user, I don't like to see spaces in filenames.

Much better than nested callbacks!

I put the calls to `get_flag` and `get_country` in separate `with` blocks controlled by the `semaphore` because it's good practice to hold semaphores and locks for the shortest possible time.

I could schedule both `get_flag` and `get_country` in parallel using `asyncio.gather`, but if `get_flag` raises an exception, there is no image to save, so it's pointless to run `get_country`. But there are cases where it makes sense to use `asyncio.gather` to hit several APIs at the same time instead of waiting for one response before making the next request.

In *flags3_asyncio.py*, the `await` syntax appears six times, and `async with` three times. Hopefully, you should be getting the hang of asynchronous programming in Python. One challenge is to know when you have to use `await` and when you can't use it. The answer in principle is easy: you `await` coroutines and other awaitables, such as `asyncio.Task` instances. But some APIs are tricky, mixing coroutines and plain functions in seemingly arbitrary ways, like the `StreamWriter` class we'll use in Example 21-14.

Example 21-9 wrapped up the *flags* set of examples. Now let's discuss the use of thread or process executors in asynchronous programming.

Delegating Tasks to Executors

One important advantage of Node.js over Python for asynchronous programming is the Node.js standard library, which provides async APIs for all I/O—not just for network I/O. In Python, if you're not careful, file I/O can seriously degrade the performance of asynchronous applications, because reading and writing to storage in the main thread blocks the event loop.

In the `download_one` coroutine of Example 21-6, I used this line to save the downloaded image to disk:

```
await asyncio.to_thread(save_flag, image, f'{cc}.gif')
```

As mentioned before, the `asyncio.to_thread` was added in Python 3.9. If you need to support 3.7 or 3.8, then replace that single line with the lines in Example 21-10.

Example 21-10. Lines to use instead of `await` `asyncio.to_thread`

```
loop = asyncio.get_running_loop()          ❶
loop.run_in_executor(None, save_flag,      ❷
                      image, f'{cc}.gif')   ❸
```

❶ Get a reference to the event loop.

❷ The first argument is the executor to use; passing `None` selects the default `Thread PoolExecutor` that is always available in the `asyncio` event loop.

❸ You can pass positional arguments to the function to run, but if you need to pass keyword arguments, then you need to resort to `functool.partial`, as described in the `run_in_executor` documentation (*https://fpy.li/21-22*).

The newer `asyncio.to_thread` function is easier to use and more flexible, as it also accepts keyword arguments.

The implementation of `asyncio` itself uses `run_in_executor` under the hood in a few places. For example, the `loop.getaddrinfo(…)` coroutine we saw in Example 21-1 is implemented by calling the `getaddrinfo` function from the `socket` module— which is a blocking function that may take seconds to return, as it depends on DNS resolution.

A common pattern in asynchronous APIs is to wrap blocking calls that are implementation details in coroutines using `run_in_executor` internally. That way, you provide a consistent interface of coroutines to be driven with `await`, and hide the threads you need to use for pragmatic reasons. The Motor (*https://fpy.li/21-23*) asynchronous driver for MongoDB has an API compatible with `async/await` that is really a façade around a threaded core that talks to the database server. A. Jesse Jiryu Davis, the lead developer of Motor, explains his reasoning in "Response to 'Asynchronous Python and Databases'" (*https://fpy.li/21-24*). Spoiler: Davis discovered that a thread pool was more performant in the particular use case of a database driver—despite the myth that asynchronous approaches are always faster than threads for network I/O.

The main reason to pass an explicit `Executor` to `loop.run_in_executor` is to employ a `ProcessPoolExecutor` if the function to execute is CPU intensive, so that it runs in a different Python process, avoiding contention for the GIL. Because of the high start-up cost, it would be better to start the `ProcessPoolExecutor` in the `supervisor`, and pass it to the coroutines that need to use it.

Caleb Hattingh—the author of *Using Asyncio in Python* (O' Reilly)—is one of the tech reviewers of this book and suggested I add the following warning about executors and *asyncio*.

Caleb's Warning about run_in_executors

Using `run_in_executor` can produce hard-to-debug problems since cancellation doesn't work the way one might expect. Coroutines that use executors give merely the pretense of cancellation: the underlying thread (if it's a `ThreadPoolExecutor`) has no cancellation mechanism. For example, a long-lived thread that is created inside a `run_in_executor` call may prevent your *asyncio* program from shutting down cleanly: `asyncio.run` will wait for the executor to fully shut down before returning, and it will wait forever if the executor jobs don't stop somehow on their own. My greybeard inclination is to want that function to be named `run_in_executor_uncancellable`.

We'll now go from client scripts to writing servers with `asyncio`.

Writing asyncio Servers

The classic toy example of a TCP server is an echo server (*https://fpy.li/21-25*). We'll build slightly more interesting toys: server-side Unicode character search utilities, first using HTTP with *FastAPI*, then using plain TCP with `asyncio` only.

These servers let users query for Unicode characters based on words in their standard names from the `unicodedata` module we discussed in "The Unicode Database" on page 151. Figure 21-2 shows a session with *web_mojifinder.py*, the first server we'll build.

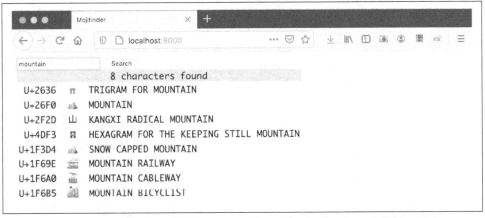

Figure 21-2. Browser window displaying search results for "mountain" from the web_mojifinder.py service.

The Unicode search logic in these examples is in the `InvertedIndex` class in the *char-index.py* module in the *Fluent Python* code repository (*https://fpy.li/code*). There's nothing concurrent in that small module, so I'll only give a brief overview in the optional box that follows. You can skip to the HTTP server implementation in "A FastAPI Web Service" on page 805.

Meet the Inverted Index

An inverted index usually maps words to documents in which they occur. In the *mojifinder* examples, each "document" is one Unicode character. The `charin dex.InvertedIndex` class indexes each word that appears in each character name in the Unicode database, and creates an inverted index stored in a `defaultdict`. For example, to index character U+0037—DIGIT SEVEN—the `InvertedIndex` initializer appends the character `'7'` to the entries under the keys `'DIGIT'` and `'SEVEN'`. After indexing the Unicode 13.0.0 data bundled with Python 3.9.1, `'DIGIT'` maps to 868 characters, and `'SEVEN'` maps to 143, including U+1F556—CLOCK FACE SEVEN OCLOCK and U+2790—DINGBAT NEGATIVE CIRCLED SANS-SERIF DIGIT SEVEN (which appears in many code listings in this book).

See Figure 21-3 for a demonstration using the entries for `'CAT'` and `'FACE'`.[9]

```
>>> from charindex import InvertedIndex
>>> idx.entries['CAT']
{'🐱', '🐈', '칻', '🔣', '🐾', '😺', '😼', '🐱', '😸', '😹', '🐈', '0 ', '😻', '😽'}
>>> len(idx.entries['FACE'])
171
>>> idx.entries['FACE'] & idx.entries['CAT']
{'🐱', '🐈', '😺', '😼', '😸', '😹', '😻', '😽', '😾', '😿'}
>>> idx.search('cat face')
{'🐱', '🐈', '😺', '😼', '😸', '😹', '😻', '😽', '😾', '😿'}
>>>
```

Figure 21-3. Python console exploring InvertedIndex attribute entries and search method.

The `InvertedIndex.search` method breaks the query into words, and returns the intersection of the entries for each word. That's why searching for "face" finds 171 results, "cat" finds 14, but "cat face" only 10.

That's the beautiful idea behind an inverted index: a fundamental building block in information retrieval—the theory behind search engines. See the English Wikipedia article "Inverted Index" (*https://fpy.li/21-27*) to learn more.

---

[9] The boxed question mark in the screen shot is not a defect of the book or ebook you are reading. It's the U +101EC—PHAISTOS DISC SIGN CAT character, which is missing from the font in the terminal I used. The Phaistos disc (*https://fpy.li/21-26*) is an ancient artifact inscribed with pictograms, discovered in the island of Crete.

A FastAPI Web Service

I wrote the next example—*web_mojifinder.py*—using *FastAPI* (*https://fpy.li/21-28*): one of the Python ASGI Web frameworks mentioned in "ASGI—Asynchronous Server Gateway Interface" on page 736. Figure 21-2 is a screenshot of the frontend. It's a super simple SPA (Single Page Application): after the initial HTML download, the UI is updated by client-side JavaScript communicating with the server.

FastAPI is designed to implement backends for SPA and mobile apps, which mostly consist of web API end points returning JSON responses instead of server-rendered HTML. *FastAPI* leverages decorators, type hints, and code introspection to eliminate a lot of the boilerplate code for web APIs, and also automatically publishes interactive OpenAPI—a.k.a. Swagger (*https://fpy.li/21-29*)—documentation for the APIs we create. Figure 21-4 shows the autogenerated /docs page for *web_mojifinder.py*.

Figure 21-4. Autogenerated OpenAPI schema for the /search endpoint.

Example 21-11 is the code for *web_mojifinder.py*, but that's just the backend code. When you hit the root URL /, the server sends the *form.html* file, which has 81 lines of code, including 54 lines of JavaScript to communicate with the server and fill a table with the results. If you're interested in reading plain framework-less JavaScript, please find *21-async/mojifinder/static/form.html* in the *Fluent Python* code repository (*https://fpy.li/code*).

To run *web_mojifinder.py*, you need to install two packages and their dependencies: *FastAPI* and *uvicorn*.[10] This is the command to run Example 21-11 with *uvicorn* in development mode:

```
$ uvicorn web_mojifinder:app --reload
```

The parameters are:

web_mojifinder:app

The package name, a colon, and the name of the ASGI application defined in it—app is the conventional name.

--reload

Make *uvicorn* monitor changes to application source files and automatically reload them. Useful only during development.

Now let's study the source code for *web_mojifinder.py*.

Example 21-11. web_mojifinder.py: complete source

```
from pathlib import Path
from unicodedata import name

from fastapi import FastAPI
from fastapi.responses import HTMLResponse
from pydantic import BaseModel

from charindex import InvertedIndex

STATIC_PATH = Path(__file__).parent.absolute() / 'static'  ❶

app = FastAPI(  ❷
    title='Mojifinder Web',
    description='Search for Unicode characters by name.',
)

class CharName(BaseModel):  ❸
    char: str
    name: str

def init(app):  ❹
    app.state.index = InvertedIndex()
    app.state.form = (STATIC_PATH / 'form.html').read_text()

init(app)  ❺
```

---

10 Instead of *uvicorn*, you may use another ASGI server, such as *hypercorn* or *Daphne*. See the official ASGI documentation page about implementations (*https://fpy.li/21-30*) for more information.

```
@app.get('/search', response_model=list[CharName])  ❻
async def search(q: str):  ❼
    chars = sorted(app.state.index.search(q))
    return ({'char': c, 'name': name(c)} for c in chars)  ❽

@app.get('/', response_class=HTMLResponse, include_in_schema=False)
def form():  ❾
    return app.state.form

# no main funcion  ❿
```

❶ Unrelated to the theme of this chapter, but worth noting: the elegant use of the overloaded / operator by pathlib.[11]

❷ This line defines the ASGI app. It could be as simple as app = FastAPI(). The parameters shown are metadata for the autogenerated documentation.

❸ A *pydantic* schema for a JSON response with char and name fields.[12]

❹ Build the index and load the static HTML form, attaching both to the app.state for later use.

❺ Run init when this module is loaded by the ASGI server.

❻ Route for the /search endpoint; response_model uses that CharName *pydantic* model to describe the response format.

❼ *FastAPI* assumes that any parameters that appear in the function or coroutine signature that are not in the route path will be passed in the HTTP query string, e.g., /search?q=cat. Since q has no default, *FastAPI* will return a 422 (Unprocessable Entity) status if q is missing from the query string.

❽ Returning an iterable of dicts compatible with the response_model schema allows *FastAPI* to build the JSON response according to the response_model in the @app.get decorator.

❾ Regular functions (i.e., non-async) can also be used to produce responses.

❿ This module has no main function. It is loaded and driven by the ASGI server—*uvicorn* in this example.

---

11 Thanks to tech reviewer Miroslav Šedivý for highlighting good places to use pathlib in code examples.

12 As mentioned in Chapter 8, *pydantic* (*https://fpy.li/21-31*) enforces type hints at runtime, for data validation.

Example 21-11 has no direct calls to `asyncio`. *FastAPI* is built on the *Starlette* ASGI toolkit, which in turn uses `asyncio`.

Also note that the body of `search` doesn't use `await`, `async with`, or `async for`, therefore it could be a plain function. I defined `search` as a coroutine just to show that *FastAPI* knows how to handle it. In a real app, most endpoints will query databases or hit other remote servers, so it is a critical advantage of *FastAPI*—and ASGI frameworks in general—to support coroutines that can take advantage of asynchronous libraries for network I/O.

 The `init` and `form` functions I wrote to load and serve the static HTML form are a hack to make the example short and easy to run. The recommended best practice is to have a proxy/load-balancer in front of the ASGI server to handle all static assets, and also use a CDN (Content Delivery Network) when possible. One such proxy/load-balancer is *Traefik* (*https://fpy.li/21-32*), a self-described "edge router" that "receives requests on behalf of your system and finds out which components are responsible for handling them." *FastAPI* has project generation (*https://fpy.li/21-33*) scripts that prepare your code to do that.

The typing enthusiast may have noticed that there are no return type hints in `search` and `form`. Instead, *FastAPI* relies on the `response_model=` keyword argument in the route decorators. The "Response Model" (*https://fpy.li/21-34*) page in the *FastAPI* documentation explains:

> The response model is declared in this parameter instead of as a function return type annotation, because the path function may not actually return that response model but rather return a dict, database object or some other model, and then use the `response_model` to perform the field limiting and serialization.

For example, in `search`, I returned a generator of `dict` items, not a list of `CharName` objects, but that's good enough for *FastAPI* and *pydantic* to validate my data and build the appropriate JSON response compatible with `response_model=list[Char Name]`.

We'll now focus on the *tcp_mojifinder.py* script that is answering the queries in Figure 21-5.

An asyncio TCP Server

The *tcp_mojifinder.py* program uses plain TCP to communicate with a client like Telnet or Netcat, so I could write it using `asyncio` without external dependencies—and without reinventing HTTP. Figure 21-5 shows text-based UI.

```
 ● ● ●                          luciano — telnet localhost 2323 — 83×30
TW-LR-MBP:~ luciano$ telnet localhost 2323
Trying 127.0.0.1...
Connected to localhost.
Escape character is '^]'.
?> fire
U+2632  ☲        TRIGRAM FOR FIRE
U+2EA3  ⺣        CJK RADICAL FIRE
U+2F55  火       KANGXI RADICAL FIRE
U+322B  ㈫       PARENTHESIZED IDEOGRAPH FIRE
U+328B  ㊋       CIRCLED IDEOGRAPH FIRE
U+4DDD  ䷝        HEXAGRAM FOR THE CLINGING FIRE
U+1F525 🔥       FIRE
U+1F692 🚒       FIRE ENGINE
U+1F6F1 🛱       ONCOMING FIRE ENGINE
U+1F702 🜂       ALCHEMICAL SYMBOL FOR FIRE
U+1F9EF 🧯       FIRE EXTINGUISHER
─────────────────────────────────────────────────── 11 found
```

Figure 21-5. Telnet session with the tcp_mojifinder.py server: querying for "fire."

This program is twice as long as *web_mojifinder.py*, so I split the presentation into
three parts: Example 21-12, Example 21-14, and Example 21-15. The top of *tcp_moji-
finder.py*—including the import statements—is in Example 21-14, but I will start by
describing the supervisor coroutine and the main function that drives the program.

Example 21-12. tcp_mojifinder.py: a simple TCP server; continues in Example 21-14

```python
async def supervisor(index: InvertedIndex, host: str, port: int) -> None:
    server = await asyncio.start_server(        ❶
        functools.partial(finder, index),       ❷
        host, port)                             ❸

    socket_list = cast(tuple[TransportSocket, ...], server.sockets)  ❹
    addr = socket_list[0].getsockname()
    print(f'Serving on {addr}. Hit CTRL-C to stop.')  ❺
    await server.serve_forever()                ❻

def main(host: str = '127.0.0.1', port_arg: str = '2323'):
    port = int(port_arg)
    print('Building index.')
    index = InvertedIndex()                     ❼
    try:
        asyncio.run(supervisor(index, host, port))  ❽
    except KeyboardInterrupt:                    ❾
        print('\nServer shut down.')

if __name__ == '__main__':
    main(*sys.argv[1:])
```

❶ This `await` quickly gets an instance of `asyncio.Server`, a TCP socket server. By default, `start_server` creates and starts the server, so it's ready to receive connections.

❷ The first argument to `start_server` is `client_connected_cb`, a callback to run when a new client connection starts. The callback can be a function or a coroutine, but it must accept exactly two arguments: an `asyncio.StreamReader` and an `asyncio.StreamWriter`. However, my `finder` coroutine also needs to get an `index`, so I used `functools.partial` to bind that parameter and obtain a callable that takes the reader and writer. Adapting user functions to callback APIs is the most common use case for `functools.partial`.

❸ `host` and `port` are the second and third arguments to `start_server`. See the full signature in the `asyncio` documentation (*https://fpy.li/21-35*).

❹ This `cast` is needed because *typeshed* has an outdated type hint for the `sockets` property of the `Server` class—as of May 2021. See Issue #5535 on *typeshed* (*https://fpy.li/21-36*).[13]

❺ Display the address and port of the first socket of the server.

❻ Although `start_server` already started the server as a concurrent task, I need to `await` on the `server_forever` method so that my `supervisor` is suspended here. Without this line, `supervisor` would return immediately, ending the loop started with `asyncio.run(supervisor(…))`, and exiting the program. The documentation for `Server.serve_forever` (*https://fpy.li/21-37*) says: "This method can be called if the server is already accepting connections."

❼ Build the inverted index.[14]

❽ Start the event loop running `supervisor`.

❾ Catch the `KeyboardInterrupt` to avoid a distracting traceback when I stop the server with Ctrl-C on the terminal running it.

---

13 Issue #5535 is closed as of October 2021, but Mypy did not have a new release since then, so the error persists.

14 Tech reviewer Leonardo Rochael pointed out that building the index could be delegated to another thread using `loop.run_with_executor()` in the `supervisor` coroutine, so the server would be ready to take requests immediately while the index is built. That's true, but querying the index is the only thing this server does, so it would not be a big win in this example.

You may find it easier to understand how control flows in *tcp_mojifinder.py* if you study the output it generates on the server console, listed in Example 21-13.

Example 21-13. tcp_mojifinder.py: this is the server side of the session depicted in Figure 21-5

```
$ python3 tcp_mojifinder.py
Building index.  ❶
Serving on ('127.0.0.1', 2323). Hit Ctrl-C to stop.  ❷
 From ('127.0.0.1', 58192): 'cat face'   ❸
   To ('127.0.0.1', 58192): 10 results.
 From ('127.0.0.1', 58192): 'fire'    ❹
   To ('127.0.0.1', 58192): 11 results.
 From ('127.0.0.1', 58192): '\x00'    ❺
Close ('127.0.0.1', 58192).        ❻
^C  ❼
Server shut down.  ❽
$
```

❶ Output by main. Before the next line appears, I see a 0.6s delay on my machine while the index is built.

❷ Output by supervisor.

❸ First iteration of a while loop in finder. The TCP/IP stack assigned port 58192 to my Telnet client. If you connect several clients to the server, you'll see their various ports in the output.

❹ Second iteration of the while loop in finder.

❺ I hit Ctrl-C on the client terminal; the while loop in finder exits.

❻ The finder coroutine displays this message then exits. Meanwhile the server is still running, ready to service another client.

❼ I hit Ctrl-C on the server terminal; server.serve_forever is cancelled, ending supervisor and the event loop.

❽ Output by main.

After main builds the index and starts the event loop, supervisor quickly displays the Serving on… message and is suspended at the await server.serve_forever() line. At that point, control flows into the event loop and stays there, occasionally coming back to the finder coroutine, which yields control back to the event loop whenever it needs to wait for the network to send or receive data.

While the event loop is alive, a new instance of the finder coroutine will be started for each client that connects to the server. In this way, many clients can be handled concurrently by this simple server. This continues until a KeyboardInterrupt occurs on the server or its process is killed by the OS.

Now let's see the top of *tcp_mojifinder.py*, with the finder coroutine.

Example 21-14. tcp_mojifinder.py: continued from Example 21-12

```python
import asyncio
import functools
import sys
from asyncio.trsock import TransportSocket
from typing import cast

from charindex import InvertedIndex, format_results  ❶

CRLF = b'\r\n'
PROMPT = b'?> '

async def finder(index: InvertedIndex,                 ❷
                 reader: asyncio.StreamReader,
                 writer: asyncio.StreamWriter) -> None:
    client = writer.get_extra_info('peername')  ❸
    while True:  ❹
        writer.write(PROMPT)  # can't await!  ❺
        await writer.drain()  # must await!  ❻
        data = await reader.readline()  ❼
        if not data:  ❽
            break
        try:
            query = data.decode().strip()  ❾
        except UnicodeDecodeError:  ❿
            query = '\x00'
        print(f' From {client}: {query!r}')  ⓫
        if query:
            if ord(query[:1]) < 32:  ⓬
                break
            results = await search(query, index, writer)  ⓭
            print(f'   To {client}: {results} results.')  ⓮

    writer.close()  ⓯
    await writer.wait_closed()  ⓰
    print(f'Close {client}.')  ⓱
```

❶ `format_results` is useful to display the results of `InvertedIndex.search` in a text-based UI such as the command line or a Telnet session.

❷ To pass `finder` to `asyncio.start_server`, I wrapped it with `functools.par tial`, because the server expects a coroutine or function that takes only the `reader` and `writer` arguments.

❸ Get the remote client address to which the socket is connected.

❹ This loop handles a dialog that lasts until a control character is received from the client.

❺ The `StreamWriter.write` method is not a coroutine, just a plain function; this line sends the `?>` prompt.

❻ `StreamWriter.drain` flushes the `writer` buffer; it is a coroutine, so it must be driven with `await`.

❼ `StreamWriter.readline` is a coroutine that returns bytes.

❽ If no bytes were received, the client closed the connection, so exit the loop.

❾ Decode the `bytes` to `str`, using the default UTF-8 encoding.

❿ A `UnicodeDecodeError` may happen when the user hits Ctrl-C and the Telnet client sends control bytes; if that happens, replace the query with a null character, for simplicity.

⓫ Log the query to the server console.

⓬ Exit the loop if a control or null character was received.

⓭ Do the actual `search`; code is presented next.

⓮ Log the response to the server console.

⓯ Close the `StreamWriter`.

⓰ Wait for the `StreamWriter` to close. This is recommended in the `.close()` method documentation (*https://fpy.li/21-38*).

⓱ Log the end of this client's session to the server console.

The last piece of this example is the `search` coroutine, shown in Example 21-15.

Example 21-15. tcp_mojifinder.py: search coroutine

```python
async def search(query: str,        ❶
                 index: InvertedIndex,
                 writer: asyncio.StreamWriter) -> int:
    chars = index.search(query)      ❷
    lines = (line.encode() + CRLF for line      ❸
                in format_results(chars))
    writer.writelines(lines)         ❹
    await writer.drain()             ❺
    status_line = f'{"─" * 66} {len(chars)} found'      ❻
    writer.write(status_line.encode() + CRLF)
    await writer.drain()
    return len(chars)
```

❶ search must be a coroutine because it writes to a StreamWriter and must use its .drain() coroutine method.

❷ Query the inverted index.

❸ This generator expression will yield byte strings encoded in UTF-8 with the Unicode codepoint, the actual character, its name, and a CRLF sequence—e.g., b'U+0039\t9\tDIGIT NINE\r\n').

❹ Send the lines. Surprisingly, writer.writelines is not a coroutine.

❺ But writer.drain() is a coroutine. Don't forget the await!

❻ Build a status line, then send it.

Note that all network I/O in *tcp_mojifinder.py* is in bytes; we need to decode the bytes received from the network, and encode strings before sending them out. In Python 3, the default encoding is UTF-8, and that's what I used implicitly in all encode and decode calls in this example.

> Note that some of the I/O methods are coroutines and must be driven with await, while others are simple functions. For example, StreamWriter.write is a plain function, because it writes to a buffer. On the other hand, StreamWriter.drain—which flushes the buffer and performs the network I/O—is a coroutine, as is StreamReader.readline—but not StreamWriter.writelines! While I was writing the first edition of this book, the asyncio API docs were improved by clearly labeling coroutines as such (*https://fpy.li/21-39*).

The *tcp_mojifinder.py* code leverages the high-level `asyncio` Streams API (*https://fpy.li/21-40*) that provides a ready-to-use server so you only need to implement a handler function, which can be a plain callback or a coroutine. There is also a lower-level Transports and Protocols API (*https://fpy.li/21-41*), inspired by the transport and protocols abstractions in the *Twisted* framework. Refer to the `asyncio` documentation for more information, including TCP and UDP echo servers and clients (*https://fpy.li/21-42*) implemented with that lower-level API.

Our next topic is `async for` and the objects that make it work.

Asynchronous Iteration and Asynchronous Iterables

We saw in "Asynchronous Context Managers" on page 790 how `async with` works with objects implementing the `__aenter__` and `__aexit__` methods returning awaitables—usually in the form of coroutine objects.

Similarly, `async for` works with *asynchronous iterables*: objects that implement `__aiter__`. However, `__aiter__` must be a regular method—not a coroutine method—and it must return an *asynchronous iterator*.

An asynchronous iterator provides an `__anext__` coroutine method that returns an awaitable—often a coroutine object. They are also expected to implement `__aiter__`, which usually returns `self`. This mirrors the important distinction of iterables and iterators we discussed in "Don't Make the Iterable an Iterator for Itself" on page 609.

The *aiopg* asynchronous PostgreSQL driver documentation (*https://fpy.li/21-43*) has an example that illustrates the use of `async for` to iterate over the rows of a database cursor:

```
async def go():
    pool = await aiopg.create_pool(dsn)
    async with pool.acquire() as conn:
        async with conn.cursor() as cur:
            await cur.execute("SELECT 1")
            ret = []
            async for row in cur:
                ret.append(row)
            assert ret == [(1,)]
```

In this example the query will return a single row, but in a realistic scenario you may have thousands of rows in response to a SELECT query. For large responses, the cursor will not be loaded with all the rows in a single batch. Therefore it is important that `async for row in cur:` does not block the event loop while the cursor may be waiting for additional rows. By implementing the cursor as an asynchronous iterator, *aiopg* may yield to the event loop at each `__anext__` call, and resume later when more rows arrive from PostgreSQL.

Asynchronous Generator Functions

You can implement an asynchronous iterator by writing a class with `__anext__` and `__aiter__`, but there is a simpler way: write a function declared with `async def` and use `yield` in its body. This parallels how generator functions simplify the classic Iterator pattern.

Let's study a simple example using `async for` and implementing an asynchronous generator. In Example 21-1 we saw *blogdom.py*, a script that probed domain names. Now suppose we find other uses for the `probe` coroutine we defined there, and decide to put it into a new module—*domainlib.py*—together with a new `multi_probe` asynchronous generator that takes a list of domain names and yields results as they are probed.

We'll look at the implementation of *domainlib.py* soon, but first let's see how it is used with Python's new asynchronous console.

Experimenting with Python's async console

Since Python 3.8 (*https://fpy.li/21-44*), you can run the interpreter with the `-m asyncio` command-line option to get an "async REPL": a Python console that imports `asyncio`, provides a running event loop, and accepts `await`, `async for`, and `async with` at the top-level prompt—which otherwise are syntax errors when used outside of native coroutines.[15]

To experiment with *domainlib.py*, go to the *21-async/domains/asyncio/* directory in your local copy of the *Fluent Python* code repository (*https://fpy.li/code*). Then run:

```
$ python -m asyncio
```

You'll see the console start, similar to this:

```
asyncio REPL 3.9.1 (v3.9.1:1e5d33e9b9, Dec  7 2020, 12:10:52)
[Clang 6.0 (clang-600.0.57)] on darwin
Use "await" directly instead of "asyncio.run()".
Type "help", "copyright", "credits" or "license" for more information.
>>> import asyncio
>>>
```

Note how the header says you can use `await` instead of `asyncio.run()`—to drive coroutines and other awaitables. Also: I did not type `import asyncio`. The `asyncio` module is automatically imported and that line makes that fact clear to the user.

---

[15] This is great for experimentation, like the Node.js console. Thanks to Yury Selivanov for yet another excellent contribution to asynchronous Python.

Now let's import *domainlib.py* and play with its two coroutines: `probe` and `multi_probe` (Example 21-16).

Example 21-16. Experimenting with domainlib.py after running `python3 -m asyncio`

```
>>> await asyncio.sleep(3, 'Rise and shine!')   ❶
'Rise and shine!'
>>> from domainlib import *
>>> await probe('python.org')   ❷
Result(domain='python.org', found=True)   ❸
>>> names = 'python.org rust-lang.org golang.org no-lang.invalid'.split()   ❹
>>> async for result in multi_probe(names):   ❺
...     print(*result, sep='\t')
...
golang.org      True   ❻
no-lang.invalid False
python.org      True
rust-lang.org   True
>>>
```

❶ Try a simple `await` to see the asynchronous console in action. Tip: `asyncio.sleep()` takes an optional second argument that is returned when you `await` it.

❷ Drive the `probe` coroutine.

❸ The `domainlib` version of `probe` returns a `Result` named tuple.

❹ Make a list of domains. The `.invalid` top-level domain is reserved for testing. DNS queries for such domains always get an NXDOMAIN response from DNS servers, meaning "that domain does not exist."[16]

❺ Iterate with `async for` over the `multi_probe` asynchronous generator to display the results.

❻ Note that the results are not in the order the domains were given to `multiprobe`. They appear as each DNS response comes back.

Example 21-16 shows that `multi_probe` is an asynchronous generator because it is compatible with `async for`. Now let's do a few more experiments, continuing from that example with Example 21-17.

---

16 See RFC 6761—Special-Use Domain Names (*https://fpy.li/21-45*).

Example 21-17. More experiments, continuing from Example 21-16

```
>>> probe('python.org')  ❶
<coroutine object probe at 0x10e313740>
>>> multi_probe(names)  ❷
<async_generator object multi_probe at 0x10e246b80>
>>> for r in multi_probe(names):  ❸
...     print(r)
...
Traceback (most recent call last):
  ...
TypeError: 'async_generator' object is not iterable
```

❶ Calling a native coroutine gives you a coroutine object.

❷ Calling an asynchronous generator gives you an `async_generator` object.

❸ We can't use a regular `for` loop with asynchronous generators because they implement `__aiter__` instead of `__iter__`.

Asynchronous generators are driven by `async for`, which can be a block statement (as seen in Example 21-16), and it also appears in asynchronous comprehensions, which we'll cover soon.

Implementing an asynchronous generator

Now let's study the code for *domainlib.py*, with the `multi_probe` asynchronous generator (Example 21-18).

Example 21-18. domainlib.py: functions for probing domains

```
import asyncio
import socket
from collections.abc import Iterable, AsyncIterator
from typing import NamedTuple, Optional


class Result(NamedTuple):  ❶
    domain: str
    found: bool


OptionalLoop = Optional[asyncio.AbstractEventLoop]  ❷


async def probe(domain: str, loop: OptionalLoop = None) -> Result:  ❸
    if loop is None:
        loop = asyncio.get_running_loop()
    try:
```

```
        await loop.getaddrinfo(domain, None)
    except socket.gaierror:
        return Result(domain, False)
    return Result(domain, True)


async def multi_probe(domains: Iterable[str]) -> AsyncIterator[Result]:  ❹
    loop = asyncio.get_running_loop()
    coros = [probe(domain, loop) for domain in domains]  ❺
    for coro in asyncio.as_completed(coros):  ❻
        result = await coro  ❼
        yield result  ❽
```

❶   NamedTuple makes the result from probe easier to read and debug.

❷   This type alias is to avoid making the next line too long for a book listing.

❸   probe now gets an optional loop argument, to avoid repeated calls to get_run
    ning_loop when this coroutine is driven by multi_probe.

❹   An asynchronous generator function produces an asynchronous generator
    object, which can be annotated as AsyncIterator[SomeType].

❺   Build list of probe coroutine objects, each with a different domain.

❻   This is not async for because asyncio.as_completed is a classic generator.

❼   Await on the coroutine object to retrieve the result.

❽   Yield result. This line makes multi_probe an asynchronous generator.

> The for loop in Example 21-18 could be more concise:
>
> ```
> for coro in asyncio.as_completed(coros):
>     yield await coro
> ```
>
> Python parses that as yield (await coro), so it works.
>
> I thought it could be confusing to use that shortcut in the first
> asynchronous generator example in the book, so I split it into two
> lines.

Given *domainlib.py*, we can demonstrate the use of the multi_probe asynchronous
generator in *domaincheck.py*: a script that takes a domain suffix and searches for
domains made from short Python keywords.

Here is a sample output of *domaincheck.py*:

```
$ ./domaincheck.py net
FOUND           NOT FOUND
=====           =========
in.net
del.net
true.net
for.net
is.net
                none.net
try.net
                from.net
and.net
or.net
else.net
with.net
if.net
as.net
                elif.net
                pass.net
                not.net
                def.net
```

Thanks to *domainlib*, the code for *domaincheck.py* is straightforward, as seen in Example 21-19.

Example 21-19. domaincheck.py: utility for probing domains using domainlib

```python
#!/usr/bin/env python3
import asyncio
import sys
from keyword import kwlist

from domainlib import multi_probe


async def main(tld: str) -> None:
    tld = tld.strip('.')
    names = (kw for kw in kwlist if len(kw) <= 4)      ❶
    domains = (f'{name}.{tld}'.lower() for name in names)   ❷
    print('FOUND\t\tNOT FOUND')      ❸
    print('=====\t\t=========')
    async for domain, found in multi_probe(domains):    ❹
        indent = '' if found else '\t\t'     ❺
        print(f'{indent}{domain}')


if __name__ == '__main__':
    if len(sys.argv) == 2:
        asyncio.run(main(sys.argv[1]))     ❻
    else:
        print('Please provide a TLD.', f'Example: {sys.argv[0]} COM.BR')
```

❶ Generate keywords with length up to 4.

❷ Generate domain names with the given suffix as TLD.

❸ Format a header for the tabular output.

❹ Asynchronously iterate over `multi_probe(domains)`.

❺ Set `indent` to zero or two tabs to put the result in the proper column.

❻ Run the `main` coroutine with the given command-line argument.

Generators have one extra use unrelated to iteration: they can be made into context managers. This also applies to asynchronous generators.

Asynchronous generators as context managers

Writing our own asynchronous context managers is not a frequent programming task, but if you need to write one, consider using the `@asynccontextmanager` (*https://fpy.li/21-46*) decorator added to the `contextlib` module in Python 3.7. That's very similar to the `@contextmanager` decorator we studied in "Using @contextmanager" on page 668.

An interesting example combining `@asynccontextmanager` with `loop.run_in_execu tor` appears in Caleb Hattingh's book *Using Asyncio in Python* (*https://fpy.li/ hattingh*). Example 21-20 is Caleb's code—with a single change and added callouts.

Example 21-20. Example using `@asynccontextmanager` and `loop.run_in_executor`

```
from contextlib import asynccontextmanager

@asynccontextmanager
async def web_page(url):            ❶
    loop = asyncio.get_running_loop()    ❷
    data = await loop.run_in_executor(   ❸
        None, download_webpage, url)
    yield data                      ❹
    await loop.run_in_executor(None, update_stats, url)  ❺

async with web_page('google.com') as data:   ❻
    process(data)
```

❶ The decorated function must be an asynchronous generator.

❷ Minor update to Caleb's code: use the lightweight `get_running_loop` instead of `get_event_loop`.

❸ Suppose `download_webpage` is a blocking function using the *requests* library; we run it in a separate thread to avoid blocking the event loop.

❹ All lines before this `yield` expression will become the `__aenter__` coroutine-method of the asynchronous context manager built by the decorator. The value of `data` will be bound to the `data` variable after the `as` clause in the `async with` statement below.

❺ Lines after the `yield` will become the `__aexit__` coroutine method. Here, another blocking call is delegated to the thread executor.

❻ Use `web_page` with `async with`.

This is very similar to the sequential `@contextmanager` decorator. Please see "Using @contextmanager" on page 668 for more details, including error handling at the `yield` line. For another example of `@asynccontextmanager`, see the `contextlib` documentation (*https://fpy.li/21-46*).

Now let's wrap up our coverage of asynchronous generator functions by contrasting them with native coroutines.

Asynchronous generators versus native coroutines

Here are some key similarities and differences between a native coroutine and an asynchronous generator function:

- Both are declared with `async def`.
- An asynchronous generator always has a `yield` expression in its body—that's what makes it a generator. A native coroutine never contains `yield`.
- A native coroutine may `return` some value other than `None`. An asynchronous generator can only use empty `return` statements.
- Native coroutines are awaitable: they can be driven by `await` expressions or passed to one of the many `asyncio` functions that take awaitable arguments, such as `create_task`. Asynchronous generators are not awaitable. They are asynchronous iterables, driven by `async for` or by asynchronous comprehensions.

Time to talk about asynchronous comprehensions.

Async Comprehensions and Async Generator Expressions

PEP 530—Asynchronous Comprehensions (*https://fpy.li/pep530*) introduced the use of `async for` and `await` in the syntax of comprehensions and generator expressions, starting with Python 3.6.

The only construct defined by PEP 530 that can appear outside an `async def` body is an asynchronous generator expression.

Defining and using an asynchronous generator expression

Given the `multi_probe` asynchronous generator from Example 21-18, we could write another asynchronous generator returning only the names of the domains found. Here is how—again using the asynchronous console launched with `-m asyncio`:

```
>>> from domainlib import multi_probe
>>> names = 'python.org rust-lang.org golang.org no-lang.invalid'.split()
>>> gen_found = (name async for name, found in multi_probe(names) if found)   ❶
>>> gen_found
<async_generator object <genexpr> at 0x10a8f9700>   ❷
>>> async for name in gen_found:   ❸
...     print(name)
...
golang.org
python.org
rust-lang.org
```

❶ The use of `async for` makes this an asynchronous generator expression. It can be defined anywhere in a Python module.

❷ The asynchronous generator expression builds an `async_generator` object— exactly the same type of object returned by an asynchronous generator function like `multi_probe`.

❸ The asynchronous generator object is driven by the `async for` statement, which in turn can only appear inside an `async def` body or in the magic asynchronous console I used in this example.

To summarize: an asynchronous generator expression can be defined anywhere in your program, but it can only be consumed inside a native coroutine or asynchronous generator function.

The remaining constructs introduced by PEP 530 can only be defined and used inside native coroutines or asynchronous generator functions.

Asynchronous comprehensions

Yury Selivanov—the author of PEP 530—justifies the need for asynchronous comprehensions with three short code snippets reproduced next.

We can all agree that we should be able to rewrite this code:

```
result = []
async for i in aiter():
```

```
    if i % 2:
        result.append(i)
```

like this:

```
result = [i async for i in aiter() if i % 2]
```

In addition, given a native coroutine fun, we should be able to write this:

```
result = [await fun() for fun in funcs]
```

 Using await in a list comprehension is similar to using asyn
cio.gather. But gather gives you more control over exception
handling, thanks to its optional return_exceptions argument.
Caleb Hattingh recommends always setting return_excep
tions=True (the default is False). Please see the asyncio.gather
documentation (https://fpy.li/21-48) for more.

Back to the magic asynchronous console:

```
>>> names = 'python.org rust-lang.org golang.org no-lang.invalid'.split()
>>> names = sorted(names)
>>> coros = [probe(name) for name in names]
>>> await asyncio.gather(*coros)
[Result(domain='golang.org', found=True),
Result(domain='no-lang.invalid', found=False),
Result(domain='python.org', found=True),
Result(domain='rust-lang.org', found=True)]
>>> [await probe(name) for name in names]
[Result(domain='golang.org', found=True),
Result(domain='no-lang.invalid', found=False),
Result(domain='python.org', found=True),
Result(domain='rust-lang.org', found=True)]
>>>
```

Note that I sorted the list of names to show that the results come out in the order they were submitted, in both cases.

PEP 530 allows the use of async for and await in list comprehensions as well as in dict and set comprehensions. For example, here is a dict comprehension to store the results of multi_probe in the asynchronous console:

```
>>> {name: found async for name, found in multi_probe(names)}
{'golang.org': True, 'python.org': True, 'no-lang.invalid': False,
'rust-lang.org': True}
```

We can use the await keyword in the expression before the for or async for clause, and also in the expression after the if clause. Here is a set comprehension in the asynchronous console, collecting only the domains that were found:

```
>>> {name for name in names if (await probe(name)).found}
{'rust-lang.org', 'python.org', 'golang.org'}
```

I had to put extra parentheses around the `await` expression due to the higher precedence of the `__getattr__` operator . (dot).

Again, all of these comprehensions can only appear inside an `async def` body or in the enchanted asynchronous console.

Now let's talk about a very important feature of the `async` statements, `async` expressions, and the objects they create. Those constructs are often used with *asyncio* but, they are actually library independent.

async Beyond asyncio: Curio

Python's `async/await` language constructs are not tied to any specific event loop or library.[17] Thanks to the extensible API provided by special methods, anyone sufficiently motivated can write their own asynchronous runtime environment and framework to drive native coroutines, asynchronous generators, etc.

That's what David Beazley did in his *Curio* (*https://fpy.li/21-49*) project. He was interested in rethinking how these new language features could be used in a framework built from scratch. Recall that `asyncio` was released in Python 3.4, and it used `yield from` instead of `await`, so its API could not leverage asynchronous context managers, asynchronous iterators, and everything else that the `async/await` keywords made possible. As a result, *Curio* has a cleaner API and a simpler implementation, compared to `asyncio`.

Example 21-21 shows the *blogdom.py* script (Example 21-1) rewritten to use *Curio*.

Example 21-21. blogdom.py: Example 21-1, now using Curio

```
#!/usr/bin/env python3
from curio import run, TaskGroup
import curio.socket as socket
from keyword import kwlist

MAX_KEYWORD_LEN = 4


async def probe(domain: str) -> tuple[str, bool]:     ❶
    try:
        await socket.getaddrinfo(domain, None)        ❷
    except socket.gaierror:
        return (domain, False)
    return (domain, True)
```

---

17 That's in contrast with JavaScript, where `async/await` is hardwired to the built-in event loop and runtime environment, i.e., a browser, Node.js, or Deno.

```
async def main() -> None:
    names = (kw for kw in kwlist if len(kw) <= MAX_KEYWORD_LEN)
    domains = (f'{name}.dev'.lower() for name in names)
    async with TaskGroup() as group:     ❸
        for domain in domains:
            await group.spawn(probe, domain)     ❹
        async for task in group:     ❺
            domain, found = task.result
            mark = '+' if found else ' '
            print(f'{mark} {domain}')

if __name__ == '__main__':
    run(main())     ❻
```

❶ probe doesn't need to get the event loop, because…

❷ …getaddrinfo is a top-level function of curio.socket, not a method of a loop object—as it is in asyncio.

❸ A TaskGroup is a core concept in *Curio*, to monitor and control several coroutines, and to make sure they are all executed and cleaned up.

❹ TaskGroup.spawn is how you start a coroutine, managed by a specific TaskGroup instance. The coroutine is wrapped by a Task.

❺ Iterating with async for over a TaskGroup yields Task instances as each is completed. This corresponds to the line in Example 21-1 using for … as_completed(…):.

❻ *Curio* pioneered this sensible way to start an asynchronous program in Python.

To expand on the last point: if you look at the asyncio code examples for the first edition of *Fluent Python*, you'll see lines like these, repeated over and over:

```
loop = asyncio.get_event_loop()
loop.run_until_complete(main())
loop.close()
```

A *Curio* TaskGroup is an asynchronous context manager that replaces several ad hoc APIs and coding patterns in asyncio. We just saw how iterating over a TaskGroup makes the asyncio.as_completed(…) function unnecessary. Another example: instead of a special gather function, this snippet from the "Task Groups" docs (*https://fpy.li/21-50*) collects the results of all tasks in the group:

```
async with TaskGroup(wait=all) as g:
    await g.spawn(coro1)
    await g.spawn(coro2)
```

```
    await g.spawn(coro3)
  print('Results:', g.results)
```

Task groups support *structured concurrency* (*https://fpy.li/21-51*): a form of concurrent programming that constrains all the activity of a group of asynchronous tasks to
a single entry and exit point. This is analogous to structured programming, which
eschewed the GOTO command and introduced block statements to limit the entry and
exit points of loops and subroutines. When used as an asynchronous context manager, a TaskGroup ensures that all tasks spawned inside are completed or cancelled,
and any exceptions raised, upon exiting the enclosed block.

 Structured concurrency will probably be adopted by asyncio in
upcoming Python releases. A strong indication appears in PEP
654–Exception Groups and except* (*https://fpy.li/pep654*), which
was approved for Python 3.11 (*https://fpy.li/21-52*). The "Motivation" section (*https://fpy.li/21-53*) mentions *Trio's* "nurseries," their
name for task groups: "Implementing a better task spawning API
in *asyncio*, inspired by Trio nurseries, was the main motivation for
this PEP."

Another important feature of *Curio* is better support for programming with coroutines and threads in the same codebase—a necessity in most nontrivial asynchronous
programs. Starting a thread with await spawn_thread(func, …) returns an Asyn
cThread object with a Task-like interface. Threads can call coroutines thanks to a
special AWAIT(coro) (*https://fpy.li/21-54*) function—named in all caps because await
is now a keyword.

Curio also provides a UniversalQueue that can be used to coordinate the work
among threads, *Curio* coroutines, and asyncio coroutines. That's right, *Curio* has
features that allow it to run in a thread along with asyncio in another thread, in the
same process, communicating via UniversalQueue and UniversalEvent. The API for
these "universal" classes is the same inside and outside of coroutines, but in a coroutine, you need to prefix calls with await.

As I write this in October 2021, *HTTPX* is the first HTTP client library compatible
with *Curio* (*https://fpy.li/21-55*), but I don't know of any asynchronous database
libraries that support it yet. In the *Curio* repository there is an impressive set of network programming examples (*https://fpy.li/21-56*), including one using *WebSocket*,
and another implementing the RFC 8305—Happy Eyeballs (*https://fpy.li/21-57*) concurrent algorithm for connecting to IPv6 endpoints with fast fallback to IPv4 if
needed.

The design of *Curio* has been influential. The *Trio* (*https://fpy.li/21-58*) framework
started by Nathaniel J. Smith was heavily inspired by *Curio*. *Curio* may also have

prompted Python contributors to improve the usability of the `asyncio` API. For example, in its earliest releases, `asyncio` users very often had to get and pass around a `loop` object because some essential functions were either `loop` methods or required a `loop` argument. In recent versions of Python, direct access to the loop is not needed as often, and in fact several functions that accepted an optional `loop` are now deprecating that argument.

Type annotations for asynchronous types are our next topic.

Type Hinting Asynchronous Objects

The return type of a native coroutine describes what you get when you `await` on that coroutine, which is the type of the object that appears in the `return` statements in the body of the native coroutine function.[18]

This chapter provided many examples of annotated native coroutines, including `probe` from Example 21-21:

```python
async def probe(domain: str) -> tuple[str, bool]:
    try:
        await socket.getaddrinfo(domain, None)
    except socket.gaierror:
        return (domain, False)
    return (domain, True)
```

If you need to annotate a parameter that takes a coroutine object, then the generic type is:

```python
class typing.Coroutine(Awaitable[V_co], Generic[T_co, T_contra, V_co]):
    ...
```

That type, and the following types were introduced in Python 3.5 and 3.6 to annotate asynchronous objects:

```python
class typing.AsyncContextManager(Generic[T_co]):
    ...
class typing.AsyncIterable(Generic[T_co]):
    ...
class typing.AsyncIterator(AsyncIterable[T_co]):
    ...
class typing.AsyncGenerator(AsyncIterator[T_co], Generic[T_co, T_contra]):
    ...
class typing.Awaitable(Generic[T_co]):
    ...
```

With Python ≥ 3.9, use the `collections.abc` equivalents of these.

---

18 This differs from the annotations of classic coroutines, as discussed in "Generic Type Hints for Classic Coroutines" on page 654.

I want to highlight three aspects of those generic types.

First: they are all covariant on the first type parameter, which is the type of the items yielded from these objects. Recall rule #1 of "Variance rules of thumb" on page 555:

> If a formal type parameter defines a type for data that comes out of the object, it can be covariant.

Second: `AsyncGenerator` and `Coroutine` are contravariant on the second to last parameter. That's the type of the argument of the low-level `.send()` method that the event loop calls to drive asynchronous generators and coroutines. As such, it is an "input" type. Therefore, it can be contravariant, per Variance Rule of Thumb #2:

> If a formal type parameter defines a type for data that goes into the object after its initial construction, it can be contravariant.

Third: `AsyncGenerator` has no return type, in contrast with `typing.Generator`, which we saw in "Generic Type Hints for Classic Coroutines" on page 654. Returning a value by raising `StopIteration(value)` was one of the hacks that enabled generators to operate as coroutines and support `yield from`, as we saw in "Classic Coroutines" on page 645. There is no such overlap among the asynchronous objects: `AsyncGenerator` objects don't return values, and are completely separate from native coroutine objects, which are annotated with `typing.Coroutine`.

Finally, let's briefly discuss the advantages and challenges of asynchronous programming.

How Async Works and How It Doesn't

The sections closing this chapter discuss high-level ideas around asynchronous programming, regardless of the language or library you are using.

Let's begin by explaining the #1 reason why asynchronous programming is appealing, followed by a popular myth, and how to deal with it.

Running Circles Around Blocking Calls

Ryan Dahl, the inventor of Node.js, introduces the philosophy of his project by saying "We're doing I/O completely wrong."[19] He defines a *blocking function* as one that does file or network I/O, and argues that we can't treat them as we treat nonblocking functions. To explain why, he presents the numbers in the second column of Table 21-1.

---

19 Video: "Introduction to Node.js" (*https://fpy.li/21-59*) at 4:55.

Table 21-1. Modern computer latency for reading data from different devices; third column shows proportional times in a scale easier to understand for us slow humans

Device	CPU cycles	Proportional "human" scale
L1 cache	3	3 seconds
L2 cache	14	14 seconds
RAM	250	250 seconds
disk	41,000,000	1.3 years
network	240,000,000	7.6 years

To make sense of Table 21-1, bear in mind that modern CPUs with GHz clocks run billions of cycles per second. Let's say that a CPU runs exactly 1 billion cycles per second. That CPU can make more than 333 million L1 cache reads in 1 second, or 4 (four!) network reads in the same time. The third column of Table 21-1 puts those numbers in perspective by multiplying the second column by a constant factor. So, in an alternate universe, if one read from L1 cache took 3 seconds, then a network read would take 7.6 years!

Table 21-1 explains why a disciplined approach to asynchronous programming can lead to high-performance servers. The challenge is achieving that discipline. The first step is to recognize that "I/O bound system" is a fantasy.

The Myth of I/O-Bound Systems

A commonly repeated meme is that asynchronous programming is good for "I/O bound systems." I learned the hard way that there are no "I/O-bound systems." You may have I/O-bound *functions*. Perhaps the vast majority of the functions in your system are I/O bound; i.e., they spend more time waiting for I/O than crunching data. While waiting, they cede control to the event loop, which can then drive some other pending task. But inevitably, any nontrivial system will have some parts that are CPU bound. Even trivial systems reveal that, under stress. In "Soapbox" on page 834, I tell the story of two asynchronous programs that struggled with CPU-bound functions slowing down the event loop with severe impact on performance.

Given that any nontrivial system will have CPU-bound functions, dealing with them is the key to success in asynchronous programming.

Avoiding CPU-Bound Traps

If you're using Python at scale, you should have some automated tests designed specifically to detect performance regressions as soon as they appear. This is critically important with asynchronous code, but also relevant to threaded Python code— because of the GIL. If you wait until the slowdown starts bothering the development team, it's too late. The fix will probably require some major makeover.

Here are some options for when you identify a CPU-hogging bottleneck:

- Delegate the task to a Python process pool.
- Delegate the task to an external task queue.
- Rewrite the relevant code in Cython, C, Rust, or some other language that compiles to machine code and interfaces with the Python/C API, preferably releasing the GIL.
- Decide that you can afford the performance hit and do nothing—but record the decision to make it easier to revert to it later.

The external task queue should be chosen and integrated as soon as possible at the start of the project, so that nobody in the team hesitates to use it when needed.

The last option—do nothing—falls in the category of technical debt (*https://fpy.li/ 21-60*).

Concurrent programming is a fascinating topic, and I would like to write a lot more about it. But it is not the main focus of this book, and this is already one of the longest chapters, so let's wrap it up.

Chapter Summary

> The problem with normal approaches to asynchronous programming is that they're all-or-nothing propositions. You rewrite all your code so none of it blocks or you're just wasting your time.
>
> —Alvaro Videla and Jason J. W. Williams, *RabbitMQ in Action*

I chose that epigraph for this chapter for two reasons. At a high level, it reminds us to avoid blocking the event loop by delegating slow tasks to a different processing unit, from a simple thread all the way to a distributed task queue. At a lower level, it is also a warning: once you write your first `async def`, your program is inevitably going to have more and more `async def`, `await`, `async with`, and `async for`. And using nonasynchronous libraries suddenly becomes a challenge.

After the simple *spinner* examples in Chapter 19, here our main focus was asynchronous programming with native coroutines, starting with the *blogdom.py* DNS probing example, followed by the concept of *awaitables*. While reading the source code of *flags_asyncio.py*, we found the first example of an *asynchronous context manager*.

The more advanced variations of the flag downloading program introduced two powerful functions: the `asyncio.as_completed` generator and the `loop.run_in_exec utor` coroutine. We also saw the concept and application of a semaphore to limit the number of concurrent downloads—as expected from well-behaved HTTP clients.

Server-side asynchronous programming was presented through the *mojifinder* examples: a *FastAPI* web service and *tcp_mojifinder.py*—the latter using just `asyncio` and the TCP protocol.

Asynchronous iteration and asynchronous iterables were the next major topic, with sections on `async for`, Python's async console, asynchronous generators, asynchronous generator expressions, and asynchronous comprehensions.

The last example in the chapter was *blogdom.py* rewritten with the *Curio* framework, to demonstrate how Python's asynchronous features are not tied to the `asyncio` package. *Curio* also showcases the concept of *structured concurrency*, which may have an industry-wide impact, bringing more clarity to concurrent code.

Finally, the sections under "How Async Works and How It Doesn't" on page 829 discuss the main appeal of asynchronous programming, the misconception of "I/O-bound systems," and dealing with the inevitable CPU-bound parts of your program.

Further Reading

David Beazley's PyOhio 2016 keynote "Fear and Awaiting in Async" (*https://fpy.li/21-61*) is a fantastic, live-coded introduction to the potential of the language features made possible by Yury Selivanov's contribution of the `async/await` keywords in Python 3.5. At one point, Beazley complains that `await` can't be used in list comprehensions, but that was fixed by Selivanov in PEP 530—Asynchronous Comprehensions (*https://fpy.li/pep530*), implemented in Python 3.6 later in that same year. Apart from that, everything else in Beazley's keynote is timeless, as he demonstrates how the asynchronous objects we saw in this chapter work, without the help of any framework—just a simple `run` function using `.send(None)` to drive coroutines. Only at the very end Beazley shows *Curio* (*https://fpy.li/21-62*), which he started that year as an experiment to see how far can you go doing asynchronous programming without a foundation of callbacks or futures, just coroutines. As it turns out, you can go very far —as demonstrated by the evolution of *Curio* and the later creation of *Trio* (*https://fpy.li/21-58*) by Nathaniel J. Smith. *Curio's* documentation has links (*https://fpy.li/21-64*) to more talks by Beazley on the subject.

Besides starting *Trio*, Nathaniel J. Smith wrote two deep blog posts that I highly recommend: "Some thoughts on asynchronous API design in a post-async/await world" (*https://fpy.li/21-65*), contrasting the design of *Curio* with that of *asyncio*,and "Notes on structured concurrency, or: Go statement considered harmful" (*https://fpy.li/21-66*), about structured concurrency. Smith also gave a long and informative answer to the question: "What is the core difference between asyncio and trio?" (*https://fpy.li/21-67*) on StackOverflow.

To learn more about the *asyncio* package, I've mentioned the best written resources I know at the start of this chapter: the official documentation (*https://fpy.li/21-1*) after the outstanding overhaul (*https://fpy.li/21-69*) started by Yury Selivanov in 2018, and Caleb Hattingh's book *Using Asyncio in Python* (O'Reilly). In the official documentation, make sure to read "Developing with asyncio" (*https://fpy.li/21-70*): documenting the *asyncio* debug mode, and also discussing common mistakes and traps and how to avoid them.

For a very accessible, 30-minute introduction to asynchronous programming in general and also *asyncio*, watch Miguel Grinberg's "Asynchronous Python for the Complete Beginner" (*https://fpy.li/21-71*), presented at PyCon 2017. Another great introduction is "Demystifying Python's Async and Await Keywords" (*https://fpy.li/21-72*), presented by Michael Kennedy, where among other things I learned about the *unsync* (*https://fpy.li/21-73*) library that provides a decorator to delegate the execution of coroutines, I/O-bound functions, and CPU-bound functions to `asyncio`, `threading`, or `multiprocessing` as needed.

At EuroPython 2019, Lynn Root—a global leader of *PyLadies* (*https://fpy.li/21-74*)— presented the excellent "Advanced asyncio: Solving Real-world Production Problems" (*https://fpy.li/21-75*), informed by her experience using Python as a staff engineer at Spotify.

In 2020, Łukasz Langa recorded a series of great videos about *asyncio*, starting with "Learn Python's AsyncIO #1—The Async Ecosystem" (*https://fpy.li/21-76*). Langa also made the super cool video "AsyncIO + Music" (*https://fpy.li/21-77*) for PyCon 2020 that not only shows *asyncio* applied in a very concrete event-oriented domain, but also explains it from the ground up.

Another area dominated by event-oriented programming is embedded systems. That's why Damien George added support for `async/await` in his *MicroPython* (*https://fpy.li/21-78*) interpreter for microcontrollers. At PyCon Australia 2018, Matt Trentini demonstrated the *uasyncio* (*https://fpy.li/21-79*) library, a subset of *asyncio* that is part of MicroPython's standard library.

For higher-level thinking about async programming in Python, read the blog post "Python async frameworks—Beyond developer tribalism" (*https://fpy.li/21-80*) by Tom Christie.

Finally, I recommend "What Color Is Your Function?" (*https://fpy.li/21-81*) by Bob Nystrom, discussing the incompatible execution models of plain functions versus async functions—a.k.a. coroutines—in JavaScript, Python, C#, and other languages. Spoiler alert: Nystrom's conclusion is that the language that got this right is Go, where all functions are the same color. I like that about Go. But I also think Nathaniel J. Smith has a point when he wrote "Go statement considered harmful" (*https://fpy.li/21-66*). Nothing is perfect, and concurrent programming is always hard.

Soapbox

How a Slow Function Almost Spoiled the uvloop Benchmarks

In 2016, Yury Selivanov released *uvloop* (*https://fpy.li/21-83*), "a fast, drop-in replacement of the built-in *asyncio* event loop." The benchmarks presented in Selivanov's blog post (*https://fpy.li/21-84*) announcing the library in 2016 are very impressive. He wrote: "it is at least 2x faster than nodejs, gevent, as well as any other Python asynchronous framework. The performance of uvloop-based asyncio is close to that of Go programs."

However, the post reveals that *uvloop* is able to match the performance of Go under two conditions:

1. Go is configured to use a single thread. That makes the Go runtime behave similarly to *asyncio*: concurrency is achieved via multiple coroutines driven by an event loop, all in the same thread.[20]

2. The Python 3.5 code uses *httptools* (*https://fpy.li/21-85*) in addition to *uvloop* itself.

Selivanov explains that he wrote *httptools* after benchmarking *uvloop* with *aiohttp* (*https://fpy.li/21-86*)—one of the first full-featured HTTP libraries built on `asyncio`:

> However, the performance bottleneck in *aiohttp* turned out to be its HTTP parser, which is so slow, that it matters very little how fast the underlying I/O library is. To make things more interesting, we created a Python binding for *http-parser* (Node.js HTTP parser C library, originally developed for *NGINX*). The library is called *httptools*, and is available on Github and PyPI.

Now think about that: Selivanov's HTTP performance tests consisted of a simple echo server written in the different languages/libraries, pounded by the *wrk* (*https://fpy.li/21-87*) benchmarking tool. Most developers would consider a simple echo server an "I/O-bound system," right? But it turned out that parsing HTTP headers is CPU bound, and it had a slow Python implementation in *aiohttp* in when Selivanov did the benchmarks in 2016. Whenever a function written in Python was parsing headers, the event loop was blocked. The impact was so significant that Selivanov went to the extra trouble of writing *httptools*. Without optimizing the CPU-bound code, the performance gains of a faster event loop were lost.

---

[20] Using a single thread was the default setting until Go 1.5 was released. Years before, Go had already earned a well-deserved reputation for enabling highly concurrent networked systems. One more evidence that concurrency doesn't require multiple threads or CPU cores.

Death by a Thousand Cuts

Instead of a simple echo server, imagine a complex and evolving Python system with tens of thousands of lines of asynchronous code, interfacing with many external libraries. Years ago I was asked to help diagnose performance problems in a system like that. It was written in Python 2.7 with the *Twisted* (*https://fpy.li/21-88*) framework—a solid library and in many ways a precursor to `asyncio` itself.

Python was used to build a façade for the web UI, integrating functionality provided by preexisting libraries and command-line tools written in other languages—but not designed for concurrent execution.

The project was ambitious; it had been in development for more than a year already, but it was not in production yet.[21] Over time, the developers noticed that the performance of the whole system was decreasing, and they were having a hard time finding the bottlenecks.

What was happening: with each added feature, more CPU-bound code was slowing down *Twisted*'s event loop. Python's role as a glue language meant there was a lot of data parsing and conversion between formats. There wasn't a single bottleneck: the problem was spread over countless little functions added over months of development. Fixing that would require rethinking the architecture of the system, rewriting a lot of code, probably leveraging a task queue, and perhaps using microservices or custom libraries written in languages better suited for CPU-intensive concurrent processing. The stakeholders were not prepared to make that additional investment, and the project was cancelled shortly afterwards.

When I told this story to Glyph Lefkowitz—founder the *Twisted* project—he said that one of his priorities at the start of an asynchronous programming project is to decide which tools he will use to farm out the CPU-intensive tasks. This conversation with Glyph was the inspiration for "Avoiding CPU-Bound Traps" on page 830.

---

21 Regardless of technical choices, this was probably the biggest mistake in this project: the stakeholders did not go for an MVP approach—delivering a Minimum Viable Product as soon as possible, and then adding features at a steady pace.

## PART V

Metaprogramming

## CHAPTER 22

Dynamic Attributes and Properties

The crucial importance of properties is that their existence makes it perfectly safe and indeed advisable for you to expose public data attributes as part of your class's public interface.

> — Martelli, Ravenscroft, and Holden, "Why properties are important"[1]

Data attributes and methods are collectively known as *attributes* in Python. A method is an attribute that is *callable*. *Dynamic attributes* present the same interface as data attributes—i.e., `obj.attr`—but are computed on demand. This follows Bertrand Meyer's *Uniform Access Principle*:

> All services offered by a module should be available through a uniform notation, which does not betray whether they are implemented through storage or through computation.[2]

There are several ways to implement dynamic attributes in Python. This chapter covers the simplest ways: the `@property` decorator and the `__getattr__` special method.

A user-defined class implementing `__getattr__` can implement a variation of dynamic attributes that I call *virtual attributes*: attributes that are not explicitly declared anywhere in the source code of the class, and are not present in the instance `__dict__`, but may be retrieved elsewhere or computed on the fly whenever a user tries to read a nonexistent attribute like `obj.no_such_attr`.

Coding dynamic and virtual attributes is the kind of metaprogramming that framework authors do. However, in Python the basic techniques are straightforward, so we can use them in everyday data wrangling tasks. That's how we'll start this chapter.

---

1 Alex Martelli, Anna Ravenscroft, and Steve Holden, *Python in a Nutshell,* 3rd ed. (O'Reilly), p. 123.

2 Bertrand Meyer, *Object-Oriented Software Construction,* 2nd ed. (Pearson), p. 57.

What's New in This Chapter

Most of the updates to this chapter were motivated by a discussion of `@func
tools.cached_property` (introduced in Python 3.8), as well as the combined use of
`@property` with `@functools.cache` (new in 3.9). This affected the code for the
`Record` and `Event` classes that appear in "Computed Properties" on page 849. I also
added a refactoring to leverage the PEP 412—Key-Sharing Dictionary (*https://fpy.li/
pep412*) optimization.

To highlight more relevant features while keeping the examples readable, I removed
some nonessential code—merging the old `DbRecord` class into `Record`, replacing
`shelve.Shelve` with a `dict`, and deleting the logic to download the OSCON dataset
—which the examples now read from a local file included in the *Fluent Python* code
repository (*https://fpy.li/code*).

Data Wrangling with Dynamic Attributes

In the next few examples, we'll leverage dynamic attributes to work with a JSON
dataset published by O'Reilly for the OSCON 2014 conference. Example 22-1 shows
four records from that dataset.[3]

Example 22-1. Sample records from osconfeed.json; some field contents abbreviated

```
{ "Schedule":
  { "conferences": [{"serial": 115 }],
    "events": [
      { "serial": 34505,
        "name": "Why Schools Don't Use Open Source to Teach Programming",
        "event_type": "40-minute conference session",
        "time_start": "2014-07-23 11:30:00",
        "time_stop": "2014-07-23 12:10:00",
        "venue_serial": 1462,
        "description": "Aside from the fact that high school programming...",
        "website_url": "http://oscon.com/oscon2014/public/schedule/detail/34505",
        "speakers": [157509],
        "categories": ["Education"] }
    ],
    "speakers": [
      { "serial": 157509,
        "name": "Robert Lefkowitz",
        "photo": null,
        "url": "http://sharewave.com/",
```

---

3 OSCON—O'Reilly Open Source Conference—was a casualty of the COVID-19 pandemic. The original 744
 KB JSON file I used for these examples is no longer online as of January 10, 2021. You'll find a copy of *oscon-
 feed.json* in the example code repository (*https://fpy.li/22-1*).

```
        "position": "CTO",
        "affiliation": "Sharewave",
        "twitter": "sharewaveteam",
        "bio": "Robert ´r0ml´ Lefkowitz is the CTO at Sharewave, a startup..." }
    ],
    "venues": [
      { "serial": 1462,
        "name": "F151",
        "category": "Conference Venues" }
    ]
  }
}
```

Example 22-1 shows 4 of the 895 records in the JSON file. The entire dataset is a single JSON object with the key "Schedule", and its value is another mapping with four keys: "conferences", "events", "speakers", and "venues". Each of those four keys maps to a list of records. In the full dataset, the "events", "speakers", and "venues" lists have dozens or hundreds of records, while "conferences" has only that one record shown in Example 22-1. Every record has a "serial" field, which is a unique identifier for the record within the list.

I used Python's console to explore the dataset, as shown in Example 22-2.

Example 22-2. Interactive exploration of osconfeed.json

```
>>> import json
>>> with open('data/osconfeed.json') as fp:
...     feed = json.load(fp)          ❶
>>> sorted(feed['Schedule'].keys())    ❷
['conferences', 'events', 'speakers', 'venues']
>>> for key, value in sorted(feed['Schedule'].items()):
...     print(f'{len(value):3} {key}')  ❸
...
  1 conferences
484 events
357 speakers
 53 venues
>>> feed['Schedule']['speakers'][-1]['name']   ❹
'Carina C. Zona'
>>> feed['Schedule']['speakers'][-1]['serial']  ❺
141590
>>> feed['Schedule']['events'][40]['name']
'There *Will* Be Bugs'
>>> feed['Schedule']['events'][40]['speakers']   ❻
[3471, 5199]
```

❶ feed is a dict holding nested dicts and lists, with string and integer values.

❷ List the four record collections inside "Schedule".

❸ Display record counts for each collection.

❹ Navigate through the nested dicts and lists to get the name of the last speaker.

❺ Get the serial number of that same speaker.

❻ Each event has a `'speakers'` list with zero or more speaker serial numbers.

Exploring JSON-Like Data with Dynamic Attributes

Example 22-2 is simple enough, but the syntax `feed['Schedule']['events'][40]['name']` is cumbersome. In JavaScript, you can get the same value by writing `feed.Schedule.events[40].name`. It's easy to implement a `dict`-like class that does the same in Python—there are plenty of implementations on the web.[4] I wrote `FrozenJSON`, which is simpler than most recipes because it supports reading only: it's just for exploring the data. `FrozenJSON` is also recursive, dealing automatically with nested mappings and lists.

Example 22-3 is a demonstration of `FrozenJSON`, and the source code is shown in Example 22-4.

Example 22-3. FrozenJSON from Example 22-4 allows reading attributes like name, and calling methods like .keys() and .items()

```
>>> import json
>>> raw_feed = json.load(open('data/osconfeed.json'))
>>> feed = FrozenJSON(raw_feed)        ❶
>>> len(feed.Schedule.speakers)        ❷
357
>>> feed.keys()
dict_keys(['Schedule'])
>>> sorted(feed.Schedule.keys())       ❸
['conferences', 'events', 'speakers', 'venues']
>>> for key, value in sorted(feed.Schedule.items()):   ❹
...     print(f'{len(value):3} {key}')
...
  1 conferences
484 events
357 speakers
 53 venues
>>> feed.Schedule.speakers[-1].name    ❺
'Carina C. Zona'
>>> talk = feed.Schedule.events[40]
>>> type(talk)                         ❻
```

---

4 Two examples are `AttrDict` (*https://fpy.li/22-2*) and `addict` (*https://fpy.li/22-3*).

```
<class 'explore0.FrozenJSON'>
>>> talk.name
'There *Will* Be Bugs'
>>> talk.speakers    ❼
[3471, 5199]
>>> talk.flavor    ❽
Traceback (most recent call last):
    ...
KeyError: 'flavor'
```

❶ Build a FrozenJSON instance from the raw_feed made of nested dicts and lists.

❷ FrozenJSON allows traversing nested dicts by using attribute notation; here we show the length of the list of speakers.

❸ Methods of the underlying dicts can also be accessed, like .keys(), to retrieve the record collection names.

❹ Using items(), we can retrieve the record collection names and their contents, to display the len() of each of them.

❺ A list, such as feed.Schedule.speakers, remains a list, but the items inside are converted to FrozenJSON if they are mappings.

❻ Item 40 in the events list was a JSON object; now it's a FrozenJSON instance.

❼ Event records have a speakers list with speaker serial numbers.

❽ Trying to read a missing attribute raises KeyError, instead of the usual AttributeError.

The keystone of the FrozenJSON class is the __getattr__ method, which we already used in the Vector example in "Vector Take #3: Dynamic Attribute Access" on page 409, to retrieve Vector components by letter: v.x, v.y, v.z, etc. It's essential to recall that the __getattr__ special method is only invoked by the interpreter when the usual process fails to retrieve an attribute (i.e., when the named attribute cannot be found in the instance, nor in the class or in its superclasses).

The last line of Example 22-3 exposes a minor issue with my code: trying to read a missing attribute should raise AttributeError, and not KeyError as shown. When I implemented the error handling to do that, the __getattr__ method became twice as long, distracting from the most important logic I wanted to show. Given that users would know that a FrozenJSON is built from mappings and lists, I think the KeyError is not too confusing.

Example 22-4. explore0.py: turn a JSON dataset into a `FrozenJSON` holding nested `FrozenJSON` objects, lists, and simple types

```
from collections import abc


class FrozenJSON:
    """A read-only façade for navigating a JSON-like object
       using attribute notation
    """

    def __init__(self, mapping):
        self.__data = dict(mapping)  ❶

    def __getattr__(self, name):  ❷
        try:
            return getattr(self.__data, name)  ❸
        except AttributeError:
            return FrozenJSON.build(self.__data[name])  ❹

    def __dir__(self):  ❺
        return self.__data.keys()

    @classmethod
    def build(cls, obj):  ❻
        if isinstance(obj, abc.Mapping):  ❼
            return cls(obj)
        elif isinstance(obj, abc.MutableSequence):  ❽
            return [cls.build(item) for item in obj]
        else:  ❾
            return obj
```

❶ Build a `dict` from the `mapping` argument. This ensures we get a mapping or something that can be converted to one. The double-underscore prefix on `__data` makes it a *private attribute*.

❷ `__getattr__` is called only when there's no attribute with that `name`.

❸ If `name` matches an attribute of the instance `__data` dict, return that. This is how calls like `feed.keys()` are handled: the keys method is an attribute of the `__data` dict.

❹   Otherwise, fetch the item with the key name from self.__data, and return the result of calling FrozenJSON.build() on that.[5]

❺   Implementing __dir__ suports the dir() built-in, which in turns supports auto-completion in the standard Python console as well as IPython, Jupyter Notebook, etc. This simple code will enable recursive auto-completion based on the keys in self.__data, because __getattr__ builds FrozenJSON instances on the fly—useful for interactive exploration of the data.

❻   This is an alternate constructor, a common use for the @classmethod decorator.

❼   If obj is a mapping, build a FrozenJSON with it. This is an example of *goose typing*—see "Goose Typing" on page 444 if you need a refresher.

❽   If it is a MutableSequence, it must be a list,[6] so we build a list by passing each item in obj recursively to .build().

❾   If it's not a dict or a list, return the item as it is.

A FrozenJSON instance has the __data private instance attribute stored under the name _FrozenJSON__data, as explained in "Private and 'Protected' Attributes in Python" on page 384. Attempts to retrieve attributes by other names will trigger __getattr__. This method will first look if the self.__data dict has an attribute (not a key!) by that name; this allows FrozenJSON instances to handle dict methods such as items, by delegating to self.__data.items(). If self.__data doesn't have an attribute with the given name, __getattr__ uses name as a key to retrieve an item from self.__data, and passes that item to FrozenJSON.build. This allows navigating through nested structures in the JSON data, as each nested mapping is converted to another FrozenJSON instance by the build class method.

Note that FrozenJSON does not transform or cache the original dataset. As we traverse the data, __getattr__ creates FrozenJSON instances again and again. That's OK for a dataset of this size, and for a script that will only be used to explore or convert the data.

---

5 The expression self.__data[name] is where a KeyError exception may occur. Ideally, it should be handled and an AttributeError raised instead, because that's what is expected from __getattr__. The diligent reader is invited to code the error handling as an exercise.

6 The source of the data is JSON, and the only collection types in JSON data are dict and list.

Any script that generates or emulates dynamic attribute names from arbitrary sources must deal with one issue: the keys in the original data may not be suitable attribute names. The next section addresses this.

The Invalid Attribute Name Problem

The `FrozenJSON` code doesn't handle attribute names that are Python keywords. For example, if you build an object like this:

```
>>> student = FrozenJSON({'name': 'Jim Bo', 'class': 1982})
```

You won't be able to read `student.class` because `class` is a reserved keyword in Python:

```
>>> student.class
  File "<stdin>", line 1
    student.class
                ^
SyntaxError: invalid syntax
```

You can always do this, of course:

```
>>> getattr(student, 'class')
1982
```

But the idea of `FrozenJSON` is to provide convenient access to the data, so a better solution is checking whether a key in the mapping given to `FrozenJSON.__init__` is a keyword, and if so, append an _ to it, so the attribute can be read like this:

```
>>> student.class_
1982
```

This can be achieved by replacing the one-liner __init__ from Example 22-4 with the version in Example 22-5.

Example 22-5. explore1.py: append an _ to attribute names that are Python keywords

```
def __init__(self, mapping):
    self.__data = {}
    for key, value in mapping.items():
        if keyword.iskeyword(key):   ❶
            key += '_'
        self.__data[key] = value
```

❶ The `keyword.iskeyword(...)` function is exactly what we need; to use it, the keyword module must be imported, which is not shown in this snippet.

A similar problem may arise if a key in a JSON record is not a valid Python identifier:

```
>>> x = FrozenJSON({'2be':'or not'})
>>> x.2be
```

```
  File "<stdin>", line 1
    x.2be
      ^
SyntaxError: invalid syntax
```

Such problematic keys are easy to detect in Python 3 because the str class provides the s.isidentifier() method, which tells you whether s is a valid Python identifier according to the language grammar. But turning a key that is not a valid identifier into a valid attribute name is not trivial. One solution would be to implement __geti tem__ to allow attribute access using notation like x['2be']. For the sake of simplicity, I will not worry about this issue.

After giving some thought to the dynamic attribute names, let's turn to another essential feature of FrozenJSON: the logic of the build class method. Fro zen.JSON.build is used by __getattr__ to return a different type of object depending on the value of the attribute being accessed: nested structures are converted to FrozenJSON instances or lists of FrozenJSON instances.

Instead of a class method, the same logic could be implemented as the __new__ special method, as we'll see next.

Flexible Object Creation with __new__

We often refer to __init__ as the constructor method, but that's because we adopted jargon from other languages. In Python, __init__ gets self as the first argument, therefore the object already exists when __init__ is called by the interpreter. Also, __init__ cannot return anything. So it's really an initializer, not a constructor.

When a class is called to create an instance, the special method that Python calls on that class to construct an instance is __new__. It's a class method, but gets special treatment, so the @classmethod decorator is not applied to it. Python takes the instance returned by __new__ and then passes it as the first argument self of __init__. We rarely need to code __new__, because the implementation inherited from object suffices for the vast majority of use cases.

If necessary, the __new__ method can also return an instance of a different class. When that happens, the interpreter does not call __init__. In other words, Python's logic for building an object is similar to this pseudocode:

```
# pseudocode for object construction
def make(the_class, some_arg):
    new_object = the_class.__new__(some_arg)
    if isinstance(new_object, the_class):
        the_class.__init__(new_object, some_arg)
    return new_object

# the following statements are roughly equivalent
```

```
        x = Foo('bar')
        x = make(Foo, 'bar')
```

Example 22-6 shows a variation of FrozenJSON where the logic of the former build class method was moved to __new__.

Example 22-6. explore2.py: using __new__ instead of build to construct new objects that may or may not be instances of FrozenJSON

```
from collections import abc
import keyword

class FrozenJSON:
    """A read-only façade for navigating a JSON-like object
       using attribute notation
    """

    def __new__(cls, arg):              ❶
        if isinstance(arg, abc.Mapping):
            return super().__new__(cls)  ❷
        elif isinstance(arg, abc.MutableSequence):  ❸
            return [cls(item) for item in arg]
        else:
            return arg

    def __init__(self, mapping):
        self.__data = {}
        for key, value in mapping.items():
            if keyword.iskeyword(key):
                key += '_'
            self.__data[key] = value

    def __getattr__(self, name):
        try:
            return getattr(self.__data, name)
        except AttributeError:
            return FrozenJSON(self.__data[name])  ❹

    def __dir__(self):
        return self.__data.keys()
```

❶ As a class method, the first argument __new__ gets is the class itself, and the remaining arguments are the same that __init__ gets, except for self.

❷ The default behavior is to delegate to the __new__ of a superclass. In this case, we are calling __new__ from the object base class, passing FrozenJSON as the only argument.

❸ The remaining lines of __new__ are exactly as in the old build method.

❹ This was where FrozenJSON.build was called before; now we just call the FrozenJSON class, which Python handles by calling FrozenJSON.__new__.

The __new__ method gets the class as the first argument because, usually, the created object will be an instance of that class. So, in FrozenJSON.__new__, when the expression super().__new__(cls) effectively calls object.__new__(FrozenJSON), the instance built by the object class is actually an instance of FrozenJSON. The __class__ attribute of the new instance will hold a reference to FrozenJSON, even though the actual construction is performed by object.__new__, implemented in C, in the guts of the interpreter.

The OSCON JSON dataset is structured in a way that is not helpful for interactive exploration. For example, the event at index 40, titled 'There *Will* Be Bugs' has two speakers, 3471 and 5199. Finding the names of the speakers is awkward, because those are serial numbers and the Schedule.speakers list is not indexed by them. To get each speaker, we must iterate over that list until we find a record with a matching serial number. Our next task is restructuring the data to prepare for automatic retrieval of linked records.

Computed Properties

We first saw the @property decorator in Chapter 11, in the section, "A Hashable Vector2d" on page 376. In Example 11-7, I used two properties in Vector2d just to make the x and y attributes read-only. Here we will see properties that compute values, leading to a discussion of how to cache such values.

The records in the 'events' list of the OSCON JSON data contain integer serial numbers pointing to records in the 'speakers' and 'venues' lists. For example, this is the record for a conference talk (with an elided description):

```
{ "serial": 33950,
  "name": "There *Will* Be Bugs",
  "event_type": "40-minute conference session",
  "time_start": "2014-07-23 14:30:00",
  "time_stop": "2014-07-23 15:10:00",
  "venue_serial": 1449,
  "description": "If you're pushing the envelope of programming...",
  "website_url": "http://oscon.com/oscon2014/public/schedule/detail/33950",
  "speakers": [3471, 5199],
  "categories": ["Python"] }
```

We will implement an Event class with venue and speakers properties to return the linked data automatically—in other words, "dereferencing" the serial number. Given an Event instance, Example 22-7 shows the desired behavior.

Example 22-7. Reading venue and speakers returns Record objects

```
>>> event  ❶
<Event 'There *Will* Be Bugs'>
>>> event.venue  ❷
<Record serial=1449>
>>> event.venue.name  ❸
'Portland 251'
>>> for spkr in event.speakers:  ❹
...     print(f'{spkr.serial}: {spkr.name}')
...
3471: Anna Martelli Ravenscroft
5199: Alex Martelli
```

❶ Given an Event instance...

❷ ...reading event.venue returns a Record object instead of a serial number.

❸ Now it's easy to get the name of the venue.

❹ The event.speakers property returns a list of Record instances.

As usual, we will build the code step-by-step, starting with the Record class and a function to read the JSON data and return a dict with Record instances.

Step 1: Data-Driven Attribute Creation

Example 22-8 shows the doctest to guide this first step.

Example 22-8. Test-driving schedule_v1.py (from Example 22-9)

```
>>> records = load(JSON_PATH)  ❶
>>> speaker = records['speaker.3471']  ❷
>>> speaker  ❸
<Record serial=3471>
>>> speaker.name, speaker.twitter  ❹
('Anna Martelli Ravenscroft', 'annaraven')
```

❶ load a dict with the JSON data.

❷ The keys in records are strings built from the record type and serial number.

❸ speaker is an instance of the Record class defined in Example 22-9.

❹ Fields from the original JSON can be retrieved as Record instance attributes.

The code for *schedule_v1.py* is in Example 22-9.

Example 22-9. schedule_v1.py: reorganizing the OSCON schedule data

```python
import json

JSON_PATH = 'data/osconfeed.json'

class Record:
    def __init__(self, **kwargs):
        self.__dict__.update(kwargs)  ❶

    def __repr__(self):
        return f'<{self.__class__.__name__} serial={self.serial!r}>'  ❷

def load(path=JSON_PATH):
    records = {}  ❸
    with open(path) as fp:
        raw_data = json.load(fp)  ❹
    for collection, raw_records in raw_data['Schedule'].items():  ❺
        record_type = collection[:-1]  ❻
        for raw_record in raw_records:
            key = f'{record_type}.{raw_record["serial"]}'  ❼
            records[key] = Record(**raw_record)  ❽
    return records
```

❶ This is a common shortcut to build an instance with attributes created from keyword arguments (detailed explanation follows).

❷ Use the `serial` field to build the custom `Record` representation shown in Example 22-8.

❸ `load` will ultimately return a `dict` of `Record` instances.

❹ Parse the JSON, returning native Python objects: lists, dicts, strings, numbers, etc.

❺ Iterate over the four top-level lists named `'conferences'`, `'events'`, `'speakers'`, and `'venues'`.

❻ `record_type` is the list name without the last character, so `speakers` becomes `speaker`. In Python ≥ 3.9 we can do this more explicitly with `collection.remove suffix('s')`—see PEP 616—String methods to remove prefixes and suffixes (*https://fpy.li/pep616*).

❼ Build the key in the format `'speaker.3471'`.

❽ Create a `Record` instance and save it in `records` with the key.

The `Record.__init__` method illustrates an old Python hack. Recall that the `__dict__` of an object is where its attributes are kept—unless `__slots__` is declared in the class, as we saw in "Saving Memory with __slots__" on page 386. So, updating an instance `__dict__` with a mapping is a quick way to create a bunch of attributes in that instance.[7]

 Depending on the application, the `Record` class may need to deal with keys that are not valid attribute names, as we saw in "The Invalid Attribute Name Problem" on page 846. Dealing with that issue would distract from the key idea of this example, and is not a problem in the dataset we are reading.

The definition of `Record` in Example 22-9 is so simple that you may be wondering why I did not use it before, instead of the more complicated `FrozenJSON`. There are two reasons. First, `FrozenJSON` works by recursively converting the nested mappings and lists; `Record` doesn't need that because our converted dataset doesn't have mappings nested in mappings or lists. The records contain only strings, integers, lists of strings, and lists of integers. Second reason: `FrozenJSON` provides access to the embedded `__data dict` attributes—which we used to invoke methods like `.keys()`—and now we don't need that functionality either.

 The Python standard library provides classes similar to `Record`, where each instance has an arbitrary set of attributes built from keyword arguments given to `__init__`: `types.SimpleNamespace` (*https://fpy.li/22-5*), `argparse.Namespace` (*https://fpy.li/22-6*), and `multiprocessing.managers.Namespace` (*https://fpy.li/22-7*). I wrote the simpler `Record` class to highlight the essential idea: `__init__` updating the instance `__dict__`.

After reorganizing the schedule dataset, we can enhance the `Record` class to automatically retrieve `venue` and `speaker` records referenced in an `event` record. We'll use properties to do that in the next examples.

Step 2: Property to Retrieve a Linked Record

The goal of this next version is: given an `event` record, reading its `venue` property will return a `Record`. This is similar to what the Django ORM does when you access a `ForeignKey` field: instead of the key, you get the linked model object.

---

7 By the way, `Bunch` is the name of the class used by Alex Martelli to share this tip in a recipe from 2001 titled "The simple but handy 'collector of a bunch of named stuff' class" (*https://fpy.li/22-4*).

We'll start with the venue property. See the partial interaction in Example 22-10 as an example.

Example 22-10. Extract from the doctests of schedule_v2.py

```
>>> event = Record.fetch('event.33950')  ❶
>>> event  ❷
<Event 'There *Will* Be Bugs'>
>>> event.venue  ❸
<Record serial=1449>
>>> event.venue.name  ❹
'Portland 251'
>>> event.venue_serial  ❺
1449
```

❶ The Record.fetch static method gets a Record or an Event from the dataset.

❷ Note that event is an instance of the Event class.

❸ Accessing event.venue returns a Record instance.

❹ Now it's easy to find out the name of an event.venue.

❺ The Event instance also has a venue_serial attribute, from the JSON data.

Event is a subclass of Record adding a venue to retrieve linked records, and a specialized __repr__ method.

The code for this section is in the *schedule_v2.py* (*https://fpy.li/22-8*) module in the *Fluent Python* code repository (*https://fpy.li/code*). The example has nearly 60 lines, so I'll present it in parts, starting with the enhanced Record class.

Example 22-11. schedule_v2.py: Record class with a new fetch method

```
import inspect  ❶
import json

JSON_PATH = 'data/osconfeed.json'

class Record:

    __index = None  ❷

    def __init__(self, **kwargs):
        self.__dict__.update(kwargs)

    def __repr__(self):
        return f'<{self.__class__.__name__} serial={self.serial!r}>'
```

```
@staticmethod   ❸
def fetch(key):
    if Record.__index is None:   ❹
        Record.__index = load()
    return Record.__index[key]   ❺
```

❶   inspect will be used in load, listed in Example 22-13.

❷   The __index private class attribute will eventually hold a reference to the dict returned by load.

❸   fetch is a staticmethod to make it explicit that its effect is not influenced by the instance or class on which it is called.

❹   Populate the Record.__index, if needed.

❺   Use it to retrieve the record with the given key.

> This is one example where the use of staticmethod makes sense. The fetch method always acts on the Record.__index class attribute, even if invoked from a subclass, like Event.fetch()— which we'll soon explore. It would be misleading to code it as a class method because the cls first argument would not be used.

Now we get to the use of a property in the Event class, listed in Example 22-12.

Example 22-12. schedule_v2.py: the Event class

```
class Event(Record):   ❶

    def __repr__(self):
        try:
            return f'<{self.__class__.__name__} {self.name!r}>'   ❷
        except AttributeError:
            return super().__repr__()

    @property
    def venue(self):
        key = f'venue.{self.venue_serial}'
        return self.__class__.fetch(key)   ❸
```

❶ Event extends Record.

❷ If the instance has a `name` attribute, it is used to produce a custom representation. Otherwise, delegate to the `__repr__` from `Record`.

❸ The `venue` property builds a key from the `venue_serial` attribute, and passes it to the `fetch` class method, inherited from `Record` (the reason for using `self.__class__` is explained shortly).

The second line of the `venue` method of Example 22-12 returns `self.__class__.fetch(key)`. Why not simply call `self.fetch(key)`? The simpler form works with the specific OSCON dataset because there is no event record with a `'fetch'` key. But, if an event record had a key named `'fetch'`, then within that specific `Event` instance, the reference `self.fetch` would retrieve the value of that field, instead of the `fetch` class method that `Event` inherits from `Record`. This is a subtle bug, and it could easily sneak through testing because it depends on the dataset.

When creating instance attribute names from data, there is always the risk of bugs due to shadowing of class attributes—such as methods—or data loss through accidental overwriting of existing instance attributes. These problems may explain why Python dicts are not like JavaScript objects in the first place.

If the `Record` class behaved more like a mapping, implementing a dynamic `__getitem__` instead of a dynamic `__getattr__`, there would be no risk of bugs from overwriting or shadowing. A custom mapping is probably the Pythonic way to implement `Record`. But if I took that road, we'd not be studying the tricks and traps of dynamic attribute programming.

The final piece of this example is the revised `load` function in Example 22-13.

Example 22-13. schedule_v2.py: the load function

```
def load(path=JSON_PATH):
    records = {}
    with open(path) as fp:
        raw_data = json.load(fp)
    for collection, raw_records in raw_data['Schedule'].items():
        record_type = collection[:-1]  ❶
        cls_name = record_type.capitalize()  ❷
        cls = globals().get(cls_name, Record)  ❸
        if inspect.isclass(cls) and issubclass(cls, Record):  ❹
            factory = cls  ❺
        else:
            factory = Record  ❻
```

```
        for raw_record in raw_records:    ❼
            key = f'{record_type}.{raw_record["serial"]}'
            records[key] = factory(**raw_record)    ❽
    return records
```

❶ So far, no changes from the load in *schedule_v1.py* (Example 22-9).

❷ Capitalize the `record_type` to get a possible class name; e.g., `'event'` becomes `'Event'`.

❸ Get an object by that name from the module global scope; get the `Record` class if there's no such object.

❹ If the object just retrieved is a class, and is a subclass of `Record`…

❺ …bind the `factory` name to it. This means `factory` may be any subclass of `Record`, depending on the `record_type`.

❻ Otherwise, bind the `factory` name to `Record`.

❼ The `for` loop that creates the `key` and saves the records is the same as before, except that…

❽ …the object stored in `records` is constructed by `factory`, which may be `Record` or a subclass like `Event`, selected according to the `record_type`.

Note that the only `record_type` that has a custom class is `Event`, but if classes named `Speaker` or `Venue` are coded, `load` will automatically use those classes when building and saving records, instead of the default `Record` class.

We'll now apply the same idea to a new `speakers` property in the `Events` class.

Step 3: Property Overriding an Existing Attribute

The name of the `venue` property in Example 22-12 does not match a field name in records of the `"events"` collection. Its data comes from a `venue_serial` field name. In contrast, each record in the `events` collection has a `speakers` field with a list of serial numbers. We want to expose that information as a `speakers` property in `Event` instances, which returns a list of `Record` instances. This name clash requires some special attention, as Example 22-14 reveals.

Example 22-14. schedule_v3.py: the speakers property

```
@property
def speakers(self):
```

```
spkr_serials = self.__dict__['speakers']  ❶
fetch = self.__class__.fetch
return [fetch(f'speaker.{key}')
        for key in spkr_serials]  ❷
```

❶ The data we want is in a `speakers` attribute, but we must retrieve it directly from the instance `__dict__` to avoid a recursive call to the `speakers` property.

❷ Return a list of all records with keys corresponding to the numbers in `spkr_serials`.

Inside the `speakers` method, trying to read `self.speakers` will invoke the property itself, quickly raising a `RecursionError`. However, if we read the same data via `self.__dict__['speakers']`, Python's usual algorithm for retrieving attributes is bypassed, the property is not called, and the recursion is avoided. For this reason, reading or writing data directly to an object's `__dict__` is a common Python metaprogramming trick.

The interpreter evaluates `obj.my_attr` by first looking at the class of `obj`. If the class has a property with the `my_attr` name, that property shadows an instance attribute by the same name. Examples in "Properties Override Instance Attributes" on page 865 will demonstrate this, and Chapter 23 will reveal that a property is implemented as a descriptor—a more powerful and general abstraction.

As I coded the list comprehension in Example 22-14, my programmer's lizard brain thought: "This may be expensive." Not really, because events in the OSCON dataset have few speakers, so coding anything more complicated would be premature optimization. However, caching a property is a common need—and there are caveats. So let's see how to do that in the next examples.

Step 4: Bespoke Property Cache

Caching properties is a common need because there is an expectation that an expression like `event.venue` should be inexpensive.[8] Some form of caching could become necessary if the `Record.fetch` method behind the `Event` properties needed to query a database or a web API.

---

8 This is actually a downside of Meyer's Uniform Access Principle, which I mentioned in the opening of this chapter. Read the optional "Soapbox" on page 879 if you're interested in this discussion.

In the first edition *Fluent Python*, I coded the custom caching logic for the speakers method, as shown in Example 22-15.

Example 22-15. Custom caching logic using hasattr disables key-sharing optimization

```python
@property
def speakers(self):
    if not hasattr(self, '__speaker_objs'):  ❶
        spkr_serials = self.__dict__['speakers']
        fetch = self.__class__.fetch
        self.__speaker_objs = [fetch(f'speaker.{key}')
                for key in spkr_serials]
    return self.__speaker_objs  ❷
```

❶ If the instance doesn't have an attribute named __speaker_objs, fetch the speaker objects and store them there.

❷ Return self.__speaker_objs.

The handmade caching in Example 22-15 is straightforward, but creating an attribute after the instance is initialized defeats the PEP 412—Key-Sharing Dictionary (*https://fpy.li/pep412*) optimization, as explained in "Practical Consequences of How dict Works" on page 102. Depending on the size of the dataset, the difference in memory usage may be important.

A similar hand-rolled solution that works well with the key-sharing optimization requires coding an __init__ for the Event class, to create the necessary __speaker_objs initialized to None, and then checking for that in the speakers method. See Example 22-16.

Example 22-16. Storage defined in __init__ to leverage key-sharing optimization

```python
class Event(Record):

    def __init__(self, **kwargs):
        self.__speaker_objs = None
        super().__init__(**kwargs)

# 15 lines omitted...
    @property
    def speakers(self):
        if self.__speaker_objs is None:
            spkr_serials = self.__dict__['speakers']
            fetch = self.__class__.fetch
            self.__speaker_objs = [fetch(f'speaker.{key}')
                    for key in spkr_serials]
        return self.__speaker_objs
```

Examples 22-15 and 22-16 illustrate simple caching techniques that are fairly common in legacy Python codebases. However, in multithreaded programs, handmade caches like those introduce race conditions that may lead to corrupted data. If two threads are reading a property that was not previously cached, the first thread will need to compute the data for the cache attribute (`__speaker_objs` in the examples) and the second thread may read a cached value that is not yet complete.

Fortunately, Python 3.8 introduced the `@functools.cached_property` decorator, which is thread safe. Unfortunately, it comes with a couple of caveats, explained next.

Step 5: Caching Properties with functools

The `functools` module provides three decorators for caching. We saw `@cache` and `@lru_cache` in "Memoization with functools.cache" on page 322 (Chapter 9). Python 3.8 introduced `@cached_property`.

The `functools.cached_property` decorator caches the result of the method in an instance attribute with the same name. For example, in Example 22-17, the value computed by the `venue` method is stored in a `venue` attribute in `self`. After that, when client code tries to read `venue`, the newly created `venue` instance attribute is used instead of the method.

Example 22-17. Simple use of a @cached_property

```
@cached_property
def venue(self):
    key = f'venue.{self.venue_serial}'
    return self.__class__.fetch(key)
```

In "Step 3: Property Overriding an Existing Attribute" on page 856, we saw that a property shadows an instance attribute by the same name. If that is true, how can `@cached_property` work? If the property overrides the instance attribute, the `venue` attribute will be ignored and the `venue` method will always be called, computing the key and running `fetch` every time!

The answer is a bit sad: `cached_property` is a misnomer. The `@cached_property` decorator does not create a full-fledged property, it creates a *nonoverriding descriptor*. A descriptor is an object that manages the access to an attribute in another class. We will dive into descriptors in Chapter 23. The `property` decorator is a high-level API to create an *overriding descriptor*. Chapter 23 will include a through explanation about *overriding* versus *nonoverriding* descriptors.

For now, let us set aside the underlying implementation and focus on the differences between `cached_property` and `property` from a user's point of view. Raymond Hettinger explains them very well in the Python docs (*https://fpy.li/22-9*):

The mechanics of cached_property() are somewhat different from property(). A regular property blocks attribute writes unless a setter is defined. In contrast, a cached_property allows writes.

The cached_property decorator only runs on lookups and only when an attribute of the same name doesn't exist. When it does run, the cached_property writes to the attribute with the same name. Subsequent attribute reads and writes take precedence over the cached_property method and it works like a normal attribute.

The cached value can be cleared by deleting the attribute. This allows the cached_property method to run again.[9]

Back to our Event class: the specific behavior of @cached_property makes it unsuitable to decorate speakers, because that method relies on an existing attribute also named speakers, containing the serial numbers of the event speakers.

@cached_property has some important limitations:

- It cannot be used as a drop-in replacement to @property if the decorated method already depends on an instance attribute with the same name.

- It cannot be used in a class that defines __slots__.

- It defeats the key-sharing optimization of the instance __dict__, because it creates an instance attribute after __init__.

Despite these limitations, @cached_property addresses a common need in a simple way, and it is thread safe. Its Python code (*https://fpy.li/22-13*) is an example of using a *reentrant lock* (*https://fpy.li/22-14*).

The @cached_property documentation (*https://fpy.li/22-15*) recommends an alternative solution that we can use with speakers: stacking @property and @cache decorators, as shown in Example 22-18.

Example 22-18. Stacking @property on @cache

```
@property    ❶
@cache       ❷
def speakers(self):
```

---

9 Source: @functools.cached_property (*https://fpy.li/22-9*) documentation. I know Raymond Hettinger authored this explanation because he wrote it as a response to an issue I filed: bpo42781—functools.cached_property docs should explain that it is non-overriding (*https://fpy.li/22-11*). Hettinger is a major contributor to the official Python docs and standard library. He also wrote the excellent "Descriptor HowTo Guide" (*https://fpy.li/22-12*), a key resource for Chapter 23.

```
        spkr_serials = self.__dict__['speakers']
        fetch = self.__class__.fetch
        return [fetch(f'speaker.{key}')
                for key in spkr_serials]
```

❶ The order is important: @property goes on top…

❷ …of @cache.

Recall from "Stacked Decorators" on page 324 the meaning of that syntax. The top three lines of Example 22-18 are similar to:

```
speakers = property(cache(speakers))
```

The @cache is applied to speakers, returning a new function. That function then is decorated by @property, which replaces it with a newly constructed property.

This wraps up our discussion of read-only properties and caching decorators, exploring the OSCON dataset. In the next section, we start a new series of examples creating read/write properties.

Using a Property for Attribute Validation

Besides computing attribute values, properties are also used to enforce business rules by changing a public attribute into an attribute protected by a getter and setter without affecting client code. Let's work through an extended example.

LineItem Take #1: Class for an Item in an Order

Imagine an app for a store that sells organic food in bulk, where customers can order nuts, dried fruit, or cereals by weight. In that system, each order would hold a sequence of line items, and each line item could be represented by an instance of a class, as in Example 22-19.

Example 22-19. bulkfood_v1.py: the simplest LineItem class

```
class LineItem:

    def __init__(self, description, weight, price):
        self.description = description
        self.weight = weight
        self.price = price

    def subtotal(self):
        return self.weight * self.price
```

That's nice and simple. Perhaps too simple. Example 22-20 shows a problem.

Example 22-20. A negative weight results in a negative subtotal

```
>>> raisins = LineItem('Golden raisins', 10, 6.95)
>>> raisins.subtotal()
69.5
>>> raisins.weight = -20  # garbage in...
>>> raisins.subtotal()    # garbage out...
-139.0
```

This is a toy example, but not as fanciful as you may think. Here is a story from the early days of Amazon.com:

> We found that customers could order a negative quantity of books! And we would credit their credit card with the price and, I assume, wait around for them to ship the books.
>
> — Jeff Bezos, founder and CEO of Amazon.com[10]

How do we fix this? We could change the interface of LineItem to use a getter and a setter for the weight attribute. That would be the Java way, and it's not wrong.

On the other hand, it's natural to be able to set the weight of an item by just assigning to it; and perhaps the system is in production with other parts already accessing item.weight directly. In this case, the Python way would be to replace the data attribute with a property.

LineItem Take #2: A Validating Property

Implementing a property will allow us to use a getter and a setter, but the interface of LineItem will not change (i.e., setting the weight of a LineItem will still be written as raisins.weight = 12).

Example 22-21 lists the code for a read/write weight property.

Example 22-21. bulkfood_v2.py: a LineItem with a weight property

```
class LineItem:

    def __init__(self, description, weight, price):
        self.description = description
        self.weight = weight     ❶
        self.price = price

    def subtotal(self):
        return self.weight * self.price
```

---

10 Direct quote by Jeff Bezos in the *Wall Street Journal* story, "Birth of a Salesman" (*https://fpy.li/22-16*) (October 15, 2011). Note that as of 2021, you need a subscription to read the article.

```
@property  ❷
def weight(self):  ❸
    return self.__weight  ❹

@weight.setter  ❺
def weight(self, value):
    if value > 0:
        self.__weight = value  ❻
    else:
        raise ValueError('value must be > 0')  ❼
```

❶ Here the property setter is already in use, making sure that no instances with negative weight can be created.

❷ @property decorates the getter method.

❸ All the methods that implement a property share the name of the public attribute: weight.

❹ The actual value is stored in a private attribute __weight.

❺ The decorated getter has a .setter attribute, which is also a decorator; this ties the getter and setter together.

❻ If the value is greater than zero, we set the private __weight.

❼ Otherwise, ValueError is raised.

Note how a LineItem with an invalid weight cannot be created now:

```
>>> walnuts = LineItem('walnuts', 0, 10.00)
Traceback (most recent call last):
    ...
ValueError: value must be > 0
```

Now we have protected weight from users providing negative values. Although buyers usually can't set the price of an item, a clerical error or a bug may create a LineItem with a negative price. To prevent that, we could also turn price into a property, but this would entail some repetition in our code.

Remember the Paul Graham quote from Chapter 17: "When I see patterns in my programs, I consider it a sign of trouble." The cure for repetition is abstraction. There are two ways to abstract away property definitions: using a property factory or a descriptor class. The descriptor class approach is more flexible, and we'll devote Chapter 23 to a full discussion of it. Properties are in fact implemented as descriptor classes themselves. But here we will continue our exploration of properties by implementing a property factory as a function.

But before we can implement a property factory, we need to have a deeper understanding of properties.

A Proper Look at Properties

Although often used as a decorator, the property built-in is actually a class. In Python, functions and classes are often interchangeable, because both are callable and there is no new operator for object instantiation, so invoking a constructor is no different from invoking a factory function. And both can be used as decorators, as long as they return a new callable that is a suitable replacement of the decorated callable.

This is the full signature of the property constructor:

```
property(fget=None, fset=None, fdel=None, doc=None)
```

All arguments are optional, and if a function is not provided for one of them, the corresponding operation is not allowed by the resulting property object.

The property type was added in Python 2.2, but the @ decorator syntax appeared only in Python 2.4, so for a few years, properties were defined by passing the accessor functions as the first two arguments.

The "classic" syntax for defining properties without decorators is illustrated in Example 22-22.

Example 22-22. bulkfood_v2b.py: same as Example 22-21, but without using decorators

```
class LineItem:

    def __init__(self, description, weight, price):
        self.description = description
        self.weight = weight
        self.price = price

    def subtotal(self):
        return self.weight * self.price

    def get_weight(self):          ❶
        return self.__weight

    def set_weight(self, value):    ❷
        if value > 0:
            self.__weight = value
        else:
            raise ValueError('value must be > 0')
```

```
weight = property(get_weight, set_weight)  ❸
```

❶ A plain getter.

❷ A plain setter.

❸ Build the `property` and assign it to a public class attribute.

The classic form is better than the decorator syntax in some situations; the code of
the property factory we'll discuss shortly is one example. On the other hand, in a class
body with many methods, the decorators make it explicit which are the getters and
setters, without depending on the convention of using `get` and `set` prefixes in their
names.

The presence of a property in a class affects how attributes in instances of that class
can be found in a way that may be surprising at first. The next section explains.

Properties Override Instance Attributes

Properties are always class attributes, but they actually manage attribute access in the
instances of the class.

In "Overriding Class Attributes" on page 391 we saw that when an instance and its
class both have a data attribute by the same name, the instance attribute overrides, or
shadows, the class attribute—at least when read through that instance.
Example 22-23 illustrates this point.

Example 22-23. Instance attribute shadows the class data attribute

```
>>> class Class:  ❶
...     data = 'the class data attr'
...     @property
...     def prop(self):
...         return 'the prop value'
...
>>> obj = Class()
>>> vars(obj)  ❷
{}
>>> obj.data  ❸
'the class data attr'
>>> obj.data = 'bar'  ❹
>>> vars(obj)  ❺
{'data': 'bar'}
>>> obj.data  ❻
'bar'
>>> Class.data  ❼
'the class data attr'
```

❶ Define Class with two class attributes: the data attribute and the prop property.

❷ vars returns the __dict__ of obj, showing it has no instance attributes.

❸ Reading from obj.data retrieves the value of Class.data.

❹ Writing to obj.data creates an instance attribute.

❺ Inspect the instance to see the instance attribute.

❻ Now reading from obj.data retrieves the value of the instance attribute. When read from the obj instance, the instance data shadows the class data.

❼ The Class.data attribute is intact.

Now, let's try to override the prop attribute on the obj instance. Resuming the previous console session, we have Example 22-24.

Example 22-24. Instance attribute does not shadow the class property (continued from Example 22-23)

```
>>> Class.prop  ❶
<property object at 0x1072b7408>
>>> obj.prop  ❷
'the prop value'
>>> obj.prop = 'foo'  ❸
Traceback (most recent call last):
  ...
AttributeError: can't set attribute
>>> obj.__dict__['prop'] = 'foo'  ❹
>>> vars(obj)  ❺
{'data': 'bar', 'prop': 'foo'}
>>> obj.prop  ❻
'the prop value'
>>> Class.prop = 'baz'  ❼
>>> obj.prop  ❽
'foo'
```

❶ Reading prop directly from Class retrieves the property object itself, without running its getter method.

❷ Reading obj.prop executes the property getter.

❸ Trying to set an instance prop attribute fails.

❹ Putting 'prop' directly in the obj.__dict__ works.

❺ We can see that obj now has two instance attributes: data and prop.

❻ However, reading obj.prop still runs the property getter. The property is not shadowed by an instance attribute.

❼ Overwriting Class.prop destroys the property object.

❽ Now obj.prop retrieves the instance attribute. Class.prop is not a property anymore, so it no longer overrides obj.prop.

As a final demonstration, we'll add a new property to Class, and see it overriding an instance attribute. Example 22-25 picks up where Example 22-24 left off.

Example 22-25. New class property shadows the existing instance attribute (continued from Example 22-24)

```
>>> obj.data   ❶
'bar'
>>> Class.data   ❷
'the class data attr'
>>> Class.data = property(lambda self: 'the "data" prop value')   ❸
>>> obj.data   ❹
'the "data" prop value'
>>> del Class.data   ❺
>>> obj.data   ❻
'bar'
```

❶ obj.data retrieves the instance data attribute.

❷ Class.data retrieves the class data attribute.

❸ Overwrite Class.data with a new property.

❹ obj.data is now shadowed by the Class.data property.

❺ Delete the property.

❻ obj.data now reads the instance data attribute again.

The main point of this section is that an expression like obj.data does not start the search for data in obj. The search actually starts at obj.__class__, and only if there is no property named data in the class, Python looks in the obj instance itself. This applies to *overriding descriptors* in general, of which properties are just one example. Further treatment of descriptors must wait for Chapter 23.

Now back to properties. Every Python code unit—modules, functions, classes, meth-ods—can have a docstring. The next topic is how to attach documentation to properties.

Property Documentation

When tools such as the console help() function or IDEs need to display the docu-mentation of a property, they extract the information from the __doc__ attribute of the property.

If used with the classic call syntax, property can get the documentation string as the doc argument:

```
weight = property(get_weight, set_weight, doc='weight in kilograms')
```

The docstring of the getter method—the one with the @property decorator itself—is used as the documentation of the property as a whole. Figure 22-1 shows the help screens generated from the code in Example 22-26.

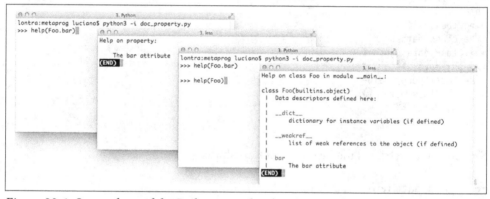

Figure 22-1. Screenshots of the Python console when issuing the commands help(Foo.bar) and help(Foo). Source code is in Example 22-26.

Example 22-26. Documentation for a property

```
class Foo:

    @property
    def bar(self):
        """The bar attribute"""
        return self.__dict__['bar']

    @bar.setter
    def bar(self, value):
        self.__dict__['bar'] = value
```

Now that we have these property essentials covered, let's go back to the issue of protecting both the `weight` and `price` attributes of `LineItem` so they only accept values greater than zero—but without implementing two nearly identical pairs of getters/setters by hand.

Coding a Property Factory

We'll create a factory to create `quantity` properties—so named because the managed attributes represent quantities that can't be negative or zero in the application. Example 22-27 shows the clean look of the `LineItem` class using two instances of `quantity` properties: one for managing the `weight` attribute, the other for `price`.

Example 22-27. bulkfood_v2prop.py: the quantity property factory in use

```
class LineItem:
    weight = quantity('weight')   ❶
    price = quantity('price')     ❷

    def __init__(self, description, weight, price):
        self.description = description
        self.weight = weight      ❸
        self.price = price

    def subtotal(self):
        return self.weight * self.price   ❹
```

❶ Use the factory to define the first custom property, `weight`, as a class attribute.

❷ This second call builds another custom property, `price`.

❸ Here the property is already active, making sure a negative or `0` `weight` is rejected.

❹ The properties are also in use here, retrieving the values stored in the instance.

Recall that properties are class attributes. When building each `quantity` property, we need to pass the name of the `LineItem` attribute that will be managed by that specific property. Having to type the word `weight` twice in this line is unfortunate:

```
    weight = quantity('weight')
```

But avoiding that repetition is complicated because the property has no way of knowing which class attribute name will be bound to it. Remember: the righthand side of an assignment is evaluated first, so when `quantity()` is invoked, the `weight` class attribute doesn't even exist.

Improving the quantity property so that the user doesn't need to retype the attribute name is a nontrivial metaprogramming problem. We'll solve that problem in Chapter 23.

Example 22-28 lists the implementation of the quantity property factory.[11]

Example 22-28. bulkfood_v2prop.py: the quantity property factory

```
def quantity(storage_name):     ❶

    def qty_getter(instance):     ❷
        return instance.__dict__[storage_name]     ❸

    def qty_setter(instance, value):     ❹
        if value > 0:
            instance.__dict__[storage_name] = value     ❺
        else:
            raise ValueError('value must be > 0')

    return property(qty_getter, qty_setter)     ❻
```

❶ The storage_name argument determines where the data for each property is stored; for the weight, the storage name will be 'weight'.

❷ The first argument of the qty_getter could be named self, but that would be strange because this is not a class body; instance refers to the LineItem instance where the attribute will be stored.

❸ qty_getter references storage_name, so it will be preserved in the closure of this function; the value is retrieved directly from the instance.__dict__ to bypass the property and avoid an infinite recursion.

❹ qty_setter is defined, also taking instance as first argument.

❺ The value is stored directly in the instance.__dict__, again bypassing the property.

❻ Build a custom property object and return it.

---

11 This code is adapted from "Recipe 9.21. Avoiding Repetitive Property Methods" from *Python Cookbook*, 3rd ed., by David Beazley and Brian K. Jones (O'Reilly).

The bits of Example 22-28 that deserve careful study revolve around the stor age_name variable. When you code each property in the traditional way, the name of the attribute where you will store a value is hardcoded in the getter and setter methods. But here, the qty_getter and qty_setter functions are generic, and they depend on the storage_name variable to know where to get/set the managed attribute in the instance __dict__. Each time the quantity factory is called to build a property, the storage_name must be set to a unique value.

The functions qty_getter and qty_setter will be wrapped by the property object created in the last line of the factory function. Later, when called to perform their duties, these functions will read the storage_name from their closures to determine where to retrieve/store the managed attribute values.

In Example 22-29, I create and inspect a LineItem instance, exposing the storage attributes.

Example 22-29. bulkfood_v2prop.py: exploring properties and storage attributes

```
>>> nutmeg = LineItem('Moluccan nutmeg', 8, 13.95)
>>> nutmeg.weight, nutmeg.price  ❶
(8, 13.95)
>>> nutmeg.__dict__  ❷
{'description': 'Moluccan nutmeg', 'weight': 8, 'price': 13.95}
```

❶ Reading the weight and price through the properties shadowing the namesake instance attributes.

❷ Using vars to inspect the nutmeg instance: here we see the actual instance attributes used to store the values.

Note how the properties built by our factory leverage the behavior described in "Properties Override Instance Attributes" on page 865: the weight property overrides the weight instance attribute so that every reference to self.weight or nut meg.weight is handled by the property functions, and the only way to bypass the property logic is to access the instance __dict__ directly.

The code in Example 22-28 may be a bit tricky, but it's concise: it's identical in length to the decorated getter/setter pair defining just the weight property in Example 22-21. The LineItem definition in Example 22-27 looks much better without the noise of the getter/setters.

In a real system, that same kind of validation may appear in many fields, across several classes, and the quantity factory would be placed in a utility module to be used over and over again. Eventually that simple factory could be refactored into a more extensible descriptor class, with specialized subclasses performing different validations. We'll do that in Chapter 23.

Now let us wrap up the discussion of properties with the issue of attribute deletion.

Handling Attribute Deletion

We can use the del statement to delete not only variables, but also attributes:

```
>>> class Demo:
...     pass
...
>>> d = Demo()
>>> d.color = 'green'
>>> d.color
'green'
>>> del d.color
>>> d.color
Traceback (most recent call last):
  File "<stdin>", line 1, in <module>
AttributeError: 'Demo' object has no attribute 'color'
```

In practice, deleting attributes is not something we do every day in Python, and the requirement to handle it with a property is even more unusual. But it is supported, and I can think of a silly example to demonstrate it.

In a property definition, the @my_property.deleter decorator wraps the method in charge of deleting the attribute managed by the property. As promised, silly Example 22-30 is inspired by the scene with the Black Knight from *Monty Python and the Holy Grail*.[12]

Example 22-30. blackknight.py

```
class BlackKnight:

    def __init__(self):
        self.phrases = [
            ('an arm', "'Tis but a scratch."),
            ('another arm', "It's just a flesh wound."),
            ('a leg', "I'm invincible!"),
            ('another leg', "All right, we'll call it a draw.")
        ]

    @property
    def member(self):
        print('next member is:')
```

---

12 The bloody scene is available on Youtube (*https://fpy.li/22-17*) as I review this in October 2021.

```
        return self.phrases[0][0]

    @member.deleter
    def member(self):
        member, text = self.phrases.pop(0)
        print(f'BLACK KNIGHT (loses {member}) -- {text}')
```

The doctests in *blackknight.py* are in Example 22-31.

Example 22-31. blackknight.py: doctests for Example 22-30 (the Black Knight never concedes defeat)

```
>>> knight = BlackKnight()
>>> knight.member
next member is:
'an arm'
>>> del knight.member
BLACK KNIGHT (loses an arm) -- 'Tis but a scratch.
>>> del knight.member
BLACK KNIGHT (loses another arm) -- It's just a flesh wound.
>>> del knight.member
BLACK KNIGHT (loses a leg) -- I'm invincible!
>>> del knight.member
BLACK KNIGHT (loses another leg) -- All right, we'll call it a draw.
```

Using the classic call syntax instead of decorators, the fdel argument configures the deleter function. For example, the member property would be coded like this in the body of the BlackKnight class:

```
    member = property(member_getter, fdel=member_deleter)
```

If you are not using a property, attribute deletion can also be handled by implementing the lower-level __delattr__ special method, presented in "Special Methods for Attribute Handling" on page 875. Coding a silly class with __delattr__ is left as an exercise to the procrastinating reader.

Properties are a powerful feature, but sometimes simpler or lower-level alternatives are preferable. In the final section of this chapter, we'll review some of the core APIs that Python offers for dynamic attribute programming.

Essential Attributes and Functions for Attribute Handling

Throughout this chapter, and even before in the book, we've used some of the built-in functions and special methods Python provides for dealing with dynamic attributes. This section gives an overview of them in one place, because their documentation is scattered in the official docs.

Special Attributes that Affect Attribute Handling

The behavior of many of the functions and special methods listed in the following sections depend on three special attributes:

__class__

A reference to the object's class (i.e., obj.__class__ is the same as type(obj)). Python looks for special methods such as __getattr__ only in an object's class, and not in the instances themselves.

__dict__

A mapping that stores the writable attributes of an object or class. An object that has a __dict__ can have arbitrary new attributes set at any time. If a class has a __slots__ attribute, then its instances may not have a __dict__. See __slots__ (next).

__slots__

An attribute that may be defined in a class to save memory. __slots__ is a tuple of strings naming the allowed attributes.[13] If the '__dict__' name is not in __slots__, then the instances of that class will not have a __dict__ of their own, and only the attributes listed in __slots__ will be allowed in those instances. Recall "Saving Memory with __slots__" on page 386 for more.

Built-In Functions for Attribute Handling

These five built-in functions perform object attribute reading, writing, and introspection:

dir([object])

Lists most attributes of the object. The official docs (https://fpy.li/22-18) say dir is intended for interactive use so it does not provide a comprehensive list of attributes, but an "interesting" set of names. dir can inspect objects implemented with or without a __dict__. The __dict__ attribute itself is not listed by dir, but the __dict__ keys are listed. Several special attributes of classes, such as __mro__, __bases__, and __name__, are not listed by dir either. You can customize the output of dir by implementing the __dir__ special method, as we saw in Example 22-4. If the optional object argument is not given, dir lists the names in the current scope.

---

13 Alex Martelli points out that, although __slots__ can be coded as a list, it's better to be explicit and always use a tuple, because changing the list in the __slots__ after the class body is processed has no effect, so it would be misleading to use a mutable sequence there.

`getattr(object, name[, default])`

Gets the attribute identified by the `name` string from the `object`. The main use case is to retrieve attributes (or methods) whose names we don't know beforehand. This may fetch an attribute from the object's class or from a superclass. If no such attribute exists, `getattr` raises `AttributeError` or returns the `default` value, if given. One great example of using `gettatr` is in the `Cmd.onecmd` method (*https://fpy.li/22-19*) in the `cmd` package of the standard library, where it is used to get and execute a user-defined command.

`hasattr(object, name)`

Returns `True` if the named attribute exists in the `object`, or can be somehow fetched through it (by inheritance, for example). The documentation (*https://fpy.li/22-20*) explains: "This is implemented by calling getattr(object, name) and seeing whether it raises an AttributeError or not."

`setattr(object, name, value)`

Assigns the `value` to the named attribute of `object`, if the `object` allows it. This may create a new attribute or overwrite an existing one.

`vars([object])`

Returns the `__dict__` of `object`; `vars` can't deal with instances of classes that define `__slots__` and don't have a `__dict__` (contrast with `dir`, which handles such instances). Without an argument, `vars()` does the same as `locals()`: returns a `dict` representing the local scope.

Special Methods for Attribute Handling

When implemented in a user-defined class, the special methods listed here handle attribute retrieval, setting, deletion, and listing.

Attribute access using either dot notation or the built-in functions `getattr`, `hasattr`, and `setattr` triggers the appropriate special methods listed here. Reading and writing attributes directly in the instance `__dict__` does not trigger these special methods —and that's the usual way to bypass them if needed.

Section "3.3.11. Special method lookup" (*https://fpy.li/22-21*) of the "Data model" chapter warns:

> For custom classes, implicit invocations of special methods are only guaranteed to work correctly if defined on an object's type, not in the object's instance dictionary.

In other words, assume that the special methods will be retrieved on the class itself, even when the target of the action is an instance. For this reason, special methods are not shadowed by instance attributes with the same name.

In the following examples, assume there is a class named Class, obj is an instance of Class, and attr is an attribute of obj.

For every one of these special methods, it doesn't matter if the attribute access is done using dot notation or one of the built-in functions listed in "Built-In Functions for Attribute Handling" on page 874. For example, both obj.attr and getattr(obj, 'attr', 42) trigger Class.__getattribute__(obj, 'attr').

__delattr__(self, name)
    Always called when there is an attempt to delete an attribute using the del statement; e.g., del obj.attr triggers Class.__delattr__(obj, 'attr'). If attr is a property, its deleter method is never called if the class implements __delattr__.

__dir__(self)
    Called when dir is invoked on the object, to provide a listing of attributes; e.g., dir(obj) triggers Class.__dir__(obj). Also used by tab-completion in all modern Python consoles.

__getattr__(self, name)
    Called only when an attempt to retrieve the named attribute fails, after the obj, Class, and its superclasses are searched. The expressions obj.no_such_attr, getattr(obj, 'no_such_attr'), and hasattr(obj, 'no_such_attr') may trigger Class.__getattr__(obj, 'no_such_attr'), but only if an attribute by that name cannot be found in obj or in Class and its superclasses.

__getattribute__(self, name)
    Always called when there is an attempt to retrieve the named attribute directly from Python code (the interpreter may bypass this in some cases, for example, to get the __repr__ method). Dot notation and the getattr and hasattr built-ins trigger this method. __getattr__ is only invoked after __getattribute__, and only when __getattribute__ raises AttributeError. To retrieve attributes of the instance obj without triggering an infinite recursion, implementations of __getattribute__ should use super().__getattribute__(obj, name).

__setattr__(self, name, value)
    Always called when there is an attempt to set the named attribute. Dot notation and the setattr built-in trigger this method; e.g., both obj.attr = 42 and setattr(obj, 'attr', 42) trigger Class.__setattr__(obj, 'attr', 42).

In practice, because they are unconditionally called and affect practically every attribute access, the __getattribute__ and __setattr__ special methods are harder to use correctly than __getattr__, which only handles nonexisting attribute names. Using properties or descriptors is less error prone than defining these special methods.

This concludes our dive into properties, special methods, and other techniques for coding dynamic attributes.

Chapter Summary

We started our coverage of dynamic attributes by showing practical examples of simple classes to make it easier to deal with a JSON dataset. The first example was the FrozenJSON class that converted nested dicts and lists into nested FrozenJSON instances and lists of them. The FrozenJSON code demonstrated the use of the __getattr__ special method to convert data structures on the fly, whenever their attributes were read. The last version of FrozenJSON showcased the use of the __new__ constructor method to transform a class into a flexible factory of objects, not limited to instances of itself.

We then converted the JSON dataset to a dict storing instances of a Record class. The first rendition of Record was a few lines long and introduced the "bunch" idiom: using self.__dict__.update(**kwargs) to build arbitrary attributes from keyword arguments passed to __init__. The second iteration added the Event class, implementing automatic retrieval of linked records through properties. Computed property values sometimes require caching, and we covered a few ways of doing that.

After realizing that @functools.cached_property is not always applicable, we learned about an alternative: combining @property on top of @functools.cache, in that order.

Coverage of properties continued with the LineItem class, where a property was deployed to protect a weight attribute from negative or zero values that make no business sense. After a deeper look at property syntax and semantics, we created a property factory to enforce the same validation on weight and price, without coding multiple getters and setters. The property factory leveraged subtle concepts—such as closures, and instance attribute overriding by properties—to provide an elegant generic solution using the same number of lines as a single hand-coded property definition.

Finally, we had a brief look at handling attribute deletion with properties, followed by an overview of the key special attributes, built-in functions, and special methods that support attribute metaprogramming in the core Python language.

Further Reading

The official documentation for the attribute handling and introspection built-in functions is Chapter 2, "Built-in Functions" (*https://fpy.li/22-22*) of *The Python Standard Library*. The related special methods and the __slots__ special attribute are documented in *The Python Language Reference* in "3.3.2. Customizing attribute access" (*https://fpy.li/22-23*). The semantics of how special methods are invoked bypassing instances is explained in "3.3.9. Special method lookup" (*https://fpy.li/22-24*). In Chapter 4, "Built-in Types," of *The Python Standard Library*, "4.13. Special Attributes" (*https://fpy.li/22-25*) covers __class__ and __dict__ attributes.

Python Cookbook, 3rd ed., by David Beazley and Brian K. Jones (O'Reilly) has several recipes covering the topics of this chapter, but I will highlight three that are outstanding: "Recipe 8.8. Extending a Property in a Subclass" addresses the thorny issue of overriding the methods inside a property inherited from a superclass; "Recipe 8.15. Delegating Attribute Access" implements a proxy class showcasing most special methods from "Special Methods for Attribute Handling" on page 875 in this book; and the awesome "Recipe 9.21. Avoiding Repetitive Property Methods," which was the basis for the property factory function presented in Example 22-28.

Python in a Nutshell, 3rd ed., by Alex Martelli, Anna Ravenscroft, and Steve Holden (O'Reilly) is rigorous and objective. They devote only three pages to properties, but that's because the book follows an axiomatic presentation style: the preceding 15 pages or so provide a thorough description of the semantics of Python classes from the ground up, including descriptors, which are how properties are actually implemented under the hood. So by the time Martelli et al., get to properties, they pack a lot of insights in those three pages—including what I selected to open this chapter.

Bertrand Meyer—quoted in the Uniform Access Principle definition in this chapter opening—pioneered the Design by Contract methodology, designed the Eiffel language, and wrote the excellent *Object-Oriented Software Construction*, 2nd ed. (Pearson). The first six chapters provide one of the best conceptual introductions to OO analysis and design I've seen. Chapter 11 presents Design by Contract, and Chapter 35 offers Meyer's assessments of some influential object-oriented languages: Simula, Smalltalk, CLOS (the Common Lisp Object System), Objective-C, C++, and Java, with brief comments on some others. Only in the last page of the book does he reveal that the highly readable "notation" he uses as pseudocode is Eiffel.

Soapbox

Meyer's Uniform Access Principle is aesthetically appealing. As a programmer using an API, I shouldn't have to care whether `product.price` simply fetches a data attribute or performs a computation. As a consumer and a citizen, I do care: in e-commerce today the value of `product.price` often depends on who is asking, so it's certainly not a mere data attribute. In fact, it's common practice that the price is lower if the query comes from outside the store—say, from a price-comparison engine. This effectively punishes loyal customers who like to browse within a particular store. But I digress.

The previous digression does raise a relevant point for programming: although the Uniform Access Principle makes perfect sense in an ideal world, in reality, users of an API may need to know whether reading `product.price` is potentially too expensive or time-consuming. That's a problem with programming abstractions in general: they make it hard to reason about the runtime cost of evaluating an expression. On the other hand, abstractions let users accomplish more with less code. It's a trade-off. As usual in matters of software engineering, Ward Cunningham's original wiki (*https:// fpy.li/22-26*) hosts insightful arguments about the merits of the Uniform Access Principle (*https://fpy.li/22-27*).

In object-oriented programming languages, application or violations of the Uniform Access Principle often revolve around the syntax of reading public data attributes versus invoking getter/setter methods.

Smalltalk and Ruby address this issue in a simple and elegant way: they don't support public data attributes at all. Every instance attribute in these languages is private, so every access to them must be through methods. But their syntax makes this painless: in Ruby, `product.price` invokes the `price` getter; in Smalltalk, it's simply `product price`.

At the other end of the spectrum, the Java language allows the programmer to choose among four access-level modifiers—including the no-name default that the Java Tutorial (*https://fpy.li/22-28*) calls "package-private."

The general practice does not agree with the syntax established by the Java designers, though. Everybody in Java-land agrees that attributes should be `private`, and you must spell it out every time, because it's not the default. When all attributes are private, all access to them from outside the class must go through accessors. Java IDEs include shortcuts for generating accessor methods automatically. Unfortunately, the IDE is not so helpful when you must read the code six months later. It's up to you to wade through a sea of do-nothing accessors to find those that add value by implementing some business logic.

Alex Martelli speaks for the majority of the Python community when he calls accessors "goofy idioms" and then provides these examples that look very different but do the same thing:[14]

```
someInstance.widgetCounter += 1
# rather than...
someInstance.setWidgetCounter(someInstance.getWidgetCounter() + 1)
```

Sometimes when designing APIs, I've wondered whether every method that does not take an argument (besides `self`), returns a value (other than `None`), and is a pure function (i.e., has no side effects) should be replaced by a read-only property. In this chapter, the `LineItem.subtotal` method (as in Example 22-27) would be a good candidate to become a read-only property. Of course, this excludes methods that are designed to change the object, such as `my_list.clear()`. It would be a terrible idea to turn that into a property, so that merely accessing `my_list.clear` would delete the contents of the list!

In the *Pingo* (*https://fpy.li/22-29*) GPIO library, which I coauthored (mentioned in "The __missing__ Method" on page 91), much of the user-level API is based on properties. For example, to read the current value of an analog pin, the user writes `pin.value`, and setting a digital pin mode is written as `pin.mode = OUT`. Behind the scenes, reading an analog pin value or setting a digital pin mode may involve a lot of code, depending on the specific board driver. We decided to use properties in Pingo because we want the API to be comfortable to use even in interactive environments like a Jupyter Notebook, and we feel `pin.mode = OUT` is easier on the eyes and on the fingers than `pin.set_mode(OUT)`.

Although I find the Smalltalk and Ruby solution cleaner, I think the Python approach makes more sense than the Java one. We are allowed to start simple, coding data members as public attributes, because we know they can always be wrapped by properties (or descriptors, which we'll talk about in the next chapter).

__new__ Is Better than new

Another example of the Uniform Access Principle (or a variation of it) is the fact that function calls and object instantiation use the same syntax in Python: `my_obj = foo()`, where `foo` may be a class or any other callable.

Other languages influenced by C++ syntax have a `new` operator that makes instantiation look different than a call. Most of the time, the user of an API doesn't care whether `foo` is a function or a class. For years I was under the impression that `property` was a function. In normal usage, it makes no difference.

---

14 Alex Martelli, *Python in a Nutshell*, 2nd ed. (O'Reilly), p. 101.

There are many good reasons for replacing constructors with factories.[15] A popular motive is limiting the number of instances by returning previously built ones (as in the Singleton pattern). A related use is caching expensive object construction. Also, sometimes it's convenient to return objects of different types, depending on the arguments given.

Coding a constructor is simpler; providing a factory adds flexibility at the expense of more code. In languages that have a new operator, the designer of an API must decide in advance whether to stick with a simple constructor or invest in a factory. If the initial choice is wrong, the correction may be costly—all because new is an operator.

Sometimes it may also be convenient to go the other way, and replace a simple function with a class.

In Python, classes and functions are interchangeable in many situations. Not only because there's no new operator, but also because there is the __new__ special method, which can turn a class into a factory producing objects of different kinds (as we saw in "Flexible Object Creation with __new__" on page 847) or returning prebuilt instances instead of creating a new one every time.

This function-class duality would be easier to leverage if PEP 8 — Style Guide for Python Code (*https://fpy.li/22-31*) did not recommend CamelCase for class names. On the other hand, dozens of classes in the standard library have lowercase names (e.g., property, str, defaultdict, etc.). So maybe the use of lowercase class names is a feature, and not a bug. But however we look at it, the inconsistent capitalization of classes in the Python standard library poses a usability problem.

Although calling a function is not different from calling a class, it's good to know which is which because of another thing we can do with a class: subclassing. So I personally use CamelCase in every class that I code, and I wish all classes in the Python standard library used the same convention. I am looking at you, collections.Order edDict and collections.defaultdict.

---

15 The reasons I am about to mention are given in the Dr. Dobbs Journal article titled "Java's new Considered Harmful" (*https://fpy.li/22-30*), by Jonathan Amsterdam and in "Consider static factory methods instead of constructors," which is Item 1 of the award-winning book *Effective Java*, 3rd ed., by Joshua Bloch (Addison-Wesley).

## CHAPTER 23

Attribute Descriptors

> Learning about descriptors not only provides access to a larger toolset, it creates a deeper understanding of how Python works and an appreciation for the elegance of its design.
>
> — Raymond Hettinger, Python core developer and guru[1]

Descriptors are a way of reusing the same access logic in multiple attributes. For example, field types in ORMs, such as the Django ORM and SQLAlchemy, are descriptors, managing the flow of data from the fields in a database record to Python object attributes and vice versa.

A descriptor is a class that implements a dynamic protocol consisting of the __get__, __set__, and __delete__ methods. The property class implements the full descriptor protocol. As usual with dynamic protocols, partial implementations are OK. In fact, most descriptors we see in real code implement only __get__ and __set__, and many implement only one of these methods.

Descriptors are a distinguishing feature of Python, deployed not only at the application level but also in the language infrastructure. User-defined functions are descriptors. We'll see how the descriptor protocol allows methods to operate as bound or unbound methods, depending on how they are called.

Understanding descriptors is key to Python mastery. This is what this chapter is about.

In this chapter we'll refactor the bulk food example we first saw in "Using a Property for Attribute Validation" on page 861, replacing properties with descriptors. This will make it easier to reuse the attribute validation logic across different classes. We'll

---

1 Raymond Hettinger, *Descriptor HowTo Guide* (*https://fpy.li/descrhow*).

tackle the concepts of overriding and nonoverriding descriptors, and realize that Python functions are descriptors. Finally we'll see some tips about implementing descriptors.

What's New in This Chapter

The Quantity descriptor example in "LineItem Take #4: Automatic Naming of Storage Attributes" on page 891 was dramatically simplified thanks to the __set_name__ special method added to the descriptor protocol in Python 3.6.

I removed the property factory example formerly in "LineItem Take #4: Automatic Naming of Storage Attributes" on page 891 because it became irrelevant: the point was to show an alternative way of solving the Quantity problem, but with the addition of __set_name__, the descriptor solution becomes much simpler.

The AutoStorage class that used to appear in "LineItem Take #5: A New Descriptor Type" on page 893 is also gone because __set_name__ made it obsolete.

Descriptor Example: Attribute Validation

As we saw in "Coding a Property Factory" on page 869, a property factory is a way to avoid repetitive coding of getters and setters by applying functional programming patterns. A property factory is a higher-order function that creates a parameterized set of accessor functions and builds a custom property instance from them, with closures to hold settings like the storage_name. The object-oriented way of solving the same problem is a descriptor class.

We'll continue the series of LineItem examples where we left off, in "Coding a Property Factory" on page 869, by refactoring the quantity property factory into a Quantity descriptor class. This will make it easier to use.

LineItem Take #3: A Simple Descriptor

As we said in the introduction, a class implementing a __get__, a __set__, or a __delete__ method is a descriptor. You use a descriptor by declaring instances of it as class attributes of another class.

We'll create a Quantity descriptor, and the LineItem class will use two instances of Quantity: one for managing the weight attribute, the other for price. A diagram helps, so take a look at Figure 23-1.

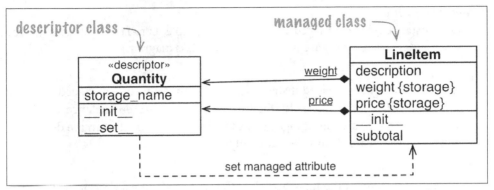

*Figure 23-1. UML class diagram for LineItem using a descriptor class named Quan
tity. Underlined attributes in UML are class attributes. Note that weight and price are
instances of Quantity attached to the LineItem class, but LineItem instances also have
their own weight and price attributes where those values are stored.*

Note that the word weight appears twice in Figure 23-1, because there are really two
distinct attributes named weight: one is a class attribute of LineItem, the other is an
instance attribute that will exist in each LineItem object. This also applies to price.

Terms to understand descriptors

Implementing and using descriptors involves several components, and it is useful to
be precise when naming those components. I will use the following terms and definitions as I describe the examples in this chapter. They will be easier to understand
once you see the code, but I wanted to put the definitions up front so you can refer
back to them when needed.

Descriptor class
  A class implementing the descriptor protocol. That's Quantity in Figure 23-1.

Managed class
  The class where the descriptor instances are declared as class attributes. In
  Figure 23-1, LineItem is the managed class.

Descriptor instance
  Each instance of a descriptor class, declared as a class attribute of the managed
  class. In Figure 23-1, each descriptor instance is represented by a composition
  arrow with an underlined name (the underline means class attribute in UML).
  The black diamonds touch the LineItem class, which contains the descriptor
  instances.

Managed instance

>One instance of the managed class. In this example, `LineItem` instances are the managed instances (they are not shown in the class diagram).

Storage attribute

>An attribute of the managed instance that holds the value of a managed attribute for that particular instance. In Figure 23-1, the `LineItem` instance attributes `weight` and `price` are the storage attributes. They are distinct from the descriptor instances, which are always class attributes.

Managed attribute

>A public attribute in the managed class that is handled by a descriptor instance, with values stored in storage attributes. In other words, a descriptor instance and a storage attribute provide the infrastructure for a managed attribute.

It's important to realize that `Quantity` instances are class attributes of `LineItem`. This crucial point is highlighted by the mills and gizmos in Figure 23-2.

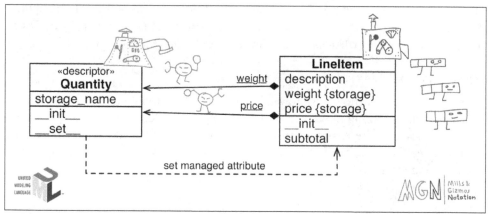

Figure 23-2. UML class diagram annotated with MGN (Mills & Gizmos Notation): classes are mills that produce gizmos—the instances. The `Quantity` mill produces two gizmos with round heads, which are attached to the `LineItem` mill: weight and price. The `LineItem` mill produces rectangular gizmos that have their own weight and price attributes where those values are stored.

Introducing Mills & Gizmos Notation

After explaining descriptors many times, I realized UML is not very good at showing relationships involving classes and instances, like the relationship between a managed class and the descriptor instances.[2] So I invented my own "language," the Mills & Gizmos Notation (MGN), which I use to annotate UML diagrams.

MGN is designed to make very clear the distinction between classes and instances. See Figure 23-3. In MGN, a class is drawn as a "mill," a complicated machine that produces gizmos. Classes/mills are always machines with levers and dials. The gizmos are the instances, and they look much simpler. When this book is rendered in color, gizmos have the same color as the mill that made it.

Figure 23-3. MGN sketch showing the LineItem class making three instances, and Quantity making two. One instance of Quantity is retrieving a value stored in a LineItem instance.

For this example, I drew LineItem instances as rows in a tabular invoice, with three cells representing the three attributes (description, weight, and price). Because Quantity instances are descriptors, they have a magnifying glass to __get__ values, and a claw to __set__ values. When we get to metaclasses, you'll thank me for these doodles.

Enough doodling for now. Here is the code: Example 23-1 shows the Quantity descriptor class, and Example 23-2 lists a new LineItem class using two instances of Quantity.

---

2 Classes and instances are drawn as rectangles in UML class diagrams. There are visual differences, but instances are rarely shown in class diagrams, so developers may not recognize them as such.

Example 23-1. bulkfood_v3.py: Quantity descriptor does not accept negative values

```
class Quantity:  ❶

    def __init__(self, storage_name):
        self.storage_name = storage_name  ❷

    def __set__(self, instance, value):  ❸
        if value > 0:
            instance.__dict__[self.storage_name] = value  ❹
        else:
            msg = f'{self.storage_name} must be > 0'
            raise ValueError(msg)

    def __get__(self, instance, owner):  ❺
        return instance.__dict__[self.storage_name]
```

❶ Descriptor is a protocol-based feature; no subclassing is needed to implement one.

❷ Each Quantity instance will have a storage_name attribute: that's the name of the storage attribute to hold the value in the managed instances.

❸ __set__ is called when there is an attempt to assign to the managed attribute. Here, self is the descriptor instance (i.e., LineItem.weight or LineItem.price), instance is the managed instance (a LineItem instance), and value is the value being assigned.

❹ We must store the attribute value directly into __dict__; calling set attr (instance, self.storage_name) would trigger the __set__ method again, leading to infinite recursion.

❺ We need to implement __get__ because the name of the managed attribute may not be the same as the storage_name. The owner argument will be explained shortly.

Implementing __get__ is necessary because a user could write something like this:

```
class House:
    rooms = Quantity('number_of_rooms')
```

In the House class, the managed attribute is rooms, but the storage attribute is number_of_rooms. Given a House instance named chaos_manor, reading and writing chaos_manor.rooms goes through the Quantity descriptor instance attached to rooms, but reading and writing chaos_manor.number_of_rooms bypasses the descriptor.

Note that __get__ receives three arguments: self, instance, and owner. The owner argument is a reference to the managed class (e.g., LineItem), and it's useful if you want the descriptor to support retrieving a class attribute—perhaps to emulate Python's default behavior of retrieving a class attribute when the name is not found in the instance.

If a managed attribute, such as weight, is retrieved via the class like Line Item.weight, the descriptor __get__ method receives None as the value for the instance argument.

To support introspection and other metaprogramming tricks by the user, it's a good practice to make __get__ return the descriptor instance when the managed attribute is accessed through the class. To do that, we'd code __get__ like this:

```python
def __get__(self, instance, owner):
    if instance is None:
        return self
    else:
        return instance.__dict__[self.storage_name]
```

Example 23-2 demonstrates the use of Quantity in LineItem.

Example 23-2. bulkfood_v3.py: Quantity descriptors manage attributes in LineItem

```python
class LineItem:
    weight = Quantity('weight')   ❶
    price = Quantity('price')   ❷

    def __init__(self, description, weight, price):   ❸
        self.description = description
        self.weight = weight
        self.price = price

    def subtotal(self):
        return self.weight * self.price
```

❶ The first descriptor instance will manage the weight attribute.

❷ The second descriptor instance will manage the price attribute.

❸ The rest of the class body is as simple and clean as the original code in *bulk-food_v1.py* (Example 22-19).

The code in Example 23-2 works as intended, preventing the sale of truffles for $0:[3]

```
>>> truffle = LineItem('White truffle', 100, 0)
Traceback (most recent call last):
  ...
ValueError: value must be > 0
```

 When coding descriptor __get__ and __set__ methods, keep in mind what the self and instance arguments mean: self is the descriptor instance, and instance is the managed instance. Descriptors managing instance attributes should store values in the managed instances. That's why Python provides the instance argument to the descriptor methods.

It may be tempting, but wrong, to store the value of each managed attribute in the descriptor instance itself. In other words, in the __set__ method, instead of coding:

```
instance.__dict__[self.storage_name] = value
```

the tempting, but bad, alternative would be:

```
self.__dict__[self.storage_name] = value
```

To understand why this would be wrong, think about the meaning of the first two arguments to __set__: self and instance. Here, self is the descriptor instance, which is actually a class attribute of the managed class. You may have thousands of LineItem instances in memory at one time, but you'll only have two instances of the descriptors: the class attributes LineItem.weight and LineItem.price. So anything you store in the descriptor instances themselves is actually part of a LineItem class attribute, and therefore is shared among all LineItem instances.

A drawback of Example 23-2 is the need to repeat the names of the attributes when the descriptors are instantiated in the managed class body. It would be nice if the LineItem class could be declared like this:

```
class LineItem:
    weight = Quantity()
    price = Quantity()

    # remaining methods as before
```

As it stands, Example 23-2 requires naming each Quantity explicitly, which is not only inconvenient but dangerous. If a programmer copying and pasting code forgets to edit both names and writes something like price = Quantity('weight'), the

---

3 White truffles cost thousands of dollars per pound. Disallowing the sale of truffles for $0.01 is left as an exercise for the enterprising reader. I know a person who actually bought an $1,800 encyclopedia of statistics for $18 because of an error in an online store (not *Amazon.com* in this case).

program will misbehave badly, clobbering the value of weight whenever the price is set.

The problem is that—as we saw in Chapter 6—the righthand side of an assignment is executed before the variable exists. The expression Quantity() is evaluated to create a descriptor instance, and there is no way the code in the Quantity class can guess the name of the variable to which the descriptor will be bound (e.g., weight or price).

Thankfully, the descriptor protocol now supports the aptly named __set_name__ special method. We'll see how to use it next.

 Automatic naming of a descriptor storage attribute used to be a thorny issue. In the first edition of *Fluent Python*, I devoted several pages and lines of code in this chapter and the next to presenting different solutions, including the use of a class decorator, and then metaclasses in Chapter 24. This was greatly simplified in Python 3.6.

LineItem Take #4: Automatic Naming of Storage Attributes

To avoid retyping the attribute name in the descriptor instances, we'll implement __set_name__ to set the storage_name of each Quantity instance. The __set_name__ special method was added to the descriptor protocol in Python 3.6. The interpreter calls __set_name__ on each descriptor it finds in a class body—if the descriptor implements it.[4]

In Example 23-3, the LineItem descriptor class doesn't need an __init__. Instead, __set_item__ saves the name of the storage attribute.

Example 23-3. bulkfood_v4.py: __set_name__ sets the name for each Quantity descriptor instance

```
class Quantity:

    def __set_name__(self, owner, name):    ❶
        self.storage_name = name            ❷

    def __set__(self, instance, value):     ❸
        if value > 0:
            instance.__dict__[self.storage_name] = value
```

---

4 More precisely, __set_name__ is called by type.__new__—the constructor of objects representing classes. The type built-in is actually a metaclass, the default class of user-defined classes. This is hard to grasp at first, but rest assured: Chapter 24 is devoted to the dynamic configuration of classes, including the concept of metaclasses.

```
            else:
                msg = f'{self.storage_name} must be > 0'
                raise ValueError(msg)

        # no __get__ needed  ❹

class LineItem:
    weight = Quantity()  ❺
    price = Quantity()

    def __init__(self, description, weight, price):
        self.description = description
        self.weight = weight
        self.price = price

    def subtotal(self):
        return self.weight * self.price
```

❶ `self` is the descriptor instance (not the managed instance), `owner` is the managed class, and `name` is the name of the attribute of `owner` to which this descriptor instance was assigned in the class body of `owner`.

❷ This is what the `__init__` did in Example 23-1.

❸ The `__set__` method here is exactly the same as in Example 23-1.

❹ Implementing `__get__` is not necessary because the name of the storage attribute matches the name of the managed attribute. The expression `product.price` gets the `price` attribute directly from the `LineItem` instance.

❺ Now we don't need to pass the managed attribute name to the `Quantity` constructor. That was the goal for this version.

Looking at Example 23-3, you may think that's a lot of code just for managing a couple of attributes, but it's important to realize that the descriptor logic is now abstracted into a separate code unit: the `Quantity` class. Usually we do not define a descriptor in the same module where it's used, but in a separate utility module designed to be used across the application—even in many applications, if you are developing a library or framework.

With this in mind, Example 23-4 better represents the typical usage of a descriptor.

Example 23-4. bulkfood_v4c.py: `LineItem` definition uncluttered; the `Quantity` descriptor class now resides in the imported `model_v4c` module

```
import model_v4c as model  ❶
```

```
class LineItem:
    weight = model.Quantity()  ❷
    price = model.Quantity()

    def __init__(self, description, weight, price):
        self.description = description
        self.weight = weight
        self.price = price

    def subtotal(self):
        return self.weight * self.price
```

❶   Import the model_v4c module where Quantity is implemented.

❷   Put model.Quantity to use.

Django users will notice that Example 23-4 looks a lot like a model definition. It's no coincidence: Django model fields are descriptors.

Because descriptors are implemented as classes, we can leverage inheritance to reuse some of the code we have for new descriptors. That's what we'll do in the following section.

LineItem Take #5: A New Descriptor Type

The imaginary organic food store hits a snag: somehow a line item instance was created with a blank description, and the order could not be fulfilled. To prevent that, we'll create a new descriptor, NonBlank. As we design NonBlank, we realize it will be very much like the Quantity descriptor, except for the validation logic.

This prompts a refactoring, producing Validated, an abstract class that overrides the __set__ method, calling a validate method that must be implemented by subclasses.

We'll then rewrite Quantity, and implement NonBlank by inheriting from Validated and just coding the validate methods.

The relationship among Validated, Quantity, and NonBlank is an application of the *template method* as described in the *Design Patterns* classic:

> A template method defines an algorithm in terms of abstract operations that subclasses override to provide concrete behavior.[5]

---

5 Gamma et al., *Design Patterns: Elements of Reusable Object-Oriented Software*, p. 326.

In Example 23-5, `Validated.__set__` is the template method and `self.validate` is the abstract operation.

Example 23-5. model_v5.py: the Validated ABC

```
import abc

class Validated(abc.ABC):

    def __set_name__(self, owner, name):
        self.storage_name = name

    def __set__(self, instance, value):
        value = self.validate(self.storage_name, value)  ❶
        instance.__dict__[self.storage_name] = value      ❷

    @abc.abstractmethod
    def validate(self, name, value):  ❸
        """return validated value or raise ValueError"""
```

❶ `__set__` delegates validation to the `validate` method…

❷ …then uses the returned `value` to update the stored value.

❸ `validate` is an abstract method; this is the template method.

Alex Martelli prefers to call this design pattern *Self-Delegation*, and I agree it's a more descriptive name: the first line of `__set__` self-delegates to `validate`.[6]

The concrete `Validated` subclasses in this example are `Quantity` and `NonBlank`, shown in Example 23-6.

Example 23-6. model_v5.py: Quantity and NonBlank, concrete Validated subclasses

```
class Quantity(Validated):
    """a number greater than zero"""

    def validate(self, name, value):  ❶
        if value <= 0:
            raise ValueError(f'{name} must be > 0')
        return value


class NonBlank(Validated):
    """a string with at least one non-space character"""
```

---

6 Slide #50 of Alex Martelli's "Python Design Patterns" talk (*https://fpy.li/23-1*). Highly recommended.

```
def validate(self, name, value):
    value = value.strip()
    if not value:  ❷
        raise ValueError(f'{name} cannot be blank')
    return value  ❸
```

❶ Implementation of the template method required by the Validated.validate abstract method.

❷ If nothing is left after leading and trailing blanks are stripped, reject the value.

❸ Requiring the concrete validate methods to return the validated value gives them an opportunity to clean up, convert, or normalize the data received. In this case, value is returned without leading or trailing blanks.

Users of *model_v5.py* don't need to know all these details. What matters is that they get to use Quantity and NonBlank to automate the validation of instance attributes. See the latest LineItem class in Example 23-7.

Example 23-7. bulkfood_v5.py: LineItem using Quantity and NonBlank descriptors

```
import model_v5 as model  ❶

class LineItem:
    description = model.NonBlank()  ❷
    weight = model.Quantity()
    price = model.Quantity()

    def __init__(self, description, weight, price):
        self.description = description
        self.weight = weight
        self.price = price

    def subtotal(self):
        return self.weight * self.price
```

❶ Import the model_v5 module, giving it a friendlier name.

❷ Put model.NonBlank to use. The rest of the code is unchanged.

The LineItem examples we've seen in this chapter demonstrate a typical use of descriptors to manage data attributes. Descriptors like Quantity are called overriding descriptors because its __set__ method overrides (i.e., intercepts and overrules) the setting of an instance attribute by the same name in the managed instance. However, there are also nonoverriding descriptors. We'll explore this distinction in detail in the next section.

Overriding Versus Nonoverriding Descriptors

Recall that there is an important asymmetry in the way Python handles attributes. Reading an attribute through an instance normally returns the attribute defined in the instance, but if there is no such attribute in the instance, a class attribute will be retrieved. On the other hand, assigning to an attribute in an instance normally creates the attribute in the instance, without affecting the class at all.

This asymmetry also affects descriptors, in effect creating two broad categories of descriptors, depending on whether the __set__ method is implemented. If __set__ is present, the class is an overriding descriptor; otherwise, it is a nonoverriding descriptor. These terms will make sense as we study descriptor behaviors in the next examples.

Observing the different descriptor categories requires a few classes, so we'll use the code in Example 23-8 as our test bed for the following sections.

 Every __get__ and __set__ method in Example 23-8 calls print_args so their invocations are displayed in a readable way. Understanding print_args and the auxiliary functions cls_name and display is not important, so don't get distracted by them.

Example 23-8. descriptorkinds.py: simple classes for studying descriptor overriding behaviors

```
### auxiliary functions for display only ###

def cls_name(obj_or_cls):
    cls = type(obj_or_cls)
    if cls is type:
        cls = obj_or_cls
    return cls.__name__.split('.')[-1]

def display(obj):
    cls = type(obj)
    if cls is type:
        return f'<class {obj.__name__}>'
    elif cls in [type(None), int]:
        return repr(obj)
    else:
        return f'<{cls_name(obj)} object>'

def print_args(name, *args):
    pseudo_args = ', '.join(display(x) for x in args)
    print(f'-> {cls_name(args[0])}.__{name}__({pseudo_args})')


### essential classes for this example ###
```

```
class Overriding:    ❶
    """a.k.a. data descriptor or enforced descriptor"""

    def __get__(self, instance, owner):
        print_args('get', self, instance, owner)    ❷

    def __set__(self, instance, value):
        print_args('set', self, instance, value)

class OverridingNoGet:    ❸
    """an overriding descriptor without ``__get__``"""

    def __set__(self, instance, value):
        print_args('set', self, instance, value)

class NonOverriding:    ❹
    """a.k.a. non-data or shadowable descriptor"""

    def __get__(self, instance, owner):
        print_args('get', self, instance, owner)

class Managed:    ❺
    over = Overriding()
    over_no_get = OverridingNoGet()
    non_over = NonOverriding()

    def spam(self):    ❻
        print(f'-> Managed.spam({display(self)})')
```

❶ An overriding descriptor class with __get__ and __set__.

❷ The print_args function is called by every descriptor method in this example.

❸ An overriding descriptor without a __get__ method.

❹ No __set__ method here, so this is a nonoverriding descriptor.

❺ The managed class, using one instance of each of the descriptor classes.

❻ The spam method is here for comparison, because methods are also descriptors.

In the following sections, we will examine the behavior of attribute reads and writes on the Managed class, and one instance of it, going through each of the different descriptors defined.

Overriding Descriptors

A descriptor that implements the __set__ method is an *overriding descriptor*, because although it is a class attribute, a descriptor implementing __set__ will override attempts to assign to instance attributes. This is how Example 23-3 was implemented. Properties are also overriding descriptors: if you don't provide a setter function, the default __set__ from the property class will raise AttributeError to signal that the attribute is read-only. Given the code in Example 23-8, experiments with an overriding descriptor can be seen in Example 23-9.

 Python contributors and authors use different terms when discussing these concepts. I adopted "overriding descriptor" from the book *Python in a Nutshell*. The official Python documentation uses "data descriptor," but "overriding descriptor" highlights the special behavior. Overriding descriptors are also called "enforced descriptors." Synonyms for nonoverriding descriptors include "nondata descriptors" or "shadowable descriptors."

Example 23-9. Behavior of an overriding descriptor

```
>>> obj = Managed()  ❶
>>> obj.over  ❷
-> Overriding.__get__(<Overriding object>, <Managed object>, <class Managed>)
>>> Managed.over  ❸
-> Overriding.__get__(<Overriding object>, None, <class Managed>)
>>> obj.over = 7  ❹
-> Overriding.__set__(<Overriding object>, <Managed object>, 7)
>>> obj.over  ❺
-> Overriding.__get__(<Overriding object>, <Managed object>, <class Managed>)
>>> obj.__dict__['over'] = 8  ❻
>>> vars(obj)  ❼
{'over': 8}
>>> obj.over  ❽
-> Overriding.__get__(<Overriding object>, <Managed object>, <class Managed>)
```

❶ Create Managed object for testing.

❷ obj.over triggers the descriptor __get__ method, passing the managed instance obj as the second argument.

❸ Managed.over triggers the descriptor __get__ method, passing None as the second argument (instance).

❹ Assigning to obj.over triggers the descriptor __set__ method, passing the value 7 as the last argument.

❺ Reading `obj.over` still invokes the descriptor `__get__` method.

❻ Bypassing the descriptor, setting a value directly to the `obj.__dict__`.

❼ Verify that the value is in the `obj.__dict__`, under the `over` key.

❽ However, even with an instance attribute named `over`, the `Managed.over` descriptor still overrides attempts to read `obj.over`.

Overriding Descriptor Without __get__

Properties and other overriding descriptors, such as Django model fields, implement both `__set__` and `__get__`, but it's also possible to implement only `__set__`, as we saw in Example 23-2. In this case, only writing is handled by the descriptor. Reading the descriptor through an instance will return the descriptor object itself because there is no `__get__` to handle that access. If a namesake instance attribute is created with a new value via direct access to the instance `__dict__`, the `__set__` method will still override further attempts to set that attribute, but reading that attribute will simply return the new value from the instance, instead of returning the descriptor object. In other words, the instance attribute will shadow the descriptor, but only when reading. See Example 23-10.

Example 23-10. Overriding descriptor without __get__

```
>>> obj.over_no_get   ❶
<__main__.OverridingNoGet object at 0x665bcc>
>>> Managed.over_no_get   ❷
<__main__.OverridingNoGet object at 0x665bcc>
>>> obj.over_no_get = 7   ❸
-> OverridingNoGet.__set__(<OverridingNoGet object>, <Managed object>, 7)
>>> obj.over_no_get   ❹
<__main__.OverridingNoGet object at 0x665bcc>
>>> obj.__dict__['over_no_get'] = 9   ❺
>>> obj.over_no_get   ❻
9
>>> obj.over_no_get = 7   ❼
-> OverridingNoGet.__set__(<OverridingNoGet object>, <Managed object>, 7)
>>> obj.over_no_get   ❽
9
```

❶ This overriding descriptor doesn't have a `__get__` method, so reading `obj.over_no_get` retrieves the descriptor instance from the class.

❷ The same thing happens if we retrieve the descriptor instance directly from the managed class.

❸ Trying to set a value to `obj.over_no_get` invokes the `__set__` descriptor method.

❹ Because our `__set__` doesn't make changes, reading `obj.over_no_get` again retrieves the descriptor instance from the managed class.

❺ Going through the instance `__dict__` to set an instance attribute named `over_no_get`.

❻ Now that `over_no_get` instance attribute shadows the descriptor, but only for reading.

❼ Trying to assign a value to `obj.over_no_get` still goes through the descriptor set.

❽ But for reading, that descriptor is shadowed as long as there is a namesake instance attribute.

Nonoverriding Descriptor

A descriptor that does not implement `__set__` is a nonoverriding descriptor. Setting an instance attribute with the same name will shadow the descriptor, rendering it ineffective for handling that attribute in that specific instance. Methods and `@functools.cached_property` are implemented as nonoverriding descriptors. Example 23-11 shows the operation of a nonoverriding descriptor.

Example 23-11. Behavior of a nonoverriding descriptor

```
>>> obj = Managed()
>>> obj.non_over   ❶
-> NonOverriding.__get__(<NonOverriding object>, <Managed object>, <class Managed>)
>>> obj.non_over = 7   ❷
>>> obj.non_over   ❸
7
>>> Managed.non_over   ❹
-> NonOverriding.__get__(<NonOverriding object>, None, <class Managed>)
>>> del obj.non_over   ❺
>>> obj.non_over   ❻
-> NonOverriding.__get__(<NonOverriding object>, <Managed object>, <class Managed>)
```

❶ `obj.non_over` triggers the descriptor `__get__` method, passing `obj` as the second argument.

❷ `Managed.non_over` is a nonoverriding descriptor, so there is no `__set__` to interfere with this assignment.

❸ The `obj` now has an instance attribute named `non_over`, which shadows the namesake descriptor attribute in the `Managed` class.

❹ The `Managed.non_over` descriptor is still there, and catches this access via the class.

❺ If the `non_over` instance attribute is deleted…

❻ …then reading `obj.non_over` hits the `__get__` method of the descriptor in the class, but note that the second argument is the managed instance.

In the previous examples, we saw several assignments to an instance attribute with the same name as a descriptor, and different results according to the presence of a `__set__` method in the descriptor.

The setting of attributes in the class cannot be controlled by descriptors attached to the same class. In particular, this means that the descriptor attributes themselves can be clobbered by assigning to the class, as the next section explains.

Overwriting a Descriptor in the Class

Regardless of whether a descriptor is overriding or not, it can be overwritten by assignment to the class. This is a monkey-patching technique, but in Example 23-12 the descriptors are replaced by integers, which would effectively break any class that depended on the descriptors for proper operation.

Example 23-12. Any descriptor can be overwritten on the class itself

```
>>> obj = Managed()  ❶
>>> Managed.over = 1  ❷
>>> Managed.over_no_get = 2
>>> Managed.non_over = 3
>>> obj.over, obj.over_no_get, obj.non_over  ❸
(1, 2, 3)
```

❶ Create a new instance for later testing.

❷ Overwrite the descriptor attributes in the class.

❸ The descriptors are really gone.

Example 23-12 reveals another asymmetry regarding reading and writing attributes: although the reading of a class attribute can be controlled by a descriptor with `__get__` attached to the managed class, the writing of a class attribute cannot be handled by a descriptor with `__set__` attached to the same class.

In order to control the setting of attributes in a class, you have to attach descriptors to the class of the class—in other words, the metaclass. By default, the metaclass of user-defined classes is `type`, and you cannot add attributes to `type`. But in Chapter 24, we'll create our own metaclasses.

Let's now focus on how descriptors are used to implement methods in Python.

Methods Are Descriptors

A function within a class becomes a bound method when invoked on an instance because all user-defined functions have a __get__ method, therefore they operate as descriptors when attached to a class. Example 23-13 demonstrates reading the `spam` method from the `Managed` class introduced in Example 23-8.

Example 23-13. A method is a nonoverriding descriptor

```
>>> obj = Managed()
>>> obj.spam    ❶
<bound method Managed.spam of <descriptorkinds.Managed object at 0x74c80c>>
>>> Managed.spam    ❷
<function Managed.spam at 0x734734>
>>> obj.spam = 7    ❸
>>> obj.spam
7
```

❶ Reading from `obj.spam` retrieves a bound method object.

❷ But reading from `Managed.spam` retrieves a function.

❸ Assigning a value to `obj.spam` shadows the class attribute, rendering the `spam` method inaccessible from the `obj` instance.

Functions do not implement __set__, therefore they are nonoverriding descriptors, as the last line of Example 23-13 shows.

The other key takeaway from Example 23-13 is that `obj.spam` and `Managed.spam` retrieve different objects. As usual with descriptors, the __get__ of a function returns a reference to itself when the access happens through the managed class. But when the access goes through an instance, the __get__ of the function returns a bound method object: a callable that wraps the function and binds the managed instance (e.g., `obj`) to the first argument of the function (i.e., `self`), like the `functools.par tial` function does (as seen in "Freezing Arguments with functools.partial" on page 247). For a deeper understanding of this mechanism, take a look at Example 23-14.

Example 23-14. method_is_descriptor.py: a Text class, derived from `UserString`

```
import collections


class Text(collections.UserString):

    def __repr__(self):
        return 'Text({!r})'.format(self.data)

    def reverse(self):
        return self[::-1]
```

Now let's investigate the `Text.reverse` method. See Example 23-15.

Example 23-15. Experiments with a method

```
>>> word = Text('forward')
>>> word                ❶
Text('forward')
>>> word.reverse()      ❷
Text('drawrof')
>>> Text.reverse(Text('backward'))   ❸
Text('drawkcab')
>>> type(Text.reverse), type(word.reverse)   ❹
(<class 'function'>, <class 'method'>)
>>> list(map(Text.reverse, ['repaid', (10, 20, 30), Text('stressed')]))   ❺
['diaper', (30, 20, 10), Text('desserts')]
>>> Text.reverse.__get__(word)   ❻
<bound method Text.reverse of Text('forward')>
>>> Text.reverse.__get__(None, Text)   ❼
<function Text.reverse at 0x101244e18>
>>> word.reverse        ❽
<bound method Text.reverse of Text('forward')>
>>> word.reverse.__self__   ❾
Text('forward')
>>> word.reverse.__func__ is Text.reverse   ❿
True
```

❶ The `repr` of a `Text` instance looks like a `Text` constructor call that would make an equal instance.

❷ The reverse method returns the text spelled backward.

❸ A method called on the class works as a function.

❹ Note the different types: a `function` and a `method`.

⑤ Text.reverse operates as a function, even working with objects that are not instances of Text.

⑥ Any function is a nonoverriding descriptor. Calling its __get__ with an instance retrieves a method bound to that instance.

⑦ Calling the function's __get__ with None as the instance argument retrieves the function itself.

⑧ The expression word.reverse actually invokes Text.reverse.__get__(word), returning the bound method.

⑨ The bound method object has a __self__ attribute holding a reference to the instance on which the method was called.

⑩ The __func__ attribute of the bound method is a reference to the original function attached to the managed class.

The bound method object also has a __call__ method, which handles the actual invocation. This method calls the original function referenced in __func__, passing the __self__ attribute of the method as the first argument. That's how the implicit binding of the conventional self argument works.

The way functions are turned into bound methods is a prime example of how descriptors are used as infrastructure in the language.

After this deep dive into how descriptors and methods work, let's go through some practical advice about their use.

Descriptor Usage Tips

The following list addresses some practical consequences of the descriptor characteristics just described:

Use property *to keep it simple*

The property built-in creates overriding descriptors implementing __set__ and __get__ even if you do not define a setter method.[7] The default __set__ of a property raises AttributeError: can't set attribute, so a property is the easiest way to create a read-only attribute, avoiding the issue described next.

---

7 A __delete__ method is also provided by the property decorator, even if no deleter method is defined by you.

Read-only descriptors require __set__

If you use a descriptor class to implement a read-only attribute, you must remember to code both __get__ and __set__, otherwise setting a namesake attribute on an instance will shadow the descriptor. The __set__ method of a read-only attribute should just raise `AttributeError` with a suitable message.[8]

Validation descriptors can work with __set__ only

In a descriptor designed only for validation, the __set__ method should check the `value` argument it gets, and if valid, set it directly in the instance __dict__ using the descriptor instance name as key. That way, reading the attribute with the same name from the instance will be as fast as possible, because it will not require a __get__. See the code for Example 23-3.

Caching can be done efficiently with __get__ only

If you code just the __get__ method, you have a nonoverriding descriptor. These are useful to make some expensive computation and then cache the result by setting an attribute by the same name on the instance.[9] The namesake instance attribute will shadow the descriptor, so subsequent access to that attribute will fetch it directly from the instance __dict__ and not trigger the descriptor __get__ anymore. The `@functools.cached_property` decorator actually produces a nonoverriding descriptor.

Nonspecial methods can be shadowed by instance attributes

Because functions and methods only implement __get__, they are nonoverriding descriptors. A simple assignment like `my_obj.the_method = 7` means that further access to `the_method` through that instance will retrieve the number 7—without affecting the class or other instances. However, this issue does not interfere with special methods. The interpreter only looks for special methods in the class itself, in other words, `repr(x)` is executed as `x.__class__.__repr__(x)`, so a __repr__ attribute defined in x has no effect on `repr(x)`. For the same reason, the existence of an attribute named __getattr__ in an instance will not subvert the usual attribute access algorithm.

The fact that nonspecial methods can be overridden so easily in instances may sound fragile and error prone, but I personally have never been bitten by this in more than 20 years of Python coding. On the other hand, if you are doing a lot of dynamic

---

8 Python is not consistent in such messages. Trying to change the `c.real` attribute of a `complex` number gets `AttributeError: readonly attribute`, but an attempt to change `c.conjugate` (a method of `complex`), results in `AttributeError: 'complex' object attribute 'conjugate' is read-only`. Even the spelling of "read-only" is different.

9 However, recall that creating instance attributes after the __init__ method runs defeats the key-sharing memory optimization, as discussed in from "Practical Consequences of How dict Works" on page 102.

attribute creation, where the attribute names come from data you don't control (as we did in the earlier parts of this chapter), then you should be aware of this and perhaps implement some filtering or escaping of the dynamic attribute names to preserve your sanity.

 The FrozenJSON class in Example 22-5 is safe from instance attribute shadowing methods because its only methods are special methods and the build class method. Class methods are safe as long as they are always accessed through the class, as I did with FrozenJSON.build in Example 22-5—later replaced by __new__ in Example 22-6. The Record and Event classes presented in "Computed Properties" on page 849 are also safe: they implement only special methods, static methods, and properties. Properties are overriding descriptors, so they are not shadowed by instance attributes.

To close this chapter, we'll cover two features we saw with properties that we have not addressed in the context of descriptors: documentation and handling attempts to delete a managed attribute.

Descriptor Docstring and Overriding Deletion

The docstring of a descriptor class is used to document every instance of the descriptor in the managed class. Figure 23-4 shows the help displays for the LineItem class with the Quantity and NonBlank descriptors from Examples 23-6 and 23-7.

That is somewhat unsatisfactory. In the case of LineItem, it would be good to add, for example, the information that weight must be in kilograms. That would be trivial with properties, because each property handles a specific managed attribute. But with descriptors, the same Quantity descriptor class is used for weight and price.[10]

The second detail we discussed with properties, but have not addressed with descriptors, is handling attempts to delete a managed attribute. That can be done by implementing a __delete__ method alongside or instead of the usual __get__ and/or __set__ in the descriptor class. I deliberately omitted coverage of __delete__ because I believe real-world usage is rare. If you need this, please see the "Implementing Descriptors" (https://fpy.li/23-2) section of the Python Data Model documentation (https://fpy.li/dtmodel). Coding a silly descriptor class with __delete__ is left as an exercise to the leisurely reader.

---

10 Customizing the help text for each descriptor instance is surprisingly hard. One solution requires dynamically building a wrapper class for each descriptor instance.

Figure 23-4. Screenshots of the Python console when issuing the commands `help(LineItem.weight)` *and* `help(LineItem)`.

Chapter Summary

The first example of this chapter was a continuation of the `LineItem` examples from Chapter 22. In Example 23-2, we replaced properties with descriptors. We saw that a descriptor is a class that provides instances that are deployed as attributes in the managed class. Discussing this mechanism required special terminology, introducing terms such as *managed instance* and *storage attribute*.

In "LineItem Take #4: Automatic Naming of Storage Attributes" on page 891, we removed the requirement that `Quantity` descriptors were declared with an explicit `storage_name`, which was redundant and error prone. The solution was to implement the `__set_name__` special method in `Quantity`, to save the name of the managed property as `self.storage_name`.

"LineItem Take #5: A New Descriptor Type" on page 893 showed how to subclass an abstract descriptor class to share code while building specialized descriptors with some common functionality.

We then looked at the different behaviors of descriptors providing or omitting the __set__ method, making the crucial distinction between overriding and nonoverriding descriptors, a.k.a. data and nondata descriptors. Through detailed testing we uncovered when descriptors are in control and when they are shadowed, bypassed, or overwritten.

Following that, we studied a particular category of nonoverriding descriptors: methods. Console experiments revealed how a function attached to a class becomes a method when accessed through an instance, by leveraging the descriptor protocol.

To conclude the chapter, "Descriptor Usage Tips" on page 904 presented practical tips, and "Descriptor Docstring and Overriding Deletion" on page 906 provided a brief look at how to document descriptors.

As noted in "What's New in This Chapter" on page 884, several examples in this chapter became much simpler thanks to the __set_name__ special method of the descriptor protocol, added in Python 3.6. That's language evolution!

Further Reading

Besides the obligatory reference to the "Data Model" chapter (*https://fpy.li/dtmodel*), Raymond Hettinger's "Descriptor HowTo Guide" (*https://fpy.li/23-3*) is a valuable resource—part of the HowTo collection (*https://fpy.li/23-4*) in the official Python documentation.

As usual with Python object model subjects, Martelli, Ravenscroft, and Holden's *Python in a Nutshell*, 3rd ed. (O'Reilly) is authoritative and objective. Martelli also has a presentation titled "Python's Object Model," which covers properties and descriptors in depth (see the slides (*https://fpy.li/23-5*) and video (*https://fpy.li/23-6*)).

Beware that any coverage of descriptors written or recorded before PEP 487 was adopted in 2016 is likely to contain examples that are needlessly complicated today, because __set_name__ was not supported in Python versions prior to 3.6.

For more practical examples, *Python Cookbook*, 3rd ed., by David Beazley and Brian K. Jones (O'Reilly), has many recipes illustrating descriptors, of which I want to highlight "6.12. Reading Nested and Variable-Sized Binary Structures," "8.10. Using Lazily Computed Properties," "8.13. Implementing a Data Model or Type System," and "9.9. Defining Decorators As Classes." The last recipe of which addresses deep issues with the interaction of function decorators, descriptors, and methods, explaining how a function decorator implemented as a class with __call__ also needs to implement __get__ if it wants to work with decorating methods as well as functions.

PEP 487—Simpler customization of class creation (*https://fpy.li/pep487*) introduced the __set_name__ special method, and includes an example of a validating descriptor (*https://fpy.li/23-7*).

Soapbox

The Design of self

The requirement to explicitly declare self as a first argument in methods is a controversial design decision in Python. After 23 years using the language, I am used to it. I think that decision is an example of "worse is better": a design philosophy described by computer scientist Richard P. Gabriel in "The Rise of Worse is Better" (*https://fpy.li/23-8*). The first priority of this philosophy is "simplicity," which Gabriel presents as:

> The design must be simple, both in implementation and interface. It is more important for the implementation to be simple than the interface. Simplicity is the most important consideration in a design.

Python's explicit self embodies that design philosophy. The implementation is simple—elegant even—at the expense of the user interface: a method signature like def zfill(self, width): doesn't visually match the invocation label.zfill(8).

Modula-3 introduced that convention with the same identifier self. But there is a key difference: in Modula-3, interfaces are declared separately from their implementation, and in the interface declaration the self argument is omitted, so from the user's perspective, a method appears in an interface declaration with the same explicit parameters used to call it.

Over time, Python's error messages related to method arguments became clearer. For a user-defined method with one argument besides self, if the user invokes obj.meth(), Python 2.7 raised:

```
TypeError: meth() takes exactly 2 arguments (1 given)
```

In Python 3, the confusing argument count is not mentioned, and the missing argument is named:

```
TypeError: meth() missing 1 required positional argument: 'x'
```

Besides the use of self as an explicit argument, the requirement to qualify every access to instance attributes with self is also criticized. See, for example, A. M. Kuchling's famous "Python Warts" post (archived (*https://fpy.li/23-9*)); Kuchling himself is not so bothered by the self qualifier, but he mentions it—probably echoing opinions from the comp.lang.python group. I personally don't mind typing the self qualifier:

it's good to distinguish local variables from attributes. My issue is with the use of `self` in the `def` statement.

Anyone who is unhappy about the explicit `self` in Python can feel a lot better by considering the baffling semantics (*https://fpy.li/23-10*) of the implicit `this` in JavaScript. Guido had some good reasons to make `self` work as it does, and he wrote about them in "Adding Support for User-Defined Classes" (*https://fpy.li/23-11*), a post on his blog, *The History of Python*.

## CHAPTER 24

Class Metaprogramming

> Everyone knows that debugging is twice as hard as writing a program in the first place.
> So if you're as clever as you can be when you write it, how will you ever debug it?
>
> —Brian W. Kernighan and P. J. Plauger, *The Elements of Programming Style*[1]

Class metaprogramming is the art of creating or customizing classes at runtime. Classes are first-class objects in Python, so a function can be used to create a new class at any time, without using the `class` keyword. Class decorators are also functions, but designed to inspect, change, and even replace the decorated class with another class. Finally, metaclasses are the most advanced tool for class metaprogramming: they let you create whole new categories of classes with special traits, such as the abstract base classes we've already seen.

Metaclasses are powerful, but hard to justify and even harder to get right. Class decorators solve many of the same problems and are easier to understand. Furthermore, Python 3.6 implemented PEP 487—Simpler customization of class creation (*https://fpy.li/pep487*), providing special methods supporting tasks that previously required metaclasses or class decorators.[2]

This chapter presents the class metaprogramming techniques in ascending order of complexity.

---

1 Quote from Chapter 2, "Expression" of *The Elements of Programming Style*, 2nd ed. (McGraw-Hill), page 10.

2 That doesn't mean PEP 487 broke code that used those features. It just means that some code that used class decorators or metaclasses prior to Python 3.6 can now be refactored to use plain classes, resulting in simpler and possibly more efficient code.

This is an exciting topic, and it's easy to get carried away. So I must offer this advice.

For the sake of readability and maintainability, you should probably avoid the techniques described in this chapter in application code.

On the other hand, these are the tools of the trade if you want to write the next great Python framework.

What's New in This Chapter

All the code in the "Class Metaprogramming" chapter of the first edition of *Fluent Python* still runs correctly. However, some of the previous examples no longer represent the simplest solutions in light of new features added since Python 3.6.

I replaced those examples with different ones, highlighting Python's new metaprogramming features or adding further requirements to justify the use of the more advanced techniques. Some of the new examples leverage type hints to provide class builders similar to the @dataclass decorator and typing.NamedTuple.

"Metaclasses in the Real World" on page 951 is a new section with some high-level considerations about the applicability of metaclasses.

Some of the best refactorings are removing code made redundant by newer and simpler ways of solving the same problems. This applies to production code as well as books.

We'll get started by reviewing attributes and methods defined in the Python Data Model for all classes.

Classes as Objects

Like most program entities in Python, classes are also objects. Every class has a number of attributes defined in the Python Data Model, documented in "4.13. Special Attributes" (*https://fpy.li/24-1*) of the "Built-in Types" chapter in *The Python Standard Library*. Three of those attributes appeared several times in this book already: __class__, __name__, and __mro__. Other class standard attributes are:

cls.__bases__
    The tuple of base classes of the class.

```
cls.__qualname__
```
The qualified name of a class or function, which is a dotted path from the global scope of the module to the class definition. This is relevant when the class is defined inside another class. For example, in a Django model class such as Ox (*https://fpy.li/24-2*), there is an inner class called Meta. The __qualname__ of Meta is Ox.Meta, but its __name__ is just Meta. The specification for this attribute is PEP 3155—Qualified name for classes and functions (*https://fpy.li/24-3*).

```
cls.__subclasses__()
```
This method returns a list of the immediate subclasses of the class. The implementation uses weak references to avoid circular references between the superclass and its subclasses—which hold a strong reference to the superclasses in their __bases__ attribute. The method lists subclasses currently in memory. Subclasses in modules not yet imported will not appear in the result.

```
cls.mro()
```
The interpreter calls this method when building a class to obtain the tuple of superclasses stored in the __mro__ attribute of the class. A metaclass can override this method to customize the method resolution order of the class under construction.

None of the attributes mentioned in this section are listed by the dir(…) function.

Now, if a class is an object, what is the class of a class?

type: The Built-In Class Factory

We usually think of type as a function that returns the class of an object, because that's what type(my_object) does: it returns my_object.__class__.

However, type is a class that creates a new class when invoked with three arguments.

Consider this simple class:

```
class MyClass(MySuperClass, MyMixin):
    x = 42

    def x2(self):
        return self.x * 2
```

Using the type constructor, you can create MyClass at runtime with this code:

```
MyClass = type('MyClass',
               (MySuperClass, MyMixin),
               {'x': 42, 'x2': lambda self: self.x * 2},
        )
```

That `type` call is functionally equivalent to the previous `class MyClass…` block statement.

When Python reads a `class` statement, it calls `type` to build the class object with these parameters:

`name`
> The identifier that appears after the `class` keyword, e.g., `MyClass`.

`bases`
> The tuple of superclasses given in parentheses after the class identifier, or `(object,)` if superclasses are not mentioned in the `class` statement.

`dict`
> A mapping of attribute names to values. Callables become methods, as we saw in "Methods Are Descriptors" on page 902. Other values become class attributes.

> The `type` constructor accepts optional keyword arguments, which are ignored by `type` itself, but are passed untouched into `__init_subclass__`, which must consume them. We'll study that special method in "Introducing `__init_subclass__`" on page 918, but I won't cover the use of keyword arguments. For more, please read PEP 487—Simpler customization of class creation (*https://fpy.li/ pep487*).

The `type` class is a *metaclass*: a class that builds classes. In other words, instances of the `type` class are classes. The standard library provides a few other metaclasses, but `type` is the default:

```
>>> type(7)
<class 'int'>
>>> type(int)
<class 'type'>
>>> type(OSError)
<class 'type'>
>>> class Whatever:
...     pass
...
>>> type(Whatever)
<class 'type'>
```

We'll build custom metaclasses in "Metaclasses 101" on page 935.

Next, we'll use the `type` built-in to make a function that builds classes.

A Class Factory Function

The standard library has a class factory function that appears several times in this book: `collections.namedtuple`. In Chapter 5 we also saw `typing.NamedTuple` and `@dataclass`. All of these class builders leverage techniques covered in this chapter.

We'll start with a super simple factory for classes of mutable objects—the simplest possible replacement for `@dataclass`.

Suppose I'm writing a pet shop application and I want to store data for dogs as simple records. But I don't want to write boilerplate like this:

```
class Dog:
    def __init__(self, name, weight, owner):
        self.name = name
        self.weight = weight
        self.owner = owner
```

Boring…each field name appears three times, and that boilerplate doesn't even buy us a nice `repr`:

```
>>> rex = Dog('Rex', 30, 'Bob')
>>> rex
<__main__.Dog object at 0x2865bac>
```

Taking a hint from `collections.namedtuple`, let's create a `record_factory` that creates simple classes like Dog on the fly. Example 24-1 shows how it should work.

Example 24-1. Testing record_factory, a simple class factory

```
>>> Dog = record_factory('Dog', 'name weight owner')    ❶
>>> rex = Dog('Rex', 30, 'Bob')
>>> rex    ❷
Dog(name='Rex', weight=30, owner='Bob')
>>> name, weight, _ = rex    ❸
>>> name, weight
('Rex', 30)
>>> "{2}'s dog weighs {1}kg".format(*rex)    ❹
"Bob's dog weighs 30kg"
>>> rex.weight = 32    ❺
>>> rex
Dog(name='Rex', weight=32, owner='Bob')
>>> Dog.__mro__    ❻
(<class 'factories.Dog'>, <class 'object'>)
```

❶ Factory can be called like `namedtuple`: class name, followed by attribute names separated by spaces in a single string.

❷ Nice `repr`.

❸ Instances are iterable, so they can be conveniently unpacked on assignment…

❹ …or when passing to functions like `format`.

❺ A record instance is mutable.

❻ The newly created class inherits from `object`—no relationship to our factory.

The code for `record_factory` is in Example 24-2.[3]

Example 24-2. record_factory.py: a simple class factory

```python
from typing import Union, Any
from collections.abc import Iterable, Iterator

FieldNames = Union[str, Iterable[str]]  ❶

def record_factory(cls_name: str, field_names: FieldNames) -> type[tuple]:  ❷

    slots = parse_identifiers(field_names)  ❸

    def __init__(self, *args, **kwargs) -> None:  ❹
        attrs = dict(zip(self.__slots__, args))
        attrs.update(kwargs)
        for name, value in attrs.items():
            setattr(self, name, value)

    def __iter__(self) -> Iterator[Any]:  ❺
        for name in self.__slots__:
            yield getattr(self, name)

    def __repr__(self):  ❻
        values = ', '.join(f'{name}={value!r}'
            for name, value in zip(self.__slots__, self))
        cls_name = self.__class__.__name__
        return f'{cls_name}({values})'

    cls_attrs = dict(  ❼
        __slots__=slots,
        __init__=__init__,
        __iter__=__iter__,
        __repr__=__repr__,
    )

    return type(cls_name, (object,), cls_attrs)  ❽
```

---

3 Thanks to my friend J. S. O. Bueno for contributing to this example.

```
def parse_identifiers(names: FieldNames) -> tuple[str, ...]:
    if isinstance(names, str):
        names = names.replace(',', ' ').split()      ❾
    if not all(s.isidentifier() for s in names):
        raise ValueError('names must all be valid identifiers')
    return tuple(names)
```

❶ User can provide field names as a single string or an iterable of strings.

❷ Accept arguments like the first two of collections.namedtuple; return a type—
i.e., a class that behaves like a tuple.

❸ Build a tuple of attribute names; this will be the __slots__ attribute of the new
class.

❹ This function will become the __init__ method in the new class. It accepts positional and/or keyword arguments.[4]

❺ Yield the field values in the order given by __slots__.

❻ Produce the nice repr, iterating over __slots__ and self.

❼ Assemble a dictionary of class attributes.

❽ Build and return the new class, calling the type constructor.

❾ Convert names separated by spaces or commas to list of str.

Example 24-2 is the first time we've seen type in a type hint. If the annotation was
just -> type, that would mean that record_factory returns a class—and it would be
correct. But the annotation -> type[tuple] is more precise: it says the returned class
will be a subclass of tuple.

The last line of record_factory in Example 24-2 builds a class named by the value of
cls_name, with object as its single immediate base class, and with a namespace
loaded with __slots__, __init__, __iter__, and __repr__, of which the last three
are instance methods.

We could have named the __slots__ class attribute anything else, but then we'd have
to implement __setattr__ to validate the names of attributes being assigned,

---

[4] I did not add type hints to the arguments because the actual types are Any. I put the return type hint because
otherwise Mypy will not check inside the method.

because for our record-like classes we want the set of attributes to be always the same and in the same order. However, recall that the main feature of __slots__ is saving memory when you are dealing with millions of instances, and using __slots__ has some drawbacks, discussed in "Saving Memory with __slots__" on page 386.

 Instances of classes created by record_factory are not serializable —that is, they can't be exported with the dump function from the pickle module. Solving this problem is beyond the scope of this example, which aims to show the type class in action in a simple use case. For the full solution, study the source code for collections.namedtuple (*https://fpy.li/24-4*); search for the word "pickling."

Now let's see how to emulate more modern class builders like typing.NamedTuple, which takes a user-defined class written as a class statement, and automatically enhances it with more functionality.

Introducing __init_subclass__

Both __init_subclass__ and __set_name__ were proposed in PEP 487—Simpler customization of class creation (*https://fpy.li/pep487*). We saw the __set_name__ special method for descriptors for the first time in "LineItem Take #4: Automatic Naming of Storage Attributes" on page 891. Now let's study __init_subclass__.

In Chapter 5, we saw that typing.NamedTuple and @dataclass let programmers use the class statement to specify attributes for a new class, which is then enhanced by the class builder with the automatic addition of essential methods like __init__, __repr__, __eq__, etc.

Both of these class builders read type hints in the user's class statement to enhance the class. Those type hints also allow static type checkers to validate code that sets or gets those attributes. However, NamedTuple and @dataclass do not take advantage of the type hints for attribute validation at runtime. The Checked class in the next example does.

 It is not possible to support every conceivable static type hint for runtime type checking, which is probably why typing.NamedTuple and @dataclass don't even try it. However, some types that are also concrete classes can be used with Checked. This includes simple types often used for field contents, such as str, int, float, and bool, as well as lists of those types.

Example 24-3 shows how to use Checked to build a Movie class.

Example 24-3. initsub/checkedlib.py: doctest for creating a `Movie` subclass of `Checked`

```
>>> class Movie(Checked):    ❶
...         title: str    ❷
...         year: int
...         box_office: float
...
>>> movie = Movie(title='The Godfather', year=1972, box_office=137)    ❸
>>> movie.title
'The Godfather'
>>> movie    ❹
Movie(title='The Godfather', year=1972, box_office=137.0)
```

❶ `Movie` inherits from `Checked`—which we'll define later in Example 24-5.

❷ Each attribute is annotated with a constructor. Here I used built-in types.

❸ `Movie` instances must be created using keyword arguments.

❹ In return, you get a nice `__repr__`.

The constructors used as the attribute type hints may be any callable that takes zero or one argument and returns a value suitable for the intended field type, or rejects the argument by raising `TypeError` or `ValueError`.

Using built-in types for the annotations in Example 24-3 means the values must be acceptable by the constructor of the type. For `int`, this means any x such that `int(x)` returns an `int`. For `str`, anything goes at runtime, because `str(x)` works with any x in Python.[5]

When called with no arguments, the constructor should return a default value of its type.[6]

This is standard behavior for Python's built-in constructors:

```
>>> int(), float(), bool(), str(), list(), dict(), set()
(0, 0.0, False, '', [], {}, set())
```

---

5 That's true for any object, except when its class overrides the `__str__` or `__repr__` methods inherited from `object` with broken implementations.

6 This solution avoids using `None` as a default. Avoiding null values is a good idea (*https://fpy.li/24-5*). They are hard to avoid in general, but easy in some cases. In Python as well as SQL, I prefer to represent missing data in a text field with an empty string instead of `None` or `NULL`. Learning Go reinforced this idea: variables and struct fields of primitive types in Go are initialized by default with a "zero value." See "Zero values" in the online *Tour of Go* (*https://fpy.li/24-6*) if you are curious.

In a Checked subclass like Movie, missing parameters create instances with default values returned by the field constructors. For example:

```
>>> Movie(title='Life of Brian')
Movie(title='Life of Brian', year=0, box_office=0.0)
```

The constructors are used for validation during instantiation and when an attribute is set directly on an instance:

```
>>> blockbuster = Movie(title='Avatar', year=2009, box_office='billions')
Traceback (most recent call last):
  ...
TypeError: 'billions' is not compatible with box_office:float
>>> movie.year = 'MCMLXXII'
Traceback (most recent call last):
  ...
TypeError: 'MCMLXXII' is not compatible with year:int
```

Checked Subclasses and Static Type Checking

In a *.py* source file with a movie instance of Movie, as defined in Example 24-3, Mypy flags this assignment as a type error:

```
movie.year = 'MCMLXXII'
```

However, Mypy can't detect type errors in this constructor call:

```
blockbuster = Movie(title='Avatar', year='MMIX')
```

That's because Movie inherits Checked.__init__, and the signature of that method must accept any keyword arguments to support arbitrary user-defined classes.

On the other hand, if you declare a Checked subclass field with the type hint list[float], Mypy can flag assignments of lists with incompatible contents, but Checked will ignore the type parameter and treat that the same as list.

Now let's look at the implementation of *checkedlib.py*. The first class is the Field descriptor, as shown in Example 24-4.

Example 24-4. initsub/checkedlib.py: the Field descriptor class

```
from collections.abc import Callable  ❶
from typing import Any, NoReturn, get_type_hints


class Field:
    def __init__(self, name: str, constructor: Callable) -> None:  ❷
        if not callable(constructor) or constructor is type(None):  ❸
            raise TypeError(f'{name!r} type hint must be callable')
        self.name = name
```

```
        self.constructor = constructor

    def __set__(self, instance: Any, value: Any) -> None:
        if value is ...:          ❹
            value = self.constructor()
        else:
            try:
                value = self.constructor(value)   ❺
            except (TypeError, ValueError) as e:    ❻
                type_name = self.constructor.__name__
                msg = f'{value!r} is not compatible with {self.name}:{type_name}'
                raise TypeError(msg) from e
        instance.__dict__[self.name] = value     ❼
```

❶ Recall that since Python 3.9, the Callable type for annotations is the ABC in collections.abc, and not the deprecated typing.Callable.

❷ This is a minimal Callable type hint; the parameter type and return type for constructor are both implicitly Any.

❸ For runtime checking, we use the callable built-in.[7] The test against type(None) is necessary because Python reads None in a type as NoneType, the class of None (therefore callable), but a useless constructor that only returns None.

❹ If Checked.__init__ sets the value as ... (the Ellipsis built-in object), we call the constructor with no arguments.

❺ Otherwise, call the constructor with the given value.

❻ If constructor raises either of these exceptions, we raise TypeError with a helpful message including the names of the field and constructor; e.g., 'MMIX' is not compatible with year:int.

❼ If no exceptions were raised, the value is stored in the instance.__dict__.

In __set__, we need to catch TypeError and ValueError because built-in constructors may raise either of them, depending on the argument. For example, float(None) raises TypeError, but float('A') raises ValueError. On the other hand, float('8') raises no error and returns 8.0. I hereby declare that this is a feature and not a bug of this toy example.

---

7 I believe that callable should be made suitable for type hinting. As of May 6, 2021, this is an open issue (*https://fpy.li/24-7*).

In "LineItem Take #4: Automatic Naming of Storage Attributes" on page 891, we saw the handy __set_name__ special method for descriptors. We don't need it in the Field class because the descriptors are not instantiated in client source code; the user declares types that are constructors, as we saw in the Movie class (Example 24-3). Instead, the Field descriptor instances are created at runtime by the Checked.__init_subclass__ method, which we'll see in Example 24-5.

Now let's focus on the Checked class. I split it in two listings. Example 24-5 shows the top of the class, which includes the most important methods in this example. The remaining methods are in Example 24-6.

Example 24-5. initsub/checkedlib.py: the most important methods of the Checked class

```
class Checked:
    @classmethod
    def _fields(cls) -> dict[str, type]:  ❶
        return get_type_hints(cls)

    def __init_subclass__(subclass) -> None:  ❷
        super().__init_subclass__()           ❸
        for name, constructor in subclass._fields().items():  ❹
            setattr(subclass, name, Field(name, constructor))  ❺

    def __init__(self, **kwargs: Any) -> None:
        for name in self._fields():           ❻
            value = kwargs.pop(name, ...)      ❼
            setattr(self, name, value)         ❽
        if kwargs:                             ❾
            self.__flag_unknown_attrs(*kwargs) ❿
```

❶ I wrote this class method to hide the call to typing.get_type_hints from the rest of the class. If I need to support Python ≥ 3.10 only, I'd call inspect.get_annotations instead. Review "Problems with Annotations at Run-time" on page 542 for the issues with those functions.

❷ __init_subclass__ is called when a subclass of the current class is defined. It gets that new subclass as its first argument—which is why I named the argument subclass instead of the usual cls. For more on this, see "__init_subclass__ Is Not a Typical Class Method" on page 923.

❸ super().__init_subclass__() is not strictly necessary, but should be invoked to play nice with other classes that might implement .__init_subclass__() in the same inheritance graph. See "Multiple Inheritance and Method Resolution Order" on page 496.

❹ Iterate over each field `name` and `constructor`...

❺ ...creating an attribute on `subclass` with that `name` bound to a `Field` descriptor parameterized with `name` and `constructor`.

❻ For each `name` in the class fields...

❼ ...get the corresponding `value` from `kwargs` and remove it from `kwargs`. Using ... (the `Ellipsis` object) as default allows us to distinguish between arguments given the value `None` from arguments that were not given.[8]

❽ This `setattr` call triggers `Checked.__setattr__`, shown in Example 24-6.

❾ If there are remaining items in `kwargs`, their names do not match any of the declared fields, and `__init__` will fail.

❿ The error is reported by `__flag_unknown_attrs`, listed in Example 24-6. It takes a `*names` argument with the unknown attribute names. I used a single asterisk in `*kwargs` to pass its keys as a sequence of arguments.

__init_subclass__ Is Not a Typical Class Method

The `@classmethod` decorator is never used with `__init_subclass__`, but that doesn't mean much, because the `__new__` special method behaves as a class method even without `@classmethod`. The first argument that Python passes to `__init_subclass__` is a class. However, it is never the class where `__init_subclass__` is implemented: it is a newly defined subclass of that class. That's unlike `__new__` and every other class method that I know about. Therefore, I think `__init_subclass__` is not a class method in the usual sense, and it is misleading to name the first argument `cls`. The `__init_suclass__` documentation (*https://fpy.li/24-8*) names the argument `cls` but explains: "...called whenever the containing class is subclassed. `cls` is then the new subclass."

---

8 As mentioned in "Loops, Sentinels, and Poison Pills" on page 725, the `Ellipsis` object is a convenient and safe sentinel value. It has been around for a long time, but recently people are finding more uses for it, as we see in type hints and NumPy.

Now let's see the remaining methods of the Checked class, continuing from Example 24-5. Note that I prepended _ to the _fields and _asdict method names for the same reason the collections.namedtuple API does: to reduce the chance of name clashes with user-defined field names.

Example 24-6. initsub/checkedlib.py: remaining methods of the Checked class

```
def __setattr__(self, name: str, value: Any) -> None:  ❶
    if name in self._fields():                          ❷
        cls = self.__class__
        descriptor = getattr(cls, name)
        descriptor.__set__(self, value)                 ❸
    else:                                               ❹
        self.__flag_unknown_attrs(name)

def __flag_unknown_attrs(self, *names: str) -> NoReturn:  ❺
    plural = 's' if len(names) > 1 else ''
    extra = ', '.join(f'{name!r}' for name in names)
    cls_name = repr(self.__class__.__name__)
    raise AttributeError(f'{cls_name} object has no attribute{plural} {extra}')

def _asdict(self) -> dict[str, Any]:  ❻
    return {
        name: getattr(self, name)
        for name, attr in self.__class__.__dict__.items()
        if isinstance(attr, Field)
    }

def __repr__(self) -> str:  ❼
    kwargs = ', '.join(
        f'{key}={value!r}' for key, value in self._asdict().items()
    )
    return f'{self.__class__.__name__}({kwargs})'
```

❶ Intercept all attempts to set an instance attribute. This is needed to prevent setting an unknown attribute.

❷ If the attribute name is known, fetch the corresponding descriptor.

❸ Usually we don't need to call the descriptor __set__ explicitly. It was necessary in this case because __setattr__ intercepts all attempts to set an attribute on the instance, including in the presence of an overriding descriptor such as Field.[9]

---

9 The subtle concept of an overriding descriptor was explained in "Overriding Descriptors" on page 898.

❹ Otherwise, the attribute `name` is unknown, and an exception will be raised by `__flag_unknown_attrs`.

❺ Build a helpful error message listing all unexpected arguments, and raise `Attribu teError`. This is a rare example of the `NoReturn` special type, covered in "NoReturn" on page 295.

❻ Create a `dict` from the attributes of a `Movie` object. I'd call this method `_as_dict`, but I followed the convention started by the `_asdict` method in `col lections.namedtuple`.

❼ Implementing a nice `__repr__` is the main reason for having `_asdict` in this example.

The `Checked` example illustrates how to handle overriding descriptors when implementing `__setattr__` to block arbitrary attribute setting after instantiation. It is debatable whether implementing `__setattr__` is worthwhile in this example. Without it, setting `movie.director = 'Greta Gerwig'` would succeed, but the `director` attribute would not be checked in any way, and would not appear in the `__repr__` nor would it be included in the `dict` returned by `_asdict`—both defined in Example 24-6.

In *record_factory.py* (Example 24-2) I solved this issue using the `__slots__` class attribute. However, this simpler solution is not viable in this case, as explained next.

Why __init_subclass__ Cannot Configure __slots__

The `__slots__` attribute is only effective if it is one of the entries in the class namespace passed to `type.__new__`. Adding `__slots__` to an existing class has no effect. Python invokes `__init_subclass__` only after the class is built—by then it's too late to configure `__slots__`. A class decorator can't configure `__slots__` either, because it is applied even later than `__init_subclass__`. We'll explore these timing issues in "What Happens When: Import Time Versus Runtime" on page 929.

To configure `__slots__` at runtime, your own code must build the class namespace passed as the last argument of `type.__new__`. To do that, you can write a class factory function, like *record_factory.py*, or you can take the nuclear option and implement a metaclass. We will see how to dynamically configure `__slots__` in "Metaclasses 101" on page 935.

Before PEP 487 (*https://fpy.li/pep487*) simplified the customization of class creation with `__init_subclass__` in Python 3.7, similar functionality had to be implemented using a class decorator. That's the focus of the next section.

Enhancing Classes with a Class Decorator

A class decorator is a callable that behaves similarly to a function decorator: it gets the decorated class as an argument, and should return a class to replace the decorated class. Class decorators often return the decorated class itself, after injecting more methods in it via attribute assignment.

Probably the most common reason to choose a class decorator over the simpler __init_subclass__ is to avoid interfering with other class features, such as inheritance and metaclasses.[10]

In this section, we'll study *checkeddeco.py*, which provides the same service as *checkedlib.py*, but using a class decorator. As usual, we'll start by looking at a usage example, extracted from the doctests in *checkeddeco.py* (Example 24-7).

Example 24-7. checkeddeco.py: creating a Movie class decorated with @checked

```
>>> @checked
... class Movie:
...     title: str
...     year: int
...     box_office: float
...
>>> movie = Movie(title='The Godfather', year=1972, box_office=137)
>>> movie.title
'The Godfather'
>>> movie
Movie(title='The Godfather', year=1972, box_office=137.0)
```

The only difference between Example 24-7 and Example 24-3 is the way the Movie class is declared: it is decorated with @checked instead of subclassing Checked. Otherwise, the external behavior is the same, including the type validation and default value assignments shown after Example 24-3 in "Introducing __init_subclass__" on page 918.

Now let's look at the implementation of *checkeddeco.py*. The imports and Field class are the same as in *checkedlib.py*, listed in Example 24-4. There is no other class, only functions in *checkeddeco.py*.

The logic previously implemented in __init_subclass__ is now part of the checked function—the class decorator listed in Example 24-8.

---

10 This rationale appears in the abstract of PEP 557–Data Classes (*https://fpy.li/24-9*) to explain why it was implemented as a class decorator.

Example 24-8. checkeddeco.py: the class decorator

```
def checked(cls: type) -> type:  ❶
    for name, constructor in _fields(cls).items():  ❷
        setattr(cls, name, Field(name, constructor))  ❸

    cls._fields = classmethod(_fields)  # type: ignore  ❹

    instance_methods = (  ❺
        __init__,
        __repr__,
        __setattr__,
        _asdict,
        __flag_unknown_attrs,
    )
    for method in instance_methods:  ❻
        setattr(cls, method.__name__, method)

    return cls  ❼
```

❶ Recall that classes are instances of type. These type hints strongly suggest this is a
   class decorator: it takes a class and returns a class.

❷ _fields is a top-level function defined later in the module (in Example 24-9).

❸ Replacing each attribute returned by _fields with a Field descriptor instance is
   what __init_subclass__ did in Example 24-5. Here there is more work to do…

❹ Build a class method from _fields, and add it to the decorated class. The type:
   ignore comment is needed because Mypy complains that type has no _fields
   attribute.

❺ Module-level functions that will become instance methods of the decorated class.

❻ Add each of the instance_methods to cls.

❼ Return the decorated cls, fulfilling the essential contract of a class decorator.

Every top-level function in *checkeddeco.py* is prefixed with an underscore, except the checked decorator. This naming convention makes sense for a couple of reasons:

- checked is part of the public interface of the *checkeddeco.py* module, but the other functions are not.
- The functions in Example 24-9 will be injected in the decorated class, and the leading _ reduces the chance of naming conflicts with user-defined attributes and methods of the decorated class.

The rest of *checkeddeco.py* is listed in Example 24-9. Those module-level functions have the same code as the corresponding methods of the Checked class of *checked-lib.py*. They were explained in Examples 24-5 and 24-6.

Note that the _fields function does double duty in *checkeddeco.py*. It is used as a regular function in the first line of the checked decorator, and it will also be injected as a class method of the decorated class.

Example 24-9. checkeddeco.py: the methods to be injected in the decorated class

```python
def _fields(cls: type) -> dict[str, type]:
    return get_type_hints(cls)

def __init__(self: Any, **kwargs: Any) -> None:
    for name in self._fields():
        value = kwargs.pop(name, ...)
        setattr(self, name, value)
    if kwargs:
        self.__flag_unknown_attrs(*kwargs)

def __setattr__(self: Any, name: str, value: Any) -> None:
    if name in self._fields():
        cls = self.__class__
        descriptor = getattr(cls, name)
        descriptor.__set__(self, value)
    else:
        self.__flag_unknown_attrs(name)

def __flag_unknown_attrs(self: Any, *names: str) -> NoReturn:
    plural = 's' if len(names) > 1 else ''
    extra = ', '.join(f'{name!r}' for name in names)
    cls_name = repr(self.__class__.__name__)
    raise AttributeError(f'{cls_name} has no attribute{plural} {extra}')

def _asdict(self: Any) -> dict[str, Any]:
    return {
        name: getattr(self, name)
        for name, attr in self.__class__.__dict__.items()
        if isinstance(attr, Field)
```

```
        }
def __repr__(self: Any) -> str:
    kwargs = ', '.join(
        f'{key}={value!r}' for key, value in self._asdict().items()
    )
    return f'{self.__class__.__name__}({kwargs})'
```

The *checkeddeco.py* module implements a simple but usable class decorator. Python's
@dataclass does a lot more. It supports many configuration options, adds more
methods to the decorated class, handles or warns about conflicts with user-defined
methods in the decorated class, and even traverses the __mro__ to collect user-
defined attributes declared in the superclasses of the decorated class. The source code
(*https://fpy.li/24-10*) of the dataclasses package in Python 3.9 is more than 1,200
lines long.

For metaprogramming classes, we must be aware of when the Python interpreter
evaluates each block of code during the construction of a class. This is covered next.

What Happens When: Import Time Versus Runtime

Python programmers talk about "import time" versus "runtime," but the terms are
not strictly defined and there is a gray area between them.

At import time, the interpreter:

1. Parses the source code of a *.py* module in one pass from top to bottom. This is
   when a SyntaxError may occur.

2. Compiles the bytecode to be executed.

3. Executes the top-level code of the compiled module.

If there is an up-to-date *.pyc* file available in the local __pycache__, parsing and
compiling are skipped because the bytecode is ready to run.

Although parsing and compiling are definitely "import time" activities, other things
may happen at that time, because almost every statement in Python is executable in
the sense that they can potentially run user code and may change the state of the user
program.

In particular, the import statement is not merely a declaration,[11] but it actually runs
all the top-level code of a module when it is imported for the first time in the process.
Further imports of the same module will use a cache, and then the only effect will be

---

11 Contrast with the import statement in Java, which is just a declaration to let the compiler know that certain
  packages are required.

binding the imported objects to names in the client module. That top-level code may do anything, including actions typical of "runtime," such as writing to a log or connecting to a database.[12] That's why the border between "import time" and "runtime" is fuzzy: the `import` statement can trigger all sorts of "runtime" behavior. Conversely, "import time" can also happen deep inside runtime, because the `import` statement and the `__import__()` built-in can be used inside any regular function.

This is all rather abstract and subtle, so let's do some experiments to see what happens when.

Evaluation Time Experiments

Consider an *evaldemo.py* script that uses a class decorator, a descriptor, and a class builder based on `__init_subclass__`, all defined in a *builderlib.py* module. The modules have several `print` calls to show what happens under the covers. Otherwise, they don't perform anything useful. The goal of these experiments is to observe the order in which these `print` calls happen.

 Applying a class decorator and a class builder with `__init_sub class__` together in single class is likely a sign of overengineering or desperation. This unusual combination is useful in these experiments to show the timing of the changes that a class decorator and `__init_subclass__` can apply to a class.

Let's start by checking out *builderlib.py*, split into two parts: Example 24-10 and Example 24-11.

Example 24-10. builderlib.py: top of the module

```
print('@ builderlib module start')

class Builder:    ❶
    print('@ Builder body')

    def __init_subclass__(cls):    ❷
        print(f'@ Builder.__init_subclass__({cls!r})')

        def inner_0(self):    ❸
            print(f'@ SuperA.__init_subclass__:inner_0({self!r})')

        cls.method_a = inner_0
```

---

12 I'm not saying opening a database connection just because a module is imported is a good idea, only pointing out it can be done.

```
    def __init__(self):
        super().__init__()
        print(f'@ Builder.__init__({self!r})')


def deco(cls):  ❹
    print(f'@ deco({cls!r})')

    def inner_1(self):  ❺
        print(f'@ deco:inner_1({self!r})')

    cls.method_b = inner_1
    return cls  ❻
```

❶ This is a class builder to implement...

❷ ...an __init_subclass__ method.

❸ Define a function to be added to the subclass in the assignment below.

❹ A class decorator.

❺ Function to be added to the decorated class.

❻ Return the class received as an argument.

Continuing with *builderlib.py* in Example 24-11...

Example 24-11. builderlib.py: bottom of the module

```
class Descriptor:  ❶
    print('@ Descriptor body')

    def __init__(self):  ❷
        print(f'@ Descriptor.__init__({self!r})')

    def __set_name__(self, owner, name):  ❸
        args = (self, owner, name)
        print(f'@ Descriptor.__set_name__{args!r}')

    def __set__(self, instance, value):  ❹
        args = (self, instance, value)
        print(f'@ Descriptor.__set__{args!r}')

    def __repr__(self):
        return '<Descriptor instance>'


print('@ builderlib module end')
```

❶ A descriptor class to demonstrate when…

❷ …a descriptor instance is created, and when…

❸ …__set_name__ will be invoked during the owner class construction.

❹ Like the other methods, this __set__ doesn't do anything except display its arguments.

If you import *builderlib.py* in the Python console, this is what you get:

```
>>> import builderlib
@ builderlib module start
@ Builder body
@ Descriptor body
@ builderlib module end
```

Note that the lines printed by *builderlib.py* are prefixed with @.

Now let's turn to *evaldemo.py*, which will trigger special methods in *builderlib.py* (Example 24-12).

Example 24-12. evaldemo.py: script to experiment with builderlib.py

```
#!/usr/bin/env python3

from builderlib import Builder, deco, Descriptor

print('# evaldemo module start')

@deco                          ❶
class Klass(Builder):          ❷
    print('# Klass body')

    attr = Descriptor()        ❸

    def __init__(self):
        super().__init__()
        print(f'# Klass.__init__({self!r})')

    def __repr__(self):
        return '<Klass instance>'


def main():                    ❹
    obj = Klass()
    obj.method_a()
    obj.method_b()
    obj.attr = 999
```

```
if __name__ == '__main__':
    main()

print('# evaldemo module end')
```

❶ Apply a decorator.

❷ Subclass `Builder` to trigger its `__init_subclass__`.

❸ Instantiate the descriptor.

❹ This will only be called if the module is run as the main program.

The `print` calls in *evaldemo.py* show a # prefix. If you open the console again and import *evaldemo.py*, Example 24-13 is the output.

Example 24-13. Console experiment with evaldemo.py

```
>>> import evaldemo
@ builderlib module start     ❶
@ Builder body
@ Descriptor body
@ builderlib module end
# evaldemo module start
# Klass body  ❷
@ Descriptor.__init__(<Descriptor instance>)  ❸
@ Descriptor.__set_name__(<Descriptor instance>,
      <class 'evaldemo.Klass'>, 'attr')
                                           ❹
@ Builder.__init_subclass__(<class 'evaldemo.Klass'>)  ❺
@ deco(<class 'evaldemo.Klass'>)  ❻
# evaldemo module end
```

❶ The top four lines are the result of `from builderlib import…`. They will not appear if you didn't close the console after the previous experiment, because *builderlib.py* is already loaded.

❷ This signals that Python started reading the body of `Klass`. At this point, the class object does not exist yet.

❸ The descriptor instance is created and bound to `attr` in the namespace that Python will pass to the default class object constructor: `type.__new__`.

❹ At this point, Python's built-in `type.__new__` has created the `Klass` object and calls `__set_name__` on each descriptor instance of descriptor classes that provide that method, passing `Klass` as the owner argument.

⑤ `type.__new__` then calls `__init_subclass__` on the superclass of `Klass`, passing `Klass` as the single argument.

⑥ When `type.__new__` returns the class object, Python applies the decorator. In this example, the class returned by `deco` is bound to `Klass` in the module namespace.

The implementation of `type.__new__` is written in C. The behavior I just described is documented in the "Creating the class object" (*https://fpy.li/24-11*) section of Python's "Data Model" (*https://fpy.li/dtmodel*) reference.

Note that the `main()` function of *evaldemo.py* (Example 24-12) was not executed in the console session (Example 24-13), therefore no instance of `Klass` was created. All the action we saw was triggered by "import time" operations: importing `builderlib` and defining `Klass`.

If you run *evaldemo.py* as a script, you will see the same output as Example 24-13 with extra lines right before the end. The extra lines are the result of running `main()` (Example 24-14).

Example 24-14. Running evaldemo.py as a program

```
$ ./evaldemo.py
[... 9 lines omitted ...]
@ deco(<class '__main__.Klass'>)   ❶
@ Builder.__init__(<Klass instance>)   ❷
# Klass.__init__(<Klass instance>)
@ SuperA.__init_subclass__:inner_0(<Klass instance>)   ❸
@ deco:inner_1(<Klass instance>)   ❹
@ Descriptor.__set__(<Descriptor instance>, <Klass instance>, 999)   ❺
# evaldemo module end
```

❶ The top 10 lines—including this one—are the same as shown in Example 24-13.

❷ Triggered by `super().__init__()` in `Klass.__init__`.

❸ Triggered by `obj.method_a()` in `main`; `method_a` was injected by `SuperA.__init_subclass__`.

❹ Triggered by `obj.method_b()` in `main`; `method_b` was injected by `deco`.

❺ Triggered by `obj.attr = 999` in `main`.

A base class with `__init_subclass__` and a class decorator are powerful tools, but they are limited to working with a class already built by `type.__new__` under the

covers. In the rare occasions when you need to adjust the arguments passed to
type.__new__, you need a metaclass. That's the final destination of this chapter—and
this book.

Metaclasses 101

> [Metaclasses] are deeper magic than 99% of users should ever worry about. If you
> wonder whether you need them, you don't (the people who actually need them know
> with certainty that they need them, and don't need an explanation about why).
>
> —Tim Peters, inventor of the Timsort algorithm and prolific Python contributor[13]

A metaclass is a class factory. In contrast with record_factory from Example 24-2, a
metaclass is written as a class. In other words, a metaclass is a class whose instances
are classes. Figure 24-1 depicts a metaclass using the Mills & Gizmos Notation: a mill
producing another mill.

Figure 24-1. A metaclass is a class that builds classes.

Consider the Python object model: classes are objects, therefore each class must be an
instance of some other class. By default, Python classes are instances of type. In other
words, type is the metaclass for most built-in and user-defined classes:

```
>>> str.__class__
<class 'type'>
>>> from bulkfood_v5 import LineItem
>>> LineItem.__class__
<class 'type'>
```

---

13 Message to comp.lang.python, subject: "Acrimony in c.l.p." (*https://fpy.li/24-12*). This is another part of the
same message from December 23, 2002, quoted in the Preface. The TimBot was inspired that day.

```
>>> type.__class__
<class 'type'>
```

To avoid infinite regress, the class of type is type, as the last line shows.

Note that I am not saying that str or LineItem are subclasses of type. What I am saying is that str and LineItem are instances of type. They all are subclasses of object. Figure 24-2 may help you confront this strange reality.

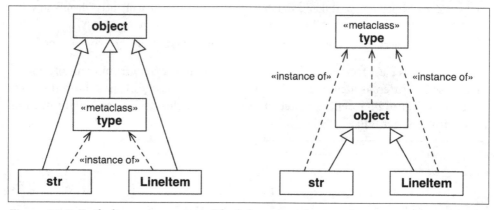

Figure 24-2. Both diagrams are true. The left one emphasizes that str, type, and LineI tem are subclasses of object. The right one makes it clear that str, object, and LineI tem are instances type, because they are all classes.

 The classes object and type have a unique relationship: object is an instance of type, and type is a subclass of object. This relationship is "magic": it cannot be expressed in Python because either class would have to exist before the other could be defined. The fact that type is an instance of itself is also magical.

The next snippet shows that the class of collections.Iterable is abc.ABCMeta. Note that Iterable is an abstract class, but ABCMeta is a concrete class—after all, Iterable is an instance of ABCMeta:

```
>>> from collections.abc import Iterable
>>> Iterable.__class__
<class 'abc.ABCMeta'>
>>> import abc
>>> from abc import ABCMeta
>>> ABCMeta.__class__
<class 'type'>
```

Ultimately, the class of ABCMeta is also type. Every class is an instance of type, directly or indirectly, but only metaclasses are also subclasses of type. That's the most important relationship to understand metaclasses: a metaclass, such as ABCMeta, inherits from type the power to construct classes. Figure 24-3 illustrates this crucial relationship.

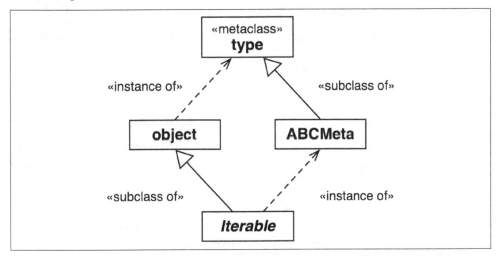

Figure 24-3. Iterable is a subclass of object and an instance of ABCMeta. Both object and ABCMeta are instances of type, but the key relationship here is that ABCMeta is also a subclass of type, because ABCMeta is a metaclass. In this diagram, Iterable is the only abstract class.

The important takeaway here is that metaclasses are subclasses of type, and that's what makes them work as class factories. A metaclass can customize its instances by implementing special methods, as the next sections demonstrate.

How a Metaclass Customizes a Class

To use a metaclass, it's critical to understand how __new__ works on any class. This was discussed in "Flexible Object Creation with __new__" on page 847.

The same mechanics happen at a "meta" level when a metaclass is about to create a new instance, which is a class. Consider this declaration:

```
class Klass(SuperKlass, metaclass=MetaKlass):
    x = 42
    def __init__(self, y):
        self.y = y
```

To process that class statement, Python calls MetaKlass.__new__ with these arguments:

meta_cls
    The metaclass itself (MetaKlass), because __new__ works as class method.

cls_name
> The string Klass.

bases
> The single-element tuple (SuperKlass,), with more elements in the case of multiple inheritance.

cls_dict
> A mapping like:
>
> ```
> {x: 42, `__init__`: <function __init__ at 0x1009c4040>}
> ```

When you implement MetaKlass.__new__, you can inspect and change those arguments before passing them to super().__new__, which will eventually call type.__new__ to create the new class object.

After super().__new__ returns, you can also apply further processing to the newly created class before returning it to Python. Python then calls Super Klass.__init_subclass__, passing the class you created, and then applies a class decorator to it, if one is present. Finally, Python binds the class object to its name in the surrounding namespace—usually the global namespace of a module, if the class statement was a top-level statement.

The most common processing made in a metaclass __new__ is to add or replace items in the cls_dict—the mapping that represents the namespace of the class under construction. For instance, before calling super().__new__, you can inject methods in the class under construction by adding functions to cls_dict. However, note that adding methods can also be done after the class is built, which is why we were able to do it using __init_subclass__ or a class decorator.

One attribute that you must add to the cls_dict before type.__new__ runs is __slots__, as discussed in "Why __init_subclass__ Cannot Configure __slots__" on page 925. The __new__ method of a metaclass is the ideal place to configure __slots__. The next section shows how to do that.

A Nice Metaclass Example

The MetaBunch metaclass presented here is a variation of the last example in Chapter 4 of *Python in a Nutshell*, 3rd ed., by Alex Martelli, Anna Ravenscroft, and Steve

Holden, written to run on Python 2.7 and 3.5.[14] Assuming Python 3.6 or later, I was able to further simplify the code.

First, let's see what the Bunch base class provides:

```
>>> class Point(Bunch):
...     x = 0.0
...     y = 0.0
...     color = 'gray'
...
>>> Point(x=1.2, y=3, color='green')
Point(x=1.2, y=3, color='green')
>>> p = Point()
>>> p.x, p.y, p.color
(0.0, 0.0, 'gray')
>>> p
Point()
```

Remember that Checked assigns names to the Field descriptors in subclasses based on class variable type hints, which do not actually become attributes on the class since they don't have values.

Bunch subclasses, on the other hand, use actual class attributes with values, which then become the default values of the instance attributes. The generated __repr__ omits the arguments for attributes that are equal to the defaults.

MetaBunch—the metaclass of Bunch—generates __slots__ for the new class from the class attributes declared in the user's class. This blocks the instantiation and later assignment of undeclared attributes:

```
>>> Point(x=1, y=2, z=3)
Traceback (most recent call last):
  ...
AttributeError: No slots left for: 'z'
>>> p = Point(x=21)
>>> p.y = 42
>>> p
Point(x=21, y=42)
>>> p.flavor = 'banana'
Traceback (most recent call last):
  ...
AttributeError: 'Point' object has no attribute 'flavor'
```

---

14 The authors kindly gave me permission to use their example. MetaBunch first appeared in a message posted by Martelli in the comp.lang.python group on July 7, 2002, with the subject line "a nice metaclass example (was Re: structs in python)" (*https://fpy.li/24-13*), following a discussion about record-like data structures in Python. Martelli's original code for Python 2.2 still runs after a single change: to use a metaclass in Python 3, you must use the metaclass keyword argument in the class declaration, e.g., Bunch(metaclass=MetaBunch), instead of the older convention of adding a __metaclass__ class-level attribute.

Now let's dive into the elegant code of MetaBunch in Example 24-15.

Example 24-15. metabunch/from3.6/bunch.py: MetaBunch metaclass and Bunch class

```python
class MetaBunch(type):  ❶
    def __new__(meta_cls, cls_name, bases, cls_dict):  ❷

        defaults = {}  ❸

        def __init__(self, **kwargs):  ❹
            for name, default in defaults.items():  ❺
                setattr(self, name, kwargs.pop(name, default))
            if kwargs:  ❻
                extra = ', '.join(kwargs)
                raise AttributeError(f'No slots left for: {extra!r}')

        def __repr__(self):  ❼
            rep = ', '.join(f'{name}={value!r}'
                            for name, default in defaults.items()
                            if (value := getattr(self, name)) != default)
            return f'{cls_name}({rep})'

        new_dict = dict(__slots__=[], __init__=__init__, __repr__=__repr__)  ❽

        for name, value in cls_dict.items():  ❾
            if name.startswith('__') and name.endswith('__'):  ❿
                if name in new_dict:
                    raise AttributeError(f"Can't set {name!r} in {cls_name!r}")
                new_dict[name] = value
            else:  ⓫
                new_dict['__slots__'].append(name)
                defaults[name] = value
        return super().__new__(meta_cls, cls_name, bases, new_dict)  ⓬


class Bunch(metaclass=MetaBunch):  ⓭
    pass
```

❶ To create a new metaclass, inherit from type.

❷ __new__ works as a class method, but the class is a metaclass, so I like to name the first argument meta_cls (mcs is a common alternative). The remaining three arguments are the same as the three-argument signature for calling type() directly to create a class.

❸ defaults will hold a mapping of attribute names and their default values.

❹ This will be injected into the new class.

⑤ Read the `defaults` and set the corresponding instance attribute with a value popped from `kwargs` or a default.

⑥ If there is still any item in `kwargs`, it means there are no slots left where we can place them. We believe in *failing fast* as best practice, so we don't want to silently ignore extra items. A quick and effective solution is to pop one item from `kwargs` and try to set it on the instance, triggering an `AttributeError` on purpose.

⑦ `__repr__` returns a string that looks like a constructor call—e.g., `Point(x=3)`, omitting the keyword arguments with default values.

⑧ Initialize namespace for the new class.

⑨ Iterate over the namespace of the user's class.

⑩ If a dunder `name` is found, copy the item to the new class namespace, unless it's already there. This prevents users from overwriting `__init__`, `__repr__`, and other attributes set by Python, such as `__qualname__` and `__module__`.

⑪ If not a dunder `name`, append to `__slots__` and save its `value` in `defaults`.

⑫ Build and return the new class.

⑬ Provide a base class, so users don't need to see `MetaBunch`.

`MetaBunch` works because it is able to configure `__slots__` before calling `super().__new__` to build the final class. As usual when metaprogramming, understanding the sequence of actions is key. Let's do another evaluation time experiment, now with a metaclass.

Metaclass Evaluation Time Experiment

This is a variation of "Evaluation Time Experiments" on page 930, adding a metaclass to the mix. The *builderlib.py* module is the same as before, but the main script is now *evaldemo_meta.py*, listed in Example 24-16.

Example 24-16. evaldemo_meta.py: experimenting with a metaclass

```
#!/usr/bin/env python3

from builderlib import Builder, deco, Descriptor
from metalib import MetaKlass  ❶

print('# evaldemo_meta module start')
```

```
@deco
class Klass(Builder, metaclass=MetaKlass):  ❷
    print('# Klass body')

    attr = Descriptor()

    def __init__(self):
        super().__init__()
        print(f'# Klass.__init__({self!r})')

    def __repr__(self):
        return '<Klass instance>'


def main():
    obj = Klass()
    obj.method_a()
    obj.method_b()
    obj.method_c()  ❸
    obj.attr = 999


if __name__ == '__main__':
    main()

print('# evaldemo_meta module end')
```

❶ Import `MetaKlass` from *metalib.py*, which we'll see in Example 24-18.

❷ Declare `Klass` as a subclass of `Builder` and an instance of `MetaKlass`.

❸ This method is injected by `MetaKlass.__new__`, as we'll see.

 In the interest of science, Example 24-16 defies all reason and applies three different metaprogramming techniques together on `Klass`: a decorator, a base class using `__init_subclass__`, and a custom metaclass. If you do this in production code, please don't blame me. Again, the goal is to observe the order in which the three techniques interfere in the class construction process.

As in the previous evaluation time experiment, this example does nothing but print messages revealing the flow of execution. Example 24-17 shows the code for the top part of *metalib.py*—the rest is in Example 24-18.

Example 24-17. metalib.py: the NosyDict class

```
print('% metalib module start')
```

```
import collections

class NosyDict(collections.UserDict):
    def __setitem__(self, key, value):
        args = (self, key, value)
        print(f'% NosyDict.__setitem__{args!r}')
        super().__setitem__(key, value)

    def __repr__(self):
        return '<NosyDict instance>'
```

I wrote the `NosyDict` class to override `__setitem__` to display each key and value as they are set. The metaclass will use a `NosyDict` instance to hold the namespace of the class under construction, revealing more of Python's inner workings.

The main attraction of *metalib.py* is the metaclass in Example 24-18. It implements the `__prepare__` special method, a class method that Python only invokes on metaclasses. The `__prepare__` method provides the earliest opportunity to influence the process of creating a new class.

> When coding a metaclass, I find it useful to adopt this naming convention for special method arguments:
>
> - Use `cls` instead of `self` for instance methods, because the instance is a class.
> - Use `meta_cls` instead of `cls` for class methods, because the class is a metaclass. Recall that `__new__` behaves as a class method even without the `@classmethod` decorator.

Example 24-18. metalib.py: the MetaKlass

```
class MetaKlass(type):
    print('% MetaKlass body')

    @classmethod            ❶
    def __prepare__(meta_cls, cls_name, bases):   ❷
        args = (meta_cls, cls_name, bases)
        print(f'% MetaKlass.__prepare__{args!r}')
        return NosyDict()   ❸

    def __new__(meta_cls, cls_name, bases, cls_dict):   ❹
        args = (meta_cls, cls_name, bases, cls_dict)
        print(f'% MetaKlass.__new__{args!r}')
        def inner_2(self):
            print(f'% MetaKlass.__new__:inner_2({self!r})')

        cls = super().__new__(meta_cls, cls_name, bases, cls_dict.data)   ❺
```

```
        cls.method_c = inner_2  ❻

        return cls  ❼

    def __repr__(cls):  ❽
        cls_name = cls.__name__
        return f"<class {cls_name!r} built by MetaKlass>"

print('% metalib module end')
```

❶ __prepare__ should be declared as a class method. It is not an instance method because the class under construction does not exist yet when Python calls __prepare__.

❷ Python calls __prepare__ on a metaclass to obtain a mapping to hold the namespace of the class under construction.

❸ Return NosyDict instance to be used as the namespace.

❹ cls_dict is a NosyDict instance returned by __prepare__.

❺ type.__new__ requires a real dict as the last argument, so I give it the data attribute of NosyDict, inherited from UserDict.

❻ Inject a method in the newly created class.

❼ As usual, __new__ must return the object just created—in this case, the new class.

❽ Defining __repr__ on a metaclass allows customizing the repr() of class objects.

The main use case for __prepare__ before Python 3.6 was to provide an OrderedDict to hold the attributes of the class under construction, so that the metaclass __new__ could process those attributes in the order in which they appear in the source code of the user's class definition. Now that dict preserves the insertion order, __prepare__ is rarely needed. You will see a creative use for it in "A Metaclass Hack with __prepare__" on page 954.

Importing *metalib.py* in the Python console is not very exciting. Note the use of % to prefix the lines output by this module:

```
>>> import metalib
% metalib module start
% MetaKlass body
% metalib module end
```

Lots of things happen if you import *evaldemo_meta.py*, as you can see in Example 24-19.

Example 24-19. Console experiment with evaldemo_meta.py

```
>>> import evaldemo_meta
@ builderlib module start
@ Builder body
@ Descriptor body
@ builderlib module end
% metalib module start
% MetaKlass body
% metalib module end
# evaldemo_meta module start    ❶
% MetaKlass.__prepare__(<class 'metalib.MetaKlass'>, 'Klass',    ❷
                        (<class 'builderlib.Builder'>,))
% NosyDict.__setitem__(<NosyDict instance>, '__module__', 'evaldemo_meta')    ❸
% NosyDict.__setitem__(<NosyDict instance>, '__qualname__', 'Klass')
# Klass body
@ Descriptor.__init__(<Descriptor instance>)    ❹
% NosyDict.__setitem__(<NosyDict instance>, 'attr', <Descriptor instance>)    ❺
% NosyDict.__setitem__(<NosyDict instance>, '__init__',
                       <function Klass.__init__ at …>)    ❻
% NosyDict.__setitem__(<NosyDict instance>, '__repr__',
                       <function Klass.__repr__ at …>)
% NosyDict.__setitem__(<NosyDict instance>, '__classcell__', <cell at …: empty>)
% MetaKlass.__new__(<class 'metalib.MetaKlass'>, 'Klass',
                    (<class 'builderlib.Builder'>,), <NosyDict instance>)    ❼
@ Descriptor.__set_name__(<Descriptor instance>,
                          <class 'Klass' built by MetaKlass>, 'attr')    ❽
@ Builder.__init_subclass__(<class 'Klass' built by MetaKlass>)
@ deco(<class 'Klass' built by MetaKlass>)
# evaldemo_meta module end
```

❶ The lines before this are the result of importing *builderlib.py* and *metalib.py*.

❷ Python invokes __prepare__ to start processing a class statement.

❸ Before parsing the class body, Python adds the __module__ and __qualname__ entries to the namespace of the class under construction.

❹ The descriptor instance is created…

❺ …and bound to attr in the class namespace.

❻ __init__ and __repr__ methods are defined and added to the namespace.

❼ Once Python finishes processing the class body, it calls MetaKlass.__new__.

❽ __set_name__, __init_subclass__, and the decorator are invoked in this order, after the __new__ method of the metaclass returns the newly constructed class.

If you run *evaldemo_meta.py* as script, main() is called, and a few more things happen (Example 24-20).

Example 24-20. Running evaldemo_meta.py as a program

```
$ ./evaldemo_meta.py
[... 20 lines omitted ...]
@ deco(<class 'Klass' built by MetaKlass>)   ❶
@ Builder.__init__(<Klass instance>)
# Klass.__init__(<Klass instance>)
@ SuperA.__init_subclass__:inner_0(<Klass instance>)
@ deco:inner_1(<Klass instance>)
% MetaKlass.__new__:inner_2(<Klass instance>)   ❷
@ Descriptor.__set__(<Descriptor instance>, <Klass instance>, 999)
# evaldemo_meta module end
```

❶ The top 21 lines—including this one—are the same shown in Example 24-19.

❷ Triggered by obj.method_c() in main; method_c was injected by Meta Klass.__new__.

Let's now go back to the idea of the Checked class with the Field descriptors implementing runtime type validation, and see how it can be done with a metaclass.

A Metaclass Solution for Checked

I don't want to encourage premature optimization and overengineering, so here is a make-believe scenario to justify rewriting *checkedlib.py* with __slots__, which requires the application of a metaclass. Feel free to skip it.

A Bit of Storytelling

Our *checkedlib.py* using __init_subclass__ is a company-wide success, and our production servers have millions of instances of Checked subclasses in memory at any one time.

Profiling a proof-of-concept, we discover that using __slots__ will reduce the cloud hosting bill for two reasons:

- Lower memory usage, as Checked instances don't need their own __dict__
- Higher performance, by removing __setattr__, which was created just to block unexpected attributes, but is triggered at instantiation and for all attribute setting before Field.__set__ is called to do its job

---

The *metaclass/checkedlib.py* module we'll study next is a drop-in replacement for *init-sub/checkedlib.py*. The doctests embedded in them are identical, as well as the *checkedlib_test.py* files for *pytest*.

The complexity in *checkedlib.py* is abstracted away from the user. Here is the source code of a script using the package:

```
from checkedlib import Checked

class Movie(Checked):
    title: str
    year: int
    box_office: float

if __name__ == '__main__':
    movie = Movie(title='The Godfather', year=1972, box_office=137)
    print(movie)
    print(movie.title)
```

That concise Movie class definition leverages three instances of the Field validating descriptor, a __slots__ configuration, five methods inherited from Checked, and a metaclass to put it all together. The only visible part of checkedlib is the Checked base class.

Consider Figure 24-4. The Mills & Gizmos Notation complements the UML class diagram by making the relationship between classes and instances more visible.

For example, a Movie class using the new *checkedlib.py* is an instance of CheckedMeta, and a subclass of Checked. Also, the title, year, and box_office class attributes of Movie are three separate instances of Field. Each Movie instance has its own _title, _year, and _box_office attributes, to store the values of the corresponding fields.

Now let's study the code, starting with the Field class, shown in Example 24-21.

The Field descriptor class is now a bit different. In the previous examples, each Field descriptor instance stored its value in the managed instance using an attribute of the same name. For example, in the Movie class, the title descriptor stored the field value in a title attribute in the managed instance. This made it unnecessary for Field to provide a __get__ method.

However, when a class like Movie uses __slots__, it cannot have class attributes and instance attributes with the same name. Each descriptor instance is a class attribute, and now we need separate per-instance storage attributes. The code uses the descriptor name prefixed with a single _. Therefore Field instances have separate name and storage_name attributes, and we implement Field.__get__.

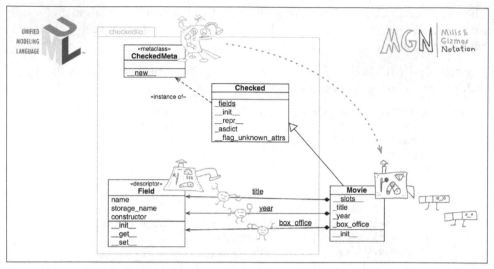

Figure 24-4. UML class diagram annotated with MGN: the `CheckedMeta` meta-mill builds the `Movie` mill. The `Field` mill builds the `title`, `year`, and `box_office` descriptors, which are class attributes of `Movie`. The per-instance data for the fields is stored in the `_title`, `_year`, and `_box_office` instance attributes of `Movie`. Note the package boundary of `checkedlib`. The developer of `Movie` doesn't need to grok all the machinery inside checkedlib.py.

Example 24-21 shows the source code for `Field`, with callouts describing only the changes in this version.

Example 24-21. metaclass/checkedlib.py: the `Field` descriptor with `storage_name` and `__get__`

```python
class Field:
    def __init__(self, name: str, constructor: Callable) -> None:
        if not callable(constructor) or constructor is type(None):
            raise TypeError(f'{name!r} type hint must be callable')
        self.name = name
        self.storage_name = '_' + name  ❶
        self.constructor = constructor

    def __get__(self, instance, owner=None):
        if instance is None:  ❷
            return self
        return getattr(instance, self.storage_name)  ❸

    def __set__(self, instance: Any, value: Any) -> None:
        if value is ...:
            value = self.constructor()
        else:
```

```
        try:
            value = self.constructor(value)
        except (TypeError, ValueError) as e:
            type_name = self.constructor.__name__
            msg = f'{value!r} is not compatible with {self.name}:{type_name}'
            raise TypeError(msg) from e
    setattr(instance, self.storage_name, value)  ❹
```

❶ Compute `storage_name` from the `name` argument.

❷ If `__get__` gets `None` as the `instance` argument, the descriptor is being read from the managed class itself, not a managed instance. So we return the descriptor.

❸ Otherwise, return the value stored in the attribute named `storage_name`.

❹ `__set__` now uses `setattr` to set or update the managed attribute.

Example 24-22 shows the code for the metaclass that drives this example.

Example 24-22. metaclass/checkedlib.py: the CheckedMeta metaclass

```
class CheckedMeta(type):

    def __new__(meta_cls, cls_name, bases, cls_dict):  ❶
        if '__slots__' not in cls_dict:  ❷
            slots = []
            type_hints = cls_dict.get('__annotations__', {})  ❸
            for name, constructor in type_hints.items():  ❹
                field = Field(name, constructor)  ❺
                cls_dict[name] = field  ❻
                slots.append(field.storage_name)  ❼

            cls_dict['__slots__'] = slots  ❽

        return super().__new__(
                meta_cls, cls_name, bases, cls_dict)  ❾
```

❶ `__new__` is the only method implemented in `CheckedMeta`.

❷ Only enhance the class if its `cls_dict` doesn't include `__slots__`. If `__slots__` is already present, assume it is the `Checked` base class and not a user-defined subclass, and build the class as is.

❸ To get the type hints in prior examples, we used `typing.get_type_hints`, but that requires an existing class as the first argument. At this point, the class we are configuring does not exist yet, so we need to retrieve the `__annotations__` directly from the `cls_dict`—the namespace of the class under construction, which Python passes as the last argument to the metaclass `__new__`.

❹ Iterate over `type_hints` to…

❺ …build a `Field` for each annotated attribute…

❻ …overwrite the corresponding entry in `cls_dict` with the `Field` instance…

❼ …and append the `storage_name` of the field in the list we'll use to…

❽ …populate the `__slots__` entry in `cls_dict`—the namespace of the class under construction.

❾ Finally, we call `super().__new__`.

The last part of *metaclass/checkedlib.py* is the `Checked` base class that users of this library will subclass to enhance their classes, like `Movie`.

The code for this version of `Checked` is the same as `Checked` in *initsub/checkedlib.py* (listed in Example 24-5 and Example 24-6), with three changes:

1. Added an empty `__slots__` to signal to `CheckedMeta.__new__` that this class doesn't require special processing.
2. Removed `__init_subclass__`. Its job is now done by `CheckedMeta.__new__`.
3. Removed `__setattr__`. It became redundant because adding `__slots__` to the user-defined class prevents setting undeclared attributes.

Example 24-23 is a complete listing of the final version of `Checked`.

Example 24-23. metaclass/checkedlib.py: the Checked base class

```python
class Checked(metaclass=CheckedMeta):
    __slots__ = ()  # skip CheckedMeta.__new__ processing

    @classmethod
    def _fields(cls) -> dict[str, type]:
        return get_type_hints(cls)

    def __init__(self, **kwargs: Any) -> None:
        for name in self._fields():
            value = kwargs.pop(name, ...)
            setattr(self, name, value)
        if kwargs:
            self.__flag_unknown_attrs(*kwargs)
```

```
def __flag_unknown_attrs(self, *names: str) -> NoReturn:
    plural = 's' if len(names) > 1 else ''
    extra = ', '.join(f'{name!r}' for name in names)
    cls_name = repr(self.__class__.__name__)
    raise AttributeError(f'{cls_name} object has no attribute{plural} {extra}')

def _asdict(self) -> dict[str, Any]:
    return {
        name: getattr(self, name)
        for name, attr in self.__class__.__dict__.items()
        if isinstance(attr, Field)
    }

def __repr__(self) -> str:
    kwargs = ', '.join(
        f'{key}={value!r}' for key, value in self._asdict().items()
    )
    return f'{self.__class__.__name__}({kwargs})'
```

This concludes the third rendering of a class builder with validated descriptors.

The next section covers some general issues related to metaclasses.

Metaclasses in the Real World

Metaclasses are powerful, but tricky. Before deciding to implement a metaclass, consider the following points.

Modern Features Simplify or Replace Metaclasses

Over time, several common use cases of metaclasses were made redundant by new language features:

Class decorators
> Simpler to understand than metaclasses, and less likely to cause conflicts with base classes and metaclasses.

__set_name__
> Avoids the need for custom metaclass logic to automatically set the name of a descriptor.[15]

---

15 In the first edition of *Fluent Python*, the more advanced versions of the LineItem class used a metaclass just to set the storage name of the attributes. See the code in the metaclasses of bulkfood in the first edition code repository (*https://fpy.li/24-14*).

`__init_subclass__`
> Provides a way to customize class creation that is transparent to the end user and even simpler than a decorator—but may introduce conflicts in a complex class hierarchy.

Built-in `dict` *preserving key insertion order*
> Eliminated the #1 reason to use `__prepare__`: to provide an `OrderedDict` to store the namespace of the class under construction. Python only calls `__prepare__` on metaclasses, so if you needed to process the class namespace in the order it appears in the source code, you had to use a metaclass before Python 3.6.

As of 2021, every actively maintained version of CPython supports all the features just listed.

I keep advocating these features because I see too much unnecessary complexity in our profession, and metaclasses are a gateway to complexity.

Metaclasses Are Stable Language Features

Metaclasses were introduced in Python 2.2 in 2002, together with so-called "new-style classes," descriptors, and properties.

It is remarkable that the `MetaBunch` example, first posted by Alex Martelli in July 2002, still works in Python 3.9—the only change being the way to specify the metaclass to use, which in Python 3 is done with the syntax `class Bunch(metaclass=Meta Bunch):`.

None of the additions I mentioned in "Modern Features Simplify or Replace Metaclasses" on page 951 broke existing code using metaclasses. But legacy code using metaclasses can often be simplified by leveraging those features, especially if you can drop support to Python versions before 3.6—which are no longer maintained.

A Class Can Only Have One Metaclass

If your class declaration involves two or more metaclasses, you will see this puzzling error message:

```
TypeError: metaclass conflict: the metaclass of a derived class
must be a (non-strict) subclass of the metaclasses of all its bases
```

This may happen even without multiple inheritance. For example, a declaration like this could trigger that `TypeError`:

```
class Record(abc.ABC, metaclass=PersistentMeta):
    pass
```

We saw that `abc.ABC` is an instance of the `abc.ABCMeta` metaclass. If that `Persistent` metaclass is not itself a subclass of `abc.ABCMeta`, you get a metaclass conflict.

There are two ways of dealing with that error:

- Find some other way of doing what you need to do, while avoiding at least one of the metaclasses involved.

- Write your own `PersistentABCMeta` metaclass as a subclass of both `abc.ABCMeta` and `PersistentMeta`, using multiple inheritance, and use that as the only metaclass for `Record`.[16]

I can imagine the solution of the metaclass with two base metaclasses implemented to meet a deadline. In my experience, metaclass programming always takes longer than anticipated, which makes this approach risky before a hard deadline. If you do it and make the deadline, the code may contain subtle bugs. Even in the absence of known bugs, you should consider this approach as technical debt simply because it is hard to understand and maintain.

Metaclasses Should Be Implementation Details

Besides `type`, there are only six metaclasses in the entire Python 3.9 standard library. The better known metaclasses are probably `abc.ABCMeta`, `typing.NamedTupleMeta`, and `enum.EnumMeta`. None of them are intended to appear explicitly in user code. We may consider them implementation details.

Although you can do some really wacky metaprogramming with metaclasses, it's best to heed the principle of least astonishment (*https://fpy.li/24-15*) so that most users can indeed regard metaclasses as implementation details.[17]

In recent years, some metaclasses in the Python standard library were replaced by other mechanisms, without breaking the public API of their packages. The simplest way to future-proof such APIs is to offer a regular class that users subclass to access the functionality provided by the metaclass, as we've done in our examples.

To wrap up our coverage of class metaprogramming, I will share with you the coolest, small example of metaclass I found as I researched this chapter.

---

16 If you just got dizzy considering the implications of multiple inheritance with metaclasses, good for you. I'd stay way from this solution as well.

17 I made a living writing Django code for a few years before I decided to study how Django's model fields were implemented. Only then I learned about descriptors and metaclasses.

A Metaclass Hack with __prepare__

When I updated this chapter for the second edition, I needed to find simple but illuminating examples to replace the *bulkfood* LineItem code that no longer require metaclasses since Python 3.6.

The simplest and most interesting metaclass idea was given to me by João S. O. Bueno—better known as JS in the Brazilian Python community. One application of his idea is to create a class that autogenerates numeric constants:

```
>>> class Flavor(AutoConst):
...     banana
...     coconut
...     vanilla
...
>>> Flavor.vanilla
2
>>> Flavor.banana, Flavor.coconut
(0, 1)
```

Yes, that code works as shown! That's actually a doctest in *autoconst_demo.py*.

Here is the user-friendly AutoConst base class and the metaclass behind it, implemented in *autoconst.py*:

```
class AutoConstMeta(type):
    def __prepare__(name, bases, **kwargs):
        return WilyDict()

class AutoConst(metaclass=AutoConstMeta):
    pass
```

That's it.

Clearly the trick is in WilyDict.

When Python processes the namespace of the user's class and reads banana, it looks up that name in the mapping provided by __prepare__: an instance of WilyDict. WilyDict implements __missing__, covered in "The __missing__ Method" on page 91. The WilyDict instance initially has no 'banana' key, so the __missing__ method is triggered. It makes an item on the fly with the key 'banana' and the value 0, returning that value. Python is happy with that, then tries to retrieve 'coconut'. Wily Dict promptly adds that entry with the value 1, returning it. The same happens with 'vanilla', which is then mapped to 2.

We've seen __prepare__ and __missing__ before. The real innovation is how JS put them together.

Here is the source code for WilyDict, also from *autoconst.py*:

```python
class WilyDict(dict):
    def __init__(self, *args, **kwargs):
        super().__init__(*args, **kwargs)
        self.__next_value = 0

    def __missing__(self, key):
        if key.startswith('__') and key.endswith('__'):
            raise KeyError(key)
        self[key] = value = self.__next_value
        self.__next_value += 1
        return value
```

While experimenting, I found that Python looked up __name__ in the namespace of the class under construction, causing WilyDict to add a __name__ entry, and increment __next_value. So I added that if statement in __missing__ to raise KeyError for keys that look like dunder attributes.

The *autoconst.py* package both requires and illustrates mastery of Python's dynamic class building machinery.

I had a great time adding more functionality to AutoConstMeta and AutoConst, but instead of sharing my experiments, I will let you have fun playing with JS's ingenious hack.

Here are some ideas:

- Make it possible to retrieve the constant name if you have the value. For example, Flavor[2] could return 'vanilla'. You can to this by implementing __geti tem__ in AutoConstMeta. Since Python 3.9, you can implement __class_geti tem__ (*https://fpy.li/24-16*) in AutoConst itself.

- Support iteration over the class, by implementing __iter__ on the metaclass. I would make the __iter__ yield the constants as (name, value) pairs.

- Implement a new Enum variant. This would be a major undertaking, because the enum package is full of tricks, including the EnumMeta metaclass with hundreds of lines of code and a nontrivial __prepare__ method.

Enjoy!

The __class_getitem__ special method was added in Python 3.9 to support generic types, as part of PEP 585—Type Hinting Generics In Standard Collections (*https://fpy.li/pep585*). Thanks to __class_getitem__, Python's core developers did not have to write a new metaclass for the built-in types to implement __getitem__ so that we could write generic type hints like list[int]. This is a narrow feature, but representative of a wider use case for metaclasses: implementing operators and other special methods to work at the class level, such as making the class itself iterable, just like Enum subclasses.

Wrapping Up

Metaclasses, as well as class decorators and __init_subclass__ are useful for:

- Subclass registration
- Subclass structural validation
- Applying decorators to many methods at once
- Object serialization
- Object-relational mapping
- Object-based persistence
- Implementing special methods at the class level
- Implementing class features found in other languages, such as traits (*https://fpy.li/24-17*) and aspect-oriented programming (*https://fpy.li/24-18*)

Class metaprogramming can also help with performance issues in some cases, by performing tasks at import time that otherwise would execute repeatedly at runtime.

To wrap up, let's recall Alex Martelli's final advice from his essay "Waterfowl and ABCs" on page 445:

> And, *don't* define custom ABCs (or metaclasses) in production code… if you feel the urge to do so, I'd bet it's likely to be a case of "all problems look like a nail"-syndrome for somebody who just got a shiny new hammer—you (and future maintainers of your code) will be much happier sticking with straightforward and simple code, eschewing such depths.

I believe Martelli's advice applies not only to ABCs and metaclasses, but also to class hierarchies, operator overloading, function decorators, descriptors, class decorators, and class builders using __init_subclass__.

Those powerful tools exist primarily to support library and framework development. Applications naturally should *use* those tools, as provided by the Python standard library or external packages. But *implementing* them in application code is often premature abstraction.

Good frameworks are extracted, not invented.[18]

—David Heinemeier Hansson, creator of Ruby on Rails

Chapter Summary

This chapter started with an overview of attributes found in class objects, such as __qualname__ and the __subclasses__() method. Next, we saw how the type built-in can be used to construct classes at runtime.

The __init_subclass__ special method was introduced, with the first iteration of a Checked base class designed to replace attribute type hints in user-defined subclasses with Field instances that apply constructors to enforce the type of those attributes at runtime.

The same idea was implemented with a @checked class decorator that adds features to user-defined classes, similar to what __init_subclass__ allows. We saw that neither __init_subclass__ nor a class decorator can dynamically configure __slots__, because they operate only after a class is created.

The concepts of "import time" and "runtime" were clarified with experiments showing the order in which Python code is executed when modules, descriptors, class decorators, and __init_subclass__ is involved.

Our coverage of metaclasses began with an overall explanation of type as a metaclass, and how user-defined metaclasses can implement __new__ to customize the classes it builds. We then saw our first custom metaclass, the classic MetaBunch example using __slots__. Next, another evaluation time experiment demonstrated how the __prepare__ and __new__ methods of a metaclass are invoked earlier than __init_subclass__ and class decorators, providing opportunities for deeper class customization.

The third iteration of a Checked class builder with Field descriptors and custom __slots__ configuration was presented, followed by some general considerations about metaclass usage in practice.

Finally, we saw the AutoConst hack invented by João S. O. Bueno, based on the cunning idea of a metaclass with __prepare__ returning a mapping that implements __missing__. In less than 20 lines of code, *autoconst.py* showcases the power of combining Python metaprogramming techniques

---

18 The phrase is widely quoted. I found an early direct quote in a post (*https://fpy.li/24-19*) in DHH's blog from 2005.

I haven't yet found a language that manages to be easy for beginners, practical for professionals, and exciting for hackers in the way that Python is. Thanks, Guido van Rossum and everybody else who makes it so.

Further Reading

Caleb Hattingh—a technical reviewer of this book—wrote the *autoslot* (*https://fpy.li/ 24-20*) package, providing a metaclass to automatically create a __slots__ attribute in a user-defined class by inspecting the bytecode of __init__ and finding all assignments to attributes of self. It's useful and also an excellent example to study: only 74 lines of code in *autoslot.py*, including 20 lines of comments explaining the most difficult parts.

The essential references for this chapter in the Python documentation are "3.3.3. Customizing class creation" (*https://fpy.li/24-21*) in the "Data Model" chapter of *The Python Language Reference*, which covers __init_subclass__ and metaclasses. The type class documentation (*https://fpy.li/24-22*) in the "Built-in Functions" page, and "4.13. Special Attributes" (*https://fpy.li/24-1*) of the "Built-in Types" chapter in the *The Python Standard Library* are also essential reading.

In the *The Python Standard Library*, the types module documentation (*https://fpy.li/ 24-24*) covers two functions added in Python 3.3 that simplify class metaprogramming: types.new_class and types.prepare_class.

Class decorators were formalized in PEP 3129—Class Decorators (*https://fpy.li/ 24-25*), written by Collin Winter, with the reference implementation authored by Jack Diederich. The PyCon 2009 talk "Class Decorators: Radically Simple" (video (*https://fpy.li/24-26*)), also by Jack Diederich, is a quick introduction to the feature. Besides @dataclass, an interesting—and much simpler—example of a class decorator in Python's standard library is functools.total_ordering (*https://fpy.li/24-27*) that generates special methods for object comparison.

For metaclasses, the main reference in Python's documentation is PEP 3115—Metaclasses in Python 3000 (*https://fpy.li/pep3115*), in which the __prepare__ special method was introduced.

Python in a Nutshell, 3rd ed., by Alex Martelli, Anna Ravenscroft, and Steve Holden, is authoritative, but was written before PEP 487—Simpler customization of class creation (*https://fpy.li/pep487*) came out. The main metaclass example in that book—MetaBunch—is still valid, because it can't be written with simpler mechanisms. Brett Slatkin's *Effective Python*, 2nd ed. (Addison-Wesley) has several up-to-date examples of class building techniques, including metaclasses.

To learn about the origins of class metaprogramming in Python, I recommend Guido van Rossum's paper from 2003, "Unifying types and classes in Python 2.2" (*https://fpy.li/24-28*). The text applies to modern Python as well, as it covers what were then called the "new-style" class semantics—the default semantics in Python 3—including descriptors and metaclasses. One of the references cited by Guido is *Putting Metaclasses to Work: a New Dimension in Object-Oriented Programming*, by Ira R. Forman and Scott H. Danforth (Addison-Wesley), a book to which he gave five stars on *Amazon.com*, adding the following review:

This book contributed to the design for metaclasses in Python 2.2

Too bad this is out of print; I keep referring to it as the best tutorial I know for the difficult subject of cooperative multiple inheritance, supported by Python via the super() function.[19]

If you are keen on metaprogramming, you may wish Python had the ultimate metaprogramming feature: syntactic macros, as offered in the Lisp family of languages and —more recently—by Elixir and Rust. Syntactic macros are more powerful and less error prone than the primitive code substitution macros in the C language. They are special functions that rewrite source code using custom syntax into standard code before the compilation step, enabling developers to introduce new language constructs without changing the compiler. Like operator overloading, syntactic macros can be abused. But as long as the community understands and manages the downsides, they support powerful and user-friendly abstractions, like DSLs (Domain-Specific Languages). In September 2020, Python core developer Mark Shannon posted PEP 638—Syntactic Macros (*https://fpy.li/pep638*), advocating just that. A year after it was initially published, PEP 638 was still in draft and there were no ongoing discussions about it. Clearly it's not a top priority for the Python core developers. I would like to see PEP 638 further discussed and eventually approved. Syntactic macros would allow the Python community to experiment with controversial new features, such as the walrus operator (PEP 572 (*https://fpy.li/pep572*)), pattern matching (PEP 634 (*https://fpy.li/pep634*)), and alternative rules for evaluating type hints (PEPs 563 (*https://fpy.li/pep563*) and 649 (*https://fpy.li/pep649*)) before making permanent changes to the core language. Meanwhile, you can get a taste of syntactic macros with the MacroPy (*https://fpy.li/24-29*) package.

---

19 I bought a used copy and found it a very challenging read.

Soapbox

I will start the last soapbox in the book with a long quote from Brian Harvey and Matthew Wright, two computer science professors from the University of California (Berkeley and Santa Barbara). In their book, *Simply Scheme: Introducing Computer Science* (MIT Press), Harvey and Wright wrote:

> There are two schools of thought about teaching computer science. We might caricature the two views this way:
>
> 1. **The conservative view**: Computer programs have become too large and complex to encompass in a human mind. Therefore, the job of computer science education is to teach people how to discipline their work in such a way that 500 mediocre programmers can join together and produce a program that correctly meets its specification.
>
> 2. **The radical view**: Computer programs have become too large and complex to encompass in a human mind. Therefore, the job of computer science education is to teach people how to expand their minds so that the programs can fit, by learning to think in a vocabulary of larger, more powerful, more flexible ideas than the obvious ones. Each unit of programming thought must have a big payoff in the capabilities of the program.
>
> —Brian Harvey and Matthew Wright, preface to *Simply Scheme*[20]

Harvey and Wright's exaggerated descriptions are about teaching computer science, but they also apply to programming language design. By now, you should have guessed that I subscribe to the "radical" view, and I believe Python was designed in that spirit.

The property idea is a great step forward compared to the accessors-from-the-start approach practically demanded by Java and supported by Java IDEs generating getters/setters with a keyboard shortcut. The main advantage of properties is to let us start our programs simply exposing attributes as public—in the spirit of *KISS*—knowing a public attribute can become a property at any time without much pain. But the descriptor idea goes way beyond that, providing a framework for abstracting away repetitive accessor logic. That framework is so effective that essential Python constructs use it behind the scenes.

Another powerful idea is functions as first-class objects, paving the way to higher-order functions. Turns out the combination of descriptors and higher-order functions enable the unification of functions and methods. A function's __get__ produces

---

20 See p. xvii. Full text available at Berkeley.edu (*https://fpy.li/24-30*).

a method object on the fly by binding the instance to the `self` argument. This is elegant.[21]

Finally, we have the idea of classes as first-class objects. It's an outstanding feat of design that a beginner-friendly language provides powerful abstractions such as class builders, class decorators, and full-fledged, user-defined metaclasses. Best of all, the advanced features are integrated in a way that does not complicate Python's suitability for casual programming (they actually help it, under the covers). The convenience and success of frameworks such as Django and SQLAlchemy owe much to metaclasses. Over the years, class metaprogramming in Python is becoming simpler and simpler, at least for common use cases. The best language features are those that benefit everyone, even if some Python users are not aware of them. But they can always learn and create the next great library.

I look forward to learning about your contributions to the Python community and ecosystem!

---

21 *Machine Beauty: Elegance and the Heart of Technology* by David Gelernter (Basic Books) opens with an intriguing discussion of elegance and aesthetics in works of engineering, from bridges to software. The later chapters are not great, but the opening is worth the price.

Afterword

> Python is a language for consenting adults.
>
> —Alan Runyan, cofounder of Plone

Alan's pithy definition expresses one of the best qualities of Python: it gets out of the way and lets you do what you must. This also means it doesn't give you tools to restrict what others can do with your code and the objects it builds.

At age 30, Python is still growing in popularity. But of course, it is not perfect. Among the top irritants to me is the inconsistent use of CamelCase, snake_case, and joinedwords in the standard library. But the language definition and the standard library are only part of an ecosystem. The community of users and contributors is the best part of the Python ecosystem.

Here is one example of the community at its best: while writing about *asyncio* in the first edition, I was frustrated because the API has many functions, dozens of which are coroutines, and you had to call the coroutines with yield from—now with await —but you can't do that with regular functions. This was documented in the *asyncio* pages, but sometimes you had to read a few paragraphs to find out whether a particular function was a coroutine. So I sent a message to python-tulip titled "Proposal: make coroutines stand out in the *asyncio* docs" (*https://fpy.li/a-1*). Victor Stinner, an *asyncio* core developer; Andrew Svetlov, main author of *aiohttp*; Ben Darnell, lead developer of Tornado; and Glyph Lefkowitz, inventor of *Twisted*, joined the conversation. Darnell suggested a solution, Alexander Shorin explained how to implement it in Sphinx, and Stinner added the necessary configuration and markup. Less than 12 hours after I raised the issue, the entire *asyncio* documentation set online was updated with the *coroutine* tags (*https://fpy.li/a-2*) you can see today.

That story did not happen in an exclusive club. Anybody can join the python-tulip list, and I had posted only a few times when I wrote the proposal. The story illustrates a community that is really open to new ideas and new members. Guido van Rossum used to hang out in python-tulip and often answered basic questions.

Another example of openness: the Python Software Foundation (PSF) has been working to increase diversity in the Python community. Some encouraging results are already in. The 2013–2014 PSF board saw the first women elected directors: Jessica McKellar and Lynn Root. In 2015, Diana Clarke chaired PyCon North America in Montréal, where about one-third of the speakers were women. PyLadies became a truly global movement, and I am proud that we have so many PyLadies chapters in Brazil.

If you are a Pythonista but you have not engaged with the community, I encourage you to do so. Seek the PyLadies or Python Users Group (PUG) in your area. If there isn't one, create it. Python is everywhere, so you will not be alone. Travel to events if you can. Join live events too. During the Covid-19 pandemic I learned a lot in the "hallway tracks" of online conferences. Come to a PythonBrasil conference—we've had international speakers regularly for many years now. Hanging out with fellow Pythonistas brings real benefits besides all the knowledge sharing. Like real jobs and real friendships.

I know I could not have written this book without the help of many friends I made over the years in the Python community.

My father, Jairo Ramalho, used to say "Só erra quem trabalha," Portuguese for "Only those who work make mistakes," great advice to avoid being paralyzed by the fear of making errors. I certainly made my share of mistakes while writing this book. The reviewers, editors, and early release readers caught many of them. Within hours of the first edition early release, a reader was reporting typos in the errata page for the book. Other readers contributed more reports, and friends contacted me directly to offer suggestions and corrections. The O'Reilly copyeditors will catch other errors during the production process, which will start as soon as I manage to stop writing. I take responsibility and apologize for any errors and suboptimal prose that remains.

I am very happy to bring this second edition to conclusion, mistakes and all, and I am very grateful to everybody who helped along the way.

I hope to see you soon at some live event. Please come say hi if you see me around!

Further Reading

I will wrap up the book with references regarding what it its to be "Pythonic"—the main question this book tried to address.

Brandon Rhodes is an awesome Python teacher, and his talk "A Python Æsthetic: Beauty and Why I Python" (*https://fpy.li/a-3*) is beautiful, starting with the use of Unicode U+00C6 (LATIN CAPITAL LETTER AE) in the title. Another awesome teacher, Raymond Hettinger, spoke of beauty in Python at PyCon US 2013: "Transforming Code into Beautiful, Idiomatic Python" (*https://fpy.li/a-4*).

The "Evolution of Style Guides" thread (*https://fpy.li/a-5*) that Ian Lee started on Python-ideas is worth reading. Lee is the maintainer of the pep8 (*https://fpy.li/a-6*) package that checks Python source code for PEP 8 compliance. To check the code in this book, I used flake8 (*https://fpy.li/a-7*), which wraps pep8, pyflakes (*https://fpy.li/a-8*), and Ned Batchelder's McCabe complexity plug-in (*https://fpy.li/a-9*).

Besides PEP 8, other influential style guides are the *Google Python Style Guide* (*https://fpy.li/a-10*) and the *Pocoo Styleguide* (*https://fpy.li/a-11*), from the team that brought us Flake, Sphinx, Jinja 2, and other great Python libraries.

The Hitchhiker's Guide to Python! (*https://fpy.li/a-12*) is a collective work about writing Pythonic code. Its most prolific contributor is Kenneth Reitz, a community hero thanks to his beautifully Pythonic requests package. David Goodger presented a tutorial at PyCon US 2008 titled "Code Like a Pythonista: Idiomatic Python" (*https://fpy.li/a-13*). If printed, the tutorial notes are 30 pages long. Goodger created both reStructuredText and docutils—the foundations of Sphinx, Python's excellent documentation system (which, by the way, is also the official documentation system (*https://fpy.li/a-14*) for MongoDB and many other projects).

Martijn Faassen tackles the question head-on in "What is Pythonic?" (*https://fpy.li/a-15*) In the python-list, there is a thread with that same title (*https://fpy.li/a-16*). Martijn's post is from 2005, and the thread from 2003, but the Pythonic ideal hasn't changed much—neither has the language, for that matter. A great thread with "Pythonic" in the title is "Pythonic way to sum n-th list element?" (*https://fpy.li/a-17*), from which I quoted extensively in the "Soapbox" on page 429.

PEP 3099 — Things that will Not Change in Python 3000 (*https://fpy.li/pep3099*) explains why many things are the way they are, even after the major overhaul that was Python 3. For a long time, Python 3 was nicknamed Python 3000, but it arrived a few centuries sooner—to the dismay of some. PEP 3099 was written by Georg Brandl, compiling many opinions expressed by the *BDFL*, Guido van Rossum. The "Python Essays" (*https://fpy.li/a-18*) page lists several texts by Guido himself.

Index

Symbols

!= (not equal to) operator, 581
!r conversion field, 12
% (modulo) operator, 5, 12
%r placeholder, 12
* (star) operator, 10, 36-37, 50-56, 240, 576-578
** (double star) operator, 80, 240
*= (star equals) operator, 53-56, 584-589
*_ symbol, 42
*_new*_, 847-849
+ operator, 10, 50-56, 570-576
+= (addition assignment) operator, 53-56, 584-589
+ELLIPSIS directive, 7
:= (Walrus operator), 26
< (less than) operator, 581
<= (less than or equal to) operator, 581
== (equality) operator, 206, 225, 581
> (greater than) operator, 581
>= (greater than or equal to) operator, 581
@ sign, 578-580
@asyncio.coroutine decorator, 781
@cached_property, 860
@contextmanager decorator, 668-673
@dataclass
    default settings, 180
    example using, 187-189
    field options, 180-183
    init-only variables, 186
    keyword parameters accepted by, 179
    post-init processing, 183-185
    typed class attributes, 185
    __hash__ method, 180
@typing.overload decorator, 524-530

[] (square brackets), 6, 26, 35, 49
\ (backslash), 26
\ line continuation escape, 26
\N{} (Unicode literals escape notation), 136
_ symbol, 41
__ (double underscore), 3
__abs__, 11
__add__, 11
__bool__, 13
__bytes__, 367
__call__, 362
__class__, 874, 912
__contains__, 7, 93
__delattr__, 876
__delete__, 883
__del__, 219
__dict__, 874
__dir__, 876
__enter__, 662
__eq__, 413-418
__exit__, 662
__format__, 367, 372, 420-427, 430
__getattribute__, 876
__getattr__, 409-413, 876
__getitem__, 5-8, 49, 405-409
__get__, 883
__hash__, 180, 413-418
__iadd__, 53
__init_subclass__, 918-925
__init__, 9, 183, 401
__invert__, 567
__iter__, 607-614
__len__, 5-8, 17, 405-409
__missing__, 91-95

__mro__, 912
__mul__, 11
__name__, 912
__neg__, 567
__post_init__, 183
__pos__, 567
__prepare__, 954-956
__repr__, 11-13, 366, 401
__setattr__, 876
__setitem__, 49
__set__, 883
__slots__, 386-390, 413, 874, 925
__str__, 13, 366
{} (curly brackets), 26
| (pipe) operator, 80, 690
|= (pipe equals) operator, 80
... (ellipsis), 7, 49

A

abc.ABC class, 451
abc.Iterable, 282
abc.Sequence, 282
ABCs (abstract base classes)
    ABC syntax details, 459
    defining and using ABCs, 453-459
    further reading on, 484
    goose typing and, 444-447
    overview of, 483
    in Python standard library, 451-453
    Soapbox discussion, 486-488
    structural typing with, 466-468
    subclassing ABCs, 449-451, 460-462
    type hints (type annotations), 278-280
    UML class diagrams, 14-15
    usage of register, 465
    virtual subclasses of ABCs, 462-465
abs built-in function, 10
actual type parameters, 548
addition assignment (+=) operator, 53-56,
    584-589
aliasing, 204-208
anonymous functions, 236, 252, 313
Any type, 266-269
AnyStr, 286
.append method, 67
apply function, 234-236
arguments
    freezing with functools.partial, 247
    key argument, 74

keyword-only arguments, 242
arrays, 23, 59-62
as keyword, 41
assignment expression (:=), 26
asynchronous generators, 238, 781
asynchronous programming
    asynchronous context managers, 790-792
    asyncio script example, 782-785
    avoiding CPU-bound traps, 830
    awaitables, 785
    benefits of, 829
    Curio project, 825-828
    delegating tasks to executors, 801-803
    enhancing asyncio downloader, 792-801
    further reading on, 832
    iteration and iterables, 815-825
    myth of I/O-bound systems, 830
    overview of, 831
    relevant terminology, 781
    significant changes to, 780
    Soapbox discussion, 834
    topics covered, 779
    type hinting asynchronous objects, 828
    writing asyncio servers, 803-815
Asynchronous Server Gateway Interface
    (ASGI), 736
asyncio package
    achieving peak performance with, 790
    documentation, 780
    downloading with, 786-790
    enhancing asyncio downloader, 792-801
    example script, 782-785
    queue implementation by, 69
    writing asyncio servers, 803-815
asyncpg, 791
attribute descriptors (see also attributes;
    dynamic attributes and properties)
    attribute validation, 884-895
    descriptor docstring and overriding dele-
        tion, 906
    descriptor usage tips, 904-906
    further reading on, 908
    methods as descriptors, 902-904
    overriding versus nonoverriding, 859,
        896-902
    overview of, 907
    purpose of, 883
    relevant terminology, 885
    significant changes to, 884

Soapbox discussion, 909
    topics covered, 883
attributes (see also attribute descriptors;
    dynamic attributes and properties)
    dynamic attribute access, 409-413
    handling attribute deletion, 872
    overriding class attributes, 391-393
    private and protected, 384-386
    properties and up-front costs, 396
    safety versus security in private, 397
    using attribute descriptors for validation,
        884-895
    using properties for attribute validation,
        861-864
    virtual attributes, 839
augmented assignment operators, 53-56,
    584-589
averages, computing, 647-649
await keyword, 785

B
backslash (\), 26
behavioral subtyping, 268
binary records, parsing with struct, 118
binary sequences, 120 (see also Unicode text
    versus bytes)
bisect module, 58
blue tool, 259
BOMs (byte-order marks), 129
bool type, 13
Boolean values, custom types and, 13
built-in functions, 238
byte sequences, 128 (see also Unicode text ver-
    sus bytes)
bytecode, disassembling, 312

C
call by sharing, 213
callable objects
    nine types of, 237-239
    user-defined, 239
    using iter() with, 602-603
Callable type, 292
card deck example, 5-8
Cartesian products, 27-29
case folding, 142
chain generator, 637
ChainMap, 95
characters

finding Unicode by name, 151-153
    numeric meaning of, 153-155
Chardet library, 129
cladistics, 446
class metaprogramming
    benefits and drawbacks of, 911
    built-in class factory, 913
    class factory function, 915-918
    classes as objects, 912
    enhancing classes with class decorators,
        926-929
    further reading on, 958
    import time versus runtime, 929-935
    __init_subclass__, 918-925
    metaclass basics, 935-946
    metaclass issues, 951-953
    metaclass solution for checkedlib.py,
        946-951
    overview of, 957
    __prepare__ method, 954-956
    significant changes to, 912
    Soapbox discussion, 960
    useful applications of metaclasses, 956
classes (see also protocols)
    as callable objects, 238
    implementing generic classes, 545-548
    topics covered, xxi
    undocumented classes, 561
classic refactoring strategy, 344-348
classmethod decorator, 371
client codes, 636
clock decorators
    class-based, 337
    parameterized, 334-336
closures (see decorators and closures)
cls.mro(), 913
cls.__bases__, 912
cls.__qualname__, 913
cls.__subclasses__(), 913
code examples, obtaining and using, xxiv
code points, 119, 161
code smells, 163, 190-192, 448
codecs, 123
Collection API, 14-15
collections.abc module
    abstract base classes defined in, 451
    ChainMap, 95
    Counter, 96
    defaultdict and OrderedDict, 85, 95

Mapping and MutableMapping ABCs, 83
  multiple inheritance in, 504
  UserDict, 97
collections.deque class, 67-70
collections.namedtuple, 5, 169-172
Command pattern, 357-359
comments and questions, xxv
comparison operators, 206, 581-584
computed properties
  caching properties with functools, 859-861
  data-driven attribute creation, 850-852
  properties that compute values, 849
  property caching, 857-859
  property overriding existing attributes, 856
  property to retrieve linked records, 852-856
concatenation, 50-56
concurrency models
  basics of concurrency, 700
  benefits of concurrency, 699
  further reading on, 738-743
  Global Interpreter Lock impact, 717-719
  Hello World example, 705-716
  indefinite loops and sentinels, 725
  multicore processors and, 729-737
  overview of, 737
  process pools, 720-729
  Python programming concepts, 703-705
  relevant terminology, 701-703
  significant changes to, 700
  Soapbox discussion, 744-746
  structured concurrency, 827
  topics covered, 700
concurrent executors
  concurrent web downloads, 748-758
  downloads with progress display and error
    handling, 766-776
  Executor.map, 762-765
  further reading on, 776
  launching processes with concur-
    rent.futures, 758-762
  overview of, 776
  purpose of, 747
  significant changes to, 747
  Soapbox discussion, 777
concurrent.futures
  downloading with, 753-755
  launching processes with, 758-762
consistent-with relationships, 268
Container interface, 15

container sequences, 22, 73
contention, 703
context managers
  @contextmanager decorator, 668-673
  asynchronous, 790-792
  asynchronous generators as, 821
  contextlib utilities, 667
  creative uses for, 662
  demonstrations of, 663-666
  methods included in interface, 662
  parenthesized in Python 3.10, 667
  purpose of, 662
contravariance (see variance)
control flow, xxi (see also asynchronous programming; concurrent executors; concurrency models; iterators; generators; with,
  match, and else blocks)
cooperative multiple inheritance, 499
copies
  deep, 211-213
  shallow, 208-211
coroutine objects, 646
coroutines
  computing running averages, 647-649
  definition of term, 702
  further reading on, 656
  generator-based, 781
  generic type hints for, 654
  Global Interpreter Lock impact, 719
  overview of, 656
  returning values from, 650-654
  significant changes to, 598
  Soapbox discussion, 658
  spinners (loading indicators) using, 710-714
  topics covered, 598
  types of, 781
  understanding classic, 645
Counter, 96
covariance (see variance)
CPU-bound systems, 830
Curio project, 825-828
curly brackets ({}), 26

D

Dask, 731
data attributes (see attributes)
data class builders
  @dataclass, 179-189
  classic named tuples, 169-172

data class as code smell, 190-192
  further reading on, 196
  main features, 167-169
  overview of, 164-167, 195
  pattern matching class instances, 192-195
  significant changes to, 164
  Soapbox discussion, 197
  topics covered, 163
  type hints, 173-179
  typed named tuples, 172
data descriptors (see overriding descriptors)
data model (see Python Data Model)
data science, 731
data structures, xxi (see also data class builders;
  dictionaries and sets; object references;
  sequences; Unicode text versus bytes)
data wrangling
  with dynamic attributes, 840-842
  flexible object creation, 847-849
  invalid attribute name problem, 846
  JSON-like data, 842-846
decimal.Decimal class, 569
decoding (see also Unicode text versus bytes)
  basics of, 123-124
  definition of, 119
  understanding encode/decode problems,
    125-131
decorator-enhanced strategy pattern, 355-357
decorators and closures
  classmethod versus staticmethod, 371
  closure basics, 313-316
  closures in lis.py, 689
  decorator basics, 306-308
  decorator execution, 308
  decorator implementation, 319-322
  decorators in Python standard library,
    322-325
  enhancing classes with class decorators,
    926-929
  further reading on, 338
  nonlocal declarations, 317-319
  overview of, 338
  parameterized decorators, 331-337
  purpose of, 305
  registration decorators, 310
  significant changes to, 306
  Soapbox discussion, 340-342
  topics covered, 305
  variable scope rules, 310-312

deep copies, 211-213
defaultdict, 85, 90
defensive programming, 87, 442-444
del statement, 219-221, 872
delegating generators, 636
deprecated collection types, 272
deque (double-ended queue), 59, 67-70
descriptor classes, 885
descriptor instances, 885
descriptors, 177, 883 (see also attribute descriptors)
design patterns (see functions, design patterns
  with first-class)
destructuring, 40
diacritics, normalization and, 144-148
dictcomps (dict comprehensions), 79
dictionaries and sets
  automatic handling of missing keys, 90-95
  consequences of how dict works, 102
  consequences of how set works, 107
  dictionary views, 101-102
  further reading on, 113
  immutable mappings, 99
  internals of, 78
  modern dict syntax, 78-81
  overview of, 112
  pattern matching with mappings, 81-83
  set operations, 107-110
  set operations on dict views, 110
  set theory, 103-106
  significant changes to, 78
  Soapbox discussion, 114
  standard API of mapping types, 83-90
  topics covered, 77
  variations of dict, 95-99
dir([object]) function, 874
dis module, 312
displays, formatting, 372-376
distributed task queues, 736
Django generic views mixins, 506-509
doctest package
  documentation, xxii
  ellipsis in, 7
double star (**) operator, 80, 240
double underscore (__), 3
double() function, 468-470
Dublin Core Schema, 187
duck typing, 87, 262, 303, 404, 429, 433, 472
dunder methods, 4

dynamic attributes and properties
  coding property factories, 869-872
  computed properties, 849-861
  data wrangling with dynamic attributes,
    840-849
  dynamic versus virtual attributes, 839
  essential attributes and functions for
    attribute handling, 873-877
  further reading on, 878
  handling attribute deletion, 872
  overview of, 877
  property class, 864-869
  significant changes to, 840
  Soapbox discussion, 879-881
  using properties for attribute validation,
    861-864
dynamic protocols, 405, 437
dynamic type, 266-269

E

ellipsis (…), 7, 49
else blocks, 691-693
emojis
  building, 118
  console font and, 136
  finding characters by name, 151-153
  in the Museum of Modern Art, 160
  increasing issues with, 162
  UCS-2 versus UTF-16 encoding, 124
  varied support for, 152
encoding (see also Unicode text versus bytes)
  basics of, 123-124
  definition of, 119
  encoding defaults, 134-139
  understanding encode/decode problems,
    125-131
equality (==) operator, 206, 225, 581
error handling, in network I/O, 766-776
execution units, 701
Executor.map, 762-765
executors, delegating tasks to, 801-803 (see also
  concurrent executors)
explicit self argument, 909

F

f-string syntax
  benefits of, 5
  delegation of formatting by, 372

string representation using special methods,
    12
fail-fast philosophy, 87, 419, 442-444
FastAPI framework, 805-808
FIFO (first in, first out), 59, 67
filter function, 27, 234-236
filtering generator functions, 624
first-class functions (see functions, as first-class
  objects)
first-class objects, 231
flake8 tool, 259
flat sequences, 22, 73
flawed typing, 296
fluentpython.com, xxiii
ForkingMixIn, 505
formal type parameters, 548
format() function, 372
forward reference problem, 542
free variables, 315, 689
frozenset, 103 (see also dictionaries and sets)
function decorators (see decorators and closures)
function parameters, introspection of, 232
function-class duality, 880
function-oriented refactoring strategy, 349-352
functional programming
  packages for, 243-249
  with Python, 250
functions
  abs built-in function, 10
  dir([object]) function, 874
  disassembling bytecode of, 312
  double() function, 468
  filter, map, and reduce functions, 27, 234
  format() function, 372
  getattr function, 875
  getattr(object, name[, default]) function,
    875
  globals() function, 353
  hasattr function, 875
  higher-order functions, 234-236
  id() function, 206
  iter() function, 600
  len() function, 6
  map function, 27
  max() function, 525
  repr() function, 366
  setattr funcion, 875

setattr(object, name, value) function, 875, 875

single dispatch generic functions, 326-331

str() function, 13, 366

super() function, 413, 490

zip() function, 418

functions, as first-class objects (see also decorators and closures)

    anonymous functions, 236

    callable objects, 237-239

    definition of term, 231

    flexible parameter handling and, 240-243

    further reading on, 250

    higher-order functions, 234-236

    overview of, 249

    packages for functional programming, 243-249

    significant changes to, 232

    Soapbox discussion, 250

    topics covered, xxi

    treating functions like objects, 232-234

    user-defined callable types, 239

functions, design patterns with first-class

    Command pattern, 357-359

    decorator-enhanced strategy pattern, 355-357

    dynamic languages and, 343

    further reading on, 360

    overview of, 359

    refactoring strategies, 344-355

    significant changes to, 344

    Soapbox discussion, 361

functions, type hints in

    annotating positional only and variadic parameters, 295

    benefits and drawbacks of, 253

    flawed typing and strong testing, 296

    further reading on, 299

    gradual typing, 254-260

    overview of, 298

    significant changes to, 254

    Soapbox discussion, 300-303

    supported operations and, 261-266

    topics covered, 254

    types usable in annotations, 266-295

functools module

    caching properties with, 859-861

    freezing arguments with, 247-249

    functools.cache decorator, 322-325

functools.lru_cache function, 325

functools.singledispatch decorator, 328-331

futures

    basics of, 755-758

    definition of term, 747

futures.as_completed, 773-776

G

garbage collection, 219-221, 226

generator expressions (genexps), 26, 29, 235, 617, 822-825

generators

    arithmetic progression generators, 619-623

    asynchronous generator functions, 816-822

    examples of, 611-614

    further reading on, 656

    generator functions in Python standard library, 238, 623-634

    generator-based coroutines, 781

    generic iterable types, 643

    humble generators, 789

    iterable reducing functions, 634-635

    versus iterators, 618

    lazy generators, 614-617

    overview of, 656

    Sentence classes with, 610

    significant changes to, 598

    Soapbox discussion, 658

    subgenerators with yield from expression, 636-643

    topics covered, 598

    when to use generator expressions, 617

    yield keyword, 611

generic classes, implementing, 545-548

generic collections

    parameterized generics and TypeVar, 282-286

    Soapbox discussion, 303

    type annotations and, 271-272

generic functions, single dispatch, 326-331

generic mapping types, 277

generic static protocols, 556-558

getattr function, 875

getattr(object, name[, default]) function, 875

gevent library, 715

Global Interpreter Lock (GIL), 66, 703, 717-719, 729, 740

globals() function, 353

goose typing

ABC syntax details, 459
ABCs in Python standard library, 451-453
abstract base classes (ABCs), 444-447
defining and using ABCs, 453-459
definition of term, 433
overview of, 448
structural typing with ABCs, 466-468
subclassing ABCs, 449-451, 460-462
usage of register, 465
virtual subclasses of ABCs, 462-465
gradual type system (see also type hints (type annotations))
abstract base classes, 278-280
Any type, 266-267
basics of, 254
Callable type, 292
further reading on, 559
generic collections, 271-272
generic mappings, 277
implementing generic classes, 545-548
implementing generic static protocols, 556-558
in practice, 255-260
Iterable, 280-282
legacy support and deprecated collection types, 272
NoReturn type, 295
Optional and Union types, 270
overloaded signatures, 524-530
overview of, 558
parameterized generics and TypeVar, 282-286
reading hints at runtime, 541-545
significant changes to, 523
simple types and classes, 269
Soapbox discussion, 561
static protocols, 287-292
subtype-of versus consistent-with relationships, 267-269
topics covered, 523
tuple types, 274-276
type casting, 538-541
TypedDict, 530
variance and, 548-555
greater than (>) operator, 581
greater than or equal to (>=) operator, 581
greenlet package, 714

H
hasattr function, 875
hash code, versus hash value, 84
hash tables, 77
hashable, definition of, 84
heapq package, 69
higher-order functions, 234-236
HTTPServer class, 505
HTTPX library, 786-790
humble generators, 789

I
I/O (input/output) (see network I/O)
id() function, 206
immutable mappings, 99
immutable sequences, 24
implicit conversion, 117
import time versus runtime, 308, 929
indefinite loops, 725
infix operators, 565, 578-580
inheritance and subclassing
best practices, 512-516
further reading on, 517
mixin classes, 502-504
multiple inheritance and method resolution order, 496-501
overview of, 516
real-world examples of, 504-511
significant changes to, 490
Soapbox discussion, 519-521
subclassing ABCs, 449-451, 460-462
subclassing built-in types, 492-496
super() function, 490-492
topics covered, 489
virtual subclasses of ABCs, 462-465
input expanding generator functions, 629
interfaces (see also goose typing; protocols)
Container interface, 15
further reading on, 484
Iterable interface, 15, 280, 438
overview of, 483
protocols as informal, 429
role in object-oriented programming, 433
significant changes to, 435
Sized interface, 15
Soapbox discussion, 486-488
topics covered, 435
typing map, 434
ways of defining and using, 433

interning, 222
invalid attribute name problem, 846
inverted indexes, 804
is operator, 206, 221
.items method, 110
iter() function, 600-603
Iterable interface, 15, 280-282, 438-440
iterables
    asynchronous, 815-825
    iterable reducing functions, 634-635
    versus iterators, 603-607
    unpacking, 35-38
iterators
    asynchronous, 815-825
    further reading on, 656
    versus generators, 618
    generic iterable types, 643
    iter() function, 600-603
    versus iterables, 603-607
    lazy sentences, 614-617
    overview of, 656
    role of, 597
    Sentence classes with __iter__, 607-614
    sequence protocol, 598-600
    significant changes to, 598
    Soapbox discussion, 658
    topics covered, 598
itertools module, 622

J

JSON-like data, 842-846

K

key argument, 74
keys
    automatic handling of missing, 90-95
    converting nonstring keys to str, 98
    hashability, 84
    persistent storage for mapping, 97
    practical consequences of using dict, 102
    preserving key insertion order, 15, 952
    sorting multiple, 244
.keys method, 110
keyword class patterns, 193
keyword-only arguments, 242
keywords
    as keyword, 41
    await keyword, 785
    lambda keyword, 236

nonlocal keyword, 317-319, 687
    reserved keywords, 683
    yield keyword, 238, 609-614, 619, 646, 649, 673
KISS principle, 429, 519, 743

L

lambda keyword, 236
lazy sentences, 614-617
Least Recently Used (LRU), 325
len() function, 6
less than (<) operator, 581
less than or equal to (<=) operator, 581
line breaks, 26
lis.py interpreter
    Environment class, 677
    evaluate function, 680-689
    imports and types, 675
    OR-patterns, 690
    parser, 675-677
    pattern matching in, 43-47
    Procedure class, 689-690
    REPL (read-eval-print-loop), 679
    Scheme syntax, 673-675
    topics covered, 673
list comprehensions (listcomps)
    asynchronous, 822-825
    building lists from cartesian products, 27
    building sequences with, 25
    versus generator expressions, 29
    local scope within, 26
    readability and, 25
    syntax tip, 26
    versus map and filter functions, 27, 235
lists
    alternatives to, 59-70
    building lists of lists, 51
    list.sort versus sorted built-in, 56-58
    mixed-bag, 74
    multiline, 26
    shallow copies of, 208-211
    versus tuples, 34
    using tuples as immutable, 32-34
locks, definition of term, 703
LRU (see Least Recently Used)

M

magic methods, 4, 19
managed attributes, 886

managed classes, 885
managed instances, 886
map function, 27, 234-236
mappings
    automatic handling of missing keys, 90-95
    case-insensitive, 502-504
    immutable mappings, 99
    mapping generator functions, 625
    merging, 80
    pattern matching with, 81-83
    standard API of mapping types, 83-90
    unpacking, 80
match blocks (see with, match, and else blocks)
match/case statement, 39, 81
mathematical vector operations, 570
max() function, 525-530
memoization, 322-325
memory, saving with __slots__, 386-390
memoryview class, 62-64
metaclasses
    basics of, 935-937
    considerations for use, 951-953
    customizing classes, 937
    definition of term, 914
    example metaclass, 938-941
    metaclass evaluation time experiment,
        941-946
    metaclass solution for checkedlib.py,
        946-951
    useful applications of, 956
metaobjects, 19
metaprogramming, xxii (see also attribute
    descriptors; class metaprogramming;
    dynamic attributes and properties)
method resolution order (MRO), 496-501
methods, as callable objects, 238 (see also
    sequences, special methods for; special
    methods)
Meyer's Uniform Access Principle, 879-880
Mills & Gizmos Notation (MGN), 887
mixin classes, 502-504
mixin methods, 504
modulo (%) operator, 5, 12
monkey-patching, 440-442, 488, 901
MRO (see method resolution order)
multicore processing
    data science, 731
    distributed task queues, 736
    increased availability of, 729

    server-side web/mobile development, 732
    system administration, 730
    WSGI application servers, 734
multiline lists, 26
multiple inheritance (see also inheritance and
    subclassing)
    method resolution order and, 496-501
    real-world examples of, 504-511
multiplication, scalar, 10, 576-578
multiprocessing package, 69, 708
mutable objects, 225 (see also object references)
mutable parameters, 214-218
mutable sequences, 24
mutable values, inserting or updating, 87-90
MutableMapping ABC, 83
Mypy type checker, 255-260
my_fmt.format() method, 5

N

name mangling, 384
namedtuple, 169-172
native coroutines
    versus asynchronous generators, 822
    definition of term, 781
    functions defined with async def, 238
    humble generators and, 789
network I/O
    downloading with asyncio, 786-790
    downloading with concurrent.futures,
        753-755
    downloads with progress display and error
        handling, 766-776
    enhancing asyncio downloader, 792-801
    essential role of concurrency in, 748-750
    myth of I/O-bound systems, 830
    role of futures, 755-758
    sequential download script, 750-753
NFC (see Normalization Form C)
nominal typing, 262
nonlocal keyword, 317-319, 687
nonoverriding descriptors, 859, 896-902
NoReturn type, 295
Normalization Form C (NFC), 140
normalized text matching, 143-148
not equal to (!=) operator, 581
numbers ABCs, 480-483
numbers package, 280
numeric protocols, 480-483
numeric tower, 280

numeric types
    checking for convertibility, 470, 482
    emulating using special methods, 9-12
    hashability of, 84
    support for, 481
NumPy, 64-67

O

object references
    aliasing, 204-208
    deep copies, 211-213
    del and garbage collection, 219-221
    distinction between objects and their
        names, 201
    function parameters as references, 213-218
    further reading on, 224
    immutability and, 221
    overview of, 223
    shallow copies, 208-211
    Soapbox discussion, 225
    variables as labels versus boxes, 202-204
objects
    callable objects, 237-239, 602-603
    first-class, 231
    flexible object creation, 847-849
    mutable, 225
    treating functions like, 232-234
    user-defined callable objects, 239
operator module, 243-247
operator overloading
    augmented assignment operators, 584-589
    basics of, 566
    further reading on, 591
    infix operator method names, 580
    infix operators, 565
    overloading * for scalar multiplication,
        576-578
    overloading + for vector addition, 570-576
    overview of, 589
    rich comparison operators, 581-584
    significant changes to, 566
    Soapbox discussion, 592
    topics covered, 566
    unary operators, 567-570
    using @ as infix operator, 578-580
Optional type, 270
OR-patterns, 690
OrderedDict, 85, 95
os functions, str versus bytes in, 157

overloaded signatures, 524-530
overriding descriptors, 859, 867, 896-902

P

parallelism, 699, 701
parameterized decorators, 331-337
parameterized types, 548
parameters
    annotating positional only and variadic
        parameters, 295
    introspection of function parameters, 232
    keyword-only, 242
    mutable, 214-218
    parameter passing, 213
    positional, 240-243
pattern matching
    *_ symbol, 42
    destructuring, 40
    in lis.py interpreter, 43-47, 673-691
    with mappings, 81-83
    match/case statement, 39
    pattern matching class instances, 192-195
    tuples and lists, 41
    type information, 42
    _ symbol, 41
patterns (see functions, design patterns with
    first-class; pattern matching)
pickle module, 97
Pingo library, 99
pipe (|) operator, 80, 690
pipe equals (|=) operator, 80
plain text, 129, 161
.pop method, 67
positional class patterns, 194
positional parameters, 240-243
positional patterns, 379
process pools
    code for multicore prime checker, 723-727
    example problem, 720
    process-based solution, 722
    thread-based nonsolution, 728
    understanding elapsed times, 722
    varying process numbers, 727
processes
    definition of term, 702
    launching with concurrent.futures, 758-762
progress displays, 766-776
Project Jupyter, 731
proper tail calls (PTC), 695-697

properties (see computed properties; dynamic attributes and properties)
property class, 864-869
protocol classes, 405
Protocol type, 287-292
protocols (see also interfaces)
  defensive programming, 442-444
  duck typing and, 404
  further reading on, 484
  implementing at runtime, 440-442
  implementing generic static protocols, 556-558
  as informal interfaces, 429
  meanings of protocol, 436
  numeric, 480-483
  overview of, 483
  sequence and iterable protocols, 438-440
  significant changes to, 435
  Soapbox discussion, 486-488
  static protocols, 405, 468-483
  topics covered, 435
PSF (see Python Software Foundation)
PUG (see Python Users Group)
PyICU, 150
PyLadies, 964
pytest package, xxii
Python
  appreciating language-specific features, xix
  approach to learning, xx-xxii
  community support for, 963
  fluentpython.com, xxiii
  functional programming with, 250
  functioning with multicore processors, 729-737
  further reading on, 964
  prerequisites to learning, xx
  target audience, xx
  versions featured, xx
Python Data Model
  further reading on, 18
  __getitem__ and __len__, 5-8
  making len work with custom objects, 17
  overview of, 3, 18
  significant changes to, 4
  Soapbox discussion, 19
  special methods overview, 15-17
  using special methods, 8-15
Python Software Foundation (PSF), 964
Python type checkers, 256

Python Users Group (PUG), 964
python-tulip list, 963
Pythonic Card Deck example, 5-8
Pythonic objects (see also objects)
  alternative constructor for, 370
  building user-defined classes, 365
  classmethod versus staticmethod, 371
  formatted displays, 372-376
  further reading on, 394
  hashable Vector2d, 376-379
  object representations, 366
  overriding class attributes, 391-393
  overview of, 393
  private and protected attributes, 384-386
  saving memory with __slots__, 386-390
  significant changes to, 366
  Soapbox discussion, 396-398
  supporting positional patterns, 379
  topics covered, 365
  Vector2d class example, 367-370
  Vector2d full listing, 380-383
Pythonic sums, 430-432
pyuca library, 150, 158

Q

quantity properties, 869-872
questions and comments, xxv
queues
  definition of term, 702
  deque (double-ended queue), 59, 67
  distributed task queues, 736
  implementing, 69

R

race conditions, 727
random.choice function, 6
recycling (see garbage collection)
reduce function, 234-236
reducing functions, 414, 634-635
refactoring strategies
  choosing the best, 352
  classic, 344-348
  Command pattern, 357-359
  decorator-enhanced pattern, 355-357
  finding strategies in modules, 353-355
  function-oriented, 349-352
reference counting, 219
registration decorators, 310, 331-334
regular expressions, str versus bytes in, 155

repr() function, 366
reserved keywords, 683
rich comparison operators, 581-584
running averages, computing, 647-649

S

S-expression, 673
salts, 85
Scheme language, 43-47, 673-675
SciPy, 64-67
scope
    dynamic scope versus lexical scope, 340-341
    function local scope, 312
    module global scope, 312
    variable scope rules, 310-312
    within comprehensions and generator
      expressions, 26
semaphores, 795-799
Sentence classes, 607-614
sentinels, 725
sequence protocol, 438-440, 598-600
sequences
    alternatives to lists, 59-70
    further reading on, 71
    list comprehensions and generator expres-
      sions, 25-30
    list.sort versus sorted built-in, 56-58
    overview of, 70
    overview of built-in, 22-24
    pattern matching with, 39-47
    significant changes to, 22
    slicing, 47-50
    Soapbox discussion, 73-75
    topics covered, 22
    tuples, 30-35
    uniform handling of, 21
    unpacking sequences and iterables, 35-38
    using + and * with, 50-56
sequences, special methods for
    applications beyond three dimensions, 400
    dynamic attribute access, 409-413
    __format__, 420-427
    further reading on, 428
    __hash__ and __eq__, 413-418
    overview of, 427
    protocols and duck typing, 404
    significant changes to, 400
    sliceable sequences, 405-409
    Soapbox discussion, 429-432

topics covered, 399
Vector implementation strategy, 400
Vector2d compatibility, 401-403
sequential.py program, 720
server-side web/mobile development, 732
servers
    Asynchronous Server Gateway Interface
      (ASGI), 736
    HTTPServer class, 505
    TCP servers, 808-815
    test servers, 769
    ThreadingHTTPServer class, 505
    Web Server Gateway Interface (WSGI), 734
    writing asyncio servers, 803-815
setattr function, 875
sets (see also dictionaries and sets)
    consequences of how set works, 107
    set comprehensions, 106
    set literals, 105
    set operations, 107-110
    set operations on dict views, 110
    set theory, 103-105
shallow copies, 208-211
shelve module, 97
simple class patterns, 192
single dispatch generic functions, 326-331
Sized interface, 15
slicing
    assigning to slices, 50
    excluding last item in, 47
    multidimensional slicing and ellipses, 49
    slice objects, 48
    sliceable sequences, 405-409
Soapbox sidebars
    @dataclass, 197
    anonymous functions, 252
    __call__, 362
    code points, 161
    data model versus object model, 19
    design patterns, 361
    duck typing, 303, 429
    dynamic scope versus lexical scope, 340-341
    equality (==) operator, 225
    explicit self argument, 909
    flat versus container sequences, 73
    __format__, 430
    function-class duality, 880
    functional programming with Python, 250
    generic collections, 303

inheritance across languages, 520
interfaces, 488
key argument, 74
lis.py and evaluate function, 697
magic methods, 19
metaobjects, 19
minimalistic iterator interface, 658
mixed-bag lists, 74
monkey-patching, 488
multilevel class hierarchies, 519
mutability, 225
non-ASCII names in source code, 160
object destruction and garbage collection, 226
operator overloading, 592
Oracle, Google, and the Timbot, 74
plain text, 161
pluggable generators, 658-660
programming language design, 960
proper tail calls (PTC), 695-697
properties and up-front costs, 396
protocols as informal interfaces, 429
Python decorators and decorator design pattern, 341
Pythonic sums, 430-432
safety versus security in private attributes, 397
static typing, 486
syntactic sugar, 114
thread avoidance, 777
threads-and-locks versus actor-style programming, 744-746
trade-offs of built-ins, 519
tuples, 73
Twisted library, 835
type hints (type annotations), 300-303
typing map, 487
undocumented classes, 561
Uniform Access Principle, 879-880
uvloop, 834
variance notation in other classes, 562
with statements, 695
sorted function, 56-58
special methods (see also sequences, special methods for)
advantages of using, 6
Boolean values of custom types, 13
calling, 8
Collection API, 14-15
emulating numeric types, 9-12
__getitem__ and __len__, 5-8
naming conventions, 3
purpose of, 3
special method names (operators excluded), 15
special method names and symbols for operators, 16
string representation, 12
spinners (loading indicators) (see also network I/O)
comparing supervisor functions, 715
created using coroutines, 710-714
created with multiprocessing package, 708
created with threading, 705-708
Global Interpreter Lock impact, 717-719
keeping alive, 719
square brackets ([]), 6, 26, 35, 49
stacked decorators, 324
star (*) operator, 10, 36-37, 50-56, 240, 576-578
star equals (*=) operator, 584-589
static duck typing, 291, 434, 517
static protocols
best practices for protocol design, 478
definition of, 437
designing, 476-478
versus dynamic protocols, 405
extending, 479
implementing generic static protocols, 556-558
limitations of runtime protocol checks, 473
numbers ABCS and numeric protocols, 480-483
runtime checkable, 470-473
Soapbox discussion, 486
supporting, 474-476
type hints (type annotations), 287-292
typed double function, 468-470
static typing, 433
staticmethod decorator, 371
storage attributes, 886
str() function, 13, 366
str.format() method, 5, 372
Strategy pattern, 344-348
strings
default sorting of, 58
dual-mode str and bytes APIs, 155-157
normalizing Unicode for reliable comparisons, 140-148

representation using special methods, 12
strong testing, 296
struct module, 118
structural typing, 466-468
structured concurrency, 827
subclassing (see inheritance and subclassing)
subgenerators, 636
subtype-of relationships, 267
super() function, 413, 490-492
syntactic sugar, 114
SyntaxError, 128
system administration, 730

T

tail call optimization (TCO), 695-697
TCP servers, 808-815
TensorFlow, 731
test servers, 769
text files, handling, 131-139 (see also Unicode
    text versus bytes)
ThreadingHTTPServer class, 505
ThreadingMixIn class, 505
threads
    definition of term, 702
    enhancing asyncio downloader, 793-801
    further reading on, 738
    Global Interpreter Lock impact, 718
    spinners (loading indicators) using, 705-708
    thread avoidance, 777
    thread-based process pools, 728
throttling, 795-799
Timsort algorithm, 74
Tkinter GUI toolkit
    benefits and drawbacks of, 515
    multiple inheritance in, 509-511
tree structures, traversing, 638-643
tuples
    classic named tuples, 169-172
    immutability and, 221
    as immutable lists, 32-34
    versus lists, 34
    nature of, 73
    as records, 30-32
    relative immutability of, 207
    simplified memory diagram for, 23
    tuple unpacking, 32
    type hints (type annotations), 274-276
    typing.NamedTuple, 172
Twisted library, 835

type casting, 538-541
type hints (type annotations)
    annotating positional only and variadic
        parameters, 295
    for asynchronous objects, 828
    basics of, 173-179
    benefits and drawbacks of, 253
    flawed typing and strong testing, 296
    further reading on, 299
    generic type hints for coroutines, 654
    gradual typing, 254-260 (see also gradual
        type system)
    overview of, 298
    significant changes to, 254
    Soapbox discussion, 300-303
    supported operations and, 261-266
    topics covered, 254
    types usable in, 266-295
typed double function, 468-470
TypedDict, 164, 530-538
Typeshed project, 281
TypeVar, 282-286
typing map, 434, 487 (see also type hints (type
    annotations))
typing module, 266
typing.NamedTuple, 172

U

UCA (see Unicode Collation Algorithm)
UCS-2 encoding, 124
UML class diagrams
    ABCs in collections.abc, 451
    annotated with MGN, 886, 947
    Command design pattern, 357
    django.views.generic.base module, 506
    django.views.generic.list module, 508
    fundamental collection types, 14
    managed and descriptor classes, 884
    MutableSequence ABC and superclasses,
        450
    Sequence ABC and abstract classes, 438
    simplified for collections.abc, 24
    simplified for MutableMapping and super-
        classes, 83
    simplified for MutableSet and superclasses,
        107
    Strategy design pattern, 344
    Tkinter Text widget class and superclasses,
        501

TomboList, 463
unary operators, 567-570
undocumented classes, 561
Unicode Collation Algorithm (UCA), 150
Unicode literals escape notation (\N{}), 136
Unicode sandwich, 131
Unicode text versus bytes
    basic encoders/decoders, 123-124
    byte essentials, 120-123
    characters and Unicode standard, 118-120
    dual-mode str and bytes APIs, 155-157
    further reading on, 158
    handling text files, 131-139
    normalizing Unicode for reliable compari-
        sons, 140-148
    overview of, 157
    significant changes to, 118
    Soapbox discussion, 160
    sorting Unicode text, 148-150
    topics covered, 117
    understanding encode/decode problems,
        125-131
    Unicode database, 151-155
UnicodeDecodeError, 126
UnicodeEncodeError, 125
Uniform Access Principle, 879-880
Union type, 270
unittest module, xxii
unpacking
    iterables and mappings, 240
    mapping unpackings, 80
    nested, 37
    sequences and iterables, 35
    using * to grab excess items, 36
    with * in function calls and sequence liter-
        als, 37
user-defined functions, 238
UserDict, 97-99
UTF-8 decoding, 129
UTF-8-SIG encoding, 130
uvloop, 834

V

variable annotations
    meaning of, 175-179
    syntax of, 174
variable scope rules, 310-312
variables
    free, 315

init-only variables, 186
    as labels versus boxes, 202-204
    lookup logic, 318
variadic parameters, 295
variance
    contravariant types, 551
    covariant types, 550
    in callable types, 293
    invariant types, 549
    overview of, 553
    relevance of, 548
    rules of thumb, 555
    variance notation in other classes, 562
vars([object]) function, 875
Vector class, multidimensional
    applications beyond three dimensions, 400
    dynamic attribute access, 409-413
    __format__, 420-427
    further reading on, 428
    __hash__ and __eq__, 413-418
    implementation strategy, 400
    overview of, 427
    protocols and duck typing, 404
    sliceable sequences, 405-409
    topics covered, 399
    Vector2d compatibility, 401-403
Vector2d
    class example, 367-370
    full listing, 380-383
    hashable, 376
vectors
    overloading + for vector addition, 570-576
    representing two-dimensional, 9-12
virtual attributes, 839
virtual subclasses, 462-465

W

Walrus operator (:=), 26
weak references, 221
Web Server Gateway Interface (WSGI), 734
web/mobile development, 732
with, match, and else blocks
    context managers and with blocks, 662-673
    else clause, 691-693
    further reading on, 694
    overview of, 693
    pattern matching in lis.py, 673-691
    purpose of with statements, 662
    significant changes to, 662

Soapbox discussion, 695-698
topics covered, 661

Y

yield from expression, 636-643

yield keyword, 238, 609-614, 619, 646, 649, 673

Z

zero-based indexing, 47
zip() function, 418

About the Author

Luciano Ramalho was a web developer before the Netscape IPO in 1995, and switched from Perl to Java to Python in 1998. He joined Thoughtworks in 2015, where he is a Principal Consultant in the São Paulo office. He has delivered keynotes, talks, and tutorials at Python events in the Americas, Europe, and Asia, and also presented at Go and Elixir conferences, focusing on language design topics. Ramalho is a fellow of the Python Software Foundation and cofounder of Garoa Hacker Clube, the first hackerspace in Brazil.

Colophon

The animal on the cover of *Fluent Python* is a Namaqua sand lizard (*Pedioplanis namaquensis*), found throughout Namibia in arid savannah and semi-desert regions.

The Namaqua sand lizard has a black body with four white stripes running down its back, brown legs with white spots, a white belly, and a long, pinkish-brown tail. It is one of the fastest of the lizards active during the day and feeds on small insects. It inhabits sparsely vegetated sand gravel flats. Female Namaqua sand lizards lay between three to five eggs in November, and these lizards spends the rest of winter dormant in burrows that they dig near the base of bushes.

The current conservation status of the Namaqua sand lizard is of "Least Concern." Many of the animals on O'Reilly covers are endangered; all of them are important to the world.

The cover illustration is by Karen Montgomery, based on a black and white engraving from Wood's *Natural History*. The cover fonts are Gilroy Semibold and Guardian Sans. The text font is Adobe Minion Pro; the heading font is Adobe Myriad Condensed; and the code font is Dalton Maag's Ubuntu Mono.

Printed in the USA
CPSIA information can be obtained
at www.ICGtesting.com
JSHW061353190224
57666JS00010B/211